Teacher's Edition

Realidades 3

      realidades.com

Digital Edition

Peggy Palo Boyles
OKLAHOMA CITY, OK

Myriam Met
ROCKVILLE, MD

Richard S. Sayers
LONGMONT, CO

PEARSON

Boston, Massachusetts | Chandler, Arizona
Glenview, Illinois | Upper Saddle River, New Jersey

Front cover, left: Young man wearing baseball jacket
Center left: City of Arts and Sciences, Valencia, Spain
Center right: Young indigenous women, Santiago de Atitlán, Guatemala
Right: Mola, a traditional decorative fabric panel from San Blas Islands, Panama

Copyright © 2014 Pearson Education, Inc., or its affiliates. All Rights Reserved. Printed in the United States of America. This publication is protected by copyright, and permission should be obtained from the publisher prior to any prohibited reproduction, storage in a retrieval system, or transmission in any form or by any means, electronic, mechanical, photocopying, recording, or likewise. For information regarding permissions, write to Rights Management & Contracts, Pearson Education, Inc., One Lake Street, Upper Saddle River, New Jersey 07458.

Pearson, Prentice Hall, Pearson Prentice Hall, PresentationExpress, and eText™ are trademarks, in the U.S. and/or other countries, of Pearson Education, Inc., or its affiliates.

ExamView® is a registered trademark of eInstruction Corporation.

Pre-AP* is a registered trademark of the College Board. Use of the trademark implies no relationship, sponsorship, endorsement, sale, or promotion on the part of Pearson Education, Inc., or its affiliates.

PEARSON

ISBN-13: 978-0-13-319953-6
ISBN-10: 0-13-319953-3

3 4 5 6 7 8 9 10   V056   17 16 15 14 13

Professional Development Handbook

Realidades 3

     realidades.com

Digital Edition

Table of Contents

realidades.com Get started on **realidades.com**!

Now that you have purchased Realidades ©2014, follow these steps to set up a new account:

a. Go to **realidades.com** and click "Register."
b. Select the account type you need.
c. Provide your School Code or use the search tool to find it.
d. Follow directions to complete registration.

For Video Modules and other implementation support, visit:

*my*PearsonTraining.com
• Video Modules and PDFs for product training

Realidades, Research, and the Standards

Realidades is based on the belief that the purpose of learning Spanish is to communicate with the people who speak it and to understand their cultures. *Realidades* presents a fresh, exciting approach to Spanish by making language learning real for today's students.

. . . .

Topics covered:

▶ *Realidades* and Research-based Instruction

▶ **Achieving the Standards with *Realidades***

Realidades and Research-based Instruction

Realidades reflects the most current research on how students learn languages and what teachers and materials need to do to help them become proficient language users. Let's take a look at some of the basic premises about language and language learning.

Communication

Communication is an authentic exchange of information for a real purpose between two or more people. By this we mean that people tell each other (through speech or writing) something the other person doesn't already know.

Communicating meaning has several aspects. Students need to listen to and read Spanish in order to interpret intended meanings. Students need to express meaning by conveying their own messages for a purpose and to a real audience. They also need to negotiate meaning through the natural give-and-take involved in understanding and making oneself understood. Research tells us that classroom activities must provide students practice in interpreting, expressing, and negotiating meaning through extensive and frequent peer interactions.

Throughout *Realidades,* students are engaged in understanding messages, in sending their own messages, and thus in communicating real ideas and real meanings for real purposes.

REALIDADES and the Common Core State Standards

The *Common Core State Standards for English Language Arts and Literacy in History/Social Studies, Science, and Technology Subjects* define general, cross-disciplinary literacy expectations to ensure that all students are prepared for success in college or workforce training programs. These Standards contain four strands: Reading, Writing, Speaking and Listening, and Language.

Teachers using *REALIDADES** can be assured that they are supporting the Common Core Standards. Look for the National Standards for Language Learning correlations within a chapter as evidence of support:
- Reading: 1.2, 2.1, 2.2, 3.1, 3.2, 4.1, 4.2, 5.1
- Writing: 1.3, 2.1, 2.2, 3.1, 3.2, 4.1, 4.2, 5.1
- Speaking and Listening: 1.1, 1.3, 2.1, 2.2, 3.2, 4.1, 5.2

© You'll also find this icon next to Common Core activities in the *¡Adelante!* section.

* Visit PearsonSchool.com/Real2014 for a correlation to the Common Core Standards.

Comprehensible input

Research states that students learn best when they have ample opportunities to internalize meanings before they have to produce them. In other words, comprehension precedes production. The term "comprehensible input" suggests that learners acquire language by understanding what they hear and read. Students need many opportunities to match what they hear with visual cues (pictures, video, or teacher pantomime) or experiences (physical actions). Reading input should be supported by a close connection between text and visuals. All these strategies for comprehensible input help students associate meaning with forms.

In keeping with this research, *Realidades* begins each chapter of Levels 1–3 with a section called *A primera vista*. These four pages of language input give students opportunities to comprehend new language before producing it. The visualized presentation of vocabulary in context, the reading input in the *Videohistoria,* and the listening input in the *A primera vista* video segment provide a wide range of comprehensible input of new language that addresses all students and all learning styles.

Practice activities

Research tells us that students need extensive practice using new language to create and convey their own messages. The *Manos a la obra* section in Levels 1–3 provides a wide range of practice activities. New vocabulary and grammar are first practiced in skill-getting activities that provide concrete practice. This basic practice helps to develop accuracy in using the language and prepares students to transition into more communicative tasks. In the transitional activities that follow the basic practice, students work with a partner or in small groups with information- or opinion-gap activities that are characteristic of real-life communication. Students then continue on to more open-ended, personalized speaking or writing tasks.

> "Communication is an authentic exchange of information for a real purpose between two or more people."

Meaningful context in language learning

All effective learning is rooted in a meaningful context. We know from research that information is most likely to be retained when it is connected to other information in a meaningful way. Thus, language learning is most successful and retention more likely when we present new language organized into topics or by situations.

Realidades is organized into themes. All material in a chapter—vocabulary, grammar, culture— is rooted in a context and used meaningfully. Students engage in communicative tasks that are relevant to their lives. Students work with readings, realia, photography, and art that are authentic to the Spanish-speaking world. The video programs and Internet links show native speakers engaged in real-life situations and experiences.

Understanding grammar

Students learn grammar most effectively when it is presented and practiced in a meaningful context and when it connects to real communication needs. Students also benefit when shown how the patterns of grammar work.

In *Realidades,* new structures are foreshadowed through lexical presentation (grammar is presented as vocabulary) in the *Vocabulario en contexto* language input section in Levels 1–3. In addition, early vocabulary activities in the *Vocabulario en uso* section have students work with the grammar lexically. This allows students to see the grammar and work with it in a meaningful context before being formally presented with the rules or paradigms.

Grammar is formally presented with clear explanations and examples in the *Gramática* section in Levels 1–3. Comparisons between English and Spanish grammar are made whenever possible. Students then practice the grammar concepts in a variety of tasks that range from concrete activities that focus primarily on the structures to more open-ended tasks that focus on communication.

To further facilitate the learning of grammar, *Realidades* offers *GramActiva*, a multi-modality approach to grammar that includes grammar videos and hands-on grammar activities. By teaching and practicing grammar through different learning styles, more students will be able to learn grammar.

Building cultural perspectives

The *Standards for Foreign Language Learning* have expanded how culture is taught in today's classroom. We want students to understand the *why* (perspectives) of culture that determines the *what* (products and practices).

The approach to culture in *Realidades* not only teaches students the *what* but asks students to explore the *why*. Cultural products, practices, and comparisons are presented throughout *Realidades* in features such as *Arte y cultura, Fondo cultural, La cultura en vivo,* and *Perspectivas del mundo hispano,* and in *Realidades 3, Puente a la cultura.* Students read information about cultures that offer different perspectives and they are asked questions that encourage them to think and make observations about cultures.

Strategies for Success

Research shows that effective learners know how to help themselves become successful learners. One way they do this is by using specific problem-solving strategies.

Realidades teaches students strategies to be effective communicators whether listening, speaking, reading, or writing. Each reading selection in Levels 1–3 is supported by a reading strategy. Each performance-based task in Levels 1–3 includes a useful strategy that connects to a step-by-step approach that helps students plan, rehearse, and present or publish. Each also includes a rubric so students know how they might be evaluated.

We know more than ever about how foreign languages are learned. *Realidades* is based on solid research in second-language acquisition, on accepted theories about the teaching of culture, and on sound pedagogical practices that are common to all disciplines. We are sure that you and your students will find this an exciting, motivating, and enormously successful approach to learning Spanish.

Achieving the Standards with *Realidades*

The *Standards for Foreign Language Learning* provide an important and useful framework to guide the teaching and learning of foreign languages. This framework should result in a new generation of language learners prepared to meet the demand for competence in other languages that our nation will face in an increasingly interdependent world.

Realidades is written based upon the Standards. This means that instruction used in *Realidades* will help students develop the competencies delineated in the *Standards for Foreign Language Learning.* Teachers will find a correlation to the Standards at the beginning of each chapter and with the notes that accompany each activity (if appropriate) in the Teacher's Edition.

Goal 1: Communication

1.1 (Interpersonal): Each chapter provides a wide range of paired and group activities. Students speak with a partner, work in small groups, and interview classmates.

1.2 (Interpretive): *Realidades* builds the interpretive listening skill through the Audio Program. This program in Levels 1–3 supports activities in the Student Edition (input checks, dictations, listening comprehension, and test preparation) and the *Writing, Audio, & Video* section of the *Communication Workbook.* The Video Program also develops listening through the different language, grammar, and storyline mystery video segments.

Realidades provides extensive support for the interpretive reading skill. Students read throughout the chapter: comprehensible input, practice activities, realia, culture notes, and reading selections. Reading is seamlessly integrated with practice and anchored in real-life contexts. Whenever possible, readings are supported by focused strategies.

1.3 (Presentational): Each chapter in Level 3 has two performance-based tasks: a speaking task and a writing task. Both presentations are supported by strategies and the speaking or writing process, step-by-step support to help students successfully complete the task.

Goal 2: Culture

2.1 (Practices and Perspectives) and **2.2** (Products and Perspectives): Each chapter in *Realidades* explores a cultural theme through a wide range of practices, products, and perspectives. Students see authentic culture through realia, art, photographs, popular sayings, tongue twisters, rhymes and songs, hands-on projects, readings, and authentic literature. In addition, the unique *Fondo cultural* readings in Levels 1–3 generally include a Standards-based critical thinking question.

Goal 3: Connections

3.1 (Cross-curricular Connections): *Realidades* integrates cross-curricular activities (*Conexiones*) within the *Manos a la obra section* in Levels 1–3. Students make connections to a variety of disciplines through activities that integrate the language of the chapter.

3.2 (Connections to Target Culture): *Realidades* exposes students to perspectives only available within the target culture through art, realia, pronunciation activities, and readings.

Goal 4: Comparisons

4.1 (Language Comparisons): *Realidades* enables students to see comparisons between languages in both the grammar explanations in the text and *GramActiva* videos, and in a unique section called *Exploración del lenguaje* in Levels 1–2. Students learn to look for language connections, to understand how language works, and to integrate these new skills as they continue in their study of Spanish.

4.2 (Cultural Comparisons): *Realidades* is rich in cultural comparisons. A unique feature called *Fondo cultural* in Levels 1–3 generally informs students about a cultural product or practice and is followed by a question that challenges students to think critically and make comparisons between cultures.

Goal 5: Communities

5.1 (Outside the Classroom): *Realidades* provides informative features called *El español en la comunidad* and *El español en el mundo del trabajo* in Levels 1–3. These sections help students see how to use Spanish beyond the classroom, in their communities, and in the world of work.

5.2 (Lifelong Learners): For a textbook to help students achieve this goal, it must motivate students to want to communicate and want to learn more about the culture. The core of *Realidades*—real language, real culture, real tasks—motivates students. The video programs and other technology support engage learners in ways that may encourage them to continue their exploration of the Spanish language and cultures.

Standards for Foreign Language Learning

Goal 1: Communicate in Languages Other Than English

- Standard 1.1: Students engage in conversation, provide and obtain information, express feelings and emotions, and exchange opinions.
- Standard 1.2: Students understand and interpret written and spoken language on a variety of topics.
- Standard 1.3: Students present information, concepts and ideas to an audience of listeners or readers on a variety of topics.

Goal 2: Gain Knowledge and Understanding of Other Cultures

- Standard 2.1: Students demonstrate an understanding of the relationship between the practices and perspectives of the culture studied.
- Standard 2.2: Students demonstrate an understanding of the relationship between the products and perspectives of the culture studied.

Goal 3: Connect with Other Disciplines and Acquire Information

- Standard 3.1: Students reinforce and further their knowledge of other disciplines through the foreign language.
- Standard 3.2: Students acquire information and recognize the distinctive viewpoints that are only available through the foreign language and its cultures.

Goal 4: Develop Insight into the Nature of Language and Culture

- Standard 4.1: Students demonstrate understanding of the nature of language through comparisons of the language studied and their own.
- Standard 4.2: Students demonstrate understanding of the concept of culture through comparisons of the cultures studied and their own.

Goal 5: Participate in Multilingual Communities at Home and Around the World

- Standard 5.1: Students use the language both within and beyond the school setting.
- Standard 5.2: Students show evidence of becoming life-long learners by using the language for personal enjoyment and enrichment.

Program Organization

R ealidades is a communication-based six-level series with a full range of print and technology components that allow teachers to meet the needs of the different students in today's Spanish classroom.

Realidades A
- Introductory section *Para empezar*
- Temas 1–4

Realidades B
- Review section *Para empezar*
- Temas 5–9

Middle School

Realidades A and *B* are separate middle school books that meet the needs of the younger learners. Each Student Edition provides the same content of *Realidades 1* but has been adapted with new art, photographs, and activities that are age-appropriate for the younger learner. Students completing *Realidades B* will make a smooth transition into *Realidades 2*.

Realidades 1
- Introductory section *Para empezar*
- Temas 1–9

Realidades 2
- Review section *Para empezar*
- Temas 1–9

High School

Each high school Student Edition provides the complete curriculum for one year of instruction. The spiraling of themes and extensive recycling of content allows for smooth articulation between levels. Students completing *Realidades 3 and 4* will have a solid foundation for advanced Spanish study.

Realidades 3
- Review section *Para empezar*
- Capítulos 1–10

Realidades 4
- Capítulos 1–12

Chapter Organization

▶ Temas

Realidades 3 is organized around ten thematic chapters that contain two separate vocabulary and grammar sections.

Tema	Capítulo
Para empezar	1. Tu vida diaria 2. Días especiales
1: Accomplishments	1: Días inolvidables
2: Artistic and Personal Expression	2: ¿Cómo te expresas?
3: Health and Exercise	3: ¿Qué haces para estar en forma?
4: Interpersonal Relationships	4: ¿Cómo te llevas con los demás?
5: The World of Work	5: Trabajo y comunidad
6: The Future	6: ¿Qué nos traerá el futuro?
7: Interpreting the Past	7: ¿Mito o realidad?
8: Encounters between Cultures	8: Encuentro entre culturas
9: Protecting the Environment	9: Cuidemos nuestro planeta
10: Rights and Responsibilities	10: ¿Cuáles son tus derechos y deberes?

▶ Chapters

Each chapter in *Realidades* is built around a clear sequence of instruction.

Chapter Section	Pedagogical support
A primera vista 1 y 2 • Vocabulario en contexto	Provides comprehensible language input for the chapter's new vocabulary and grammar within an authentic context. Input includes words, dialogues, narration, visuals, and audio. Students' language production focuses on comprehension and limited production.
Manos a la obra 1 y 2 • Vocabulario en uso • Gramática	Provides productive language practice with a variety of concrete, transitional, and open-ended activities. The activities develop all four language skills and focus on relevant language tasks. Many activities build off of authentic documents, *realia*, and photographs.
¡Adelante! • Puente a la cultura • ¿Qué me cuentas? • Presentación oral/escrita • Lectura	Provides culminating theme-based activities that have students apply what they have learned. The section features a culturally-based reading, listening and integration activities, performance-based speaking and writing tasks, and authentic literature.
Repaso del capítulo • Vocabulario y gramática • Preparación para el examen	Provides complete support for the end-of-chapter assessment. Two pages summarize what students need to know (vocabulary and grammar). The next two pages outline the proficiency and culture sections of the test by describing the task, providing a practice task, and referring students to chapter activities for review.

Articulation

Realidades 1

Realidades offers a completely articulated Scope and Sequence across all levels. The recursive themes allow for the recycling, review, and reteaching of vocabulary and grammar.

Realidades 1

Tema	Capítulo	

Para empezar
- En la escuela: greetings; introductions; leave-takings; numbers; time; body parts
- En la clase: classroom, dates, asking for help
- El tiempo: weather, seasons

A / **B**

1: Mis amigos y yo

1A ¿Qué te gusta hacer?
Vocabulary: activities and expressions for saying what you like and don't like to do
Grammar: infinitives; making negative statements

1B Y tú, ¿cómo eres?
Vocabulary: adjectives and vocabulary to ask about and describe someone's personality
Grammar: adjectives; definite and indefinite articles; word order

2: La escuela

2A Tu día en la escuela
Vocabulary: classroom items and furniture; parts of the classroom; prepositions of location
Grammar: subject pronouns; the present tense of -ar verbs

2B Tu sala de clases
Vocabulary: classroom items and furniture; parts of the classroom; prepositions of location
Grammar: the verb estar; plurals of nouns and articles

3: La comida

3A ¿Desayuno o almuerzo?
Vocabulary: foods; beverages; adverbs of frequency; expressions to show surprise
Grammar: present tense of -er and -ir verbs; me gusta(n), me encanta(n)

3B Para mantener la salud
Vocabulary: food; beverages; expressions to discuss health; expressions to discuss preferences, agreement, disagreement, and quantity; adjectives to describe food
Grammar: the plural of adjectives; the verb ser

4: Los pasatiempos

4A ¿Adónde vas?
Vocabulary: leisure activities; places; expressions to tell where and with whom you go; expressions to talk about when things are done
Grammar: the verb ir; interrogative words

4B ¿Quieres ir conmigo?
Vocabulary: leisure activities; feelings; expressions for extending, accepting, and declining invitations; expressions to tell when something happens
Grammar: ir + a + infinitive; the verb jugar

5: Fiesta en familia

5A Una fiesta de cumpleaños
Vocabulary: family and parties
Grammar: the verb tener; possessive adjectives

5B ¡Vamos a un restaurante!
Vocabulary: describing people and ordering a meal
Grammar: the verb venir; the verbs ser and estar

6: La casa

6A En mi dormitorio
Vocabulary: bedroom items; electronic equipment; colors; adjectives to describe things
Grammar: comparisons and superlatives; stem-changing verbs: poder and dormir

6B ¿Cómo es tu casa?
Vocabulary: rooms in a house and household chores
Grammar: affirmative tú commands; the present progressive tense

7: De compras

7A ¿Cuánto cuesta?
Vocabulary: clothing; shopping; numbers 200–1,000
Grammar: stem-changing verbs: pensar, querer, and preferir; demonstrative adjectives

7B ¡Qué regalo!
Vocabulary: places to shop; gifts; accessories; buying and selling
Grammar: preterite of -ar, -car, and -gar verbs; direct object pronouns lo, la, los, las

8: Experiencias

8A De vacaciones
Vocabulary: vacation places; activities; modes of transportation
Grammar: preterite of -er and -ir verbs; preterite of ir; the personal a

8B Ayudando en la comunidad
Vocabulary: recycling and volunteer work; places in a community
Grammar: the verb decir; indirect object pronouns; preterite of hacer and dar

9: Medios de comunicación

9A El cine y la televisión
Vocabulary: television shows; movie genres; giving opinions
Grammar: acabar de + infinitive; gustar and similar verbs

9B La tecnología
Vocabulary: computers; communication; computer-related activities
Grammar: the verbs pedir and servir; saber and conocer

Realidades A

Realidades A and *B* provide the same Scope and Sequence as *Realidades 1*.

Realidades A covers the same content as the *Para empezar* section and *Temas* 1–4.

Tema	Capítulo	
Para empezar	• En la escuela: greetings; introductions; leave-takings; numbers; time; body parts • En la clase: classroom, dates, asking for help • El tiempo: weather, seasons	
	A	**B**
1: Mis amigos y yo	**1A ¿Qué te gusta hacer?** Vocabulary: activities and expressions for saying what you like and don't like to do Grammar: infinitives; making negative statements	**1B Y tú, ¿cómo eres?** Vocabulary: adjectives and vocabulary to ask about and describe someone's personality Grammar: adjectives; definite and indefinite articles; word order
2: La escuela	**2A Tu día en la escuela** Vocabulary: classroom items and furniture; parts of the classroom; prepositions of location Grammar: subject pronouns; the present tense of -ar verbs	**2B Tu sala de clases** Vocabulary: classroom items and furniture; parts of the classroom; prepositions of location Grammar: the verb estar; plurals of nouns and articles
3: La comida	**3A ¿Desayuno o almuerzo?** Vocabulary: foods; beverages; adverbs of frequency; expressions to show surprise Grammar: present tense of -er and -ir verbs; me gusta(n), me encanta(n)	**3B Para mantener la salud** Vocabulary: food; beverages; expressions to discuss health; expressions to discuss preferences, agreement, disagreement, and quantity; adjectives to describe food Grammar: the plural of adjectives; the verb ser
4: Los pasatiempos	**4A ¿Adónde vas?** Vocabulary: leisure activities; places; expressions to tell where and with whom you go; expressions to talk about when things are done Grammar: the verb ir; interrogative words	**4B ¿Quieres ir conmigo?** Vocabulary: leisure activities; feelings; expressions for extending, accepting, and declining invitations; expressions to tell when something happens Grammar: ir + a + infinitive; the verb jugar

Realidades B

Realidades B provides a review section called *Para empezar* and continues with *Temas* 5–9.

Tema	Capítulo	
5: Fiesta en familia	**5A Una fiesta de cumpleaños** Vocabulary: family and parties Grammar: the verb tener; possessive adjectives	**5B ¡Vamos a un restaurante!** Vocabulary: describing people and ordering a meal Grammar: the verb venir; the verbs ser and estar
6: La casa	**6A En mi dormitorio** Vocabulary: bedroom items; electronic equipment; colors; adjectives to describe things Grammar: comparisons and superlatives; stem-changing verbs: poder and dormir	**6B ¿Cómo es tu casa?** Vocabulary: rooms in a house and household chores Grammar: affirmative tú commands; the present progressive tense
7: De compras	**7A ¿Cuánto cuesta?** Vocabulary: clothing; shopping; numbers 200–1,000 Grammar: stem-changing verbs: pensar, querer, and preferir; demonstrative adjectives	**7B ¡Qué regalo!** Vocabulary: places to shop; gifts; accessories; buying and selling Grammar: preterite of -ar, -car, and -gar verbs; direct object pronouns lo, la, los, las
8: Experiencias	**8A De vacaciones** Vocabulary: vacation places; activities; modes of transportation Grammar: preterite of -er and -ir verbs; preterite of ir; the personal a	**8B Ayudando en la comunidad** Vocabulary: recycling and volunteer work; places in a community Grammar: the verb decir; indirect object pronouns; preterite of hacer and dar
9: Medios de comunicación	**9A El cine y la televisión** Vocabulary: television shows; movie genres; giving opinions Grammar: acabar de + infinitive; gustar and similar verbs	**9B La tecnología** Vocabulary: computers; communication; computer-related activities Grammar: the verbs pedir and servir; saber and conocer

▶ Scope and Sequence

Realidades 2 uses a recursive Scope and Sequence that revisits the themes from *Realidades A, B,* or *1.* This natural recycling allows for important review and reteaching. In addition, students expand their vocabulary, grammar, and cultural understanding as they revisit each theme in greater depth.

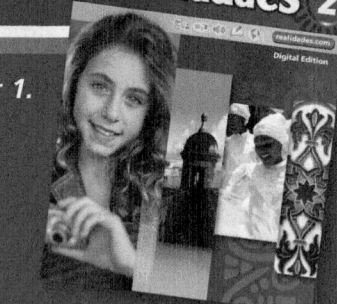

Realidades 2

Tema	Capítulo	
Para empezar	A. ¿Cómo eres tú? *Repaso:* describing people; asking for information; nationalities; adjective agreement; the verb *ser* B. ¿Qué haces? *Repaso:* leisure activities; seasons of the year; regular *-ar, -er,* and *-ir* verbs	
	A	**B**
1: Tu día escolar	**1A ¿Qué haces en la escuela?** Vocabulary: classroom items, activities, and rules Grammar: *(Repaso)* stem-changing verbs; affirmative and negative words	**1B ¿Qué haces después de las clases?** Vocabulary: extracurricular activities Grammar: making comparisons; *(Repaso)* the verbs *saber* and *conocer; hace* + time expressions
2: Un evento especial	**2A ¿Cómo te preparas?** Vocabulary: daily routines, getting ready for an event Grammar: reflexive verbs; *(Repaso)* the verbs *ser* and *estar;* possessive adjectives *mío, tuyo, suyo*	**2B ¿Qué ropa compraste?** Vocabulary: shopping vocabulary, prices, money Grammar: *(Repaso)* the preterite of regular verbs; demonstrative adjectives
3: Tú y tu comunidad	**3A ¿Qué hiciste ayer?** Vocabulary: running errands; locations in a downtown; items purchased Grammar: *(Repaso)* direct object pronouns; the irregular preterite of the verbs *ir, ser, hacer, tener, estar, poder*	**3B ¿Cómo se va . . . ?** Vocabulary: places in a city or town; driving terms; modes of transportation Grammar: *(Repaso)* direct object pronouns: *me, te, nos;* irregular affirmative *tú* commands; *(Repaso)* present progressive: irregular forms
4: Recuerdos del pasado	**4A Cuando éramos niños** Vocabulary: toys; play terms; describing children Grammar: the imperfect tense: regular verbs and irregular verbs; *(Repaso)* indirect object pronouns	**4B Celebrando los días festivos** Vocabulary: expressions describing etiquette; holiday and family celebrations Grammar: the imperfect tense: describing a situation; reciprocal actions
5: En las noticias	**5A Un acto heroico** Vocabulary: natural disasters; emergencies; rescues; heroes Grammar: the imperfect tense: other uses; the preterite of the verbs *oír, leer, creer,* and *destruir*	**5B Un accidente** Vocabulary: parts of the body; accidents; events in the emergency room Grammar: the irregular preterites: *venir, poner; decir, traer;* the imperfect progressive and preterite
6: La televisión y el cine	**6A ¿Viste el partido en la televisión?** Vocabulary: watching television programs; sporting events Grammar: the preterite of *-ir* stem-changing verbs; other reflexive verbs	**6B ¿Qué película has visto?** Vocabulary: movies; making a movie Grammar: verbs that use indirect objects; the present perfect
7: Buen provecho	**7A ¿Cómo se hace la paella?** Vocabulary: cooking expressions; food; appliances; following a recipe; giving directions in a kitchen Grammar: negative *tú* commands; the impersonal *se*	**7B ¿Te gusta comer al aire libre?** Vocabulary: camping and cookouts; food Grammar: *Usted* and *ustedes* commands; uses of *por*
8: Cómo ser un buen turista	**8A Un viaje en avión** Vocabulary: visiting an airport; planning a trip; traveling safely Grammar: the present subjunctive; irregular verbs in the subjunctive	**8B Quiero que disfrutes de tu viaje** Vocabulary: staying in a hotel; appropriate tourist behaviors; traveling in a foreign city Grammar: the present subjunctive with impersonal expressions; the present subjunctive of stem-changing verbs
9: ¿Cómo será el futuro?	**9A ¿Qué profesión tendrás?** Vocabulary: professions; making plans for the future; earning a living Grammar: the future tense; the future tense of irregular verbs	**9B ¿Qué haremos para mejorar el mundo?** Vocabulary: environment; environmental issues and solutions Grammar: the future tense: other irregular verbs; the present subjunctive with expressions of doubt

Realidades 3

Realidades 3 offers ten thought-provoking thematic chapters that integrate rich vocabulary groups and a thorough presentation of grammar. Chapter activities combine communication, culture, and cross-curricular content with authentic literature and poetry.

Realidades 3

Capítulo	Each thematic chapter is divided into two sections. Each of these sections (1 and 2) present and practice vocabulary and grammar.	
Para empezar	1. Tu vida diaria *Repaso:* daily routines; school life; leisure activities; present tense verbs; reflective verbs 2. Días especiales *Repaso:* weekend activities; celebrations; special events; verbs like *gustar:* possessive adjectives	
	①	**②**
1: Un día inolvidable	Vocabulary: hiking objects, activities, and perils; weather Grammar: *(Repaso)* preterite verbs with the spelling change *i–y; (Repaso)* preterite of irregular verbs; *(Repaso)* preterite of verbs with the spelling change *e–i* and *o–u*	Vocabulary: getting ready for an athletic or academic competition; emotional responses to competition; awards and ceremonies Grammar: *(Repaso)* the imperfect; uses of the imperfect
2: ¿Cómo te expresas?	Vocabulary: describing art and sculpture; tools for painting; describing what influences art Grammar: *(Repaso)* the preterite vs. the imperfect; *estar* + participle	Vocabulary: musical instruments; describing dance; describing drama Grammar: *(Repaso) ser* and *estar;* verbs with special meanings in the preterite vs. the imperfect
3: ¿Qué haces para estar en forma?	Vocabulary: nutrition; illnesses and pains; medicine; habits for good health Grammar: *(Repaso)* affirmative *tú* commands; *(Repaso)* affirmative and negative commands with *Ud.* and *Uds.*	Vocabulary: exercises; getting and staying in shape; health advice Grammar: *(Repaso)* the subjunctive: regular verbs; *(Repaso)* the subjunctive: irregular verbs; *(Repaso)* the subjunctive with stem changing *-ar* and *-er* verbs
4: ¿Cómo te llevas con los demás?	Vocabulary: personality traits; interpersonal behavior; friendship Grammar: *(Repaso)* the subjunctive with verbs of emotion; *(Repaso)* the uses of *por* and *para*	Vocabulary: expressing and resolving interpersonal problems; interpersonal relationships Grammar: commands with *nosotros;* possessive pronouns
5: Trabajo y comunidad	Vocabulary: after-school work; describing a job Grammar: *(Repaso)* the present perfect; *(Repaso)* the past perfect	Vocabulary: volunteer activities; the benefits and importance of volunteer work Grammar: the present perfect subjunctive; demonstrative adjectives and pronouns
6: ¿Qué nos traerá en el futuro?	Vocabulary: jobs and professions; qualities of a good employee Grammar: *(Repaso)* the future; *(Repaso)* the future of probability	Vocabulary: technology; inventions; jobs in the future Grammar: the future perfect; *(Repaso)* the use of direct and indirect object pronouns
7: ¿Mito o realidad?	Vocabulary: archaeological terms and activities; describing archaeological sites Grammar: the present and past subjunctive in expressions of doubt	Vocabulary: myths and legends; ancient beliefs; pre-Columbian scientific discoveries Grammar: the subjunctive in adverbial clauses
8: Encuentro entre culturas	Vocabulary: architecture and history of Spain Grammar: the conditional	Vocabulary: Spain in the Americas; the encounter between Cortés and the Aztecs; family heritage Grammar: the past subjunctive; the past subjunctive with *si* clauses
9: Cuidemos nuestro planeta	Vocabulary: caring for the environment Grammar: present subjunctive with conjunctions (*mientras, tan pronto como,* etc.); relative pronouns *que, quien, lo que*	Vocabulary: environmental issues; endangered animals Grammar: present subjunctive with other conjunctions (*a menos que, sin que, para que,* etc.)
10: ¿Cuáles son tus derechos y responsabilidades?	Vocabulary: rights and responsibilties Grammar: the passive voice: *ser* + past participle; the present vs. the past subjunctive	Vocabulary: government; the role of government; individual rights Grammar: the past perfect subjunctive; the conditional perfect

Realidades 4 offers twelve thought-provoking thematic chapters that integrate unique and thorough scope and sequence, careful progression of activities, and a wealth of authentic literature, songs, and paintings by renowned artists from the Spanish-speaking world.

Realidades 4

Capítulo	Each thematic chapter is divided into two sections. Each of these parts (1 and 2) present and practice vocabulary and grammar.	
	Primera parte	**Segunda parte**
1: Esas modas que van y vienen	Vocabulary: fashion trends and fads Grammar: the preterit tense; the imperfect tense	Vocabulary: the influence of fashion on cars Grammar: preterit vs. imperfect
2: La tecnología y el progreso	Vocabulary: environmental issues affecting your world Grammar: uses of *ser, estar,* and *haber;* the future tense	Vocabulary: professions and activities in the future Grammar: the subjunctive in noun clauses
3: Los derechos humanos	Vocabulary: human rights and foreign policy Grammar: indirect commands	Vocabulary: the work of charitable organizations Grammar: direct and indirect object pronouns and the personal *a; gustar* and similar verbs
4: El individuo y la perso-nalidad	Vocabulary: personality and routines Grammar: reflexive constructions	Vocabulary: discussing personality Grammar: agreement, form, and position of adjectives; the past participle and the present perfect indicative and subjunctive
5: Las relaciones personales	Vocabulary: styles of communication and relationships with friends and family Grammar: subjunctive vs. indicative in adjective clauses	Vocabulary: feelings and qualities Grammar: the future perfect and the pluperfect tenses; comparisons with nouns, adjectives, verbs, and adverbs; superlatives
6: El mundo del espectáculo	Vocabulary: entertainers and shows Grammar: subjunctive vs. indicative in adverbial clauses	Vocabulary: music, musicians, and musical events Grammar: formal and informal commands; subjunctive with *ojalá, tal vez,* and *quizá(s)*
7: La diversidad humana	Vocabulary: equality of opportunity Grammar: review of the preterit and imperfect; *hacer* and *desde* in time expressions	Vocabulary: ethnic and gender diversity Grammar: *por* and *para;* verbs that require a preposition before an infinitive
8: Las artes culinarias y la nutrición	Vocabulary: foods and their preparation Grammar: the imperfect subjunctive	Vocabulary: foods and nutrition Grammar: the conditional and conditional perfect; the indicative or subjunctive in *si*-clauses
9: Nuestra compleja sociedad	Vocabulary: crime and personal safety Grammar: the pluperfect subjunctive	Vocabulary: social problems and personal excesses Grammar: uses of *se* with impersonal and passive constructions; indefinite and negative expressions
10: El empleo y la economía	Vocabulary: career choices and the interview process Grammar: indirect speech	Vocabulary: talking about finances Grammar: the relative pronouns *que, quien,* and *lo que* and the relative adjective *cuyo/a(s);* the relative pronouns *el / la cual* and *los / las cuales*
11: El tiempo libre	Vocabulary: outdoor activities and sports Grammar: sequence of tenses with the subjunctive	Vocabulary: what you do in your free time Grammar: uses of definite and indefinite articles; uses of the infinitive and the -ing (-*ndo*) form of the verb
12: Temas que no pasan de moda	Vocabulary: 21st Century advances and challenges Grammar: *se* for unplanned events	Vocabulary: how life will be in the future Grammar: the passive voice; diminutives and augmentatives

Integrating 21st Century Skills in the Spanish Classroom

Spanish teachers recognize the need for students to interact effectively with the many Spanish speakers in the United States and across the globe. Today's world languages curriculum and instruction are based upon the 5Cs (Communication, Cultures, Connections, Comparisons, and Communities) with the goal of building communicative proficiency and cultural understanding. World languages learners are 21st Century Learners.

However, as today's students enter into an increasingly global economy, it is important that they have a diverse range of skills to succeed. The Partnership for 21st Century Skills, a national organization that advocates for 21st century readiness for every student, has developed a Framework for 21st Century Learning. This document fuses the traditinoal 3Rs with what they call the 4Cs:

- Critical thinking and problem solving
- Communication
- Collaboration
- Creativity and innovation

World Languages 21st Century Skills Map

The American Council on the Teaching of Foreign Languages (ACTFL) has worked with the Partnership for 21st Century Skills to create a 21st Century Skills Map that describes the integration of World Languages and 21st Century Skills. This map provides concrete examples of how 21st Century Skills can be integrated into all world language classrooms.

By combining the 5Cs of the National Standards for Foreign Language Learning with the 4Cs from the Partnership for 21st Century Skills, world languages teachers now have a unique opportunity. As schools, districts, and states expand assessment and instruction to focus on 21st Century Skills, we can further prepare students for their future. The 4Cs can be seamlessly integrated on a daily basis within the world languages classroom.

Realidades and the 21st Century World Languages Classroom

Teachers using *Realidades* will easily be able to integrate 21st Century Skills into daily instruction due to the series' pedagogical framework, the alignment of assessment and instruction, and the integration of print and digital resources. In *Realidades*:

- Each chapter is built around thematic instruction based upon real-world tasks and authentic sources.
- Instruction is learner-centered; students take responsibility for the learning and creation of new content.
- Technology is integrated with instruction and assessment to support and enhance learning.
- Instruction and assessment are differentiated to meet the needs of individual learners.
- Assessment is focused on what students can do with the language; students know what they will be asked to do and how they will be assessed.
- Instruction and assessment of culture focuses on the relationship between the products, practices, and perspectives of the target culture as well as comparisons between cultures.
- Students explore opportunities to use the language outside of the classroom.

Realidades and the 4 Cs

Realidades provides a wide range of resources, activities, and assessments that support the 4Cs. At the beginning of each *Tema* in the Teacher's Edition for Levels 1–3, the "b" page contains a chart with recommended activities and assessments in each chapter that build the skills outlined on the 21st Century Skills Map for World Languages.

For further information about the Partnership for 21st Century Skills, please visit their Web site: www.p21.org.

Program Components

Realidades offers a wide range of program components to support the diverse students in today's Spanish classroom! To provide more teaching and learning options, program components are available in three convenient formats: print, DVD, or online at **realidades.com**.

For the Student

Student Edition ONLINE, DVD, PRINT

- eText on DVD-ROM and online contains embedded audio and video files plus flashcards.

Workbooks ONLINE, DVD, PRINT

Leveled Vocabulary and Grammar Workbook

PART 1: GUIDED WORKBOOK
- Vocabulary clip art and study sheets
- Step-by-step grammar activities
- Simplified reading, speaking, and writing activities

PART 2: CORE WORKBOOK
- Focused practice for vocabulary and grammar
- End-of-chapter Crossword Puzzle and Organizer

Communication Workbook with Test Preparation

PART 1: WRITING, AUDIO, AND VIDEO ACTIVITIES
- Additional writing practice
- Student response pages for the Audio Program and *Videodocumentario* video segments

PART 2: TEST PREPARATION
- Thematic readings that prepare students for standardized assessments
- Reading Skills Study Sheets
- Integrated Performance Assessments (IPA)

Realidades para hispanohablantes Workbook
- All-Spanish companion worktext to Student Edition
- Grammar explanations in Spanish
- More practice for language mechanics, usage, vocabulary, grammar, reading, and writing

Readers PRINT

Lecturas
- Sixteen readings per level

Grammar Study Guide PRINT
- Laminated cards summarize grammar for Levels 3–4

realidades.com

Students have complete access to all these digital assets on their account:

Student Edition
- eText with embedded audio and video files plus flashcards

DK Bilingual Visual Dictionary
- eText with over 6,000 vocabulary items organized by topics

DK Reference Atlas
- Complete overview of Spanish-speaking world

Mapa global interactivo
- Links to locations and activities from across the Spanish-speaking world using KMZ files and activities

Videos
Videodocumentario: Theme-based culture videos

¡Pura vida!: Episode-based video series filmed in Costa Rica

Tutorials: Grammar videos with comparisons to English

Videomodelos: Videos that model interpersonal speaking tasks

Audio
- All audio for Student Edition and workbooks
- *Canciones de hip hop* (downloadable)

Animations
- Animated Grammar

Assignable content
- Auto-graded review with Study Plans
- Auto-graded activities from eText, Instant Check, and workbooks
- Interactive auto-graded games for fun, end-of-chapter review
- Teacher-graded RealTalk! speaking activities
- Teacher-graded speaking, writing, and culture activities from eText and workbooks

Assignable assessments
- Quizzes
- Quizzes with Study Plans
- Chapter Tests
- Cumulative Tests
- Integrated Performance Assessments

For the Teacher

PLANNING AND INSTRUCTION

Interactive Teacher's Edition with Resource Library DVD-ROM DVD
- Interactive Teacher's Editions (TE)
- PDF files of resources
- Point-of-use links in TE to PDF file of resources

▢ Activities and Tools for Interactive Whiteboards and Grammar Activities ONLINE DVD
- Interactive practice activities for vocabulary and grammar
- Teaching suggestions, extensions, and answers
- Downloadable SMART Notebook Files
- Use with or without a SMART Interactive Whiteboard
- Over 6,000 images from DK Bilingual Visual Dictionary in Image Gallery
- DVD includes DK dictionary eText

PresentationExpress™ Premium DVD-ROM DVD
Presentation tool that includes:
- Vocabulary images and clip art
- Student Edition audio files
- DK Bilingual Visual Dictionary eText
- GramActiva videos
- Animated Verbs
- Transparencies

Transparencies (on PresentationExpress™ Premium DVD-ROM) ONLINE DVD
- Vocabulario en contexto
- Answer Keys to Student Edition
- Maps, Graphs, Realia, and Rapid Review
- Fine Art Transparencies
- Answer Keys to Workbooks

▶ Video Programs ONLINE DVD
Video Program
- ¡Adelante!: Theme-based videodocumentarios
- ¡Pura vida!: Episode-based video series filmed in Costa Rica

Videomodelos Video Program
- Videos model speaking tasks

◀» Audio Program ONLINE DVD
All audio is available on a single DVD organized by chapter using mp3 files or on realidades.com:
- Vocabulario en contexto
- Communication Workbook Audio activities
- Student Edition Escuchar activities
- En voz alta
- Listening section of Examen del capítulo

Teacher's Resource Book ONLINE PRINT DVD
Includes by chapter:
- Components Overview
- Theme Project
- School-to-Home Letter
- Input Script
- Audio and Video Script
- Lecturas Teacher's Guide
- Communicative Pair Activities
- Situation Cards
- GramActiva Blackline Masters
- Vocabulary Clip Art
- Answer Keys for Workbooks
- 21st Century Skills Rubrics

Pre-AP* Resource Book ONLINE PRINT DVD
- Strategies for building Pre-AP® skills at all levels
- Activities to practice for AP® Spanish Language and Culture Examination

ASSESSMENT AND REMEDIATION

Assessment Program ONLINE PRINT DVD
- Use for core assessment

realidades.com
- Pruebas for Vocabulary Recognition: auto-graded
- Pruebas with Study Plans for Vocabulary Production and Grammar: auto-graded with built-in remediation and retesting
- Examen del capítulo: auto- and teacher-graded
- (Talk!) RealTalk! Speaking Tasks: Presentación oral, Examen del capítulo, Integrated Performance Assessments

Alternate Assessment Program ONLINE PRINT DVD
- For students needing adapted assessment or retesting

Assessment Program: Realidades para hispanohablantes ONLINE PRINT DVD
- For heritage learners

Communication Workbook with Test Preparation ONLINE PRINT DVD
- Integrated Performance Assessments

ExamView® Assessment Suite CD-ROM
- Four editable test banks per chapter: two for core assessment, one for heritage learners, one for Pre-AP® learners
- Test banks available in realidades.com Question Library

Getting Started

Students get started in *Realidades 3* with these colorful reference and introductory sections:

▶ **Mapas**

▶ **Getting Started on realidades.com**

▶ **Para empezar**

▶ **A ver si recuerdas**

Mapas

Colorful atlas pages support geography skills.

Students can explore more online:
🌐 *Mapa global interactivo*
📖 Reference Atlas

Getting Started on realidades.com

Students get a complete overview of online resources available on **realidades.com**.

Para empezar

This bridge section provides a basic review of key content from *Realidades 2*.

Basic Review

The quick review covers concepts from the second year.

A ver si recuerdas

This section helps students review the key vocabulary and grammar learned in first- and second-year Spanish as it relates to the themes for the upcoming chapter.

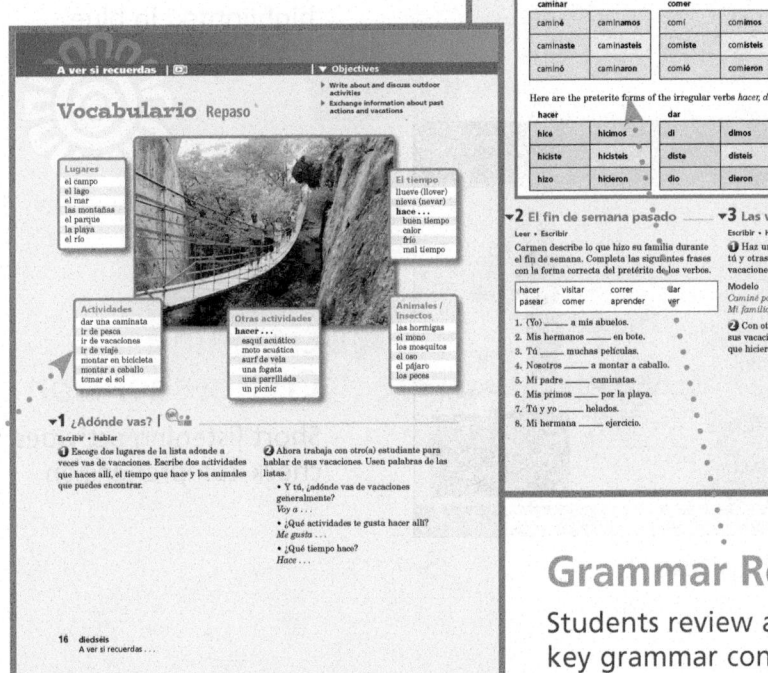

Vocabulary Review

Thematic vocabulary is reviewed using a graphic organizer.

Grammar Review

Students review and practice key grammar concepts.

Chapter Organization

All content and activities available online.

Chapter Sequence

▶ Vocabulario en contexto

▶ Vocabulario en uso

▶ Gramática y vocabulario en uso

▶ ¡Adelante!

▶ Repaso del capítulo

Chapter Opener Capítulo 1

A primera vista 1 and 2

Vocabulario en contexto

This four-page section gives students a "first look" at the new vocabulary and grammar through comprehensible input that integrates visuals and text with audio and video. There are two *A primera vista* sections per chapter.

Visualized Vocabulary

New words are presented visually and in context.

Language Input

Input continues with visuals accompanied by narrative. All new vocabulary words and grammar are highlighted in blue.

◄))Listening Comprehension

Short listening activities check comprehension.

Reading and Language Input

The input of new vocabulary and grammar continues using longer narratives such as a story, realia, or a dialogue. New content is highlighted in blue.

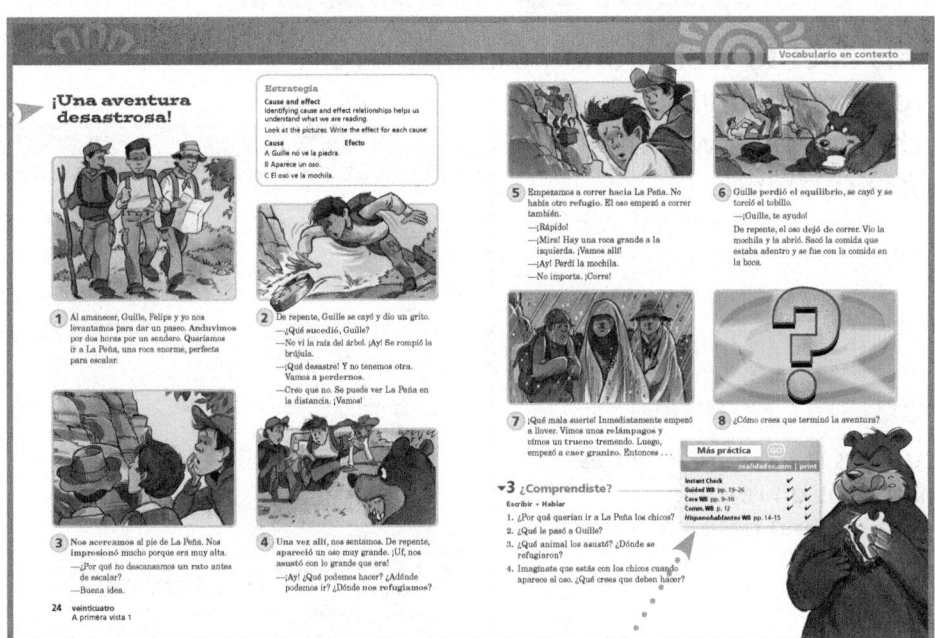

More Practice

Extra practice is available in the workbooks and online.

Reading Comprehension

Questions check students' comprehension of the story while practicing the new vocabulary and grammar.

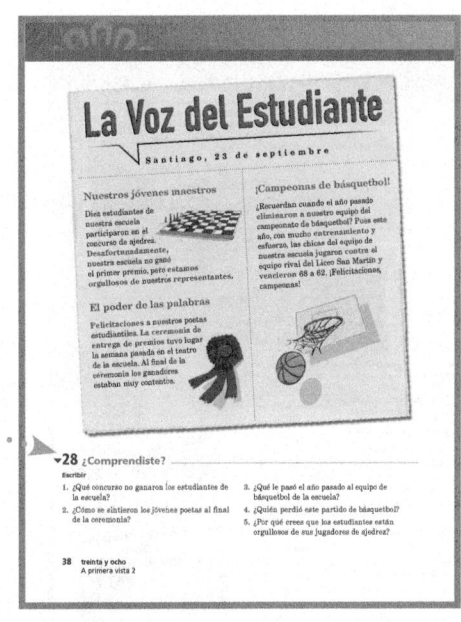

Chapter Organization

Manos a la obra 1 and 2

Vocabulario en uso

Students "get to work" using the chapter's new vocabulary and grammar. Each chapter has two *Manos a la obra* sections.

Focused Practice

Students start with activities that focus on reading, listening, and basic writing.

▶️ **Modelo** Students can view videos that model the conversation.

🗣️ Paired students can record their conversations online!

Paired Practice

Students transition to paired practice activities that focus on the new vocabulary.

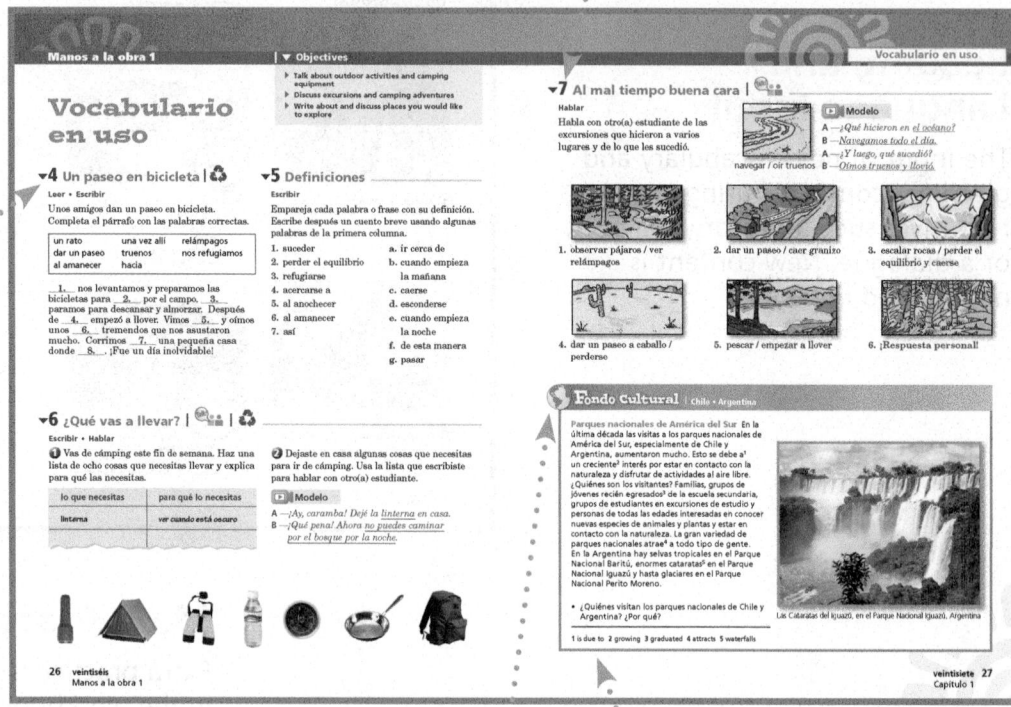

Integrated Culture

Cultural notes are embedded throughout the chapter.

Grammar Integrated with Communication

The complete grammar presentation features clear explanations and examples.

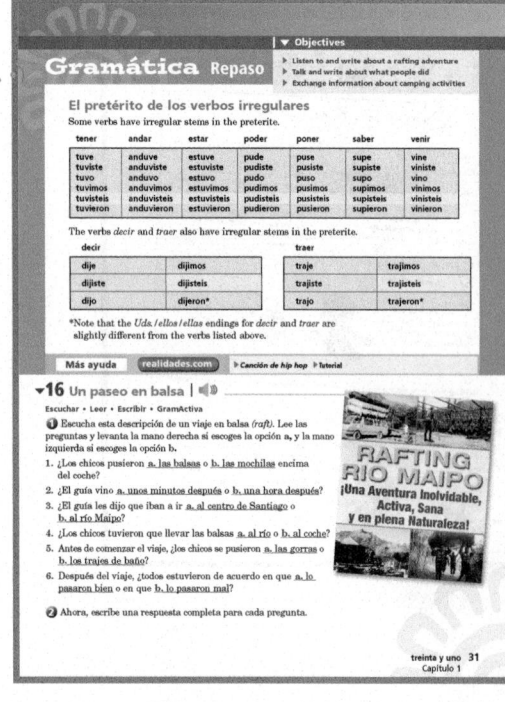

Interactive Geography

Students expand their geography skills using our online *Mapa global interactivo* activities.

Gramática y vocabulario en uso

Language and Culture

Culture is woven together with language practice.

Connections to Other Disciplines

Cross-curricular connections are integrated into the language practice.

▼11 Las estrellas del sur

Leer • Hablar

Cuando miras el cielo en una noche clara puedes ver muchas estrellas. Pero no todos ven las mismas estrellas. Lee este párrafo para aprender un poco más sobre las estrellas del hemisferio sur.

Conexiones | Las ciencias

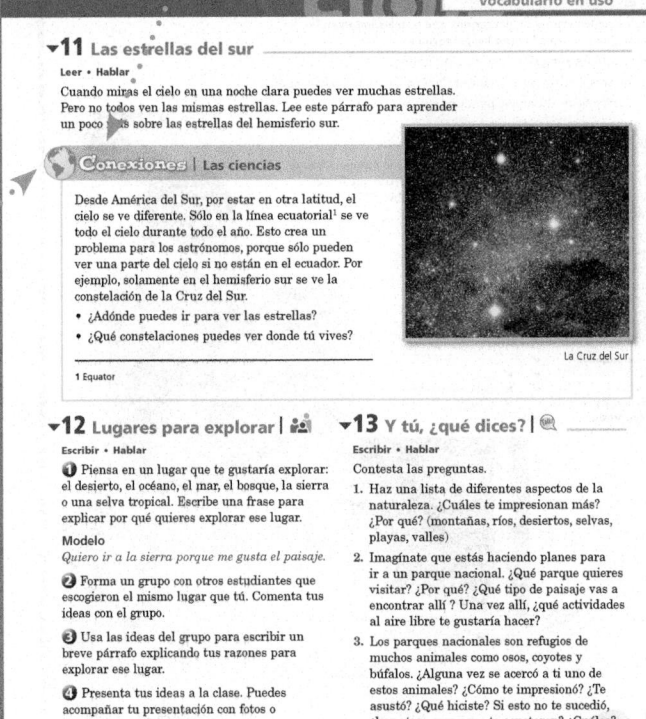

Desde América del Sur, por estar en otra latitud, el cielo se ve diferente. Sólo en la línea ecuatorial[1] se ve todo el cielo durante todo el año. Esto crea un problema para los astrónomos, porque sólo pueden ver una parte del cielo si no están en el ecuador. Por ejemplo, solamente en el hemisferio sur se ve la constelación de la Cruz del Sur.

- ¿Adónde puedes ir para ver las estrellas?
- ¿Qué constelaciones puedes ver donde tú vives?

La Cruz del Sur

1 Equator

▼12 Lugares para explorar | 👥

Escribir • Hablar

❶ Piensa en un lugar que te gustaría explorar: el desierto, el océano, el mar, el bosque, la sierra o una selva tropical. Escribe una frase para explicar por qué quieres explorar ese lugar.

Modelo
Quiero ir a la sierra porque me gusta el paisaje.

❷ Forma un grupo con otros estudiantes que escogieron el mismo lugar que tú. Comenta tus ideas con el grupo.

❸ Usa las ideas del grupo para escribir un breve párrafo explicando tus razones para explorar ese lugar.

❹ Presenta tus ideas a la clase. Puedes acompañar tu presentación con fotos o ilustraciones de ese lugar.

▼13 Y tú, ¿qué dices? | 💬

Escribir • Hablar

Contesta las preguntas.

1. Haz una lista de diferentes aspectos de la naturaleza. ¿Cuáles te impresionan más? ¿Por qué? (montañas, ríos, desiertos, selvas, playas, valles)

2. Imagínate que estás haciendo planes para ir a un parque nacional. ¿Qué parque quieres visitar? ¿Por qué? ¿Qué tipo de paisaje vas a encontrar allí ? Una vez allí, ¿qué actividades al aire libre te gustaría hacer?

3. Los parques nacionales son refugios de muchos animales como osos, coyotes y búfalos. ¿Alguna vez se acercó a ti uno de estos animales? ¿Cómo te impresionó? ¿Te asustó? ¿Qué hiciste? Si esto no te sucedió, ¿hay otras cosas que te asustaron? ¿Cuáles? Relata una ocasión en que algo te asustó y describe tu reacción.

▼24 Una caminata por Torres del Paine

Leer • Escribir

Imagínate que fuiste con unos(as) amigos(as) a hacer una excursión como la que se describe en este anuncio turístico. Escribe tres frases para describir lo que pasó en cada actividad.

Modelo
El primer día dimos una caminata muy larga.

▼25 Los Ecocamps de Torres del Paine

Leer • Escribir

Lee el texto sobre el Parque Nacional Torres del Paine y los Ecocamps y contesta las siguientes preguntas.

El Parque Nacional Torres del Paine, situado en la zona patagónica de Chile, es uno de los lugares más hermosos de nuestro planeta. Los senderos del parque ofrecen vistas magníficas del paisaje patagónico: montañas, bosques, ríos, glaciares, lagos y abundante flora y fauna. Este parque, remoto y misterioso, atrae a miles de turistas y aventureros de todo el mundo que vienen cada año a hacer caminatas, montar a caballo o navegar. Y la gran demanda por visitar el parque ha generado problemas serios de impacto ecológico y en la calidad de los servicios turísticos en general.

Una solución a este problema ha sido cambiar los hoteles por "Ecocamps", tiendas de acampar modernas, cómodas y transportables. Los "Ecocamps" permiten a los visitantes estar más cerca de la naturaleza y producen menos basura que los hoteles.

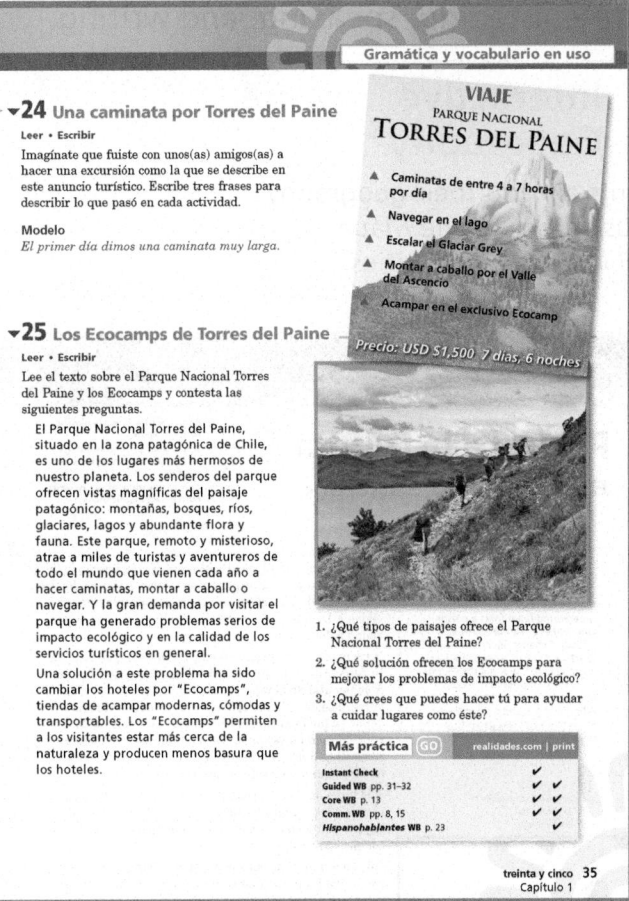

VIAJE
PARQUE NACIONAL
TORRES DEL PAINE

- ▲ Caminatas de entre 4 a 7 horas por día
- ▲ Navegar en el lago
- ▲ Escalar el Glaciar Grey
- ▲ Montar a caballo por el Valle del Ascencio
- ▲ Acampar en el exclusivo Ecocamp

Precio: USD $1,500 7 días, 6 noches

1. ¿Qué tipos de paisajes ofrece el Parque Nacional Torres del Paine?
2. ¿Qué solución ofrecen los Ecocamps para mejorar los problemas de impacto ecológico?
3. ¿Qué crees que puedes hacer tú para ayudar a cuidar lugares como éste?

Más práctica GO | realidades.com | print

Instant Check		✔
Guided WB pp. 31–32	✔	✔
Core WB p. 13	✔	✔
Comm. WB pp. 8, 15	✔	✔
Hispanohablantes WB p. 23		✔

Integrated Poetry and Song Lyrics

The pronunciation section in each chapter features poetry or song lyrics.

▼ En voz alta | 💬

¿Sabes cómo terminó el partido? Platko volvió al juego. Su equipo ganó uno de los encuentros más emocionantes de la historia del fútbol.

El equipo de Barcelona tiene unos cánticos[1] que son conocidos en todo el mundo. Se cantan en catalán, el idioma de la región de Cataluña. La mayoría de los cánticos utilizan melodías de música conocidas. Uno se puede imaginar que los aficionados de Barcelona cantaron estos cánticos muchas veces durante este partido inolvidable.

Escucha los cánticos, unos traducidos al español, y trata de repetirlos. Luego, contesta las preguntas.

- ¿Qué palabras o frases se repiten? ¿Cuál es el efecto de esta repetición?
- ¿Cuál de los tres cánticos está en catalán? En tu opinión, ¿qué significa?

Cánticos del Fútbol Club Barcelona

Cántico 1
1899, nació el club que llevo
en el corazón,
azulgrana[2] son los colores,
¡Fútbol Cluuub Barcelooona!
Le le le le le leeee,
le le le le le leeee,
¡Fútbol Cluuub Barcelooona!

Cántico 2
O le le le, o la la la
Ser del Barça es, el mejor
que hay

Cántico 3
Força Barça!

1 cheers 2 blue and scarlet

¿Recuerdas?
En América Latina y en partes de España, la c antes de las vocales e e i, y la z antes de una vocal se pronuncian como la s en inglés de la palabra *sink*. En otras regiones de España esas letras se parecen al sonido de *th* en la palabra *think*. Pronuncia estas palabras usando los dos sonidos de la letra c y escucha la diferencia: *nació, Barcelona*.

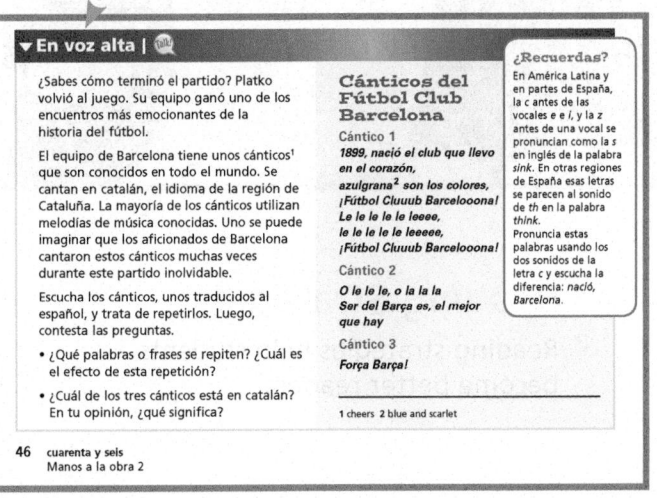

¡Adelante!

Each chapter culminates with rich and varied activities that feature cultural readings, literature, listening, speaking, and writing.

Interactive Geography

Students expand their geography skills using our online *Mapa global interactivo* activities.

Building a Bridge to Culture

High-interest cultural readings deepen cultural perspectives.

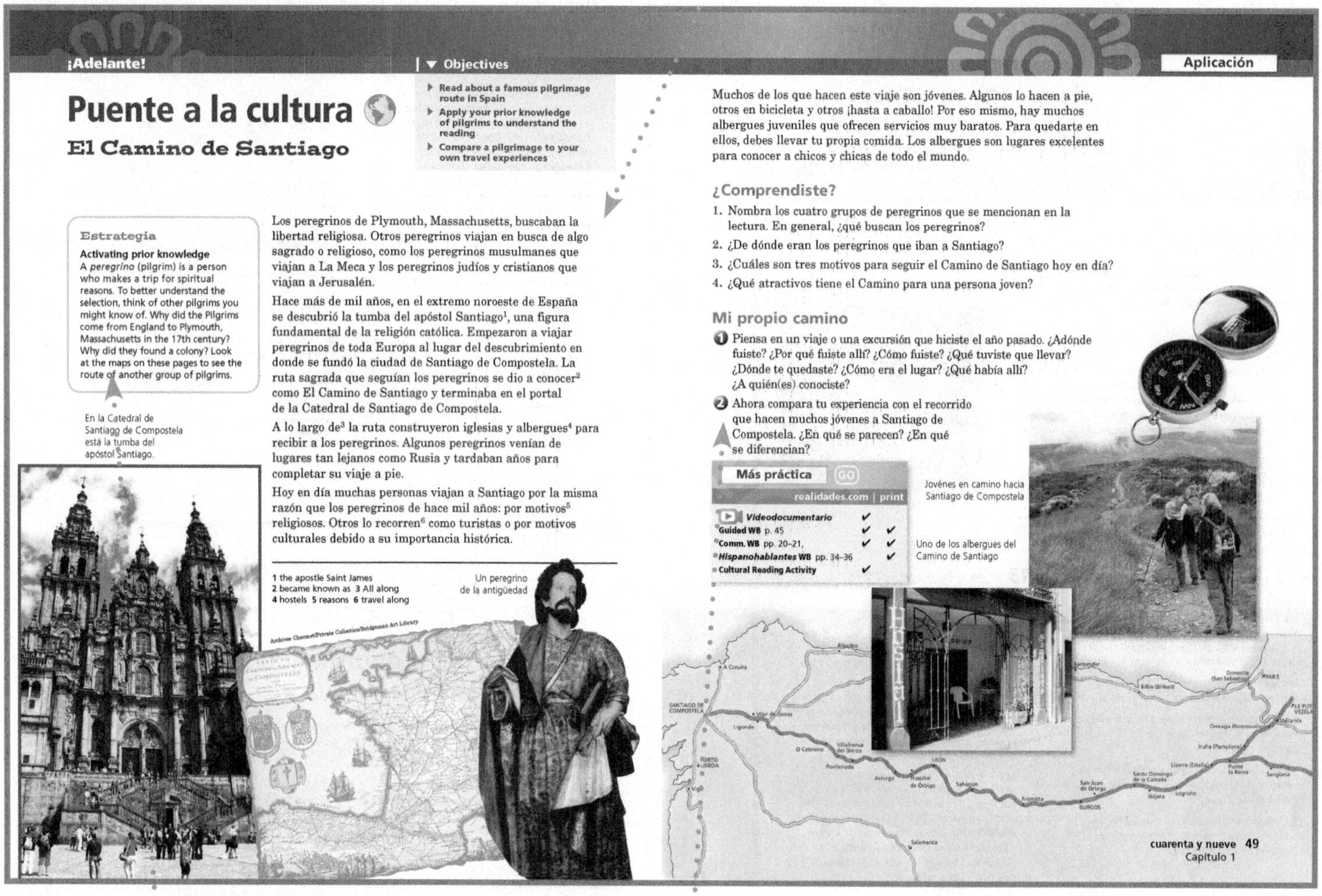

¡Adelante!

Puente a la cultura

El Camino de Santiago

▼ Objectives

▶ Read about a famous pilgrimage route in Spain

▶ Apply your prior knowledge of pilgrims to understand the reading

▶ Compare a pilgrimage to your own travel experiences

Estrategia

Activating prior knowledge
A *peregrino* (pilgrim) is a person who makes a trip for spiritual reasons. To better understand the selection, think of other pilgrims you might know of. Why did the Pilgrims come from England to Plymouth, Massachusetts in the 17th century? Why did they found a colony? Look at the maps on these pages to see the route of another group of pilgrims.

En la Catedral de Santiago de Compostela está la tumba del apóstol Santiago.

Los peregrinos de Plymouth, Massachusetts, buscaban la libertad religiosa. Otros peregrinos viajan en busca de algo sagrado o religioso, como los peregrinos musulmanes que viajan a La Meca y los peregrinos judíos y cristianos que viajan a Jerusalén.

Hace más de mil años, en el extremo noroeste de España se descubrió la tumba del apóstol Santiago[1], una figura fundamental de la religión católica. Empezaron a viajar peregrinos de toda Europa al lugar del descubrimiento en donde se fundó la ciudad de Santiago de Compostela. La ruta sagrada que seguían los peregrinos se dio a conocer[2] como El Camino de Santiago y terminaba en el portal de la Catedral de Santiago de Compostela.

A lo largo de[3] la ruta construyeron iglesias y albergues[4] para recibir a los peregrinos. Algunos peregrinos venían de lugares tan lejanos como Rusia y tardaban años para completar su viaje a pie.

Hoy en día muchas personas viajan a Santiago por la misma razón que los peregrinos de hace mil años: por motivos[5] religiosos. Otros lo recorren[6] como turistas o por motivos culturales debido a su importancia histórica.

1 the apostle Saint James
2 became known as 3 All along
4 hostels 5 reasons 6 travel along

Un peregrino de la antigüedad

Aplicación

Muchos de los que hacen este viaje son jóvenes. Algunos lo hacen a pie, otros en bicicleta y otros ¡hasta a caballo! Por eso mismo, hay muchos albergues juveniles que ofrecen servicios muy baratos. Para quedarte en ellos, debes llevar tu propia comida. Los albergues son lugares excelentes para conocer a chicos y chicas de todo el mundo.

¿Comprendiste?

1. Nombra los cuatro grupos de peregrinos que se mencionan en la lectura. En general, ¿qué buscan los peregrinos?
2. ¿De dónde eran los peregrinos que iban a Santiago?
3. ¿Cuáles son tres motivos para seguir el Camino de Santiago hoy en día?
4. ¿Qué atractivos tiene el Camino para una persona joven?

Mi propio camino

1 Piensa en un viaje o una excursión que hiciste el año pasado. ¿Adónde fuiste? ¿Por qué fuiste allí? ¿Cómo fuiste? ¿Qué tuviste que llevar? ¿Dónde te quedaste? ¿Cómo era el lugar? ¿Qué había allí? ¿A quién(es) conociste?

2 Ahora compara tu experiencia con el recorrido que hacen muchos jóvenes a Santiago de Compostela. ¿En qué se parecen? ¿En qué se diferencian?

Más práctica GO

realidades.com | print

▶ *Videodocumentario*	✔	
Guided WB p. 45	✔	✔
Comm. WB pp. 20–21,	✔	✔
Hispanohablantes WB pp. 34–36	✔	
● *Cultural Reading Activity*	✔	

Jóvenes en camino hacia Santiago de Compostela

Uno de los albergues del Camino de Santiago

cuarenta y nueve 49
Capítulo 1

Reading Strategies

Reading strategies help students become better readers.

Comprehension Checks

Follow-up questions check students' comprehension.

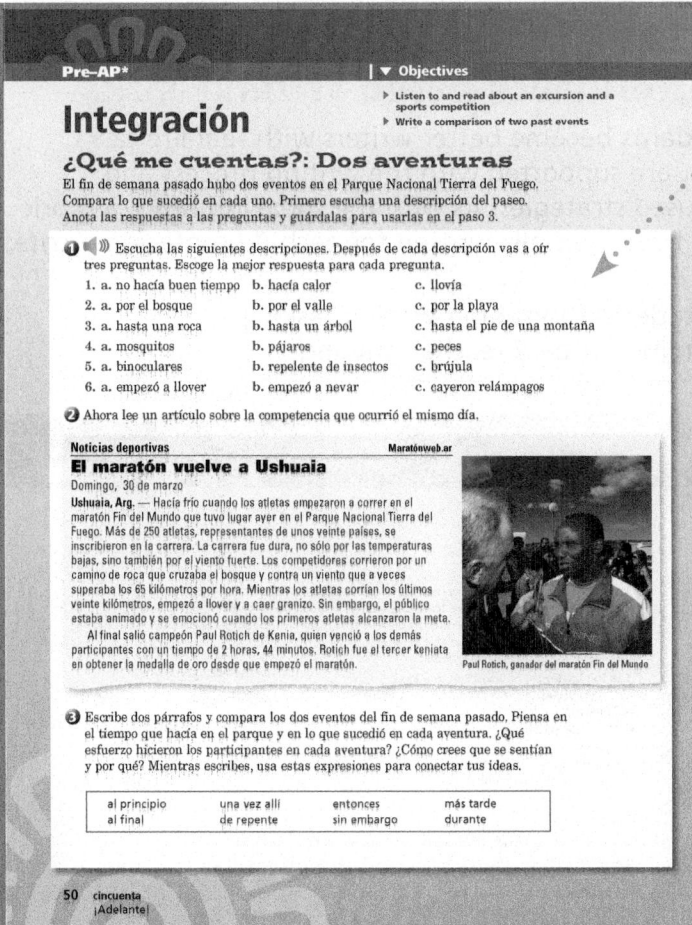

 ## Integrated Skills Activity

Students expand multiple skills as they write or speak on current topics using information from audio recordings and authentic readings.

 Common Core: Speaking

Performance-based Speaking Task

Real-life speaking tasks are supported by strategies and a step-by-step process that helps all students to be successful. A rubric for this task appears at the bottom of the page.

Students can record their speaking using RealTalk!

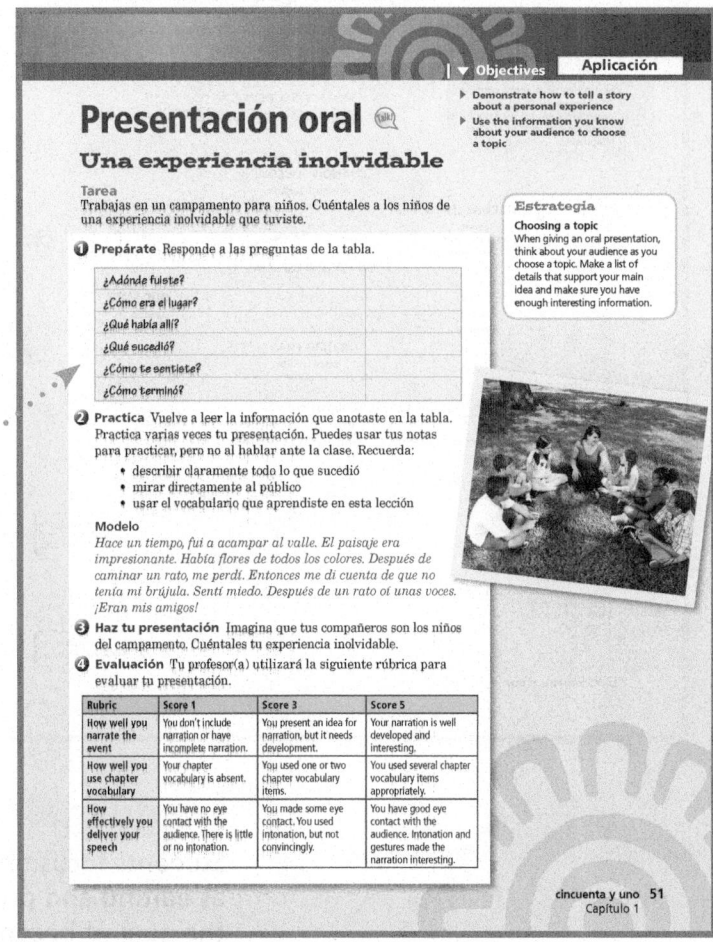

 **Common Core: Writing**

Performance-based Writing Tasks

Students become better writers with real-life tasks that are supported with the writing process and focused strategies. As with the speaking tasks, a rubric has been specially written for each *Presentación escrita*.

Students can submit writing tasks online for easy teacher grading!

| ▼ Objectives | Aplicación |

▶ Narrate a special experience in the past tense
▶ Add details in order to improve the story

Presentación escrita

Aventuras bajo el sol

Estrategia

Adding details
Adding details to our writing makes it more interesting. If you say *"oí un ruido y me asusté,"* the reader cannot imagine the setting very well. But if you write: *"En la oscuridad de la noche, sentí un ruido como de un trueno . . . comencé a gritar,"* your reader will have a better picture of what happened.

Imagínate que acabas de participar en una de las actividades que muestran las fotos de este capítulo. Escribe un cuento sobre esa aventura. ¿Quiénes participaron? ¿Cómo era el lugar? ¿Qué querían ver? ¿Cómo lo pasaron? ¿Fue emocionante? ¿Cómo te sentiste al final?

1 Antes de escribir

Usa una red de palabras para organizar tus ideas.

- **CUÁNDO SUCEDIÓ** — el verano pasado
- **ENTRENAMIENTO** — correr, levantar pesas
- **DÓNDE SUCEDIÓ** — valle
- **UN EVENTO ESPECIAL**
- **EQUIPO** — brújula, linternas
- **LO QUE SENTÍ** — miedo
- **CÓMO ERA** — emocionante

2 Borrador

Escribe tu borrador. Usa el pretérito y el imperfecto y el vocabulario de esta lección. Escribe tus ideas en orden lógico, así tu cuento va a ser más interesante y más fácil de entender.

Modelo

Topic sentence: What is the composition about?

Hace dos semanas yo fui con mis amigos a escalar una montaña. Me entrené dos meses: todas las tardes corría media hora y levantaba pesas. . . .

Details about the topic: preparing for the trip.

Description of the trip: how it was and how I felt.

Al llegar al pie de la montaña, me di cuenta de lo alta que era. Iba a ser una dura prueba. Comenzamos a escalar la montaña con cuidado. Después de cuatro horas de esfuerzo alcanzamos nuestra meta. Desde lo alto . . . .

Al final de esta aventura estuve muy contenta . . . .

Conclusion ties everything together.

3 Redacción/Revisión

Después de escribir el primer borrador de la composición, trabaja con otro(a) estudiante para intercambiar los trabajos y leerlos. Decidan qué aspectos son más efectivos. Fíjense en cómo el escritor del modelo incluyó detalles en su composición. Cada persona puede decir qué se puede hacer para mejorar la composición que leyó.

Haz lo siguiente: Subraya con una línea los verbos en pretérito y con dos líneas los verbos en imperfecto.

- ¿Hay concordancia *(agreement)* entre cada sujeto y verbo?
- ¿El pretérito y el imperfecto están empleados correctamente?

Hace dos semanas yo ~~fuer~~ fui con mis amigos a escalar una montaña. Me entrené dos meses; todas las tardes ~~corría~~ corrió media hora y levantaba pesas.

4 Publicación

Antes de crear la versión final, lee de nuevo tu borrador y repasa los siguientes puntos:

- ¿Sigue mi cuento un orden lógico?
- ¿Tiene un argumento, con un principio, un cuerpo y un final?
- ¿Hay otros detalles que debo poner en mi composición? ¿Hay algo que debo quitar?

Después de revisar el borrador, escribe tu composición en limpio.

5 Evaluación

Se utilizará la siguiente rúbrica para evaluar tu presentación.

Rubric	Score 1	Score 3	Score 5
Completion of task	You don't highlight any special event.	Your idea for narration is present but needs development.	Your special event is clearly narrated and made prominent.
Organization and level of detail	Your ideas aren't presented in logical order nor with detail.	You have some organizational problems. One or two details are provided.	Your organization is easy to follow. You use good details.
Sentence structure	Your sentences are run-on or are fragmented with many errors.	You use sentences consistently, but with some errors.	Your sentence structure is correct with few errors.

52 cincuenta y dos
¡Adelante!

cincuenta y tres 53
Capítulo 1

Language Arts Skills

Students focus on writing skills such as editing and proofreading with the goal of becoming better writers.

Interactive Geography

Students expand their geography skills using our online *Mapa global interactivo* activities.

Strategy

Reading strategies support comprehension.

¡Adelante!

▼ Objectives
- ▶ Read and understand a Mexican legend
- ▶ Make predictions to increase interest
- ▶ Discuss legends that explain natural phenomena

Aplicación

Lectura
El Iztaccíhuatl y el Popocatépetl

Estrategia

Making predictions
Making predictions about what will happen in a story allows us to focus on what we read and increases our interest in the story.
- Do you know any stories that explain a natural phenomenon?
- Look at the picture of the volcanoes. What do you think this story will explain?

Al leer

El cuento que vas a leer es una leyenda mexicana que relaciona una historia de amor con dos volcanes en México. Copia la gráfica organizadora de la página 57. Mientras lees la selección, llena todos los espacios de la gráfica con la información del cuento.

Mientras lees, presta atención a los siguientes puntos:
- el conflicto entre las dos familias
- la relación entre los personajes principales y la naturaleza

Hace mucho tiempo, en la gran ciudad de Teotihuacán, había un rey tolteca que tenía una hija muy hermosa. El pelo de la princesa era tan negro y suave como una noche de verano, sus ojos eran tan grandes y oscuros como las aguas de un lago secreto y su sonrisa era tan bonita que decían que el sol miraba a las montañas todas las mañanas para ser el primero en verla.

Muchos príncipes ricos y famosos venían de todas partes de la región tolteca para ganar el amor de la princesa, pero ella no se enamoraba de ninguno. El rey, que quería para su hija un esposo rico de buena posición en la sociedad tolteca, ya estaba impaciente. A veces le preguntaba a la princesa qué esperaba.

—No sé —contestaba la muchacha—. Sólo sé que mi esposo va a ser alguien que voy a amar desde el principio y para siempre.

Un día llegó a la ciudad un príncipe chichimeca. Los chichimecas no tenían una civilización tan espléndida como la de los toltecas. Vivían de la caza[1] y la pesca en las montañas. Los toltecas pensaban que los chichimecas vivían como perros, y se reían de ellos.

1 hunting

Príncipe chichimeca

El príncipe chichimeca venía para visitar el gran mercado de Teotihuacán, donde vendían hermosísimos objetos de oro, ropa de brillantes colores, animales exóticos y muchas otras cosas.

Ese mismo día, la princesa tolteca estaba en el mercado comprando canastas[2], telas y alfombras para su palacio. Pasó que, de repente, entre toda la gente y el ruido del mercado, el príncipe y la princesa se fijaron[3] uno en el otro. Sin una palabra, desde el principio y para siempre, el príncipe y la princesa se enamoraron.

Los dos sabían muy bien que su amor era prohibido. Cada uno debía casarse con alguien de su pueblo y su clase: la princesa tolteca con un príncipe tolteca y el príncipe chichimeca con una princesa chichimeca.

2 large round basket 3 they noticed

Aplicación

Las señoras que acompañaban[4] a la princesa se dieron cuenta de lo que pasaba, y rápidamente llevaron a la princesa a su palacio. El príncipe también regresó al suyo en las montañas. Trató de olvidar a la bella princesa, pero no pudo.

Después de un tiempo, el príncipe decidió volver a Teotihuacán, a pedir la mano de la princesa. Un día se vistió de su ropa más fina y fue al palacio del rey tolteca. Allí mandó[5] a sus mensajeros a hablar con el rey para pedirle a su hija como esposa.

Cuando oyó las palabras de los mensajeros del príncipe, el rey tembló[6] de furia y gritó:
—¡Mi hija sólo se va a casar con un príncipe tolteca, nunca con un chichimeca que vive en las montañas como un animal!

4 escorted 5 sent 6 shook

Princesa tolteca

cincuenta y cinco **55**
Capítulo 1

Authentic Literature

Students read a wide range of authentic literature.

🄫 **Common Core: Reading**

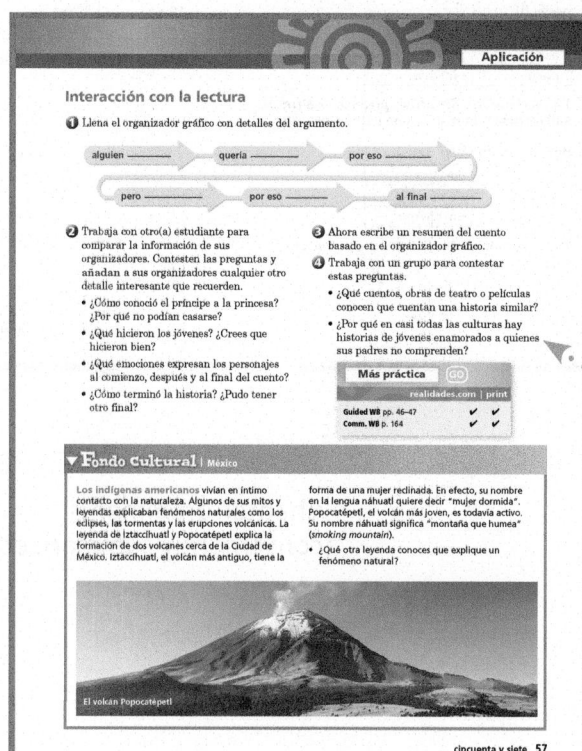

Aplicación

Interacción con la lectura

❶ Llena el organizador gráfico con detalles del argumento.

alguien ——— quería ——— por eso ———
pero ——— por eso ——— al final ———

❷ Trabaja con otro(a) estudiante para comparar la información de sus organizadores. Contesten las preguntas y añadan a sus organizadores cualquier otro detalle interesante que recuerden.
- ¿Cómo conoció el príncipe a la princesa? ¿Por qué no podían casarse?
- ¿Qué hicieron los jóvenes? ¿Crees que hicieron bien?
- ¿Qué emociones expresan los personajes al comienzo, después y al final del cuento?
- ¿Cómo terminó la historia? ¿Pudo tener otro final?

❸ Ahora escribe un resumen del cuento basado en el organizador gráfico.

❹ Trabaja con un grupo para contestar estas preguntas.
- ¿Qué cuentos, obras de teatro o películas conocen que cuentan una historia similar?
- ¿Por qué en casi todas las culturas hay historias de jóvenes enamorados a quienes sus padres no comprenden?

Más práctica GO
realidades.com | print
Guided WB pp. 46-47 ✔ ✔
Comm. WB p. 164 ✔

▼ Fondo Cultural | México

Los indígenas americanos vivían en íntimo contacto con la naturaleza. Algunos de sus mitos y leyendas explicaban fenómenos naturales como los eclipses, las tormentas y las erupciones volcánicas. La leyenda de Iztaccíhuatl y Popocatépetl explica la formación de dos volcanes cerca de la Ciudad de México. Iztaccíhuatl, el volcán más antiguo, tiene la

forma de una mujer reclinada. En efecto, su nombre en la lengua náhuatl quiere decir "mujer dormida". Popocatépetl, el volcán más joven, es todavía activo. Su nombre náhuatl significa "montaña que humea" (*smoking mountain*).
- ¿Qué otra leyenda conoces que explique un fenómeno natural?

El volcán Popocatépetl

cincuenta y siete **57**
Capítulo 1

Comprehension Checks

A variety of questions check students' comprehension of and reaction to the literature.

Repaso del capítulo

These four pages provide complete review and preparation for the chapter test.

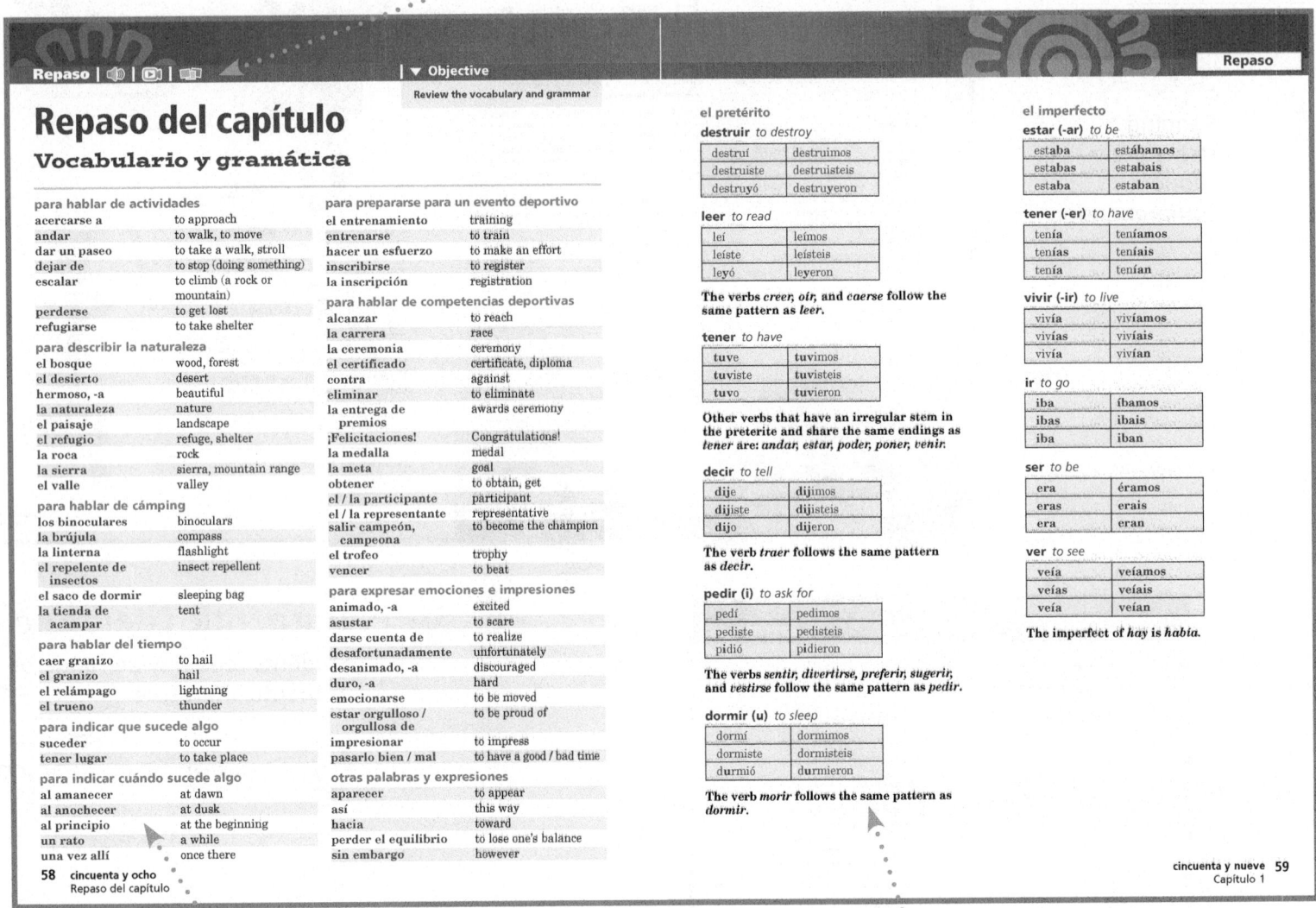

Repaso | 🔊 | ▶️ | 🖥️   ▼ Objective
Review the vocabulary and grammar

Repaso del capítulo
Vocabulario y gramática

para hablar de actividades
acercarse a	to approach
andar	to walk, to move
dar un paseo	to take a walk, stroll
dejar de	to stop (doing something)
escalar	to climb (a rock or mountain)
perderse	to get lost
refugiarse	to take shelter

para describir la naturaleza
el bosque	wood, forest
el desierto	desert
hermoso, -a	beautiful
la naturaleza	nature
el paisaje	landscape
el refugio	refuge, shelter
la roca	rock
la sierra	sierra, mountain range
el valle	valley

para hablar de cámping
los binoculares	binoculars
la brújula	compass
la linterna	flashlight
el repelente de insectos	insect repellent
el saco de dormir	sleeping bag
la tienda de acampar	tent

para hablar del tiempo
caer granizo	to hail
el granizo	hail
el relámpago	lightning
el trueno	thunder

para indicar que sucede algo
suceder	to occur
tener lugar	to take place

para indicar cuándo sucede algo
al amanecer	at dawn
al anochecer	at dusk
al principio	at the beginning
un rato	a while
una vez allí	once there

para prepararse para un evento deportivo
el entrenamiento	training
entrenarse	to train
hacer un esfuerzo	to make an effort
inscribirse	to register
la inscripción	registration

para hablar de competencias deportivas
alcanzar	to reach
la carrera	race
la ceremonia	ceremony
el certificado	certificate, diploma
contra	against
eliminar	to eliminate
la entrega de premios	awards ceremony
¡Felicitaciones!	Congratulations!
la medalla	medal
la meta	goal
obtener	to obtain, get
el / la participante	participant
el / la representante	representative
salir campeón, campeona	to become the champion
el trofeo	trophy
vencer	to beat

para expresar emociones e impresiones
animado, -a	excited
asustar	to scare
darse cuenta de	to realize
desafortunadamente	unfortunately
desanimado, -a	discouraged
duro, -a	hard
emocionarse	to be moved
estar orgulloso / orgullosa de	to be proud of
impresionar	to impress
pasarlo bien / mal	to have a good / bad time

otras palabras y expresiones
aparecer	to appear
así	this way
hacia	toward
perder el equilibrio	to lose one's balance
sin embargo	however

el pretérito

destruir *to destroy*
destruí	destruimos
destruiste	destruisteis
destruyó	destruyeron

leer *to read*
leí	leímos
leíste	leísteis
leyó	leyeron

The verbs *creer, oír,* and *caerse* follow the same pattern as *leer.*

tener *to have*
tuve	tuvimos
tuviste	tuvisteis
tuvo	tuvieron

Other verbs that have an irregular stem in the preterite and share the same endings as *tener* are: *andar, estar, poder, poner, venir.*

decir *to tell*
dije	dijimos
dijiste	dijisteis
dijo	dijeron

The verb *traer* follows the same pattern as *decir.*

pedir (i) *to ask for*
pedí	pedimos
pediste	pedisteis
pidió	pidieron

The verbs *sentir, divertirse, preferir, sugerir,* and *vestirse* follow the same pattern as *pedir.*

dormir (u) *to sleep*
dormí	dormimos
dormiste	dormisteis
durmió	durmieron

The verb *morir* follows the same pattern as *dormir.*

el imperfecto

estar (-ar) *to be*
estaba	estábamos
estabas	estabais
estaba	estaban

tener (-er) *to have*
tenía	teníamos
tenías	teníais
tenía	tenían

vivir (-ir) *to live*
vivía	vivíamos
vivías	vivíais
vivía	vivían

ir *to go*
iba	íbamos
ibas	ibais
iba	iban

ser *to be*
era	éramos
eras	erais
era	eran

ver *to see*
veía	veíamos
veías	veíais
veía	veían

The imperfect of *hay* is *había.*

58 cincuenta y ocho
Repaso del capítulo

cincuenta y nueve **59**
Capítulo 1

Repaso

Vocabulary List
Chapter vocabulary is listed as language functions and with English translations.

Grammar Summary
Chapter grammar is conveniently summarized.

Test Preparation:
Vocabulary and Grammar

This page practices new content using an achievement test format.

Instant Check

End-of-chapter activity provides extra practice.

Review Games

Online interactive games make review fun!

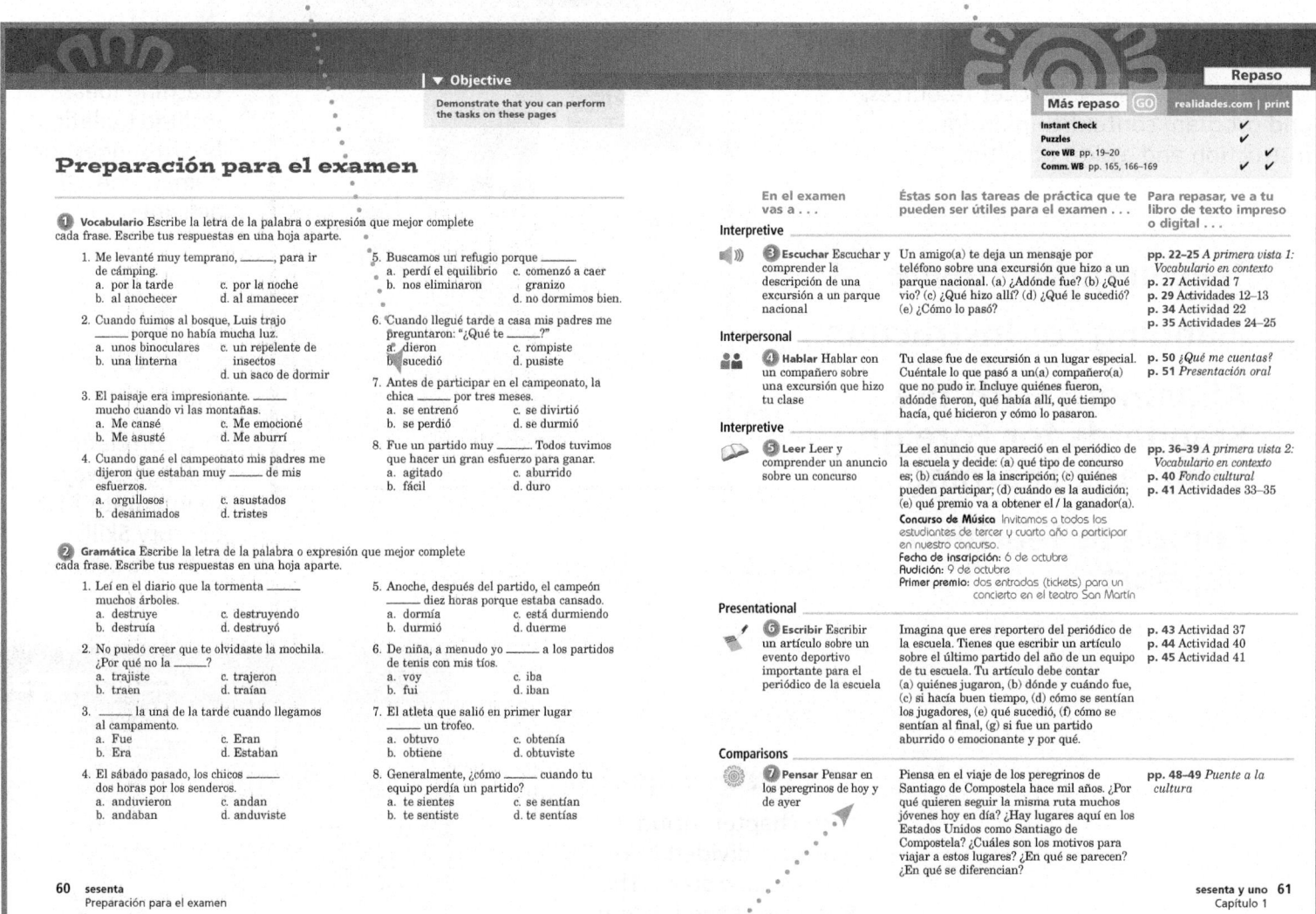

▼ Objective

Demonstrate that you can perform the tasks on these pages

Repaso

Más repaso GO realidades.com | print

Instant Check	✔
Puzzles	✔
Core WB pp. 19–20	✔
Comm. WB pp. 165, 166–169	✔ ✔

Preparación para el examen

1 Vocabulario Escribe la letra de la palabra o expresión que mejor complete cada frase. Escribe tus respuestas en una hoja aparte.

1. Me levanté muy temprano, _____, para ir de cámping.
   a. por la tarde   c. por la noche
   b. al anochecer   d. al amanecer

2. Cuando fuimos al bosque, Luis trajo _____ porque no había mucha luz.
   a. unos binoculares   c. un repelente de insectos
   b. una linterna   d. un saco de dormir

3. El paisaje era impresionante. _____ mucho cuando vi las montañas.
   a. Me cansé   c. Me emocioné
   b. Me asusté   d. Me aburrí

4. Cuando gané el campeonato mis padres me dijeron que estaban muy _____ de mis esfuerzos.
   a. orgullosos   c. asustados
   b. desanimados   d. tristes

5. Buscamos un refugio porque _____.
   a. perdí el equilibrio   c. comenzó a caer granizo
   b. nos eliminaron   d. no dormimos bien.

6. Cuando llegué tarde a casa mis padres me preguntaron: "¿Qué te _____?"
   a. dieron   c. rompiste
   b. sucedió   d. pusiste

7. Antes de participar en el campeonato, la chica _____ por tres meses.
   a. se entrenó   c. se divirtió
   b. se perdió   d. se durmió

8. Fue un partido muy _____. Todos tuvimos que hacer un gran esfuerzo para ganar.
   a. agitado   c. aburrido
   b. fácil   d. duro

2 Gramática Escribe la letra de la palabra o expresión que mejor complete cada frase. Escribe tus respuestas en una hoja aparte.

1. Leí en el diario que la tormenta _____ muchos árboles.
   a. destruye   c. destruyendo
   b. destruía   d. destruyó

2. No puedo creer que te olvidaste la mochila. ¿Por qué no la _____?
   a. trajiste   c. trajeron
   b. traen   d. traían

3. _____ la una de la tarde cuando llegamos al campamento.
   a. Fue   c. Eran
   b. Era   d. Estaban

4. El sábado pasado, los chicos _____ dos horas por los senderos.
   a. anduvieron   c. andan
   b. andaban   d. anduviste

5. Anoche, después del partido, el campeón _____ diez horas porque estaba cansado.
   a. dormía   c. está durmiendo
   b. durmió   d. duerme

6. De niña, a menudo yo _____ a los partidos de tenis con mis tíos.
   a. voy   c. iba
   b. fui   d. iban

7. El atleta que salió en primer lugar _____ un trofeo.
   a. obtuvo   c. obtenía
   b. obtiene   d. obtuviste

8. Generalmente, ¿cómo _____ cuando tu equipo perdía un partido?
   a. te sientes   c. se sentían
   b. te sentiste   d. te sentías

60 sesenta
Preparación para el examen

En el examen vas a . . .	Éstas son las tareas de práctica que te pueden ser útiles para el examen . . .	Para repasar, ve a tu libro de texto impreso o digital . . .
Interpretive		
3 Escuchar Escuchar y comprender la descripción de una excursión a un parque nacional	Un amigo(a) te deja un mensaje por teléfono sobre una excursión que hizo a un parque nacional. (a) ¿Adónde fue? (b) ¿Qué vio? (c) ¿Qué hizo allí? (d) ¿Qué le sucedió? (e) ¿Cómo lo pasó?	pp. 22–25 *A primera vista 1: Vocabulario en contexto* p. 27 Actividad 7 p. 29 Actividades 12–13 p. 34 Actividad 22 p. 35 Actividades 24–25
Interpersonal		
4 Hablar Hablar con un compañero sobre una excursión que hizo tu clase	Tu clase fue de excursión a un lugar especial. Cuéntale lo que pasó a un(a) compañero(a) que no pudo ir. Incluye quiénes fueron, adónde fueron, qué había allí, qué tiempo hacía, qué hicieron y cómo lo pasaron.	p. 50 *¿Qué me cuentas?* p. 51 *Presentación oral*
Interpretive		
5 Leer Leer y comprender un anuncio sobre un concurso	Lee el anuncio que apareció en el periódico de la escuela y decide: (a) qué tipo de concurso es; (b) cuándo es la inscripción; (c) quiénes pueden participar; (d) cuándo es la audición; (e) qué premio va a obtener el / la ganador(a). **Concurso de Música** Invitamos a todos los estudiantes de tercer y cuarto año a participar en nuestro concurso. **Fecha de inscripción:** 6 de octubre **Audición:** 9 de octubre **Primer premio:** dos entradas (tickets) para un concierto en el teatro San Martín	pp. 36–39 *A primera vista 2: Vocabulario en contexto* p. 40 *Fondo cultural* p. 41 Actividades 33–35
Presentational		
6 Escribir Escribir un artículo sobre un evento deportivo importante para el periódico de la escuela	Imagina que eres reportero del periódico de la escuela. Tienes que escribir un artículo sobre el último partido del año de un equipo de tu escuela. Tu artículo debe contar (a) quiénes jugaron, (b) dónde y cuándo fue, (c) si hacía buen tiempo, (d) cómo se sentían los jugadores, (e) qué sucedió, (f) cómo se sentían al final, (g) si fue un partido aburrido o emocionante y por qué.	p. 43 Actividad 37 p. 44 Actividad 40 p. 45 Actividad 41
Comparisons		
7 Pensar Pensar en los peregrinos de hoy y de ayer	Piensa en el viaje de los peregrinos de Santiago de Compostela hace mil años. ¿Por qué quieren seguir la misma ruta muchos jóvenes hoy en día? ¿Hay lugares aquí en los Estados Unidos como Santiago de Compostela? ¿Cuáles son los motivos para viajar a estos lugares? ¿En qué se parecen? ¿En qué se diferencian?	pp. 48–49 *Puente a la cultura*

sesenta y uno 61
Capítulo 1

Test Preparation:
Proficiency and Culture

This page prepares students for the proficiency and culture sections of the chapter test. Students are told how they will be tested, what the task might be like, and how to review.

Using the Teacher's Edition

realidades.com

Use the Lesson Plans, teacher resources, and program content to plan for instruction and assign activities.

▶ **Teaching the Theme**

▶ **Planning for Instruction**

▶ **Alignment with the Standards for Foreign Language Learning**

▶ **Complete Teaching Support**

Teaching the Theme

The Teacher's Edition provides complete planning support for teaching the themes.

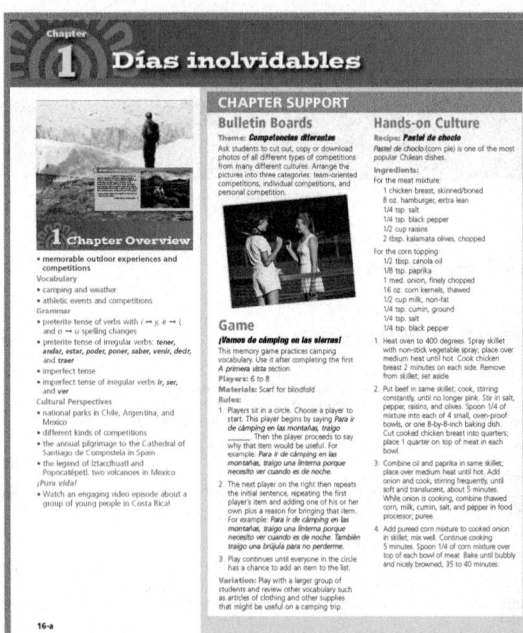

Chapter Support

Time-saving teaching ideas include bulletin board suggestions, games, and other activities.

21st Century Skills

This correlation highlights ways to integrate 21st Century Skills into instruction.

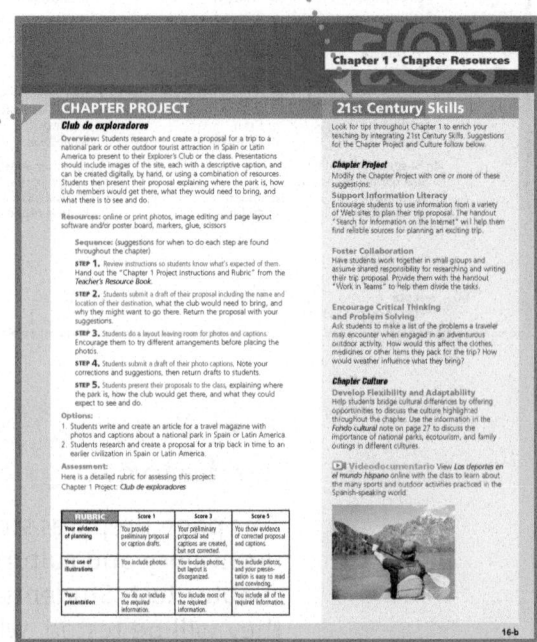

Chapter Project

Each chapter includes a project divided into manageable steps. The Rubric is at the bottom of the page as well as in the Teacher's Resource Book and in the Assessment Program.

Planning for Instruction

The Teacher's Edition provides six pages of planning support interleaved at the beginning of each chapter.

Chapter Overview

This section gives a quick overview of each chapter.

Program Resources

This section shows all the program resources available for this chapter. All resources are conveniently referenced at point of use in the chapter.

Lesson Plans

Lesson Plans are provided for instruction on the regular or block schedule.

Lesson plans are also available on **realidades.com.**

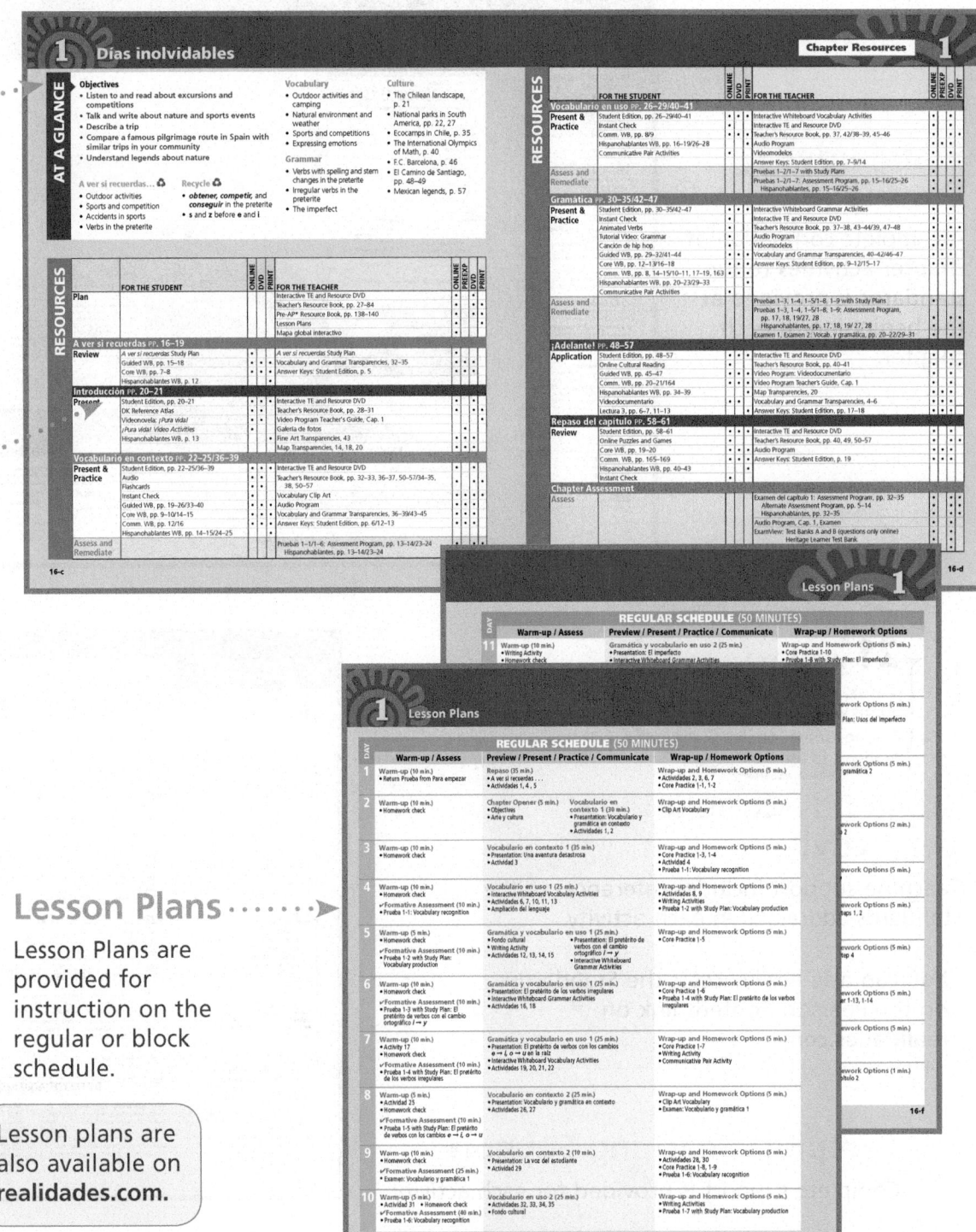

Alignment with the Standards for Foreign Language Learning

Realidades is fully aligned with the Standards for Foreign Language Learning. Correlations to the standards are provided throughout the Teacher's Edition.

Standards Correlation

A complete correlation of chapter activities to the standards is provided at the beginning of each chapter.

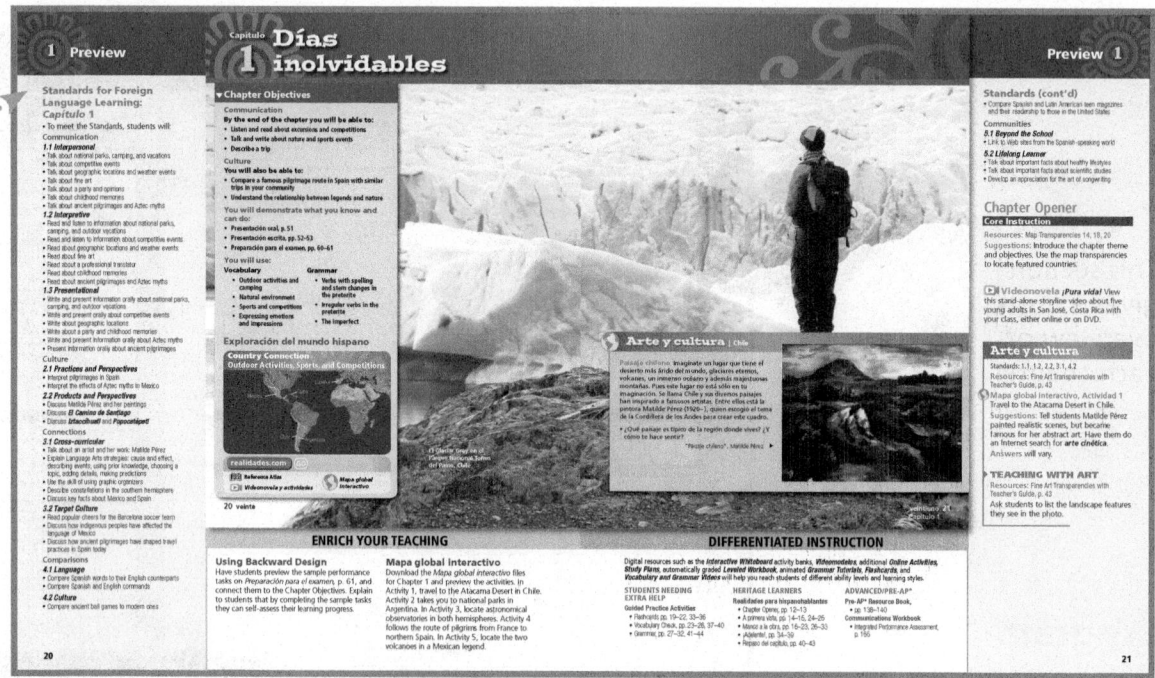

Standards Correlation per Activity

Teaching support includes references to the standards addressed in each activity.

You can also easily access the Standards on the Pearson Content link on **realidades.com**.

Complete Teaching Support

Complete support is provided for each activity.

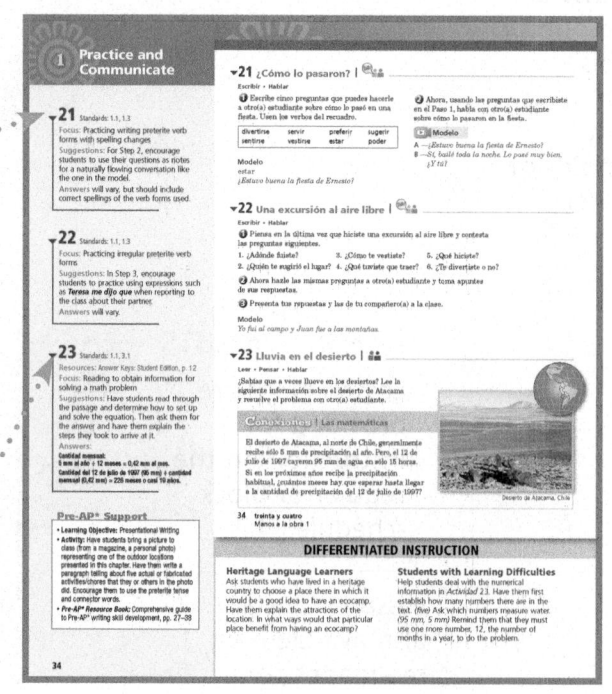

Complete Teaching Support

Realidades provides teachers with complete instructional support in both print and technology formats.

Chapter Objectives

Each chapter provides a well-organized structure, clear student outcomes based upon the standards, and a variety of activities that develop all language skills.

> ### Objectives
> - Listen to and read about activities people like and don't like to do
> - Talk and write about what you and others like and don't like to do
> - Describe your favorite activities and ask others about theirs
> - Describe dances and music from the Spanish-speaking world and compare them to dances you know
> - Compare favorite activities of Spanish-speaking teens to those of teens in the United States

Assessment

Teachers are provided with multiple print and technology tools that measure student progress in listening, speaking, reading, and writing. The program also offers an Integrated Performance Assessment for each chapter.

✔ASSESSMENT

Prueba 1A-2 with Study Plan (online only)

Quiz: Vocabulary Production
Prueba 1A-2: pp. 15–16

Más repaso GO

Instant Check
Puzzles
Core WB pp. 20–21
Comm. WB pp. 117, 118–120

Presentación oral (Talk?)

A mí me gusta mucho . . .

Task
You are a new student at school and have been asked to tell the class a little bit about your likes and dislikes.

Differentiated Instruction

Realidades provides teaching suggestions to help all students learn Spanish. Each level also provides differentiated assessment.

DIFFERENTIATED INSTRUCTION

Students with Learning Difficulties
Have students review the *Repaso del capítulo* and create flashcards for any words that they do not know. Pair them with a student who is more confident with the vocabulary to practice. Before the test, provide students with a practice test, so they can become comfortable with the format.

Heritage Language Learners
Have students write a few paragraphs telling about their perfect day: What activities are they going to do? Whom are they going to invite? What activities do they like the most? Encourage them to use as many vocabulary words from this chapter as they can.

DIFFERENTIATED ASSESSMENT

CORE ASSESSMENT
- **Assessment Program:** Examen del capítulo 1A, pp. 19–25
- **Audio Program DVD:** Cap. 1A, Track 23
- **ExamView:** Chapter Test, Test Banks A and B
ADVANCED/PRE-AP*
- **ExamView:** Pre-AP* Test Bank
- **Pre-AP* Resource Book,** pp. 61–65

STUDENTS NEEDING EXTRA HELP
- **Alternate Assessment Program:** Examen del capítulo 1A
- **Audio Program DVD:** Cap. 1A, Track 23
HERITAGE LEARNERS
- **Assessment Program:** Realidades para hispanohablantes: Examen del capítulo 1A
- **ExamView:** Heritage Learner Test Bank

Instructional Planning and Support

Realidades provides complete planning and teaching support. The Teacher's Edition, the Interactive Teacher's Edition and Resources DVD, the PresentationEXPRESS™ DVD, **realidades.com**, and other program components provide time-saving teaching tools to help you teach all your students.

Assessment

An assessment program in a second language classroom should be based on the premise that the main purpose of learning a language is to communicate in a meaningful and culturally appropriate way. As you begin to teach a unit of instruction, you might want to start by asking a few key questions: What do I expect my students to learn? What do I want them to be able to do? How can I assess what I am looking for in student performance?

Topics covered:

▶ Assessing Student Progress

▶ Purposes of Assessment

▶ Forms of Assessment

▶ *Realidades* and the ACTFL Performance Guidelines

▶ Integrating Technology with Assessment

▶ Assessment Resources in *Realidades*

> 66 Performance assessment does not determine *who* is best but helps learners *do* their best. 99
> —*Challenge for a New Era;*
> *Nebraska K–12 Foreign*
> *Language Frameworks*

Assessing Student Progress

The role of assessment in the world languages classroom is to provide both the teacher and students with a measure of progress toward achieving predetermined outcomes. It is an integral and ongoing part of the learning process. Here are key factors to consider as you develop curriculum that aligns assessment with instruction:

- Focus assessment on what students can do in the language (not just what they know).
- Performance tasks should be based upon real-world, authentic activities.
- Consider the principles of backward design to align assessment with instruction: determine outcomes, decide upon the evidence of transfer (performance tasks), and then create the learning activities.
- Give students multiple opportunities to show what they can do with the language that take into consideration cultures, learning styles, languages, and individual abilities.
- Use rubrics to evaluate performance tasks. This tool measures specific criteria against a defined scale. Provide the rubric to students in advance of the performance task.
- Provide students with anchors, or representative samples, of the performance task so that they can better understand the desired outcomes.
- Utilize both formative and summative assessments to provide ongoing feedback to students.
- Provide opportunities for students to self-evaluate and reflect upon their learning and progress.

Purposes of Assessment

The following chart outlines the various purposes for assessment:

Purposes of Assessment	
Entry-level assessment	• Analyzes students' ability to communicate as a basis for placing students at an appropriate level in an established world languages program
Formative assessment	• Provides real-time feedback during the instructional process • Can take many different forms in the classroom • Helps the teacher and student determine the next steps to further learning • Takes place prior to the summative assessment
Summative assessment	• Documents and judges students' learning or success at a point in time such as the end of a unit, chapter, or course of study

Forms of Assessment

Achievement tests determine what students know by evaluating them on specific, previously learned material, such as the names of items of clothing or the conjugation of *-ar* verbs. Students are tested on discrete bits of information. Achievement tests are used to measure the incremental steps involved in learning a second language—for example, to cover what was taught in a specific chapter. Achievement may be quizzed or tested with some frequency as proof of regular progress for both student and teacher.

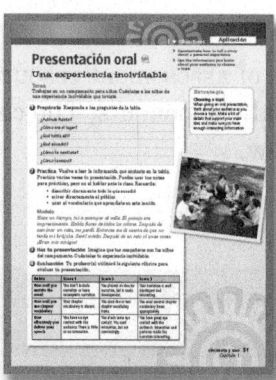

Performance-based speaking task in *Realidades 3 Capítulo 1*

Performance-based assessment measures what students can do with this knowledge and how well they can perform in the language. These tests do not involve testing specific items; rather they are performance-based, checking how well students integrate what they have learned. Their characteristic open-endedness permits students to use what they know to receive or communicate a message, since the emphasis is on communication needs. Performance-based assessment addresses this question: How well and at what level can the student use the language to receive and express meaningful communication?

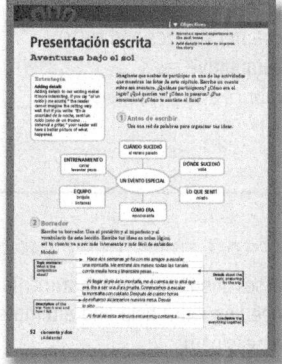

Performance-based writing task in *Realidades 3 Capítulo 1*

Assessment

Realidades and the ACTFL Performance Guidelines

The ACTFL Performance Guidelines for K–12 Learners describe the language proficiency of learners in Standards-based language programs such as *Realidades*. They are organized around three Modes of Communication: Interpersonal, Interpretive, and Presentational and provide for three Benchmark Levels: Novice, Intermediate, and Pre-Advanced.

Realidades has been carefully written to provide activities that develop and assess the Modes of Communication at levels appropriate to the students' proficiency. The last page in each chapter of Levels 1–3, called *Preparación para el examen*, provides an overview of the chapter outcomes and performance tasks organized around the three Modes. The Communication Workbook features an Integrated Performance Assessment (IPA) as an alternate assessment resource.

Assessment Resources in *Realidades*

Realidades offers a wide range of assessment resources found in various print and digital components. The chart on page T37 provides an overview.

Integrating Technology with Assessment

There are many opportunities to use the technology in *Realidades* to assess student performance. These include:

 RealTalk! Use the RealTalk tool in **realidades.com** to evaluate your students' interpersonal and presentation skills.

 Online Games Who says learning can't be fun? Each chapter within **realidades.com** offers three games that help students monitor their learning.

 Interactive Whiteboard Activities Get your students talking using the *¡Cuéntame!* and *Encuesta* Interactive Whiteboard Activities.

Assessment Programs

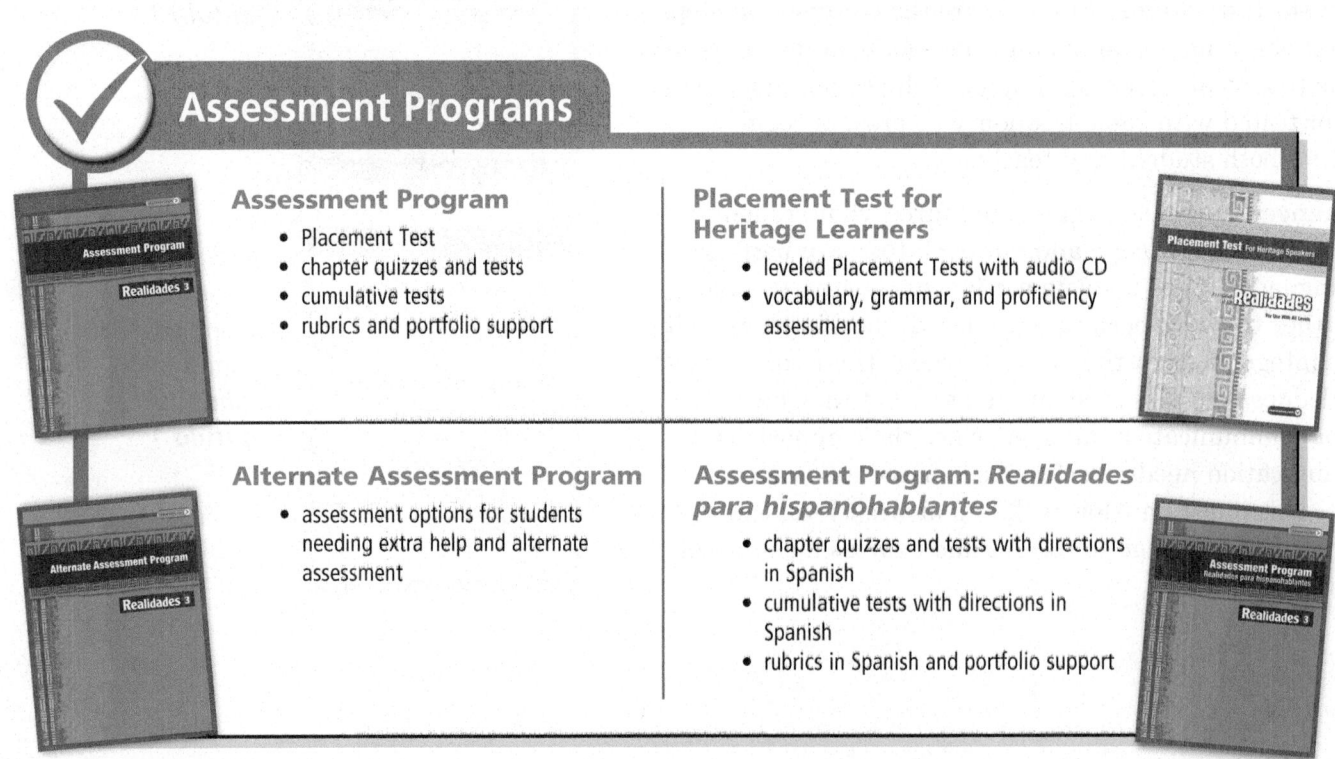

Assessment Program
- Placement Test
- chapter quizzes and tests
- cumulative tests
- rubrics and portfolio support

Placement Test for Heritage Learners
- leveled Placement Tests with audio CD
- vocabulary, grammar, and proficiency assessment

Alternate Assessment Program
- assessment options for students needing extra help and alternate assessment

Assessment Program: *Realidades para hispanohablantes*
- chapter quizzes and tests with directions in Spanish
- cumulative tests with directions in Spanish
- rubrics in Spanish and portfolio support

Assessment Resources in *Realidades*

Assessment Resources

	Self-Evaluation	Formative	Summative: Achievement	Summative: Performance
Student Edition				
Actividades (various)		X		X
Presentación oral				X
Presentación escrita				X
Preparación para el examen				X
realidades.com				
Actividades with (Talk!)	X	X		X
Presentación oral with (Talk!)				X
Instant Checks	X	X		
Online Games	X			
Chapter Quizzes with Study Plans		X		
Chapter Tests with (Talk!)			X	X
Integrated Performance Assessments with (Talk!)				X
Assessment Programs				
Placement Tests				X
Chapter Quizzes		X		
Chapter Part Tests		X		
Chapter Tests			X	X
Cumulative Tests			X	X
Rubrics				X
Chapter Checklist and Self-Assessment Worksheet	X			
Communication Workbook				
Audio and Writing Activities		X		
Practice Tests				X
Integrated Performance Assessments				X
Teacher Resource Book				
Communicative Pair Activities		X		
Situation Cards				X
Pre-AP® Resource Book				
Activities				X
Interactive Whiteboard Activities				
Vocabulary and Grammar		X		X
ExamView® Computer Test Generator				
Test Banks			X	

Differentiated Instruction

All students are capable of and can benefit from learning a second language. However, today's students bring into the classroom a wide range of needs, interests, motivations, home languages, and literacy levels. This diversity presents heightened challenges to both curriculum and instruction. It should be clearly acknowledged that individual needs of some students require additional specialized support. However, the goal of a comprehensive program remains the provision of teaching all students to develop proficiency in Spanish. All students should have access to a communicative and culturally rich program in addition to whatever specialized intervention may be required. *Realidades* has been developed especially to meet the diverse needs of students in Spanish classrooms.

Topics covered:

- ▷ Success in Teaching All Students
- ▷ Effective Instructional Strategies
- ▷ Teaching Today's Students
- ▷ Teaching Spanish to Students with Learning Disabilities
- ▷ Accommodating Instruction
- ▷ Accommodations for Students with Special Needs
- ▷ Accommodation in *Realidades*
- ▷ Teaching Heritage Learners
- ▷ Teaching Heritage Learners with *Realidades para hispanohablantes*
- ▷ Teaching Heritage Learners with *Realidades 3*
- ▷ Teaching All Students: Summary

Success in Teaching All Students

All students are able to access learning when teachers provide curriculum and instruction in ways that allow all learners in the classroom to participate and achieve the instructional and behavioral goals of general education, as well as those of the core curriculum. Success is achieved in classrooms that consistently and systematically integrate instructional strategies that are responsive to the needs of all learners with a special focus on students that need extra help—students with learning difficulties, heritage learners, and students who are eligible for and receiving special education services.

Effective Instructional Strategies

Here are general strategies that deliver effective instruction for all learners in the Spanish classroom.

- **Clarify the objectives for a chapter.** Students need to understand the outcomes for which they will be assessed.
- **Provide "thinking time" before students have to talk.** You may want to ask a question and then count to 10 before expecting a response. If a student is struggling, state that you want him/her to think about it, and indicate that you'll be back for the response in a minute. Move on to another student, and then return to the student for his/her response.

- **Write all assignments on the board.** Assignments given both verbally and visually are clearer to all students.

- **Use visuals throughout the lesson.** Present vocabulary visually. Use charts to present grammar. Use video that provides visual support (such as vocabulary words highlighted on the screen) and grammar videos that visualize grammar patterns. Use graphic organizers whenever possible. Connect communicative tasks to photos, art, and realia.

- **Assist in time management.** When requiring students to complete projects or long-term assignments, provide a calendar that breaks down requirements by due dates. Many students experience significant difficulties in self-managing the time needed to complete complex projects.

- **Build in opportunities for reteaching and practicing vocabulary words and grammar.** Students need many opportunities to learn new concepts and need to practice in a variety of formats.

- **Build vocabulary skills by teaching the patterns of language.** Teach the meaning of prefixes, suffixes, and the role of cognates. Point out connections between English, Spanish, and Latin.

- **Work with students based on their strengths rather than their weaknesses.** Allow students to experience success by using their strengths while working on areas of weakness.

- **Consider alternative means for demonstrating understanding.** Think beyond the common modes of reading and writing. Students could present information orally, create a poster or visual representation of work, record their ideas on an audio file, or act out their understanding.

- **Have students begin all work in class.** Prior to class dismissal, check to ensure that each student has a good start and understands what is expected.

> **❝** All students are capable of and can benefit from learning a second language. **❞**

- **Assign work using the Calendar on *realidades.com* or create a class Web page.** Homework assignments could be posted and easily accessed by parents and students outside of school hours.

Teaching Today's Students

The strategies presented on these pages provide an overview of instructional strategies that are effective with all learners. Today's students need instruction that enables them to see how learning is relevant, that helps them organize their time and learning, that provides focus on what is important (either within instructional materials or with classroom activities), that provides multiple opportunities to learn utilizing different modalities, and that assures students know what is expected of them whether in the classroom or for homework.

Teaching Spanish to Students with Learning Disabilities

There are many reasons why students may experience difficulties in learning a second language. In general, these difficulties may be characterized by the inability to spell or read well, problems with auditory discrimination and in understanding auditory input, and difficulty with abstract thinking. Research by Ganchow and Sparks (1991) indicates that difficulties with one's first language are a major factor in foreign language learning difficulties.

It is not always evident which students will experience difficulties with learning a second language. Many times these students are bright and outgoing. They may have experienced reading or spelling problems in elementary school, but they have learned to compensate over time. Ask students what problems they may have experienced with their first language, especially in the areas of reading and dictation.

Accommodating Instruction

Students with learning disabilities can develop a level of proficiency in a second language with some modifications to instruction and testing. These learners benefit from a highly structured approach that teaches new content in context and in incremental amounts. Teach, practice, and assess using multi-sensory strategies. Many students benefit when instruction combines seeing, hearing, saying, and writing. For example, a teacher would first show a visual of a word and say it aloud. This is followed by using the new word in context. The teacher then writes the word on the board. Students would say the word aloud with the teacher. They then write it down and say it aloud again. In subsequent days, many students benefit from frequent reviews of learned auditory materials.

Accommodations for Students with Special Needs

Here are suggestions for instruction for students with special needs. For additional support, see the *Realidades* Alternate Assessment Program.

Hearing impairments

- Help students comprehend oral information or instructions. Provide written directions/materials and/or visual cues to support what is presented orally. Face the students when speaking, repeat as needed, and speak clearly. Seat these students in the front of the classroom. Provide outlines of lectures or oral presentations. Have another student take notes and make copies of notes available to all students. Use the audio and video scripts of the *Realidades* Audio or Video Program. Utilize the close-captioned version of the Video Program.

- Allow students to refer to their textbooks or to other written materials during oral presentations.

- Limit background noises that may distract students. Avoid seating these students where they may hear extraneous noise.

- Change listening activities and assessments to reading/writing activities. In activities that require aural/oral skills, let students demonstrate skills through alternative responses such as writing.

- Provide access to the audio and video materials. Students can download all Student Edition audio material from **realidades.com.** The eText provides pronunciation support for all vocabulary, access to all Student Edition listening activities, and access to the vocabulary and grammar videos.

Visual perception problems

- Help students access information provided visually. Allow for preferred seating in the front of the class, including providing space for a guide dog, if necessary. Avoid seating students where they will be distracted by extraneous auditory or visual stimuli. Give students additional time to review visual input prior to an oral or written task. Highlight important information by providing key words, visuals, and simple outlines.

- Provide support for accessing printed information. Make sure the print is easy to read. The readings should be designed to maximize readability: easy-to-read font, layout, and design. Teach reading strategies that highlight the visual aspects of a selection: text organization, use of visuals, titles and headers, and the use of color. Provide copies of reading selections with additional support: underline key words/sentences/concepts or magnify the text in duplication.

- Teach, practice, and assess using multi-sensory strategies.

ADHD/ADD

- Provide additional support that enables students to focus. Present information in small "chunks." This includes new content, short instructions or directions, and shorter assignments, or break assignments into steps. Limit extraneous auditory and visual stimulation. Provide visual and written support for aural instructions or input. Repeat and explain (again) as needed. Provide outlines of oral presentations. Support readings with strategies similar to those for students with visual perception problems. Use graphic organizers.

- Verify that students "got it." Check that students are looking at you (eye contact) when providing oral instructions. Ask students to repeat what you just told them. Move closer to students to increase attention. Provide preferential seating that allows you to monitor students' focus and attention. Allow extra wait time when students are responding.

- Provide a variety of different learning activities that reach different learning styles. This will also allow for frequent changes of activities within a class. Provide for hands-on activities, vocabulary clip art, and grammar manipulatives.

- Use technology to provide interactive learning. These students will benefit from using the online resources at **realidades.com.**

- Be predictable. Establish a daily routine for managing the classroom and be consistent. Avoid surprises with these students.

- Help students organize themselves and their learning. Ask students to maintain notebooks that are organized by dividers. Provide study guides, summary sheets, and organizers for daily or weekly assignments.

DIFFERENTIATED INSTRUCTION

Accommodation in *Realidades*

Realidades 3 **provides a wide range of support for accommodating instruction.**

Student Edition
- clean design and layout of pages
- visualized presentation of vocabulary
- step-by-step scaffolding of activities
- online vocabulary and grammar tutorials and extra practice at **realidades.com**

Teacher's Edition
- Differentiated Instruction article
- Differentiated Instruction suggestions

Leveled Vocabulary and Grammar Workbook: Guided Practice
- vocabulary clip art to create flashcards
- focused vocabulary practice
- simplified grammar instruction
- Answer Key in Teacher's Resource Book

Alternate Assessment Program
- additional suggestions for accommodating assessment
- for students needing extra help

Teaching Heritage Learners

A diverse background

Those who have a home language other than English bring a wider range of language abilities to the classroom. These abilities range from minimal functioning in the language to complete fluency and literacy. It is important for teachers to assess the language skills of the different heritage learners in the classroom. This diversity includes:

- Students who are able to understand the spoken language, but are unable to respond in the language beyond single-word answers.

- Students who are able to understand the language and communicate at a minimal level. These students may be able to read some items, but because of their limited vocabulary, they may not comprehend much information. They may write what they are able to sound out, but errors are evident.

- Students who can speak the language fluently but who have little to no experience with the language in its written form.

- Students who have come to the United States from non-English-speaking countries. They can understand and speak the language fluently; however, their reading and writing skills may be limited due to lack of a formal education in their country of origin.

- Fluent bilingual students who can understand, speak, read, and write another language very well and have possibly received formal instruction in that language in the United States or in another country.

Program goals

Heritage learners bring rich home language experiences to the classroom that can serve as a foundation for learning. Because of their language background, these students have the potential to be bilingual, biliterate, and bicultural. Heritage learners need to be exposed to a program that can improve and maintain the home language. Students need to study the grammar and focus on vocabulary development. Emphasis should be placed on building reading and writing skills. It is important that students develop a sensitivity to when standard and non-standard language should be employed and comfortably adjust their language accordingly. In addition, students should be exposed to the diverse cultures within the Spanish-speaking community while developing a sense of pride in their own heritage. Heritage learners need to reach a high level of proficiency and accuracy that will ensure success at the advanced level of language study and testing. These students should also be ready to transition into a focused study of Spanish in specific professional areas.

Focus on individual needs

Due to their diverse backgrounds, heritage learners differ greatly in language skills and may need individualized instruction. In many of today's classrooms, teachers encounter classes that contain a mixture of beginning-level students and heritage learners. These groups need different materials, different instructional approaches, and different objectives. Here are several strategies that may be helpful for heritage learners:

- Build upon their background knowledge. Develop instructional units around themes and topics that relate to their life experiences. Encourage students to use these experiences as the foundation for building language skills through vocabulary development, reading, and writing.

- Help students connect aural with written language. If students don't understand a word in a reading, have them read it aloud or ask a friend or teacher to read it aloud. Often they can recognize the word once they hear it. Allow for opportunities for students to follow along as a story is read aloud.

- Use strategies that are effective in a language arts classroom, such as building schema, teaching language-learning strategies, using graphic organizers, and incorporating pre- and post-reading tasks. Use the writing process to develop good writers.

- Encourage students to begin communicating, especially in writing. Have them write down their thoughts in the way they sound to them. Then have students work with the teacher or another student for corrections. Students can also look through textbooks and dictionaries to assist with error correction.

- Maintain high standards. Require students to focus on accuracy and proficient communication. Many heritage learners experience frustration with reading and writing in the home language when they have good aural/oral skills. Building language skills takes time.

Teaching Heritage Learners with *Realidades 3*

Realidades 3 offers ideal support for teaching heritage learners at the novice level of proficiency. The Student Edition, the *Realidades para hispanohablantes* all-Spanish worktext, and the varied assessment options offer a rich and varied curriculum. In addition, the Pre-AP* support in each chapter of the Student Edition will lay the foundation for success on the AP* Language Examination.

Teaching All Students: Summary

The diverse needs of today's Spanish students pose a challenge to teachers, curriculum developers, and school administrators as they design programs to ensure that all students develop language proficiency. With *Realidades,* teachers have at their disposal a variety of materials and strategies to enable them to provide access to Spanish for all learners. Clearly, some students will require additional tutoring and specialized services to reach their full learning potential. However, the activities and materials that accompany *Realidades,* coupled with instructional strategies described within this article, constitute a viable framework for reaching and teaching all learners.

Teaching Heritage Learners with *Realidades para hispanohablantes*

Realidades 3 provides extensive support for teaching heritage learners.

Student Edition
- focused vocabulary and grammar
- integrated language and culture
- extensive reading and writing
- test preparation

Realidades para hispanohablantes

- all-Spanish companion worktext
- all-Spanish grammar explanations
- companion pages for each section of Student Edition
- increased emphasis on reading and writing
- accompanying Teacher's Guide

Assessment Program: *Realidades para hispanohablantes*
- direction lines in Spanish
- complete assessment support
- rubrics in Spanish

Instructional Planning and Support

For more issues online, see
*my*PearsonTraining.com

Today's Spanish classroom is a vibrant and interactive learning community, integrating language with culture. Teachers are planning for instruction that is communicative, motivating, and real for *all* students. They are incorporating a wide range of strategies, activities, and technology to achieve clearly defined teaching objectives. This section provides an overview of instructional strategies that will help teachers achieve these goals.

Creating a Communicative Learning Community

A communicative classroom is built upon activities that enable students to use language in meaningful and purposeful ways. One of the challenges is to get students ready, willing, and able to communicate. Here are several strategies that can be built into communicative tasks to help all students be successful.

Teach and use learning strategies

Research states that successful language students use a wide range of learning strategies. In contrast, unsuccessful students employ fewer strategies and tend to give up quickly. Strategies are inherently student-centered and when employed by learners, allow them to become more independent and more successful. Learning strategies enable students to:

- Learn and recall information more efficiently
- Interpret and comprehend language when reading or writing
- Speak more effectively
- Write more effectively
- Take more risks and be more positive
- Work more cooperatively with others

Use activities based upon multiple intelligences

The Multiple Intelligences Theory tells us that students learn in different ways. If new material is presented in a variety of formats, more students will likely learn and be able to demonstrate proficiency with the new material. Howard Gardner in 1983 proposed the theory of Multiple Intelligences in his book *Frames of Mind*. This theory states that a person has many different ways of acquiring and demonstrating intelligence. Some people remember just about anything if learned to the tune of a jingle or chant, while someone else may be able to grasp an idea, concept, or grammatical point if presented as a graph, chart, or picture.

Gardner presents the notion that there is no "general intelligence," but rather that the mind is organized around distinct functional capacities, which he defines as "intelligences." Though each of the intelligences is developed independently of the others over the course of a lifetime, they usually work together and do not often appear in isolation. Gardner has identified and labeled eight main styles of acquiring and demonstrating knowledge; those eight intelligences are:

- Verbal/Linguistic
- Visual/Spatial
- Bodily/Kinesthetic
- Logical/Mathematical
- Interpersonal/Social
- Intrapersonal/Introspective
- Musical/Rhythmic
- Naturalist

In this Teacher's Edition, you will find frequent specific suggestions for accommodating and teaching to the Multiple Intelligences. This is not meant to be construed as a paradigm for labeling every student in your class. On the contrary, they are presented as tools to help more students access content while recognizing that they are intelligent in many ways and that their overall "intelligence" is based upon the sum of all their intelligences.

Scaffolded tasks

Step-by-step support builds success.

▼12 Lugares para explorar | 👥

Escribir • Hablar

❶ Piensa en un lugar que te gustaría explorar: el desierto, el océano, el mar, el bosque, la sierra o una selva tropical. Escribe una frase para explicar por qué quieres explorar ese lugar.

Modelo
Quiero ir a la sierra porque me gusta el paisaje.

❷ Forma un grupo con otros estudiantes que escogieron el mismo lugar que tú. Comenta tus ideas con el grupo.

❸ Usa las ideas del grupo para escribir un breve párrafo explicando tus razones para explorar ese lugar.

❹ Presenta tus ideas a la clase. Puedes acompañar tu presentación con fotos o ilustraciones de ese lugar.

Activities that incorporate critical thinking tend to be more interesting for students as they are guided to think differently in ways such as:

- ☐ use or apply
- ☐ illustrate/sketch/diagram
- ☐ compare and contrast
- ☐ analyze
- ☐ categorize
- ☐ create
- ☐ organize/prepare
- ☐ evaluate
- ☐ revise
- ☐ value

Provide activities that require critical thinking

All students learn more effectively when activities help them make connections and see and use information in new and different ways. Critical thinking skills can be used as tools for learning and are easily integrated in a variety of tasks beginning in the first year of language study in both communication and culture activities.

Scaffold communicative tasks

Communicating in a second language is a complicated task. There are mental steps that take place as a student attempts to communicate a message. Activities that help students get through these mental steps allow students to be successful. This "scaffolded" support is provided throughout *Realidades*.

For example, in preparing for a speaking task, students think through what they might want to say using a chart. In writing, they might fill out a word web before attempting the first draft. By providing a scaffold that asks students to think, plan, process, and then communicate, more students will become effective communicators.

The Role of Grammar in a Communicative Classroom

In a proficiency-based curriculum, vocabulary and grammar are viewed as tools that students need in order to communicate, rather than as ends in themselves.

Input grammar in context

For students to internalize grammar, it needs to be presented in a meaningful context. For example, students can grasp the concept of the preterite more easily if it is presented within a topic, like shopping. As the teacher presents clothing and store vocabulary, she can tell the class what items of clothing she or another person bought, when it was purchased, and how much was paid. As the teacher points to a picture of a sweater on an overhead transparency or clip art or an actual sweater, she begins with comprehensible input that uses the *yo* form of the preterite: *Ayer, yo fui de compras y compré un suéter nuevo. Y pagué veinte dólares. No es mucho, ¿verdad?* Repetition of the input can continue with other articles of clothing, allowing students to easily deduce and internalize the meaning of *compré* and *pagué*. The teacher then begins to ask students questions using *compraste* and *pagaste* and makes summary comments about what is said in the class, drawing other students into the discussion as she introduces other preterite forms. As students begin to internalize these forms and the chapter vocabulary, they begin to make simple statements or ask questions to a partner about shopping for clothing.

Input grammar in small, manageable chunks

Present new grammar in manageable chunks that can be immediately practiced. In the example above, students can use a few preterite forms of *comprar* and *pagar* as they talk about shopping. Additional *-ar* verbs and other preterite forms can be added as students become comfortable using *comprar* and *pagar*.

Input grammar in readings

Grammar input can also take place through reading. As students read sentences, short paragraphs, and dialogues with supporting contextual and visual cues, they can understand new grammatical forms. Through carefully planned out questions asked by their teacher, students can be led to explain grammatical concepts.

Teach what is needed for the immediate communication objectives

Teach students the grammar needed to accomplish the communicative objective. This allows students to learn the concept in context and practice. For example, if you teach *pensar* or *querer* in connection with a theme, don't give students an additional list of all *ie* stem-changing verbs. Rather, teach additional *ie* verbs in later chapters as they connect to the themes.

Practice grammar in a variety of activities

Just as there are several ways to provide input, there are many useful methods for practicing grammar. This practice can involve hands-on activities and games that let students manipulate grammatical structures. Grammar practice is effectively integrated into communicative activities such as surveys, Venn diagrams, and paired and group activities. In addition, practice can involve activities on **realidades.com** where students can practice grammar again and again at their own pace.

Grammar and communication

Grammar can be successfully integrated in a communicative classroom with activities that deal with grammatical accuracy at different levels. When presented in meaningful contexts, in manageable chunks, and with presentation and practice that incorporate a variety of activities, students will develop increasing accuracy with grammar.

Pair and Group Activities in a Communicative Classroom

Benefits of group work

Effective group work develops a friendly and cooperative atmosphere by giving students a chance to get to know each other better. This sense of camaraderie leads to a more relaxed classroom in which students are more willing to talk and to participate. Group work also allows more opportunity for "student talk," thereby increasing the quantity of student practice in the target language.

Grouping options and techniques

The communicative activities in a Spanish classroom allow for a variety of grouping options.

The most common option is random grouping that includes pairing up two students or creating small groups of three to five students. Some possible ways to randomly group students include:

- Count off by going left to right or up and down in rows.
- Write on pieces of paper vocabulary words (English/Spanish), countries/capitals, opposites, colors, or categories that can be matched up, in a bag. Have students draw a piece of paper and find their partner(s).
- Order students along a continuum by birthday, height, phone numbers, etc.
- Place numbers or a deck of cards in a hat, bag, or box and have students draw.
- Turn to the student to the left or right, front or back.

Another grouping option is to place students by their ability level. Homogeneous grouping allows students of similar ability to work together. In this case, teachers assign tasks based upon the ability level of the group. Advanced students are given a more challenging task. Other students are given tasks that they can successfully complete. Heterogeneous grouping places students of varying abilities together. This allows for stronger students to help weaker students.

Grouping students by interest level is another option to consider. Students could group themselves for an activity or longer project based upon mutual interest.

Planning and facilitating an effective group activity

- Make sure that the task involves a true exchange of information.
- Think through the language functions and content information to make certain students can complete the task.
- Prepare all materials in advance and anticipate questions.
- Explain the task before the students break up into groups. Be sure to model the task if necessary.
- Determine in advance how students will be evaluated and share those criteria with the class.
- Allow adequate time for the task. Make sure at least three quarters of the students at different ability levels can complete it. Tell students how much time they have and stick to the plan.
- Encourage students to stay on task by walking around the class and monitoring the groups.
- Build into your grading system a way to include group participation and staying on task.
- Develop some sort of follow-up upon completion of the task.

Error correction

As students work in groups, they will be making mistakes. Here are strategies that can help students focus on accuracy while doing group work.

- Listen for common errors while monitoring the class. If the error is one of vocabulary usage or grammar, discuss the error with the class and do some focused practice once the task is completed. If the error is one of meaning (very common in beginning writing), have the class work together to determine how best to express the message.
- If you want to correct an individual student error, correct the student only after he or she has spoken. Restate the student's response using the correction in your restatement.

Integrating Technology in the Classroom

For the Teacher

Realidades provides many time-saving digital resources to help teachers plan, teach, assess, and remediate or enrich instruction.

	Teacher Resources	eText	realidades.com	DVD
Planning	• Interactive Teacher's Edition (ITE) with Resource Library		•	ITE with Resource Library
	• Teacher Resources (PDF files)		•	ITE with Resource Library
	• Lesson Plans (PDF files with links)		•	
	• DK Bilingual Visual Dictionary (enrichment)		•	Activities and Tools for Interactive Whiteboards DVD-ROM
Review	• *Un poco más de repaso*		•	
A ver si recuerdas	• *A ver si recuerdas* with Study Plan		•	
Chapter Opener	• Fine Art and Map Transparencies		•	PresentationExpress™ Premium DVD-ROM
Vocabulario en contexto	• Audio	•	•	Audio Program, PresentationExpress™ Premium DVD-ROM
	• Transparencies, Clip Art		•	PresentationExpress™ Premium DVD-ROM
	• *Prueba:* Voc. Recognition Quiz		•	ITE with Resource Library
Vocabulario en uso	• Interactive Whiteboard Vocabulary Activities		•	Activities and Tools for Interactive Whiteboards DVD-ROM
	• *Videomodelos* Videos	•	•	*Videomodelos* Video Program
	• Audio	•	•	Audio Program
	• *Prueba:* Voc. Production Quiz with Study Plan		•	ITE with Resource Library
Gramática y vocabulario en uso	• Interactive Whiteboard Grammar Activities		•	Activities and Tools for Interactive Whiteboards DVD-ROM
	• Tutorial Videos		•	
	• Animated Verbs	•	•	PresentationExpress™ Premium DVD-ROM
	• *Videomodelos* Videos	•	•	*Videomodelos* Video Program
	• Audio	•	•	PresentationExpress™ DVD, Audio Program
	• Transparencies		•	PresentationExpress™ Premium DVD-ROM
	• *Canciones de hip hop*		•	
	• *Prueba:* Grammar Quiz with Study Plan		•	ITE with Resource Library
¡Adelante!	• *¡Pura vida!*	•	•	*¡Pura vida!* Video Program on DVD
	• *Videodocumentario* Videos		•	
Repaso del capítulo	• Integrated Performance Assessment		•	ITE with Resource Library
	• Situation Cards		•	ITE with Resource Library
	• *Examen del capítulo*		•	ITE with Resource Library
	• ExamView® Assessment Suite			ExamView® Assessment Suite CD-ROM

For the Student

Realidades is ready for today's digital learner! Through **realidades.com,** students can access a wide array of interactive online activities and multimedia resources. They can monitor their own progress, complete graded assignments and assessments, record speaking tasks, explore the Spanish-speaking world, and much more! Here is a list of the resources available for students on **realidades.com.**

	Student Resources	Auto-graded	Teacher-graded
Chapter Opener	*Mapa global interactivo*		•
	eText *Actividades*	•	•
	DK Reference Atlas		
Vocabulario en contexto	eText *Actividades*	•	•
	Flashcards	•	
	Instant Check	•	
	Workbook activities	•	•
	Quiz	•	•
	Additional practice	•	
Vocabulario en uso	eText *Actividades*	•	
	Videomodelos		
	RealTalk! speaking tasks		•
	Workbook activities	•	•
	Quiz with Study Plans	•	
	Communicative Pair Activities		•
Gramática y vocabulario en uso	eText *Actividades*	•	•
	Tutorials, Animated Verbs		
	Canciones de hip hop		
	Instant Check	•	
	Workbook activities	•	•
	RealTalk! speaking tasks		•
	Quizzes with Study Plans	•	
	Additional practice	•	
¡Adelante!	eText *Actividades*	•	•
	Presentación oral		•
	Culture Reading Activity		•
	Workbook activities	•	•
	Videodocumentario and *Actividades*	•	•
	DK Bilingual Visual Dictionary		
Repaso del capítulo	eText *Actividades*	•	•
	Games and Puzzles	•	
	Instant Check and Self-Test	•	
	Workbook activities	•	
	Situation Cards		•
	Integrated Performance Assessment		•
	Examen del capítulo	•	•

Bibliography

realidades.com

Go online for links to state and national professional organizations, regional conferences, Web sites of interest, and Listservs.

Assessment

Boyles, Peggy. "Assessing the Speaking Skill in the Classroom: New Solutions to an Ongoing Problem." *Northeast Conference Reports: Testing, Teaching, and Assessment,* ed. Charles R. Hancock. Lincolnwood, IL: National Textbook Company, 1994.

Cooper, Thomas C., Daniel J. Yanosky II, and Joseph M. Wisenbaker. "Foreign Language Learning and SAT Verbal Scores Revisited." *Foreign Language Annals,* Summer 2008.

James, W. "Formative Assessment: Why, What, and Whether," from *Transformative Assessment,* W. James. Popham, Chapter 1. ASCD Member Book, 2008.

Liskin-Gasparro, Judith. "Assessment: From Content Standards to Student Performance." *National Standards. A Catalyst for Reform,* ed. Robert Lafayette. Lincolnwood, IL: National Textbook Co., 1996.

National K–12 Foreign Language Resource Center. "National Assessment Summit Papers", *New Visions in Action,* Iowa State University, 2005.

New Visions in Action: National Assessment Summit Papers, ed. Marcia Harmon Rosenbusch, National K–12 Foreign Language Resource Center, Iowa State University, 2005.

Pettigrew, Frances and Ghislaine Tulou. "Performance Assessment for Language Students." *Language Learners of Tomorrow: Process and Promise,* ed. Margaret Ann Kassen. Lincolnwood, IL: National Textbook Co., 1999.

Tomlinson, Carol Ann. "Learning to Love Assessment." *Educational Leadership,* Jan. 2008.

Block Scheduling

Blaz, Deborah. *Teaching Foreign Languages on the Block.* Larchmont, NY: Eye on Education, 1998.

Canady, R. L., and M. D. Rettig. *Block Scheduling: A Catalyst for Change in High Schools.* Larchmont, NY: Eye on Education, 1995.

———. *Teaching on the Block: Strategies for Engaging Active Learners.* Larchmont, NY: Eye on Education, 1996.

Culture

Byram, Michael. *Teaching and Assessing Intercultural Competence.* Clevedon, U.K.: Multilingual Matters, 1997.

Fantini, Alvino. "Comparisons: towards the Development of Intercultural Competence." *Foreign Language Standards: Linking Theory, Research, and Practice,* ed. June Phillips. Lincolnwood, IL: National Textbook Co., 1999.

Galloway, Vicki. "Bridges and Boundaries: Growing the Cross-Cultural Mind." *Language Learners of Tomorrow: Process and Promise.* Lincolnwood, IL: National Textbook Co., 1999.

Heusvinkveld, Paula R., ed. *Pathways to Culture.* Yarmouth, ME: Intercultural Press, Inc. 1997.

Koning, Patricia. "Let's Go to the Movies." *The Language Editor,* Vol. 6, Issue 4 (2011): 32–36.

Curriculum and Instruction

ACTFL Performance Guidelines for K–12 Learners. Yonkers, NY: ACTFL, 1999.

"Challenge for a New Era." *Nebraska K–12 Foreign Language Frameworks.* Lincoln: Nebraska Department of Education, 1996.

Chamot, Anna U. "Reading and Writing Processes: Learning Strategies in Immersion Classrooms." *Language Learners of Tomorrow: Process and Promise,* ed. Margaret Ann Kassen. Lincolnwood, IL: National Textbook Company, 1999.

Davis, Robert. "Group Work is NOT Busy Work: Maximizing Success of Group Work in the L2 Classroom." *Foreign Language Annals,* Vol. 30 (1997): 265–279.

Ferguson, Susan. "Breathing Life Into Foreign Language Reading," *Educational Leadership,* Vol. 63 No. 2 (2005): 63–65.

Foreign Language Framework for California Public Schools Kindergarten Through Grade Twelve. Sacramento: California State Department of Education, 2002.

Guntermann, G., ed. *Teaching Spanish with the Five C's: A Blueprint for Success.* New York: Harcourt College Publishers, 2000.

Hall, Joan Kelly. "The Communication Standards." *Foreign Language Standards: Linking Theory, Research, and Practice,* ed. June Phillips. Lincolnwood, IL: National Textbook Co., 1999.

Jackson, Claire, et al. *Articulation & Achievement: Connecting Standards, Performance, and Assessment in Foreign Language.* New York: College Board of Publications, 1996.

Klee, Carol A. "Communication as an Organizing Principle in the National Standards: Sociolinguistic Aspects of Spanish Language Teaching." *Hispania.* Vol. 81 (2) (1998), pp. 339–351.

Krashen, Stephen. *Principles and Practice in Second Language Acquisition.* Oxford: Pergamon Press, 1982.

Met, Myriam, with J. Phillips. *Curriculum Handbook.* Association for Supervision and Curriculum Development, 1999.

———. "Making Connections." *Foreign Language Standards: Linking Theory, Research, and Practice,* ed. June Phillips. Lincolnwood, IL: National Textbook Co., 1999.

Moeller, Aleidine. "Optimizing Student Success: Focused Curriculum, Meaningful Assessment, and Effective Instruction," *The 2005 Report of the Central States Conference on the Teaching of Foreign Languages. The Year of Languages: Challenges, Changes, and Choices,* ed. Peggy Boyles and Paul Sandrock. Eau Claire, WI: Crown Prints. 2005.

National K–12 Foreign Language Resource Center. "A Guide to Aligning Curriculum with the Standards." Ames: Iowa State University, 1996.

———. *Bringing the Standards into the Classroom: A Teacher's Guide.* Ames: Iowa State University, 1997.

Patrick, Paula. "The Keys to the Classroom." *The ACTFL Guide for Professional Language Education.* ACTFL, 2007.

Standards for Foreign Language Learning in the 21st Century: Including Chinese, Classical Languages, French, German, Italian, Japanese, Portuguese, Russian, and Spanish. Lawrence, KS: Allen Press, 1999.

VanPatten, Bill and Wong, Wynne. "The Evidence is IN: Drills are OUT." *Foregin Language Annals,* Fall 2003.

Zaslow, Brandon. "Teaching Language for Proficiency: From Theory to Practice (An Instructional Framework)." Unpublished document. School of Education, University of California, Los Angeles, 2001.

Heritage Learners

Blanco, George. "El hispanohablante y la gramática." *Bilingual Research Journal* 18 (1995): 23–46.

Colombi, Cecilia M. and Francisco X. Alarcón, eds. *La enseñanza del español a hispanohablantes: Praxis y teoría.* Boston: Houghton Mifflin Co., 1997.

Rodríguez-Pino, Cecilia, and Daniel Villa. "A Student-Centered Spanish for Native Speakers Program: Theory, Curriculum Design, and Outcome Assessment." *Faces in a Crowd: The Individual Learner in Multisection Courses,* ed. Carol Klee. Boston: Heinle and Heinle, 1994.

Miller, Barbara L., and John B. Webb, eds. *Teaching Heritage Language Learners: Voices from the Classroom,* ACTFL Series. Princeton: Princeton University, 2000.

Methodology

Hadley, Alice Omaggio. *Teaching Language in Context,* 3rd ed. Boston: Heinle and Heinle, 2001.

Hall, Joan Kelly. *Methods for Teaching Foreign Languages: Creating a Community of Learners in the Classroom.* Upper Saddle River, NJ: Merrill Prentice Hall, 2001.

Hamilton, Heidi E., Crane, Cori, Bartoshesky, Abigal. "Doing Foreign Language: Bringing Concordia Language Villages into Language Classrooms." Pearson Education, Inc. 2005.

Lee, James, and Bill Van Patten. *Making Communicative Language Teaching Happen.* New York: McGraw Hill, 1995.

Oxford, Rebecca L. *Language Learning Strategies: What Every Teacher Should Know.* New York: Newbury House, 1990.

Shrum, Judith, and Eileen Glisan. *Teacher's Handbook: Contextualized Language Instruction.* Boston: Heinle and Heinle, 1994.

Multiple Intelligences

Armstrong, Thomas. *Multiple Intelligences in the Classroom.* Alexandria, VA: Association for Supervision and Curriculum Development, 1994.

Gardner, Howard. *Frames of Mind: The Theory of Multiple Intelligences.* New York, NY: Basic Books, 1983.

Lazear, David. *Seven Pathways of Learning: Teaching Students and Parents about Multiple Intelligences.* Tucson, AZ: Zephyr Press, 1994.

Middle School

Raven, Patrick T. and Jo Anne S. Wilson. "Middle-School Foreign Language: What Is It? What Should It Be?" *Visions and Reality in Foreign Language Teaching: Where We Are, Where We Are Going,* ed. William N. Hatfield. Lincolnwood, IL: National Textbook Co., 1993.

Verkler, Karen W. "Middle School Philosophy and Second Language Acquisition Theory: Working Together for Enhanced Proficiency." *Foreign Language Annals,* Vol. 27 (1994): 19–42.

Differentiated Instruction & Inclusion

Ganschow, Leonore, and Richard Sparks. "A Screening Instrument for the Identification of Foreign Language Learning Problems." *Foreign Language Annals,* Vol. 24 (1991): 383–398.

———, and James Javorsky, John Patton, Jane Pohlman, Richard Sparks. "Test Comparisons among Students Identified as High-Risk, Low-Risk, and Learning Disabled in High School Foreign Language Courses," *The Modern Language Journal,* Vol. 76 (1992): 142–159.

Sax Mabbott, Ann. "An Exploration of Reading Comprehension, Oral Reading Errors, and Written Errors by Subjects Labeled Learning Disabled." *Foreign Language Annals,* Vol. 27 (1994): 294–324.

Sheppard, Marie. "Proficiency as an Inclusive Orientation: Meeting the Challenge of Diversity." *Reflecting on Proficiency from the Classroom Perspective,* ed. June Phillips. Lincolnwood, IL: National Textbook Co., 1993.

Tomlinson, Carol Ann and McTighe, Jay. "Integrating Differentiated Instruction & Understanding by Design." ASCD Publication, 2006.

Treviño, María. "Inclusion in the languages other than English classroom." *LOTE CED Communiqué,* Issue 9. Austin, TX: 2003.

Technology

Moore, Zena T. "Technology and Teaching Culture: What Spanish Teachers Do. *Foreign Language Annals,* Vol. 39, No. 4, pp. 579–593.

Muyskens, Judith Ann., ed. *New Ways of Learning and Teaching: Focus on Technology and Foreign Language Education.* Boston: Heinle and Heinle, 1997.

21st Century Skills

Simplicio, Joseph S.C. *Educating the 21st Century Student.* Bloomington, IN: AuthorHouse, 2007.

Trilling, Bernie and Charles Fadel. *21st Century Skills: Learning for Life in Our Times.* San Francisco, CA: Jossey-Bass, 2009.

Understanding by Design

Wiggins, Grant and McTighe, Jay. *Understanding by Design,* 2nd edition. ASCD Publication, 2005.

Index of Cultural References

The numbers following each entry indicate the pages on which a reference to that topic is made; an *i* following a number indicates that the reference appears on that page in an illustration, photograph, or artwork; an *m* indicates that the reference appears in a map.

Realidades 3

realidades.com

Digital Edition

Peggy Palo Boyles
OKLAHOMA CITY, OK

Myriam Met
ROCKVILLE, MD

Richard S. Sayers
LONGMONT, CO

PEARSON

Boston, Massachusetts | Chandler, Arizona
Glenview, Illinois | Upper Saddle River, New Jersey

Front cover, left: Young man wearing baseball jacket
Center left: City of Arts and Sciences, Valencia, Spain
Center right: Young indigenous women, Santiago de Atitlán, Guatemala
Right: Mola, a traditional decorative fabric panel from San Blas Islands, Panama

Acknowledgments appear on pages 560–561, which constitute an extension of this copyright page.

ISBN-13:   978-0-13-319967-3
ISBN-10:   0-13-319967-3

PEARSON

3 4 5 6 7 8 9 10   V011   17 16 15 14 13

Realidades

      realidades.com

Digital Edition

Realidades Authors

Peggy Palo Boyles

During her foreign language career of over thirty years, Peggy Palo Boyles has taught elementary, secondary, and university students in both private and public schools. She is currently an independent consultant who provides assistance to schools, districts, universities, state departments of education, and other organizations of foreign language education in the areas of curriculum, assessment, cultural instruction, professional development and program evaluation. She is also a part-time instructor at Oklahoma State University. She was a member of the ACTFL Performance Guidelines for the K–12 Learners task force and served as a Senior Editor for the project. She currently serves on the Advisory Committee for the ACTFL Assessment for Performance and Proficiency of Languages (AAPPL). Peggy is a Past-President of the National Association of District Supervisors of Foreign Language (NADSFL) and was a recipient of ACTFL's K–12 Steiner Award for Leadership in K–12 Foreign Language Education. Peggy lives in Oklahoma City, OK with her husband, Del. Their son, Ryan, works at the University of Texas at Arlington.

Myriam Met

For most of her professional life, Myriam (Mimi) Met has worked in the public schools, first as a high school teacher in New York, then as K–12 supervisor of language programs in the Cincinnati Public Schools, and finally as a Coordinator of Foreign Language in Montgomery County (MD) Public Schools. She is currently a Senior Research Associate at the National Foreign Language Center, University of Maryland, where she works on K–12 language policy and infrastructure development. Mimi Met has served on the Advisory Board for the National Standards for Foreign Language Learning, on the Executive Council of ACTFL, and as President of the National Association of District Supervisors of Foreign Languages (NADSFL). She has been honored by ACTFL with the Steiner Award for Leadership in K–12 Foreign Language Education and the Papalia Award for Excellence in Teacher Education.

Richard S. Sayers

Rich Sayers has been an educator in world languages since 1978. He taught Spanish at Niwot High School in Longmont, CO for 18 years, where he taught levels 1 through AP Spanish. While at Niwot High School, Rich served as department chair, district foreign language coordinator, and board member of the Colorado Congress of Foreign Language Teachers. Rich has also served on the Board of the Southwest Conference on Language Teaching. In 1991, Rich was selected as one of the Disney Company's Foreign Language Teacher Honorees for the American Teacher Awards. Rich has served as a world languages consultant for Pearson since 1996. He is currently the Curriculum Specialist Manager for Pearson in the Mountain Region.

National Consultants

María R. Hubbard
Braintree, MA

Patrick T. Raven
Milwaukee, WI

¡Bienvenidos!

Welcome back to **Realidades 3!** Throughout the year your Spanish skills will improve as the themes, topics, and language become more complex. In addition, your understanding of the rich cultures in the Spanish-speaking world will increase as you explore the cultural topics in each chapter.

In **Realidades 3,** you'll:

- review vocabulary and grammar
- learn additional vocabulary and grammar
- expand your listening, speaking, reading, and writing skills
- connect Spanish with science, math, history, and geography
- read about people, places, and traditions from the Spanish-speaking world
- read authentic short stories, poems, autobiographies, legends, and song lyrics
- communicate about what's important to you: friends, relationships, leisure activities, and future plans
- communicate about contemporary topics: health, history, government, the arts, and the environment
- develop a strong foundation for the study of the Spanish language and culture

Throughout **Realidades 3,** you'll find a wide range of support to help you communicate more effectively.

Para empezar Realidades 3 begins with a review chapter that focuses on the basics from second year. You may remember this vocabulary and grammar. If not, use the activities in the textbook and on **realidades.com** for extra practice.

A ver si recuerdas Each chapter begins with a review section that provides a quick summary of the vocabulary and grammar from first and second year Spanish that connects with the upcoming chapter. This material isn't tested, but it might be something you'll use as you communicate.

Grammar Summaries and Glossaries At the end of the book, you'll find vocabulary and grammar reference sections from all levels of **Realidades.** These will be a useful tool as you need to look up information.

realidades.com Be sure to use the online activities as a review or extra practice.

Estrategia Be sure to use all the different strategies you learned in the previous levels: using cognates, using visuals, using graphic organizers, using prior knowledge, etc.

Online Resources with realidades.com

REALIDADES includes lots of online resources to help you learn Spanish! You can easily link to all of them when you log on to your Home Page within realidades.com. Your teacher will assign some activities, such as the ones in the workbooks. Others you can access on your own.

You'll find these resources highlighted on the pages of your print or online Student Edition with technology icons. Here's a list of the different icons used.

 Bilingual Visual Dictionary Quick link to eText dictionary featuring more than 6,000 visualized words

Reference Atlas Quick links to the countries in the online atlas

 Mapa global interactivo Links to GIS showing locations across the Spanish-speaking world

 Videos

Videocultura Cultural overview of each theme

¡Pura vida! Series with episodes filmed in Costa Rica

Grammar Tutorials Clear explanations of grammar with comparison to English

Animated Verbs Animations that highlight verb conjugations

Videodocumentarios Short documentaries that connect to each chapter theme

 Modelo *Videomodelos*
Video models of speaking activities

 Audio Audio files for vocabulary, listening practice, and pronunciation

 Canciones de hip hop Songs to help practice new vocabulary and grammar

 **Flashcards** Practice for the new vocabulary

 RealTalk! Speak-and-record tool for speaking activities

 Más práctica GO **Online practice**

Instant Check Short activities that check your progress right away

Guided Workbook Step-by-step vocabulary and grammar practice

Core Workbook Vocabulary and grammar exercises

Communication Workbook Listening, video, and writing activities

Cultural Reading Activity Questions for the *Puente a la cultura* reading

Puzzles End-of-chapter games

Getting Started on realidades.com

At the beginning of the year, you'll want to get registered on realidades.com. Your teacher will help you get started. If you log on to realidades.com using a non-school computer, be sure to check out the System Requirements to make sure you are using compatible browsers and have the needed software.

realidades.com Home Page

After you register, you'll land on your realidades.com Home Page. Here you'll be able to access assignments, grades, and study resources. You'll also be able to communicate with your teacher.

 You'll find everything that's in the book online as eText.

RealTalk!

You'll be able to record many of your speaking activities using RealTalk! You can use the microphone in your computer or a headset with microphone. If you want, you can download and save your recording.

Mapa global interactivo

Build your geography skills and learn about more locations throughout the Spanish-speaking world. You can download .kmz files from realidades.com and link to sites using Google Earth™ or other geographic information systems.

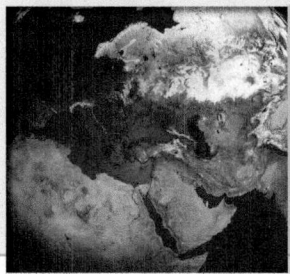

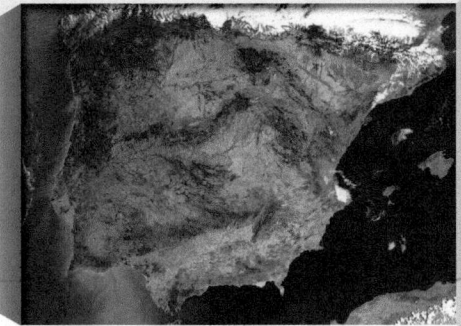

Tabla de materias

Para empezar

Capítulo 1 Días inolvidables

Capítulo 2 ¿Cómo te expresas?

Capítulo 3 ¿Qué haces para estar en forma?

Capítulo 4 ¿Cómo te llevas con los demás?

Capítulo 5 Trabajo y comunidad

Capítulo 6 ¿Qué nos traerá el futuro?

Capítulo 7 ¿Mito o realidad?

Capítulo 8 Encuentro entre culturas

Capítulo 9 Cuidemos nuestro planeta

Capítulo 10 ¿Cuáles son tus derechos y deberes?

Apéndices

México

Cabo San Lucas, Baja California, México

Morelia, México

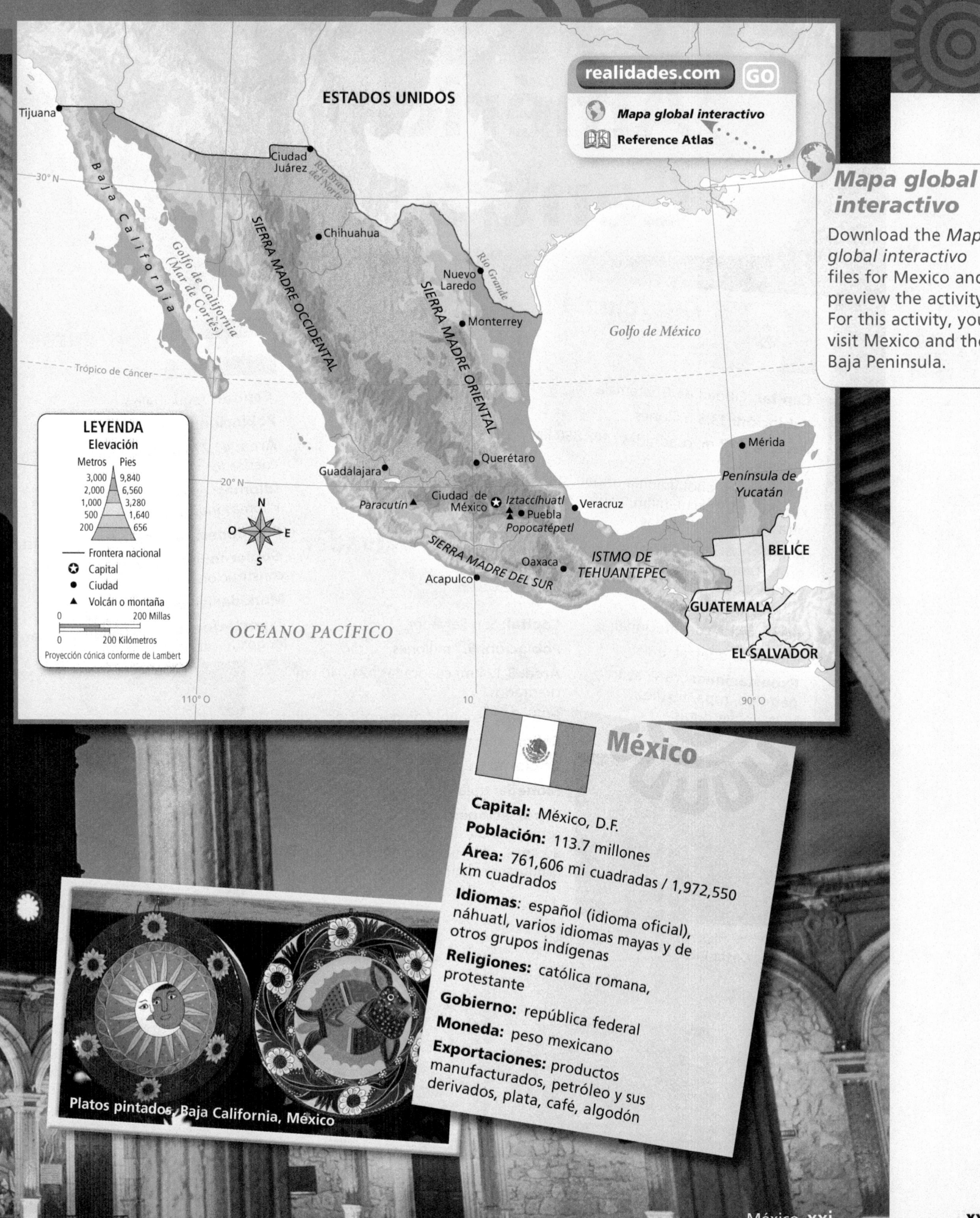

ESTADOS UNIDOS

Tijuana

Ciudad Juárez

Río Bravo del Norte

30° N

Chihuahua

Baja California

Golfo de California (Mar de Cortés)

SIERRA MADRE OCCIDENTAL

Nuevo Laredo

Río Grande

SIERRA MADRE ORIENTAL

Monterrey

Golfo de México

Trópico de Cáncer

Mapa global interactivo

Download the *Mapa global interactivo* files for Mexico and preview the activity. For this activity, you visit Mexico and the Baja Peninsula.

Mérida

Península de Yucatán

20° N

Guadalajara

Querétaro

Paracutín ▲

Ciudad de México ⭐

Iztaccíhuatl ▲
▲ Puebla
Popocatépetl

Veracruz

LEYENDA
Elevación

Metros	Pies
3,000	9,840
2,000	6,560
1,000	3,280
500	1,640
200	656

—— Frontera nacional
⭐ Capital
● Ciudad
▲ Volcán o montaña

0 ————— 200 Millas
0 ————— 200 Kilómetros

Proyección cónica conforme de Lambert

N O E S

SIERRA MADRE DEL SUR

Oaxaca

ISTMO DE TEHUANTEPEC

BELICE

Acapulco

GUATEMALA

OCÉANO PACÍFICO

EL SALVADOR

110° O

10

90° O

México

Capital: México, D.F.

Población: 113.7 millones

Área: 761,606 mi cuadradas / 1,972,550 km cuadrados

Idiomas: español (idioma oficial), náhuatl, varios idiomas mayas y de otros grupos indígenas

Religiones: católica romana, protestante

Gobierno: república federal

Moneda: peso mexicano

Exportaciones: productos manufacturados, petróleo y sus derivados, plata, café, algodón

Platos pintados, Baja California, México

América Central

Guatemala

Capital: Ciudad de Guatemala

Población: 13.8 millones

Área: 42,043 mi cuadradas / 108,890 km cuadrados

Idiomas: español (idioma oficial), quiché, kaqchiquel, kekchi, mam, garifuna, xinca y otras lenguas indígenas

Religiones: católica romana, protestante, creencias tradicionales mayas

Gobierno: república democrática constitucional

Moneda: quetzal, dólar

Exportaciones: café, azúcar, petróleo, ropa, textiles, plátano, verduras

El Salvador

Capital: San Salvador

Población: 6.1 millones

Área: 8,124 mi cuadradas / 21,040 km cuadrados

Idiomas: español (idioma oficial), nahua

Religiones: católica romana, protestante

Gobierno: república

Moneda: dólar

Exportaciones: elaboración de productos con materiales fabricados en el extranjero, equipos, café, azúcar, camarón, textiles, productos químicos, electricidad

Honduras

Capital: Tegucigalpa

Población: 8.1 millones

Área: 43,278 mi cuadradas / 112,090 km cuadrados

Idiomas: español (idioma oficial), idiomas indígenas

Religiones: católica romana, protestante

Gobierno: república democrática constitucional

Moneda: lempira

Exportaciones: café, plátano, camarón, langosta, carne, cinc, madera

San José, Costa Rica

Lago Atitlán, Guatemala

MÉXICO

Parque
Nacional Tikal

Lago de
Petén
Itzá

BELICE

Golfo de
Honduras

Lago de
Izabal

San Pedro Sula

GUATEMALA

Quetzaltenango

Ciudad de
Guatemala

Copán

Santa Rosa de Copán

HONDURAS

Antigua

Cerro El Pital

Volcán de
Santa Ana

Santa Ana

Tegucigalpa

San
Salvador

Santa Rosa
de Lima

CORDILLERA
ISABELIA

La Libertad

EL SALVADOR

Golfo de
Fonseca

Lago de
Managua

NICARAGUA

CORDILLERA CHONTALEÑA

Managua

Masaya

Granada

Lago de
Nicaragua

Los Chiles

COSTA RICA

San José

Puerto Limón

Golfo de
Nicoya

OCÉANO PACÍFICO

Mar
Caribe

JAM

Canal de
Panamá

Colón

Ciudad de
Panamá

PANAMÁ

Golfo de
Panamá

Golfo
Dulce

Parque
Nacional
Darién

8° N

COLOMBIA

92° O

84° O

80° O

realidades.com **GO**

🌐 *Mapa global interactivo*

📖 Reference Atlas

LEYENDA
Elevación

Metros	Pies
3,000	9,840
2,000	6,560
1,000	3,280
500	1,640
200	656

— Frontera nacional
⊛ Capital
• Ciudad
▲ Volcán o montaña
■ Zona arqueológica

0 ____ 100 Millas
0 ____ 100 Kilómetros

Proyección azimutal
equivalente de Lambert

Mapa global interactivo

Download the *Mapa global interactivo* files for Central America and preview the activities. In Activity 1, explore Guatemala and visit Lake Atitlán. In Activity 2, you visit El Salvador and its active volcano. In Activity 3, visit Honduras and explore its many islands. For Activity 4, you travel to Nicaragua and see Lake Nicaragua. In Activity 5, you explore Costa Rica's wetlands and rain forest preserves. In Activity 6, you visit Panama and explore its many rivers.

Nicaragua

Capital: Managua

Población: 5.7 millones

Área: 49,998 mi cuadradas / 129,494 km cuadrados

Idiomas: español (idioma oficial), inglés, miskito y otras lenguas indígenas

Religiones: católica romana, protestante

Gobierno: república

Moneda: córdoba oro

Exportaciones: café, camarón, langosta, algodón, tabaco, carne, azúcar, plátano, oro

Costa Rica

Capital: San José

Población: 4.6 millones

Área: 19,730 mi cuadradas / 51,100 km cuadrados

Idiomas: español (idioma oficial) e inglés

Religiones: católica romana, protestante

Gobierno: república democrática

Moneda: colón de Costa Rica

Exportaciones: café, plátano, azúcar, textiles, componentes electrónicos

Panamá

Capital: Ciudad de Panamá

Población: 3.5 millones

Área: 30,193 mi cuadradas / 78,200 km cuadrados

Idiomas: español (idioma oficial) e inglés

Religiones: católica romana, protestante

Gobierno: democracia constitucional

Moneda: balboa, dólar

Exportaciones: plátano, azúcar, camarón, café

El Caribe

Punta Cana, República Dominicana

La Habana, Cuba

ESTADOS
UNIDOS

Golfo de
México

ISLAS BAHAMAS

N
O E
S

24° N

Trópico de Cáncer

Estrecho de la Florida

La Habana

OCÉANO
ATLÁNTICO

CUBA

Isla de la
Juventud

Santiago
de Cuba

Guantánamo

REPÚBLICA
DOMINICANA

20° N

Bahía de
Samaná

PUERTO
RICO
(E.E.U.U.)

VIEQUES

HAITÍ

Santo
Domingo

San Juan

Ponce

El Yunque

JAMAICA

LEYENDA
Elevación

Metros	Pies
3,000	9,840
2,000	6,560
1,000	3,280
500	1,640
200	656

— Frontera nacional
Ⓢ Capital
● Ciudad
▲ Volcán o montaña

0   100 Millas
0   100 Kilómetros

Proyección azimutal
equivalente de Lambert

Mar Caribe

80° O

12° N

Mapa global interactivo

Download the *Mapa global interactivo* files for the Caribbean and preview the activities. In Activity 1, learn about the island nation of Cuba and its wetlands. For Activity 2, you explore the Dominican Republic with its rain forest and sandy beaches. In Activity 3, visit the U.S. territory of Puerto Rico and Mona Island.

República Dominicana

Capital: Santo Domingo

Población: 10 millones

Área: 18,815 mi cuadradas / 48,730 km cuadrados

Idiomas: español (idioma oficial)

Religiones: católica romana, protestante

Gobierno: democracia representativa

Moneda: peso dominicano

Exportaciones: ferroníquel, azúcar, oro, plata, cacao, tabaco, carne

Puerto Rico

Capital: San Juan

Población: 4 millones

Área: 3,515 mi cuadradas / 9,104 km cuadrados

Idiomas: español e inglés (idiomas oficiales)

Religiones: católica romana, protestante

Gobierno: estado libre asociado de Estados Unidos

Moneda: dólar estadounidense

Exportaciones: productos químicos, productos electrónicos, ropa, atún enlatado, concentrados de bebidas, equipo médico

Cuba

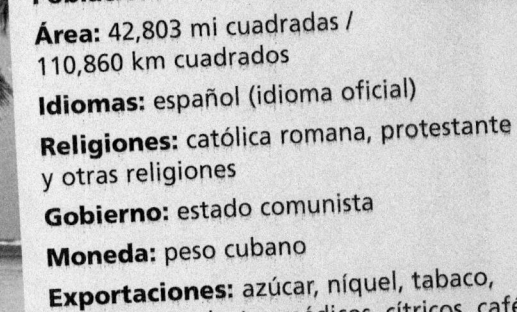

Capital: La Habana

Población: 11.1 millones

Área: 42,803 mi cuadradas / 110,860 km cuadrados

Idiomas: español (idioma oficial)

Religiones: católica romana, protestante y otras religiones

Gobierno: estado comunista

Moneda: peso cubano

Exportaciones: azúcar, níquel, tabaco, mariscos, productos médicos, cítricos, café

El Caribe **XXV**

América del Sur
(Parte norte)

Ecuador

Capital: Quito

Población: 15 millones

Área: 109,483 mi cuadradas / 283,560 km cuadrados

Idiomas: español (idioma oficial), quechua y otros idiomas indígenas

Religiones: católica romana

Gobierno: república

Moneda: dólar

Exportaciones: petróleo, plátano, atún, camarón, cacao, oro, madera tropical

Colombia

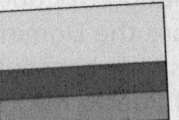

Capital: Bogotá

Población: 44.7 millones

Área: 439,736 mi cuadradas / 1,138,910 km cuadrados

Idiomas: español (idioma oficial)

Religiones: católica romana

Gobierno: república

Moneda: peso colombiano

Exportaciones: textiles, petróleo, carbón, café, oro, esmeraldas, plátano, flores, productos de farmacia, azúcar

Perú

Capital: Lima

Población: 29.2 millones

Área: 496,226 mi cuadradas / 1,285,220 km cuadrados

Idiomas: español y quechua (idiomas oficiales), aymara y otras lenguas indígenas

Religiones: católica romana y otras religiones

Gobierno: república constitucional

Moneda: nuevo sol

Exportaciones: oro, cinc, cobre, pescado y productos de pescado, textiles

Mujer de los Andes, Perú

Mapa global interactivo

Download the *Mapa global interactivo* files for the northern part of South America and preview the activities. In Activity 1, you visit Colombia and the *cordilleras* of the Andes. In Activity 2, travel to Ecuador and its capital of Quito high in the Andes. In Activity 3, visit Peru with its mountains and beaches. In Activity 4, travel through Venezuela with its varied topography of islands, coastlines, and mountains. And in Activity 5, visit landlocked Bolivia and its two capitals, Sucre and La Paz.

realidades.com GO

🌐 *Mapa global interactivo*

📖 Reference Atlas

LEYENDA
Elevación

Metros	Pies
3,000	9,840
2,000	6,560
1,000	3,280
500	1,640
200	656

— Frontera nacional
⊛ Capital
● Ciudad
▲ Volcán o montaña
■ Zona arqueológica

0   400 Millas
0   400 Kilómetros

Proyección azimutal
equivalente de Lambert

Bolivia

Capitales: La Paz, Sucre

Población: 10.1 millones

Área: 424,164 mi cuadradas / 1,098,580 km cuadrados

Idiomas: español, quechua, aymara (idiomas oficiales)

Religiones: católica romana, protestante

Gobierno: república

Moneda: boliviano

Exportaciones: soya, gas natural, cinc, madera, oro

Venezuela

Capital: Caracas

Población: 27.6 millones

Área: 352,144 mi cuadradas / 912,050 km cuadrados

Idiomas: español (idioma oficial), otras lenguas indígenas

Religiones: católica romana, protestante

Gobierno: república federal

Moneda: bolívar fuerte

Exportaciones: petróleo y productos derivados, plátano, acero, aluminio, energía hidroeléctrica

América del Sur
(Parte sur)

 **Chile**

Capital: Santiago

Población: 16.9 millones

Área: 292,260 mi cuadradas / 756,950 km cuadrados

Idiomas: español (idioma oficial)

Religiones: católica romana, protestante

Gobierno: república

Moneda: peso chileno

Exportaciones: cobre, pescado, hierro, yodo, fruta, madera, papel y pulpa, productos químicos

 **Paraguay**

Capital: Asunción

Población: 6.5 millones

Área: 157,047 mi cuadradas / 406,750 km cuadrados

Idiomas: español y guaraní (idiomas oficiales)

Religiones: católica romana, protestante

Gobierno: república constitucional

Moneda: guaraní

Exportaciones: azúcar, carne, tapioca, energía hidroeléctrica

La Boca, Buenos Aires, Argentina

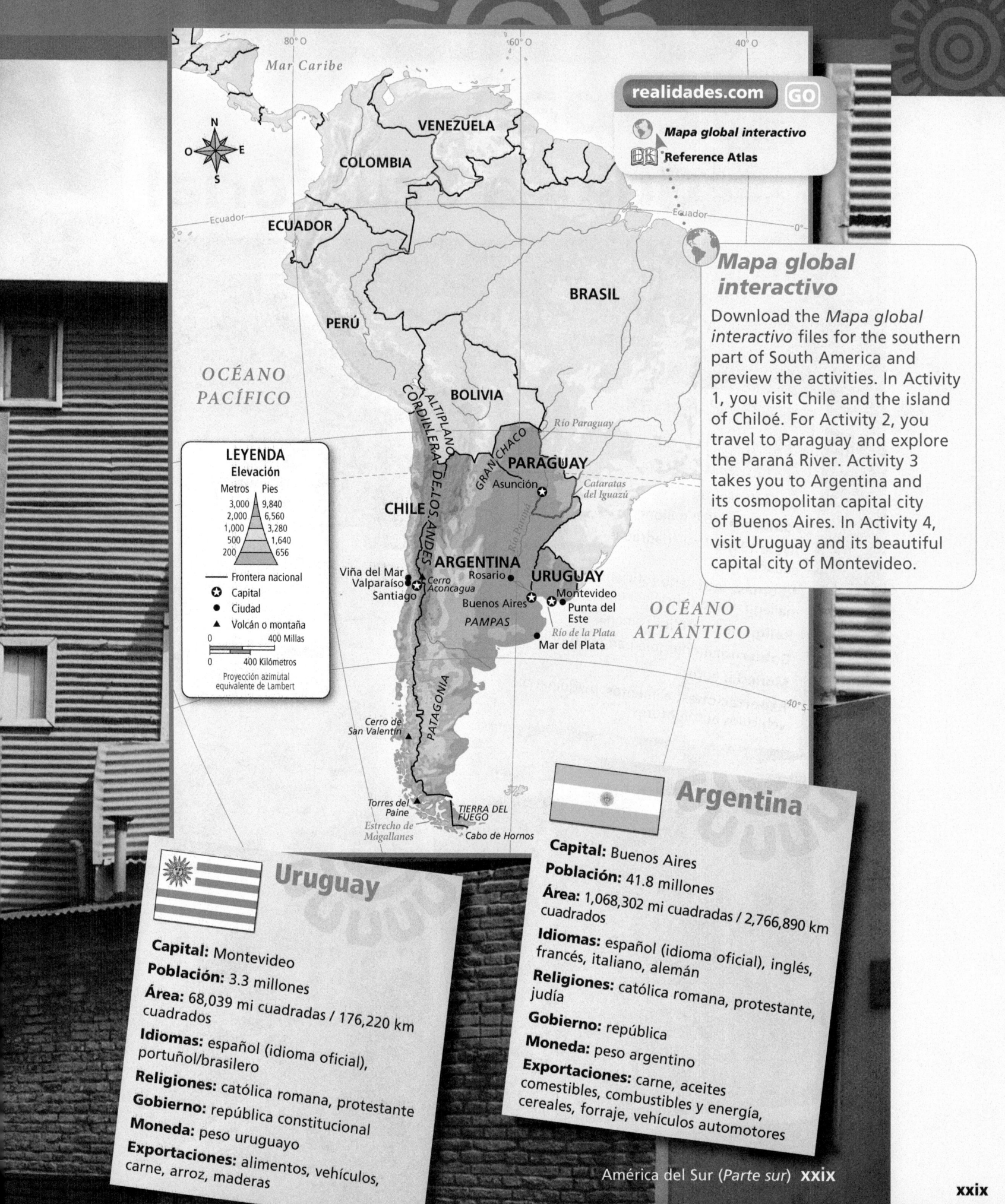

80° O   60° O   40° O

Mar Caribe

VENEZUELA

COLOMBIA

realidades.com GO

🌎 *Mapa global interactivo*

📖▶ Reference Atlas

Ecuador   Ecuador   0°

ECUADOR

BRASIL

PERÚ

Mapa global interactivo

Download the *Mapa global interactivo* files for the southern part of South America and preview the activities. In Activity 1, you visit Chile and the island of Chiloé. For Activity 2, you travel to Paraguay and explore the Paraná River. Activity 3 takes you to Argentina and its cosmopolitan capital city of Buenos Aires. In Activity 4, visit Uruguay and its beautiful capital city of Montevideo.

OCÉANO PACÍFICO

BOLIVIA

Río Paraguay

GRAN CHACO

ALTIPLANO

CORDILLERA DE LOS ANDES

PARAGUAY

Asunción ✪   *Cataratas del Iguazú*

CHILE

Río Paraná

LEYENDA
Elevación

Metros	Pies
3,000	9,840
2,000	6,560
1,000	3,280
500	1,640
200	656

—— Frontera nacional
✪ Capital
● Ciudad
▲ Volcán o montaña

0 ————— 400 Millas
0 ————— 400 Kilómetros

Proyección azimutal equivalente de Lambert

ARGENTINA

Viña del Mar
Valparaíso ●   *Cerro Aconcagua* ▲
Santiago ✪

Rosario ●

URUGUAY

Montevideo ✪
Buenos Aires ✪   ● Punta del Este

PAMPAS

Río de la Plata

OCÉANO ATLÁNTICO

● Mar del Plata

40° S

PATAGONIA

Cerro de San Valentín ▲

Torres del Paine ▲   TIERRA DEL FUEGO

Estrecho de Magallanes   Cabo de Hornos

Argentina

Capital: Buenos Aires

Población: 41.8 millones

Área: 1,068,302 mi cuadradas / 2,766,890 km cuadrados

Idiomas: español (idioma oficial), inglés, francés, italiano, alemán

Religiones: católica romana, protestante, judía

Gobierno: república

Moneda: peso argentino

Exportaciones: carne, aceites comestibles, combustibles y energía, cereales, forraje, vehículos automotores

Uruguay

Capital: Montevideo

Población: 3.3 millones

Área: 68,039 mi cuadradas / 176,220 km cuadrados

Idiomas: español (idioma oficial), portuñol/brasilero

Religiones: católica romana, protestante

Gobierno: república constitucional

Moneda: peso uruguayo

Exportaciones: alimentos, vehículos, carne, arroz, maderas

América del Sur (*Parte sur*) **xxix**

España
Guinea Ecuatorial

El pueblo blanco de Casares, España

España

Capital: Madrid

Población: 46.8 millones

Área: 194,897 mi cuadradas / 504,782 km cuadrados

Idiomas: castellano (oficial); catalán, gallego, vasco (oficiales regionalmente)

Religiones: católica romana

Gobierno: monarquía parlamentaria

Moneda: euro

Exportaciones: alimentos, maquinaria, vehículos automotores

Museo Guggenheim, Bilbao, España

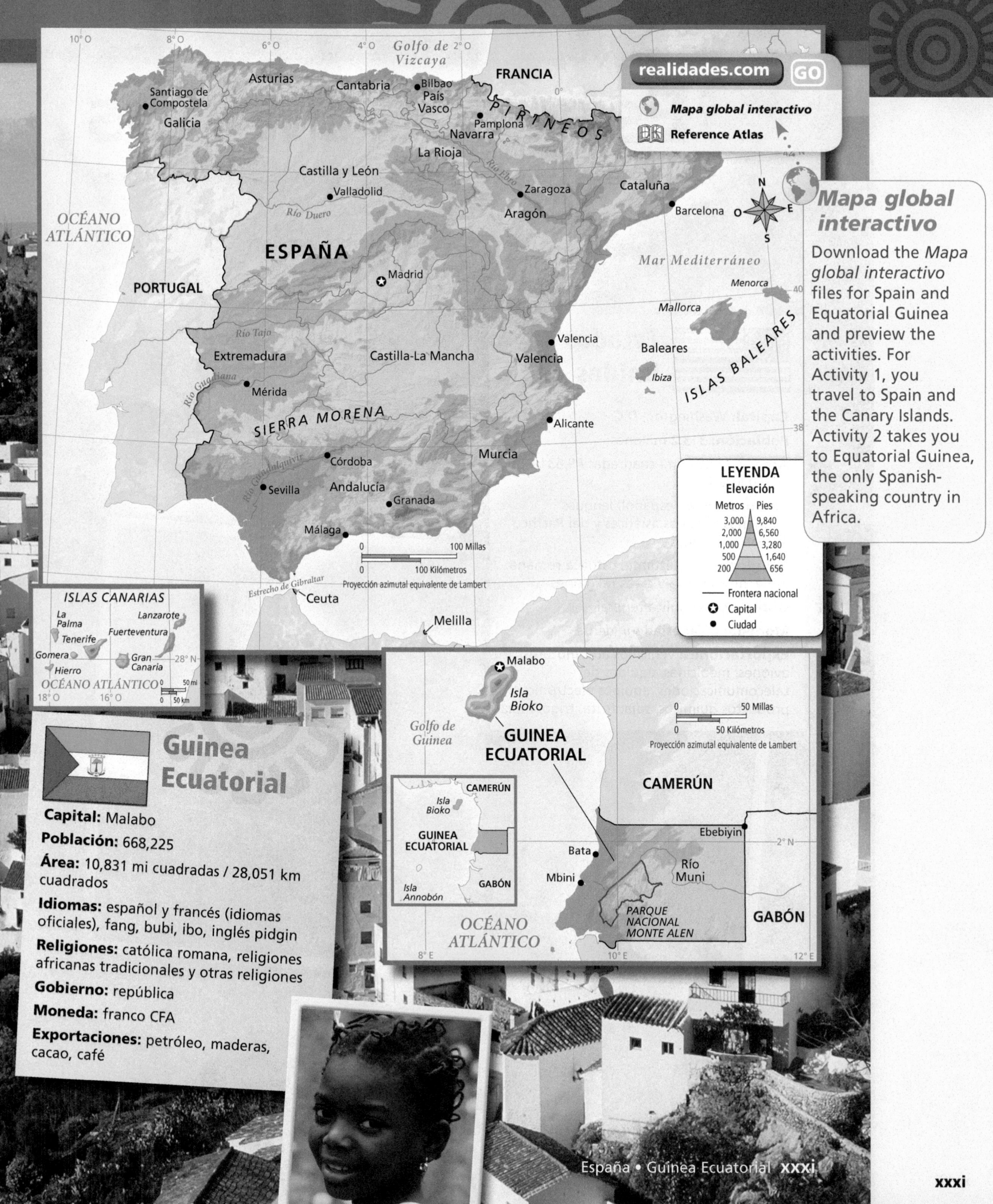

ESPAÑA

PORTUGAL

OCÉANO ATLÁNTICO

Golfo de Vizcaya

FRANCIA

PIRINEOS

Santiago de Compostela
Galicia
Asturias
Cantabria
Bilbao
País Vasco
Pamplona
Navarra
La Rioja
Castilla y León
Valladolid
Río Duero
Río Ebro
Zaragoza
Aragón
Cataluña
Barcelona

Río Tajo

Madrid

Extremadura
Mérida
Río Guadiana

Castilla-La Mancha

SIERRA MORENA

Córdoba
Sevilla
Río Guadalquivir
Andalucía
Granada
Málaga

Murcia
Alicante
Valencia
Valencia

Mar Mediterráneo

Menorca
Mallorca
Baleares
Ibiza
ISLAS BALEARES

Estrecho de Gibraltar
Ceuta
Melilla

0   100 Millas
0   100 Kilómetros
Proyección azimutal equivalente de Lambert

realidades.com **GO**

🌐 *Mapa global interactivo*

📖 Reference Atlas

Mapa global interactivo

Download the *Mapa global interactivo* files for Spain and Equatorial Guinea and preview the activities. For Activity 1, you travel to Spain and the Canary Islands. Activity 2 takes you to Equatorial Guinea, the only Spanish-speaking country in Africa.

LEYENDA
Elevación

Metros	Pies
3,000	9,840
2,000	6,560
1,000	3,280
500	1,640
200	656

—— Frontera nacional
⭐ Capital
● Ciudad

ISLAS CANARIAS

La Palma
Lanzarote
Tenerife
Fuerteventura
Gomera
Gran Canaria
Hierro

OCÉANO ATLÁNTICO

0   50 mi
0   50 km

Guinea Ecuatorial

Capital: Malabo

Población: 668,225

Área: 10,831 mi cuadradas / 28,051 km cuadrados

Idiomas: español y francés (idiomas oficiales), fang, bubi, ibo, inglés pidgin

Religiones: católica romana, religiones africanas tradicionales y otras religiones

Gobierno: república

Moneda: franco CFA

Exportaciones: petróleo, maderas, cacao, café

Malabo
Isla Bioko
Golfo de Guinea
GUINEA ECUATORIAL
CAMERÚN
Ebebiyin
Bata
Mbini
Río Muni
GABÓN
PARQUE NACIONAL MONTE ALEN
OCÉANO ATLÁNTICO

CAMERÚN
Isla Bioko
GUINEA ECUATORIAL
Isla Annobón
GABÓN

0   50 Millas
0   50 Kilómetros
Proyección azimutal equivalente de Lambert

Estados Unidos

Jackson Hole, Wyoming

Estados Unidos

Capital: Washington, D.C.

Población: 313.2 millones

Área: 3,717,813 mi cuadradas / 9,631,418 km cuadrados

Idiomas: inglés, español, lenguas indígenas, lenguas asiáticas y del Pacífico Sur, otras lenguas

Religiones: protestante, católica romana, judía, musulmana y otras religiones

Gobierno: república federal

Moneda: dólar estadounidense

Exportaciones: vehículos automotores, aviones, medicinas, equipos de telecomunicaciones, equipos electrónicos, productos químicos, soja, fruta, trigo, maíz

Puente Golden Gate, San Francisco, California

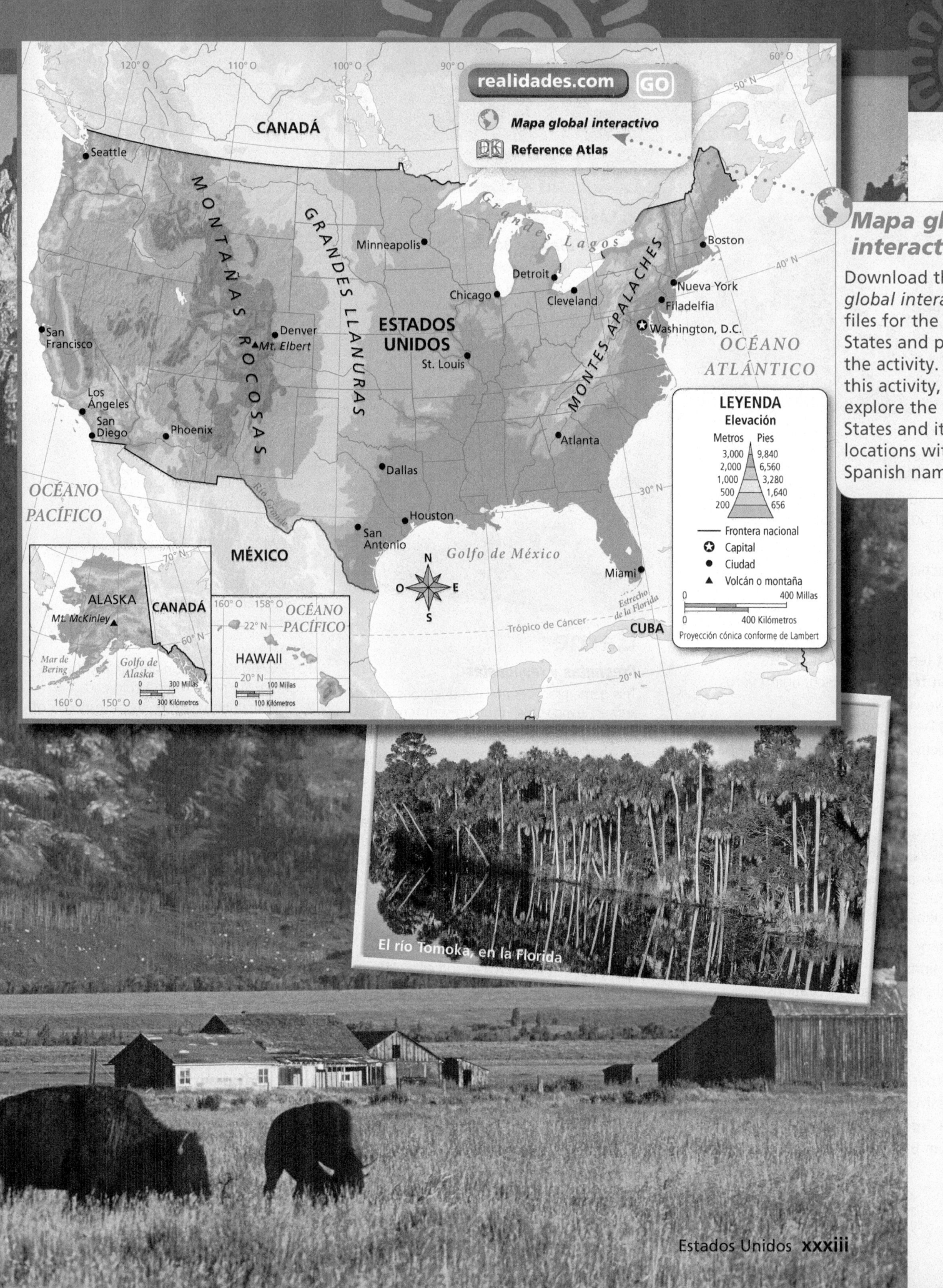

realidades.com **GO**

🌐 *Mapa global interactivo*

📖 Reference Atlas

CANADÁ

Seattle

MONTAÑAS ROCOSAS

GRANDES LLANURAS

Minneapolis

Grandes Lagos

Detroit

Chicago

Cleveland

Boston

MONTES APALACHES

Nueva York

Filadelfia

Washington, D.C.

ESTADOS UNIDOS

San Francisco

Denver

▲Mt. Elbert

St. Louis

OCÉANO ATLÁNTICO

Los Ángeles

San Diego

Phoenix

Atlanta

OCÉANO PACÍFICO

Río Grande

Dallas

Houston

San Antonio

Golfo de México

Miami

MÉXICO

Estrecho de la Florida

CUBA

Trópico de Cáncer

LEYENDA
Elevación

Metros	Pies
3,000	9,840
2,000	6,560
1,000	3,280
500	1,640
200	656

── Frontera nacional

✪ Capital

● Ciudad

▲ Volcán o montaña

0   400 Millas

0   400 Kilómetros

Proyección cónica conforme de Lambert

ALASKA

CANADÁ

Mt. McKinley ▲

Mar de Bering

Golfo de Alaska

OCÉANO PACÍFICO

HAWAII

0   300 Millas
0   300 Kilómetros

0   100 Millas
0   100 Kilómetros

Mapa global interactivo

Download the *Mapa global interactivo* files for the United States and preview the activity. In this activity, you explore the United States and its many locations with Spanish names.

El río Tomoka, en la Florida

Estados Unidos **xxxiii**

1 Tu vida diaria

- school and
  non-school daily activities

Vocabulary
- daily activities
- household chores
- errands

Grammar
- **present** tense of irregular verbs
- present tense of stem-changing verbs
- reflexive verbs

Cultural Perspectives
- daily activities of young people in Spain

2 Días especiales

- weekend activities
  and special events
  and celebrations

Vocabulary
- entertainment
- special events and celebrations
- television and movies
- travel

Grammar
- verbs that conjugate like *gustar*
- possessive adjectives

Cultural Perspectives
- skiing in Bariloche, Argentina

CHAPTER SUPPORT

Bulletin Boards

Theme: *Días especiales*

Ask students to cut out, copy, or download photos or pictures of special celebrations and holidays in different countries. They can also include their own photos. Cluster pictures by country.

Game

Preguntas y respuestas

This game practices making questions and answers, using verbs in the present tense.

Players: the entire class

Materials: 3" x 5" index cards, cut in half, small paper bag

Steps:

1. Give students two halves of an index card and ask them to write a question in the present tense on one half and an answer on the other. Questions can be funny, silly, or serious. The answers should include as many details as possible. For example:
   Q: ¿Cómo ayudas a tu mamá cuando regresas de la escuela?
   A: Voy al supermercado con ella y la ayudo a cocinar.
2. Place answers in a bag and mix them up.
3. Each student selects a card from the bag.
4. The first player reads his / her question aloud. A student who thinks he / she has the correct answer reads it to the class. If correct, this student reads the next question. If incorrect, another player reads an answer. If, after three tries, no one presents the correct answer, the player who wrote the original question says the answer and chooses someone to read the next question.
5. The game is over when all questions are read.

Hands-on Culture

Craft: *Piñata*

A *piñata* is a decorated container filled with candy and toys that is suspended from a height. Children take turns trying to break it open with a stick while blindfolded. The *piñata* is a Mexican custom that has existed for many centuries. Original *piñatas* were made of clay, and then replaced by cardboard.

Materials:

    medium-size round balloon
    string and scissors
    newspapers
    white liquid glue and water
    old tablespoon for measuring
    small bowl for glue
    bowl to hold the balloon
    brush for glue
    tissue paper in assorted colors
    wrapped candy and/or small toys
    masking tape (optional)

Steps:

1. Blow up the balloon and tie it with a string. Do not cut the string ends.
2. In a small bowl, dilute six tablespoons of white liquid glue with three tablespoons of water.
3. Tear off small pieces of tissue paper. Brush diluted glue over the balloon, a small section at a time, and paste on the paper pieces. Overlap the pieces and brush more glue on top. Continue to cover the balloon, making large patches of different colors, overlapping them at edges. Hold the balloon in empty bowl while you work so that it won't roll. Leave a 2" patch uncovered around the knot. Then turn the balloon right side up, knotted end down, and cover the top.
4. Use the string to hang the balloon upside down. Let dry overnight.
5. Paste two more layers of paper pieces on the balloon, letting it dry overnight between each layer.
6. Cut the knotted end off, pull the balloon out and discard it.
7. Fill the piñata with wrapped candies. Paste tissue paper pieces to cover the opening. Let dry.
8. Paint and decorate the *piñata*.
9. Use the strings to hang up the *piñata* outside.

CHAPTER PROJECT

La entrevista

Overview: Students write a television script for an interview program about all the things a student does everyday from the time he / she wakes up. They also create a time schedule showing all the things the interviewee (a student) does. They then perform the interview and record it for the class to view.

Resources: design tools for print or screen, poster board, markers, video equipment

Sequence: (suggestions for when to do each step are found throughout the unit)

STEP 1. Review instructions so students know what is expected of them. Hand out the "*Para empezar* Project Instructions and Rubric" from the *Teacher's Resource Book*.

STEP 2. Students write a rough draft of their interview. They then exchange scripts with a partner for peer editing. Students make corrections based on their partner's comments.

STEP 3. Students create a time schedule. The time schedule should show the different things the student says he / she does during the day. After completing the schedules, students could add illustrations to make it more interesting.

STEP 4. Students rehearse their interview with a partner. Partners give students feedback about the content, accuracy, and presentation of the subject.

STEP 5. Students record their interview. Show videos to the class.

Options:

1. Students present their interviews to the class "live" instead of recording them.
2. Students give a presentation of the everyday activities of a student.

Assessment:

Here is a detailed rubric for assessing this project:
Preliminary Unit Project: *La entrevista*

RUBRIC	Score 1	Score 3	Score 5
Your evidence of planning	You do not include a written draft.	Your draft is written, but not corrected.	You provide evidence of corrected draft.
Your use of illustrations	You do not include a time schedule.	Your time schedule is difficult to read, incomplete, and / or inaccurate.	Your time schedule is easy to read, complete, and accurate.
Your interview presentation	You do not include the majority of the required elements.	You include some of the following: greeting, questions, answers, and descriptions.	You include the following: greeting, questions, answers, and descriptions.

21st Century Skills

Look for tips throughout *Para empezar* to enrich your teaching by integrating 21st Century Skills. Suggestions for the Chapter Project and Culture follow below.

Chapter Project

Modify the Chapter Project with one or more of these suggestions:

Enhance Communication

As students begin preparations for the Chapter Project, provide them with the handout "Ask Questions." Have them also make a list of the interrogative words and phrases they know in Spanish. Make sure they integrate what they have learned from the handout, along with their Spanish interrogative words and phrases, into their script for the student interview.

Foster Collaboration

Encourage students to work with a partner or in a small group to share the responsibility of preparing the interview questions. They should take turns playing the role of interviewer and interviewee by asking and answering the questions they created as a rehearsal for the recording of the interview.

Promote Social and Cross Cultural Skills

Have students interview an older family member or a person in their community from another culture about a similar daily time schedule. They can conduct the interview in English, then report back to the class in Spanish. Have students circulate around the room to compare their schedules with the schedules they have gathered from people outside the class. What are the similarities and differences?

Chapter Culture

Develop Critical Thinking and Problem Solving

Have students compare their responses to the question in the *Fondo cultural* note on page xxxiv with a partner. What similarities or differences are there between their responses? Ask them to consider what these similarities or differences might be attributed to: culture? economics? other influences? Ask them to identify the most important element to them from the list (friends, family, health, etc.), and to comment on their choices.

AT A GLANCE

Objectives

- Talk about your daily life
- Write about leisure and after-school activities
- Talk about school and non-school daily activities
- Describe your day before and after school
- Talk about weekend activities
- Discuss special events, celebrations, and vacations

Recycle ♻

- Foods and beverages
- Health and exercise

Vocabulary

- Daily activities (school related and non-school related)
- Help around the house and errands
- Entertainment, television, and movies
- Events and celebrations
- Traveling

Grammar

- Irregular verbs
- Stem-changing verbs in the present tense
- Reflexive verbs
- Verbs that conjugate like *gustar*
- Possessive adjectives

Culture

- Daily activities of young people, p. xxxiv
- Skiing in Bariloche, p. 12

RESOURCES

	FOR THE STUDENT	ONLINE	DVD	PRINT	FOR THE TEACHER	ONLINE	PREEXP	DVD	PRINT
Plan					Interactive TE and Resources DVD	•		•	
					Teacher's Resource Book, pp. 1–12	•		•	•
					Lesson Plans	•			•
					Mapa global interactivo	•			

Introducción PP. **xxxiv–1**

	FOR THE STUDENT	ONLINE	DVD	PRINT	FOR THE TEACHER	ONLINE	PREEXP	DVD	PRINT
Present	Student Edition, pp. xxxiv–1	•	•	•	Interactive TE and Resources DVD	•		•	
	DK Reference Atlas	•	•		Teacher's Resource Book, pp. 2–5	•		•	•
	Hispanohablantes WB, p. viii			•	Galería de fotos		•		
					Map Transparencies, 20	•	•	•	

Tu vida diaria PP. **2–7**

	FOR THE STUDENT	ONLINE	DVD	PRINT	FOR THE TEACHER	ONLINE	PREEXP	DVD	PRINT
Present & Practice	Student Edition, pp. 2–7	•	•	•	Interactive Whiteboard Grammar Activities	•		•	
	Audio	•	•		Interactive TE and Resources DVD	•		•	
	Flashcards	•	•		Teacher's Resource Book, pp. 6, 8–9	•		•	•
	Instant Check	•			Communicative Pair Activities, p. 10	•		•	•
	Guide WB, pp. 1–10	•	•	•	Audio Program	•	•	•	•
	Core WB, pp. 1–3	•	•	•	Vocabulary and Grammar Transparencies, 23–26	•	•	•	
	Comm. WB, pp. 1–3, 6	•	•	•	Answer Keys: Student Edition, pp. 1–2	•	•	•	
	Hispanohablantes WB, pp. 1–5			•					
	Communicative Pair Activities	•							
Assess and Remediate					Prueba P–1 with Study Plan	•			
					Prueba P–1: Assessment Program, pp. 8–9 Hispanohablantes, pp. 8–9	•		•	•

RESOURCES

FOR THE STUDENT	ONLINE	DVD	PRINT	FOR THE TEACHER	ONLINE	PREEXP	DVD	PRINT
Días especiales PP. **8–13**								
Present & Practice Student Edition, pp. 8–13	•	•	•	Interactive Whiteboard Grammar Activities	•		•	
Instant Check	•			Interactive TE and Resources DVD	•		•	
Tutorial Video: Grammar	•			Teacher's Resource Book, pp. 7, 9	•		•	•
Guided WB, pp. 11–14	•	•	•	Audio Program	•	•	•	
Core WB, pp. 4–6	•	•	•	Vocabulary and Grammar Transparencies, 4, 18, 27–31	•	•	•	
Comm. WB, pp. 4–5	•	•	•	Answer Keys: Student Edition, pp. 3–4	•	•	•	
Hispanohablantes WB, pp. 6–9			•					
Assess and Remediate				Prueba P–2 with Study Plan	•			
				Prueba P–2: Assessment Program, pp. 10–11	•		•	•
				Hispanohablantes, pp. 10–11	•		•	•
Presentación oral, Presentación escrita PP. **14–15**								
Application Student Edition, pp. 14–15	•	•	•	Interactive TE and Resources DVD	•		•	
Hispanohablantes WB, pp. 10–11			•					

REGULAR SCHEDULE (50 MINUTES)

DAY	Warm-up / Assess	Preview / Present / Practice / Communicate	Wrap-up / Homework Options
1	**Warm-up (10 min.)** • Chapter Opener • Arte y cultura	**Tu vida diaria (35 min.)** • Presentation: Tu vida diaria • Actividad 1 • Presentation: Gramática-Repaso • Interactive Whiteboard Grammar Activities • Actividades 3, 4, 5, 6 • Audio Activity 1 • Presentation: Gramática-Repaso	**Wrap-up and Homework Options (5 min.)** • Actividades 2, 7, 8, 9 • Core Practice P-1 • Clip Art Vocabulary
2	**Warm-up (10 min.)** • Homework check	**Tu vida diaria (35 min.)** • Actividad 10 • Audio Activity 2 • Presentation: Gramática-Repaso • Actividad 11 • Audio Activity 3 • Communicative Pair Activity	**Wrap-up and Homework Options (5 min.)** • Actividad 12 • Core Practice P-2, P-3 • Prueba P-1 with Study Plan
3	**Warm-up (10 min.)** • Homework check ✔**Formative Assessment** • Prueba P-1 with Study Plan	**Días especiales (35 min.)** • Presentation: Días especiales • Actividad 13 • Actividades 15, 16 • Audio Activity 4 • Presentation: Gramática-Repaso • Interactive Whiteboard Grammar Activities • Actividades 17, 18 • Audio Activity 5	**Wrap-up and Homework Options (5 min.)** • Actividad 14 • Core Practice P-4 • Prueba P-2 with Study Plan
4	**Warm-up (10 min.)** • Homework check ✔**Formative Assessment** • Prueba P-2 with Study Plan	**Días especiales (20 min.)** • Presentation: Gramática-Repaso • Actividades 19, 20, 21 • Fondo cultural **Assessment (15 min.)** • Presentación oral • Communicative Pair Activity	**Wrap-up and Homework Options (5 min.)** • Core Practice P-5 • Presentación oral
5	**Warm-up (3 min.)** ✔**Formative Assessment (32 min.)** • Presentación oral	✔**Formative Assessment (14 min.)** • Presentación escrita	**Wrap-up and Homework Options (1 min.)** • Presentación escrita

DAY

BLOCK SCHEDULE (90 MINUTES)

Warm-up / Assess	Preview / Present / Practice / Communicate	Wrap-up / Homework Options
1 **Warm-up** (10 min.) • Chapter Opener • Arte y cultura	**Tu vida diaria** (25 min.) • Presentation: Tu vida diaria • Actividad 1 • Presentation: Gramática-Repaso • Interactive Whiteboard Grammar Activities • Actividades 3, 4, 5, 6 • Audio Activity 1 • Presentation: Gramática-Repaso • Actividades 8, 9, 10 • Audio Activity 2 • Presentation: Gramática-Repaso • Actividad 11 • Audio Activity 3 • Communicative Pair Activity	**Wrap-up and Homework Options** (5 min.) • Actividades 2, 7, 12 • Core Practice: P-1, P-2, P-3 • Clip Art Vocabulary • Prueba P-1 with Study Plan
2 **Warm-up** (10 min.) • Actividad 6 • Homework check ✔**Formative Assessment** • Prueba P-1 with Study Plan	**Días especiales** (60 min.) • Presentation: Días especiales • Actividades 13, 15, 16 • Audio Activity 4 • Presentation: Gramática-Repaso • Interactive Whiteboard Grammar Activities • Actividades 17, 18 • Audio Activity 5 • Presentation: Gramática-Repaso • Actividades 20, 21 **Assessment** (15 min.) • Presentación oral	**Wrap-up and Homework Options** (5 min.) • Actividades 14, 19 • Core Practice: P-4, P-5 • Presentación oral • Prueba P-2 with Study Plan
3 **Warm-up** (10 min.) • Actividad 10 • Homework check ✔**Formative Assessment** • Prueba P-2 with Study Plan	✔**Formative Assessment** (60 min.) • Presentación oral • Presentación escrita	**Wrap-up and Homework Options** (20 min.) • Fondo cultural • Communicative Pair Activity

Standards for Foreign Language Learning: *Para empezar*

- To achieve the goals of the Standards, students will:

Communication

1.1 Interpersonal
- Talk about the activities of Spanish young people
- Talk about daily routines, pastimes, and chores
- Talk about TV programs, entertainment, special days, and vacations
- Talk about Bariloche, Argentina

1.2 Interpretive
- Read about the activities of Spanish young people
- Read and listen to information about daily routines, pastimes, and household chores
- Read and listen to information about TV programs, entertainment, special days, and vacations
- Read about Bariloche, Argentina
- Read about speech and composition preparation

1.3 Presentational
- Write and present information orally about daily routines, pastimes, and household chores
- Write and present information orally about TV programs, entertainment, special days, and vacations
- Write about activities for visiting foreign students

Culture

2.1 Practices and Perspectives
- Understand lifestyles and values of Spanish and Venezuelan young people
- Understand the vacation practices of Spanish-speaking peoples

2.2 Products and Perspectives
- Learn about the ski resort of Bariloche, Argentina

Connections

3.1 Cross-curricular
- Learn key facts about Spanish youth
- Learn key facts about an Argentine town
- Learn Language Arts Strategies: evaluate your lead

3.2 Target Culture
- Read poetry from Spain by Rafael Alberti
- Learn how indigenous peoples have affected the language of Mexico
- Learn how ancient pilgrimages have shaped travel practices in Spain today

Comparisons

4.1 Language
- Compare the use of **encantar, gustar, importar,** and **interesar** to that of their English counterparts
- Compare Spanish words to their English counterparts

4.2 Culture
- Compare the activities of young people in Spain to those in the United States

Communities

5.1 Beyond the School
- Link to Web sites from the Spanish-speaking world

Para empezar

▼ Chapter Objectives

Communication

By the end of *Para empezar* you will be able to:
- Talk about your daily life
- Write about leisure and after-school activities

You will demonstrate what you know and can do:
- Presentación oral, p. 14
- Presentación escrita, p. 15

You will also learn to:

 1 Tu vida diaria
- Talk about school and non-school daily activities
- Describe your day before and after school

 2 Días especiales
- Talk about weekend activities
- Discuss special events, celebrations, and vacations

realidades.com GO

📖 Reference Atlas   🌎 **Mapa global interactivo**

Arte y cultura | España

Vida diaria de los jóvenes ¿Qué cosas son importantes para los jóvenes de España? Según una encuesta *(survey)*, para los jóvenes españoles son importantes los amigos, la familia, la salud, la libertad[1], las cosas que tienen, el tiempo libre, los estudios, la situación económica y el trabajo. ¿Qué hacen en su tiempo libre? Los días de semana practican deportes, estudian instrumentos musicales o idiomas, escuchan música, ven la televisión o usan la computadora. Los fines de semana salen con sus amigos, van al cine o a bailar.

- ¿En qué te pareces y en qué te diferencias de los jóvenes que respondieron a la encuesta?

---
1 freedom

Un grupo de chicas juega al fútbol en Cuzco, Perú.

ENRICH YOUR TEACHING

Using Backward Design
Have students preview the *Presentación oral* and *Presentación escrita* tasks on pages 14–15 and connect them to the Chapter Objectives. Explain to students that by completing these sample tasks they can self-assess their learning progress.

Mapa global interactivo
Download the *Mapa global interactivo* files for *Para empezar* and preview the activity. For this activity, travel to Bariloche, the gateway to Patagonia in Argentina.

 PresentationExpress™
See pp. xxxiv-c–xxxiv-d

Chapter Opener

Core Instruction

Para empezar is designed to give a quick re-entry into the new school year by allowing students to talk about what they enjoy doing. It reviews fundamental structures and basic vocabulary. Additional review of vocabulary and structures will be woven throughout the book in the *A ver si recuerdas* sections as well as in the regular chapters. You may also want to incorporate any favorite activities or materials from *Realidades* 1 and 2 that deal with the same topics or structures.

Suggestions: Introduce yourself to students who don't know you. Provide a brief description of yourself (where you are from and some activities you enjoy). Then have each student turn to a partner he or she doesn't know, to find out his or her name, some favorite activities.

Arte y cultura

Standards: 1.1, 1.2, 2.1, 3.1, 4.2

Suggestions: After students read the information silently, guide them to answer the question by saying: *¿Hay cosas que son importantes para los jóvenes españoles que no son importantes para ti? ¿Cuáles son?*

Answers will vary.

CULTURE NOTE

Soccer has the number 1 ranking as the world's most popular sport. According to FIFA, the international governing body for the game of soccer, there are over 270 million male and female players and officials involved in the game of soccer worldwide. This represents almost four per cent of the world's population.

uno **1**
Para empezar

DIFFERENTIATED INSTRUCTION

Digital resources such as the *Interactive Whiteboard* activity banks, *Videomodelos*, additional *Online Activities*, *Study Plans*, automatically graded *Leveled Workbook*, animated *Grammar Tutorials*, *Flashcards*, and *Vocabulary and Grammar Videos* will help you reach students of different ability levels and learning styles.

STUDENTS NEEDING EXTRA HELP

Guided Practice Activities
• Flashcards, pp. 1–2
• Vocabulary Check, pp. 3–4
• Grammar, pp. 5–14

HERITAGE LEARNERS

Realidades para hispanohablantes
• Chapter Opener, pp. x–1
• Tu vida diaria, pp. 2–5
• Días especiales, pp. 6–9
• Presentación oral, p. 10
• Presentación escrita, p. 11

Communications Workbook
• Integrated Performance Assessment, p. 162

Tu vida diaria

Core Instruction

Standards: 1.2

Resources: Voc. and Gram. Transparency 23; Teacher's Resource Book: Input Script, p. 6, Audio Script, p. 8; Audio Program DVD: Para empezar, Track 1

INTERACTIVE WHITEBOARD
Grammar Activities PE

Focus: Reviewing daily routines, pastimes

Suggestions: After students have read the conversations, say the activities aloud and have volunteers pantomime the actions.

BELLRINGER REVIEW

Show Voc. and Gram. Transparency 23. Have students mention activities that Ana and Tomás do daily.

1 Standards: 1.1, 1.2

Resources: Answer Keys: Student Edition, p. 1

Focus: Demonstrating reading comprehension

Suggestions: Have students write down words and phrases to answer the questions. Have them use these notes as they answer orally in complete sentences.

Common Errors: Students may forget to change first-person forms to the third-person when answering. Model correct verb forms and have students repeat.

Answers:
1. Ana hace la cama, toma el desayuno, pone los libros en la mochila y sale de casa.
2. Su actividad favorita es jugar al fútbol.
3. A veces va al gimnasio con sus amigos.
4. Hace su tarea.
5. Dicen que él cocina muy bien.

2 Standards: 1.3

Focus: Practicing daily-routine and pastime vocabulary

Suggestions: Encourage students to include details, such as times and descriptive adjectives, in their answers.

Answers will vary.

▼ **Objectives**
▶ Talk and write about your daily routine
▶ Discuss school and extracurricular activities

1 Tu vida diaria

—Hola, Ana. Tengo que escribir un artículo para la revista de la escuela sobre la vida diaria de los estudiantes. ¿Puedes responder a unas preguntas?

—¡Por supuesto!

—¿Qué haces generalmente por la mañana, antes de salir para la escuela?

—Hago la cama, tomo el desayuno, pongo los libros en la mochila y salgo de casa a las 7:30.

—¿Y en tu tiempo libre?

—Juego al fútbol . . . mi actividad favorita.

—Hola Tomás, ¿puedes contestar unas preguntas sobre lo que haces después de la escuela?

—Hmm, . . . A veces voy con mis amigos al gimnasio a hacer ejercicio.

—¿Y cuándo haces la tarea?

—Hago la tarea por la tarde, antes de ayudar a mi mamá con los quehaceres de la casa.

—¿Cómo ayudas a tu mamá?

—Voy al supermercado con ella y la ayudo a cocinar. Me encanta hacer la cena y todos en mi familia dicen que cocino muy bien.

▼1 Cada día

Leer • Hablar

Contesta las preguntas sobre Ana y Tomás.
1. ¿Qué hace Ana por la mañana?
2. ¿Cuál es la actividad favorita de Ana?
3. ¿Adónde va a veces Tomás? ¿Con quién?
4. ¿Qué hace Tomás antes de ayudar a su mamá con los quehaceres de la casa?
5. ¿Qué dicen en la familia de Tomás acerca de cómo cocina él?

▼2 Tu vida diaria

Escribir

¿Qué haces durante el día? Completa las frases con lo que haces en un día típico.
1. Voy . . .
2. Hago . . .
3. Tomo . . .
4. Juego . . .
5. Pongo . . .
6. Salgo . . .
7. Miro . . .
8. Ayudo . . .
9. Estudio . . .
10. Escucho . . .

DIFFERENTIATED INSTRUCTION

Multiple Intelligences

Bodily/Kinesthetic: Have students group themselves, pantomime an action, and conjugate one verb accordingly. For example, one student pantomimes and says: *Yo tomo el desayuno.* Another joins him or her and they say: *Nosotros tomamos el desayuno.* Another addresses them and says: *Uds. toman el desayuno,* and so on.

Advanced Learners

Have students interview a classmate on the subject of his or her daily activities on a typical day. Then ask them to convert the interviewee's answers to the third-person and present an oral report of the person's typical day.

Gramática Repaso

Verbos irregulares

Remember that some verbs in Spanish are irregular in the first person singular of the present tense. Look at the following examples. Note that other verbs you know that are conjugated like *conocer* are *obedecer, ofrecer,* and *parecer.*

conocer	conozco	salir	salgo
dar	doy	traer	traigo
hacer	hago	ver	veo
poner	pongo	caer	caigo
saber	sé		

Also, there are some verbs in Spanish that are irregular in all the persons of the present tense:

ser

soy	somos
eres	sois
es	son

ir

voy	vamos
vas	vais
va	van

decir

digo	decimos
dices	decís
dice	dicen

estar

estoy	estamos
estás	estáis
está	están

oír

oigo	oímos
oyes	oís
oye	oyen

tener

tengo	tenemos
tienes	tenéis
tiene	tienen

| **Más ayuda** | **realidades.com** | ▶ Tutorials |

▼3 ¿Qué haces tú? |

Hablar

No todas las personas hacen las mismas actividades durante el día. Trabaja con otro(a) estudiante para hablar sobre las actividades que hacen usando los verbos del recuadro. Usen *¿qué?, ¿cómo?, ¿cuándo?, ¿dónde?, ¿para qué?, ¿a qué hora?,* y *¿por qué?* para hacer las preguntas.

▶ **Modelo**

A —*¿A qué hora desayunas?*

B —*Yo desayuno a las ocho de la mañana.*

comer	ir de compras	tomar el desayuno
estudiar	hacer la tarea	ir a la escuela
ir al gimnasio	hacer/practicar un	llegar
ver la tele	deporte	tomar (lecciones)
salir de paseo	hablar por teléfono	navegar en la Red

tres **3**
Para empezar

Practice and Communicate PE

Gramática Repaso

Core Instruction

Resources: Voc. and Gram. Transparency 24

Suggestions: Conduct a rapid interchange, moving through the class with questions to which students invent answers on the spot:
—*María, ¿de dónde sales por la mañana?*
—*Salgo de la casa.*
—*Pedro, ¿de dónde sale María?*
—*Sale de la casa.*
—*¿Y tú? ¿De dónde sales por la tarde?*
—*Salgo de la escuela.*
—*Y Pedro, ¿qué pones en la mochila?*
—*Pongo mis libros.*

▼3 Standards: 1.1

Focus: Practicing verbs that are irregular in the first person

Suggestions: Have students conduct the activity twice, switching roles, so that each partner can practice the first-person forms.

Answers will vary.

Extension: Ask students questions about their partner's activities, and then about their own:
—*Belinda, ¿qué dice Tomás sobre la tarea?*
—*Tomás hace su tarea después de la cena.*
—*¿Y tú? ¿Cuándo haces tu tarea?*
—*Yo hago mi tarea antes de la cena.*

Teacher-to-Teacher

Have students socialize on the first day of class by interviewing four classmates. Ask them to find out the names, ages, favorite classes, and favorite activities of the people to whom they speak. Encourage students to take notes. Call on volunteers to report their findings to the class.

Additional Resources

• Communication Wbk.: Audio Act. 1, p. 1
• Teacher's Resource Book: Audio Script, p. 8
• Audio Program DVD: Para empezar, Track 2

ENRICH YOUR TEACHING

Culture Note

In most places in Latin America, school sports are not as heavily funded and organized as they are in United States schools. However, this doesn't mean young people there don't play league sports. Rather, sports enthusiasts belong to neighborhood teams sponsored by local merchants or parents' organizations.

21st Century Skills

Initiative and Self-Direction Direct students to the online tutorials available in **realidades.com** for self-directed review of the grammar topics recycled in this chapter. These tools will help them monitor their own understanding and learning needs. Remind them that each tutorial is followed by a quick comprehension check.

4 Standards: 1.2

Resources: Teacher's Resource Book: Audio Script, p. 8; Audio Program DVD: Para empezar, Track 3; Answer Keys: Student Edition, p. 1

Focus: Practicing daily-routine vocabulary

Suggestions: Before playing the audio for Step 2, ask questions with **quién:** *¿Quién corta el césped?* Have students respond with complete sentences.

Answers:

1. F	4. F
2. F	5. C
3. F	6. F

5 Standards: 1.1, 1.3

Focus: Practicing daily-routine vocabulary

Suggestions: Encourage students to use Elena's account in *Actividad* 4 as a model for their own accounts of household chores.

Answers will vary.

6 Standards: 1.1, 1.3

Focus: Practicing daily-routine vocabulary

Suggestions: Point out to students that they should concentrate on verbs involved in performing the activity, in order to adequately describe it. For **lavar el coche,** for example, suitable verbs might be **llenar** or **usar.**

Answers will vary.

Teacher-to-Teacher

Time pair work and group work activities with a kitchen timer. When the alarm sounds, stop the activity, address any questions students may have, and move on. Timed activities will help you greatly in designing and sticking to your lesson plans.

▼4 Elena y su familia |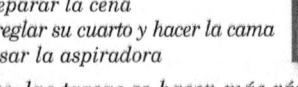

Leer • Escuchar

① Lee la siguiente descripción de Elena de los quehaceres que hace cada miembro de su familia.

En mi familia todos ayudamos con los quehaceres de la casa. Cada uno de nosotros tiene una tarea específica. Como nuestros horarios son diferentes, nunca estamos todos trabajando al mismo tiempo. Las tareas que tenemos son:

Mamá:
- *preparar el almuerzo*
- *limpiar la cocina y el baño*
- *lavar la ropa*

Papá:
- *hacer el desayuno*
- *cortar el césped*
- *lavar el coche*

Yo:
- *arreglar mi cuarto y hacer la cama*
- *dar de comer al perro*
- *poner la mesa*

Mi hermano mayor:
- *preparar la cena*
- *arreglar su cuarto y hacer la cama*
- *pasar la aspiradora*

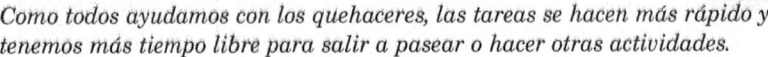

Como todos ayudamos con los quehaceres, las tareas se hacen más rápido y tenemos más tiempo libre para salir a pasear o hacer otras actividades.

② Escribe los números del 1 al 6 en una hoja. Escucha las frases y escribe *C* si la frase es cierta y *F* si es falsa.

▼5 En tu familia | 👥

Escribir • Hablar

① Escribe una breve descripción sobre quiénes hacen los quehaceres en tu casa y qué hace cada uno. Escribe la información en forma de frase.

② Trabaja con un(a) compañero(a) para comparar las descripciones que escribieron. Decidan qué actividades tienen en común y por qué.

▼6 Tu actividad favorita | 👥

Escribir • Hablar

① Decide cuál es tu actividad favorita del día y descríbela. No digas qué actividad es.

Modelo
Leo mis libros y escribo cosas.

② En grupo, cada uno(a) lee su descripción. El resto debe adivinar de qué actividad se trata.

Modelo
Tu actividad favorita es hacer la tarea.

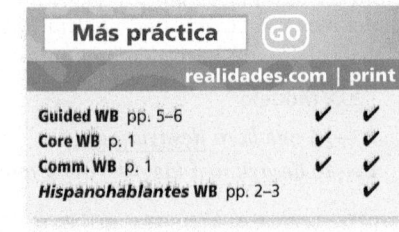

Más práctica	GO
realidades.com	print

Guided WB pp. 5–6	✔	✔
Core WB p. 1	✔	✔
Comm. WB p. 1	✔	✔
Hispanohablantes WB pp. 2–3		✔

DIFFERENTIATED INSTRUCTION

Students with Learning Difficulties

Have students work with partners who are kinesthetic learners. The partners can pantomime doing household chores while students name the chore being pantomimed.

Advanced Learners

Have students with cameras create photo essays of people, preferably their families, doing household chores. Each picture of a chore should be accompanied by a one-sentence caption saying who is doing the chore.

Gramática Repaso

Presente de los verbos con cambios de raíz

Remember that in Spanish there are three groups of stem-changing verbs. The stem change occurs in all forms except the *nosotros(as)* and *vosotros(as)* forms. Here are the present-tense forms of *perder (ie)*, *poder (ue)* and *pedir (i)*.

perder (e → ie)

pierdo	perdemos
pierdes	perdéis
pierde	pierden

poder (o → ue)

puedo	podemos
puedes	podéis
puede	pueden

pedir (e → i)

pido	pedimos
pides	pedís
pide	piden

Other verbs like *perder* are: *empezar, querer, preferir, pensar, divertirse, despertarse, sentirse, mentir, cerrar, comenzar, entender.*

Other verbs like *poder* are: *jugar (u → ue), contar, costar, encontrar, recordar, volar, dormir, volver, devolver, acostarse, almorzar.*

Other verbs like *pedir* are *servir, repetir, reír, sonreír, seguir, vestirse.*

Más ayuda	realidades.com	▶ Tutorial

▼7 Vida deportiva

Leer

Lee lo que escribió Carmen sobre su equipo de fútbol. Completa el párrafo con la forma correcta del verbo apropiado en el presente.

Después de la escuela yo __1.__ (*preferir / dormir*) ir al club para jugar al fútbol. Mis compañeras y yo __2.__ (*recordar / jugar*) bastante bien pero nuestra entrenadora __3.__ (*poder / pensar*) que el equipo rival __4.__ (*empezar / jugar*) mejor. A veces nosotras __5.__ (*perder / servir*) un partido, pero cuando nuestro equipo __6.__ (*poder / comenzar*) meter un gol es fabuloso.

▼8 Actividades de la semana

Escribir

Usa los verbos del recuadro para completar las frases según tu experiencia.

servir	querer	perder	jugar
dormir	poder	sentirse	preferir

1. Después de la escuela, mis amigos . . .
2. Para el almuerzo, mi mamá . . .
3. A veces, mis amigos y yo . . .
4. Cuando mi equipo favorito . . .
5. Muchas veces yo . . . pero no . . .

cinco **5**
Para empezar

Gramática Repaso

Core Instruction

Resources: Voc. and Gram. Transparency 25

♻ Un poco más de repaso

Suggestions: Ask students to write sentences that contain two verbs from each of the three lists in the *Gramática*. Tell them not to use **nosotros** or **vosotros** forms.

▼7 Standards: 1.2

Resources: Answer Keys: Student Edition, p. 1

Focus: Practicing verbs with stem changes in the present tense

Suggestions: Remind students to pay attention to the subject of each sentence before they write their answer.

Answers:
1. prefiero
2. jugamos
3. piensa
4. juega
5. perdemos
6. puede

▼8 Standards: 1.3

Focus: Practicing verbs with stem changes in the present tense

Suggestions: Encourage students to refer as often as necessary to the verb conjugations in the *Gramática* while they complete the activity.

Answers will vary.

Additional Resources

- Communication Wbk.: Audio Act. 2, p. 2
- Teacher's Resource Book: Audio Script, pp. 8–9
- Audio Program DVD: Para empezar, Track 4

ENRICH YOUR TEACHING

Teacher-to-Teacher

Have students get acquainted with the book at the outset of the school year. Make a list of features for students to find as quickly as they can. These might include: maps of the Spanish-speaking world, English-Spanish and Spanish-English vocabulary lists, a ¿Recuerdas? box, a Go Online feature, a *Repaso* section, the first *Lectura,* and so on. Have students write down the page numbers of the various features. This could be done as a whole-class activity or as a race between groups of students.

9
Standards: 1.2, 1.3

Focus: Practicing review vocabulary and structures via reading and response

Common Errors: Some students may forget to make the spelling changes when they use forms of verbs that have them. Point out that the spelling changes affect the pronunciation of the forms as well. Model correct pronunciation where the spelling changes occur. Have students repeat, or correct their spelling if the error was written.

Suggestions: Help students focus on the content of the reading by having them copy the chart to their own paper before they read.

Answers will vary.

BELLRINGER REVIEW

Write logical sentences by unscrambling these words and conjugating the verb appropriately.
1) una ensalada/preferir/mis amigos/para el almuerzo
2) ocho horas/dormir/mi hermanito/todos los días
3) a veces/arroz con pollo/servir/mi mamá

10
Standards: 1.3

Focus: Using new vocabulary and structures in sentences

Suggestions: Point out to students that they can skip around when choosing their cues. They don't have to use the cues in a straight, horizontal line.

Answers will vary.

Block Schedule

After students have written their paragraphs, put them in pairs. Have each student exchange paragraphs. The partner is to write six *Cierto/Falso* statements about the information. Each student reads the statements to the partner who will agree or correct the incorrect information.

---

9 Roberto y Lucas

Leer • Escribir

1 Imagina que conoces a dos hermanos muy diferentes entre sí *(from each other)*. Observa las fotos y lee el texto que las acompaña.

Roberto y Lucas son hermanos. Ellos son muy diferentes entre sí. Los fines de semana, Roberto empieza el día temprano; duerme solamente hasta las siete de la mañana. A las ocho, juega al fútbol con sus amigos y a las diez vuelve a casa. Lucas prefiere levantarse tarde porque se acuesta muy tarde. No entiende cómo su hermano puede levantarse temprano. A Lucas le gusta tocar la guitarra y escribir canciones. Sonríe mucho cuando escucha música, porque le encanta. Cuando Lucas toca la guitarra muy alto *(loudly)*, Roberto se vuelve loco. Lucas se vuelve loco cuando Roberto enciende la luz y lo despierta. A los dos hermanos les gusta ir al cine y navegar en la Red. Los dos son muy amables pero no se entienden muy bien.

2 ¿Eres más similar a Roberto o a Lucas? Indica con una *X* quién hace cada una de estas actividades y si tú también las haces. Luego, escribe un párrafo comparándote a ti mismo con Roberto y Lucas.

Actividad	Roberto	Lucas	Yo
jugar al fútbol			
tocar la guitarra			
sonreír al escuchar música			
preferir levantarse tarde			
encender la luz temprano			

Modelo
Lucas y yo preferimos escuchar música que hacer deportes.

10 ¿Y qué haces tú?

Escribir

Imagina que estás en una reunión de amigos y comienzan a hablar de lo que hacen. Escribe frases usando las palabras de las tres columnas.

Modelo
yo / cortarse / el pelo
Yo me corto el pelo todos los meses.

A	B	C
yo	ayudar	autobús
tú	correr	de paseo
Carlos	desayunar	en el parque
nosotros	hacer	quehaceres
ustedes	salir	tarea de la escuela
mis amigos	tomar	temprano / tarde

Más práctica	GO

realidades.com | print

Guided WB pp. 7–8	✔	✔
Core WB p. 2	✔	✔
Comm. WB p. 2	✔	✔
***Hispanohablantes* WB** p. 4		✔

6 seis
Tu vida diaria

DIFFERENTIATED INSTRUCTION

Students with Learning Difficulties

Help students orientate themselves when using the chart in *Actividad 9*. Slide your finger across the first row of the chart and explain that all the information in that row has to do with playing football. Repeat this procedure for each row of the chart.

Students with Special Needs

Provide hearing-impaired students with a seat near the speakers, or with headphones if possible, whenever conducting recorded listening activities.

Gramática Repaso

Los verbos reflexivos

To say that people do something to or for themselves, you use reflexive verbs. A reflexive verb has two parts: a reflexive pronoun (*me, te, se, nos, os*) and a verb form. Here are all the present-tense forms of *levantarse*:

me levanto	**nos** levantamos
te levantas	**os** levantáis
se levanta	**se** levantan

Many reflexive verbs in Spanish describe daily routine actions: *acostarse (ue), afeitarse, arreglarse, bañarse, cepillarse, despertarse (ie), ducharse, lavarse, pintarse, ponerse, secarse, vestirse (i).*

Except for *se*, the reflexive pronouns are the same as the indirect object pronouns. They usually come before the verb, but they may also be attached to an infinitive.

Me lavo la cara.   Voy a **lavarme** la cara.

Remember that with reflexive verbs, you usually use the definite article with parts of the body or articles of clothing.

Me pongo **la** chaqueta.   Me cepillo **los** dientes.

| **Más ayuda** **realidades.com** ▶ Tutorial |

▼ 11 Lo opuesto a ti

Escribir

Imagina que tienes hermanos(as) muy diferentes a ti. Lo que a ti te gusta hacer, a ellos(as) no. Escribe frases comparándose.

Modelo
secarse el pelo
Mi hermana no se seca el pelo antes de salir de la casa pero yo sí.

1. lavarse la cara
2. cepillarse los dientes
3. vestirse con ropa moderna
4. cortarse el pelo todos los meses
5. despertarse
6. acostarse

▼ 12 A las 7:00 . . .

Escribir

Describe lo que haces cada mañana desde que abres los ojos hasta que sales para ir a la escuela.

Modelo
7:00: Me despierto. 7:05: Me levanto de la cama.

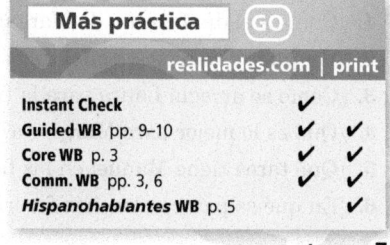

Más práctica GO
realidades.com | print
Instant Check ✔
Guided WB pp. 9–10 ✔ ✔
Core WB p. 3 ✔ ✔
Comm. WB pp. 3, 6 ✔ ✔
Hispanohablantes WB p. 5 ✔

siete 7
Para empezar

Gramática Repaso

Core Instruction

Resources: Voc. and Gram. Transparency 26

♻ Un poco más de repaso

Suggestions: Use the reflexive verbs in sentences about what you are going to do tomorrow. Have students respond by saying that they perform the action every day. —*Mañana, voy a despertarme a las seis y media.* —*Yo me despierto a las seis y media todos los días.* Pantomime the action and have students do likewise.

▼ 11 Standards: 1.3

Resources: Answer Keys: Student Edition, p. 2

Focus: Practicing reflexive verbs

Suggestions: Point out to students that for this activity, all reflexive pronouns should precede the verb.

Answers: Family members will vary. Students will use the following verb forms (with singular subjects).

1. se lava   3. se viste   5. se despierta
2. se cepilla   4. se corta   6. se acuesta

▼ 12 Standards: 1.1, 1.3

Focus: Practicing reflexive verbs

Suggestions: Have students list all their morning activities. Suggest that they refer to the *Gramática* for reminders. Then have them convert their list into a final draft that includes the times and complete sentences. As they make their final draft they can include other activities that were not in their lists.

Answers will vary.

Additional Resources

• Communication Wbk.: Audio Act. 3, p. 3
• Teacher's Resource Book: Audio Script, p. 9, Communicative Pair Activity BLM, p. 10
• Audio Program DVD: Para empezar, Track 5

✔ ASSESSMENT

Prueba P-1 with Study Plan (online only)

Prueba: Tu vida diaria
• Prueba P-1: pp. 8–9

ENRICH YOUR TEACHING

Teacher-to-Teacher

Conduct an information exchange. Prepare a worksheet with students' names in the left column and in the right column a list of daily activities with their times of day, such as *almorzar a la una.* Give each student a slip of paper with a daily activity and time from the right column of the worksheet written on it. Have students complete the worksheet by circulating around the room and asking each other questions about the right column: *¿Tú almuerzas a la una?* The first to match all the names and daily activities on his or her worksheet wins.

PE Practice and Communicate

Días especiales

Core Instruction

Standards: 1.2

Resources: Voc. and Gram. Transparencies 4, 27; Teacher's Resource Book: Input Script, p. 7, Audio Script, p. 9; Audio Program DVD: Para empezar, Track 6

INTERACTIVE WHITEBOARD

Grammar Activities PE

Focus: Reviewing celebrations and special events

Suggestions: Use *Vocabulary and Grammar Transparency* 27 to aid understanding as students read the information. Then show *Vocabulary and Grammar Transparency* 4. Enter the names *Margarita, Laura,* and *Manuel* at the tops of the first three columns. Leave the fourth column empty. Ask guiding questions to elicit information about each of the three people and record students' answers in the appropriate column. For example, if you ask *¿A quién le gustan las celebraciones para los acontecimientos importantes?* students should say *a Manuel.* Under *Manuel* on the chart, write *celebraciones.* Continue until all information for each person is recorded.

▼13 Standards: 1.2, 1.3

Resources: Answer Keys: Student Edition, p. 3

Focus: Demonstrating reading comprehension

Suggestions: Ask students to answer the questions in complete sentences, using their own words as much as possible.

Answers:

1. El día favorito de Margarita es el día de su cumpleaños. El de Manuel es el día que la familia entera se reúne.
2. Se reúnen para celebrar algún acontecimiento importante, como una boda o una graduación.
3. Se arregla con sus amigas en la casa de una de ellas.
4. Lo mejor para Margarita es pasar la noche bailando con sus amigos.
5. Manuel tiene que cuidar a sus hermanos y primos más pequeños.
6. En los dos días favoritos, la gente baila. También los días se parecen en que pasan sólo una vez al año.

▼ **Objectives**
▶ Write and talk about special events and activities
▶ Exchange information about favorite movies, TV programs, and sports
▶ Write about and discuss vacations

2 Días especiales

Todos los años, la revista *Familia* hace una encuesta. A continuación aparecen algunas de las respuestas más interesantes a la encuesta "¿Cuál es tu día de fiesta favorito?".

Margarita: ▶

"Mi día de fiesta favorito es el día de mi cumpleaños. Siempre hacemos una fiesta. Mis padres y yo decoramos la casa con globos y luces. Mi mamá siempre me prepara un pastel. Pero lo mejor es que todos mis amigos vienen y traen música y nos pasamos la noche bailando".

◀ **Laura:**

"Lo que más me gusta es el baile de la escuela de fin de año. Me gusta porque puedo charlar con mis amigos y bailar. Además me encanta arreglarme para la fiesta.

Con mis amigas siempre nos reunimos en una de las casas para prepararnos e ir juntas a la fiesta".

Manuel: ▶

"Mi día preferido es el día que la familia entera se reúne para celebrar algún evento importante, como una boda o una graduación. La abuela prepara una gran cena pero todos ayudamos con algo. Yo tengo la tarea de cuidar a mis primos y hermanos más pequeños".

▼13 Los días de fiesta

Leer • Escribir

Contesta las preguntas sobre los jóvenes de la encuesta.

1. ¿Cuál es el día favorito de Margarita? ¿Y el de Manuel?
2. ¿Por qué se reúnen Manuel y sus parientes?
3. ¿Cómo se arregla Laura para la fiesta de fin de año de la escuela?
4. ¿Qué es lo mejor para Margarita?
5. ¿Qué tarea tiene Manuel en las fiestas?
6. ¿En qué se parecen los días favoritos de Margarita y Laura?

DIFFERENTIATED INSTRUCTION

Heritage Language Learners

Invite students to share information about special days they celebrate with their families. What is the occasion? What activities take place? Are there decorations? Are any special foods prepared?

Students with Learning Difficulties

As students read the information about each person, point to appropriate parts of the accompanying photo to help them associate words and meanings.

Practice and Communicate **PE**

▼14 Actividades de una joven |

Leer • Escribir • Hablar

1 Lucía participa en una encuesta. Lee la siguiente gráfica que indica cuántas veces Lucía realiza cada actividad.

Actividad	1 a 3 veces por semana	1 vez al mes	1 a 3 veces al año	Nunca
ir a bailar		X		
practicar deportes	X			
ir al cine		X		
ver la televisión	X			
ir de compras	X			
ir a una fiesta de sorpresa			X	
tocar un instrumento musical	X			
celebrar un día especial		X		
reunirse con amigos	X			
ir de vacaciones			X	
tener una cita		X		
ir a una boda				X
hacer un concurso		X		
hacer una audición		X		
ir a un desfile		X		
ver fuegos artificiales				X
hacer un picnic			X	

2 Copia la gráfica y úsala para hacer la encuesta a tres estudiantes.

▶ **Modelo**

A —¿Cuántas veces al mes o al año vas a bailar?
B —Voy a bailar tres veces al año.

3 Con los resultados que obtengas, escribe cinco frases sobre las actividades de tus compañeros.

▼15 Tu día favorito

Leer • Escribir

1 Piensa en cuál es tu día de fiesta favorito y contesta las siguientes preguntas.

1. ¿Celebras con tu familia o con tus amigos?
2. ¿Te preparas para ese día durante la semana?
3. ¿Qué haces para celebrarlo?
4. ¿Es un día importante para otras personas?

2 Basándote en tus respuestas, escribe un párrafo para describir tu día favorito del año y decir cuál es. Cuenta lo que ocurre ese día.

▼14 Standards: 1.1, 1.3

Focus: Practicing vocabulary related to celebrations and special events

Suggestions: Explain that for Step 2, students should write the names of each student they interview in the appropriate space, rather than using Xs.

Answers will vary.

▼15 Standards: 1.3

Focus: Practicing vocabulary related to celebrations and special events

Suggestions: Remind students before they complete Step 2, that the first sentence of their paragraph should announce which favorite day they are going to describe.

Answers will vary.

Extension: Invite volunteers to read their completed paragraphs to the class.

Culture Note

In Mexico, a girl's fifteenth birthday celebration, her *quinceañera,* is often one of the biggest of her life. (The term *quinceañera* is used to refer to the girl herself, as well as to the celebration.) It is often a huge family affair. Traditionally, this day marks the transition from girlhood to womanhood. Depending on the family, it may begin with a religious celebration, often a Catholic Mass. Urban families might lease a banquet hall and have a formal gala dinner. Rural families might have a more casual celebration, perhaps outdoors, with plenty of food, music, and relaxing fun for everyone.

ENRICH YOUR TEACHING

Teacher-to-Teacher

Have students write a note describing themselves (name, favorite classes, and activities). Then have them write four questions to ask someone in the class. Place the notes in a box and have students randomly draw a note. Have them read the information then respond in writing to the questions and return the note to the appropriate person.

21st Century Skills

Communication Ask students to bring into class a picture or a drawing of a favorite holiday occasion they have celebrated with their family and friends. Working in small groups, have them name the occasion, the people in attendance, special food and preparations, and any other details they would like to share with their classmates about the celebration.

▼**16 Las películas**

Leer • Escribir

❶ Una actividad que le gusta hacer a casi todo el mundo es ir al cine. Lee lo
que dicen estos jóvenes venezolanos de la película *El señor de los anillos* y
contesta las preguntas que siguen.

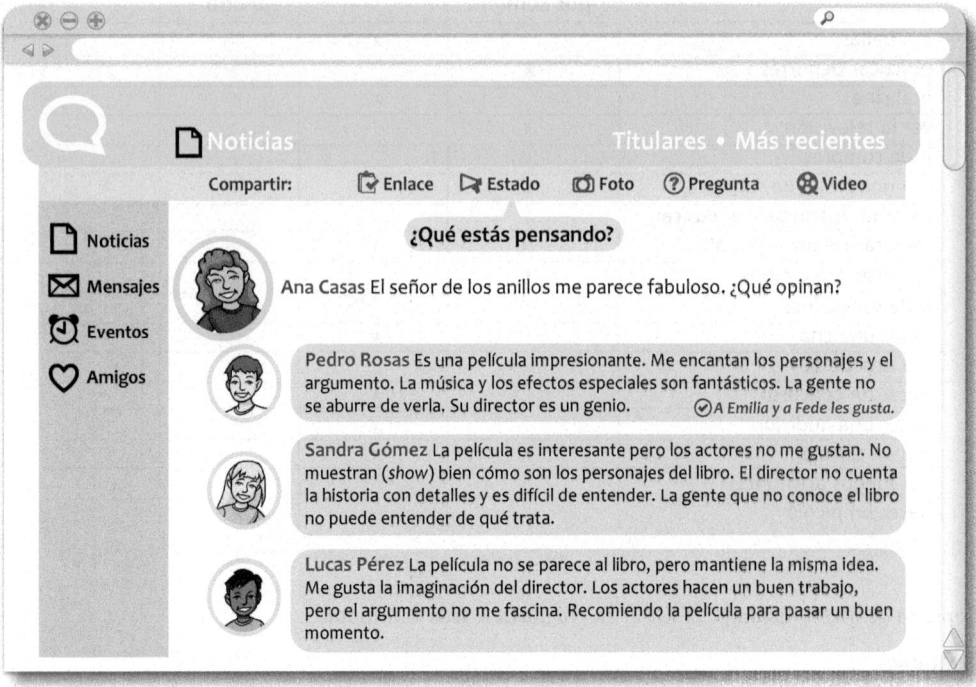

1. Nombra tres cosas que le gustan a Pedro de la película.

2. ¿Qué cree Sandra sobre cómo la película se compara al libro?

3. Nombra una cosa que le gusta y una cosa que no le gusta a Lucas.

❷ Piensa en una película que te gusta mucho o que no te gusta
nada. Escribe una descripción de la película. Puedes usar las
palabras del recuadro.

inolvidable	despacio(a)
típico(a)	divertido(a)
estupendo(a)	emocionante
bello(a)	exagerado(a)
artístico(a)	horrible
talentoso(a)	violento(a)

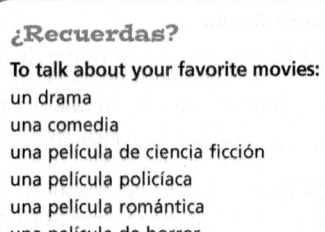

¿Recuerdas?

To talk about your favorite movies:
un drama
una comedia
una película de ciencia ficción
una película policíaca
una película romántica
una película de horror

10 diez
Días especiales

DIFFERENTIATED INSTRUCTION

Students with Learning Difficulties

Make a set of index cards containing the
adjectives in Step 2 of *Actividad* 16. Go through
the movie section of a local newspaper. Help
students match the various adjectives with
appropriate movies. Then ask them to make a
sentence about each movie using the adjective
on the card.

Advanced Learners

Ask students to write their own opinion about
a film they have recently seen. Have them use
the opinions in *Actividad* 16 as models.

Gramática Repaso

Verbos que se conjugan como *gustar*

You already know several verbs that always use the indirect object pronouns *me, te, le, nos, os, les*:

encantar	*to love*	importar	*to matter*
gustar	*to like*	interesar	*to be interested in*

These verbs all use the same construction: indirect object pronoun + verb + subject.

Me gusta el fútbol.   ¿**Te interesan** las pinturas?

Remember, in the sentences above, the verb forms *gusta* (singular) and *interesan* (plural) agree with the subjects *fútbol* and *pinturas*. The words *me* and *te* are indirect object pronouns.

Más ayuda   **realidades.com**   ▸**Tutorial**

▾**17 Los programas de televisión** |

Hablar

¿Qué programas te gustan? Trabaja con un(a) compañero(a) para hablar sobre sus programas favoritos. Usa *gustar, encantar,* e *interesar*.

▸ **Modelo**

A —*¿Te interesan los programas de noticias?*

B —*Sí, me interesan mucho. Me gusta saber lo que pasa en el mundo.*

o: —*No, no me gustan porque son aburridos.*

Estudiante A

1. los programas educativos
2. los programas de la vida real
3. los programas de dibujos animados
4. los programas de deportes
5. las telenovelas

Estudiante B

¡Respuesta personal!

▾**18 Programas de deportes** |

Hablar

Trabaja con otro(a) estudiante para hacer y contestar preguntas sobre tus deportes favoritos. Usa los verbos *gustar, encantar, importar* e *interesar*.

▸ **Modelo**

A — *¿Te gusta jugar al béisbol?*

B — *Sí, me encanta jugar al béisbol.*

Más práctica GO

realidades.com | print

Guided WB pp. 11–12	✔	✔
Core WB p. 4	✔	✔
Comm. WB p. 4	✔	✔
Hispanohablantes WB pp. 6–8		✔

once **11**
Para empezar

ENRICH YOUR TEACHING

Culture Note

The use of social media sites on the Internet has grown exponentially in the Spanish-speaking world. By 2011, more than 130 million accounts had been registered in Spain and Latin America in one social network alone. Besides Facebook and *Facebook en español,* other popular social media sites include Tuenti and Orkut.

21st Century Skills

Technology Literacy Discuss with students the issue of digital versus print sources of information about movies or other entertainment materials. Do they ever read reviews about movies they are interested in via websites, blogs, or Facebook pages? Do they ever read a printed review in the arts section of a newspaper? Ask them for their opinions about the advantages and disadvantages of both mediums for obtaining entertainment news, for example.

Practice and Communicate PE

Gramática Repaso

Core Instruction

Resources: Voc. and Gram. Transparency 29

Suggestions: Have students practice the verbs by talking about things that please, enchant, interest, or matter to them. Remind them that in a sentence such as: *Me gusta el perro,* the subject is **perro.** The construction moves in the opposite direction from the English sentence "I like the dog."

BELLRINGER REVIEW

Label two columns on the board:
Divertido/Aburrido
Brainstorm as a class to place different types of TV shows in the appropriate column to reflect the class opinion.

▾**17** Standards: 1.1

Focus: Practicing verbs like ***gustar***

Suggestions: Tell Student B to "bounce" the question back to Student A with a question such as: *¿Y a ti?* or *¿Y qué piensas tú?* This way both students can practice the verbs like ***gustar*** in a natural, flowing conversation.

Answers will vary.

▾**18** Standards: 1.1

Focus: Practicing verbs like ***gustar***

Suggestions: Suggest that students talk about sports they enjoy watching as well as those they enjoy playing, so they can extend the activity for further practice.

Answers will vary.

Additional Resources

• Communication Wbk.: Audio Act. 4, p. 4
• Teacher's Resource Book: Audio Script, p. 9
• Audio Program DVD: Para empezar, Track 7

11

Gramática Repaso

Core Instruction

Resources: Voc. and Gram. Transparency 30

♻ Un poco más de repaso

Suggestions: Have students practice the possessive adjectives by describing their own home, then that of a friend or relative. Ask guiding questions to elicit the various pronouns: —¿Y cómo es el jardín de tu abuelo? —Su jardín es muy hermoso.

▼19 Standards: 1.2

Resources: Answer Keys: Student Edition, p. 4

Focus: Practicing possessive adjectives

Suggestions: Have students scan the entire postcard first for meaning before they begin to write their answers.

Answers:

1. mi	6. mis
2. nuestro	7. Mis
3. nuestros	8. mi
4. Nuestro	9. su
5. nuestras	10. sus

Fondo cultural

Standards: 1.1, 1.2

Resources: Map Transparency 18

🌐 Mapa global interactivo, Actividad Visit Bariloche, the gateway to Patagonia in Argentina.

Suggestions: Before students read the information, show Map Transparency 18 and point out Bariloche, Argentina. It is a bit more than halfway down the length of Argentina, in the Andes Mountains, near the Chilean border.

Answers will vary.

Additional Resources

• Communication Wbk.: Audio Act. 5, p. 5
• Teacher's Resource Book: Audio Script, p. 9
• Audio Program DVD: Para empezar, Track 8

Gramática Repaso

Adjetivos posesivos

Remember that possessive adjectives in Spanish agree in gender and number with the nouns they describe. They are placed in front of the noun.

Singular		Plural	
mi, tu, su, nuestro, vuestro	vuelo	mis, tus, sus, nuestros, vuestros	vuelos
mi, tu, su, nuestra, vuestra	maleta	mis, tus, sus, nuestras, vuestras	maletas

Since *su* and *sus* have many meanings, use the prepositional phrase *de* + name/pronoun instead for clarity or emphasis.

Sus pantalones son elegantes.
¿Los pantalones **de ella**?
No, los **de usted**.

Más ayuda	realidades.com	▶ Tutorials

▼19 ¡A esquiar!

Leer • Escribir

Pablo sale mañana para esquiar con su familia en Bariloche, Argentina. Él está muy emocionado (excited) y escribe cómo se siente en su diario. Lee lo que escribe y llena los espacios con la forma correcta del adjetivo posesivo apropiado.

Mañana voy con 1._____ familia a esquiar en Bariloche. Estamos un poco nerviosos porque 2._____ vuelo sale muy temprano y todavía tenemos que recoger 3._____ boletos en el aeropuerto. 4._____ agente de viajes nos dice que 5._____ reservaciones están confirmadas, y yo le creo.

Estoy muy emocionado con esquiar. ¡Hace una semana que están hechas 6._____ maletas! 7._____ padres y 8._____ hermana mayor tienen maletas muy grandes a causa de 9._____ ropa. Mi hermano menor también lleva una maleta grande a causa de 10._____ juguetes... ¡tiene muchos!

🌐 Fondo Cultural | Argentina

Esquiar en Bariloche Cuando hay nieve, mucha gente aprovecha (takes advantage) para practicar su deporte preferido: esquiar. En Bariloche, Argentina, se encuentra uno de los centros de esquí más famosos de Latinoamérica. Esquiadores de todas partes del mundo, tanto profesionales como principiantes (beginners), llegan a este lugar cada año. Aquí pueden disfrutar de modernas pistas de esquí y también de los impresionantes paisajes (scenery) que hay a su alrededor. Bariloche es un lugar ideal para hacer deportes y conocer las bellezas naturales que nos ofrece nuestro planeta.

• ¿En qué otros países hispanobablantes es posible esquiar? ¿En qué países hace demasiado calor?

12 doce
Días especiales

DIFFERENTIATED INSTRUCTION

Students with Learning Difficulties

Have students work with single objects and pairs of similar objects, such as a pencil and a pair of pencils. Hand the object or objects to various individuals or pairs and ask students to say sentences such as: *Son sus lápices. Son mis lápices. Es mi lápiz. Es tu lápiz.*

Advanced Learners

Have students pretend they are on a trip to a vacation spot of their choice in Spain or Latin America. Ask them to research the place and write a postcard as if they were there, telling about some of its attractions. Tell them to use at least two possessive adjectives.

▼20 Días de vacaciones

Leer • Escribir

❶ Lee esta tarjeta postal que Rosa le escribe a una amiga sobre sus vacaciones de verano.

SALUDOS DE MIAMI

Querida Sara:

¿Cómo estás? Te escribo desde la playa, en Miami. ¡Me encanta estar de vacaciones! Todos los días me levanto tarde, desayuno y voy a la playa con mi familia. Mis hermanos y yo nos bañamos en el mar todo el día, y a veces salimos a dar vueltas por la ciudad en nuestras bicicletas. Mi hermano también se encuentra con sus amigos. Todas las noches, después de cenar, voy con mi hermano y sus amigos al cine o a comer helado. Nuestro hotel también es fantástico. Hay un vendedor que vende artesanías en la playa y me encanta mirar sus aretes de plata. ¡Qué divertido!

Saludos,

Rosa

Sara Ponce
3600 Mesa Way
Tucson, AZ

❷ Haz una lista de las cosas que hace Rosa en sus vacaciones.

Modelo
Rosa le escribe una tarjeta postal a su amiga.

▼21 Unas preguntas sobre tus vacaciones

Escribir • Hablar

❶ Piensa en las cosas que haces durante tus vacaciones. En una hoja de papel escribe las respuestas a estas preguntas.

1. ¿Qué haces durante tus vacaciones?
2. ¿Te quedas en la ciudad todo el tiempo?
3. ¿Viajas con tu familia o amigos a algún lugar? ¿Adónde?
4. ¿Qué haces generalmente en un día de vacaciones?
5. ¿A qué hora te levantas? ¿Y a qué hora te acuestas?
6. ¿Qué lugar te gusta más para irte de vacaciones?

❷ Trabaja con otro(a) estudiante para hablar sobre las vacaciones. Usen las preguntas anteriores como modelo para su conversación. Escriban las respuestas y un párrafo sobre las vacaciones.

Más práctica	GO
realidades.com	print

Instant Check	✔	
Guided WB pp. 13–14	✔	✔
Core WB pp. 5–6	✔	✔
Comm. WB p. 7	✔	✔
Hispanohablantes **WB** p. 9		✔

Practice and Communicate ⬤ PE

▼20 Standards: 1.2

Resources: Voc. and Gram. Transparency 31

Focus: Practicing possessive adjectives

Suggestions: Instruct students to mention with whom Rosa does the activities, so they practice using plural possessive adjectives.

Answers will vary.

▼21 Standards: 1.1, 1.3

Focus: Practicing vocabulary related to vacation and travel

Suggestions: Have students who may not go on vacations themselves write about their partner's vacation or that of someone they know.

Answers will vary.

ENRICH YOUR TEACHING

Culture Note

The founding of Bariloche, Argentina is attributed to a man named Carlos Weitherholdt. He built a house and began regular trade in wool, leather, potatoes, cheese, butter, and other products. German influence can still be seen in some of the architecture in the older parts of the town.

21st Century Skills

Communication Have students write an e-mail or a postcard to a friend in which they describe their summer vacation. Direct them to use the questions in *Actividad* 21 to guide their writing. Students can use the postcard in *Actividad* 20 as a model for their correspondence.

✓ASSESSMENT

Prueba P-2 with Study Plan (online only)

Prueba: Días especiales
• Prueba P-2: pp. 10–11

Common Core: Speaking

Presentación oral

Core Instruction

Standards: 1.2, 1.3, 3.1

Focus: Preparing and delivering an oral presentation

Suggestions: Help students decide on which task they will do. Review the four-step approach with them. Review the rubric with the class (see *Assessment* below) to explain how you will grade the performance task. Encourage them to use a graphic organizer, such as a column chart or a concept web in Step 1, as an aid to organizing their ideas.

Portfolio

Make video or audio recordings of student presentations in class, or assign the RealTalk activity so they can record their presentations online. Include the recording in their portfolios.

Additional Resources

Student Resources: Realidades para hispanohablantes, p. 10

Presentación oral

Mi vida

Tarea

Imagínate que tienes que hacer una presentación oral en español. Escoge uno de estos aspectos de tu vida.

* Un día en la escuela. ¿Qué haces antes de ir a la escuela? ¿Te diviertes en tu escuela? ¿Cómo son tus amigos? ¿Qué actividades haces después de la escuela?
* Tu película o programa de televisión favorito. ¿Quiénes son los personajes del programa o de la película? ¿Qué problemas tienen? ¿Qué hacen para resolverlos?
* El deporte que practicas. ¿Por qué te gusta ese deporte? ¿Con quiénes practicas ese deporte? ¿Dónde lo practicas? ¿Qué se necesita para ser un buen jugador?

Estudiantes comen pizza después de l en la República Dominicana.

① **Prepárate** Contesta las preguntas o escribe frases y palabras que te van a ayudar a hacer tu presentación.

② **Practica** Vuelve a leer la información que escribiste y piensa cómo la vas a presentar. Puedes usar tus notas para practicar, pero no al hablar ante la clase. Después, vas a ir donde están los estudiantes que hablarán del mismo tema para practicar cada presentación. Contesta las preguntas que te hacen los estudiantes de tu grupo sobre tu presentación.

③ **Haz tu presentación** Habla de tu tema con tu grupo como ayuda para pensar en más ideas. Al final, cada estudiante debe presentar el tema ante la clase.

④ **Evaluación** Tu profesor(a) utilizará la siguiente rúbrica para evaluar tu presentación.

Rubric	Score 1	Score 3	Score 5
How well you organize your ideas	You have too few ideas. Your ideas aren't organized.	Some organizational problems make your speech hard to follow.	You organize ideas well, making your speech easy to follow.
How well you use details	You include no details in your speech.	You include one or two interesting details, but need more.	Good use of details makes your speech interesting.
How effectively you deliver your speech	You read your speech and make no eye contact with your audience.	You make some eye contact, and you use some intonation.	Your eye contact is good. Your intonation helps get your message across.

14 catorce
Días especiales

DIFFERENTIATED INSTRUCTION

21st Century Skills

Initiative and Self-Direction Ask students to review the rubrics on pages 14 and 15. Have them discuss with a partner why their teacher gives them rubrics, and how are they supposed to be used. Students should choose one of the rubrics to start with the outcome, figure out what they might need to do to get the best grade possible, and develop a plan to achieve that goal.

☑ ASSESSMENT

Presentación oral

Review the rubric with students. Go over the descriptions of the different levels of performance. After assessing students, help individuals understand how their performance could be improved. (See Teacher's Resource Book for suggestions on using rubrics in assessment.)

Presentación escrita

Actividades en mi comunidad

Tarea

Imagínate que tienes que hacer una página Web describiendo las actividades que hacen los jóvenes de tu ciudad. Imagina que la leen jóvenes de otros países que planean visitar los Estados Unidos y necesitan saber qué cosas pueden hacer en tu ciudad.

> **Estrategia**
> Evaluate your lead sentence to see whether added details might help to generate more interest in your topic. Make notes to suggest areas for further development, and jot down ideas that will make the paragraphs and the information more appealing.

1 **Antes de escribir** Piensa en los siguientes temas:

- gimnasios
- cines y teatros
- restaurantes
- lugares para bailar o ir de compras
- escuelas de música, idiomas, computación

2 **Borrador** Escribe tu borrador de la página Web. Usa la información de arriba. Piensa en las ilustraciones que acompañan la página Web.

3 **Redacción/Revisión** Trabaja con otro(a) estudiante para intercambiar los borradores de las páginas Web y leerlos. Habla de qué se puede hacer para mejorarlos.

- ¿Incluye la página Web información sobre los temas de la sección *Antes de escribir?*
- ¿Usaste correctamente verbos y adjetivos posesivos?

Las actividades de los jóvenes

4 **Publicación** Revisa otra vez tu borrador y escribe el texto de la página Web en una hoja grande de papel para hacer un póster. Añade fotos o ilustraciones.

5 **Evaluación** Tu profesor(a) utilizará la siguiente rúbrica para evaluar tu presentación.

Rubric	Score 1	Score 3	Score 5
Completion of task	Your Web page is incomplete.	Your Web page is complete, but some parts still need work.	Your Web page is complete and carefully revised.
Effective development	Your topic is undeveloped.	You have some ideas that enhance your topic.	Your ideas are all well developed and enhance your topic.
Grammar, spelling, mechanics	You make too many grammar, spelling, and/or mechanics errors.	You make some grammar, spelling, and/or mechanics errors.	You make very few grammar, spelling, and/or mechanics errors.

ENRICH YOUR TEACHING

21st Century Skills

Information Literacy Ask students to use information from a variety of online sources to plan their *Actividades en mi comunidad* Web site. Have them find reliable sources that provide accurate information about the things to do in the local area. Encourage students to include this information in their materials for the *Presentación escrita* Web page in class.

Writing

 Common Core: Writing

Presentación escrita

Expository
Standards: 1.2, 1.3, 3.1

Focus: Combining review vocabulary and structures in a written presentation

Suggestions: Explain the criteria you will use to evaluate students' compositions. (See Step 5, *Evaluación,* in the Student Edition, and *Assessment* below.)

Direct students' attention to the *Estrategia.* Point out that to evaluate their lead, they can simply ask classmates and other students for their opinions on the activities that they want to include on their Web page. If the people they ask don't think an activity is interesting, they should abandon that idea and think of another activity for their Web page. Point out also that talking with other people this way often generates new and better ideas. Students should write down ideas that they like and try to include them in their Web page.

In Step 2, students should concentrate on the layout of their Web page and fitting in the information they want to include.

In Step 3, students should pay closer attention to the written portions of their Web page, in particular to their use of verbs and possessive adjectives.

Evaluation

Steps 4 and 5 overlap. Students will need evaluation by you, their peers, or self-evaluation to fine-tune their drafts.

Portfolio

Keep students' final drafts in their portfolios as a writing sample.

Additional Resources

Student Resources: Realidades para hispanohablantes, p. 11

✓ ASSESSMENT

Presentación escrita
Review the rubric with students. Go over the descriptions of the different levels of performance. After assessing students, help individuals understand how their performance could be improved. (See Teacher's Resource Book for suggestions on using rubrics in assessment.)

Días inolvidables

1 Chapter Overview

- **memorable outdoor experiences and competitions**

Vocabulary
- camping and weather
- athletic events and competitions

Grammar
- preterite tense of verbs with $i \rightarrow y$, $e \rightarrow i$, and $o \rightarrow u$ spelling changes
- preterite tense of irregular verbs: *tener, andar, estar, poder, poner, saber, venir, decir,* and *traer*
- imperfect tense
- imperfect tense of irregular verbs *ir, ser,* and *ver*

Cultural Perspectives
- national parks in Chile, Argentina, and Mexico
- different kinds of competitions
- the annual pilgrimage to the Cathedral of Santiago de Compostela in Spain
- the legend of Iztaccíhuatl and Popocatépetl, two volcanoes in Mexico

¡Pura vida!
- Watch an engaging video episode about a group of young people in Costa Rica!

CHAPTER SUPPORT

Bulletin Boards

Theme: *Competencias diferentes*

Ask students to cut out, copy or download photos of all different types of competitions from many different cultures. Arrange the pictures into three categories: team-oriented competitions, individual competitions, and personal competition.

Game

¡Vamos de cámping en las sierras!

This memory game practices camping vocabulary. Use it after completing the first *A primera vista* section.

Players: 6 to 8

Materials: Scarf for blindfold

Rules:

1. Players sit in a circle. Choose a player to start. This player begins by saying *Para ir de cámping en las montañas, traigo _____.* Then the player proceeds to say why that item would be useful. For example: *Para ir de cámping en las montañas, traigo una linterna porque necesito ver cuando es de noche.*

2. The next player on the right then repeats the initial sentence, repeating the first player's item and adding one of his or her own plus a reason for bringing that item. For example: *Para ir de cámping en las montañas, traigo una linterna porque necesito ver cuando es de noche. También traigo una brújula para no perderme.*

3. Play continues until everyone in the circle has a chance to add an item to the list.

Variation: Play with a larger group of students and review other vocabulary such as articles of clothing and other supplies that might be useful on a camping trip.

Hands-on Culture

Recipe: *Pastel de choclo*

Pastel de choclo (corn pie) is one of the most popular Chilean dishes.

Ingredients:

For the meat mixture:
    1 chicken breast, skinned/boned
    8 oz. hamburger, extra lean
    1/4 tsp. salt
    1/4 tsp. black pepper
    1/2 cup raisins
    2 tbsp. kalamata olives, chopped

For the corn topping:
    1/2 tbsp. canola oil
    1/8 tsp. paprika
    1 med. onion, finely chopped
    16 oz. corn kernels, thawed
    1/2 cup milk, non-fat
    1/4 tsp. cumin, ground
    1/4 tsp. salt
    1/4 tsp. black pepper

1. Heat oven to 400 degrees. Spray skillet with non-stick vegetable spray; place over medium heat until hot. Cook chicken breast 2 minutes on each side. Remove from skillet; set aside.

2. Put beef in same skillet; cook, stirring constantly, until no longer pink. Stir in salt, pepper, raisins, and olives. Spoon 1/4 of mixture into each of 4 small, oven-proof bowls, or one 8-by-8-inch baking dish. Cut cooked chicken breast into quarters; place 1 quarter on top of meat in each bowl.

3. Combine oil and paprika in same skillet; place over medium heat until hot. Add onion and cook, stirring frequently, until soft and translucent, about 5 minutes. While onion is cooking, combine thawed corn, milk, cumin, salt, and pepper in food processor; puree.

4. Add pureed corn mixture to cooked onion in skillet; mix well. Continue cooking 5 minutes. Spoon 1/4 of corn mixture over top of each bowl of meat. Bake until bubbly and nicely browned, 35 to 40 minutes.

CHAPTER PROJECT

Club de exploradores

Overview: Students research and create a proposal for a trip to a national park or other outdoor tourist attraction in Spain or Latin America to present to their Explorer's Club or the class. Presentations should include images of the site, each with a descriptive caption, and can be created digitally, by hand, or using a combination of resources. Students then present their proposal explaining where the park is, how club members would get there, what they would need to bring, and what there is to see and do.

Resources: online or print photos, image editing and page layout software and/or poster board, markers, glue, scissors

Sequence: (suggestions for when to do each step are found throughout the chapter)

STEP 1. Review instructions so students know what's expected of them. Hand out the "Chapter 1 Project Instructions and Rubric" from the *Teacher's Resource Book*.

STEP 2. Students submit a draft of their proposal including the name and location of their destination, what the club would need to bring, and why they might want to go there. Return the proposal with your suggestions.

STEP 3. Students do a layout leaving room for photos and captions. Encourage them to try different arrangements before placing the photos.

STEP 4. Students submit a draft of their photo captions. Note your corrections and suggestions, then return drafts to students.

STEP 5. Students present their proposals to the class, explaining where the park is, how the club would get there, and what they could expect to see and do.

Options:
1. Students write and create an article for a travel magazine with photos and captions about a national park in Spain or Latin America.
2. Students research and create a proposal for a trip back in time to an earlier civilization in Spain or Latin America.

Assessment:
Here is a detailed rubric for assessing this project:
Chapter 1 Project: *Club de exploradores*

RUBRIC	Score 1	Score 3	Score 5
Your evidence of planning	You provide preliminary proposal or caption drafts.	Your preliminary proposal and captions are created, but not corrected.	You show evidence of corrected proposal and captions.
Your use of illustrations	You include photos.	You include photos, but layout is disorganized.	You include photos, and your presentation is easy to read and convincing.
Your presentation	You do not include the required information.	You include most of the required information.	You include all of the required information.

21st Century Skills

Look for tips throughout Chapter 1 to enrich your teaching by integrating 21st Century Skills. Suggestions for the Chapter Project and Culture follow below.

Chapter Project

Modify the Chapter Project with one or more of these suggestions:

Support Information Literacy
Encourage students to use information from a variety of Web sites to plan their trip proposal. The handout "Search for Information on the Internet" will help them find reliable sources for planning an exciting trip.

Foster Collaboration
Have students work together in small groups and assume shared responsibility for researching and writing their trip proposal. Provide them with the handout "Work in Teams" to help them divide the tasks.

Encourage Critical Thinking and Problem Solving
Ask students to make a list of the problems a traveler may encounter when engaged in an adventurous outdoor activity. How would this affect the clothes, medicines or other items they pack for the trip? How would weather influence what they bring?

Chapter Culture

Develop Flexibility and Adaptability
Help students bridge cultural differences by offering opportunities to discuss the culture highlighted throughout the chapter. Use the information in the *Fondo cultural* note on page 27 to discuss the importance of national parks, ecotourism, and family outings in different cultures.

▶◀ **Videodocumentario** View *Los deportes en el mundo hispano* online with the class to learn about the many sports and outdoor activities practiced in the Spanish-speaking world.

AT A GLANCE

Objectives

- Listen to and read about excursions and competitions
- Talk and write about nature and sports events
- Describe a trip
- Compare a famous pilgrimage route in Spain with similar trips in your community
- Understand legends about nature

A ver si recuerdas...

- Outdoor activities
- Sports and competition
- Accidents in sports
- Verbs in the preterite

Recycle ♻

- **obtener**, **competir**, and **conseguir** in the preterite
- **s** and **z** before **e** and **i**

Vocabulary

- Outdoor activities and camping
- Natural environment and weather
- Sports and competitions
- Expressing emotions

Grammar

- Verbs with spelling and stem changes in the preterite
- Irregular verbs in the preterite
- The imperfect

Culture

- The Chilean landscape, p. 21
- National parks in South America, pp. 22, 27
- Ecocamps in Chile, p. 35
- The International Olympics of Math, p. 40
- F.C. Barcelona, p. 46
- El Camino de Santiago, pp. 48–49
- Mexican legends, p. 57

RESOURCES

FOR THE STUDENT	ONLINE	DVD	PRINT	FOR THE TEACHER	ONLINE	PREEXP	DVD	PRINT
Plan				Interactive TE and Resource DVD	•		•	
				Teacher's Resource Book, pp. 27–84	•		•	•
				Pre-AP* Resource Book, pp. 138–140	•		•	•
				Lesson Plans	•			•
				Mapa global interactivo	•			

A ver si recuerdas PP. 16–19

	FOR THE STUDENT	ONLINE	DVD	PRINT	FOR THE TEACHER	ONLINE	PREEXP	DVD	PRINT
Review	A ver si recuerdas Study Plan	•			A ver si recuerdas Study Plan	•			
	Guided WB, pp. 15–18	•	•	•	Vocabulary and Grammar Transparencies, 32–35	•	•	•	
	Core WB, pp. 7–8	•	•	•	Answer Keys: Student Edition, p. 5	•	•	•	
	Hispanohablantes WB, p. 12			•					

Introducción PP. 20–21

	FOR THE STUDENT	ONLINE	DVD	PRINT	FOR THE TEACHER	ONLINE	PREEXP	DVD	PRINT
Present	Student Edition, pp. 20–21	•	•	•	Interactive TE and Resource DVD	•		•	
	DK Reference Atlas	•	•		Teacher's Resource Book, pp. 28–31	•		•	•
	Videonovela: ¡Pura vida!	•	•		Video Program Teacher's Guide, Cap. 1				•
	¡Pura vida! Video Activities	•			Galería de fotos		•		
	Hispanohablantes WB, p. 13			•	Fine Art Transparencies, 43	•	•	•	
					Map Transparencies, 14, 18, 20	•	•	•	

Vocabulario en contexto PP. 22–25/36–39

	FOR THE STUDENT	ONLINE	DVD	PRINT	FOR THE TEACHER	ONLINE	PREEXP	DVD	PRINT
Present & Practice	Student Edition, pp. 22–25/36–39	•	•	•	Interactive TE and Resource DVD	•		•	
	Audio	•	•		Teacher's Resource Book, pp. 32–33, 36–37, 50–57/34–35, 38, 50–57	•		•	•
	Flashcards	•	•						
	Instant Check	•			Vocabulary Clip Art	•	•	•	
	Guided WB, pp. 19–26/33–40	•	•	•	Audio Program	•	•	•	
	Core WB, pp. 9–10/14–15	•	•	•	Vocabulary and Grammar Transparencies, 36–39/43–45	•	•	•	
	Comm. WB, pp. 12/16	•	•	•	Answer Keys: Student Edition, pp. 6/12–13	•	•	•	
	Hispanohablantes WB, pp. 14–15/24–25			•					
Assess and Remediate					Pruebas 1–1/1–6: Assessment Program, pp. 13–14/23–24	•		•	•
					Hispanohablantes, pp. 13–14/23–24	•		•	•

RESOURCES

Vocabulario en uso PP. 26–29/40–41

Present & Practice

FOR THE STUDENT	ONLINE	DVD	PRINT
Student Edition, pp. 26–29/40–41	•	•	•
Instant Check	•		
Comm. WB, pp. 8/9	•	•	•
Hispanohablantes WB, pp. 16–19/26–28			•
Communicative Pair Activities	•		

FOR THE TEACHER	ONLINE	PREEXP	DVD	PRINT
Interactive Whiteboard Vocabulary Activities	•		•	
Interactive TE and Resource DVD	•		•	
Teacher's Resource Book, pp. 37, 42/38–39, 45–46	•		•	•
Audio Program	•	•	•	
Videomodelos	•		•	
Answer Keys: Student Edition, pp. 7–9/14	•	•	•	•

Assess and Remediate

FOR THE TEACHER	ONLINE	PREEXP	DVD	PRINT
Pruebas 1–2/1–7 with Study Plans	•			
Pruebas 1–2/1–7: Assessment Program, pp. 15–16/25–26	•		•	•
Hispanohablantes, pp. 15–16/25–26	•		•	•

Gramática PP. 30–35/42–47

Present & Practice

FOR THE STUDENT	ONLINE	DVD	PRINT
Student Edition, pp. 30–35/42–47	•	•	•
Instant Check	•		
Animated Verbs	•		
Tutorial Video: Grammar	•		
Canción de hip hop	•		
Guided WB, pp. 29–32/41–44	•	•	•
Core WB, pp. 12–13/16–18	•	•	•
Comm. WB, pp. 8, 14–15/10–11, 17–19, 163	•	•	•
Hispanohablantes WB, pp. 20–23/29–33			•
Communicative Pair Activities	•		

FOR THE TEACHER	ONLINE	PREEXP	DVD	PRINT
Interactive Whiteboard Grammar Activities	•		•	
Interactive TE and Resource DVD	•		•	
Teacher's Resource Book, pp. 37–38, 43–44/39, 47–48	•		•	•
Audio Program	•	•	•	
Videomodelos	•	•	•	
Vocabulary and Grammar Transparencies, 40–42/46–47	•	•	•	
Answer Keys: Student Edition, pp. 9–12/15–17	•	•	•	

Assess and Remediate

FOR THE TEACHER	ONLINE	PREEXP	DVD	PRINT
Pruebas 1–3, 1–4, 1–5/1–8, 1–9 with Study Plans	•			
Pruebas 1–3, 1–4, 1–5/1–8, 1–9: Assessment Program, pp. 17, 18, 19/27, 28	•		•	•
Hispanohablantes, pp. 17, 18, 19/ 27, 28	•		•	•
Examen 1, Examen 2: Vocab. y gramática, pp. 20–22/29–31	•		•	•

¡Adelante! PP. 48–57

Application

FOR THE STUDENT	ONLINE	DVD	PRINT
Student Edition, pp. 48–57	•	•	•
Online Cultural Reading	•		
Guided WB, pp. 45–47	•	•	•
Comm. WB, pp. 20–21/164	•	•	•
Hispanohablantes WB, pp. 34–39			•
Videodocumentario	•	•	
Lectura 3, pp. 6–7, 11–13			•

FOR THE TEACHER	ONLINE	PREEXP	DVD	PRINT
Interactive TE and Resource DVD	•		•	
Teacher's Resource Book, pp. 40–41	•		•	•
Video Program: Videodocumentario	•		•	
Video Program Teacher's Guide, Cap. 1	•		•	
Map Transparencies, 20	•	•	•	
Vocabulary and Grammar Transparencies, 4–6	•	•	•	
Answer Keys: Student Edition, pp. 17–18	•	•	•	

Repaso del capítulo PP. 58–61

Review

FOR THE STUDENT	ONLINE	DVD	PRINT
Student Edition, pp. 58–61	•	•	•
Online Puzzles and Games	•		
Core WB, pp. 19–20	•	•	•
Comm. WB, pp. 165–169	•	•	•
Hispanohablantes WB, pp. 40–43			•
Instant Check	•		

FOR THE TEACHER	ONLINE	PREEXP	DVD	PRINT
Interactive TE and Resource DVD	•		•	
Teacher's Resource Book, pp. 40, 49, 50–57	•		•	•
Audio Program	•	•	•	
Answer Keys: Student Edition, p. 19	•	•	•	

Chapter Assessment

Assess

FOR THE TEACHER	ONLINE	PREEXP	DVD	PRINT
Examen del capítulo 1: Assessment Program, pp. 32–35	•		•	•
Alternate Assessment Program, pp. 5–14	•		•	•
Hispanohablantes, pp. 32–35	•		•	•
Audio Program, Cap. 1, Examen	•		•	
ExamView: Test Banks A and B (questions only online)	•		•	
Heritage Learner Test Bank	•		•	
Pre-AP* Test Bank	•		•	

REGULAR SCHEDULE (50 MINUTES)

DAY	Warm-up / Assess	Preview / Present / Practice / Communicate		Wrap-up / Homework Options
1	**Warm-up** (10 min.) • Return Prueba from Para empezar	**Repaso** (35 min.) • A ver si recuerdas . . . • Actividades 1, 4 , 5		**Wrap-up and Homework Options** (5 min.) • Actividades 2, 3, 6, 7 • Core Practice 1-1, 1-2
2	**Warm-up** (10 min.) • Homework check	**Chapter Opener** (5 min.) • Objetives • Arte y cultura	**Vocabulario en contexto 1** (30 min.) • Presentation: Vocabulario y gramática en contexto • Actividades 1, 2	**Wrap-up and Homework Options** (5 min.) • Clip Art Vocabulary
3	**Warm-up** (10 min.) • Homework check	**Vocabulario en contexto 1** (35 min.) • Presentation: Una aventura desastrosa • Actividad 3		**Wrap-up and Homework Options** (5 min.) • Core Practice 1-3, 1-4 • Actividad 4 • Prueba 1-1: Vocabulary recognition
4	**Warm-up** (10 min.) • Homework check ✔**Formative Assessment** (10 min.) • Prueba 1-1: Vocabulary recognition	**Vocabulario en uso 1** (25 min.) • Interactive Whiteboard Vocabulary Activities • Actividades 6, 7, 10, 11, 13 • Ampliación del lenguaje		**Wrap-up and Homework Options** (5 min.) • Actividades 8, 9 • Writing Activities • Prueba 1-2 with Study Plan: Vocabulary production
5	**Warm-up** (5 min.) • Homework check ✔**Formative Assessment** (10 min.) • Prueba 1-2 with Study Plan: Vocabulary production	**Gramática y vocabulario en uso 1** (25 min.) • Fondo cultural • Writing Activity • Actividades 12, 13, 14, 15	• Presentation: El pretérito de verbos con el cambio ortográfico $i \rightarrow y$ • Interactive Whiteboard Grammar Activities	**Wrap-up and Homework Options** (5 min.) • Core Practice 1-5
6	**Warm-up** (10 min.) • Homework check ✔**Formative Assessment** (10 min.) • Prueba 1-3 with Study Plan: El pretérito de verbos con el cambio ortográfico $i \rightarrow y$	**Gramática y vocabulario en uso 1** (25 min.) • Presentation: El pretérito de los verbos irregulares • Interactive Whiteboard Grammar Activities • Actividades 16, 18		**Wrap-up and Homework Options** (5 min.) • Core Practice 1-6 • Prueba 1-4 with Study Plan: El pretérito de los verbos irregulares
7	**Warm-up** (10 min.) • Activity 17 • Homework check ✔**Formative Assessment** (10 min.) • Prueba 1-4 with Study Plan: El pretérito de los verbos irregulares	**Gramática y vocabulario en uso 1** (25 min.) • Presentation: El pretérito de verbos con los cambios $e \rightarrow i, o \rightarrow u$ en la raíz • Interactive Whiteboard Vocabulary Activities • Actividades 19, 20, 21, 22		**Wrap-up and Homework Options** (5 min.) • Core Practice 1-7 • Writing Activity • Communicative Pair Activity
8	**Warm-up** (5 min.) • Actividad 25 • Homework check ✔**Formative Assessment** (10 min.) • Prueba 1-5 with Study Plan: El pretérito de verbos con los cambios $e \rightarrow i, o \rightarrow u$	**Vocabulario en contexto 2** (25 min.) • Presentation: Vocabulario y gramática en contexto • Actividades 26, 27		**Wrap-up and Homework Options** (5 min.) • Clip Art Vocabulary • Examen: Vocabulario y gramática 1
9	**Warm-up** (10 min.) • Homework check ✔**Formative Assessment** (25 min.) • Examen: Vocabulario y gramática 1	**Vocabulario en contexto 2** (10 min.) • Presentation: La voz del estudiante • Actividad 29		**Wrap-up and Homework Options** (5 min.) • Actividades 28, 30 • Core Practice 1-8, 1-9 • Prueba 1-6: Vocabulary recognition
10	**Warm-up** (5 min.) • Actividad 31 • Homework check ✔**Formative Assessment** (40 min.) • Prueba 1-6: Vocabulary recognition	**Vocabulario en uso 2** (25 min.) • Actividades 32, 33, 34, 35 • Fondo cultural		**Wrap-up and Homework Options** (5 min.) • Writing Activities • Prueba 1-7 with Study Plan: Vocabulary production

REGULAR SCHEDULE (50 MINUTES)

DAY	Warm-up / Assess	Preview / Present / Practice / Communicate	Wrap-up / Homework Options
11	**Warm-up** (10 min.) • Writing Activity • Homework check ✔**Formative Assessment** (10 min.) • Prueba 1-7 with Study Plan: Vocabulary production	**Gramática y vocabulario en uso 2** (25 min.) • Presentation: El imperfecto • Interactive Whiteboard Grammar Activities • Actividades 36, 37, 38 • Writing Activity	**Wrap-up and Homework Options** (5 min.) • Core Practice 1-10 • Prueba 1-8 with Study Plan: El imperfecto
12	**Warm-up** (10 min.) • Writing Activity • Homework check ✔**Formative Assessment** (10 min.) • Prueba 1-8 with Study Plan: El imperfecto	**Gramática y vocabulario en uso 2** (25 min.) • Presentation: Usos del imperfecto • Actividades 39, 40 • El español en el mundo del trabajo	**Wrap-up and Homework Options** (5 min.) • Core Practice 1-10 • Prueba 1-9 with Study Plan: Usos del imperfecto • En voz alta
13	**Warm-up** (10 min.) • Actividad 43 • Homework check ✔**Formative Assessment** (10 min.) • Prueba 1-9 with Study Plan: Usos del imperfecto	**Gramática y vocabulario en uso 2** (25 min.) • Actividad 44 • Audio and Writing Activities • Communicative Pair Activity • Actividades 39, 40	**Wrap-up and Homework Options** (5 min.) • Examen: Vocabulario y gramática 2
14	**Warm-up** (10 min.) • Homework check ✔**Formative Assessment** (30 min.) • Examen: Vocabulario y gramática 2	**¡Adelante!** (8 min.) • Presentación oral: Step 1	**Wrap-up and Homework Options** (2 min.) • Presentación oral: Step 2
15	**Warm-up** (10 min.) • Presentación oral: Step 2	**¡Adelante!** (35 min.) • Presentación oral: Step 3	**Wrap-up and Homework Options** (5 min.) • El Camino de Santiago • ¿Comprendiste?
16	**Warm-up** (10 min.) • El Camino de Santiago: ¿Comprendiste? • Homework check	**¡Adelante!** (30 min.) • ¿Qué me cuentas? 1, 2, 3 • View Video	**Wrap-up and Homework Options** (5 min.) • Presentación escrita: Steps 1, 2
17	**Warm-up** (10 min.) • Homework check	**¡Adelante!** (15 min.) • Presentación escrita: Step 3 **Repaso** (20 min.) • Preparación para el examen: Actividades 3, 6	**Wrap-up and Homework Options** (5 min.) • Presentación escrita: Step 4 • Fondo cultural
18	**Warm-up** (10 min.) • Homework check	**¡Adelante!** (35 min.) • Lectura • Interacción con la lectura	**Wrap-up and Homework Options** (5 min.) • Core Practice: Organizer 1-13, 1-14 • Instant Check
19	**Warm-up** (20 min.) • Preparación para el examen: Actividades 1, 2 • Homework check	**Repaso** (25 min.) • Preparación para el examen: Actividades 4, 5, 7 • Other review	**Wrap-up and Homework Options** (5 min.) • Examen del capítulo
20	**Warm-up** (5 min.) • Answer questions ✔**Summative Assessment** (44 min.) • Examen del capítulo		**Wrap-up and Homework Options** (1 min.) • A ver si recuerdas: Capítulo 2

BLOCK SCHEDULE (90 MINUTES)

DAY	Warm-up / Assess	Preview / Present / Practice / Communicate	Wrap-up / Homework Options
1	**Warm-up (10 min.)** • Return Prueba from Para empezar	**A ver si recuerdas (30 min.)** • Presentation: Vocabulario p. 16 • Actividad 1 • Presentation: Gramática p. 17 • Actividades 2, 3 • Presentation: Vocabulario p. 18 • Actividades 4, 5 • Presentation: Gramática p. 19 • Actividades 6, 7 **Vocabulario en contexto 1 (35 min.)** • Objectives • Arte y cultura • Presentation: Vocabulario y gramática en contexto • Actividades 1, 2 • Presentation: ¡Una aventura desastrosa! • Actividad 3 **Vocabulario en uso 1 (10 min.)** • Actividades 4, 5	**Wrap-up and Homework Options (5 min.)** • Core Practice 1-1 to 1-4 • Clip Art Vocabulary • Prueba 1-1: Vocabulary recognition
2	**Warm-up (10 min.)** • Vocabulario y gramática en contexto • ¡Una aventura desastrosa! • Homework check ✔**Formative Assessment (10 min.)** • Prueba 1-1: Vocabulary recognition	**Vocabulario en uso 1 (65 min.)** • Actividades 6, 7, 10, 11, 13 • Interactive Whiteboard Vocabulary Activities • Ampliación del lenguaje • Fondo cultural • Communicative Pair Activity	**Wrap Up and Homework Options (5 min.)** • Writing Activities • Prueba 1-2 with Study Plan: Vocabulary production
3	**Warm-up (10 min.)** • Writing Activity • Homework check **Vocabulario en uso 1 (20 min.)** • Actividad 12 ✔**Formative Assessment (10 min.)** • Prueba 1-2 with Study Plan: Vocabulary production	**Gramática y vocabulario en uso 1 (45 min.)** • Presentation: El pretérito de verbos con el cambio ortográfico $i \rightarrow y$ • Interactive Whiteboard Grammar Activities • Actividades 14, 15 • Presentation: El pretérito de verbos irregulares • Actividades 16, 17, 18 • Actividades 24, 25	**Wrap-up and Homework Options (5 min.)** • Core Practice 1-5, 1-6 • Pruebas 1-3, 1-4 with Study Plans: El pretérito de verbos con el cambio ortográfico $i \rightarrow y$, El pretérito de verbos irregulares
4	**Warm-up (10 min.)** • Writing Activity • Homework check ✔**Formative Assessment: (20 min.)** • Pruebas 1-3, 1-4 with Study Plans: El pretérito de verbos con el cambio ortográfico $i \rightarrow y$, El pretérito de verbos irregulares	**Gramática y vocabulario en uso 1 (40 min.)** • Presentation: El pretérito de verbos con los cambios $e \rightarrow i, o \rightarrow u$ en la raíz • Interactive Whiteboard Grammar Activities • Actividades 19, 20, 21, 22, 23 • Writing Activity • Communicative Pair Activity **Vocabulario en contexto 2 (15 min.)** • Presentation: Vocabulario y gramática en contexto • Actividades 26, 27	**Wrap-up and Homework Options (5 min.)** • Core Practice 1-7 • Prueba 1-5 with Study Plan: El pretérito de verbos con los cambios $e \rightarrow i, o \rightarrow u$ en la raíz • Examen: Vocabulario y gramática 1
5	**Warm-up (10 min.)** • Homework check ✔**Formative Assessment Options: (40 min.)** • Prueba 1-5 with Study Plan: El pretérito de verbos con los cambios $e \rightarrow i, o \rightarrow u$ en la raíz • Examen: Vocabulario y gramática 1	**Vocabulario en contexto 2 (25 min.)** • Presentation: La voz del estudiante • Actividades 28, 29, 30, 31 **Vocabulario en uso 2 (10 min.)** • Actividad 32 • Interactive Whiteboard Vocabulary Activities • Fondo cultural	**Wrap-up and Homework Options (5 min.)** • Core Practice 1-8, 1-9 • Prueba 1-6: Vocabulary recognition
6	**Warm-up (10 min.)** • Homework check ✔**Formative Assessment (10 min.)** • Prueba 1-6: Vocabulary recognition	**Gramática y vocabulario en uso 2 (65 min.)** • Actividades 33, 34, 35 • Presentation: El imperfecto • Interactive Whiteboard Grammar Activities • Actividades 36, 37, 38	**Wrap-up and Homework Options (5 min.)** • Core Practice 1-10 • Pruebas 1-7, 1-8 with Study Plans: Vocabulary production, El imperfecto

BLOCK SCHEDULE (90 MINUTES)

DAY	Warm-up / Assess	Preview / Present / Practice / Communicate	Wrap-up / Homework Options
7	**Warm-up** (10 min.) • Writing Activity • Homework check ✔**Formative Assessment** (20 min.) • Pruebas 1-7, 1-8 with Study Plans: Vocabulary production, El imperfecto	**Gramática y vocabulario en uso 2** (40 min.) • Presentation: Usos del imperfecto • Interactive Whiteboard Grammar Activities • Actividades 39, 40, 41 • El español en el mundo del trabajo **¡Adelante!** (15 min.) • Presentación oral: Steps 1, 2	**Wrap-up and Homework Options** (5 min.) • Presentación oral: Step 2
8	**Warm-up** (15 min.) • Actividad 43 • Homework check ✔**Formative Assessment** (40 min.) • Presentación oral: Step 3	**Gramática y vocabulario en uso 2** (30 min.) • En voz alta • Actividades 42, 43, 44 • Communicative Pair Activity	**Wrap-up and Homework Options** (5 min.) • Core Practice 1-11, 1-12 • Prueba 1-9 with Study Plan: Usos del imperfecto • Examen: Vocabulario y gramática 2
9	**Warm-up** (10 min.) • Writing Activity • Homework check ✔**Formative Assessment Options:** (30 min.) • Prueba 1-9 with Study Plan: Usos del imperfecto • Examen: Vocabulario y gramática 2	**¡Adelante!** (45 min.) • El Camino de Santiago • ¿Comprendiste? • ¿Qué me cuentas? 1, 2, 3 • View Video • Video Activities • Presentación escrita: Step 1	**Wrap-up and Homework Options** (5 min.) • Presentación escrita: Step 2 • Preparación para el examen: Actividades 1, 2
10	**Warm-up** (20 min.) • Presentación escrita: Step 3 • Homework check	**¡Adelante!** (35 min.) • Lectura • Interacción con la lectura • Fondo cultural **Repaso** (30 min.) • Preparación para el examen: Actividades 3, 6 • Preparación para el examen: Actividades 4, 5, 7	**Wrap-up and Homework Options** (5 min.) • Presentación escrita: Step 4 • Core Practice: Organizer 1-13, 1-14 • Instant Check • Preparación para el examen: Actividades 4, 5, 7 • Examen del capítulo
11	**Warm-up** (10 min.) • Homework check ✔**Summative Assessment** (45 min.) • Examen del capítulo	**Theme Game** (20 min.) **A ver si recuerdas – Capítulo 2** (10 min.) • Presentation: Vocabulario • Presentation: Gramática	**Wrap-up and Homework Options** (5 min.) • A ver si recuerdas – Capítulo 2 • Actividades 1–6

1 Recycle

Vocabulario Repaso

Core Instruction

Standards: 1.1, 1.2

Resources: Voc. and Gram. Transparency 32

♻ Un poco más de repaso

Suggestions: Before presenting the material in this review section, consider testing your students' command of the material by assigning the Study Plan. Students will automatically be given additional practice of the material they have not yet mastered, and you can focus your review based on the class's overall performance on the post-test.

Show the blank organizer and have students copy it on a sheet of paper. With the book closed, students work in groups of two and list as many words as they can remember in each category.

1 Standards: 1.1, 1.3

Focus: Practicing review vocabulary

Suggestions: Remind students to use the word web as a source for ideas. Encourage them to use vocabulary and expressions that they might know which are not on the list.

Common Errors: Following English logic, some students may talk about weather conditions attempting to use **estar** + adjective when **hacer** + noun would more commonly be used in Spanish. Provide repeated models of the **hacer** construction.

Extension: Have students take notes on what their partner says and later use the notes to write a paragraph with complete sentences.

Answers will vary.

Vocabulario Repaso

Lugares
el campo
el lago
el mar
las montañas
el parque
la playa
el río

El tiempo
llueve (llover)
nieva (nevar)
hace . . .
buen tiempo
calor
frío
mal tiempo

Actividades
dar una caminata
ir de pesca
ir de vacaciones
ir de viaje
montar en bicicleta
montar a caballo
tomar el sol

Otras actividades
hacer . . .
esquí acuático
moto acuática
surf de vela
una fogata
una parrillada
un picnic

Animales / Insectos
las hormigas
el mono
los mosquitos
el oso
el pájaro
los peces

▼1 ¿Adónde vas? | 🗣

Escribir • Hablar

❶ Escoge dos lugares de la lista adonde a veces vas de vacaciones. Escribe dos actividades que haces allí, el tiempo que hace y los animales que puedes encontrar.

❷ Ahora trabaja con otro(a) estudiante para hablar de sus vacaciones. Usen palabras de las listas.

• Y tú, ¿adónde vas de vacaciones generalmente?
Voy a . . .

• ¿Qué actividades te gusta hacer allí?
Me gusta . . .

• ¿Qué tiempo hace?
Hace . . .

16 dieciséis
A ver si recuerdas . . .

Block Schedule

Have students break into groups of four. Taking turns, each student has to stand up and pantomine a vocabulary word from the word web. The other students in the group have to guess the word. Alternate students acting out words until all the words have been used or you call time.

DIFFERENTIATED INSTRUCTION

Heritage Language Learners

Assign students one or more of the following from the *Actividades* list: **dar un(a), ir de, montar en/a,** or **tomar.** Ask them to think of as many expressions as they can that begin with their assigned word(s), such as **dar una vuelta, ir de compras, montar en bicicleta,** or **tomar precauciones.**

Advanced Learners

Have students apply the same expressions to other situations: *¿Adónde vas los fines de semana?*

Gramática Repaso

El pretérito de los verbos

You use the preterite to talk about things that happened in the past. Here are the regular preterite forms of verbs ending in -ar, -er, and -ir:

caminar

caminé	caminamos
caminaste	caminasteis
caminó	caminaron

comer

comí	comimos
comiste	comisteis
comió	comieron

vivir

viví	vivimos
viviste	vivisteis
vivió	vivieron

Here are the preterite forms of the irregular verbs *hacer*, *dar*, and *ver*:

hacer

hice	hicimos
hiciste	hicisteis
hizo	hicieron

dar

di	dimos
diste	disteis
dio	dieron

ver

vi	vimos
viste	visteis
vio	vieron

▼2 El fin de semana pasado

Leer • Escribir

Carmen describe lo que hizo su familia durante el fin de semana. Completa las siguientes frases con la forma correcta del pretérito de los verbos.

hacer	visitar	correr	dar
pasear	comer	aprender	ver

1. (Yo) _____ a mis abuelos.
2. Mis hermanos _____ en bote.
3. Tú _____ muchas películas.
4. Nosotros _____ a montar a caballo.
5. Mi padre _____ caminatas.
6. Mis primos _____ por la playa.
7. Tú y yo _____ helados.
8. Mi hermana _____ ejercicio.

▼3 Las vacaciones

Escribir • Hablar

❶ Haz una lista de ocho actividades que tú y otras personas hicieron durante las vacaciones pasadas.

Modelo

Caminé por la playa.
Mi familia y yo hicimos un picnic en el campo.

❷ Con otro(a) estudiante hablen de sus vacaciones. Comparen las actividades que hicieron.

Recycle 1

Gramática Repaso

Core Instruction

Resources: Voc. and Gram. Transparency 33

♻ Un poco más de repaso

Suggestions: Refer students who are having difficulty with the preterite of verbs to the *GramActiva* video from Level 2 Chapter 2B, and to the online tutorials. Allow students a few minutes to read through the grammar review on their own. Continue by using verbal cues to elicit preterite forms of regular verbs such as *ayer, anoche, la semana pasada,* or *el año pasado.*

▼2 Standards: 1.2

Resources: Answer Keys: Student Edition, p. 5

Focus: Practicing regular preterite verb forms

Suggestions: After students complete the activity, have them check their answers with a partner.

Common Errors: Students commonly confuse first- and third-person preterite endings. Provide them with this mnemonic device: The first-person endings are -*e* as in the English first-person **"me"** and -*i* as in English first-person **"I."**

Answers:

1. visité
2. pasearon
3. viste
4. aprendimos
5. dio
6. corrieron
7. comimos
8. hizo

▼3 Standards: 1.1, 1.3

Focus: Reviewing regular preterite verb forms

Suggestions: Remind students that they can use the verbs on p. 16 to complete this activity.

Answers will vary.

Extension: Ask students to write a list of activities they did at another time in the past: *ayer en la clase...; el fin de semana pasado....*

ENRICH YOUR TEACHING

Teacher-to-Teacher

Have students work in pairs to practice preterite verb forms. Student A cues Student B by asking if he or she is doing something in the present. Student B gives a negative response, adds that he or she did that thing yesterday, and asks Student A another question:

A —¿Hablas con Rita hoy?

B —No, pero hablé con ella ayer.

B —¿Vemos una película en clase hoy?

A —No, pero vimos una película en clase ayer.

Vocabulario Repaso

Core Instruction

Standards: 1.1, 1.2

Resources: Voc. and Gram. Transparency 34

♻ Un poco más de repaso

Suggestions: Have students use the vocabulary to talk about the photos. Help them expand on their statements with questions such as *¿A cuántos jugadores ves en la foto?* For names of parts of the body, use a picture from a magazine or bring in a doll. Point to various parts of the body and have students name them.

BELLRINGER REVIEW

Show Transparency 34. Have students write a three-sentence mini-story for each of the three photos.

---

4 Standards: 1.1, 1.2

Focus: Practicing review vocabulary

Suggestions: Model intonation as necessary and encourage students to speak with intonation that is appropriate for the sentence.

Answers will vary.

Extension: Have each student write two sentences that are similar to the exercise items: one about a positive occurrence and one about a negative one. Then have partners take turns reading and reacting to their sentences.

---

5 Standards: 1.2, 1.3

Resources: Answer Keys: Student Edition, p. 5

Focus: Practicing review vocabulary

Suggestions: Have students check their answers with a partner orally. Reading the items aloud will provide additional pronunciation practice.

Answers:

1. a   2. d   3. b   4. e   5. c

Extension: Invite students who wrote stories to read them aloud. Encourage those who wrote dialogues to act them out with you or a partner.

Vocabulario Repaso

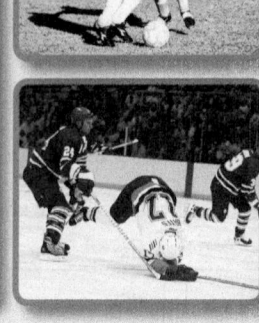

Deportes

correr
esquiar
jugar al fútbol
montar en monopatín
nadar
navegar
patinar

Reacciones

¡Fantástico!
¡Genial!
¡Increíble!
Lo siento.
¡Qué lástima!
¡Qué pena!
¡Uy!

Competencias

el campeón, la campeona
el campeonato
la competencia
competir
el concurso
el equipo
el jugador, la jugadora
el partido
el premio
el tanteo

Acciones

ganar
jugar
participar
perder
practicar

El cuerpo

el brazo   el músculo
el codo   el pie
el dedo   la pierna
el hueso   la rodilla
la mano   el tobillo
la muñeca

Accidentes

caerse
cortarse
lastimarse
romperse
torcerse

▼4 El campeonato |

Leer • Hablar

Trabaja con otro(a) estudiante para leer y reaccionar a los comentarios siguientes.

▶ **Modelo**

A —Perdimos el partido.
B —*¡Qué lástima!*

1. ¡Ganamos cinco a cero!
2. El jugador se cayó y se lastimó.
3. Me torcí el tobillo.
4. Nuestro equipo quedó campeón.
5. Les metimos tres goles.
6. ¡Perdimos el campeonato!
7. Hoy llovió y no pudimos jugar.

18   dieciocho
A ver si recuerdas . . .

▼5 Definiciones

Leer • Escribir

Empareja cada definición con la palabra correspondiente. Luego, escribe un diálogo o un cuento usando cuatro de las palabras o expresiones de la segunda columna.

1. una parte del cuerpo que usas para jugar al fútbol
2. un grupo de personas que juegan un partido
3. la persona que siempre gana una competencia
4. lo que dices si te caes
5. un tipo de accidente

   a. el pie
   b. el campeón / la campeona
   c. torcerse la muñeca
   d. un equipo
   e. ¡Uy!

DIFFERENTIATED INSTRUCTION

Students with Special Needs

Students with hearing disabilities may not be able to distinguish between the sounds of *-car* and *-gar*, or between *-qué* and *-gué.* Such minimal pairs may require exaggerated emphasis on the first consonant sound.

Students with Learning Difficulties

Using vocabulary clip art, have students sort vocabulary into appropriate categories: *la rodilla* goes in *partes del cuerpo* and so on.

Gramática Repaso

El pretérito de los verbos *ir* y *ser*, y de los verbos que terminan en *-car*, *-gar* y *-zar*

The preterite forms of *ir* and *ser* are exactly the same.

Carlos **fue** de vacaciones a las montañas. (*ir*)
Mi equipo **fue** campeón escolar el año pasado. (*ser*)

fui	fuimos
fuiste	fuisteis
fue	fueron

Remember that verbs ending in *-car*, *-gar*, or *-zar* have a spelling change in the *yo* form in the preterite. The other forms of these verbs are regular.

buscar	yo bus**qué**	investigar	yo investi**gué**	almorzar	yo almor**cé**
chocar	yo cho**qué**	navegar	yo nave**gué**	comenzar	yo comen**cé**
practicar	yo practi**qué**	jugar	yo ju**gué**	cruzar	yo cru**cé**
practicar	yo sa**qué**	llegar	yo lle**gué**	empezar	yo empe**cé**

▼6 El partido ayer

Leer • Escribir

En una hoja de papel escribe los números del 1 al 8. Completa las siguientes frases sobre el partido de ayer con el pretérito de *ser* o *ir*. Indica si usaste una forma del verbo *ser* o del verbo *ir*.

Modelo
Yo no *fui* al partido ayer. *(Ir)*

1. El partido de fútbol _____ ayer por la noche.
2. Todos los padres _____ al estadio.
3. Tú _____ el mejor jugador del equipo.
4. El partido _____ muy emocionante.
5. Este equipo _____ campeón hace dos años.
6. Durante el partido, nosotros _____ a comprar unas salchichas.
7. El partido duró más de tres horas. _____ muy largo.
8. Después del partido, los campeones _____ a celebrar a un restaurante.

▼7 La tarea

Leer • Escribir

Luisa no pudo hacer la tarea. Completa esta nota que le escribió a su profesora con la forma correcta del verbo apropiado.

Estimada Srta. Herrera:
Perdón, yo no pude hacer la tarea, por eso no la ___1.___ *(entregar / llegar)*. Ayer pensaba jugar al tenis pero no ___2.___ *(caminar / jugar)*. Por la mañana ___3.___ *(salir / llegar)* al club deportivo. Después ___4.___ *(buscar / pintar)* mi raqueta y la ___5.___ *(llevar / sacar)* del bolso. Cuando yo ___6.___ *(ganar / empezar)* a jugar ___7.___ *(comenzar / ir)* a llover. Entonces ___8.___ *(cantar / tropezar)* y me lastimé la mano. Esta nota la escribió mi hermano.
Gracias, Luisa

Más práctica GO

realidades.com | print

A ver si recuerdas with Study Plan ✔
Guided WB pp. 15–18 ✔ ✔
Core WB pp. 7–8 ✔ ✔
Hispanohablantes WB p. 12 ✔

diecinueve **19**
Capítulo 1

ENRICH YOUR TEACHING

Teacher-to-Teacher
It is always a good idea for students to continue to review the irregular preterite forms. Many students find it useful to create a section of their notebooks that contains the conjugations of the more common irregular verbs. They can add to the list throughout the year and it can serve as a convenient reference.

21st Century Skills
Initiative and Self-Direction Direct students to the resources available at **realidades.com** for a self-directed review of the grammar topics recycled in this chapter. Students can expand their learning by doing the additional vocabulary and grammar activities.

Gramática Repaso

Core Instruction

Resources: Voc. and Gram. Transparency 35

♻ *Un poco más de repaso*

Suggestions: Refer students who are having difficulty with the preterite of irregular verbs, and with verbs with spelling changes in the preterite, to the *GramActiva* videos from Level 1 Chapters 7A and 8A, and to the online tutorials. Assign one verb from the charts to each student and ask them to use their verb in two sentences with two different subjects. Ask students to spell the ending of each verb form.

▼6 Standards: 1.2

Resources: Answer Keys: Student Edition, p. 5
Focus: Practicing preterite of *ir* and *ser*
Suggestions: Have students read their completed activity items aloud.
Answers:

1. fue/ser
2. fueron/ir
3. fuiste/ser
4. fue/ser
5. fue/ser
6. fuimos/ir
7. Fue/ser
8. fueron/ir

Common errors: Students tend to misspell *fueron*. Remind them there is no *"i"* in *fue* or *fueron*.

Extension: Ask students to use *ser* and *ir* to create and share two additional sentences about yesterday's soccer match.

▼7 Standards: 1.2

Resources: Answer Keys: Student Edition, p. 5
Focus: Reviewing preterite verb forms with spelling changes
Suggestions: Point out the reason for the spelling change in *-car* and *-gar* verbs: it allows the *c* and *g* consonants to retain their "hard" sound before the vowel *e*.
Answers:

1. entregué
2. jugué
3. salí
4. busqué
5. saqué
6. empecé
7. comenzó
8. tropecé

✓ ASSESSMENT

A ver si recuerdas with Study Plan (online only)
After reviewing material on these pages, assign the *A ver si recuerdas* Study Plan to evaluate students' mastery of the material. Additional practice is available online.

Capítulo 1 Días inolvidables

Capítulo
1

Standards for Foreign Language Learning: *Capítulo* 1

• To meet the Standards, students will:

Communication

1.1 Interpersonal

• Talk about national parks, camping, and vacations
• Talk about competitive events
• Talk about geographic locations and weather events
• Talk about fine art
• Talk about a party and opinions
• Talk about childhood memories
• Talk about ancient pilgrimages and Aztec myths

1.2 Interpretive

• Read and listen to information about national parks, camping, and outdoor vacations
• Read and listen to information about competitive events
• Read about geographic locations and weather events
• Read about fine art
• Read about a professional translator
• Read about childhood memories
• Read about ancient pilgrimages and Aztec myths

1.3 Presentational

• Write and present information orally about national parks, camping, and outdoor vacations
• Write and present orally about competitive events
• Write about geographic locations
• Write about a party and childhood memories
• Write and present information orally about Aztec myths
• Present information orally about ancient pilgrimages

Culture

2.1 Practices and Perspectives

• Interpret pilgrimages in Spain
• Interpret the effects of Aztec myths in Mexico

2.2 Products and Perspectives

• Discuss Matilde Pérez and her paintings
• Discuss *El Camino de Santiago*
• Discuss *Iztaccíhuatl* and *Popocatépetl*

Connections

3.1 Cross-curricular

• Talk about an artist and her work: Matilde Pérez
• Explain Language Arts strategies: cause and effect, describing events, using prior knowledge, choosing a topic, adding details, making predictions
• Use the skill of using graphic organizers
• Describe constellations in the southern hemisphere
• Discuss key facts about Mexico and Spain

3.2 Target Culture

• Read popular cheers for the Barcelona soccer team
• Discuss how indigenous peoples have affected the language of Mexico
• Discuss how ancient pilgrimages have shaped travel practices in Spain today

Comparisons

4.1 Language

• Compare Spanish words to their English counterparts
• Compare Spanish and English commands

4.2 Culture

• Compare ancient ball games to modern ones

▼ Chapter Objectives

Communication

By the end of the chapter you will be able to:

• Listen and read about excursions and competitions
• Talk and write about nature and sports events
• Describe a trip

Culture

You will also be able to:

• Compare a famous pilgrimage route in Spain with similar trips in your community
• Understand the relationship between legends and nature

You will demonstrate what you know and can do:

• Presentación oral, p. 51
• Presentación escrita, pp. 52–53
• Preparación para el examen, pp. 60–61

You will use:

Vocabulary	Grammar
• Outdoor activities and camping	• Verbs with spelling and stem changes in the preterite
• Natural environment	• Irregular verbs in the preterite
• Sports and competitions	• The imperfect
• Expressing emotions and impressions	

Exploración del mundo hispano

Country Connection
Outdoor Activities, Sports, and Competitions

España
Cuba
México
Chile — Argentina

realidades.com [GO]

[ ] Reference Atlas
▶ Videonovela y actividades

🌐 Mapa global interactivo

20 veinte

El Glaciar Grey en el Parque Nacional Torres del Paine, Chile

ENRICH YOUR TEACHING

Using Backward Design

Have students preview the sample performance tasks on *Preparación para el examen*, p. 61, and connect them to the Chapter Objectives. Explain to students that by completing the sample tasks they can self-assess their learning progress.

Mapa global interactivo

Download the *Mapa global interactivo* files for Chapter 1 and preview the activities. In Activity 1, travel to the Atacama Desert in Chile. Activity 2 takes you to national parks in Argentina. In Activity 3, locate astronomical observatories in both hemispheres. Activity 4 follows the route of pilgrims from France to northern Spain. In Activity 5, locate the two volcanoes in a Mexican legend.

Arte y cultura | Chile

Paisaje chileno Imagínate un lugar que tiene el desierto más árido del mundo, glaciares eternos, volcanes, un inmenso océano y además majestuosas montañas. Pues este lugar no está sólo en tu imaginación. Se llama Chile y sus diversos paisajes han inspirado a famosos artistas. Entre ellos está la pintora Matilde Pérez (1920–), quien escogió el tema de la Cordillera de los Andes para crear este cuadro.

• ¿Qué paisaje es típico de la región donde vives? ¿Y cómo te hace sentir?

"Paisaje chileno", Matilde Pérez ▶

veintiuno. **21**
Capítulo 1

Standards (cont'd)
• Compare Spanish and Latin American teen magazines and their readership to those in the United States

Communities
5.1 Beyond the School
• Link to Web sites from the Spanish-speaking world

5.2 Lifelong Learner
• Talk about important facts about healthy lifestyles
• Talk about important facts about scientific studies
• Develop an appreciation for the art of songwriting

PresentationExpress™
See pp. 16c–16d

Chapter Opener
Core Instruction

Resources: Map Transparencies 14, 18, 20
Suggestions: Introduce the chapter theme and objectives. Use the map transparencies to locate featured countries.

Videonovela *¡Pura vida!* View this stand-alone storyline video about five young adults in San José, Costa Rica with your class, either online or on DVD.

Arte y cultura

Standards: 1.1, 1.2, 2.2, 3.1, 4.2
Resources: Fine Art Transparencies with Teacher's Guide, p. 43
Mapa global interactivo, Actividad 1 Travel to the Atacama Desert in Chile.
Suggestions: Tell students Matilde Pérez painted realistic scenes, but became famous for her abstract art. Have them do an Internet search for *arte cinética*.
Answers will vary.

▶ TEACHING WITH ART
Resources: Fine Art Transparencies with Teacher's Guide, p. 43
Ask students to list the landscape features they see in the photo.

DIFFERENTIATED INSTRUCTION

Digital resources such as the *Interactive Whiteboard* activity banks, *Videomodelos*, additional *Online Activities*, *Study Plans*, automatically graded *Leveled Workbook*, animated *Grammar Tutorials*, *Flashcards*, and *Vocabulary and Grammar Videos* will help you reach students of different ability levels and learning styles.

STUDENTS NEEDING EXTRA HELP
Guided Practice Activities
• Flashcards pp. 19–22, 33–36
• Vocabulary Check, pp. 23–26, 37–40
• Grammar, pp. 27–32, 41–44

HERITAGE LEARNERS
Realidades para hispanohablantes
• Chapter Opener, pp. 12–13
• A primera vista, pp. 14–15, 24–25
• Manos a la obra, pp. 16–23, 26–33
• ¡Adelante!, pp. 34–39
• Repaso del capítulo, pp. 40–43

ADVANCED/PRE-AP*
Pre-AP* Resource Book,
• pp. 138–140
Communications Workbook
• Integrated Performance Assessment, p. 165

Vocabulario en contexto

Core Instruction

Standards: 1.1, 1.2

Resources: Teacher's Resource Book: Input Script, p. 32, Clip Art, pp. 50–57, Audio Script, p. 36; Voc. and Gram. Transparencies 36–37; Audio Program DVD: Cap. 1, Tracks 1, 3

Focus: Presenting new vocabulary and using grammar lexically in context

Suggestions: These two pages present new vocabulary and grammar in context using visuals. Each page can be presented separately, but they complement each other. The presentation of new content will continue on the following two pages (pp. 24–25) through the use of a story. Use the audio to present new vocabulary. Have students read along as you play it. Ask what each item is used for. Check comprehension by asking questions. See the Input Script in the *Teacher's Resource Book* for examples.

BELLRINGER REVIEW

Ask students to refer to pp. xxviii–xxix to locate Chile on the map and share facts about the country. (Use Map Transparency *América del Sur/parte sur.*)

1 Standards: 1.2

Resources: Teacher's Resource Book: Audio Script, p. 36; Audio Program DVD: Cap. 1, Track 2; Answer Keys: Student Edition, p. 6

Focus: Practicing listening comprehension of new vocabulary

Suggestions: Use the audio or read the script aloud to students.

Common Errors: Remind students not to try to understand every word they hear during listening comprehension activities. They should let the language "flow through" as a stream.

Answers:

1. lógica	3. lógica	5. lógica
2. ilógica	4. ilógica	

▶ **Read, listen to, and understand information about**
- **camping activities**
- **features of the natural environment**

Vocabulario en contexto

Los parques nacionales de Chile ofrecen una gran oportunidad para explorar **la naturaleza**. Todos los años, miles de jóvenes vienen a acampar en **los bosques, valles**, montañas, lagos y **desiertos** de este país **hermoso**.

"Hola, me llamo Fernando y soy chileno. El verano pasado, mi familia y yo fuimos de cámping a **la sierra**. Lo pasamos bien. ¡**El paisaje** era impresionante! Como ves, tuvimos que llevar mucho **equipo**".

la linterna

la tienda de acampar

el repelente de insectos

la brújula

el saco de dormir

los binoculares

▼1 Equipo de cámping | 🔊

Escuchar

En una hoja de papel escribe los números del 1 al 5. Vas a escuchar a unos jóvenes hablar sobre el equipo de cámping. Escucha cada frase y escribe si es lógica o ilógica.

22 veintidós
A primera vista 1

DIFFERENTIATED INSTRUCTION

Heritage Language Learners

Invite students to research information they have about camping abroad. They might describe national parks or comment on differences between the camping experience in the United States and in other places.

Students with Learning Disabilities

Remind students that the new vocabulary is presented in blue. Use the visuals and context to determine meaning.

Language Input 1

66 Éstas son las fotos que sacamos durante nuestro viaje a la sierra.

1 Dimos un paseo por los senderos al amanecer. Llevamos binoculares para observar los pájaros.

2 También fuimos de pesca. Es un deporte muy tranquilo. Mucha gente dice que es aburrido, pero a mí me encanta.

3 También dimos un paseo a caballo. Así se puede explorar mejor el valle.

4 Otra actividad que nos gustó mucho fue escalar rocas. No es peligroso si te preparas bien.

5 Al anochecer hicimos una fogata. ¿Qué comimos? ¡Pescado, por supuesto! 99

▼2 El viaje | ◀))

Escuchar

En una hoja de papel escribe los números del 1 al 5. Escucha cada frase y escribe *C* (cierto) o *F* (falso) según las fotos.

veintitrés **23**
Capítulo 1

---

2 Standards: 1.2

Resources: Teacher's Resource Book: Audio Script, p. 36; Voc. and Gram. Transparency 37; Audio Program DVD: Cap. 1, Track 4; Answer Keys: Student Edition, p. 6

Focus: Practicing listening comprehension of new vocabulary

Suggestions: Use the audio or the script. Remind students that this listening activity is based on the vocabulary on p. 23.
Answers:

1. C	4. F
2. C	5. F
3. C	

Extension: On the board, copy as models two or three statements from the Audio Script. Have each student write two statements like the models, one true and one false. Ask volunteers to read aloud one of their statements. After each statement, ask another volunteer to determine whether it is *cierto* or *falso.*

Pre-AP* Support

- **Learning Objective:** Interpersonal Speaking
- **Activity:** Ask students to make up a mini-story using one of the photos as an illustration. They should give names to the people and create sentences using the preterite to relate their story. Have students share their story with classmates.
- **Pre-AP* Resource Book:** Comprehensive guide to Pre-AP* vocabulary skill development, pp. 51–57

Teacher-to-Teacher

Have students write a note to a friend asking for advice on what they need for a camping trip, focusing on basic needs such as clothing, food, and shelter. Have them exchange notes with a classmate who will write a response. Ask students to hand in the notes if you wish to assess the activity.

ENRICH YOUR TEACHING

Culture Note

Ecotourism has become an important industry in Latin America. The beauty and variety of climate, landscape, flora, and fauna attract visitors from around the world. In recent years, countries such as Costa Rica, Venezuela, and Brazil have become internationally renowned ecotourism hotspots.

21st Century Skills

Critical Thinking and Problem-Solving
Have teams of students discuss which outdoor activities are most popular in their area. What national or state parks are nearby? What problems might arise with an increase in popularity of outdoor activities in these parks? Why? How could these problems be avoided or minimized?

23

BELLRINGER REVIEW

On the board, begin a word web with the expression *ir de cámping* at the center. Invite students to share what they know about camping and to tell about outdoor experiences they have had. Add camping and outdoors-related vocabulary that students use to the web.

Vocabulario en contexto

Core Instruction

Standards: 1.2, 3.1

Resources: Teacher's Resource Book: Input Script, p. 33, Clip Art, pp. 50–57, Audio Script, pp. 36–37; Voc. and Gram. Transparencies 38–39; Audio Program DVD: Cap. 1, Track 5

Focus: Presenting additional vocabulary; extending presentation of vocabulary and grammar in the context of a story

Suggestions:

Pre-reading: Direct attention to the *Estrategia.* Have students talk about their reasons for writing each *efecto.*

Reading: Have students read along as they listen. Have them look at each of the visuals to aid comprehension. Allow them to listen more than once. Model pronunciation of the words in boldface. Check comprehension by asking questions. See the Input Scripts in the *Teacher's Resource Book* for specific questions.

Post-reading: Complete *Actividad* 3 to check comprehension.

Extension: Have students rewrite the story as a third-person narrative.

Block Schedule

Divide students into groups of three. Give each group a number from 1 to 7 that represents a scene in *Una aventura desastrosa*. The group has five minutes to present that scene for the class. They are also to create the scene for panel 8. Have each group present their scene sequentially as the story is retold. Then have each group present panel 8. The class can vote on the most creative ending!

¡Una aventura desastrosa!

Estrategia

Cause and effect
Identifying cause and effect relationships helps us understand what we are reading.

Look at the pictures. Write the effect for each cause:

Causa	Efecto
A Guille no ve la piedra.	
B Aparece un oso.	
C El oso ve la mochila.	

1 Al amanecer, Guille, Felipe y yo nos levantamos para dar un paseo. **Anduvimos** por dos horas por un sendero. Queríamos ir a La Peña, una roca enorme, perfecta para escalar.

2 De repente, Guille se cayó y dio un grito.

—¿Qué **sucedió**, Guille?

—No vi la raíz del árbol. ¡Ay! Se rompió la brújula.

—¡Qué desastre! Y no tenemos otra. Vamos a **perdernos**.

—Creo que no. Se puede ver La Peña en la distancia. ¡Vamos!

3 Nos acercamos al pie de La Peña. Nos **impresionó** mucho porque era muy alta.

—¿Por qué no descansamos **un rato** antes de escalar?

—Buena idea.

4 **Una vez allí**, nos sentamos. De repente, **apareció** un oso muy grande. ¡Uf, nos **asustó** con lo grande que era!

—¡Ay! ¿Qué podemos hacer? ¿Adónde podemos ir? ¿Dónde **nos refugiamos**?

24 veinticuatro
A primera vista 1

DIFFERENTIATED INSTRUCTION

Students with Special Needs

Help visually impaired students deal with the information on these two pages by asking other volunteers to describe each panel. Remind them to include details about the weather, location, colors, and the expressions on the boys' faces.

Advanced Learners

Have students prepare descriptions of the story in their own words describing as accurately as possible the elements and actions in each picture. Partners then take turns giving their descriptions of the pictures in random order. The listener identifies which picture is being described.

5 Empezamos a correr **hacia** La Peña. No había otro **refugio**. El oso empezó a correr también.

—¡Rápido!

—¡Mira! Hay una roca grande a la izquierda. ¡Vamos allí!

—¡Ay! Perdí la mochila.

—No importa. ¡Corre!

6 Guille **perdió el equilibrio**, se cayó y se torció el tobillo.

—¡Guille, te ayudo!

De repente, el oso **dejó de correr**. Vio la mochila y la abrió. Sacó la comida que estaba adentro y se fue con la comida en la boca.

7 ¡Qué mala suerte! Inmediatamente empezó a llover. Vimos unos **relámpagos** y oímos un **trueno** tremendo. Luego, empezó a **caer granizo**. Entonces . . .

8 ¿Cómo crees que terminó la aventura?

> **Más práctica** **GO**
>
> realidades.com | print
>
> | Instant Check | ✔ | |
> |---|---|---|
> | **Guided WB** pp. 19–26 | ✔ | ✔ |
> | **Core WB** pp. 9–10 | ✔ | ✔ |
> | **Comm. WB** p. 12 | ✔ | ✔ |
> | *Hispanohablantes* **WB** pp. 14–15 | | ✔ |

▼**3** ¿Comprendiste?

Escribir • Hablar

1. ¿Por qué querían ir a La Peña los chicos?
2. ¿Qué le pasó a Guille?
3. ¿Qué animal los asustó? ¿Dónde se refugiaron?
4. Imagínate que estás con los chicos cuando aparece el oso. ¿Qué crees que deben hacer?

3 Standards: 1.1, 1.2, 1.3

Resources: Voc. and Gram. Transparencies 38–39; Answer Keys: Student Edition, p. 6

Focus: Demonstrating comprehension of a story

Suggestions: As students answer the questions, have them also supply the number of the picture in which the information for their answer is presented.

Answers:

1. Querían escalar la roca enorme. (panel 1)
2. Guille se cayó y dio un grito. Rompió la brújula. (panel 2)
3. Un oso los asustó. Se refugiaron en una roca grande. (panel 4)
4. Answers will vary.

Extension: Ask students to write down one question they have about the story. This may involve story elements such as plot or characters, or it may be a question about new words or structures. Invite them to take turns reading their questions. As much as possible, allow other students to answer the questions.

Teacher-to-Teacher

Asking students to visualize parts of a story is a good way to help them understand new material. During a second or third presentation, ask students to close their eyes and visualize scenes as they listen. Then ask them to describe what they visualized. Doing this regularly helps students improve their memories by creating mental "corners" or "places" in which to store information.

Chapter Project

Give students copies of the Chapter Project outline and rubric from the *Teacher's Resource Book*. Explain the task to them, and have them perform Step 1. (For more information, see p. 16-b.)

ENRICH YOUR TEACHING

Culture Note

A backpacking trip to the mountains in the southern part of South America would probably include sightings of the guanaco or its cousin the vicuña. These wild herd animals are related to the camel, but smaller. The llama and the alpaca, domestic animals used in the Andes, are descendants of the guanaco.

21st Century Skills

Develop Flexibility and Adaptability
Ask students working in small groups to turn their imagined ending to the story into a Spanish interview program about outdoors survival adventures called *¡Sobrevivientes!* Have one of the students interview the others in the group, who will play the characters in the story, offer their version of the events, and explain how their adventure ended.

☑ASSESSMENT

Prueba: **Comprensión del vocabulario 1**
• Prueba 1-1: pp. 13–14

▶ Talk about outdoor activities and camping equipment
▶ Discuss excursions and camping adventures
▶ Write about and discuss places you would like to explore

Vocabulario en uso

INTERACTIVE WHITEBOARD
Vocabulary Activities 1-1

4 Standards: 1.2

Resources: Answer Keys: Student Edition, p. 7
Focus: Using new words and expressions in a cloze exercise
Recycle: reflexive pronouns, preterite forms
Suggestions: Refer students to pp. 22–25 for vocabulary.
Answers:

1. Al amanecer   5. relámpagos
2. dar un paseo   6. truenos
3. Una vez allí   7. hacia
4. un rato   8. nos refugiamos

5 Standards: 1.2, 1.3

Resources: Answer Keys: Student Edition, p. 7
Focus: Practicing new vocabulary
Suggestions: Ask students to check their answers with a partner.
Answers:

1.g 2.c 3.d 4.a 5.e 6.b 7.f

6 Standards: 1.1, 1.3, 3.1

Resources: Answer Keys: Student Edition, p. 7
Focus: Practicing new vocabulary
Recycle: expressions with the infinitive
Suggestions: Point out that only seven camping items are pictured. Students must come up with their own eighth item in Step 1.
Answers:

tienda de acampar; dormir y descansar
binoculares; ver animales
agua; beber
brújula; no perderme
sartén; cocinar pescado
mochila; llevar cosas
Answers will vary.

▼4 Un paseo en bicicleta |

Leer • Escribir

Unos amigos dan un paseo en bicicleta. Completa el párrafo con las palabras correctas.

un rato	una vez allí	relámpagos
dar un paseo	truenos	nos refugiamos
al amanecer	hacia	

  __1.__ nos levantamos y preparamos las bicicletas para __2.__ por el campo. __3.__ paramos para descansar y almorzar. Después de __4.__ empezó a llover. Vimos __5.__ y oímos unos __6.__ tremendos que nos asustaron mucho. Corrimos __7.__ una pequeña casa donde __8.__. ¡Fue un día inolvidable!

▼6 ¿Qué vas a llevar? |  |

Escribir • Hablar

❶ Vas de cámping este fin de semana. Haz una lista de ocho cosas que necesitas llevar y explica para qué las necesitas.

lo que necesitas	para qué lo necesitas
linterna	ver cuando está oscuro

▼5 Definiciones

Escribir

Empareja cada palabra o frase con su definición. Escribe después un cuento breve usando algunas palabras de la primera columna.

1. suceder
2. perder el equilibrio
3. refugiarse
4. acercarse a
5. al anochecer
6. al amanecer
7. así

a. ir cerca de
b. cuando empieza la mañana
c. caerse
d. esconderse
e. cuando empieza la noche
f. de esta manera
g. pasar

❷ Dejaste en casa algunas cosas que necesitas para ir de cámping. Usa la lista que escribiste para hablar con otro(a) estudiante.

▶ Modelo

A —¡Ay, caramba! Dejé la linterna en casa.
B —¡Qué pena! Ahora no puedes caminar por el bosque por la noche.

DIFFERENTIATED INSTRUCTION

Students with Learning Difficulties

For *Actividad* 4, have students copy the word bank to their papers. As they complete each item, tell them to check off or cross out the item they used from the word bank in order to minimize their choices for the remaining items.

Advanced Learners

Have students use the preterite to write their own paragraph about a real or imagined outdoor experience. Invite them to read their paragraphs aloud in a small group and discuss similarities and differences among their outdoor experiences.

7 Al mal tiempo buena cara |

Hablar

Habla con otro(a) estudiante de las excursiones que hicieron a varios lugares y de lo que les sucedió.

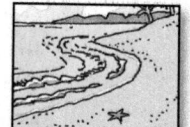

navegar / oír truenos

▶ Modelo

A —¿Qué hicieron en _el océano?_
B —_Navegamos todo el día._
A —¿Y luego, qué sucedió?
B —_Oímos truenos y llovió._

1. observar pájaros / ver relámpagos

2. dar un paseo / caer granizo

3. escalar rocas / perder el equilibrio y caerse

4. dar un paseo a caballo / perderse

5. pescar / empezar a llover

6. ¡Respuesta personal!

Fondo Cultural | Chile • Argentina

Parques nacionales de América del Sur En la última década las visitas a los parques nacionales de América del Sur, especialmente de Chile y Argentina, aumentaron mucho. Esto se debe a[1] un creciente[2] interés por estar en contacto con la naturaleza y disfrutar de actividades al aire libre. ¿Quiénes son los visitantes? Familias, grupos de jóvenes recién egresados[3] de la escuela secundaria, grupos de estudiantes en excursiones de estudio y personas de todas las edades interesadas en conocer nuevas especies de animales y plantas y estar en contacto con la naturaleza. La gran variedad de parques nacionales atrae[4] a todo tipo de gente. En la Argentina hay selvas tropicales en el Parque Nacional Baritú, enormes cataratas[5] en el Parque Nacional Iguazú y hasta glaciares en el Parque Nacional Perito Moreno.

• ¿Quiénes visitan los parques nacionales de Chile y Argentina? ¿Por qué?

Las Cataratas del Iguazú, en el Parque Nacional Iguazú, Argentina

1 is due to **2** growing **3** graduated **4** attracts **5** waterfalls

veintisiete **27**
Capítulo 1

Practice and Communicate 1

7 Standards: 1.1
Resources: Answer Keys: Student Edition, p. 8
Focus: Practicing new vocabulary and preterite forms
Suggestions: Direct students to use the pictures and clues to guide them.
Answers:
1. ¿Qué hicieron en el bosque?/Observamos los pájaros./Vimos relámpagos.
2. ¿...en el valle?/Dimos un paseo./Cayó granizo.
3. ¿...en la sierra? Escalamos rocas./Perdimos el equilibrio y nos caímos.
4. ¿...en el desierto?/Dimos un paseo a caballo./Nos perdimos.
5. ¿...en el lago?/Pescamos./Empezó a llover.
6. Answers will vary.

BELLRINGER REVIEW

Have students refer to the pictures in Actividad 7 and be prepared to say what the weather might be like in each location. (Ex. _En la playa, hace sol._)

Fondo cultural

Standards: 1.2, 3.1
Resources: Answer Keys: Student Edition, p. 8
Mapa global interactivo, Actividad 2 Explore a glacier and a tropical national park in Argentina.
Suggestions: After students read the paragraph, ask them to talk about activities in which visitors to national parks frequently engage.
Answers:
Los parques atraen a todo tipo de gente: familias, grupos de jóvenes recién egresados de la escuela secundaria, estudiantes en excursiones de estudio y personas de todas las edades.
A los visitantes les interesa conocer nuevas especies de animales y plantas y ponerse en contacto con la naturaleza. También quieren disfrutar de actividades al aire libre.

ENRICH YOUR TEACHING

Culture Note

One of Venezuela's national parks, Canaima, is the home of the world's highest waterfall, **El Salto Ángel** (Angel Falls). It plunges off a **tepuy,** a flat-topped mountain, to fall for more than 2,400 feet. There are more than 100 **tepuys** in the area of **el Salto Ángel,** all with vertical sides of sandstone shaped by heavy rainfalls.

21st Century Skills

Technology Literacy Have students research the national parks of Chile and Argentina. Ask them to brainstorm the list of keywords they will use in their search. How can they decide which websites will give them reliable and accurate information?

▼ Ampliación del lenguaje

Ir de . . .

Muchas acciones en español se pueden expresar usando *ir de* más un sustantivo *(noun)* de la misma familia que el verbo. Por ejemplo:

ir de pesca	pescar
ir de paseo	pasear

Como puedes ver, el sustantivo *pesca* y el verbo *pescar* pertenecen a la misma familia de palabras.

¿Puedes adivinar *(guess)* cuáles son los verbos que corresponden a las siguientes expresiones con *ir de . . .* ?

ir de compras
ir de caza *(hunting)*
ir de visita
ir de viaje

▼ 8 ¿Qué pasó?

Leer • Escribir

Imagina lo que pasó en cada situación y escribe una frase usando los verbos entre paréntesis.

Modelo
Fuimos de pesca el sábado. *(perder)*
Perdimos el equilibrio en el bote y nos caímos al agua.

1. Mis padres fueron de paseo. *(acercarse)*
2. Mi hermana fue de compras. *(pasarlo bien)*
3. Fui de viaje con mi familia. *(impresionar)*
4. Fuimos de caza al amanecer. *(asustar)*
5. Mis abuelos fueron de visita. *(perderse)*

▼ 9 ¡Fue un desastre!

Escribir

Acabas de regresar de una excursión de cámping desastrosa. Quieres escribir un mensaje electrónico a un(a) amigo(a) para decirle cómo lo pasaste. Escribe cinco frases para describir tu experiencia. Escoge entre las siguientes palabras y expresiones:

una vez allí	aparecer	dejar de
caer granizo	llover	relámpago
trueno	así	impresionar
perderse	refugiarse	

Modelo
Durante toda la noche cayó granizo sobre la tienda de acampar.

▼ 10 Juego

Hablar • Escuchar

Trabaja con un grupo de cuatro estudiantes y escojan uno de los mensajes electrónicos que escribieron para la Actividad 9. Actúen el mensaje mientras otro grupo cuenta lo que pasó.

DIFFERENTIATED INSTRUCTION

▾11 Las estrellas del sur

Leer • Hablar

Cuando miras el cielo en una noche clara puedes ver muchas estrellas. Pero no todos ven las mismas estrellas. Lee este párrafo para aprender un poco más sobre las estrellas del hemisferio sur.

 Conexiones | Las ciencias

La Cruz del Sur

Desde América del Sur, por estar en otra latitud, el cielo se ve diferente. Sólo en la línea ecuatorial[1] se ve todo el cielo durante todo el año. Esto crea un problema para los astrónomos, porque sólo pueden ver una parte del cielo si no están en el ecuador. Por ejemplo, solamente en el hemisferio sur se ve la constelación de la Cruz del Sur.

- ¿Adónde puedes ir para ver las estrellas?
- ¿Qué constelaciones puedes ver donde tú vives?

_____

1 Equator

▾12 Lugares para explorar |

Escribir • Hablar

❶ Piensa en un lugar que te gustaría explorar: el desierto, el océano, el mar, el bosque, la sierra o una selva tropical. Escribe una frase para explicar por qué quieres explorar ese lugar.

Modelo
Quiero ir a la sierra porque me gusta el paisaje.

❷ Forma un grupo con otros estudiantes que escogieron el mismo lugar que tú. Comenta tus ideas con el grupo.

❸ Usa las ideas del grupo para escribir un breve párrafo explicando tus razones para explorar ese lugar.

❹ Presenta tus ideas a la clase. Puedes acompañar tu presentación con fotos o ilustraciones de ese lugar.

▾13 Y tú, ¿qué dices? |

Escribir • Hablar

Contesta las preguntas.

1. Haz una lista de diferentes aspectos de la naturaleza. ¿Cuáles te impresionan más? ¿Por qué? (montañas, ríos, desiertos, selvas, playas, valles)

2. Imagínate que estás haciendo planes para ir a un parque nacional. ¿Qué parque quieres visitar? ¿Por qué? ¿Qué tipo de paisaje vas a encontrar allí? Una vez allí, ¿qué actividades al aire libre te gustaría hacer?

3. Los parques nacionales son refugios de muchos animales como osos, coyotes y búfalos. ¿Alguna vez se acercó a ti uno de estos animales? ¿Cómo te impresionó? ¿Te asustó? ¿Qué hiciste? Si esto no te sucedió, ¿hay otras cosas que te asustaron? ¿Cuáles? Relata una ocasión en que algo te asustó y describe tu reacción.

veintinueve 29
Capítulo 1

ENRICH YOUR TEACHING

Culture Note
The beautiful colored lights of the aurora borealis sometimes appear in the night sky of the Northern Hemisphere. The aurora australis is found in the Southern Hemisphere. Both phenomena occur when electrons and protons from the sun are drawn toward the poles by Earth's magnetic field.

21st Century Skills

Communication Encourage students to articulate their thoughts and ideas clearly and effectively as they respond to the questions in _Actividades_ 12 and 13. Ask them to pay special attention to the adjectives and descriptive phrases they could use to make their descriptions more vivid. Students will use both oral and written communication skills in these activities.

Practice and Communicate ① 1

▾11 Standards: 1.1, 1.2, 3.1

Focus: Reading about the constellations in different latitudes

Suggestions: Remind students that cognates, such as _latitud_ and _ecuatorial,_ are a valuable aid to understanding new material.

Answers will vary.

🌐 **Mapa global interactivo, Actividad 3** See the location of astronomical observatories in both hemispheres.

BELLRINGER REVIEW

Have students share what is studied in various science classes (_biología, química, ciencias naturales_). List on the board.

▾12 Standards: 1.1, 1.3, 3.1

Focus: Speaking, listening, and writing to contribute to group reports

Suggestions: Encourage students to use a graphic organizer such as a concept web to help them develop their presentation.

Answers will vary.

▾13 Standards: 1.1, 1.2, 1.3, 3.1

Focus: Discussing and writing about personal experiences and opinions

Suggestions: Assign or have students choose one or more of the options, depending on time and ability. Option 3 is the most challenging.

Answers will vary.

Additional Resources
- Communication Wbk.: Audio Act. 1, p. 8
- Teacher's Resource Book: Audio Script, p. 37; Communicative Pair Activity BLM, p. 42
- Audio Program DVD: Cap. 1, Track 6

✔ASSESSMENT

Prueba 1-2 with Study Plan (online only)

Prueba: Aplicación del vocabulario 1
- Prueba 1-2: pp. 15–16

29

Practice and Communicate

Gramática (Repaso)

Core Instruction

Resources: Voc. and Gram. Transparency 40

INTERACTIVE WHITEBOARD
Grammar Activities 1-1

♻ Un poco más de repaso

Suggestions: Point out the *i* to *y* changes in the paradigm. Have students write out the verbs that follow the same pattern.

▼14 Standards: 1.2

Resources: Answer Keys: Student Edition, p. 9

Focus: Practicing verbs with spelling changes in the preterite

Suggestions: Ask volunteers to spell aloud the verb forms they wrote.

Answers:

Step 1

1. dimos	5. oímos	8. Cayó
2. oyó	6. se cayó	9. destruyó
3. creyó	7. empezó	10. corrimos
4. vimos		

Step 2

Answers will vary.

▼15 Standards: 1.2

Resources: Teacher's Resource Book: Audio Script, p. 37; Audio Program DVD: Cap. 1, Track 7; Answer Keys: Student Edition, p. 9

Focus: Practicing listening comprehension and writing accuracy

Answers:

Step 1

1. se cayeron	3. destruyó	5. creyó
2. oímos	4. leyó	

Step 2

1. Tres árboles se cayeron.
2. Uno de los árboles destruyó un puente.
3. La hermana no creyó el cuento. Ella no estaba allí.

✓ ASSESSMENT

Prueba 1-3 with Study Plan (online only)

Prueba: El pretérito de verbos con el cambio *i → y*
• Prueba 1-3: p. 17

30

Gramática Repaso

▸ Talk and write about outdoor adventures
▸ Listen to and write about what happened

El pretérito de los verbos con el cambio ortográfico *i → y*

Verbs ending in *-uir*, such as *destruir*, have a spelling change in the preterite. The *i* becomes *y* in the *Ud. / él / ella* and *Uds. / ellos / ellas* forms.

destruí	destruimos
destruiste	destruisteis
destruyó	destruyeron

Note that the *i* is only accented in the *yo* form.

Other verbs, such as *leer*, *creer*, *oír*, and *caerse*, follow a similar pattern.

leí	leímos
leíste	leísteis
leyó	leyeron

In these verbs, the *i* is always accented.

Más ayuda **realidades.com** ▸ Tutorial

▼14 En el bosque | 👥

Leer • Escribir • Hablar

❶ En una hoja de papel escribe los números del 1 al 10. Completa este cuento con el pretérito del verbo apropiado.

El verano pasado, Tomás y yo __1.__ (*dar / leer*) un paseo por el bosque. Nos sentamos a descansar, cuando de repente, Tomás __2.__ (*creer / oír*) un ruido arriba de un árbol. Tomás __3.__ (*creer / caerse*) que era un mono, pero cuando nos acercamos al árbol, nosotros no __4.__ (*ver / comer*) ni __5.__ (*oír / destruir*) nada. Pero entonces, Tomás perdió el equilibrio y __6.__ (*creer / caerse*). Afortunadamente, no se lastimó mucho. Un poco después __7.__ (*empezar / hacer*) a llover. __8.__ (*caer / leer*) granizo y la violenta tormenta __9.__ (*creer / destruir*) muchos árboles. Nosotros __10.__ (*correr / vivir*) a refugiarnos pero . . .

❷ Ahora, con otro(a) estudiante, escribe un final para el cuento.

▼15 Después de la tormenta | 🔊

Escuchar • Leer • Escribir

❶ En una hoja de papel escribe los números del 1 al 5. Escucha lo que pasó después de una tormenta y escribe los verbos que completan el párrafo.

Ayer, después de la tormenta, __1.__ tres árboles en el parque. Hicieron un ruido tremendo. Nosotros estábamos en el lago, pero lo __2.__ claramente. Uno de los árboles __3.__ un puente. Esta mañana, mi hermana __4.__ la noticia en el periódico. Ella no estaba con nosotros en el lago y no __5.__ el cuento hasta que vio la noticia.

❷ Ahora escribe las respuestas a estas preguntas sobre la tormenta.

1. ¿Cuántos árboles se cayeron?
2. ¿Qué destruyó uno de los árboles?
3. ¿Quién no creyó este cuento? ¿Por qué?

Más práctica (GO) **realidades.com | print**

Instant Check	✔	
Guided WB pp. 27–28	✔	✔
Core WB p. 11	✔	✔
Comm. WB p. 13	✔	✔
Hispanohablantes WB pp. 16–20		✔

DIFFERENTIATED INSTRUCTION

Heritage Language Learners

Have students review the irregular preterite forms in the *Gramática* on p. 31 in groups. Ask them to work together to think of other words that have irregular preterite forms and write the forms in tables like the one in the *Gramática*. Encourage them to check their spelling using the Student Edition or an online dictionary.

Advanced Learners

Have students write five sentences that use verbs with the *i* to *y* change in the preterite. Ask them to read their sentences aloud to a partner. The partner who listens writes down the preterite verb he or she hears in each sentence. Partners can then check their spelling of the preterite verb forms with each other.

Gramática Repaso

| ▼ Objectives
▶ Listen to and write about a rafting adventure
▶ Talk and write about what people did
▶ Exchange information about camping activities

El pretérito de los verbos irregulares

Some verbs have irregular stems in the preterite.

tener	andar	estar	poder	poner	saber	venir
tuve	anduve	estuve	pude	puse	supe	vine
tuviste	anduviste	estuviste	pudiste	pusiste	supiste	viniste
tuvo	anduvo	estuvo	pudo	puso	supo	vino
tuvimos	anduvimos	estuvimos	pudimos	pusimos	supimos	vinimos
tuvisteis	anduvisteis	estuvisteis	pudisteis	pusisteis	supisteis	vinisteis
tuvieron	anduvieron	estuvieron	pudieron	pusieron	supieron	vinieron

The verbs *decir* and *traer* also have irregular stems in the preterite.

decir	
dije	dijimos
dijiste	dijisteis
dijo	dijeron*

traer	
traje	trajimos
trajiste	trajisteis
trajo	trajeron*

*Note that the *Uds./ellos/ellas* endings for *decir* and *traer* are slightly different from the verbs listed above.

Más ayuda   **realidades.com**   ▶ *Canción de hip hop*   ▶ *Tutorial*

▼16 Un paseo en balsa |

Escuchar • Leer • Escribir • GramActiva

❶ Escucha esta descripción de un viaje en balsa *(raft)*. Lee las preguntas y levanta la mano derecha si escoges la opción **a**, y la mano izquierda si escoges la opción **b**.

1. ¿Los chicos pusieron a. las balsas o b. las mochilas encima del coche?

2. ¿El guía vino a. unos minutos después o b. una hora después?

3. ¿El guía les dijo que iban a ir a. al centro de Santiago o b. al río Maipo?

4. ¿Los chicos tuvieron que llevar las balsas a. al río o b. al coche?

5. Antes de comenzar el viaje, ¿los chicos se pusieron a. las gorras o b. los trajes de baño?

6. Después del viaje, ¿todos estuvieron de acuerdo en que a. lo pasaron bien o en que b. lo pasaron mal?

❷ Ahora, escribe una respuesta completa para cada pregunta.

RAFTING RIO MAIPO
¡Una Aventura Inolvidable, Activa, Sana y en plena Naturaleza!

treinta y uno **31**
Capítulo 1

ENRICH YOUR TEACHING

Teacher-to-Teacher

English speakers often wonder why there are two forms of "you" in Spanish. Explain that the answer begins with Latin's second-person plural: **vos.** In the fourth century, the Romans began to use this form as a sign of respect for individuals. The custom carried over to languages that evolved from Latin. (Spanish **vosotros** is a vestige, although it is a plural form.) In the eighteenth century, Spain's upper classes refined rules of address for individuals. **Vos** (a singular form) became **vuestra merced,** which underwent such variations as **vuesarcé** and **ucé** until it became **usted.** This was later used by the nobility with the third-person singular verb forms.

▼ **17** Standards: 1.3

Resources: Answer Keys: Student Edition, p. 10

Focus: Writing preterite verb forms

Suggestions: Tell students that, besides targeting verb forms, this activity examines their comprehension of the sentence parts that they must put together.

Answers:

1. Yo no pude venir.
2. Nosotros trajimos la comida.
3. Perla se puso el traje de baño.
4. Raúl y Silvia estuvieron muy ocupados.
5. Tú viniste en bicicleta.
6. Todos dijimos "¡Claro que sí!"

BELLRINGER REVIEW

Form groups of six students. Taking turns around the circle, each student uses one of the forms of *decir* in the preterite to say what different people said about the past summer's activities.

▼ **18** Standards: 1.1, 1.2

Focus: Asking and answering questions in the preterite

♻ *Un poco más de repaso*

Recycle: time expressions, daily routines

Suggestions: Tell students they should listen carefully to their partner's question, and answer using the same verb that the question contained.

Answers will vary.

✓ **ASSESSMENT**

Prueba 1-4 with Study Plan (online only)

Prueba: El pretérito de los verbos irregulares
• Prueba 1-4: p. 18

▼ **17** Una invitación a la playa

Escribir

Carolina invitó a sus amigos a ir con ella a la playa. Describe cómo respondió cada amigo(a) usando el pretérito del verbo entre paréntesis y las palabras apropiadas del recuadro.

Modelo

José *(venir)* / después de un rato.
José *vino después de un rato*.

el traje de baño	muy ocupados(as)	venir	en bicicleta	la comida	"¡Claro que sí!"

1. Yo no *(poder)*
2. Nosotros *(traer)*
3. Perla *(ponerse)*
4. Raúl y Silvia *(estar)*
5. Tú *(venir)*
6. Todos *(decir)*

▼ **18** En el Campamento "Amistad"

Leer • Hablar

Los consejeros del Campamento "Amistad" hablan de las actividades que hicieron los niños. Trabaja con otro(a) estudiante para hablar del horario. Puedes usar los verbos *andar, estar, poder, poner, venir, tener* y *traer*.

▶ **Modelo**

A —¿Dónde estuvo Daniel a las 11:00?
B —Estuvo en la piscina.
A —¿Qué tuvo que hacer Julián a la 1:00?
B —Tuvo que servir la comida.

Horario del grupo "Los piratas" para el 15 de julio					
Nombre	9:00 a 10:30	11:00 a 12:30	1:00 a 1:15	3:00 a 5:00	6:00 a 7:00
Daniel	campo de deportes/jugar al fútbol	piscina/traer el traje de baño	comedor/lavar los platos	playa/bucear	sala/usar la computadora
Marta	campo de deportes/jugar al tenis	piscina/traer las toallas	comedor/traer el pan	lago/navegar	sala/poner flores
Estela	campo de deportes/jugar al tenis	bosque/andar por los senderos	comedor/poner la mesa	campo/montar a caballo	jardín/traer los binoculares
Julián	en cama/enfermo	lago/navegar	comedor/servir la comida	playa/nadar	playa/hacer una fogata

Más práctica GO
realidades.com | print

Instant Check	✔	
Guided WB pp. 29–30	✔	✔
Core WB p. 12	✔	✔
Comm. WB p. 14	✔	✔
Hispanohablantes **WB** pp. 21–22		✔

DIFFERENTIATED INSTRUCTION

Heritage Language Learners

Have students list in chronological order five activities that they did today before they arrived to Spanish class. Have them exchange lists with a partner and check each other's work for errors in spelling or placement of accent marks.

Students with Learning Difficulties

Help students better understand the schedule in *Actividad* 18. Reproduce the schedule on the board with clock faces at the top to show the time periods. Point out that the time gets later as students read from left to right in the schedule.

Gramática Repaso

▼ Objectives
▶ Talk and write about past family trips
▶ Exchange information about parties and excursions
▶ Write about excursions and places in Chile

El pretérito de los verbos con los cambios e → i, o → u en la raíz

Stem changing *-ir* verbs in the present tense also have a stem change in the preterite tense. The changes are *e → i* and *o → u* and take place in the *Ud. / él / ella* and *Uds. / ellos / ellas* forms only.

Here are the preterite forms of *pedir, sentir,* and *dormir:*

pedí	pedimos	sentí	sentimos	dormí	dormimos
pediste	pedisteis	sentiste	sentisteis	dormiste	dormisteis
pidió	pidieron	sintió	sintieron	durmió	durmieron

Other verbs like *pedir (i)* and *sentir (i)* are: *divertirse, preferir, sugerir, vestirse.*
Another verb like *dormir (u)* is: *morir.*

Más ayuda | **realidades.com** | ▶ Tutorial

▼19 ¿Qué pasó en el picnic?

Leer • Escribir

La familia Suárez hizo un picnic en la playa. Completa las frases con el pretérito del verbo apropiado.

1. Yo *(preferir / dormir)* dar un paseo por la playa.
2. Mis hermanitos *(morirse / pedir)* de miedo cuando hicieron moto acuática.
3. Fuimos de pesca y *(morirse / divertirse)* mucho.

4. Mamá hizo una fogata y *(sentir / servir)* pescado.
5. Mi hermanita *(pedir / dormir)* más postre.
6. Después de comer mis hermanos y yo *(dormir / servir)* una siesta.
7. Después de nadar en la playa, nosotros *(vestirse / divertirse)* rápidamente y regresamos a casa.

▼20 ¿Cómo lo pasaron? |

Hablar

Una semana después, los hermanos Suárez fueron de cámping por cinco días. Habla con otro(a) estudiante de su experiencia.

▶ **Modelo**
¿A qué hora? / dormirse
A —¿A qué hora *se durmieron?*
B —*Se durmieron a las siete.*

Estudiante A

1. ¿Por dónde? / andar los hermanos
2. ¿Dónde? / dormir los hermanos
3. ¿Qué? / ponerse el hermano menor
4. ¿Qué? / traer los chicos para beber
5. ¿Dónde? / divertirse más

Estudiante B

treinta y tres **33**
Capítulo 1

Practice and Communicate  1

Gramática Repaso

Core Instruction

Resources: Voc. and Gram. Transparency 42

INTERACTIVE WHITEBOARD
Grammar Activities 1-1

♻ Un poco más de repaso

Suggestions: Use *Vocabulary & Grammar Transparency* 42 to reinforce the preterite forms.

▼19 Standards: 1.2

Resources: Answer Keys: Student Edition, p. 11
Focus: Practicing preterite verb forms with spelling changes
Suggestions: Have students write the answers. Then call on volunteers to read the answers aloud and spell the verb forms. Write the answers on the board.

Answers:
1. preferí
2. se murieron
3. nos divertimos
4. sirvió
5. pidió
6. dormimos
7. nos vestimos

Common errors: Students often forget the third-person stem change. Review this change using the transparency.

▼20 Standards: 1.1

Resources: Answer Keys: Student Edition, p. 11
Focus: Practicing preterite verb forms with spelling changes
Suggestions: Remind students to use the pictures to help them answer the questions.

Answers:
1. —¿Por dónde anduvieron los hermanos?
   —Anduvieron por el sendero.
2. —¿Dónde durmieron los hermanos?
   —Durmieron en una tienda de acampar.
3. —¿Qué se puso el hermano menor?
   —Se puso una camiseta, un pantalón y un par de botas.
4. —¿Qué trajeron los chicos para beber?
   —Trajeron agua para beber.
5. —¿Dónde se divirtieron más?
   —Se divirtieron más en el bosque.

ENRICH YOUR TEACHING

Teacher-to-Teacher

Students can create a conversation that revolves around a bad experience with a food server. For example, Student A tells B how the server kept bringing the wrong food, how the food was overcooked, and so on. Student B can ask for more details with questions such as *¿Y después? ¿Qué pidieron Uds. de postre?*

21st Century Skills

Initiative and Self-Direction Remind students of the various digital tools available in **realidades.com** to help them monitor their own understanding and learning needs, such as the eText with embedded audio files and online tutorials.

21 Standards: 1.1, 1.3

Focus: Practicing writing preterite verb forms with spelling changes

Suggestions: For Step 2, encourage students to use their questions as notes for a naturally flowing conversation like the one in the model.

Answers will vary, but should include correct spellings of the verb forms used.

22 Standards: 1.1, 1.3

Focus: Practicing irregular preterite verb forms

Suggestions: In Step 3, encourage students to practice using expressions such as *Teresa me dijo que* when reporting to the class about their partner.

Answers will vary.

23 Standards: 1.1, 3.1

Resources: Answer Keys: Student Edition, p. 12

Focus: Reading to obtain information for solving a math problem

Suggestions: Have students read through the passage and determine how to set up and solve the equation. Then ask them for the answer and have them explain the steps they took to arrive at it.

Answers:

Cantidad mensual:
5 mm al año ÷ 12 meses = 0,42 mm al mes.
Cantidad del 12 de julio de 1997 (95 mm) ÷ cantidad mensual (0,42 mm) = 226 meses o casi 19 años.

Pre-AP* Support

- **Learning Objective:** Presentational Writing
- **Activity:** Have students bring a picture to class (from a magazine, a personal photo) representing one of the outdoor locations presented in this chapter. Have them write a paragraph telling about five actual or fabricated activities/chores that they or others in the photo did. Encourage them to use the preterite tense and connector words.
- **Pre-AP* Resource Book:** Comprehensive guide to Pre-AP* writing skill development, pp. 27–38

▼21 ¿Cómo lo pasaron?

Escribir • Hablar

❶ Escribe cinco preguntas que puedes hacerle a otro(a) estudiante sobre cómo lo pasó en una fiesta. Usen los verbos del recuadro.

divertirse	servir	preferir	sugerir
sentirse	vestirse	estar	poder

Modelo
estar
¿Estuvo buena la fiesta de Ernesto?

❷ Ahora, usando las preguntas que escribiste en el Paso 1, habla con otro(a) estudiante sobre cómo lo pasaron en la fiesta.

▶ **Modelo**

A —*¿Estuvo buena la fiesta de Ernesto?*
B —*Sí, bailé toda la noche. Lo pasé muy bien. ¿Y tú?*

▼22 Una excursión al aire libre

Escribir • Hablar

❶ Piensa en la última vez que hiciste una excursión al aire libre y contesta las preguntas siguientes.

1. ¿Adónde fuiste? 3. ¿Cómo te vestiste? 5. ¿Qué hiciste?
2. ¿Quién te sugirió el lugar? 4. ¿Qué tuviste que traer? 6. ¿Te divertiste o no?

❷ Ahora hazle las mismas preguntas a otro(a) estudiante y toma apuntes de sus respuestas.

❸ Presenta tus repuestas y las de tu compañero(a) a la clase.

Modelo
Yo fui al campo y Juan fue a las montañas.

▼23 Lluvia en el desierto

Leer • Pensar • Hablar

¿Sabías que a veces llueve en los desiertos? Lee la siguiente información sobre el desierto de Atacama y resuelve el problema con otro(a) estudiante.

Conexiones | Las matemáticas

El desierto de Atacama, al norte de Chile, generalmente recibe sólo 5 mm de precipitación al año. Pero, el 12 de julio de 1997 cayeron 95 mm de agua en sólo 15 horas.

Si en los próximos años recibe la precipitación habitual, ¿cuántos meses hay que esperar hasta llegar a la cantidad de precipitación del 12 de julio de 1997?

Desierto de Atacama, Chile

34 treinta y cuatro
Manos a la obra 1

DIFFERENTIATED INSTRUCTION

Heritage Language Learners

Ask students who have lived in a heritage country to choose a place there in which it would be a good idea to have an ecocamp. Have them explain the attractions of the location. In what ways would that particular place benefit from having an ecocamp?

Students with Learning Difficulties

Help students deal with the numerical information in *Actividad 23.* Have them first establish how many numbers there are in the text. *(five)* Ask which numbers measure water. *(95 mm, 5 mm)* Remind them that they must use one more number, 12, the number of months in a year, to do the problem.

Practice and Communicate 1

▼24 Una caminata por Torres del Paine

Leer • Escribir

Imagínate que fuiste con unos(as) amigos(as) a hacer una excursión como la que se describe en este anuncio turístico. Escribe tres frases para describir lo que pasó en cada actividad.

Modelo
El primer día dimos una caminata muy larga.

▼25 Los Ecocamps de Torres del Paine

Leer • Escribir

Lee el texto sobre el Parque Nacional Torres del Paine y los Ecocamps y contesta las siguientes preguntas.

El Parque Nacional Torres del Paine, situado en la zona patagónica de Chile, es uno de los lugares más hermosos de nuestro planeta. Los senderos del parque ofrecen vistas magníficas del paisaje patagónico: montañas, bosques, ríos, glaciares, lagos y abundante flora y fauna. Este parque, remoto y misterioso, atrae a miles de turistas y aventureros de todo el mundo que vienen cada año a hacer caminatas, montar a caballo o navegar. Y la gran demanda por visitar el parque ha generado problemas serios de impacto ecológico y en la calidad de los servicios turísticos en general.

Una solución a este problema ha sido cambiar los hoteles por "Ecocamps", tiendas de acampar modernas, cómodas y transportables. Los "Ecocamps" permiten a los visitantes estar más cerca de la naturaleza y producen menos basura que los hoteles.

VIAJE
PARQUE NACIONAL
TORRES DEL PAINE

▲ Caminatas de entre 4 a 7 horas por día

▲ Navegar en el lago

▲ Escalar el Glaciar Grey

▲ Montar a caballo por el Valle del Ascencio

▲ Acampar en el exclusivo Ecocamp

Precio: USD $1,500 7 días, 6 noches

1. ¿Qué tipos de paisajes ofrece el Parque Nacional Torres del Paine?

2. ¿Qué solución ofrecen los Ecocamps para mejorar los problemas de impacto ecológico?

3. ¿Qué crees que puedes hacer tú para ayudar a cuidar lugares como éste?

Más práctica GO		realidades.com | print
Instant Check	✔	
Guided WB pp. 31–32	✔	✔
Core WB p. 13	✔	✔
Comm. WB pp. 8, 15	✔	✔
Hispanohablantes WB p. 23		✔

▼24 Standards: 1.2, 1.3

Focus: Practicing new vocabulary and preterite forms

Suggestions: Have students tell about what they themselves did on the trip, what one other person did, and what the whole group did.

Answers will vary.

▼25 Standards: 1.1, 1.2, 3.1

Resources: Answer Keys: Student Edition, p. 12

Focus: Developing reading comprehension and critical thinking

Suggestions: Have students read the passage at least twice to comprehend the main idea and important details. Ask them to write their answers in one or more complete sentences.

Common Errors: Some students tend to answer every question that begins with *¿Qué crees...?* or *¿Crees que...?* with *Creo que...*. Point out that, although grammatically correct, it is not necessary and can become monotonous.

Answers:
1 Ofrece montañas, bosques, ríos, glaciares y lagos.
2. Los Ecocamps producen menos basura que los hoteles.
3. Answers will vary.

Additional Resources

- Communication Wbk.: Audio Act. 2, p. 8
- Teacher's Resource Book: Audio Script, pp. 37–38, Communicative Pair Activity BLM, pp. 43–44
- Audio Program DVD: Cap. 1, Track 9

ENRICH YOUR TEACHING

Culture Note

The Atacama desert extends from the Pacific Ocean to the Andes Mountains. It is 600 miles long and a little less than 100 miles wide in most places. It is the most arid place on Earth—so arid, in fact, that scientists believe it may have a lot in common with Mars. A robot that will be sent to Mars is being tested in the Atacama desert.

21st Century Skills

Critical Thinking and Problem Solving
Encourage students to exercise sound reasoning and use their reading strategies when reading these short Spanish passages. Remind them to preview the comprehension questions first before reading *Los Ecocamps de Torres del Paine*.

✔ASSESSMENT

Prueba 1-5 with Study Plan (online only)

Prueba: El pretérito de verbos con los cambios *e → i, o → u*
- Prueba 1-5: p. 19

Examen: Vocabulario y gramática 1
- Examen 1: pp. 20–22
- ExamView: Examen 1

35

Vocabulario en contexto

Standards: 1.1, 1.2

Resources: Teacher's Resource Book: Input Script, p. 34, Clip Art, pp. 50–57, Audio Script, p. 38; Voc. and Gram. Transparencies 43–44; Audio Program DVD: Cap. 1, Tracks 10–11

Focus: Presenting new vocabulary and using grammar lexically in context

Suggestions: Have students read along as you play the audio to present the new vocabulary. Model the pronunciation of the new vocabulary words. Have students repeat in chorus. Make sure they read the information on the poster. Check for comprehension by asking questions. See the Input Scripts in the *Teacher's Resource Book* for specific questions.

BELLRINGER REVIEW

Working in pairs, have students alternate saying the following numbers represented in Spanish: Sept. 15, $750.00, 6:30 PM, July 4, $1500.00, 15:30.

▼26 Standards: 1.2

Resources: Answer Keys: Student Edition, p. 12

Focus: Practicing reading comprehension of new vocabulary

Suggestions: Remind students to look at the race poster.

Common Errors: Remind students that names of days and months are not capitalized in Spanish. Also remind them that when working with numbers in Spanish, the functions of commas and periods in Spanish are exactly the opposite of what they are in English.

Answers:

1. 4 de agosto
2. cuatro
3. $1.200.00
4. 9:30
5. $120.00

A primera vista 2 | 🔊 | 🖼

▼ Objectives

▶ Read, listen to, and understand information about
  • athletic events
  • other kinds of competitions
  • goals and prizes

Vocabulario en contexto

—Mira, no sabía que el 4 de agosto es la carrera de San Cristóbal. ¿Quieres participar?

—¡Claro! ¿Dónde tiene lugar?

—En Ecatepec. No está muy lejos.

—Entonces me voy a inscribir hoy mismo.

5 KM. CARRERA ATLÉTICA SAN CRISTÓBAL

El Consejo de Participación Ciudadana en coordinación con el Club de Atletismo los invitan a participar

FECHA: Domingo 4 de agosto
HORA: A partir de las 9:00 A.M.
LUGAR: Explanada del Palacio Municipal de Ecatepec, Edo. de México

INSCRIPCIONES

En deportes "Maxi Diablo"   *la inscripción*
(Av. Morelos #129 San Cristóbal Centro)
teléfono: 555-02-54

Y en la oficina del H.C.P.C. (centro cívico)

Donativo de inscripción: $40.00
(para gastos del evento)

¡Medallas a los primeros 500 participantes!

participantes

CATEGORÍAS Y PREMIOS

	chicos (14 a 18 años) 9:00 horas	chicas (14 a 18 años) 9:30 horas	hombres (mayores de 18 años) 9:00 horas	mujeres (mayores de 18 años) 9:30 horas
1°	$1000.00	$1000.00	$1.200.00	$1.200.00
2°	$700.00	$700.00	$1000.00	$1000.00
3°	$400.00	$400.00	$700.00	$700.00

▼26 ¿Qué dice el anuncio?

Leer

Lee el anuncio de la carrera atlética y completa las frases.

1. La carrera atlética tiene lugar el (*8 de abril* / *4 de agosto*).

2. Hay (*tres* / *cuatro*) categorías de participantes.

3. El premio de primer lugar para la categoría de hombres es de (*$1200* / *$1000*).

4. La carrera para chicas entre 14 y 18 años tiene lugar a las (*9:00* / *9:30*).

5. Si quieres participar con dos amigos(as), la inscripción les cuesta (*$100.00* / *$120.00*).

DIFFERENTIATED INSTRUCTION

Students with Learning Difficulties

Help students interpret the information in the *categorías y premios* part of the poster. Ask volunteers to read each of the categories separately from top to bottom. Point out that the information in each of these vertical sections pertains to one age and gender group.

Advanced Learners/Pre-AP*

Have students write an interview with the person who came in last in the race. They can use some of the same questions asked of the winner, but challenge them to invent one or two that an interviewer might ask someone who didn't win.

Después de la carrera, una reportera del periódico de la escuela entrevistó a Héctor Díaz, el campeón de la competencia.

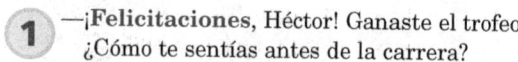
el trofeo

1 —¡**Felicitaciones**, Héctor! Ganaste el trofeo. ¿Cómo te sentías antes de la carrera?

—Estaba muy **animado,** porque sabía que podía ganar. Ésa era mi **meta: salir campeón** y **obtener** el trofeo.

2 —¿Cómo te preparaste?

—**Me di cuenta** de que para **alcanzar** mi meta, debía **hacer un esfuerzo.** Estuve dos meses **entrenándome.** Corría cinco veces por semana. Comía bien y bebía mucho líquido.

3 —¿Fue una carrera muy **dura**?

—Sí, **al principio** iba en tercer lugar. **Sin embargo,** no estaba **desanimado.** Hice un esfuerzo y gané. **Me emocioné** mucho al final.

la medalla

el certificado

▼**27 ¿Qué dice el campeón?** 🔊

Escuchar

Numera una hoja del 1 al 6. Escucha las frases. Escribe *C* (cierto) o *F* (falso) para cada frase.

treinta y siete **37**
Capítulo 1

▼**27** Standards: 1.2

Resources: Voc. and Gram. Transparency 44; Teacher's Resource Book: Audio Script, p. 38; Audio Program DVD: Cap. 1, Track 12; Answer Keys: Student Edition, p. 12

Focus: Practicing listening comprehension of new vocabulary

Suggestions: Before using the audio or the script for this activity, allow students a few minutes to reread p. 37.

Answers:

1. F 2. F 3. F 4. C 5. F 6. F

Extension: Read the script or play the audio again. Ask students to correct the false statements.

Chapter Project

Students can perform Step 3 at this point. (For more information, see p. 16-b.)

ENRICH YOUR TEACHING

Culture Note

Over 500 years ago, the Incas relied on runners to maintain their hold over a huge empire. Runners brought messages and materials along a network of almost 20,000 miles of roads. These men would run for a distance and be relieved by a fresh runner. That way, news could cross the empire in a few days.

Teacher-to-Teacher

For many students, listening comprehension is the most difficult language skill to master. Once you and your students are ready to begin a listening activity, allow students a few seconds of silence in order to mentally prepare themselves. Don't begin until classroom noise and other distractions have settled down.

Vocabulario en contexto

Standards: 1.1, 1.2

Resources: Teacher's Resource Book: Input Script, p. 35, Clip Art, pp. 50–57, Audio Script, p. 38; Voc. and Gram. Transparency 45; Audio Program DVD: Cap. 1, Track 13

Focus: Extending presentation of vocabulary and grammar in context

Suggestions:

Pre-reading: Have students use the titles and pictures to predict what each story is about.

Reading: Play the audio or read aloud from the script. Have students read along as they listen. Allow them to listen more than once.

Post-reading: Check comprehension by asking questions.

▼**28** Standards: 1.3

Resources: Answer Keys: Student Edition, p. 13

Focus: Demonstrating comprehension of school newspaper articles

Suggestions: Have students give the answers orally before writing them. If they have difficulty, rephrase the question, embedding the answer. For item 1, for example, ask: *¿Qué concurso no ganaron los estudiantes: el concurso de ajedrez o el partido de básquetbol?*

Answers:

1. Los estudiantes de la escuela no ganaron el concurso de ajedrez.
2. Los jóvenes poetas estaban muy contentos al final de la ceremonia.
3. El año pasado eliminaron al equipo de básquetbol.
4. Las chicas del equipo del Liceo San Martín perdieron el partido de básquetbol.
5. Answers will vary.

Pre-AP* Support

- **Learning Objective:** Interpretive: Print and Audio
- **Activity:** This activity helps students practice key print and audio interpretative skills. Have students follow along as you read the selection aloud or play the audio. Have students create multiple choice questions to check their comprehension. Then, have them confirm their answers by reading the text.
- **Pre-AP* Resource Book:** Comprehensive guide to Pre-AP* vocabulary skill development, pp. 51–57

38

La Voz del Estudiante

Santiago, 23 de septiembre

Nuestros jóvenes maestros

Diez estudiantes de nuestra escuela participaron en el concurso de ajedrez. **Desafortunadamente,** nuestra escuela no ganó el primer premio, pero **estamos orgullosos** de nuestros **representantes.**

El poder de las palabras

Felicitaciones a nuestros poetas estudiantiles. La **ceremonia de entrega de premios** tuvo lugar la semana pasada en el teatro de la escuela. Al final de la ceremonia los **ganadores** estaban muy contentos.

¡Campeonas de básquetbol!

¿Recuerdan cuando el año pasado **eliminaron** a nuestro equipo del campeonato de básquetbol? Pues este año, con mucho **entrenamiento y esfuerzo,** las chicas del equipo de nuestra escuela jugaron **contra** el equipo rival del Liceo San Martín y **vencieron** 68 a 62. ¡Felicitaciones, campeonas!

▼**28** **¿Comprendiste?**

Escribir

1. ¿Qué concurso no ganaron los estudiantes de la escuela?
2. ¿Cómo se sintieron los jóvenes poetas al final de la ceremonia?
3. ¿Qué le pasó el año pasado al equipo de básquetbol de la escuela?
4. ¿Quién perdió este partido de básquetbol?
5. ¿Por qué crees que los estudiantes están orgullosos de sus jugadores de ajedrez?

38 treinta y ocho
A primera vista 2

DIFFERENTIATED INSTRUCTION

Heritage Language Learners

Ask students to think of other information that could be included in one of the articles from *La voz del estudiante.* Encourage them to invent names for teams and individual players, and include details about highlights during an event. Have them rewrite the article incorporating their new information.

Advanced Learners

Invite students to write their own brief articles for a school newspaper. They should report on an actual recent competitive event or awards ceremony at your school. Collaborative efforts can be combined into a Spanish-language school newspaper. Have students place sketches where photos would go.

▼29 ¡Salimos campeonas! 🔊

Escuchar

Escucha las siguientes frases e indica a qué dibujo se refiere cada una. Cada dibujo puede referirse a más de una frase.

> **Estrategia**
>
> **Order of events**
> Trying to determine the order of events in a story will help you understand it better. When you listen to a story in Spanish, pay attention to words such as *antes, al principio, durante, después, más tarde,* and *finalmente* to determine the sequence.

▼30 Ordena tus notas

Leer • Pensar

Imagínate que eres reportero(a) de *La Voz del Estudiante.* Acabas de tomar unas notas sobre el partido de básquetbol, pero tus notas no están en orden. Ordena las frases y escríbelas según la secuencia de los dibujos.

• Durante el partido tuvimos que hacer un gran esfuerzo porque el otro equipo era muy bueno.

• Más tarde, tuvimos un empate de 42 a 42.

• Cuando nos dieron el trofeo, todas nos emocionamos mucho.

• Antes del partido, nuestra entrenadora nos hizo practicar con la pelota.

• Finalmente, pudimos vencer a nuestras rivales 68 a 62.

▼31 Evalúa las actividades | 🗣

Hablar

En el periódico se habla de tres actividades en las que participan los estudiantes. Con un(a) compañero(a), da tu opinión de las actividades. Usa:

Prefiero . . .

No disfruto mucho . . .

No me gusta . . .

Sólo me gusta observar . . .

Más práctica	GO	
realidades.com	print	
Instant Check	✔	
Guided WB pp. 33–40	✔	✔
Core WB pp.14–15	✔	✔
Comm. WB p. 16	✔	✔
Hispanohablantes WB pp. 24–25		✔

treinta y nueve **39**
Capítulo 1

29 Standards: 1.2, 3.1

Resources: Teacher's Resource Book: Audio Script, p. 38; Audio Program DVD: Cap. 1, Track 14; Answer Keys: Student Edition, p. 13

Focus: Practicing listening comprehension of new vocabulary and structures

Suggestions: Review the *Estrategia* with students before beginning the activity.

Answers:
1. 1   2. 3   3. 2   4. 3   5. 1   6. 2

30 Standards: 1.2

Resources: Answer Keys: Student Edition, p. 13

Focus: Sequencing events to demonstrate comprehension

Suggestions: Encourage students to use the transitions in the *Estrategia* as they sequence the events.

Answers:
Antes del partido, nuestra entrenadora nos hizo practicar con la pelota. Durante el partido tuvimos que hacer un gran esfuezo porque el otro equipo era muy bueno. Más tarde, tuvimos un empate de 42 a 42. Finalmente, pudimos vencer a nuestras rivales 48 a 46. Cuando nos dieron el trofeo, todas nos emocionamos mucho.

31 Standards: 1.1

Focus: Using new vocabulary in context

Suggestions: Remind students that the expressions they are using to begin their sentences introduce statements of opinion.

Answers will vary.

ENRICH YOUR TEACHING

Teacher-to-Teacher

After students complete and check *Actividad* 29, ask them to say which elements in each picture helped them decide on the answer.

21st Century Skills

Media Literacy Have students discuss how media messages are conveyed in a student newspaper like *La voz del estudiante* on page 38. Who is the intended audience? What is the purpose of each article? How is this newspaper similar to or different from their school newspaper?

✔**ASSESSMENT**

Prueba: Comprensión del vocabulario 2
• Prueba 1-6: pp. 23–24

▶ Talk and write about sports competitions and prizes
▶ Listen to a report about a tennis competition
▶ Write about and discuss a sports event

1 Practice and Communicate

INTERACTIVE WHITEBOARD
Vocabulary Activities 1-2

32 Standards: 1.2

Resources: Answer Keys: Student Edition, p. 14

Focus: Using new words and expressions in a cloze exercise

Suggestions: Encourage students to quickly read over the entire passage first in order to have an idea of what it is about.

Answers:

1. representantes
2. meta
3. Desafortunadamente
4. eliminaron
5. desanimados
6. Sin embargo
7. se dio cuenta
8. alcanzar
9. orgulloso
10. animados

BELLRINGER REVIEW

Unscramble the following words for prizes:
fotroe   icerfcatido   demalal   olrfes
(**Answers:** *trofeo/certificado/medalla/ flores*)

Fondo cultural

Standards: 1.2, 3.1, 4.2

Suggestions: Many high-level competitions use the word "Olympic" in their title. Ask students why they think this is so. They might say it's because the Olympic Games are the height of sports competition, because there are participants from many different places, and so on. What are some competitions in which they participate?

Answers will vary.

Note Both *Matemática* and *Matemáticas* are correct uses of this noun.

Vocabulario en uso

▼32 El concurso

Leer • Escribir

Completa los párrafos con las palabras de los recuadros.

desafortunadamente	eliminaron	desanimados	meta	representantes

Los __1.__ de mi escuela organizaron un concurso de música. Su __2.__ era obtener suficiente dinero para construir un nuevo teatro. Todos los padres de la escuela participaron. Vendieron refrescos y galletas. __3.__ nuestra banda no llegó a los finales y nos __4.__ de la competencia. Todos nos sentimos muy __5.__.

animados	orgulloso	sin embargo	se dio cuenta	alcanzar

__6.__, al día siguiente, tuvimos una gran sorpresa. El director de la escuela __7.__ de que con la venta de galletas pudimos __8.__ nuestra meta. Después, dijo que estaba muy __9.__ de los esfuerzos de nuestro equipo. Esta vez, todos nos sentimos muy __10.__.

▼ Fondo Cultural | El mundo hispano

La Olimpíada Iberoamericana de Matemática
Cada año, chicos y chicas de América Latina y España participan en la Olimpíada Iberoamericana de Matemática. Es una competencia para jóvenes de escuela secundaria. Las olimpíadas tienen como meta estimular el estudio de las matemáticas y el desarrollo[1] de jóvenes con talento para esta ciencia, a través de[2] la resolución ingeniosa de problemas matemáticos en un tiempo limitado.

¿Dónde y cuándo? La Olimpíada Iberoamericana de Matemática tiene lugar cada año en un país diferente de América Latina o en España, en el mes de septiembre. Otros países del mundo también tienen olimpíadas de matemáticas.

• ¿Puedes pensar en una competencia similar en los Estados Unidos?

_____

1 development **2** through

XVII OLIMPÍADA IBEROAMERICANA DE MATEMÁTICA

Block Schedule

Inside-Outside Circles. Have each student write two questions to ask a partner on a sheet of paper or index card that relate to an event or competition. Have students count off by twos. One partner goes to the "inside circle" and faces out. The second partner goes to the "outside circle" and faces in. The partners ask their questions and after about one minute, you call time and everyone moves two spaces. Repeat.

DIFFERENTIATED INSTRUCTION

Heritage Language Learners

Ask students to research the *Olimpíada Iberoamericana de Matemática* on the Internet. Have them prepare brief reports in which they share the information they find, such as where the next event will be held and what kinds of events it will involve.

Advanced Learners

Invite students to browse through sports magazines or sports-related websites and describe situations and events they see in pictures about competitive events. Encourage them to talk about the events in the past tense.

33 La entrega de premios | 💬 | ♻

Hablar

Di qué premios obtuvieron los atletas en la ceremonia de entrega de premios.

Modelo

el atleta que salió en tercer lugar
El atleta que salió en tercer lugar obtuvo una camiseta.

¿Recuerdas?
El verbo *obtener* tiene las mismas terminaciones en el pretérito que *tener*.

1. el equipo campeón
2. el atleta que ganó la carrera
3. el atleta que salió en segundo lugar
4. todos los participantes
5. los entrenadores

34 El campeonato de tenis | 🔊

Escuchar • Escribir

Escucha el reportaje sobre el campeonato de tenis. Luego contesta las preguntas.

1. ¿Cuándo tuvo lugar el campeonato?
2. ¿Cómo fue el partido?
3. ¿Cuándo hizo un gran esfuerzo María?
4. ¿Quién ganó?

5. ¿Qué recibió como premio la campeona?
6. ¿Cómo se sintieron las dos tenistas al final?

35 El festival deportivo | 💬👥

Escribir • Hablar

1 Imagina que fuiste a un festival deportivo en el que había partidos de diferentes deportes, comida y premios. Un(a) estudiante te entrevista para aprender un poco más del festival. Contesta sus preguntas.

1. ¿Cuándo y dónde tuvo lugar el festival?
2. ¿Cuánto costó la inscripción?
3. ¿Qué eventos deportivos había?
4. ¿En cuáles participaste tú?
5. ¿Jugaste con un equipo? ¿Contra quién jugaste?
6. ¿Participaste en alguna carrera?
7. ¿Ganaste algún premio? Si es así, ¿qué ganaste?
8. ¿Cómo se sintieron los participantes después de la ceremonia de entrega de premios?
9. ¿Cómo lo pasaste?

2 Trabaja con otro(a) estudiante para hacer y contestar preguntas sobre el festival.

Un partido de béisbol en Cuba

---

33 Standards: 1.1

Resources: Answer Keys: Student Edition, p. 14
Focus: Practicing new vocabulary
Recycle: irregular preterite stems, sports
Suggestions: First refer students to the *¿Recuerdas?* before doing the exercise.

Answers:

1. obtuvo un trofeo
2. obtuvo una medalla
3. obtuvo una medalla
4. obtuvieron un certificado
5. obtuvieron flores

34 Standards: 1.2, 1.3

Resources: Teacher's Resource Book: Audio Script, p. 38; Audio Program DVD: Cap. 1, Track 15; Answer Keys: Student Edition, p. 14
Focus: Practicing and reviewing new vocabulary and preterite forms

Answers:

1. Tuvo lugar el 25 de agosto.
2. El partido fue muy largo y duro.
3. Hizo un gran esfuerzo en el último set.
4. María ganó el partido.
5. Recibió un trofeo de plata.
6. Se sintieron muy orgullosas.

35 Standards: 1.1, 1.2, 1.3

Focus: Practicing new vocabulary and preterite forms
Suggestions: Encourage students to write their answers based on real events.
Answers will vary.

Additional Resources

- Communication Wbk.: Audio Act. 3, p. 9
- Teacher's Resource Book: Audio Script, p. 39, Communicative Pair Activity BLM, pp. 45–46
- Audio Program DVD: Cap. 1, Track 16

ENRICH YOUR TEACHING

Culture Note

Point out that the suffix *ibero-* is often used in words having to do with Spain and the Spanish-speaking world. *América Latina* is often called *Iberoamérica,* and Spain itself is sometimes still referred to as *Iberia.* These appellations tend to be used by Spaniards rather than Latin Americans. *Iberia* and its variations come from the name the ancient Greeks gave to the peninsula comprising what are now Spain and Portugal *(la Península Ibérica).* The Greeks got the name *Iberia* from a river on the peninsula that they called the Iber River, which many believe to be the Ebro, one of Spain's major rivers.

Gramática Repaso

Core Instruction

Standards: 4.1

Resources: Voc. and Gram. Transparency 46

INTERACTIVE WHITEBOARD

Grammar Activities 1-2

 Un poco más de repaso

Suggestions: Refer students to the ¿Recuerdas? Challenge them to create sentences in the imperfect that use the expressions listed there.

BELLRINGER REVIEW

Have students write the infinitive form of four verbs in Spanish to represent what they used to do in elementary school.

36 Standards: 1.2

Resources: Answer Keys: Student Edition, p. 15

Focus: Practicing the imperfect tense in a cloze exercise

Recycle: regular and irregular verbs, imperfect tense

Suggestions: Before students write their answers, ask them to point out expressions in the exercise that are similar to those in the ¿Recuerdas? above.

Answers:

1. era
2. tenía
3. íbamos
4. leía/sacaba
5. leía/sacaba
6. pedían
7. molestaba
8. devolvían
9. enojaba
10. eran

Manos a la obra 2

▼ Objectives
▶ Talk and write about childhood activities
▶ Discuss activities you used to do

Gramática Repaso

El imperfecto

Use the imperfect tense to talk about actions that happened regularly. In English you often say "used to" or "would" to express this idea.

Todos los meses, mi escuela **organizaba** una carrera. Nuestro equipo nunca **perdía**.

¿Recuerdas?

Expresiones como *generalmente, a menudo, muchas veces, todos los días, siempre* y *nunca* indican el uso del imperfecto.

estar

estaba	estábamos
estabas	estabais
estaba	estaban

tener

tenía	teníamos
tenías	teníais
tenía	tenían

vivir

vivía	vivíamos
vivías	vivíais
vivía	vivían

• Stem-changing verbs do not have a stem change in the imperfect.

Quería participar en el campeonato pero no **me sentía** bien.

The verbs *ir, ser,* and *ver* are the only irregular verbs in the imperfect. Here are their forms:

ir

iba	íbamos
ibas	ibais
iba	iban

ser

era	éramos
eras	erais
era	eran

ver

veía	veíamos
veías	veíais
veía	veían

• The imperfect form of *hay* is *había* ("there was / were, there used to be").

Generalmente, no **había** muchos participantes en el campeonato.

| Más ayuda | realidades.com | ▶*Canción de hip hop* ▶*Tutorial* |

▼36 Recuerdos de mi niñez |

Leer • Escribir

Completa los párrafos con la forma del imperfecto del verbo apropiado de cada recuadro.

ir	tener	ser	leer	sacar

Cuando yo ___1.___ niño, me gustaba mucho leer. Yo ___2.___ una colección de más de cien libros. Todos los sábados, mi hermana y yo ___3.___ a la biblioteca. Generalmente, mi hermana ___4.___ libros de historia. Yo, en cambio, ___5.___ los libros de aventura.

molestar	devolver	pedir	enojar	ser

A veces, mis amigos me ___6.___ prestado un libro. A mí no me ___7.___ compartir los libros, pero cuando ellos no los ___8.___, entonces yo me ___9.___ mucho. Los libros ___10.___ mis mejores amigos.

42 cuarenta y dos
Manos a la obra 2

DIFFERENTIATED INSTRUCTION

Students with Learning Difficulties

Some students may need extra help in order to understand verb form paradigms like those in the *Gramática* on this page. Copy some of the paradigms on the board, including the subject pronouns, so students can associate subjects with verb forms.

Advanced Learners/Pre-AP*

Invite students to prepare and deliver a short presentation in which they practice using the imperfect. They can tell about a situation that occurred regularly in the past, such as a summer camp they attended, a vacation spot their family repeatedly visited, a pastime they engaged in, or a class they attended in grade school.

Practice and Communicate **1**

▼37 Campeonatos escolares |

Leer • Hablar

Marilú recuerda los deportes y las actividades que hacía de niña en la escuela primaria. Después de leer su descripción, trabaja con otro(a) estudiante para hacer y contestar preguntas sobre los recuerdos de Marilú.

66Cuando yo asistía a la escuela primaria, jugaba con un equipo de fútbol que siempre vencía a los demás. Mis compañeras y yo nos entrenábamos todos los días y nuestros entrenadores nos ayudaban mucho. Nuestros padres siempre nos animaban para alcanzar nuestra meta, que era hacer el mejor esfuerzo posible para ganar.

Un año, salimos campeonas de todo el estado y nos dieron un trofeo.

—¡Felicitaciones campeonas! —nos decían todos durante la entrega de premios. Nos emocionamos mucho99.

▶ Modelo

A —¿A qué deporte jugaba Marilú de niña?
B —Marilú jugaba al fútbol.

▼38 ¿Qué hacías de niño(a)? | |

Escribir • Hablar

❶ Escribe una descripción de tu vida cuando eras niño(a). Incluye:

- los juegos
- los deportes
- la familia
- los programas de televisión
- la comida
- los(as) amigos(as)

❷ Ahora, pregúntale a otro(a) estudiante si hacía las mismas cosas que tú. Toma notas de sus respuestas.

▶ Modelo

A —De niño(a) yo leía libros de cuentos. ¿Tú también leías libros de cuentos?
B —Sí, a mí me gustaba leer libros de cuentos.

❸ Preséntale a la clase una comparación entre tu vida de niño(a) y la de tu compañero(a).

Modelo

Los dos comíamos cosas dulces. Yo prefería chocolate y él prefería helado.

Más práctica	GO
realidades.com	print	

Instant Check	✔	
Guided WB pp. 41–42	✔	✔
Core WB p. 16	✔	✔
Comm. WB p. 17	✔	✔
Hispanohablantes **WB** pp. 26–30		✔

---

37 Standards: 1.1, 1.2

Focus: Practicing the imperfect tense through reading and discussion

Suggestions: Before students work in pairs, ask them to look through Marilú's description for verbs that are in the preterite rather than the imperfect. Discuss the difference between actions that happened at one specific time in the past and those that happened regularly.

Answers will vary.

Extension: Ask students to write their questions about Marilú's description on slips of paper. Place the slips in a hat or other container. Have students take turns drawing one question at a time, reading it aloud, and answering it orally.

38 Standards: 1.1, 1.3

Focus: Practicing the imperfect verb forms in context

Recycle: games and pastimes, food, family members

Suggestions: In Step 1, tell students they should write at least one sentence about each of the items. Point out that, as students are interviewing each other in Step 2, they should take notes they can use in Step 3.

Answers will vary.

Chapter Project

Students can perform Step 4 at this point. Be sure they understand your corrections and suggestions. (For more information, see p. 16-b.)

✓ASSESSMENT

Prueba 1-8 with Study Plan (online only)

Prueba: El imperfecto
• Prueba 1-8: p. 27

ENRICH YOUR TEACHING

Teacher-to-Teacher

Students enjoy talking about movie or TV characters. Have them choose one such character and prepare a brief description, telling about where the character lived, what he or she was like, what activities he or she did, and what makes this character stand out.

21st Century Skills

Initiative and Self-Direction Remind students of the various digital tools available in **realidades.com** to help them monitor their own understanding and learning needs, such as the eText with embedded audio files, audio activities, and online tutorials.

Gramática _{Repaso}

Core Instruction

Resources: Voc. and Gram. Transparency 47

INTERACTIVE WHITEBOARD
Grammar Activities 1-2

♻ Un poco más de repaso

Suggestions: Ask for additional examples of each use of the imperfect.

39 Standards: 1.3

Focus: Practicing the imperfect

Recycle: household chores, leisure activities

Suggestions: After students write their sentences, have them share their recollections with the class.

Answers will vary.

40 Standards: 1.1, 1.2, 1.3

Focus: Practicing new vocabulary and past tenses through speaking and writing in context

Suggestions: Tell students that the event they choose to talk about with their partners can be real or imaginary. In Step 2, encourage students to write in complete sentences in paragraph form.

Answers: will vary.

Alternative Assessment: Use the written report from Step 2 of *Actividad* 40 to assess students' writing skills. Students' oral presentations of their reports can likewise be used to assess speaking skills.

Pre-AP* Support

- **Learning Objective:** Interpersonal Speaking
- **Activity:** This *Entrevista* activity helps students practice key interpersonal skills. Remind students to practice strategies for effectively sustaining conversations.
- **Pre-AP* Resource Book:** Comprehensive guide to Pre-AP* speaking skill development, pp. 39–50

| ▼ Objectives
▶ Write about regular past actions
▶ Talk and write about athletes and competitions

Gramática Repaso

Usos del imperfecto

You have learned to use the imperfect to describe something that used to take place regularly. You also use the imperfect

- to describe people, places, and situations in the past.
  Hacía mucho calor. El estadio **estaba** lleno. Los espectadores **gritaban**.

- to talk about a past action that was continuous or that kept happening.
  Los atletas **se entrenaban** en el gimnasio.

- to describe the date, time, age, and weather in the past.
  Era el 5 de noviembre. **Eran** las seis de la mañana pero ya **hacía** calor.

| **Más ayuda** | **realidades.com** | ▶ Tutorials |

▼39 Los sábados del pasado | ♻

Escribir

Cuando eras pequeño(a), ¿cómo pasabas los sábados?

Usa *ir*, *ver* o *ser* en cada respuesta.

Modelo

A veces, yo . . .
A veces, yo iba al supermercado con mi mamá.

1. Por las mañanas, mis hermanos y yo . . .
2. Por las tardes, yo . . .
3. Muchas veces, yo . . .
4. Mis padres . . .
5. Los quehaceres . . .
6. Por la tarde, mis amigos . . .

▼40 Entrevista |

Hablar • Escribir

❶ Entrevista a un(a) compañero(a). Hazle preguntas sobre alguna competencia a la que asistió o en la que participó. Toma notas de sus respuestas.

1. ¿Dónde tuvo lugar la competencia de . . . ?
2. ¿A qué hora era?
3. ¿Cómo era el auditorio / estadio / salón / gimnasio?
4. ¿Quiénes eran los participantes?
5. ¿Quiénes asistieron al evento?
6. ¿Cómo se sintió el público?
7. ¿Qué premios entregaron a los ganadores?
8. ¿Cómo se sentían los ganadores después de recibir sus premios?

❷ Escribe un reportaje basado en las notas de la entrevista que hiciste. Luego, lee tu reportaje a la clase.

44 cuarenta y cuatro
Manos a la obra 2

DIFFERENTIATED INSTRUCTION

Students with Learning Difficulties

Help students better understand the concept of completed actions vs. continuous actions in the past. Have them first focus on a completed action they did earlier in the day: "I ate breakfast." Then ask them to think of something that was happening while they performed that action: "It was raining." Translate their sentences to Spanish.

Advanced Learners

Have students prepare and present brief oral presentations about an important event they experienced in the past. Their presentations should include the imperfect and preterite tenses. They should use the imperfect to "set the scene" of the event and to describe people, places, or things, and the preterite to tell about the event itself.

▼41 Una atleta olímpica | ♻

Leer • Escribir

❶ Completa la biografía de la atleta olímpica Jennifer Rodríguez con el pretérito o el imperfecto del verbo entre paréntesis.

> **¿Recuerdas?**
> Los verbos *competir* y *conseguir* tienen el cambio e → i en el pretérito.

De niña, Jennifer (1976–) __1.__ *(ser)* muy atlética. Ella __2.__ *(ser)* la primera atleta de origen hispanohablante que __3.__ *(ganar)* dos medallas en los Juegos Olímpicos de Invierno en las carreras de patinaje de velocidad.

Cuando __4.__ *(ser)* pequeña, Jennifer __5.__ *(comenzar)* a patinar sobre ruedas. __6.__ *(demostrar)* tanto entusiasmo y agilidad que sus padres __7.__ *(decidir)* inscribirla en clases cuando __8.__ *(tener)* sólo 4 años.

Un año más tarde, Jennifer __9.__ *(competir)* en patinaje artístico y de velocidad y __10.__ *(vencer)* a otros niños de su edad.

En 1996, Jennifer __11.__ *(comenzar)* a practicar el patinaje sobre hielo. En 1998, Jennifer __12.__ *(conseguir)* la cuarta posición en la carrera de 3,000 metros en los Juegos Olímpicos de Invierno, en Nagano.

En los Juegos Olímpicos de Invierno de Salt Lake City, Jennifer __13.__ *(subir)* al podio por primera vez, al obtener dos medallas de bronce en patinaje de velocidad sobre hielo en las categorías de 1,000 y 1,500 metros. En 2005, Jennifer sale campeona mundial de patinaje de velocidad. En 2010 participa en los Juegos Olímpicos de Invierno de Vancouver (Canadá) y en la Copa del Mundo de Patinaje.

Jennifer Rodríguez

❷ Contesta las preguntas sobre Jennifer Rodríguez.

1. ¿Por qué sus padres inscribieron a Jennifer en clases de patinaje?

2. ¿Por qué crees que Jennifer pudo comenzar a competir sólo años después de comenzar a patinar sobre hielo?

3. ¿Qué características personales crees que ayudaron a Jennifer a triunfar?

4. ¿Qué importancia tienen las medallas olímpicas de Jennifer para otros jóvenes hispanohablantes de los Estados Unidos?

5. ¿Qué edad tenía Jennifer cuando compitió en los Juegos Olímpicos de Invierno en Nagano?

6. ¿Conoces a otros(as) campeones(as) olímpicos(as) de habla hispana? ¿Qué hacen?

El español en el mundo del trabajo

El español y el fútbol americano

"Hoy en día, muchos latinoamericanos que viven en los Estados Unidos disfrutan del fútbol americano. Algunas cadenas[1] de televisión transmiten sus programas sobre fútbol americano también en español. Mi labor es traducir[2] lo que dicen los jugadores y locutores. Pero ese deporte no se practica mucho en América Latina ni en España, por eso a veces es difícil buscar la palabra que exprese en español la jugada, el error o la regla que no existe en nuestro idioma. Muchas veces hay que inventar la palabra o expresión que necesitamos. Traducir es hacer que dos culturas distintas puedan conversar . . . hasta de deportes".

1 networks 2 translate

Practice and Communicate ①

▼41 Standards: 1.2, 1.3

Resources: Answer Keys: Student Edition, p. 15

Focus: Practicing the preterite and imperfect tenses in a cloze exercise; writing to demonstrate comprehension of a reading passage

Recycle: sports, personality traits

Suggestions: After students complete the activity on their own, have them take turns reading through it aloud together. Have them give their reasons for choosing the preterite or imperfect. In Step 2, point out to students that not all the questions have explicit answers. They must use their critical thinking skills and background knowledge to answer questions 2, 3, 4, and 6.

Answers:

1. **era**	8. **tenía**
2. **fue**	9. **compitió**
3. **ganó**	10. **venció**
4. **era**	11. **comenzó**
5. **comenzó**	12. **consiguió**
6. **Demostró**	13. **subió**
7. **decidieron**	

Step 2

1. Jennifer demostró mucho entusiasmo y agilidad al patinar sobre ruedas.

2–4. Answers will vary.

5. Tenía 22 años.

6. Answers will vary.

BELLRINGER REVIEW

Have students write two sentences telling what was going on in the classroom when they entered today.

▼ El español en el mundo del trabajo

Core Instruction

Standards: 1.2, 5.2

Suggestions: Explain that translation *(la traducción)* rests in the domains of reading and writing. Most translators *(los traductores)* read in the foreign language and write the translation in their own language. Interpretation *(la interpretación)* is a more immediate oral activity. Interpreters *(los intérpretes)* listen to the foreign language and speak the interpretation in their own language.

ENRICH YOUR TEACHING

Culture Note

The 1992 Summer Olympics cost the city of Barcelona $10 billion. A quarter of this sum was used to modernize the city, especially the old waterfront area. The Games earned only $3 billion, but the publicity led to an enormous increase in tourism, and the improved roads, housing, and transportation have benefited the citizens.

21st Century Skills

Critical Thinking and Problem Solving
Encourage students to watch and/or listen online to a soccer game in Spanish and try to determine the Spanish expressions used for certain sports terms, such as *goal, penalty kick, score a point,* or *goalie.* What similarities can they find between these English and Spanish terms?

▼42 Standards: 1.2, 1.3

Resources: Answer Keys: Student Edition, p. 16

Focus: Practicing the preterite and imperfect tenses in a cloze exercise

Suggestions: Point out that the information in *En voz alta* continues the story of the same soccer match.

Answers:

Step 1

1.	Era	6.	eran	11.	paró
2.	Llovía	7.	eran	12.	dio
3.	hacía	8.	comenzó	13.	tuvo
4.	Era	9.	iba	14.	llegó
5.	Jugaban	10.	parecía	15.	estaban

Step 2

1. El partido tuvo lugar el 28 de mayo de 1928 en Santander, España.

2–4. Answers will vary.

En voz alta
Core Instruction

Standards: 1.2, 3.1, 3.2, 5.2

Resources: Teacher's Resource Book: Audio Script, p. 39; Audio Program DVD: Cap. 1, Track 17

Suggestions: Have students silently read the information. Ask comprehension questions: *¿Cuántos años tiene el equipo de Barcelona? ¿Qué dice el primer cántico acerca de la relación entre el equipo y los aficionados?*

Direct student's attention to the information in the *¿Recuerdas?* Allow them a few minutes to practice with a partner. Explain that Catalan uses the *s* sound for the letter *c* before *e* and *i*. In Catalan, the *cedilla*, *ç* is also pronounced like the *s* in English.

You may want to share with the class the second cheer in Catalan and discuss the similarities between the two versions: *O le le , o la la, ser de Barça es, el millor que hi ha.*

Discuss with the class the second comprehension question. Brainstorm possible meanings for the Catalan phrase *Força Barça*, then explain that it means "force" or "strength to Barça." In English, a similar cheer would be "Go Barça!"

Chapter Project

Students can perform Step 5 at this point. Record their presentations for inclusion in their portfolio. (For more information, see p. 16-b.)

▼42 Un partido inolvidable

Leer • Escribir

❶ Completa esta descripción de un famoso partido de fútbol que tuvo lugar en 1928 en Santander, una ciudad en el norte de España, con el pretérito o el imperfecto del verbo entre paréntesis.

1. *(ser)* el 28 de mayo de 1928. **2.** *(llover)* y **3.** *(hacer)* viento. **4.** *(ser)* un día muy especial para Santander. **5.** *(jugar)* el Barcelona y La Real Sociedad. Platko y Samitier **6.** *(ser)* las grandes estrellas del Barcelona. Las estrellas de la Real **7.** *(ser)* Zaldúa y Cholín.

Por fin **8.** *(comenzar)* el partido. En un momento en que la Real **9.** *(ir)* hacia el área del Barcelona, Cholín avanzó[1] hasta el arco[2]. Cuando el gol **10.** *(parecer)* inevitable, el guardameta[3] Platko se arrojó[4]

sobre el pie de Cholín y **11.** *(parar)* la pelota. Sin embargo, el pie de Cholín **12.** *(dar)* contra la cabeza de Platko, quien **13.** *(tener)* que salir del campo, con la frente[5] llena de sangre. A los pocos minutos se **14.** *(llegar)* al descanso, con un empate de cero a cero. Los aficionados del Barcelona **15.** *(estar)* desanimados. ¿Cómo podían ganar el campeonato sin Platko, su gran guardameta?

5 forehead

❷ Ahora, contesta las preguntas.

1. ¿Dónde y cuándo tuvo lugar el partido?

2. ¿Crees que Platko era valiente? ¿Por qué?

3. ¿Qué pensaban los aficionados del Barcelona sobre Platko? ¿Cómo lo sabes?

4. ¿Alguna vez te sentiste como los aficionados del Barcelona? ¿Por qué?

1 moved forward 2 goal 3 goalkeeper 4 leaped

▼ En voz alta |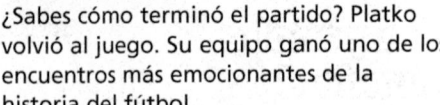

¿Sabes cómo terminó el partido? Platko volvió al juego. Su equipo ganó uno de los encuentros más emocionantes de la historia del fútbol.

El equipo de Barcelona tiene unos cánticos[1] que son conocidos en todo el mundo. Se cantan en catalán, el idioma de la región de Cataluña. La mayoría de los cánticos utilizan melodías de música conocidas. Uno se puede imaginar que los aficionados de Barcelona cantaron estos cánticos muchas veces durante este partido inolvidable.

Escucha los cánticos, unos traducidos al español, y trata de repetirlos. Luego, contesta las preguntas.

• ¿Qué palabras o frases se repiten? ¿Cuál es el efecto de esta repetición?

• ¿Cuál de los tres cánticos está en catalán? En tu opinión, ¿qué significa?

Cánticos del Fútbol Club Barcelona

Cántico 1

1899, nació el club que llevo en el corazón,
azulgrana[2] son los colores,
¡Fútbol Cluuub Barcelooona!
Le le le le le leeee,
le le le le le leeeee,
¡Fútbol Cluuub Barcelooona!

Cántico 2

O le le le, o la la la
Ser del Barça es, el mejor que hay

Cántico 3

Força Barça!

1 cheers 2 blue and scarlet

¿Recuerdas?

En América Latina y en partes de España, la *c* antes de las vocales *e* e *i*, y la *z* antes de una vocal se pronuncian como la *s* en inglés de la palabra *sink*. En otras regiones de España esas letras se parecen al sonido de *th* en la palabra *think*.

Pronuncia estas palabras usando los dos sonidos de la letra *c* y escucha la diferencia: *nació, Barcelona.*

46 cuarenta y seis
Manos a la obra 2

DIFFERENTIATED INSTRUCTION

Heritage Language Learners

Have students pick a sport and recall the most thrilling game they ever saw, either live or on TV. Ask them to write about the game's most exciting moment or moments and to describe in detail one or two events that made the game so thrilling.

Students with Learning Difficulties

On the board, create a T-chart. Label the left side **pretérito** and the right side **imperfecto.** Write a few examples of one-time, completed actions on the left and longer, "background" actions on the right. Allow students to use the chart as a reference as they complete *Actividad* 42.

▼43 Una competencia artística

Escribir

Fuiste a una competencia artística y tuviste que escribir un informe para presentar en tu clase. Usa los dibujos para escribir lo que sucedió. Usa las formas correctas del pretérito y del imperfecto.

Estrategia

Describing events
When you describe a sequence of events, it is useful to write words such as *primero* (first), *luego* (next), *después* (then), *al final* (finally) to describe the order in which these events have occurred.

1.
2.
El Palacio de las Artes
3.
4.
5.

6.
7.
8.
9.
10.

▼44 Un cuento en grupo | (Talk?)

Escribir • Hablar

❶ Usa tu imaginación para completar este cuento con cuatro de tus compañeros(as). Traten de incorporar en su cuento el vocabulario y la gramática que aprendieron en este capítulo.

1. Había una vez un(a) . . .
2. Era una persona muy . . . y . . .
3. Vivía en . . . con su(s) . . . y su(s) . . .
4. Siempre le gustaba . . . y . . .
5. Un día, al amanecer, (nombre) fue . . .
6. Era un lugar . . . y . . .
7. De repente, oyó / vio . . .
8. ¡Era un(a) . . . !
9. Cuando el / la . . . se acercó, (nombre) empezó a . . .
10. Pero entonces, se dio cuenta de . . . y . . . a pasear por . . .
11. Al final, (nombre) . . .
12. Fue una aventura muy . . .

❷ Trabajen en grupo para leer, comentar y corregir el cuento que escribieron. ¿Usaron el pretérito y el imperfecto correctamente? ¿Incorporaron el vocabulario del capítulo? Añadan más detalles si es necesario.

❸ Presenten su cuento a la clase. La clase va a votar por el cuento más imaginativo, el más divertido y el mejor cuento de horror.

Más práctica (GO)

realidades.com | print

Instant Check	✔	
Guided WB pp. 43–44	✔	✔
Core WB pp. 17–18	✔	✔
Comm. WB pp. 10–11, 18–19, 163	✔	✔
Hispanohablantes WB pp. 31–33		✔

Practice and Communicate ①

▼43 Standards: 1.3, 3.1

Resources: Answer Keys: Student Edition, p. 16

Focus: Combining learned vocabulary and structures in a written presentation

Suggestions: Direct students' attention to the transitions in the *Estrategia*. Before they write, have them practice these and other transitions orally by telling about what they did in Spanish class yesterday and using the sequencing transitions to connect their ideas.

Answers:

Reports will vary, but should include some or all of the following phrases, based on the pictured items:

1. las tres y cuarto
2. El Palacio de las Artes
3. la participante
4. el cantante
5. el pianista
6. entusiasmados
7. aplaudir
8. el trofeo
9. el certificado
10. las seis y media

▼44 Standards: 1.1, 1.2, 1.3

Focus: Combining learned vocabulary and structures in a group-planned story

Suggestions: Remind students that an important component of this activity is that they include in their stories all of the twelve numbered items in the correct order. Explain that this will be a factor in how they evaluate each other's stories in Step 3. Their stories should also refer in some way to the picture.

Answers will vary.

Additional Resources

- Communication Wbk.: Audio Act. 4–5, pp. 10–11
- Teacher's Resource Book: Audio Script, p. 39, Communicative Pair Activity BLM, pp. 47–48
- Audio Program DVD: Cap. 1, Tracks 18–19

✓ASSESSMENT

Prueba 1-9 with Study Plan (online only)

Prueba: Usos del imperfecto
- Prueba 1-9: p. 28

Examen: Vocabulario y gramática 2
- Examen 2: pp. 29–31
- ExamView: Examen 2

ENRICH YOUR TEACHING

Teacher-to-Teacher

For *Actividad 44*, give groups the option of presenting their story in the form of a skit with a narrator and actors. Kinesthetic learners will enjoy the skit format. Acting out a scene that a narrator describes in words is similar to TPR and will help reinforce meaning.

21st Century Skills

Collaboration Have students clearly define and assign the tasks for each person in the *Un cuento en grupo* activity. Teams work well together if they know what they want to accomplish and when each person has an equal role.

47

Puente a la cultura

El Camino de Santiago

Objectives
▶ Read about a famous pilgrimage route in Spain
▶ Apply your prior knowledge of pilgrims to understand the reading
▶ Compare a pilgrimage to your own travel experiences

BELLRINGER REVIEW

On the board, draw a simple compass rose and use it to review direction words, such as *norte, sur, este, oeste,* and the intermediate points. Point to a place on the compass rose and ask students to say which direction it is.

Puente a la cultura

Core Instruction

Standards: 3.1

Focus: Reading to learn about culture

Suggestions:

Pre-reading: Ask a volunteer to read the title of the passage aloud. Read the *Estrategia* aloud together and have students answer the questions. Have students read the captions and describe what they see in the pictures.

Reading: Encourage students to read once through the entire passage silently, without stopping at problem words or to ask questions. Then have them read it again, stopping after each paragraph to address comprehension issues.

Post-reading: Ask the *¿Comprendiste?* questions to check comprehension.

Country Connection
Core Instruction

Standards: 1.1, 1.2, 1.3, 2.1, 2.2, 3.1

Resources: Map Transparency 20

Mapa global interactivo, Actividad 4
Follow the route of pilgrims from France to northern Spain.

Suggestions:

Use *Map Transparency* 20 to help students become further acquainted with Spain. Point out that it is comprised of 17 *regiones autónomas,* including *las Islas Canarias* and *las Islas Baleares.* Remind students that, besides the *castellano* they are learning, four other languages are spoken in Spain: *vascuence* in *el País Vasco, catalán* in *Cataluña, valenciano* in *la Comunidad Valenciana,* and *gallego* in *Galicia,* the region in which Santiago de Compostela is located.

Estrategia

Activating prior knowledge
A *peregrino* (pilgrim) is a person who makes a trip for spiritual reasons. To better understand the selection, think of other pilgrims you might know of. Why did the Pilgrims come from England to Plymouth, Massachusetts in the 17th century? Why did they found a colony? Look at the maps on these pages to see the route of another group of pilgrims.

En la Catedral de Santiago de Compostela está la tumba del apóstol Santiago.

Los peregrinos de Plymouth, Massachusetts, buscaban la libertad religiosa. Otros peregrinos viajan en busca de algo sagrado o religioso, como los peregrinos musulmanes que viajan a La Meca y los peregrinos judíos y cristianos que viajan a Jerusalén.

Hace más de mil años, en el extremo noroeste de España se descubrió la tumba del apóstol Santiago[1], una figura fundamental de la religión católica. Empezaron a viajar peregrinos de toda Europa al lugar del descubrimiento en donde se fundó la ciudad de Santiago de Compostela. La ruta sagrada que seguían los peregrinos se dio a conocer[2] como El Camino de Santiago y terminaba en el portal de la Catedral de Santiago de Compostela.

A lo largo de[3] la ruta construyeron iglesias y albergues[4] para recibir a los peregrinos. Algunos peregrinos venían de lugares tan lejanos como Rusia y tardaban años para completar su viaje a pie.

Hoy en día muchas personas viajan a Santiago por la misma razón que los peregrinos de hace mil años: por motivos[5] religiosos. Otros lo recorren[6] como turistas o por motivos culturales debido a su importancia histórica.

1 the apostle Saint James
2 became known as 3 All along
4 hostels 5 reasons 6 travel along

Un peregrino de la antigüedad

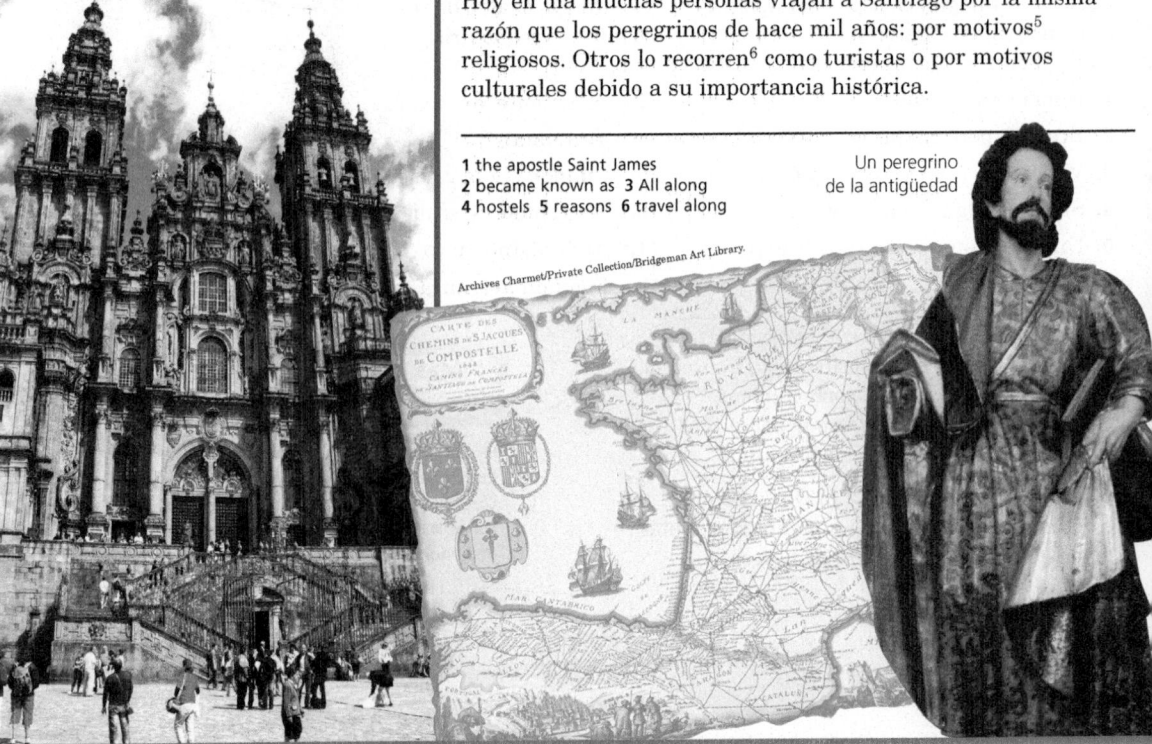

Archives Charmet/Private Collection/Bridgeman Art Library.

DIFFERENTIATED INSTRUCTION

Heritage Language Learners

Ask students to research and report on a pilgrimage that takes place in Latin America or the southwestern United States. They might also report on a major shrine, such as the *Basílica de la Virgen de Guadalupe* in Mexico City.

Advanced Learners

Invite students to research *el Camino de Santiago* and report back to the class. They can look for information such as the names and locations of *albergues juveniles,* the costs and procedures involved when staying there, tour groups, and distances between towns along the pilgrimage.

Muchos de los que hacen este viaje son jóvenes. Algunos lo hacen a pie, otros en bicicleta y otros ¡hasta a caballo! Por eso mismo, hay muchos albergues juveniles que ofrecen servicios muy baratos. Para quedarte en ellos, debes llevar tu propia comida. Los albergues son lugares excelentes para conocer a chicos y chicas de todo el mundo.

¿Comprendiste?

1. Nombra los cuatro grupos de peregrinos que se mencionan en la lectura. En general, ¿qué buscan los peregrinos?

2. ¿De dónde eran los peregrinos que iban a Santiago?

3. ¿Cuáles son tres motivos para seguir el Camino de Santiago hoy en día?

4. ¿Qué atractivos tiene el Camino para una persona joven?

Mi propio camino

1 Piensa en un viaje o una excursión que hiciste el año pasado. ¿Adónde fuiste? ¿Por qué fuiste allí? ¿Cómo fuiste? ¿Qué tuviste que llevar? ¿Dónde te quedaste? ¿Cómo era el lugar? ¿Qué había allí? ¿A quién(es) conociste?

2 Ahora compara tu experiencia con el recorrido que hacen muchos jóvenes a Santiago de Compostela. ¿En qué se parecen? ¿En qué se diferencian?

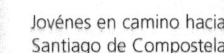

Más práctica GO

realidades.com | print

▶ *Videodocumentario*	✔	
Guided WB p. 45	✔	✔
Comm. WB pp. 20–21,	✔	✔
Hispanohablantes WB pp. 34–36		✔
Cultural Reading Activity	✔	

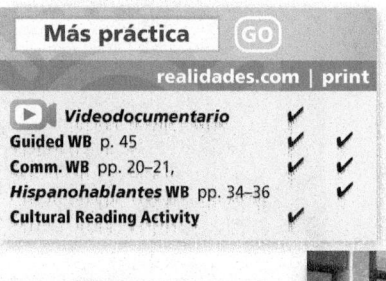

Jóvenes en camino hacia Santiago de Compostela

Uno de los albergues del Camino de Santiago

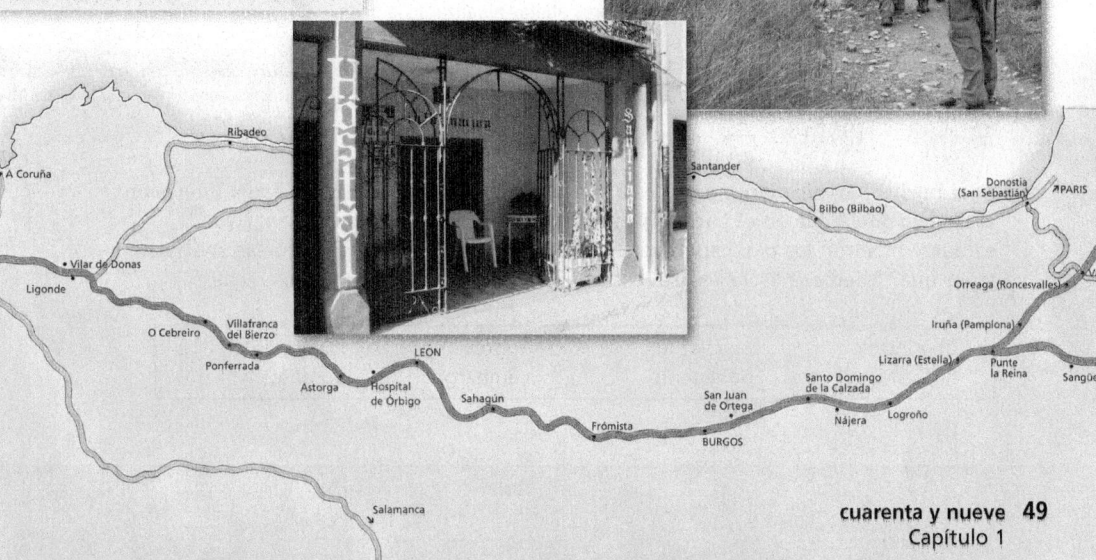

Ribadeo
A Coruña
Santander
Donostia (San Sebastián) ► PARIS
Bilbo (Bilbao)
DE ELA
Vilar de Donas
Orreaga (Roncesvalles)
Ligonde
O Cebreiro
Villafranca del Bierzo
Iruña (Pamplona)
PORTO ↓LISBOA
Ponferrada
LEÓN
Lizarra (Estella)
Punte la Reina
Sangües
igo
Astorga
Hospital de Órbigo
Sahagún
San Juan de Ortega
Santo Domingo de la Calzada
Nájera
Frómista
Logroño
BURGOS
Salamanca

cuarenta y nueve **49**
Capítulo 1

ENRICH YOUR TEACHING

Culture Note

According to legend, Saint James was killed in Palestine in 44 A.D. Disciples took his body to Spain and buried it in a hidden place. In 813, a hermit reportedly saw a star shining on a field, and this led to the discovery of the tomb. The place was named **Campus Stellae,** which was transformed to **Compostela.**

21st Century Skills

Information Literacy Have students research in the library or on Internet the route the pilgrims follow on **El Camino de Santiago.** What towns and cities are along the route? How far is the entire trip? Where do travelers stay along the route?

Culture 1

¿Comprendiste? Standards: 1.3

Resources: Answer Keys: Student Edition, p. 17

Focus: Demonstrating reading comprehension

Suggestions: Ask students to paraphrase the sections of text that contain their answers, rather than reading them verbatim.

Answers:

1. Los cuatro grupos de peregrinos mencionados son: los de Plymouth, Massachusetts, los peregrinos musulmanes, los peregrinos judíos y los peregrinos cristianos. Buscan algo sagrado o religioso.
2. Los peregrinos que iban a Santiago eran de toda Europa.
3. Tres motivos para seguir el Camino de Santiago hoy en día pueden ser motivos religiosos, turísticos y culturales.
4. Los atractivos que tiene el camino para los jóvenes son los albergues juveniles que ofrecen servicios muy baratos.

Mi propio camino Standards: 1.3, 2.1, 3.1, 3.2, 4.2

Focus: Comparing personal travel experience to the ancient practice of making pilgrimages in Spain

Suggestions: Students should discuss the questions in pairs or small groups.

Answers will vary.

Portfolio

Invite students to organize their responses to *Mi propio camino* and write them in paragraph form. Keep the paragraphs in students' portfolios as a writing sample.

▶ Videodocumentario

Core Instruction

Standards: 1.2

Resources: Teacher's Resource Book: Video Script, p. 41; Video Program: Cap. 1

View *Los deportes en el mundo hispano* with the class, either online in **realidades.com** or using the DVD. See the *Video Teacher's Guide* for additional suggestions.

Additional Resources

Student Resource: Realidades para hispanohablantes, pp. 34–36; Guided WB, p. 45; Communication Wbk., pp. 20–21

49

¿Qué me cuentas?

Core Instruction

Standards: 1.1, 1.2, 1.3

Resources: Teacher's Resource Book: Audio Script, p. 40; Audio Program DVD: Cap. 1, Track 20; Answer Keys: Student Edition, p.17

Focus: Practicing listening and reading comprehension of new vocabulary and grammar; using information to write a cohesive and coherent reaction.

AP* Skills: Integration of listening, reading, and writing to comprehend and synthesize information from spoken and written sources.

Suggestions: For Step 1, use the audio or read the descriptions aloud. Allow students to hear both descriptions twice through: the first time to write their answers, the second time to check them.

For Step 2, have students identify significant details as they read and then summarize the main points of the article.

Encourage students to use each of the suggested expressions in their written responses for Step 3.

Answers:

Step 1

1. a **2.** b **3.** c **4.** a **5.** b **6.** a

Steps 2–3

Answers will vary.

Extension: As students do Step 2, have them also write three multiple-choice questions about the article, like the ones they answered in Step 1. Remind them to make their distractors (the incorrect answers) different from the correct answers. Have them ask their questions orally before they begin Step 3.

Block Schedule

True/False Quiz. Have students work in pairs to create a series of ten statements that are *cierto* or *falso* about the article. Have them partner with another pair and read their statements. The team has to determine whether the other pair's statements are *cierto* or *falso*.

Additional Resources

Student Resource: Realidades para hispanohablantes, p. 37

Pre–AP*

| ▼ Objectives

▶ Listen to and read about an excursion and a sports competition

▶ Write a comparison of two past events

Integración

¿Qué me cuentas?: Dos aventuras

El fin de semana pasado hubo dos eventos en el Parque Nacional Tierra del Fuego. Compara lo que sucedió en cada uno. Primero escucha una descripción del paseo. Anota las respuestas a las preguntas y guárdalas para usarlas en el paso 3.

❶ 🔊))) Escucha las siguientes descripciones. Después de cada descripción vas a oír tres preguntas. Escoge la mejor respuesta para cada pregunta.

1. a. no hacía buen tiempo   b. hacía calor   c. llovía
2. a. por el bosque   b. por el valle   c. por la playa
3. a. hasta una roca   b. hasta un árbol   c. hasta el pie de una montaña
4. a. mosquitos   b. pájaros   c. peces
5. a. binoculares   b. repelente de insectos   c. brújula
6. a. empezó a llover   b. empezó a nevar   c. cayeron relámpagos

❷ Ahora lee un artículo sobre la competencia que ocurrió el mismo día.

Noticias deportivas   **Maratónweb.ar**

El maratón vuelve a Ushuaia

Domingo, 30 de marzo

Ushuaia, Arg. — Hacía frío cuando los atletas empezaron a correr en el maratón Fin del Mundo que tuvo lugar ayer en el Parque Nacional Tierra del Fuego. Más de 250 atletas, representantes de unos veinte países, se inscribieron en la carrera. La carrera fue dura, no sólo por las temperaturas bajas, sino también por el viento fuerte. Los competidores corrieron por un camino de roca que cruzaba el bosque y contra un viento que a veces superaba los 65 kilómetros por hora. Mientras los atletas corrían los últimos veinte kilómetros, empezó a llover y a caer granizo. Sin embargo, el público estaba animado y se emocionó cuando los primeros atletas alcanzaron la meta.

Al final salió campeón Paul Rotich de Kenia, quien venció a los demás participantes con un tiempo de 2 horas, 44 minutos. Rotich fue el tercer keniata en obtener la medalla de oro desde que empezó el maratón.

Paul Rotich, ganador del maratón Fin del Mundo

❸ Escribe dos párrafos y compara los dos eventos del fin de semana pasado. Piensa en el tiempo que hacía en el parque y en lo que sucedió en cada aventura. ¿Qué esfuerzo hicieron los participantes en cada aventura? ¿Cómo crees que se sentían y por qué? Mientras escribes, usa estas expresiones para conectar tus ideas.

al principio	una vez allí	entonces	más tarde
al final	de repente	sin embargo	durante

50 cincuenta
¡Adelante!

DIFFERENTIATED INSTRUCTION

Heritage Language Learners

After students complete Step 2 on p. 50, ask them to think of a sporting or other event they have witnessed that was affected by unexpected weather. Have them tell what happened. Encourage them to use both the preterite and imperfect tenses.

Multiple Intelligences

Interpersonal/Social: For Step 3, help students think about how the people in Steps 1 and 2 felt. Ask them to recall a similar experience of their own. Encourage them to imagine the sensory details, including sights, sounds, and smells that will help them remember how they felt under similar circumstances.

Presentación oral

Una experiencia inolvidable

Tarea
Trabajas en un campamento para niños. Cuéntales a los niños de una experiencia inolvidable que tuviste.

1 Prepárate Responde a las preguntas de la tabla.

¿Adónde fuiste?	
¿Cómo era el lugar?	
¿Qué había allí?	
¿Qué sucedió?	
¿Cómo te sentiste?	
¿Cómo terminó?	

2 Practica Vuelve a leer la información que anotaste en la tabla. Practica varias veces tu presentación. Puedes usar tus notas para practicar, pero no al hablar ante la clase. Recuerda:

- describir claramente todo lo que sucedió
- mirar directamente al público
- usar el vocabulario que aprendiste en esta lección

Modelo
Hace un tiempo, fui a acampar al valle. El paisaje era impresionante. Había flores de todos los colores. Después de caminar un rato, me perdí. Entonces me di cuenta de que no tenía mi brújula. Sentí miedo. Después de un rato oí unas voces. ¡Eran mis amigos!

3 Haz tu presentación Imagina que tus compañeros son los niños del campamento. Cuéntales tu experiencia inolvidable.

4 Evaluación Tu profesor(a) utilizará la siguiente rúbrica para evaluar tu presentación.

Rubric	Score 1	Score 3	Score 5
How well you narrate the event	You don't include narration or have incomplete narration.	You present an idea for narration, but it needs development.	Your narration is well developed and interesting.
How well you use chapter vocabulary	Your chapter vocabulary is absent.	You used one or two chapter vocabulary items.	You used several chapter vocabulary items appropriately.
How effectively you deliver your speech	You have no eye contact with the audience. There is little or no intonation.	You made some eye contact. You used intonation, but not convincingly.	You have good eye contact with the audience. Intonation and gestures made the narration interesting.

Estrategia

Choosing a topic
When giving an oral presentation, think about your audience as you choose a topic. Make a list of details that support your main idea and make sure you have enough interesting information.

cincuenta y uno **51**
Capítulo 1

Speaking (1)

ⓒ Common Core: Speaking

Presentación oral

Core Instruction
Standards: 1.1, 1.2, 1.3, 3.1
Resources: Voc. and Gram. Transparency 4
Focus: Preparing and delivering an oral presentation
Suggestions: Review the task and the rubric with students. Before they write their questions, direct students' attention to the *Estrategia*. Do a presentation of your own (called an anchor) to model a top-scoring presentation.

Pre-AP* Support

- **Learning Objective:** Presentational Speaking
- **Activity:** Remind students to focus on the presentational speaking skills used in this task such as fluency, pronunciation, and comprehensibility.
- **Pre-AP* Resource Book:** Comprehensive guide to Pre-AP* speaking skill development, pp. 39–50

Portfolio
Make audio or video recordings of student oral presentations in class, or assign the RealTalk activity so they can record their presentations online. Include the recording in their portfolios.

Additional Resources
Student Resource: Realidades para hispanohablantes, p. 38

ENRICH YOUR TEACHING

Teacher-to-Teacher
Record your own model presentation online. This way, students can view the model as often as they wish while they prepare and practice their presentations. Some students show a marked improvement when they have a readily accessible model to study. Remind them that it is only a model and that their presentations should not include any content taken directly from it.

21st Century Skills

Communication As they do this *Presentación oral* task, students should try to use sensory information (sights, sounds, and smells, etc.) to provide additional detail and interest as they describe their unforgettable summer camp experience.

✓ASSESSMENT

Presentación oral
- Assessment Program: Rubrics, p. T28
  Review the rubric with students. Go over the descriptions of the different levels of performance. After assessing students, help individuals understand how their performance could be improved. (See Teacher's Resource Book for suggestions on using rubrics in assessment.)

Language Arts Connection: Creative Writing

Standards: 3.1

Explain to students that the five-step writing process presented on these two pages will be used consistently throughout *Realidades*. Point out that this is the same process they most likely use for writing assignments in their Language Arts classes. They can apply the skills and strategies they learn there to their writing in Spanish and vice versa.

© Common Core: Writing

Presentación escrita

Core Instruction

Standards: 1.3, 3.1

Resources: Voc. and Gram. Transparency 5

Focus: Combining learned vocabulary and structures in a written presentation

Suggestions: Explain at the start the criteria you will use to evaluate students' compositions. (See Step 5, *Evaluación* and *Assessment* on the next page.)

During Step 1, circulate and consult with students. Use questions and suggestions to help them limit their topic. For example, a student will have trouble bringing life to a composition on a topic as broad as *un verano en Chiapas.* Help him or her narrow the topic to one important or interesting incident that happened that summer.

During Step 2, direct students' attention to the *Estrategia*. Point out that focusing on details requires them to stretch their vocabulary and grammar skills because they will include more ideas and images in their sentences.

Pre-AP* Support

- **Learning Objective:** Presentational Writing
- *Pre-AP* Resource Book:* Comprehensive guide to Pre-AP* writing skill development, pp. 27–38

52

Presentación escrita

Aventuras bajo el sol

> **Estrategia**
>
> **Adding details**
> Adding details to our writing makes it more interesting. If you say *"oí un ruido y me asusté,"* the reader cannot imagine the setting very well. But if you write: *"En la oscuridad de la noche, sentí un ruido como de un trueno . . . comencé a gritar,"* your reader will have a better picture of what happened.

Imagínate que acabas de participar en una de las actividades que muestran las fotos de este capítulo. Escribe un cuento sobre esa aventura. ¿Quiénes participaron? ¿Cómo era el lugar? ¿Qué querían ver? ¿Cómo lo pasaron? ¿Fue emocionante? ¿Cómo te sentiste al final?

1 Antes de escribir

Usa una red de palabras para organizar tus ideas.

2 Borrador

Escribe tu borrador. Usa el pretérito y el imperfecto y el vocabulario de esta lección. Escribe tus ideas en orden lógico, así tu cuento va a ser más interesante y más fácil de entender.

Modelo

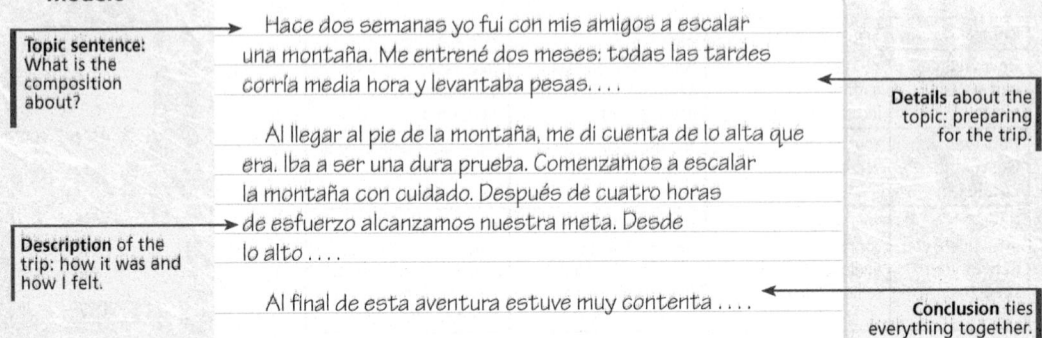

52 cincuenta y dos
¡Adelante!

DIFFERENTIATED INSTRUCTION

Heritage Language Learners

These students are sometimes used as reference sources by those who are not heritage speakers. This arrangement can be beneficial to both parties, and many heritage language learners are happy to provide help. Set limits, however, to make sure their own work is not unduly interrupted.

Students with Learning Difficulties

To stress the importance of details in a narrative, ask students to "freeze" the action of the characters in their minds, as if they had pressed the "pause" button on a video or DVD. While the characters are frozen tell them to concentrate on the details in the scene, such as clothing and background objects.

③ Redacción/Revisión

Después de escribir el primer borrador de la composición, trabaja con otro(a) estudiante para intercambiar los trabajos y leerlos. Decidan qué aspectos son más efectivos. Fíjense en cómo el escritor del modelo incluyó detalles en su composición. Cada persona puede decir qué se puede hacer para mejorar la composición que leyó.

Haz lo siguiente: Subraya con una línea los verbos en pretérito y con dos líneas los verbos en imperfecto.

- ¿Hay concordancia *(agreement)* entre cada sujeto y verbo?
- ¿El pretérito y el imperfecto están empleados correctamente?

> fui
> Hace dos semanas yo ~~fueron~~ con mis
> amidos a escalar una montaña. Me <u>entrené</u> dos
> corría
> meses: todas las tardes ~~corrían~~ media hora y
> <u>levantaba</u> pesas.

④ Publicación

Antes de crear la versión final, lee de nuevo tu borrador y repasa los siguientes puntos:
- ¿Sigue mi cuento un orden lógico?
- ¿Tiene un argumento, con un principio, un cuerpo y un final?
- ¿Hay otros detalles que debo poner en mi composición? ¿Hay algo que debo quitar?

Después de revisar el borrador, escribe tu composición en limpio.

⑤ Evaluación

Se utilizará la siguiente rúbrica para evaluar tu presentación.

Rubric	Score 1	Score 3	Score 5
Completion of task	You don't highlight any special event.	Your idea for narration is present but needs development.	Your special event is clearly narrated and made prominent.
Organization and level of detail	Your ideas aren't presented in logical order nor with detail.	You have some organizational problems. One or two details are provided.	Your organization is easy to follow. You use good details.
Sentence structure	Your sentences are run-on or are fragmented with many errors.	You use sentences consistently, but with some errors.	Your sentence structure is correct with few errors.

Suggestions (Cont'd):
During Step 3, encourage students to add details to their writing, focusing on sentence structure and transitions as they work in added details. During their peer consultations, remind them to follow the suggestions shown. Remind them that now is the time to think about a title to give their finished work.

Evaluation: Steps 4 and 5 overlap. Students will need evaluation by you, their peers, or self-evaluation to fine-tune and polish their drafts.

Portfolio

Keep students' final drafts in their portfolios as a writing sample.

Teacher-to-Teacher

e-amigos: Pair students to be *e-amigos.* Have them use e-mail to send each other the compositions they wrote for the *Presentación escrita.* Ask students to include an introduction to the composition and ask their partner's opinion of the story. Have students print out their e-mails or send them to you for review.

Additional Resources

Student Resource: Realidades para hispanohablantes, p. 39

ENRICH YOUR TEACHING

21st Century Skills

Communication Students will have to use their written language for the purpose of narrating a special experience in the past. Have students create a list of words and expressions that signal sequence of events, such as *primero, después, luego,* and *finalmente.* These can serve as good transitions between the events in their story.

✓ASSESSMENT

Presentación escrita
- Assessment Program: Rubrics, p. T29
  Review the rubric with students. Go over the descriptions of the different levels of performance. After assessing students, help individuals understand how their performance could be improved. (See Teacher's Resource Book for suggestions on using rubrics in assessment.)

53

▶ Read and understand a Mexican legend
▶ Make predictions to increase interest
▶ Discuss legends that explain natural phenomena

Ⓒ Common Core: Reading

Lectura

Core Instruction

Standards: 1.2, 1.3, 2.2, 3.1, 3.2, 5.2

Focus: Reading an extended passage

🌐 **Mapa global interactivo, Actividad 5**
Locate two Mexican volcanoes, which are the source of a popular legend.

Suggestions:

Pre-reading: Read aloud the title of the passage. Model the pronunciation of the names *Iztaccíhuatl* and *Popocatépetl* and have students repeat. Ask if anyone knows from what Native American culture these unusual names come. If necessary, explain that they are *náhuatl* names. *Náhuatl* is the language of the Aztecs. Before the arrival of the conquistadors, the Aztecs had a great civilization that included the area around what is today Mexico City. Tell students they will come across other *náhuatl* words as they read the selection.

Ask students to share what they know about the two volcanoes near Mexico city named *Iztaccíhuatl* and *Popocatépetl.* Tell them they are going to read an Aztec legend that explains how these two mountains were created and got their names.

Before reading, direct students' attention to the *Estrategia* and to the *Al leer* section. Have them answer the questions there and copy the graphic organizer from p. 57.

BELLRINGER REVIEW

Have students share the name of a legend that they remember from childhood and a one-sentence description of what happened in it.

Block Schedule

After reading the *Lectura,* assign each student a paragraph for which he or she must write four questions. Have students circulate around the class asking and answering the questions related to each of their paragraphs. This should help students comprehend the story in more detail.

Lectura
El Iztaccíhuatl y el Popocatépetl

> ### Estrategia
>
> **Making predictions**
> Making predictions about what will happen in a story allows us to focus on what we read and increases our interest in the story.
>
> • Do you know any stories that explain a natural phenomenon?
> • Look at the picture of the volcanoes. What do you think this story will explain?

Al leer

El cuento que vas a leer es una leyenda mexicana que relaciona una historia de amor con dos volcanes en México. Copia la gráfica organizadora de la página 57. Mientras lees la selección, llena todos los espacios de la gráfica con la información del cuento.

Mientras lees, presta atención a los siguientes puntos:

• el conflicto entre las dos familias

• la relación entre los personajes principales y la naturaleza

---

Hace mucho tiempo, en la gran ciudad de Teotihuacán, había un rey tolteca que tenía una hija muy hermosa. El pelo de la princesa era tan negro y suave como una noche de verano, sus ojos eran tan grandes y oscuros como las aguas de un lago secreto y su sonrisa era tan bonita que decían que el sol miraba por las montañas todas las mañanas para ser el primero en verla.

Muchos príncipes ricos y famosos venían de todas partes de la región tolteca para ganar el amor de la princesa, pero ella no se enamoraba de ninguno. El rey, que quería para su hija un esposo rico de buena posición en la sociedad tolteca, ya estaba impaciente. A veces le preguntaba a la princesa qué esperaba.

—No sé —contestaba la muchacha—. Sólo sé que mi esposo va a ser alguien que voy a amar desde el principio y para siempre.

Un día llegó a la ciudad un príncipe chichimeca. Los chichimecas no tenían una civilización tan espléndida como la de los toltecas. Vivían de la caza[1] y la pesca en las montañas. Los toltecas pensaban que los chichimecas vivían como perros, y se reían de ellos.

---

1 hunting

DIFFERENTIATED INSTRUCTION

Students with Special Needs

To help the hearing-impaired understand these names, say them aloud slowly several times (note that final *-l* is hardly pronounced): Popocatépetl (poh-poh-ca-TEH-pehtl), Iztaccíhuatl (is-tahs-IH-wahtl), Teotihuacán (tah-oh-tee-hwah-KAHN), chichimeca (chee-chee-MEH-kuh), náhuatl (NAH-wahtl).

Advanced Learners

Invite students to write a narrative about a volcanic eruption from the point of view of a Toltec or Chichimec person. Encourage them to try to portray the emotions such a person might feel at such a moment.

Príncipe chichimeca

Las señoras que acompañaban[4] a la princesa se dieron cuenta de lo que pasaba, y rápidamente llevaron a la princesa a su palacio. El príncipe también regresó al suyo en las montañas. Trató de olvidar a la bella princesa, pero no pudo.

Después de un tiempo, el príncipe decidió volver a Teotihuacán, a pedir la mano de la princesa. Un día se vistió de su ropa más fina y fue al palacio del rey tolteca. Allí mandó[5] a sus mensajeros a hablar con el rey para pedirle a su hija como esposa.

Cuando oyó las palabras de los mensajeros del príncipe, el rey tembló[6] de furia y gritó: —¡Mi hija sólo se va a casar con un príncipe tolteca, nunca con un chichimeca que vive en las montañas como un animal!

---

4 escorted **5** sent **6** shook

El príncipe chichimeca venía para visitar el gran mercado de Teotihuacán, donde vendían hermosísimos objetos de oro, ropa de brillantes colores, animales exóticos y muchas otras cosas.

Ese mismo día, la princesa tolteca estaba en el mercado comprando canastas[2], telas y alfombras para su palacio. Pasó que, de repente, entre toda la gente y el ruido del mercado, el príncipe y la princesa se fijaron[3] uno en el otro. Sin una palabra, desde el principio y para siempre, el príncipe y la princesa se enamoraron.

Los dos sabían muy bien que su amor era prohibido. Cada uno debía casarse con alguien de su pueblo y su clase: la princesa tolteca con un príncipe tolteca y el príncipe chichimeca con una princesa chichimeca.

---

2 large round basket **3** they noticed

Princesa tolteca

cincuenta y cinco **55**
Capítulo 1

ENRICH YOUR TEACHING

Suggestions (Cont'd):

Post-reading: Once students have read and discussed the passage section by section, allow them time for another silent reading. This allows them to apply their prior knowledge about the topic, as well as the information they have learned from class discussion. During a final silent reading, students can approach the passage with more confidence and iron out any final comprehension problems they may have.

Pre-AP* Support

- **Learning Objective:** Presentational Speaking (Cultural Comparison)
- **Background:** This task prepares students for the Spoken Presentational Communication tasks that focus on cultural comparisons.
- **Activity:** Have students prepare a two-minute (maximum) presentation on the following topic: Different views about the natural world are reflected in the legends of different cultures. Students may use the Mexican legend in this reading as a basis for the comparison. They should then comment on a legend they know from another culture, explaining the similarities and differences between the two.
- **Pre-AP* Resource Book:** Comprehensive guide to Pre-AP* speaking skill development, pp. 39–50

Additional Resources

Student Resource: Guided WB: Lectura, pp. 46–47

Cuando la princesa oyó todo esto, se sintió muy triste. Le tenía mucho respeto a su papá, pero sabía que no podía vivir sin el amor del príncipe chichimeca. Salió de su palacio y se reunió con el príncipe para decirle que sí quería casarse con él. Se fueron a las montañas, y esa noche se casaron.

Al día siguiente, la princesa regresó a Teotihuacán y le dijo a su padre que ya era la esposa del príncipe chichimeca. Le pidió perdón y esperó la comprensión de su padre. Pero el rey estaba furioso: —¿Cómo pudiste hacerme eso? —le preguntó a su hija—. ¡Vete de aquí y no vuelvas nunca! ¡Y no le pidas ni comida ni casa a ningún tolteca, que no te va a dar nada! ¡Lo prohíbo!

Lo mismo le pasó al príncipe cuando volvió a su palacio. Su padre le gritó: —¿Te casaste con una tolteca? ¡Ya no eres mi hijo, ni eres chichimeca! ¡No esperes nunca la ayuda de ningún chichimeca!

Con el corazón muy triste, el príncipe y la princesa se reunieron y empezaron a buscar dónde vivir en las montañas. Nadie los quería ayudar o darles un lugar para descansar y refugiarse de los vientos fríos. Comían sólo hierbas[7] y frutas, porque el príncipe no tenía nada con qué cazar o pescar. Poco a poco, los esposos se estaban muriendo.

Una noche muy fría y larga, el príncipe se dio cuenta de que pronto se iban a morir los dos. Estaban en un valle pequeño desde donde podían ver la ciudad de Teotihuacán. La princesa pensaba en su casa, y el príncipe la miraba con tristeza y amor, sabiendo lo que pensaba.

—Mi bella princesa —le dijo—, ya nos vamos a morir. Nos vamos a separar ahora en este mundo para estar siempre juntos en el otro. Duerme por última vez en mis brazos esta noche. En la mañana, tú te vas a ir a la montaña más baja que mira sobre tu ciudad, y yo me voy a ir a la montaña más alta que también mira sobre tu ciudad. Allí vamos a descansar, allí te voy a cuidar para siempre y nuestros espíritus[8] van a ser un solo espíritu. Al día siguiente los dos se separaron, y cada uno empezó a subir su montaña. La princesa subió la montaña Iztaccíhuatl y el príncipe subió la montaña Popocatépetl.

Cuando la princesa llegó a la cumbre[9] de su montaña, se durmió y la nieve la cubrió[10]. El príncipe se puso de rodillas, mirando hacia la princesa y la nieve también lo cubrió.

De esta manera podemos ver hoy al príncipe y a la princesa, en la cumbre del Iztaccíhuatl y el Popocatépetl. A veces hay grandes ruidos desde muy dentro del Popocatépetl. Es el príncipe llorando por su princesa.

---

7 grass **8** spirits, souls **9** summit **10** covered

DIFFERENTIATED INSTRUCTION

Students with Learning Difficulties

Help students deal with long reading passages by "jigsawing" the reading process. Divide the passage into sections and have individuals or pairs work on reading comprehension for their assigned section only. Then have students meet and share what they have learned about their section.

Advanced Learners

Mt. Popocatéptl erupted in 1997 and again in 2000. Encourage students to research and report on these eruptions and on the status of the volcano today.

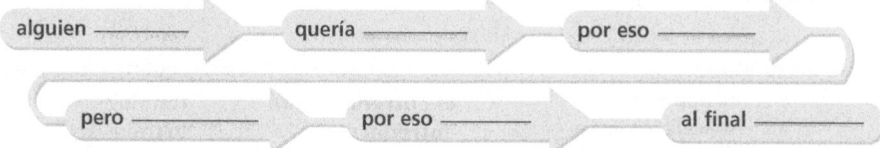

Interacción con la lectura

1 Llena el organizador gráfico con detalles del argumento.

alguien _____ → quería _____ → por eso _____ →

→ pero _____ → por eso _____ → al final _____

2 Trabaja con otro(a) estudiante para comparar la información de sus organizadores. Contesten las preguntas y **añadan** a sus organizadores cualquier otro detalle interesante que recuerden.

- ¿Cómo conoció el príncipe a la princesa? ¿Por qué no podían casarse?
- ¿Qué hicieron los jóvenes? ¿Crees que hicieron bien?
- ¿Qué emociones expresan los personajes al comienzo, después y al final del cuento?
- ¿Cómo terminó la historia? ¿Pudo tener otro final?

3 Ahora escribe un resumen del cuento basado en el organizador gráfico.

4 Trabaja con un grupo para contestar estas preguntas.

- ¿Qué cuentos, obras de teatro o películas conocen que cuentan una historia similar?
- ¿Por qué en casi todas las culturas hay historias de jóvenes enamorados a quienes sus padres no comprenden?

Más práctica GO

realidades.com | print

Guided WB pp. 46–47	✔	✔
Comm. WB p. 164	✔	✔

▼ Fondo Cultural | México

Los **indígenas americanos** vivían en íntimo contacto con la naturaleza. Algunos de sus mitos y leyendas explicaban fenómenos naturales como los eclipses, las tormentas y las erupciones volcánicas. La leyenda de Iztaccíhuatl y Popocatépetl explica la formación de dos volcanes cerca de la Ciudad de México. Iztaccíhuatl, el volcán más antiguo, tiene la forma de una mujer reclinada. En efecto, su nombre en la lengua náhuatl quiere decir "mujer dormida". Popocatépetl, el volcán más joven, es todavía activo. Su nombre náhuatl significa "montaña que humea" (*smoking mountain*).

- ¿Qué otra leyenda conoces que explique un fenómeno natural?

El volcán Popocatépetl

cincuenta y siete **57**
Capítulo 1

ENRICH YOUR TEACHING

Culture Note

Perhaps the most famous volcano in Mexico is Parícutin. It was born in 1943, when a farmer discovered a crack in his cornfield. Soon ashes covered the area. A year later, the village of San Salvador Parícutin had been overrun by lava. The last eruption was in 1952. By then the volcano had grown to an altitude of 424 meters, or about 1,300 feet.

21st Century Skills

Information Literacy Have students do online research about other legends that try to explain a natural phenomenon. They can research legends from any ancient civilizations they have previously studied, or legends from indigenous groups in the world today.

Review Activities

Para hablar de actividades al aire libre, cámping y el tiempo/Para describir la naturaleza/Para indicar que sucede algo y cuándo sucede algo: Show a five-minute segment of an adventure film or recorded TV show set in the outdoors. Tell students to open their books to this page. Ask them to think of ways to use as many vocabulary items as they can to talk about what they saw. Play the segment again, pausing frequently to allow students to make their comments. Ask questions to elicit words and expressions they have not yet included in their comments.

Make It a Game: The above review strategy can also be set up as a game. Divide the class into two teams. Choose two students as neutral "readers." After showing the recorded segment, give teams ten minutes to use as many vocabulary items as they can in comments about the segment. Have them write their comments as a single list of sentences. Only accurate and sensible comments count. Collect the two lists, and have the readers take turns reading one comment at a time. Keep a tally. The team that uses the most vocabulary items wins.

Para prepararse para un evento deportivo/Para hablar de competencias deportivas/Para expresar emociones e impresiones

Have pairs of students create comic strips about a character or characters involved in a sporting event. Their strips should include at least one scene each involving training, the event itself, and a victory or awards ceremony. The strips should include narrative lines and speech and/or thought balloons for the characters. Display completed comic strips in the classroom.

Otras palabras y expresiones: Students can use these words and expressions as they do the review activities for the other categories.

Repaso del capítulo
Vocabulario y gramática

para hablar de actividades
acercarse a	to approach
andar	to walk, to move
dar un paseo	to take a walk, stroll
dejar de	to stop (doing something)
escalar	to climb (a rock or mountain)
perderse	to get lost
refugiarse	to take shelter

para describir la naturaleza
el bosque	wood, forest
el desierto	desert
hermoso, -a	beautiful
la naturaleza	nature
el paisaje	landscape
el refugio	refuge, shelter
la roca	rock
la sierra	sierra, mountain range
el valle	valley

para hablar de cámping
los binoculares	binoculars
la brújula	compass
la linterna	flashlight
el repelente de insectos	insect repellent
el saco de dormir	sleeping bag
la tienda de acampar	tent

para hablar del tiempo
caer granizo	to hail
el granizo	hail
el relámpago	lightning
el trueno	thunder

para indicar que sucede algo
suceder	to occur
tener lugar	to take place

para indicar cuándo sucede algo
al amanecer	at dawn
al anochecer	at dusk
al principio	at the beginning
un rato	a while
una vez allí	once there

58 cincuenta y ocho
Repaso del capítulo

para prepararse para un evento deportivo
el entrenamiento	training
entrenarse	to train
hacer un esfuerzo	to make an effort
inscribirse	to register
la inscripción	registration

para hablar de competencias deportivas
alcanzar	to reach
la carrera	race
la ceremonia	ceremony
el certificado	certificate, diploma
contra	against
eliminar	to eliminate
la entrega de premios	awards ceremony
¡Felicitaciones!	Congratulations!
la medalla	medal
la meta	goal
obtener	to obtain, get
el / la participante	participant
el / la representante	representative
salir campeón, campeona	to become the champion
el trofeo	trophy
vencer	to beat

para expresar emociones e impresiones
animado, -a	excited
asustar	to scare
darse cuenta de	to realize
desafortunadamente	unfortunately
desanimado, -a	discouraged
duro, -a	hard
emocionarse	to be moved
estar orgulloso / orgullosa de	to be proud of
impresionar	to impress
pasarlo bien / mal	to have a good / bad time

otras palabras y expresiones
aparecer	to appear
así	this way
hacia	toward
perder el equilibrio	to lose one's balance
sin embargo	however

DIFFERENTIATED INSTRUCTION

Multiple Intelligences
Verbal/Linguistic: Ask a volunteer with good acting skills to say the items in the **emociones e impresiones** list and exaggerate the corresponding intonation. Have the other students repeat chorally, imitating the intonation.

Students with Learning Difficulties
Given the importance of the element of time when dealing with the past tenses, students may find it easier to retain vocabulary—and use the proper tense—if they add a few words when reviewing the lists of preterite and imperfect verbs. For example: *Yo leí un libro ayer. ¿Qué tiempo hacía ayer?*

el pretérito

destruir *to destroy*

destruí	destruimos
destruiste	destruisteis
destruyó	destruyeron

leer *to read*

leí	leímos
leíste	leísteis
leyó	leyeron

The verbs *creer*, *oír*, and *caerse* follow the same pattern as *leer*.

tener *to have*

tuve	tuvimos
tuviste	tuvisteis
tuvo	tuvieron

Other verbs that have an irregular stem in the preterite and share the same endings as *tener* are: *andar, estar, poder, poner, venir.*

decir *to tell*

dije	dijimos
dijiste	dijisteis
dijo	dijeron

The verb *traer* follows the same pattern as *decir*.

pedir (i) *to ask for*

pedí	pedimos
pediste	pedisteis
pidió	pidieron

The verbs *sentir, divertirse, preferir, sugerir,* and *vestirse* follow the same pattern as *pedir*.

dormir (u) *to sleep*

dormí	dormimos
dormiste	dormisteis
durmió	durmieron

The verb *morir* follows the same pattern as *dormir*.

el imperfecto

estar (-ar) *to be*

estaba	estábamos
estabas	estabais
estaba	estaban

tener (-er) *to have*

tenía	teníamos
tenías	teníais
tenía	tenían

vivir (-ir) *to live*

vivía	vivíamos
vivías	vivíais
vivía	vivían

ir *to go*

iba	íbamos
ibas	ibais
iba	iban

ser *to be*

era	éramos
eras	erais
era	eran

ver *to see*

veía	veíamos
veías	veíais
veía	veían

The imperfect of *hay* is *había.*

Pretérito e imperfecto

At random, say one preterite or imperfect form of any verb. Ask students to say as much as they can about that verb form and the verb to which it belongs. For example:

Teacher: *pedí*

Student A: *Es el pretérito de pedir.*

Student B: *Es la primera persona: Yo pedí.*

Student C: *Las formas de la tercera persona son irregulares: pidió, pidieron.*

Student D: *Las demás formas en el pretérito son pediste, pedimos y pedisteis.*

Student E: *Las formas del imperfecto son pedía, pedías, pedía...*

This "working backward" approach to reviewing verb forms challenges students and encourages them to look back through the chapter for answers.

Alternative Assessment Options

The above activity can be used as a way to assess students' assimilation of the chapter grammar points.

Portfolio

Invite students to review the activities they completed in this chapter, including written reports, posters or other visuals, tapes of oral presentations, and other projects. Have them select one or two items that they feel best demonstrate their achievements in Spanish. Include these products in students' portfolios. Have them include this with the Chapter Checklist and Self-Assessment Worksheet.

Additional Resources

Student Resources: Realidades para hispanohablantes, pp. 40–41

Teacher Resources:

- Teacher's Resource Book: Situation Cards, p. 49, Clip Art, pp. 50–57

- Assessment Program: Chapter Checklist and Self-Assessment Worksheet, pp. T49–T50

¡Pura vida! is a storyline video that is independent of chapter content and an ideal support for expanding listening skills. The 14 episodes are available within **realidades.com** or on a separate DVD. Student activities and Teacher support are also assignable within **realidades.com**.

ENRICH YOUR TEACHING

Teacher-to-Teacher

Try "jigsawing" the verb form review from the column on this page. Give one different verb form to each student and allow them five minutes to work. Each student comes up with as much information as he or she can about the assigned verb form and the verb to which it belongs. Then students come together to share their information. Listeners can fill in information they think is missing.

1 Review

Performance Tasks

Standards: 1.1, 1.2, 1.3, 2.1

Student Resource: Realidades para hispanohablantes, pp. 42–43

Teacher Resources: Teacher's Resource Book: Audio Script, p. 40; Audio Program DVD: Cap. 1, Track 22; Answer Keys: Student Edition, p. 19

1. Vocabulario

Suggestions: Encourage students to review the vocabulary from the *A primera vista* sections on pp. 22–25 and 36–38 before they complete the activity.

Answers:

1. d	5. c
2. b	6. b
3. c	7. a
4. a	8. d

2. Gramática

Suggestions: Remind students that the main ideas of the grammar presentations in *Capítulo* 1 were the forms and uses of the preterite and the imperfect.

Answers:

1. d	5. b
2. a	6. c
3. b	7. a
4. a	8. d

Preparación para el examen

1 **Vocabulario** Escribe la letra de la palabra o expresión que mejor complete cada frase. Escribe tus respuestas en una hoja aparte.

1. Me levanté muy temprano, _____, para ir de cámping.
   - a. por la tarde
   - b. al anochecer
   - c. por la noche
   - d. al amanecer

2. Cuando fuimos al bosque, Luis trajo _____ porque no había mucha luz.
   - a. unos binoculares
   - b. una linterna
   - c. un repelente de insectos
   - d. un saco de dormir

3. El paisaje era impresionante. _____ mucho cuando vi las montañas.
   - a. Me cansé
   - b. Me asusté
   - c. Me emocioné
   - d. Me aburrí

4. Cuando gané el campeonato mis padres me dijeron que estaban muy _____ de mis esfuerzos.
   - a. orgullosos
   - b. desanimados
   - c. asustados
   - d. tristes

5. Buscamos un refugio porque _____.
   - a. perdí el equilibrio
   - b. nos eliminaron
   - c. comenzó a caer granizo
   - d. no dormimos bien.

6. Cuando llegué tarde a casa mis padres me preguntaron: "¿Qué te _____?"
   - a. dieron
   - b. sucedió
   - c. rompiste
   - d. pusiste

7. Antes de participar en el campeonato, la chica _____ por tres meses.
   - a. se entrenó
   - b. se perdió
   - c. se divirtió
   - d. se durmió

8. Fue un partido muy _____. Todos tuvimos que hacer un gran esfuerzo para ganar.
   - a. agitado
   - b. fácil
   - c. aburrido
   - d. duro

2 **Gramática** Escribe la letra de la palabra o expresión que mejor complete cada frase. Escribe tus respuestas en una hoja aparte.

1. Leí en el diario que la tormenta _____ muchos árboles.
   - a. destruye
   - b. destruía
   - c. destruyendo
   - d. destruyó

2. No puedo creer que te olvidaste la mochila. ¿Por qué no la _____?
   - a. trajiste
   - b. traen
   - c. trajeron
   - d. traían

3. _____ la una de la tarde cuando llegamos al campamento.
   - a. Fue
   - b. Era
   - c. Eran
   - d. Estaban

4. El sábado pasado, los chicos _____ dos horas por los senderos.
   - a. anduvieron
   - b. andaban
   - c. andan
   - d. anduviste

5. Anoche, después del partido, el campeón _____ diez horas porque estaba cansado.
   - a. dormía
   - b. durmió
   - c. está durmiendo
   - d. duerme

6. De niña, a menudo yo _____ a los partidos de tenis con mis tíos.
   - a. voy
   - b. fui
   - c. iba
   - d. iban

7. El atleta que salió en primer lugar _____ un trofeo.
   - a. obtuvo
   - b. obtiene
   - c. obtenía
   - d. obtuviste

8. Generalmente, ¿cómo _____ cuando tu equipo perdía un partido?
   - a. te sientes
   - b. te sentiste
   - c. se sentían
   - d. te sentías

DIFFERENTIATED INSTRUCTION

Students with Learning Difficulties

Before students complete the tasks, have them review the *Vocabulario* on p. 58 and make flashcards for any words that they do not know. Have them use the cards for practice in pairs with partners who are more confident.

Advanced Learners

Ask students to serve as tutors for classmates who are struggling. Give tutors specific targets to work on. Some students may consider these requests an unfair imposition and extra work. Consider these feelings, while at the same time working towards maintaining an atmosphere of cooperation.

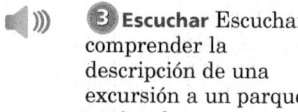
Más repaso (GO) realidades.com | print

Instant Check	✔	
Puzzles	✔	
Core WB pp. 19–20		✔
Comm. WB pp. 165, 166–169	✔	✔

En el examen vas a . . .	Éstas son las tareas de práctica que te pueden ser útiles para el examen . . .	Para repasar, ve a tu libro de texto impreso o digital . . .

Interpretive

 3 Escuchar Escuchar y comprender la descripción de una excursión a un parque nacional

Un amigo(a) te deja un mensaje por teléfono sobre una excursión que hizo a un parque nacional. (a) ¿Adónde fue? (b) ¿Qué vio? (c) ¿Qué hizo allí? (d) ¿Qué le sucedió? (e) ¿Cómo lo pasó?

pp. 22–25 *A primera vista 1: Vocabulario en contexto*
p. 27 Actividad 7
p. 29 Actividades 12–13
p. 34 Actividad 22
p. 35 Actividades 24–25

Interpersonal

 4 Hablar Hablar con un compañero sobre una excursión que hizo tu clase

Tu clase fue de excursión a un lugar especial. Cuéntale lo que pasó a un(a) compañero(a) que no pudo ir. Incluye quiénes fueron, adónde fueron, qué había allí, qué tiempo hacía, qué hicieron y cómo lo pasaron.

p. 50 *¿Qué me cuentas?*
p. 51 *Presentación oral*

Interpretive

5 Leer Leer y comprender un anuncio sobre un concurso

Lee el anuncio que apareció en el periódico de la escuela y decide: (a) qué tipo de concurso es; (b) cuándo es la inscripción; (c) quiénes pueden participar; (d) cuándo es la audición; (e) qué premio va a obtener el / la ganador(a).

Concurso de Música Invitamos a todos los estudiantes de tercer y cuarto año a participar en nuestro concurso.
Fecha de inscripción: 6 de octubre
Audición: 9 de octubre
Primer premio: dos entradas (tickets) para un concierto en el teatro San Martín

pp. 36–39 *A primera vista 2: Vocabulario en contexto*
p. 40 *Fondo cultural*
p. 41 Actividades 33–35

Presentational

 6 Escribir Escribir un artículo sobre un evento deportivo importante para el periódico de la escuela

Imagina que eres reportero del periódico de la escuela. Tienes que escribir un artículo sobre el último partido del año de un equipo de tu escuela. Tu artículo debe contar (a) quiénes jugaron, (b) dónde y cuándo fue, (c) si hacía buen tiempo, (d) cómo se sentían los jugadores, (e) qué sucedió, (f) cómo se sentían al final, (g) si fue un partido aburrido o emocionante y por qué.

p. 43 Actividad 37
p. 44 Actividad 40
p. 45 Actividad 41

Comparisons

 7 Pensar Pensar en los peregrinos de hoy y de ayer

Piensa en el viaje de los peregrinos de Santiago de Compostela hace mil años. ¿Por qué quieren seguir la misma ruta muchos jóvenes hoy en día? ¿Hay lugares aquí en los Estados Unidos como Santiago de Compostela? ¿Cuáles son los motivos para viajar a estos lugares? ¿En qué se parecen? ¿En qué se diferencian?

pp. 48–49 *Puente a la cultura*

sesenta y uno **61**
Capítulo 1

3. Escuchar

Suggestions: Use the audio or read from the script.

◀))) **Answers:**

a. Fue al Parque Nacional Torres del Paine.
b. Vio valles y montañas altísimas.
c. Hizo caminatas y montó a caballo.
d. Perdió el equilibrio y se cayó del caballo.
e. Lo pasó muy bien.

4. Leer

Suggestions: Tell students to refer to pp. 22–25 and 36–38 if they have questions about vocabulary in the announcement.

Answers:

a. Es un concurso de música.
b. La inscripción es el 6 de octubre.
c. Todos los estudiantes de tercer y cuarto año pueden participar.
d. La audición es el 9 de octubre.
e. El (la) ganador(a) va a obtener dos entradas para un concierto en el teatro San Martín.

5. Escribir

Suggestions: Encourage students to put their thoughts in a graphic organizer before writing.

Answers will vary.

6. Hablar

Suggestions: As students take turns telling about their excursions, encourage the listeners to help the speakers by asking questions.

Answers will vary.

7. Pensar

Suggestions: Ask students to write down the answers and be ready to share them with the class.

Answers will vary.

DIFFERENTIATED ASSESSMENT

CORE ASSESSMENT

- **Assessment Program:** Examen del capítulo 1, pp. 32–35
- **Audio Program DVD:** Cap. 1, Track 23
- **ExamView:** Chapter Test, Test Banks A and B

ADVANCED/PRE-AP*

- **ExamView:** Pre-AP* Test Bank
- **Pre-AP* Resource Book,** pp. 138–140

STUDENTS NEEDING EXTRA HELP

- **Alternate Assessment Program:** Examen del capítulo 1
- **Audio Program DVD:** Cap. 1, Track 23

HERITAGE LEARNERS

- **Assessment Program: Realidades para hispanohablantes:** Examen del capítulo 1
- **ExamView: Heritage Learner Test Bank**

② ¿Cómo te expresas?

② Chapter Overview

- **different artistic expressions and how to appreciate them**

Vocabulary
- types of art and how to describe them
- music, drama and dance performances

Grammar
- preterite vs. imperfect
- *estar* + past participle
- *ser* and *estar*
- verbs with different meanings in the imperfect and the preterite

Cultural Perspectives
- artistic expressions and artists in the Spanish-speaking world
- the art of Mexican artists Diego Rivera and David Alfaro Siqueiros
- the origins of *salsa*
- the Spanish *zarzuela*
- the world of Francisco de Goya

¡Pura vida!
- Watch an engaging video episode about a group of young people in Costa Rica!

CHAPTER SUPPORT

Bulletin Boards

Theme: *Las artes*

Ask students to cut out, draw, or download pictures of artists from different Spanish-speaking countries and of their work. Cluster photos into categories: painting, sculpture, dance, music, and literature.

Game

Veo, veo. ¿Qué ves?

Use this traditional children's game to practice art-related vocabulary in the *Manos a la obra* 1 section.

Players: entire class

Materials: Poster of a painting from a Spanish or Latin American artist.

Rules:
1. Students write their names on scraps of paper and place them in a paper bag.
2. Shake the paper bag to mix up the names. Then call on a volunteer to come to the front of the class and draw a name from the paper bag.
3. Students take turns asking the volunteer questions in order to guess an object from the painting that the volunteer has chosen.
   Student 1: Veo, veo.
   Student 2: ¿Qué ves?
   Student 1: Una cosa.
   Student 2: ¿De qué color?
   Student 1: Verde.
   Student 2: ¿Está en primer plano?
   Student 1: Sí.
   Student 2: Es una manzana.
   Student 1: Sí.
4. When a student correctly guesses the object in the painting, he or she becomes the new volunteer. Play continues until every student has had a chance to ask one or two questions.

Hands-on Culture

Craft: *Una máscara de tigre*

In Mexico, the art of making tiger or jaguar masks has its roots in pre-Hispanic theatrical performances. The character of the tiger or jaguar is extremely popular and important in many Mexican festivals and pageants. Tiger masks are typically painted yellow with black spots in keeping with the coloring of the real animal.

Materials: water, white flour (one part flour to one part water), newspaper (uncut), aluminum foil, masking tape, strips of newspaper (about 1 inch wide), acrylic or poster paint, brushes

Directions:
1. Prepare paste by mixing flour and water in a large bowl until it makes a smooth paste.
2. Make a mold by forming a large round or oval shape out of balled-up sheets of dry newspaper. Next, cover the front of this shape with aluminum foil, smoothing it down so it forms to your shape. Use more balled-up newspaper to form facial features on your mold. Attach them to the aluminum foil with masking tape.
3. Dip the newspaper strips, one at a time, into the paste. Lay the coated newspaper on the mold. Smooth out the wrinkles and continue to place coated newspaper strips over the surface until it is completely covered. Continue until you have put 3 to 4 layers of newspaper strips on your mold. Allow the mask to dry for about 24 hours.
4. When the mask is dry, pull the balled-up newspaper out of it. The aluminum foil will remain attached to your mask as a lining. Paint the mask yellow and add black spots. Cut holes for the eyes and mouth.

CHAPTER PROJECT

Escultura personal

Overview: Students create a sculpture that will represent their personality. First they draw a draft and write how the design relates to them. Then they create the sculpture. It might be done with clay, papier-mâché, carved soap, cardboard, or other scrap materials found at home. Have them paint it or decorate it according to their taste. Finally, they give an oral presentation of the piece, explaining how it relates to them or represents them.

Resources: paper, clay, cardboard, soap, paint, markers, scrap materials found at home. Remind students that there are no restrictions on materials, as long as they are safe.

Sequence: (suggestions for when to do each step are found throughout the chapter)

STEP 1. Review instructions so students know what is expected of them. Hand out the "Chapter 2 Project Instructions and Rubric" from the *Teacher's Resource Book*.

STEP 2. On a sheet of paper students draw a rough draft of their sculpture and write a few paragraphs explaining how it relates to their personality. Return their draft and text with suggestions. For vocabulary and grammar practice, ask partners to present their sketches and text to each other.

STEP 3. Students create their sculpture, based on their previous drafts. Encourage them to try different materials for their work and to use as much vocabulary as possible from *Capítulo* 2 in their written text.

STEP 4. Students submit a draft of their text, explaining how the sculpture relates to their personality. Write your corrections and suggestions, then return drafts to students.

STEP 5. Students present their sculpture to the class, using their notes to explain how it relates to them.

Options:

1. Students create a collage to represent aspects of their personality.
2. Students create a brochure about an artist of their choice.

Assessment:

Here is a detailed rubric for assessing this project:

Chapter 2 Project: *Escultura personal*

RUBRIC	Score 1	Score 3	Score 5
Your evidence of planning	You present no draft or written text.	Your draft or text is missing.	You show evidence of a corrected draft.
Your use of materials	You provide little or no decoration.	Your structure or decoration is missing.	Your piece is well done.
Your presentation	Your presentation is short and does not relate to the sculpture.	You describe part of the sculpture.	You describe in detail your relationship with the sculpture.

21st Century Skills

Look for tips throughout Chapter 2 to enrich your teaching by integrating 21st Century Skills. Suggestions for the Chapter Project and Culture follow below.

Chapter Project

Modify the Chapter Project with these suggestions:

Encourage Information Literacy
Encourage students to go online and research artists who have created self portraits or autobiographical sculptures to see how they define themselves through a variety of media. The handout "Search for Information on the Internet" will help them find reliable sources and museum Web sites to view a variety of artwork.

Foster Creativity and Innovation
Encourage students to be creative with the materials they choose to make their sculptures. Remind them of the possibilities of *collage*, such as embedding beads, small stones, or pieces of wood into their sculptures, or of using a combination of media in the same sculpture.

Enhance Communication
As students prepare to present their projects, provide them with the handout "Give an Effective Presentation" to remind them of the importance of body language, tone of voice, eye contact, and other strategies for delivering an effective presentation.

Chapter Culture

Develop Social and Cross Cultural Skills
Help students bridge cultural differences by offering opportunities to discuss the culture highlighted throughout the chapter. Use the teaching suggestions in the *Fondo cultural* features to discuss cultural perspectives in the artistic expression of different artists and performers of the Spanish-speaking world.

▶️ **Videodocumentario** View *El arte en el mundo hispano* online with the class to hear different Spanish-speaking artists share their inspirations for their own work.

2 ¿Cómo te expresas?

Objectives
- Listen to and read about art and music
- Talk and write about music and theater
- Discuss and explain art school activities
- Compare how artists express their ideas
- Understand the context of an artist
- Understand cross-cultural perspectives

A ver si recuerdas...

- Arts and artists
- Colors and materials
- In the theater
- Adjectives
- Nouns and superlatives

Recycle ♻

- Preterite and imperfect
- The letters *b* and *v*

Vocabulary
- Art forms, genres, materials and professions
- Works of art and artists
- Performing arts: music, dance, stage

Grammar
- Preterite vs. imperfect
- Verb *estar* + participle
- *Ser* and *estar*
- Verbs with different meanings in the imperfect and preterite

Culture
- Picasso and cubism, p. 67
- Dina Bursztyn, p. 70
- Carlos Enríquez, Diego Rivera, Osvaldo Guayasamín, p. 71
- Miró and Dalí, p. 74
- Diego Rivera, p. 75
- David Alfaro Siqueiros, p. 78
- Lila Downs, p. 84
- Dancing *salsa*, p. 91
- The *zarzuela*, p. 93
- Francisco de Goya, pp. 94–95
- Esmeralda Santiago, p. 103

RESOURCES

FOR THE STUDENT	ONLINE	DVD	PRINT	FOR THE TEACHER	ONLINE	PREEXP	DVD	PRINT
Plan				Interactive TE and Resource DVD	•		•	
				Teacher's Resource Book, pp. 85–141	•		•	•
				Pre-AP* Resource Book, pp. 141–143	•		•	•
				Lesson Plans	•			•
				Mapa global interactivo	•			
A ver si recuerdas PP. 62–65								
Review								
A ver si recuerdas Study Plan	•			*A ver si recuerdas* Study Plan	•			
Guided WB, pp. 48–51	•	•	•	Vocabulary and Grammar Transparencies, 49–52	•	•	•	
Core WB, pp. 21–22	•	•	•	Fine Art Transparencies, 47	•	•	•	
Hispanohablantes WB, p. 44			•	Answer Keys: Student Edition, p. 20	•	•	•	
Introducción PP. 66–67								
Present								
Student Edition, pp. 66–67	•	•	•	Interactive TE and Resource DVD	•		•	
DK Reference Atlas	•	•		Teacher's Resource Book, pp. 86–89	•		•	•
Videonovela: ¡Pura vida!	•	•		Video Program Teacher's Guide, Cap. 2				•
¡Pura vida! Video Activities	•			Galería de fotos		•		
Hispanohablantes WB, p. 45			•	Fine Art Transparencies, 48	•	•	•	
				Map Transparencies, 14, 16–20, 22	•	•	•	
Vocabulario en contexto PP. 68–71/82–85								
Present & Practice								
Student Edition, pp. 68–71/82–85	•	•	•	Interactive TE and Resource DVD	•		•	
Audio	•	•		Teacher's Resource Book, pp. 90–91, 94–95, 110–116/92–93, 96–97, 110–116	•		•	•
Flashcards	•	•		Vocabulary Clip Art				•
Instant Check	•			Audio Program	•	•	•	
Guided WB, pp. 52–58/63–70	•	•	•	Vocabulary and Grammar Transparencies, 53–56/59–62	•	•	•	
Core WB, pp. 23–24/28–29	•	•	•	Fine Art Transparencies, 12, 19, 32, 39–40, 55	•	•	•	
Comm. WB, pp. 26/29	•			Answer Keys: Student Edition, pp. 20–21/28	•	•	•	
Hispanohablantes WB, pp. 46–47/56–57			•					
Assess and Remediate				Pruebas 2–1/2–5: Assessment Program, pp. 37–38/46–47 Hispanohablantes, pp. 37–38/46–47	•		•	•

RESOURCES

FOR THE STUDENT	ONLINE	DVD	PRINT	FOR THE TEACHER	ONLINE	PREEXP	DVD	PRINT
Vocabulario en uso PP. 72–75/86–87								
Present & Practice Student Edition, pp. 72–75/86–87	•	•	•	Interactive Whiteboard Vocabulary Activities	•		•	
Instant Check	•			Interactive TE and Resource DVD	•		•	
Comm. WB, pp. 22/24	•	•	•	Teacher's Resource Book, pp. 95, 101–102/97, 105–106	•		•	•
Hispanohablantes WB, pp. 48–49/58–59			•	Audio Program	•	•	•	
Communicative Pair Activities	•			Videomodelos	•		•	
				Fine Art Transparencies, 16, 20, 40, 56, 72	•	•	•	
				Answer Keys: Student Edition, pp. 22–24/29	•	•	•	•
Assess and Remediate				Pruebas 2–2/2–6 with Study Plans	•			
				Pruebas 2–2/2–6: Assessment Program, pp. 39–40/48–49	•		•	•
				Hispanohablantes, pp. 39–40/48–49	•		•	•
Gramática PP. 76–81/88–93								
Present & Practice Student Edition, pp. 76–81/88–93	•	•	•	Interactive Whiteboard Grammar Activities	•		•	
Instant Check	•			Interactive TE and Resource DVD	•		•	
Animated Verbs	•			Teacher's Resource Book, pp. 95/97–98, 103–104, 107–108	•		•	•
Tutorial Video: Grammar	•			Audio Program	•	•	•	
Canción de hip hop	•			Videomodelos	•	•	•	
Guided WB, pp. 59–62/71–74	•	•	•	Vocabulary and Grammar Transparencies, 57–58/63–64	•	•	•	
Core WB, pp. 25–27/30–32	•	•	•	Fine Art Transparencies, 42, 64, 70	•	•	•	
Comm. WB, pp. 23, 27–28, 170/24–25, 30–33	•	•	•	Answer Keys: Student Edition, pp. 24–27/29–32	•	•	•	•
Hispanohablantes WB, pp. 50–55/60–65			•					
Communicative Pair Activities	•							
Assess and Remediate				Pruebas 2–3, 2–4/2–7, 2–8 with Study Plans	•			
				Pruebas 2–3, 2–4/2–7, 2–8: Assessment Program, pp. 41, 42/50, 51	•		•	•
				Hispanohablantes, pp. 41, 42/50, 51	•		•	•
				Examen 1, Examen 2: Vocab. y gramática, pp. 43–45/52–54	•		•	•
¡Adelante! PP. 94–103								
Application Student Edition, pp. 94–103	•	•	•	Interactive TE and Resource DVD	•		•	
Online Cultural Reading	•			Teacher's Resource Book, pp. 98, 100	•		•	•
Guided WB, pp. 75–77	•	•	•	Video Program: Videodocumentario	•		•	
Comm. WB, pp. 34–35, 171	•	•	•	Video Program Teacher's Guide, Cap. 2	•		•	
Hispanohablantes WB, pp. 67–71			•	Vocabulary and Grammar Transparencies, 4, 12	•	•	•	
Videodocumentario	•	•		Map Transparencies, 16	•	•	•	
Lecturas 3, pp. 42–45, 51			•	Fine Art Transparencies, 11, 17, 27–30	•	•	•	
				Answer Keys: Student Edition, p. 33	•	•	•	
Repaso del capítulo PP. 104–107								
Review Student Edition, pp. 104–107	•	•	•	Interactive TE and Resource DVD	•		•	
Online Puzzles and Games	•			Teacher's Resource Book, pp. 99, 109–116	•		•	•
Core WB, pp. 33–34	•	•	•	Audio Program	•	•	•	
Comm. WB, pp. 172–175	•	•	•	Answer Keys: Student Edition, p. 34	•	•	•	
Hispanohablantes WB, pp. 72–75			•					
Instant Check	•							
Chapter Assessment								
Assess				Examen del capítulo 2: Assessment Program, pp. 55–58	•		•	•
				Alternate Assessment Program, pp. 15–24	•		•	•
				Hispanohablantes, pp. 55–58	•		•	•
				Audio Program, Cap. 2, Examen	•		•	
				ExamView: Test Banks A and B (questions only online)	•		•	
				Heritage Learner Test Bank	•		•	
				Pre-AP* Test Bank	•		•	

REGULAR SCHEDULE (50 MINUTES)

DAY	Warm-up / Assess	Preview / Present / Practice / Communicate	Wrap-up / Homework Options
1	**Warm-up** (10 min.) • Return Examen del capítulo: Capítulo 1	**Repaso** (35 min.) • A ver si recuerdas . . . • Actividades 5	**Wrap-up and Homework Options** (5 min.) • Core Practice 2-1, 2-2
2	**Warm-up** (10 min.) • Homework check	**Chapter Opener** (10 min.) • Objectives • Arte y cultura **Vocabulario en contexto 1** (25 min.) • Presentation: Vocabulario y gramática en contexto • Actividades 1, 2	**Wrap-up and Homework Options** (5 min.) • Clip Art Vocabulary
3	**Warm-up** (10 min.) • Homework check	**Vocabulario en contexto 1** (35 min.) • Presentation: Entrevista con Dina Bursztyn • Actividad 3 • Presentation: Artistas latinoamericanos • Actividades 4, 5	**Wrap-up and Homework Options** (5 min.) • Core Practice 2-3, 2-4 • Actividad 6 • Prueba 2-1: Vocabulary recognition
4	**Warm-up** (10 min.) • Homework check ✔**Formative Assessment** (10 min.) • Prueba 2-1: Vocabulary recognition	**Vocabulario en uso 1** (25 min.) • Interactive Whiteboard Vocabulary Activities • Actividades 7, 8, 9, 10 • Ampliación del lenguaje	**Wrap-up and Homework Options** (5 min.) • Actividades 11, 12 • Writing Activities • Prueba 2-2 with Study Plan: Vocabulary production
5	**Warm-up** (10 min.) • Homework check ✔**Formative Assessment** (10 min.) • Prueba 2-2 with Study Plan: Vocabulary production	**Gramática y vocabulario en uso 1** (25 min.) • Actividad 13 • Presentation: Pretérito vs. imperfecto • Interactive Whiteboard Grammar Activities • Actividades 15, 16 • Writing Activity	**Wrap-up and Homework Options** (5 min.) • Core Practice 2-5
6	**Warm-up** (10 min.) • Actividad 14 • Homework check	**Gramática y vocabulario en uso 1** (35 min.) • Actividades 17, 18 • Communicative Pair Activity • Presentation: *Estar* + participio • Interactive Whiteboard Grammar Activities • Actividad 19	**Wrap-up and Homework Options** (5 min.) • Writing Activity • Prueba 2-3 with Study Plan: Pretérito vs. imperfecto
7	**Warm-up** (10 min.) • Fondo cultural • Homework check ✔**Formative Assessment** (10 min.) • Prueba 2-3 with Study Plan: Pretérito vs. imperfecto	**Gramática y vocabulario en uso 1** (25 min.) • Actividades 20, 21, 22 • El español en la comunidad • Communicative Pair Activity	**Wrap-up and Homework Options** (5 min.) • Core Practice 2-6, 2-7 • Prueba 2-4 with Study Plan: *Estar* + participio
8	**Warm-up** (15 min.) • Writing Activity • Homework check ✔**Formative Assessment** (10 min.) • Prueba 2-4 with Study Plan: *Estar* + participio	**Vocabulario en contexto 2** (20 min.) • Presentation: Vocabulario y gramática en contexto • Actividades 23, 24	**Wrap-up and Homework Options** (5 min.) • Clip Art Vocabulary • Examen: Vocabulario y gramática 1
9	**Warm-up** (5 min.) • Homework check ✔**Formative Assessment** (30 min.) • Examen: Vocabulario y gramática	**Vocabulario en contexto 2** (10 min.) • Presentation: Espectáculos del mundo latino • Actividad 25	**Wrap-up and Homework Options** (5 min.) • Actividad 26 • Core Practice 2-8, 2-9 • Prueba 2-5: Vocabulary recognition
10	**Warm-up** (20 min.) • Actividad 25 • Homework check ✔**Formative Assessment** (10 min.) • Prueba 2-5: Vocabulary recognition	**Vocabulario en uso 2** (15 min.) • Actividades 30, 31 • Interactive Whiteboard Vocabulary Activities	**Wrap-up and Homework Options** (5 min.) • Actividades 28, 29 • Prueba 2-6 with Study Plan: Vocabulary production

REGULAR SCHEDULE (50 MINUTES)

DAY	Warm-up / Assess	Preview / Present / Practice / Communicate	Wrap-up / Homework Options
11	**Warm-up** (10 min.) • Writing Activity • Homework check ✔**Formative Assessment** (10 min.) • Prueba 2-6 with Study Plan: Vocabulary production	**Gramática y vocabulario en uso 2** (25 min.) • Presentation: *Ser y estar* • Interactive Whiteboard Grammar Activities • Actividades 32, 33, 34 • Communicative Pair Activity	**Wrap-up and Homework Options** (5 min.) • Actividad 35 • Core Practice 2-10 • Prueba 2-7 with Study Plan: *Ser y estar*
12	**Warm-up** (10 min.) • Writing Activity • Homework check ✔**Formative Assessment** (10 min.) • Prueba 2-7 with Study Plan: *Ser y estar*	**Gramática y vocabulario en uso 2** (25 min.) • Presentation: Verbos con distinto sentido en el pretérito y en el imperfecto • Interactive Whiteboard Grammar Activities • Actividades 36, 37	**Wrap-up and Homework Options** (5 min.) • Core Practice 2-11, 2-12 • Prueba 2-8 with Study Plan: Verbos con distinto sentido en el pretérito y en el imperfecto
13	**Warm-up** (10 min.) • Homework check ✔**Formative Assessment** (10 min.) • Prueba 2-8 with Study Plan: Verbos con distinto sentido en el pretérito y en el imperfecto	**Gramática y vocabulario en uso 2** (25 min.) • Actividades 38, 39 • Fondo cultural • Communicative Pair Activity	**Wrap-up and Homework Options** (5 min.) • Examen: Vocabulario y gramática 2
14	**Warm-up** (8 min.) • Homework check ✔**Formative Assessment** (30 min.) • Examen: Vocabulario y gramática 2	**¡Adelante!** (10 min.) • Presentación oral: Steps 1, 2	**Wrap-up and Homework Options** (2 min.) • Presentación oral: Step 2
15	**Warm-up** (10 min.) • Presentación oral: Step 2	**¡Adelante!** (35 min.) • Presentación oral: Step 3	**Wrap-up and Homework Options** (5 min.) • El mundo de Francisco de Goya • ¿Comprendiste?
16	**Warm-up** (15 min.) • El mundo de Francisco de Goya: ¿Comprendiste? • Homework check	**¡Adelante!** (30 min.) • Escribe tu opinión • ¿Qué me cuentas? 1, 2, 3 • View Video	**Wrap-up and Homework Options** (5 min.) • Presentación escrita: Steps 1, 2
17	**Warm-up** (10 min.) • Homework check	**¡Adelante!** (15 min.) • Presentación escrita: Step 3 **Repaso** (20 min.) • Preparación para el examen: Actividades 3, 4	**Wrap-up and Homework Options** (5 min.) • Presentación escrita: Step 4
18	**Warm-up** (10 min.) • Homework check	**¡Adelante!** (35 min.) • Lectura • ¿Comprendiste? • Fondo cultural	**Wrap-up and Homework Options** (5 min.) • Core Practice: Organizer 2-13, 2-14 • Instant Check
19	**Warm-up** (20 min.) • Preparación para el examen: Actividades 1, 2 • Homework check	**Repaso** (25 min.) • Preparación para el examen: Actividades 5, 6, 7 • Other review	**Wrap-up and Homework Options** (5 min.) • Examen del capítulo
20	**Warm-up** (5 min.) • Answer questions ✔**Summative Assessment** (44 min.) • Examen del capítulo		**Wrap-up and Homework Options** (1 min.) • A ver si recuerdas: Capítulo 3

BLOCK SCHEDULE (90 MINUTES)

DAY	Warm-up / Assess	Preview / Present / Practice / Communicate	Wrap-up / Homework Options
1	**Warm-up (35 min.)** • Return Examen del capítulo: Capítulo 1 • A ver si recuerdas . . . • Actividad 5 • Homework check	**Chapter Opener (10 min.)** • Objectives • Arte y cultura **Vocabulario en contexto 1 (30 min.)** • Presentation: Vocabulario y gramática en contexto • Actividades 1, 2 • Presentation: Entrevista con Dina Bursztyn • Actividad 3 • Presentation: Artistas latinoamericanos • Actividades 4, 5 **Vocabulario en uso 1 (10 min.)** • Actividades 6, 7	**Wrap-up and Homework Options (5 min.)** • Core Practice 2-3, 2-4 • Clip Art Vocabulary • Prueba 2-1: Vocabulary recognition
2	**Warm-up (15 min.)** • Actividad 8 • Homework check ✓**Formative Assessment (10 min.)** • Prueba 2-1: Vocabulary recognition	**Vocabulario en uso 1 (60 min.)** • Actividades 9, 10, 11, 12, 13 • Interactive Whiteboard Vocabulary Activities • Ampliación del lenguaje • Communicative Pair Activity	**Wrap-up and Homework Options (5 min.)** • Writing Activities • Prueba 2-2 with Study Plan: Vocabulary production
3	**Warm-up (15 min.)** • Writing Activity • Homework check ✓**Formative Assessment (10 min.)** • Prueba 2-2 with Study Plan: Vocabulary production	**Gramática y vocabulario en uso 1 (60 min.)** • Presentation: Pretérito vs. imperfecto • Interactive Whiteboard Grammar Activities • Actividades 14, 15, 16, 18 • Fondo cultural • Audio and Writing Activities	**Wrap-up and Homework Options (5 min.)** • Core Practice 2-5 • Prueba 2-3 with Study Plan: Pretérito vs. imperfecto
4	**Warm-up (10 min.)** • Actividad 17 • Homework check ✓**Formative Assessment (10 min.)** • Prueba 2-3 with Study Plan: Pretérito vs. imperfecto	**Gramática y vocabulario en uso 1 (50 min.)** • Presentation: *Estar* + participio • Interactive Whiteboard Grammar Activities • Actividades 19, 20, 21, 22 • El español en la comunidad • Communicative Pair Activity **Vocabulario en contexto 2 (15 min.)** • Presentation: Vocabulario y gramática en contexto • Actividades 23, 24	**Wrap-up and Homework Options (5 min.)** • Core Practice 2-6, 2-7 • Prueba 2-4 with Study Plan: *Estar* + participio • Examen: Vocabulario y gramática 1
5	**Warm-up (10 min.)** • Writing Activity • Homework check ✓**Formative Assessment Options (40 min.)** • Prueba 2-4 with Study Plan: *Estar* + participio • Examen: Vocabulario y gramática 1	**Vocabulario en contexto 2 (20 min.)** • Presentation: Espectáculos del mundo latino • Actividades 25, 26, 27 **Vocabulario en uso 2 (15 min.)** • Actividades 30, 31 • Interactive Whiteboard Vocabulary Activities	**Wrap-up and Homework Options (5 min.)** • Core Practice 2-8, 2-9 • Prueba 2-5: Vocabulary recognition
6	**Warm-up (20 min.)** • Actividades 28, 29 • Homework check ✓**Formative Assessment (10 min.)** • Prueba 2-5: Vocabulary recognition	**Gramática y vocabulario en uso 2 (55 min.)** • Presentation: *Ser* y *estar* • Actividades 32, 33, 34, 35 • Interactive Whiteboard Grammar Activities • Fondo cultural • En voz alta • Writing Activities	**Wrap-up and Homework Options (5 min.)** • Core Practice 2-10 • Pruebas 2-6, 2-7 with Study Plans: Vocabulary production, *ser* y *estar*

BLOCK SCHEDULE (90 MINUTES)

DAY	Warm-up / Assess	Preview / Present / Practice / Communicate	Wrap-up / Homework Options
7	**Warm-up** (10 min.) • Homework check ✔**Formative Assessment** (20 min.) • Pruebas 2-6, 2-7 with Study Plans: Vocabulary production, *ser* y *estar*	**Gramática y vocabulario en uso 2** (40 min.) • Presentation: Verbos con distinto sentido en el pretérito y en el imperfecto • Interactive Whiteboard Grammar Activities • Actividades 36, 37, 38, 39 • Fondo cultural **¡Adelante!** (15 min.) • Presentación oral: Steps 1, 2	**Wrap-up and Homework Options** (5 min.) • Presentación oral: Step 2
8	**Warm-up** (10 min.) • Writing Activity • Homework check ✔**Formative Assessment** (40 min.) • Presentación oral: Step 3	**Gramática y vocabulario en uso 2** (20 min.) • Communicative Pair Activity **¡Adelante!** (15 min.) • Presentation: El mundo de Francisco de Goya	**Wrap-up and Homework Options** (5 min.) • Core Practice 2-11, 2-12 • Prueba 2-8 with Study Plan: Verbos con distinto sentido en el pretérito y en el imperfecto • Examen: Vocabulario y gramática 2
9	**Warm-up** (10 min.) • Homework check ✔**Formative Assessment Options** (30 min.) • Prueba 2-8 with Study Plan: Verbos con distinto sentido en el pretérito y en el imperfecto • Examen: Vocabulario y gramática 2	**¡Adelante!** (45 min.) • El mundo de Francisco de Goya • ¿Comprendiste? • Escribe tu opinión • ¿Qué me cuentas? 1, 2, 3 • Presentación escrita: Step 1 • Video • Video Activities	**Wrap-up and Homework Options** (5 min.) • Presentación escrita: Step 2 • Preparación para el examen: Actividades 1, 2
10	**Warm-up** (20 min.) • Presentación escrita: Step 3 • Homework check	**¡Adelante!** (35 min.) • Lectura • ¿Comprendiste? • Fondo cultural **Repaso** (30 min.) • Preparación para el examen: Actividades 3, 4, 6	**Wrap-up and Homework Options** (5 min.) • Presentación escrita: Step 4 • Core Practice: Organizer 2-13, 2-14 • Instant Check • Preparación para el examen: Actividades 5, 7 • Examen del capítulo
11	**Warm-up** (30 min.) • Homework check ✔**Summative Assessment** (30 min.) • Examen del capítulo	**Theme Game** (15 min.) **A ver si recuerdas – Capítulo 3** (10 min.) • Presentation: Vocabulario • Presentation: Gramática	**Wrap-up and Homework Options** (5 min.) • A ver si recuerdas – Capítulo 3 • Actividades 1–6 • Core Practice 3-1, 3-2

2 Recycle

A ver si recuerdas | ▷

▼ **Objectives**
▸ Discuss and express opinions about paintings
▸ Read and write about art and artists

Vocabulario Repaso

Core Instruction

Standards: 1.1, 2.2

Resources: Voc. and Gram. Transparency 49; Fine Art Transparencies with Teacher's Guide, p. 47

Suggestions: Before presenting the material in this review section, consider testing your students' command of the material by assigning the Study Plan. Students will automatically be given additional practice of the material they have not yet mastered, and you can focus your review based on the class's overall performance on the post-test.

Call out vocabulary items from the six categories in random order. Have a volunteer use the item you call out to make a statement about one or both of the paintings.

1 Standards: 1.1

Focus: Practicing review vocabulary

Suggestions: For Step 1, make sure students choose vocabulary from various categories, rather than just one or two. Point out that the sentence starters in Steps 2 and 3 are suggestions. Encourage students to experiment with other ways to incorporate the vocabulary in their paired discussion about the paintings.

Answers will vary.

Extension: During their discussion in pairs, ask students to write down their partner's comments about the paintings. Then have students take turns reporting their partners' comments to the class: *Victoria cree que el cuadro de Picasso es....*

Teaching with Art

Resources: Fine Art Transparencies with Teacher's Guide p. 47

To guide the discussion of the two paintings, ask: *¿Cuál de los dos cuadros tiene un estilo más realista? ¿Puedes explicar tu respuesta? ¿Qué elementos tienen en común los cuadros? ¿Cuál de los dos cuadros prefieres? ¿Por qué?*

Block Schedule

Have a pair of students pantomime two people with contrasting characteristics. The class should guess what is being portrayed using comparatives, superlatives, and adjective agreement.

62

Vocabulario Repaso

el arte y los artistas
el / la artista
el cuadro
dibujar
el estilo
la estatua
el museo
pintar
el pintor, la pintora

color y luz
amarillo, -a
anaranjado, -a
azul
blanco, -a
claro, -a
gris
marrón
morado, -a
negro, -a
oscuro, -a
pastel
rojo, -a
rosado, -a
verde
vivo, -a

opiniones
a mí también / tampoco
creo que . . .
estoy / no estoy de acuerdo
me parece que . . .
me gusta / no me gusta
no estoy seguro, -a
para mí, ti . . .
¿qué te parece?

"Paisaje Juan les Pins", (1920), Pablo Picasso
Oil on canvas, 52 x 70 cm. Musée Picasso, Paris, France. © 2009 Estate of Pablo Picasso/Artists Rights Society (ARS), New York. Photo: R. G. Ojeda/Réunion des Musées Nationaux/Art Resource, NY.

"Paisaje hondureño de San Antonio de Oriente", (1957), José Antonio Velásquez
Oil on canvas. 26" x 37". Collection of the Art Museum of the Americas. Organization of American States.

materiales
el oro
el papel
la piedra
el plástico
la plata

descripciones
aburrido, -a
bonito, -a
complicado, -a
divertido, -a
exagerado, -a
fascinante
feo, -a
horrible
interesante
mejor
moderno, -a
peor
realista
sencillo, -a
serio, -a
triste

comparaciones
más / menos . . . que
mejor / peor . . . que
tan . . . como

▼1 El arte |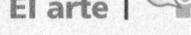

Escribir • Hablar

1 Haz una lista de diez palabras que describan estas obras de arte.

2 Usa la información que escribiste para describir las pinturas a tu compañero(a). Usa como guía las siguientes preguntas: ¿Cómo son? ¿Qué representan?

> *El cuadro de . . . es . . .*
> *El cuadro de . . . muestra . . .*

3 Intercambia opiniones con tu compañero(a).

• Pregúntale su opinión.
"¿Cuál de los cuadros . . . ?"

• Expresa tu opinión.
Yo creo que el cuadro de . . . es . . .
No estoy de acuerdo . . . porque . . .

62 sesenta y dos
A ver si recuerdas . . .

DIFFERENTIATED INSTRUCTION

Students with Learning Difficulties

Have students create their own visual clues to reinforce new vocabulary. As they choose and list adjectives in *Actividad* 1, encourage them to utilize simple drawings, colored pencils, or colored chalk to help reinforce the meanings of the descriptive words they have chosen.

Advanced Learners

Have students write a paragraph describing the scene in the Picasso painting. Encourage them to study the painting closely in order to find real-world elements that Picasso chose to portray in an unusual way. For example, the wavy lines in the upper right most likely portray the sea. What do they think some of the other shapes and colors represent?

Gramática Repaso

Concordancia y comparación de adjetivos

Adjectives agree in gender and number with the persons or things they describe. Masculine adjectives usually end in -o and feminine adjectives usually end in -a.

> una estatua **moderna**   un cuadro **moderno**

- Adjectives that end in -e or in a consonant may be either feminine or masculine.

> un cuadro **interesante**   una estatua **gris**

- Adjectives that end in -ista may be either masculine or feminine.

> un dibujo **realista**   una pintora **surrealista**

- To form the feminine form of adjectives that end in -or, add -a at the end.

> un niño **trabajador**   una niña **trabajadora**

- If an adjective describes a combination of masculine and feminine nouns, the masculine plural ending is used.

> Ese cuadro y esa estatua no son **feos**.

To express a comparison of similarity, use *tan* + adjective + *como*.

> El cuadro de Picasso es **tan bonito como** el cuadro de Velásquez.

To express a comparison of difference, use *más / menos* + adjective + *que*.

> El cuadro de Picasso me parece **más / menos interesante que** el de Velásquez.

- The adjectives *bueno(a)*, *malo(a)*, *viejo(a)*, and *joven* have irregular comparative forms. The words *más / menos* are not used.

bueno(a)	**mejor (que)**	viejo(a)	**mayor (que)**
malo(a)	**peor (que)**	joven	**menor (que)**

▼2 El museo de arte

Leer • Escribir

Dos amigos fueron al museo. Completa lo que dijeron con la forma correcta de los adjetivos del recuadro.

complicado	moderno	plástico
exagerado	fascinante	

A —Ayer fui a un museo de arte __1.__ y vi unos cuadros __2.__ . Me gustaron mucho. Sin embargo, las estatuas de __3.__ son __4.__ .

B —¿Sí? Pues yo no entiendo el arte moderno. El estilo moderno es __5.__ y tienes que pensar para comprenderlo.

▼3 En mi opinión

Escribir

Usa los siguientes adjetivos para escribir cinco frases que comparen el cuadro de Velásquez con el de Picasso en la página 62. Usa *más / menos . . . que* o *tan . . . como*, según sea necesario.

inteligente	moderno	sencillo
serio	realista	bonito

Modelo
El cuadro de Velásquez me parece tan interesante como el cuadro de Picasso.

Gramática Repaso

Core Instruction

Resources: Voc. and Gram. Transparency 50

Suggestions: Refer students who are having difficulty with comparisons to the *GramActiva* video from Level 2 Chapter 1B, and to the online tutorial. After students review the *Gramática*, write several different adjectives on the board, one at a time. Point to one adjective and say different nouns. Have students use the adjective to modify each noun, making sure it agrees in gender and number each time.

▼2 Standards: 1.2

Resources: Answer Keys: Student Edition, p. 20

Focus: Reviewing adjective agreement

Suggestions: Remind students that in noun phrases such as *museo de arte,* they must consider which noun is being modified in order to know which adjective form to use. In this case, since both nouns are masculine, the same adjective form can be used for either noun. But in a noun phrase such as *sala de cuadros,* they must decide whether they are modifying *sala* or *cuadros.*

Answers:
1. moderno   4. exageradas
2. fascinantes   5. complicado
3. plástico

▼3 Standards: 1.3, 2 .2

Focus: Reviewing comparison of adjectives

Suggestions: Since students are comparing one *cuadro* with another each time, the adjective forms for the activity will all be masculine singular. This allows students to focus on the constructions *más/menos...que* and *tan...como.*

Answers will vary.

ENRICH YOUR TEACHING

Teacher-to-Teacher

Display several works of art of varying styles and periods. These might be reproductions of paintings or photographs of sculptures, ceramics, or other kinds of art. Ask students to select two works of art to compare and not to reveal their choices to anyone. Have them write sentences describing and comparing the two works of art, but not to mention either of them by name. Invite students to take turns sharing their sentences. Ask the rest of the class to decide which two works of art are being described and compared.

Vocabulario Repaso

BELLRINGER REVIEW

Use the verbs in the *reacciones* section of the vocabulary to help students review the preterite. Assign each student a subject pronoun to work with, such as *nosotros* or *tu amigo y tú.* Have students use their subject and one or more of the verbs to create and share sentences about an entertainment event: *¿Tu amigo y tú se aburrieron en el concierto?*

Vocabulario Repaso

Core Instruction

Standards: 1.1

Resources: Voc. and Gram. Transparency 51

Suggestions: Begin by having students use the vocabulary to talk about the photos. Then play *5 preguntas*—a shortened version of 20 Questions. Each student chooses a word or expression and takes a turn at being "it." Other students ask up to five *Si/No* questions to try to determine what the word is: *¿Es una persona? ¿Esta persona canta?*

4 Standards: 1.2, 1.3

Resources: Answer Keys: Student Edition, p. 20

Focus: Practicing review vocabulary

Suggestions: Tell students to look over the complete *mensaje* in Step 1 before writing their answers.

Answers:
Step 1

1.	argumento	4.	actor
2.	comedia	5.	galán
3.	drama	6.	aplaudió

Step 2

Answers will vary.

Extension: Help students practice the vocabulary under the *reacciones* and *comentarios* categories. Have them write and read aloud dialogues of two to three lines in which two people talk about an entertainment event. Provide a model like the following:

—*Anoche vi una obra de teatro inolvidable.*

—*¿Sí? ¿Te divertiste?*

—*¡Muchísimo! Después, aplaudí durante cinco minutos con todo el público.*

en el teatro
la actuación
el argumento
la comedia
el concierto
el drama
los efectos especiales
el ensayo
la escena
la luz
la obra de teatro

en el concierto
el auditorio
la banda
la canción
el coro
la música
la orquesta
la voz

participantes
el actor, la actriz
el bailarín, la bailarina
el / la cantante
el crítico, la crítica
el director, la directora
el galán
el músico, la música
el personaje

actividades
bailar
cantar
ensayar
hacer el papel de . . .
hacer el papel principal
tener éxito
tocar . . .
        la guitarra
        el piano

reacciones
aburrirse
aplaudir
divertirse
dormirse
gritar

comentarios
emocionante
estar basado, -a en . .
flojo, -a
increíble
inolvidable
largo, -a
más o menos
talentoso, -a

▼4 En el teatro

Leer • Escribir

① Completa el siguiente mensaje que te dejó una amiga sobre una noche en el teatro. Usa las palabras del recuadro.

galán	aplaudió	comedia
drama	argumento	actor

Anoche fui al teatro. Desde el principio, el **1.** de la obra me pareció muy divertido. Prefiero ir al teatro a reír con una **2.** que llorar con un **3.** . El **4.** que hacía el papel del **5.** tuvo una actuación extraordinaria. Al final, el público **6.** por más de cinco minutos.

② Usa las palabras del vocabulario para escribir una descripción de estas personas. Trata de incluir información sobre lo que hace la persona y dónde lo hace.

Modelo
un actor
Un actor hace el papel de un personaje en una película o una obra de teatro.

1. un(a) músico(a)   3. un(a) cantante

2. un(a) crítico(a)   4. un bailarín, una bailarina

64 sesenta y cuatro
A ver si recuerdas . . .

DIFFERENTIATED INSTRUCTION

Heritage Language Learners

Have students write a description of a performing arts event that they have seen either in the United States or in their heritage country. Encourage them to use specific descriptive language in order to elaborate on each detail presented. Those who have not recently seen a performing arts event can describe one they would most like to see.

Multiple Intelligences

Musical/Rhythmic: Encourage students to prepare a short selection of music to share with the class. They might play an instrument, sing a song, or bring in a favorite recording. Use these as the basis for the descriptions and comparisons in *Actividad 6* on p. 65.

Gramática Repaso

Comparación de sustantivos y el superlativo

To make a comparison or differentiation between two nouns, use *más/menos* + noun + *que*.

> Hoy hay **menos gente que** ayer en el teatro.

To make a comparison between two similar nouns, use: *tanto(a)* + noun + *como*. Since *tanto* is an adjective, it should agree with the noun in both gender (masculine or feminine) and number (singular or plural).

> Hoy hay **tanto público como** ayer en el teatro.
> Hoy hay **tantas personas como** ayer en el teatro.

The superlative is used to say something is the "most" or the "least." To express a superlative comparison use: *el/la/los/las* + noun + *más/menos* + adjective.

> **El concierto más emocionante** fue el de ayer.
> Para mí, **la obra menos divertida** es "Algún día".

- When *mejor* and *peor* are used as superlatives, the following construction is used: *el/la/los/las* + *mejor(es)/peor(es)* + noun.

> Pienso que Alejandra Ruiz es **la mejor bailarina.**
> ¡Ustedes son **los peores cantantes!**

- The preposition *de* is used after the adjective when the superlative comparison occurs within a group or category.

> El concierto de ayer fue **el más emocionante de** todos.

▼5 ¿Qué opinas? |

Hablar

Un(a) compañero(a) y tú van a expresar su opinión sobre los siguientes temas.

▶ **Modelo**
la mejor película del año
A —*Para ti, ¿cuál fue la mejor película del año?*
B —*Para mí, la mejor película fue "Frida".*

a. el mejor actor de teatro
b. la peor actriz de Hollywood
c. la canción más romántica de este año
d. el baile que les gusta más a los jóvenes
e. el programa de tele más aburrido de la semana

▼6 La fiesta

Escribir

Escribe comparaciones entre dos artistas o grupos de música. Usa los siguientes temas.

- número de canciones que grabaron
- talento que tienen
- instrumentos que tocan

Modelo
Shakira tiene más canciones que Selena.

Más práctica	GO

realidades.com | print

A *ver si recuerdas* with Study Plan	✔	
Guided WB pp. 48–51	✔	✔
Core WB pp. 21–22	✔	✔
Hispanohablantes WB p. 44		✔

sesenta y cinco **65**
Capítulo 2

ENRICH YOUR TEACHING

Teacher-to-Teacher

Ask students to form small groups based on topics of shared interest. Have them talk about their common interest and create a few comparative and superlative statements about it to share with the class.

21st Century Skills

Initiative and Self-Direction Direct students to the online tutorials available in **realidades.com** for self-directed review of the grammar topics recycled in this chapter. Students can expand their own learning by reviewing the related English grammar first, then proceed to the new Spanish grammar point.

Recycle 2

Gramática Repaso

Core Instruction

Resources: Voc. and Gram. Transparency 52
Suggestions: Refer students who are having difficulty with superlatives to the *GramActiva* video from Level 1 Chapter 6A, and to the online tutorial. On the board, write the frames for the two constructions:

más/menos + noun + que

el/la/los/las + noun + más/menos + adj.

Fill the frames with different nouns and adjectives from p. 50 that make sense and have students create sentences using the results: *Hay más público que actores en el teatro. Los bailarines son los más talentosos de todos.*

▼5 Standards: 1.3
Focus: Reviewing noun comparisons
Suggestions: For further practice, have students think of additional categories for their comparisons.
Answers will vary.

▼6 Standards: 1.1
Focus: Reviewing comparatives
Suggestions: Partners might share opinions or discuss their differing opinions. After they have gone through the list together, invite them to share their opinions with the rest of the class.
Answers will vary.

Extension: Ask students to collect the opinions of the class and compile the information in a chart. Consider keeping this chart and bringing it out again a few months from now to see how students' opinions have changed.

☑ ASSESSMENT

A ver si recuerdas with Study Plan (online only)
After presenting the review material on these pages, assign the *A ver si recuerdas* Study Plan to evaluate students' mastery of the material. Additional practice for students who need it is available online.

Standards for Foreign Language Learning: *Capítulo* 2

- To meet the Standards, students will:

Communication

1.1 Interpersonal
- Talk about the style, features, tools, and media used in the creation of works of visual, literary, and performing art
- Talk about important artists and art museums
- Talk about events in the past

1.2 Interpretive
- Read and listen to information about the style, features, tools, and media used in the creation of works of visual, literary, and performing art
- Read and listen to information about important artists
- Read about the suffix *-ismo*
- Read about a family party
- Read about art museums, arts and entertainment reviews
- Read about events in the past
- Read song lyrics by Juan Luis Guerra

1.3 Presentational
- Write about the style, tools, and media used in the creation of visual, literary, and performing art
- Write and present information orally about artists
- Write arts and entertainment reviews and write about their contents
- Present orally about "the artist of the millennium"
- Write a review of a student audition

Culture

2.1 Practices and Perspectives
- Explain the practices and perspectives of important Latin American and Spanish figures in the visual, literary, and performing arts

2.2 Products and Perspectives
- Discuss the work of important Latin American and Spanish figures in the visual, literary, and performing arts
- Talk about Museo del Barrio and its cultural roots
- Talk about the popular TV show *Sábado Gigante*
- Describe *salsa* music
- Discuss the song lyrics of Juan Luis Guerra
- Talk about a Spanish version of *El Rey León*

Connections

3.1 Cross-curricular
- Talk about key facts about the fine arts
- Talk about key facts about the Mexican Revolution
- Talk about key facts about the history of Spain
- Discuss Language Arts strategies: using illustrations, using context clues, using visuals, organizing information, categorizing, monitoring your reading
- Discuss the Language Arts skill of using graphic organizers

3.2 Target Culture
- Read the titles of works of art
- Read a famous slogan from the Mexican Revolution
- Read an advertisement for El Museo del Barrio
- Read about the cultural significance of the term *salsa*
- Read song lyrics by Juan Luis Guerra
- Read an excerpt from a work by Esmeralda Santiago

Comparisons

4.1 Language
- Compare Spanish words to their English counterparts
- Compare Spanish comparatives, superlatives to English
- Compare the uses of English and Spanish past tenses

Capítulo 2 ¿Cómo te expresas?

▼ Chapter Objectives

Communication
By the end of the chapter you will be able to:
- Listen and read about art and music
- Talk and write about music and theater performances
- Discuss and explain art school activities

Culture
You will also be able to:
- Compare how artists express their ideas
- Understand the historical context of a famous artist
- Understand the perspective of a person living between cultures

You will demonstrate what you know and can do:
- Presentación oral, p. 97
- Presentación escrita, pp. 98–99
- Preparación para el examen, pp. 106–107

You will use:

Vocabulary
- Art forms, genres, materials and professions
- Works of art and artists
- Performing arts: Music, dance, stage

Grammar
- Preterite vs. imperfect
- Verb *estar* + participle
- *Ser* and *estar*
- Verbs with different meanings in the imperfect and preterite

Exploración del mundo hispano

Country Connection
Art and Artists

Nueva York
España
Cuba
México
El Salvador
Puerto Rico
Colombia
Ecuador
Chile
Argentina

realidades.com GO

📖 Reference Atlas
▶ Videonovela y actividades

🌎 Mapa global interactivo

Clase de música del proyecto juvenil
Por mi Barrio en San Salvador, El Salvador

ENRICH YOUR TEACHING

Using Backward Design
Have students preview the sample performance tasks on *Preparación para el examen,* p. 107, and connect them to the Chapter Objectives. Explain to students that by completing the sample tasks, they can self-assess their learning progress.

Mapa global interactivo
Download the *Mapa global interactivo* files for Chapter 2 and preview the activities. Activity 1 takes you to the Picasso Museum in Málaga, Spain. In Activity 2, you explore the world of Salvador Dalí in Spain. In Activity 3, discover the theaters of Madrid, Spain. In Activity 4, look at migration patterns from Puerto Rico to the United States.

4.2 Culture
• Compare growing up in one culture to growing up in more than one culture

Communities

5.1 Beyond the School
• Link to Web sites from the Spanish-speaking world

5.2 Lifelong Learner
• Develop an appreciation for artistic role models
• Develop an appreciation for the fine arts
• Recognize sources of artistic inspiration
• Discuss how culture impacts personality

 **PresentationExpress™**
See pp. 62c–62d

Chapter Opener
Core Instruction

Resources: Map Transparencies, 14, 16–20, 22

Suggestions: Introduce students to the theme and objectives of the chapter.

▶ **Videonovela** *¡Pura vida!* View this stand-alone storyline video about five young adults in San José, Costa Rica with your class, either online or on DVD.

Arte y cultura

Standards: 1.1, 1.2, 2.2, 3.1

Resources: Fine Art Transparencies with Teacher's Guide, p. 48

🌐 **Mapa global interactivo, Actividad 1** Locate the Picasso Museum in Málaga, Spain.

Suggestions: Have volunteers point to various parts of the painting and say what they think they portray. Review the vocabulary of colors, shapes, and physical location so students are better able to describe the artwork.

Answers will vary, but may include American cubists such as Stuart Davis, Alfred Maurer, or Max Weber.

▶ **TEACHING WITH ART**
Resources: Fine Art Transparencies with Teacher's Guide, p. 48

Arte y cultura | España

Picasso y el cubismo Si observas con atención esta pintura del artista español Pablo Picasso (1881–1973), te vas a dar cuenta de que el artista representa a la modelo, a la izquierda, y al pintor, a la derecha, con formas geométricas. A esta forma de expresión se la conoce como cubismo, un movimiento artístico que comenzó en Francia entre 1907 y 1914, y que tuvo una gran importancia en Europa y los Estados Unidos.

• ¿Conoces un artista de los Estados Unidos que usa formas geométricas en sus obras?

▼ "El pintor y su modelo", (1928), Pablo Picasso
Oil on canvas, 51 1/8 x 64 1/4 inches. The Sidney and Harriet Janis Collection, #644.19. © 2009 Estate of Pablo Picasso/Artists Rights Society (ARS), New York. Photo: ©The Museum of Modern Art/Scala/Art Resource, NY.

sesenta y siete **67**
Capítulo 2

DIFFERENTIATED INSTRUCTION

Digital resources such as the *Interactive Whiteboard* activity banks, *Videomodelos*, additional *Online Activities*, *Study Plans*, automatically graded *Leveled Workbook*, animated *Grammar Tutorials*, *Flashcards*, and *Vocabulary and Grammar Videos* will help you reach students of different ability levels and learning styles.

STUDENTS NEEDING EXTRA HELP

Guided Practice Activities
• Flashcards, pp. 52–54, 63–66
• Vocabulary Check, pp. 55–58, 67–70
• Grammar, pp. 59–62, 71–74

HERITAGE LEARNERS

Realidades para hispanohablantes
• Chapter Opener, pp. 44–45
• A primera vista, pp. 46–47, 56–57
• Manos a la obra, pp. 48–55, 58–65
• ¡Adelante!, pp. 66–71
• Repaso del capítulo, pp. 72–75

ADVANCED/PRE-AP*

Pre-AP* Resource Book,
• pp. 141–143

Communications Workbook
• Integrated Performance Assessment, p. 172

Vocabulario en contexto

Core Instruction

Standards: 1.1, 1.2, 2.2, 3.1, 3.2

Resources: Teacher's Resource Book: Input Script, p. 90, Clip Art, pp. 110–116, Audio Script, p. 94; Voc. and Gram. Transparencies, p. 53; Audio Program DVD: Cap. 2, Tracks 1, 3; Fine Art Transparencies with Teacher's Guide, p. 39

Focus: Presenting new vocabulary and using grammar lexically in context

Suggestions: Use the Input Script from the *Teacher's Resource Book* as a source of ideas for presentation of new vocabulary and comprehensible input. Use pantomime to clarify the meaning of the adjectives *sentado(a)* and *parado(a).* For objects, use TPR. Name an object on the transparency and ask a volunteer to come and point to it. Point out that *mural, famoso(a), abstracto(a), expresar,* and *representar* are cognates.

BELLRINGER REVIEW

Show the Fine Art Transparency, *"El pintor y su modelo"* by Picasso and lead a class discussion about how many people they believe they are seeing in the painting. Mention/Point out body parts to confirm.

1 Standards: 1.2

Resources: Teacher's Resource Book: Audio Script, p. 94; Audio Program DVD: Cap. 2, Track 2; Answer Keys: Student Edition, p. 20

Focus: Practicing listening comprehension of new vocabulary

Suggestions: Before engaging students in the listening activity, give them a few minutes to read over and study p. 68 silently. Then play the audio or read the script aloud.

Answers:

1. C	4. C
2. F	5. C
3. F	6. C

Read, listen to, and understand information about
▶ different types of art
▶ art materials
▶ works of art

Vocabulario en contexto

Los estudiantes de la escuela Simón Bolívar de Caracas, Venezuela, querían decorar la cafetería de su escuela. Para esto, decidieron pintar un mural en una pared de la cafetería. Antes de comenzar a pintar, los estudiantes se reunieron en el taller de arte para planear lo que querían hacer.

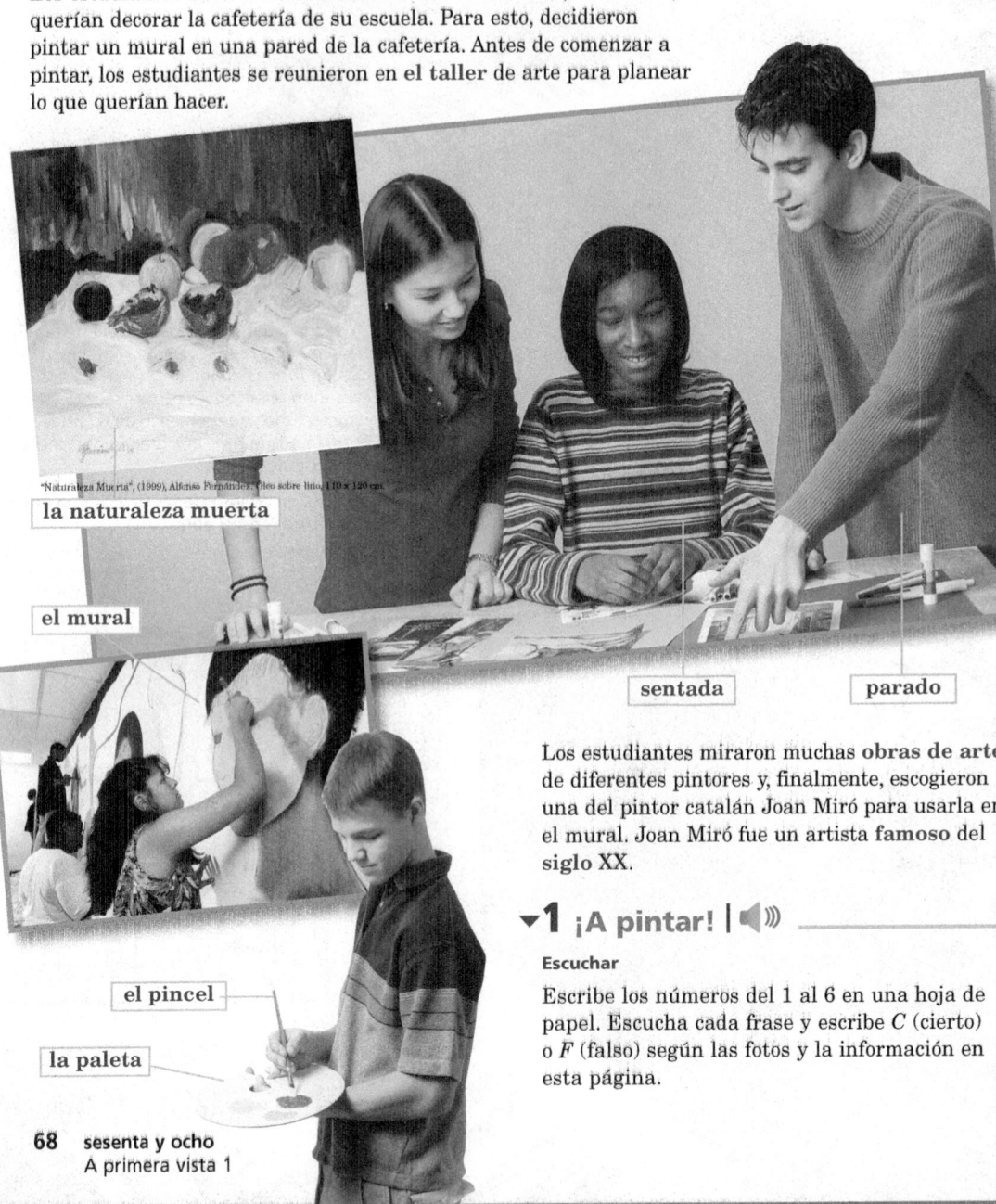

"Naturaleza Muerta", (1999), Alfonso Fernández. Oleo sobre lina, 110 x 120 cm.

la naturaleza muerta

el mural

sentada   **parado**

el pincel

la paleta

Los estudiantes miraron muchas **obras de arte** de diferentes pintores y, finalmente, escogieron una del pintor catalán Joan Miró para usarla en el mural. Joan Miró fue un artista **famoso** del **siglo XX**.

▼1 ¡A pintar! | 🔊

Escuchar

Escribe los números del 1 al 6 en una hoja de papel. Escucha cada frase y escribe *C* (cierto) o *F* (falso) según las fotos y la información en esta página.

68   sesenta y ocho
A primera vista 1

DIFFERENTIATED INSTRUCTION

Advanced Learners

Ask students to work together to draw and label the floor plan of the art room in your school. Encourage them to include details such as furniture, art supplies, and the various types of art that are currently on display or projects that are in progress. Then have them share the floor plan with the rest of the class. They can point out the various features of the room, tell where each of them works when they are in art class, and talk about art projects they may be currently involved in. Listeners can join in and talk about their own experiences in the art room.

Éstas son algunas de las obras de Miró que los estudiantes miraron cuando estaban buscando un cuadro para su mural.

1 Cuando era joven, Miró pintaba con un estilo realista, como podemos ver en el paisaje "La granja", de 1922. En este paisaje se ve en primer plano un árbol entre una casa y un establo (*stable*). Al fondo del cuadro vemos el cielo y la luna.

fondo

primer plano

¹"La Granja", (1922), Joan Miró

2 En esta pintura de 1919, el joven Miró hizo su propio **retrato**, es decir, pintó su autorretrato.

la pintura

el autorretrato

²"Autorretrato", (1919), Joan Miró

3 Más tarde, el estilo de Miró se vuelve mucho menos realista, como se ve en este "Interior holandés", de 1928.

³"Interior holandés", (1928), Joan Miró

¹ Oil on canvas, National Gallery of Art, Washington DC, USA/© 2009 Successió Miró/Artists Rights Society (ARS), New York/ADAGP, Paris. Photo: Index/The Bridgeman Art Library

² Oil on canvas. © 2009 Successió Miró/Artists Rights Society (ARS), New York/ADAGP, Paris. Photo: J. G. Berizzi. Musée Picasso, Paris, France.

³ Oil on canvas, 36 1/8 x 28 3/4 inches. Mrs. Simon Guggenheim Fund, #163.1945, The Museum of Modern Art© 2009 Successió Miró/Artists Rights Society (ARS), New York/ADAGP, Paris. Photo: Scala/Art Resource, NY.

4 Cuando ya era un artista famoso, Miró comenzó su obra de **escultor**. Esta **escultura** es **abstracta**, no vemos claramente lo que **representa**, pero sus colores vivos **expresan** sentimientos de alegría.

"Pair of lovers with almond blossom games", 1975, Joan Miró. Painted synthetic resin, 273 x 127 x 140 cm./300 x 160 x 140 cm/ Fundació Joan Miró, Barcelona/© 2009 Successió Miró/Artists Rights Society (ARS), New York/ ADAGP, Paris. Photo: Jaume Blassi.

▼**2 El guía del museo** | 🔊

Escuchar

Escucha la descripción que hace un guía de museo de las obras de arte que aparecen en la página. Señala cada obra que describe.

sesenta y nueve 69
Capítulo 2

2 Standards: 1.2

Resources: Voc. and Gram. Transparency 54; Teacher's Resource Book: Audio Script, p. 94; Audio Program DVD: Cap. 2, Track 4; Answer Keys: Student Edition, p. 21

Focus: Practicing listening comprehension of new vocabulary

Suggestions: Use the audio or read the script. Allow students to listen more than once. Pause to monitor students, making sure they are identifying the correct works of art.

Answers:
1. 1   3. 3   5. 4
2. 3   4. 2

Extension: Have students write their own set of four comments, one for each work of art pictured on the page. Then have them work in pairs. One student reads his or her comments aloud while the partner identifies which work of art is being described.

Block Schedule

Have students draw a self-portrait modeled after Miró's or in a different style. Then place students in groups of four or five and have each member of the group ask a question about the self-portrait.

Pre-AP* Support

- **Learning Objective:** Interpersonal Speaking
- **Activity:** Have students work in pairs to recreate the interview with Dina Bursztyn on p. 70. One student is the interviewer and the other plays the role of the artist. Have students record their interviews to be used in following classes as a class dictation activity.
- **Pre-AP* Resource Book:** Comprehensive guide to Pre-AP* vocabulary skill development, pp. 51–57

ENRICH YOUR TEACHING

Culture Note

In addition to being a painter and sculptor, Joan Miró was also a printmaker. In 1938, he completed *The Black and Red Series,* a series of eight etchings. Now at the Museum of Modern Art in New York, the series shows the unique characteristics of this printing process.

21st Century Skills

Technology Literacy Have students research other works by Joan Miró on the Internet. What keywords will they use in their search? Ask them to investigate different styles and mediums employed by the artist, as well as any works by Miró in museums in their area.

Vocabulario en contexto

Core Presentation

Standards: 1.2, 2.1, 2.2, 3.1, 5.2

Resources: Teacher's Resource Book: Input Script, p. 91, Clip Art, pp. 110–116, Audio Script, pp. 94–95; Voc. and Gram. Transparency 55; Audio Program DVD: Cap. 2, Track 5; Fine Art Transparencies with Teacher's Guide, p. 12

Focus: Extending presentation of vocabulary and grammar in the context of an interview

Suggestions:

Pre-reading: Direct students' attention to the *Estrategia*. Remind them that, with the amount of Spanish they now know, they can use context clues as they read, in much the same way as they do in English.

Reading: Allow students time to read the interview silently first. Then play the audio or read the interview aloud, with students reading along as they listen. Allow them to listen more than once. Another option after silent reading is to have volunteers take turns reading the parts of the interviewer and Dina Bursztyn.

Post-reading: Complete *Actividad* 3 to check comprehension.

3 Standards: 1.2, 1.3

Resources: Answer Keys: Student Edition, p. 21

Focus: Demonstrating comprehension of the reading passage

Suggestions: Have students share their written answers. Use items 3–5 as a springboard to discussion about art.

Answers:

1. La artista usó barro para hacer la escultura.
2. La tía Fanny influyó mucho en Dina Bursztyn porque pintaba y tenía obras de cerámica en su casa.
3–5. Answers will vary.

Chapter Project

Give students copies of the Chapter Project outline and rubric from the *Teacher's Resource Book*. Explain the task to them, and have them perform Step 1. (For more information, see p. 62-b.)

Entrevista con Dina Bursztyn

Dina Bursztyn es una escultora que nació en Mendoza, Argentina, y vive en Nueva York. Escribe poesía y cuentos y trabaja la **cerámica** para hacer murales y esculturas en distintos lugares de la ciudad.

¿Qué material prefiere para expresarse?
"Principalmente el barro[1], pero también me gusta escribir y pintar".

*¿Qué artista la **inspiró**?*
"Mi mayor **fuente de inspiración** fue mi tía Fanny. Ella pintaba y tenía obras de cerámica en su casa. **Influyó** mucho en mí y empecé a moldear[2]. A los cinco años ya llevaba siempre un poco de plastilina[3] en los bolsillos[4]".

¿De qué está hecha esta escultura?
"*Lady Dreams* está hecha de barro".

*¿Qué representa **la figura** de* Lady Dreams*?*
"Es una suma de **las imágenes** de mis sueños[5]. También hice otras *Ladies*".

*¿Por qué escogió **el tema** de las* Ladies*?*
"Porque siempre me interesaron los mitos[6] y pensé que necesitaba crear nuevos mitos. Entonces decidí crear mi propia mitología".

1 clay 2 to mold 3 modeling clay 4 pockets
5 dreams 6 myths

> **Nota**
> The preterite form of the verb *influir* is similar to the preterite of the verb *destruir: influí, influiste, influyó, influyeron.*

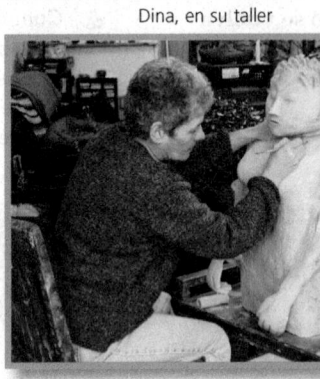

Dina, en su taller

Lady Dreams

> **Estrategia**
> **Context clues**
> When you read, try to determine the meaning of words you don't understand by using context clues. Sometimes words in the same sentence or surrounding sentences will give you the meaning of the word you don't know. For example, if you do not know the meaning of the word barro, you may determine that it is a material for making sculptures by looking at the context.

▼3 Lo que nos dice *Lady Dreams*

Leer • Escribir

1. ¿Qué materiales crees que usó la artista para hacer la escultura *Lady Dreams*?
2. ¿Por qué fue importante la tía Fanny para Dina?
3. ¿Te gusta esta escultura? ¿Por qué?
4. ¿Qué representa *Lady Dreams* para ti?
5. ¿Alguna vez alguien te inspiró a pintar o dibujar algo? Cuenta esa experiencia.

70 setenta
A primera vista 1

DIFFERENTIATED INSTRUCTION

Heritage Language Learners

Have students conduct an interview with a Spanish-speaking professional whose work they respect. Encourage them to prepare questions and to record the interview. Invite them to share the interview with the class.

Students with Learning Difficulties

Direct students to read for specific information about each of the artists presented. Have them create a simple chart with the following headings: ***nombre del artista, país, material, tema.*** Then have students fill in the chart with key points found in the reading.

Artistas latinoamericanos

Durante el siglo XX América Latina tuvo numerosos artistas que, **a través de** sus diferentes estilos, expresaron en sus obras la rica cultura de sus países.

1 El pintor cubano Carlos Enríquez vivió en París en los años 20 y recibió la influencia del **movimiento** surrealista. Sus paisajes **muestran** la naturaleza y la luz intensa de los países del Caribe.

"Paisaje criollo", (1941), Carlos Enríquez
Oil on composition board. 17 1/2" x 23 5/8". Gift of Dr. C. M. Ramírez Corria. (604.1942). The Museum of Modern Art/Licensed by SCALA/Art Resource, NY.

2 El movimiento muralista mexicano muestra un país en el que se mezclan la cultura indígena y la española.

"Hombre controlando el universo", (1934), (detalle del mural) Diego Rivera
© 2009 Banco de México Diego Rivera & Frida Kahlo Museums Trust, México, D.F./Artists Rights Society (ARS), New York/Corbis.

Diego Rivera (en la foto con su esposa, la pintora Frida Kahlo) fue el artista más importante del muralismo mexicano.

3 El pintor ecuatoriano Oswaldo Guayasamín mostró en su obra la cultura de los indígenas de América Latina y cómo vivían muchos de ellos.

"La madre y el niño", (1989), Oswaldo Guayasamín
Photo Nicolas Osorio Ruiz. Museo Fundación Guayasamín, Quito, Ecuador.

▼4 ¿De quién es? |

Leer • Escuchar

Mira las ilustraciones y lee sus descripciones. Escucha las frases; ¿a qué ilustración se refieren?

▼5 Mi favorita | 🗣️👥

Hablar

Escoge la obra de arte que más te gusta de esta página y descríbesela a otro(a) estudiante. Explícale por qué te gusta más que las otras.

Más práctica	GO
**realidades.com	print**	
Instant Check	✔
Guided WB pp. 52–58	✔ ✔
Core WB pp. 23–24	✔ ✔
Comm. WB p. 26	✔ ✔
Hispanohablantes WB pp. 46–47	✔

setenta y uno **71**
Capítulo 2

Language Input **2**

Vocabulario en contexto

Core Instruction

Standards: 1.2, 2.1, 2.2, 3.1, 5.2

Resources: Teacher's Resource Book: Input Script, p. 91, Clip Art, pp. 110–116, Audio Script, p. 95; Voc. and Gram. Transparency 56; Audio Program DVD: Cap. 2, Track 6; Fine Art Transparencies with Teacher's Guide, pp. 19, 32, 55

Focus: Extending presentation of vocabulary and grammar in context

Suggestions: Have students read silently before volunteers read each section aloud.

▼4 Standards: 1.1, 1.2

Resources: Teacher's Resource Book: Audio Script, p. 95; Audio Program DVD: Cap. 2, Track 7; Fine Art Transparencies with Teacher's Guide, pp. 19, 32, 55; Answer Keys: Student Edition, p. 21

Focus: Practicing listening comprehension of new vocabulary

Suggestions: Play the audio or read the script aloud.

Answers:
1. Paisaje criollo
2. Hombre controlando el universo
3. La madre y el niño
4. Hombre controlando el universo
5. La madre y el niño

▼5 Standards: 1.1

Resources: Fine Art Transparencies with Teacher's Guide, pp. 19, 32, 55

Focus: Practicing new vocabulary and structures in a topical conversation

Suggestions: Encourage students to talk about color and light as well as the subject matter of the paintings.

Answers will vary.

✔ASSESSMENT

Prueba: Comprensión del vocabulario 1
• Prueba 2-1: pp. 37–38

ENRICH YOUR TEACHING

Culture Note

Another category of sculpture in Dina Bursztyn's work is her "contemporary artifacts," objects that are both ancient and modern, bridging time and cultures. Some examples of these "machines" include a *Cell Phone to Talk to Oneself,* a *Computer to Slow Down,* and a *Mailbox for Unwritten Letters.*

21st Century Skills

Communication Encourage students to articulate their thoughts and ideas clearly and effectively as they discuss their favorite work of art with each other in *Actividad* 5. Ask them to discuss the style, colors, or medium used by the artist, or the message expressed in their favorite work.

71

▼ Objectives
▸ Discuss art materials and details in paintings
▸ Talk about famous painters
▸ Write about artists and what influences them

2 Practice and Communicate

INTERACTIVE WHITEBOARD
Vocabulary Activities 2-1

6
Standards: 1.2, 1.3

Resources: Answer Keys: Student Edition, p. 22

Focus: Using new words and expressions in sentences

Suggestions: Use the Transparencies to review visualized vocabulary. Leave them on the projector as a visual reference while students work.

Answers:
1. un taller
2. una naturaleza muerta
3. Un siglo
4. inspiración
5. mural

BELLRINGER REVIEW

Write these words on the board and have the class brainstorm items made from these materials: *el oro, la piedra, el plástico, la plata.*

7
Standards: 1.1

Resources: Answer Keys: Student Edition, p. 22

Focus: Practicing new vocabulary

Suggestions: Make sure partners switch roles, so both can practice explaining the uses of the various items.

Answers:
1. A —El pintor usa una paleta y un pincel, ¿no?
   B —Sí, los usa para mezclar los colores.
2. A —Una escultora usa piedra, ¿no?
   B —Sí, la usa para crear una escultura.
3. A —Un(a) poeta usa papel y lápiz, ¿no?
   B —Sí, los usa para escribir sus poesías.
4. A —Un escritor usa una computadora, ¿no?
   B —Sí, la usa para escribir cuentos.

Ampliación del lenguaje
Core Instruction

Standards: 1.2, 4.1

Resources: Answer Keys: Student Edition, p. 22

Focus: Understanding the suffix **-ismo**

Suggestions: Ask students to brainstorm other words they have heard that contain the **-ismo** suffix, such as **idealismo** or **modernismo.**

Answers:
impresionismo, realismo

72

Vocabulario en uso

▼6 Definiciones

Leer • Escribir

Completa cada frase con una palabra o expresión apropiada del recuadro. Luego, escribe frases usando las palabras del recuadro.

| una naturaleza muerta | inspiración | un taller | mural | un siglo |

1. Los artistas generalmente trabajan en _____ .
2. Un cuadro que representa objetos, frutas o comida es _____ .
3. _____ son cien años.
4. Un artista necesita _____ para crear su obra.
5. Cuando la pintura se hace en una pared, se llama _____ .

▼7 ¿La paleta o el pincel? |

Hablar

En el taller de arte, los estudiantes usan diferentes materiales para crear sus obras. Habla con un(a) compañero(a) para explicar lo que usa cada artista y para qué lo usa.

▶ **Modelo**

los niños ✂

A —*Los niños usan tijeras, ¿no?*

B —*Sí, las usan para cortar papel.*

Estudiante A

1. pintor
2. escultora
3. poeta
4. escritor

Estudiante B

¡Respuesta personal!

▼ Ampliación del lenguaje

El sufijo *-ismo* se usa para nombrar una doctrina o un movimiento artístico. Para hablar de los pintores que hacen pinturas *románticas,* usamos la palabra *romanticismo.* Otros ejemplos son:

cubo → **cubismo**   futuro → **futurismo**   surreal → **surrealismo**

Completa cada frase.

Un pintor dijo que quería pintar la *impresión* que tenía del paisaje, por eso llamaron al movimiento __1.__ . Otros querían pintar la vida *real,* y llamaron a su movimiento __2.__ .

DIFFERENTIATED INSTRUCTION

Multiple Intelligences
Visual/Spatial: Have students create a painting or drawing in the style of Miró, Picasso, Velázquez, or one of the other artists discussed in the chapter. Use these "original" works of art to supplement partner discussions in *Actividad 9* on p. 73.

Advanced Learners
Have students prepare and present detailed descriptions of artistic processes such as writing a story, making a ceramic sculpture, painting a mural, or writing a song. Ask them to describe the process step by step. Remind them to use sequencing words such as **primero, segundo, después,** and **finalmente** to help listeners understand their presentations.

▼8 La inspiración de un joven artista

Leer • Escribir

Lee la siguiente entrevista con el pintor chileno Alfonso Fernández. Después, observa el cuadro de este artista y contesta las preguntas.

¿Qué te gustaba hacer cuando eras joven?
"Desde joven me gustaba dibujar más que salir a bailar. Hasta los 15 años, los temas históricos fueron mi fuente de inspiración".

¿Qué artista influyó en tu obra y por qué?
"Cuando empecé a estudiar arte me inspiré en la obra del famoso pintor español Goya, porque a través de su obra criticó el momento político y cultural en que vivió".

¿De qué época era Goya?
"Goya era del siglo XIX".

¿En qué se parece tu obra a la de Goya?
"Goya, como yo, representó al pueblo *(common people)* en su obra".

¿Qué consejo le puedes dar a un joven artista?
"Es importante expresar tus sentimientos en tu obra".

"Naturaleza muerta",
(1999),
Alfonso Fernández
Óleo sobre lino, 110 x 120 cm.
1999.

1. ¿Qué temas inspiraban a Fernández cuando era joven?

2. Más tarde, ¿qué artista influyó en su arte? ¿Cuándo vivió ese artista? ¿En qué se parecen el arte de ese artista y el de Fernández?

3. ¿Qué cree Fernández que debe hacer un joven artista?

4. ¿Tú te expresas a través del arte? ¿Cómo? ¿A través del dibujo, de la pintura o de la escultura? ¿Cuáles son tus fuentes de inspiración?

▼9 Describe el cuadro

Hablar

Diego Rodríguez de Silva y Velázquez (1599–1660) fue el pintor de la corte del rey Felipe IV de España. "Las Meninas", un retrato de la familia real, es su obra maestra. Trabaja con otro(a) estudiante para hablar de los detalles de este cuadro.

 **Modelo**

A —*¿Qué se ve <u>a la derecha de la niña rubia</u>?*

B —*Se ve <u>la figura de un perro sentado</u>.*

"Las Meninas", (1656), Diego Velázquez
Oil on canvas (1656). 318 x 270 cm. Inv. 1174. Museo Nacional
del Prado, Madrid, Spain © Lessing/Art Resource, NY.

Estudiante A

1. en el centro, a la izquierda
2. al fondo, en la puerta
3. en primer plano
4. a la izquierda de la niña rubia
5. en la pared del fondo

Estudiante B

el pintor, parado con los pinceles y la paleta
una niña rubia de pelo largo
un hombre
un cuadro
una joven que le ofrece algo

setenta y tres   **73**
Capítulo 2

ENRICH YOUR TEACHING

Culture Note

Even master painters are influenced and inspired by others. Pablo Picasso, for example, was clearly influenced by the work of other Spanish masters. The connection between Picasso's portraits, such as "Lady in Blue," and the work of Diego de Silva y Velázquez is evident.

Similarly, much of the work during Picasso's Blue Period is reminiscent of the paintings of El Greco in terms of composition and style. The link between Picasso's "Guernica" and Goya's theme of the horror of war is also clear.

10 Standards: 1.1

10 Standards: 1.1

Resources: Fine Art Transparencies with Teacher's Guide, p. 16

Focus: Using new vocabulary and structures in a guessing game

Suggestions: If possible, have students refer to the transparencies for this activity. Otherwise have them refer to the photos in the student book. Have them look over the questions in *Actividad* 11 before they begin the game.

Answers will vary.

11 Standards: 1.2, 1.3, 2.1, 2.2, 3.1, 3.2

Resources: Fine Art Transparencies with Teacher's Guide, p. 40; Answer Keys: Student Edition, p. 24

Focus: Practicing and demonstrating comprehension of new vocabulary and structures

Suggestions: Have students answer the questions in Step 2 as a list first, before attempting to organize this information into a written comparison.

Answers:
1. Los dos artistas son de España.
2. Pintaron en el siglo XX.
3–6. Answers will vary.
7. Es arte surrealista (abstracto).
8–9. Answers will vary.

Country Connection
Core Instruction

Standards: 3.1

Ask students to research on the Internet the hometowns of Joan Miró (*Barcelona, Cataluña*) and Salvador Dalí (*Figueras, Cataluña*). Have them locate these places on a map.

🌐 **Mapa global interactivo, Actividad 2**
Explore the world of Salvador Dalí in Spain.

Teacher-to-Teacher

Have students write a note in which they express their preference for one of the two paintings in *Actividad* 11. They will then exchange notes with a partner who will respond in writing to the preference that was stated.

74

▼**10** Juego |

Hablar

Escoge una de las obras de arte que se encuentran en las páginas 69 y 71. No se la muestres a tu compañero(a). Tu compañero(a) te va a hacer preguntas como las que están al final de la Actividad 11 y va a intentar adivinar la obra. ¡Después, cambien los papeles!

▼**11 Los mundos de Miró y de Dalí** | 🌐

Leer • Escribir

① Lee este artículo sobre los artistas surrealistas Joan Miró y Salvador Dalí.

El movimiento surrealista empezó poco después de la Primera Guerra Mundial. Los pintores del surrealismo se inspiraban en temas de su propia imaginación. Querían capturar en sus cuadros ideas e imágenes del subconsciente *(subconscious)*, como las que vemos en los sueños. El español Salvador Dalí (1904–1989) fue uno de los pintores más famosos de este grupo. Su cuadro "La persistencia de la memoria", que aparece en esta página, es un ejemplo del estilo surrealista.

Como muchos otros artistas, el español Joan Miró (1893–1983) se fue a París a principios de los años veinte. Allí lo influyeron los surrealistas, aunque su estilo es más abstracto que el de Salvador Dalí. Además, Miró usa colores vivos y figuras que recuerdan a los dibujos de los niños. Su obra es una fiesta de imaginación y colores. Un ejemplo es su cuadro "Escaleras cruzan el cielo azul en una rueda de fuego".

② Ahora contesta las siguientes preguntas sobre estos dos artistas y los cuadros de esta página. Usa las respuestas para escribir una comparación de los dos cuadros.

1. ¿De qué país son estos artistas?
2. ¿En qué siglo pintaron?
3. En cada cuadro, ¿qué se ve en primer plano? ¿Qué se ve al fondo?
4. ¿Qué se ve a la izquierda?

5. ¿Qué colores usa más cada artista?
6. ¿Cómo son las figuras, realistas o más abstractas?
7. ¿Qué tipo de arte es?
8. ¿Cómo te hace sentir este arte?
9. ¿Te gusta alguno de los cuadros? ¿Por qué?

74 setenta y cuatro
Manos a la obra 1

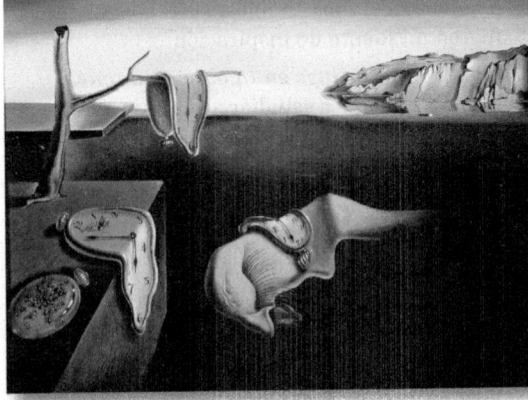

"La persistencia de la memoria", (1931), Salvador Dalí
Oil on canvas, 9 1/2 x 13 in. (24.1 x 33 cm). Given anonymously. © 2009 Salvador Dalí, Gala-Salvador Dalí Foundation/Artists Rights Society (ARS), New York.† A.K.G., Berlin/Photo: SuperStock.

"Escaleras cruzan el cie azul en una rueda de fuego", (1953), Joan N
© Dennis Hallinan/Alamy Ladders Cro Blue Sky in a Wheel of Fire by Joan M

DIFFERENTIATED INSTRUCTION

Heritage Language Learners

Students may have spelling difficulty with words involving the letters **b** and **v**. Have them identify words containing these letters. Some examples might include **obra, dibujo, abstracto(a), cubismo,** and **movimiento.** Have students separate the words into two columns and quiz each other on proper spelling.

Students with Learning Difficulties

Before they answer the questions in *Actividad* 11, have students brainstorm a bank of applicable nouns and adjectives to describe each of the paintings presented. Review the meanings of these descriptive words and have students use their word banks when answering the questions.

▼12 Diego Rivera: Arte y revolución

Leer • Escribir

Estrategia

Using illustrations
The details in a painting or illustration can give you clues about the main theme of a text. Observe the painting on the right. What does it tell you about the main theme of this article?

La obra del pintor mexicano Diego Rivera (1886–1957) muestra una preocupación por los ideales de la Revolución Mexicana. Lee el siguiente artículo sobre una de las figuras principales de la obra de Rivera y contesta las preguntas.

"Emiliano Zapata" (panel de un mural), (1931), Diego Rivera

Fresco, 7' 9 3/4" x 6' 2", Abby Aldrich Rockefeller Fund, #1631.1940. © 2009 Banco de México Diego Rivera & Frida Kahlo Museums Trust, México, D.F./Artists Rights Society (ARS), New York. Photo: © The Museum of Modern Art/Scala/Art Resource, NY.

Conexiones | El arte y la historia

Diego Rivera creía que el arte debe ayudar a los campesinos[1] a entender su propia historia. Este panel titulado "Emiliano Zapata" representa a Zapata, el líder de los campesinos durante la Revolución Mexicana. Con el famoso lema[2] "tierra y libertad", Zapata luchó[3] por una reforma agraria a principios del siglo XX.

Diego Rivera pensaba que Zapata era un verdadero héroe de la Revolución. En este panel, que es parte de un mural del Palacio Nacional de la Ciudad de México, vemos a Zapata en primer plano y a sus revolucionarios campesinos detrás de él. En la mano derecha lleva una hoz[4] y con la mano izquierda sujeta[5] un caballo. A sus pies hay un hombre muerto.

1 peasants 2 motto 3 fought 4 sickle 5 restrains

Observa los detalles del panel.

1. ¿Quién es la figura central en esta composición? ¿Cómo está vestido?
2. ¿Qué representa el caballo blanco?
3. ¿Qué representa la hoz?
4. ¿Qué comunica Rivera con los hombres que están al fondo?
5. ¿Qué representa el hombre muerto a los pies de Zapata?
6. ¿Qué crees que sucedió en esta escena?

▼13 Nuestra obra de arte |

Escribir • Dibujar • Hablar

Trabaja con un(a) compañero(a) para escoger un tema histórico que les gustaría pintar. Escriban una descripción de su pintura. Si es posible, hagan un dibujo de lo que van a pintar. Usen por lo menos tres símbolos (symbols) para representar el tema que escogieron. Luego, presenten la descripción a la clase. Incluyan la siguiente información:

- el título
- el tema y por qué lo escogieron
- qué o a quién van a mostrar en primer plano
- qué o a quién van a mostrar al fondo
- qué representan los símbolos que incluyeron

setenta y cinco **75**
Capítulo 2

▼12 Standards: 1.2, 1.3, 2.2, 3.1, 3.2

Resources: Fine Art Transparencies with Teacher's Guide, p. 56; Answer Keys: Student Edition, p. 24

Focus: Reading about a historical person and event in the context of a mural painting

Suggestions: Point out to students that carefully studying the panel will help them understand the second paragraph.

Answers
1. Es Emiliano Zapata. Está vestido de blanco.
2–6. Answers will vary.

▼13 Standards: 1.1, 1.3

Focus: Discussing, planning, and reporting on a painting about a historical event

Suggestions: Ask students to make their drawings large enough for everyone to see. Point out that they will be using the future tense. Ask: *¿Qué pondrás en primer plano? ¿Y en el fondo? ¿Qué tendrá tu pintura?*

Answers will vary.

Pre-AP* Support

- **Learning Objective:** Interpretative: Print and Audio
- **Activity:** As a pre-reading activity, distribute the questions accompanying *Actividad* 11. With books closed show Fine Arts Transparency 16 as you read aloud the first paragraph. Show Fine Arts Transparency 40 as you read the second paragraph. Then, ask them to answer the questions. Finally, have students follow along in their texts as you read the selection again to confirm their answers.
- **Pre-AP* Resource Book:** Comprehensive guide to Pre-AP* communication skill development, pp. 10–18, 19–26

Additional Resources

- Communication Wbk.: Audio Act. 1, p. 22
- Teacher's Resource Book: Audio Script, p. 95, Communicative Pair Activity BLM, pp. 101–102
- Audio Program DVD: Cap. 2, Track 8

✓ASSESSMENT

Prueba 2-2 with Study Plan (online only)

Prueba: Aplicación del vocabulario 1
- Prueba 2-2: pp. 39–40

ENRICH YOUR TEACHING

Culture Note

In 1920, Diego Rivera traveled to Italy to study the frescoes of the Renaissance. The fresco technique involves painting directly onto plaster that has been freshly applied to a wall. As the plaster dries into a hard surface, the color of the paint becomes fixed. Rivera was especially influenced by the Italian Renaissance painter Giotto.

21st Century Skills

Collaboration Have students evenly divide up the tasks of writing, drawing, and presenting in *Actividad* 13 so they can better accomplish the work. Partners work well together if they know what they want to accomplish and when each person has an equal role.

Practice and Communicate

Gramática Repaso

Core Instruction

Resources: Voc. and Gram. Transparency 57

INTERACTIVE WHITEBOARD

Grammar Activities 2-1

♻ Un poco más de repaso

Suggestions: After presenting the *Gramática* information to students, direct their attention to the *¿Recuerdas?* Ask students to explain why each expression takes the tense that it does. For example, *generalmente* takes the imperfect tense because it introduces either a habitual action in the past or background details in the past. Have them give examples.

▼14 Standards: 1.2

Resources: Answer Keys: Student Edition, p. 24

Focus: Practicing uses of the preterite and imperfect tenses

Suggestions: Remind students that sometimes expressions like those in the *¿Recuerdas?* will help them determine which tense to use.

Answers:

1. tomaba
2. me inscribí
3. fue
4. Eran/llegamos
5. trabajó
6. llevaba
7. visitaban
8. gustaban

Extension: After students have completed the activity, have them compare answers and discuss the reasons for their choices.

▼15 Standards: 1.1

Resources: Answer Keys: Student Edition, p. 25

Focus: Practicing the preterite and imperfect tenses in a guided conversation

Recycle: Time expressions, things to do on a trip

Suggestions: Before doing the activity, ask: *Las actividades ocurrieron a una hora específica en el pasado. Por eso, ¿qué tiempo verbal tenemos que usar?*
(el pretérito)

Gramática Repaso

> **Talk about activities in the past**
> **Listen to art-related activities in the past**

Pretérito vs. *imperfecto*

When speaking about the past, you can use either the preterite or the imperfect, depending on the sentence and the meaning you wish to convey. Compare:

> Este fin de semana **tomé** una clase de cerámica. Cuando **era** niño, **tomaba** clases de escultura.

- Use the preterite to tell about past actions that happened and are complete.

  > El sábado, la clase **empezó** a las 10 de la mañana.

- Use the imperfect to tell about habitual actions in the past.

  > Cuando **era** niño, las clases **empezaban** a las 5 de la tarde.

- Use the preterite to give a sequence of actions in the past.

  > Cuando **llegamos**, la profesora **sacó** su pintura y sus pinceles y **empezó** a pintar.

¿Recuerdas?

Las expresiones como *generalmente, a menudo* y *muchas veces* se usan frecuentemente en frases que tienen verbos en imperfecto.

Las expresiones como *ayer, la semana pasada* y *una vez* se usan en frases que llevan verbos en pretérito.

- Use the imperfect to give background details such as time, location, weather, mood, age, and physical and mental descriptions.

  > **Eran** las dos de la tarde. **Estábamos** en el parque. **Era** un día de otoño. Todos **estábamos** muy contentos.

- Use the preterite and the imperfect together when an action (preterite) interrupts another that is taking place in the past (imperfect).

  > **Estábamos** en el taller cuando **entró** el profesor.

- Use the imperfect when two or more actions are taking place simultaneouly in the past.

  > Mientras los niños **pintaban,** el profesor **observaba** las pinturas.

▼14 Una familia de artistas

Leer • Escribir

La familia Gutiérrez, desde que eran niños, participan en muchos proyectos de arte. Completa estas frases con el tiempo verbal correcto.

1. Cuando era niño *(tomé / tomaba)* clases de pintura todas las tardes.

2. Este fin de semana, *(me inscribí / me inscribía)* en un concurso de cerámica.

3. La semana pasada, mi hermano Juan *(fue / iba)* a pintar en la playa.

4. *(Eran / Fueron)* las dos de la tarde cuando nosotros *(llegué / llegamos)* a la clase de escultura.

5. Ayer, mi mamá *(trabajó / trabajaba)* varias horas en un retrato.

6. Todos los años, nuestra tía nos *(llevó / llevaba)* a ver su taller.

7. Generalmente, mis padres *(visitaron / visitaban)* el museo todos los fines de semana.

8. Y a ti, ¿qué te *(gustaban / gustaron)* más de niño(a), las clases de pintura o las clases de música?

DIFFERENTIATED INSTRUCTION

Students with Learning Difficulties

Students may have difficulty making the distinction between past actions that have been completed and past actions that are habitual or ongoing. Have students attempt to dramatize the examples in *Actividad 14.* Explain that the examples that are "easier" to act out (because the action is completed) require **el pretérito.**

Advanced Learners/Pre-AP*

Ask students to prepare a narration about a situation, real or imagined, in the past. It should include a mixture of the preterite and imperfect tenses. Allow them to prepare their narrative either as notes or as a paragraph to be read aloud. Remind them to improve their narrative by using expressions like those in the *¿Recuerdas?*

▼15 ¿Qué pasó en el museo? |  | ♻

Hablar

Con otro(a) estudiante, hablen de la visita de la clase al museo, la semana pasada.

1. la maestra / ir a comprar los boletos / 11:20
2. ustedes / comenzar la visita / 11:30
3. Juan y Lucía / perderse en el museo / 12:00

▶ Modelo

ustedes / llegar al museo / 11:15
A —*¿Cuándo llegaron al museo?*
B —*Eran las 11:15 cuando llegamos.*

4. la maestra / darse cuenta / 12:20
5. tú / encontrar a Juan y a Lucía / 1:00
6. ustedes / salir del museo / 2:30

▼16 ¿Imperfecto o pretérito? | 👥 | ◀))

Escuchar • Escribir • Hablar • GramActiva

En una hoja de papel, haz una tabla de dos columnas. Escribe *Pretérito* en la columna de la izquierda e *Imperfecto* en la columna de la derecha. Vas a escuchar una historia con los verbos en infinitivo. Cada vez que escuches un verbo, decide si debe ir en pretérito o imperfecto y escríbelo en la columna correcta. Luego, habla con otro(a) estudiante sobre las formas que escogieron.

▼17 Vida de artista: Remedios Varo

Escribir

Completa esta corta biografía de la artista surrealista Remedios Varo con los verbos entre paréntesis. Usa la forma apropiada del pretérito o del imperfecto.

María de los Remedios Varo y Uranga __1.__ *(nacer)* el 16 de diciembre de 1908, en Anglés, un pequeño pueblo al norte de Barcelona, España. __2.__ *(ser)* hija de Rodrigo Varo y de Ignacia Uranga. Su padre __3.__ *(ser)* ingeniero. __4.__ *(construir)* canales. A causa de su trabajo, Rodrigo Varo __5.__ *(llevar)* a su familia por muchas partes de España y del Norte de África.

Desde joven, a Remedios le __6.__ *(gustar)* pintar. Como otros artistas y escritores españoles de su generación, ella __7.__ *(viajar)* a París en 1930 en búsqueda de nuevas ideas. Allí __8.__ *(encontrar)* una fuente de inspiración en el movimiento surrealista. Los surrealistas __9.__ *(tratar)* de expresar imágenes del subconsciente. En 1936, a causa de la Guerra Civil española, Remedios __10.__ *(tener)* que buscar refugio en México. Allí, Remedios __11.__ *(crear)* algunas de las obras más originales de la pintura moderna.

"Still Life Reviving", (1963), Remedios Varo
© 2009 Artists Rights Society (ARS), New York/VEGAP, Madrid.

setenta y siete 77
Capítulo 2

ENRICH YOUR TEACHING

Culture Note

In Spain and some countries in Latin America, people traditionally use two family names or surnames. The first **apellido** is the father's family name, and the second is the mother's. The two **apellidos** may be separated by **y,** as is the case for Remedios Varo y Uranga, hyphenated, or just used together.

21st Century Skills

Initiative and Self-Direction Remind students of the various digital tools available in **realidades.com** to help them monitor their own understanding and learning needs, such as the eText with embedded audio files and online tutorials.

▼15 Standards: 1.1

(Cont'd)

Answers

1. A —¿Cuándo fue la maestra a comprar los boletos?
   B —Eran las 11:20 cuando fue.
2. A —¿Cuándo comenzaron ustedes la visita?
   B —Eran las 11:30 cuando comenzamos.
3. A —¿Cuándo se perdieron Juan y Lucía en el museo?
   B —Eran las 12:00 cuando se perdieron.
4. A —¿Cuándo se dio cuenta la maestra?
   B —Eran las 12:20 cuando se dio cuenta.
5. A —¿Cuándo encontraste a Juan y a Lucía?
   B —Era la 1:00 cuando los encontré.
6. A —¿Cuándo salieron ustedes del museo?
   B —Eran las 2:30 cuando salimos.

▼16 Standards: 1.2

Resources: Teacher's Resource Book: Audio Script, p. 95; Audio Program DVD: Cap. 2, Track 9; Answer Keys: Student Edition, p. 25

Focus: Determining use of the preterite versus the imperfect tense

Suggestions: Use the audio or read the script. Allow students to listen more than once.

Answers:

Pretérito	Imperfecto
llegó	iba
llegó	estaba
encontró	Eran
oyó	dormían
vio	

▼17 Standards: 1.2, 2.2, 3.1

Resources: Fine Art Transparencies with Teacher's Guide, p. 70; Answer Keys: Student Edition, p. 26

Focus: Practicing using the preterite vs. the imperfect tense

Suggestions: Have students read through the entire biography once before writing their answers.

Answers:

1. nació
2. Era
3. era
4. Construía
5. llevó
6. gustaba
7. viajó
8. encontró
9. trataban
10. tuvo
11. creó

▼18 Escena en el parque | (talk)

▼18 Standards: 1.1

Resources: Answer Keys: Student Edition, p. 26

Focus: Practicing using the preterite vs. the imperfect tense

Suggestions: After students answer the questions, encourage them to talk about the picture further by describing the people's clothes.

Answers will vary, but should contain the following tense usage and information.

1. Eran las dos de la tarde.
2. Era probablemente el verano. Hacía buen tiempo y la gente estaba vestida de ropa de verano.
3. Las niñas saltaban a la cuerda cuando llegó la mamá.
4. El perro robó las salchichas porque tenía hambre.
5. Carlos se enojó. Él también tenía hambre.
6. Eva se reía.
7. Luis le sacaba una foto.
8. El policía se acostó debajo de un árbol para tomar una siesta.

Fondo cultural

Standards: 1.1, 1.2, 2.2, 3.1, 5.2

Resources: Fine Art Transparencies with Teacher's Guide, p. 64

Suggestions: Remind students that all details in a mural like this one by Siqueiros are present for a reason. As they answer the questions, ask them to elaborate on details with questions such as the following: *¿Por qué muestra el artista a tantas personas en el mural? ¿Qué cosa llevan los hombres en la mano? ¿Piensas que la presencia de las mujeres es importante? ¿Por qué?*

Answers will vary.

78

▼18 Escena en el parque | (talk)

Hablar

Contesta las preguntas para describir lo que pasó en el parque.

1. ¿Qué hora era?
2. ¿Qué estación del año crees que era, probablemente? ¿Cómo lo sabes?
3. ¿Qué hacían las niñas cuando llegó la mamá?
4. ¿Quién robó las salchichas? ¿Por qué?
5. ¿Cómo se sentía Carlos? ¿Por qué?
6. ¿Qué hacía Eva?
7. ¿Qué hacía Luis mientras su papá leía?
8. ¿Quién se acostó debajo de un árbol? ¿Por qué?

▼ Fondo Cultural | México

David Alfaro Siqueiros A principios del siglo XX, ocurrían muchos cambios sociales en México. En 1910, terminó el régimen de Porfirio Díaz, quien fue Presidente de México durante 30 años, y comenzó la Revolución Mexicana.

Junto a Rivera y Orozco, David Alfaro Siqueiros (1898–1974) fue uno de los grandes artistas del muralismo mexicano, el movimiento artístico que se inspiró en los ideales de la Revolución.

A través de su obra, Siqueiros nos habla de los tiempos en que vive el país, de los cambios que ocurren. Sus murales nos muestran una nueva realidad en la que los pobres son las figuras centrales de la historia de México.

• ¿Quiénes crees que son las personas que muestra el mural? ¿Cómo están representados?

• ¿Qué nos dice este mural sobre la Revolución Mexicana?

"Del Porfirismo a la Revolución", (1906–1913), David Alfaro Siqueiros
Museo Nacional de Historia, Castillo de Chapultepec, Mexico City, D.F., México.
© 2009 Artists Rights Society (ARS), New York/ SOMAAP, Mexico City. Photo: Schalkwijk/Art Resource, NY.

Más práctica (GO)		realidades.com	print
Instant Check	✔	
Guided WB pp. 59–60	✔	✔
Core WB p. 25	✔	✔
Comm. WB pp. 22, 27, 170	✔	✔
Hispanohablantes **WB** pp. 48–53		✔

78 setenta y ocho
Manos a la obra 1

DIFFERENTIATED INSTRUCTION

Heritage Language Learners

Have students tell about family gatherings in their heritage country. For what types of events do families typically get together? What foods, decorations, and activities are usually involved?

Students with Learning Difficulties

Before completing the chart in *Actividad* 19 on p. 79, have students brainstorm and list the infinitive forms of verbs that would be applicable to the picture. Then lead them through the process outlined in the *Gramática*. Model, step-by-step, the conversion of each verb into the appropriate past participle form.

Gramática

▼ **Objectives**

▶ **Listen to the description of a family portrait**
▶ **Write about a description of a scene**
▶ **Talk about art museums and artists**

Practice and Communicate ②

Estar + participio

Many adjectives in Spanish are actually past participles of verbs. Recall that to form a past participle you add *-ado* to the root of *-ar* verbs and *-ido* to the root of *-er* and *-ir* verbs.

decorar decorado	conocer conocido	preferir preferido

- The past participle is frequently used with *estar* to describe conditions that are the result of a previous action. In those cases, the past participle agrees with the subject in gender and number.

    El pintor está sentado.   Las paredes estaban pintadas.

- Recall that there are a number of cases in which the past participle is irregular.

abrir: abierto	poner: puesto	decir: dicho	resolver: resuelto	escribir: escrito
romper: roto	hacer: hecho	ver: visto	morir: muerto	volver: vuelto

Más ayuda	**realidades.com**	▶ *Canción de hip hop* ▶ *Tutorial*

▼19 Retrato de familia | 🔊

Escuchar

Rosario describe un retrato de una fiesta familiar. ¿Quiénes estaban allí? ¿Cómo estaban? En una hoja de papel, copia la siguiente tabla. Escucha la descripción del retrato y escribe cómo estaban las siguientes personas y cosas.

¿Quién? o ¿Qué?	¿Cómo estaban?
Yo	
Mi padrino	
Mi papá	
Mi tía Luisa	
Mi primo Jorge	
La mesa	
Los refrescos	
Los niños	
Mis primos más pequeños	

ENRICH YOUR TEACHING

Culture Note

Like Diego Rivera, David Alfaro Siqueiros was trained in the classic technique of fresco painting. However, Siqueiros was also known for his innovations to the technique. In addition to painting on non-conventional surfaces such as concrete and cement, Siqueiros used non-traditional oil-based paints or airbrushing to cover large areas quickly. In addition to his own painting, Siqueiros taught many other artists. One of his most famous pupils was Jackson Pollock, a painter who went on to develop his own, original technique.

Gramática

Core Instruction

Resources: Voc. and Gram. Transparency 58

INTERACTIVE WHITEBOARD
Grammar Activities 2-1

Suggestions: Point out that, just as Spanish uses past participles ending in **-ado** or **-ido** as adjectives, English also uses past participles ending in *-ed* and *-en* as adjectives: *a heated room, a typed memo, a driven student, a given answer*.

▼19 Standards: 1.2

Resources: Teacher's Resource Book: Audio Script, p. 95; Audio Program DVD: Cap. 2, Track 10; Answer Keys: Student Edition, p. 27

Focus: Practicing listening comprehension

Suggestions: Use the audio or the script. Allow students to listen more than once. Remind them to use the picture to help them.

Common Errors: In the *estar* + **participle** construction, students often forget to make the participle agree in number and gender with the subject. Correct this error with visual cues. Hold up two fingers to cue plural. Prepare a pair of flashcards with masculine and feminine symbols to cue gender.

Answers:

1. estaba sentada
2. estaba parado
3. estaba sentado
4. estaba parada
5. estaba vestido de Superman
6. estaba puesta
7. estaban servidos
8. estábamos muy cansados
9. estaban dormidos

Chapter Project

Students can perform Step 2 at this point. Be sure they understand your corrections and suggestions. (For more information, see p. 62-b.)

Additional Resources

- Communication Wbk.: Audio Act. 2, p. 23
- Teacher's Resource Book: Audio Script, p. 95; Communicative Pair Activity BLM, pp. 103–104
- Audio Program DVD: Cap. 2, Track 11

20 Standards: 1.1

Resources: Answer Keys: Student Edition, p. 27
Focus: Practicing using **estar + past participle**

Suggestions: Point out to students that all of their sentences should begin with **Cuando llegué a su taller....** Therefore, they should use **estar + past participle** for all the verbs in the second part of the sentence.

Answers will vary. Endings for past participles will vary with number and gender: **abierto, dormido, hecho, roto, escondido, encendido, parado.**

21 Standards: 1.2, 1.3, 2.2, 3.1, 5.2

Resources: Fine Art Transparencies with Teacher's Guide, p. 42
Focus: Reading about an artist and planning an assemblage for a piece of artwork

Suggestions: Show students other examples of installations (collections of objects brought together by an artist) to help guide them in their discussion of the medium. Many photos of these, by Pepón Osorio and other artists, are available online and in art books and magazines.

Answers will vary.

▼20 En el cuarto de la pintora

Hablar

Una artista te invitó a visitar su taller. Describe la escena que viste cuando llegaste. Usa el participio pasado de los siguientes verbos: *abrir, dormir, hacer, romper, esconder, encender, parar.*

 **Modelo**

Cuando llegué a su taller, el niño estaba sentado.

▼21 Pepón Osorio, artista entre dos culturas

Leer • Escribir

¿Cómo refleja un artista una vida entre dos culturas? Lee este artículo para aprender un poco más sobre la vida y el arte de Pepón Osorio, un artista puertorriqueño. Después contesta las preguntas.

Conexiones | El arte

Pepón Osorio nació en 1955, en Santurce, Puerto Rico. A los 20 años vino a Nueva York para empezar su carrera de artista. Osorio cree que los artistas deben hacer trabajos que muestren su época y su país de origen. Su obra representa frecuentemente su niñez y adolescencia en Puerto Rico, y su experiencia multicultural como artista puertorriqueño en Nueva York. Dice que los puertorriqueños son multiculturales porque viven en dos culturas, la puertorriqueña y la neoyorkina.

Osorio hace montajes[1] de cosas que encuentra. En "100% Boricua"[2], Osorio mezcla recuerdos turísticos de Nueva York con banderas puertorriqueñas y otros objetos típicos del Caribe.

Su objetivo es reunir los elementos de toda una comunidad en un solo lugar.

---

1 assemblages 2 *Boricua* is a term Puerto Ricans use to describe themselves as natives to the island.

"100% Boricua", (1991), Pepón Osorio

Wood, glass, plexiglass, paper, fabric, metal, plastic. 79 3/8 x 33 1/2 x 20 1/2 inches. Collection Walker Art Center, Minneapolis. Gift of the Peter Norton Family Foundation, 1992.

1 Observa el montaje de Osorio. ¿Cómo es un montaje similar a otras obras de arte? ¿Cómo es diferente?

2 Ahora vas a planear tu propio montaje. Piensa en varios objetos que representan parte de tu historia. Escribe un corto párrafo describiendo cada objeto y explicando por qué es importante para ti. Dale un título y preséntalo a la clase.

80 ochenta
Manos a la obra 1

DIFFERENTIATED INSTRUCTION

Multiple Intelligences

Visual/Spatial: Have students select and collect objects to create their own **montajes.** Then have them explain the meaning and rationale behind the objects they have selected.

Advanced Learners

Have students create a report that compares two different kinds of visual art. They may compare two different media, such as sculpture and paintings, or two different schools, such as surrealist and kinesthetic. Ask them to research and organize their report of one of the media or styles for a class presentation.

22 Una visita a El Museo del Arte |

Leer • Hablar

1 Lee el siguiente anuncio de El Museo del Arte y contesta las preguntas:

• ¿Dónde está El Museo del Arte?

• ¿Qué artistas presenta?

• Observa la foto en el anuncio. ¿De quién crees que es el retrato?

• ¿Qué puedes aprender de los artistas si vas a la exposición?

2 Trabaja con otro(a) estudiante para representar una visita a un museo. Hablen del museo y de las obras que tiene (autorretratos, esculturas, cerámica). Describan qué es lo que les gusta o no les gusta (tema, forma, colores). Digan cuál es su obra favorita y expliquen por qué.

Frida Kahlo | Diego Rivera
y el Arte Mexicano del Siglo XX

del 3 de agosto al 18 de noviembre

• *Sus retratos y autorretratos*
• *Sus fuentes de inspiración*
• *El movimiento que los influyó*

El Museo del Arte
Avenida Juárez, 500

El español en la comunidad

El Museo del Barrio En 1969, un grupo de educadores, artistas y representantes puertorriqueños fundaron El Museo del Barrio en Harlem del Este. Su objetivo era ayudar a mantener la cultura, las tradiciones y el idioma de los puertorriqueños, y en general, de todos los latinoamericanos de Nueva York.

El Museo ha influido en la población hispanohablante de Nueva York gracias a sus programas educativos para la comunidad. Los estudiantes universitarios pueden hacer prácticas *(internships)* en El Museo y ser guías de visitas, ayudar a realizar talleres de orientación sobre arte y ayudar a los maestros de arte a preparar sus clases.

El Museo del Barrio es una de las instituciones culturales de la población hispanohablante más importantes de los Estados Unidos. Sirve de puente de comunicación entre los diferentes grupos latinoamericanos de Nueva York y también entre la cultura hispanohablante y la anglosajona. Ése fue el sueño de sus fundadores.

• Imagínate que vas a trabajar durante el verano en El Museo del Barrio como voluntario(a). ¿Qué trabajo quieres hacer? ¿En qué crees que puedes ayudar?

• Identifica otros ejemplos de instituciones culturales que representen a las comunidades hispanohablantes en los Estados Unidos.

Más práctica (GO)   realidades.com | print

Instant Check		
Guided WB pp. 61–62	✓	✓
Core WB pp. 26–27	✓	✓
Comm. WB p. 28	✓	✓
Hispanohablantes WB pp. 53–55		✓

Practice and Communicate (2)

22 Standards: 1.1, 1.2, 1.3, 3.2

Resources: Answer Keys: Student Edition, p. 27

Focus: Reading, responding, and role-playing

Suggestions: Ask partners to present to the class the conversation they come up with for Step 2.

Answers:

Está en la avenida Juárez.
Presenta a Frida Kahlo y a Diego Rivera.
Es de Frida Kahlo.
Se puede aprender sobre sus fuentes de inspiración y el movimiento que los influyó.

El español en la comunidad

Core Instruction

Standards: 1.1, 1.2, 5.1, 5.2

Suggestions: Have students imagine that they are starting up a museum from scratch. Ask them to think about and discuss questions such as: *¿Dónde va a estar nuestro museo? ¿Cuáles son los gastos* (expenses) *necesarios para empezar y mantener un museo? ¿De dónde van a venir los fondos necesarios? ¿Qué servicios va a ofrecer el museo? ¿Cómo vamos a atraer* (attract) *al público?*

✓ASSESSMENT

Prueba 2-4 with Study Plan (online only)

Prueba: *Estar* + participio
• Prueba 2-4: p. 42

Examen: Vocabulario y gramática 1
• Examen 1: pp. 43–45
• ExamView: Examen 1

ENRICH YOUR TEACHING

Culture Note

Across the United States, there are many museums and resources for Spanish and Latin American art. Some examples include the San José Center for Latino Arts, The Florida Museum of Hispanic and Latin American Art in Miami, and the Latino Museum of History, Art and Culture in Los Angeles.

21st Century Skills

Social and Cross Cultural Skills Encourage students to investigate another museum or cultural institution that represents the Spanish-speaking communities in the United States. Have them gather information about current exhibits, any outreach programs they have, and the Spanish-speaking communities they serve. How does it compare to the *Museo del Barrio* in New York City?

Vocabulario en contexto

Core Instruction

Standards: 1.2, 3.1

Resources: Teacher's Resource Book: Input Script, p. 92, Clip Art, pp. 110–116, Audio Script, p. 96; Voc. and Gram. Transparencies 59–60; Audio Program DVD: Cap. 2, Tracks 12, 14

Focus: Presenting new vocabulary and using grammar lexically in context

Suggestions: Use the Input Script from the *Teacher's Resource Book* as a source of ideas for presentation of new vocabulary as comprehensible input. Pantomime to clarify the meaning of words and expressions such as *pararse, exagerar, el aplauso,* and *los pasos de una danza.* Show *Vocabulary & Grammar Transparency* 59 and ask volunteers to point to *la trompeta, el tambor,* and *el micrófono.*

23 Standards: 1.2

Resources: Teacher's Resource Book: Audio Script, p. 96; Audio Program DVD: Cap. 2, Track 13; Answer Keys: Student Edition, p. 28

Focus: Practicing listening comprehension of new vocabulary

Suggestions: Before engaging students in the listening activity, give them a few minutes to silently read and study the reviews on p. 82. Tell them that the information they will hear refers to the *Semana Cultural* announcement. Then play the audio or use the script to read the activity aloud.

Answers:

1. F	3. C	5. F
2. F	4. F	6. F

Block Schedule

Have students work in pairs to write a short review for a cultural event similar to the models shown. Ask students to read them to the class imitating a critic.

A primera vista 2 | 🔊 | 🖥️

▼ **Objectives**
▶ Read, listen to, and understand information about
• music, drama, and dance performances
• art reviews

Vocabulario en contexto

Aquí tienes algunas **reseñas** que aparecieron en el periódico sobre las actividades de la Semana Cultural.

1 El actor que **actuó** en "Sueño de una noche de verano" y que **interpretó** el papel de Puck fue muy cómico. Al **exagerar** tanto los **gestos**, se pareció a un político. El público se rió mucho.

SEMANA CULTURAL
PROGRAMA

"Sueño de una noche de verano"
de William Shakespeare
Teatro Estudiantil
Martes 20, 9:00 p.m.

Conjunto musical "Los Salseros de Hoy"
Miércoles 21, 7:00 p.m.

Taller de danza
Presentación de danza clásica y moderna
Jueves 23, 8:00 p.m.

Lectura de poemas de autores latinoamericanos
Viernes 24, 6:00 p.m.

2 El **conjunto** de salsa "Los Salseros de Hoy" estuvo sensacional. Interpretó "Burbujas de amor" con **entusiasmo**. Muchos jóvenes bailaron al **ritmo de las canciones".

▼23 La semana cultural | 🔊

Escuchar

Escucha cada frase sobre el programa y levanta una mano si es cierta y dos manos si es falsa.

el micrófono

la trompeta

el tambor

Hector Silveira y su Orquesta

82 ochenta y dos
A primera vista 2

DIFFERENTIATED INSTRUCTION

Students with Learning Difficulties

Use concrete objects and listening samples to reinforce the meaning of new vocabulary. For example, play a song from a *conjunto de salsa* so that students can hear the *ritmo.* Read aloud a poem written by *un(a) poeta.* Encourage students to bring in programs from cultural events that they have attended.

Advanced Learners

Have students work in groups to create a series of narrated pantomimes that use the vocabulary presented on pp. 82–83. Ask them to choose one student in each group as the narrator. The other members act out the actions or scenes that the narrator describes. Have them present their narrated pantomimes to the class.

3 Felicitaciones a los bailarines que **realizaron una interpretación** hermosa del "Lago de los Cisnes". El aplauso del público fue impresionante y muchas personas se **pararon** con entusiasmo.

el aplauso

danza clásica

4 Los jóvenes en el auditorio se **identificaron** con la interpretación de *hip hop* del Grupo de Danza Moderna. Algunos quisieron aprender sus **movimientos** rápidos y sus **pasos** complicados pero no pudieron.

el escenario

5 La poeta Sandra Cisneros leyó los poemas en voz alta y las palabras **sonaron a** música. Todos queríamos escuchar más.

lectura de poemas

▼**24** Lo que dijo la prensa | ◀))

Escuchar • Hablar

Escucha cada fragmento y di a qué reseña se refiere.

ochenta y tres **83**
Capítulo 2

▼**24** Standards: 1.2

Resources: Voc. and Gram. Transparencies 59–60; Teacher's Resource Book: Audio Script, p. 96; Audio Program DVD: Cap. 2, Track 15; Answer Keys: Student Edition, p. 28

Focus: Practicing listening comprehension of new vocabulary

Suggestions: Use the audio or the script. Allow students to listen more than once. Pause to monitor students, making sure they are identifying the correct review.

Answers:
1. 5
2. 4
3. 2
4. 1
5. 3

Extension: Clarify the meaning of the expression **identificarse con.** Use *Voc. and Gram. Transparency* 60 as well as magazine or newspaper ads and pictures that show contrasting types of art, such as ballet vs. salsa, poetry vs. fiction, or classical music vs. hip hop. Show two contrasting art types at once and ask: *¿Con qué danza te identificas?* Students answer with **Me identifico con ....**

BELLRINGER REVIEW

Write these words above columns on the board: *la danza, la música instrumental, cantante, pintor, director, escultor.* As a class brainstorm, write the names of famous people under the appropriate category.

Teacher-to-Teacher

Encourage students to bring in CD covers, posters, magazines, and ads that demonstrate their own artistic preferences. These can be used as props throughout this chapter to aid in question-and-answer sessions and discussions about the varying types of art and students' responses to them.

Chapter Project

Students can perform Step 3 at this point. (For more information, see p. 62-b.)

ENRICH YOUR TEACHING

Culture Note

There are many different styles of the dance we call *salsa.* The Puerto Rican Style is known for its footwork; the New York Style shows the influence of disco; the Los Angeles Style is influenced by West Coast Swing. The Cuban Style stresses the "one" and "three" beats of the music, and the rhythms are faster.

21st Century Skills

Critical Thinking and Problem Solving
Encourage students to listen to salsa music online. Have them try to identify the instruments they hear in the music. Are there similarities between salsa music and other dance music they know? What are the similarities and differences?

Vocabulario en contexto

Core Instruction

Standards: 1.2, 2.2, 3.1

Resources: Teacher's Resource Book: Input Script, p. 93, Clip Art, pp. 110–116, Audio Script, pp. 96–97; Voc. and Gram. Transparencies 61–62; Audio Program DVD: Cap. 2, Track 16

Focus: Extending presentation of vocabulary and grammar in the context of reviews of the arts

Suggestions:

Pre-reading: Have students read just the titles of the four reviews. Ask them to name the kinds of art that they expect the reviews to be about.

Reading: Allow students time to read the reviews silently. Then play the audio and have students read along as they listen. Allow them to listen more than once.

Post-reading: Ask students to write down two statements about two different cultural events on pp. 84–85. Each statement should tell something that happened at the chosen event or describe how it happened. Have students take turns reading one statement at a time. Listeners identify which event is being talked about:

A: *Este cantante cantó canciones con títulos en inglés.*

B: *Es el concierto de Marc Anthony.*

Then check comprehension by having students complete *Actividades* 26 and 27.

Pre-AP* Support

- **Learning Objective:** Interpersonal Writing
- **Activity:** Have students imagine they attended one of the four events described in *Espectáculos del mundo latino.* Based on the review, have them write an email to their parents or to a friend describing the event: where and when it occurred, who or what they saw, who did they go with, and their general impressions about the artist and the occasion.
- *Pre-AP* Resource Book:* Comprehensive guide to Pre-AP* writing development, pp. 27–38

Teacher-to-Teacher

To focus on the role of the *tango* and the *flamenco* in the Hispanic culture, show the *¡Adelante!* video for this chapter. Play the video with and without sound to allow students to focus on the verbal and nonverbal signals in communication.

Espectáculos del mundo latino

¿Alguna vez buscaste información sobre un **espectáculo** en una revista, en un periódico o en la Red? Las reseñas te pueden ayudar a encontrar las películas, las obras de teatro y las exposiciones que más te interesan. ¿Qué dicen estas reseñas?

LILA DOWNS ACTÚA EN EL TEATRO MELICO SALAZAR DE SAN JOSÉ

La cantante mexicana Lila Downs dio su primer concierto en Costa Rica. Nacida en Oaxaca y criada entre los EE. UU. y México, Downs es la autora de la **letra** y la **melodía** de sus canciones que combinan la música popular mexicana con poemas indígenas y el Jazz. En esta ocasión, cantó sus canciones más conocidas, entre ellas "Burn It Blue", canción de la película *Frida*.

Museo Vivo del Tango

Museo Vivo del Tango dedicó la semana a la música argentina

El Museo Vivo del Tango en Buenos Aires ofreció un espectáculo original de gran esplendor. Los que más se destacaron fueron un cantante y el Tango Ballet, quienes después de actuar, enseñaron a los visitantes los pasos básicos del tango.

DIFFERENTIATED INSTRUCTION

Heritage Language Learners

Have students compose two newspaper clips reporting on a favorite artist's exhibition or performance. Explain that one clip would appear in the newspaper before the event, and the other clip would appear after the event. Remind students to keep the time frame consistent whether they are reporting on a future or past event.

Students with Learning Difficulties

Have students preview the sentences in *Actividad 26* on p. 85 prior to reading *Espectáculos del mundo latino.* After they have read the selection and answered true or false, have them locate and point to the sentence in the reading that proves their answer is correct.

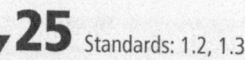

Language Input 2

Recuerdan a *Lope de Vega*

La Compañía de Danza Contemporánea de León presentó "Poeta del cielo y de la tierra", basada en la obra de Lope de Vega. Los bailarines representaron con sus movimientos y gestos la obra de este **escritor** español, que se caracteriza por combinar lo trágico y lo cómico.

Marc Anthony
Llenó el Madison Square Garden

Una vez más, se vendieron todas las **entradas** para el concierto de Marc Anthony en el Madison Square Garden. Después de interpretar sus éxitos en inglés *"You sang to me"* y *"My baby you"*, el público se unió a Anthony para cantar sus éxitos en español y bailar al **compás** de su música.

▼25 El mundo del espectáculo | 🔊

Escuchar • Escribir

Escribe los números del 1 al 5 en una hoja de papel. Escucha las siguientes preguntas y escribe la respuesta correcta.

▼26 ¿Es cierto?

Leer

Lee las frases y escribe *C* (cierto) o *F* (falso) según lo que leíste en "Espectáculos del mundo latino".

1. En el Museo Vivo del Tango, los visitantes aprenden a bailar salsa.
2. Marc Anthony sólo canta canciones en inglés.
3. Lila Downs escribe la letra y la melodía de sus canciones.
4. A través de su obra, Lope de Vega combina lo trágico y lo cómico.

▼27 Quisiera ir

Escribir

Después de leer estas reseñas, escribe una frase para cada una, diciendo por qué sí o por qué no te gustaría ir a ese espectáculo.

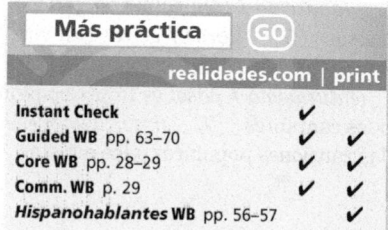

Más práctica	GO
realidades.com | print	
Instant Check	✔
Guided WB pp. 63–70	✔ ✔
Core WB pp. 28–29	✔ ✔
Comm. WB p. 29	✔ ✔
Hispanohablantes WB pp. 56–57	✔

25 Standards: 1.2, 1.3

Resources: Voc. and Gram. Transparencies 61–62; Teacher's Resource Book: Audio Script, p. 97; Audio Program DVD: Cap. 2, Track 17; Answer Keys: Student Edition, p. 28

Focus: Demonstrating comprehension of arts reviews

Suggestions: Remind students that answers to the questions they hear are found in the reviews on pp. 84–85.

Answers:
1. Es cantante.
2. Era escritor.
3. Está en Buenos Aires.
4. Se presentó en el Madison Square Garden.
5. El público bailó.

26 Standards: 1.2

Resources: Answer Keys: Student Edition, p. 28

Focus: Demonstrating comprehension of arts reviews

Suggestions: Have students check their answers with a partner and correct the false statements.

Answers:
1. F   2. F   3. C   4. C

27 Standards: 1.3

Focus: Expressing personal opinions in writing

Suggestions: Invite students to share and support their opinion with a partner.

Answers will vary.

ENRICH YOUR TEACHING

Culture Note

Born in France, Carlos Gardel (the "Father of Tango") moved to Argentina as a young child. He went on to become one of the foremost interpreters of the Argentine tango ballad, as well as a motion picture actor. Gardel appeared in many feature films produced for Spanish-speaking audiences, such as the 1934 film *El Tango en Broadway*.

21st Century Skills

Media Literacy Have students discuss how media messages are conveyed in announcements for cultural events, such as those on pages 84–85. What is the purpose of each announcement? Who is the intended audience? How are these articles similar to or different from the announcements they see in their own local newspapers?

✔ ASSESSMENT

Prueba: Comprensión del vocabulario 2
• Prueba 2-5: pp. 46–47

2 Practice and Communicate

▼ Objectives
▶ Read and write about different forms of entertainment
▶ Discuss a performance
▶ Talk about your favorite music

Vocabulario en uso

INTERACTIVE WHITEBOARD
Vocabulary Activities 2-2

28 Standards: 1.2, 3.1

Resources: Answer Keys: Student Edition, p. 29

Focus: Categorizing new vocabulary

Suggestions: When checking answers with students, ask them to say why the word they chose does not belong with the others.

Answers:

1. d
2. a
3. d
4. c
5. d
6. c

BELLRINGER REVIEW

Have students unscramble these words to make a logical sentence.

los / rió / exageró / la / se / mucho / el / gestos / político / gente / y

(**Answer:** *El político exageró los gestos y la gente se rió mucho.*)

---

29 Standards: 1.2, 2.2

Resources: Answer Keys: Student Edition, p. 29

Focus: Practicing new vocabulary in a cloze activity

Suggestions: Remind students that looking over the entire review first will give them an idea of what it is about and help them select the correct answers.

Answers:

1. se identifica
2. las actuaciones
3. se destacan
4. cómico
5. gestos
6. entusiasmo
7. interpretan
8. actuar

Extension: Invite students to work in groups. Have them choose a popular TV show they all know and make critical comments about it.

▼28 ¡Quita la palabra!

Leer • Escribir

Escribe en una hoja de papel los números del 1 al 6. Para cada grupo de palabras, escribe en la hoja la letra de la palabra que no está relacionada con las otras. Después, haz una lista de las palabras que no están relacionadas con las demás y escribe una frase con cada una.

1. a. la melodía   b. el ritmo   c. el compás   d. el gesto
2. a. el poema   b. la danza   c. el paso   d. bailar
3. a. la actuación   b. el gesto   c. interpretar   d. el conjunto
4. a. el escenario   b. realizar   c. la entrada   d. la interpretación
5. a. el escritor   b. el poeta   c. el poema   d. el micrófono
6. a. el tambor   b. la trompeta   c. el actor   d. el piano

▼29 Una reseña

Leer • Escribir

Loreto Michea, un crítico, escribe sobre el popular programa de tele, *Sábado Gigante*. Completa la reseña con la palabra correcta.

"Sábado Gigante no es sólo un programa familiar. Es un lugar donde la audiencia ___1.___ *(actúa / se identifica)* con otros hispanohablantes, sin importar en qué lugar de América viven. Pero los concursos, la música, el humor, ___2.___ *(los pasos / las actuaciones)* y las entrevistas, no son los elementos del programa que más ___3.___ *(se destacan / se exageran)*. Don Francisco, su presentador, es la clave *(key)*. Es un actor muy ___4.___ *(aburrido / cómico)* y energético que utiliza sus ___5.___ *(libros / gestos)*, su voz y su picardía *(wit)* para divertir al público. Su ___6.___ *(entusiasmo / paso)* es impresionante, y cuando los cantantes ___7.___ *(interpretan / actúan)* las canciones populares o los artistas

Don Francisco, el presentador del programa *Sábado Gigante*

aparecen en el escenario para ___8.___ *(exagerar / actuar)*, la energía de don Francisco inspira al público."

DIFFERENTIATED INSTRUCTION

Students with Learning Difficulties

Encourage students to bring in examples of their own favorite music. After copying the chart in *Actividad* 31 on p. 87, guide students to take appropriate notes for each of the songs they hear. Have them use these to conduct the partner conversations.

Advanced Learners/Pre-AP*

Challenge students to write six sentences, one for each item in *Actividad* 28. Each sentence should use all of the words in the row—including the word that does not belong—in a way that makes sense.

Practice and Communicate 2

▼30 Un espectáculo de flamenco |

Escribir • Hablar

Imagina que estuviste en el espectáculo de flamenco de la ilustración y describe la escena. Escribe frases en pretérito o imperfecto. Puedes usar las palabras y frases del recuadro. Luego, otro(a) estudiante te va a hacer preguntas sobre lo que escribiste.

el fondo	al frente
al lado	a la izquierda
el micrófono	los bailarines
tocar la guitarra	cantar
el cantante	sentado
parado	el paso
el escenario	

▶ **Modelo**

A — *Vi un espectáculo en el escenario.*
B — *¿Qué clase de espectáculo fue?*
A — *Fue un espectáculo de flamenco.*

▼31 ¡Viva la música! |

Escribir • Hablar

❶ ¿Cuál es tu álbum de música favorito? ¿Por qué? Piensa en algunas palabras que describan los diferentes elementos de tu canción o álbum de música favorito. En una hoja de papel, dibuja y completa una tabla como la siguiente.

Elemento	Álbum de música/Canción
el compás / el ritmo	
la melodía	
la voz	
los instrumentos	
la letra	
el tema	

Estudiante A

¿Qué te parece . . . ?
¿Cómo suena . . . ?
¿Cómo es . . . ?
¿Qué canción tiene mejor . . . ?

Estudiante B

interesante	largo(a)
original	corto(a)
alegre	alto(a)
aburrido(a)	bajo(a)
tradicional	rápido(a)
	lento(a)

❷ Habla con otro(a) estudiante sobre tu canción o álbum de música favorito. Usa las palabras que escribiste en la tabla.

▶ **Modelo**

A —*¿Qué te parece la melodía de la primera canción del álbum de música de Shakira?*
B —*La melodía es muy original, me gusta mucho.*
A —*¿Cómo suenan las guitarras en esta canción?*
B —*Suenan demasiado alto, no se oye la voz.*

ochenta y siete **87**
Capítulo 2

▼30 Standards: 1.1

Focus: Using new vocabulary and structures in a guided conversation

Suggestions: Encourage students to build more than one question-and-answer exchange around each word or expression. Make sure they switch roles, so that all students have a chance to practice both asking and answering.

Answers will vary.

▼31 Standards: 1.1, 3.1

Focus: Practicing new vocabulary in a guided conversation

Suggestions: Explain to students that they should choose just one favorite album or song.

Common Errors: Some students make the assumption that all Spanish nouns ending in *-a* are feminine. Remind them that many nouns ending in *-a,* such as **el tema, el programa,** and **el problema,** are masculine.

Answers will vary.

Teacher-to-Teacher

Invite students to share with the class a favorite art work (part of a song, a poem or a rap, or a scene from a film) and then tell about what it means to them. Aside from any English involved, their presentations should be in Spanish. Then take the assignment one step further: request that they spend equal time showing and telling about an art form or artist from the Spanish-speaking world.

Additional Resources

- Communication Wbk.: Audio Act. 3, p. 24
- Teacher's Resource Book: Audio Script. p. 97, Communicative Pair Activity BLM, pp. 105–106
- Audio Program DVD: Cap. 2, Track 18

✓ASSESSMENT

Prueba 2-6 with Study Plan (online only)

Prueba: Aplicación del vocabulario 2
- Prueba 2-6: pp. 48–49

ENRICH YOUR TEACHING

Culture Note

Flamenco is an art form comprised of three parts: the dance, the song, and the music of the guitar. Flamenco enjoyed its "Golden Age" in the late nineteenth and early twentieth century. During this era, the art was developed in Spain's many **cafés cantantes** or musical cafés.

21st Century Skills

Social and Cross Cultural Skills Have students investigate online music-sharing sites and find the most popular songs of the Latin genre. Have them choose a song and describe its elements, as they did in *Actividad* 31. How does this song compare to their favorite songs?

Gramática *Repaso*

Core Instruction

Standards: 4.1

Resources: Voc. and Gram. Transparency 63

INTERACTIVE WHITEBOARD
Grammar Activities 2-2

♻ Un poco más de repaso

Suggestions: Give other examples where the adjective has different meanings when used with **ser** or **estar:**

El niño es (está) malo. The boy is bad (sick).
Las manzanas son (están) verdes. The apples are green (unripe).

32 Standards: 1.2

Resources: Answer Keys: Student Edition, p. 29

Focus: Practicing uses of **ser** and **estar** in a cloze exercise

Suggestions: Once they are finished, encourage students to check their answers against the rules in the *Gramática* and make any necessary changes.

Common Errors: Correct usage of **ser** and **estar** is difficult for any English speaker learning Spanish. Tell students that correct usage will come with patience and practice.

Answers:

1. es	4. son	7. están
2. está	5. están	8. estamos
3. es	6. son	9. están

33 Standards: 1.2

Resources: Teacher's Resource Book: Audio Script, p. 97; Audio Program DVD: Cap. 2, Track 19; Answer Keys: Student Edition, p. 30

Focus: Listening for and using forms of **ser** and **estar**

Suggestions: Make sure students answer in complete sentences.

Answers:

1. Es argentino.
2. Es músico.
3. Está en Chicago para dar un concierto.
4. Los otros miembros del conjunto están con él.
5. El cantante es colombiano.
6. El concierto es mañana por la noche.
7. Está un poco nervioso.

Gramática Repaso

▶ **Listen to an interview with an artist**
▶ **Describe a performance**
▶ **Write and illustrate a haiku**

Ser y estar

Remember that *ser* and *estar* both mean "to be." They are used in different situations and have different meanings.

Use *ser:*

- to describe permanent characteristics of objects and people

  Esa canción **es** muy original.

- to indicate origin, nationality, or profession

  Mi tía **es** escritora. **Es** de Madrid.

- to indicate when and where something takes place

  El concierto **es** el viernes. **Es** en el teatro.

- to indicate possession

  La guitarra **es** de Elisa.

Use *estar:*

- to describe temporary characteristics, emotional states, or conditions

  El teatro **está** cerrado a esta hora.
  Los actores **están** muy nerviosos.

- to indicate location

  El conjunto **está** en el escenario.

- to form the progressive tense

  El bailarín **está** interpretando a Cabral.

Some adjectives have different meanings depending on whether they are used with *ser* or with *estar*.

La bailarina **es bonita**. *The dancer is pretty. (She's a pretty person.)*
La bailarina **está** muy **bonita** hoy. *The dancer looks pretty today. (She doesn't always look this pretty.)*
El cómico **es aburrido**. *(He is boring.)* El cómico **está aburrido**. *(He is bored.)*
El cantante **es rico**. *(He is wealthy.)* El postre **está rico**. *(It tastes very good.)*

Más ayuda   **realidades.com**   ▶ **Tutorial**

▼**32** Invitación a Caras y Caretas

Leer • Escribir

El secretario del club de teatro mandó esta invitación por correo electrónico. Completa la invitación con la forma correcta de *ser* o *estar*.

¡Atención compañeros y compañeras!
El jueves a las 3:30 __1.__ la reunión de Caras y Caretas. Nuestro club __2.__ en la sala 28, en el segundo piso. Caras y Caretas __3.__ un club que trabaja para realizar comedias y tragedias de España y América Latina. Los miembros __4.__ estudiantes, profesores y otros que __5.__ interesados en hacer teatro. Los invitados de honor __6.__ Raúl Moreno y Eva Díaz, dos jóvenes poetas mexicanos que ahora __7.__ estudiando en Nueva York. Nosotros __8.__ muy orgullosos de la obra de estos jóvenes. Todos ustedes __9.__ invitados a conocerlos. ¡Los esperamos!

88 ochenta y ocho
Manos a la obra 2

DIFFERENTIATED INSTRUCTION

Heritage Language Learners

Have students draft an e-mail message extending an invitation to a performing arts event in their heritage country. Instruct students to identify their audience. They might be writing to a close friend or to the entire mailing list of the performing arts institution. Remind them to tailor their language accordingly.

Students with Learning Difficulties

Have students write the verb forms **es** and **está** on two separate index cards. Help them reinforce the distinction between the forms of these two verbs that both mean "to be." Provide sentences in which students must fill in the blank by holding up the appropriate card. Ask them to explain each choice.

▼33 Entrevista en la radio | 🔊

Escuchar

Escucha la entrevista en la radio con Carlos Galán y luego contesta las preguntas.

1. ¿De dónde es Carlos?
2. ¿Cuál es su profesión?
3. ¿Por qué está en Chicago?
4. ¿Quiénes están con Carlos?
5. ¿Quién es colombiano?
6. ¿Cuándo es el concierto?
7. ¿Cómo se siente Carlos?

▼35 Poeta por un día | Talk? 👥

Escribir • Dibujar • Hablar

Los poemas haiku tienen tres líneas. La primera tiene 5 sílabas, la segunda tiene 7 y la tercera tiene 5. Por lo general, hablan de la naturaleza, escenas de la vida, las artes y los sentimientos que inspiran. Los sentimientos se expresan de una manera breve y sencilla.

❶ Piensa en un lugar, cosa o situación que te gusta o no te gusta. Por ejemplo, un baile, una fiesta, un museo. ¿Qué sientes cuando estás allí? Mira el ejemplo e inspírate para escribir tu propio haiku. Usa el presente de *ser* o *estar* para escribir tus frases, y no olvides que necesitas 5, 7 y 5 sílabas.

❷ Después de escribir tu haiku, haz un dibujo para ilustrarlo.

❸ Ahora estás listo(a) para presentar tu haiku a la clase. Explica en qué te inspiraste para escribirlo y muestra la ilustración.

▼34 Escena de teatro | Talk? 👥

Leer • Escribir • Hablar

Tú y otro(a) estudiante están hablando de una visita que hicieron al teatro. Túrnense para combinar palabras o expresiones de las dos listas y escriban frases completas con el imperfecto de *ser* o *estar*. Usen las formas correctas de los adjetivos.

▶ Modelo

el cantante / alto y guapo

A —¿*Cómo era el cantante?*
B —*El cantante era alto y guapo.*

1. las bailarinas   a. muy difícil
2. el micrófono   b. nervioso
3. el teatro   c. en la calle Bolívar
4. los pasos del tango d. muy bonito
5. la melodía   e. el viernes a las ocho
6. el concierto   f. entusiasmado con el espectáculo
7. los actores
8. nosotros   g. alto
                       h. fondo del escenario
                       i. argentino

En el museo
las estatuas me miran.
Estoy perdido.

Más práctica GO   realidades.com | print

Instant Check	✔	
Guided WB pp. 71–72	✔	✔
Core WB p. 30	✔	✔
Comm. WB pp. 30–31	✔	✔
***Hispanohablantes* WB** pp. 58–61	✔	

ochenta y nueve **89**
Capítulo 2

Practice and Communicate ②

▼34 Standards: 1.1

Resources: Answer Keys: Student Edition, p. 31

Focus: Determining use of the preterite forms of *ser* and *estar*

Suggestions: Have partners share their exchanges with the class. Ask which rule determined their use of *ser* or *estar.*

Answers will vary. The following are sensible uses of the cues given:

1. A —¿De qué nacionalidad eran las bailarinas?
   B —Eran argentinas.
2. A —¿Dónde estaba el micrófono?
   B —Estaba al fondo del escenario.
3. A —¿Dónde estaba el teatro?
   B —Estaba en la calle Bolívar.
4. A —¿Cómo eran los pasos del tango?
   B —Eran muy difíciles.
5. A —¿Cómo era la melodía?
   B —Era muy bonita.
6. A —¿De qué era el concierto?
   B —Era de música argentina.
7. A —¿Cómo eran los actores?
   B —Eran muy altos.
8. A —¿Cómo nos sentíamos?
   B —Estábamos entusiasmados con el espectáculo.

▼35 Standards: 1.2, 1.3, 3.1

Focus: Practicing using the preterite vs. the imperfect tense

Suggestions: Display students' finished haikus in the classroom.

Answers will vary.

Chapter Project

Students can perform Step 4 at this point. Be sure they understand your corrections and suggestions. (For more information, see p. 62-b.)

ENRICH YOUR TEACHING

Culture Note

Haiku grew out of a Japanese style of poetry in which people would play a kind of word game. Today the formalized style of haiku has spread and gained popularity around the world, and haiku can be found written in a multitude of languages, including Spanish.

21st Century Skills

Communication As students create their haiku poems, they should try to incorporate simple yet vivid images in their descriptions. Each line can have a separate purpose: first they could state their location, then make an observation, then finish with a personal comment.

✔ASSESSMENT

Prueba 2-7 with Study Plan (online only)

Prueba: *Ser y estar*
• Prueba 2-7: p. 50

Gramática

Core Instruction

Standards: 4.1

Resources: Voc. and Gram. Transparency 64

INTERACTIVE WHITEBOARD
Grammar Activities 2-2

Suggestions: Ask students to write other sentences that use the five verbs in the two tenses. Since meaning is the key here, allow them to think of an idea in English first if necessary, and then convert the idea to a Spanish sentence.

36 Standards: 1.2, 1.3

Resources: Answer Keys: Student Edition, p. 32

Focus: Practicing verbs whose meanings change depending on tense

Suggestions: Have students do the activity on their own. Then have volunteers take turns reading it aloud. Ask each volunteer to say in English what the sentence means, based on the Spanish verb form he or she chose.

Answers:

Step 1

1. conocía
2. conocí
3. quería
4. podía
5. sabía
6. pudo
7. quería
8. quise

Step 2

1. La conoció el verano pasado.
2. Rita dijo que quería comer algo.
3. Ricardo estaba enojado porque Rita tenía una cita con otro muchacho.

Teacher-to-Teacher

Have students work in pairs to select a song in Spanish and create a list of similarities and differences to a similar song in English. Have them play both songs for the class, present their findings, and encourage the class to add to the list.

▼ Objectives
▶ Talk about music and dancing
▶ Discuss a theater review
▶ Write about a performance you attended

Gramática

Verbos con distinto sentido en el pretérito y en el imperfecto

A few Spanish verbs have different meanings in the imperfect and the preterite tenses.

	IMPERFECT	PRETERITE
saber	*knew*	*found out, learned*
	¿Sabías que el concierto empezaba tarde?	Sí, supe ayer que empezaba tarde.
conocer	*knew (somebody)*	*met (somebody) for the first time*
	Pedro conocía muy bien a esa actriz.	Luis la conoció el año pasado.
querer	*wanted to*	*tried to*
	Luis quería comprar las entradas hoy.	Yo quise comprarlas, pero me enfermé.
no querer	*didn't want to*	*refused to*
	No querían ver esa obra de teatro.	No quisieron ver esa obra de teatro.
poder	*was able to, could*	*managed to, succeeded in*
	Ella podía aprender la letra de la canción.	Ella pudo aprender la letra de esa canción.

Más ayuda **realidades.com** ▶ *Canción de hip hop* ▶ *Tutorial*

▼36 Una cita con Rita

Leer • Escribir

1 A veces las citas no resultan como queremos. Lee estos párrafos sobre la cita que Ricardo tuvo con Rita y complétalo con el pretérito o el imperfecto de los verbos entre paréntesis.

Yo no __1.__ (conocer) bien a Rita. Era sólo nuestra segunda cita. Recuerdo que la __2.__ (conocer) el verano pasado en una clase de danza. Ella __3.__ (querer) aprender salsa, pero no __4.__ (poder) seguir bien los pasos. Yo le pregunté si __5.__ (saber) los movimientos de baile. Ella me dijo que no. Entonces, yo la ayudé y al final ella __6.__ (poder) aprenderlos.

Cuando salimos de la escuela de danza, Rita me dijo que __7.__ (querer) comer algo. Después, me dijo que ya era tarde y que tenía una cita con otro muchacho. Me invitó a ir con ellos, pero yo no __8.__ (querer) ir. Ya estaba bastante enojado. ¡Nunca más salí con ella!

2 Ahora, responde a las siguientes preguntas.

1. ¿Cuándo conoció Ricardo a Rita?
2. ¿Qué pasó cuando salieron de la escuela de danza?
3. ¿Por qué estaba enojado Ricardo?

DIFFERENTIATED INSTRUCTION

Heritage Language Learners

Have students write out the lyrics to a favorite Spanish-language song on poster board or chart paper. Invite them to read the lyrics aloud for the class and explain unfamiliar vocabulary, then play the song so their classmates can listen and read along.

Students with Special Needs

Help students with hearing impairments experience the rhythms of salsa, merengue, and tango by exhibiting video or live examples of the dances associated with these musical genres. Encourage students to move, clap, or drum to the beat of the movements they are seeing.

▼ Fondo Cultural | Cuba • Estados Unidos

La salsa tiene origen en el *son*, una mezcla de ritmos africanos y europeos que nació en Cuba. Al principio, el *son* se interpretaba con tambores y maracas. Luego se añadieron otros instrumentos como el bajo *(bass)* y la guitarra. El término *salsa* empezó a usarse en los años sesenta en Nueva York y sirve para definir una música que es mezcla del *son* cubano y otros ritmos del Caribe. La salsa es uno de los bailes más populares en los Estados Unidos.

• ¿Qué nombres de cantantes o grupos de salsa conoces?

• ¿Por qué crees que la salsa tiene tanto éxito en los Estados Unidos?

Fondo cultural

Standards: 1.1, 1.2, 2.2, 3.1

Suggestions: Ask if any students know how to dance *salsa* and if they would volunteer to give a demonstration. Extend this invitation to any colleagues. Some students or teachers might even be willing to give a *salsa* lesson, which would provide an excellent context for real-life use of chapter vocabulary related to dance and music.

Answers will vary.

▼ 37 Y tú, ¿qué dices? | 🗨

Escribir • Hablar

1. Piensa en un momento en que quisiste hacer algo pero no pudiste. ¿Qué fue?
2. ¿Hay algo que nunca pudiste hacer bien? ¿Por qué no podías hacerlo?
3. ¿Qué poemas o canciones sabías de niño(a)? ¿Los sabías de memoria?
4. Piensa en una ocasión en que no quisiste hacer algo. ¿Qué fue?
5. ¿Conocías ya a muchos(as) de tus compañeros(as) cuando empezaste esta clase?
6. ¿Conociste a alguien famoso(a) alguna vez? ¿A quién? ¿Cómo sabías que era famoso(a)?

▼ 37
Standards: 1.1, 1.3

Focus: Practicing verbs whose meanings change depending on tense

Suggestions: As students hold their discussions based on the questions, have them write down any of their partner's responses that strike them as interesting. After the paired discussions, have students share with the class one interesting fact that they learned about their partner.

Answers will vary.

▼ En voz alta | 🗨

Juan Luis Guerra creció escuchando la música popular de la República Dominicana y a los Beatles en la radio. Más tarde, asistió al Conservatorio Nacional y al Berklee College of Music de Massachusetts, donde recibió la influencia del jazz. Con todas esas experiencias, Guerra comenzó a componer[1] canciones de merengue, el popular ritmo dominicano, que eran perfectas para bailar pero que tenían una música, y sobre todo una letra, mucho más rica y compleja[2] que la de los merengues tradicionales.

Escucha este fragmento de la letra de una canción de Juan Luis Guerra y luego trata de repetirla en voz alta.

---
1 compose 2 complex

¿Recuerdas?

En español, las letras b y v se pronuncian igual. Al principio de una palabra, el sonido es similar a la b en boy. En otras posiciones, el sonido es más suave.

"Amigos"
de Juan Luis Guerra

Yo soy tu amigo cuando a nadie le interesas
tan sólo llámame
y enseguida tocaré a tu puerta.
Yo soy tu amigo cuando buscas y no
encuentras tan sólo llámame
y estaré a tu lado cuando quieras.
Somos el viento que despierta el alba
dos nubes blancas bajo la ventana
yo soy tu carga que no pesa nada
tú eres el río donde bebo el agua.
Tómalo todo, pide lo que quieras
haz el camino y seguiré tus huellas.

noventa y uno 91
Capítulo 2

En voz alta
Core Instruction

Standards: 1.2, 3.1, 2.2, 3.2, 5.2

Resources: Map Transparency 16; Teacher's Resource Book: Audio Script, pp. 97–98; Audio Program DVD: Cap. 2, Track 20

Suggestions: Show *Map Transparency* 16 and ask a volunteer to locate *la República Dominicana*.

Before having students recite the lyrics, direct their attention to the information in the ¿*Recuerdas?* Allow them a few minutes to practice with a partner. Invite students to talk about how the images in the third stanza demonstrate friendship.

ENRICH YOUR TEACHING

Culture Note

Merengue is a rural music with roots in the Dominican Republic. Traditionally bands were composed of an accordion, a saxophone, a bass, a **tambora** drum, and a **guayano**—a metal scraper. Today however, merengue bands often achieve a big-band sound through the use of multiple saxophones, electric guitars, keyboards, and synthesizers.

21st Century Skills

Critical Thinking and Problem Solving
Encourage students to find other songs by Juan Luis Guerra and choose their favorite bachata or merengue. Then have them research a salsa performer such as Rubén Blades, also known for the rich lyrics and complex arrangements of his songs, and choose their favorite. What are the similarities between these two types of music? What are the differences?

38 Standards: 1.1, 1.2, 1.3, 2.2, 3.1

Resources: Answer Keys: Student Edition, p. 32

Focus: Reading and answering questions about a musical theater review from Spain

Suggestions: Before students read the review, direct their attention to the *Estrategia*. Remind them that using context clues will keep them reading and prevent them from getting stuck on unfamiliar words. Using context clues develops their skills in reading Spanish faster than consulting a dictionary because they are using what they already know and making associations between words and ideas.

Have students read the review silently and answer the questions on their own. Encourage them to paraphrase information drawn directly from the review, rather than stating it verbatim. Then go through the questions with the whole class. Ask students to read their answers aloud.

Answers:

1. Se habla de una obra teatral musical. Es una buena adaptación.
2. Answers will vary.
3. Se agregaron más canciones y algunas escenas dramáticas.
4. Mencionan el grandísimo escenario, los actores, el colorido vestuario y los efectos especiales.
5–6. Answers will vary.

Extension: When discussing students' answers for the questions, ask if anyone knows the original storyline of *El Rey León*. Ask any students who do to retell the story in the past tense.

Pre-AP* Support

- **Learning Objective:** Interpretative Print
- **Activity:** As a pre-reading activity, have students prepare the following T-chart on a blank piece of paper. Have the class decide on several questions that they believe will be answered in the movie review. Then, read aloud to the class the review presented in *Actividad* 38 and ask students to take notes in column 2 as they hear their questions answered. Discuss with the class.

Preguntas sobre la reseña de El Rey León	Respuestas

- ***Pre-AP* Resource Book:** Comprehensive guide to Pre-AP* communication skill development, pp. 19–26, 39–50

Estrategia

Context clues
When you read, look for cognates (words similar to English), which will make reading easier. Then, if you do not recognize a word, look at the words around it to try and guess what it means.

▼38 Una reseña de teatro

Leer • Escribir • Hablar

Lee esta reseña de una obra musical presentada en Madrid, que fue adaptada de una película estadounidense, y luego contesta las preguntas.

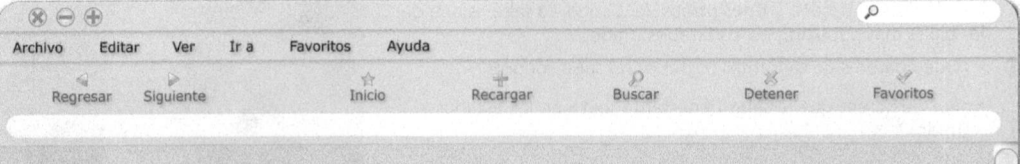

Reseña de un musical

El Rey León

Siempre asusta el hecho de ver convertida una buena película en un musical. Sin embargo, en este caso se trata de una buena adaptación. A pesar de que se hicieron varios cambios con respecto a la película, son cambios que mejoran la adaptación musical. Por ejemplo, se agregaron más canciones y algunas escenas dramáticas. Sin dudas, el musical El Rey León es un gran éxito en España. Es la primera vez en la historia de este musical que se adapta la versión en español.

El teatro Lope de Vega tuvo que ser remodelado para poder instalar el grandísimo escenario para este impresionante musical de éxito internacional. Los 53 actores que trabajan en El Rey León bailan, cantan y entretienen al público con esta obra que parece hecha a medida[1] para convertirse en musical. El espectáculo lo completa el colorido vestuario[2] y los efectos especiales, que hacen que el público se sienta en la sabana[3] de África. Además, esta es la primera vez que se representa en español. ¡Hakuna Matata!

1 made to measure 2 colorful wardrobe 3 savannah

1. ¿De qué tipo de espectáculo se habla en el artículo? ¿Qué dice sobre la adaptación de *El Rey León*?

2. ¿Crees que es una buena idea convertir una película en obra teatral? ¿Por qué?

3. ¿Qué cambios tiene este musical con respecto a la película?

4. ¿Qué elementos positivos del musical menciona el artículo?

5. ¿Sabes cuál es el argumento de la obra? ¿Por qué crees que el escritor de la reseña no dice cuál es el argumento o dónde ocurre la acción?

6. ¿Crees que la persona que escribió la reseña está a favor o en contra de esta comedia musical? ¿Por qué?

DIFFERENTIATED INSTRUCTION

Heritage Language Learners

Have students give a brief commentary on an adaptation or translation that they have seen or read. They might choose a book that has been made into a movie, or the Spanish-language version of an English-language film, for example. Ask them to include a brief synopsis and tell which version they enjoyed more.

Students with Learning Difficulties

Have students identify and copy key words in each of the questions following *El Rey León*. Then have them locate these key words in the reading passage. Encourage them to use this connection to help find the answers to each question.

39 Los críticos

Escribir • Hablar

1 Trabaja con otro(a) estudiante. Escojan un espectáculo que vieron, que les gustó o que no les gustó. Escriban una lista de datos del espectáculo incluyendo los siguientes:

- tipo de espectáculo (obra de teatro de la escuela, película, pieza de baile o musical, programa de televisión)
- el autor o la autora
- los personajes (cómo eran, la ropa que usaban, quiénes los representaban)
- el argumento
- dónde ocurría la acción
- la interpretación de los actores principales (cómica, aburrida)
- el orden de los sucesos
- con qué personajes se identificaron
- cómo reaccionó el público cuando terminó (lloró, se rió, aplaudió)

El tenor Juan Diego Flórez en un concierto en Moscú

2 Escriban una reseña usando los datos que juntaron. Si es posible, acompañen la reseña con fotos o anuncios del espectáculo.

Modelo
La obra de teatro "Romeo y Julieta" es un drama de William Shakespeare. Los personajes principales son . . . El problema es que . . . La acción tiene lugar en . . . En general, nos gustó . . . Muchas personas dijeron que la actriz se identificó bien . . . Pero otras dijeron que exageraba . . .

Más práctica (GO)

realidades.com | print

Instant Check	✔	
Guided WB pp. 73–74	✔	✔
Core WB pp. 31–32	✔	✔
Comm. WB pp. 24–25, 32–33	✔	✔
Hispanohablantes WB pp. 62–65		✔

3 Trabajen con otra pareja y lean su reseña. Si ellos también vieron el espectáculo, ¿están de acuerdo con Uds.? Si no vieron el espectáculo, ¿qué más quieren saber? Luego hagan lo mismo con la reseña de la otra pareja.

Fondo Cultural | España

La zarzuela ¿Ópera . . . opereta . . . obra musical de Broadway? Se parece un poco a cada una de estas formas musicales, pero es una expresión de la cultura, la historia y las costumbres de España. La zarzuela nació en el siglo XVII. En el siglo XIX se construyeron los dos teatros más famosos de la zarzuela en Madrid, el Teatro de La Zarzuela (1856) y el Teatro Apolo (1873–1929), y las compañías comenzaron a visitar América Latina. Su popularidad aumentó *(increased)* en el siglo XX, cuando varias zarzuelas se llevaron al cine.

Generalmente, la zarzuela tiene partes cantadas y partes habladas. Puede ser cómica o trágica, y muchas veces el argumento es romántico.

- ¿Qué películas u obras de teatro similares a la zarzuela conoces? ¿Por qué crees que la zarzuela se hizo tan popular? Sugiere dos ideas.

noventa y tres 93
Capítulo 2

ENRICH YOUR TEACHING

Puente a la cultura

Core Instruction

Standards: 1.2, 1.3, 2.1, 2.2, 3.1, 5.2

Resources: Fine Art Transparencies with Teacher's Guide, pp. 27–30

Focus: Reading to learn about the life and work of Spanish artist Francisco de Goya

Suggestions:

Pre-reading: Direct students' attention to the *Estrategia*. Use the questions there and the title of the selection to help students predict what the reading is about. Ask them to write down their predictions and to return to them as they read in order to verify whether or not they were correct. As you discuss the photos, have volunteers read the captions aloud.

Reading: Encourage students to read through the entire passage once silently, without stopping at problem words or to ask questions. Then ask volunteers to read sections aloud. Remind students to use background knowledge, cognates, and context clues to help them understand unfamiliar words and expressions as they read.

Post-reading: Ask students to comment on the predictions they wrote down in the *Pre-reading*. Ask questions such as: *¿Tus predicciones eran correctas? ¿Tuviste que cambiar alguna predicción? ¿Cómo? ¿Leíste algo en este artículo que no esperabas? ¿Qué fue? ¿Qué más te gustaría saber sobre Francisco de Goya?*

Common Errors: Point out to students the word *obra* in the first paragraph. Ask a volunteer to read aloud the sentence in which it is used. Explain that *obra* can refer to one single work, such as a painting, or to the work of an artist's entire life, as it does here.

BELLRINGER REVIEW

Show Fine Art Transparency, *"Duquesa de Alba"* by Goya. Have students write a short paragraph telling what the woman might be doing and why.

Teacher-to-Teacher

Have students visit the official Museo del Prado Web site to find more information about Goya and his paintings.

Puente a la cultura

El mundo de Francisco de Goya

▼ Objectives

▶ Read about a famous Spanish painter
▶ Use visuals as an aid to understand the reading
▶ Relate a painter's life to his/her work

Estrategia

Using visuals
Looking at the visuals before reading a selection allows us to better understand it. What do you notice about the paintings on this page and the next one? What might your observations tell you about what you will read about the painter?

"Duquesa de Alba", (1795), Francisco de Goya
194 x 130 cm. Madrid, the Dukes of Alba's collection.

Francisco de Goya nació en 1746 en España. Murió en Francia en 1828, a los 82 años de edad y sordo[1], a causa de una misteriosa enfermedad. Goya es uno de los artistas más conocidos de todos los tiempos. Su obra es extensa y muy variada. Realizó murales religiosos, retratos de la corte española, dibujos de toros, cuadros sobre la guerra, y hasta sus propias pesadillas[2] que pintó en las paredes de su casa.

Uno de sus grandes triunfos artísticos fue llegar a ser Pintor de Cámara[3], o sea el pintor oficial de los reyes. Goya pintó retratos de la familia real y de otros personajes de la corte madrileña[4]. De esta época[5] son muy conocidos los retratos que hizo de la Duquesa de Alba, según algunos, una de las mujeres más hermosas de su época. Durante 18 años, Goya trabajó para la Real Fábrica de Tapices[6] de Santa Bárbara. Allí se dedicó a dibujar bocetos[7] de escenas alegres y pintorescas, que representaban la vida cotidiana[8] en Madrid. Estos bocetos luego aparecían en tapices que adornaban las paredes de los palacios reales.

1 deaf 2 nightmares 3 Chamber Painter 4 Court of Madrid 5 period 6 Royal Tapestry Factory 7 sketches 8 everyday

"El quitasol", (1777), Francisco de Goya
Oil on canvas, 104 x 152 cm. Museo Nacional del Prado, Madrid, Spain.

DIFFERENTIATED INSTRUCTION

Students with Learning Difficulties

Students may be overwhelmed by the amount of information contained in the biography of Francisco de Goya. To help organize this information, have them isolate the dates included in this passage. Then have them organize the dates into a timeline, adding a short caption to each significant date.

Advanced Learners

Ask students to summarize the selection by paraphrasing each paragraph in Spanish. Suggest that they begin each paraphrase with phrases such as *El primer párrafo dice que...* or *Esta parte se trata de....*

La pintura de Goya cambió con el tiempo para mostrar los sucesos que ocurrían en su país. Los españoles lucharon[9] durante siete años contra las tropas francesas que Napoleón envió para invadir España. La obra más famosa de Goya sobre el tema de la guerra[10] contra Francia es el cuadro "El 3 de mayo de 1808".

Al final de su vida, Goya estuvo muy enfermo. Sus obras de esta época se llaman las Pinturas Negras, ya que Goya representaba imágenes de pesadillas, como monstruos, en pinturas que eran oscuras.

Los cuadros de Goya están en los museos más importantes del mundo. Para celebrar los 250 años del nacimiento del pintor, el Museo del Prado de Madrid organizó una gran exposición en 1996. La obra de Goya es todavía muy popular hoy en día. ¿Por qué crees que es así?

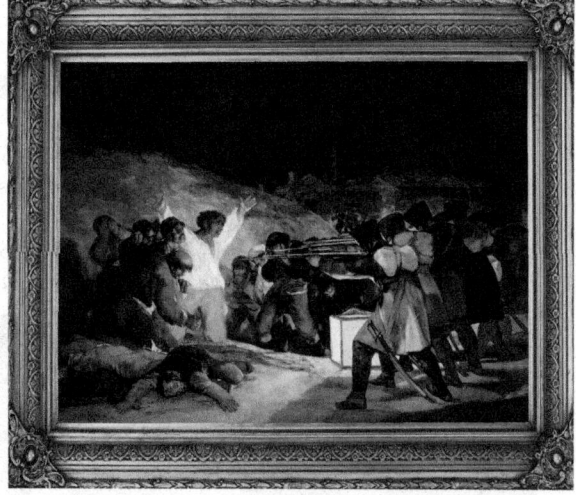

"El 3 de mayo de 1808", (1814), Francisco de Goya
Oil on canvas, 8 ft. 9 in. x 13 ft. 4 in. Museo Nacional del Prado, Madrid. Copyright Lessing/Art Resource, NY.

9 fought 10 war

¿Comprendiste?

1. ¿Cuándo, en qué lugar y cómo se celebraron los 250 años del nacimiento de Goya?

2. ¿Por qué podemos decir que las pinturas de la página 94 son representativas de las obras de Goya cuando era Pintor de Cámara?

3. La pintura de Goya cambió según las diferentes épocas de su vida. Da dos ejemplos y explica cómo se relacionan esas pinturas con los cambios en su vida.

4. El artículo dice que Goya es uno de los artistas más conocidos de todos los tiempos. ¿Cuáles son las razones de su éxito como pintor?

Escribe tu opinión

Acabas de leer sobre los diferentes períodos de la pintura de Goya. Basado(a) en la información que leíste y las obras que ves aquí, escribe si te gustaría ver más obras de Goya, como el retrato de la "Duquesa de Alba" o "El sueño de la razón produce monstruos".

"El sueño de la razón produce monstruos", (1799), Francisco de Goya
Plate 43 of 'Los Caprichos', published c. 1810 (color engraving). Bibliotheque de Nationale, Paris, France. Archives Charmet. Bridgeman Art Library, London.

Más práctica	GO
realidades.com | print	

▶ *Videodocumentario*	✔	
Guided WB p. 75	✔	✔
Comm. WB pp. 34–35	✔	✔
Hispanohablantes **WB** pp. 66–68		✔
Cultural Reading Activity	✔	

noventa y cinco **95**
Capítulo 2

▼**¿Comprendiste?** Standards: 1.2, 1.3

Resources: Fine Art Transparencies with Teacher's Guide, pp. 27–30; Answer Keys: Student Edition, p. 33

Focus: Demonstrating reading comprehension

Suggestions: Have pairs of students answer the questions and write responses.

Answers:

1. **Los 250 años del nacimiento de Goya se celebraron en 1996 con una gran exposición en el Museo del Prado de Madrid.**
2. **La pintura de la Duquesa de Alba es de un personaje de la corte madrileña. "El quitasol" es del mismo estilo realista.**
3–4. **Answers will vary.**

▼**Escribe tu opinión**

Standards: 1.3, 3.1

Focus: Using new vocabulary and structures in a written response to a reading

Suggestions: Tell students to include one or two statements supporting their opinion.

Answers will vary.

Teaching with Art

Ask students to choose one of the paintings and not to reveal their choice to anyone. Tell them they can do one of two things:

A. Write an imaginary character sketch of one of the persons in the painting. Do not name the person, but include details about his or her life at or before the moment frozen in the painting.

B. Write a monologue that shows the thoughts going through the mind of one of the persons in the painting.

▶ Videodocumentario

Core Instruction

Standards: 1.2

Resources: Teacher's Resource Book: Video Script, p. 100; Video Program: Cap. 2

View *El arte en el mundo hispano* with the class, either online in **realidades.com** or using the DVD. See the *Video Teacher's Guide* for additional suggestions.

Additional Resources

Student Resource: Realidades para hispanohablantes, pp. 66–68; Guided WB, p. 75; Communication Wbk., pp. 34–35

ENRICH YOUR TEACHING

Culture Note

The ***Real Fábrica de Tapices de Santa Bárbara*** was created in 1720 under the order of Felipe V. Goya painted for the factory from 1775 until 1800. His "cartoons" served as models for the tapestries. At times, the tapestry workers ran into difficulty transferring Goya's intricate cartoons onto fabric. In some cases, Goya had to change his original designs to suit the medium.

21st Century Skills

Critical Thinking and Problem Solving Have students research museums with artwork by Francisco de Goya in the United States. Ask them to identify two. Have them choose one of the museums and briefly describe their holdings by the painter. Does the collection include paintings, etchings, or other art forms?

¿Qué me cuentas?

Core Instruction

Standards: 1.1, 1.2, 2.2, 3.1, 5.2

Resources: Fine Art Transparencies with Teacher's Guide, pp. 11, 17; Teacher's Resource Book: Audio Script, p. 98; Audio Program DVD: Cap. 2, Track 23; Answer Keys: Student Edition, p. 33

Focus: Practicing listening and reading comprehension of new vocabulary and grammar; using information to write a cohesive and coherent reaction.

AP* Skills: Integration of listening, reading, and writing to comprehend and synthesize information from spoken and written sources.

Suggestions: For Step 1, use the audio or read the descriptions aloud. Allow students to hear both descriptions twice through: the first time to write their answers, the second time to check them.

For Step 2, have students identify significant details as they read and then summarize the main points of the article.

In Step 3, students may need some guidance in order to discuss what they think the artists wanted to express. Circulate and listen to their discussions. If necessary, help them with questions containing embedded answers: *¿Piensas que la pintura de Botero expresa la confusión o la alegría de estar en casa? ¿Y la de Dalí?*

Answers:

Step 1

1. **Dalí**	5. **Botero**
2. **Dalí**	6. **Botero**
3. **Botero**	7. **Dalí**
4. **Dalí**	8. **Botero**

Steps 2–3

Answers will vary.

Block Schedule

Ask each student to create a *naturaleza muerta* using colors, shapes, and images that reflect his or her personal style. Encourage creativity. Upon completion, give the painting to another student who will describe it.

Additional Resources

Student Resource: Realidades para hispanohablantes, p. 69

Pre–AP*

| ▼ **Objectives**
▶ Listen to and read descriptions of paintings and the art genre of still life
▶ Discuss two paintings

Integración 🗨️

¿Qué me cuentas?: Naturaleza muerta

Compara el cuadro de naturaleza muerta de Botero con el de Dalí. Primero escucha unas descripciones de los cuadros. Guarda lo que escribes para usarlo en el paso 3.

1 🔊 Vas a escuchar unas descripciones sobre los dos cuadros de esta página. Escribe cada descripción e indica si pertenece al cuadro de Botero o de Dalí.

"Naturaleza muerta con sopa verde", (1972), Fernando Botero
© Fernando Botero, courtesy, Marlborough Gallery, New York.

"Naturaleza muerta, viva", (1956), Salvador Dalí
Oil on canvas, 49 1/4 x 63 inches. Collection of The Salvador Dalí Museum, St. Petersburg, Florida. © 2009 Salvador Dalí, Gala-Salvador Dalí Foundation/Artists Rights Society (ARS), New York.

2 Ahora lee la información sobre el género de naturaleza muerta.

La pintura de naturaleza muerta tiene como fuente de inspiración los objetos inanimados de la vida diaria. El pintor puede tener diferentes metas. Algunos artistas quieren hacer una representación detallada de la realidad y se concentran en la técnica de la pintura. Cuando pintan, destacan detalles en la imagen, como la textura de los objetos o los efectos de la luz. A veces los artistas quieren comunicar un mensaje e incluyen objetos simbólicos. Por ejemplo, los libros o mapas simbolizan la educación. Las frutas cortadas o flores marchitas[1] pueden simbolizar la muerte. A través de los siglos, los artistas han interpretado este género según las ideas de los movimientos artísticos de su época[2].

1 withered 2 era

3 Habla con otro estudiante y comparen el cuadro de Botero y el de Dalí. Piensen en los títulos. ¿Por qué se llaman así? Observen las pinturas y compárenlas según el tema, los colores, las imágenes y lo que quiere expresar el artista. Expliquen cómo el artista adapta su estilo, realista o surrealista, al género de la naturaleza muerta. Usen las frases siguientes para unir sus ideas.

Por un lado . . . *(on the one hand)*	Esto me parece más . . .	Sin embargo . . .
Por otra parte . . . *(on the other hand)*	En primer lugar . . .	En contraste . . .

DIFFERENTIATED INSTRUCTION

Heritage Language Learners

Have students add a second layer to their oral presentations. In addition to explaining why a particular heritage country artist should be voted **Artista del Año.** Have them explain why a major competitor to this artist is not as qualified to receive the distinction.

Students with Learning Difficulties

Students may have difficulty organizing and recalling information for their oral presentations. To support them, have students provide you with a written copy of their presentation materials prior to the actual oral presentation. Use this information to provide guiding questions or cues if necessary.

Presentación oral

"Artista del Año"

Tarea
Imagínate que en tu clase van a seleccionar a un(a) artista como candidato(a) al premio "Artista del Año". Puede ser un(a) pintor(a), un actor, una actriz, o un(a) cantante que te guste. Explica quién debe ser el / la candidato(a) y por qué.

1 Prepárate Escoge tu artista preferido(a). Completa una tabla como ésta sobre tu candidato(a). Recuerda que puedes usar tus notas para prepararte, pero no al hacer la presentación oral.

> **Estrategia**
>
> **Organize information**
> Organize the key points you may want to talk about by listing them in a chart. This will help you give a more effective presentation.

Nombre	
Tipo de artista	
Puntos positivos	
Experiencia	
Originalidad, personalidad	

2 Practica Haz tu presentación ante el grupo. Al final, se va a hacer una votación para escoger un(a) ganador(a). Recuerda que debes:
- incluir el nombre del / de la artista, su especialidad y lo que hizo
- describir los puntos positivos del / de la candidato(a)
- decir claramente por qué debe ganar el premio
- usar el vocabulario de este capítulo

3 Haz tu presentación Haz tu presentación ante la clase. Al final, todos los estudiantes votan para elegir al / a la "Artista del Milenio".

4 Evaluación Tu profesor(a) utilizará la siguiente rúbrica para evaluar tu presentación.

Los cantantes colombianos Shakira (arriba) y Juanes (abajo)

Rubric	Score 1	Score 3	Score 5
How well you provide information	You lack vital information, such as the artist's identity.	Your vital information about the artist is present.	Your information about the artist is clearly presented.
How well you support your opinion	You have little or no convincing evidence.	Your supporting evidence is present, but not developed.	Your supporting evidence is clear and convincing.
How effectively you deliver your speech	You have no eye contact with the audience.	You make some eye contact. You use intonation, but not convincingly.	You make good eye contact with the audience. You have good intonation and gestures.

© **Common Core: Speaking**

Presentación oral

Core Instruction
Standards: 1.1, 1.2, 1.3, 3.1
Resources: Voc. and Gram. Transparency 4
Focus: Preparing and delivering an oral presentation

Suggestions: Review the task and the rubric with students. Help students decide what type of information to put in the various categories of the chart. In **Puntos positivos,** they can focus on the artist's artistic qualities. For **Experiencia,** they might list the work they know of from that artist. For **Originalidad, personalidad,** they can tell what they know about the artist's personal life.

Pre-AP* Support
- **Learning Objective:** Presentational Speaking
- **Activity:** Remind students to focus on the presentational speaking skills used in this task such as fluency, pronunciation, and comprehensibility.
- *Pre-AP* Resource Book:* Comprehensive guide to Pre-AP* speaking skill development, pp. 39–50

Portfolio
Make audio or video recordings of student presentations in class, or assign the RealTalk activity so they can record their presentations online. Include the recording in their portfolios.

Additional Resources
Student Resource: Realidades para hispanohablantes, p. 70

ENRICH YOUR TEACHING

Teacher-to-Teacher
Some students experience stress when asked to make oral presentations to the class. Allow them, at least occasionally, to record their presentations. This reduces stress for them and provides you with a handy tool for assessment.

21st Century Skills
Media Literacy As they do this *Presentación oral* task, student should try to incorporate different types of media into their presentation, including visuals, audio, or video representations of their artist candidate. Have students determine the best media to represent their artist.

✓ASSESSMENT

Presentación oral
- Assessment Program: Rubrics, p. T29
  Review the rubric with students. Go over the descriptions of the different levels of performance. After assessing students, help individuals understand how their performance could be improved. (See Teacher's Resource Book for suggestions on using rubrics in assessment.)

▼ Objectives
▸ Write an evaluation about a student's audition
▸ Categorize information for clarity

2 Writing

Language Arts Connection: Persuasive Writing

Remind students that in their Language Arts classes they were taught effective use of transitions in writing. As they revise their drafts in Step 3, tell them to include transitions that will warn the reader that they are changing from one main idea to another. As part of the revision process, have partners comment on one another's use of transitions.

 Common Core: Writing

Presentación escrita

Core Instruction

Standards: 1.3, 3.1

Resources: Voc. and Gram. Transparency 12

Focus: Combining learned vocabulary and structures in a written presentation

Suggestions: Explain at the start the criteria you will use to evaluate students' compositions. (See Step 5, *Evaluación*, in the Student Edition.)

First, direct students' attention to the *Estrategia*. Remind them that using a graphic organizer will help them prepare their evaluations. Then show *Voc. and Gram. Transparency* 12. Model filling in the information about an imaginary candidate. Make statements about the candidate's capabilities and ask students where the information should go in the web: *Sol Herrera es una buena escritora. Escribió dos cuentos cortos. Estos cuentos están publicados en revistas.* Once students determine that this information goes in the *Nombre, arte* and *Experiencia* sections of the web, fill it in on the transparency image. Together with students, read through the information about the imaginary candidate Vicky Lagardera in the web shown on this page. Answer any questions they may have about the graphic organizer.

Block Schedule

Encourage students to use the graphic organizer. You might have students work in small groups and share their notes.

You might ask a few students to present their notes using an overhead transparency.

98

Presentación escrita

El mejor candidato

Imagínate que te piden que escribas sobre la audición de un(a) artista y que digas por qué deben aceptarlo(a) en una escuela famosa. Haz un informe para explicar por qué crees que será un(a) buen(a) estudiante.

Estrategia

Categorizing
When writing a report you must include the greatest amount of information in the clearest way possible. If you organize the information into categories and write everything about one topic before going to the next one, the reader will have no trouble understanding your report.

1 Antes de escribir

Contesta estas preguntas:

- ¿Qué tipo de artista es y qué experiencia tuvo? ¿Tuvo actuaciones en público? ¿Cuándo?
- Si canta, ¿sabe la letra?, ¿sigue la música? Si baila, ¿sabe los pasos?, ¿sigue el ritmo? Si hace teatro, ¿representa bien al personaje?, ¿sabe los diálogos?
- ¿Qué aptitudes naturales tiene el(la) estudiante?

Antes de escribir tu composición, usa un organizador gráfico como éste para ordenar tus ideas.

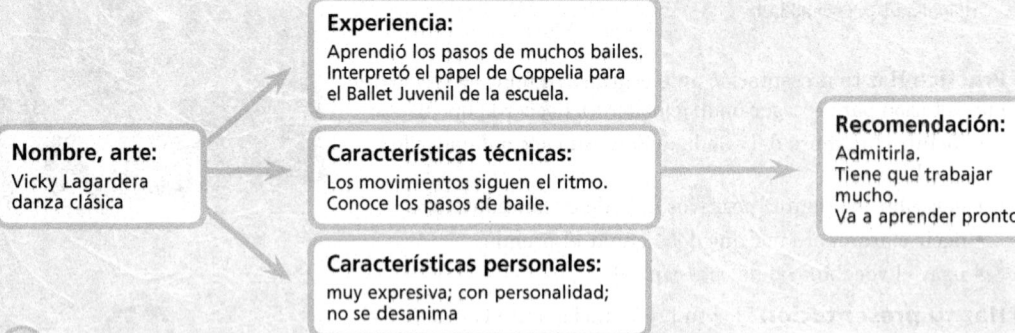

2 Borrador

Escribe tu borrador. Escribe un informe con toda la información del organizador gráfico. Más tarde lo podrás revisar.

Modelo

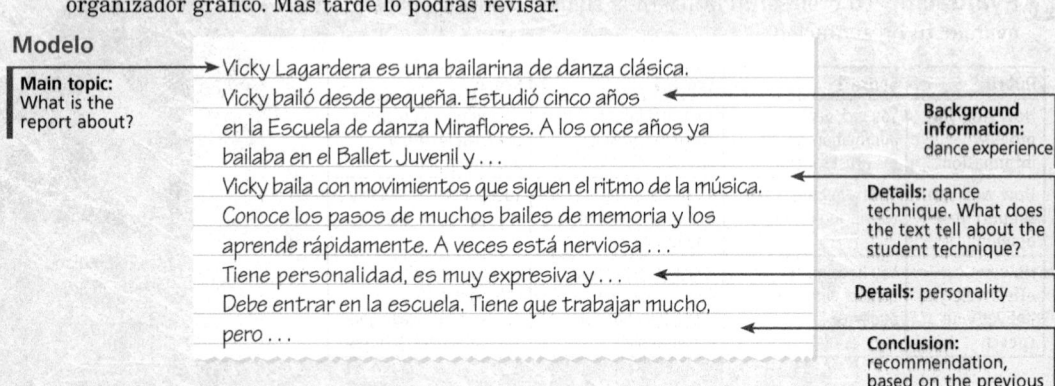

98 noventa y ocho
¡Adelante!

DIFFERENTIATED INSTRUCTION

Heritage Language Learners

Have students identify one or two specific elements of Spanish grammar that they find challenging in their writing. Direct them to focus on these specific points while revising their written presentations.

Advanced Learners

Encourage students to interview the person they are evaluating. They can ask the person for hard facts about his or her artistic experience, such as publications or exhibits. They can also ask the artist to assess his or her own strong points. They can then translate at least some of this information to Spanish and use it in their evaluations.

③ Redacción/Revisión

Después de escribir el primer borrador, trabaja con otro(a) estudiante para intercambiar los trabajos y leerlos. Luego, hagan sugerencias para mejorar sus informes.

- ¿Seguiste el plan que hiciste en tu organizador gráfico? ¿Escribiste todas las ideas que querías expresar?
- ¿Están bien organizados los párrafos? ¿Comunicaste claramente la información?
- ¿Usaste los verbos y los tiempos verbales correctos?

Haz lo siguiente: Verifica si usaste correctamente los verbos en pretérito o imperfecto.

> bailó   Estudió
> Vicky ~~bailó~~ desde pequeña. ~~Estudiaba~~ cinco
> años en la Escuela de danza Miraflores. A los
>   bailaba
> once años ya ~~bailó~~ en el Ballet Juvenil y . . .

④ Publicación

Antes de crear la versión final, lee de nuevo el informe y repasa los siguientes puntos:

- ¿Explica mi informe claramente lo que pienso del / de la estudiante que quiere entrar en la escuela?
- ¿Usé el vocabulario apropiado para este tema?
- ¿Debo añadir detalles importantes?

⑤ Evaluación

Se utilizará la siguiente rúbrica para evaluar tu presentación.

Rubric	Score 1	Score 3	Score 5
How well you organize information	Your vital information about the candidate is missing.	You present vital information but it's unorganized.	Your information is clearly presented and organized.
How well you support your choice	You have few or no convincing details about the candidate.	Your details convince us to vote for the candidate.	Your details about the candidate are organized and convincing.
Sentence structure/ grammar, spelling, mechanics	Your sentences are run-on or are fragmented with many errors.	You use sentences effectively, but with a few errors.	Your sentence structure is varied with very few errors.

Suggestions (Cont'd)

Then, have them create on their own paper a similar, empty web and use it to prepare their evaluations of their own candidates. Once students have a rough draft ready, read through the model on this page together. Help them see how information from the web on p. 98 was incorporated into this draft and to note the additional information that was added. Point out the use of past tenses and complete sentences. Encourage them to work toward similar organization, level of detail, and language use as they revise their own drafts.

Evaluation

Steps 4 and 5 overlap. Students will need evaluation by you, their peers, or self-evaluation to fine-tune and polish their drafts.

Pre-AP* Support

- **Learning Objective:** Presentational Writing
- **Pre-AP* Resource Book:** Comprehensive guide to Pre-AP* writing skills development, pp. 27–38

Portfolio

Keep students' final drafts in their portfolios as a writing sample.

Additional Resources

Student Resource: Realidades para hispanohablantes, p. 71

ENRICH YOUR TEACHING

Teacher-to-Teacher

As students review each other's work, encourage them to begin their critiques with a positive comment or two. Remind them of how much more readily they themselves respond to positive criticism than to negative comments. Ask them to provide suggestions and additions in a constructive way.

21st Century Skills

Initiative and Self-Direction Have students review the rubrics they have been given (pp. 97, 99). Ask them to discuss with a partner why their teacher gives them rubrics; how are they supposed to be used? Have them work with the rubric on this page to start with the outcome, figure out what they might need to do to get the best grade possible, and develop a plan to achieve that goal.

✓ ASSESSMENT

Presentación escrita

- Assessment Program: Rubrics, p. T29
  Review the rubric with students. Go over the descriptions of the different levels of performance. After assessing students, help individuals understand how their performance could be improved. (See Teacher's Resource Book for suggestions on using rubrics in assessment.)

Ⓒ **Common Core: Reading**

Lectura

Core Instruction

Standards: 1.1, 1.2, 1.3, 2.1, 2.2, 3.1, 3.2, 4.1, 4.2, 5.2

Resources: Map Transparency 16

Focus: Reading an extended passage

Suggestions:

Pre-reading: Ask a volunteer to read the title of the passage aloud. Ask students what they think is meant by the expression *Fragmento de.* If they don't know, explain that the selection is a fragment or excerpt from a longer work.

Before reading, direct students' attention to the *Estrategia* and to the *Al leer* sections. Have them answer the questions and copy the graphic organizer from this page.

Consider having students read the information about the author of the autobiography in the *Fondo cultural* on p. 103 before they read the selection itself. Ask them to use what they learn from that, as well as the title of the selection and the photos, to answer the question *¿De qué tratará esta lectura?*

Block Schedule

After reading the *Lectura*, ask each student to play the role of Esmeralda and do a short reading from this autobiography, perhaps one paragraph in length. Explain how it is common for authors to do "readings" of their work. Have students focus on pronunciation and personal expression, imagining how the author herself might read the selected excerpt.

▼ Objectives
▶ Read an excerpt of an autobiography
▶ Monitor reading to increase understanding
▶ Give your opinion about the advantages of living between two cultures

Lectura

Fragmento de

Cuando era puertorriqueña

Estrategia

Monitoring your reading
When you are reading a long selection, stop after each paragraph to ask yourself questions such as: What is the main idea of this paragraph? How does this idea relate to the title or the topic of the reading? This strategy will help you understand better what you are reading.

Al leer

Vas a leer un fragmento de una autobiografía. Se trata de Esmeralda Santiago, una joven puertorriqueña que emigró con su familia a Nueva York. Esmeralda da una audición en la famosa escuela secundaria Performing Arts. Mientras lees, anota en una tabla los siguientes puntos:

Qué hace y cómo se siente Esmeralda	
antes de la audición	
durante la audición	
después de la audición	

—¡Las pruebas son en menos de un mes! Tienes que aprender una escena dramática, y la vas a realizar enfrente de un jurado[1]. Si lo haces bien, y tus notas aquí son altas, puede ser que te admitan a la escuela.

El Mister Barone se encargó de prepararme para la prueba. Seleccionó un soliloquio de una obra de Sidney Howard titulada *The Silver Cord*, montada[2] por primera vez en 1926, pero la acción de la cual acontecía en una sala de estrado en Nueva York, alrededor del año 1905.

—Mister Gatti, el maestro de gramática, te dirigirá . . . Y Missis Johnson te hablará acerca de lo que te debes de poner y esas cosas.

Mi parte era la de Cristina, una joven casada confrontando a su suegra[3]. Aprendí el soliloquio fonéticamente, bajo la dirección de Mister Gatti. Mis primeras palabras eran: "You belong to a type that's very common in this country, Mrs. Phelps, a type of self-centered, self-pitying, son-devouring tigress, with unmentionable proclivities suppressed on the side".

—No tenemos tiempo de aprender lo que quiere decir cada palabra —dijo Mister Gatti—. Sólo asegúrate de que las pronuncies todas.

Yo había soñado[4] con este momento durante varias semanas. Más que nada, quería impresionar al jurado con mi talento para que me aceptaran en Performing Arts High School y para poder salir de Brooklyn todos los días, y un día nunca volver.

Pero en cuanto me enfrenté con las tres mujeres bien cuidadas que formaban el jurado de la audición, se me olvidó el inglés que había aprendido y las lecciones que Missis Johnson me había inculcado sobre cómo portarme como una dama. En la agonía de contestar sus preguntas incomprensibles, puyaba[5] mis manos hacia aquí y hacia allá, formando palabras con mis dedos porque no me salían por la boca.

—¿Por qué no nos dejas oír tu soliloquio ahora? —preguntó la señora de los lentes colgantes.

Me paré como asustada, y mi silla cayó patas arriba como a tres pies de donde yo estaba

---

1 jury panel **2** put on stage **3** mother-in-law **4** The usage of *había* with the past participle expresses what a person *had* done. *Había soñado* = I had dreamed **5** moved, pushed

---

DIFFERENTIATED INSTRUCTION

Heritage Language Learners

After previewing the selection, have students practice and present a "dramatic reading" of this literature excerpt. Tell them to imagine that their version will be broadcast on the radio. Encourage students to assume different roles, characterizations, voices, and intonations.

Students with Learning Difficulties

As students read the excerpt aloud, model for them the appropriate intonation or expression. Have students repeat and imitate your exaggerated intonation to help support the meaning of the narrative.

parada. La fui a buscar, deseando con toda mi alma que un relámpago entrara por la ventana y me hiciera cenizas allí mismo.

—No te aflijas —dijo la señora—. Sabemos que estás nerviosa.

Cerré los ojos y respiré profundamente, caminé al centro del salón y empecé mi soliloquio.

—Llu bilón tú é tayp dats beri cómo in dis contri Missis Felps. É tayp of selfcente red self pí tí in són de baurin taygrés huid on menshonabol proclibétis on de sayd.

A pesar de las instrucciones de Mister Gatti de hablar lentamente y pronunciar bien las palabras aunque no las entendiera, recité mi monólogo de tres minutos en un minuto sin respirar ni una vez.

Las pestañas[6] falsas de la señora bajita parecían haber crecido de sorpresa. La cara serena de la señora elegante temblaba con risa controlada.

La señora alta vestida de pardo me dio una sonrisa dulce.

—Gracias, querida. ¿Puedes esperar afuera un ratito?

Resistí el deseo de hacerle reverencia. El pasillo era largo, con paneles de madera angostos pegados verticalmente entre el piso y el cielo raso. Lámparas con bombillas grandes y redondas colgaban de cordones largos, creando charcos amarillos en el piso pulido. Unas muchachas como de mi edad estaban sentadas en sillas a la orilla del corredor, esperando su turno. Me miraron de arriba a abajo cuando salí, cerrando la puerta tras de mí. Mami se paró de su silla al fondo del corredor. Se veía tan asustada como me sentía yo.

—¿Qué te pasó?

—Na'[7]—no me atreví a hablar, porque si empezaba a contarle lo que había sucedido, empezaría a llorar enfrente de las otras personas, cuyos ojos me seguían como si

---

6 eyelashes 7 nothing

ENRICH YOUR TEACHING

Culture Note

The theme of remaining and retaining one's self in the context of a new country and culture is a popular one in contemporary U.S. literature. Some notable examples include Nicholasa Mohr's *El Bronx Remembered,* and Julia Álvarez's *How the García Girls Lost Their Accents.*

21st Century Skills

Critical Thinking and Problem Solving Encourage students to use their reading strategies when reading *Cuando era puertorriqueña.* Remind them to preview the comprehension questions first, then have them focus their attention on the use of dialogue and first person narrative as they read the story.

Suggestions (Cont'd)

Reading: While reading the selection together with students, pause frequently to address comprehension issues that students may bring up. Ask your own comprehension questions to help them focus on the main idea and important details of each section. Here are some possible comprehension issues on pp. 100–101 for which you can provide some guidance:

- p. 100: Ask a volunteer to read aloud the excerpt that the author had to recite for her audition. Ask: *¿Este ejemplo de inglés es fácil o difícil?* Ask them to consider how much more difficult it would be for a person like the author, whose first language isn't English.
- p. 101, column 1: Tell students that the expression *No te aflijas* means the same as *No te preocupes.*
- p. 101, column 1: Explain that the paragraph beginning with *—Llu bilón…* is the phonetic rendition of English that the author refers to on the previous page. Read this aloud for students.
- p. 101, columns 1-2: Help students understand by pantomiming the actions in passages such as *La cara serena de la señora elegante temblaba…* and *…hacerle reverencia.*

Teacher-to-Teacher

Students may need some guidance in order to appreciate the humor in this selection. Point out humorous parts by asking questions such as *¿Piensan que el fragmento de una obra de teatro que eligieron los maestros de Esmeralda era adecuado (adequate) para su audición? ¿Por qué?/¿Por qué no? ¿Qué pasó cuando Esmeralda se levantó para decir su soliloquio? ¿Cómo se sintió ella? ¿Esmeralda dijo su soliloquio rápida o lentamente? ¿Cómo lo sabes?*

Suggestions (Cont'd)

Reading: Additional comprehension issues are as follows:

- p. 101, column 2: Help students through the passage about light by telling them that the key word in the passage, ***charco,*** means "puddle" or "pool."

- p. 101, column 2: Point out that ***na*** is Esmeralda's shortened, slang form of ***nada***.

- p. 102, column 1: Guide students to see the humor in Esmeralda's saying ***¡Presente! quiero decir, aquí...*** Say: *Primero, Esmeralda habla en español, pero quiere hablar en inglés. Entonces trata de corregirse* (correct herself). *¿Qué piensan que quería decir la segunda vez?* ("Here")

- p. 103: Point out the use of the participles ***jugando*** and ***chapurreando*** in participial phrases. Remind students that they reviewed this type of usage before the reading.

Pre-AP* Support

- **Learning Objective:** Presentational Speaking (Cultural Comparison)

- **Background:** This task prepares students for the Spoken Presentational Communication tasks that focus on cultural comparisons.

- **Activity:** Have students prepare a two-minute (maximum) presentation on the following topic: Strategies for adapting to a new culture can be varied and unexpected. Students may use Esmeralda Santiago's experiences as described in the reading as a basis for the comparison. They should comment on a cross-cultural or adaptation experience they have had or may have read about, explaining the similarities and differences between the two.

- ***Pre-AP* Resource Book:** Comprehensive guide to Pre-AP* speaking skill development, pp. 39–50

Teacher-to-Teacher

e-amigos: Have students send their e-amigos a paragraph summarizing their responses to the question in item 4 of *¿Comprendiste?* Encourage students to express their feelings in an honest and sincere way. Have students print out their e-mails or send them to you for review.

Additional Resources

Student Resource: Guided Practice: Lectura, pp. 76–77

---

buscando señas de lo que les esperaba. Caminamos hasta la puerta de salida—. Tengo que esperar aquí un momentito.

—¿No te dijeron nada?

—No. Sólo que espere aquí.

Nos recostamos contra la pared. Enfrente de nosotras había una pizarra de corcho con recortes de periódico acerca de graduados de la escuela. En las orillas, alguien había escrito en letras de bloque, "P.A." y el año cuando el actor, bailarín o músico se había graduado. Cerré mis ojos y traté de imaginar un retrato de mí contra el corcho y la leyenda "P.A. '66" en la orilla.

La puerta al otro lado del pasillo se abrió, y la señora vestida de pardo sacó la cabeza.

—¿Esmeralda?

—¡Presente! quiero decir, aquí —alcé la mano.

Me esperó hasta que entré al salón. Había otra muchacha adentro, a quien me presentó como Bonnie, una estudiante en la escuela.

—¿Sabes lo que es una pantomima? —preguntó la señora. Señalé con la cabeza que sí—. Bonnie y tú son hermanas decorando el árbol de Navidad.

Bonnie se parecía mucho a Juanita Marín, a quien yo había visto por última vez cuatro años antes. Decidimos dónde poner el árbol invisible, y nos sentamos en el piso y actuamos como que estábamos sacando las decoraciones de una caja y colgándolas en las ramas.

Mi familia nunca había puesto un árbol de Navidad, pero yo me acordaba de cómo una vez yo ayudé a Papi a ponerle luces de colores alrededor de una mata de berenjenas[8] que dividía nuestra parcela de la de Doña Ana.

Empezamos por abajo, y le envolvimos el cordón eléctrico con las lucecitas rojas alrededor de la mata hasta que no nos quedaba más. Entonces Papi enchufó otro cordón eléctrico con más luces, y seguimos envolviéndolo hasta que las ramas se doblaban con el peso y la mata parecía estar prendida en llamas.

En un ratito se me olvidó dónde estaba, y que el árbol no existía, y que Bonnie no era mi hermana. Hizo como que me pasaba una decoración bien delicada y, al yo extender la mano para cogerla, hizo como que se me cayó y se rompió. Me asusté de que Mami entraría gritándonos que le habíamos roto una de sus figuras favoritas. Cuando empecé a recoger los fragmentos delicados de cristal invisible, una voz nos interrumpió y dijo:

—Gracias.

Bonnie se paró, sonrió y se fue.

La señora elegante estiró su mano para que se la estrechara.

—Notificaremos a tu escuela en unos días. Mucho gusto en conocerte.

Le estreché la mano a las tres señoras, y salí sin darles la espalda, en una neblina silenciosa, como si la pantomima me hubiera quitado la voz y el deseo de hablar.

De vuelta a casa, Mami me preguntaba qué había pasado, y yo le contestaba, "Na'. No pasó na'," avergonzada de que, después de tantas horas de práctica con Missis Johnson, Mister Barone y Mister Gatti, después del gasto de ropa y zapatos nuevos, después de que Mami

---

8 eggplant bush

DIFFERENTIATED INSTRUCTION

Heritage Language Learners

Have students research and locate a Spanish-language play whose theme they find interesting. Have them design and rehearse a scene from this play. Remind them to consider characterization, costume, and movement. Encourage students to perform the scene for the class.

Advanced Learners

Invite students who enjoyed this selection to read the rest of Santiago's *Cuando era puertorriqueña.* If more than one student is interested, encourage them to form their own book club to discuss the book.

tuvo que coger el día libre sin paga para llevarme hasta Manhattan, después de todo eso, no había pasado la prueba y nunca jamás saldría de Brooklyn.

Epílogo: Un día de éstos

Diez años después de mi graduación de Performing Arts High School, volví a visitar la escuela. Estaba viviendo en Boston, una estudiante becada en la universidad Harvard. La señora alta y elegante de mi prueba se había convertido en mi mentora durante mis tres años en la escuela. Después de mi graduación, se había casado con el principal de la escuela.

—Me acuerdo del día de tu prueba —me dijo, su cara angular soñadora, sus labios jugando con una sonrisa que todavía parecía tener que controlar.

¿Comprendiste?

En parejas, revisen la tabla que completaron y luego contesten estas preguntas:

1. ¿Crees que Esmeralda se preparó bien para su audición? ¿Por qué sí o por qué no?

2. ¿Cuál fue la verdadera razón por la que la aceptaron?

3. Muchos jóvenes inmigrantes se sienten atrapados *(trapped)* entre dos culturas. ¿Cómo creía Esmeralda que podía salir de esa situación?

4. Y tú, ¿tuviste alguna vez una experiencia similar a la de Esmeralda? ¿Sentiste alguna vez que no te identificabas con un grupo? Si es así, ¿cómo resolviste el problema?

Me había olvidado de la niña flaca y trigueña[9] con el pelo enrizado, el vestido de lana y las manos inquietas. Pero ella no. Me dijo que el jurado tuvo que pedirme que esperara afuera para poderse reír, ya que les parecía tan cómico ver a aquella chica puertorriqueña de catorce años chapurreando[10] un soliloquio acerca de una suegra posesiva durante el cambio de siglo, las palabras incomprensibles porque pasaban tan rápido.

—Admiramos el valor necesario para pararte al frente de nosotras y hacer lo que hiciste.

—¿Quiere decir que me aceptaron en la escuela no porque tenía talento, sino porque era atrevida?

Nos reímos juntas.

---

9 dark haired **10** babbling

5. En tu opinión, ¿cuál es el significado del título del libro? ¿Siente la autora que ahora, como estadounidense, ya no es puertorriqueña?

Más práctica GO

realidades.com | print

Guided WB pp. 76-77	✔	✔
Comm. WB p. 171	✔	✔
Cultural Reading Activity	✔	

 Fondo Cultural | Puerto Rico • Estados Unidos

Esmeralda Santiago (1940–) nació en Puerto Rico y emigró con su familia a Nueva York. Fue a la escuela The High School for Performing Arts, de la cual salió con una beca *(scholarship)* para estudiar en Harvard. Dos de sus libros, *Cuando era puertorriqueña* y *Casi una mujer* son autobiográficos. Describen el proceso de adaptación a otra cultura de una joven inmigrante. Aunque escribe desde el punto de vista de otra cultura, muchos de sus lectores se identifican con sus experiencias y sentimientos.

• ¿Cuál es una ventaja *(advantage)* de vivir entre dos culturas?

Esmeralda Santiago

ciento tres 103
Capítulo 2

¿Comprendiste? Standards: 1.1, 1.2, 1.3
Suggestions:

Post-reading: After students revisit their chart and make changes or additions, have them share the information they included. Ask volunteers which parts of the selection help them answer the *¿Comprendiste?* questions.

Answers will vary. For question 2, guide students to see the importance of the part of the selection in which Esmeralda loses herself in her memories during the pantomime. Ask a volunteer to read that part aloud. Say: *Estos dos recuerdos* (memories) *deben ser importantes porque interrumpen la acción del cuento. ¿Piensas que estos recuerdos tuvieron un efecto sobre su actuación en la pantomima? ¿Qué efecto?*

Fondo cultural
Standards: 1.2, 3.1, 4.2
Suggestions: Point out to students that this information sheds light on Santiago's purpose for writing the selection. Remind them that considering the author's purpose is a key factor in understanding what they read. Ask: *¿Cómo te puede ayudar esta información para responder a la pregunta número 5 de* ¿Comprendiste?
Answers will vary.

Mapa global interactivo, Actividad 4 Look at migration patterns from Puerto Rico to the United States.

Teacher-to-Teacher
The excerpt by Santiago might serve as a starting point for healthy discussions between students of varying cultural backgrounds. Encourage, but never force, students to talk with each other about their cultural similarities and differences.

For Further Reading:
Student Resources: Lecturas 3: "El mural," pp. 42–45, "Lamento," p. 51

Culture Note
In 1936, the High School for Music and Art was founded by New York City mayor Fiorello H. LaGuardia. Its mission was to provide talented students with access to artistic training. Today's facility, The LaGuardia High School for Music and Art and Performing Arts, opened its doors in 1984, just steps away from Lincoln Center.

21st Century Skills
Social and Cross Cultural Skills Have students interview people from their community who may have the experience of living between two cultures. What cultures are represented? How do their experiences compare to those of Esmeralda Santiago in *Cuando era puertorriqueña?*

Repaso del capítulo
Vocabulario y gramática

Review Activities

Formas, géneros y materiales de arte/ Profesiones artísticas: Have partners play ***Diez preguntas.*** One partner chooses a word or expression from these vocabulary categories. The other partner asks up to ten ***sí/no*** questions to try to determine what the word or expression is. Once the vocabulary item is determined or the asker is stumped, partners switch roles.

Para describir una obra de arte: Ask students to go back through the works of art shown in this chapter of the Student Edition or on the *Fine Arts Transparencies.* Have them take turns asking and answering questions about the works of art:

A: *¿Qué fue la fuente de inspiración para esta pintura?*
B: *Pienso que fue la alegría de estar en casa.*

En el escenario/Sobre la actuación: Ask pairs of students to make a labeled sketch or computer-generated representation of a theater with actors on stage and an audience. Have them present these to other pairs, pointing out the various parts and people of the theater. For the ***Sobre la actuación*** category, they can make comments about the actors and the audience: *Este señor se identifica con el galán.*

Otras palabras y expresiones: Students can use these words and expressions as they do the review activities for the other categories.

Sobre la música y la danza: Have pairs of students take turns giving each other TPR commands: *Toca la trompeta. Muéstrame unos pasos de tango. Canta … .*

Pretérito e imperfecto: You will need a small foam or paper cube. Write the numbers 1–4 on four of the sides. Sides 5–6 will not count. Sides 1–4 refer to the rules in the ***Pretérito e imperfecto*** chart.

Divide the class into two teams. Rotate through each team so that only one student speaks for the team at a time. However, the team's "speaker" can consult with teammates for up to thirty seconds before responding.

formas de arte

la cerámica	pottery
la escultura	sculpture
el mural	mural
la pintura	painting

géneros de arte

el autorretrato	self-portrait
la naturaleza muerta	still life
el retrato	portrait

materiales de arte

la paleta	palette
el pincel	brush

profesiones artísticas

el / la escritor(a)	writer
el / la escultor(a)	sculptor
el / la poeta	poet

para describir una obra de arte

abstracto, -a	abstract
expresar(se)	to express (oneself)
famoso, -a	famous
la figura	figure
el fondo	background
la fuente de inspiración	source of inspiration
la imagen	image
influir (i→y)	to influence
inspirar	to inspire
la obra de arte	work of art
el primer plano	foreground
representar	to represent
el sentimiento	feeling
el siglo	century
el tema	subject

en el escenario

el aplauso	applause
la entrada	ticket
el escenario	stage
el espectáculo	show
el micrófono	microphone

otras palabras y expresiones

a través de	through
mostrar(ue)	to show
parado, -a	to be standing
pararse	to stand up
parecerse (a)	to look, seem (like)
el poema	poem
realizar	to perform, to accomplish
la reseña	review
sentado, -a	to be seated
sonar (ue) (a)	to sound like
el taller	workshop
volverse (ue)	to become

sobre la música y la danza

clásico, -a	classical
el compás	rhythm
el conjunto	band
la danza	dance
la letra	lyrics
la melodía	melody
el movimiento	movement
el paso	step
el ritmo	rhythm
el tambor	drum
la trompeta	trumpet

sobre la actuación

actuar	to perform
destacar(se)	to stand out
el entusiasmo	enthusiasm
exagerar	to exaggerate
el gesto	gesture
identificarse con	to identify oneself with
la interpretación	interpretation
interpretar	to interpret

DIFFERENTIATED INSTRUCTION

Students with Special Needs

Provide concrete objects or listening examples to assist visually impaired students in their review of vocabulary from the chapter. Examples might include actual art pieces, art materials, as well as audio recordings of musical or dramatic performances.

Advanced Students

Have students use their creativity to make a video about a group of artists. Challenge them to incorporate all of the vocabulary on this page in their script. Remind them that there are many ways to do this. Some words might be seen on a sign in the background, others might occur in a letter someone reads, still others in a narration.

pretérito e imperfecto

Use the **preterite** to tell about an action that happened once and was completed. Ayer escribí un poema.	Use the **imperfect** to tell about habitual actions in the past. A menudo cantábamos juntos.	Use the **imperfect** to give background details, like time, date and weather. Eran las ocho y hacía mucho frío.	Use the **preterite** and the **imperfect** together when an action interrupts another that is taking place in the past. Caminábamos por el parque cuando empezó a llover.

estar + participio

The **past participle** is frequently used with the verb *estar*.			
El teatro **está cerrado**.		El tren **está parado**.	
In the following cases, the **past participle** is irregular.			
hacer: **hecho**	cubrir: **cubierto**	morir: **muerto**	escribir: **escrito**
abrir: **abierto**	decir: **dicho**	poner: **puesto**	volver: **vuelto**
descubrir: **descubierto**	romper: **roto**	ver: **visto**	resolver: **resuelto**

ser y estar

Remember that *ser* and *estar* both mean **to be** in English, but have different meanings in Spanish.	Use *ser*: to describe permanent characteristics La actriz es bonita. to tell the date Mañana es miércoles. to indicate possession Los pinceles son de Luis.	Use *estar*: to describe temporary characteristics El escenario está oscuro. to indicate location Están sobre la mesa. to form the progressive tenses Estoy dibujando un retrato.	Some adjectives have different meanings depending on whether they are used with *ser* or *estar*. Los niños están aburridos. *(The children are bored.)* Los niños son aburridos. *(Children are boring.)*

verbos con significados diferentes en el pretérito y en el imperfecto

The following Spanish verbs have different meanings in the imperfect and the preterite tenses.	
Yo **conocía** ese cuadro. *(I knew about that painting.)*	Él **conoció** a su maestro en Perú. *(He met his teacher in Perú.)*
No **sabíamos** que era tan tarde. *(We didn't know it was so late.)*	Nunca **supe** dónde estaba. *(I never found out where he/she was.)*
Ellos **querían** viajar hoy. *(They wanted to travel today.)*	Sofía **quiso ir**, pero perdió el avión. *(Sofía tried to go, but she missed the plane.)*
Antes **no podía** dibujar. *(Before, I couldn't draw.)*	Nunca **pude** dibujar. *(I was never able to draw.)*

ciento cinco **105**
Capítulo 2

(Cont'd):
Team A rolls the cube and has thirty seconds to come up with a sentence that follows the rule that was rolled. If they do, they earn a point. If their sentence is incorrect or time runs out, play passes to Team B. The team with the best score out of 21 wins.

Estar + *participio:* Have students work in pairs. Each partner writes down five sentences about actions completed in the past tense: *Carla abrió la ventana*. They then take turns reading one sentence at a time to each other. The listener comes up with a sentence based on the one he or she hears, that uses **estar +** *participio: La ventana está abierta.*

Ser y estar: Play a game that is set up the same way as the one for *Pretérito e imperfecto.* For rule number 4 in the chart, allow teams double the time (one minute) to come up with two sentences that contrast two different meanings of an adjective based on its use with **ser** and **estar.**

Verbos con significados diferentes en el pretérito y en el imperfecto: Have students write their own exercises modeled after *Actividad* 36 on p. 90. Their exercises need not be in story form; a numbered list is fine. Have them take each other's quizzes, and check and discuss answers.

Portfolio

Invite students to review the activities they completed in this chapter, including written reports, presentations, or other projects. Have them select one or two items to include in their portfolios with the Chapter Checklist and Self-Assessment Worksheet.

Additional Resources

Student Resource: Realidades para hispanohablantes, pp. 72–73

Teacher Resources:
- Teacher's Resource Book: Situation Cards, p. 109, Clip Art, pp. 110–116
- Assessment Program: Chapter Checklist and Self-Assessment Worksheet, pp. T49–T50

▶ *¡Pura vida!* is a storyline video that expands listening skills and is available within **realidades.com** or on DVD. Student activities and Teacher support are also assignable within **realidades.com**.

ENRICH YOUR TEACHING

Teacher-to-Teacher

After students review the vocabulary on the previous page, organize a "vocabulary bee." Have all students stand in a circle around the room. Give a student one item from the list. He or she has ten seconds to come up with a Spanish definition or explanation of the vocabulary or use it correctly in a sentence that clearly shows an understanding of its meaning. Students who make a mistake or run out of time sit down. The last student standing is the winner of the bee.

Performance Tasks

Standards: 1.1, 1.2, 1.3, 3.1

Student Resource: Realidades para hispanohablantes, pp. 74–75

Teacher Resources: Teacher's Resource book: Audio Script, p. 99; Audio Program DVD: Cap. 2, Track 25; Answer Keys: Student Edition, p. 34

1. Vocabulario

Suggestions: Encourage students to review the vocabulary from the *A primera vista* sections on pp. 68–71 and 82–85 before they complete the activity.

Answers:

1. b	5. b
2. c	6. c
3. c	7. c
4. d	8. a

2. Gramática

Suggestions: Remind students of the main points of the grammar presentations in *Capítulo* 2:

• uses of the preterite and the imperfect tenses
• constructions with **estar** + past participle
• uses of **ser** vs. **estar**
• adjectives that have different meanings when used in conjunction with the imperfect or the preterite tense

Answers:

1. d	5. a
2. a	6. a
3. d	7. d
4. a	8. c

Preparación para el examen

1 **Vocabulario** Escribe la letra de la palabra o expresión que mejor complete cada frase. Escribe tus respuestas en una hoja aparte.

1. El surrealismo fue _____ de inspiración de los pintores Miró y Dalí.
   a. el espectáculo   c. la melodía
   b. la fuente   d. la reseña

2. El actor principal _____ por su actuación y entusiasmo.
   a. se interpretó   c. se destacó
   b. se volvió   d. se inspiró

3. Si quieres bailar salsa, necesitas aprender _____ .
   a. la letra   c. los pasos
   b. los gestos   d. la actuación

4. La familia es _____ principal de muchos cuadros de Botero.
   a. el estilo   c. la forma
   b. el fondo   d. el tema

5. Picasso fue un pintor del _____ XX.
   a. estilo   c. año
   b. siglo   d. ritmo

6. Cuando termina una obra se oye _____ .
   a. un paso   c. un aplauso
   b. el micrófono   d. la paleta

7. La paleta de ese pintor _____ colores vivos como el rojo y el anaranjado.
   a. actúa   c. muestra
   b. interpreta   d. realiza

8. Los actores no dijeron nada pero se expresaron muy bien con _____ exagerados.
   a. gestos   c. escenarios
   b. poemas   d. compases

2 **Gramática** Escribe la letra de la palabra o expresión que mejor complete cada frase. Escribe tus respuestas en una hoja aparte.

1. La semana pasada _____ en una clase de cerámica.
   a. me inscribo   c. me inscribe
   b. me inscribía   d. me inscribí

2. No te van a oír bien porque el micrófono está _____ .
   a. roto   c. rompiendo
   b. rotas   d. romper

3. El museo estaba _____ todos los sábados.
   a. abrí   c. abiertos
   b. abriendo   d. abierto

4. Marta siempre _____ nerviosa antes de un ensayo.
   a. está   c. es
   b. están   d. era

5. Ayer, a causa de los truenos, yo no _____ dormir en toda la noche.
   a. pude   c. puedo
   b. podía   d. pudo

6. ¿Dónde _____ a tu mejor amigo?
   a. conociste   c. conocías
   b. conoces   d. conocieron

7. Nos perdimos porque no _____ bien la ciudad.
   a. conocemos   c. conocías
   b. conocimos   d. conocíamos

8. Yo _____ esta mañana que la función tuvo mucho éxito.
   a. sabía   c. supe
   b. sabe   d. saben

DIFFERENTIATED INSTRUCTION

Heritage Language Learners

Have students create a brochure for their own "virtual museum." Encourage them to select artists and works from the chapter, from their own areas of interest, or from their heritage country. Remind students to tailor the language of their descriptions to the appropriate audience.

Students with Learning Difficulties

In reviewing the vocabulary and grammar of the chapter, use gestures and facial expressions to support students in their choice of the correct answer. Use TPR to support meaning of the vocabulary choices.

Instant Check	✔	
Puzzles	✔	
Core WB pp. 33–34		✔
Comm. WB pp. 172, 173–175	✔	✔

En el examen vas a . . .	Éstas son las tareas de práctica que te pueden ser útiles para el examen . . .	Para repasar, ve a tu libro de texto impreso o digital . . .

Interpretive

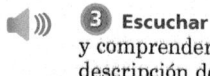 ③ **Escuchar** Escuchar y comprender la descripción de un cuadro

El guía de un museo está describiendo uno de los cuadros de la galería de arte moderno. (a) ¿Qué tipo de pintura describe? (b) ¿Quién es el pintor? (c) ¿Qué se ve en primer plano? (d) ¿Qué se ve al fondo? (e) ¿Cómo son los colores?

pp. 68–69 *A primera vista 1: Vocabulario en contexto*
p. 73 Actividades 8–9
p. 74 Actividad 11
p. 75 Actividades 12, 13

Interpersonal

 ④ **Hablar** Hablar de las actividades que tienen lugar en una escuela de arte

Un nuevo estudiante visita por primera vez tu escuela de arte. Tu tarea es mostrarle los talleres de la escuela y explicarle lo que pasa en cada clase. Incluye en tu descripción (a) las clases que ofrecen, (b) los materiales que necesitan para cada clase, (c) las actividades que hacen en cada clase, (d) las obras que los estudiantes realizan en cada clase.

p. 68 *A primera vista 1: Vocabulario en contexto*
p. 72 Actividad 7

Interpretive

 ⑤ **Leer** Leer y comprender las notas de un álbum musical

Lee la reseña sobre un álbum musical y di (a) ¿cuál es el tipo de música del álbum musical?, (b) ¿qué cosas le gustaron al crítico?, (c) ¿qué no le gustó?, (d) ¿qué cree que puede ser mejor?

pp. 82–85 *A primera vista 2: Vocabulario en contexto*
p. 86 Actividad 29
p. 87 Actividad 31
pp. 92–93 Actividades 38–39

La letra de las canciones del conjunto Sol y salsa suena a poesía. Pero creo que la interpretación puede ser mejor. El ritmo que da el tambor se destaca del de la trompeta y va bien con todo el conjunto. Me gustó mucho la melodía de la primera canción. Cuando tocan la trompeta en algunas canciones, creo que exageran. Se ve que el conjunto se inspiró mucho al tocar la música.

Presentational

 ⑥ **Escribir** Escribir una reseña sobre una obra de teatro que presentaron en tu escuela

Trabajas como reportero(a) para el periódico de la escuela y tienes que escribir una reseña sobre una obra de teatro. Incluye (a) el nombre de la obra, (b) los actores principales, (c) una breve descripción del argumento, (d) la actuación de los protagonistas.

pp. 84–85 *A primera vista 2: Vocabulario en contexto*
p. 89 Actividad 34
pp. 92–93 Actividades 38–39

Cultures

 ⑦ **Pensar** Demostrar cómo las artes pueden expresar las perspectivas y actitudes del artista

Piensa en las obras de Goya, Dalí o Botero. ¿Como usaron su arte para expresar sus actitudes y sus perspectivas sobre lo que pasaba en sus vidas? ¿De qué manera expresan los jóvenes de hoy sus actitudes por el arte?

pp. 86–87 Actividades 29–31
p. 89 Actividad 35
pp. 94–95 *Puente a la cultura*

ciento siete **107**
Capítulo 2

3. Escuchar

Suggestions: Use the audio or read from the script.

◀)) **Answers:**
a. un paisaje
b. Pablo Picasso
c. una casa y árboles
d. el mar Mediterráneo
e. los colores no son vivos

4. Hablar

Suggestions: Point out that this activity involves pair work. One partner should act as the new student, asking questions and making comments. The other should act as the student showing him or her around. The result is a dialogue.

Answers will vary.

5. Leer

Suggestions: Tell students to refer to pp. 68–71 and 82–85 if they have questions about vocabulary in the music review.

Answers:
(a) salsa
(b) el ritmo del tambor y la melodía de la primera canción
(c) la trompeta en algunas canciones
(d) la interpretación

6. Escribir

Suggestions: Encourage students to organize their thoughts in a list like the one on p. 93 before writing their reviews.

Answers will vary.

7. Pensar

Suggestions: Encourage students to put their thoughts down using a T-chart. They can label the columns *Goya, Dalí, Botero* and *artistas jóvenes.*

Answers will vary.

DIFFERENTIATED ASSESSMENT

CORE ASSESSMENT
- **Assessment Program:** Examen del capítulo 2, pp. 55–58
- **Audio Program DVD:** Cap. 2, Track 26
- **ExamView:** Chapter Test, Test Banks A and B

ADVANCED/PRE-AP*
- **ExamView Pre-AP* Test Bank**
- **Pre-AP* Resource Book,** pp. 141–143

STUDENTS NEEDING EXTRA HELP
- **Alternate Assessment Program:** Examen del capítulo 2
- **Audio Program DVD:** Cap. 2, Track 26

HERITAGE LEARNERS
- **Assessment Program: Realidades para hispanohablantes:** Examen del capítulo 2
- **ExamView Heritage Learner Test Bank**

3 Chapter Overview

- **health and nutrition**

Vocabulary
- symptoms and remedies
- health food, nutrition, and fitness

Grammar
- affirmative and negative *tú* commands
- commands with *Ud.* and *Uds.*
- subjunctive of regular, irregular, and stem-changing verbs

Cultural Perspectives
- art of Rufino Tamayo
- medicinal plants in Latin America
- eating habits of young Spaniards
- physical education in Spain
- ancient sports in Mexico and Central America
- Spanish and Latin American teen magazines
- habits related to food and fitness
- sports in ancient American civilizations

¡Pura vida!
- Watch an engaging video episode about a group of young people in Costa Rica!

CHAPTER SUPPORT

Bulletin Boards

Theme: *Pirámide de alimentos*

Ask students to cut out or draw the appropriate food groups to include in the new food pyramid that they will create on the bulletin board. The left column of the pyramid should have: *pan, cereales, arroz, pasta*. Under the next two categories, they will place *vegetales* on the left side and *frutas* on the right. They will place *grasas, aceites* under the thinnest column. Products such as *leche, yogur, quesos* will be placed in the blue column, and *carne, pollo, pescado, huevos, guisantes* will be on the last column. This will be a visual guide of a healthy and complete diet.

Hands-on Culture

Recipe: *Yogur de frutas helado*

This Mexican recipe provides a simple and healthy way to enjoy a nutritious dessert.

Ingredients: 2 cups of lowfat yogurt (vanilla or other flavors), 2 pears or apples, 4 tablespoons of honey, 4 small serving bowls

Peel and cut the fruit into small cubes. Discard the seeds.

Fill each container halfway with yogurt.

Add the fruit to each container.

Add a tablespoon of honey.

Mix the contents in each container.

Place the bowls in the refrigerator.

Game

Síntomas y remedios

Play this game in Capítulo 3, after students have learned vocabulary related to symptoms and remedies.

Players: entire class

Materials: index cards, pen, a show box

Rules:
1. Students write names of symptoms on index cards and place them in a shoe box.

2. Shake the box to mix up the index cards. Then call on a volunteer to come to the front of the class. The volunteer draws an index card from the box and acts out the symptom.

3. Students take turns guessing the correct symptom. Once they guess the symptom they must provide a remedy or solution to alleviate it.
   Student 1: ¿Tienes gripe?
   Student 2: Sí.
   Student 1: Entonces debes tomar antibióticos.

4. The student that guesses the symptom and provides the correct remedy becomes the new volunteer. Play continues until every student has had a chance to ask one or two questions.

Variation: Instead of physical ailments, students will act out emotional states such as *"estoy en la luna," "me caigo de sueño,"* and so on.

CHAPTER PROJECT

Buenos hábitos

Overview: Students create a proposal for a complete health program that consists of three parts: 1. a healthy diet, 2. a physical exercise routine, and 3. the selection of a song in Spanish to accompany their routine. They should include in their proposals the name of the artist and the country of origin. Students can create their health program digitally or by hand, or by using a combination of resources. Students then give an oral presentation of their complete program to the class.

Resources: online or print photos, image editing and page layout software and/or poster board, markers, glue, and an audio device.

Sequence: (suggestions for when to do each step are found throughout the chapter)

STEP 1. Review sections of the chapter and instructions, so students know what is expected of them. Hand out the "Chapter 3 Project Instructions and Rubric" from the *Teacher's Resource Book*.

STEP 2. Students submit a draft of the appropriate diet and matching exercises. Return the drafts with your suggestions. For vocabulary and grammar practice, ask partners to present their drafts to each other.

STEP 3. Students do a layout leaving room for photos or drawings and descriptions.

STEP 4. Students submit completed health programs.

STEP 5. Students present their health programs to the class, play the accompanying song and explain why their program promotes health.

Options:
1. Students can modify and adapt their exercise programs for body building (after appropriate research).
2. Students feature only one aspect of the health program.

Assessment:

Here is a detailed rubric for assessing this project.

Chapter 3 Project: *Buenos hábitos*

RUBRIC	Score 1	Score 3	Score 5
Your evidence of planning	You have no written draft or poster layout.	Either your draft or your layout is missing.	You show evidence of corrected draft and layout.
Your use of illustrations	You have no music or song.	You are missing data about the artist.	You include music and artist's data.
Your presentation	Your presentation is weak.	Your diet and exercise program don't complement each other.	You present a coordinated program.

21st Century Skills

Look for tips throughout Chapter 3 to enrich your teaching by integrating 21st Century Skills. Suggestions for the Chapter Project and Culture follow below.

Chapter Project

Modify the Chapter Project with these suggestions:

Encourage Media Literacy

Ask students to go online to their favorite video-sharing site and view models of exercise programs. The handout "Analyze Media Content" will help them determine the best way to present their proposed diet and exercise plan.

Foster Creativity and Innovation

Encourage students to be creative in selecting the Spanish song to accompany their presentation. What is the role of music and exercise? What songs are used during professional sports games in this country? If they cannot find a Spanish song, encourage them to write their own song or rap.

Enhance Communication

Provide students with the handout "Give an Effective Presentation" to remind them of the importance of body language, tone of voice, eye contact in a presentation.

Chapter Culture

Develop Flexibility and Adaptability

Help students bridge cultural differences by offering opportunities to discuss alternative vs. traditional medicine, as presented in the *Fondo cultural* on p. 120.

▶ **Videodocumentario** View *¿Qué haces para estar saludable?* online with the class to learn more about eating and exercise habits and medical care in the Spanish-speaking world.

AT A GLANCE

Objectives
- **Listen to and read about health advice and nutrition**
- **Talk and write about healthy eating habits and exercise**
- **Give advice to others about healthy lifestyles**
- **Compare an ancient game with a modern game**
- **Understand the connection between healthy habits and lifestyle in Spanish-speaking countries**

A ver si recuerdas... ♻
- Fruits and vegetables
- Descriptions
- Breakfast, lunch, dinner
- Direct object pronouns
- Indirect object pronouns

Recycle ♻
- Pronunciation of the letter *d* between vowels

Vocabulary
- Symptoms and remedies
- Parts of the body
- Health, food, and nutrition
- Physical fitness and exercise
- Moods

Grammar
- Affirmative and negative *tú* commands
- Affirmative and negative *Ud.* and *Uds.* commands
- Subjunctive verbs

Culture
- Rufino Tamayo, p. 113
- Healing plants in Latin America, p. 120
- Eating habits of Spanish teenagers, p. 124
- World Health Day, p. 129
- Physical education in Spain, p. 131
- Mayan ball game, pp. 140–141
- Teen magazines, p. 149

RESOURCES

FOR THE STUDENT	ONLINE	DVD	PRINT	FOR THE TEACHER	ONLINE	PREEXP	DVD	PRINT
Plan				Interactive TE and Resource DVD	•		•	
				Teacher's Resource Book, pp. 143–203	•		•	•
				Pre-AP* Resource Book, pp. 144–146	•		•	•
				Lesson Plans	•			•
				Mapa global interactivo	•			
A ver si recuerdas PP. 108–111								
Review	*A ver si recuerdas* Study Plan	•			*A ver si recuerdas* Study Plan	•			
	Guided WB, pp. 78–81	•	•	•	Vocabulary and Grammar Transparencies, 2, 66–69	•	•	•	
	Core WB, pp. 35–36	•	•	•	Answer Keys: Student Edition, pp. 35–36	•	•	•	
	Hispanohablantes WB, p. 76			•					
Introducción PP. 112–113								
Present	Student Edition, pp. 112–113	•	•	•	Interactive TE and Resource DVD	•		•	
	DK Reference Atlas	•	•		Teacher's Resource Book, pp. 144–147	•		•	•
	Videonovela: ¡Pura vida!	•	•		Video Program Teacher's Guide, Cap. 3				•
	¡Pura vida! Video Activities	•			Galería de fotos		•		
	Hispanohablantes WB, p. 77			•	Fine Art Transparencies, 66	•	•	•	
					Map Transparencies, 14, 20	•	•	•	
Vocabulario en contexto PP. 114–117/126–129								
Present & Practice	Student Edition, pp. 114–117/126–129	•	•	•	Interactive TE and Resource DVD	•		•	
	Audio	•	•		Teacher's Resource Book, pp. 148–149, 152–153,	•		•	•
	Flashcards	•	•		168–175/150–151, 153–155, 168–175				
	Instant Check	•			Vocabulary Clip Art	•	•	•	•
	Guided WB, pp. 82–90/97–104	•	•	•	Audio Program	•	•	•	
	Core WB, pp. 37–38/42–43	•	•	•	Vocabulary and Grammar Transparencies, 70–72/76–79	•	•	•	
	Comm. WB, pp. 40/44	•	•	•	Answer Keys: Student Edition, pp. 36–38/41–42	•	•	•	
	Hispanohablantes WB, pp. 78–79/88–89			•					
Assess and Remediate					Pruebas 3–1/3–6 Assessment Program, pp. 59–60/69–70	•		•	•
					Hispanohablantes, pp. 59–60/69–70	•		•	•

RESOURCES

FOR THE STUDENT	ONLINE	DVD	PRINT	FOR THE TEACHER	ONLINE	PREEXP	DVD	PRINT
Vocabulario en uso PP. **118–120/130–131**								
Present & Practice Student Edition, pp. 118–120/130–131	•	•	•	Interactive Whiteboard Vocabulary Activities	•		•	
Instant Check	•			Interactive TE and Resource DVD	•		•	
Comm. WB, pp. 36/37	•	•	•	Teacher's Resource Book, pp. 153, 159–162/155, 163–164	•		•	•
Hispanohablantes WB, pp. 80–82/90–92			•	Audio Program	•	•	•	
Communicative Pair Activities	•			Videomodelos	•		•	
				Vocabulary and Grammar Transparencies, 72/78	•	•	•	
				Answer Keys: Student Edition, pp. 38–40/42–43	•	•	•	•
Assess and Remediate				Pruebas 3–2/3–7 with Study Plans	•			
				Pruebas 3–2/3–7: Assessment Program, pp. 61–62/71–72	•		•	•
				Hispanohablantes, pp. 61–62/71–72	•		•	•
Gramática PP. **121–125/132–139**								
Present & Practice Student Edition, pp. 121–125/132–139	•	•	•	Interactive Whiteboard Grammar Activities	•		•	
Instant Check	•			Interactive TE and Resource DVD	•		•	
Animated Verbs	•			Teacher's Resource Book, pp. 153, 161–162/155–156, 165–166	•		•	•
Tutorial Video: Grammar	•			Audio Program	•	•	•	
Canción de hip hop	•			Videomodelos	•		•	
Guided WB, pp. 91–96/105–110	•	•	•	Map Transparencies, 20/ 80–82	•		•	
Core WB, pp. 39–41/44–46	•	•	•	Vocabulary and Grammar Transparencies, 40, 73–75	•		•	
Comm. WB, pp. 37, 41–43/38–39, 45–47, 176	•	•	•	Answer Keys: Student Edition, pp. 40–41/43–47	•	•	•	
Hispanohablantes WB, pp. 83–87/93–97			•					
Communicative Pair Activities	•							
Assess and Remediate				Pruebas 3–3, 3–4, 3–5/3–8, 3–9, 3–10 with Study Plans	•			
				Pruebas 3–3, 3–4, 3–5/3–8, 3–9, 3–10 Assessment Program, pp. 63, 64, 65/73, 74, 75	•		•	•
				Hispanohablantes, pp. 63, 64, 65/73, 74, 75	•		•	•
				Examen 1, Examen 2: Vocab. y gramática, pp. 66–68/76–78	•		•	•
¡Adelante! PP. **140–149**								
Application Student Edition, pp. 140–149	•	•	•	Interactive TE and Resource DVD	•		•	
Online Cultural Reading	•			Teacher's Resource Book, pp. 156, 158	•		•	•
Guided WB, pp. 111–113	•	•	•	Video Program: Videodocumentario	•		•	
Comm. WB, pp. 48–49, 177	•	•	•	Video Program Teacher's Guide, Cap. 3	•		•	
Hispanohablantes WB, pp. 98–103			•	Vocabulary and Grammar Transparencies, 4	•	•	•	
Videodocumentario	•	•		Answer Keys: Student Edition, pp. 47–48	•	•	•	
Lecturas 3, pp. 54–60			•					
Repaso del capítulo PP. **150–153**								
Review Student Edition, pp. 150–153	•	•	•	Interactive TE and Resource DVD	•		•	
Online Puzzles and Games	•			Teacher's Resource Book, pp. 157, 167–175	•		•	
Core WB, pp. 47–48	•	•	•	Audio Program	•	•	•	
Comm. WB, pp. 178–182	•	•	•	Answer Keys: Student Edition, p. 48	•	•	•	
Hispanohablantes WB, pp. 104–107			•					
Instant Check	•							
Chapter Assessment								
Assess				Examen del capítulo 3: Assessment Program, pp. 79–82	•		•	•
				Alternate Assessment Program, pp. 25–34	•		•	•
				Hispanohablantes, pp. 79–82	•		•	•
				Audio Program, Cap. 3, Examen	•		•	
				ExamView: Test Banks A and B (questions only online)	•		•	
				Heritage Learner Test Bank	•		•	
				Pre–AP* Test Bank	•		•	

REGULAR SCHEDULE (50 MINUTES)

DAY	Warm-up / Assess	Preview / Present / Practice / Communicate	Wrap-up / Homework Options
1	**Warm-up (10 min.)** • Return Examen del capítulo: Capítulo 2	**Repaso (35 min.)** • A ver si recuerdas . . .	**Wrap-up and Homework Options (5 min.)** • Core Practice 3-1, 3-2
2	**Warm-up (10 min.)** • Homework check	**Chapter Opener (10 min.)** • Objectives • Arte y cultura **Vocabulario en contexto 1 (25 min.)** • Presentation: Vocabulario y gramática en contexto • Actividades 1, 2	**Wrap-up and Homework Options (5 min.)** • Clip Art Vocabulary
3	**Warm-up (10 min.)** • Homework check	**Vocabulario en contexto 1 (35 min.)** • Presentation: La alimentación de los jóvenes • Actividades 3, 5	**Wrap-up and Homework Options (5 min.)** • Core Practice 3-3, 3-4 • Prueba 3-1: Vocabulary • Actividad 6 recognition
4	**Warm-up (10 min.)** • Actividad 4 • Homework check ✔**Formative Assessment (10 min.)** • Prueba 3-1: Vocabulary recognition	**Vocabulario en uso 1 (25 min.)** • Actividades 7, 8, 9, 10 • Interactive Whiteboard Vocabulary Activities • Ampliación del lenguaje	**Wrap-up and Homework Options (5 min.)** • Writing Activities • Prueba 3-2 with Study Plan: Vocabulary production
5	**Warm-up (10 min.)** • Homework check ✔**Formative Assessment (10 min.)** • Prueba 3-2 with Study Plan: Vocabulary production	**Gramática y vocabulario en uso 1 (25 min.)** • Fondo cultural • Presentation: Mandatos afirmativos con *tú* • Interactive Whiteboard Grammar Activities • Actividades 11, 12 • Writing Activity	**Wrap-up and Homework Options (5 min.)** • Core Practice 3-5 • Prueba 3-3 with Study Plan: Presentation: Mandatos afirmativos con *tú*
6	**Warm-up (10 min.)** • Homework check ✔**Formative Assessment (10 min.)** • Prueba 3-3 with Study Plan: Mandatos afirmativos con *tú*	**Gramática y vocabulario en uso 1 (25 min.)** • Presentation: Mandatos negativos con *tú* • Interactive Whiteboard Grammar Activities • Actividades 13, 14 • Communicative Pair Activity	**Wrap-up and Homework Options (5 min.)** • Core Practice 3-6 • Prueba 3-4 with Study Plan: Mandatos negativos con *tú*
7	**Warm-up (10 min.)** • Writing Activity • Homework check ✔**Formative Assessment (10 min.)** • Prueba 3-4 with Study Plan: Mandatos negativos con *tú*	**Gramática y vocabulario en uso 1 (25 min.)** • Presentación: Mandatos afirmativos y negativos con *Ud.* y *Uds.* • Interactive Whiteboard Grammar Activities • Actividades 15, 16, 17, 20 • Writing Activity	**Wrap-up and Homework Options (5 min.)** • Core Practice 3-7 • Actividad 18 • Prueba 3-5 with Study Plan: Mandatos afirmativos y negativos con *Ud.* y *Uds.*
8	**Warm-up (10 min.)** • Actividad 19 • Homework check ✔**Formative Assessment (10 min.)** • Prueba 3-5 with Study Plan: Mandatos afirmativos y negativos con *Ud.* y *Uds.*	**Vocabulario en contexto 2 (25 min.)** • Presentation: Vocabulario y gramática en contexto • Actividades 21, 22, 23	**Wrap-up and Homework Options (5 min.)** • Clip Art Vocabulary • Examen: Vocabulario y gramática 1
9	**Warm-up (10 min.)** • Clip Art Vocabulary ✔**Formative Assessment (25 min.)** • Examen: Vocabulario y gramática 1	**Vocabulario en contexto 2 (10 min.)** • Presentation: ¿Qué me aconsejas? • Actividad 24 • Presentation: Día Mundial de la Salud	**Wrap-up and Homework Options (5 min.)** • Core Practice 3-8, 3-9 • Prueba 3-6: Vocabulary recognition
10	**Warm-up (10 min.)** • Homework check • Actividades 25, 26 ✔**Formative Assessment (10 min.)** • Prueba 3-6: Vocabulary recognition	**Vocabulario en uso 2 (25 min.)** • Actividades 27, 28, 29 • Interactive Whiteboard Vocabulary Activities • Fondo cultural • Audio and Video Activities	**Wrap-up and Homework Options (5 min.)** • Writing Activities • Prueba 3-7 with Study Plan: Vocabulary production

REGULAR SCHEDULE (50 MINUTES)

DAY	Warm-up / Assess	Preview / Present / Practice / Communicate	Wrap-up / Homework Options
11	**Warm-up (10 min.)** • Writing Activity • Homework check ✔**Formative Assessment (10 min.)** • Prueba 3-7 with Study Plan: Vocabulary production	**Gramática y vocabulario en uso 2 (25 min.)** • Presentation: El subjuntivo: Verbos regulares • Interactive Whiteboard Grammar Activities • Actividades 30, 31, 32 • El español en el mundo del trabajo	**Wrap-up and Homework Options (5 min.)** • Core Practice 3-10 • Prueba 3-8 with Study Plan: El subjuntivo: Verbos regulares
12	**Warm-up (10 min.)** • Actividad 33 • Homework check ✔**Formative Assessment (10 min.)** • Prueba 3-8 with Study Plan: El subjuntivo: Verbos regulares	**Gramática y vocabulario en uso 2 (25 min.)** • Presentation: El subjuntivo: Verbos irregulares • Actividades 34, 35, 37 • Presentation: El subjuntivo: Verbos con cambio de raíz • Interactive Whiteboard Grammar Activities • Actividad 39	**Wrap-up and Homework Options (5 min.)** • Actividad 36 • Core Practice 3-11, 3-12 • Prueba 3-9, 3-10 with Study Plans
13	**Warm-up (10 min.)** • Actividad 38 • Homework check ✔**Formative Assessment (15 min.)** • Pruebas 3-9, 3-10 with Study Plans	**Gramática y vocabulario en uso 2 (20 min.)** • Actividad 40 • En voz alta • Communicative Pair Activity	**Wrap-up and Homework Options (5 min.)** • Examen: Vocabulario y gramática 2
14	**Warm-up (5 min.)** • Writing Activity ✔**Formative Assessment (30 min.)** • Examen: Vocabulario y gramática 2	**¡Adelante! (10 min.)** • Presentación oral: Step 1	**Wrap-up and Homework Options (5 min.)** • Presentación oral: Step 2
15	**Warm-up (10 min.)** • Presentación oral: Step 2	**¡Adelante! (35 min.)** • Presentación oral: Step 3	**Wrap-up and Homework Options (5 min.)** • Un juego muy antiguo • ¿Comprendiste? • Usa tus conocimientos
16	**Warm-up (15 min.)** • Un juego muy antiguo: ¿Comprendiste? • Homework check	**¡Adelante! (30 min.)** • ¿Qué me cuentas? 1, 2, 3 • View Video • View Activities 1, 2, 3	**Wrap-up and Homework Options (5 min.)** • Presentación escrita: Steps 1, 2
17	**Warm-up (10 min.)** • Video Activity 4	**¡Adelante! (15 min.)** • Presentación escrita: Step 3 **Repaso (20 min.)** • Preparación para el examen: Actividades 3, 4	**Wrap-up and Homework Options (5 min.)** • Presentación escrita: Step 4 • Fondo cultural
18	**Warm-up (10 min.)** • Homework check	**¡Adelante! (35 min.)** • Lectura • Interacción con la lectura	**Wrap-up and Homework Options (5 min.)** • Core Practice: Organizer 3-13, 3-14 • Instant Check
19	**Warm-up (20 min.)** • Preparación para el examen: Actividades 1, 2 • Homework check	**Repaso (25 min.)** • Preparación para el examen: Actividades 5, 6, 7 • Other review	**Wrap-up and Homework Options (5 min.)** • Examen del capítulo
20	**Warm-up (5 min.)** • Answer questions ✔**Summative Assessment (44 min.)** • Examen del capítulo		**Wrap-up and Homework Options (1 min.)** • A ver si recuerdas: Capítulo 4 • Actividades 1-4, 6

BLOCK SCHEDULE (90 MINUTES)

DAY	Warm-up / Assess	Preview / Present / Practice / Communicate	Wrap-up / Homework Options
1	**Warm-up** (35 min.) • Return Examen del capítulo: Capítulo 2 • A ver si recuerdas . . . • Actividad 7 • Homework check	**Chapter Opener** (10 min.) • Objectives • Arte y cultura **Vocabulario en contexto 1** (30 min.) • Presentation: Vocabulario y gramática en contexto • Actividades 1, 2 • Presentation: La alimentación de los jóvenes • Actividades 3, 4, 5 **Vocabulario en uso 1** (10 min.) • Actividades 7, 8	**Wrap-up and Homework Options** (5 min.) • Core Practice 3-3, 3-4 • Clip Art Vocabulary • Prueba 3-1: Vocabulary recognition
2	**Warm-up** (15 min.) • Actividad 6 • Homework check ✔**Formative Assessment** (10 min.) • Prueba 3-1: Vocabulary recognition	**Vocabulario en uso 1** (60 min.) • Actividades 9, 10 • Interactive Whiteboard Vocabulary Activities • Ampliación del lenguaje • Fondo cultural • Writing or Audio Activities • Communicative Pair Activity	**Wrap-up and Homework Options** (5 min.) • Writing Activities • Prueba 3-2 with Study Plan: Vocabulary production
3	**Warm-up** (10 min.) • Writing Activity • Homework check ✔**Formative Assessment** (10 min.) • Prueba 3-2 with Study Plan : Vocabulary production	**Gramática y vocabulario en uso 1** (65 min.) • Presentation: Mandatos afirmativos con *tú* • Interactive Whiteboard Grammar Activities • Actividades 11, 12 • Presentation: Mandatos negativos con *tú* • Actividades 13, 14 • Writing Activities	**Wrap-up and Homework Options** (5 min.) • Core Practice 3-5, 3-6 • Pruebas 3-3, 3-4 with Study Plans: Mandatos afirmativos con *tú*, Mandatos negativos con *tú*
4	**Warm-up** (10 min.) • Homework check ✔**Formative Assessment** (20 min.) • Pruebas 3-3, 3-4 with Study Plans: Mandatos afirmativos con *tú*, Mandatos negativos con *tú*	**Gramática y vocabulario en uso 1** (35 min.) • Presentation: Mandatos afirmativos y negativos con *Ud.* y *Uds.* • Interactive Whiteboard Grammar Activities • Actividades 15, 16, 17, 20 • Communicative Pair Activity **Vocabulario en contexto 2** (20 min.) • Presentation: Vocabulario y gramática en contexto • Actividades 21, 22, 23	**Wrap-up and Homework Options** (5 min.) • Actividades 18, 19 • Core Practice 3-7 • Prueba 3-5 with Study Plan: Mandatos afirmativos y negativos con *Ud.* y *Uds.* • Examen: Vocabulario y gramática 1
5	**Warm-up** (10 min.) • Homework check ✔**Formative Options** (40 min.) • Prueba 3-5 with Study Plan: Mandatos afirmativos y negativos con *Ud.* y *Uds.* • Examen: Vocabulario y gramática 1	**Vocabulario en contexto 2** (25 min.) • Presentation: ¿Qué me aconsejas? • Actividades 24, 25, 26 **Vocabulario en uso 2** (10 min.) • Actividad 29 • Interactive Whiteboard Vocabulary Activities • Fondo cultural	**Wrap-up and Homework Options** (5 min.) • Core Practice 3-8, 3-9 • Prueba 3-6: Vocabulary recognition

BLOCK SCHEDULE (90 MINUTES)

DAY	Warm-up / Assess	Preview / Present / Practice / Communicate	Wrap-up / Homework Options
6	**Warm-up** (15 min.) • Actividad 28 • Homework check ✔**Formative Assessment** (10 min.) • Prueba 3-6: Vocabulary recognition	**Gramática y vocabulario en uso 2** (60 min.) • Actividad 27 • Presentation: El subjuntivo: Verbos regulares • Interactive Whiteboard Grammar Activities • Actividades 30, 31, 32 • Fondo cultural • El español en el mundo del trabajo	**Wrap-up and Homework Options** (5 min.) • Core Practice 3-10 • Pruebas 3-7, 3-8 with Study Plans: Vocabulary production, El subjuntivo: Verbos regulares
7	**Warm-up** (15 min.) • Actividad 33 • Homework check ✔**Formative Assessment** (20 min.) • Pruebas 3-7, 3-8 with Study Plans: Vocabulary production, El subjuntivo: Verbos regulares	**Gramática y vocabulario en uso 2** (40 min.) • Presentation: Subjuntivo: Verbos irregulares • Presentation: Subjuntivo: Verbos con cambio de raíz • Interactive Whiteboard Grammar Activities • Actividades 34, 35, 37 • Actividad 38 **¡Adelante!** (15 min.) • Presentación oral: Steps 1, 2	**Wrap-up and Homework Options** (5 min.) • Presentación oral: Step 2
8	**Warm-up** (15 min.) • Actividad 36 • Homework check ✔**Formative Assessment** (40 min.) • Presentación oral: Step 3	**Gramática y vocabulario en uso 2** (30 min.) • En voz alta • Actividades 39, 40 • Communicative Pair Activity	**Wrap-up and Homework Options** (5 min.) • Core Practice 3-11, 3-12 • Prueba 3-9 with Study Plan: El subjuntivo: Verbos irregulares • Prueba 3-10 with Study Plan: El subjuntivo: Verbos con cambio de raíz • Examen: Vocabulario y gramática 2
9	**Warm-up** (10 min.) • Homework check ✔**Formative Assessment Options** (30 min.) • Prueba 3-9 with Study Plan: El Subjuntivo: Verbos irregulares • Prueba 3-10 with Study Plan: El Subjuntivo: Verbos con cambio de raíz • Examen: Vocabulario y gramática 2	**¡Adelante!** (45 min.) • Presentation: Un juego muy antiguo • ¿Comprendiste? • Usa tus conocimientos • ¿Qué me cuentas? 1, 2, 3 • View Video • Video Activities • Presentación escrita: Step 1	**Wrap-up and Homework Options** (5 min.) • Presentación escrita: Step 2 • Preparación para el examen: Actividades 1, 2
10	**Warm-up** (20 min.) • Presentación escrita: Step 3 • Homework check	**¡Adelante!** (35 min.) • Lectura • Interacción con la lectura • Fondo cultural **Repaso** (30 min.) • Preparación para el examen: Actividades 3, 4, 6	**Wrap-up and Homework Options** (5 min.) • Presentación escrita: Step 4 • Core Practice: Organizer 3-13, 3-14 • Instant Check • Preparación para el examen: Actividades 5, 7 • Examen del capítulo
11	**Warm-up** (15 min.) • Homework check ✔**Summative Assessment** (45 min.) • Examen del capítulo	**Theme Game** (15 min.) **A ver si recuerdas – Capítulo 4** (10 min.) • Presentation: Vocabulario • Presentation: Gramática	**Wrap-up and Homework Options** (5 min.) • A ver si recuerdas – Capítulo 4 • Actividades 1–6 • Core Practice 4-1, 4-2

3 Recycle

Vocabulario Repaso

Core Instruction

Standards: 1.1, 1.2

Resources: Voc. and Gram. Transparency 66

Suggestions: Before presenting the material in this review section, consider testing your students' command of the material by assigning the Study Plan. Students will automatically be given additional practice of the material they have not yet mastered, and you can focus your review based on the class's overall performance on the post-test.

Give students a few minutes to "create" a meal comprised of at least five of the foods from the lists. Then have them take turns describing and commenting on their "creations": *Es mi desayuno de sábado. Es muy sabroso. Tiene dos salchichas de cerdo, dos huevos fritos y pan tostado sin mantequilla. A veces como unas papas fritas. Para beber, hay café con leche y jugo de naranja.*

1 Standards: 1.1, 1.3

Resources: Voc. and Gram. Transparency 2

Focus: Practicing review vocabulary

Suggestions: Some students may ask for suggestions on recipes they can use for Step 1. Suggest Mexican recipes with which many students will be familiar, such as **huevos rancheros, guacamole,** and **tacos.**

Answers will vary.

2 Standards: 1.1

Focus: Practicing review vocabulary

Suggestions: Encourage students to use words from the *descripciones* category when talking about foods they like and dislike.

Answers will vary.

Block Schedule

Write each vocabulary word per category on individual slips of paper and place in a bag. Per category, ask a student to draw a word and act it out. Have the class guess the word being acted out.

Vocabulario Repaso

las frutas y las verduras
- el aguacate
- el ajo
- la cebolla
- las cerezas
- el durazno
- la ensalada
- las fresas
- los frijoles
- los guisantes
- las judías verdes
- la lechuga
- el maíz
- el melón
- la papa
- la piña
- la sandía
- la sopa de verduras
- el tomate
- las uvas
- la zanahoria

descripciones
- bueno, -a / malo, -a para la salud
- caliente
- congelado, -a
- delicioso, -a
- dulce
- enlatado, -a
- fresco, -a
- frito, -a
- grasoso, -a
- horrible
- picante
- ¡Qué asco!
- rico, -a
- sabroso, -a

actividades
- añadir
- comer
- cortar
- probar (ue)
- servir (i)

para el desayuno
- el azúcar
- el cereal
- desayunar
- el huevo
- el pan con mantequilla
- el pan tostado
- las salchichas
- el tocino
- el yogur

para el almuerzo o la cena
- almorzar (ue)
- el arroz
- el bistec
- el camarón
- la carne de res
- cenar
- la chuleta de cerdo
- los dulces
- los espaguetis
- la galleta
- el helado
- los mariscos
- la paella
- el pastel
- el pavo
- el pescado
- el pollo
- el postre

▼1 Lista de ingredientes | 👥

Escribir • Hablar

1 Haz una lista de los ingredientes que se necesitan para preparar una comida mexicana y otra lista de los ingredientes para una comida estadounidense.

2 Con otro(a) estudiante, comparen sus listas. Trabajen juntos para preparar un menú para una comida completa.

▼2 Las comidas |

Escribir • Hablar

Escribe una lista de tus comidas favoritas y otra de las comidas que no te gustan. Usa la lista para hablar con tu compañero(a) de las comidas que les gustan y que no les gustan y de sus hábitos alimenticios *(eating habits)*. Hablen de lo que comen y por qué, cuándo y cómo lo comen.

Modelo
Me gusta el yogur. Lo como con cereal todos los días en el desayuno porque es bueno para la salud.

108 ciento ocho
A ver si recuerdas . . .

DIFFERENTIATED INSTRUCTION

Students with Learning Difficulties

Point to objects in the classroom and ask questions with embedded direct object pronouns. Students will restate the pronouns in their responses: Teacher: *El libro, ¿lo ves?* Student: *Sí, lo veo.* Teacher: *El reloj, ¿lo oyes?* Student: *Sí, lo oigo.*

Advanced Learners

Have students work together to create a menu for the restaurant of their dreams. Menus should include at least three different main entrées, as well as beverages and side dishes. Ask them to be creative and dream up a restaurant that they would regularly go to. They can also describe the décor.

Gramática Repaso

Pronombres de complemento directo

Direct object pronouns tell who or what receives the action of the verb. They are used to replace a noun, in order not to repeat it. Remember that when the direct object is a person or group of people, you use the personal *a* before it.

—¿Probaste el pescado?   —¿Ves mucho a tus amigas?
—Sí, **lo** probé.   —Sí, **las** veo todos los días.

Here all the direct object pronouns:

me	nos
te	os
lo / la	los / las

• Direct object pronouns generally go before the main verb. If there is a *no* before the verb, the pronoun goes between *no* and the verb.

—Antonio comió las uvas. **Las** comió en el desayuno. Yo no **las** comí.

• If the verb is followed by an infinitive or a present participle (present progressive), the direct object pronoun may go before the main verb or be attached to the infinitive or participle.

—¿Vas a comer el helado?   —Estoy comiéndo**lo** ahora.
—**Lo** estoy comiendo ahora.   —No, no **lo** quiero comer. / —No, no quiero comer**lo**.

▼3 Al restaurante |

Leer • Hablar

Trabaja con otro(a) estudiante. Imaginen que él (ella) fue a un restaurante con su familia. Hablen del menú y de la comida que probaron.

▶ **Modelo**

las salchichas / mi hermano
A —¿Alguien probó las salchichas?
B —Sí, mi hermano las probó.

1. los espaguetis / mi papá
2. el helado de chocolate / mi hermanita
3. la sopa de pollo / todos
4. los pasteles / nadie
5. la chuleta de cerdo / yo
6. los huevos con tocino / mi hermanita y yo
7. el yogur de durazno / mi mamá y mi papá

▼4 La cena

Leer • Escribir

Algunos estudiantes planean una cena. Lee lo que preguntan y escribe una respuesta apropiada. Usa el pronombre de complemento directo que corresponda.

Modelo

A —¿Quién va a preparar arroz?
B —Lo va a preparar Luisa.
o: —Luisa va a prepararlo.

1. ¿Cómo vas a preparar las verduras?
2. ¿Quién va a comprar el pescado?
3. ¿Cuándo vamos a preparar la ensalada?
4. ¿Quién está cortando la fruta?
5. ¿Quieres preparar el postre?
6. ¿Quién está cortando las zanahorias?

ciento nueve 109
Capítulo 3

Gramática Repaso

Core Instruction

Standards: 4.1

Resources: Voc. and Gram. Transparency 67

Suggestions: Refer students who are having difficulty with direct object pronouns to the *GramActiva* videos from L2 Chapters 3A and 3B, and to the online tutorials. Cue students with sentences containing direct objects that are nouns. Have them restate each sentence, changing the direct object to a pronoun.

▼3 Standards: 1.1

Resources: Answer Keys: Student Edition, p. 35

Focus: Reviewing direct object pronouns

Suggestions: Have students switch roles, so both partners can practice asking and answering the questions.

Answers:

Student A's questions follow the pattern in the model. Student B's answers are as follows:

1. **Sí, mi papá los probó.**
2. **Sí, mi hermanita lo probó.**
3. **Sí, todos la probamos (probaron).**
4. **No, nadie los probó.**
5. **Sí, yo la probé.**
6. **Sí, mi hermanita y yo los probamos.**
7. **Sí, mi mamá y mi papá lo probaron.**

▼4

Resources: Answer Keys: Student Edition, p. 35

Focus: Reviewing direct object pronouns

Suggestions: After students complete the activity, have them take turns reading the questions and their answers aloud.

Answers will vary but should contain the following information:

1. **las voy a preparar/voy a prepararlas**
2. **lo va a comprar/va a comprarlo**
3. **la vamos a preparar/vamos a prepararla**
4. **la está cortando/está cortándola**
5. **lo quiero preparar/quiero prepararlo**
6. **las está cortando/está cortándolas**

ENRICH YOUR TEACHING

Teacher-to-Teacher

Students tend to confuse direct and indirect object pronouns, especially when the objects are people. This *Gramática* review focuses mainly on things as direct objects. For further review of direct objects as people, ask questions such as the following and have students respond using a direct object pronoun:

¿Viste a [name of student(s)] ayer?

¿Conocen ustedes al (a la) señor(a) [name of teacher]?

¿Conoces a los (las) señores(as) [names of teachers]?

109

| ▼ Objectives
▶ Discuss and illustrate how you feel when you are ill
▶ Read and write about illnesses and accidents

3 Recycle

Vocabulario Repaso

Core Instruction

Standards: 1.1

Resources: Voc. and Gram. Transparency 68

Suggestions: Have students choose one word or expression to pantomime from the *Vocabulario*. Have them take turns presenting their pantomimes, while others say what they are doing: *A Norberto le duele el brazo. Julia tiene frío. Miguel está tomando una pastilla.* Do your own pantomimes of words and expressions that students do not elicit.

Vocabulario Repaso

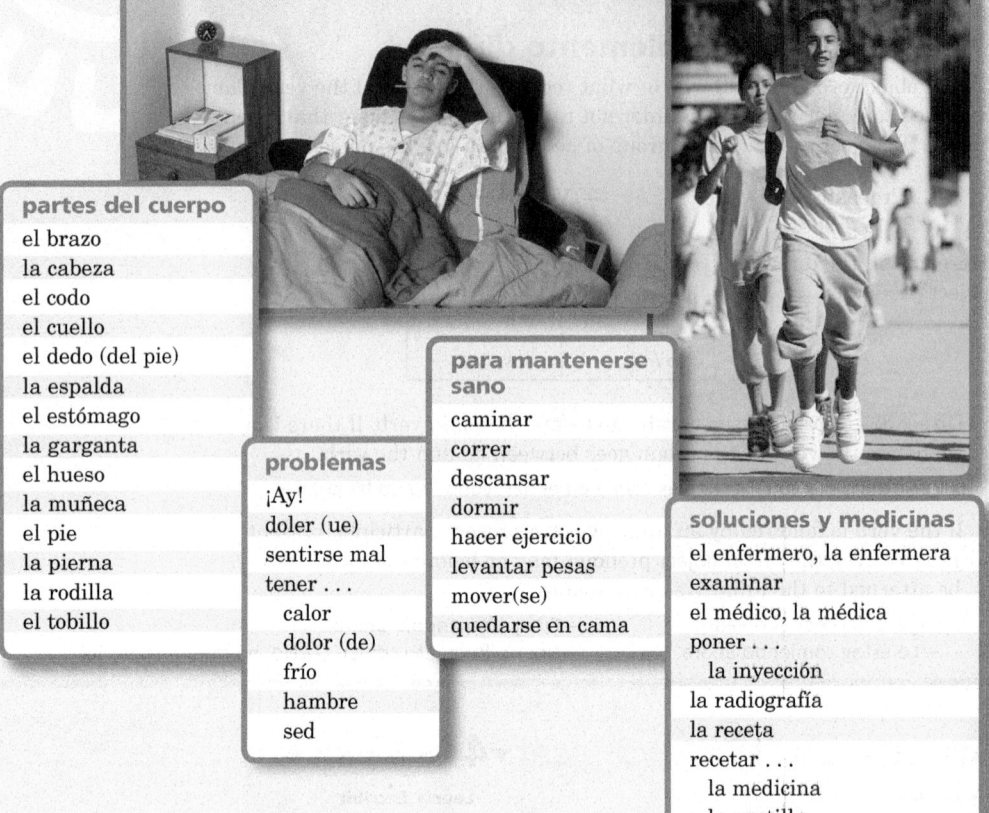

partes del cuerpo
- el brazo
- la cabeza
- el codo
- el cuello
- el dedo (del pie)
- la espalda
- el estómago
- la garganta
- el hueso
- la muñeca
- el pie
- la pierna
- la rodilla
- el tobillo

problemas
- ¡Ay!
- doler (ue)
- sentirse mal
- tener . . .
  - calor
  - dolor (de)
  - frío
  - hambre
  - sed

para mantenerse sano
- caminar
- correr
- descansar
- dormir
- hacer ejercicio
- levantar pesas
- mover(se)
- quedarse en cama

soluciones y medicinas
- el enfermero, la enfermera
- examinar
- el médico, la médica
- poner . . .
  - la inyección
  - la radiografía
  - la receta
- recetar . . .
  - la medicina
  - la pastilla
- recomendar (ie)

5 Standards: 1.1, 1.3

Focus: Practicing review vocabulary

Suggestions: Allow students to talk about real or imaginary illnesses they have had. Have them use the past tenses. They can also talk about an illness of another person, such as a family member, friend, or pet, in order to practice third-person forms.

Answers will vary.

Common Errors: Some students will consistently use possessive pronouns to identify parts of the body: *mi mano; mi estómago.* Remind them that, unlike English, Spanish usually uses the definite article with parts of the body. Model as necessary: *la mano; el estómago.*

▼5 Enfermo de nuevo

Dibujar • Escribir • Hablar

❶ Haz un dibujo sobre la última vez que estuviste enfermo(a). Luego, escribe:

- qué te pasaba
  Me sentía . . .
  Me dolía(n) (mucho / un poco) . . .

- qué te recomendó o recetó el médico
  Me recetó . . .
  Me recomendó . . .

- qué hiciste tú
  Tuve que . . .
  Debí . . .

❷ Muestra tu dibujo a dos estudiantes. Describe cómo te sentiste. Los(as) otros(as) estudiantes pueden hacerte preguntas.

  ¿Por cuánto tiempo . . . ?

  ¿También tuviste que . . . ?

110 ciento diez
  A ver si recuerdas . . .

DIFFERENTIATED INSTRUCTION

Heritage Language Learners

Students may use English or other alternative terms they have learned in place of some of the Spanish vocabulary: "prescription" instead of *receta;* "X-ray" (or *rayo equis*) instead of *radiografía.* Model the appropriate terms as necessary and have students repeat.

Multiple Intelligences

Musical/Rhythmic: Select a musically gifted volunteer and have him or her lead the class in a simple rap using the vocabulary for parts of the body. For example: *El brazo, el codo y la mu-ñe-ca. La cabeza, el cuello y la es-pal-da.* The rapper and the class should point to the parts of their bodies as they hear the words.

Gramática Repaso

Pronombres de complemento indirecto

Indirect object pronouns indicate to whom or for whom an action is performed.

El médico **le** recetó unas pastillas a Eva.

Here are the indirect object pronouns:

me	nos
te	os
le	les

- Sometimes you can use *a + Ud. / él / ella* or a noun to clarify to whom the indirect pronouns *le* and *les* refer.

  El médico **le** dio una inyección **a ella**.
  ¿Quién **les** trajo las medicinas **a ustedes**?
  La enfermera **le** trajo la radiografía **al doctor**.

- If a verb is followed by an infinitive or a present participle (present progressive), the indirect object pronoun may go before the main verb or be attached to the infinitive or participle.

  Le tienen que hacer una radiografía a mi perro.   **Les** estoy dando las medicinas.
  Tienen que hacer**le** una radiografía a mi perro.   Estoy dándo**les** las medicinas.

- Remember that indirect object pronouns are used with verbs like *gustar*, *encantar*, and *doler*.

  Me duele el brazo.   A los niños no **les** gustan las inyecciones.

▼6 Un accidente

Leer • Escribir

Unos(as) amigos(as) hablan de un accidente y de lo que les recetó el médico. Completa las oraciones con el pronombre de complemento indirecto *(me, te, le, nos, os, les)* que corresponda.

1. Yo no me puedo mover. _____ duele todo.
2. El médico va a poner_____ una inyección a José y a mí.
3. Y a Clara, ¿qué _____ recetó el doctor?
4. Ella se siente bien, a ella no _____ recetó nada.
5. Mi hermana está en cama. Yo _____ estoy dando las medicinas.
6. ¿Y a ti _____ duele el brazo?
7. No, a mí ahora empezaron a doler_____ las piernas.

▼7 Una nota

Leer • Escribir

Completa este mensaje con los pronombres correctos.

¿Cómo estás? Hace una semana que a mi hermana Teresa y a mí __1.__ duele la cabeza. A mí el médico __2.__ recomendó usar anteojos. __3.__ pregunté si tenía que llevarlos todo el tiempo y __4.__ dijo que sí. A Teresa no __5.__ dio nada.

Más práctica	**GO**

realidades.com | print

A ver si recuerdas with Study Plan ✔
Guided WB pp. 78–81   ✔ ✔
Core WB pp. 35–36   ✔ ✔
Hispanohablantes **WB** p. 36   ✔

Recycle 3

Gramática Repaso

Core Instruction

Resources: Voc. and Gram. Transparency 69

Suggestions: Refer students who are having difficulty with indirect object pronouns to the *GramActiva* video from L2 Chapter 4A, and to the online tutorials. Have students pass around an object, such as a book. Have them use *dar* to tell about what they did, are doing, or will do: *Carlos me dio el libro. Le voy a dar el libro a María.* Change the number of recipients and guide students with questions as necessary:

¿Qué está haciendo Guillermo?
Está dándoles el libro a Gloria y a Ana.

▼**6** Standards: 1.2

Resources: Answer Keys: Student Edition, p. 36

Focus: Reviewing indirect object pronouns

Suggestions: Remind students first to identify the indirect object in each item. This will help them determine which pronoun to use.

Answers:

1. Me
2. nos
3. le
4. le
5. le
6. te
7. me

▼**7** Standards: 1.2

Resources: Answer Keys: Student Edition, p. 36

Focus: Reviewing indirect object pronouns

Suggestions: Ask a volunteer to read the completed message aloud, so students can check their answers.

Answers:

1. nos
2. me
3. Le
4. me
5. le

ENRICH YOUR TEACHING

Teacher-to-Teacher

Give students sentences containing nouns and ask them to change all the nouns to pronouns. Remind them that subject pronouns are often eliminated completely in Spanish:

La profesora hablaba a los estudiantes./Les hablaba.

21st Century Skills

Initiative and Self-Direction Direct students to the online tutorials available in **realidades.com** for self-directed review of the grammar topics recycled in this chapter. Students can expand their own learning by reviewing the related English grammar first, then proceed to the new Spanish grammar point.

✔ASSESSMENT

A *ver si recuerdas* with Study Plan (online only)

After presenting the review material on these pages, assign the *A ver si recuerdas* Study Plan to evaluate students' mastery of the material. Additional practice for students who need it is available online.

Standards for Foreign Language Learning: *Capítulo 3*

• To meet the Standards, students will:

Communication

1.1 Interpersonal
• Talk about menus, nutrition, and the preparation and quality of foods
• Talk about physical and mental health, exercise, illnesses, and remedies
• Talk about ancient Central American ball games
• Talk about Spanish and Latin American teen magazines

1.2 Interpretive
• Read and listen to information about menus, nutrition, and the preparation and quality of foods
• Read and listen to information about physical and mental health, exercise, illnesses, and remedies
• Read about word families
• Read about the career of a bilingual student advisor
• Read about ancient Central American ball games
• Read about Spanish and Latin American teen magazines
• Read lyrics from a Mexican *corrido*

1.3 Presentational
• Write about menus, nutrition, and the preparation and quality of foods
• Write about physical and mental health, exercise, illnesses, and remedies
• Write about planning a party
• Write about ancient Central American ball games

Culture

2.1 Practices and Perspectives
• Explain the use of natural remedies in Latin America
• Explain the physical education system in Spanish schools
• Explain the practice of ball games in ancient Central America
• Explain teen reading habits in Spain and Latin America

2.2 Products and Perspectives
• Describe a Spanish nutrition study
• Discuss *corridos* and the Mexican Revolution
• Talk about Spanish and Latin American teen magazines

Connections

3.1 Cross-curricular
• Talk about key facts about health, nutrition, remedies, and physical education
• Talk about key facts about the career of a bilingual student advisor
• Talk about key facts about ancient Mexico and modern Spain
• Discuss Language Arts Strategies: using prior knowledge, speech projection, persuasive writing, cause and effect

3.2 Target Culture
• Read a Spanish nutrition study report
• Read an article excerpt from a Spanish magazine
• Read song lyrics from a Mexican *corrido*

Comparisons

4.1 Language
• Compare Spanish words to their English counterparts
• Compare Spanish and English commands

Capítulo 3 ¿Qué haces para estar en forma?

▼ Chapter Objectives

Communication

By the end of the chapter you will be able to:
• Listen and read about health advice and nutrition
• Talk and write about healthy eating habits and exercise
• Give advice to others about healthy lifestyles

Culture

You will also be able to:
• Compare an ancient game with a modern game
• Understand the connection between healthy habits and lifestyle in Spanish-speaking countries

You will demonstrate what you know and can do:
• Presentación oral, p. 143
• Presentación escrita, pp. 144–145
• Preparación para el examen, pp. 152–153

You will use:

Vocabulary
• Symptoms and remedies
• Parts of the body
• Health, food, and nutrition
• Physical fitness and exercise
• Moods

Grammar
• Affirmative and negative commands with *tú*
• Affirmative and negative commands with *Ud.* and *Uds.*
• Subjunctive: Regular, stem-changing verbs, irregular verbs

Exploración del mundo hispano

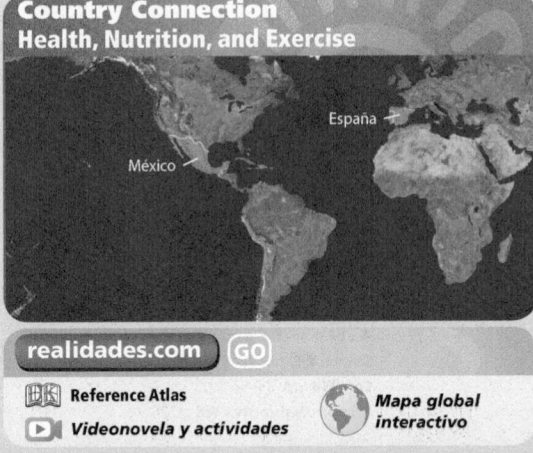

Country Connection
Health, Nutrition, and Exercise

España

México

realidades.com [GO]

📖 Reference Atlas
▶ Videonovela y actividades

🌎 Mapa global interactivo

112 ciento doce

Puesto de frutas y verduras en un mercado de Guanajuato, México

ENRICH YOUR TEACHING

Using Backward Design

Have students preview the sample performance tasks on *Preparación para el examen*, p. 153, and connect them to the Chapter Objectives. Explain to students that by completing the sample tasks, they can self-assess their learning progress.

Mapa global interactivo

Download the *Mapa global interactivo* files for Chapter 3 and preview the activities. Use Activity 1 to explore the Amazon Rain Forest. In Activity 2, discover the ruins of Chichén Itzá, where Mayans played ball games.

Standards (cont'd)

4.2 Culture
• Compare ancient Central American ball games to modern ones
• Compare Spanish and Latin American teen magazines and their readership to those in the United States

Communities

5.1 Beyond the School
• Link to Web sites from the Spanish-speaking world

5.2 Lifelong Learner
• Discuss important facts about healthy lifestyles
• Discuss important facts about scientific studies
• Develop an appreciation for the art of songwriting

▷ **Videonovela** *¡Pura vida!* View this stand-alone storyline video about five young adults in San José, Costa Rica with your class, either online or on DVD.

◉ **PresentationExpress™**
See pp. 108c–108d

Chapter Opener

Core Instruction

Resources: Map Transparencies 14, 20
Suggestions: Introduce students to the chapter theme and objectives.

Arte y cultura

Standards: 1.2, 3.1
Resources: Fine Art Transparencies with Teacher's Guide, p. 66
Suggestions: Ask: *¿Qué frutas se ven en la pintura? ¿Las comes tú?*
Answers will vary, but may include mango, guava, papaya, and kiwi.

▷ **TEACHING WITH ART**
Resources: Fine Art Transparencies with Teacher's Guide, p. 66

Arte y cultura | México

Las frutas de Tamayo Rufino Tamayo (1899–1991) fue un gran pintor y muralista mexicano que nació en Oaxaca, un estado conocido por sus deliciosas frutas. Cuando Tamayo era niño, su familia vendía frutas en un mercado y él aprendió mucho de ellas. Su forma, variedad y color lo fascinaban. Sabía cuándo tenían calidad y cuándo estaban listas para comer. Él pintó muchas frutas. Decía que su único lenguaje era la pintura porque estaba hecha de formas, como las frutas.

• ¿Qué frutas conoces que no se producen aquí y las traen de otros países? ¿Sabes de dónde las traen?

"Sandías", Rufino Tamayo ▶
© D.R. Rufino Tamayo/Herederos/México/2010/Fundación Olga y Rufino Tamayo, A.C./Christie's Images/Corbis.

ciento trece **113**
Capítulo 3

DIFFERENTIATED INSTRUCTION

Digital resources such as the *Interactive Whiteboard* activity banks, *Videomodelos*, additional *Online Activities*, *Study Plans*, automatically graded *Leveled Workbook*, animated *Grammar Tutorials*, *Flashcards*, and *Vocabulary and Grammar Videos* will help you reach students of different ability levels and learning styles.

STUDENTS NEEDING EXTRA HELP
Guided Practice Activities
• Flashcards, pp. 82–86, 97–100
• Vocabulary Check, pp. 87–90, 101–104
• Grammar, pp. 91–96, 105–110

HERITAGE LEARNERS
Realidades para hispanohablantes
• Chapter Opener, pp. 76–77
• A primera vista, pp. 78–79, 88–89
• Manos a la obra, pp. 80–87, 90–97
• ¡Adelante!, pp. 98–103
• Repaso del capítulo, pp. 104–107

ADVANCED/PRE-AP*
Pre-AP* Resource Book,
• pp. 144–146
Communications Workbook
• Integrated Performance Assessment, p. 178

Vocabulario en contexto

Core Instruction

Standards: 1.1, 1.2, 3.1

Resources: Teacher's Resource Book: Input Script, p. 148, Clip Art, pp. 168–175, Audio Script, p. 152; Voc. and Gram. Transparencies 70–71; Audio Program DVD: Cap. 3, Tracks 1, 3

Focus: Presenting new vocabulary and using grammar lexically in context

Suggestions: You may want to use the Input Script from the *Teacher's Resource Book* as a source of ideas for presentation of new vocabulary and comprehensible input. Meaning for most of the vocabulary in this lesson can be clarified either by pantomime or by TPR commands, and having students point to the objects named on *Vocabulary & Grammar Transparency* 71.

1

Standards: 1.2

Resources: Teacher's Resource Book: Audio Script, p. 152; Audio Program DVD: Cap. 3, Track 2; Answer Keys: Student Edition, p. 36

Focus: Practicing listening comprehension of new vocabulary

Suggestions: Point out to students that *Actividad* 1 focuses on the information on p. 114. Before they listen, allow students a few minutes to read over and study this page. Then play the audio or use the script to read the activity aloud.

Answers:

1. C	3. F	5. F
2. C	4. C	6. F

Block Schedule

Have the class stand up. Call out different vocabulary words from these two pages and have students act them out. Call them out quickly and repeat words twice or three times for reinforcement. A quick pace will make the activity fun.

Vocabulario en contexto

| ▼ **Objectives**
▶ Read, listen to, and understand information about
 • symptoms and remedies
 • health, food, and nutrition

A nadie le gusta ir al médico, pero cuando estamos enfermos vamos inmediatamente a visitarlo: queremos que nos devuelva la salud en un minuto para poder seguir con nuestra vida normal. Cuando vamos al médico, a veces nos sentimos como niños que quieren la ayuda de sus papás.

Clínica de Medicina Familiar
Dr. Raúl López

Estornudo mucho. Creo que tengo una alergia.

Estoy resfriada.

Tengo fiebre de 38° (grados centígrados). Creo que tengo gripe.

Me duele el oído.

Carlitos, te duele el pecho, ¿no?, y tienes una tos muy fuerte. ¡Pobrecito!

▼1 ¿Quién está enfermo(a)? | 🔊

Escuchar

Escribe los números del 1 al 6 en una hoja. Escucha las siguientes frases y escribe *C* (cierto) o *F* (falso).

DIFFERENTIATED INSTRUCTION

Heritage Language Learners

Invite a student with outstanding pronunciation skills to take turns with you, randomly naming the vocabulary items during the presentation. This way, students will be exposed to variations in the pronunciation of the words and expressions.

Advanced Learners

Have students prepare and perform a skit set in a doctor's waiting room. Characters should include a doctor, a nurse, and at least two patients with different illnesses.

LA NUTRICIÓN

Los siguientes alimentos son nutritivos y por eso son importantes para tu alimentación.

los huevos y la leche
La leche tiene calcio y ayuda a tener huesos fuertes. Los huevos tienen muchas proteínas y aunque son muy buen alimento, no debes comer demasiados.

las espinacas[1]
Las espinacas contienen un alto nivel de hierro.

el cereal y el pan
El cereal y algunas clases de pan tienen mucha fibra. Los dos alimentos tienen carbohidratos.

las piñas y las naranjas
Tienen muchas vitaminas. Es bueno comer de todas las frutas con frecuencia.

los cacahuates
Tienen mucha grasa, carbohidratos y proteínas, por lo que dan energía, pero no debes comer muchos.

1 spinach

el jarabe

la aspirina

el antibiótico

¡Ay!, doctor, me duele el estómago. Anoche comí cuatro bolsas de papas fritas y dos hamburguesas.

Tome esta medicina, pero no la tome con el estómago vacío. Y, por favor, evite comer comida basura.

▼2 La receta del doctor | 🔊

Escuchar

Dibuja una tabla con dos columnas. En una columna, escribe *problemas de los pacientes* y en la otra, *receta del doctor*. Escucha lo que dicen el doctor López y sus pacientes y completa la tabla.

ciento quince **115**
Capítulo 3

---

2 Standards: 1.2

Resources: Teacher's Resource Book: Audio Script, p. 152; Audio Program DVD: Cap. 3, Track 4; Answer Keys: Student Edition, p. 37

Focus: Practicing listening comprehension of new vocabulary

Suggestions: Use the audio or the script. Allow students to listen more than once. Pause frequently to allow them to write the information. Then have students work in pairs to check their answers and each other's comprehension. One partner reads items from the *problemas de los pacientes* side of the chart in random order. The other responds with the appropriate *receta*.

Answers:

problemas de los pacientes
dolor de cabeza, está resfriado, no puede dormir
tos, dolor de garganta
fiebre, dolor de oído
quiere ser fuerte

receta del doctor
tomar aspirina antes de acostarse
tomar jarabe dos veces al día
tomar antibiótico
tomar vitaminas, hacer ejercicio, no comer comida basura

Extension: Have students work in pairs to come up with another idea for a patient's complaint and a doctor's prescription.

Note: The term "comida basura" is not used in all Spanish-speaking countries. Tell your students they may also say "comida rápida" to refer to junk food.

Pre-AP* Support

- **Learning Objective:** Interpretive: Audio
- **Activity:** Have pairs of students write a dialog between a doctor and a patient highlighting vocabulary from this chapter. In addition, have each pair write three multiple-choice questions to accompany their dialog. Have them record their dialog as well as their questions. Redistribute the recordings to other pairs. Ask each pair of other students to listen to the dialog and answer the questions.
- *Pre-AP* Resource Book:* Comprehensive guide to Pre-AP* vocabulary skill development, pp. 51–57

ENRICH YOUR TEACHING

Culture Note

Two grains have been Latin American staples for centuries. Quinoa (KEEN-wah) was grown by the Incas; amaranth (AH-mah-rahnth) by the Aztecs. Both are highly nutritious. Moreover, they can be grown in poor soil and arid climates. Both can now be found in many United States supermarkets.

21st Century Skills

Technology Literacy Have students research and come up with a list of two or three useful Internet resources for supporting sound nutritional practices, such as sites providing calorie counts for items in fast food restaurants, and the like.

Vocabulario en contexto

Core Instruction

Standards: 1.2, 3.1

Resources: Teacher's Resource Book: Input Script, p. 149, Clip Art, pp. 168–175, Audio Script, pp. 152–153; Voc. and Gram. Transparency 72; Audio Program DVD: Cap. 3, Track 5

Focus: Extending presentation of vocabulary and grammar in the context of dietary information

Suggestions:

Pre-reading: Direct students' attention to the food label and ask them to use it as a clue to predict the main idea of the information on this page.

Reading: Allow students time to read the information silently first. Then play the audio or read the information aloud, with students reading along as they listen. Allow them to listen more than once.

Post-reading: Use gestures, explanations, and demonstrations to clarify the meaning of new vocabulary.

3 Standards: 1.2, 1.3

Resources: Answer Keys: Student Edition, p. 37

Focus: Demonstrating comprehension of the reading passage

Suggestions: Have students answer the questions in pairs, so they can share strategies for learning new words and structures as well as practice writing skills.

Answers will vary in structure but contain the following ideas:

1. **Debemos leer la etiqueta para saber si debemos incluir esa comida en nuestra dieta.**
2. **Una dieta equilibrada es comer de todos los grupos de alimentos todos los días.**
3. **Debemos comer a horarios regulares y evitar muchas meriendas para tener una alimentación saludable.**
4. **Answers will vary.**
5. **Una ración tiene 160 calorías. Tiene 5 gramos de proteína.**

La alimentación de los jóvenes

A veces no es tan fácil saber qué alimentos tienen mucha azúcar o demasiada grasa. Lee las etiquetas (*labels*) de la comida que compras para saber si la debes incluir en tu dieta.

ARROZ CON FRIJOLES NEGROS

Datos de Nutrición
Tamaño por Ración 1/4 Taza (45g)
Raciones por Envase 5

Cantidad por Ración

Calorías 160   Cal. Grasa 0

	%Valor Diario*
Grasa Total 0g	0%
Grasa Sat. 0g	0%
Colesterol 0mg	0%
Sodio 445mg	19%
Carb. Total 34g	11%
Fibra Dietética 3g	10%
Azúcares 1g	
Proteínas 5g	

Vitamina A 0% • Vitamina C 0%
Calcio 0% • Hierro 6%

* Los porcentajes de Valores Diarios están basados en una dieta de 2,000 calorías. Sus valores diarios pueden ser mayores o menores dependiendo de sus necesidades calóricas.

	Calorías	2,000	2,500
Grasa Total	Menos de	65g	80g
Grasa Sat.	Menos de	20g	25g
Colest.	Menos de	300mg	300mg

¿Por qué es importante una alimentación saludable?

Una alimentación saludable es la mejor manera de:
• Tener energía todo el día y estar bien para hacer deporte y otras actividades.
• Recibir las vitaminas y el hierro que necesitas.
• Alcanzar tu estatura apropiada si no eres adulto.
• Mantener el mejor peso para tu edad y tu estatura.
• Evitar hábitos alimenticios malos.

¿Qué significa una alimentación saludable?

• Comer comidas a horarios regulares y evitar muchas meriendas.
• Mantener una dieta equilibrada, es decir, comer de todos los grupos de alimentos todos los días.
• No saltar comidas y evitar la comida basura.
• Comer cuando tienes hambre y parar cuando te sientes lleno(a).

▼3 ¿Comprendiste?

Escribir

1. ¿Por qué debemos leer la etiqueta antes de comprar un alimento?
2. ¿Qué significa una "dieta equilibrada"?
3. ¿Cuándo debemos comer? ¿Por qué?
4. ¿Cuál de estos consejos te parece más difícil de seguir? ¿Por qué?
5. Según la información de la etiqueta, ¿cuántas calorías tiene una ración de arroz con frijoles negros? ¿Cuántos gramos de proteínas tiene una ración?

116 ciento dieciséis
A primera vista 1

DIFFERENTIATED INSTRUCTION

Heritage Language Learners

Ask students to tell about foods that they eat at home that are not usually part of the local United States diet. Or, in the case of foods that have become fast food, such as the *taco,* ask them to talk about how the fast-food version differs from the version they may eat at home.

Multiple Intelligences

Naturalist: Ask students to describe fruits and vegetables only in terms of touch, smell, and taste. Ask them to imagine the taste, smell, or texture and weight of each as they describe it or hear it described. Encourage them to use the Spanish they know: *El limón no es dulce.* Provide adjectives such as *ácido* if requested.

▼4 La intrusa | ♻

Leer • Escribir

Escribe en una hoja de papel los números del 1 al 6. Para cada grupo de palabras, escribe la palabra o frase que no está relacionada con las otras. Luego, escribe una frase con cada una de las palabras que escribiste.

1. a. la dieta   b. los hábitos alimenticios   c. la alimentación   d. las alergias
2. a. la fiebre   b. la merienda   c. la tos   d. estornudar
3. a. lleno   b. vacío   c. equilibrado   d. las proteínas
4. a. el peso   b. la edad   c. el oído   d. la estatura
5. a. el calcio   b. el pecho   c. la cabeza   d. el oído
6. a. la comida basura b. saludable   c. nutritiva   d. la dieta equilibrada

Consejos para una alimentación saludable

1 🍴 No saltes comidas. Planea tus comidas y meriendas.
  • Come dos o tres meriendas al día para mantener la energía y un peso saludable.

2 🍴 Aprende maneras simples y saludables de preparar alimentos.
  • Evita freír los alimentos. Es mejor hervirlos, asarlos, prepararlos al horno o cocinarlos en el microondas.
  • Evita añadir mantequilla a la comida.

3 🍴 La energía que da el azúcar se gasta pronto.
  • Evita tomar refrescos o bebidas que tienen mucha azúcar. Come pocos postres y dulces.

4 🍴 Presta atención a tu cuerpo y a lo que comes.
  • Come despacio. Tu cuerpo necesita unos 20 minutos para sentirse lleno.
  • Come comidas calientes y alimentos con mucha fibra.
  • No comas comida basura. Escoge alimentos nutritivos.

5 🍴 Evita pensar en las dietas.
  • Lo importante es comer todo tipo de alimentos, sin exagerar.
  • Tú eres más importante que tu peso o tu estatura. ¡Créelo!

▼5 ¿Saludable o no? | 🔊

Leer • Escuchar

Lee este artículo. Luego escucha las frases y escribe *C* (cierto) o *F* (falso) según los "Consejos para una alimentación saludable".

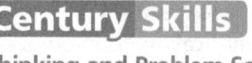

Más práctica	GO

realidades.com | print

Instant Check	✔	
Guided WB pp. 82–90	✔	✔
Core WB pp. 37–38	✔	✔
Comm. WB p. 40	✔	✔
Hispanohablantes WB pp. 78–79		✔

ciento diecisiete **117**
Capítulo 3

ENRICH YOUR TEACHING

Culture Note

Chili peppers are a staple not only in Mexican food. After salt, they are the world's most common form of seasoning. There are many kinds of chilis and many different tastes, some spicy enough to burn your mouth, others milder. And with twice the Vitamin C of most citrus fruits, chilis are nutritious.

21st Century Skills

Critical Thinking and Problem Solving
Encourage students to use their reading strategies when reading *La alimentación de los jóvenes* and *Consejos para una alimentación saludable*. Students should pay attention to the format of each reading to aid their comprehension. Are there headings or subheadings that organize each reading? What is the purpose of bulleted lists or visuals? What are the verb forms used? Who is the target audience?

Language Input 3

BELLRINGER REVIEW

On the board, write food categories such as *verduras, carnes,* and *frutas.* Ask pairs of students to list as many foods as they can under each category.

4 Standards: 3.1

Resources: Answer Keys: Student Edition, p. 38
Focus: Demonstrating comprehension of new vocabulary through categorizing
Suggestions: Ask students to explain why each odd item does not belong: *Para el número 1, las palabras de las letras a, b y c se tratan de lo que comemos, pero las alergias son problemas de la salud.*
Answers:

1. las alergias   4. el oído
2. la merienda   5. el calcio
3. las proteínas   6. la comida basura

5 Standards: 1.2, 3.1

Resources: Teacher's Resource Book: Audio Script, p. 153; Audio Program DVD: Cap. 3, Track 6; Answer Keys: Student Edition, p. 38
Focus: Practicing reading and listening comprehension
Suggestions: Allow students to listen to the audio more than once.
Answers:

1. F   2. F   3. C   4. C   5. C

Chapter Project

Give students copies of the Chapter Project outline and rubric from the *Teacher's Resource Book*. Explain the task to them, and have them perform Step 1. (For more information, see p. 108-b.)

✔ASSESSMENT

Prueba: Comprensión del vocabulario 1
• Prueba 3-1: pp. 59–60

3 Practice and Communicate

▶ Talk about symptoms and remedies
▶ Discuss healthy eating choices
▶ Write about food and recipes

Vocabulario en uso

INTERACTIVE WHITEBOARD
Vocabulary Activities 3-1

6 Standards: 1.2

Resources: Voc. and Gram. Transparency 72; Answer Keys: Student Edition, p. 38

Focus: Practicing new vocabulary in a cloze exercise

Suggestions: Have students briefly read the entire paragraph once for meaning before they write their answers.

Answers:

1. Tenía tos
2. Aunque
3. tenía fiebre
4. grados centígrados
5. tengo gripe
6. antibióticos

BELLRINGER REVIEW

Have students list three reasons they might go to the doctor.

7 Standards: 1.1, 3.1

Resources: Answer Keys: Student Edition, p. 39

Focus: Practicing new vocabulary

Suggestions: Encourage partners to ask questions and explain their answers. Remind students that everything is relative: an occasional serving of cookies and milk might be considered healthy or at least not unhealthy, but eating such foods every day is not a healthy dietary habit. Ask students to include comments about quantity and frequency as they talk about the pictures.

Answers will vary but should contain the following information:

1. Hamburguesa con papas fritas y refresco: contienen proteína y carbohidratos. No son saludables.
2. Ensalada de espinacas: contiene fibra y hierro. Es saludable.
3. Cereal con leche: contiene proteína, carbohidratos, calcio y fibra. Es nutritivo y saludable.
4. Galleta y refresco: contienen carbohidratos. No son saludables.

▼6 Llegó el otoño | ♻

Leer • Escribir

En el otoño los estudiantes comienzan sus clases y todo el mundo estornuda. Completa esta carta que le escribió un estudiante a su profesor con las palabras o frases del recuadro.

grados centígrados	tengo gripe
antibióticos	aunque
tenía fiebre	tenía tos

Profesor:

No puedo ir a la escuela hoy. __1.__ anoche. __2.__ tomé un jarabe que me recetó el doctor, no pude dormir. Hoy por la mañana tenía mucho frío, mi mamá me puso el termómetro debajo del brazo y me dijo que __3.__ porque tenía 39 __4.__.

Ella cree que yo __5.__. En vez de recetarme __6.__, la doctora recomienda que yo descanse mucho y que beba mucha agua. ¡Siempre me pasa lo mismo en otoño! Espero regresar a clase pronto.

Tomás

▼7 Contiene un alto nivel de . . . |

Hablar

Mira las ilustraciones y explica a otro(a) estudiante lo que come cada uno de estos jóvenes y por qué es saludable o no es saludable. Usa las palabras del recuadro.

proteína	fibra	nutritivo	calcio	hierro	carbohidratos	contener

1. 2. 3. 4.

DIFFERENTIATED INSTRUCTION

Multiple Intelligences

Logical/Mathematical: Bring in empty food cans and boxes. Have students review the nutrition facts information on the labels and note the amounts of **proteína, calcio, fibra, carbohidratos,** and **hierro** in each food. Ask them to make statements comparing the nutritional contents of different foods.

Students with Learning Difficulties

Review the concept of cognates and point out examples such as **alimentación** or **nutrición** on these two pages. Ask students to name other words they see that look like English words. Help students recognize a cognate like **proteína** by writing it on the board and covering the **a.**

▼ Ampliación del lenguaje

Familias de palabras

Las familias de palabras son grupos de palabras que tienen la misma raíz *(root)*. Muchas veces podemos saber el significado *(meaning)* de una palabra si conocemos otras palabras de la misma familia. Observa la relación entre las siguientes palabras y completa las frases.

Verbos	Sustantivos	Adjetivos
alimentar	alimentación	alimenticio
equilibrar	equilibrio	equilibrada
nutrir	nutrición	nutritivo
pesar	peso	pesado

1. Para obtener una buena _____, debemos comer alimentos nutritivos.

2. Tenemos un buen hábito _____ cuando no nos alimentamos con comida basura.

▼8 Preparándose para la carrera |

Leer • Hablar • Escribir

Trabaja con otro(a) estudiante para terminar el cuento sobre este atleta. Usa por lo menos cinco palabras del recuadro.

estar resfriado	nivel	hierro	energía
carbohidratos	hábitos	aunque	evitar

Rafa era un atleta fuerte, de peso apropiado para su edad. Iba a participar en una carrera. Tenía el estómago vacío y quería comer . . .

▼9 ¿Qué puedo hacer? | Talk! 👥

Hablar

Túrnate con otro(a) compañero(a) para representar la conversación entre un(a) estudiante y su maestro(a).

▶ **Modelo**

Estudiante —*Me duele la cabeza.*
Maestro(a) —*Debes tomar una aspirina.*

Estudiante

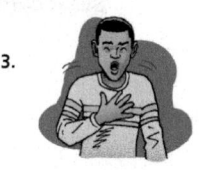

1.
2.
3.
4.
5.

Maestro(a)

Debes . . .
Tienes que . . .
Puedes tomar . . .
El médico te puede recetar . . .

ciento diecinueve **119**
Capítulo 3

ENRICH YOUR TEACHING

Teacher-to-Teacher

Invite students to view one or more segments of popular TV shows with a medical theme. Play the segments without sound. Pause frequently and ask students to comment on the action, describe some of the ailments of the patients, and discuss the actions of doctors and nurses. Another alternative is to play Spanish-language versions of these shows, available on cable channels or online, and show students all or part of an episode with sound.

3 Practice and Communicate

BELLRINGER REVIEW

Have students refer to a metric-standard U.S. English conversion table and ask questions that help them understand the physical size and nature of measurements: *¿Cuántas libras hay en un kilo? ¿Cuántos gramos hay en una onza?*

10 Standards: 1.1, 1.2, 1.3, 3.1

Focus: Using new vocabulary and structures in a contextual discussion

Suggestions: First, have partners work together to clear up any comprehension problems with the recipe. Remind students that for Step 2, they should discuss a recipe that involves several ingredients.

Answers will vary.

Fondo cultural

Standards: 1.1, 1.2, 2.1, 3.1
Resources: Answer Keys: Student Edition, p. 40

Mapa global interactivo, Actividad 1
Look at the extent and importance of the Amazon Rain Forest.

Suggestions: Use the *Fondo cultural* information to launch a discussion about the growing popularity of natural remedies. Have students consult a bilingual dictionary for names of natural remedies with which they are familiar. Possibilities include *la equinácea* (echinacea), *el ajo* (garlic), and *el hipericón (todabuena)* (St. John's wort). Ask questions such as: *¿Para qué se usa ese remedio? ¿Cómo se toma? ¿En qué forma? ¿Cuándo se toma?*

Answers:
• Usan la manzanilla. Usan el girasol.
• Answers will vary.

Additional Resources

• Communication Wbk.: Audio Act. 1, p. 36
• Teacher's Resource Book: Audio Script, p. 153, Communicative Pair Activity BLM, pp. 159–160
• Audio Program DVD: Cap. 3, Track 7

✔ASSESSMENT

Prueba 3-2 with Study Plan (online only)

Prueba: Aplicación del vocabulario 1
• Prueba 3-2: pp. 61–62

120

▼10 Una receta saludable |

Leer • Hablar • Escribir

1 Ésta es una receta para preparar un postre nutritivo. Léela y explica a otro(a) estudiante por qué la receta es saludable. Habla de los ingredientes que tiene y de los que no tiene.

Modelo
El postre tiene avena. La avena es un cereal y tiene fibra, que es saludable.

2 Ahora, piensen en una comida que les gusta y escriban cinco ingredientes que contiene. Luego escriban tres frases que describen el valor *(value)* nutritivo de la comida.

Avena[1] con fresas

Ingredientes

4 tazas de leche sabor a fresa	1 taza llena de avena
azúcar al gusto	1 cucharada de vainilla
1 raja de canela[2]	10 fresas en pedazos

Preparación:
Calentar la leche a fuego bajo, junto con el azúcar y la canela, hasta que hierva. Añadir la avena y mover la mezcla hasta que se cocine. Quitarla del fuego, añadir la vainilla, y dejarla en la olla unos diez minutos. Servirla con fresas.

1 oatmeal **2** stick of cinnamon

🌎 Fondo Cultural | El mundo hispano

Las plantas medicinales En América Latina, es muy común tomar remedios naturales para resolver problemas menores de salud, como la tos, la fiebre y los dolores de estómago o de cabeza. Generalmente estos remedios son plantas que usan los indígenas de la región por sus efectos saludables y curativos[1]. Muchas de estas plantas medicinales se preparan como una infusión o té para beber. Algunos ejemplos de plantas medicinales son la manzanilla[2], que se usa para los dolores de estómago, el girasol[3], para la tos y cuando estás resfriado, y la menta[4], para los dolores de cabeza y estómago. Estos remedios naturales se venden en ferias y mercados al aire libre en toda América Latina.

• ¿Qué remedios naturales usan los indígenas de América Latina para el dolor de estómago? ¿Y para la tos?

• ¿Qué remedios naturales usan en tu familia y comunidad?

1 curative **2** chamomile **3** sunflower **4** mint

Unas plantas medicinales

120 ciento veinte
Manos a la obra 1

DIFFERENTIATED INSTRUCTION

Heritage Language Learners
Invite students to share their knowledge about folk remedies. Ask guiding questions, such as: *¿Cómo se llama el remedio? ¿Para qué se usa? Si es una planta, ¿dónde se encuentra? ¿Cómo se administra el remedio?*

Students with Learning Difficulties
Learners who have difficulty remembering the irregular *tú* commands may be helped by memorizing classic *refranes,* such as: *Dime con quien andas, y te diré quien eres. Haz bien y no mires a quien. Pon el burro delante, para que no se espante.*

Gramática Repaso

▼ Objectives
▶ Give informal advice about symptoms and remedies
▶ Give instructions to follow a recipe

Mandatos afirmativos con *tú*

To tell a friend or close family member to do something, use the *tú* command form. To give an affirmative command in the *tú* form, use the present indicative Ud. / él / ella form. This rule also applies to stem-changing verbs.

caminar → camina	comer → come	abrir → abre
jugar → juega	volver → vuelve	pedir → pide

- Some verbs have irregular *tú* commands.

decir → **di**	hacer → **haz**	ir → **ve**	mantener → **mantén**	poner → **pon**
salir → **sal**	ser → **sé**	tener → **ten**	venir → **ven**	

- Attach reflexive, direct, and indirect object pronouns to the end of affirmative commands. Add an accent mark to show that the stress remains in the same place.

    ¡Toma esas vitaminas! **¡Tómalas** ahora mismo!
    Siéntate aquí.

Más ayuda   **realidades.com**   ▶ *Canción de hip hop* ▶ *Tutorials*

▼11 Respuestas para todo

Leer • Escribir

Verónica siempre tiene una respuesta para todos los problemas. Completa lo que dice con el mandato del verbo apropiado.

1. ¿Te duelen las piernas? _____ ejercicio. *(hacer / correr)*

2. ¿Estás muy cansada? _____ un rato. *(descansar / jugar)*

3. ¿Quieres mantener tu peso? _____ la comida basura. *(comprar / evitar)*

4. ¿Tienes malos hábitos alimenticios? _____ una dieta equilibrada. *(mantener / recetar)*

5. ¿Te sientes mal? _____ al médico. *(ayudar / ir)*

6. ¿Quieres sentirte mejor? _____ bien todos los días. *(comer / pedir)*

7. ¿No tienes energía? _____ unas vitaminas en la farmacia. *(comprar / ver)*

8. ¿Estás triste? _____ con tus amigos para divertirte. *(salir / buscar)*

▼12 ¿Cómo se prepara?

Leer • Hablar • Escribir

❶ Lee la receta de la Actividad 10 y después explica a otro(a) estudiante cómo se prepara usando mandatos con *tú*.

Modelo
Primero, compra los ingredientes.

❷ Ahora, escribe cómo preparar otra receta que conoces. Usa mandatos con *tú*.

Más práctica (GO)

realidades.com | print

Instant Check	✔	
Guided WB pp. 91–92	✔	✔
Core WB p. 39	✔	✔
Comm. WB pp. 36, 41	✔	✔
Hispanohablantes WB pp. 80–83	✔	

Practice and Communicate ③

Gramática Repaso

Core Instruction

Standards: 4.1

Resources: Voc. and Gram. Transparency 73

INTERACTIVE WHITEBOARD
Grammar Activities 3-1

Suggestions: Model a series of commands for a volunteer to carry out. Then have pairs of students take turns giving each other commands.

▼11 Standards: 1.2

Resources: Voc. and Gram. Transparency 40

Focus: Practicing commands with *tú*

Suggestions: Remind students that some verbs in the activity have irregular forms.

Answers:

1. Haz	3. Evita	5. Ve	7. Compra
2. Descansa	4. Mantén	6. Come	8. Sal

▼12 Standards: 1.1, 1.2, 1.3

Focus: Practicing commands with *tú*

Suggestions: In Step 1, students should change the infinitives to affirmative commands with *tú*.

Answers will vary.

Pre-AP* Support

- **Learning Objective:** Presentational Speaking
- **Activity:** Have pairs of students bring in a utensil (spatula, etc.). Ask each pair to prepare instructions for its use. Have a class member join them at the front of the class to follow the *tú* commands as they alternate giving instructions.
- *Pre-AP* Resource Book:* Comprehensive guide to Pre-AP* communication skill development, pp. 10–18, 39–50

✓ ASSESSMENT

Prueba 3-3 with Study Plan (online only)

Prueba: Mandatos afirmativos con *tú*
- Prueba 3-3: p. 63

ENRICH YOUR TEACHING

Teacher-to-Teacher

Have students invent and deliver "command circuits." These are a series of commands given to a partner, beginning and ending at one point. A typical command circuit might read as follows:

Levántate. / Camina a la ventana. / Ábrela. / Ahora ciérrala. / Vuelve a tu pupitre. / Siéntate.

21st Century Skills

Initiative and Self-Direction Remind students of the various digital tools available in **realidades.com** to help them monitor their own understanding and learning needs, such as the online tutorials with comprehension check exercises.

Gramática (Repaso)

Core Instruction

Resources: Voc. and Gram. Transparency 74

INTERACTIVE WHITEBOARD
Grammar Activities 3-1

Suggestions: Remind students that, for negative commands, regular **-ar** verb endings are used with **-er** and **-ir** verbs, and regular **-er/-ir** endings are used with **-ar** verbs.

13 Standards: 1.2

Resources: Answer Keys: Student Edition, p. 40
Focus: Practicing negative commands with **tú**
Suggestions: Have students check their answers by reading each completed item aloud.
Answers:

1. hables	3. llegues	5. entregues
2. juegues	4. vayas	6. seas

14 Standards: 3.1

Resources: Answer Keys: Student Edition, p. 40
Focus: Practicing commands with **tú**
Suggestions: After pairs have taken turns giving commands, have students switch partners, so that they may hear a larger variety of commands.
Answers will vary. The affirmative and negative command forms are:
come, no comas; haz, no hagas; ve, no vayas; pon(te), no (te) pongas; evita, no evites; mantén, no mantengas; sal, no salgas.

✓ ASSESSMENT

Prueba 3-4 with Study Plan (online only)
Prueba: Mandatos negativos con tú
• Prueba 3-4: p. 64

Gramática Repaso

Mandatos negativos con *tú*

To form negative *tú* commands with regular verbs, drop the *-o* of the present tense *yo* form and add the following endings:

hablar	hablo → habl + **es**	**No hables** ahora.
comer	como → com + **as**	**No comas** tanto.
abrir	abro → abr + **as**	**No abras** la boca.

• The same rule applies to verbs whose present tense *yo* form ends in *-go, -zco, -yo,* and *-jo.*

No **salgas** si estás enferma.
No les **ofrezcas** comida basura a tus amigos.
No **escojas** comida con mucha grasa.

• The following verbs have irregular negative *tú* command forms.

dar → **no des**	ir → **no vayas**
estar → **no estés**	ser → **no seas**

• Verbs ending in *-car, -gar,* and *-zar* have the following spelling changes in the negative *tú* commands in order to keep the original sound.

sacar *(c → qu)*	saqu + es	**No saques** la basura.
llegar *(g → gu)*	llegu + es	**No llegues** tarde.
cruzar *(z → c)*	cruc + es	**No cruces** aquí.

• If you are using reflexive or object pronouns with negative commands, place them after *no.*

Estás enfermo. No **te** levantes de la cama.
No comas el pastel. No **lo** comas.

Más ayuda	**realidades.com**	▸ Tutorial

▼13 Lo que no debes hacer

Leer • Escribir

Luis sacó malas notas. Ayúdale a sacar mejores notas. Completa las frases con el mandato del verbo apropiado.

1. No _____ cuando la maestra está explicando algo. *(hablar / comer)*

2. No _____ con otro estudiante en clase. *(jugar / escribir)*

3. No _____ tarde a la clase. *(hacer / llegar)*

4. No _____ a la escuela sin hacer la tarea. *(ir / lavar)*

5. No _____ tu tarea sin leerla antes. *(entregar / comprar)*

6. No _____ tan impaciente. *(ser / tomar)*

▼14 Cuida tu salud |

Hablar

Tu amiga siempre está enferma. Dale siete consejos usando los verbos del recuadro. Usa mandatos afirmativos y negativos.

comer	hacer	ir	poner(se)	evitar	mantener	salir

Modelo
tomar
¡Toma tu medicina!

Más práctica	GO

realidades.com | print

Instant Check	✔	
Guided WB pp. 93–94	✔	✔
Core WB p. 40	✔	✔
Comm. WB p. 42	✔	✔
Hispanohablantes WB p. 84		✔

122 ciento veintidós
Manos a la obra 1

DIFFERENTIATED INSTRUCTION

Heritage Language Learners

Ask students to work in pairs to write sentences that demonstrate double negatives, such as **No digas nada.** Encourage them to see how many negatives they can work into a coherent sentence: **No digas nada de nada a nadie nunca.** Invite them to share their sentences with the class.

Advanced Learners/Pre-AP*

Have students choose a goal that they would like to achieve, such as keeping fit or driving safely. Ask them to create advice sheets consisting of affirmative and negative commands with **tú** that they would give to someone in order to help them achieve this goal.

Gramática Repaso

| ▼ Objectives |
- ▸ Discuss good eating habits
- ▸ Read and write about a doctor's advice
- ▸ Write and talk about healthy living

Mandatos afirmativos y negativos con *Ud.* y *Uds.*

To give commands to people other than *tú* and to more than one person, use the *Ud.* and *Uds.* commands. To form a command with *Ud.*, remove the *-s* from a negative *tú* command form. To form a command with *Uds.*, replace the *-s* of a negative *tú* command with an *-n.*

No hables.	Hable (Ud.).	Hablen (Uds.).
No traigas la receta.	Traiga (Ud.) la receta.	Traigan (Uds.) la receta.
No vayas al consultorio.	Vaya (Ud.) al consultorio.	Vayan (Uds.) al consultorio.

- To form negative *Ud.* and *Uds.* commands just add *no* before the command.

  Coma frutas, pero **no coma** muchos dulces.   **No salten** comidas.

- Attach reflexive, direct, and indirect object pronouns to the end of affirmative *Ud.* and *Uds.* commands. Add an accent mark to show that the stress remains in the same place. In negative commands, add the pronoun between *no* and the verb.

  ¡Tomen esas pastillas! **¡Tómenlas** ahora mismo!   **Lleve** la receta. Por favor, **llévela.**

  ¡Cepíllese los dientes después de comer!   **No le pidan** dulces. **Pídanle** fruta.

Más ayuda	realidades.com	▸ *Canción de hip hop* ▸ *Tutorials*

▼15 Qué dicen todos?

Escribir • Hablar

❶ ¿Qué mandatos se oyen en diferentes lugares? Trabaja con otro(a) estudiante para escribir un mandato afirmativo y un mandato negativo con *Ud.* o *Uds.* para cada uno de los siguientes lugares.

1. en el consultorio del doctor
2. en la biblioteca
3. en el gimnasio
4. en la clase de español
5. en una fiesta
6. en la cocina
7. en una tienda de ropa

Modelo
en la sala
Apaguen el televisor.
No apaguen el televisor.

¡Corran! ¡Corran! ¡Rápido! ¡A ganar!

❷ Ahora, cada pareja debe leer sus mandatos a la clase, y los demás deben decir si la frase está correcta. Si está correcta la frase, y si no la tiene escrita otra pareja, gana un punto la pareja que la escribió. Gana la pareja que reúne más puntos.

ciento veintitrés   123
Capítulo 3

ENRICH YOUR TEACHING

Teacher-to-Teacher

If you had students create command circuits as suggested on p. 121, have them go through them again now with a partner. Then ask them to create new command circuits that include negative commands.

21st Century Skills

Media Literacy Have students find examples of command forms used in Spanish language advertisements. Discuss why media messages use the command forms to express their intentions. What is the purpose of an advertisement? Who is the intended audience? When might they use the *tú* or *Ud./Uds.* forms?

Practice and Communicate ③

Gramática Repaso

Core Instruction

Standards: 4.1

Resources: Voc. and Gram. Transparency 75

INTERACTIVE WHITEBOARD
Grammar Activities 3-1

Suggestions: Remind students that, just as negative **tú** commands, endings for negative **Ud.** and **Uds.** commands are also "switched." Regular **-ar** verb endings are used with **-er** and **-ir** verbs, and regular **-er/-ir** endings are used with **-ar** verbs.

▼15 Standards: 1.1, 1.2, 1.3

Focus: Practicing commands with **Ud. / Uds.**

Suggestions: Students sometimes become frustrated trying to remember the command forms. Encourage them by telling them that they will learn to use the correct forms through patience and practice until the correct form "sounds right." This activity provides excellent practice, since it forces students to focus on the "switched" endings.

Answers will vary.

Chapter Project

Students can perform Step 2 at this point. Be sure they understand your corrections and suggestions. (see p. 108-b.)

16 Standards: 1.1

Focus: Practicing commands with *tú, Ud.,* and *Uds.*

Suggestions: Remind students that their commands can be negative or affirmative.

Answers will vary.

Extension: After some practice, add an element of spontaneity. After each student responds, have him or her toss a foam ball or a wadded-up sheet of paper to any other student in the group, who must say the next command.

17 Standards: 1.1, 1.2, 3.1

Focus: Reading about an actual study of dietary habits conducted in Spain

Suggestions: Have students phrase their recommendations as if they were directly addressing the students in Ávila. For Advanced Learners, have students research the use and formation of *vosotros* commands to address the class accordingly, as though they were making suggestions directly to young people in Spain.

Answers will vary.

Country Connection
Core Instruction

Standards: 3.1

Resources: Map Transparency 20

Suggestions: Have students locate Ávila on *Vocabulary & Grammar Transparency 20* or another map of Spain. It is about 75 kilometers west-northwest of Madrid, in the autonomous region of Castilla y León. Tell students that Ávila is surrounded by a historic Romanesque wall and contains many other treasures that date back to the eleventh century. Ávila was the home of the Spanish kings until the court was moved to Madrid. A mountain range and province also bear the same name.

124

▼16 Juego | 🧑‍🤝‍🧑

Escribir • Hablar • GramActiva

Formen grupos de cuatro estudiantes. Cada estudiante escribe un mandato en infinitivo en un pedazo de papel y lo mete en una caja. Los estudiantes se turnan para sacar un papel de la caja. El(La) que saca el papel, lee el mandato. El(La) segundo(a) estudiante forma un mandato con *tú*. El(La) siguiente forma el mandato con *Uds.* y el(la) último(a) añade un pronombre de complemento directo o indirecto a uno de los dos mandatos. Los mandatos pueden ser negativos o afirmativos.

Modelo
Comer manzanas verdes
No comas las manzanas verdes.
No coman las manzanas verdes.
No las comas.

▼17 Hábitos alimenticios de los jóvenes | 💬

Leer • Hablar

Lee este artículo sobre los hábitos alimenticios de los estudiantes españoles.

Conexiones | Las ciencias

El Centro de Salud de Ávila, en España, estudió los hábitos alimenticios de los estudiantes de 15 años. Los científicos que hicieron la encuesta piensan que es importante conocer los hábitos alimenticios que adquieren *(adopt)* los jóvenes, pues muchos los conservan toda la vida.

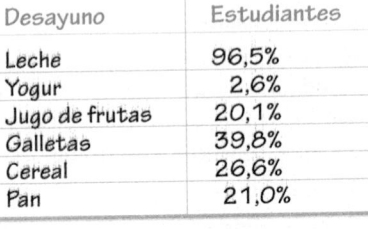

Desayuno	Estudiantes
Leche	96,5%
Yogur	2,6%
Jugo de frutas	20,1%
Galletas	39,8%
Cereal	26,6%
Pan	21,0%

Al final del estudio, los científicos dijeron que estaban preocupados, pues los estudiantes no estaban recibiendo en el desayuno todo el alimento que sus cuerpos necesitan para las actividades del día. Muchos científicos piensan que el desayuno es la comida más importante del día, pero el estudio de Ávila nos dice que el 38 por ciento de los estudiantes sólo toma líquidos en el desayuno.

- Observa la tabla de resultados y di a la clase qué otros alimentos deben comer los estudiantes de Ávila para tener más energía durante el día. Explica lo que tiene cada alimento (calcio, vitaminas, fibra, carbohidratos, grasa, hierro, energía) y por qué es bueno comerlo.

124 ciento veinticuatro
Manos a la obra 1

DIFFERENTIATED INSTRUCTION

Heritage Language Learners

Have students write short descriptions of their favorite breakfast food(s) and breakfast habits. Do they eat different foods on school days and on weekends? If students have lived in a heritage country, ask them to compare and contrast the foods they ate there with those they eat now.

Multiple Intelligences

Logical/Mathematical: Have volunteers poll small groups in the class to find out what they eat for breakfast. Have them conduct their interviews in Spanish. Then have them compare their results and present their findings in a graphic organizer.

18 Un consejo para cada persona | ♻

Leer • Escribir

¿Qué consejos les da la doctora a estos pacientes? Empareja cada frase de la columna A con un consejo de la columna B. Luego escribe un mandato con *Ud.* o *Uds.* para dar el consejo en cada caso.

Modelo
Tengo mucha sed. / tomar agua
Tome un vaso de agua.

Columna A

1. Necesitamos estar en forma.
2. No tenemos energía.
3. Tengo tos y dolor de cabeza.
4. El médico dice que necesito más calcio.
5. Creo que tengo fiebre.
6. Nos sentimos mal porque comimos mucha grasa y azúcar.

Columna B

a. ponerse el termómetro
b. tomar bastante yogur y leche
c. evitar la comida basura y los refrescos
d. tener una dieta equilibrada y no tomar muchos refrescos
e. tomar un jarabe y una aspirina
f. comprar vitaminas con hierro

▼19 Una gran fiesta

Escribir

Imagínate que tú y seis de tus amigos(as) están planeando una fiesta en tu casa. Escribe un mensaje electrónico a tus amigos y explícales qué deben hacer. Usa los verbos del recuadro.

| llegar | traer | comprar | invitar | decorar | hacer |

▼20 Guía para una vida sana |

Hablar • Escribir

❶ Vas a escribir una guía para una vida sana. Trabaja con un grupo de estudiantes. Hagan una lista de ideas sobre lo que es importante hacer y evitar para mantener la salud.

❷ Escriban cinco frases para la guía usando la lista de ideas. Usen mandatos con *Ud.*

Modelo
No ponga mucha sal en la comida.

❸ Lean a la clase la guía que escribieron. Intercambien ideas sobre lo que recomendaron. Digan qué ideas son buenas para todas las personas, cuáles sólo sirven para los jóvenes y cuáles sólo para las personas mayores, y expliquen por qué.

Más práctica (GO)

realidades.com | print

Instant Check	✔	
Guided WB pp. 95–96	✔	✔
Core WB p. 41	✔	✔
Comm. WB pp. 37, 43	✔	✔
Hispanohablantes WB pp. 85–87		✔

Practice and Communicate ③

▼18 Standards: 1.2, 3.1

Resources: Answer Keys: Student Edition, p. 41

Focus: Practicing new vocabulary and command forms

Suggestions: Remind students that the subject in Column A determines to whom to address their commands.

Answers:

1. **Tengan una dieta equilibrada y no tomen muchos refrescos.**
2. **Compren vitaminas con hierro.**
3. **Tome un jarabe y una aspirina.**
4. **Tome bastante yogur y leche.**
5. **Póngase el termómetro.**
6. **Eviten la comida basura y los refrescos.**

▼19 Standards: 1.3

Focus: Writing commands in the context of an e-mail

Suggestions: Encourage students to include some negative commands.

Answers will vary.

▼20 Standards: 1.1, 1.3, 3.1

Focus: Practicing writing commands and new vocabulary in context

Suggestions: Have students work on their own to write sentences in Step 2.

Answers will vary.

Additional Resources

- Communication Wbk.: Audio Act. 2, p. 37
- Teacher's Resource Book: Audio Script, p. 153, Communicative Pair Activity BLM, pp. 161–162
- Audio Program DVD: Cap. 3, Track 8

ENRICH YOUR TEACHING

Culture Note

Although dietary habits in Spain have changed recently, much as they have in the United States, many people still enjoy a sweet breakfast of **churros y chocolate.** This is a cup of very thick hot chocolate and a small bundle of deep-fried dough sticks, whose texture resembles that of doughnuts.

21st Century Skills

Creativity and Innovation Have students browse online recipes in Spanish and work in pairs to change the ingredients to create a healthier version of the dish.

✓ASSESSMENT

Prueba 3-5 with Study Plan (online only)

Prueba: Mandatos con *Ud.* y *Uds.*
- Prueba 3-5: p. 65

Examen: Vocabulario y gramática 1
- Examen 1: pp. 66–68
- ExamView: Examen 1

Vocabulario en contexto

▶ Read, listen to, and understand information about
• physical fitness equipment
• exercises to stay fit
• giving advice

Core Instruction

Standards: 1.2, 3.1

Resources: Teacher's Resource Book: Input Script, p. 150, Clip Art, pp. 168–175, Audio Script, pp. 153–154; Voc. and Gram. Transparencies 76–77; Audio Program DVD: Cap. 3, Tracks 9, 11

Focus: Presenting new vocabulary and using grammar lexically in context

Suggestions: Have students read along as you present the new vocabulary by playing the audio or reading aloud. Use the pictures on *Vocabulary & Grammar Transparency* 76 and clarify the meaning of new vocabulary via pantomime. Check comprehension by asking questions. See the Input Scripts in the *Teacher's Resource Book* for specific questions.

▼**21** Standards: 1.2

Resources: Teacher's Resource Book: Audio Script, p. 154; Audio Program DVD: Cap. 3, Track 10; Answer Keys: Student Edition, p. 41

Focus: Practicing listening comprehension of new vocabulary

Suggestions: Before engaging students in the listening activity, give them a few minutes to read over and study the advertisement for **Club Deportivo Las Fuentes.** Tell them to compare the information they hear to what they see in this announcement.

Answers:
1. F   3. F   5. C
2. C   4. F

Extension: After completing the activity, ask students to correct the false answers.

Block Schedule

Have students work in groups of 4 to 5 and create a brief speech by a fitness trainer giving tips for maintaining a healthy body. Use five expressions from this page and have the group act them out in front of the class.

Vocabulario en contexto

Estar en forma no es sólo tener mucho **músculo** y poca grasa en el cuerpo. Algunas personas hacen ejercicios como entrenamiento para una competencia o porque el médico les dice que lo necesitan. Pero muchos más hacen ejercicio para eliminar **el estrés** y dar a su cuerpo **fuerza** y energía. Estar en forma es también sentirse bien con uno mismo, estar saludable.

Para estar en forma

hacer ejercicios de step

hacer flexiones

hacer cinta

hacer ejercicios aeróbicos

hacer yoga

hacer bicicleta

hacer abdominales

¿Se siente débil? ¿Quiere estar más fuerte?
Nunca es tarde para estar en forma

CLUB DEPORTIVO LAS FUENTES

◆ sala de pesas
◆ equipo para hacer bicicleta
◆ piscina
◆ baños sauna y jacuzzi
◆ clases de ejercicios aeróbicos y artes marciales
◆ entrenadores profesionales

Inscríbase hoy mismo y obtenga un 20% de descuento.
Tel. 555-242 677 Independencia #125

▼**21 El Club Deportivo** | 🔊

Leer • Escuchar • Escribir

Escribe en una hoja los números del 1 al 5. Escucha lo que explica esta chica a su amiga sobre el Club Deportivo Las Fuentes y escribe *C* (cierto) o *F* (falso) en cada caso.

126 ciento veintiséis
A primera vista 2

DIFFERENTIATED INSTRUCTION

Heritage Language Learners

Have students list four favorite sports from their heritage country and then compare notes to see which two are the most popular. Encourage them to revise their lists during the discussion. Have them write a few lines explaining why they like or dislike one of those sports.

Advanced Learners

Ask students to work in a small group to prepare and present a TV commercial for a health club. Individuals can act as trainers or clients and do "sound bites" about the club's features and equipment and about correct and incorrect ways to do various exercises. Invite the group to record their commercial on video.

Para hacer ejercicio

flexionar

estirar

1 Antes de comenzar una sesión de ejercicio, es importante tener unos minutos para estirarse. Es necesario que flexiones y estires los músculos para evitar **calambres.**

2 Debemos comenzar a correr despacio, para evitar calambres. Después de un tiempo, podemos correr más rápido.

3 Es importante no hacer demasiado ejercicio sin descansar. Debemos siempre cuidar nuestro **corazón** y saber cuándo debemos parar.

4 Igualmente, al terminar el ejercicio, debe haber un tiempo para **relajarse** y **respirar** normalmente. ¡Ah, qué bien se siente uno después del entrenamiento!

▼22 El anuncio | 🔊 | 💬 _____

Escuchar • Hablar

Escucha el anuncio por radio de un club deportivo y busca las fotos de estas páginas que correspondan a los servicios que se anuncian. Luego, di qué ejercicios de estas páginas no están en el anuncio del club deportivo.

▼23 Mis favoritos | 👥 _____

Escribir • Hablar

En una hoja, haz una lista de tres ejercicios que te gusta hacer que se mencionan en estas páginas y los tres servicios del club deportivo que más te gustaría usar. Comparte tu lista con otro(a) estudiante de la clase.

ciento veintisiete 127
Capítulo 3

22 Standards: 1.2

Resources: Teacher's Resource Book: Audio Script, p. 154; Audio Program DVD: Cap. 3, Track 12; Answer Keys: Student Edition, p. 41

Focus: Practicing listening comprehension of new vocabulary

Suggestions: To avoid confusion, remind students that the word *ejercicios* in the instructions refers to physical exercises, not the language activities on these pages. Play the audio or use the script. Allow students to listen more than once. Pause to monitor students, making sure they are identifying the correct illustrations.

Answers:

Photos: hacer yoga/hacer cinta/hacer bicicleta Exercises not included: hacer flexiones/hacer abdominales/hacer ejercicios de step/hacer ejercicios aeróbicos

BELLRINGER REVIEW

Working in pairs, ask students to come up with at least three suggestions for maintaining good health.

23 Standards: 1.1

Resources: Voc. and Gram. Transparencies 76–77

Focus: Listing and reading new vocabulary in the context of personal preferences

Suggestions: Encourage students to demonstrate or describe the exercises they choose in order to demonstrate comprehension of the vocabulary.

Answers will vary.

ENRICH YOUR TEACHING

Culture Note

Physical fitness is part of daily life in Latin America. In Buenos Aires, Argentina there are over 7000 gyms where members take exercise classes or work out, alone or with a personal trainer. Over 50% of Argentineans are involved in physical activity, either at a gym or outdoors. The most popular outdoor activities include running, bicycling, rollerblading and soccer.

21st Century Skills

Communication Have pairs of students discuss which sports and outdoor activities are most popular in their school. What gyms or sports complexes are nearby? Where do people go running, walking, or biking? What team sports are played and where?

Vocabulario en contexto

Core Instruction

Standards: 1.1, 1.2, 3.1

Resources: Teacher's Resource Book: Input Script, p. 151, Clip Art, pp. 168–175, Audio Script, pp. 154–155; Voc. and Gram. Transparencies 78–79; Audio Program DVD: Cap. 3, Tracks 13, 15

Focus: Extending presentation of vocabulary and grammar in context

Suggestions:

Pre-reading: Have students close their books. Show *Vocabulary & Grammar Transparency* 78. Tell students that one person in each of the pictures has a problem and ask if they can identify it.

Reading: Allow students time to read the presentation silently first, including the Web page on p. 129. Then play the audio and have students read along as they listen. Allow them to listen more than once.

Post-reading: Check comprehension by asking questions. See the Input Script in the *Teacher's Resource Book* for specific questions.

---

24 Standards: 1.2

Resources: Teacher's Resource Book: Audio Script, pp. 154–155; Audio Program DVD: Cap. 3, Track 14; Answer Keys: Student Edition, p. 42

Focus: Practicing listening comprehension of new vocabulary and structures

Suggestions: Allow students to listen to the activity once through first. Then play the audio again, pausing after each item so students can write their answers.

Answers:

1.	B	4.	M
2.	M	5.	B
3.	B	6.	M

Extension: After completing the activity, ask students to replace any bad advice they heard with helpful advice.

¿QUÉ ME ACONSEJAS? Cuando tenemos problemas, muchas veces les pedimos consejos a nuestros(as) amigos(as). Mira las ilustraciones y lee lo que les dijeron estas personas a sus amigos(as) para ayudarles con sus problemas.

▼**24 Escoge un buen consejo** | 🔊 ───────────

Escuchar

Escribe los números del 1 al 6 en una hoja. Escucha lo que aconsejan estas personas y escribe si es un buen consejo *(B)* o un mal consejo *(M)*.

128 ciento veintiocho
A primera vista 2

DIFFERENTIATED INSTRUCTION

Heritage Language Learners

Invite students who have lived in a heritage country to tell about comic strips that are popular there. Ask questions to guide them: *¿Cómo se llaman los personajes importantes? ¿Cómo son? ¿Quién lee la tira cómica típicamente? ¿Se publica en un diario o en una revista?*

Students with Learning Difficulties

Make photocopies of *Vocabulary & Grammar Transparency* 78. Have students use these to cut out the dialogue balloons. Make other copies in which the dialogue balloons have been blanked out by covering them with a piece of paper. Give students sets of dialogue balloons and dialogue-less comic strips. Have them match the dialogues to the pictures.

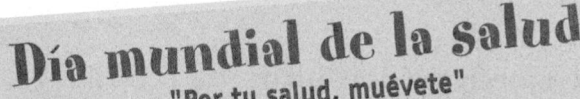

Día mundial de la salud
"Por tu salud, muévete"
7 de abril

LA ACTIVIDAD FÍSICA Y LOS JÓVENES

Según la OMS (Organización Mundial de la Salud), el ejercicio es muy importante para la salud de los jóvenes. La práctica regular del ejercicio o del deporte ayuda a los niños y a los jóvenes a **desarrollar** y mantener saludables los huesos y los músculos. También ayuda a cuidar el peso, a reducir las grasas y al buen funcionamiento del corazón.

Los juegos, los deportes y otras actividades físicas permiten a los jóvenes expresarse, tener **confianza en sí mismos** y desarrollar sentimientos de éxito. Estos efectos positivos reducen el estrés de la vida de los jóvenes de hoy.

▼**25** ¿Comprendiste?
Escribir • Hablar

1. ¿Por qué es buena la práctica regular de ejercicios?

2. ¿Cuáles son cuatro beneficios de hacer ejercicio?

3. ¿Cuáles son algunos efectos positivos de reducir el estrés con el ejercicio?

4. ¿Estás de acuerdo con que los juegos y deportes permiten a los jóvenes expresarse? Explica tu respuesta.

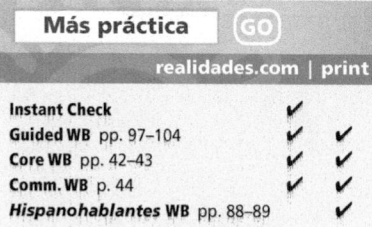

Más práctica	GO
realidades.com | print	

Instant Check	✔	
Guided WB pp. 97–104	✔	✔
Core WB pp. 42–43	✔	✔
Comm. WB p. 44	✔	✔
Hispanohablantes **WB** pp. 88–89		✔

▼**26** Tu propia experiencia |
Leer • Hablar

Lee las frases y dile a otro(a) estudiante cuándo tienes los problemas de los que se habla aquí.

Me caigo de sueño . . .
Estoy de mal humor . . .
Me preocupo . . .
No tengo energía . . .
Estoy estresado(a) . . .
No puedo concentrarme . . .
Me quejo . . .

Modelo
Me siento fatal <u>si no duermo bien</u>.

ciento veintinueve **129**
Capítulo 3

---

25 Standards: 1.1, 1.2, 3.1
Resources: Answer Keys: Student Edition, p. 42
Focus: Demonstrating comprehension of new vocabulary
Suggestions: Have students discuss answers with a partner first.
Answers:
1. Es muy importante para la salud.
2. Ayuda a los niños y a los jóvenes a desarrollar y mantener saludables los huesos y los músculos. También ayuda a cuidar el peso, a reducir las grasas y al buen funcionamiento del corazón.
3. Permite a una persona expresarse, tener confianza en sí mismo y desarrollar sentimientos de éxito.
4. Answers will vary.

26 Standards: 1.1
Focus: Demonstrating comprehension of new vocabulary
Suggestions: If students don't have the problem specified, ask them to make a negative statement followed by an additional comment: *Nunca me preocupo mucho. Preocuparse mucho no resuelve ningún problema.*
Answers will vary.

Pre-AP* Support

- **Learning Objective:** Interpersonal Writing
- **Activity:** Use the phrases in Activity 26, *Tu propia experiencia*, to write an e-mail to a friend about the things that are causing stress in your life. Be sure to ask your friend at least one question about his or her stressful problems so they can respond.
- **Pre-AP* Resource Book:** Comprehensive guide to Pre-AP* writing skill development, pp. 27–38

Chapter Project
Students can perform Step 3 at this point. (For more information, see p. 108-b.)

ENRICH YOUR TEACHING

Culture Note

In a Spanish custom of long ago, girls played a game called ***echar los estrechos*** (pick your dear one) on the last day of each year. They wrote their names on pieces of paper and put them in a bag. Then they wrote the names of boys they knew or wished they knew and put them in

another bag. The girls drew pairs of papers and read aloud the names of each couple. If a pair of people named were already in a relationship, it was thought good luck. If they weren't, it was thought (or hoped!) that they would be before long.

✓ASSESSMENT

Prueba: Comprensión del vocabulario 2
• Prueba 3-6: pp. 67–70

▶ Read and write about doing exercise
▶ Discuss and give advice about health and fitness

Vocabulario en uso

BELLRINGER REVIEW

Use *Vocabulary & Grammar Transparencies* 70–72 for a quick review of vocabulary from pp. 114–116. Ask: *¿Cuáles son algunos malos hábitos alimenticios?¿Y algunos buenos?* Reviewing this information will help students with Step 2 of *Actividad* 27.

▼**27 En la clase de ejercicios aeróbicos**

Leer • Escribir

1 Imagina que te inscribes en una clase de ejercicios aeróbicos. Describe cómo se siente cada estudiante usando las expresiones del recuadro.

No aguanto más	No tengo energía	No me puedo concentrar
o	o	o
Me siento fatal	Me caigo de sueño	Estoy en la luna

▼**27** Standards: 1.2

Resources: Voc. and Gram. Transparency 78; Answer Keys: Student Edition, p. 42

Focus: Demonstrating comprehension of new words and expressions

Suggestions: Show *Vocabulary & Grammar Transparency* 78 for students to use as a reference as they do Step 1.

Answers:

Step 1
Some expressions are similar, and their use may vary. The following are suggestions.

1. No tengo energía.
2. Estoy en la luna.
3. No aguanto más.
4. No me puedo concentrar.
5. Me caigo de sueño.
6. Me siento fatal.

Step 2
Answers will vary.

Extension: After completing the activity, invite pairs of students to role-play one or more of the exchanges from Step 1 for the class. Encourage them to use appropriate intonation for the various expressions.

2 Escribe cinco consejos para los estudiantes de esta clase.

Modelo
Deben tomar vitaminas y desayunar mejor.

130 ciento treinta
Manos a la obra 2

Teacher-to-Teacher

Ask students to write a note in which they complain about being out of shape. In the note, have them describe how they feel, tell why they are in such bad shape, and ask for advice about how to return to a healthier lifestyle. Have them exchange notes with a classmate who will respond with suggestions for meeting the need.

DIFFERENTIATED INSTRUCTION

Students with Learning Difficulties

Before students complete *Actividad* 27, remind them that the third suggested sentence, **No me puedo concentrar** can also be stated **No puedo concentrarme.** They may have less difficulty understanding the alternative construction.

Advanced Learners

Ask students to work in a small group to prepare a brief skit set in a physical education class. One student can be the instructor leading an exercise session. The others can be students in the class, some having success and others having problems. Invite the group to present the skit to the class.

▼28 Nuestra entrenadora

Leer • Escribir

Completa esta descripción de una entrenadora con las palabras apropiadas del recuadro. Usa la forma apropiada de los verbos.

consejos	exigir	confianza en sí misma
débiles	corazón	estirar y flexionar
desarrollar		

Nuestra entrenadora es una atleta que sabe mantenerse en forma y tiene mucha __1.__. Durante las prácticas, ella nos __2.__ mucho. Primero tenemos que __3.__ los músculos. Luego levantamos pesas para __4.__ más músculos en los brazos. Nuestra entrenadora siempre nos da __5.__, como "Hagan ejercicio todos los días para cuidar su __6.__". Ella no quiere que seamos __7.__.

▼29 El deportista |

Hablar

Éstas son las sugerencias que un(a) estudiante deportista le da a su amigo(a). Trabaja con otro(a) estudiante y escojan los mejores consejos para cada pregunta.

▶ **Modelo**

estar en forma
A —¿Cómo se puede estar en forma?
B —Se debe hacer ejercicio.

Estudiante A

¿Cómo se puede . . . ?
1. evitar los calambres
2. quitar el mal humor
3. cuidar el corazón
4. hacer más fuertes los músculos del estómago
5. tener brazos menos débiles

Estudiante B

Se debe . . .
Se recomienda . . .

▼ Fondo Cultural | España

La educación física en España es parte del programa de educación en las escuelas. Sin embargo, en los últimos años muchos estudiantes comenzaron a ir a los clubes deportivos para hacer ejercicio. ¿Por qué? Las escuelas no tienen los equipos deportivos necesarios o estos equipos son muy antiguos.

Muchos profesores de educación física están preocupados por la situación. En primer lugar, dicen ellos, los estudiantes deben tener el equipo necesario para las clases de educación física en su escuela, donde sus profesores pueden decirles qué ejercicios son mejores para su edad. En segundo lugar, muchos jóvenes tienen lesiones (injuries) cuando usan equipos deportivos que no conocen, sin la ayuda de un entrenador.

• ¿Qué crees que se debe hacer en las escuelas de España para mejorar esa situación? Compara su situación con la de tu escuela.

ENRICH YOUR TEACHING

Culture Note

About 80 percent of the people in the world rely on plants to treat illnesses. Even the other 20 percent use many prescription drugs that are plant-based. Aspirin, for example, is based on a substance found in willow bark. Plants in the rain forests of the Americas play an important part in the discovery and development of new drugs.

21st Century Skills

Technology Literacy Have students prepare a multimedia presentation in which they show how physical education class in their school is similar to and different from physical education in a school in Spain. Students can use the information in *Fondo cultural* as a basis for their comparison.

▼28 Standards: 1.2

Resources: Answer Keys: Student Edition, p. 43

Focus: Using new vocabulary

Suggestions: Encourage students to begin by scanning the complete paragraph.

Answers:

1. confianza en sí misma
2. exige
3. estirar y flexionar
4. desarrollar
5. consejos
6. corazón
7. débiles

▼29 Standards: 1.1

Resources: Answer Keys: Student Edition, p. 43

Focus: Practicing new vocabulary in a guided conversation

Suggestions: Have students switch roles to practice both parts of the dialogue.

Answers will vary.

Probable answers:

1. Se debe/Se recomienda estirar (flexionar).
2. … hacer yoga.
3. … hacer bicicleta.
4. … hacer abdominales.
5. … levantar pesas.

Fondo cultural

Standards: 1.1, 1.2, 3.1

Suggestions: Ask: ¿Qué problema tienen muchas escuelas españolas? ¿Qué hacen los estudiantes para resolverlo?

Answers will vary.

Additional Resources

• Communication Wbk.: Audio Act. 3, p. 37
• Teacher's Resource Book: Audio Script, p. 155, Communicative Pair Activity BLM, pp. 163–164
• Audio Program DVD: Cap. 3, Track 16

✓ ASSESSMENT

Prueba 3-7 with Study Plan (online only)

Prueba: Aplicación del vocabulario 2
• Prueba 3-7: pp. 71–72

3 Practice and Communicate

Gramática Repaso

Core Instruction

Resources: Voc. and Gram. Transparency 80

INTERACTIVE WHITEBOARD

Grammar Activities 3-2

Suggestions: Point out that the endings used for regular verbs in the subjunctive are the same as those used for negative command forms. Refer students to pp. 122–123 for these endings.

30 Standards: 1.2

Resources: Answer Keys: Student Edition, p. 43

Focus: Practicing forms of the present subjunctive with regular verbs

Suggestions: Ask students to pay attention to the reason for using the subjunctive in each case as they work. Then have volunteers read each sentence of the completed activity aloud, including the correct verb form.

Common Errors: Since English contains only a few vestiges of the subjunctive (such as "If I were you…"), some students have difficulty remembering to use it in Spanish. Help them by providing more examples in Spanish that require the subjunctive.

Answers:

1. comience   4. hagan
2. corran   5. estiremos
3. hablen   6. subamos

Extension: As students read through the completed activity aloud, ask them to state the reason why the subjunctive is required in each case.

Gramática Repaso

▼ **Objectives**
▶ Read and write about a fitness class
▶ Give advice about exercise and health

El subjuntivo: Verbos regulares

To say that one person wants, suggests, or demands that someone else do something, use the *subjunctive mood*. A sentence that includes the subjunctive form has two parts, the main clause and the subordinate clause, connected by the word *que*.

Quiero que respires lentamente.   **Sugiero que bebas** agua antes de correr.
El entrenador **exige que** los atletas **estiren** los músculos.

You can also suggest more general or impersonal ideas using expressions such as *es necesario . . .*, *es bueno . . .*, and *es importante . . .*, followed by *que* and a form of the present subjunctive.

Es necesario que hagas ejercicio.   **Es importante que** los jóvenes **coman** bien.

To form the subjunctive, drop the *-o* ending to the *yo* form of the present tense, and add the present subjunctive endings to the stem of the verb.

saltar		conocer		decir	
salte	saltemos	conozca	conozcamos	diga	digamos
saltes	saltéis	conozcas	conozcáis	digas	digáis
salte	salten	conozca	conozcan	diga	digan

Verbs ending in *-car*, *-gar*, and *-zar* have a spelling change in order to keep the pronunciation consistent.

buscar (c → qu)		pagar (g → gu)		cruzar (z → c)	
busque	busquemos	pague	paguemos	cruce	crucemos
busques	busquéis	pagues	paguéis	cruces	crucéis
busque	busquen	pague	paguen	cruce	crucen

Más ayuda   **realidades.com**   ▶**Tutorial**

▼30 Una clase inolvidable

Leer • Escribir

¿Tuviste alguna vez una instructora de ejercicios aeróbicos que te exigía mucho? Completa la descripción con el verbo apropiado en subjuntivo.

La instructora exige que la clase ___1.___ *(comenzar / cruzar)* a tiempo y que los estudiantes ___2.___ *(correr / comer)* durante diez minutos antes de comenzar la sesión. Ella no permite que ellos ___3.___ *(tocar / hablar)* durante la clase. A ella tampoco le gusta que ___4.___ *(hacer / tener)* ruido cuando da la clase. Prefiere que nos ___5.___ *(estirar / cruzar)* y que ___6.___ *(apagar / subir)* escaleras para tener más energía antes de la clase.

DIFFERENTIATED INSTRUCTION

Heritage Language Learners

Have students listen to conversations between family members and focus on words or phrases in the subjunctive mood. Ask them to estimate how frequently the subjunctive is used in a brief conversation. Have them write down as many of the words as they can remember. Check for spelling and structure.

Students with Learning Difficulties

Before beginning the grammar presentation on this page, remind students that they have already seen these spelling changes in other grammatical forms. On the board, write the preterite forms of *sacar, llegar,* and *empezar.* Highlight the spelling changes in the **yo** form and remind students of the spelling change rules.

▼31 ¿Qué ejercicios hago? |  | ♻

Hablar

Imagínate que eres el(la) entrenador(a) de la escuela. Habla con otro(a) estudiante para aconsejarle algo. Usen las siguientes expresiones.

▶ **Modelo**

Me duele(n) . . . / Es necesario que . . . .

A —*Me duelen las piernas cuando corro.*

B —*Es necesario que estires los músculos antes de correr.*

Estudiante A

1. ¿Qué hago para . . . ?
2. No puedo . . .
3. Estoy muy . . .
4. Quiero desarrollar . . .
5. Necesito . . .
6. Tengo . . .

Estudiante B

Te sugiero que . . .

Es importante que . . .

Para que estés más tranquilo(a), te aconsejo que . . .

Lo mejor es que practiques . . .

Es muy bueno que vayas a . . .

Para evitar los calambres quiero que . . .

El español en el mundo del trabajo

La consejera bilingüe

De niña, María Romero Thomas hablaba sólo español en su casa e inglés en la escuela. Sus padres le decían que ella no podía olvidar la cultura de sus abuelos mexicanos, pero que debía integrarse *(to integrate)* y tener éxito en la cultura estadounidense. María quiso ayudar a otros a alcanzar también esa meta y decidió estudiar para ser una consejera escolar.

La función de un(a) consejero(a) escolar es muy importante para los estudiantes y para la comunidad. Estos(as) profesionales se dedican a dar apoyo a los chicos y a guiarlos al elegir la carrera que van a seguir. También aconsejan sobre temas de salud, cómo

coordinar el estudio con otras actividades como recreación, trabajo y ejercicios, en las relaciones con su familia y amigos, cómo mantener un buen estado de ánimo, y cómo desarrollar sus aptitudes en la escuela. Si ven que los chicos se sienten mal, no se pueden concentrar o están muy estresados, les recomiendan ir al médico, tener una alimentación saludable y cosas que pueden hacer para relajarse.

Al comienzo de los años ochenta, María Romero Thomas se convirtió en *(became)* la primera consejera bilingüe del Sequoia Union High School District, en California. En esos años, viajaba de una escuela a otra para implementar el primer programa bilingüe del distrito. También hablaba con los padres sobre la importancia que tenía para sus hijos recibir una buena educación.

Hoy en día, hay cientos de consejeros bilingües en los distritos escolares de los Estados Unidos que ayudan a los niños hispanohablantes a vivir entre dos culturas.

ciento treinta y tres **133**
Capítulo 3

ENRICH YOUR TEACHING

Culture Note

For a great many Spanish-speaking people the notion of "bilingualism" has nothing to do with English. In Mexico alone, more than a hundred languages are spoken, from the **nahuatl** of the Aztecs to **amuzgo** to **zoque.** About eight percent of those who speak an indigenous language are bilingual in Spanish. Consider all

of Central and South America and the Caribbean, and the number of known languages rises to almost a thousand. Indigenous languages are so important in some countries that they have been given official standing equal to Spanish. Examples include **guaraní** in Paraguay and **quechua** in Peru.

Practice and Communicate ③

▼31 Standards: 1.1

Focus: Using the subjunctive with regular verbs in a guided conversation

Recycle: parts of the body; ***poder* +** infinitive

Suggestions: Allow students a few minutes on their own to prepare the problems they are going to talk about when they play the role of Student A. As they practice the dialogue together, encourage those playing the role of Student B to respond as quickly and naturally as possible with a suggestion that makes sense.

Answers will vary.

▼ El español en el mundo del trabajo

Core Instruction

Standards: 1.2, 3.1, 5.1

Suggestions: Ask students, including Heritage Language Learners who may have known a bilingual advisor, to talk about their experiences with him or her. Ask: *¿Cómo ayudaba el (la) consejero(a) a los estudiantes? ¿Tenía interacción con los profesores también? ¿Y con los padres? ¿Cuáles eran algunas de sus tareas?* Then ask students: *¿Les interesa tener una carrera como consejero(a) bilingüe? ¿Por qué? ¿Por qué no?*

Teacher-to-Teacher

Prepare (or ask Advanced Learners to prepare) two sets of notecards. One set contains subordinate clauses in which the verb is in the infinitive in parentheses *...que (estudiar) mucho.* The other set is a mixture of main clauses, some that require the subjunctive in the subordinate clause and some that do not, such as **Es evidente que...** or **Veo que....** Students can take turns drawing one card from each pile, determining whether or not the subjunctive is needed in the subordinate clause, and if so, what its form is. Then have them read the complete complex sentence aloud: *Veo que estudias mucho.*

133

32 Standards: 1.1

Resources: Answer Keys: Student Edition, p. 44

Focus: Practicing the subjunctive with regular verbs in a guided conversation

Suggestions: Remind students that the words and expressions in the word bank are to be used to begin the main clause in Student B's sentences.

Answers: Student B's sentences will vary, but should make use of the following subjunctive forms:

saques	añadas	conozcas
pongas	tomes	hagas
respires	hagas	

33

Resources: Answer Keys: Student Edition, p. 44

Focus: Practicing the subjunctive with regular verbs in the context of giving advice

Suggestions: Challenge students to be creative with their mixing and matching from the three columns, in order to make as many sentences as they can.

Answers will vary.

Students should choose from the following subjunctive verb forms, depending on the subject of each subordinate *(que)* clause:

limpies/limpie/limpiemos/limpien
llegues/llegue/lleguemos/lleguen
laves/lave/lavemos/laven
expliques/explique/expliquemos/expliquen
muestres/muestre/mostremos/muestren
te preocupes/se preocupe/nos preocupemos/se preocupen
tengas/tenga/tengamos/tengan
aprendas/aprenda/aprendamos/aprendan

Prueba 3-8 with Study Plan (online only)

Prueba: El subjuntivo: Verbos regulares
• Prueba 3-8: p. 73

134

▼**32** ¿Qué le aconsejas? | 🗣️👥 _____

Hablar

Tu amigo(a) siempre se queja de sus problemas. ¿Qué le aconsejas en cada caso? Trabaja con otro(a) estudiante para darle consejos. Usa la forma correcta del subjuntivo y las expresiones del recuadro.

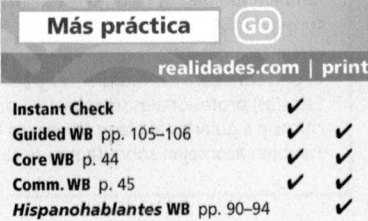

sugiero	recomiendo	quiero	es importante	es necesario

▶ **Modelo**

Me caigo de sueño. / descansar un poco
A —*Me caigo de sueño.*
B —*Sugiero que descanses un poco.*

Estudiante A

1. Siempre estoy en la luna.
2. Quiero hacer más fuertes mi corazón y los músculos de mis piernas.
3. No tengo energía.
4. Estoy aburrido(a).
5. No aguanto más los juegos de mis amigos.
6. Siempre tengo sed.
7. Como demasiada comida basura.
8. Necesito hacer más ejercicio.

Estudiante B

sacar . . . de la biblioteca
poner . . .
respirar lentamente . . .
añadir más . . .
tomar . . .
hacer . . .
conocer . . .
hacer . . . y ejercicios . . .

¡Respuesta personal!

▼**33** En el club atlético Sol y Salud _____

Escribir

Trabajas en un club atlético y tienes que darles consejos a los miembros del club y a las personas que trabajan contigo. Combina palabras de las tres columnas para hacer frases con el subjuntivo.

Modelo

Queremos / Roberto / enseñar
Queremos que Roberto enseñe la clase de ejercicios aeróbicos.

Es importante que . . .	los entrenadores	limpiar
Sugerimos que . . .	tú	llegar a tiempo
Es mejor que . . .	David y Rita	lavar
(No) Queremos que . . .	nadie	explicar
Es necesario que . . .	ustedes	mostrar cómo
Exigimos que . . .	Julieta	no preocuparse por
	los profesores	(no) tener
	todos	aprender

Más práctica	GO

realidades.com | print

Instant Check	✔	
Guided WB pp. 105–106	✔	✔
Core WB p. 44	✔	✔
Comm. WB p. 45	✔	✔
Hispanohablantes **WB** pp. 90–94		✔

134 ciento treinta y cuatro
Manos a la obra 2

DIFFERENTIATED INSTRUCTION

Students with Learning Difficulties

Ask students to search for a picture in which two or more people are interacting socially. Have them write sentences using the subjunctive that the people in the picture might be saying to one another. Ask students to cut their sentences out in the shape of dialogue balloons and paste them to the picture.

Advanced Learners/Pre-AP*

Ask students to write ten affirmative commands about eating well and keeping fit. Have them exchange sentences with a partner. Partners take turns changing the commands into suggestions, demands, or requirements that take the subjunctive: *Deja de comer comida basura./Es mejor que dejes de comer comida basura.*

Gramática Repaso

▼ Objectives
▶ Read and write about giving advice
▶ Discuss ways to solve problems

El subjuntivo: Verbos irregulares

The following verbs are irregular in the present subjunctive:

dar	estar	haber	ir	saber	ser
dé	esté	haya	vaya	sepa	sea
des	estés	hayas	vayas	sepas	seas
dé	esté	haya	vaya	sepa	sea
demos	estemos	hayamos	vayamos	sepamos	seamos
deis	estéis	hayáis	vayáis	sepáis	seáis
den	estén	hayan	vayan	sepan	sean

▼34 Cambiar los hábitos

Leer • Escribir

Rocío y Manuel están estresados. Escoge el verbo correcto y completa las recomendaciones que les dio el consejero.

1. Es importante que Manuel _____ yoga dos veces por semana. (cambiar / hacer)

2. Les aconsejo que _____ más confianza en sí mismos. (ser / tener)

3. Recomiendo que los dos _____ caminatas por el campo. (eliminar / dar)

4. Es bueno que ustedes _____ de vacaciones al campo. (ir / cambiar)

5. Rocío, te recomiendo que _____ más paciente con Manuel. (estar / ser)

6. Por último, sugiero que cada uno _____ sus propios amigos. (perder / tener)

▼35 Carta a la consejera sentimental

Leer • Escribir

Completa esta correspondencia entre una joven y una consejera con las palabras apropiadas del recuadro.

decir	llegar	relajarse	hacer
estar	ser	haber	darse

Querida Ana:

Mis padres siempre me exigen demasiado. Quieren que yo siempre les __1__ adónde voy y me exigen que __2__ a casa antes de las 9 de la noche. Casi todos los días tenemos algún problema.

¡No aguanto más!

Frustrada en Quito

Querida Frustrada:

Primero, te aconsejo que __3__. Es importante que __4__ un esfuerzo para comprender lo que quieren tus padres. Ellos quieren que __5__ segura (safe). Aunque tú quieres salir con tus amigos, es necesario que __6__ responsable. No es bueno que __7__ problemas en tu casa, y te recomiendo que __8__ cuenta de lo que haces. Sé paciente y trata de hablar con tus padres y las cosas van a mejorar.

Ana

Practice and Communicate ③

Gramática Repaso

Core Instruction

Resources: Voc. and Gram. Transparency 81

INTERACTIVE WHITEBOARD
Grammar Activities 3-2

Suggestions: Challenge students to create sentences using subjunctive verb forms that you call out.

▼34 Standards: 1.2

Resources: Answer Keys: Student Edition, p. 45

Focus: Practicing forms of the present subjunctive with irregular verbs

Suggestions: Review with students the verbs in the main clause that require the subjunctive in the subordinate clause.

Answers:

1. haga
2. tengan
3. den
4. vayan
5. seas
6. tenga

▼35 Standards: 1.2

Resources: Answer Keys: Student Edition, p. 45

Focus: Practicing the subjunctive with irregular verbs in a cloze exercise

Suggestions: Encourage students to look for expressions such as **querer que** and **es necesario que.** Remind them that these expressions are markers for the subjunctive.

Answers:

1. diga
2. llegue
3. te relajes
4. hagas
5. estés
6. seas
7. haya
8. te des

ENRICH YOUR TEACHING

Teacher-to-Teacher

Invent a few scenarios in which you briefly describe an imaginary problem and ask for advice. Problem scenarios might include being tired all the time, or questions about how to create a healthy meal for guests.

21st Century Skills

Productivity and Accountability Have students create a class checklist of Spanish learning goals for the year using the subjunctive after expressions such as, *es importante que, es bueno que,* etc. Students should revisit the goals regularly through the term to track their progress.

Chapter Project

Students can perform Step 4 at this point. Be sure they understand your corrections and suggestions. (For more information, see p. 108-b.)

36 Standards: 1.2, 1.3

Resources: Answer Keys: Student Edition, p. 46

Focus: Practicing new vocabulary and structures via letter reading and writing

Suggestions: Encourage students to build sentences around the *sugerencias* before they organize them into a response.

Answers will vary.

Verb forms for the *sugerencias* are as follows:

cambies
estés
salgas
tengas
camines

37 Standards: 1.2

Resources: Answer Keys: Student Edition, p. 46

Focus: Practicing new vocabulary and structures in guided conversations

Suggestions: Have groups conduct the activity in round-robin fashion. Rotate around the circle with a different student presenting the problem each time, with others eliciting possible solutions.

Answers will vary.

Students may use the following vocabulary and subjunctive forms:

1. Tengo calambres. 3. Estoy de mal humor.
2. Me caigo de sueño. 4. Estoy estresado(a).

vayas, conozcas, estés, tengas, seas, sepa

136

▼36 Querida Laura . . .

Leer • Escribir

Muchos jóvenes le escriben a Laura, la escritora de la columna de consejos de una revista de Madrid. Lee la carta que una joven le escribió a Laura y luego escribe la respuesta de Laura. Usa expresiones como: *te recomiendo, te sugiero, es necesario, es bueno, es importante* y la lista de sugerencias. Pon los verbos en el subjuntivo.

Querida Laura:

Me encanta la clase de yoga. Siempre me siento mejor y me relajo después de ir. Pero el problema es que no tengo tiempo. Tengo mucha tarea y también estudio piano. ¿Cómo me puedo relajar y estar tranquila si no puedo ir a yoga?

Ocupada de Burgos

Querida Ocupada de Burgos:

Si tienes tanto trabajo y no puedes ir a tu clase de yoga, te recomiendo que . . .

Sugerencias
• cambiar el horario
• estar ocupada
• salir con los(as) amigos(as)
• tener tiempo para relajarse
• caminar todos los días

▼37 Intercambio de ideas |

Hablar

Imagina que tú eres la persona de los dibujos. Tus compañeros(as) te van a dar sugerencias o consejos para ayudarte a resolver tus problemas. Usen los verbos del recuadro.

 **Modelo**

A— *Estoy muy aburrido, nunca hago nada interesante.*

B— *Es importante que salgas más.*

C— *Es bueno que conozcas más gente.*

ir	conocer	estar	tener	ser	saber

1. 2.

3. 4.

Más práctica	GO

realidades.com | print

Instant Check	✓	
Guided WB pp. 107–108	✓	✓
Core WB p. 45	✓	✓
Comm. WB p. 46	✓	✓
***Hispanohablantes* WB** p. 95		✓

DIFFERENTIATED INSTRUCTION

Heritage Language Learners

Advice is often given in the form of popular sayings. Cite a few examples, such as **Barriga llena, corazón contento** or **Todo lo que brilla no es oro.** Have students ask family members what their favorite saying is and write them down. Encourage them to find out if there are similar sayings in English.

Students with Special Needs

Have visually impaired students sit with a partner who can help them complete *Actividad* 37 by explaining the scene in each of the pictures.

Gramática Repaso

▼ Objectives
▶ Read and write about leading a healthy lifestyle
▶ Discuss suggestions for staying healthy and exercising

El subjuntivo: Verbos con cambio de raíz

In the present subjunctive, stem-changing -ar and -er verbs have the stem change in all forms except *nosotros* and *vosotros*.

jugar (u → ue)

juegue	juguemos
juegues	juguéis
juegue	jueguen

pensar (e → ie)

piense	pensemos
pienses	penséis
piense	piensen

entender (e → ie)

entienda	entendamos
entiendas	entendáis
entienda	entiendan

- Other verbs you know that follow these patterns are:
  - o → ue: *contar, poder, volver, costar, probar(se), llover, doler*
  - e → ie: *querer, sentarse, calentar, despertar(se), empezar, entender*

Stem-changing e → ie, e → i, and o → ue verbs that end in -ir have a stem change in all forms of the subjunctive.

sentirse (e → ie)

me sienta	nos sintamos
te sientas	os sintáis
se sienta	se sientan

pedir (e → i)

pida	pidamos
pidas	pidáis
pida	pidan

dormir (o → ue)

duerma	durmamos
duermas	durmáis
duerma	duerman

- Other verbs you know that follow these patterns are:
  - e → ie: *divertirse, preferir*
  - e → i: *reír, repetir, servir, vestir(se), seguir, conseguir*
  - o → ue: *morir*

▼38 ¿Qué recomienda la entrenadora?

Leer • Escribir

Estás en un gimnasio y la entrenadora te recomienda varias cosas. Lee lo que dice la entrenadora y escoge el verbo apropiado para completar las frases en subjuntivo.

1. Es importante que _____ mis consejos. *(sentir / seguir)*
2. Sugiero que _____ ocho horas cada noche. *(pedir / dormir)*
3. Es importante que no _____ durante las clases de ejercicio. *(sentarse / practicar)*
4. Quiero que _____ bicicleta tres veces por semana. *(repetir / hacer)*
5. También es bueno que _____ al tenis una o dos veces por semana. *(pensar / jugar)*
6. Te aconsejo que _____ con ropa cómoda. *(seguir / vestirse)*
7. Quiero que _____ durante la clase. *(concentrarse / reír)*
8. Es necesario que _____ cuántas flexiones haces. *(contar / cantar)*

ciento treinta y siete **137**
Capítulo 3

ENRICH YOUR TEACHING

Teacher-to-Teacher
Supply blank index cards and have pairs of students make flashcards for stem-changing verbs. They should write one verb form on each card. On the back of each card they can write the infinitive, tense, and mood. For example, "*jugar*—present subjunctive." This will help users reorganize the cards into sets.

21st Century Skills
Initiative and Self-Direction The verb charts available to students in **realidades.com** will help students monitor their own understanding as they review the stem-changing verbs in the subjunctive. They can also find additional verb conjugation practice online.

BELLRINGER REVIEW
Briefly review the indicative forms of stem-changing verbs. On the board write paradigms for some of the verbs in the *Gramática* on this page. Leave some forms out of each paradigm and ask students to supply them, either by spelling them aloud or filling in the paradigm.

Gramática [Repaso]

Core Instruction
Resources: Voc. and Gram. Transparency 82

INTERACTIVE WHITEBOARD
Grammar Activities 3-2

Suggestions: On the board, list *...que yo ___, ...que tú ___, ...que Ud./él/ella ___, ...que nosotros(as) ___,* and *...que Uds./ellos/ellas ___.* Point to these phrases at random and call out an infinitive from the *Gramática*. Ask students to supply and spell aloud the correct subjunctive form.

▼38 Standards: 1.2
Resources: Answer Keys: Student Edition, p. 46
Focus: Practicing stem-changing subjunctive verb forms
Suggestions: Remind students to be extra careful with spelling, since that is the focus of the activity.

Answers:
1. sigas
2. duermas
3. te sientes
4. hagas
5. juegues
6. te vistas
7. te concentres
8. cuentes

Pre-AP* Support
- **Learning Objective:** Interpersonal Speaking
- **Activity:** Working with a partner, have students use the information from Activity 36 as a model to role-play a conversation between a stressed client and a life-coach. One student will request advice for his or her stress-related problem, while the other will offer suggestions using expressions like: *te recomiendo, es necesario, es bueno,* and verbs in the subjunctive. Students may prepare a brief outline of their conversation before their role-play.
- *Pre-AP* Resource Book:* Comprehensive guide to Pre-AP* communication skill development, pp. 10–18, 39–50

39 Standards: 1.1, 1.3, 3.1

Resources: Answer Keys: Student Edition, p. 47

Focus: Practicing new vocabulary and structures via writing and guided conversation

Suggestions: In Step 1, make sure students understand from the model that the two cues should be combined to make one sentence. Remind them that the subordinate *(que)* clause of each sentence should contain a subject of their choice and a subjunctive verb form. In Step 2, encourage Student B to explain in one or more sentences why he or she agrees or disagrees with the original comment.

Answers will vary.

Students should use the following expressions and subjunctive verbs:

1. **Es bueno que durmamos…**
2. **Es mejor que perdamos…**
3. **Es bueno que pidamos…**
4. **Es bueno que volvamos…**
5. **Es importante que nos acostemos…**
6. **Es necesario que juguemos…**
7. **Es necesario que entendamos…**
8. **Es importante que sigamos…**

Extension: Ask partners to report to the class on their opinions regarding a healthy lifestyle. Create a class profile by recording the information on the board.

En voz alta
Core Instruction

Standards: 1.2, 2.2, 3.2, 5.2

Resources: Teacher's Resource Book: Audio Script, p. 156; Audio Program DVD: Cap. 3, Track 18

Suggestions: Have students read the information and the song silently. Have them find the rhyming words and note the pattern. Explain to students that the fighting during the Mexican Revolution started in 1910 and ended about 1920. Discuss with the class what they imagine life would have been like during that time. Ask comprehension questions: *¿Cómo son los corridos? ¿Cuáles son los temas principales? ¿Por qué cantaron corridos durante la Revolución?*

Before having students read the song aloud, direct their attention to the information in the *¿Recuerdas?* Allow them a few minutes to practice with a partner.

Answers: valiente, popular, bonita

138

Escribir • Hablar

❶ Con otro(a) estudiante, hagan una lista de buenos consejos para llevar una vida más saludable.

Modelo
importante / comer
Es importante que comamos verduras todos los días.

1. bueno / dormir
2. mejor / perder
3. bueno / pedir
4. bueno / volver
5. importante / acostarse
6. necesario / jugar
7. necesario / entender
8. importante / seguir

❷ Léele las sugerencias que escribiste a otro(a) estudiante, quien va a decidir si está de acuerdo o no y por qué.

▶ **Modelo**

A —*Es importante que comamos verduras todos los días.*

B —*Estoy de acuerdo.*

o: —*No estoy de acuerdo. Es más importante que comamos comida con menos grasa.*

▼ En voz alta |

Lee un fragmento de un corrido mexicano, un tipo de canción poética popular de México. Las letras y melodías de estas canciones son sencillas. Obtuvieron popularidad durante la Revolución Mexicana ya que servían para contar noticias, hechos importantes e historias de amor y pena. "La Adelita", uno de los más populares, cuenta de una mujer que se enamoró de un sargento y lo siguió a la guerra. La canción también representa a muchas mujeres que seguían a las tropas, les preparaban comida y cuidaban a heridos y enfermos.

Ahora, escucha la canción y trata de repetirla en voz alta.

• ¿Qué palabras que describen a Adelita pueden describir a las mujeres de la Revolución Mexicana?

¿Recuerdas?

Cuando la consonante *d* va entre vocales, su sonido es similar a la *th* en inglés de la palabra *the*.

Pronuncia estas palabras: *Adelita, acampado, además, quedar.*

La Adelita

En lo alto de la abrupta serranía[1]
acampado se encontraba un regimiento
y una joven que valiente lo seguía
locamente enamorada del sargento.

Popular entre la tropa era Adelita
la mujer que el sargento idolatraba
que además de ser valiente era bonita
que hasta el mismo coronel la respetaba.

Y se oía…
que decía…
aquel que tanto la quería…,

Y si acaso yo muero en la guerra
y mi cuerpo en la tierra va a quedar,
Adelita por Dios te lo ruego
que por mi amor no vayas a llorar.

1 mountainous country

DIFFERENTIATED INSTRUCTION

Heritage Language Learners
Have small groups review the words in *Actividad* 39 and brainstorm other words and phrases that they know are often or always used with the subjunctive. Have the groups compare lists. Then have each group write a sentence for each of the words.

Students with Learning Difficulties
Unfamiliar phrasing can make *"La Adelita"* difficult to understand. To help students follow the story told in the lyrics, have small groups rephrase each verse to retell the story in their own words.

▼40 Cómo te beneficia el ejercicio |

Leer • Hablar

❶ Lee este artículo que explica diferentes clases de ejercicio y los beneficios que tienen.

DANZA AERÓBICA

Más danza y ritmos latinos

Este tipo de danza comienza con un calentamiento de músculos. Incluye ritmos latinos y no tiene saltos.

Beneficios: Ayuda a la coordinación.

CARDIO TRAINING

Pon tu corazón en forma y, con él, todo tu organismo

Es el mejor ejercicio para estar en forma. Comienza con un calentamiento, sigue con una actividad física más intensa, como los saltos, y termina con una fase de descanso, para llevar el ritmo cardíaco a la normalidad.

Beneficios: Ayuda a la capacidad cardiovascular y todas las funciones del organismo.

ZUMBA

Ejercicio aeróbico, pero con pasos de baile

La zumba mezcla pasos de bailes como la samba, el *hip-hop*, la salsa y el merengue. Para hacer zumba, hay que seguir el ritmo de la música con movimientos repetitivos. Es como bailar y hacer aerobic a la vez.

Beneficios: Hace más fuertes los músculos, mejora la coordinación.

❷ Con otros estudiantes, hablen de cada uno de los tipos de ejercicio. ¿Están de acuerdo con lo que dice el artículo? ¿Qué otros beneficios les gustaría añadir?

❸ Y a ti, ¿cuál de las clases de ejercicio te gustaría tomar? Explica tu respuesta.

❹ Hagan recomendaciones a otros jóvenes. Usen formas del subjuntivo.

Modelo

Sugiero que hagas danza aeróbica si te gusta bailar. Es importante que vayas a clases de cardio training *si quieres ser deportista profesional.*

Más práctica	GO	
realidades.com	print	
Instant Check	✔	
Guided WB pp. 109–110	✔	✔
Core WB p. 46	✔	✔
Comm. WB pp. 38–39, 47, 176	✔	✔
Hispanohablantes **WB** pp. 96–97		✔

ciento treinta y nueve **139**
Capítulo 3

▼**40** Standards: 1.1, 1.2, 3.1

Focus: Practicing new vocabulary and structures through reading and discussion

Suggestions: Have students read the article silently twice before opening the discussion. As they discuss the article, encourage them to paraphrase parts that support the comments they make. As students complete Step 4, ask: *¿Han cambiado sus opiniones o recomendaciones desde que empezamos este capítulo? ¿De qué manera?*

Answers will vary.

Additional Resources

- Communication Wbk.: Audio Act. 4–5, pp. 38–39
- Teacher's Resource Book: Audio Script, p. 155–156, Communicative Pair Activity BLM, pp. 165–166
- Audio Program DVD: Cap. 3, Tracks 17, 19

Chapter Project

Students can perform Step 5 at this point. Make audio or video recordings of their presentations for inclusion in their portfolio. (For more information, see p. 108-b.)

ENRICH YOUR TEACHING

Culture Note

The *corrido* is a type of ballad that often tells the stories of heroes, natural disasters, and events. The genre originated in Mexico in the early 1800s, and was especially popular during the Mexican Revolution when it was used to spread news. The *corridos* carried on the oral tradition, and thus preserved stories.

21st Century Skills

Technology Literacy Encourage students to find online Web sites that play Mexican *corridos* and find a musical rendition of *"Adelita"* if possible. You may also ask them to listen to the lyrics of another traditional *corrido* and list any words and expressions they recognize. Are there similarities between the music of *corridos* and other folk music they know? What are the differences?

✓**ASSESSMENT**

Prueba 3-10 with Study Plan (online only)

Prueba: El subjuntivo: Verbos con cambio de raíz
- Prueba 3-10: p. 75

Examen: Vocabulario y gramática 2
- Examen 2: pp. 76–78
- ExamView: Examen 2

▼ Objectives
▶ Read about an ancient team sport played by the Native Americans in Mexico and Central America
▶ Use prior knowledge to increase comprehension

Puente a la cultura

Un juego muy antiguo

Puente a la cultura

Core Instruction

Standards: 1.1, 1.2, 2.1, 2.2, 3.1, 5.2

Focus: Reading to learn about ball games played by ancient peoples in Mexico

Suggestions:

Pre-reading: On the board, set up an **SQA** chart. This is a three-column chart with the columns labeled **Sé, Quiero saber,** and **Aprendí.** Have students duplicate the chart on their own paper. Direct their attention to the *Estrategia.* Help them access their prior knowledge on the topic by discussing the questions there. They can fill in the **Sé** column of their charts with this information. In the **Quiero saber** column, have them write at least three questions—things they would like to learn from reading **Un juego muy antiguo.**

Reading: As students read, remind them to use background knowledge, cognates, and context clues to understand unfamiliar words and expressions. Help them resolve comprehension problems by asking **si/no** or embedded-answer questions.

Post-reading: Ask: *¿Encontraste las respuestas a todas tus preguntas en la lectura?* Have students fill in the **Aprendí** column of their **SQA** charts with any answers to the questions they wrote in the **Quiero saber** column, as well as other interesting facts they have learned.

Country Connection

Core Instruction

Standards: 3.1

Mapa global interactivo, Actividad 2 Discover the ruins of Chichén Itzá, where Mayans played ball games.

Suggestions: Remind students that the ancient ruins found at these places are some of Mexico's major historical and tourist attractions. Assign, or ask students to choose, one of the ancient sites and research it in an encyclopedia or on the Internet. Have them report back at least three interesting facts.

Estrategia

Using your prior knowledge
What do you know about competitive games in Roman and Greek times? Have you heard of the origin of games like baseball or basketball?

Remember that retrieving information you already know about the topic of your reading is always useful to help you better understand it.

Ilustración del antiguo juego olmeca de pelota

La historia del juego de pelota comenzó hace unos 3,000 años alrededor del golfo de México. Los olmecas inventaron este deporte pero otros pueblos conocidos de Mesoamérica, como los mayas y los aztecas, también lo jugaban. El juego de pelota era uno de los eventos más importantes en el Nuevo Mundo.

Llamado *ullamalitzi* por los aztecas, el juego de pelota fue el primer deporte que se jugó en grupo. En la sociedad indígena, estos eventos sociales eran tanto actos religiosos como espectáculos para el público. Los pueblos indígenas creían que los dioses, la naturaleza y el ser humano no podían separarse. La vida, la astronomía y las matemáticas, la organización política y social, el arte, las guerras y hasta los deportes se relacionaban con la religión. Se cree que, para los pueblos indígenas, en el juego de pelota la competencia entre dos equipos representaba la lucha entre el Sol y otros astros[1]. Según los mayas, los dioses miraban el juego desde arriba[2]. Por eso, aunque todos podían ver el juego, solamente jugaban los nobles y los atletas entrenados por los sacerdotes[3].

Hasta hoy se han descubierto más de 600 canchas[4] de pelota en México. Todas tenían dos paredes, una en cada lado, con un anillo de piedra en el centro de cada una. Algunas eran tan grandes como una cancha de fútbol moderna. Las paredes estaban decoradas con escenas del juego.

Para jugar se necesitaba una pelota de caucho[5] que pesaba unas 8 libras[6] y era tan grande como una pelota de básquetbol.

1 heavenly bodies 2 above 3 priests
4 courts 5 rubber 6 pounds

Mesoamérica va desde México hasta Panamá

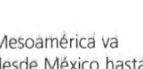

140 ciento cuarenta
¡Adelante!

DIFFERENTIATED INSTRUCTION

Multiple Intelligences

Bodily/Kinesthetic: Reinforce the link between the reading and the sports context. Assign sports words by handing out papers with the words. Ask students to act out the word they received. The rest of the class calls out the appropriate sports word each time.

Advanced Learners

Encourage students to prepare more elaborate reports about the ancient site they chose in the *Country Connection.* Invite them to work together to create a bulletin board display or a graphic presentation using computer software.

La pelota no podía tocar el suelo[7] y los jugadores no podían tocarla con las manos. Usaban la cabeza, los codos, las caderas[8] y las rodillas para pasar la pelota a través de uno de los anillos.

Los atletas llevaban cascos[9] y ropa de cuero para protegerse. También llevaban uniformes especiales que se cree que formaban parte de las ceremonias religiosas anteriores al juego.

Anillo para el juego

La cancha más grande se encuentra en Chichén Itzá, México

---

7 ground **8** hips **9** helmets

¿Comprendiste?

1. ¿Por qué crees que los sacerdotes eran los que entrenaban a los jugadores indígenas?

2. ¿Por qué el juego de pelota tiene un significado especial? Da una explicación de origen histórico y otra de origen religioso.

3. Di dos razones por las que crees que el juego de pelota se jugaba en la sociedad indígena, y compáralas con las que la gente tiene ahora para jugar deportes.

4. ¿A qué deportes actuales se parece más el juego de pelota? ¿En qué se parecen?

Usa tus conocimientos

Imagínate que eres uno de los sacerdotes que van a entrenar a los nobles y los atletas. Piensa en una vez que te entrenaste para algo y escribe cinco ideas para explicarles cómo entrenarse, lo que es importante que hagan, cómo son las competiciones y qué deben evitar hacer.

Cerámica maya del juego de pelota

Más práctica	GO

realidades.com | print

▶ *Videodocumentario*	✔	
Instant Check	✔	
Guided WB p. 111	✔	✔
Comm. WB pp. 48–49	✔	✔
Hispanohablantes **WB** pp. 98–100	✔	
Cultural Reading Activity	✔	

ciento cuarenta y uno **141**
Capítulo 3

ENRICH YOUR TEACHING

Culture Note
The ancient Mexicans discovered a way to process rubber around 1600 B.C. by harvesting latex from the rubber tree *(castilla elástica)*. They used it to make sandals and for waterproofing, among other things, but they generally considered rubber a ritual material.

21st Century Skills
Critical Thinking and Problem Solving Have students research the Aztec game of *ullamalitzi* and other sports of the ancient civilizations of Mexico and Central America. What was the relationship between religion and sports in the ancient civilizations? How has this relationship between religion and sports evolved in today's civilization?

▼ **¿Comprendiste?** Standards: 1.1, 1.2, 3.1, 4.2

Resources: Answer Keys: Student Edition, p. 47

Focus: Demonstrating reading comprehension

Suggestions: Encourage students to support their opinions with information from the reading and their own background knowledge.

Answers:
1. Los sacerdotes eran los que entrenaban a los jugadores porque los eventos sociales eran como actos religiosos para el público.
2. El juego de pelota fue el primer deporte que se jugó en grupo. Según los mayas, los dioses miraban el juego.
3–4. **Answers will vary.**

▼ **Usa tus conocimientos** Standards: 1.3, 3.1

Focus: Using new vocabulary and structures in a written response to a reading

Suggestions: Have students use evidence from the reading and from the pictures on these pages to help them formulate their advice. Encourage them to use the chapter vocabulary to advise the players to train for strength and endurance and to avoid injury.

Answers will vary.

Portfolio
Invite students to organize their responses to *Usa tus conocimientos* and write them down in paragraph form. Keep the paragraphs in students' portfolios as a writing sample.

◼ Videodocumentario
Core Instruction

Standards: 1.2

Resources: Teacher's Resource Book: Video Script, p. 158; Video Program: Cap 3

View *¿Qué haces para estar saludable?* with the class, either online in **realidades.com** or using the DVD. See the *Video Teacher's Guide* for additional suggestions.

Additional Resources
Student Resource: Realidades para hispanohablantes, pp. 98–100; Guided Practice Activities, p. 110; Communication Wbk., pp. 48–49

3 Integrated Skills

Pre–AP*

| ▼ Objectives
▶ Listen to and read about exercise routines and nutrition choices
▶ Write about nutrition advice

¿Qué me cuentas?

Core Instruction

Standards: 1.1, 1.2, 1.3

Resources: Teacher's Resource Book: Audio Script, p. 156; Audio Program DVD: Cap. 3, Track 20; Answer Keys: Student Edition, p. 48

Focus: Practicing listening and reading comprehension of new vocabulary and grammar; using information to write a cohesive and coherent reaction.

AP* Skills: Integration of listening, reading, and writing to comprehend and synthesize information from spoken and written sources.

Suggestions: For Step 1, use the audio or read the descriptions aloud. Allow students to hear both descriptions twice through: the first time to write their answers, the second time to check them.

For Step 2, have students summarize the main points and make inferences to show that they understand what they have read.

Encourage students to express their own opinions in addition to using information from the reading in their written responses for Step 3.

Answers:
Step 1

1. a	4. a
2. c	5. c
3. c	6. c

Steps 2–3
Answers will vary.

Additional Resources

Student Resource: Realidades para hispanohablantes, p. 101

Block Schedule

In groups of two, ask students to draw a story sequence cartoon that uses the content of the chapter. Have them give this drawing to another pair of students who are to describe it. This description can be evaluated by the pair who drew the cartoon.

Integración

¿Qué me cuentas?: ¿Al club o a comer?

Tres amigos quieren hacer ejercicio y mejorar su estado físico. ¿Qué les aconsejas? Primero escucha la conversación y luego lee unas recomendaciones. Anota las respuestas a las preguntas y guárdalas para usarlas en el paso 3.

1 🔊))) Vas a escuchar un cuento acerca de tres amigos que se reúnen para hacer ejercicio. Después de cada parte vas a oír tres preguntas. Escoge la respuesta correcta.

1. a. al club deportivo b. a un restaurante c. al doctor
2. a. para respirar b. para dormir bien c. para tener músculos fuertes
3. a. las flexiones b. los abdominales c. los ejercicios aeróbicos
4. a. se sentía fatal b. se caía de sueño c. tenía hambre
5. a. flexiones b. yoga c. ir juntos al club
6. a. para hacer lo mismo que Manu b. para estar en la luna c. para relajarse, divertirse y estar de buen humor

2 Ahora lee las recomendaciones para seguir una dieta sana.

Aliméntate bien y entrénate mejor

¿Cuáles son tus razones para entrenar?
¿Sabías que una dieta apropiada mejora tu entrenamiento?

Me entreno para estar más fuerte.
Levantar pesas quema muchas calorías y los músculos usan aún más calorías para recuperarse. Por eso, es importante que consumas más calorías de las que usas. Tu dieta debe tener alimentos ricos en proteínas, como la carne, los huevos y los lácteos[1]. Un plan de comidas ideal tiene 55% de proteínas, 25% de carbohidratos y 20% de grasas.

Me entreno para aliviar el estrés.
Para reducir los efectos del estrés, es recomendado que incluyas entre 60% y 75% de alimentos crudos[2]. Escoge frutas y verduras frescas que tengan vitaminas B y C. También es necesario que comas carbohidratos ricos en fibra. Toma agua y evita el café, el té, las gaseosas y los alimentos procesados.

Me entreno para proteger el corazón.
Es importante que mantengas una dieta equilibrada. No consumas más calorías de las que quemas. Evita las grasas saturadas, pero sí incluye las grasas saludables como el aceite de oliva. No pongas demasiada sal a las comidas y evita las gaseosas porque tienen mucho sodio[3]. Consume alimentos ricos en fibra: frutas, verduras, granos[4]. Si te gustan los lácteos, escoge los que son bajos en grasa.

[1] dairy [2] raw [3] sodium [4] grains

3 Escribe unos consejos para Manuel, Vicky y Paula. Aconséjales una dieta que corresponda a sus metas de entrenamiento. Incluye los alimentos que deben comer. Usa estas expresiones para conectar tus ideas.

así	para	es importante que
aunque	por eso	es mejor que

142 ciento cuarenta y dos
¡Adelante!

DIFFERENTIATED INSTRUCTION

Heritage Language Learners

Ask students to write a short description of a very special lunch (such as a picnic or a barbecue) that they have had with their families or friends. Have them describe the food, the setting, and anything else that made the occasion special.

Students with Learning Difficulties

Public speaking, such as the *Presentación oral* on p. 143, can be stressful for some students. Suggest that speakers pause at the end of each sentence and take a deep breath and that they use gestures to emphasize parts of what they say. Humor, and an informal approach to the subject matter are other means of reducing stress.

Presentación oral

Una vida más sana

▶ Demonstrate how to give advice about leading a healthy lifestyle
▶ Pay attention to your posture to give an effective presentation

Tarea
Tu escuela va a organizar un evento para que los estudiantes aprendan a tener una vida más sana. A ti te toca hacer una presentación. Busca materiales y haz un cartel.

① Prepárate Escoge un tema y prepara un cartel.

temas	cartel
el ejercicio	deportes y tipos de ejercicio
los alimentos	alimentos nutritivos
las recetas, cómo preparar la comida	recetas saludables

② Practica Vuelve a leer la información de tu cartel. Practica varias veces tu presentación para recordar los detalles. Usa mandatos con *Uds.* o recomendaciones con el subjuntivo para explicar a tus compañeros qué deben hacer. Recuerda:

- hablar con voz clara y mirar al público directamente
- hablar de cada uno de los temas en orden y explicar por qué es importante para la salud
- dar alguna recomendación

Modelo
Mi presentación es acerca de cómo tener una vida más sana. Voy a hablarles de qué ejercicios hacer para estar saludable. El ejercicio sirve para estar en forma. Hagan ejercicio por lo menos tres veces por semana.

③ Haz tu presentación Imagina que estás en un auditorio. Habla claro y en voz alta. Explica el tema y muestra el cartel. Al final, pregunta a los estudiantes si tienen un comentario que hacer.

④ Evaluación Tu profesor(a) utilizará la siguiente rúbrica para evaluar tu presentación.

Estrategia

Making an oral presentation
When making an oral presentation make sure you face your audience at all times. You may look at the front, middle, and back rows. Remember to speak loudly enough for all to hear, and speak clearly.

Rubric	Score 1	Score 3	Score 5
How well your information is organized	Your ideas are undeveloped with incorrect or no transitions.	Some of your ideas are undeveloped. Your transitions are confusing.	Your ideas are well developed with clear transitions.
How effective you deliver your speech	You make no eye contact with the audience. You have little intonation.	You make some eye contact and use intonation.	You make good eye contact and use intonation.
How effectively you use your visuals	Your visuals don't communicate the message.	You use visuals, but not effectively.	Your visuals are very helpful and are used effectively.

Presentación oral

Core Instruction
Standards: 1.2, 1.3, 3.1

Focus: Preparing and delivering an oral presentation

Suggestions: Review the task and the rubric with students. Before students begin practicing in Step 2, direct their attention to the *Estrategia*. Encourage them to practice at home before a mirror or with a partner in class to develop their public speaking skills.

Portfolio
Make video or audio recordings of student presentations in class, or assign the RealTalk activity so they can record their presentations online. Include the recording in their portfolios.

Pre-AP* Support
- **Learning Objective:** Presentational Speaking
- **Activity:** Remind students to focus on the presentational speaking skills used in this task such as fluency, pronunciation, and comprehensibility.
- *Pre-AP* Resource Book:* Comprehensive guide to Pre-AP* speaking skill development, pp. 39–50

Teacher-to-Teacher
Some students may prefer to use a computer and project their poster. Remind students that skillful use of visuals during a presentation is a valuable asset in many professions.

Additional Resources
Student Resource: Realidades para hispanohablantes, p. 102

☑ ASSESSMENT
Presentación oral
- Assessment Program: Rubrics, p. T30
Review the rubric with students. Go over the descriptions of the different levels of performance. After assessing students, help individuals understand how their performance could be improved. (See Teacher's Resource Book for suggestions on using rubrics in assessment.)

ENRICH YOUR TEACHING

Teacher-to-Teacher
E-amigos: Have students send their *e-amigos* a message expressing their preferences and choices for a healthy lifestyle. Ask them to include questions about what their *e-amigos* do to satisfy the basic needs of health.

21st Century Skills

Flexibility and Adaptability Students will have to adapt to a variety of roles in this *Presentación oral* project. As writers, they will develop a series of persuasive suggestions for leading a healthier lifestyle. As artists, they will search for images to illustrate a poster they will design. And finally, as presenters, they will present their project effectively to the class.

3 Writing

Language Arts Connection: Persuasive Writing

Standards: 3.1

Help students apply the knowledge they have about writing a persuasive essay to Spanish. Have them do their planning in Step 1 in small groups. Guide them with comments and questions such as the following:

1. ¿Quién es tu público? Es preferible elegir a un grupo específico, como los jóvenes de esta escuela, los atletas o los jóvenes que comen mucha comida basura. Si conoces bien a tu público, vas a saber mejor lo que tienes que decirle.

2. Hay que prestar atención a las palabras que usas. La condición física, por ejemplo, puede ser un tema delicado para mucha gente. Para persuadir a la gente, es muy importante que no la ofendas.

 Common Core: Writing

Presentación escrita

Core Instruction

Standards: 1.3, 3.1

Resources: Voc. and Gram. Transparency 4

Focus: Combining learned vocabulary and structures in a written presentation

Suggestions: Explain at the start the criteria you will use to evaluate students' compositions. (See Step 5, *Evaluación*, in the Student Edition, and *Assessment* on p. 145.)

Direct students' attention to the *Estrategia*. Ask them to share additional background information they have learned in Language Arts courses about persuasive writing. Then show *Vocabulary & Grammar Transparency* 4. Have students begin a similar chart on their own paper. Guide them to add other points and to develop each point with specific details. For Step 2, remind students that their persuasive essay should build through at least three arguments. They should save their strongest argument for last, rather than "bringing out the big guns" at the beginning of the article.

Presentación escrita

Por una vida más saludable

Estrategia

Persuasive writing
Use persuasive writing to convince an audience about something. Use words that clearly express your opinion about an issue. Always include facts and examples to support your opinions. A persuasive composition is always addressed to a specific audience. Therefore, it is important to choose words, tone and style that are directed to your audience.

Imagina que trabajas para una revista y te piden que escribas un artículo sobre cómo las personas pueden llevar una vida más saludable. Presenta razones para persuadir a las personas de que cambien sus hábitos para estar más saludables.

1 Antes de escribir

Piensa en los elementos que ayudan a llevar una vida saludable. Describe por qué son importantes y qué ocurre si no se ponen en práctica. Crea una tabla como la de abajo.

Para llevar una vida saludable	Ventajas y problemas que se evitan
• mantener una dieta equilibrada	• se evitan las enfermedades • el cuerpo se mantiene sano
• mantenerse en forma	

2 Borrador

Escribe un artículo dirigido a un público específico. Usa la escritura persuasiva. Pon las ideas de tu tabla en una composición, usando el vocabulario de este capítulo, el subjuntivo con expresiones impersonales y los mandatos.

Modelo

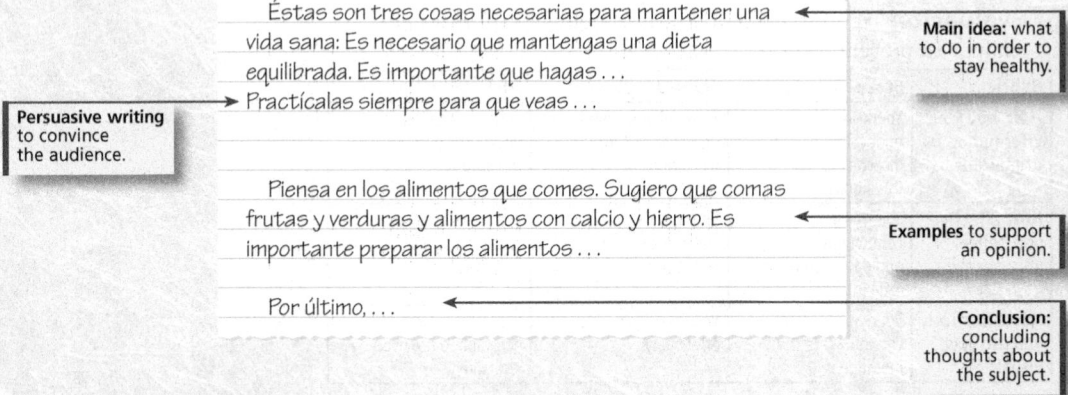

Éstas son tres cosas necesarias para mantener una vida sana: Es necesario que mantengas una dieta equilibrada. Es importante que hagas...
Practícalas siempre para que veas...

Main idea: what to do in order to stay healthy.

Persuasive writing to convince the audience.

Piensa en los alimentos que comes. Sugiero que comas frutas y verduras y alimentos con calcio y hierro. Es importante preparar los alimentos...

Examples to support an opinion.

Por último,...

Conclusion: concluding thoughts about the subject.

144 ciento cuarenta y cuatro
¡Adelante!

DIFFERENTIATED INSTRUCTION

Students with Learning Difficulties

Some students may need help understanding how to use various types of graphic organizers. Show them how the table on this page works by pointing out the titles at the top and explaining the cause-and-effect relationship between the information on the left and that on the right.

Advanced Learners

Encourage students to use their skills in Spanish to incorporate into their articles even more strategies for effective persuasive writing. Have them study persuasive articles in both English and Spanish as models.

Writing ③

③ Redacción/Revisión

Después de escribir el primer borrador, trabaja con otro(a) estudiante para intercambiar los trabajos y leerlos. Después de leer el trabajo de tu compañero(a), sugiere cómo puede mejorarlo y dile que haga lo mismo con el tuyo. Revisen si:

- la composición se enfoca en consejos para la salud
- para persuadir al público se usan mandatos y se dan razones
- se usan expresiones impersonales para enfatizar los consejos

Haz lo siguiente: Subraya con una línea los verbos en subjuntivo, con dos líneas los mandatos, y encierra en un círculo las expresiones impersonales.

> Éstas son tres cosas necesarias para
>
> mantener una vida sana: (Es necesario) que
> mantengas
> ~~mantienes~~ una dieta equilibrada.(Es importante)
> que hagas ...
> Practícalas
> ~~Practícala~~ siempre para ...

④ Publicación

Antes de hacer la versión final, lee de nuevo tu borrador y repasa los siguientes puntos:

- ¿Di suficientes razones para apoyar mis ideas?
- ¿Usé el vocabulario apropiado para convencer al público de que lea la revista donde van a publicar el artículo?

Después de revisar el borrador, escribe una copia en limpio de tu composición.

⑤ Evaluación

Se utilizará la siguiente rúbrica para evaluar tu presentación.

Rubric	Score 1	Score 3	Score 5
Completion of task	You are missing important parts of the article.	Parts of your article are missing or incorrect.	You include all parts and it is effectively organized.
Ability to persuade	Your lack of information organization makes message unclear.	Your message is present, but sometimes unconvincing.	Your information creates a clear message.
Sentence structure/ grammar, spelling, mechanics	Your sentences are run-on or are fragmented with many grammar, spelling, and mechanics errors.	You use sentences convincingly, but with some grammar, spelling, and/or mechanics errors.	Your sentence structure is correct and varied with very few grammar, spelling, and mechanics errors.

ciento cuarenta y cinco **145**
Capítulo 3

Suggestions (Cont'd)

Once students have a rough draft ready, read through the model on this page together. Help them see how information from the chart on p. 144 was incorporated into this draft and to note the additional information that was added. Point out the use of imperative and subjunctive verb forms. Encourage them to work toward similar organization, level of detail, and language use as they revise their own drafts.

For Step 3, encourage students to focus on sentence structure, transitions, and correct use of commands and the subjunctive. Have them follow the suggestions shown.

Evaluation

Steps 4 and 5 overlap. Students will need some evaluation by you or peers or some self-evaluation to fine-tune and polish their drafts.

Pre-AP* Support

- **Learning Objective:** Presentational Writing
- **Activity:** As a warm-up to the *Presentación escrita*, have students write a short blog about the things that cause stress in their lives. Have them describe what they do to prevent stress from taking over their lives.
- **Pre-AP* Resource Book:** Comprehensive guide to Pre-AP* writing skill development, pp. 27–38

Portfolio

Keep students' final drafts in their portfolios as a writing sample.

Additional Resources

Student Resource: Realidades para hispanohablantes, p. 103

ENRICH YOUR TEACHING

Teacher-to-Teacher

As students develop their persuasive articles, remind them that they use elements of persuasion every day. Ask them to talk about times they themselves have persuaded someone to act or think a certain way and to analyze the techniques they used.

21st Century Skills

Communication Students will have to use their written language for the purpose of persuading magazine readers to lead a healthier lifestyle. Have students create a list of persuasive phrases and expressions to use in their article to make their arguments more forceful and convincing.

✓ ASSESSMENT

Presentación escrita

- Assessment Program: Rubrics, p. T30

Review the rubric with students. Go over the descriptions of the different levels of performance. After assessing students, help individuals understand how their performance could be improved. (See Teacher's Resource Book for suggestions on using rubrics in assessment.)

3 Reading

© Common Core: Reading

Lectura

Core Instruction

Standards: 1.2, 3.1

Resources: Voc. and Gram. Transparency 4
Focus: Reading an extended passage
Suggestions:

Pre-reading: Before reading, direct students' attention to the *Al leer* section and to the *Estrategia*. Have them answer the questions from there and copy the graphic organizer from p. 149.

Point out that each section is organized the same way, with the titles *Meta, ¡Lógralo!,* and *Nuestros consejos.* Explain that in this case *meta* means "goal" or "objective."

Ask volunteers to read the title and subtitles aloud. Based on these and the photos throughout the article, have them predict to which bulleted item on p. 146 each section of the article refers. For example: *La sección Muy limpios debe tratarse de la higiene personal y la salud.*

Ask students to name the items in the photos throughout the article. If they can't name an item, ask them to scan that section of the article to see if they can find it.

Block Schedule

Working in pairs, have students create a short article about a health tip following the models in the *Lectura*. Be sure they include an illustration and post it on the bulletin board.

Lectura
¡Cambia tus hábitos!

> ### Estrategia
>
> **Cause and effect**
> Our personality and the way we eat, sleep, or react to fear can affect our health. If we change our bad habits, we will be healthier and more productive persons. While you read this magazine article, look for other examples of cause and effect. For example, what happens if you do not eat well, you do not drink enough water, or if you do not sit correctly and comfortably?

▼ Objectives

- ▶ Read about healthy eating habits
- ▶ Identify cause and effect to increase understanding
- ▶ Compare Spanish-language teen magazines with similar ones in the U.S.

Al leer

Nuestra vida está llena de actos que repetimos todos los días, por ejemplo, comer, dormir o estudiar. Vas a leer un artículo con recomendaciones sobre cómo cambiar tus malos hábitos para llevar una vida más saludable. Copia la tabla de la página 149. Mientras lees los artículos, llena los espacios de la gráfica con causas y efectos que encuentres en el texto.

Presta atención a los siguientes puntos:

- la importancia de tener buenos hábitos alimenticios
- la higiene personal y la salud
- cómo cuidar tu espalda aprendiendo a sentarte bien

Aliméntate bien

Meta: "Voy a desayunar todos los días".

Saltarte el desayuno no te sirve para nada. Empieza tu día con algo ligero[1], para poner a funcionar tu metabolismo. No sólo da energía sino que despierta al organismo y acelera la quema de calorías durante todo el día.

¡Lógralo!

Desayuna algo aunque sea ligero, como un jugo de naranja o una fruta, pan tostado con mermelada, cereal con leche o yogur, té o un buen vaso de leche.

Nuestros consejos:

Si tienes prisa: bebe el jugo mientras caminas a la escuela.
También puedes llevar un yogur que trae una porción de cereal.

---

1 light

DIFFERENTIATED INSTRUCTION

Heritage Language Learners

Ask students to interview family members about their breakfast habits and those of other relatives or friends. How many eat a nutritious breakfast? How many have changed their eating habits over the years? Do they now eat a better breakfast than they used to, or one that is worse? Why?

Students with Learning Difficulties

If students have difficulty with the cause and effect concept in the *Estrategia,* you may wish to help them by asking guiding questions that will help them focus on the concept in English. For example: What happens if you don't allow enough time to complete a school project?

No comas comida basura

Meta: "No voy a comer tantos dulces en la escuela".

Seguro que a la hora del recreo quieres comer chocolate o una bolsa de papas fritas. Mejor escoge alimentos que echen a andar tu motor. Si comes un almuerzo nutritivo, tu rendimiento físico y mental va a ser mucho mejor y no te vas a dormir en las últimas clases.

¡Lógralo!

Lleva de tu casa zanahorias o pepinos². Las palomitas de maíz³ y las frutas deshidratadas son una buena opción en lugar de comidas fritas.

Nuestros consejos:

¡No lleves dinero! Así evitas la tentación de comprar comida basura.

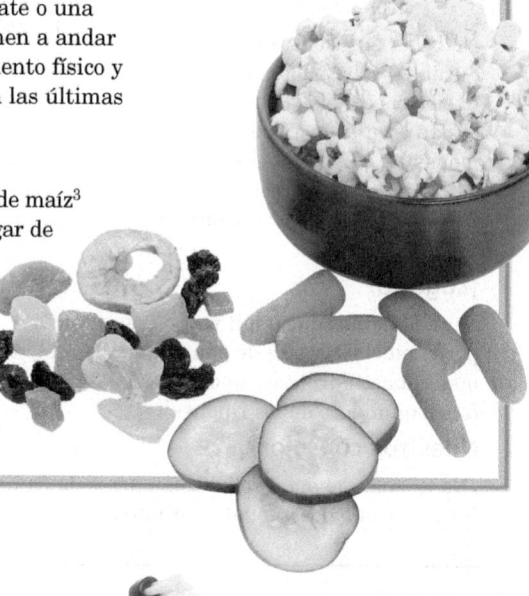

---

2 cucumbers **3** popcorn

Muy limpios

Meta: "Siempre me voy a lavar las manos y los dientes".

Muchas enfermedades del estómago son producidas por las bacterias que recogemos durante el día en nuestras actividades diarias. El simple hecho de abrir la puerta para salir del baño después de lavarte las manos, ya implica una contaminación de gérmenes. Y de la boca ni hablemos, ¿quién quiere verte con el frijol entre los dientes?

¡Lógralo!

El jabón más efectivo para eliminar las bacterias en las manos es un gel que no se enjuaga⁴. Llévalo en tu mochila y úsalo cada vez que vayas al baño. En cuanto a los dientes, lávalos después de cada comida.

Nuestros consejos:

Compra un cepillo de dientes de viaje (algunos incluyen una crema de dientes pequeña) y llévalo en tu mochila junto con un hilo dental. ¿Se te olvidó lavarte los dientes o no tuviste tiempo? Usa una pastilla de menta o un chicle con clorofila para evitar el mal aliento.

---

4 rinse off

Reading (3)

Suggestions (Cont'd)

Remind students that cognates and context clues can help them understand difficult passages as they read. Help them focus on cognates by saying words in English and asking them to scan a given section for the Spanish cognate. For example: *¿Cómo se dice "dehydrated" en español? Busquen en la sección* No comas comida basura. *(deshidratadas)*

Reading: Allow students time to read the entire selection on their own silently. You might assign this task for homework. This will allow you to capitalize on class time to read it again together with students. When reading together, pause frequently to address comprehension issues that students may bring up and to allow them to fill in their *Causa/Efecto* charts from p. 149. Ask your own comprehension questions to help them focus on the main idea and important details of each section. Here are some possible comprehension issues on pp. 146–147 on which you can provide some guidance:

• p. 146: *Lee la parte* Meta. *¿A qué se refiere* (refer) *la expresión "algo ligero," a la comida o al sueño? (a la comida)*

¿A qué se refiere la palabra "organismo," a un hábito alimenticio o al cuerpo? (al cuerpo)

• p. 147: *Lee la parte* No comas comida basura. *¿A qué se refiere la expresión "rendimiento físico," a tu nivel de energía o los ingredientes de una comida? (a tu nivel de energía)*

• p. 147: *Lee la parte* Muy limpios. *¿Qué quiere decir la expresión "Y de la boca ni hablemos," que la boca tiene o no tiene gérmenes? (que tiene gérmenes)*

ENRICH YOUR TEACHING

Teacher-to-Teacher

While reading and working through comprehension problems with students, don't forget to also focus on the content of a passage. Ask students to comment on what they are reading. For example, in the *Muy limpios* section, ask: *¿Quiénes ya usan jabón que no se enjuaga?*

21st Century Skills

Technology Literacy Have students use the digital technology within **realidades.com** to access extra reading support. Computer corrected activities use different reading strategies to help students build their vocabulary and progress at their own pace through the reading.

Suggestions (Cont'd)
Reading:

- p. 148: *Lee la parte* Más H₂O. *En la primera frase, la que empieza con "No beber …," ¿cuál es el sujeto?* (No beber suficientes líquidos durante el día) *¿Qué quiere decir esta frase en inglés?* (usando un participio presente: Not drinking enough water during the day) *¿Cuál es la palabra opuesta de "hidratado"? Adivina. Busca una pista en la sección* No comas comida basura *en la página 147.* (deshidratado)
- p. 148: *Lee la parte* ¿Una siesta? *El artículo da tres categorías de causas posibles para la falta de energía después de las clases. ¿Cuáles son?* (causas fisiológicas, emocionales o relacionadas con el estilo de vida)
- p. 148: *Lee la parte* Siéntate bien. *¿Qué parte del cuerpo tienes que pegar al asiento para sentarte bien?* (toda la espalda)

Pre-AP* Support

- **Learning Objective:** Interpretive: Print and Audio
- **Activity:** Divide the class into groups of five and assign one of the sub-titled sections to each in the group. Have each student write three true/false statements about his or her section and make four copies. Each student distributes his or her questions to other group members. Then each student will read aloud his or her section to his or her group (with textbooks closed) and allow them time to respond to the true/false statements about that section. Confirm answers.
- *Pre-AP* Resource Book:* Comprehensive guide to Pre-AP* reading skill development, pp. 19–26

Additional Resources
Student Resources: Guided Practice: Lectura, pp. 111–112

Block Schedule
Bring in magazines from different Spanish-speaking countries. Have students work with a partner and find an ad related to health. Have them explain the ad to another group. Is it an effective ad?

Más H₂O

Meta: "Ahora sí voy a tomar agua".

No beber suficientes líquidos durante el día puede hacer que te sientas cansado. Los refrescos te dan energía pero sólo por un momento, luego te sientes igual de cansado; los refrescos *light* tampoco ayudan, por el contrario, te quitan energía.

¡Lógralo!

Ya te lo hemos dicho mil veces: debes tomar por lo menos 8 vasos de agua al día. No sólo te mantienen hidratado, sino que ayudan al buen funcionamiento de los riñones[1].

Nuestros consejos:

¿No te gusta el agua sola? Toma jugos de fruta fresca o leche descremada durante el día.

---

1 kidneys

¿Una siesta?

Meta: "Ya no voy a dormir cuando llegue de la escuela".

Nadie en tu casa entiende por qué cuando regresas de la escuela lo primero que haces es dormirte. Las causas pueden ser fisiológicas (como los niveles hormonales de la tiroides), emocionales (demasiado estrés), o estar relacionadas con tu estilo de vida (no dormir bien en las noches). Lo que debes hacer son unos cuantos ajustes en tu dieta diaria para combatir el cansancio.

¡Lógralo!

Si te sientes cansado, evita completamente las galletas, el pan dulce, los dulces, los refrescos y los jugos de fruta envasados, ya que contienen azúcares simples que te quitan energía; también evita la cafeína. Lo ideal es que comas proteínas con vegetales (como un pescado hervido con verduras).

Nuestros consejos:

Trata de hacer un poco de ejercicio para subir tus niveles de energía. O pon un disco compacto y ponte a bailar en tu cuarto.

Siéntate bien

Meta: "Me voy a sentar derecho en la silla".

No es nada fácil sentarte derecho por más de diez minutos, pero si sigues sentándote así, hundiéndote en[2] tu asiento de clases, tu cuerpo y sobre todo tu espalda se acostumbrarán y es probable que no se corrijan.

¡Lógralo!

Pega bien toda la espalda —baja, alta y lumbar— al asiento. Asegúrate de que tus pies estén bien apoyados en el piso y mantén las piernas juntas.

Nuestros consejos:

¿Se te hace muy difícil? Imagina que tienes un hilo que jala tu columna[3] hacia arriba para mantenerla derecha.

2 sinking yourself into 3 a string that pulls your spine

DIFFERENTIATED INSTRUCTION

Heritage Language Learners
Have students discuss commands that their parents frequently give them at home. Ask volunteers to make signs of the four or five most common ones. Post these around the room in appropriate places. For example, *Siéntate bien* might be posted on the front wall.

Advanced Learners
Have students create a glossary of unfamiliar vocabulary for the article that lists items of students' choosing, along with a definition in Spanish. They can arrive at their definitions via discussion or by using a Spanish dictionary. Encourage them to paraphrase dictionary definitions and write them in their own words.

Interacción con la lectura

1 Trabaja con un grupo de estudiantes para hacer una tabla de *causa y efecto.* Cada estudiante va a añadir las relaciones de causa y efecto que escribió mientras leía el artículo.

2 Contesten las siguientes preguntas sobre el artículo y, si notan relaciones de causa y efecto que aún no incluyeron en la tabla, añádanlas.

- ¿Crees que los jóvenes en general tienen hábitos saludables? Explica tu respuesta.
- ¿Qué recomendaciones del artículo te parecen mejores o más prácticas?
- ¿Hay alguna recomendación con la que no estás de acuerdo? ¿Por qué?
- Según este artículo, ¿qué tipo de comidas y bebidas debes evitar para tener más energía? ¿Cuáles debes comer o beber?

3 Trabaja con un grupo para hablar sobre estos temas. Hablen con la clase de lo que piensan sobre las causas y los efectos.

Causa	Efecto

▼ Fondo Cultural | El mundo hispano

Revistas para jóvenes Al igual que en los Estados Unidos, en España y América Latina hay muchas revistas para jóvenes. En ellas puedes encontrar los temas que les interesan a los chicos y a las chicas de esos países, cómo se visten, qué música prefieren, y cuáles son sus sueños.

Si quieres leer más artículos relacionados con la salud, si te gustan los temas culturales y científicos o quieres mantenerte al día en deportes, música, libros o cine, existe un gran número de esas revistas que te pueden interesar. Éstas son algunas de ellas: *Generación 21* de Ecuador, *Revista 15 a 20* de México, y *Okapi* y *Muy Junior* de España.

- ¿Te interesa la moda o la música de otros países?
- ¿Crees que los jóvenes de otros países tienen gustos *(taste)* similares con respecto a la moda o la música? ¿Por qué?

Más práctica	GO
**realidades.com	print**	
Guided WB pp. 112–113	✔ ✔
Comm. WB p. 177	✔ ✔
Cultural Reading Activity	✔

ciento cuarenta y nueve **149**
Capítulo 3

▼ Interacción con la lectura
Suggestions:
Post-reading: After students revisit their *Causa/Efecto* charts and make changes or additions, have them share the information they included. Ask volunteers to read aloud or paraphrase the parts of the article that support their choices for the chart and that help them answer the *Interacción con la lectura questions.*
Answers will vary.

Fondo cultural
Suggestions: Ask: *¿Qué revistas estadounidenses para jóvenes puedes nombrar? ¿Cuáles de estas revistas se parecen a las que ves en el* Fondo cultural? *¿Qué revistas para jóvenes lees? ¿Qué secciones de estas revistas te gustan más?* If possible, obtain some copies of the Spanish-language magazines shown and mentioned to put on display for students to peruse. Heritage language learners may have copies of Spanish-language magazines that they are willing to lend or contribute to the class.
Answers will vary.

Teacher-to-Teacher
A comparison of Spanish-language teen magazines to ones in English from the United States will provide students with valuable cultural insight. Ask students to analyze which topics are the same in the two groups of magazines. Which are noticeably different? How are the advertisements similar or different?

For Further Reading
Student Resource:
AP* Literature Author: Horacio Quiroga, *Lecturas 3:* "La gama ciega," pp. 54–60

ENRICH YOUR TEACHING

Culture Note
The first printing press in the Americas was established in Mexico City. At the request of Juan de Zumárraga, first Bishop of Mexico, a publishing house in Sevilla set up a branch in Mexico City. The first book printed there, in 1539, was an edition of the *Breve y más compendiosa doctrina cristiana en lengua mexicana y castellana.*

21st Century Skills
Social and Cross Cultural Skills To expand on the suggestions for the *Fondo cultural,* have students work in small groups to review copies of the Spanish language teen magazines. Have them compare their impressions about commonalities and differences between teenagers in different countries, as illustrated by these magazines.

Review Activities

Los síntomas y las medicinas: Ask students to sort the vocabulary in this section into smaller categories of their choice. Have them use a graphic organizer, such as a columnar chart or a word web. Ask them to share their work and discuss their reasons for assigning a particular item to a category.

Partes del cuerpo: Have students sketch a basic human figure and label the parts of the body. Encourage them to include labels for other parts of the body that they previously learned, or terms such as ***columna (vertebral)*** that they learned about in the chapter.

Actividades relacionadas con la salud/La nutrición: Have students sit in a circle. Give a foam ball to a student and say one of the words from the ***actividades*** or ***nutrición*** categories. The student has ten seconds to use the word in a sentence, then tosses the ball randomly to another student in the circle and says another word from the lists. The student catching the ball uses that word in a sentence, announces the next word, and tosses the ball again. Continue until all the words in the list have been covered at least once.

Para estar en forma/Estados de ánimo: Ask pairs of students to work together using TPR commands to demonstrate comprehension of these sections of the vocabulary: *Flexiona la rodilla derecha. Ahora estírala.*

Expresiones útiles: Students can use these words and expressions as they go over the review activities for the other categories.

Teacher-to-Teacher

e-amigos: Have e-*amigos* play the role of a patient and receptionist at a doctor's office. Ask them to write an e-mail describing their symptoms and asking for an appointment. They should respond by asking appropriate questions and proposing a date and time for the appointment. Encourage students to continue the exchange until they have answered all questions and made the appointment. Have students print out their e-mails or send them to you for review.

Repaso del capítulo
Vocabulario y gramática

los síntomas y las medicinas

la alergia	allergy
el antibiótico	antibiotic
la aspirina	aspirin
estar resfriado, -a	to have a cold
estornudar	to sneeze
la fiebre	fever
el grado centígrado	centigrade degree
la gripe	flu
el jarabe	syrup
la tos	cough

partes del cuerpo

el corazón	heart
el músculo	muscle
el oído	ear
el pecho	chest

actividades relacionadas con la salud

aconsejar	to advise
contener	to contain
desarrollar	to develop
evitar	to avoid
exigir	to demand
incluir	to include
quejarse	to complain
saltar (una comida)	to skip (a meal)
tomar	to take, to drink

para estar en forma

abdominales	crunches
el calambre	cramp
débil	weak
ejercicios aeróbicos	aerobics
estar en forma	to be fit
estirar	to stretch
flexionar	to flex, to stretch
fuerte	strong
la fuerza	strength
hacer bicicleta	to use a stationary bike
hacer cinta	to use a treadmill
hacer flexiones	to do push-ups
relajar(se)	to relax
respirar	to breathe
yoga	yoga

la nutrición

la alimentación	nutrition, feeding
los alimentos	food
apropiado, -a	appropriate
el calcio	calcium
el carbohidrato	carbohydrate
la comida basura	junk food
la dieta	diet
la edad	age
la energía	energy
equilibrado, -a	balanced
la estatura	height
la fibra	fiber
el hábito alimenticio	eating habit
el hierro	iron
lleno, -a	full
la merienda	snack
nutritivo, -a	nutritious
el peso	weight
la proteína	protein
saludable	healthy
vacío, -a	empty
la vitamina	vitamin

expresiones útiles

aguantar	to endure, to tolerate
aunque	despite, even when
el consejo	advice
la manera	way
el nivel	level

estados de ánimo

caerse de sueño	to be exhausted, sleepy
concentrarse	to concentrate
confianza en sí mismo, -a	self-confidence
estar de buen / mal humor	to be in a good / bad mood
estar en la luna	to be daydreaming
el estrés	stress
estresado, -a	stressed out
preocuparse	to worry
sentirse fatal	to feel awful

DIFFERENTIATED INSTRUCTION

Students with Learning Difficulties
Suggest that students review the vocabulary lists in sets of three words or phrases, saying them out loud while cycling through them several times. This will also help them remember the gender of each word.

Advanced Students
Tell students to bring in a magazine photo of a scene in a hospital or doctor's waiting room, or in a gym. Have them describe the people in the scene. Then have them write a short conversation between two or more of the people.

Mandatos afirmativos y negativos

Regular and stem-changing verbs, and verbs ending in -*car*, -*gar*, and -*zar*

	tú	Ud.	Uds.
evitar	evit**a**, no evit**es**	(no) evit**e**	(no) evit**en**
volver	vuelv**e**, no vuelv**as**	(no) vuelv**a**	(no) vuelv**an**
abrir	abr**e**, no abr**as**	(no) abr**a**	(no) abr**an**
sacar	sac**a**, no sa**ques**	(no) sa**que**	(no) sa**quen**
llegar	lleg**a**, no lle**gues**	(no) lle**gue**	(no) lle**guen**
cruzar	cruz**a**, no cru**ces**	(no) cru**ce**	(no) cru**cen**

Irregular verbs

	tú	Ud.	Uds.
decir	**di, no digas**	**(no) diga**	**(no) digan**
poner	**pon, no pongas**	**(no) ponga**	**(no) pongan**
ir	**ve, no vayas**	**(no) vaya**	**(no) vayan**
hacer	**haz, no hagas**	**(no) haga**	**(no) hagan**
tener	**ten, no tengas**	**(no) tenga**	**(no) tengan**
mantener	**mantén, no mantengas**	**(no) mantenga**	**(no) mantengan**
ser	**sé, no seas**	**(no) sea**	**(no) sean**
salir	**sal, no salgas**	**(no) salga**	**(no) salgan**

Placement of pronouns

Attach reflexive or object pronouns at the end of affirmative commands.
With negative commands, place them after the word *no*.

Toma esas vitaminas.	¡Tómalas ahora mismo!	No las tomes.

El subjuntivo: Verbos regulares y verbos con cambios de raíz

saltar

salt**e**	salt**emos**
salt**es**	salt**éis**
salt**e**	salt**en**

poder (o → ue)

p**ue**da	p**o**damos
p**ue**das	p**o**dáis
p**ue**da	p**ue**dan

pedir (e → i)

p**i**da	p**i**damos
p**i**das	p**i**dáis
p**i**da	p**i**dan

El subjuntivo: Verbos irregulares

dar

dé	demos
des	déis
dé	den

haber

haya	hayamos
hayas	hayáis
haya	hayan

ir

vaya	vayamos
vayas	vayáis
vaya	vayan

estar

esté	estemos
estés	estéis
esté	estén

ser

sea	seamos
seas	seáis
sea	sean

saber

sepa	sepamos
sepas	sepáis
sepa	sepan

ENRICH YOUR TEACHING

Teacher-to-Teacher

Have students write the infinitives of the verbs with irregular imperative forms on slips of paper and place them in a hat or other container. Have a playing cube ready. Explain that rolling an even number means *afirmativo* and rolling an odd number means *negativo.* Students take turns rolling the cube, drawing a verb, and using it in either an affirmative or negative command.

Mandatos afirmativos y negativos: Have individual students write a series of commands that a partner will carry out. The commands will tell the partner how to draw something. The drawing might consist of geometric shapes or of something realistic, such as a landscape or floor plan. Then have students follow their own commands carefully, in order to create the drawing. Ask them to keep this drawing out of sight. Finally, have pairs sit back-to-back, each with pencil and paper. Students take turns reading their complete list of commands, while the partner attempts to draw based on what he or she hears. Students compare their drawings to the originals to see how well they created and followed the commands.

El subjuntivo: Have students list at least five typical health or lifestyle complaints. Have them exchange lists with a partner and write solutions to the problems with complete sentences containing the subjunctive. As a guide, write the following information on the board: Main Clause (indicative) + *que* + Subordinate Clause (subjunctive). This activity can be used to assess students' assimilation of rules for basic formation and use of the subjunctive.

Portfolio

Invite students to review the activities and projects they completed in this chapter. Have them select one or two items that they feel best demonstrate their achievements in Spanish. Include these products in students' portfolios with their Chapter Checklist and Self-Assessment Worksheet.

Additional Resources

Student Resources: Realidades para hispanohablantes, pp. 104–105

Teacher Resources:

• Teacher's Resource Book: Situation Cards, p. 167, Clip Art, pp. 168–175

• Assessment Program: Chapter Checklist and Self-Assessment Worksheet, pp. T49–T50

▶ *¡Pura vida!* is a storyline video that is independent of chapter content and an ideal support for expanding listening skills. The 14 episodes are available within **realidades.com** or on a separate DVD. Student activities and Teacher support are also assignable within **realidades.com**.

3 Review

Performance Tasks

Standards: 1.1, 1.2, 1.3, 2.2

Student Resource: Realidades para hispanohablantes, pp. 106–107

Teacher Resources: Teacher's Resource Book: Audio Script, p. 157; Audio Program DVD: Cap. 3, Track 22; Answer Keys: Student Edition, p. 48

1. Vocabulario

Suggestions: Encourage students to review the vocabulary from the *A primera vista* sections on pp. 114–116 and 126–129 before they complete the activity.

Answers:

1.	b	5.	b
2.	b	6.	b
3.	c	7.	a
4.	a	8.	d

2. Gramática

Suggestions: Remind students of the main points of the grammar presentations in *Capítulo* 3:

- affirmative commands with **tú**
- negative commands with **tú**
- affirmative and negative commands with **Ud.** and **Uds.**
- the subjunctive: regular verbs
- the subjunctive: irregular verbs
- the subjunctive: stem-changing verbs

Answers:

1.	b	5.	d
2.	a	6.	a
3.	a	7.	c
4.	c	8.	d

Preparación para el examen

1 Vocabulario Escribe la letra de la palabra o expresión que mejor complete cada frase. Escribe tus respuestas en una hoja aparte.

1. El médico le aconseja a Lucía que coma queso y tome leche todos los días porque contienen _____.
   a. comida basura   c. dulces
   b. calcio   d. fibra

2. Estoy enfermo(a) cuando _____.
   a. hago yoga   c. hago ejercicio
   b. tengo fiebre   d. tengo sueño

3. Te voy a recetar _____ para la tos.
   a. una gripe   c. un jarabe
   b. carbohidratos   d. una aspirina

4. Para evitar los calambres les recomiendo que _____.
   a. estiren los músculos   c. hagan flexiones
   b. hagan abdominales   d. corran rápido

5. Si _____, te aconsejo que hagas yoga.
   a. estás en la luna   c. haces cinta
   b. estás estresado   d. te caes de sueño

6. Doctor, _____ y tengo dolor de cabeza.
   a. tengo el oído   c. me duele la gripe
   b. me duele el pecho   d. estoy en forma

7. Tengo fiebre, cuando _____.
   a. tengo 39° centígrados   c. tengo calambres
   b. evito los antibióticos   d. mantengo mi dieta

8. ¡No aguanto más! significa que _____.
   a. estás muy contento(a)   c. tienes energía
   b. te gusta hacer ejercicio   d. estás muy estresado(a)

2 Gramática Escribe la letra de la palabra o expresión que mejor complete cada frase. Escribe tus respuestas en una hoja aparte.

1. Jorge, no _____ al gimnasio hoy. Está cerrado.
   a. vas   c. ve
   b. vayas   d. vayan

2. Sra. Díaz, por favor _____ las vitaminas allí.
   a. ponga   c. pongan
   b. pon   d. pones

3. El doctor me aconseja que _____ una dieta equilibrada.
   a. mantenga   c. mantengo
   b. mantén   d. mantener

4. ¿Estás estresado? _____ con tus amigos para divertirte.
   a. Salgas   c. Sal
   b. Sales   d. Salgan

5. Es importante que ustedes _____ de buen humor durante las clases de yoga.
   a. estemos   c. estamos
   b. están   d. estén

6. ¡Tomen las vitaminas! ¡_____ por la mañana!
   a. Tómenlas   c. Tómalas
   b. Tómenlo   d. Tómenlos

7. Niños, ¡_____ comida basura a la escuela!
   a. no traen   c. no traigan
   b. no traiga   d. no traes

8. Quiero que tú me _____ las reglas del club.
   a. explicas   c. explique
   b. expliquen   d. expliques

DIFFERENTIATED INSTRUCTION

Heritage Language Learners

Have students create a brochure for their own "virtual museum." Encourage them to select artists and works from the chapter, from their own areas of interest, or from their heritage country. Remind students to tailor the language of their descriptions to the appropriate audience.

Students with Learning Difficulties

In reviewing the vocabulary and grammar of the chapter, use gestures and facial expressions to support students in their choice of the correct answer. Use TPR to support meaning of the vocabulary choices.

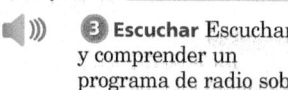

	Más repaso GO realidades.com | print	
Instant Check	✔	
Puzzles	✔	
Core WB pp. 47–48		✔
Comm. WB pp. 178, 179–182	✔	✔

En el examen vas a . . .	Éstas son las tareas de práctica que te pueden ser útiles para el examen . . .	Para repasar, ve a tu libro de texto impreso o digital . . .
Interpretive		
❸ **Escuchar** Escuchar y comprender un programa de radio sobre consejos para la salud	En este programa de radio, varias personas llaman al Dr. Salvavidas para pedirle consejos. (a) ¿Qué síntomas tiene cada uno?, (b) ¿Qué tienen que tomar?, (c) ¿Qué más les aconseja el doctor?	**pp. 114–117** *A primera vista 1: Vocabulario en contexto* **p. 115** Actividad 2 **p. 119** Actividad 9
Presentational		
❹ **Hablar** Aconsejar a otros sobre los hábitos alimenticios	La directora de la guardería infantil de tu barrio te pide que vengas a hablarles a los niños sobre lo importante que es tener buenos hábitos alimenticios. Haz cinco recomendaciones.	**pp. 114–117** *A primera vista 1* **p. 116** Actividad 3 **p. 118** Actividad 7 **p. 124** Actividad 17 **p. 125** Actividades 18 y 20
Interpretive		
❺ **Leer** Leer y entender un anuncio	Lucía quiere aprender a preparar alimentos nutritivos y tomar clases para tener músculos fuertes. Lee el anuncio que ella vio y dile: (a) por qué le recomiendas las clases de ejercicio y (b) por qué debe tomar las clases para preparar alimentos. **Centro Fuente de la Salud** Si estás estresado(a) y no puedes concentrarte, tenemos clases de ejercicios para ayudar a relajarte. Aprende a tener una alimentación equilibrada. Prepara galletas nutritivas y bebidas que dan energía.	**pp. 126–129** *A primera vista 2: Vocabulario en contexto* **p. 136** Actividad 36 **p. 139** Actividad 40
Presentational		
❻ **Escribir** Escribir una carta para dar consejos	Tu trabajo en una revista es contestar las cartas que mandan los jóvenes. En una carta, un chico te dice que siempre se siente cansado y de mal humor. Escríbele una respuesta con por lo menos cuatro consejos.	**p. 121** Actividad 11 **p. 125** Actividad 18 **p. 129** Actividad 25 **p. 135** Actividad 35 **p. 136** Actividad 36
Cultures • Comparisons		
❼ **Pensar** Pensar en los antiguos juegos de los olmecas de Mesoamérica	En tu clase puedes ganar "puntos extra" si compartes algo que aprendiste en otra clase. ¿Cómo puedes explicar el juego de pelota de los olmecas de hace 3,000 años? ¿Hoy en día hay algún juego similar? Descríbelo.	**pp. 140–141** *Puente a la cultura*

ciento cincuenta y tres **153**
Capítulo 3

Review side column

3. Escuchar
Suggestions: Play the audio or read from the script.

🔊 **Answers:**
(a) A la señorita Juana Durante le duele el estómago después del almuerzo. El señor David Ríos tiene fiebre y tos, le duelen la garganta y el pecho.
(b) La señorita Juana Durante debe cambiar sus hábitos alimenticios. El señor David Ríos debe ir al médico inmediatamente.
(c) La señorita Juana Durante debe comer más frutas y verduras y menos comida basura. El señor David Ríos debe ir al médico porque necesita antibióticos.

4. Hablar
Suggestions: Remind students that they should tailor their verb forms to the situation. Have Advanced Learners use the **vosotros** forms.

5. Leer
Suggestions: Tell students to refer to pp. 114–116 and 126–129 if they have questions about vocabulary in the review.

6. Escribir
Suggestions: Remind students that they can use either commands or sentences with the subjunctive for their advice.

7. Pensar
Suggestions: Suggest that students begin with a description of the ball game. They can then refer to this in order to compare the ancient game to modern ones.

DIFFERENTIATED ASSESSMENT

CORE ASSESSMENT
- **Assessment Program:** Examen del capítulo 3, pp. 79–82
- **Audio Program DVD:** Cap. 3, Track 23
- **ExamView:** Chapter Test, Test Banks A and B

ADVANCED/PRE-AP*
- **ExamView Pre-AP* Test Bank**
- **Pre-AP* Resource Book,** pp. 144–146

STUDENTS NEEDING EXTRA HELP
- **Alternate Assessment Program:** Examen del capítulo 3
- **Audio Program DVD:** Cap. 3, Track 23

HERITAGE LEARNERS
- **Assessment Program: Realidades para hispanohablantes:** Examen del capítulo 3
- **ExamView Heritage Learner Test Bank**

4 Chapter Overview

- **relationships with friends and family**
Vocabulary
- personality traits and conflicts
- friends and family relationships

Grammar
- subjunctive mode with verbs of emotion
- uses of *por* and *para*
- commands with *nosotros*
- use of possesive pronouns

Cultural Perspectives
- love and friendship celebrations in the Spanish-speaking world
- depictions of family life in the art of Carmen Lomas Garza and Pablo Picasso
- love expressed through the arts in the Spanish-speaking world

¡Pura vida!
- Watch an engaging video episode about a group of young people in Costa Rica!

CHAPTER SUPPORT

Bulletin Boards

Theme: *La amistad a través del mundo*

Ask students to cut out, copy, or download photos from around the world showing manifestations of friendship among teenagers in different Spanish-speaking countries and cultures. Cluster photos into categories of countries and/or cultures so that similarities and differences are evident.

Hands-on Culture

Art: *Mural de la amistad*

In many Latin American countries, murals are used to decorate the walls of public buildings. In schools, murals are used by students to express themselves and their feelings about events such as **el Día de la amistad.**

Materials: butcher paper, pencils, paint brushes, paint of different colors, tape

Directions:

1. Divide students into four groups. Ask each group to brainstorm a list of ideas about the meaning of friendship. Then, each group chooses the idea they are going to depict in the mural.

2. Students exchange ideas on how they are going to draw their mural. Then, they draw their mural in pencil on two large pieces of butcher paper that have been taped together.

3. Students paint their mural.

4. Display the murals on the walls of the classroom or around the school. Each group explains its mural to the class.

5. The class chooses a student from each group to organize a tour of the murals for students from other classes who might be interested.

Game

Busquemos el lado positivo

This game practices using positive and negative words to describe friendships and family relationships. Play it to review the vocabulary from *Capítulo 4*.

Players: the entire class, playing in pairs

Materials: index cards and colored pencils or markers

Rules:

1. On the board write positive and negative words and expressions from *Capítulo 4*. Write positive words such as **sincero(a)**, **comprensivo(a)**, **pedir perdón**, **perdonar**, **reaccionar**, **alegrarse** on the right column. On the left column, write negative words, such as **vanidoso(a)**, **conflicto**, **estar equivocado(a)**, **criticar.**

2. Ask students to write the words on their index cards, one on each card. Words from the left column should be written in blue and those from the right column should be in red.

3. Select a scorekeeper and divide the class into teams A and B. Each team A player chooses a card and thinks of a sentence that uses the negative or positive word and that can be converted to a positive or negative sentence.

4. Students go in row order, team A players alternating with players from team B. Team A player: *Una amiga que es **vanidosa** piensa sólo en ella misma.* Then, he or she says the opposite word: **considerada.** Team B player: *Es mejor ser amiga de alguien que es considerada y piensa en los demás.* This correct answer gives team B a turn.

5. Teams receive 1 point for each vocabulary word they use, as well as 1 point for each correct sentence. Each time they use a new word, the corresponding card is set aside.

6. If a team cannot make a sentence, it loses its turn. No word or sentence can be repeated. The team with the most points wins.

Variation: Players can use more than one vocabulary word in each sentence. For each additional word, they receive a point.

CHAPTER PROJECT

Anuncio ilustrado "Busco nuevos(as) amigos(as)"

Overview: Students create an illustrated ad to look for new school friends in Latin America or Spain. The ad is for the bulletin board of the school where they will be studying in summer. It should include the name of the student, his/her age, grade, phone number or email address, and photo.

Students include photos or magazine clippings with captions of two of their hobbies and two of their favorite class subjects. In a paragraph, they write why they want a new friend, two personality traits they like from a new friend, and two activities they would like to do with their new friend. Students then present their ad to the class and describe the information.

Resources: online or print photos, image layout and page layout software, and/or construction paper, scissors, glue and markers

Sequence: (suggestions for when to do each step are found throughout the chapter)

STEP 1. Review instructions so students know what is expected of them. Hand out the "Chapter 4 Project Instructions and Rubric" from the Teacher's Resource Book.

STEP 2. Students submit a draft of their ad. Return the drafts with your suggestions. For vocabulary and grammar practice, ask partners to present their drafts to each other.

STEP 3. Students do layouts, setting space for paragraphs, photos, and captions. Encourage them to try different arrangements before writing the paragraphs.

STEP 4. Students submit a draft of the personal descriptions. Note your corrections and suggestions, then return drafts to students.

STEP 5. Students present their posters to the class, explaining what kind of person is going to answer their ad.

Options:

1. Students create an ad for a newspaper instead of a bulletin board.
2. Students create an ad to look for a pen pal through a Web site.

Assessment:

Here is a detailed rubric for assessing this project:

Chapter 4 Project: *Anuncio ilustrado "Busco nuevos(as) amigos(as)"*

RUBRIC	Score 1	Score 3	Score 5
Your evidence of planning	You provide no ad layout or written draft.	You provide layout and written draft, but it is not corrected.	You show evidence of corrected draft and layout.
Your use of illustrations	You do not include photos or clippings.	You include clippings and photos but layout is unorganized.	Your ad is easy to read and photos and clippings are consistent with text.
Your presentation	You include little of the required information.	You include most of the required information.	You include all the required information.

21st Century Skills

Look for tips throughout Chapter 4 to enrich your teaching by integrating 21st Century Skills. Suggestions for the Chapter Project and Culture follow below.

Chapter Project

Modify the Chapter Project with these suggestions:

Foster Media Literacy

Discuss with students the purpose of their advertisement. What words, expressions, or visuals might best support this purpose for the target audience? What are the best media to use to convey their message?

Encourage Critical Thinking and Problem Solving

After students complete their projects, have them work together to group the students portrayed in the ads as possible roommates. Which groups of students have similar interests, likes and dislikes, eating/sleeping habits, etc.? Which pairs of students would or would not make compatible roommates?

Enhance Communication

As students prepare to present their project to the class, provide them with the handout "Give an Effective Presentation" to remind them of the importance of body language, tone of voice, eye contact, and other strategies for delivering an effective presentation.

Chapter Culture

Develop Flexibility and Adaptability

Help students bridge cultural differences by offering them opportunities to discuss the different cultural perspectives about the relationships between friends and family. After reading the *Fondo cultural* on page 178, discuss the contrasts between the image of society and family life presented in soap operas and *telenovelas*.

▶ **Videodocumentario** View *Una amistad entre hermanos* online with the class to learn more about family relationships in the Spanish-speaking world.

4 ¿Cómo te llevas con los demás?

Objectives

- Listen and read about relationships
- Talk and write about conflicts
- Express opinions and emotions while discussing problems
- Understand the relationship between emotions and art in the Hispanic world
- Compare the relationships between teens and their parents in Mexico with your own experience

A ver si recuerdas...

- Activities
- Time
- Quantities
- Use of reflexive verbs
- Reciprocal pronouns

Recycle...

- Possessive adjectives
- The letter *j*

Vocabulary

- Personality traits
- Relationships
- Emotions and conflicts

Grammar

- Subjunctive with verbs of emotion
- Uses of *por* and *para*
- *Nosotros* commands
- Possessive pronouns

Culture

- Pablo Picasso, p. 159
- Spanish youth, p. 166
- *Día de la Rosa y del Libro* in Barcelona, p. 167
- Opinions of Mexican teens about family relationships, pp. 176–177
- The soap opera in Latin America, p. 178
- Carmen Lomas Garza, p. 179
- Paulina Rubio, p. 183
- Love in the arts, pp. 186–187
- Poetry readings, p. 195

	FOR THE STUDENT	ONLINE	DVD	PRINT	FOR THE TEACHER	ONLINE	PREEXP	DVD	PRINT
Plan					Interactive TE and Resource DVD	•		•	
					Teacher's Resource Book, pp. 205–260	•		•	•
					Pre-AP* Resource Book, pp. 147–149	•		•	•
					Lesson Plans	•		•	
					Mapa global interactivo	•			
A ver si recuerdas PP. 154–157									
Review	*A ver si recuerdas* Study Plan	•			*A ver si recuerdas* Study Plan	•			
	Guided WB, pp. 114–117	•	•	•	Vocabulary and Grammar Transparencies, 2, 84–87	•	•	•	
	Core WB, pp. 49–50	•	•	•	Answer Keys: Student Edition, pp. 49–50	•	•	•	
	Hispanohablantes WB, p. 108			•					
Introducción PP. 158–159									
Present	Student Edition, pp. 158–159	•	•	•	Interactive TE and Resource DVD	•		•	
	DK Reference Atlas	•	•		Teacher's Resource Book, pp. 206–209	•		•	•
	Videonovela: ¡Pura vida!	•	•		Video Program Teacher's Guide, Cap. 4				
	¡Pura vida! Video Activities	•			Galería de fotos		•		
	Hispanohablantes WB, p. 109			•	Fine Art Transparencies, 49	•	•	•	
					Map Transparencies, 14, 15, 19, 20, 22	•	•	•	
Vocabulario en contexto PP. 160–163/174–177									
Present & Practice	Student Edition, pp. 160–163/174–177	•	•	•	Interactive TE and Resource DVD	•		•	
	Audio	•	•		Teacher's Resource Book, pp. 210–211, 214–215, 229–235/212–213, 215–217, 229–235	•		•	•
	Flashcards	•	•						
	Instant Check	•			Vocabulary Clip Art	•	•	•	•
	Guided WB, pp. 118–124/129–136	•	•	•	Audio Program	•	•	•	
	Core WB, pp. 51–52/56–57	•	•	•	Vocabulary and Grammar Transparencies, 88–90/93–95	•	•	•	
	Comm. WB, pp. 54/58	•	•	•	Answer Keys: Student Edition, pp. 50–51/55	•	•	•	
	Hispanohablantes WB, pp. 110–111/120–121			•					
Assess and Remediate					Pruebas 4–1/4–5: Assessment Program, pp. 83–84/92–93	•		•	•
					Hispanohablantes, pp. 83–84/92–93	•		•	•

RESOURCES

Vocabulario en uso PP. 164–167/178–181

Present & Practice — For the Student

FOR THE STUDENT	ONLINE	DVD	PRINT
Student Edition, pp. 164–167/178–181	•	•	•
Instant Check	•		
Comm. WB, pp. 50/51	•	•	•
Hispanohablantes WB, pp. 112–115/122–124			•
Communicative Pair Activities	•		

Present & Practice — For the Teacher

FOR THE TEACHER	ONLINE	PREEXP	DVD	PRINT
Interactive Whiteboard Vocabulary Activities	•		•	
Interactive TE and Resource DVD	•			
Teacher's Resource Book, pp. 215, 221/217, 224–225	•		•	•
Audio Program	•	•	•	
Videomodelos	•		•	
Fine Art Transparencies, 37	•	•	•	
Map Transparencies, 20	•	•	•	
Answer Keys: Student Edition, pp. 51–52/55–57	•	•	•	•

Assess and Remediate — For the Teacher

FOR THE TEACHER	ONLINE	PREEXP	DVD	PRINT
Pruebas 4–2/4–6 with Study Plans	•			
Pruebas 4–2/4–6: Assessment Program, pp. 85–86/94–95	•		•	•
Hispanohablantes, pp. 85–86/94–95	•		•	•

Gramática PP. 168–173/182–185

Present & Practice — For the Student

FOR THE STUDENT	ONLINE	DVD	PRINT
Student Edition, pp. 168–173/182–185	•	•	•
Instant Check	•		
Animated Verbs	•		
Tutorial Video: Grammar	•		
Canción de hip hop	•		
Guided WB, pp. 125–128/137–140	•	•	•
Core WB, pp. 53–55/58–60	•	•	•
Comm. WB, pp. 50, 55–57, 183/52–53, 59–60	•	•	•
Hispanohablantes WB, pp. 115–119/125–129			•
Communicative Pair Activities	•		

Present & Practice — For the Teacher

FOR THE TEACHER	ONLINE	PREEXP	DVD	PRINT
Interactive Whiteboard Grammar Activities	•		•	
Interactive TE and Resource DVD	•			
Teacher's Resource Book, pp. 215, 221–223/217–218, 226–227	•		•	•
Audio Program	•	•	•	
Videomodelos	•	•	•	
Vocabulary and Grammar Transparencies, 91–92/96–97	•	•	•	
Answer Keys: Student Edition, pp. 53–54/57–59	•	•	•	

Assess and Remediate — For the Teacher

FOR THE TEACHER	ONLINE	PREEXP	DVD	PRINT
Pruebas 4–3, 4–4/4–7, 4–8 with Study Plans	•			
Pruebas 4–3, 4–4/4–7, 4–8: Assessment Program, pp. 87, 88; 96, 97	•		•	•
Hispanohablantes, 87, 88; 96, 97	•		•	•
Examen 1, Examen 2: Vocab. y gramática, pp. 89–91/98–100	•		•	•

¡Adelante! PP. 186–195

Application — For the Student

FOR THE STUDENT	ONLINE	DVD	PRINT
Student Edition, pp. 186–195	•	•	•
Online Cultural Reading	•		
Guided WB, pp. 141–143	•	•	•
Comm. WB, pp. 61–63, 184	•	•	•
Hispanohablantes WB, pp. 130–135			•
Videodocumentario	•	•	
Lecturas 3, pp. 4–5, 8–10, 22–25			•

Application — For the Teacher

FOR THE TEACHER	ONLINE	PREEXP	DVD	PRINT
Interactive TE and Resource DVD	•		•	
Teacher's Resource Book, pp. 218, 220	•		•	•
Video Program: Videodocumentario	•		•	
Video Program Teacher's Guide, Cap. 4	•		•	
Vocabulary and Grammar Transparencies, 4	•	•	•	
Fine Art Transparencies, 50–57	•	•	•	
Map Transparencies, 20	•	•	•	
Answer Keys: Student Edition, p. 59	•	•	•	

Repaso del capítulo PP. 196–199

Review — For the Student

FOR THE STUDENT	ONLINE	DVD	PRINT
Student Edition, pp. 196–199	•	•	•
Online Puzzles and Games	•		
Core WB, pp. 61–62	•	•	•
Comm. WB, pp. 185–188	•	•	•
Hispanohablantes WB, pp. 136–139			•
Instant Check	•		

Review — For the Teacher

FOR THE TEACHER	ONLINE	PREEXP	DVD	PRINT
Interactive TE and Resource DVD	•		•	
Teacher's Resource Book, pp. 208, 228–235	•		•	
Audio Program	•	•	•	
Answer Keys: Student Edition, p. 60	•	•	•	

Chapter Assessment

Assess — For the Teacher

FOR THE TEACHER	ONLINE	PREEXP	DVD	PRINT
Examen del capítulo 4: Assessment Program, pp. 101–104	•		•	•
Alternate Assessment Program, pp. 35–44	•		•	•
Hispanohablantes, pp. 101–104	•		•	•
Audio Program, Cap. 4, Examen	•		•	
ExamView: Test Banks A and B (questions only online)	•		•	
Heritage Learner Test Bank	•		•	
Pre-AP* Test Bank	•		•	

REGULAR SCHEDULE (50 MINUTES)

DAY	Warm-up / Assess	Preview / Present / Practice / Communicate		Wrap-up / Homework Options
1	**Warm-up** (10 min.) • Return Examen del capítulo: Capítulo 3	**Repaso** (35 min.) • A ver si recuerdas . . . • Actividad 5		**Wrap-up and Homework Options** (5 min.) • Core Practice 4-1, 4-2
2	**Warm-up** (10 min.) • Homework check	**Chapter Opener** (10 min.) • Objectives • Arte y cultura	**Vocabulario en contexto 1** (25 min.) • Presentation: Vocabulario y gramática en contexto • Actividades 1, 2	**Wrap-up and Homework Options** (5 min.) • Clip Art Vocabulary
3	**Warm-up** (10 min.) • Homework check	**Vocabulario en contexto 1** (30 min.) • Presentation: Prueba de la amistad • Actividad 3, 4	**Vocabulario en uso 1** (5 min.) • Actividad 6	**Wrap-up and Homework Options** (5 min.) • Core Practice 4-3, 4-4 • Prueba 4-1: Vocabulary recognition
4	**Warm-up** (10 min.) • Homework check ✔**Formative Assessment** (10 min.) • Prueba 4-1: Vocabulary recognition	**Vocabulario en uso 1** (25 min.) • Actividades 5, 7, 8 • Interactive Whiteboard Vocabulary Activities • Ampliación del lenguaje		**Wrap-up and Homework Options** (5 min.) • Actividades 9, 10 • Writing Activities • Prueba 4-2 with Study Plan: Vocabulary production
5	**Warm-up** (10 min.) • Fondo cultural • Homework check ✔**Formative Assessment** (10 min.) • Prueba 4-2 with Study Plan: Vocabulary production	**Gramática y vocabulario en uso 1** (25 min.) • Presentation: El subjuntivo con verbos de emoción • Interactive Whiteboard Grammar Activities • Actividades 11, 13, 14, 15 • Writing Activity		**Wrap-up and Homework Options** (5 min.) • Core Practice 4-5
6	**Warm-up** (10 min.) • Actividad 12 • Homework check	**Gramática y vocabulario en uso 1** (35 min.) • Actividad 16 • Communicative Pair Activity • Presentation: Los usos de *por* y *para*	• Interactive Whiteboard Grammar Activities • Actividad 18	**Wrap-up and Homework Options** (5 min.) • Writing Activity • Prueba 4-3 with Study Plan: El subjuntivo con verbos de emoción
7	**Warm-up** (10 min.) • Homework check ✔**Formative Assessment** (10 min.) • Prueba 4-3 with Study Plan: El subjuntivo con verbos de emoción	**Gramática y vocabulario en uso 1** (25 min.) • Actividades 17, 19, 20, 21 • Communicative Pair Activity		**Wrap-up and Homework Options** (5 min.) • Core Practice 4-6, 4-7 • Prueba 4-4: Los usos de *por* y *para*
8	**Warm-up** (15 min.) • Writing Activity • Homework check ✔**Formative Assessment** (10 min.) • Prueba 4-4 with Study Plan: Los usos de *por* y *para*	**Vocabulario en contexto 2** (20 min.) • Presentation: Vocabulario y gramática en contexto • Actividad 22		**Wrap-up and Homework Options** (5 min.) • Clip Art Vocabulary • Examen: Vocabulario y gramática 1
9	**Warm-up** (5 min.) • Homework check ✔**Formative Assessment** (30 min.) • Examen: Vocabulario y gramática 1	**Vocabulario en contexto 2** (10 min.) • Presentation: Hagamos las paces • Actividad 23		**Wrap-up and Homework Options** (5 min.) • Conflictos: causas y soluciones • Core Practice 4-8, 4-9
10	**Warm-up** (20 min.) • Conflictos: causas y soluciones • Actividad 24 • Homework check ✔**Formative Assessment** (10 min.) • Prueba 4-5: Vocabulary recognition	**Vocabulario en uso 2** (15 min.) • Fondo cultural • Actividades 28, 29 • Interactive Whiteboard Vocabulary Activities		**Wrap-up and Homework Options** (5 min.) • Actividades 26, 27 • Prueba 4-6 with Study Plan: Vocabulary production

REGULAR SCHEDULE (50 MINUTES)

DAY	Warm-up / Assess	Preview / Present / Practice / Communicate	Wrap-up / Homework Options
11	**Warm-up (10 min.)** • Actividad 25 • Homework check ✔**Formative Assessment (10 min.)** • Prueba 4-6 with Study Plan: Vocabulary production	**Gramática y vocabulario en uso 2 (25 min.)** • Actividades 30, 32 • Presentation: Mandatos con *nosotros* • Interactive Whiteboard Grammar Activities • Actividades 33, 35 • Communicative Pair Activity	**Wrap-up and Homework Options (5 min.)** • Actividad 34 • Core Practice 4-10 • Prueba 4-7 with Study Plan: Mandatos con *nosotros*
12	**Warm-up (10 min.)** • Writing Activity • Homework check ✔**Formative Assessment (10 min.)** • Prueba 4-7 with Study Plan: Mandatos con *nosotros*	**Gramática y vocabulario en uso 2 (25 min.)** • Presentation: Pronombres posesivos • Interactive Whiteboard Grammar Activities • Actividades 36, 37, 38 • El español en el mundo del trabajo	**Wrap-up and Homework Options (5 min.)** • Core Practice 4-11, 4-12 • Prueba 4-8 with Study Plan: Pronombres posesivos
13	**Warm-up (10 min.)** • Homework check ✔**Formative Assessment (10 min.)** • Prueba 4-8 with Study Plan: Pronombres posesivos	**Gramática y vocabulario en uso 2 (25 min.)** • En voz alta • Communicative Pair Activity	**Wrap-up and Homework Options (5 min.)** • Examen: Vocabulario y gramática 2
14	**Warm-up (8 min.)** • Writing Activity ✔**Formative Assessment (30 min.)** • Examen: Vocabulario y gramática 2	**¡Adelante! (10 min.)** • Presentación oral: Steps 1, 2	**Wrap-up and Homework Options (5 min.)** • Presentación oral: Step 2
15	**Warm-up (10 min.)** • Presentación oral: Step 2	**¡Adelante! (35 min.)** • Presentación oral: Step 3	**Wrap-up and Homework Options (5 min.)** • El amor en las artes • ¿Comprendiste?
16	**Warm-up (15 min.)** • El amor en las artes: ¿Comprendiste? • Homework check	**¡Adelante! (30 min.)** • ¿Qué me cuentas? 1, 2, 3 • View Video • Video Activities 1, 2, 3	**Wrap-up and Homework Options (5 min.)** • Presentación escrita: Steps 1, 2
17	**Warm-up (10 min.)** • Video Activity 4	**¡Adelante! (15 min.)** • Presentación escrita: Step 3 **Repaso (20 min.)** • Preparación para el examen: Actividades 3, 4	**Wrap-up and Homework Options (5 min.)** • Presentación escrita: Step 4
18	**Warm-up (10 min.)** • Homework check	**¡Adelante! (35 min.)** • Lectura • ¿Comprendiste? • Fondo cultural	**Wrap-up and Homework Options (5 min.)** • Core Practice: Organizer 4-13, 4-14 • Instant Check
19	**Warm-up (20 min.)** • Preparación para el examen: Actividades 1, 2 • Homework check	**Repaso (25 min.)** • Preparación para el examen: Actividades 5, 6, 7 • Other review	**Wrap-up and Homework Options (5 min.)** • Examen del capítulo
20	**Warm-up (5 min.)** • Answer questions ✔**Summative Assessment (44 min.)** • Examen del capítulo		**Wrap-up and Homework Options (1 min.)** • A ver si recuerdas: Capítulo 5 • Actividades 1, 2, 4, 6, 7

4 Lesson Plans

BLOCK SCHEDULE (90 MINUTES)

DAY	Warm-up / Assess	Preview / Present / Practice / Communicate	Wrap-up / Homework Options
1	**Warm-up (35 min.)** • Return Examen del capítulo: Capítulo 3 • A ver si recuerdas . . . • Actividad 5 • Homework check	**Chapter Opener (10 min.)** • Objectives • Arte y cultura **Vocabulario en contexto 1 (30 min.)** • Presentation: Vocabulario y gramática en contexto • Actividades 1, 2 • Presentation: Prueba de la amistad • Actividades 3, 4 **Vocabulario en uso 1 (10 min.)** • Actividades 6, 7 • Interactive Whiteboard Vocabulary Activities	**Wrap-up and Homework Options (5 min.)** • Core Practice 4-3, 4-4 • Clip Art Vocabulary • Prueba 4-1: Vocabulary recognition
2	**Warm-up (15 min.)** • Actividad 5 • Homework check ✔**Formative Assessment (10 min.)** • Prueba 4-1: Vocabulary recognition	**Vocabulario en uso 1 (60 min.)** • Actividades 8, 9, 10 • Ampliación del lenguaje • Fondo cultural • Communicative Pair Activity • Audio Activity	**Wrap-up and Homework Options (5 min.)** • Writing Activities • Prueba 4-2 with Study Plan: Vocabulary production
3	**Warm-up (15 min.)** • Writing Activity • Homework check ✔**Formative Assessment (10 min.)** • Prueba 4-2 with Study Plan: Vocabulary production	**Gramática y vocabulario en uso 1 (60 min.)** • Presentation: El subjuntivo con verbos de emoción • Interactive Whiteboard Grammar Activities • Actividades 11, 12, 13, 14, 15 • Audio and Writing Activities	**Wrap-up and Homework Options (5 min.)** • Core Practice 4-5 • Prueba 4-3 with Study Plan: El subjuntivo con verbos de emoción
4	**Warm-up (10 min.)** • Actividad 16 • Homework check ✔**Formative Assessment (10 min.)** • Prueba 4-3 with Study Plan: El subjuntivo con verbos de emoción	**Gramática y vocabulario en uso 1 (50 min.)** • Presentation: Los usos de *por* y *para* • Interactive Whiteboard Grammar Activities • Actividades 18, 19, 20, 21 • Communicative Pair Activity **Vocabulario en contexto 2 (15 min.)** • Presentation: Vocabulario y gramática en contexto • Actividad 22	**Wrap-up and Homework Options (5 min.)** • Core Practice 4-6, 4-7 • Prueba 4-4: Los usos de *por* y *para* • Examen: Vocabulario y gramática 1
5	**Warm-up (15 min.)** • Actividad 16 • Homework check ✔**Formative Assessment (40 min.)** • Prueba 4-4 with Study Plan: Los usos de *por* y *para* • Examen: Vocabulario y gramática 1	**Vocabulario en contexto 2 (20 min.)** • Presentation: Hagamos las paces • Actividad 23 • Presentation: Conflictos: causas y soluciones • Actividad 24 **Vocabulario en uso 2 (10 min.)** • Actividad 25 • Fondo cultural • Interactive Whiteboard Vocabulary Activities	**Wrap-up and Homework Options (5 min.)** • Core Practice 4-8, 4-9 • Prueba 4-5: Vocabulary recognition
6	**Warm-up (20 min.)** • Actividades 26, 27 • Homework check ✔**Formative Assessment (10 min.)** • Prueba 4-5: Vocabulary recognition	**Gramática y vocabulario en uso 2 (55 min.)** • Actividades 28, 29, 30, 32 • Presentation: Mandatos con *nosotros* • Interactive Whiteboard Grammar Activities • Actividades 33, 34, 35	**Wrap-up and Homework Options (5 min.)** • Core Practice 4-10 • Pruebas 4-6, 4-7 with Study Plans: Vocabulary production, Mandatos con *nosotros*

BLOCK SCHEDULE (90 MINUTES)

DAY	Warm-up / Assess	Preview / Present / Practice / Communicate	Wrap-up / Homework Options
7	**Warm-up** (15 min.) • Actividad 31 • Homework check ✔**Formative Assessment** (20 min.) • Pruebas 4-6, 4-7 with Study Plans: Vocabulary production, Mandatos con *nosotros*	**Gramática y vocabulario en uso 2** (35 min.) • En voz alta • Presentation: Pronombres posesivos • Interactive Whiteboard Grammar Activities • Actividades 36, 37, 38 • El español en la comunidad **¡Adelante!** (15 min.) • Presentación oral: Steps 1, 2	**Wrap-up and Homework Options** (5 min.) • Presentación oral: Step 2
8	**Warm-up** (15 min.) • Writing Activity • Homework check ✔**Formative Assessment** (40 min.) • Presentación oral: Step 3	**Gramática y vocabulario en uso 2** (15 min.) • Communicative Pair Activity **¡Adelante!** (15 min.) • Presentation: El amor en las artes	**Wrap-up and Homework Options** (5 min.) • Core Practice 4-11, 4-12 • Prueba 4-8: Pronombres posesivos • Examen: Vocabulario y gramática 2
9	**Warm-up** (10 min.) • Homework check ✔**Formative Assessment** (30 min.) • Prueba 4-8: Pronombres posesivos • Examen: Vocabulario y gramática 2	**¡Adelante!** (45 min.) • El amor en las artes • ¿Comprendiste? • ¿Qué me cuentas? 1, 2, 3 • Presentación escrita: Step 1 • View Video • Video Activities	**Wrap-up and Homework Options** (5 min.) • Presentación escrita: Step 2 • Preparación para el examen: Actividades 1, 2
10	**Warm-up** (20 min.) • Presentación escrita: Step 3 • Homework check	**¡Adelante!** (40 min.) • Lectura • ¿Comprendiste? • Fondo cultural **Repaso** (25 min.) • Preparación para el examen: Actividades 3, 4, 6	**Wrap-up and Homework Options** (5 min.) • Presentación escrita: Step 4 • Core Practice: Organizer 4-13, 4-14 • Instant Check • Preparación para el examen: Actividades 5, 7 • Examen del capítulo
11	**Warm-up** (15 min.) • Homework check ✔**Summative Assessment** (45 min.) • Examen del capítulo	**Theme Game** (15 min.) **A ver si recuerdas – Capítulo 5** (10 min.) • Presentation: El amor en las artes • Presentation: Vocabulario • Presentation: Gramática	**Wrap-up and Homework Options** (5 min.) • A ver si recuerdas – Capítulo 5 • Actividades 1, 2, 4, 6, 7 • Core Practice 5-1, 5-2

4 Recycle

Vocabulario Repaso

Core Instruction

Standards: 1.1, 1.2

Resources: Voc. and Gram. Transparency 84

Suggestions: Before presenting the material in this review section, consider testing your students' command of the material by assigning the Study Plan. Students will automatically be given additional practice of the material they have not yet mastered, and you can focus your review based on the class's overall performance on the post-test.

Ask students to think of one person they know well. Have them tell at least two facts about the person, using vocabulary from the three categories. Tell students that vocabulary from the **actividades** and **tiempo** categories might be used in the same sentence: *Mi hermana Jane es una persona sociable. Le gusta escribir cartas a sus amigas durante sus viajes.*

Vocabulario Repaso

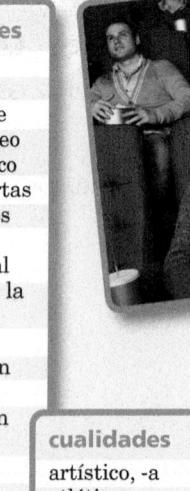

actividades

charlar
divertirse
encontrarse
enviar correo
 electrónico
escribir cartas
jugar juegos
llevarse
 bien / mal
navegar en la
 Red
participar
pasarlo bien
pasear
quedarse en
 casa
reunirse
reírse
salir

cualidades

artístico, -a	nervioso, -a
atlético, -a	reservado, -a
bien educado, -a	serio, -a
cortés	simpático, -a
divertido, -a	sociable
elegante	talentoso, -a
estudioso, -a	tranquilo, -a
gracioso, -a	
inteligente	

tiempo

antes (de)
después (de)
hasta
los días de
 semana
los fines de
 semana
los días festivos
durante
por la mañana
por la tarde
por la noche

1
Standards: 1.1, 1.3, 3.1

Resources: Voc. and Gram. Transparency 2

Focus: Practicing review vocabulary

Suggestions: Remind students that when making their Venn diagrams in Step 1, they should fill in the overlapping parts of the diagram with qualities their friends have in common.

Common Errors: Students may forget to make an adjective agree in number and gender with the noun it modifies. Correct the error by modeling the correct form of the noun phrase and having students repeat. You can also use visual cues: hold up two fingers to elicit plural; have a flash card ready with the masculine symbol on one side and the feminine symbol on the other, and hold this up to elicit the appropriate gender.

Answers will vary.

▼1 Cualidades que admiras |

Escribir • Hablar

❶ Escoge cinco cualidades para describir a tus amigos(as). Haz una lista. Compara tu lista con la de un(a) compañero(a). Luego, hagan juntos un diagrama de Venn para ver qué cualidades comparten sus amigos(as).

❷ Con tu compañero(a) hablen de las cualidades que comparten sus amigos(as) y digan por qué son importantes para ustedes.

Modelo
Nos gustan las personas divertidas porque siempre lo pasamos bien con ellas.

154 ciento cincuenta y cuatro
 A ver si recuerdas . . .

Block Schedule

Ask each student to write a sentence of up to eight words that uses a reflexive verb in the present, past, or future tense with student(s) in the class as the subject. Put the papers in a bag. Create two teams. Alternate with individual students acting out the sentences. Allow a team up to 30 seconds to guess the sentence. Keep track of the time per sentence. The team with the lowest time wins.

154

DIFFERENTIATED INSTRUCTION

Heritage Language Learners

Invite students with exemplary pronunciation to read the vocabulary aloud as a pronunciation model. Point out any regional differences between certain pronunciations, such as /y/ or /zh/ for **ll** in the phrase **llevarse bien.**

Advanced Learners

Much of the review vocabulary can be applied to an animal, such as a pet, as well as a person. Ask students to use the vocabulary to write a brief paragraph about a pet or other animal they know: *Mi perro Jake es muy gracioso. Los fines de semana, vamos al parque y nos divertimos mucho jugando con su pelota.*

Gramática Repaso

Otros usos de los verbos reflexivos

A verb is reflexive in Spanish when the subject receives the action of the verb. In English this is implied by the endings -*self* and -*selves*. In Spanish the reflexive pronouns are *me, te, se, nos, os, se*.

Ella **se** levanta.	She gets (**herself**) up.
Nosotros **nos** paramos.	We stand (**ourselves**) up.

- Many reflexive verbs in Spanish describe daily routine actions. Some verbs of this type include *despertarse* (to wake up), *ducharse* (to take a shower), *peinarse* (to comb oneself), *vestirse* (to get dressed), and *acostarse* (to go to bed).

- Other reflexive verbs describe a physical or emotional state. Verbs of this type include *divertirse* (to enjoy oneself) and *sentirse* (to feel an emotion).

- Some reflexive verbs describe a change of state and they carry the added meaning of "to get" or "to become."

Me enojé.	I became angry (got mad).	Se puso muy nervioso.	He became very nervous.
¿Te aburriste?	Did you get bored?	Se cansan.	They get (become) tired.

- Some verbs have a different meaning when used reflexively.

ir	to go	**irse**	to leave	**dormir**	to sleep	**dormirse**	to fall asleep
parecer	to seem	**parecerse a**	to look like	**quedar**	to be located	**quedarse**	to stay
quitar	to take away	**quitarse**	to take off	**volver**	to return	**volverse**	to become
perder	to lose	**perderse**	to get lost				

- Other verbs such as *darse cuenta de* (to realize), *quejarse* (to complain), and *portarse bien* (to behave) are always reflexive.

- Placement of reflexive pronouns with commands and the present participle follow the same rules that apply to placement of direct and indirect object pronouns.

Más ayuda	**realidades.com**	▶Tutorial

▼2 En familia

Escribir

Completa este párrafo con los verbos del recuadro para describir lo que hace una familia los sábados.

quedarse	levantarse	irse
quejarse	cansarse	

Los sábados todos __1.__ temprano. Mi hermano y mi papá __2.__ con sus amigos a jugar al fútbol. Por la tarde, si hace buen tiempo, nadie quiere __3.__ en casa. Todos vamos al parque a correr. A veces, después de correr, yo __4.__ un poco pero nunca __5.__. Después de todo, lo pasamos muy bien.

▼3 Los sábados

Escribir

Combina palabras de las dos listas para escribir lo que tú y tus amigos hacen los sábados.

Modelo
los chicos / reunirse
Los chicos se reúnen en la plaza.

1. mi amigo y yo	acostarse
2. tú	divertirse
3. los chicos	aburrirse
4. yo	quedarse
5. mi amiga	irse

Recycle 4

Gramática Repaso

Core Instruction

Standards: 1.4

Resources: Voc. and Gram. Transparency 85

Suggestions: Refer students who are having difficulty with reflexive verbs to the *GramActiva* video from L2 Chapter 2A, and to the online tutorial. Show *Vocabulary & Grammar Transparency* 85. Point to the images of the various activities and have students say what is happening.

▼2 Standards: 1.2

Resources: Answer Keys: Student Edition, p. 49

Focus: Reviewing reflexive verbs

Suggestions: Remind students that the verbs in the word bank are in the infinitive form, and therefore the reflexive pronoun *se* is attached to the end. They must detach the pronoun and adapt it and the verb form to suit the subject of the sentence, if necessary (see item 3).

Answers:
1. se levantan (nos levantamos)
2. se van
3. quedarse
4. me canso
5. me quejo

▼3 Standards: 1.3

Resources: Answer Keys: Student Edition, p. 49

Focus: Reviewing reflexive verbs

Suggestions: Challenge students to compete with a partner and see who can come up with the most sentences in five minutes.

Answers will vary. Students may use the following verb forms:
1. nos acostamos/nos divertimos/nos aburrimos/nos quedamos/nos vamos
2. te acuestas/te diviertes/te aburres/te quedas/te vas
3. se acuestan/se divierten/se aburren/se quedan/se van
4. me acuesto/me divierto/me aburro/me quedo/me voy
5. se acuesta/se divierte/se aburre/se queda/se va

ENRICH YOUR TEACHING

Teacher-to-Teacher

Using video with the sound off is a good way to elicit different structures or vocabulary from students. For reflexive verbs, show a video segment from a film, a TV show, or a commercial, in which characters are going through part of a daily routine. As students watch, they say sentences about the actions, using reflexive verbs.

4 Recycle

Vocabulario Repaso

Core Instruction

Standards: 1.1, 1.2

Resources: Voc. and Gram. Transparency 86

Suggestions: Hold a "gripe session" in which students think about a minor annoyance at school, work, or home. Ask them to prepare a few sentences about the annoyance, using vocabulary from as many of the categories as possible, and then share their gripe with the class.

4 Standards: 1.3

Focus: Practicing review vocabulary

Suggestions: Ask students to share what they have written. Encourage those listening to respond with an additional comment that makes sense, such as: *¡Uf! A mí también me molesta.*

Answers will vary.

5 Standards: 1.1

Resources: Answer Keys: Student Edition, p. 50

Focus: Practicing review vocabulary

Suggestions: Encourage students to speak with the intonation appropriate to the expression they are using.

Answers will vary. The following are suggestions:

1. ¡Déjame en paz!
2. A mí no me gusta lavar la ropa.
3. A mí tampoco.
4. Quédate tranquilo.
5. ¡Yo también!
6. Me estás volviendo loco(a).
7. Me estás poniendo nervioso(a).

Vocabulario Repaso

defectos
aburrido, -a
desordenado, -a
impaciente
infantil
mal educado, -a
perezoso, -a
tonto, -a

acciones
discutir
emocionarse
enojarse
gritar
importar
llorar
mentir
molestar
pelearse

reacciones
¡ay!
¡basta!
¡déjame en paz!
¡tú tampoco!
¡uf!
¡yo también!
a mí no . . .
a mí sí . . .
a mí también . . .
a mí tampoco . . .

expresiones
hablar mal (de)
llegar tarde
no pensar (en)
ponerse . . .
    furioso, -a
    nervioso, -a
quedarse
    tranquilo, -a
tener paciencia
volverse
    loco, -a

▼4 Lo que no me gusta

Escribir

Completa las frases siguientes para describir qué cosas te molestan de tus amigos(as).

Modelo
Me pongo nervioso(a) cuando . . .
Me pongo nervioso(a) cuando mi amiga no me llama.

1. Me molesta cuando . . .
2. No me gusta nada cuando . . .
3. Me enojo cuando . . .
4. Me pongo furioso(a) cuando . . .
5. Me vuelvo loco(a) cuando . . .

▼5 Reacciona

Hablar

Trabaja con otro(a) estudiante para leer y reaccionar a los siguientes comentarios. Usa la lista de reacciones de arriba.

▶ Modelo

A —Me gusta cuando la profesora está contenta con mi trabajo.
B —*A mí también.*

1. ¡Vamos! ¡Levántate, perezoso!
2. ¿Me ayudas a lavar la ropa?
3. No me gustan las fresas.
4. ¡Ten cuidado! ¡Ve más despacio!
5. ¿Al cine? ¡Sí, yo quiero ir!
6. Tengo prisa. Tenemos que llegar a las tres.
7. ¿Ya estudiaste para el examen? Dicen que va a ser difícil.

156 ciento cincuenta y seis
A ver si recuerdas . . .

DIFFERENTIATED INSTRUCTION

Multiple Intelligences

Interpersonal/Social: As you discuss conflicts and emotions, ask students to try to see situations from other people's points of view and to attempt to understand how they think and feel. Invite them to share their ideas with the class.

Students with Learning Difficulties

Help students understand the concept of reciprocal actions. Invite pairs to briefly act out situations greeting someone or having a disagreement. Explain that the situations are reciprocal because both people participate. Explain that the English words "each other" signal reciprocal actions.

Gramática Repaso

Pronombres reflexivos en acciones recíprocas

To tell what people do to or for one another use the reciprocal pronouns *nos* and *se* before the first and third person plural of certain verbs.

Mis hermanos y yo no **nos** peleamos nunca.
Alonso y Fernanda **se** llaman todos los días, pero **se** ven muy poco.

In the case of a verbal phrase with an infinitive or a present participle, you may place the reciprocal pronoun either before the conjugated verb or attached to the infinitive or participle. Remember to place an accent in the third to last syllable when you add the reciprocal pronoun to a present participle.

Vamos a ver**nos** mañana.
Nos vamos a ver mañana

Rodrigo y Luisa estaban abrazánd**ose** en el jardín.
Rodrigo y Luisa **se** estaban abrazando en el jardín.

Here are some examples of reflexive verbs that are used reciprocally:

abrazarse	comprenderse	entenderse	leerse	pelearse
ayudarse	conocerse	escribirse	llamarse	saludarse
besarse	contarse	hablarse	llevarse bien / mal	verse

▼6 ¿La pareja ideal?

Leer • Escribir

Romina siempre está hablando de la relación de su hermana Analía con su novio Nicolás. Completa las siguientes frases con el verbo que corresponda, en la forma correcta. Luego, resume en una frase qué opinas tú de la relación de esta pareja.

Analía y Nicolás . . .

1. _____ *(escribirse / ayudarse)* mensajes todas las mañanas.

2. _____ *(entenderse / hablarse)* muy bien y son muy felices.

3. Nunca _____ *(besarse / pelearse)* ni tienen opiniones diferentes.

4. Siempre _____ *(comprenderse / enojarse)* y _____ *(ayudarse / conocerse)*.

5. _____ *(llamarse / leerse)* todas las noches y hablan horas por teléfono.

6. _____ *(entenderse / verse)* todos los viernes y los sábados.

7. _____ *(conocerse / contarse)* desde hace muchos años.

8. _____ *(llevarse / saludarse)* muy bien.

Más práctica GO

realidades.com | print

A ver si recuerdas with Study Plan ✔
Guided WB pp. 114–117 ✔ ✔
Core WB pp. 49–50 ✔ ✔
Hispanohablantes WB p. 108 ✔

ciento cincuenta y siete **157**
Capítulo 4

Gramática Repaso

Core Instruction

Resources: Voc. and Gram. Transparency 87

Suggestions: Refer students who are having difficulty with the concept of reciprocal actions to the *GramActiva* video from L2 Chapter 4B, and to the online tutorials. Ask students to create sentences using verbs from the list at the end of the *Gramática*. If a sentence contains a verb phrase, have students practice using it both ways: with the reciprocal pronoun before the conjugated verb and with the pronoun attached to the end of the infinitive or present participle.

▼6
Standards: 1.3

Resources: Answer Keys: Student Edition, p. 50

Focus: Reviewing reciprocal pronouns

Suggestions: Once students have written their answers, encourage them to read all the items through like a story, in order to be better able to comment on the relationship between Analía and Nicolás.

Answers:

1. Se escriben
2. Se entienden
3. se pelean
4. se comprenden/se ayudan
5. Se llaman
6. Se ven
7. Se conocen
8. Se llevan

Extension: Have students share the comments they wrote about the relationship between Analía and Nicolás. Encourage them to support their opinion with an additional comment.

ENRICH YOUR TEACHING

Teacher-to-Teacher

The vocabulary on these two pages is suitable to the complaints, discomforts, and frustrations that many of your students go through daily. Encourage them to think of expressions such as *¡Uf!*, *¡Basta!*, and *¡Déjame en paz!* at trying times to promote connections between genuine emotion and language.

21st Century Skills

Initiative and Self-Direction Direct students to the various digital tools available in **realidades.com** to help them monitor their own understanding and learning needs, such as the online tutorials with comprehension check exercises. Students can review the related English grammar first, and then proceed to the new Spanish grammar point.

✓ASSESSMENT

A ver si recuerdas with Study Plan (online only)

After presenting the review material on these pages, assign the *A ver si recuerdas* Study Plan to evaluate students' mastery of the material. Additional practice for students who need it is available online.

157

Standards for Foreign Language Learning: *Capítulo* 4

• To meet the Standards, students will:

Communication

1.1 Interpersonal
• Talk about friendship, interpersonal relationships, personality traits, emotions, customary behavior, conflict resolution
• Talk about known artists, musicians, and poets
• Talk about soap operas and poetry readings

1.2 Interpretive
• Read and listen to information about friendship, interpersonal relationships, personality traits, emotions, customary behavior, conflict resolution, family routines
• Read about known artists, musicians, and poets
• Read about word families
• Read about soap operas and poetry readings
• Read about bilingual children

1.3 Presentational
• Write about friendship, interpersonal relationships, personality traits, emotions, conflict resolution
• Write about a trip and a day out
• Recite song lyrics by Paulina Rubio
• Write about the theme of love in art
• Present information orally about student council
• Write about known poets and their work

Culture

2.1 Practices and Perspectives
• Explain artistic life in Puerto Rico
• Interpret Spanish personality demographics and Mexican family dynamics
• Explain the impact of love in Spanish-speaking cultures and their art
• Explain the practice of poetry readings in Spanish

2.2 Products and Perspectives
• Talk about known artists, musicians, and poets
• Talk about *telenovelas*

Connections

3.1 Cross-curricular
• Talk about psychology, conflict resolution, and interpersonal dynamics
• Talk about known artists, musicians, and poets
• Work with percentages in surveys
• Describe holidays in Spain and Latin America
• Describe the history of the handshake
• Describe Spanish cities
• Discuss Language Arts strategies: compare and contrast, getting into your character, describing relationships, identifying and understanding figurative language
• Discuss conflict in fiction and drama

3.2 Target Culture
• Read a Spanish youth survey
• Read song lyrics by Paulina Rubio
• Read poetry by known poets

Comparisons

4.1 Language
• Compare Spanish words to their English counterparts
• Compare English and Spanish reflexive verbs
• Compare *por* and *para* with English
• Compare *nosotros* commands with English

▼ Chapter Objectives

Communication

By the end of the chapter you will be able to:
• Listen and read about friendship and family relationships
• Talk and write about conflicts and solutions
• Express opinions and emotions while discussing problems

Culture

You will also be able to:
• Understand the relationship between emotions and art in the Hispanic world
• Compare the relationships between teens and their parents in Mexico with your own experience

You will demonstrate what you know and can do:
• Presentación oral, p. 189
• Presentación escrita, pp. 190–191
• Preparación para el examen, p. 199

You will use:

Vocabulary
• Personality traits
• Relationships
• Emotions and conflicts

Grammar
• Subjunctive with verbs of emotion
• Uses of *por* and *para*
• *Nosotros* commands
• Possessive pronouns

Exploración del mundo hispano

Country Connection
Relationships with Friends and Family

Estados Unidos
España
México
Uruguay
Argentina

realidades.com GO

📖 Reference Atlas
▶ Videonovela y actividades

🌐 Mapa global interactivo

Una familia en Buenos Aires, Argentina

ENRICH YOUR TEACHING

Using Backward Design
Have students preview the sample performance tasks on *Preparación para el examen*, p. 199, and connect them to the Chapter Objectives. Explain to students that by completing the sample tasks, they can self-assess their learning progress.

Mapa global interactivo
Download the *Mapa global interactivo* files for Chapter 4 and preview the activities. In Activity 1, you travel the length of Judith Baca's mural wall in Los Angeles, CA. In Activity 2, you visit places where poet Pablo Neruda lived in Chile.

4.2 Culture
- Compare Spanish and U.S. teen profiles
- Compare U.S. holidays and TV shows with those in Spanish-speaking countries
- Compare works of art

Communities

5.1 Beyond the School
- Link to Web sites from the Spanish-speaking world

5.2 Lifelong Learner
- Describe their own personalities
- Discuss techniques for conflict resolution
- Develop an appreciation for poetry

▶ **Videonovela** *¡Pura vida!* View this stand-alone storyline video about five young adults in San José, Costa Rica with your class, either online or on DVD.

◉ **PresentationExpress™**
See pp. 154c–154d

Chapter Opener

Core Instruction

Resources: Map Transparencies 14, 15, 19, 20, 22

Suggestions: Introduce students to the theme of the chapter and go over the objectives. Point out that they will learn language to help them deal with their own feelings and those of others. They will also learn about how people in other cultures deal with friends and family.

Arte y cultura

Standards: 1.1, 1.2, 2.1, 2.2, 3.1

Resources: Fine Art Transparencies with Teacher's Guide, p. 49

Suggestions: After students have read the information, ask: *¿Qué detalles nos muestran quién es la madre y quién es el hijo en la pintura?*

Arte y cultura | España

Madre e hijo La relación entre madre e hijo puede ser una relación muy íntima y especial. El artista español Pablo Picasso tiene una serie de cuadros de varios períodos y estilos que muestran las figuras de una madre y un hijo. En este cuadro se ve la influencia del arte africano. Las caras de las figuras se parecen a máscaras *(masks)* africanas. ¿Qué elementos usa Picasso para comunicar la relación entre estas dos personas?

- ¿Conoces a otro(a) artista que muestre relaciones entre familias? Descríbelo(a).

"Madre e hijo", (1907), Pablo Picasso ▶
© 2009 Estate of Pablo Picasso/Artists Rights Society (ARS), New York. Photo: © Réunion des Musées Nationaux/Art Resource, NY.

ciento cincuenta y nueve **159**
Capítulo 4

DIFFERENTIATED INSTRUCTION

Digital resources such as the *Interactive Whiteboard* activity banks, *Videomodelos*, additional *Online Activities*, *Study Plans*, automatically graded *Leveled Workbook*, animated *Grammar Tutorials*, *Flashcards*, and *Vocabulary and Grammar Videos* will help you reach students of different ability levels and learning styles.

STUDENTS NEEDING EXTRA HELP

Guided Practice Activities
- Flashcards, pp. 118–120, 129–132
- Vocabulary Check, pp. 121–124, 133–136
- Grammar, pp. 125–128, 137–140

HERITAGE LEARNERS

Realidades para hispanohablantes
- Chapter Opener, pp. 108–109
- A primera vista, pp. 110–111, 120–121
- Manos a la obra, pp. 112–119, 122–129
- ¡Adelante!, pp. 130–135
- Repaso del capítulo, pp. 136–139

ADVANCED/PRE-AP*

Pre-AP* Resource Book,
- pp. 147–149

Communications Workbook
- Integrated Performance Assessment, p. 185

Vocabulario en contexto

Standards: 1.1, 1.2

Resources: Teacher's Resource Book: Input Script, p. 210, Clip Art, pp. 229–235, Audio Script, p. 214; Voc. and Gram. Transparencies 88–89; Audio Program DVD: Cap. 4, Tracks 1, 3

Focus: Presenting new vocabulary and using grammar lexically in context

Suggestions: You may want to use the Input Script from the *Teacher's Resource Book* as a source of ideas for presentation of new vocabulary and comprehensible input. Many meanings for the vocabulary in this lesson must be taught either via situations or by explanation. When explaining, use Spanish that students will readily understand:

Una persona egoísta sólo piensa en sí misma.

La joven de la foto es honesta, ¿verdad? Devuelve a su amigo el dinero que dejó caer.

1 Standards: 1.2

Resources: Teacher's Resource Book: Audio Script, p. 214; Audio Program DVD: Cap. 4, Track 2; Answer Keys: Student Edition, p. 50

Focus: Practicing listening comprehension of new vocabulary

Suggestions: Before playing the audio or reading the script aloud, allow students to read over the selections for each item. Make sure they understand they will be drawing a conclusion about each speaker's personality.

Answers:

1. b	4. a
2. b	5. a
3. b	6. b

Block Schedule

In pairs, have students write a sentence describing each of the personality traits on p. 160. Have them work with another pair, reading the descriptions to the other students who must guess the new vocabulary word.

160

▶ Read, listen to, and understand information about
• love and friendship
• personality traits

Vocabulario en contexto

¿Cuántas personas conoces en la escuela? ¿Cuántos amigos tienes? ¿Cómo te relacionas con ellos? Pueden ser muchas o pocas, pero no todas las personas que conoces son tus amigos. Los amigos son el mejor regalo que podemos recibir. ¡Ojalá que tengas muchos amigos!

Un(a) buen(a) amigo(a) es . . .

Un(a) buen(a) amigo(a) no es . . .

cariñosa(o)

Te comprendo.

comprensivo(a)

honesta(o)

egoísta

celoso(a)

vanidosa(o)

entrometido(a)

chismosa(o)

▼1 Todo el mundo dice . . . | ◄»)

Escuchar

Escucha lo que opinan algunos(as) chicos(as) sobre sus compañeros(as) y escoge la palabra que mejor describa cómo son.

1. Antonio es
   a. celoso　　b. generoso

2. Mónica es
   a. chismosa　　b. comprensiva

3. Francisco es
   a. honesto　　b. cariñoso

4. Luis es
   a. vanidoso　　b. entrometido

5. Irene es
   a. honesta　　b. egoísta

6. Mario es
   a. generoso　　b. egoísta

DIFFERENTIATED INSTRUCTION

Students with Learning Difficulties

Invite students to summarize what is happening in each picture on p. 160 and to use this summary to figure out the meaning of each vocabulary word. For example: *La mujer abraza y le sonríe al niño. Creo que "cariñoso(a)" quiere decir* nice o caring.

Advanced Learners

Ask pairs of students to stretch their creativity by preparing two different pantomimes that show the meaning of each vocabulary item on this page. Have pairs present their pantomimes in random order. Those watching must guess which characteristic the partners are trying to portray.

La amistad y el amor son temas muy importantes entre los estudiantes de la escuela Las Américas en Montevideo, Uruguay. Averigua qué piensan algunos estudiantes sobre estos temas.

1 "Un amigo es alguien en quien puedes **confiar** o que sabe **guardar** bien **un secreto**. Es alguien que **se alegra** contigo en los momentos felices y **te apoya** en los momentos tristes. En pocas palabras, es alguien que se preocupa por ti".
Ricardo Rodríguez

2 "Para mí la amistad es muy importante. Mis amigos y yo **tenemos mucho en común**. Nos gusta el cine y el fútbol. Por eso lo pasamos muy bien **juntos**. También nos tenemos **confianza** para contarnos nuestros problemas. **Espero** que seamos amigos para toda la vida".
Teresa Soto

3 "Mi mejor amiga es muy **sincera**. A veces **me sorprende** cuando dice lo que realmente piensa. Pero yo sé que es muy **considerada** y que trata de no lastimar mis sentimientos con sus opiniones".
Celina Lugo

4 "Mis compañeros y yo nos llevamos bien, pero sólo dos de ellos, Julián y Mario, son mis amigos **íntimos**. Nos conocemos desde niños y sé que puedo **contar con** ellos para todo. A veces **temo** que nuestra amistad se rompa porque soy un poco chismoso. Pero mis amigos me dicen que no **desconfían** de mí. Me alegro de que me **acepten tal como soy**".
Raúl Gutiérrez

▼2 **El (La) profesor(a) ideal**

Escribir • Hablar

¿Cuáles son para ti las cinco cualidades (qualities) más importantes que debe tener un(a) buen(a) profesor(a)? Haz una lista e intercámbiala con tus compañeros(as).

ciento sesenta y uno **161**
Capítulo 4

ENRICH YOUR TEACHING

Culture Note
Explain that, as in the United States, Spanish-speaking people have varying attitudes toward punctuality. Some are sticklers and others have a more relaxed attitude. Arriving "fashionably late" to social occasions is usually considered acceptable behavior and rarely causes annoyance.

21st Century Skills

Technology Literacy Have students research social networks that use Spanish as the target language. What keywords will they use in their search? Which social networks are most popular in different parts of the Spanish-speaking world? How do they compare to the social networks they use?

Vocabulario en contexto

Core Instruction

Standards: 1.1, 1.2

Resources: Teacher's Resource Book: Input Script, p. 211, Clip Art, pp. 229–235, Audio Script, pp. 214–215; Voc. and Gram. Transparency 90; Audio Program DVD: Cap. 4, Track 4

Focus: Extending presentation of vocabulary and grammar in the context of a friendship survey

Suggestions:

Pre-reading: Tell students that the survey is much like those they have probably seen in teen and fashion magazines. If possible, display another example of such a magazine survey. Clarify the meaning of **tener celos** and **cambias de opinión** using explanation or pantomime, or by setting up a situation. For **cualidades** and **amable**, point out the English cognates "qualities" and "amiable." Have students copy the answer grid to their own paper before taking the survey.

Reading: Allow students time to read the twenty questions silently. Then play the audio or read the information aloud, with students reading along and marking their answers on their papers as they listen. In order to make the survey more interesting and enjoyable, postpone reading the *Resultados* section until students have completed the survey.

Post-reading: Have students use the completed survey as a vehicle for a discussion about friendship. Ask: *¿Estás de acuerdo con estas cualidades para ser un buen amigo? Explica tus respuestas. ¿Crees que hay otras cualidades que deben formar parte de esta prueba?*

Pre-AP* Support

- **Learning Objective:** Interpersonal Writing
- **Activity:** Have students write an e-mail to a good friend in which they express how much they value his or her friendship. Use the card in Activity 3 as a model.
- *Pre-AP* Resource Book:* Comprehensive guide to Pre-AP* writing skill development, pp. 27–38

Chapter Project

Give students copies of the Chapter Project outline and rubric from the *Teacher's Resource Book.* Explain the task to them, and have them perform Step 1. (For more information, see p. 154-b.)

Prueba de la amistad

Anímate a hacer la prueba de la amistad y averigua si tienes cualidades como amigo(a).

¿Sabes ser amigo(a)?

1. ¿Eres considerado(a) con los demás?
2. Cuando te peleas, ¿te quedas enojado(a) poco tiempo?
3. Si haces un error, ¿dices "lo siento"?
4. ¿Te llevas bien con muchas personas?
5. ¿Tratas de ser amable y de ayudar a la gente?
6. ¿Te parece tonto tener celos de tu mejor amigo(a)?
7. ¿Sabes escuchar a la gente?
8. ¿Cambias de opinión frecuentemente?
9. Si dos amigos(as) tienen un secreto, ¿tratas de guardarlo(a) y no ser entrometido(a)?
10. Si un(a) amigo(a) no sabe qué hacer, ¿tratas de darle un buen consejo?

	Sí	No
1		
2		
3		
4		
5		
6		
7		
8		
9		
10		
Total		

Resultados

Por cada sí que respondiste, cuenta dos puntos.

Entre 15 y 20 puntos: Sabes ser un(a) buen(a) amigo(a). Eres una persona muy generosa y eso hace que tus amigos(as) te quieran.

Entre 10 y 15 puntos: Tienes muchas cosas que son necesarias para ser un(a) buen(a) amigo(a), pero también algunas que no te permiten tener amistad con algunas personas. Prefieres que tus amigos(as) piensen y sean como tú. Es mejor que seas comprensivo(a) y te preocupes más por los demás.

Menos de 10 puntos: Te es difícil tener amigos(as). Eres un poco egoísta y no haces muchos esfuerzos por llevarte bien con los demás. Recuerda que la amistad es un regalo y es mejor que cambies un poco.

162 ciento sesenta y dos
A primera vista 1

DIFFERENTIATED INSTRUCTION

Students with Learning Difficulties

Use the *Resultados* section of the *Prueba de la amistad* to review the subjunctive in context. Ask students to identify where the subjunctive is used. Challenge them to explain why the subjunctive is used in these cases and assist as needed.

Advanced Learners

Invite students to evaluate how well the questions in the *Prueba de la amistad* indicate whether or not a person is a good friend. Ask when a *no* answer might not necessarily indicate a poor quality in a friend. Encourage students to suggest other questions to add to the test.

▼3 Para mi mejor amiga . . . | (Talk!)

Leer • Hablar

Lee la tarjeta que Elena le mandó a Clarita y responde a las preguntas siguientes.

1. ¿Te parece que Elena y Clarita son buenas amigas? ¿Por qué?
2. Según lo que dice en la tarjeta, ¿te parece que Clarita es chismosa? ¿Por qué?
3. ¿Qué hizo Clarita que muestra su amistad por Elena?
4. ¿Qué hizo Elena que muestra su amistad por Clarita?

Para alguien que es...

buena, cariñosa, sincera, considerada, amable, honesta, comprensiva, divertida, generosa...

...y lo más importante de todo, ¡ES MI MEJOR AMIGA!

Querida Clarita:

Gracias por tus consejos y por guardar mi secreto. Para mí tu amistad es muy importante y tú siempre me apoyas cuando tengo un problema.
¡Eres la mejor amiga del mundo!

Besos,
Elena

▼4 ¿Lógico o no? | (Talk!) | ◀))

Escuchar • Escribir • Hablar

❶ En una hoja de papel escribe los números del 1 al 6. Escucha las frases y junto a cada número escribe si la frase es lógica o no. Si la frase no es lógica, corrígela.

❷ Escribe cinco frases que no sean lógicas sobre la amistad. Léeselas a tu compañero(a). Tu compañero(a) debe corregirlas para que sean lógicas.

Más práctica	(GO)
realidades.com | print	
Instant Check	✔	
Guided WB pp. 118–124	✔	✔
Core WB pp. 51–52	✔	✔
Comm. WB p. 54	✔	✔
Hispanohablantes WB pp. 110–111	✔	

ciento sesenta y tres **163**
Capítulo 4

Language Input ④

3 Standards: 1.1, 1.2

Resources: Answer Keys: Student Edition, p. 51

Focus: Demonstrating reading comprehension of a friendship card and personal message

Suggestions: Read the card and have students answer the questions on their own first. Then have them discuss their work with a partner.

Answers:
1. Sí. (Reasons will vary.)
2. No. Clarita le guardó un secreto a Elena.
3. Le guardó un secreto, le dio consejos y siempre la apoya cuando tiene un problema.
4. Le mandó la tarjeta y le dijo que era su mejor amiga.

4 Standards: 1.1, 1.2, 1.3

Resources: Teacher's Resource Book: Audio Script, p. 215; Audio Program DVD: Cap. 4, Track 5; Answer Keys: Student Edition, p. 51

Focus: Practicing listening comprehension and writing

Suggestions: Tell students they will be listening to statements about personal qualities. Allow them to listen to the audio more than once. If students have difficulty writing the illogical statements in Step 2, suggest that they begin with a logical statement and change either the verb or the quality in order to make it illogical.

Answers:
1. ilógica
2. lógica
3. lógica
4. ilógica
5. ilógica
6. lógica

ENRICH YOUR TEACHING

Teacher-to-Teacher

Invite students to use the materials of their choice, including computers, to create cards or e-cards. Their cards can be on any theme, including birthday, thank you, get well, or friendship. Encourage each student to have a friend or relative in mind as he or she makes the card, and to send it to that person.

21st Century Skills

Critical Thinking and Problem Solving
Working in small groups, have students analyze the survey and set the items in order of importance. Which one would be, in their opinion, the most important quality for being a good friend? Which one would not be as important? Why? Have the groups compare their answers after their discussion.

✔ASSESSMENT

Prueba: Comprensión del vocabulario 1
• Prueba 4-1: pp. 83–84

163

▶ Read and write about relationships and personality traits
▶ Discuss friendships and family relationships
▶ Talk about your views of friendship and those of young people in Spain

INTERACTIVE WHITEBOARD
Vocabulary Activities 4-1

Vocabulario en uso

5 Standards: 1.2

Resources: Answer Keys: Student Edition, p. 51

Focus: Demonstrating comprehension of new vocabulary

Recycle: Subjunctive forms

Suggestions: Remind students that the items, when put together, form a letter. Tell them to scan all the items first, so that they understand the situation before attempting to complete the activity.

Answers:

1. Me preocupa
2. Es una lástima
3. Es una lástima
4. Me enoja
5. Espero
6. Es triste
7. Ojalá
8. Espero

▼5 Una carta para alguien que fue mi amigo | ♻

Leer • Escribir

Federico y Roberto eran amigos íntimos hasta que se pelearon. Roberto no confía en los consejos de Federico. Cree que está celoso por su relación con Teresa, que es amiga de los dos. Lee estas frases de una carta que le escribió Federico a Roberto. Escoge las palabras que completan mejor cada frase.

1. (*Me preocupa / Me alegro de*) que no me aceptes tal como soy.
2. (*Es una lástima / Me alegro de*) que desconfíes de mí.
3. (*Es una lástima / Es bueno*) que no me comprendas.
4. (*Me alegro de / Me enoja*) que siempre cambies de opinión.
5. (*Me sorprende / Espero*) que sepas que no tengo celos.
6. (*Es triste / Es bueno*) que no nos llevemos bien.
7. (*Me alegro de / Ojalá*) que no rompamos nuestra amistad.
8. (*Espero / Temo*) que todos salgamos juntos otra vez.

6 Standards: 1.1

Resources: Answer Keys: Student Edition, p. 52

Focus: Practicing new vocabulary in guided conversations

Suggestions: Point out to students that the picture clues are only to elicit the various personality traits. Student B's response can be affirmative or negative. Encourage Student B to respond honestly.

Make sure students switch roles, so everyone has a chance to practice both parts of the dialogue.

Answers:

Student B's responses will vary. The following are possibilities for Student A's questions:

1. —Eres generoso(a), ¿verdad?
2. —... comprensivo(a), ...
3. —... honesto(a), ...
4. —... egoísta/vanidoso(a), ...
5. —... chismoso(a), ...

▼6 ¿Cómo te relacionas con los demás? |

Hablar

Trabaja con otro(a) estudiante para hablar de su relación con los amigos. Usen las ilustraciones.

 ▶ **Modelo**

A —*Eres cariñoso(a), ¿verdad?*
B —*¡Claro que sí!, soy muy cariñoso(a).*
o: —*No, no lo soy.*
o: —*Pues, sí, a veces.*

Estudiante A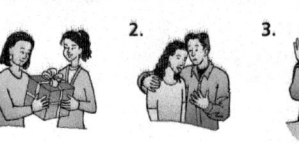

1. 2. 3. 4. 5.

Estudiante B

¡Respuesta personal!

Teacher-to-Teacher

Tell students they are moving to a new community and have been given the name of a teen who lives there. Have them write a letter to socialize with this person and to seek information about the community. They should give basic information about themselves. Have them exchange notes and write responses. Collect the notes for assessment.

DIFFERENTIATED INSTRUCTION

Multiple Intelligences

Bodily/Kinesthetic: Invite students to incorporate actions or gestures into their descriptions in *Actividad 6.*

Advanced Learners/Pre-AP*

Have students write a brief sketch of a character from a popular film or TV show. Ask them not to give away the title of the film or show or name the character, but to describe only his or her personality. Have students share their character sketches. Those listening can try to guess who the character is.

▼7 Amistad y cualidades | 💬👥 _____

Escribir • Hablar

① Escribe un verbo o una expresión que relacionas con cada una de estas cualidades.

Modelo
amable
ayudar a los demás

1. vanidoso(a)   3. entrometido(a)   5. sincero(a)
2. perezoso(a)   4. celoso(a)   6. considerado(a)

② Trabaja con otro(a) estudiante para hablar de las cualidades y verbos o expresiones que relacionas con la amistad.

▶ Modelo

A —¿*Te gusta estar con personas amables?*
B —*Sí, porque siempre se preocupan por los demás.*

③ Ahora tú y tu compañero(a) deben escoger una cualidad y escribir un párrafo sobre una persona que tenga esa cualidad.

Modelo

Luisa es muy amable porque . . .

▼ Ampliación del lenguaje

Familias de palabras

Las familias de palabras son grupos de palabras relacionadas *(related)* por tener una misma raíz. Conocer familias de palabras nos ayuda a comprender mejor el significado individual de cada palabra. Para ampliar tu vocabulario debes aprender a reconocer *(recognize)* palabras que tienen la misma raíz, por ejemplo, *celos* y *celoso*.

Lee las familias de palabras de la tabla. Piensa en palabras que conoces, que pertenecen a esas familias. Escribe en una hoja de papel las palabras que faltan para llenar los recuadros.

Luego, completa las frases utilizando la palabra correcta:

1. Carlos cuenta muchos _____, por eso todos dicen que es un _____.

Sustantivos	Adjetivos	Verbos
1. comprensión		comprender
2. alegría	alegre	
3. chisme	chismoso(a)	chismosear
4. consideración		considerar
5. sorpresa	sorprendido(a)	sorprenderse
6. reconciliación	reconciliado(a)	reconciliarse

2. Me encanta ir a las fiestas con María, pues es muy _____. Siempre me da _____ estar con ella.

3. Mi amigo se _____ mucho cuando le hicimos una fiesta _____.

ENRICH YOUR TEACHING

Teacher-to-Teacher

Consistent work with word families is an excellent way for students to increase their vocabularies on their own. Suggest that they devote an entire section of their notebooks to a word family chart like the one they began in the *Ampliación del lenguaje.* Each week, encourage them to spend a few minutes adding words they have learned to families that already exist on their chart or sitting with a dictionary and building new word families around words of their choice.

Practice and Communicate ④

▼7 Standards: 1.1, 1.3
Focus: Using new vocabulary and structures in conversation and writing

Suggestions: As students share their work in Step 2, encourage them to use additional verbs and expressions that pertain to each character trait. Point out that the more verbs and expressions they can think of, the more they will have to say about the person they write about in Step 3.

Answers will vary.

Ampliación del lenguaje
Core Instruction

Standards: 1.2, 3.1, 4.1

Resources: Answer Keys: Student Edition, p. 52

Focus: Understanding and using word families

Suggestions: Encourage students to copy the chart into their notebooks and make their additions there. Have them leave room, both horizontally and vertically, so they can add more word families and parts of speech at a later date.

Answers:

Chart
1. **comprensivo (a)**
2. **alegrar**
4. **considerado (a)**

Sentences
1. **chismes/chismoso**
2. **alegre/alegría**
3. **sorprendió/sorpresa**

Extension: Ask students to add a fourth column to their charts and title it ***Adverbios.*** Using background knowledge and dictionaries, have them work together to add adverbs to the word families on the chart. Model adding one adverb, such as ***sorprendentemente.*** Remind students that almost all Spanish adverbs end with the suffix **-mente.** Point out that not all word families in the chart will have an accompanying adverb.

▼8 Los jóvenes viéndose a sí mismos |

Leer • Hablar • Escribir

Se hizo la siguiente encuesta a jóvenes de España, para saber qué
piensan sobre las cualidades de sinceridad, solidaridad y generosidad.
Lee los resultados.

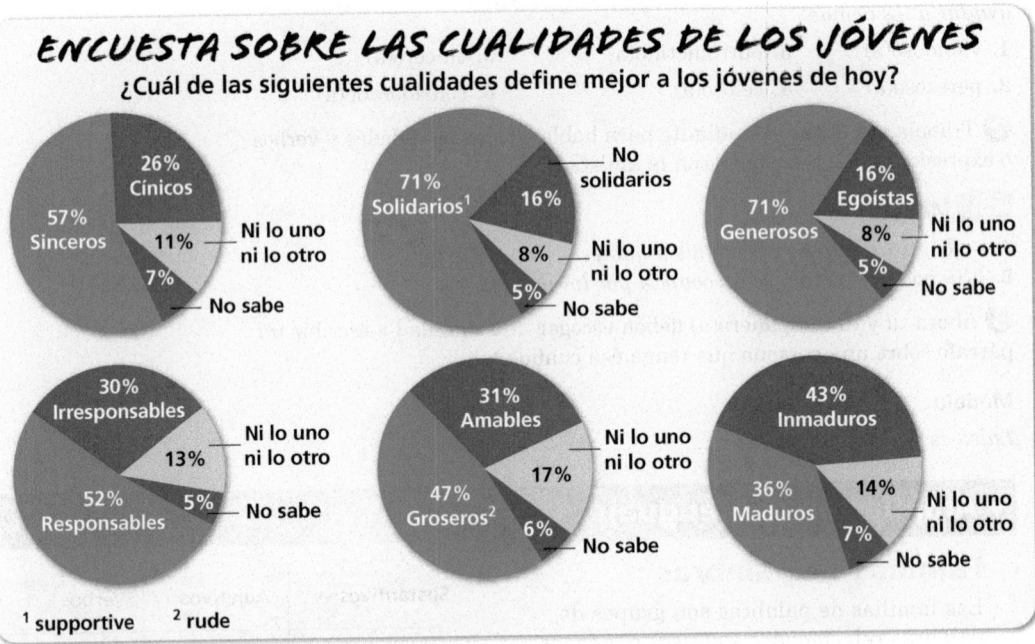

ENCUESTA SOBRE LAS CUALIDADES DE LOS JÓVENES
¿Cuál de las siguientes cualidades define mejor a los jóvenes de hoy?

- 26% Cínicos
- 57% Sinceros
- 11%
- 7%
- No sabe

- 71% Solidarios[1]
- No solidarios 16%
- 8% — Ni lo uno ni lo otro
- 5% — No sabe

- 16% Egoístas
- 71% Generosos
- 8% — Ni lo uno ni lo otro
- 5% — No sabe

- 30% Irresponsables
- 13% — Ni lo uno ni lo otro
- 52% Responsables
- 5% — No sabe

- 31% Amables
- Ni lo uno ni lo otro
- 47% Groseros[2]
- 17%
- 6% — No sabe

- 43% Inmaduros
- 36% Maduros
- 14% — Ni lo uno ni lo otro
- 7% — No sabe

[1] supportive   [2] rude

Conexiones | Las matemáticas

Trabaja con un grupo para hacer una encuesta a tus compañeros(as) y
comparar las respuestas de los jóvenes españoles con las de tu clase.

❶ Escojan un grupo de cualidades y pregúntenles a sus compañeros(as)
si piensan que describen a los jóvenes de hoy.

❷ Pasen los resultados a porcentajes para poder compararlos con la
encuesta española.

Recuerden que, para pasar los resultados de una encuesta a porcentajes,
deben seguir los siguientes pasos:

Tomar el número de respuestas que quieren convertir y dividirlo por el
número total de entrevistados. Luego, multiplicar el resultado por 100.

❸ Comenten los resultados de las encuestas. ¿Los jóvenes de España son
más o menos sinceros / solidarios / generosos que los de su clase?

BELLRINGER REVIEW

On the board, write numerical sentences
and have students read them aloud.
For example, "26 ÷ 100 = 0.26 (26%)"
reads: *Veintiséis dividido por cien son
cero punto veintiséis (o veintiséis por
ciento).*

8 Standards: 1.1, 1.2, 3.1, 3.2

Focus: Connecting new vocabulary and
structures to a math context through
surveys

Suggestions: For Step 1, have students
form questions to ask the class, such as
(for the first survey): *¿Te consideras una
persona sincera?* Have students answer
each question clearly, restating the
character trait to avoid confusion: *Sí, soy
sincero(a).* Have them write their answers
on blind ballots—folded slips of paper
collected in a hat or other container. Ask
volunteers to count the ballots for each
question and tally the results on the board.

Common Errors: Without guidance,
students would use the standard definite
articles **el** and **la** instead of the neutral
form **lo** in expressions like **ni lo uno ni lo
otro.** Use this opportunity to habituate
them to the sound and practice of using
the neutral **lo.**

Answers will vary.

DIFFERENTIATED INSTRUCTION

Students with Learning Difficulties
Prepare students to understand and manipulate
the information in the pie charts in *Actividad* 8.
Explain that each piece of a pie chart represents
a percentage or part of the total number of
responses. The total of all the pieces adds up
to 100 percent, which is represented by the
complete circle.

Advanced Learners
Once groups complete their surveys, invite
students to present visually the information
that they have collected. They might show
comparisons of percentages from each study
through bar graphs or other graphic organizers.

▼ Fondo Cultural | El mundo hispano

El Día de la Rosa y del Libro Muchas tradiciones de los países hispanohablantes celebran el amor y la amistad. Por ejemplo, en Cataluña, España, el 23 de abril se celebra el Día de la Rosa y del Libro. Ese día los chicos la regalan a su novia una rosa roja, y las chicas la regalan a su novio un libro.

En algunos países latinoamericanos el Día de San Valentín, en lugar de ser el "Día de los Enamorados", es el "Día de la Amistad", y los amigos y familiares se hacen regalos y se escriben postales.

• ¿Tú celebras un día del amor o de la amistad? ¿Cómo lo celebras?

• Dibuja una tarjeta de San Valentín para alguien especial.

Feliz Día de la Amistad

▼9 Retrato de una amistad

Escribir

Describe una relación muy importante para ti. Puede ser tu relación con un(a) amigo(a), un(a) primo(a), un familiar u otro adulto a quien quieras mucho. Describe cómo es esa amistad. Usa estos verbos como guía para escribir tu párrafo.

• conocerse
• escribirse
• contar con
• llamarse por teléfono
• enviarse mensajes electrónicos

• confiar
• apoyarse
• ayudarse
• llevarse bien
• tener en común

Modelo

Carlos y yo nos conocimos en . . . Vivíamos en el mismo barrio, pero cuando yo tenía 11 años, mi familia y yo tuvimos que irnos a . . . Ahora . . .

▼10 Un personaje

Escribir

Cuenta un hecho o describe a un personaje de un libro o película que sea un buen ejemplo de alguna de estas cualidades.

a. cariñoso(a)   **b.** chismoso(a)   **c.** comprensivo(a)   **d.** honesto(a)

Incluye:
• sus cualidades
• cómo trata a las otras personas
• ejemplos de sus acciones

Modelo

Uno de los personajes se llama Luis. Es muy amable, generoso y divertido. Sus amigos tienen mucha confianza en él.

ciento sesenta y siete **167**
Capítulo 4

Practice and Communicate   4

Fondo cultural

Standards: 1.1, 1.2, 4.2
Resources: Map Transparency 20
Suggestions: Have students locate *Cataluña* on *Map Transparency* 20. Ask: *¿Qué piensas de la costumbre del Día de la Rosa y del Libro? Imagínate que vives en Barcelona, España. ¿Te gustaría recibir un libro o una rosa en este día? ¿Cómo te sentirías?* Ask students what they think are the differences between Valentine's Day in the United States and in Latin America.

▼9 Standards: 1.3

Focus: Using new vocabulary and structures in writing
Suggestions: Remind students to use the present tense to describe the relationship and past tenses to tell about its history and how it developed.

▼10 Standards: 1.3

Focus: Using new vocabulary and structures to describe a fictional character
Suggestions: Ask students to share their descriptions.

Additional Resources

• Communication Wbk: Audio Act. 1, p. 50
• Teacher's Resource Book: Audio Script, p. 215, Communicative Pair Activity BLM, p. 221
• Audio Program DVD: Cap. 4, Track 6

ENRICH YOUR TEACHING

Teacher-to-Teacher

In some subtle ways, functioning in a foreign language is like becoming a slightly different person. By Spanish 3, some students are becoming aware of how careful attention to the demands of Spanish causes them to think in different ways. You may find students in your class who are capable of talking in Spanish about topics they would not normally broach in English. This can be one of the greatest rewards a student earns after several years of language study. Praise and encourage students who demonstrate this.

✓ASSESSMENT

Prueba 4-2 with Study Plan (online only)

Prueba: Aplicación del vocabulario 1
• Prueba 4-2: pp. 85–86

167

4 Practice and Communicate

Gramática Repaso

Core Instruction

Resources: Voc. and Gram. Transparency 91

INTERACTIVE WHITEBOARD
Grammar Activities 4-1

Suggestions: Have students use the phrases in sentences with the subjunctive. Reinforce the idea of using the subjunctive with verbs of emotion by having students "act out" the expressions.

11 Standards: 1.1, 1.2, 1.3

Resources: Teacher's Resource Book: Audio Script, p. 215; Audio Program DVD: Cap. 4, Track 7; Answer Keys: Student Edition, p. 53

Focus: Practicing the subjunctive

Suggestions: Have volunteers write their sentences on the board with all the markings.

Answers:

Step 1
1. Temo que Luis (vaya) solo a la fiesta.
2. Me preocupa que Carmen todavía no (esté) en su casa.
3. Espero alegrar a Renata con el regalo.
4. Siento no poder ir al cine con tus amigos.
5. Ojalá que me (acepten) tal como soy.

Step 2
1. subjuntivo después de un verbo de emoción con cambio de sujeto
2. subjuntivo después de un verbo de emoción con cambio de sujeto
3. infinitivo con un solo sujeto
4. infinitivo con un solo sujeto
5. subjuntivo después de la expresión de emoción *ojalá*

12 Standards: 1.2

Resources: Answer Keys: Student Edition, p. 53

Focus: Practicing the subjunctive

Suggestions: Have students scan the letter before writing their answers.

Answers:

1. sea
2. se cuenten
3. desconfíe
4. tenga
5. lleve
6. se sienta

168

Gramática

▼ Objectives
▶ Listen to a description of friendship
▶ Discuss emotions and problems in relationships
▶ Talk about the practice of shaking hands

El subjuntivo con verbos de emoción

As you already know, we use the subjunctive after verbs indicating suggestions, desire, or demands. The subjunctive is also used after verbs and impersonal phrases indicating emotion, such as *ojalá que, temo que, tengo miedo de que, me alegro de que, me molesta que, me sorprende que, siento que,* and *es triste que,* and *es bueno que,* among others. A sentence in the subjunctive mode has two parts, the main clause and the subordinate clause. Both clauses are connected by the word *que*.

Tememos que nuestros amigos **desconfíen** de nuestras palabras.

When the sentence has only one subject, we usually use the infinitive instead of the subjunctive.

Siento no **pasar** (yo) más tiempo con mis amigas.
Siento que ellas no **pasen** más tiempo conmigo.

Más ayuda **realidades.com** ▶*Canción de hip hop* ▶*Tutorial*

▼ 11 Una amiga muy cariñosa | _____

Escuchar • Escribir • Hablar • GramActiva

Alina es una amiga muy cariñosa, aunque a veces se preocupa demasiado por todos. Escribe los números del 1 al 5 en una hoja de papel. Presta atención a lo que dice Alina y escribe las frases que escuchas.

❶ Subraya con una línea los verbos en indicativo en cada frase. Subraya con dos líneas los verbos en infinitivo y encierra en un círculo los verbos en subjuntivo.

❷ Explica por qué se usó el infinitivo, el indicativo o el subjuntivo.

▼ 12 Una relación complicada _____

Leer • Escribir

Soledad, una joven chilena, le escribió una carta a la consejera sentimental de una revista para jóvenes. Soledad se está llevando muy mal con su hermana y no sabe qué hacer. Completa la carta con el subjuntivo de los verbos del recuadro.

ser	desconfiar	sentirse
contarse	tener	llevar

Querida Consejera:
Te escribo porque mi hermana Tatiana y yo nos estamos llevando muy mal. Me preocupa que nuestra relación ya no __1.__ como antes. Creo que es importante que dos hermanas __2.__ sus problemas y sus secretos. Pero ahora temo que ella __3.__ de mí. Tatiana tiene doce años. Yo tengo quince años. A ella le molesta que yo __4.__ otros amigos de mi edad y no le gusta que yo no la __5.__ con nosotros cada vez que salimos. Es una lástima que ella __6.__ celosa de mis amigos. ¿Qué me aconsejas?

DIFFERENTIATED INSTRUCTION

Students with Learning Difficulties
Prepare students for the discussion of main and subordinate clauses with the subjunctive. On the board, write English sentences, such as *She's angry that you're late. I'm afraid that we have bad news.* Explain the concepts of subject and verb and point them out in each clause.

Advanced Learners
Ask students to write the impersonal phrases that indicate emotion (see *Actividad* 13) on slips of paper and place them in a hat or other container. They can make several duplicate slips for each phrase. Have students sit in a circle and take turns drawing a phrase and using it in a sentence with the subjunctive.

13 Díganlo de dos maneras |

Hablar

Trabaja con un(a) compañero(a) para hablar de las relaciones con sus amigos. Tú dices frases generales usando el infinitivo y tu compañero(a) te contesta usando el subjuntivo.

▶ **Modelo**

importante / guardar secretos
me molesta / mi amigo(a) no . . .
A —*Es importante guardar secretos.*
B —*Sí, y me molesta que mi amigo(a) no guarde mis secretos.*

Estudiante A

1. bueno / tener mucho en común con los amigos
2. malo / tener celos de los amigos
3. importante / aceptar a los demás tal como son
4. triste / desconfiar de los amigos íntimos
5. difícil / tener buenas relaciones con los amigos

Estudiante B

a. siento / mi amigo(a) y yo no . . .
b. me sorprende / mi amigo(a) . . .
c. me preocupa / tú no me . . .
d. siento / mi amigo(a) . . .
e. ojalá / todos nosotros . . .

14 Apoya a tus amigos |

Escribir • Hablar

❶ Con un(a) compañero(a) hagan una lista de ocho problemas que generalmente ocurren entre amigos o familiares.

Modelo
se pelean

❷ Habla con tu compañero(a) de los problemas que incluyeron en la lista. Tu compañero(a) va a responder a cada problema con una expresión de emoción. Luego intercambien papeles.

▶ **Modelo**

A —*Siempre me peleo con [nombre], él (ella) no me entiende.*
B —*Siento mucho que él (ella) no te entienda.*

15 Standards: 1.1, 1.3

Focus: Using the subjunctive in interviews and oral presentations

Suggestions: Ask the student pairs to prepare the chart on their own paper and to work out any comprehension problems they have with the questions in Step 1, before they interview classmates.

Answers will vary.

16 Standards: 1.1, 1.2, 3.1

Focus: Reading about and discussing the custom of the handshake and its origins

Suggestions: After students have read the information once, ask them to list the cognates that helped them understand the reading. They should mention words such as *personas, historiadores, estatua,* and *costumbre.*

Answers will vary.

▼15 ¿Qué te parece?

Escribir • Hablar

❶ Trabaja con un(a) compañero(a) para entrevistar a cuatro estudiantes con las siguientes preguntas. Copien la tabla y complétenla con las respuestas de sus compañeros(as).

• ¿Cómo te gusta que sea tu mejor amigo(a)?

• ¿Qué no te gusta que haga tu mejor amigo(a)?

• ¿Qué te preocupa que opinen tus amigos(as) de ti?

• ¿Qué puede destruir una amistad?

• ¿Cuál es tu mejor cualidad como amigo(a)?

❷ Luego, preparen una presentación para hacer ante la clase. Basándose en los resultados de la encuesta, expliquen qué cualidades y acciones pueden ayudar a una amistad o destruirla.

	Marisa	Rafa	Luis	Ana
¿Cómo te gusta que sea...?	generoso(a), comprensivo(a)			
¿Qué no te gusta...?	que no me tenga confianza			
¿Qué te preocupa...?				
¿Qué puede destruir...?				
¿Cuál es tu mejor...?				

▼16 Dar la mano

Leer • Hablar

¿Sabes de dónde sale la costumbre de dar la mano para saludarse? Lee este artículo para enterarte.

Conexiones | Las ciencias sociales

Nadie sabe realmente cuándo o por qué las personas comenzaron a darse la mano para saludarse. Algunos historiadores creen que todo comenzó hace 3800 años, en Babilonia. El primer día de cada año, el rey tenía que "darle la mano" a la estatua de un dios para recibir el poder *(power)*.

Otros piensan que la costumbre comenzó por otra razón. Dicen que cuando dos desconocidos se encontraban en un camino o en un lugar fuera de la ciudad, se daban la mano derecha para mostrar que no tenían armas. En esos tiempos, como las mujeres no usaban armas, sólo los hombres se daban la mano.

• ¿Cómo saludas a tus amigos? ¿Y a tus familiares? ¿Les das la mano? ¿Cuándo le das la mano a alguien y cuándo lo (la) abrazas?

• ¿Conoces otros gestos o palabras de saludo? ¿Sabes cuál es su origen? Explícalo a la clase.

Más práctica GO

realidades.com | print

Instant Check	✔	
Guided WB pp. 125–126	✔	✔
Core WB p. 53	✔	✔
Comm. WB p. 55	✔	✔
Hispanohablantes WB pp. 112–117	✔	

170 ciento setenta
Manos a la obra 1

DIFFERENTIATED INSTRUCTION

Heritage Language Learners

Ask students to talk about how their family members use handshakes, kisses, or hugs to greet each other and friends, or to say good-bye. Encourage them to compare these practices with greeting and leave-taking customs in the United States.

Students with Learning Difficulties

Refer students to the list of uses for *por* and *para* as they complete *Actividad* 17. Encourage them to identify the point that explains each use of *por* and *para.*

Gramática Repaso

▼ Objectives
▶ Write and talk about friendship
▶ Discuss a conflict from different points of view

Los usos de *por* y *para*

Both *por* and *para* are prepositions. Their usages are quite different.

Use *por* to indicate:

- length of time or distance

    Estuvieron discutiendo **por** una hora.

- place where an action takes place

    Ayer caminamos **por** el parque.

- an exchange

    Cambiamos la silla vieja **por** una nueva.

- reason or motive

    Se pelearon **por** un programa de televisión.

- substitution or action on someone's behalf

    Los padres hacen mucho **por** sus hijos.

- means of communication / transportation

    Ayer hablé con Analía **por** teléfono.

Also use *por* in certain expressions:

por ejemplo	por lo general
por la mañana (tarde, noche)	por primera (segunda, tercera) vez
por favor	por supuesto
por eso	

Use *para* to indicate:

- purpose (in order to)

    Salí temprano **para** ver a mis amigos.

- destination

    En unos minutos nos vamos **para** la playa.

- a point in time, deadline

    Debemos terminar el trabajo **para** el lunes.

- use, purpose

    Las tijeras sirven **para** cortar.

- opinion

    Para mí, no hay nada mejor que viajar.

Más ayuda   **realidades.com**   ▶ **Tutorial**

▼17 Cosas de amigas

Leer • Escribir

Dos amigas están hablando. Completa las frases con *por* o *para*, según el contexto.

A —¡Claro que sí!   **1.**   supuesto que quiero ir a la fiesta. Mañana   **2.**   la tarde vamos a llamar a los chicos   **3.**   ver si quieren ir con nosotras.

B —¿Qué te parece si hacemos la tarea de español antes? No quiero perderme la fiesta   **4.**   tener que estudiar.

A —Sí, podemos pasar   **5.**   la casa de Anita   **6.**   preparar la tarea todas juntas.

▼18 Por dónde y para qué |

Escribir • Hablar

Escribe una descripción de un viaje que hiciste y léela a un(a) compañero(a). Usa *por* y *para*. Habla de:

- tiempo
- lugar
- razón o motivo
- destino
- medio de transporte
- uso

Modelo

Viajamos a Canadá por tren. Fuimos para . . .

Practice and Communicate (4)

Gramática Repaso

Core Instruction

Standards: 4.1

Resources: Voc. and Gram. Transparency 92

INTERACTIVE WHITEBOARD
Grammar Activities 4-1

Suggestions: Encourage students to think of other ways to help remember some of the uses of **por** and **para.** As an example, point out that in general, when they want to say "in order to," the Spanish word they use is **para;** when they want to say "by," the word is **por.**

▼17 Standards: 1.2

Resources: Answer Keys: Student Edition, p. 54

Focus: Practicing **por** and **para** in a cloze exercise

Suggestions: Ask volunteers to supply other sample sentences for each of the usage rules for **por** and **para.**

Answers:

1. Por	3. para	5. por
2. por	4. por	6. para

▼18 Standards: 1.3

Focus: Practicing **por** and **para** via sentence writing

Suggestions: Ask students to read their completed sentences aloud in random order. Listeners can say the rule behind each use of **por** and **para.**

ENRICH YOUR TEACHING

Culture Note

For most Spanish speakers, a greeting includes saying hello as well as some physical gesture. Shaking hands is common. Women often kiss each other on the cheek. Men and women who are close friends or family also often hug and give a light kiss on the cheek.

21st Century Skills

Social and Cross-Cultural Skills Have students identify how people of different cultures use different gestures or oral expressions to greet each other or say good-bye. Do they use handshakes, hugs, or kisses? What are common expressions between friends, family members, or work associates? Have students incorporate the new gestures or Spanish expressions they learn into their interactions with their classmates.

Pre-AP* Support

- **Learning Objective:** Presentational Writing
- **Activity:** Have students write an imaginative (perhaps nonsensical) story about an incident that occurs between two friends. The story should highlight vocabulary learned in this chapter and—as a primary requirement—use *por* and/or *para* a minimum of five times. Have students share their stories.
- **Pre-AP* Resource Book:** Comprehensive guide to Pre-AP* writing skill development, pp. 27–38

BELLRINGER REVIEW

Review *gustar* with various combinations of subjects and indirect object pronouns. On the board, write a model such as *A mí me gustan las galletitas.* Ask students to point out the subject *(las galletitas)* and the indirect object pronoun *(me).* Tell students you will use pictures to cue these two parts of the sentence. Use transparencies or pictures from books or magazines as visual cues. Display different combinations of pictures to elicit sentences such as *A ellas les gusta la película; A nosotros nos gustan los coches,* and so on.

19 Standards: 1.1, 1.3

Focus: Practicing *por* and *para* in sentence completions

Suggestions: Remind students to write all their sentences about the same two real or imaginary people, so that the completed activity creates a story. If they opt to write about real people they know, ask them to be considerate and sensitive to the feelings of others.

Answers will vary.

Extension: Ask students to develop their completed sentences into a comic strip about the two friends.

20 Standards: 1.1, 1.3, 3.1

Focus: Using the subjunctive in traded dictations and writing

Suggestions: Allow students time to figure out individually what they plan to say for Step 1. This will ensure that they use varied and original ideas. As they fill out the Venn diagram in Step 2, have them check to see how well their partner took down the dictation and make any necessary corrections.

Answers will vary.

▼19 Por eso, para ellos . . . |

Hablar • Escribir

Trabaja con un(a) compañero(a). Inventen una historia entre dos amigos(as) imaginarios(as) completando estas frases.

- Por lo general, ellos se divierten . . .
- La semana pasada se pelearon por . . .
- Estuvieron discutiendo por . . .
- Para [nombre] es importante . . .
- Por eso, (no) les gusta . . .
- Para llevarse bien necesitan . . .
- Por supuesto, no siempre . . .

▼20 ¿Tienes buenos amigos? |

Hablar • Escribir

❶ Trabaja con un(a) compañero(a). Completa las frases para decir lo que piensas de tus amigos(as), mientras tu compañero(a) las escribe. Luego, tu compañero(a) completa las frases y tú las escribes.

1. Me alegro de que . . .
2. Es una lástima que . . .
3. Me preocupa que . . .
4. Me parece importante que . . .
5. Me gusta que . . .

6. Es bueno que . . .
7. Quiero que . . .
8. Temo que . . .
9. ¡Ojalá que mis amigos(as) siempre . . . !
10. Es verdad que . . .

❷ Completen el diagrama de Venn con lo que piensan.

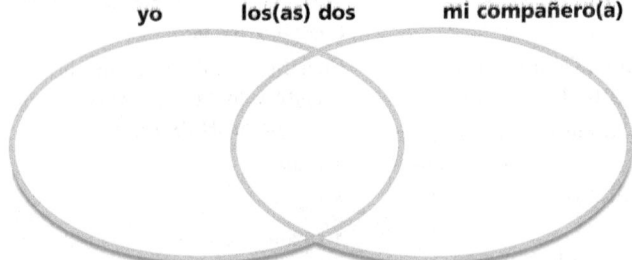

yo   los(as) dos   mi compañero(a)

❸ Escriban un breve *(short)* informe con la información de su diagrama de Venn.

Modelo
Mi compañera Marisa y yo hablamos sobre la amistad. Las dos nos alegramos de tener muchos amigos.

DIFFERENTIATED INSTRUCTION

Students with Learning Difficulties

As students complete *Actividad* 19, model correct forms for completing the sentences. For example: *Por lo general, ellos se divierten jugando con su gato/nadando en el lago/ jugando cartas.* Ask students to follow your model but change the content of the message.

Advanced Learners

Ask students to invent personal bios for a dating service. Their bios should use the new vocabulary and the subjunctive to provide a character sketch of an imaginary person and to explain what he or she wants and expects out of a relationship.

21 ¡No me vas a creer . . . !

Leer • Escribir • Hablar

Muchas veces, cuando hay un problema entre amigos(as), cada persona cree que tiene la razón. Por eso, es mejor escuchar lo que tiene que decir la otra persona.

1 Lee los relatos que hacen Luis y Manuel del mismo problema y contesta las preguntas.

1. ¿Por qué crees que Luis está tan enojado?
2. ¿Te parece sincero el relato que hace Manuel?
3. ¿Qué crees que debió hacer cada uno de los cuatro personajes para evitar este problema?
4. ¿Qué deben hacer ahora para resolver el problema que tienen?

Según Luis...

> Manuel era mi amigo más íntimo hasta ayer, pero me di cuenta de que es un entrometido. Ya no puedo confiar en él. Mi prima Laura me dijo que Manuel fue a pasear ayer con Clara, mi novia, y que los vio abrazándose. Lo llamé y le dije que estaba sorprendido de saber que salió con mi novia y que temo que nuestra amistad se rompa.

Según Manuel...

> Me sorprende que Luis esté celoso de mí. Él sabe que somos amigos desde primer grado, que nos contamos nuestros secretos y nos apoyamos en todo. ¿Cómo puede sentir celos de mí? Clara me llamó porque quería pedirme un consejo sobre un problema que tenía. Ella es muy cariñosa y al saludarnos nos abrazamos, como siempre lo hacemos. Me preocupa que este problema pueda terminar con nuestra amistad.

2 Escribe una frase sobre cada uno de los cuatro personajes que participan en la historia, usando las palabras del recuadro.

cariñoso(a)	celoso(a)	entrometido(a)
comprensivo(a)	honesto(a)	sincero(a)

3 Imagina que eres Clara. Relata lo que sucedió desde su punto de vista.

Modelo

No me gusta que Luis esté enojado. Yo llamé a Manuel para hablar sobre un problema que tuve . . .

Más práctica GO

realidades.com | print

Instant Check	✔	
Guided WB pp. 127–128	✔	✔
Core WB pp. 54–55	✔	✔
Comm. WB pp. 50, 56–57, 183	✔	✔
Hispanohablantes WB pp. 118–119		✔

ciento setenta y tres **173**
Capítulo 4

Practice and Communicate 4

21 Standards: 1.2, 1.3

Focus: Using new vocabulary and structures to read, talk, and write

Suggestions: After students have read the two accounts silently in Step 1, ask volunteers to read each one aloud. For Step 2, point out that some of the words might be used in sentences in the indicative mood describing the people; others might be used in sentences with the subjunctive, suggesting how the people should act. Have students read their completed sentences aloud and elaborate on them orally. For Step 3, have students read aloud their completed accounts by Clara.

Chapter Project

Students can perform Step 3 at this point. (For more information, see p. 154-b.)

Block Schedule

Have students write a short note to a personal advice columnist describing a "personal problem." Have them sign using a fake name. Collect the questions and distribute them to different students. Each student is to write a response and then read the question and response aloud.

Additional Resources

• Communication Wbk.: Audio Act. 2, p. 50
• Teacher's Resource Book: Audio Script, p. 215, Communicative Pair Activity BLM, pp. 222–223
• Audio Program DVD: Cap. 4, Track 8

ENRICH YOUR TEACHING

Teacher-to-Teacher

Students will learn to use prepositions more quickly if you embed the practice in a humorous context. For **por** and **para,** suggest that pairs of students prepare and present humorous dialogues in which they use the two words as often and as creatively as possible.

21st Century Skills

Critical Thinking and Problem Solving Have students analyze the problem between Luis and Manuel in *Actividad* 21. Imagine they are playing the role of a judge in a dispute between the two friends. Have them ask a question to Luis and to Manuel to better clarify each friend's point of view, then propose a solution.

✔ ASSESSMENT

Prueba 4-4 with Study Plan (online only)

Prueba: Los usos de *por* y *para*
• Prueba 4-4: p. 88

Examen: Vocabulario y gramática 1
• Examen 1: pp. 89–91
• ExamView: Examen 1

173

▶ Read, listen to, and understand information about
- conflicts and how to resolve them
- friends and family relationships

Vocabulario en contexto

Core Instruction

Standards: 1.1, 1.2, 3.1

Resources: Teacher's Resource Book: Input Script, p. 212, Clip Art, pp. 229–235, Audio Script, pp. 215–216; Voc. and Gram. Transparency 93; Audio Program DVD: Cap. 4, Track 9

Focus: Presenting new vocabulary and using grammar lexically in context

Suggestions: Refer students to the *Estrategia*. Have them respond to the questions there by talking about the pictures and writing down their predictions about the story. Then allow students time to read the presentation silently. Have students revisit the predictions they made about the story. Ask questions such as the following: *¿Todas tus predicciones resultaron correctas? ¿Qué partes del cuento son distintas de tus predicciones?*

BELLRINGER REVIEW

Have students look at the photo on page 169 and write a short dialogue.

Block Schedule

Divide students into pairs. Assign each group a scene to reenact from p. 175. You might assign each pair scene 3, 4, or 5 so that all the scenes are covered. Have them practice and then reenact the scene in front of the class. Remind them to focus on intonation, expression, and correct pronunciation.

Vocabulario en contexto

¿Qué pasa cuando se rompe la **armonía** de una amistad por causa de **un malentendido**? Lee este cuento para ver cómo **resolvieron** sus problemas estos jóvenes.

Estrategia

Using illustrations to predict the outcome
Before reading a text, look at the illustrations. What do you think is going to happen? What details in the illustrations support your prediction? After reading, compare your prediction with what happened at the end of the story.

1 Julio y Andrés eran amigos íntimos. Tenían mucho en común, por ejemplo, a los dos les gustaba mucho el fútbol. Un día se enteraron de que la entrenadora buscaba un nuevo capitán del equipo. Los dos amigos querían ser capitán.

Ojalá que sea yo, pero si escoge a Andrés, lo voy a apoyar en todo.

Espero que me escoja a mí.

2 Al día siguiente, Andrés se encontró con la entrenadora y ella le preguntó si quería ser capitán o si podía recomendar a alguien. Andrés le dijo que sí, pero cuando quiso recomendar también a su amigo, la entrenadora no le **hizo caso** y lo escogió a él como capitán, sin darle **una explicación**.

174 ciento setenta y cuatro
A primera vista 2

DIFFERENTIATED INSTRUCTION

Heritage Language Learners

Remind students of strategies they can use to monitor and improve their reading comprehension. Have them pause after each section of the reading and answer *¿Qué pasó?* If they can't answer, ask them to reread the section.

Students with Learning Difficulties

Remind students that new vocabulary in the reading is identified in bold. Review the meaning of new words and phrases with them before they begin to read.

3 Cuando Julio se enteró de que Andrés era el capitán del equipo, se fue a hablar con la entrenadora.

Julio: Sra. Torres, ¿por qué escogió a Andrés?

Sra Torres: Porque me dijo que él quería ser capitán y nadie más quería serlo.

Julio: ¡Qué va! ¿Cómo se atrevió él a decir eso? Está equivocada, yo también quería ser capitán del equipo.

Sra. Torres: Entonces pónganse de acuerdo entre ustedes.

4 Más tarde, Julio llamó a Andrés por teléfono.

Julio: Andrés, eres un egoísta, sólo piensas en ti mismo. ¿Por qué no le dijiste a la Sra. Torres que yo también quería ser capitán?

Andrés: No me acuses, yo no tengo la culpa de que no te escogió . . .

Julio: ¡No me hables más!

5 Unos días después, Andrés tuvo la oportunidad de darle a Julio una explicación de lo que realmente ocurrió.

Andrés: Julio, entiendo por qué estás enojado, pero yo no tengo la culpa. Cuando fui a sugerirle tu nombre, la Sra. Torres me dijo que yo era el capitán.

Julio: Tienes razón, reconozco que fue un malentendido. Te pido perdón.

Andrés: Te perdono. Hagamos las paces, entonces.

Julio: De acuerdo.

▼**22 Amigos en conflicto** | 🔊

Escuchar

Escribe los números del 1 al 6 en una hoja. Vas a escuchar frases sobre el problema entre Andrés y Julio. Escribe *C* (cierto) o *F* (falso) para cada frase.

Language Input 4

▼**22** Standards: 1.2

Resources: Voc. and Gram. Transparency 93; Teacher's Resource Book: Audio Script, p. 216; Audio Program DVD: Cap. 4, Track 10; Answer Keys: Student Edition, p. 55

Focus: Practicing listening comprehension of new vocabulary

Suggestions: Display *Vocabulary & Grammar Transparency 93* as a reference as students complete the activity. Allow them to listen to the audio once through first. Then play it again, pausing after each item, so they can write their answers.

Answers:

1. F	4. C
2. C	5. F
3. F	6. F

ENRICH YOUR TEACHING

Culture Note

Although United States football *(el fútbol americano)* and other sports are slowly starting to gain more popularity in Latin America, soccer *(el fútbol)* continues to dominate. Besides the top-level professional *fútbol* leagues based in major cities of each country, there are also many intra-urban leagues—teams from various neighborhoods within a city. Games between neighborhood teams attract large, enthusiastic crowds. Some neighborhoods have healthy *fútbol* rivalries that go back many decades.

Vocabulario en contexto

Core Instruction

Standards: 1.1, 1.2, 3.1

Resources: Teacher's Resource Book: Input Script, p. 213, Clip Art, pp. 229–235, Audio Script, pp. 216–217; Voc. and Gram. Transparencies 94–95; Audio Program DVD: Cap. 4, Tracks 11–12

Focus: Extending presentation of vocabulary and grammar in context

Suggestions:

Pre-reading: Point out that **conflictos, criticar, ignorar, reaccionar, reconciliar,** and **colaborar** are cognates. Explain that the verb **mejorar** comes from the adjective and adverb **mejor,** which students have already learned. Write on the board **mejorar = hacer mejor** and use **mejorar** in a model sentence such as *La situación se mejoró cuando hablamos del problema.*

Reading: Have students read along as you play the audio or as you read aloud. Make sure students read the *Nota* on the next page. Use **ignorar** in model sentences like the following to demonstrate the two meanings: *Mi madre me ignora cuando grito. Mi padre no puede resolver el conflicto porque ignora los detalles.*

Post-reading: Discuss the charts and questionnaires with students and ask questions to check comprehension.

▼**23** Standards: 1.3

Resources: Answer Keys: Student Edition, p. 55

Focus: Demonstrating comprehension of new words and expressions

Suggestions: Encourage students to cite facts from the surveys that support their answers to the questions.

Answers:
1. Muchos conflictos ocurren cuando hay diferencias de opinión entre miembros de una familia. Answers will vary.
2. Los miembros de una familia deben pensar en los demás y colaborar para tener una buena relación.
3-5. Answers will vary.

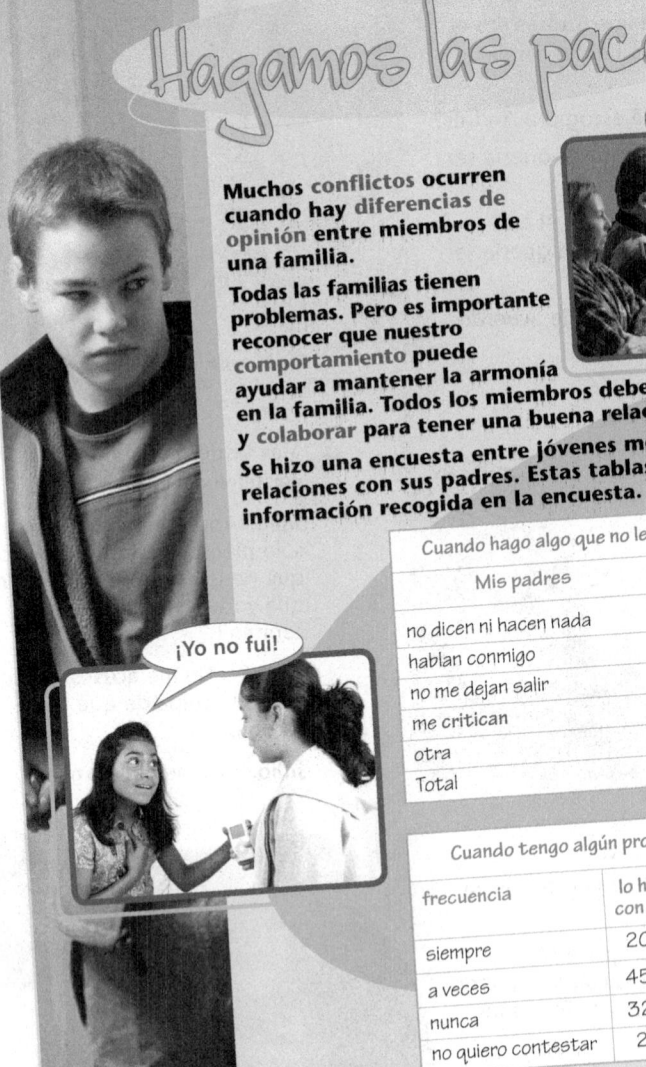

Hagamos las paces

¿Cómo te atreves a llegar a esta hora?

Muchos conflictos ocurren cuando hay diferencias de opinión entre miembros de una familia.

Todas las familias tienen problemas. Pero es importante reconocer que nuestro comportamiento puede ayudar a mantener la armonía en la familia. Todos los miembros deben pensar en los demás y colaborar para tener una buena relación.

Se hizo una encuesta entre jóvenes mexicanos sobre sus relaciones con sus padres. Estas tablas muestran la información recogida en la encuesta.

¡Yo no fui!

Cuando hago algo que no les gusta a mis padres . . .

Mis padres	Porcentaje
no dicen ni hacen nada	9.8 %
hablan conmigo	67.7 %
no me dejan salir	4.6 %
me critican	9.3 %
otra	8.6 %
Total	100.0 %

Cuando tengo algún problema con mis padres . . .

frecuencia	lo hablo con papá	lo hablo con mamá	lo hablo con los dos
siempre	20.0%	45.9%	16.1%
a veces	45.3%	40.0%	39.7%
nunca	32.5%	12.7%	36.0%
no quiero contestar	2.2%	1.4%	8.2%

▼**23 La armonía en la familia**

Escribir • Hablar

1. Según el artículo, ¿por qué a veces hay problemas en una familia? ¿Estás de acuerdo con esta opinión?

2. ¿Cuáles son algunas de las cosas que el artículo recomienda hacer para tener más armonía en una familia?

3. ¿Crees que por lo general las familias de esta encuesta se comunican bien o mal? ¿Por qué?

4. ¿Cómo podemos evitar conflictos?

5. Si tenemos diferencias de opinión o peleas con nuestra familia, ¿qué debemos hacer?

176 ciento setenta y seis
A primera vista 2

DIFFERENTIATED INSTRUCTION

Heritage Language Learners

Draw students' attention to the title *Hagamos las paces.* Invite them to share with the class other expressions that they might use to encourage harmony within their family, such as **Ya dejemos de pelear, reconciliémonos, perdón,** or **discúlpame.**

Advanced Learners

Invite students to conduct a survey similar to the one shown on p. 177. Ask them to tally the results of their surveys and to translate these into percentages, as they did on p. 166. Have them compare the results of their class with those of the students surveyed in Spain.

Conflictos:
causas y soluciones

Las preguntas de estas tablas nos pueden ayudar a saber qué hacer para **mejorar** nuestras **relaciones con las personas** que más nos **quieren**[1].

[1] The verb *querer* in this context means "to love" or "to like."

¿Te molesta cuando tus amigos . . .

	nunca	a veces	siempre
te **ignoran**?	❏	❏	❏
cuentan tus secretos a otros?	❏	❏	❏
no te **hacen caso**?	❏	❏	❏
tienen celos?	❏	❏	❏
no se alegran de tus éxitos?	❏	❏	❏
sólo piensan en sí mismos?	❏	❏	❏

¿Cómo reaccionas cuando tienes una pelea con un(a) amigo(a)?

	Sí	No
Gritas.	❏	❏
Dejas de hablarle.	❏	❏
Tratas de reconciliarte.	❏	❏
Lo(la) criticas.	❏	❏
Ignoras el problema.	❏	❏
Le **pides perdón**.	❏	❏

¿Cómo te reconcilias con tus padres?

	Sí	No
Hablamos del problema para resolverlo juntos.	❏	❏
Nos ponemos de acuerdo.	❏	❏
Hacemos las paces.	❏	❏
Reconocemos que estábamos equivocados.	❏	❏
Guardamos silencio hasta que pase el momento.	❏	❏

Nota

La palabra *ignorar* tiene más de un significado. Quiere decir "no prestar atención" o "no hacer caso" y, en un contexto diferente, puede significar "no saber algo".

▼24 Amistad y conflicto | Talk!

Hablar

Trabaja con un grupo para comparar sus respuestas a las preguntas siguientes.

1. ¿Qué nos molesta?
2. ¿Por qué nos enojamos con nuestros padres?
3. ¿Qué no nos gusta que hagan nuestros amigos?
4. ¿Qué hacemos para resolver conflictos?

Más práctica	GO
realidades.com | print	

Instant Check	✔	
Guided WB pp. 129–136	✔	✔
Core WB pp. 56–57	✔	✔
Comm. WB p. 58	✔	✔
Hispanohablantes WB pp. 120–121		✔

ciento setenta y siete **177**
Capítulo 4

Language Input 4

24 Standards: 1.1

Focus: Using new vocabulary in a guided discussion

Suggestions: Have students answer the questions individually first. Then have them meet and take turns sharing their answers. Encourage them to listen carefully to each other and to ask each other additional questions for clarification.

Answers will vary.

Pre-AP* Support

- **Learning Objective:** Interpretive: Print and Audio
- **Activity:** Show Voc. and Gram. Transparency 93. Have students work with a partner to create a dialogue that could be taking place between the two characters. As they say their dialogues aloud, other class members guess which frame their dialogue is illustrating.
- *Pre-AP* Resource Book:* Comprehensive guide to Pre-AP* vocabulary skill development, pp. 51–57

Chapter Project

Students can perform Step 4 at this point. Be sure they understand your corrections and suggestions. (For more information, see p. 154-b.)

Teacher-to-Teacher

Have students respond to the survey on p. 177. Then have students engage in a blog to express the feelings they have in the various situations described in the survey.

ENRICH YOUR TEACHING

Culture Note

As in most cultures, the family forms the most important social unit for Latin Americans. The concept of family might be considered a bit different from that in the United States. In Spain and Latin America, *familia* almost always includes not only the immediate family, but grandparents, aunts, uncles, and cousins as well. In Spanish-speaking countries, it is more common for members of three generations to live together in the same house than it is in the United States.

✓ASSESSMENT

Prueba 4-5

Prueba: Comprensión del vocabulario 2
- Prueba 4-5: pp. 92–93

▶ **Read and write about conflicts and solutions**
▶ **Discuss relationships, problems, and reactions**
▶ **Describe the family relationships portrayed in a painting**

INTERACTIVE WHITEBOARD
Vocabulary Activities 4-2

25 Standards: 1.2, 3.1

Resources: Answer Keys: Student Edition, p. 55

Focus: Demonstrating comprehension of new words and expressions

Suggestions: Point out that each possible answer has two phrases that best complete the sentence.

Answers:

1. **b**
2. **c**
3. **b**
4. **a**
5. **c**

Extension: Have students create their own sentences in which key vocabulary words are omitted, as in *Actividad* 25. They can exchange their sentences and have classmates complete them.

Fondo cultural

Standards: 1.1, 1.2, 2.1, 2.2, 4.2

Suggestions: After students read the information, ask them to compare and contrast the concept of Latin American *telenovelas* with that of U.S. soap operas. Ask: *¿En qué se parecen una telenovela y una* soap opera? *¿En qué se diferencian? ¿Una* soap opera *dura un año o más de un año? ¿Se parecen los personajes y los argumentos?¿En qué son diferentes?*

Answers will vary.

Manos a la obra 2

Vocabulario en uso

▼25 Los opuestos

Leer • Escribir

Completa las frases con la mejor selección de palabras opuestas *(opposite)*.

1. Es mejor vivir en _____ con nuestra familia y evitar los _____ .
   a. *pelea / comportamiento*   b. *armonía / conflictos*   c. *diferencia de opinión / paces*

2. El día que _____ estaban muy enojados, pero después _____ .
   a. *hicieron caso / ignoraron*   b. *perdonaron / acusaron*   c. *se pelearon / se reconciliaron*

3. Tú _____ , no sabes lo que dices. Alicia no quería _____ , sólo ayudarte.
   a. *haces las paces / se pelea*   b. *estás equivocado / criticarte*   c. *prestas atención / ignorarte*

4. Yo siempre _____ a lo que dice mi hermano y hago lo que nos pide, pero Pedro muchas veces lo _____ .
   a. *hago caso / ignora*   b. *me reconcilio / se pelea*   c. *pido perdón / acusa*

5. Amalia siempre _____ y ayuda a todo el mundo, pero su hermano es un egoísta que sólo _____ .
   a. *acusa / se reconcilia*   b. *critica / colabora*   c. *piensa en los demás / piensa en sí mismo*

▼ Fondo Cultural | El mundo hispano

La telenovela es la versión latinoamericana de la *soap opera* y generalmente la ponen entre las 8 y las 11 de la noche. El argumento es siempre una historia de amor, con personajes muy buenos o muy malos que se pelean en cada programa sin resolver sus problemas. La telenovela dura menos de un año y tiene un final emocionante, donde se resuelven los conflictos, los buenos triunfan y la muchacha y el muchacho se casan.

• ¿Qué programas similares conoces? ¿A qué hora los ponen?

• Describe un episodio de una telenovela que conoces. ¿Cuál era el conflicto? ¿Hubo un malentendido o una pelea? ¿Cómo reaccionaron los personajes? ¿Se reconciliaron al final?

Los actores Fernando Colunga y Lucero, de la telenovela mexicana "Soy tu dueña"

DIFFERENTIATED INSTRUCTION

Heritage Language Learners

Have students write a brief scene from a *telenovela* they know or one of their invention. The script should include one of the features mentioned in the *Fondo cultural*. Encourage them to perform their scenes for the class. Remind them that *telenovelas* are usually quite dramatic. Encourage them to "ham it up!"

Advanced Learners/Pre-AP*

Ask students to prepare a general overview of a soap opera they know. Have them describe the setting, the main characters, and some long- and short-term conflicts. If students are also familiar with any *telenovelas,* have them include an overview for these programs too.

▼26 Más consejos, ¡por favor! | 👥 | ♻

Leer • Escribir

❶ Un chico que participó en un salón de chat escribió este mensaje. Completa el mensaje con las palabras del recuadro.

hace caso	piensa en sí mismo	¡Qué va!	colabora	peleas

Estoy colaborando con un grupo de estudiantes para hacer un informe, pero uno de mis compañeros es muy egoísta. Cuando nos debemos reunir, dice que no puede porque tiene un partido de fútbol o clases de tenis. ¡No __1.__ en nada! ¡Este chico sólo __2.__! Ya tuvimos varias __3.__ porque temo que recibamos una mala nota, pero no __4.__ y siempre que le pedimos algo él responde: " __5.__ ".

❷ Con otro(a) estudiante, da un buen consejo a la persona que escribió el mensaje.

▼27 Lomas Garza: La gran familia chicana

Leer • Escribir • Pensar

La obra de Carmen Lomas Garza es como un retrato de familia de la comunidad chicana, es decir, mexicano-americana, de los Estados Unidos.

Conexiones | El arte

Carmen Lomas Garza (1948 –) es una artista chicana de Texas. Lomas Garza se inspiró en el Movimiento Chicano de los años sesenta, y desde entonces trata de representar en su obra la cultura de los chicanos. En sus cuadros, Lomas Garza ilustra las costumbres, las fiestas y la vida interesante y complicada de las personas que viven entre dos culturas, la mexicana y la estadounidense. Observa su cuadro "Cascarones" (*Eggshells*), de 1989, y responde a las preguntas.

"Cascarones", (1989),
Carmen Lomas Garza

Gouache painting. 15 x 20 inches.
© 1989 Carmen Lomas Garza. Photo by: Wolfgang Dietze. Collection of Gilbert Cardenas, Notra Dame, IN.

• ¿Te parece que hay armonía o conflicto en esta familia?

• ¿Por qué crees que hay una figura más grande que las otras en el cuadro? ¿Qué quiso expresar la pintora con ese detalle?

• Imagínate algo que pasa entre los miembros de esta familia. Usa las siguientes palabras para contar lo que sucede:

colaborar	hacer caso	malentendido	explicación	comportamiento

ciento setenta y nueve **179**
Capítulo 4

Practice and Communicate ④

26 Standards: 1.2

Resources: Answer Keys: Student Edition, p. 56

Focus: Practicing new vocabulary in a cloze exercise

Recycle: Past tenses, subjunctive

Suggestions: Explain to students that a clear understanding of the character description in the first part of the message will help them fill in the blanks in the second part. For Step 2, encourage students to use expressions that take the subjunctive.

Answers:
1. colabora
2. piensa en sí mismo
3. peleas
4. hace caso
5. ¡Qué va!

BELLRINGER REVIEW

Have students unscramble these letters to form words for family members:

aleuba   ineto   damarsart   hormone

(**Answers:** *abuela, nieto, madrastra, hermano*)

27 Standards: 1.1, 1.2, 2.1, 2.2, 3.1

Resources: Fine Art Transparencies with Teacher's Guide, p. 37

Focus: Practicing reading comprehension in a passage about an artist

Suggestions: Remind students that they can refer to *Capítulo* 2 if they need to review the fine art vocabulary used in the reading passage.

Answers will vary.

ENRICH YOUR TEACHING

Culture Note

Besides her paintings, Carmen Lomas Garza also makes prints, installations (mixed-media artworks in three dimensions, often incorporating movement), and paper and metal cutouts. Her installations tend to focus on the Day of the Dead (**el Día de los Muertos**), a Mexican feast day celebrated on November 1. Behind all of Garza's artwork lies pride in her Chicana heritage.

28 Standards: 1.1

Resources: Answer Keys: Student Edition, p. 56

Focus: Practicing new vocabulary and structures in a guided conversation

Suggestions: Remind students that the *¡Respuesta personal!* at the end of Student B's cues is an invitation for them to invent their own reactions as well as to practice those cues.

Answers will vary. Student B can use the following verb forms:

me alegro
me enojo
doy/pido una explicación
lloro
me pongo (feliz, furioso(a), contento(a))
reconozco el error/pido perdón
digo "¡Qué va!"/ "Yo no fui"

29 Standards: 1.1, 1.2

Focus: Using new vocabulary and structures in a dramatization

Suggestions: As students are preparing the paper slips for the drawing, ask them to read all of the items and think about the dramatization they will do if they select it.

Answers will vary.

30 Standards: 1.1

Focus: Using new vocabulary and structures in a guided conversation

Suggestions: Encourage students to supply their own personal reasons for disagreements with people they know.

Answers will vary.

▼28 ¿Cómo reaccionas cuando . . . ? |

Hablar

Con un(a) compañero(a), habla sobre tu comportamiento en las situaciones siguientes.

▶ **Modelo**

tu amigo te ignora
A —¿Cómo reaccionas cuando tu amigo te ignora?
B —Generalmente le pido una explicación.

Estudiante A

1. tu amigo dice que estás equivocado(a)
2. tu hermano(a) te acusa de algo
3. tus padres te critican
4. tus padres te preguntan "¿por qué?"
5. alguien no te hace caso
6. alguien no quiere hacer las paces

Estudiante B

alegrarse
enojarse
dar / pedir una explicación
llorar
ponerse (feliz, furioso, contento)
reconocer el error / pedir perdón
decir "¡Qué va!" / "Yo no fui"
¡Respuesta personal!

▼29 Juego | 👥

Escribir • Hablar

Trabaja con un grupo y pide a cada persona que escriba una de las siguientes frases en un pedazo de papel. Luego, pónganlos todos en una caja o bolsa y tomen turnos para sacarlos. Actúa durante 20 segundos la frase que sacaste. ¡Sé dramático(a)!

1. Explícale a tu padre por qué llegaste tarde anoche.
2. Tuviste una pelea y te das cuenta de que estabas equivocado(a). ¿Qué haces?
3. Crees que tu maestro(a) está equivocado(a). ¿Qué dices / haces? Sé muy cortés.
4. Tú y tu amigo(a) se pelearon. Hay que reconciliarse. ¿Qué dices para reconciliarte?
5. Tu hermano(a) te acusa de algo que tú no hiciste. ¿Cómo reaccionas? ¿Qué dices?
6. Tu hermano(a) menor se portó mal en la tienda. ¿Qué le dices?

▼30 Diferencias de opinión |

Hablar

Trabaja con otro(a) estudiante y explícale por qué a veces peleas con estas personas. Usa las palabras del recuadro. Después, intercambien papeles.

criticar	acusar de	ignorar	atreverse
reconocer	tener la culpa	hacer	

Modelo

hermano mayor
Peleo con mi hermano mayor cuando <u>no me deja escuchar sus discos compactos</u>.

1. papá
2. mamá
3. hermano(a)
4. hermano(a) menor
5. mejor amigo(a)
6. primo(a)
7. compañero(a) de clase

180 ciento ochenta
Manos a la obra 2

DIFFERENTIATED INSTRUCTION

Heritage Language Learners

Have students write a paragraph about one aspect of their family that they really enjoy. They might write about a relationship with a certain family member, a special family tradition, a celebration, or a memory that is important to them. Allow students to write about a close, personal friend as an option.

Advanced Learners

Ask students to interview students and teachers from other classes about their conflicts with others and how they resolve them. Have them prepare their interviews in advance by writing four or five questions they will ask. They can conduct their interviews in English and report back to the class in Spanish.

Practice and Communicate 4

▼31 Encuesta: ¿Para qué necesitas permiso?

Leer • Escribir

Lee en la tabla la información recogida en una encuesta que se hizo entre jóvenes mexicanos con respecto a sus padres. Después, contesta las preguntas.

Actividades	Prohibido	Necesito permiso	Yo decido		No aplica	No contestó	Total
			Chicos	Chicas			
Tener novio(a)	9.3%	33.0%	35.2%	16.5%	5.2%	0.8%	100%
Salir con amigos	5.5%	65.1%	19.9%	7.4%	1.8%	0.3%	100%
Vestir como tú quieres	2.9%	10.5%	43.3%	42.0%	0.9%	0.4%	100%
Llegar tarde a casa	15.2%	60.1%	16.7%	5.0%	2.6%	0.4%	100%
Ponerte aretes	45.5%	8.0%	9.7%	6.1%	30.2%	0.5%	100%

1. ¿Qué actividad se prohíbe más? ¿Cuál se prohíbe menos?
2. ¿Qué información de la tabla te sorprende? ¿Por qué?
3. Mira la columna con el título "Yo decido". ¿Qué te dice esa información?
4. Un(a) chico(a) tiene prohibido llegar tarde a casa pero nunca hace caso. ¿Cómo crees que van a reaccionar los padres?
5. ¿Qué puede hacer después ese(a) chico(a) para resolver el conflicto con sus padres?
6. Si ese(a) mismo(a) chico(a) llegó tarde a casa porque no pasó el autobús, ¿crees que los padres deben enojarse? ¿Por qué?

▼32 Los conflictos | 👥

Pensar • Escribir • Hablar

1. Escribe una lista de, por lo menos, tres conflictos o malentendidos que suceden a veces en una familia. Por ejemplo: alguien no arregló su cuarto o alguien llegó muy tarde a casa.
2. ¿Quiénes son las personas que participan en cada conflicto?
3. ¿Qué pueden hacer para mejorar la situación?
4. Con otro(a) estudiante, representen el conflicto ante la clase.
5. Basado(a) en los consejos del cartel, sugiere una solución para uno de los conflictos.

PARA RESOLVER UN CONFLICTO
◄ 1. hablen para resolver el problema
2. sugieran soluciones posibles ▲
3. sean sinceros ▲
4. expliquen lo que pasó ►

ciento ochenta y uno **181**
Capítulo 4

31 Standards: 1.2, 1.3, 2.1, 3.1, 3.2
Resources: Answer Keys: Student Edition, p. 57
Focus: Practicing new vocabulary and structures via reading and discussion of a survey
Suggestions: When students have had some time to study the chart, ask additional questions: *¿Qué porcentaje de los jóvenes necesita permiso para salir con amigos?* (65.1)
Answers:
1. Más: Ponerte aretes. Menos: vestir como tú quieres.
2–6. Answers will vary.

32 Standards: 1.3
Focus: Practicing new vocabulary and structures through reading, writing, and dramatization
Suggestions: For item 3, ask students to think of their own ways to resolve the problems. Remind them that they do not need to have personal experience with some of the ways they mention.
Answers will vary.

Additional Resources
• Communication Wbk.: Audio Act. 3, p. 51
• Teacher's Resource Book: Audio Script, p. 217, Communicative Pair Activity BLM, pp. 224–225
• Audio Program DVD: Cap. 4, Track 13

ENRICH YOUR TEACHING

Culture Note
Young single adults in much of Latin America tend to live with their parents longer than their counterparts in the United States. Reasons for this vary. Sometimes they are economical; sometimes they have to do with employment; but in many cases they spring from cultural traditions that place a high value on a strong bond between the generations within a family. As in all cultures, such traditions and values are changing.

✓ASSESSMENT
Prueba 4-6 with Study Plan (online only)
Prueba: Aplicación del vocabulario 2
• Prueba 4-6: pp. 94–95

181

Gramática

Core Instruction

Standards: 4.1

Resources: Voc. and Gram. Transparency 96

INTERACTIVE WHITEBOARD
Grammar Activities 4-2

Suggestions: Have students write more examples using the **vamos a + infinitive** construction. Ask them to include some suggestions that use stem-changing verbs and one or more of the pronouns referred to in the *Gramática*. Have them take turns reading their suggestions aloud. Ask volunteers to convert each one to the **nosotros** command form with correct spelling and pronoun placement.

▼33 Standards: 1.2

Resources: Answer Keys: Student Edition, p. 57

Focus: Practicing **nosotros** commands

Suggestions: Ask students to practice the **nosotros** commands, but remind them that the **vamos a + infinitive** construction is also an option for the items.

Answers will vary.
1. **Hablemos, veamos**
2. **Pidámosle, prometamos**
3. **Ignoremos, perdonémosla**
4. **Démosle, terminemos**
5. **Atrevámonos**
6. **Pongámonos de acuerdo**

▼34 Standards: 1.2

Resources: Answer Keys: Student Edition, p. 57

Focus: Practicing new vocabulary and structures in guided conversations

Suggestions: Have groups conduct the activity in round-robin fashion.

Answers will vary. The following verb forms will be used:

compremos refrescos, lleguemos a casa, compremos las entradas, pongámonos de acuerdo, vistámonos, colaboremos, bañémonos, disfrutemos, escojamos, salgamos, comamos, lleguemos al cine

---

Manos a la obra 2

Gramática

| ▼ Objectives
▸ Read and write about conflict resolution
▸ Discuss suggestions for doing activities with other people

Mandatos con *nosotros*

There are two ways to suggest that others do some activity with you *(Let's . . .)*.

You can use the construction *Vamos a +* infinitive.

> Vamos a hacer las paces.
> *Let's make up.*

You can also use a command with a *nosotros* form. The *nosotros* command form is the same as the *nosotros* form of the present subjunctive.

> Resolvamos el conflicto.
> No reaccionemos tan rápido.

Remember that stem-changing verbs whose infinitive ends in *-ir* have a stem change of $e \rightarrow i$, or $o \rightarrow u$ in the *nosotros* form.

> Pidamos perdón por el malentendido.
> No durmamos al aire libre.

Verbs whose infinitive ends in *-car, -gar,* or *-zar* have a spelling change in the *nosotros* form of the present subjunctive, and consequently of the *nosotros* command.

> No critiquemos a nuestros padres.
> Empecemos a pensar un poco en ellos.

Direct and indirect object pronouns are attached at the end of affirmative *nosotros* commands, but precede the negative *nosotros* command form.

> Celebremos la amistad. Celebrémosla.
> Digámosle todo. No le mintamos.

When attaching reflexive or reciprocal pronouns at the end of a *nosotros* command, drop the final *-s* of the command before the pronoun.

> ¡Alegrémonos con sus éxitos!
> Atrevámonos a darles nuestras opiniones.

Más ayuda **realidades.com** ▸ *Canción de hip hop* ▸ *Tutorial*

▼33 Encontremos la solución

Leer • Escribir

Miriam y Leonor se pelearon con Tamara, su hermana mayor. Completa las frases con el mandato con *nosotros* del verbo apropiado para saber qué sugieren para reconciliarse con Tamara.

1. _____ *(acusar / hablar)* con papá y _____ *(ver / ignorar)* cómo reacciona.
2. _____ *(pedirle / criticar)* perdón y _____ *(perder / prometer)* no mentir nunca más.
3. _____ *(mejorar / ignorar)* todo y _____ *(decirle / perdonarla)*.
4. _____ *(darle / reaccionar)* una explicación y _____ *(terminar / reaccionar)* la pelea.
5. _____ *(atreverse / colaborar)* a decirle que nosotras tuvimos la culpa.
6. ¡_____ *(pelear / ponerse de acuerdo)* pronto!

▼34 Un plan para el sábado

Escribir

Imagina que el sábado quieres ir al cine con tu hermano. Haz un plan de diez pasos para sugerirle lo que quieres que hagan juntos. Puedes usar las palabras del recuadro.

comprar refrescos	vestirse	escoger
llegar a casa	colaborar	salir
comprar entradas	bañarse	comer
ponerse de acuerdo	disfrutar	llegar al cine

Modelo
escoger
Primero, escojamos qué película vamos a ver.

DIFFERENTIATED INSTRUCTION

Heritage Language Learners

Provide extra support to students as you discuss the letters *j* and *h* in *¿Recuerdas?* Although they rarely mispronounce Spanish words with *h*, students often make errors in spelling these words. Briefly review common errors that you see, such as misspelling ***a ver*** and ***haber.***

Students with Special Needs

Pair advanced learners with visually impaired students in order to complete *Actividad* 35. The former can describe the actions shown in each scene. Their partners can then suggest other activities to do.

35 ¿Y ahora qué hacemos?

Hablar

Raúl y Rosalía nunca se ponen de acuerdo. Con otro(a) estudiante, hagan los papeles de Raúl y Rosalía. Uno(a) sugiere lo que aparece en el dibujo y el (la) otro(a) sugiere hacer otra cosa.

▶ Modelo

A —*Caminemos por el parque.*
B —*Dijeron que va a llover.*
  Volvamos a casa.

1.

2.

3.

▼ En voz alta |

La compañía discográfica EMI Latin unió en un solo disco compacto las voces de los más famosos cantantes populares de España y Latinoamérica. El objetivo del disco, *Voces unidas*, era celebrar la estrecha relación que existe entre los pueblos hispanohablantes, pues estos pueblos son como una gran familia. Escucha este fragmento de la canción "Será entre tú y yo", de la cantante mexicana Paulina Rubio. Luego trata de repetirla en voz alta.

Paulina Rubio

"Será entre tú y yo"
de Paulina Rubio

**Mostremos
respeto a la adversidad
a la competencia, fidelidad[1],
fuerza espiritual unida al cuerpo,
lleguemos unidos a la final.
Juntemos los sueños que hay de ganar
y así llegarán los himnos[2] al cielo.
Quieres llegar, tu fuerza seré yo.
Quieres volar[3] al infinito,
juntos será.**

---

1 loyalty 2 hymns 3 to fly

> **¿Recuerdas?**
>
> En español la letra *j* se pronuncia como la letra *h* en la palabra *hat* pero con un sonido más fuerte. Escucha y repite estas palabras: *juntos, juntemos.*
>
> En español la letra *h* casi nunca suena: *hacer, himnos.*

Más práctica	**GO**

realidades.com | print

Instant Check	✔	
Guided WB pp. 137–138	✔	✔
Core WB p. 58	✔	✔
Comm. WB p. 59	✔	✔
Hispanohablantes WB pp. 122–126	✔	

ciento ochenta y tres **183**
Capítulo 4

---

35 Standards: 1.1

Resources: Answer Keys: Student Edition, p. 58

Focus: Practicing *nosotros* commands in guided conversations

Suggestions: Have students practice the exchanges with their partner. Then ask pairs of volunteers to present one of the exchanges to the class.

Answers for Student B will vary. The following are suggestions for Student A:

1. Vamos de compras.
2. Hagamos ejercicio.
3. Demos un paseo y saquemos unas fotos.

En voz alta
Core Instruction

Standards: 1.2, 1.3, 2.2, 3.1, 3.2, 5.2

Resources: Teacher's Resource Book: Audio Script, p. 217; Audio Program DVD: Cap. 4, Track 14

Suggestions: Have students read the information and the song silently. Ask comprehension questions: *¿Qué piensas del objetivo del disco Voces unidas? ¿Por qué son los pueblos hispanohablantes como una gran familia? ¿Qué piensas de este fragmento de la canción?*

Before having students recite the song, direct their attention to the information in the *¿Recuerdas?* and have them listen to the audio. Then allow them a few minutes to practice with a partner.

Pre-AP* Support

- **Learning Objective:** Interpretive: Print and Audio
- **Activity:** Have students listen to the song *"Será entre tú y yo"* from the audio program. Have them raise their hands when they hear an example of a *nosotros* command. Then have them listen to the song again while they follow along in their book.
- *Pre-AP* Resource Book:* Comprehensive guide to Pre-AP* communication skill development, pp. 10–18, 39–50

✓ ASSESSMENT

Prueba 4-7 with Study Plan (online only)

Prueba: Mandatos con *nosotros*
• Prueba 4-7: p. 96

ENRICH YOUR TEACHING

Culture Note

The popularity of many types of Latin music continues to grow worldwide. So much so that in 2000, the first Latin Grammy Awards ceremony was held. The Latin Grammy honors artistic and technical achievements in Latin American music, awards excellence, and provides greater exposure to Latin American recording artists.

21st Century Skills

Communication Have students work in small groups to create an announcement in their favorite social network for an upcoming school event (dance, athletic competition, fundraiser, etc.). The announcement should include at least five suggested activities using *nosotros* commands.

Gramática

Core Instruction

Resources: Voc. and Gram. Transparency 97

INTERACTIVE WHITEBOARD
Grammar Activities 4-2

Suggestions: On the board, write this model: *Aquellas llaves son tuyas. Aquí tengo las mías.* Ask students to refer to other individual objects or groups of objects around the classroom and make similar pairs of sentences using possessive adjectives and pronouns.

36 Standards: 1.2

Resources: Answer Keys: Student Edition, p. 58

Focus: Practicing possessive pronouns in a cloze exercise

Suggestions: Have students first read through the entire letter for meaning. Ask them to identify the noun that is replaced by each possessive pronoun.

Answers:
1. mías
2. míos
3. mía
4. suyo
5. tuyos

37 Standards: 1.1

Resources: Answer Keys: Student Edition, p. 59

Focus: Practicing possessive pronouns

Suggestions: Have students practice third-person forms by reporting to the class on their partner's statements.

Answers will vary, but students will use the following possessive forms:

mi ropa: la tuya, la mía
mi perro: el tuyo, el mío
mi computadora: la tuya, la mía
nuestro coche: el tuyo, el nuestro
mis comidas favoritas: las tuyas, las mías
mis abuelos: los tuyos, los míos
mi hermano(a): el (la) tuyo(a), el (la) mío(a)
mi familia: la tuya, la mía
nuestros(as) amigos(as): los (las) tuyos(as), los (las) míos(as)

Gramática

Pronombres posesivos

To form the possessive pronouns, use the long form of possessive adjectives preceded by the definite article. Both the article and the possessive must agree in number and gender with the noun they replace.

> Mis padres son muy serios. ¿Y los tuyos?
> Los míos son bastante divertidos.
>
> Tu familia es muy pequeña. La mía es bastante grande.

We often omit the article between the verb *ser* and the possessive pronoun.

> Esas maletas son nuestras.
> Mi hermano siempre dice que toda la culpa es mía.

¿Recuerdas?

The long form possessive adjectives are used for clarity or emphasis.

1st, 2nd, and 3rd Person Sing.

mío(s)	mía(s)	*my, mine*
tuyo(s)	tuya(s)	*your, yours*
suyo(s)	suya(s)	*your, yours his, her, hers*

1st, 2nd, and 3rd Person Plural

nuestro(s)	nuestra(s)	*our, ours*
vuestro(s)	vuestra(s)	*your, yours*
suyo(s)	suya(s)	*your, yours their, theirs*

▼36 ¿Cuándo vamos al cine?

Leer • Escribir

Débora se enojó con Pablo porque él no pudo ir al cine con ella y le escribió una carta diciéndoselo. Entonces, Pablo le escribió una carta para reconciliarse. Completa la carta de Pablo con las formas correctas de los pronombres posesivos del recuadro. Algunas se pueden usar más de una vez.

tuyo	mío	suyo

> Querida Débora:
>
> Leí tu carta. Entiendo tus razones pero yo tengo las __1.__ para no ir al cine.
>
> Tus padres te dejan ir al cine siempre, pero los __2.__ nunca me dejan.
>
> Ayer tu mamá llamó a la __3.__ para pedirle que me dejara ir a tu casa,
>
> pero mi mamá dijo que su coche no funciona. Tu mamá dijo que podía llevarme
>
> en el __4.__, pero mi mamá no quiso. Yo quiero mucho a mis padres, pero me
>
> gustaría que fueran como los __5.__. Espero que me perdones. Creo que el
>
> sábado que viene sí me van a dejar ir contigo. ¡Nos vamos a divertir!
>
> Pablo

DIFFERENTIATED INSTRUCTION

Students with Learning Difficulties

Write on the board the following sentences: *These are my books. These are mine.* Guide students to understand that *mine* is a pronoun that takes the place of *my books.* Point out that English, like Spanish, uses different words for possessive adjectives and pronouns. (my/mine, your/yours, and so on.)

Advanced Learners

As students complete *Actividad* 36, ask them to tell why each form is correct. Have them say to which noun each possessive pronoun refers, identifying its number and gender. Then ask students to add two more sentences containing possessive pronouns from Pablo's letter.

▼**37** Los míos, los tuyos, los nuestros |

Hablar

Con otro(a) estudiante, hablen sobre los siguientes aspectos de su vida.

- mi computadora
- mis comidas favoritas
- mi familia
- mi ropa
- nuestro coche
- mis abuelos
- nuestros(as) amigos(as)
- mi perro

▶ **Modelo**

mis padres

A —*Mis padres son serios, pero comprensivos. ¿Cómo son los tuyos?*

B —*Los míos son muy generosos, y siempre piensan en los demás.*

▼**38** Retrato de familia |

Escribir • Hablar

❶ Piensa en una familia de una película, un libro o un programa de televisión que conoces. Imagina que eres un miembro de esa familia. Contesta las siguientes preguntas acerca de tu familia imaginaria.

1. ¿Cómo es tu familia? (cuántos son, quiénes son, cómo es cada uno)

2. ¿Quién piensa siempre en los demás y quién piensa más en sí mismo?

3. ¿Quién se pelea con los demás? ¿Quién trata de mantener la armonía?

4. ¿Cómo resuelven los conflictos?

5. ¿Qué te gusta más de tu familia?

❷ Basado(a) en las respuestas a las preguntas anteriores, escribe una descripción de tu familia imaginaria.

❸ Con otro(a) estudiante, hablen de las descripciones que escribieron y comparen sus familias imaginarias.

El español en la comunidad

Niños bilingües

En muchas familias latinas de los Estados Unidos los niños aprenden el nuevo idioma más rápido que los adultos, y son los traductores de la familia.

A veces, esto ayuda a la armonía de la familia, pues todos colaboran para adaptarse a la nueva cultura. Pero otras veces hay conflictos, porque los padres sienten que pierden control sobre los hijos y los hijos piensan que sus padres no los entienden.

Ahora que tú sabes hablar español, puedes ser útil para tu comunidad traduciendo para los nuevos estudiantes hispanohablantes.

Más práctica

realidades.com | print

Instant Check	✔	
Guided WB pp. 139–140	✔	✔
Core WB pp. 59–60	✔	✔
Comm. WB pp. 52–53, 60–61	✔	✔
Hispanohablantes WB pp. 127–129		✔

Practice and Communicate ④

38 Standards: 1.2, 1.3

Focus: Practicing possessive pronouns

Suggestions: Have students begin their family descriptions by identifying themselves: *Me llamo Joselito. Soy el hijo menor de la familia Cartwright....*

Answers will vary.

▼ El español en la comunidad

Core Instruction

Standards: 1.2, 5.1

Suggestions: Ask students to consider what it would be like to be a parent or child in a bilingual family. If your class includes heritage language speakers, they may have a lot to offer to this discussion.

Chapter Project

Students can perform Step 5 at this point. Make audio or video recordings of their presentations for inclusion in their portfolio. (For more information, see p. 154-b.)

Additional Resources

- Communication Wbk.: Audio Act. 4–5, pp. 52–53
- Teacher's Resource Book: Audio Script, pp. 217–218, Communicative Pair Activity BLM, pp. 226–227
- Audio Program DVD: Cap. 4, Tracks 15–16

☑**ASSESSMENT**

Prueba 4-8 with Study Plan (online only)

Prueba: Pronombres posesivos
- Prueba 4-8: p. 97

Examen: Vocabulario y gramática 2
- Examen 2: pp. 98–100
- ExamView: Examen 2

185

ENRICH YOUR TEACHING

Culture Note

Spanish is quickly becoming an important part of many communities in the United States. According to one study, the Hispanic population has grown faster over the past two decades than that of any immigrant group in the history of the United States. Experts predict that this rapid growth will probably continue for several decades.

21st Century Skills

Initiative and Self-Direction Remind students of the various digital tools available in **realidades.com** to help them monitor their own understanding and learning needs, such as the online tutorials with comprehension check exercises.

Puente a la cultura

Puente a la cultura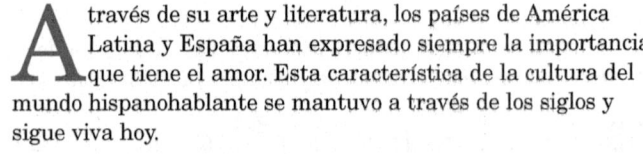

El amor en las artes

Core Instruction

Standards: 1.1, 1.2, 1.3, 2.1, 2.2, 3.1, 3.2

Resources: Fine Art Transparencies with Teacher's Guide, p. 57

Focus: Reading to learn about the theme of love depicted in the fine arts of Latin America and Spain

Suggestions:

Pre-reading: Refer students to the *Estrategia.* Ask them to apply their background knowledge about poetry, music, and visual arts with which they are familiar. Talk about what different kinds of love are expressed in the art they know and how it is expressed.

Reading: Encourage students to read through the entire passage once silently, without stopping at problem words or to ask questions. Remind them to use background knowledge, cognates, and context clues to help them understand unfamiliar words and expressions.

Post-reading: Ask volunteers to paraphrase the main idea and important details from the three main sections of the reading, including the introduction.

Estrategia

Compare and contrast
To compare, look for ways that people, events, things, or ideas are the same. To contrast, think about ways they are different. Think about their use, color, size, and shape, or other characteristics.

"Madre y niño", (1926), Diego Rivera*

*© 2009 Banco de México Diego Rivera & Frida Kahlo Museums Trust, México, D.F./Artists Rights Society (ARS), New York. Photo: © Art Resource, NY.

A través de su arte y literatura, los países de América Latina y España han expresado siempre la importancia que tiene el amor. Esta característica de la cultura del mundo hispanohablante se mantuvo a través de los siglos y sigue viva hoy.

El amor en la pintura

Quizá el sentimiento de amor más importante en la cultura latinoamericana y española es el amor a la madre. Además de poemas y estatuas, el amor a la madre ha inspirado a muchos pintores. Uno de ellos es Diego Rivera (1886–1957). Este famoso pintor y muralista disfrutaba pintando mujeres con niños, especialmente mujeres indígenas a quienes presentaba con hermosos niños, y vestidas de brillantes colores.

La pintura en murales ha sido otra forma de expresión artística del amor, el amor a la comunidad. Judith Francisca Baca es una artista de California que ha fundado programas de creación de murales. Con su arte ha ayudado a embellecer la comunidad, a hacer conocer otras culturas y a alentar[1] a miles de jóvenes a interesarse en las artes. En la creación de uno de sus murales, *"The Great Wall"*, participaron más de 400 jóvenes de 14 a 21 años de edad.

1 to encourage

"The Great Wall of Los Angeles", (1976–1984), Judith Baca

Country Connection

Core Instruction

Standards: 3.1

Mapa global interactivo, Actividad 1 Travel the length of Judith Baca's mural wall in Los Angeles, CA.

Suggestions:

Display *Map Transparency* 20. Point out the Spanish cities mentioned in the reading. Assign a different city to small groups. Ask them to research their city and report back to the class with three facts about its history, important industries, and famous sites.

Teacher-to-Teacher

e-amigos: Have students choose an expression of love or friendship from a Spanish-language song. Ask them to send their *e-amigos* the quote and comment on the feelings expressed.

DIFFERENTIATED INSTRUCTION

Students with Special Needs

Pair advanced learners with visually impaired students. Advanced learners can describe the Diego Rivera painting, focusing on how the painter demonstrates the love between mother and child. Advanced learners will also benefit from this analysis of the artwork.

Advanced Learners

Ask students to prepare an oral report about an important poem, song, or painting from the Spanish-speaking world that has love as a theme. This might be a work of art they have studied in earlier chapters of *Realidades*. Have them tell about the kind of love expressed and how it is expressed.

Culture 4

El amor en la música

La música es otra de las artes que se han usado para expresar el amor. Se escucha siempre en los grandes festivales y eventos patrióticos, en las elegantes bodas, en paseos y en funerales.

Agustín Lara (1897–1970), uno de los grandes compositores mexicanos, compuso la letra y la melodía de más de 600 canciones y sus éxitos suman cientos. La fuente de inspiración de la mayoría de sus canciones fue el amor a la mujer, ya que su vida estuvo llena de romances. Pero Agustín también fue un enamorado de España y dedicó canciones a las ciudades de Sevilla, Toledo, Navarra, Murcia, Valencia y Madrid. Su canción "Granada" ha dado la vuelta al mundo en las voces de los más famosos artistas.

Amor

Juana de Ibarourou

El amor es fragante como un ramo de rosas.
Amando se poseen todas las primaveras.
Eros[2] trae en su aljaba[3] las flores olorosas
De todas las umbrías[4] y todas las praderas.

2 god of love 3 quiver 4 shady places

El amor en la poesía

De todas las formas de expresar el amor en la literatura, quizás la más apropiada es la poesía. Un ejemplo es la obra de la gran poeta uruguaya Juana de Ibarourou (1892–1979). Cuando Juana tenía 22 años publicó *Lenguas de diamante*, su primer libro de poesía, con el que obtuvo un éxito instantáneo. Su poesía se caracteriza por un ritmo armonioso, un amor ingenuo y transparente, sin tonos dramáticos o angustiosos[1]. Sus temas incluyen el amor, la maternidad, la belleza física y la naturaleza. 1 anguished

¿Comprendiste?

1. Según el artículo, ¿en qué manifestaciones del arte de los países hispanohablantes se nota la importancia del amor? Da algunos ejemplos.

2. En el artículo se dice que el amor a la madre es el sentimiento más importante en la cultura hispanohablante. ¿Qué lugar crees que tiene en tu cultura? ¿Por qué?

3. Da ejemplos de otros sentimientos de amor que pueden expresarse en las artes.

4. Piensa en una expresión de amor de una canción, un poema o una pintura que conozcas. Escribe una composición para comparar tu ejemplo con el del artículo y di en qué se parecen y en qué se diferencian.

Más práctica GO

realidades.com | print

▶ *Videodocumentario*	✔	
Guided WB p. 141	✔	✔
Comm. WB pp. 61, 62–63		✔
Hispanohablantes **WB** pp. 130–132		✔
Cultural Reading Activity	✔	

ciento ochenta y siete **187**
Capítulo 4

ENRICH YOUR TEACHING

Culture Note

Although Mother's Day **(el Día de la Madre)** is celebrated in much of Latin America as it is in the United States, it is especially important in Mexico. There, it is celebrated on May 10, and schools are closed. During the weeks before the holiday, Mexican students spend time rehearsing elaborate performances they will put on.

21st Century Skills

Technology Literacy Encourage students to do online research on the artists, poets, and musicians featured in this cultural reading. They can search the keywords: *Agustín Lara, Diego Rivera, Judith Francisca Baca,* or *Juana de Ibarbourou*. Have students identify another work from one of these artists that represents another interpretation of love.

▼ ¿Comprendes? Standards: 1.2, 1.3, 2.1, 2.2, 3.1, 5.2

Resources: Answer Keys: Student Edition, p. 59

Focus: Demonstrating reading comprehension

Suggestions: Have students read aloud or paraphrase the sections of the reading that support their answers to the first question. Use the other questions as a vehicle for discussion with the whole class.

Answers:
1. Se nota en la pintura, en la música y en la poesía. Unos ejemplos son las pinturas y los murales de Diego Rivera, las canciones de Agustín Lara y la poesía de Juana de Ibarbouru.
2–4. Answers will vary.

Teaching with Art

Resources: Fine Art Transparencies with Teacher's Guide, p. 57

Suggestions: Help students talk about the Rivera painting by asking: *¿Te gusta esta pintura? ¿Por qué? ¿Por qué no? ¿Qué te dice la pintura sobre el tema del amor?*

▶ Videodocumentario

Core Instruction

Standards: 1.2

Resources: Teacher's Resource Book: Video Script, p. 220; Video Program: Cap. 4

View *Una amistad entre hermanos* with the class to learn more about family relationships. Access the video online in **realidades.com** or use the DVD. See the *Video Teacher's Guide* for additional suggestions.

Block Schedule

After the class has completed the reading, assign each student the number 1, 2, or 3. Each number represents a topic in the reading (1–*pintura*; 2–*música*; 3–*poesía*). Students are to write four questions about their section. Randomly create groups of 1s, 2s, and 3s. In these groups, have them ask each other their questions.

Additional Resources

Student Resource: Realidades para hispanohablantes, pp. 130–132; Guided Practice Activities, p. 141; Communication Wbk., pp. 62–63

187

¿Qué me cuentas?

Core Instruction

Standards: 1.1, 1.2, 1.3

Resources: Teacher's Resource Book: Audio Script, p. 218; Audio Program DVD: Cap. 4, Track 17; Answer Keys: Student Edition, p. 59

Focus: Practicing listening and reading comprehension of new vocabulary and grammar; using information to write a cohesive and coherent reaction.

AP* Skills: Integration of listening, reading, and writing to comprehend and synthesize information from spoken and written sources.

Suggestions:

For Step 1, use the audio or read the descriptions aloud. Allow students to hear both descriptions twice through: the first time to write their answers, the second time to check them.

For Step 2, have students summarize the main points and make inferences to show that they understand what they have read.

Encourage students to express their own opinions in addition to using information from the reading in their written responses for Step 3.

Answers:

Step 1

1. b	3. b	5. a
2. a	4. a	6. b

Steps 2–3
Answers will vary.

Teacher-to-Teacher

Have students imagine they had an argument with their best friend. Have them write a note to the friend to explain how upset they are, to tell how important their friendship is, and to apologize for the dispute. Have students exchange the notes with another student who will respond in the role of the best friend. Ask students to focus on how a friendship satisfies their basic needs.

Additional Resources

Student Resource: Realidades para hispanohablantes, p. 133

Integración (Talk!)

¿Qué me cuentas?: Conflictos con y sin solución

¿Qué consejos das a los demás? Primero escucha una versión de un conflicto que pasó entre dos jóvenes. Anota las respuestas a las preguntas y guárdalas para usarlas en el paso 3.

1 🔊 Vas a escuchar lo que ocurrió entre Laura y Enrique. Después de cada descripción, vas a oír dos preguntas. Escoge la respuesta correcta para cada pregunta.

1. **a.** fueron a ver una película en el cine   **b.** fueron a dar un paseo por el barrio

2. **a.** tres meses   **b.** nueve meses

3. **a.** de que la cena no estaba hecha   **b.** de que no tenía su bolsa

4. **a.** Regresó al parque para ver si encontraba la bolsa.   **b.** Fue a la casa de Enrique para ver si él tenía la bolsa.

5. **a.** a Enrique con otra chica   **b.** a una chica con su bolsa

6. **a.** que lo perdonaba   **b.** "¡Adiós!"

2 Ahora lee la carta que escribió Enrique.

Diana dice
CONSEJOS DE AMOR

DIFERENCIA DE OPINIÓN

Estimada Diana:
Necesito que me ayude con un problema. Mi amiga Laura y yo llevamos tres meses de novios. Es una chica fantástica y me encanta pasar tiempo con ella. Pero la verdad es que soy joven (tengo sólo 16 años), y todavía me gusta conocer a personas nuevas. Hace poco, pasé un día entero con Laura y nos divertimos mucho, pero por la noche tenía una cita con una amiga nueva. Fui con ella al parque para conversar cuando de repente pasó Laura y nos vió. Se enojó y salió corriendo. Laura ya no contesta mis llamadas ni me habla en el colegio. Normalmente es una chica muy comprensiva. Quiero reconciliarme con ella, pero temo que ella ya no confíe en mí. No creo que la culpa es mía, y quiero que hagamos las paces. ¿Qué hago?
—*Malentendido en Santiago*

3 Habla con un(a) compañero(a) sobre el conflicto entre Laura y Enrique. ¿Qué opinan de cada joven? ¿Qué aconsejan a Enrique? ¿Está equivocado? ¿Debe pedirle perdón a Laura? ¿Y qué aconsejan a Laura? ¿Debe confiar en Enrique? ¿Deben seguir de novios? Presenten sus recomendaciones a la clase. Si no están de acuerdo, expliquen sus diferencias de opinión. Usen las siguientes expresiones para conectar sus ideas.

cuando	entonces	porque	es importante que	es una lástima que

DIFFERENTIATED INSTRUCTION

Heritage Language Learners

Some students with a particularly strong command of spoken Spanish may be able to skip Step 1 of the *Presentación oral* on the next page and offer problems and solutions orally without writing them down.

Students with Learning Difficulties

Before students begin the first part of *¿Qué me cuentas?*, review the directions, emphasizing that they will hear three descriptions and two questions after each description. Suggest that after answering questions 1 and 2, they put down their pencils and listen to the next description. The same applies after questions 3 and 4, and 5 and 6.

Presentación oral

Una sesión del consejo estudiantil

Tarea

Los consejos estudiantiles *(student councils)* son grupos de estudiantes que ayudan a resolver problemas en la escuela. Trabaja con un grupo para representar ante la clase una sesión del consejo estudiantil.

❶ **Prepárate** Al reunirse el consejo, algunos miembros deben presentar un problema y otros deben hacer sugerencias sobre cómo resolverlo. Anoten sus ideas en una tabla como ésta.

Problemas	Soluciones posibles
•	•
•	•

❷ **Practica** Uno(a) de ustedes explica un problema y otro(a) sugiere soluciones. Lean lo que escribieron en la tabla y asignen turnos para que todos presenten por lo menos un problema o una solución.

Modelo
Miembro del consejo 1: *El problema que quiero presentar es el siguiente: Los estudiantes de los grados 10 y 11 siempre discuten en el gimnasio. Todos quieren jugar al básquetbol a la vez.*
Miembro del consejo 2: *Hablemos con el director para que tengamos recreos más largos y a horas diferentes.*
Miembro del consejo 3: *Pongámonos de acuerdo con ellos y tomemos turnos para usar el gimnasio.*

❸ **Haz tu presentación** Hagan la representación ante la clase. El estudiante que presenta el problema puede ponerse de pie.

❹ **Evaluación** Tu profesor(a) utilizará la siguiente rúbrica para evaluar tu presentación.

Estrategia

Getting into your character
In some cases, your oral presentation will require you to act something out. Keep in mind the character you are representing and try to act, look, and speak in the same way your character would.

For this oral presentation, remember that your character is not in front of your class, but solving a school problem at a student council meeting.

Rubric	Score 1	Score 3	Score 5
How well you presented a problem	You presented no problem, or your problem could not be understood.	You mentioned a problem but it wasn't clearly presented.	Your problem was clearly and completely presented.
How well you presented solutions	You offered no solutions.	You offered some solutions, but they need development.	Your solutions were clearly and completely presented.
How well you portrayed your characters	Your speakers said very little. You offered no character portrayal.	Your speakers read their lines.	Your speakers clearly portrayed realistic characters.

Speaking (4)

Ⓒ **Common Core: Speaking**

Presentación oral

Core Instruction

Standards: 1.1, 1.3, 3.1

Resources: Voc. and Gram. Transparency 4

Focus: Preparing and delivering an oral presentation

Suggestions: Review the task and the four-step approach with students. Review the rubric with the class (see *Assessment* below). Before students begin practicing in Step 2, direct their attention to the *Estrategia*. Encourage them to practice at home before a mirror or with a partner in class to develop their drama skills.

Portfolio

Make video or audio recordings of student presentations in class, or assign the RealTalk activity so they can record their presentations online. Include the recording in their portfolios.

Pre-AP* Support

- **Learning Objective:** Presentational Speaking
- **Activity:** Remind students to focus on the presentational speaking skills used in this task such as fluency, pronunciation, and comprehensibility.
- **Pre-AP* Resource Book:** Comprehensive guide to Pre-AP* speaking skill development, pp. 39–50

Block Schedule

You might want to set up the presentation in a way similar to a trial as seen on Court TV. Videotape each scene and encourage one of the students to "introduce" each episode.

Additional Resources

Student Resource: Realidades para hispanohablantes, p. 134

ENRICH YOUR TEACHING

21st Century Skills

Collaboration Have students clearly define the tasks they need to accomplish for this "mock" student council presentation. Have them evenly divide up the tasks so each person has an equal role in defining the problem, determining the solution, and presenting to the class.

✓ASSESSMENT

Presentación oral
- Assessment Program: Rubrics, p. T30
  Review the different levels of performance. After assessing students, help individuals understand how their performance could be improved. (See Teacher's Resource Book for suggestions on using rubrics in assessment.)

4 Writing

Language Arts Connection: Expository Writing

Standards: 3.1

Ask students to revisit stories they have read in their Language Arts classes. Have them study scenes in which two characters interact and ask: *¿Cómo se portan los dos personajes cuando hay un conflicto? ¿Cómo nos demuestran sus cualidades? ¿Cómo influyeron las cualidades de los personajes en la resolución del conflicto?*

 Common Core: Writing

Presentación escrita

Core Instruction

Standards: 1.2, 1.3, 3.1

Resources: Voc. and Gram. Transparency 4

Focus: Combining learned vocabulary and structures in a written presentation

Suggestions: Begin by explaining the criteria you will use to evaluate students' compositions. (See Step 5, *Evaluación*, in the Student Edition, and *Assessment* on the following page.)

Direct students' attention to the *Estrategia*. Ask them to consider how a character's actions, words, and thoughts are closely linked to what he or she is like. Ask: *Si un personaje es entrometido, ¿qué va a hacer si ve a dos personas que hablan? Si un personaje es comprensivo, ¿qué va a hacer si un amigo le pide perdón?* On their own paper, have students begin a chart like the one shown on this page. Point out that for this assignment, students need to tell about an event that happened between the two characters that helps readers better see what they are like.

Block Schedule

Collect the first drafts and write sentences that show examples of errors. Distribute these to pairs of students to find and fix the errors. Do not identify which papers the errors came from. This will help them become more aware of common errors and assist them with self-editing.

190

▼ Objectives
- ▶ Write a description of a relationship
- ▶ Use the character's actions to describe them

Presentación escrita
Una relación

> **Estrategia**
>
> **Describing relationships**
> Good writers help readers deduce the relationships between characters from their actions, words, and thoughts. Think about what caused the conflicts or friendships between the people you will write about. How did their actions, thoughts, or words cause a reaction from other characters? Why?

Piensa en algún cuento sobre la amistad entre dos personas. Escribe una composición sobre los personajes. Describe cómo son, qué cosas tienen en común, en qué son diferentes y cómo es su relación.

1 Antes de escribir

Para ayudarte a recordar a los personajes de tu composición, puedes hacerte las siguientes preguntas.

- ¿Quiénes eran los personajes? ¿Qué cualidades tenían?
- ¿Qué cosas tenían en común? ¿En qué se diferenciaban?
- ¿Tuvieron algún problema? ¿Cómo lo resolvieron?

Completa la tabla para preparar tu composición. En la primera columna, apunta los nombres de los personajes. En la segunda, haz una lista de sus cualidades. En la tercera, apunta las acciones de los personajes que contribuyen *(contribute)* a la armonía o al conflicto. En la cuarta, describe por qué los personajes hacen lo que hacen y, finalmente, en la quinta, saca conclusiones sobre cómo sus acciones y cualidades influyen en la relación que tienen.

2 Borrador

Escribe tu borrador. Para empezar, describe a los personajes. Luego cuenta qué problema tuvieron y cómo lo resolvieron. Por último, saca conclusiones sobre la relación.

Personajes	Cualidades	Acciones	¿Por qué?	¿Cómo influyen en la relación?
Sandra	generosa, alegre, habla mucho, hace bromas	dijo que había copiado un examen	hacía muchos chistes	
Paola	callada, honesta	le dijo a Sandra que hablara con la profesora	sabía que era un malentendido	

Modelo

Presenting the main characters: Describe the characters using specific words.

Sandra y Paola son amigas. Sandra es generosa y alegre. Paola es callada y honesta. Le preocupa que Sandra tenga problemas por hacer muchos chistes. Alguien le contó a la profesora que Sandra copió en la prueba. Paola estaba segura de que era un chiste. Luego . . .

Main conflict: Describe the characters' actions.

Conflict resolution: Explain the consequences of the characters' actions.

Sandra fue a hablar con la profesora para resolver el malentendido.

Creo que estas chicas tienen una buena amistad. Lo que hizo Paola muestra que piensa en los demás, y que Sandra le hizo caso muestra que tiene confianza en su amiga.

Conclusion: Draw conclusions about the relationship.

190 ciento noventa
¡Adelante!

DIFFERENTIATED INSTRUCTION

Heritage Language Learners

Students may sometimes confuse the letters **b** and **v** in their writing since these letters are often pronounced the same way in Spanish. As part of the revision process, have students use a dictionary to be sure that they have spelled all words with **b** and **v** correctly.

Advanced Learners

Ask students to write a short scene or part of a scene from a play in which two characters are in conflict. Students do not have to resolve the conflict in this scene. Have them share their scenes with other students, who tell what the characters are like, based on what they do, say, or think in the scene.

3 Redacción/Revisión

Después de escribir el borrador, intercambia tu trabajo con el de un(a) compañero(a) y hagan sugerencias para mejorarlo. Revisen si:

- usaron palabras específicas para describir a los personajes
- hay concordancia *(agreement)* entre sustantivos, adjetivos, verbos y pronombres

Haz lo siguiente: Subraya con una línea los sustantivos, con dos líneas los adjetivos y encierra en un círculo los verbos. Asegúrate de que en cada oración haya concordancia.

> Sandra es generosa y alegre. Paola es callada y honesta. Le preocupan que Sandra tenga problemas por hacer muchos chistes. Alguien le contó a la profesora que Sandra copió en la prueba.
>
> *callada* *preocupa*

4 Publicación

Antes de hacer la versión final, lee tu borrador y repasa los siguientes puntos:

- ¿Describí claramente a los personajes?
- ¿Expliqué el conflicto y las acciones de los personajes?
- ¿Corresponde la conclusión a la descripción de los personajes?

Después de revisar el borrador, escribe una copia en limpio y ponle un título.

5 Evaluación

Se utilizará la siguiente rúbrica para evaluar tu presentación.

Rubric	Score 1	Score 3	Score 5
Your completion of task	Your lack of information or organization makes the writing unclear.	You offer descriptions, but important information is missing.	Choice and organization of information creates a convincing message.
Your description of characters	Your characters are not identified or described.	Your character descriptions need more development.	Your characters are clearly portrayed.
Sentence structure/ grammar, spelling, mechanics	Your sentences are run-on or are fragmented. There are many grammar, spelling, and mechanics errors.	You use sentences consistently. Some grammar, spelling, and/ or mechanics errors are present.	You use correct structure. There are few grammar, spelling, and mechanics errors.

Suggestions (Cont'd):
Once students have a rough draft ready, read through the model on this page together. Help them see how information from the chart on the previous page was incorporated into this draft and note the additional information that was added. Point out uses of the subjunctive and of **por** and **para.** Encourage them to work toward similar organization, level of detail, and language use as they revise their own drafts.

Common Errors: Students often have difficulty effectively organizing their writing. Guide them to follow these steps in their composition:

A. Give a general description of the characters.

B. Introduce a conflict.

C. Show how the characters acted in the conflict.

D. Show how the conflict was resolved.

Evaluation

Steps 4 and 5 overlap. Students will need some evaluation by you, their peers, or some self-evaluation to polish their drafts.

Portfolio

Keep students' final drafts in their portfolios as a writing sample.

Pre-AP* Support

- **Learning Objective:** Presentational Writing
- **Activity:** As a warm-up to the *Presentación escrita*, ask students to brainstorm a list of five or more qualities of a healthy friendship and five or more qualities of an unhealthy relationship.
- **Pre-AP* Resource Book:** Comprehensive guide to Pre-AP* writing skill development, pp. 27–38

Additional Resources

Student Resource: Realidades para hispanohablantes, p. 135

ENRICH YOUR TEACHING

21st Century Skills

Media Literacy Have the students brainstorm a list of famous relationships as seen in modern day television shows, movies, or books they all know. Discuss how each relationship is portrayed in the media (in the spoken language, gestures or body language, conflicts, music, etc.) and how the media may influence how we perceive each relationship.

✓ ASSESSMENT

Presentación escrita

- Assessment Program: Rubrics, p. T31
  Review the different levels of performance. After assessing students, help individuals understand how their performance could be improved. (See Teacher's Resource Book for suggestions on using rubrics in assessment.)

Common Core: Reading

Lectura

Core Instruction

Standards: 1.2, 2.1, 2.2, 3.1, 3.2, 5.2

Resources: Fine Art Transparencies with Teacher's Guide, p. 50

Mapa global interactivo, Actividad 2 Visit places where poet Pablo Neruda lived in Chile.

Focus: Reading poems and analyzing figurative language

Suggestions:

Pre-reading: Before reading, direct students' attention to the *Al leer* section and to the *Estrategia*. Address any difficulties they may have understanding the concepts of **la metáfora** and **el símil,** and provide additional examples as necessary. Copy the graphic organizer from p. 195 and read the instructions that accompany it. Tell students that they will first work with a partner to record the examples of figurative language they find. Later, the class will compile their findings.

Reading: Have students work in pairs to read each poem using this procedure:

• Read the poem silently.

• Discuss comprehension problems, find examples of figurative language, and record these on the chart.

• Read the poem again silently.

Besides the instances of figurative language mentioned in the *¿Comprendiste?* on the next page, the following are other instances found in *Poema No. 15* that students should notice:

Metáfora

mariposa en arrullo (line 10)

Símil

Eres como la noche (line 15)

BELLRINGER REVIEW

As a class, brainstorm a list of words to describe personality traits of good friends. (*honesto, cariñoso,* etc.)

Additional Resources

Student Resource: Guided Practice: Lectura, pp. 142–143

Lectura

La poesía, expresión de amor y amistad

▼ Objectives

▶ Read about poems of love and friendship
▶ Identify figurative language to understand a poem
▶ Express your opinion about rap and rap poetry readings

Estrategia

Identifying and understanding figurative language When somebody says *He ruffled his friend's feathers,* do you think that the friend is a bird? Of course not. This is a figurative language expression that means "to bother" or "to annoy". To identify figurative language, pay attention to phrases that connect two different kinds of things, for example *cheeks like roses,* or *life is a river.* Then, to figure out what the poet is trying to communicate, think what characteristics of one of the things can be used to describe the other.

Al leer

En la cultura del mundo hispanohablante la poesía es una de las formas preferidas para expresar lo que sentimos. Para crear sus poemas, los poetas usan figuras retóricas *(figures of speech)* como la metáfora y el símil.

El símil es una comparación que se hace entre dos cosas usando la palabra *como.* Por ejemplo, el poeta Pablo Neruda habla de un "silencio claro como una lámpara". Con las metáforas también se hacen comparaciones entre dos cosas, pero sin usar la palabra *como.* Por ejemplo, cuando el poeta llama a la mujer que ama "mariposa de sueño", la está comparando con una mariposa. Copia la tabla de la página 195. Mientras lees los poemas, completa los espacios en blanco de la tabla.

Presta atención a los siguientes puntos:

• cómo los poemas expresan amor o amistad
• el uso de las metáforas y los símiles
• las imágenes que usa el o la poeta

Poema No. 15

Pablo Neruda

Me gustas cuando callas[1] porque estás como ausente[2],
y me oyes desde lejos, y mi voz no te toca.
Parece que los ojos se te hubieran volado[3] y
parece que un beso te cerrara la boca.

Como todas las cosas están llenas de mi alma[4]
emerges de las cosas, llena del alma mía.
Mariposa de sueño[5], te pareces a mi alma,
y te pareces a la palabra melancolía.

Me gustas cuando callas y estás como distante.
Y estás como quejándote, mariposa en arrullo[6].
Y me oyes desde lejos, y mi voz no te alcanza:
déjame que me calle con el silencio tuyo.

Déjame que te hable también con tu silencio
claro como una lámpara, simple como un anillo.
Eres como la noche, callada y constelada.
Tu silencio es de estrella, tan lejano y sencillo.

Me gustas cuando callas porque estás como ausente.
Distante y dolorosa como si hubieras muerto.
Una palabra entonces, una sonrisa bastan[7]. Y
estoy alegre, alegre de que no sea cierto.

---

1 you are quiet **2** absent **3** had flown **4** soul
5 dream butterfly **6** cooing **7** suffice

DIFFERENTIATED INSTRUCTION

Heritage Language Learners

Have students select a Latin American artist whose works express love or friendship. They may choose a poem, a song, or a piece of visual art. Ask them to write a paragraph about how the artist expresses his or her love or friendship. Have them also mention what they like and don't like about the work.

Multiple Intelligences

Visual/Spatial: Invite students to close their eyes as you read the poems out loud. Then invite them to share the mental images that the poets' words evoked.

Homenaje a los padres chicanos

Abelardo Delgado

Con el semblante[1] callado,
con el consejo bien templado[2],
demandando siempre respeto,
con la mano ampollada[3] y el orgullo repleto,
así eres tú y nosotros te hablamos este día,
padre, papá, apá, jefito, dad, daddy . . . father,
como acostumbremos llamarte, eres el mismo.
La cultura nuestra dicta[4]
        que el cariño que te tenemos
lo demostremos poco
        y unos hasta creemos
que father's day
        es cosa de los gringos
            pero no . . ,
tu sacrificio es muy sagrado
para dejarlo pasar hoy en callado.
Tu sudor[5] es agua bendita[6]
y tu palabra sabia[7],
derecha como esos surcos[8]
que con fe unos labran[9] día tras día,
nos sirve de alimento espiritual
y tu sufrir por tierras
y costumbres extrañas,
tu aguante[10], tu amparo[11], tu apoyo,
todo eso lo reconocemos y lo agradecemos
y te llamamos hoy con fuerza
        para que oigas

aun si[12] ya estás muerto,
        aun si la carga fue mucha
o la tentación bastante
        y nos abandonaste
aun si estás en la cárcel[13]
o en un hospital . . .
óyeme, padre chicano, oye también a mis
hermanos, hoy y siempre, papá, te veneramos.

---

1 face 2 tempered 3 blistered 4 dictates 5 sweat
6 holy water 7 wise 8 grooves 9 plow 10 endurance
11 protection 12 even if 13 jail

¿Comprendiste?

Trabaja con un grupo para hablar de las poesías y contestar estas preguntas:

1. ¿Qué quiere decir el poeta con "Me gusta cuando callas porque estás como ausente"?
2. ¿Qué te parece que quiere decir Neruda con "tu silencio claro como una lámpara, simple como un anillo"?
3. ¿Por qué se alegra el poeta en la última estrofa del "Poema No. 15"?
4. ¿Qué crees que quiere decir Delgado con "con la mano ampollada y el orgullo repleto"?
5. Describe las características de los padres que admira Delgado.

ENRICH YOUR TEACHING

Culture Note

Pablo Neruda (1904–1973), a Chilean poet and diplomat, won the Nobel Prize for Literature in 1971. He was politically active, holding various positions as Chilean consul to Burma, Argentina, and Mexico. In 1943, he was elected to the Chilean Senate. Much of Neruda's writing reflects political struggles, and he became known as the people's poet. Neruda is also greatly admired for his love poems. His poetry is more widely read than that of any other Latin American poet.

Suggestions (Cont'd):

Reading: Besides the instances of figurative language mentioned in the *¿Comprendiste?* on the next page, the following are other instances that students should notice:

El amor en preguntas:

Metáfora

volver a nacer (line 5)

inventar la gente (line 6)

crecer otra vez (line 9)

Point out that these are all metaphors the poet uses to describe what one must do to love and be loved. None of them are meant to be taken literally; instead they refer metaphorically to actions of the spirit.

Como tú:

Metáfora

el paisaje celeste de los días de enero (lines 3–4)

Mi sangre bulle (line 5)

Símil

la poesía es como el pan (line 9)

AP* Literature: Gustavo Adolfo Bécquer is an AP* Literature author. You may want to suggest that students read additional works by this author.

Teaching with Art

Resources: Fine Art Transparencies with Teacher's Guide, p. 50

Suggestions: To guide discussion of the painting, ask: Who is present in the painting? What are the decorations like? What story does the picture tell? What feelings does the artist convey, and how? For more ideas, see the *Fine Art Transparencies Teacher's Guide*.

Rimas

Gustavo Adolfo Bécquer

XXI

¿Qué es poesía? —dices mientras clavas[1]
  en mi pupila tu pupila azul—.
¿Qué es poesía? ¿Y tú me lo preguntas?
  Poesía . . . eres tú.

XXIII

Por [2] una mirada, un mundo;
por una sonrisa, un cielo,
por un beso . . . , ¡yo no sé
qué te diera[3] por un beso!

XXVIII

Los suspiros[4] son aire y van al aire.
Las lágrimas[5] son agua y van al mar.
Dime, mujer: cuando el amor se
olvida, ¿sabes tú a dónde va?

---

1 fix **2** in exchange for **3** I would give **4** sighs **5** tears

El amor en preguntas

Elizabeth Torres *15 años*

¿Qué me hace falta para amar?
¿Qué es necesario para ser amado,
para entender la vida y saber soñar?
Tengo acaso que obtener permisos,
girar el mundo,
volver a nacer,
inventar la gente,
dar para merecer[1],
responder preguntas,
crecer[2] otra vez?

¿O se necesita estar inspirado,
abarcar[3] el mundo,
ser iluminado?

Estallar[4] el alma . . .
¡sólo para amar!

---

1 to deserve **2** to grow **3** to cover **4** to burst

194 ciento noventa y cuatro
¡Adelante!

Como tú

Roque Dalton

Yo, como tú,
amo el amor, la vida, el dulce encanto
de las cosas, el paisaje
celeste de los días de enero.

También mi sangre bulle[1]
y río por los ojos que
han conocido el brote[2] de las lágrimas.

Creo que el mundo es bello,
que la poesía es como el pan, de todos.

Y que mis venas[3] no terminan en mí
sino en la sangre unánime
de los que luchan por la vida,
el amor,
las cosas,
el paisaje y el pan,
la poesía de todos.

---

1 boils **2** outpouring **3** veins

"La salchichona", (1917), Pablo Picasso
Oil on canvas, 116 x 89 cm. Musée Picasso, Barcelona, Spain. © 2009 Estate of Pablo Picasso/Artists Rights Society (ARS), New York. Photo: Giraudon/Art Resource, NY.

DIFFERENTIATED INSTRUCTION

Heritage Language Learners

Invite students with exemplary pronunciation to read aloud one stanza of each poem. After each reading, point out words that are linked together in spoken language. For example, in the first line of **Rimas**, the **e** sound in **qué** is elided with the first sound of the next word, **es.**

Advanced Learners

Ask students to read another poem by one of the poets studied and give a brief interpretation of its meaning and its use of figurative language.

Interacción con la lectura

METÁFORA	SÍMIL
_____	_____
_____	_____
_____	_____
_____	_____
_____	_____

Trabaja con la clase para completar una tabla como la de arriba y comentar lo que cada poeta quiere decir.

- Identifiquen y apunten todas las metáforas y símiles que encuentren en los poemas.
- Hablen acerca de lo que quiere trasmitir el poeta con cada uno(a).

Más práctica GO

realidades.com | print

Guided WB pp. 142–143	✔	✔
Comm. WB p. 184	✔	✔
Cultural Reading Activity	✔	

¿Comprendiste?

1. ¿Cuál es el tema de cada poema?
2. Según Bécquer, ¿la poesía está en las palabras de un poema? ¿Estás de acuerdo con el poeta? ¿Por qué?
3. En la "Rima XXVIII", ¿qué comparación hace el autor entre los suspiros, las lágrimas y el amor?
4. Después de leer el poema de Elizabeth Torres, ¿crees que es necesario hacer cosas extraordinarias para ser amado por las otras personas? ¿Por qué?
5. ¿Qué quiere decir Roque Dalton cuando escribe "mis venas no terminan en mí"?
6. ¿Cuál de los poemas te gustó más? ¿Por qué?
7. Forma un grupo con tres compañeros(as) para dar su opinión sobre estos temas:

- ¿Qué medios usan los jóvenes para expresar sus sentimientos? Hagan una lista.
- ¿De qué manera esas expresiones de sentimientos benefician a la comunidad?

▼ Fondo Cultural | El mundo hispano

La lectura de poemas por sus propios autores es una costumbre muy popular en bibliotecas y librerías de toda España y América Latina. De igual manera, en los Estados Unidos se realiza una actividad cultural similar; en muchos centros comunitarios[1] se hacen concursos de poesía y rap, en los cuales los poetas leen sus obras ante el público. Por ejemplo, en la Ciudad de Nueva York, el *Nuyorican Poet's Cafe*, organiza concursos literarios y lecturas en español y en inglés.

- Muchas personas creen que el rap es una forma de poesía. ¿Estás de acuerdo? ¿Por qué?
- ¿Te interesa asistir a un concurso en el que los poetas de rap recitan sus poemas? ¿Por qué?
- ¿Te interesa asistir a un concurso de poesía que no sea rap? ¿Por qué?

1 community centers

ciento noventa y cinco **195**
Capítulo 4

▼ Interacción con la lectura Standards: 1.1, 1.2, 3.1

Resources: Voc. and Gram. Transparency 4
Suggestions:

Post-reading: Have students compile the examples of figurative language they and their partners have found into a class chart. Use this activity as a basis for further discussion of the poems.

▼ ¿Comprendiste? Standards: 1.1, 1.2, 1.3, 3.2

Focus: Demonstrating reading comprehension and understanding of figurative language

Suggestions: For item 7, ask the small groups to divide the task in such a way that everyone participates in reporting orally.

Answers will vary.

Fondo cultural

Standards: 1.1, 1.2, 2.1

Suggestions: After reading and discussing the information, ask interested students to work together to prepare and present a poetry reading. Students can research Spanish-language poetry at libraries and on the Internet, then present readings of the poems. Encourage them to accompany each reading with a brief interpretation of the poem's meaning.

Answers will vary.

For Further Reading

Student Resource: Lecturas 3: "Los abuelos de Chiquitín y Chiquitán," pp. 4–5, "La verdadera historia del pastor y el lobo," pp. 8–10

AP* Literature Author: Pablo Neruda, Lecturas 3: "Sonetos de amor," pp. 22–25

ENRICH YOUR TEACHING

Culture Note

As students read about love in Spanish literature, explain the origins of the appellation "Don Juan." Never an actual person, Don Juan is a legendary character of Spanish folklore. The earliest-known dramatization of a Don Juan story, *El burlador de Sevilla,* was written by Tirso de Molina in 1630.

21st Century Skills

Technology Literacy Have students use the digital technology within **realidades.com** to access extra reading support. Computer corrected activities use reading strategies to help students build their vocabulary and progress at their own pace through the reading.

4 Review

Review Activities

Cualidades: Have students create a T-chart with the left column titled **Cualidades positivas** and the right titled **Cualidades negativas.** Ask them to sort the vocabulary from the **cualidades** list into these two categories and to write a brief Spanish definition for each word.

Sustantivos: Build a story using the nouns in this section of the *Vocabulario*. Have students sit in a circle. One student begins the story with a sentence that includes the word **amistad.** The student to his or her left continues by repeating that sentence and adding another that uses the word **armonía,** and so on. A variation on this is to write the words on slips of paper and place them in a hat or other container. This is passed around the circle. Students must build the story by adding a sentence that includes the word they draw from the hat.

Verbos: Have students work in pairs to invent mini-dialogues that use the verbs in the list. Each dialogue should use at least one of the verbs. Encourage them to use the verbs in different tenses, in the subjunctive, and with different subjects, in order to practice with different forms.

Expresiones: Play charades using the expressions from this list. Write the expressions on slips of paper and place them in a hat or other container. Students take turns drawing an expression and getting its meaning across to the others any way they can without speaking or writing. Use body language and strategies of traditional charades such as tugging at the ear to mean **suena como** or holding up two fingers to mean **dos palabras,** or invent your own rules.

El subjuntivo con verbos de emoción: On the board, write several subordinate **(que)** clauses, using a variety of verbs in the subjunctive. Vary the subjects of your clauses in order to use different verb forms. Precede each subordinate clause with a blank: ___ *que vayas.* ___ *que Uds. vayan a llegar tarde.* Have students supply verbs or expressions of emotion that make sense: *Te sugiero que vayas. Temo que Uds. vayan a llegar tarde.*

Repaso del capítulo
Vocabulario y gramática

cualidades

amable	kind
cariñoso, -a	loving, affectionate
celoso, -a	jealous
chismoso, -a	gossipy
comprensivo, -a	understanding
considerado, -a	considerate
egoísta	selfish
entrometido, -a	meddlesome, interfering
honesto, -a	honest
íntimo, -a	intimate
sincero, -a	sincere
vanidoso, -a	vain, conceited

sustantivos

la amistad	friendship
la armonía	harmony
el comportamiento	behavior
la confianza	trust
el conflicto	conflict
la cualidad	quality
la explicación	explanation
el malentendido	misunderstanding
la pelea	fight
el secreto	secret

verbos

acusar	to accuse
alegrarse	to be delighted
apoyar(se)	to support, to back (each other)
atreverse	to dare
colaborar	to collaborate
confiar (i → í)	to trust
contar con	to count on
criticar	to criticize
desconfiar (i → í)	to mistrust
esperar	to hope (for)
estar equivocado, -a	to be mistaken
guardar (un secreto)	to keep (a secret)
ignorar	to ignore
mejorar	to improve

pedir perdón	to ask for forgiveness
perdonar	to forgive
ponerse de acuerdo	to reach an agreement
reaccionar	to react
reconciliarse	to become friends again
reconocer (c → zc)	to admit, recognize
resolver (o → ue)	to resolve
sorprender(se)	to (be) surprised
temer	to fear

expresiones

aceptar tal como (soy)	to accept (me) the way (I am)
cambiar de opinión	to change one's mind
la diferencia de opinión	difference of opinion
hacer caso	to pay attention / to obey
hacer las paces	to make peace (with)
juntos, -as	together
ojalá	I wish, I hope
pensar en sí mismo(a)	to think of oneself
¡Qué va!	No way!
tener en común	to have in common
tener celos	to be jealous
tener la culpa	to be guilty
¡Yo no fui!	It was not me!

DIFFERENTIATED INSTRUCTION

Students with Learning Difficulties

Whenever possible, provide students with memory clues for retaining vocabulary. For example, say: "**Egoísta** looks like the English word 'egotistic.' Someone who is egotistic thinks a lot of him or herself and is probably selfish." Invite students to share their own memory devices.

Advanced Learners

Have students write a short letter to a friend that uses vocabulary and structures from the chapter. Letters can be one of two types: either thanking the friend for his or her positive role in resolving a problem, or reproaching the friend for an undesirable action. Have students look back through the chapter for models of similar letters, such as the ones on pp. 163 and 173.

El subjuntivo con verbos de emoción

Use the *subjunctive* following verbs indicating suggestions, desire or demands. **Te sugiero** que **vengas**. **Esperamos** que **llueva**. **Nos exigió** que **estudiemos**. **¡Ojalá** que **se diviertan!**	Use the *subjunctive* after verbs and impersonal phrases indicating emotion. **Tememos** que nuestros amigos **desconfíen** de nosotros. **Es una lástima** que no **hagan** las paces.	When the sentence has only one subject, we usually use the *infinitive* instead of the subjunctive. **Espero ir** mañana al cine. **Espero ver** esa película.

Los usos de *por* y *para*

Use *por* to indicate: length of time or distance, where an action takes place, an exchange, a reason or motive, an action on behalf of someone, a means of communication or transportation. Bailamos **por** varias horas. Busqué **por** todos los pasillos. Te cambio el café **por** un dulce. Me puse muy feliz **por** tu llegada. Fue a una marcha **por** la paz. Mandó la carta **por** avión.	Use *por* in certain expressions: **por** ejemplo **por** eso (tanto) **por** la (mañana, tarde, noche) **por** favor **por** lo general **por** primera (segunda, tercera, última) vez **por** supuesto	Use *para* to indicate: purpose, destination, a point in time, use, opinion. Estudio **para** tener un buen futuro. Salimos **para** la ciudad dentro de una hora. **Para** las ocho ya estaban allí. Ponte la chaqueta **para** no tener frío. **Para** ustedes todo es divertido.

Mandatos con *nosotros*

Regular verbs		Stem-changing verbs whose infinitive ends in *–ir*		Verbs ending in *–car*, *–gar*, and *–zar*	
olvidar	**olvidemos**	ped**ir**	**pidamos**	criti**car**	**critiquemos**
pensar	**pensemos**	dorm**ir**	**durmamos**	pa**gar**	**paguemos**
reconocer	**reconozcamos**			empe**zar**	**empecemos**

Direct and **indirect pronouns** are attached at the end of affirmative *nosotros* commands but precede the negative *nosotros* command form. **Digámosle toda** la verdad. No **les mintamos**.	To attach **reflexive** or **reciprocal pronouns** at the end of a *nosotros* command, drop the final *–s* of the command before the pronoun. **Alegrémonos** con nuestro éxito. **Abracémonos** uno al otro.

Pronombres posesivos

To form the **possesive pronouns,** use the long form possessive adjectives preceded by the definite article. Mis padres son muy serios. ¿Y **los suyos**? Su vestido es grande. **El nuestro** es pequeño. We often omit the article between the verb *ser* and the possessive pronoun. Esas maletas **son nuestras,** pero la mochila **es suya**.

Los usos de por y para: Have pairs write their own fill-in-the-blank quiz on the uses of *por* and *para*. Their quizzes should contain ten sentences in which one of the words is required. Tell students to include a variety of items in order to target the various rules of usage. They should make two copies, and they should also create an answer key. Then have pairs exchange their quizzes with another pair, take each other's quizzes, and check their work.

Mandatos con nosotros: Have students write three problems that need solving, such as *Mi computadora no funciona bien.* Have partners take turns reading these to each other and replying with a *nosotros* command that makes sense: *Llamemos a un técnico de computadoras.*

Pronombres posesivos: Have students create two sets of note cards. One set names individuals or groups of people, such as **María** or **los abuelos.** The other set names single or multiple nouns, such as **los problemas** or **el secreto.** Collect the cards and shuffle each set. Have students take turns drawing one card from each pile and making a sentence with a possessive pronoun: *María/los problemas: Los problemas son suyos.*

Portfolio

Invite students to review the activities and projects they completed in this chapter. Have them select one or two items that they feel best demonstrate their achievements in Spanish. Include these products in students' portfolios with the Chapter Checklist and Self-Assessment Worksheet.

Additional Resources

Student Resources: Realidades para hispanohablantes, pp. 136–137

Teacher Resources:
- Teacher's Resource Book: Situation Cards, p. 228, Clip Art, pp. 229–235
- Assessment Program: Chapter Checklist and Self-Assessment Worksheet, pp. T49–T50

¡Pura vida! is a storyline video that is independent of chapter content and an ideal support for expanding listening skills. The 14 episodes are available within **realidades.com** or on a separate DVD. Student activities and Teacher support are also assignable within **realidades.com**.

ENRICH YOUR TEACHING

Teacher-to-Teacher

By creating their own tools for learning, students can benefit twice: once as they are creating the tool and again as they are using it. When asking students to make tools such as flashcards, for example, make sure that your instructions are clear and give several examples so students understand exactly what is needed.

21st Century Skills

Initiative and Self-Direction Remind students of the various digital tools available in **realidades.com** to help them monitor their own understanding and learning needs, such as the online tutorials with comprehension check exercises, interactive puzzles, flashcards, and practice tests.

Performance Tasks

Standards: 1.1, 1.2, 1.3, 2.1

Student Resource: Realidades para hispanohablantes, pp. 138–139

Teacher Resources: Teacher's Resource Book: Audio Script, p. 219; Audio Program DVD: Cap. 4, Track 19; Answer Keys: Student Edition, p. 60

1. Vocabulario

Suggestions: Encourage students to review the vocabulary from the *A primera vista* sections on pp. 160–162 and 174–177 before they complete the activity.

Answers:

1. a   5. c
2. b   6. b
3. d   7. d
4. b   8. a

2. Gramática

Suggestions: Remind students of the main points of the grammar presentations in *Capítulo* 4:

• the subjunctive with verbs of emotion
• uses of **por** and **para**
• **nosotros** commands
• possessive pronouns

Answers:

1. c   5. a
2. a   6. d
3. b   7. b
4. b   8. a

Preparación para el examen

1 Vocabulario Escribe la letra de la palabra o expresión que mejor complete cada frase. Escribe tus respuestas en una hoja aparte.

1. Mis sobrinos siempre me besan y me abrazan. Son muy _____.
   a. cariñosos   c. entrometidos
   b. sinceros   d. honestos

2. Cuando dos amigos se reconcilian, _____.
   a. piensan en sí mismos   c. piensan en los demás
   b. hacen las paces   d. tienen la culpa

3. Una persona _____ no sabe guardar secretos.
   a. vanidosa   c. celosa
   b. egoísta   d. chismosa

4. Beto y Graciela son _____. Nunca mienten.
   a. armonía   c. amables
   b. sinceros   d. comprensivos

5. Cuando acusé a mi amigo de romper mi cámara, él me contestó, "_____. ¡Yo no fui!"
   a. ¡Qué lástima!   c. ¡Qué va!
   b. ¡Ojalá!   d. ¡Tienes razón!

6. Mis padres nunca me _____. Me aceptan tal como soy.
   a. hacen caso   c. temen
   b. critican   d. piden perdón

7. Mis amigos y yo tenemos _____. Nos gusta montar en monopatín y jugar videojuegos.
   a. celos   c. muchas peleas
   b. mucha confianza   d. mucho en común

8. El cariño y la confianza son dos _____ importantes en una amistad.
   a. cualidades   c. consejos
   b. conflictos   d. explicaciones

2 Gramática Escribe la letra de la palabra o expresión que complete mejor cada frase. Escribe tus respuestas en una hoja aparte.

1. Me molesta que ustedes _____ tan chismosos.
   a. son   c. sean
   b. seas   d. es

2. Ojalá que ella me _____.
   a. perdone   c. perdona
   b. perdonado   d. perdonando

3. Es triste _____ nuestra amistad.
   a. rompa   c. roto
   b. romper   d. rompo

4. Fernando y Pedro _____ todos los días.
   a. nos escribíamos   c. les escribí
   b. se escribían   d. se escribió

5. Mis hermanas y yo _____ contábamos todos los secretos.
   a. nos   c. se
   b. me   d. lo

6. Después de pelearse con su mejor amigo, Jorge le dijo: "_____ las paces".
   a. hacíamos   c. hicimos
   b. hacemos   d. hagamos

7. "¿Nos reconciliamos?", preguntó Ana. "Sí, _____," contestó Gaby.
   a. reconciliarme   c. reconciliémosnos
   b. reconciliémonos   d. reconciliamos

8. Mis padres son muy comprensivos. ¿Cómo son _____?
   a. los tuyos   c. las tuyas
   b. tuyos   d. tuyas

DIFFERENTIATED INSTRUCTION

Heritage Language Learners

Remind students to take their time during both the chapter review and the actual exam. Point out that, even though they may have the necessary language skills to do well, they will have a higher chance of success if they read carefully and follow all directions.

Students with Learning Difficulties

Review test-taking strategies to prepare students for the exam. Remind them to read the directions before they begin each section. Practice using the process of elimination in items that resemble multiple-choice items on a test. Remind students that when deciding between two possible answers, first instincts are often correct.

Más repaso GO realidades.com | print

Instant Check	✔	
Puzzles	✔	
Core WB pp. 61–62		✔
Comm. WB pp. 185, 186–188	✔	✔

En el examen vas a . . .	Éstas son las tareas de práctica que te pueden ser útiles para el examen . . .	Para repasar, ve a tu libro de texto impreso o digital . . .
Interpretive		
❸ **Escuchar** Escuchar y comprender la descripción de un buen amigo o de una buena amiga	El locutor de un canal de televisión entrevistó a varios jóvenes sobre lo que piensan de sus amigos. Escucha lo que dijo cada joven y, según lo que dijo, decide: (a) qué cualidades tiene su mejor amigo(a); (b) qué le molesta de su amigo(a); (c) qué tienen en común.	**pp. 160–163** *A primera vista 1: Vocabulario en contexto* **pp. 164–165** Actividades 6–7 **p. 166** Actividad 8
Interpersonal		
❹ **Hablar** Expresar opiniones y emociones sobre el comportamiento de otra persona	Estás cuidando a tu hermano menor que a veces se porta bien y a veces bastante mal. Dile a tu hermano lo que piensas y sientes acerca de su comportamiento. Usa por lo menos cinco frases. Por ejemplo, puedes decir: *Me alegro de que no tengas celos de nuestra hermanita. Es triste que no le hagas caso a mamá.*	**p. 168** *El subjuntivo con verbos de emoción* **p. 169** Actividades 13–14 **p. 171** Actividad 17 **p. 181** Actividades 31–32
Interpretive		
❺ **Leer** Leer y comprender un mensaje en un salón de chat	Lee este mensaje que una joven puso en un salón de chat. Decide por qué tiene tantos conflictos con sus amigos y qué debe hacer para mejorar su relación con ellos. **No entiendo por qué mis amigos están enojados conmigo. Ana dice que nunca le presto mis revistas. Lucía está enojada porque le conté a su mamá que sacó una mala nota. Luis está furioso porque llegué dos horas tarde al cine y no pudimos ver la película. En fin, ¡mi vida es un desastre! ¿Qué puedo hacer?**	**p. 161** *A primera vista 1: Vocabulario en contexto* **p. 168** Actividad 12 **p. 173** Actividad 21 **pp. 174–176** *A primera vista 2: Vocabulario en contexto*
Presentational		
❻ **Escribir** Escribir sobre un conflicto entre amigos(as)	Escribe sobre un conflicto que ocurre entre dos amigos(as) en una película que viste o entre amigos(as) de la vida real. Explica por qué se rompe la armonía y cómo se reconcilian esas personas.	**p. 170** Actividad 15 **p. 172** Actividad 20 **p. 173** Actividad 21 **p. 179** Actividad 26 **p. 181** Actividad 32
Comparisons		
❼ **Pensar** Pensar en cómo se relacionan los jóvenes con sus familias	En México se hizo una serie de encuestas sobre la vida de los jóvenes y sus familias. Piensa en la información que leíste sobre este tema en el capítulo y compara las respuestas de los jóvenes mexicanos con tu propia experiencia.	**pp. 176–177** Actividades 23–24 **p. 181** Actividad 31

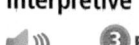 *3. Escuchar*

Suggestions: Use the audio or read from the script.

Answers:

Jorge:

a. Su mejor amigo es muy comprensivo. Lo acepta tal como es y siempre puede contar con él.
b. A veces es un poco entrometido y quiere saber todo lo que hace.
c. A los dos les gusta jugar al béisbol.

Cristina:

a. Su mejor amiga es muy sincera y considerada. Siempre le da consejos y nunca la critica.
b. A veces es un poco vanidosa.
c. Las dos toman clases de danza clásica y también les gusta mucho hacer yoga.

4. Hablar

Suggestions: Tell students to first write down five good and bad ways in which the little brother behaves. Then they can more easily come up with their comments about his behavior.

Answers will vary.

5. Leer

Suggestions: Tell students to refer to pp. 160–162 and 174–177 if they have questions about vocabulary in the review.

Answers will vary, but should make use of these subjunctive forms:

prestes/no cuentes/llegues/puedas

6. Escribir

Suggestions: Remind students to be sensitive to the privacy of others if they choose to write about real-life events.

Answers will vary.

7. Pensar

Suggestions: Have students share their thoughts with each other and compare their perceptions about young people and family life in the United States.

Answers will vary.

DIFFERENTIATED ASSESSMENT

CORE ASSESSMENT
- **Assessment Program DVD:** Cap. 2, Examen del capítulo 4, pp. 101–104
- **Audio Program DVD:** Cap. 4, Track 20
- **ExamView:** Chapter Test, Test Banks A and B

ADVANCED/PRE-AP*
- **ExamView:** Pre-AP* Test Bank
- **Pre-AP* Resource Book,** pp. 147–149

STUDENTS NEEDING EXTRA HELP
- **Alternate Assessment Program:** Examen del capítulo 4
- **Audio Program DVD:** Cap. 4, Track 20

HERITAGE LEARNERS
- **Assessment Program: Realidades para hispanohablantes:** Examen del capítulo 4
- **ExamView:** Heritage Learner Test Bank

Trabajo y comunidad

5 Chapter Overview

- **jobs and volunteer work**

Vocabulary:
- jobs and job skills
- interviewing techniques
- volunteer work

Grammar:
- present perfect
- pluperfect
- present perfect subjunctive
- demonstrative adjectives and pronouns

Cultural Perspectives:
- the importance of finding a job or profession
- the meaning of work for young people in Latin America
- the Hispanic Heritage Foundation
- work as seen through the art of Diego Rivera
- Hispanic contributions to American society

¡Pura vida!
- Watch an engaging video episode about a group of young people in Costa Rica!

CHAPTER SUPPORT

Bulletin Boards

Theme: *Trabajo y comunidad*

Ask students to cut out, copy, or download photos of people from different professions and jobs, including volunteer work. They should also include a photo of something related to each profession or job, such as a photo of a doctor along with a photo of a hospital or a patient.

Hands-on Culture

Recipe: *Mate*

Mate is a very popular drink in Argentina. Most of the *gauchos,* Argentinian cowboys, drink mate in the afternoon.

Ingredients: 1/2 oz. *mate* powder, 1 cup water, hot but not boiling, pinch of sugar

Supplies: *kettle, mate* gourd or large cup; small paper cups, *bombilla* (silver sipping straw with strainer at bottom) and/or paper straws

1. Put *mate* and sugar in the *mate* gourd (or cup) and add a cup of hot water.
2. Let the *mate* powder steep for 3-5 minutes before drinking through a *bombilla* or straw. Keep straws away from the grounds at bottom.
3. Tell students that the Argentines sit in a circle and pass the *mate* clockwise. When more water is needed, the *cebador* (server) adds hot water from the kettle.
4. Pour the *mate* into small paper cups.

Game

Rueda de palabras

This memory game practices vocabulary about work and community using a spinner. Use it toward the end of *Trabajo y comunidad,* after students have practiced the vocabulary of the chapter.

Players: entire class

Materials: spinner, pen

Rules:

1. Fill in spinner sections with the six vocabulary categories used in *Repaso del capítulo, Vocabulario y gramática.* Omit the *Acciones* and *Expresiones* categories.

2. Select a scorekeeper and divide the class into four groups. Have each group choose a writer.

3. Spin the spinner and announce the category. Groups have 3 minutes to write down all the Spanish words they can think of that fit the category. Words cannot be repeated from category to category.

Spinner category: *En el trabajo*

Team writes: *el anuncio clasificado, los beneficios, la clienta, la compañía, el gerente, el puesto, el salario, la solicitud de empleo, la computación, la recepcionista*

4. When time is up, groups take turns reading their lists one word at a time. Groups that have the same word cross it from their lists. When a category is exhausted, a tally is taken. The team with the largest number of words wins the round and spins for the next category.

5. Play until all six categories have been used.

Variation: Each team writes sentences with the words they wrote for each category. The more correct sentences they write in a given time, the more points they score.

CHAPTER PROJECT

Álbum de mis amigos en el futuro

Overview: Students create six pages for a scrapbook featuring photos or illustrations of their friends along with a brief description of what professions or jobs they think their friends are going to have in the future. They then give an oral presentation of their scrapbook, describing one of their friends and predicting his or her future profession or job.

Resources: construction paper, digital or print photos of friends, drawing paper, colored pencils, markers, glue, scissors

Sequence: (suggestions for when to do each step appear throughout the chapter)

STEP 1. Review instructions so students know what is expected of them. Hand out the "Chapter 5 Project Instructions and Rubric" from the *Teacher's Resource Book*.

STEP 2. Students submit a rough sketch of their scrapbook pages. Return the sketches with your suggestions. For vocabulary and grammar practice, ask pairs to present their drafts to each other.

STEP 3. Students do layouts. Encourage them to try different arrangements before writing descriptions.

STEP 4. Students submit a draft of their descriptions. Note your corrections and suggestions, then return the drafts to students.

STEP 5. Students complete and present their scrapbook to the class. They should describe one of the people in the photos or illustrations and say what profession or job they think he or she is going to have in the future.

Options:

1. Students write and create a poster with photos or descriptions about the future professions and jobs of their friends.
2. Students write a composition about the future professions and jobs of their best friends.

Assessment:

Here is a detailed rubric for assessing this project:

Chapter 5 Project: *Álbum de mis amigos en el futuro*

RUBRIC	Score 1	Score 3	Score 5
Your evidence of planning	You provide no preliminary sketch or description drafts.	Your preliminary sketch and descriptions are created, but not corrected.	You show evidence of corrected sketch and descriptions.
Your use of illustrations	You include no photos or illustrations.	You provide photos or illustrations but don't organize them.	You provide well organized photos and illustrations.
Your presentation	You do not include the required information.	You include most of the required information.	You include all of the required information.

21st Century Skills

Look for tips throughout Chapter 5 to enrich your teaching by integrating 21st Century Skills. Suggestions for the Chapter Project and Culture follow below.

Chapter Project

Modify the Chapter Project with these suggestions:

Encourage Information Literacy

Encourage students to use information from a variety of Web sites to find the appropriate job descriptions for their friends' future jobs. The handout "Search for Information on the Internet" will help them find reliable sources that describe popular professions and job postings in Spanish.

Foster Creativity and Innovation

Have students design a unique matching game to match professions to people. Have them describe and illustrate several professions in Spanish, along with some people, their personalities, and their likes/dislikes. Have small groups work together to match the people with the most appropriate profession.

Enhance Communication

As students prepare to present their project to the class, provide them with the handout "Give an Effective Presentation" to remind them of the importance of body language, tone of voice, eye contact, and other strategies for delivering an effective presentation.

Chapter Culture

Develop Flexibility and Adaptability

Help students bridge cultural differences by offering them opportunities to discuss the culture highlighted throughout the chapter, such as the meaning of work for young people in Latin America, as seen in the *Fondo cultural* on p. 212.

▶ **Videodocumentario** View *Un voluntario en la comunidad* online with the class to learn more about a young Dominican boy and his volunteer work in a local community center.

AT A GLANCE

Objectives

- Listen to and read about job interviews and classified ads
- Talk and write about applying for a job
- Exchange information about your skills, background experience, and job opportunities
- Understand the influence of Hispanics in the U.S.
- Compare a Mayan folktale with myths in the U.S.

A ver si recuerdas... ♻

- Work
- Community
- Present participle
- Reflexive pronouns with direct/indirect pronouns

Recycle ♻

- *r* between two vowels

Vocabulary

- Jobs and activities in the workplace
- Personal qualities and skills needed
- Volunteer and community work
- Job interviews

Grammar

- Present perfect
- Pluperfect
- Present perfect subjunctive
- Demonstrative adjectives and pronouns

Culture

- Community gardens in Latin America, p. 205
- The meaning of work for the young people in Latin America, p. 212
- The Hispanic Heritage Foundation, p. 216
- José Gálvez, photographer, p. 226
- Silvio Rodríguez, p. 231
- Spanish in the U.S., pp. 232–233
- Community centers, p. 241

RESOURCES

	FOR THE STUDENT	ONLINE	DVD	PRINT	FOR THE TEACHER	ONLINE	PREEXP	DVD	PRINT
Plan					Interactive TE and Resource DVD	•		•	
					Teacher's Resource Book, pp. 1–60	•		•	•
					Pre-AP* Resource Book, pp. 150–152	•		•	•
					Lesson Plans	•			•
					Mapa global interactivo	•			

A ver si recuerdas PP. 200–203

	FOR THE STUDENT	ONLINE	DVD	PRINT	FOR THE TEACHER	ONLINE	PREEXP	DVD	PRINT
Review	*A ver si recuerdas* Study Plan	•			*A ver si recuerdas* Study Plan	•			
	Guided WB, pp. 144–147	•	•	•	Vocabulary and Grammar Transparencies, 4, 99–102	•	•	•	
	Core WB, pp. 63–64	•	•	•	Answer Keys: Student Edition, p. 62	•	•	•	
	Hispanohablantes WB, p. 140			•					

Introducción PP. 204–205

	FOR THE STUDENT	ONLINE	DVD	PRINT	FOR THE TEACHER	ONLINE	PREEXP	DVD	PRINT
Present	Student Edition, pp. 204–205	•	•	•	Interactive TE and Resource DVD	•		•	
	DK Reference Atlas	•	•		Teacher's Resource Book, pp. 2–5	•		•	•
	Videonovela: ¡Pura vida!	•	•		Video Program Teacher's Guide, Cap. 5				•
	¡Pura vida! Video Activities	•			Galería de fotos		•		
	Hispanohablantes WB, p. 141			•	Fine Art Transparencies, 67	•	•	•	
					Map Transparencies, 14–16, 20, 22	•	•	•	

Vocabulario en contexto PP. 206–209/220–223

	FOR THE STUDENT	ONLINE	DVD	PRINT	FOR THE TEACHER	ONLINE	PREEXP	DVD	PRINT
Present & Practice	Student Edition, pp. 206–209/220–223	•	•	•	Interactive TE and Resource DVD	•		•	
	Audio	•	•		Teacher's Resource Book, pp. 6–7, 10–11, 27–34/8–9, 12–14, 27–34	•		•	•
	Flashcards	•	•						
	Instant Check	•			Vocabulary Clip Art	•	•	•	
	Guided WB, pp. 148–156/161–168	•	•	•	Audio Program	•	•	•	
	Core WB, pp. 65–66/70–71	•	•	•	Vocabulary and Grammar Transparencies, 103–106/109–112	•	•	•	
	Comm. WB, pp. 68/72	•	•	•	Answer Keys: Student Edition, pp. 63–64/67–68	•	•	•	
	Hispanohablantes WB, pp. 142–143/152–153			•					
Assess and Remediate					Pruebas 5–1/5–5: Assessment Program, pp. 105–106/114–115 Hispanohablantes, pp. 105–106/114–115	•	•	•	•

	FOR THE STUDENT	ONLINE	DVD	PRINT	FOR THE TEACHER	ONLINE	PREEXP	DVD	PRINT
Vocabulario en uso PP. 210–213/224–226									
Present & Practice	Student Edition, pp. 210–213/224–226	•	•	•	Interactive Whiteboard Vocabulary Activities	•		•	
	Instant Check	•			Interactive TE and Resource DVD	•		•	
	Comm. WB, pp. 64/65	•	•	•	Teacher's Resource Book, pp. 11–12, 18–19/14, 22–23	•		•	•
	Hispanohablantes WB, pp. 144–145/154–156			•	Audio Program	•	•	•	
	Communicative Pair Activities	•			Videomodelos	•		•	
					Answer Keys: Student Edition, pp. 64–65/68–70	•	•	•	•
Assess and Remediate					Pruebas 5–2/5–6 with Study Plans	•			
					Pruebas 5–2/5–6: Assessment Program, pp. 107–108/116–117 Hispanohablantes, pp. 107–108/116–117	• •		• •	• •
Gramática PP. 214–219/227–231									
Present & Practice	Student Edition, pp. 214–219/227–231	•	•	•	Interactive Whiteboard Grammar Activities	•		•	
	Instant Check	•			Interactive TE and Resource DVD	•		•	
	Animated Verbs	•			Teacher's Resource Book, pp. 12, 20–21/14–15, 24–25	•		•	•
	Tutorial Video: Grammar	•			Audio Program	•	•	•	
	Canción de hip hop	•			Videomodelos	•	•	•	
	Guided WB, pp. 157–160/169–172	•	•	•	Vocabulary and Grammar Transparencies, 107–108/113–114	•	•	•	
	Core WB, pp. 67–69/72–74	•	•	•	Answer Keys: Student Edition, pp. 65–66/70–71	•	•	•	
	Comm. WB, pp. 64, 69–71, 189/66–67, 73–74	•	•	•					
	Hispanohablantes WB, pp. 146–151/157–161			•					
	Communicative Pair Activities	•							
Assess and Remediate					Pruebas 5–3, 5–4/5–7, 5–8 with Study Plans	•			

					Pruebas 5–3, 5–4/5–7, 5–8: Assessment Program,
					    pp. 109, 110/118, 119
					    Hispanohablantes, pp. 109, 110/118, 119
						
						•
						•
								
								•
								•
									
									•
									•

					Examen 1, Examen 2: Vocab. y gramática, pp. 111–113/120–122	•		•	•
¡Adelante! PP. 232–241									
Application	Student Edition, pp. 232–241	•	•	•	Interactive TE and Resource DVD	•		•	
	Online Cultural Reading	•			Teacher's Resource Book, pp. 15, 17	•		•	•
	Guided WB, pp. 173–175	•	•	•	Video Program: Videodocumentario	•		•	
	Comm. WB, pp. 76–77, 190	•	•	•	Video Program Teacher's Guide, Cap. 5	•		•	
	Hispanohablantes WB, pp. 162–167			•	Vocabulary and Grammar Transparencies, 4, 12	•	•	•	
	Videodocumentario	•	•		Map Transparencies, 14, 16	•	•	•	
	Lecturas 3, pp. 14–15, 46–50			•	Answer Keys: Student Edition, pp. 72–73	•	•	•	
Repaso del capítulo PP. 242–245									
Review	Student Edition, pp. 242–245	•	•	•	Interactive TE and Resource DVD	•		•	
	Online Puzzles and Games	•			Teacher's Resource Book, pp. 16, 26–34	•		•	•
	Core WB, pp. 75–76	•	•	•	Audio Program	•	•	•	
	Comm. WB, pp. 191–194	•	•	•	Answer Keys: Student Edition, p. 73	•	•	•	
	Hispanohablantes WB, pp. 168–171			•					
	Instant Check	•							
Chapter Assessment									

Assess					Examen del capítulo 5: Assessment Program, pp. 123–126
					    Alternate Assessment Program, pp. 45–54
					    Hispanohablantes, pp. 123–126
						•
						•
						•
								•
								•
								•
									•
									•
									•

					Audio Program, Cap. 5, Examen	•		•	

					ExamView: Test Banks A and B (questions only online)
					    Heritage Learner Test Bank
					    Pre-AP* Test Bank
						•
						•
						•			

REGULAR SCHEDULE (50 MINUTES)

DAY	Warm-up / Assess	Preview / Present / Practice / Communicate	Wrap-up / Homework Options
1	**Warm-up (10 min.)** • Return Examen del capítulo: Capítulo 4	**Repaso (35 min.)** • A ver si recuerdas . . . • Actividades 3, 5	**Wrap-up and Homework Options (5 min.)** • Core Practice 5-1, 5-2
2	**Warm-up (10 min.)** • Homework check	**Chapter Opener (10 min.)** • Objectives • Arte y cultura **Vocabulario en contexto 1 (25 min.)** • Presentation: Vocabulario y gramática en contexto • Actividades 1, 2	**Wrap-up and Homework Options (5 min.)** • Clip Art Vocabulary
3	**Warm-up (10 min.)** • Homework check	**Vocabulario en contexto 1 (30 min.)** • Presentation: Tú y tus habilidades; Los anuncios clasificados • Actividades 3, 4, 5 **Vocabulario en uso 1 (5 min.)** • Actividad 6	**Wrap-up and Homework Options (5 min.)** • Core Practice 5-3, 5-4 • Prueba 5-1: Vocabulary recognition
4	**Warm-up (10 min.)** • Homework check ✔**Formative Assessment (10 min.)** • Prueba 5-1: Vocabulary recognition	**Vocabulario en uso 1 (25 min.)** • Actividades 7, 8, 9, 10 • Interactive Whiteboard Vocabulary Activities • Ampliación del lenguaje	**Wrap-up and Homework Options (5 min.)** • Actividad 13 • Writing Activities • Prueba 5-2 with Study Plan: Vocabulary production
5	**Warm-up (10 min.)** • Fondo cultural • Homework check ✔**Formative Assessment (10 min.)** • Prueba 5-2 with Study Plan: Vocabulary production	**Gramática y vocabulario en uso 1 (25 min.)** • Actividades 11, 12, 14 • Presentation: El presente perfecto • Interactive Whiteboard Grammar Activities	**Wrap-up and Homework Options (5 min.)** • Core Practice 5-5
6	**Warm-up (10 min.)** • Actividad 16 • Homework check	**Gramática y vocabulario en uso 1 (35 min.)** • Actividades 15, 17 • En voz alta • Fondo cultural • Communicative Pair Activity	**Wrap-up and Homework Options (5 min.)** • Writing Activity • Prueba 5-3 with Study Plan: El presente perfecto
7	**Warm-up (5 min.)** • Homework check ✔**Formative Assessment (10 min.)** • Prueba 5-3 with Study Plan: El presente perfecto	**Gramática y vocabulario en uso 1 (30 min.)** • Presentation: El pluscuamperfecto • Interactive Whiteboard Grammar Activities • Actividades 18, 19, 20, 21 • Communicative Pair Activity	**Wrap-up and Homework Options (5 min.)** • Core Practice 5-6, 5-7 • Prueba 5-4 with Study Plan: El pluscuamperfecto
8	**Warm-up (10 min.)** • Actividad 22 • Homework check ✔**Formative Assessment (10 min.)** • Prueba 5-4 with Study Plan: El pluscuamperfecto	**Vocabulario en contexto 2 (25 min.)** • Presentation: Vocabulario y gramática en contexto • Actividades 23, 24	**Wrap-up and Homework Options (5 min.)** • Clip Art Vocabulary • Examen: Vocabulario y gramática 1
9	**Warm-up (5 min.)** • Homework check ✔**Formative Assessment (30 min.)** • Examen: Vocabulario y gramática 1	**Vocabulario en contexto 2 (10 min.)** • Presentation: Se buscan voluntarios • Presentation: ¿A quién van a escoger?	**Wrap-up and Homework Options (5 min.)** • Actividad 25 • Core Practice 5-8, 5-9 • Prueba 5-5: Vocabulary recognition
10	**Warm-up (20 min.)** • Actividades 26, 27 • Homework check ✔**Formative Assessment (10 min.)** • Prueba 5-5: Vocabulary recognition	**Vocabulario en uso 2 (15 min.)** • Actividades 30, 32 • Interactive Whiteboard Vocabulary Activities	**Wrap-up and Homework Options (5 min.)** • Actividades 28, 29 • Prueba 5-6 with Study Plan: Vocabulary production

REGULAR SCHEDULE (50 MINUTES)

DAY	Warm-up / Assess	Preview / Present / Practice / Communicate	Wrap-up / Homework Options
11	**Warm-up** (10 min.) • Fondo cultural • Homework check ✔**Formative Assessment** (10 min.) • Prueba 5-6 with Study Plan: Vocabulary production	**Gramática y vocabulario en uso 2** (25 min.) • Actividades 31, 33 • Presentation: El presente perfecto del subjuntivo • Interactive Whiteboard Grammar Activities • Fondo cultural • Actividad 35	**Wrap-up and Homework Options** (5 min.) • Actividad 34 • Core Practice 5-10 • Prueba 5-7 with Study Plan: El presente perfecto del subjuntivo
12	**Warm-up** (15 min.) • Actividad 36 • Homework check ✔**Formative Assessment** (10 min.) • Prueba 5-7 with Study Plan: El presente perfecto del subjuntivo	**Gramática y vocabulario en uso 2** (20 min.) • Presentation: Los adjetivos y los pronombres demostrativos • Interactive Whiteboard Grammar Activities • Actividades 37, 39	**Wrap-up and Homework Options** (5 min.) • Core Practice 5-11, 5-12 • Prueba 5-8 with Study Plan: Los adjetivos y los pronombres demostrativos
13	**Warm-up** (10 min.) • Fondo cultural • Homework check ✔**Formative Assessment** (10 min.) • Prueba 5-8 with Study Plan: Los adjetivos y los pronombres demostrativos	**Gramática y vocabulario en uso 2** (25 min.) • Actividad 38 • Communicative Pair Activity • El español en la comunidad	**Wrap-up and Homework Options** (5 min.) • Examen: Vocabulario y gramática 2
14	**Warm-up** (5 min.) • Writing Activity ✔**Formative Assessment** (30 min.) • Examen: Vocabulario y gramática 2	**¡Adelante!** (10 min.) • Presentación oral: Step 1, 2	**Wrap-up and Homework Options** (5 min.) • Presentación oral: Step 2
15	**Warm-up** (10 min.) • Presentación oral: Step 2	**¡Adelante!** (35 min.) • Presentación oral: Step 3	**Wrap-up and Homework Options** (5 min.) • Estados Unidos . . . en español • Escribe tu opinión • ¿Comprendiste?
16	**Warm-up** (15 min.) • Estados Unidos . . . en español: ¿Comprendiste? • Homework check	**¡Adelante!** (30 min.) • ¿Qué me cuentas? 1, 2, 3 • View Video • Video Activities 1, 2, 3	**Wrap-up and Homework Options** (5 min.) • Presentación escrita: Steps 1, 2
17	**Warm-up** (10 min.) • Video Activity 4	**¡Adelante!** (15 min.) • Presentación escrita: Step 3 **Repaso** (20 min.) • Preparación para el examen: Actividades 3, 4	**Wrap-up and Homework Options** (5 min.) • Presentación escrita: Step 4
18	**Warm-up** (10 min.) • Homework check	**¡Adelante!** (35 min.) • Lectura • Interacción con la lectura • Fondo cultural	**Wrap-up and Homework Options** (5 min.) • Core Practice: Organizer 5-13, 5-14 • Instant Check
19	**Warm-up** (20 min.) • Preparación para el examen: Actividades 1, 2 • Homework check	**Repaso** (25 min.) • Preparación para el examen: Actividades 5, 6, 7 • Other review	**Wrap-up and Homework Options** (5 min.) • Examen del capítulo
20	**Warm-up** (5 min.) • Answer questions ✔**Summative Assessment** (44 min.) • Examen del capítulo		**Wrap-up and Homework Options** (1 min.) • A ver si recuerdas: Capítulo 6 • Actividades 4, 5, 8

BLOCK SCHEDULE (90 MINUTES)

DAY	Warm-up / Assess	Preview / Present / Practice / Communicate	Wrap-up / Homework Options
1	**Warm-up (35 min.)** • Return Examen del capítulo: Capítulo 4 • A ver si recuerdas . . . • Actividad 3, 5 • Homework check	**Chapter Opener (10 min.)** • Objectives • Arte y cultura **Vocabulario en contexto 1 (40 min.)** • Presentation: Vocabulario y gramática en contexto • Actividades 1, 2 • Presentation: Tú y tus habilidades • Actividades 3, 4 • Presentation: Los anuncios clasificados • Actividad 5	**Wrap-up and Homework Options (5 min.)** • Core Practice 5-3, 5-4 • Clip Art Vocabulary • Prueba 5-1: Vocabulary recognition
2	**Warm-up (15 min.)** • Actividad 8 • Homework check ✓**Formative Assessment (10 min.)** • Prueba 5-1: Vocabulary recognition	**Vocabulario en uso 1 (60 min.)** • Actividades 6, 7, 9, 10, 11, 12, 13 • Interactive Whiteboard Vocabulary Activities • Fondo cultural • Ampliación del lenguaje	**Wrap-up and Homework Options (5 min.)** • Writing Activities • Prueba 5-2 with Study Plan: Vocabulary production
3	**Warm-up (15 min.)** • Writing Activity • Homework check ✓**Formative Assessment (10 min.)** • Prueba 5-2 with Study Plan: Vocabulary production	**Gramática y vocabulario en uso 1 (60 min.)** • Presentation: El presente perfecto • Actividades 14, 15, 17 • Interactive Whiteboard Grammar Activities • En voz alta • Fondo cultural • Audio or Writing Activities	**Wrap-up and Homework Options (5 min.)** • Core Practice 5-5 • Prueba 5-3 with Study Plan: El presente perfecto
4	**Warm-up (10 min.)** • Actividad 16 • Homework check ✓**Formative Assessment (10 min.)** • Prueba 5-3 with Study Plan: El presente perfecto	**Gramática y vocabulario en uso 1 (45 min.)** • Presentation: El pluscuamperfecto • Interactive Whiteboard Grammar Activities • Actividades 18, 20, 21, 22 • Communicative Pair Activity **Vocabulario en contexto 2 (20 min.)** • Presentation: Vocabulario y gramática en contexto • Actividades 23, 24	**Wrap-up and Homework Options (5 min.)** • Core Practice 5-6, 5-7 • Prueba 5-4 with Study Plan: El pluscuamperfecto • Examen: Vocabulario y gramática 1

5	**Warm-up (10 min.)**
	• Actividad 19
	• Homework check
	✓**Formative Assessment (40 min.)**
	• Prueba 5-4 with Study Plan: El
	  pluscuamperfecto
	• Examen: Vocabulario y gramática 1
		Vocabulario en contexto 2 (25 min.)
		• Presentation: Se buscan voluntarios hispanohablantes para
		  ayudar a inmigrantes
		• Actividades 25, 26
		• Presentation: ¿A quién van a escoger?
		• Actividad 27
		Vocabulario en uso 2 (10 min.)
		• Actividad 30
		• Interactive Whiteboard Vocabulary Activities
			Wrap-up and Homework Options (5 min.)
			• Core Practice 5-8, 5-9
			• Prueba 5-5: Vocabulary recognition

BLOCK SCHEDULE (90 MINUTES)

DAY	Warm-up / Assess	Preview / Present / Practice / Communicate	Wrap-up / Homework Options
6	**Warm-up (20 min.)** • Actividad 28, 29 • Homework check ✔**Formative Assessment (10 min.)** • Prueba 5-5: Vocabulary recognition	**Gramática y vocabulario en uso 2 (55 min.)** • Actividades 31, 32, 33 • Fondo cultural • Presentation: El presente perfecto del subjuntivo • Interactive Whiteboard Grammar Activities • Actividades 34, 35, 36	**Wrap-up and Homework Options (5 min.)** • Core Practice 5-10 • Pruebas 5-6, 5-7 with Study Plans: Vocabulary production, El presente perfecto del subjuntivo
7	**Warm-up (15 min.)** • Writing Activity • Homework check ✔**Formative Assessment (20 min.)** • Pruebas 5-6, 5-7 with Study Plans: Vocabulary production, El presente perfecto del subjuntivo	**Gramática y vocabulario en uso 2 (35 min.)** • Presentation: Los adjetivos y los pronombres demostrativos • Interactive Whiteboard Grammar Activities • Actividades 37, 38, 39 • El español en la comunidad • Fondo cultural **¡Adelante! (15 min.)** • Presentación oral: Steps 1, 2	**Wrap-up and Homework Options (5 min.)** • Presentación oral: Step 2
8	**Warm-up (15 min.)** • Writing Activity • Homework check	**¡Adelante! (40 min.)** • Presentación oral: Step 3 **Gramática y vocabulario en uso 2 (15 min.)** • Communicative Pair Activity **¡Adelante! (15 min.)** • Presentation: Estados Unidos . . . en español	**Wrap-up and Homework Options (5 min.)** • Core Practice 5-11, 5-12 • Prueba 5-8: Los adjetivos y los pronombres demostrativos • Examen: Vocabulario y gramática 2
9	**Warm-up (10 min.)** • Homework check ✔**Formative Assessment Options (30 min.)** • Prueba 5-8 with Study Plan: Los adjetivos y los pronombres demostrativos • Examen: Vocabulario y gramática 2	**¡Adelante! (45 min.)** • Estados Unidos . . . en español • ¿Comprendiste? • Escribe tu opinión • View Video • Video Activities • ¿Qué me cuentas? 1, 2, 3 • Presentación escrita: Step 1	**Wrap-up and Homework Options (5 min.)** • Presentación escrita: Step 2 • Preparación para el examen: Actividades 1, 2
10	**Warm-up (20 min.)** • Presentación escrita: Step 3 • Homework check	**¡Adelante! (40 min.)** • Lectura • Interacción con la lectura • Fondo cultural **Repaso (25 min.)** • Preparación para el examen: Actividades 3, 4, 6	**Wrap-up and Homework Options (5 min.)** • Presentación escrita: Step 4 • Core Practice: Organizer 5-13, 5-14 • Instant Check • Preparación para el examen: Actividades 5, 7 • Examen del capítulo
11	**Warm-up (15 min.)** • Homework check ✔**Summative Assessment (45 min.)** • Examen del capítulo	**Theme Game (15 min.)** **A ver si recuerdas – Capítulo 6 (10 min.)** • Presentation: Vocabulario • Presentation: Gramática	**Wrap-up and Homework Options (5 min.)** • A ver si recuerdas – Capítulo 6 • Actividades 4, 5, 8 • Core Practice 6-1, 6-2

5 Recycle

Vocabulario *Repaso*

Vocabulario *Repaso*

Core Instruction

Standards: 1.1, 1.2

Resources: Voc. and Gram. Transparency 99

Suggestions: Before presenting the material in this review section, consider testing your students' command of the material by assigning the Study Plan. Students will automatically be given additional practice of the material they have not yet mastered, and you can focus your review based on the class's overall performance on the post-test.

On the board, write the following sentence: *En el (la) lugar, conozco a un(a) trabajo muy cualidad que acción.* Have students fill in the blanks with items from the four categories of the *Vocabulario* to create sentences that make sense: *En la biblioteca, conozco a una empleada muy ordenada que usa la computadora.*

trabajos
el / la agente de viajes
el / la atleta
el bombero,
   la bombera
el cajero, la cajera
el camarero,
   la camarera
el científico,
   la científica
el / la dentista
el / la detective
el empleado,
   la empleada
el entrenador,
   la entrenadora
el fotógrafo
   la fotógrafa
el locutor,
   la locutora
el / la piloto
el reportero,
   la reportera
el vendedor,
   la vendedora

cualidades
animado, -a
artístico, -a
atlético, -a
bien educado, -a
cortés
interesante
obediente
ordenado, -a
paciente
trabajador, -a
tranquilo, -a

lugares
el banco
la biblioteca
el centro comercial
el cine
la escuela
la estación de
   servicio
la farmacia
el gimnasio
la guardería
   infantil
la librería
el museo
el restaurante
el supermercado
el teatro
la tienda

acciones
cortar el césped
cuidar niños
decorar
dibujar
hablar por teléfono
lavar el coche
lavar los platos
limpiar
pasar la aspiradora
pasear perros
sacar fotos
tocar un instrumento
usar la computadora

1

Standards: 1.1, 1.3

Resources: Voc. and Gram. Transparency 4

Focus: Practicing review vocabulary

Suggestions: Use *Vocabulary & Grammar Transparency 4* to help students create a T-chart. Encourage students to base their discussion on real-life situations as much as possible. If a job they actually have is not included in the *Vocabulario,* have them find out the Spanish term for it either in a bilingual dictionary or by asking heritage speakers. For Step 3, point out that students should be commenting on the jobs their partners wrote about.

Answers will vary.

▼1 El trabajo | 🗣👥

Hablar • Escribir

❶ Describe en qué trabajas ahora y qué trabajos has tenido antes.

❷ Ahora, escribe en una hoja de papel dos trabajos que te gustaría hacer y dos que no te gustaría hacer. Junto a cada trabajo, pon lo que tienes que hacer, las cualidades que se necesitan y el lugar donde se hace el trabajo.

❸ Con otro(a) estudiante, hagan y contesten preguntas sobre por qué les gustarían o no les gustarían los trabajos que escribieron.

▶ **Modelo**
A—*Me gustaría ser reportero.*
B—*¿Por qué?*
A—*Un reportero escribe sobre cosas que pasan. Para ser reportero, debes saber escribir bien y sacar fotos.*

DIFFERENTIATED INSTRUCTION

Students with Special Needs
Help hearing impaired students complete Step 3 of *Actividad* 1, by having them work with a partner and write out the dialogue instead of speaking it.

Advanced Learners
Have students choose one *lugar* from the *Vocabulario* and prepare a brief oral presentation telling about the different kinds of jobs encountered there, actions typically done, and one desirable quality for people to have who work there.

Gramática Repaso

El participio presente

The present participle conveys a sense of ongoing action. To form the present participle add -*ando* to the stem of -*ar* verbs and -*iendo* to the stem of -*er* and -*ir* verbs.

trabajar	trabaj**ando**
hacer	hac**iendo**
recibir	recib**iendo**

• Verbs that have irregular third person forms in the preterite undergo the same change in the present participle.

dormir	durmiendo
pedir	pidiendo
decir	diciendo
reír	riendo

• The verbs *ir* and *oír* and verbs ending in -*aer*, -*eer*, and -*uir* have present participles that end in -*yendo*.

ir	yendo
oír	oyendo
caer	cayendo
leer	leyendo
destruir	destruyendo

• The present participle is used together with a form of *estar* to form the progressive tense:

¡No me molestes! **Estoy leyendo**.
Estábamos durmiendo cuando llamaste.

• Reflexive or object pronouns can be placed before the form of *estar*, or they can be attached to the end of the present participle. If they are attached to the present participle, a written accent is needed.

Ahora **me** estoy **bañando**. / Estoy **bañándome**.
Las está **ayudando**. / Está **ayudándolas**.

Más ayuda | **realidades.com** | ▶ **Tutorials**

▼2 ¿Qué está pasando?

Escribir

Escribe lo que está sucediendo en la clase en este momento. Nombra a las personas que están haciendo las siguientes actividades. Usa el presente progresivo en tus frases.

| leer | darle | observar | mirar | dormirse | decirme |

Modelo
mirar
La profesora está mirando a la clase.

▼3 ¿Quién está haciéndolo? | 💬

Hablar

Indica quién está haciendo cada cosa en tu clase en este momento.

Modelo
escribir en su cuaderno
Laura y Miguel están escribiendo en su cuaderno.
o: *Nadie está escribiendo en su cuaderno.*

1. ayudar a otro estudiante
2. recoger los papeles del piso
3. limpiar su escritorio
4. leer el libro de español
5. poner sus cosas en la mochila

doscientos uno **201**
Capítulo 5

Gramática Repaso

Core Instruction

Resources: Voc. and Gram. Transparency 100
Suggestions: Refer students who are having difficulty with the present progressive and the present participle to the *GramActiva* video from L2 Chapter 3B, and to the online tutorial. Have students practice with present participles by contrasting the simple present with the present progressive tense. Ask them to tell about actions they do regularly and then say whether or not they are doing them at this moment: *Escucho música a menudo, pero no estoy escuchando música en este momento.*

▼**2** Standards: 1.3
Resources: Answer Keys: Student Edition, p. 62
Focus: Reviewing present participles
Suggestions: Have students switch roles, so both partners can practice asking and answering the questions.
Answers will vary, but students will use the following present participles:

leyendo	mirando
dándole	durmiéndose
observando	diciéndome

▼**3** Standards: 1.1
Resources: Answer Keys: Student Edition, p. 62
Focus: Reviewing present participles
Suggestions: Ask students to use compound subjects in some of their answers, so that they can practice with plural forms of the present progressive tense.
Answers will vary, but students will use the following present participles:

1. ayudando
2. recogiendo
3. limpiando
4. leyendo
5. poniendo

ENRICH YOUR TEACHING

Teacher-to-Teacher

Remind students that Spanish speakers use the present progressive in slightly different situations than do English speakers. Unless the action is happening right at the moment, Spanish speakers generally use the simple present tense. However, to emphasize that an action is taking place now, the present progressive can be used. Many English speakers tend to overuse the present progressive when speaking Spanish. Encourage students to avoid this habit and use the simple present.

5 Recycle

Vocabulario Repaso

Vocabulario Repaso

Core Instruction

Standards: 1.1, 1.2

Resources: Voc. and Gram. Transparency 101

Suggestions: Have students sit in a circle. Give one student a foam ball and have him or her give a definition of a vocabulary item that you choose from one of the lists. That student tosses the ball to another and names an item from a different *Vocabulario* category. The student who catches the ball gives a brief definition of that item and tosses the ball to another student, and so on.

▼4 Standards: 1.3

Focus: Practicing review vocabulary

Suggestions: If students finish the task early, encourage them to add an extra *trabajo* done at a given location.

Answers will vary.

Extension: Have students trade their chart with a partner. The partner reports orally on the information he or she sees there: *Marina dice que en el hospital uno juega con los niños enfermos.*

▼5 Standards: 1.1

Focus: Practicing review vocabulary

Suggestions: Make sure students switch roles in order to practice both parts of the dialogue. Remind them to include the personal *a* when referring to the people they are helping.

Answers will vary.

actividades
asistir a
ayudar a los demás
colaborar
conseguir
dar . . .
   ayuda
   dinero
   juguetes
   ropa
ganar dinero
hacer trabajo
   voluntario
investigar
llenar
pagar
participar
permitir
planear
recoger basura
registrar

personas
los ancianos
la gente pobre
el niño, la niña
el paramédico,
   la paramédica
la víctima
el voluntario,
   la voluntaria

lugares
el aeropuerto
la agencia de viajes
el club atlético
el consultorio
el laboratorio
el mercado
el quiosco
el salón de belleza

desastres
el accidente
la explosión
el huracán
el incendio
la inundación
el terremoto
la tormenta

expresiones
¿cómo se hace . . . ?
ganarse la vida
no te olvides de . . .
seguir una
   carrera

▼4 Para la comunidad

Escribir

Haz una tabla como la de abajo. Escribe tres lugares de tu comunidad donde se pueda hacer trabajo voluntario. Al lado de cada lugar escribe qué trabajo se puede hacer y para qué o quién.

Lugar	Trabajo	Para quién / qué
el hospital	jugar	los niños enfermos

▼5 Trabajo voluntario | 🗨️👥

Hablar

Tu compañero(a) trabaja como voluntario(a).

1 Pregúntale:
- dónde trabaja
- qué hace allí
- a quién ayuda

2 Tu compañero(a) te invita a trabajar con él (ella). Acepta la invitación o da una excusa.

DIFFERENTIATED INSTRUCTION

Heritage Language Learners

Invite students who have lived in a heritage country to tell about volunteer work there. Encourage them to tell about the qualities needed in a person who does that kind of work.

Students with Learning Difficulties

If students have difficulty completing the chart independently, provide them with a partially completed chart and give some clues to help them finish it. For example, complete the *Lugar* column and then ask: *¿Qué trabajo se puede hacer allí?*

Gramática Repaso

Dónde van los pronombres reflexivos y de complemento

Reflexive pronouns, as well as direct and indirect object pronouns, may be placed either before a verb or after it.

• When there are two verbs, as with a participle or an infinitive, the pronoun may come either before the first verb or after the second verb.

> Estamos divirtiéndo**nos** mucho.
> **Nos** estamos divirtiendo mucho.
> Voy a acostar**me** temprano.
> **Me** voy a acostar temprano.

• If the sentence is negative, place the pronoun between no and the verb.

> No **me** estoy aburriendo.
> No **las** voy a comprar.

• In affirmative commands, pronouns are attached to the end of the verb.

> Carlos, despiér**tate**.
> Chicos, láven**se** las manos.
> ¿Los niños? Cuída**los**.
> ¿El parque? Límpie**lo**.

• In negative commands, place the pronoun between *no* and the verb.

> Esa película es mala. No **la** veas.

• Notice that written accent marks must often be added when a pronoun is attached to a verb.

> Recoge la basura.   **Recógela.**
> Estoy lavando los platos.   Estoy **lavándolos**.

▼ 6 Según el director

Leer • Escribir

El señor Díaz es el director de un centro de ayuda y da muchos mandatos. Usa los verbos y el pronombre apropiado para completar los mandatos que les dio a sus voluntarios.

recoger limpiar servir abrir ayudar lavarse

Modelo
¿Los libros? _____ en la biblioteca.
¿Los libros? Pónganlos en la biblioteca.

1. ¿La comida? _____ al mediodía y _____ las manos antes de servirla.
2. ¿Las ventanas? No _____ ahora.
3. ¿La basura? No _____ ahora.
4. ¿Los niños? _____ con la tarea.
5. ¿El comedor? _____ después del almuerzo.

▼ 7 Metas personales

Escribir

Escribe cinco metas (*goals*) que quieres alcanzar (*reach*) este año. Usa los pronombres apropiados.

Modelo
No voy a quejarme. / No me voy a quejar.
Quiero ayudar a los niños. / Quiero ayudarlos.

Más práctica   GO
**realidades.com	print**

A ver si recuerdas with Study Plan ✔
Guided **WB** pp. 144–147   ✔   ✔
Core **WB** pp. 63–64   ✔   ✔
Hispanohablantes **WB** p. 140   ✔

doscientos tres 203
Capítulo 5

Gramática Repaso

Core Instruction

Resources: Voc. and Gram. Transparency 102

Suggestions: Refer students who are having difficulty with the placement of pronouns to the online tutorials. Say sentences that contain direct or indirect objects as nouns. Ask students to say each sentence again, changing the direct and/or indirect object to a pronoun. Include affirmative and negative commands in your sentences:

Teacher: *Lee el libro* or *No leas el libro.*
Student: *(No) Lo estoy leyendo/Estoy leyéndolo.*

▼ 6 Standards: 1.2

Resources: Answer Keys: Student Edition, p. 62

Focus: Reviewing pronoun placement

Suggestions: Remind students to include an accent mark in the appropriate syllable whenever necessary.

Answers:
1. **Sírvanla, lávense**
2. **las abran**
3. **la recojan**
4. **Ayúdenlos**
5. **Límpienlo**

▼ 7 Standards: 1.3

Focus: Reviewing pronoun placement

Common Errors: Since students are concentrating on positioning the pronouns, they may forget to make them agree in number and gender. When checking answers aloud, provide a correct model as necessary and have students repeat.

Suggestions: Have students write the sentences twice, with the pronouns in the alternative positions, whenever possible.

Answers will vary.

ENRICH YOUR TEACHING

Teacher-to-Teacher

Assign a different everyday object to each student. Have them write as many commands as they can telling one person typical things to do and not do with the object, using a direct object pronoun each time: *la botella—Ábrela. Ciérrala. Llénala. Vacíala. Lávala. Recíclala. No la tires a la basura.*

21st Century Skills

Initiative and Self-Direction Direct students to the online tutorials available in **realidades.com** for self-directed review of the grammar topics recycled in this chapter. Students can expand their own learning by reviewing the related English grammar first, and then proceeding to the new Spanish grammar point.

✓ ASSESSMENT

A ver si recuerdas with Study Plan (online only)

After reviewing the material on these pages, assign the *A ver si recuerdas* Study Plan to evaluate students' mastery of the material. Additional practice is available online.

203

Standards for Foreign Language Learning: *Capítulo* 5

• To meet the Standards, students will:

Communication

1.1 Interpersonal
• Talk about work, job searches, and employment types
• Talk about personality traits
• Talk about community gardens
• Talk about emergencies, volunteer community organizations, and community activism
• Talk about songs with social content
• Talk about the Spanish-speaking community in the U.S.

1.2 Interpretive
• Read and listen to information about jobs
• Read and listen to information about personality traits
• Read about community gardens
• Read and listen to information about emergencies, volunteer organizations, and community activism
• Read about noun suffixes
• Read about known artists and poets
• Read about the contributions of the Spanish-speaking community in the U.S.
• Read about the Peace Boat program
• Read about songs with social content
• Read about campaigning for a public office
• Read fiction by María Luisa Góngora Pacheco

1.3 Presentational
• Write about work, job searches, and employment
• Write about what is happening right now
• Write about personality traits and personal goals
• Recite a poem by Antonio Machado
• Write about volunteer community organizations
• Write about the Spanish-speaking community in the U.S.
• Present a campaign speech
• Write a cover letter for a job solicitation

Culture

2.1 Practices and Perspectives
• Explain community gardens in Latin America
• Explain teenage employment in Latin America
• Explain the contributions of the Spanish-speaking community in the U.S.
• Explain the Peace Boat Program
• Explain Latin American folk music
• Explain the role of indigenous Latin American writers

2.2 Products and Perspectives
• Discuss the poetry of Antonio Machado and the stories of María Luisa Góngora Pacheco
• Talk about the murals and paintings of Diego Rivera
• Talk about community organizations

Connections

3.1 Cross-curricular
• Discuss key facts about community activities
• Discuss key facts about Latin American teenagers
• Discuss poetry, fiction, music, and visual art
• Discuss Spanish-speaking public figures
• Discuss key facts about the Peace Boat Program
• Discuss Language Arts strategies: scanning, reading for comprehension, using visual aids, writing to persuade, using context clues

3.2 Target Culture
• Read a poem excerpt by Antonio Machado
• Read a story by María Luisa Góngora Pacheco

▼ Chapter Objectives

Communication

By the end of the chapter you will be able to:
• Listen to and read about job interviews and classified ads
• Talk and write about applying for a job
• Exchange information about your skills, background experience, and job opportunities

Culture

You will also be able to:
• Understand the influence of Hispanics in the U.S.
• Compare a Mayan folktale with myths and stories in the U.S.

You will demonstrate what you know and can do:
• Presentación oral, p. 235
• Presentación escrita, pp. 236–237
• Preparación para el examen, pp. 244–245

You will use:

Vocabulary	Grammar
• Jobs and activities in the workplace	• Present perfect
• Personal qualities and skills needed	• Pluperfect
• Volunteer and community work	• Present perfect subjunctive
• Job interviews	• Demonstrative adjectives and pronouns

Exploración del mundo hispano

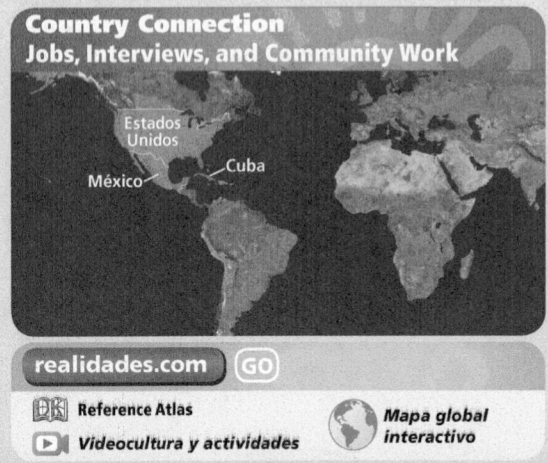

Country Connection
Jobs, Interviews, and Community Work

Estados Unidos
México
Cuba

realidades.com GO

📖 Reference Atlas
▶️ Videocultura y actividades
🌎 Mapa global interactivo

Proyecto de ayuda a la comunidad en Miami, Florida

ENRICH YOUR TEACHING

Using Backward Design
Have students preview the sample performance tasks on *Preparación para el examen*, p. 245, and connect them to the Chapter Objectives. Explain to students that by completing the sample tasks they can self-assess their learning progress.

Mapa global interactivo
Download the *Mapa global interactivo* file for Chapter 5 and preview the activity. For this activity, visit the site of Diego Rivera's work.

Arte y cultura | El mundo hispano

Jardines comunitarios En algunos pueblos de América Latina, muchas de las casas tienen pequeños jardines. A veces, dos o más casas comparten un jardín y las familias trabajan juntas para cuidarlo. Pueden sembrar (*plant*) plantas o flores, como los girasoles (*sunflowers*) que ves en este cuadro de Diego Rivera (1886–1957).

• ¿Hay un jardín en tu comunidad que se comparta entre familias? ¿Qué plantas o flores tiene?

"Muchacha con Girasoles", (1941), Diego Rivera ▶

doscientos cinco **205**
Capítulo 5

Standards (cont'd)

Comparisons
4.1 Language
• Compare Spanish words to their English counterparts
• Compare the English pluperfect tense to the Spanish *pluscuamperfecto*
• Compare the Spanish present perfect subjunctive to its expression in English

4.2 Culture
• Compare Latin American community gardens, teenage employment, and songs to those in the U.S.
• Compare centers in the U.S. Spanish-speaking community to those of society in general

Communities
5.1 Beyond the School
• Discuss community activities and volunteer work
• Discuss job solicitation skills
• Link to Web sites from the Spanish-speaking world

5.2 Lifelong Learner
• Develop an appreciation for poetry and fiction
• Discuss the value of community activity
• Discuss campaigning for a public office

○ **PresentationExpress™**
See pp. 200c–200d

Chapter Opener

Core Instruction

Resources: Map Transparencies 14, 15, 16, 20, 22
Suggestions: Discuss the chapter theme and objectives with students.

▶ **Videocultura** *¡Pura vida!* View this stand-alone storyline video about five young adults in San José, Costa Rica with your class, either online or on DVD.

Arte y cultura

Standards: 1.1, 1.2, 2.1, 3.1, 4.2
Resources: Fine Art Transparencies with Teacher's Guide, p. 67
Suggestions: Ask students if they are familiar with a community garden.

TEACHING WITH ART
Resources: Fine Art Transparencies with Teacher's Guide, p. 67

DIFFERENTIATED INSTRUCTION

Digital resources such as the *Interactive Whiteboard* activity banks, *Videomodelos*, additional *Online Activities*, *Study Plans*, automatically graded *Leveled Workbook*, animated *Grammar Tutorials*, *Flashcards*, and *Vocabulary and Grammar Videos* will help you reach students of different ability levels and learning styles.

STUDENTS NEEDING EXTRA HELP

Guided Practice Activities
• Flashcards, pp. 148–152, 161–164
• Vocabulary Check, pp. 153–156, 165–168
• Grammar, pp. 157–160, 169–172

HERITAGE LEARNERS

Realidades para hispanohablantes
• Chapter Opener, pp. 140–141
• A primera vista, pp. 142–143, 152–153
• Manos a la obra, pp. 144–151, 154–161
• ¡Adelante!, pp. 162–167
• Repaso del capítulo, pp. 168–171

ADVANCED/PRE-AP*

Pre-AP* Resource Book,
• pp. 150–152

Communications Workbook
• Integrated Performance Assessment, p. 191

5 Language Input

Vocabulario en contexto

Core Instruction

Standards: 1.1, 1.2

Resources: Teacher's Resource Book: Input Script, p. 6, Clip Art, pp. 27–34, Audio Script, p. 10; Voc. and Gram. Transparencies 103–104; Audio Program DVD: Cap. 5, Tracks 1, 3

Focus: Presenting new vocabulary and using grammar lexically in context

Suggestions: *El/la salvavidas* is another common form of *el/la salvavida.* Some heritage speakers may be more familiar with the former version. For visualized vocabulary such as *la salvavida, la recepcionista, la clienta,* and *el mensajero,* point to the image on *Vocabulary & Grammar Transparencies* 103–104, say the word, and have students repeat. Meaning of other vocabulary can be clarified through demonstration or explanations in Spanish. For example: *El salario es el dinero que gana una persona cuando trabaja.*

BELLRINGER REVIEW

Write these places on the board:

un hospital	*una escuela primaria*
una biblioteca	*un parque*

Working in pairs, have students brainstorm types of voluntary activities that one can do at any two of the places listed and share with the class.

Teacher-to-Teacher

Have students brainstorm a list of businesses where speaking Spanish would be a valuable asset. Lists may include airline companies, travel agencies, FBI, CIA, radio and television, etc. Divide the class into groups and have them research how they could request information about possible employment opportunities. You might ask students to follow through and inquire about specific information and share their results with the class. You might create a bulletin board based on their research.

▼ Objectives

▶ Read, listen to, and understand information about
  • getting a job
  • skills and abilities needed to perform a job
  • interviewing techniques

Vocabulario en contexto

¿Has trabajado alguna vez? ¿Qué trabajo has tenido? Muchas personas **suelen** usar sus **habilidades** y sus cualidades para encontrar un trabajo que les guste, como es el caso de Miguel. A Miguel le encantan los deportes. Este verano había decidido conseguir un trabajo. Buscó en el periódico algunos trabajos que le parecieron interesantes. Sigamos a Miguel en su búsqueda.

1 Primero, **se presentó** para un trabajo en un club deportivo.

la salvavida

la recepcionista

Club Deportivo Buena Vista

2 Luego, tuvo una **entrevista** con el gerente del club, pero no consiguió **el puesto** porque no tenía experiencia en **computación.**

¿Sabes trabajar con programas de computadora?

206 doscientos seis
A primera vista 1

DIFFERENTIATED INSTRUCTION

Students with Learning Difficulties

Help students improve their reading comprehension by discussing the boldfaced vocabulary items prior to reading each paragraph. After previewing the vocabulary, have them predict what information will be discussed in the paragraph. After reading, help them confirm and correct their predictions.

3 Miguel también se había entrevistado para un trabajo de **niñero**, pero era **a tiempo completo** y él buscaba un trabajo **a tiempo parcial**.

4 En el periódico había visto un trabajo de **consejero** a tiempo parcial, pero **el salario** era muy bajo.

5 Miguel **siguió solicitando** trabajo por varios días. Finalmente, después de una entrevista con el dueño, el Sr. Urbina, Miguel encontró trabajo en una tienda de equipo deportivo. A Miguel le gusta ayudar a los clientes y le encanta el horario flexible.

el dueño
la clienta
el mensajero

▼1 ¿Dónde hay trabajo? 🔊

Escuchar • Hablar

Primero, escucha las frases e indica sobre qué ilustración habla cada una. Luego, di por qué Miguel consiguió o no consiguió ese puesto.

▼2 Las búsquedas de Miguel

Escribir

En una hoja de papel, escribe los números del 1 al 4. Lee cada una de estas frases y escribe *C* (cierto) o *F* (falso). Vuelve a escribir cada frase falsa para que sea verdadera.

1. Miguel encontró trabajo como recepcionista.
2. Miguel se entrevistó para trabajar de niñero.
3. Miguel solicitó trabajos por varios días.
4. Miguel buscaba un trabajo a tiempo completo.

doscientos siete 207
Capítulo 5

Language Input 5

1 Standards: 1.2

Resources: Voc. and Gram. Transparency 104; Teacher's Resource Book: Audio Script, p. 10; Audio Program DVD: Cap. 5, Track 2; Answer Keys: Student Edition, p. 63

Focus: Practicing listening comprehension of new vocabulary

Suggestions: Use the audio or the script. Allow students to listen more than once. Remind them not to try to listen to every word, but rather for key words that will help them determine the main idea. Pause frequently to allow them to write the information.

Answers:
1. 4/El salario era muy bajo.
2. 3/El trabajo era a tiempo completo.
3. 2/No tenía experiencia en computación.
4. 5/A Miguel le gusta ayudar a los clientes y el horario es flexible.

2 Standards: 1.2

Resources: Answer Keys: Student Edition, p. 63

Focus: Demonstrating comprehension of new vocabulary

Suggestions: Make sure students understand that the statements pertain to the narration on pp. 206–207. Encourage them to read about Miguel again before completing the activity.

Answers:
1. F/ Miguel encontró trabajo como empleado en una tienda de equipo deportivo.
2. C
3. C
4. F/ Miguel buscaba un trabajo a tiempo parcial.

Teacher-to-Teacher

Have students do a search under categories like bilingual employment possibilities to find professional organizations to request information about possible employment opportunities. Web sites that may be helpful include: HispanicJobs.com, LatPro.com, and Bilingual.Jobs.com. In addition, the federal government posts many bilingual jobs at FederalJobSearch.com.

ENRICH YOUR TEACHING

Culture Note

Point out that many Latin American and Spanish work schedules differ from those in the United States. The workday starts later, the lunch break is longer, and the day ends later. Although the total hours worked are about the same, they are more spread out. Many workers still go home to have lunch together with their families. A work day that ends later coincides with the custom in many countries of eating dinner at a later hour than in the United States, often as late as ten o'clock.

Vocabulario en contexto

Core Presentation

Standards: 1.2

Resources: Teacher's Resource Book: Input Script, p. 7, Clip Art, pp. 27–34, Audio Script, pp. 10–11; Voc. and Gram. Transparency 105; Audio Program DVD: Cap. 5, Tracks 3, 5

Focus: Extending presentation of vocabulary and grammar

Suggestions:

Pre-reading: Save the reading of *Los anuncios clasificados* until after students have completed *Actividades* 3 and 4.

Reading: Tell students not to fill out the **encuesta** until they have completed *Actividad* 3.

Post-reading: Use gestures, explanations, and demonstrations to clarify the meaning of the new vocabulary.

3 Standards: 1.1, 1.2

Focus: Demonstrating comprehension of a questionnaire

Suggestions: Encourage students to answer honestly. Tell them that more than one answer is possible for each question.

Answers will vary.

4 Standards: 1.2

Resources: Teacher's Resource Book: Audio Script, p. 11; Audio Program DVD: Cap. 5, Track 4; Answer Keys: Student Edition, p. 64

Focus: Demonstrating listening comprehension of new vocabulary

Suggestions: Tell students to refer to the jobs shown on pp. 206–207.

Answers:
Sentences about each job will vary. Students should refer to the following jobs:

1. mensajero
2. salvavida
3. un puesto en el club
4. niñero
5. consejera
6. salvavidas

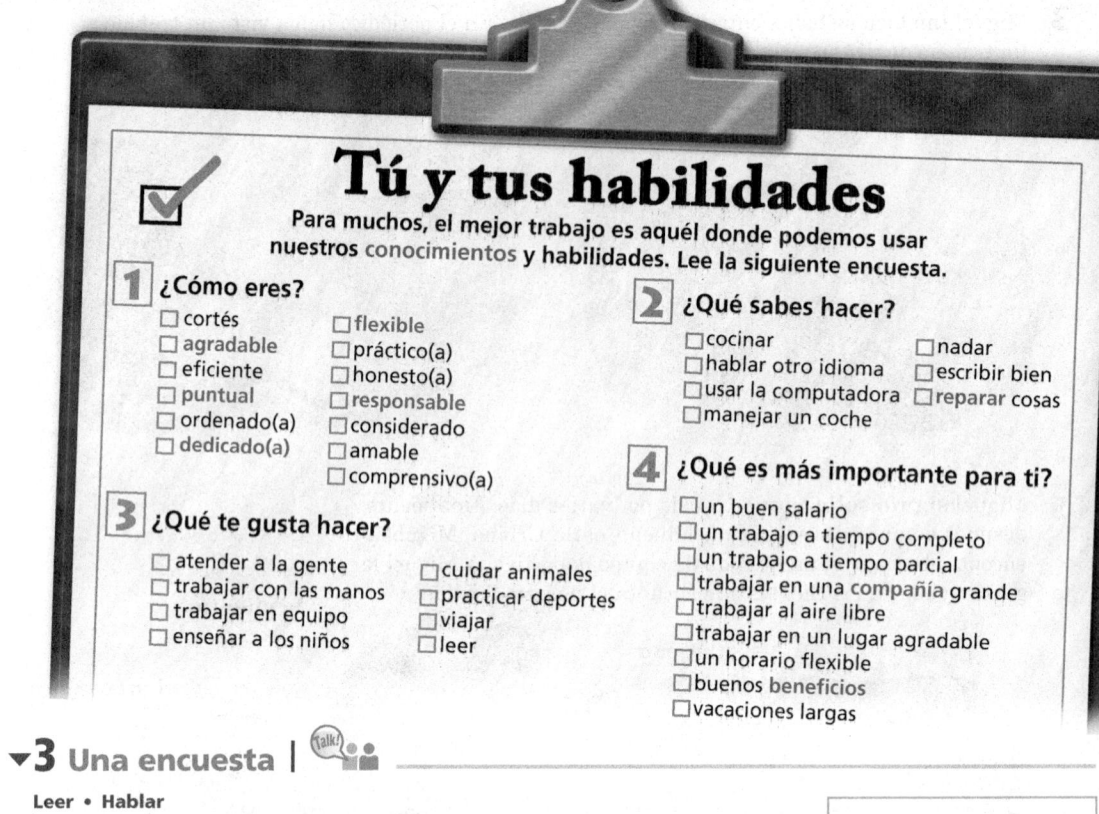

Tú y tus habilidades

Para muchos, el mejor trabajo es aquél donde podemos usar nuestros conocimientos y habilidades. Lee la siguiente encuesta.

1 ¿Cómo eres?
- ☐ cortés
- ☐ agradable
- ☐ eficiente
- ☐ puntual
- ☐ ordenado(a)
- ☐ dedicado(a)
- ☐ flexible
- ☐ práctico(a)
- ☐ honesto(a)
- ☐ responsable
- ☐ considerado
- ☐ amable
- ☐ comprensivo(a)

2 ¿Qué sabes hacer?
- ☐ cocinar
- ☐ hablar otro idioma
- ☐ usar la computadora
- ☐ manejar un coche
- ☐ nadar
- ☐ escribir bien
- ☐ reparar cosas

3 ¿Qué te gusta hacer?
- ☐ atender a la gente
- ☐ trabajar con las manos
- ☐ trabajar en equipo
- ☐ enseñar a los niños
- ☐ cuidar animales
- ☐ practicar deportes
- ☐ viajar
- ☐ leer

4 ¿Qué es más importante para ti?
- ☐ un buen salario
- ☐ un trabajo a tiempo completo
- ☐ un trabajo a tiempo parcial
- ☐ trabajar en una compañía grande
- ☐ trabajar al aire libre
- ☐ trabajar en un lugar agradable
- ☐ un horario flexible
- ☐ buenos beneficios
- ☐ vacaciones largas

▼3 Una encuesta

Leer • Hablar

❶ Escribe tus respuestas a la encuesta en una tabla como ésta.

❷ Túrnate con otro(a) estudiante para hacer y contestar preguntas sobre la información de la encuesta. Usen sus tablas.

▶ Modelo

A —*¿Cómo eres?*
B —*Soy puntual y eficiente.*

Soy . . .
Sé . . .
Me gusta . . .
Para mí es importante . . .

▼4 Conseguir trabajo es un tremendo trabajo

Escuchar • Escribir

Los estudiantes de la clase de Marcos no saben cuál es el mejor trabajo para ellos. Escribe en una hoja de papel los números del 1 al 6. Escucha lo que cada estudiante dice sobre sus habilidades y sus cualidades y decide cuál es el mejor trabajo para cada uno(a). Luego, describe en una frase cada trabajo que escribiste. Di de qué se trata ese trabajo y dónde se puede hacer.

Modelo
cajero
Un cajero trabaja en una tienda o en un supermercado.

208 doscientos ocho
A primera vista 1

DIFFERENTIATED INSTRUCTION

Students with Learning Difficulties

For *Actividad* 4, help students with listening comprehension by playing each speaker's statement once, then pointing out key vocabulary that students should listen for before playing it a second time.

Advanced Learners

Have students create their own classified ads to advertise different job openings. Direct them to use the advertising language in **Los anuncios clasificados** as models for their own work. After checking their work for grammar and spelling, students can present their ads to the rest of the class.

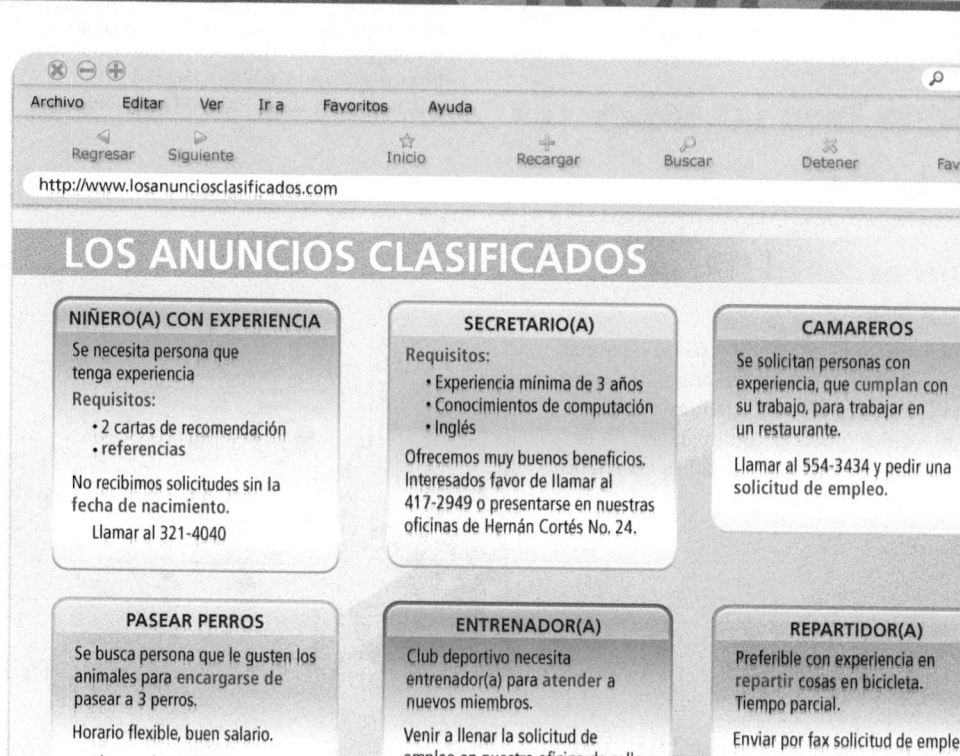

LOS ANUNCIOS CLASIFICADOS

http://www.losanunciosclasificados.com

NIÑERO(A) CON EXPERIENCIA

Se necesita persona que tenga experiencia

Requisitos:
• 2 cartas de recomendación
• referencias

No recibimos solicitudes sin la fecha de nacimiento.

Llamar al 321-4040

SECRETARIO(A)

Requisitos:
• Experiencia mínima de 3 años
• Conocimientos de computación
• Inglés

Ofrecemos muy buenos beneficios. Interesados favor de llamar al 417-2949 o presentarse en nuestras oficinas de Hernán Cortés No. 24.

CAMAREROS

Se solicitan personas con experiencia, que cumplan con su trabajo, para trabajar en un restaurante.

Llamar al 554-3434 y pedir una solicitud de empleo.

PASEAR PERROS

Se busca persona que le gusten los animales para encargarse de pasear a 3 perros.

Horario flexible, buen salario.

Llamar al 462-9032

ENTRENADOR(A)

Club deportivo necesita entrenador(a) para atender a nuevos miembros.

Venir a llenar la solicitud de empleo en nuestra oficina de calle Colón #452

REPARTIDOR(A)

Preferible con experiencia en repartir cosas en bicicleta. Tiempo parcial.

Enviar por fax solicitud de empleo.

Fax 771-7171

▼5 ¿Comprendes?

Leer • Escribir

1. ¿Qué requisitos se solicitan generalmente en un anuncio clasificado?

2. ¿Qué cualidades se buscan generalmente en un empleado? ¿Por qué?

3. ¿Por qué es importante cumplir con el trabajo en un empleo?

4. Escoge tres de los trabajos y explica de qué se encargan las personas que hacen esos trabajos.

Más práctica GO

realidades.com | print

Instant Check	✔	
Guided WB pp. 148–156	✔	✔
Core WB pp. 65–66	✔	✔
Comm. WB p. 68	✔	✔
Hispanohablantes WB pp. 142–143		✔

doscientos nueve **209**
Capítulo 5

5 Standards: 1.2, 1.3

Resources: Voc. and Gram. Transparency 106

Focus: Demonstrating reading comprehension of classified ads

Suggestions: Before having students complete the activity, allow them to review the classified ads on p. 209.

Answers will vary. For item 1, students may mention: *una carta de recomendación, referencias, experiencia,* and so on.

Pre-AP* Support

• **Learning Objective:** Interpersonal Speaking

• **Activity:** Have pairs of students prepare and present mini-dialogues. One partner plays the role of an applicant and asks questions about the job. The other plays the prospective employer and answers the questions.

• *Pre-AP* Resource Book:* Comprehensive guide to Pre-AP* vocabulary skill development, pp. 51–57

Chapter Project

Give students copies of the Chapter Project outline and rubric from the *Teacher's Resource Book*. Explain the task to them, and have them perform Step 1. (For more information, see p. 200-b.)

Teacher-to-Teacher

Have students select one of the ads on p. 209. Have them write an e-mail in which they request specific information about the job such as hours, pay, qualifications, etc. Have them "send" their e-mail to a classmate who will then "send" a written response.

☑ASSESSMENT

Prueba: Comprensión del vocabulario 1
• Prueba 5-1: pp. 105–106

ENRICH YOUR TEACHING

Culture Note

In Buenos Aires, Argentina, a common, after-school and weekend job for many young people is that of merchandise stocker. Companies hire young people to travel from store to store and stock candy, gum and other items at franchise sales displays in supermarkets and department stores. Workers usually work in teams of two.

21st Century Skills

Technology Literacy Have students research Web sites in Spanish that provide classified ads for jobs. What keywords will they use in their search? Once their search is underway, ask students to make a short list of job postings they find appealing. What is most attractive about these jobs? What qualifications would they need in order to apply?

5 Practice and Communicate

▶ Listen to a description of and write about a workplace
▶ Discuss skills and qualities needed
▶ Talk and write about jobs and preferences

Vocabulario en uso

▼ 6 ¿Quiénes son? | ◀»

Escuchar • Escribir

La ilustración a la derecha muestra las personas que trabajan en la florería de la mamá de Laura. Escucha a Laura describir lo que hace cada persona. Identifica quién es cada persona en la ilustración. Luego, escribe dos detalles acerca de cada una.

6 Standards: 1.2

Resources: Teacher's Resource Book: Audio Script, pp. 11–12; Audio Program DVD: Cap. 5, Track 6; Answer Keys: Student Edition, p. 64

Focus: Practicing listening comprehension of new vocabulary

Suggestions: Before students listen to the statements, have them look at the drawing.

Answers:
1. la Sra. Bonilla (mamá): dueña, tiene muchos clientes, amable
2. Celia (hermana): la gerente, responsable, puntual y dedicada
3. Jorge (hermano menor): repartidor, está reparando su bicicleta
4. Laura (yo): niñera, me gusta visitar a mamá
5. Eduardo (tío): mensajero, ayuda mucho a mamá

▼ 7 Consejos para conseguir un trabajo

Leer • Escribir

Tu amigo(a) busca trabajo. Dale consejos, usando la palabra que mejor complete la definición en la frase.

una referencia	requisitos	habilidades	suelen	conocimientos

1. En general, los _____ para conseguir trabajo son: ser paciente, tener habilidades para hacer el trabajo y prepararse para la entrevista.

2. Tienes _____ sobre cine, parece que has visto todas las películas. Quizás te den trabajo en una tienda de videos.

3. ¿Qué puedes hacer bien en este trabajo? ¿Tienes las _____ que se necesitan para hacerlo?

4. A veces en una entrevista te piden _____, como el nombre de una persona que te conoce.

5. Las entrevistas _____ ser formales. Debes vestirte bien.

BELLRINGER REVIEW

Ask students to choose one of these stores you have listed on the board:

Taquería   Zapatería   Dulcería
Librería   Pastelería   Florería

Then, working in pairs, ask their partner what two activities the worker might be doing there. (Ex. Partner A: *En la taquería, ¿qué está haciendo el cocinero?* Partner B: *Está cocinando la carne de res.*)

7 Standards: 1.2

Resources: Answer Keys: Student Edition, p. 65

Focus: Practicing new vocabulary

Suggestions: Have students review the vocabulary on pp. 206–209 before completing the activity.

Answers:
1. requisitos   4. una referencia
2. conocimientos   5. suelen
3. habilidades

▼ 8 ¿Qué quieren decir? | 👥

Escribir • Hablar

Escribe cinco palabras del vocabulario de las páginas 206–209 en una hoja de papel, y en otra, escribe una definición para cada una. Túrnate con otro(a) estudiante para leer las definiciones de cada uno(a) y digan de qué palabra se trata.

210 doscientos diez
Manos a la obra 1

8 Standards: 1.1, 1.3

Focus: Practicing new vocabulary in a paired matching activity

Suggestions: Tell students to trade only the definitions with their partners.

Answers will vary.

DIFFERENTIATED INSTRUCTION

Students with Learning Difficulties

Before playing the audio selection for *Actividad 6*, help students preview some of the target language for which they will be listening. Discuss the illustration with them. Point out and briefly describe the characters, and invite students to add details.

Advanced Learners/Pre-AP*

Some students may enjoy creating informal quizzes and exercises for other students. Monitor their work carefully for spelling, grammar, and punctuation. Help them write clear and concise instructions, and teach them over time to make their activities neither too difficult nor too easy for their peers.

▼9 ¿En qué te gustaría trabajar? | |

Hablar

Imagina que solicitas un puesto de trabajo. Con otro(a) estudiante, piensen en varios trabajos a tiempo parcial, digan cuáles les gustaría hacer y por qué. Decidan qué tipo de trabajo les gustaría más conseguir.

▶ Modelo

A —Dime, ¿qué te gustaría más, trabajar de gerente o de consejero de campamento?

B —Me gustaría trabajar de gerente porque soy responsable. Y a ti, ¿qué te gustaría hacer?

A —A mí me gustaría trabajar como consejero de campamento. Me gusta mucho trabajar con niños.

Estudiante A

1.
2.
3.
4.

Estudiante B

¡Respuesta personal!

▼10 ¿A quién conoces? |

Hablar

Trabaja con otro(a) estudiante. Lean la lista de trabajos y túrnense para hacer preguntas y responderlas.

agente de viajes	reportero(a)	salvavida
gerente	camarero(a)	fotógrafo(a)
bombero(a)	locutor(a)	dentista

▶ Modelo

A —¿A quién conoces que trabaje de locutor?
B —El hermano de María es locutor.
A —¿De qué se encarga él en su trabajo?

Estudiante A

1. ¿A quién conoces que trabaje de (en) . . . ?
2. ¿De qué se encarga esa persona en su trabajo?
3. ¿Qué cualidades y habilidades tiene esa persona?
4. ¿Cuándo suele trabajar?

Estudiante B

¡Respuesta personal!

9 Standards: 1.1

Focus: Using new vocabulary and structures in a guided conversation
Recycle: constructions with *gustar*
Suggestions: As you go over the model with students, point out the way in which Student B politely bounces Student A's question back after answering it. Remind students that there are many ways to sustain a conversation. Encourage them to be creative and try different ways whenever they practice dialogues in which the roles are switched.
Common Errors: Some students will try to change *salvavida* to *"salvavido"* in an attempt to give it a masculine gender form. Tell them that, just as with the word *artista,* the word ends in *-a* when applied to either gender. Point out that it is a compound word made from a form of *salvar* plus *vida.*
Answers will vary.
Student A might inquire about the following jobs based on the picture clues:
1. ...de niñero(a) o de mensajero(a)?
2. ...de salvavida o de recepcionista?
3. ...de repartidor(a) o de vendedor(a)?
4. ...de vendedor(a) o de cajero(a)?

10 Standards: 1.1

Focus: Practicing new vocabulary and structures in a guided conversation
Suggestions: Have students take turns reading the questions aloud and answering them. Encourage them to help each other when they have difficulty answering.
Answers will vary.

ENRICH YOUR TEACHING

Teacher-to-Teacher

When students work with partners to practice dialogues and target language, end the activity by inviting pairs to present their dialogues if time allows. When practicing with the understanding that they will make a presentation, many students are inclined to extend their conversations and stretch their abilities.

21st Century Skills

Communication Have pairs of students discuss which part-time jobs are most popular for young people in their community. Where do young people work in the summer or after school? Which jobs are popular with girls or with boys? What job do they currently have or would like to have?

11 Standards: 1.1, 1.2, 3.1

Focus: Practicing new vocabulary and structures through reading and response

Suggestions: Refer students to the *Estrategia*. Remind them that classified ads are written for the convenience of the reader: they are categorized, and the information is presented in a similar order each time. Have them scan the ads with these things in mind.

Answers will vary.

Fondo cultural

Standards: 1.1, 1.2, 2.1, 4.2

Suggestions: After students have read the information, ask: *¿Cuál es la edad oficial para poder empezar a trabajar en los Estados Unidos? En general, ¿qué creen los padres latinoamericanos que es más importante para los jóvenes: que estudien o que ganen dinero? ¿Cómo gastan los jóvenes latinoamericanos el dinero que ganan? ¿Piensan que lo gastan de la misma manera que los jóvenes de los Estados Unidos?*

Answers will vary.

12 Standards: 1.1, 1.3

Focus: Practicing new vocabulary and structures by writing a classified ad

Suggestions: For Step 2, have students build their interviews around an ad that another group wrote.

Answers will vary.

---

11 El mejor trabajo para ti

Leer • Escribir • Hablar

SECRETARIO(A) RECEPCIONISTA
Requisitos indispensables: Experiencia mínima de 2 años, extremadamente responsable y puntual, 2 cartas de recomendación con número telefónico, nivel intermedio de inglés y de preferencia domicilio particular cercano a nuestra zona en Distrito Federal, México.

MENSAJERO(A) / REPARTIDOR(A)
Se necesitan personas activas, excelente orientación de servicio, con iniciativa y muy responsables, para cumplir funciones de mensajero(a) y repartidor(a) motorizado(a). Se requiere la licencia de manejar correspondiente. Enviar currículum. Santiago, Chile

EMPLEADO(A) DOMÉSTICO(A)
Agencia Doña Miriam necesita urgente niñeros(as) y personas para trabajar en casas y cocinar. Salarios C$1000 a C$2000. Tel 249-3736. Nicaragua

SALVAVIDAS
AQUASWIM SL necesita 25 salvavidas para trabajar la temporada de verano en la Comunidad de Madrid. Si estás interesado(a) en trabajar con nosotros, ponte en contacto llamando al tlf. 605587464. España

▼ Fondo Cultural | El mundo hispano

El trabajo y la juventud En América Latina, la edad oficial para poder empezar a trabajar suele ser 15 años. Pero socialmente no se ve bien que un joven trabaje porque los padres piensan que interfiere con la vida escolar. En todo caso, se ven jóvenes haciendo trabajos a tiempo parcial, tales como llenar bolsas para los clientes en el supermercado o servir en los restaurantes de comida rápida. Los jóvenes usan el dinero de sus salarios para salir a divertirse o comprarse cosas.

• ¿Qué piensa la gente en los Estados Unidos de los jóvenes que tienen un trabajo a tiempo parcial?

❶ Haz una lista de las habilidades y cualidades necesarias para cada trabajo mencionado en los anuncios clasificados.

❷ Escoge un anuncio y escribe un mínimo de cinco preguntas para hacer una entrevista a una persona que se presenta para el puesto. Puedes preguntar datos como el horario que puede trabajar, el salario, su experiencia anterior y sus habilidades.

❸ Entrevista a otro(a) estudiante para ese puesto. Luego, cambien de papeles.

▶ Modelo

Para el puesto de secretaria:
A —*¿Trabajó usted de secretaria antes?*
B —*Sí, trabajo en una compañía desde el verano pasado.*
A —*¿Sigue trabajando allí?*
B —*Sí, pero el horario no es muy flexible.*
A —*¿Qué habilidades tiene?*
B —*Sé computación, hablo español e inglés y escribo bien en los dos idiomas.*

212 doscientos doce
Manos a la obra 1

DIFFERENTIATED INSTRUCTION

Heritage Language Learners
Invite students who have lived in heritage countries to share their background knowledge about typical employment for young people there. Encourage them to tell about the duties, schedules, and pay rates of the various kinds of jobs.

Students with Learning Difficulties
Give each student a photocopy of one of the classified ads. Have them use a colored highlighter to shade the key words and phrases in their ad. Then have them exchange ads with a partner and analyze the partner's markings. Finally, have them scan an unmarked ad and orally share the key information.

▼12 Un anuncio clasificado |

Hablar • Escribir

❶ Trabaja con cuatro estudiantes para escribir un anuncio clasificado. Sigan los siguientes pasos.

- Escojan un trabajo que puede hacer un estudiante y digan de qué se va a encargar.

- Determinen el horario y si el trabajo es a tiempo completo o a tiempo parcial.

- Incluyan los beneficios y el salario.

- Hagan una lista de los requisitos y de lo que el (la) candidato(a) debe llevar a la entrevista.

- Escriban el anuncio.

❷ La clase va a participar en una feria de trabajo (*job fair*). Cada grupo va a poner su anuncio clasificado en las paredes de la clase. Los estudiantes van a escoger un anuncio y turnarse para hacer los papeles de la persona que hace la entrevista y el (la) candidato(a).

▼13 Y tú, ¿qué dices? |

Hablar • Escribir

1. ¿Tienes un trabajo después de las clases? ¿Qué haces? ¿Tienes un horario flexible?

2. En tu opinión, ¿cuáles son tus habilidades? Haz una lista.

3. ¿Cuáles son algunos beneficios de tener un trabajo a tiempo parcial?

4. ¿Trabajaste alguna vez como niñera(o) o salvavida? ¿Sigues haciendo ese trabajo? ¿Por qué?

5. ¿Qué tres consejos puedes dar a un(a) estudiante de tu clase que busca trabajo?

6. Escribe un párrafo en el que describas otro trabajo que hiciste y si cumpliste con lo que te pidieron. Explica qué te gustó más de ese trabajo.

▼ Ampliación del lenguaje

Muchos sustantivos (*nouns*) que terminan con el sufijo *-ero, -era* se refieren a profesiones relacionadas con los sustantivos de los que se derivan.
Por ejemplo, el sustantivo *niñera(o)* nombra a la persona que cuida a niños.
Lee las palabras de la tabla siguiente y luego completa las frases.

Sustantivo	Profesión
mensaje	mensaj**ero**(a)
caja	caj**ero**(a)
consejo	consej**ero**(a)
carta	cart**ero**(a)
leche	lech**ero**(a)
niño	niñ**ero**(a)

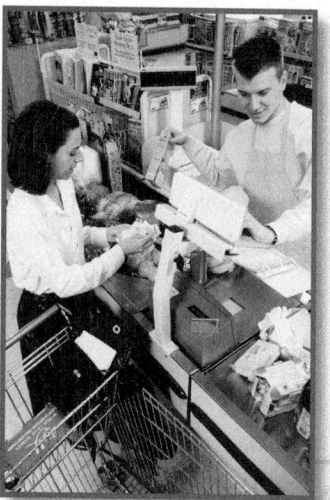

Cristina me escribió una __1.__ hace una semana. El __2.__ la dejó hoy en mi buzón.

Después de comprar la comida en el supermercado, fuimos a pagar a la __3.__ . El __4.__ tomó nuestro dinero y puso la comida en unas bolsas.

doscientos trece 213
Capítulo 5

ENRICH YOUR TEACHING

Teacher-to-Teacher
Group projects like the **feria de trabajo** in *Actividad* 12 elicit language that goes far beyond the task at hand. In order to work together, students will need to make affirmative and negative commands and to use the subjunctive in order to express necessities and preferences. Monitor them as they work and provide models of language that will help them in task-oriented communication.

Practice and Communicate   5

▼13   Standards: 1.1, 1.3
Focus: Practicing new vocabulary and structures through discussion and writing
Suggestions: Have students discuss the questions orally first. This will prepare them for writing their answers. For item 1, be prepared to help students name their job in Spanish. You might have to consult a dictionary, a colleague, or another source.
Answers will vary.
Extension: Assign two or more students to be reporters of the **feria de trabajo** in *Actividad* 12. The group can videotape the various interviews and present them in the format of a news feature about the **feria.** Ask them to provide a brief introduction and a conclusion.

Ampliación del lenguaje
Core Instruction
Standards: 1.2, 4.1

Resources: Answer Keys: Student Edition, p. 65
Focus: Understanding the noun suffixes **-ero** and **-era**
Suggestions: For each example, ask students to use both the noun and the noun + **-ero(a)** suffix in a sentence: *Un cartero reparte cartas.*
Answers:
1. **carta**
2. **cartero**
3. **caja**
4. **cajero**

Additional Resources
- Communication Wbk.: Audio Act. 1, p. 64
- Teacher's Resource Book: Audio Script, p. 12, Communicative Pair Activity BLM, pp. 18–19
- Audio Program DVD: Cap. 5, Track 7

✓ASSESSMENT
Prueba 5-2 with Study Plan (online only)
Prueba: Aplicación del vocabulario 1
- Prueba 5-2: pp. 107–108

213

Gramática Repaso

Core Instruction

Standards: 4.1

Resources: Voc. and Gram. Transparency 107

INTERACTIVE WHITEBOARD
Grammar Activities 5-1

Suggestions: Ask students to write complete, original sentences in the present perfect tense using the irregular past participles shown in the *Gramática*.

▼14 Standards: 1.2

Resources: Answer Keys: Student Edition, p. 65
Focus: Practicing the present perfect tense in a cloze exercise

Suggestions: Have students check their answers by reading each completed item aloud. Remind them that the initial *h-* in the forms of **haber** is always silent.

Answers:
1. ha ido
2. he respondido
3. me he puesto
4. ha dicho
5. he dado
6. ha leído

Chapter Project

Students can perform Step 2 at this point. Be sure they understand your corrections and suggestions. (For more information, see p. 200-b.)

Gramática Repaso

▶ Read and write about a job interview
▶ Discuss personal job experiences
▶ Write about your personal qualities and skills

El presente perfecto

To form the present perfect tense, combine the present tense of the verb *haber* with a past participle. You generally use the Spanish present perfect in the same way you use its English equivalent.

No **he reparado** la bicicleta todavía.
I haven't repaired the bicycle yet.

¿Qué trabajos **has tenido**?
What jobs have you had?

Here are the present perfect forms of *hablar*.

he hablado	hemos hablado
has hablado	habéis hablado
ha hablado	han hablado

- Recall that to form the past participle of a verb in Spanish, you add *-ado* to the stem of *-ar* verbs and *-ido* to the stem of *-er* and *-ir* verbs.

hablar → habl**ado**   comer → com**ido**
vivir → viv**ido**

- Verbs that have two vowels in the infinitive form (except for *ui*) require an accent mark on the *i* in the past participle.

caer → caído	oír → oído
traer → traído	reír → reído
leer → leído	creer → creído

- Many Spanish verbs have irregular past participles. You have already learned some of these.

abrir → **abierto**	resolver → **resuelto**
decir → **dicho**	romper → **roto**
escribir → **escrito**	ser → **sido**
morir → **muerto**	ver → **visto**
poner → **puesto**	

- Place negative words, object pronouns, and reflexive pronouns before the form of *haber*.

No he repartido las flores todavía.

Mi profesora **me** ha escrito una carta de recomendación.

El dueño **se** ha ido temprano a la oficina.

Más ayuda   **realidades.com**   ▶ *Canción de hip hop* ▶ *Tutorial*

▼14 Después de la entrevista

Leer • Escribir

Tamara y Juan fueron a una entrevista de trabajo. Completa la conversación que tuvieron con el presente perfecto de los verbos del recuadro.

decir	ir	dar	ponerse	leer	responder

—Juan, ¿cómo te __1.__ esta mañana en la entrevista?

—Creo que no muy bien, Tamara. No __2.__ a todas las preguntas.

—Yo tampoco. Además, __3.__ muy nerviosa. El gerente quería gente con mucha experiencia.

—Sí, Tamara. Él me __4.__ que buscaba jóvenes muy ordenados, puntuales y responsables.

—Yo le __5.__ mis referencias, pero él no las __6.__. Dijo que no las necesitaba.

—Bueno, a ver qué pasa . . .

DIFFERENTIATED INSTRUCTION

Students with Learning Difficulties

Allow students who have difficulty reciting in front of others to record their recitations of the Machado poem on p. 215. You may wish to have them recite only one stanza of the poem.

Advanced Learners

Have students use the present perfect tense to tell about five things they have done that qualify them either for the job they actually have or for a job they would like to have: *Quiero ser cajera. He trabajado de cajera en la tienda de mis padres. Mi papá me ha enseñado a usar la caja....*

▾15 Juego | 👥

Escribir • Hablar • GramActiva

Vas a jugar con los(as) compañeros(as) de tu clase.

❶ Escribe siete preguntas para saber si tus compañeros(as) han hecho o no cosas como *trabajar en un parque de diversiones*. Para hacer tus preguntas, usa el presente perfecto de los verbos.

❷ Con otro(a) estudiante, haz y contesta las preguntas. Para conectar tus respuestas, puedes usar las siguientes palabras o expresiones.

no . . . todavía	muchas veces	varias veces	casi siempre
casi nunca	de vez en cuando	algunas veces	una vez

❸ La clase forma dos círculos concéntricos con los estudiantes cara a cara. Al oír música, los estudiantes se mueven a la derecha. Al parar la música, deben parar y hacerle una pregunta al (a la) estudiante que tienen enfrente usando el presente perfecto. Al terminar el juego, el profesor te va a hacer preguntas sobre las respuestas de tus compañeros(as).

▼ En voz alta | 🗣

El poeta español Antonio Machado (1875–1939) escribió poemas sencillos y hermosos que comenzaron a aparecer en España en 1901. En sus poemas, Machado parece estar hablando de sus experiencias y de las de todo el pueblo[1] español al mismo tiempo. Sus poemas hacen homenaje[2] al hombre común y su voz es a menudo la de todo el pueblo. Es por esto que todavía es el poeta de su época que más lectores ha tenido.

En *Soledades* y *Campos de Castilla*, Machado hace un retrato cariñoso pero crítico de la España de su época. El poema al que pertenecen estos fragmentos es un ejemplo de la manera en que Machado retrataba al hombre común. Lee los versos y trata de repetirlos en voz alta.

---

1 people 2 pay tribute to

- ¿Crees que el autor del poema es una persona mayor o un joven? Explica por qué.
- ¿Cómo te sientes después de leer los fragmentos del poema? ¿Qué frases te hablan de cómo ve la vida el poeta?

▶ **Modelo**

A —¿Has trabajado en un parque de diversiones alguna vez?

B —Sí, trabajé una vez en el verano.

¿Recuerdas?

Cuando la consonante *r* va entre vocales, su sonido es similar a la "dd" en la palabra inglesa *ladder*. Repite estas palabras del poema: *veredas, mares, caravanas*.

"He andado muchos caminos"
de Antonio Machado

He andado muchos caminos,
he abierto muchas veredas[3],
he navegado en cien mares,
y atracado[4] en cien riberas[5] . . .

Y en todas partes he visto
gentes que danzan o juegan,
cuando pueden, y laboran
sus cuatro palmos[6] de tierra.

Son buenas gentes que viven,
laboran, pasan y sueñan,
y un día como tantos,
descansan bajo la tierra.

"Antonio Machado",
Ignacio Rived

---

3 trails 4 moored 5 shores 6 spans

doscientos quince **215**
Capítulo 5

Practice and Communicate 5

15 Standards: 1.1, 1.3

Focus: Practicing the present perfect tense through questions and answers

Suggestions: By Step 3, students should be ready to ask one of the questions they wrote or responded to in the earlier steps. Since they have had some practice, encourage them to invent new, spontaneous questions when they are in the double-circle formation.

Answers will vary.

En voz alta
Core Instruction

Standards: 1.2, 1.3, 2.2, 3.1, 3.2, 5.2

Resources: Teacher's Resource Book: Audio Script, p. 12; Audio Program DVD: Cap. 5, Track 9

Suggestions: Have students read the information and the poem silently. Ask comprehension questions: *Según el texto, de todos los poetas españoles de la época de Machado, ¿quién ha tenido el mayor número de lectores? ¿A qué obra pertenecen los fragmentos del texto?*

Before having students recite the poem, direct their attention to the information in the *¿Recuerdas?* Have students repeat your models of words with the intervocalic *r* sound, such as the names of jobs they studied in the *Ampliación del lenguaje* on p. 213: **mensajera, cajero, consejero, cartero, lechero,** and **niñera.** Then allow them a few minutes to practice reciting the poem excerpt with a partner.

Answers will vary.

Extension: Antonio Machado is an **AP* Literature** author. You may want to suggest that students read additional works by this Spanish poet.

ENRICH YOUR TEACHING

Culture Note

Antonio Machado belongs to the Generation of 1898, a group of Spanish writers whose work is marked by reflections on personal and national identity. In Machado's lifetime, Spain underwent enormous political upheaval—revolution, loss of its remaining colonial empire, and a civil war that drove Machado to die in exile.

Teacher-to-Teacher

Many students take pleasure in the practice and perfection of the sounds of a new language. Encourage them by setting up a regularly scheduled recital period. Aside from pronunciation practice, regular recitals or readings of poetry, song lyrics, or fiction excerpts strengthen students' reading skills.

Block Schedule

After completing *En voz alta*, have students write their own version of the first stanza of the poem. Model it after the Machado poem using the present perfect tense as he did. Have students read their poems aloud in small groups.

16 Standards: 1.2, 1.3

Focus: Practicing the present perfect tense through reading and writing about jobs and job qualifications

Suggestions: Remind students that in real life a paragraph like the one they are writing has the value of creating a favorable first impression.

Answers will vary.

17 Standards: 1.2, 1.3

Focus: Practicing the present perfect tense in guided conversations

Suggestions: For Step 3, remind students that most Spanish speakers would address each other with **Ud.** rather than **tú** during an interview.

Answers will vary.

Fondo cultural

Standards: 1.1, 1.2

Suggestions: After students have read the information, ask them to name other prominent people of Spanish or Latin American heritage in the United States. Have them tell what each person does or has done.

Answers will vary.

216

▼16 ¿Cómo te describes a ti mismo?

Leer • Escribir

Imagina que estás buscando trabajo y lees en el periódico este anuncio clasificado. Para contestar al anuncio, escribe un breve párrafo sobre tus cualidades y las cosas que has hecho hasta ahora. Si no te interesa este trabajo, escoge uno de los trabajos que se anuncian en la página 209.

> Se busca joven responsable y cortés p-
> trabajar en un campamento de verano. De
> gustarle la naturaleza y los niños.
> Enviar breve párrafo describiendo sus cualida
> y lo que ha hecho en materia de trabajo
> estudio.

Modelo

Mi nombre es Enrique y he trabajado con niños desde los 12 años. Siempre he sido responsable, puntual y he cumplido con mi trabajo.

▼17 Preparación para una entrevista |

Escribir • Hablar

❶ Haz una lista de cinco cosas que has hecho para prepararte para una entrevista.

Modelo
He leído los anuncios clasificados.

❷ Piensa en un trabajo específico y escribe cinco preguntas que puedan hacerte en la entrevista.

❸ Ensaya la entrevista con otro(a) estudiante.

Más práctica	GO

realidades.com | print

Instant Check	✔	
Guided WB pp. 157–158	✔	✔
Core WB p. 67	✔	✔
Comm. WB pp. 69, 189	✔	✔
***Hispanohablantes* WB** pp. 144–148	✔	

▼ Fondo cultural | Estados Unidos

La Fundación de Herencia Hispana (*Hispanic Heritage Foundation*) es una organización establecida para promover una mayor comprensión de las contribuciones que han hecho los hispanoamericanos en los Estados Unidos. Cada año, la Fundación premia a hispanoamericanos prominentes, entre ellos, científicos, artistas, atletas y, últimamente, a jóvenes hispanos. Los ganadores suelen ser profesionales y líderes que se han destacado en su campo profesional y estudiantes que han demostrado excelencia académica, participación activa en la comunidad, y orgullo cultural. Uno de los ganadores del premio fue el matemático y profesor Richard A. Tapia. Otros ganadores han sido America Ferrera (actriz), Sandra Benítez (literatura) y Cuauhtémoc Blanco (deportes).

• ¿Qué otros premios conoces que reconozcan a personas que se han destacado en sus profesiones?

La actriz America Ferrera

216 doscientos dieciséis
Manos a la obra 1

DIFFERENTIATED INSTRUCTION

Heritage Language Learners

Have students pretend they are announcers presenting a Hispanic Heritage Award to an accomplished member of the Hispanic American community in the United States. Encourage them to use target language from the chapter. Provide feedback on errors they may make.

Students with Learning Difficulties

Have students work with a partner to complete Steps 1 and 2 of *Actividad* 17. Allow partners to prepare one set of questions that can be used twice.

Gramática Repaso

El pluscuamperfecto

You use the pluperfect tense to describe an action in the past that occurred *before* another action in the past. To form the pluperfect tense, combine the imperfect tense of the verb *haber* with a past participle. You generally use the Spanish pluperfect in the same way you use its English equivalent.

Cuando llegué a la oficina, el gerente ya **había leído** mis cartas de recomendación.

When I arrived in the office, the manager had already read my letters of recommendation.

Después de la entrevista, yo estaba muy nerviosa porque la dueña de la compañía me **había pedido** referencias.

After the interview, I was feeling nervous because the owner of the company had asked me for references.

Here are the pluperfect forms of *hablar:*

había hablado	habíamos hablado
habías hablado	habíais hablado
había hablado	habían hablado

Más ayuda | **realidades.com** | ▶ Tutorials

▼18 En la agencia de empleos

Leer • Escribir

Jorge y Agustín fueron a una agencia de empleos a pedir trabajo. Completa las siguientes frases con los verbos del recuadro en la forma correcta del pluscuamperfecto.

encargarse	tener	escribir	llenar
pedir	atender	cumplir	solicitar

1. Antes de ir a la agencia, Jorge y Agustín _____ varias solicitudes de empleo.

2. Antes de llenar las solicitudes, Agustín ya _____ una lista de sus habilidades.

3. El año pasado, durante varios meses, Jorge _____ de cuidar niños.

4. Estaban sorprendidos porque la recepcionista los _____ muy rápido.

5. Poco después de entrar a la oficina, el gerente les _____ cartas de recomendación y les _____ referencias.

6. En un momento durante la entrevista, les preguntó qué salario ellos _____ en sus otros trabajos.

7. Cuando terminó la entrevista, la recepcionista ya _____ con su trabajo.

doscientos diecisiete 217
Capítulo 5

Practice and Communicate 5

Gramática Repaso

Core Instruction

Standards: 4.1

Resources: Voc. and Gram. Transparency 108

INTERACTIVE WHITEBOARD
Grammar Activities 5-1

Suggestions: Tell students you will say two events that happened in the past. Ask them to combine your two sentences into one using the pluperfect tense.

Teacher: *Primero, entré en la cocina. Después, sonó el teléfono.*

Student: *Había entrado en la cocina cuando sonó el teléfono.*

▼18 Standards: 1.2

Resources: Answer Keys: Student Edition, p. 66

Focus: Practicing the pluperfect tense in a cloze exercise

Suggestions: Remind students to look over the exercise carefully first in order to decide how best to use the answers in the word bank.

Common Errors: Some students will try to make the past participle agree in number with the subject: *habían idos.* Remind them that the verb *haber* is the only part of the verb phrase that must agree in number with the subject: *habían ido.*

Answers:
1. habían llenado
2. había escrito
3. se había encargado
4. había atendido
5. había solicitado/había pedido
6. habían tenido
7. había cumplido

Extension: For extra practice, have students rewrite the subordinate clauses of the sentences using the preterite tense. For example: *Jorge y Agustín llenaron varias solicitudes de empleo.*

ENRICH YOUR TEACHING

Teacher-to-Teacher

Set up a situation, such as a family going to bed at night. Use an adverbial clause such as ***antes de acostarse....*** Ask students to tell one thing that each member of the family had done before retiring. Then have them write sentences using the pluperfect: *Antes de acostarse, papá había apagado las luces.*

21st Century Skills

Initiative and Self-Direction Remind students of the various digital tools available in **realidades.com** to help them monitor their own understanding and learning needs, such as the online tutorials with comprehension check exercises, the flashcards, and the audio files.

19 Standards: 1.2

Resources: Answer Keys: Student Edition, p. 66

Focus: Practicing formation of the pluperfect tense

Suggestions: Point out that for this activity, students already know the tense they need to use each time. All they need to focus on is choosing the correct verb and forming the pluperfect tense correctly. Ask volunteers to take turns reading the completed story aloud, so students have a chance to concentrate on meaning.

Answers:

1. había buscado
2. había conseguido
3. había preparado
4. había estado
5. se había presentado
6. se había levantado
7. había andado
8. había querido

20 Standards: 1.1, 1.3

Focus: Practicing the pluperfect tense through writing

Suggestions: Invite students to use this activity as an opportunity to get to know someone better. Suggest that they learn something about a parent or other family member by using him or her as the subject of their paragraph in Step 2.

Answers will vary.

▼**19** Trabajos en bicicleta

Leer • Escribir

Ayer Andrés empezó a trabajar. Lee lo que le sucedió y completa el relato con el pluscuamperfecto del verbo apropiado.

Andrés ___1.___ *(buscar / creer)* trabajo por mucho tiempo. Finalmente ___2.___ *(destruir / conseguir)* un trabajo como mensajero en bicicleta, en la compañía donde trabajaba su amigo Luis. Ayer era su primer día. Él ___3.___ *(preparar / comer)* sus cosas desde el día anterior para no llegar tarde. Esa mañana, Luis lo ___4.___ *(oír / estar)* esperando en la parada del autobús para irse juntos a trabajar. Como Andrés no llegaba, Luis lo llamó a la casa. Andrés nunca antes ___5.___ *(presentarse / entrar)* tarde a una cita. La mamá le dijo que Andrés ___6.___ *(levantarse / acostarse)* hacía diez minutos y se estaba duchando. Luis se fue entonces solo en autobús. Cuando llegó a la compañía, Andrés ya estaba allí. Él ___7.___ *(correr / andar)* en bicicleta hasta allí. Más tarde, Andrés le explicó que ___8.___ *(caer / querer)* dar una buena impresión el primer día.

▼**20** Una persona que trabaja |

Escribir • Hablar

❶ Piensa en una persona que conozcas bien y que tenga un trabajo. Haz una línea de tiempo como la de abajo para indicar qué había hecho esa persona antes de conseguir este trabajo. Responde a las siguientes preguntas como ayuda.

• ¿De qué trabaja esa persona ahora?
• ¿Qué trabajo o responsabilidades tenía el año pasado?
• ¿De qué otras responsabilidades se había encargado antes?

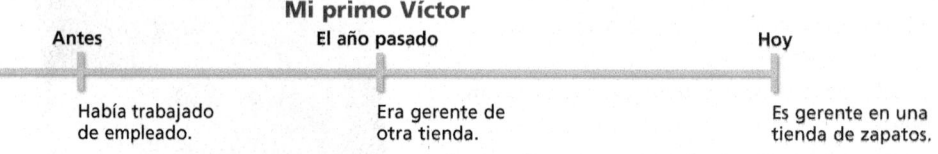

Mi primo Víctor

Antes	El año pasado	Hoy
Había trabajado de empleado.	Era gerente de otra tienda.	Es gerente en una tienda de zapatos.

❷ Escribe un párrafo describiendo a esta persona y sus experiencias en el mundo del trabajo.

❸ Intercambia papeles con otro(a) estudiante. Háganse preguntas sobre las experiencias de la persona que han descrito.

DIFFERENTIATED INSTRUCTION

Students with Special Needs

Ask an advanced learner to describe the Rivera painting on p. 219 in detailed language for visually impaired students.

Advanced Learners

Ask students to interview their parents or other adults about things they had already done by the time they were the student's age. Then have students report back to the class in Spanish. For example: *Antes de tener dieciséis años, mi mamá había viajado en avión.*

▼21 Mi trabajo el año pasado |

Hablar

Habla con otro(a) estudiante y dile tres cosas que hiciste durante el año pasado. Luego, dile si habías hecho lo mismo antes del año pasado.

▶ **Modelo**

A —*El año pasado ganamos el campeonato de fútbol.*

B —*¿Habían ganado el campeonato antes?*

▼22 El trabajo en el arte

Leer • Escribir

El tema del trabajo siempre estuvo presente en la obra de Diego Rivera, el gran pintor de México.

Conexiones | El arte

En los años 1920, el tema principal de la pintura de Diego Rivera fue los campesinos mexicanos. Sin embargo, en los Estados Unidos Rivera pintó obras en las que el trabajador estadounidense era el tema central. Ya en 1930, Rivera había pintado obras importantes en San Francisco y era un artista conocido en los Estados Unidos.

Henry Ford, el dueño de la compañía Ford, y su hijo Edsel, pidieron a Rivera que pintara un mural en el Detroit Institute of Arts. Rivera comenzó a pintarlo en 1932. Había escogido a los trabajadores de Ford como tema de su obra.

Desde 1930, las ideas políticas que Rivera expresaba en sus obras habían causado muchas críticas. Cuando terminó su obra del Detroit Institute en 1933, muchos la criticaron por esa razón. Pero gracias al apoyo de Edsel Ford, el mural sigue hoy en su lugar.

- Mira el detalle *(detail)* del mural que aparece en esta página. ¿Qué crees que nos quiere decir el artista?

- ¿Conoces otro artista al que han criticado por las ideas políticas que expresa en sus obras? ¿Qué piensas tú sobre su obra?

Detalle del mural del Detroit Institute of Arts

Detroit Industry, (1933), Diego Rivera. © 2010 Banco de México Diego Rivera & Frida Kahlo Museums Trust, México, D.F./Artists Rights Society (ARS)/ Detroit Institute of the Arts/Bridgeman Art Library.

Más práctica	GO
**realidades.com	print**	
Instant Check	✔	
Guided WB pp. 159–160	✔	✔
Core WB pp. 68–69	✔	✔
Comm. WB pp. 64, 70–71	✔	✔
Hispanohablantes WB pp. 149–151		✔

doscientos diecinueve **219**
Capítulo 5

ENRICH YOUR TEACHING

219

Vocabulario en contexto

Core Instruction

Standards: 1.1, 1.2, 5.1

Resources: Teacher's Resource Book: Input Script, p. 8, Clip Art, pp. 27–34, Audio Script, pp. 12–13; Voc. and Gram. Transparencies 109–110; Audio Program DVD: Cap. 5, Tracks 10, 12

Focus: Presenting new vocabulary and using grammar lexically in context

Suggestions: Have students read along as you present the new vocabulary by playing the audio or reading the text aloud. Use the pictures on *Vocabulary & Grammar Transparencies* 109–110 and questions with embedded answers to elicit the vocabulary from students: *¿Este hombre está en el centro de la comunidad o en el comedor de beneficencia?* Check for comprehension by asking other questions. See the Input Scripts in the *Teacher's Resource Book* for specific questions.

BELLRINGER REVIEW

Have the class brainstorm a list of "needs" that a community might have following a natural disaster.

▼23 Standards: 1.2

Resources: Teacher's Resource Book: Audio Script, p. 13; Audio Program DVD: Cap. 5, Track 11; Answer Keys: Student Edition, p. 67

Focus: Practicing listening comprehension of new vocabulary

Suggestions: Ask students to tell about what they see happening in the photos on this page and what they think typically happens in each place. Guide them with questions as necessary: *¿Quién come en el comedor de beneficencia?*

Answers:

1. el comedor de beneficencia
2. el centro recreativo
3. el centro de la comunidad
4. el hogar de ancianos
5. el centro de rehabilitación

| ▼ **Objectives**

▶ **Read, listen to, and understand information about**
- **volunteer work opportunities in your community**
- **how you can help your community**

Vocabulario en contexto

¿Has trabajado como voluntario? Ojalá lo hayas hecho, si no, nunca es tarde para ayudar a otros. Hay organizaciones en tu comunidad que buscan proteger y beneficiar a otras personas. Aquí tienes algunos lugares donde puedes colaborar como voluntario y ayudar.

el centro de rehabilitación

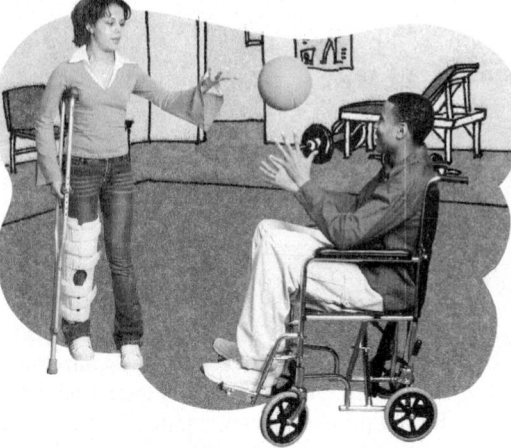

el hogar de ancianos

el centro recreativo

el comedor de beneficencia

el centro de la comunidad

▼23 Dónde buscar ayuda | 🔊

Escuchar • Escribir

Escribe los números del 1 al 5 en una hoja. Escucha la descripción de estos lugares y escribe el nombre del lugar.

220 doscientos veinte
A primera vista 2

DIFFERENTIATED INSTRUCTION

Heritage Language Learners

Have students create original announcements to post on the *Boletín de la Comunidad.* Encourage them to consider volunteer opportunities in their community and in places they have visited. Provide feedback on errors in Spanish and then invite them to share their work with the class.

Advanced Learners

Ask small groups of students to obtain leaflets or flyers from community organizations, preferably in Spanish. Have students scan the papers for words and pictures that relate to the new vocabulary, cut them out, and create a collage.

Language Input 5

Boletín de la Comunidad
marzo-abril

Queremos dar las gracias a todos los que han colaborado como voluntarios este mes. Esperamos que ésta haya sido una buena experiencia. Éstas son algunas de las actividades que **organizamos:**

¡Ayuda ahora!

1 Jóvenes de la escuela La Libertad participaron en la marcha para juntar fondos (obtener dinero) para las víctimas de los huracanes del mes pasado.

2 Los jóvenes de la escuela Simón Bolívar participaron en una manifestación en contra de la contaminación del medio ambiente. Luego sembraron flores para apoyar la causa.

donar

sembrar

Sembrar flores

Se Aceptan DONACIONES

3 La organización Hermanos solicita suéteres y abrigos para la gente sin hogar que no tiene un lugar donde vivir.

¿Quieren ayudar a conseguir abrigos? A mí me es imposible, tengo que estudiar.

A mí me encantaría, me gusta ayudar a los demás.

Me interesaría . . . ¿Qué tengo que hacer?

▼24 ¿Vas a ser voluntario?

Escribir

En el boletín se habla de diferentes proyectos de trabajo voluntario. Imagínate que te invitan a participar en ellos este sábado. Completa la tabla con las actividades del boletín según tu disponibilidad (*availability*) e interés.

Me es imposible . . .	Me encantaría . . .	Me interesaría . . .

doscientos veintiuno **221**
Capítulo 5

24 Standards: 1.2, 1.3

Focus: Writing new vocabulary

Suggestions: Explain to students that there are a variety of ways to talk about the different projects. They should study the presentation text on this page to decide on the phrasing they will use in their chart.

Answers will vary.

Extension: Have students talk about the information on their charts and add a sentence elaborating on each entry: *Me es imposible participar en la manifestación. Tengo que ayudar a mi padre.*

ENRICH YOUR TEACHING

Teacher-to-Teacher
Take advantage of the community-oriented context of this part of the chapter to get students out and learning about organizations in their own community. Encourage them to visit places where volunteer work is done and to look for brochures and other print material in Spanish.

21st Century Skills

Technology Literacy Have students use the digital technology within **realidades.com** to access and manage the audio files, videos, and activities that support learning the new vocabulary.

Vocabulario en contexto

Core Instruction

Standards: 1.1, 1.2, 3.1, 5.1

Resources: Teacher's Resource Book: Input Script, p. 9, Clip Art, pp. 27–34, Audio Script, pp. 13–14; Voc. and Gram. Transparencies 111–112; Audio Program DVD: Cap. 5, Tracks 13, 15

Focus: Extending presentation of vocabulary and grammar in context

Suggestions:

Pre-reading: Present the readings on this and the next page one at a time, along with their respective activities.

Reading: Allow students time to read each presentation silently first before they listen to the audio.

Post-reading: Check comprehension by asking questions.

▼**25** Standards: 1.2, 1.3

Resources: Answer Keys: Student Edition, p. 67

Focus: Writing answers to demonstrate comprehension of a reading

Suggestions: Have students share and discuss their answers.

Answers:

1. Pueden ayudarlos a llenar los formularios y a estudiar para el examen de ciudadanía.
2–4. Answers will vary.

▼**26** Standards: 1.2

Resources: Teacher's Resource Book: Audio Script, p. 13; Audio Program DVD: Cap. 5, Track 14; Answer Keys: Student Edition, p. 67

Focus: Practicing listening comprehension of new vocabulary and structures

Suggestions: Before students hear the conversation, have them read items 1–4 and the choices offered in parentheses. In this way they will be better prepared for the task and know what to listen for.

Answers:

1. solicitar la ciudadanía
2. llenar los formularios
3. la historia del país
4. es imposible

Se buscan voluntarios hispanohablantes para ayudar a inmigrantes

★★★★★★★★★★★★★★★★★★★★★★

¿No sabes qué hacer con tu tiempo libre? Ayuda a un inmigrante a hacerse **ciudadano**.

Buscamos voluntarios para dar clases a inmigrantes. El objetivo de las clases es **educar** a los inmigrantes para conseguir **la ciudadanía**.

¿Qué hacen los voluntarios en las clases?

Un **abogado**[1] explica **las leyes de inmigración** y luego, los voluntarios ayudan a las personas a **llenar los formularios** y a estudiar para **el examen de ciudadanía**.

Para más información, visítanos en Roosevelt Ave. y 84th St., Queens, NY

---

1 lawyer

▼**25** ¿Comprendiste?

Escribir • Hablar

1. ¿Qué pueden hacer los voluntarios para beneficiar a los inmigrantes?

2. ¿Te interesaría ayudar a los inmigrantes? ¿Qué conocimientos crees que se necesitan para ayudarlos a obtener la ciudadanía?

3. ¿Por qué es importante que los inmigrantes comprendan las leyes antes de obtener la ciudadanía?

4. ¿Crees que todos debemos ayudar y educar a las personas que lo necesitan? ¿Por qué?

222 doscientos veintidós
A primera vista 2

▼**26** Ayuda a inmigrantes | 🔊

Escuchar

Escucha la conversación de unos jóvenes voluntarios. Luego, completa cada frase según lo que dijeron los jóvenes.

1. Un abogado explicó cómo (*llenar los formularios / solicitar la ciudadanía*).

2. Los voluntarios ayudaron a (*hacer el examen / llenar los formularios*).

3. Paola tuvo que estudiar (*las leyes de inmigración / la historia del país*).

4. A Luis le (*es imposible / encantaría*) ayudar en las clases para inmigrantes.

DIFFERENTIATED INSTRUCTION

Heritage Language Learners

Ask students to research the United States citizenship test on the Internet. Then have them prepare a mini-lesson in which they act as volunteer teachers for Spanish-speaking immigrants and the rest of the class acts as the immigrants.

Students with Learning Difficulties

Have students list the main ideas from the paragraphs about the candidates on this page. This will help them focus on key language for the *Actividad* 27. Allow them to refer to their lists as they complete the activity.

¿A quién van a escoger?

La Sociedad de Beneficencia Manuel García

La Sociedad es una organización que tiene un hogar de ancianos y un hospital para niños. Cada cuatro años se hace una campaña para elegir (*elect*) un presidente. Lee sobre los candidatos de este año y sus causas, es decir, lo que piensan que es más importante.

Soy María Luna de Soto. Estoy a favor de proteger los derechos de todos los niños, por eso quiero que haya más programas de servicio social. Debemos garantizar los fondos para comprar medicinas para nuestros ciudadanos más jóvenes, los niños, y buscar voluntarios que ayuden a las personas que lo necesitan. Es injusto que sólo algunas personas reciban cuidado y ayuda.

Soy Mauricio Gutiérrez. Pienso que ser presidente de la Sociedad de Beneficencia es una gran responsabilidad. Estoy a favor de comprar equipo médico y garantizar así una mejor atención a la salud de nuestros pacientes. También quiero construir un centro recreativo junto al hogar de ancianos. Me parece justo que los ancianos tengan un lugar donde descansar y recibir todo el cuidado que ellos necesitan.

▼27 ¿Quién está a favor de esto? 🔊

Escuchar

En una hoja, escribe los números del 1 al 6. Después de leer sobre los dos candidatos, escucha estas frases y escribe *Mauricio* o *María* según quién haya expresado esa idea.

Más práctica GO

realidades.com | print

Instant Check	✔	
Guided WB pp. 161–168	✔	✔
Core WB pp. 70–71	✔	✔
Comm. WB p. 72	✔	✔
Hispanohablantes WB pp. 152–153		✔

doscientos veintitrés **223**
Capítulo 5

Language Input 5

▼27 Standards: 1.2

Resources: Teacher's Resource Book: Audio Script, p. 14; Audio Program DVD: Cap. 5, Track 16; Answer Keys: Student Edition, p. 68

Focus: Practicing listening comprehension of new vocabulary and structures

Suggestions: Prepare students for the listening activity by asking comprehension questions about the main points of each candidate's statements.

Answers:
1. María
2. Mauricio
3. María
4. Mauricio
5. María
6. María

Pre-AP* Support

- **Learning Objective:** Interpretive: Print and Audio
- **Activity:** *Actividad* 27 helps students practice key audio and print interpretive skills. Ask students to follow along as you read the selection aloud or play the audio. Have students create three multiple-choice questions to check their comprehension. Then, have them confirm their answers by reading the text.
- *Pre-AP* Resource Book:* Comprehensive guide to Pre-AP* communication skill development, pp. 10–18, 19–26

Chapter Project

Students can perform Step 4 at this point. Be sure they understand your corrections and suggestions. (For more information, see p. 200-b.)

ENRICH YOUR TEACHING

Culture Note

Many volunteer organizations protect the rights and aid in the welfare of children throughout Latin America and Spain. Some of them are worldwide organizations, while others are based in individual countries. Some examples are the Homeless Children's Network, Amnesty International, and Doctors Without Borders.

Teacher-to-Teacher

Invite volunteers to perform dramatic readings of the paragraphs about María Luna de Soto and Mauricio Gutiérrez. After they read their speeches, invite the class to ask questions about their positions on issues mentioned in the paragraph. Readers can improvise their answers.

✓ ASSESSMENT

Prueba: Comprensión del vocabulario 2
- Prueba 5-5: pp. 114–115

28 Standards: 1.2

Resources: Answer Keys: Student Edition, p. 68

Focus: Practicing new vocabulary in a cloze exercise

Recycle: preterite tense, imperfect tense

Suggestions: Encourage students to read the entire paragraph before filling in the blanks. When they have finished, have students read the paragraph again and make sure they understand Rocío's description of her efforts.

Answers:

1. responsabilidad
2. ciudadana
3. campaña
4. servicio social
5. dona
6. juntar fondos
7. sociedad
8. comedores de beneficencia
9. donen
10. construir
11. gente sin hogar

BELLRINGER REVIEW

Have students write the appropriate preterite form for the following verbs:

saber (yo)	buscar (Uds.)
pensar (él)	pedir (nosotros)
decidir (tú)	

29 Standards: 1.2, 1.3, 3.1

Resources: Answer Keys: Student Edition, p. 69

Focus: Demonstrating comprehension of new vocabulary through reading and responding to questions

Recycle: *nosotros* forms of *-ar* verbs

Suggestions: After students have read the announcement, ask them to discuss whether they think the ad is successful in its objective.

Answers:

1. La responsabilidad de los ciudadanos es la de votar.
2. El objetivo principal es juntar fondos para la campaña para votar.
3. Beneficia a los ancianos para que entiendan sus derechos y ayuda a los inmigrantes a solicitar la ciudadanía.
4. Answers will vary.

Manos a la obra 2

▼ Objectives
▶ Read and write about helping people in need
▶ Talk about community work and social services
▶ Discuss what can be done to help your community

Vocabulario en uso

▼28 Ayudar es fácil |

Leer • Escribir

Completa la entrevista con la estudiante Rocío Hernández sobre su campaña.

servicio social	campaña	ciudadana
dona	responsabilidad	juntar fondos

Cuando supe que 24,000 personas en el mundo mueren de hambre cada día y que el 75% son niños, pensé que era mi __1.__, como __2.__ del mundo, ayudar a eliminar el hambre. Decidí crear una __3.__ de __4.__ en mi escuela con el nombre de "Ayudachicos". Allí buscamos diferentes maneras de ayudar. Por ejemplo, encontramos un sitio en la Red que se llama "Hunger Site". Cada vez que haces un clic, se __5.__ comida a los ciudadanos de un país pobre. También hicimos una marcha para __6.__ que luego enviamos a UNICEF.

comedores de beneficencia	gente sin hogar	construir
donen	sociedad	

Además, escribimos a varias compañías de comida enlatada[1] para que donen parte de sus productos a la __7.__ de Aldeas Infantiles SOS. En nuestro pueblo, pedimos donaciones de comida y las llevamos a los __8.__. Ahora, vamos a solicitar a arquitectos y a compañías de construcción que __9.__ materiales y proyectos de construcción a "Hábitat para la humanidad", que se encarga de __10.__ casas para la __11.__.

[1] canned food

▼29 Jóvenes ciudadanos |

Leer • Escribir

Lee este anuncio de una organización que beneficia a la comunidad y responde a las preguntas.

1. Según el anuncio, ¿cuál es la responsabilidad de los ciudadanos?
2. Observa el título *(title)* de este proyecto. ¿Cuál es el objetivo principal de esta organización?
3. ¿A qué dos grupos beneficia esta organización? ¿Cómo los ayuda?
4. ¿Te interesaría participar en este proyecto? ¿Estás a favor o en contra de su causa? ¿Por qué?

224 doscientos veinticuatro
Manos a la obra 2

¡CAMPAÑA PARA VOTAR

¿Quiere cumplir con su responsabilidad como ciudadan_

- **Educamos a los ancianos a entender sus derechos.**
- **Ayudamos a los inmigrantes a solicitar la ciudadanía.**
- **Juntamos fondos para la campaña.**

Reuniones cada jueves a las 5:00 PM
931 E. Market St. Salinas, CA 93905

Proyecto ¡Vote!
Beneficiamos a la sociedad.

DIFFERENTIATED INSTRUCTION

Students with Learning Difficulties

To help students complete *Actividad* 28, encourage them to read each sentence and fill in the blank with a word or phrase that they think would make sense. Then have them search the choices for a word or phrase that is similar to their own idea.

Advanced Learners

Have students contact a community organization that employs Spanish speakers as staff or volunteers. Ask students to arrange for someone from the organization to speak to the class about volunteer work and areas in which Spanish-speaking volunteers are needed.

▼30 El servicio social |

Hablar

Habla con un(a) compañero(a) sobre el servicio social.

▶ **Modelo**

A —*¿Te interesaría hacer servicio social en una escuela primaria?*

B —*Sí, me encantaría porque me gusta encargarme de los niños.*

o: —*No, me es imposible porque tengo miedo de hablar frente a un grupo.*

Estudiante A

1.   2.   3.

4.   5.   6.

Estudiante B

Me encantaría
Me interesaría
No me gustaría
Me es imposible
¡Respuesta personal!

▼31 Compañeros voluntarios . . . |

Pensar • Escribir • Hablar • Dibujar

❶ Haz una lista de cinco acciones que benefician a la sociedad, tales como *donar ropa a la gente sin hogar*.

❷ En grupos de cuatro estudiantes, hablen de las acciones que todos escribieron. ¿Cuáles creen que son las cinco más importantes? ¿Por qué?

▶ **Modelo**

A —*Es importante donar ropa a la gente sin hogar.*
B —*Estoy de acuerdo, pero para mí es más importante que los niños tengan comida.*

❸ En grupo, escriban las acciones en orden de importancia (1 = lo más importante; 5 = lo menos importante). Escojan las tres acciones que a ustedes les parecen más importantes y hagan un cartel para animar a otros(as) jóvenes a hacer trabajo voluntario.

doscientos veinticinco **225**
Capítulo 5

Practice and Communicate   5

▼30 Standards: 1.1

Resources: Answer Keys: Student Edition, p. 69

Focus: Using new vocabulary in guided conversations

Suggestions: Have partners practice all the dialogues, switching roles. Then ask them to choose one dialogue to present to the class.

Answers will vary. Student A will use the following vocabulary:

1. un hogar de ancianos
2. un centro de rehabilitación
3. un centro de la comunidad
4. un centro recreativo
5. un comedor de beneficencia
6. un jardín comunitario

▼31 Standards: 1.1, 1.3

Focus: Practicing new vocabulary via discussion and writing an announcement

Suggestions: Remind students that expressions such as *es importante que* take the subjunctive. Point out that their announcement in Step 3 should include either subjunctive expressions, infinitive expressions, or imperatives.

Answers will vary.

ENRICH YOUR TEACHING

Teacher-to-Teacher

If your school has a charitable organization or a club that contributes to such efforts, ask your students to create a Spanish-language poster for it. Obtain permission to place several of these on the school grounds. The posters will help the organization, and your students will benefit from the experience.

21st Century Skills

Communication Have students work together to identify different volunteer opportunities in their own community, or in different parts of the world. They can connect via technology to learn more about projects that interest them in their own communities, or in a Spanish-speaking country.

32 Standards: 1.2

Resources: Teacher's Resource Book: Audio Script, p. 14; Audio Program DVD: Cap. 5, Track 17; Answer Keys: Student Edition, p. 70

Focus: Practicing listening comprehension of new vocabulary

Suggestions: First, allow students to listen to the audio and read the sentences. Then play it again, pausing after each item, so they can write their answers.

Answers:

1. la compañía "El Salvador"
2. un millón de bolívares
3. es nuestra responsabilidad
4. los ancianos de esta ciudad
5. siente la responsabilidad de ayudar a todos los ciudadanos

33 Standards: 1.1, 1.2

Focus: Practicing new vocabulary and structures by responding to questions

Suggestions: Remind students that when talking about opinions and values, the subjunctive is often required.

Answers will vary.

Fondo cultural

Standards: 1.1, 1.2, 2.1, 3.1, 5.1

Suggestions: Ask students to research José Gálvez and his work on the Internet and hold a follow-up discussion in which they tell about their findings.

Answers will vary.

Additional Resources

• Communication Wbk.: Audio Act. 3, p. 65
• Teacher's Resource Book: Audio Script, p. 14, Communicative Pair Activity BLM, pp. 22–23
• Audio Program DVD: Cap. 5, Track 18

✓ASSESSMENT

Prueba 5-6 with Study Plan (online only)

Prueba: Aplicación del vocabulario 2
• Prueba 5-6: pp. 116–117

226

▼32 Un reportaje especial | 🔊

Escuchar • Escribir

Imagina que estás en Caracas, Venezuela y que escuchas este reportaje en la radio. Completa las frases siguientes con la información del reportaje. Luego, usa esta información para hacer un resumen.

1. Sepúlveda es dueño de _____.

2. Donó _____.

3. La campaña se llama "Educar _____".

4. La escuela va a beneficiar a _____.

5. Sepúlveda decide ayudar porque _____.

▼33 Y tú, ¿qué dices? | 💬

Escribir • Hablar

1. ¿Qué servicios sociales hay en la comunidad donde vives? ¿A quién(es) beneficia(n)? En tu opinión, ¿cuál es el más importante? ¿Por qué?

2. ¿En cuál de estos servicios sociales participas o has participado? Si no has participado en ninguno, ¿en cuál te gustaría participar?

3. Piensa en tus habilidades o conocimientos. ¿Cómo los puedes usar para mejorar tu comunidad?

4. Imagina que vas a crear una organización de servicio social. ¿Qué organización puede beneficiar más a tu comunidad? ¿Por qué?

▼ Fondo Cultural | Estados Unidos

José Gálvez, fotógrafo En todos los tiempos, los artistas han utilizado el arte como una forma de protesta social. Hoy en día puedes ver arte de artistas chicanos que expresan posiciones a favor de algo o en su contra.

José Gálvez creció en Tucson, Arizona. Era fotógrafo para los periódicos *The Arizona Daily Star* y *The Los Angeles Times.* Siempre tenía su cámara y siempre estaba preparado para capturar la experiencia de la comunidad hispanohablante. En 1984 ganó el Premio Pulitzer por una serie de fotos sobre la experiencia mexicano-americana en Los Ángeles. Aunque ha visto muchos cambios en su vida, dice que una cosa que no cambia en la comunidad mexicano-americana es "el respeto por la familia y la herencia mexicana". Dice, "ésta es mi cultura y estoy muy orgulloso de ella".

• Compara la protesta social de los artistas con la de las personas que participan en una marcha o una manifestación. ¿En qué se parecen y en qué son diferentes?

• Habla con otros(as) estudiantes sobre personas que han logrado cambios con protestas sociales.

José Gálvez

226 **doscientos veintiséis**
Manos a la obra 2

DIFFERENTIATED INSTRUCTION

Heritage Language Learners

Students may be familiar with additional expressions of emotion that require the present perfect subjunctive. Invite them to share other expressions that are not listed in *Capítulo* 4 by using them in sentences.

Multiple Intelligences

Musical/Rhythmic: Help students obtain first-hand knowledge about Latin American musicians whose work has a social message. Have them listen to a song of your choice by the contemporary Mexican band Los Tigres del Norte and discuss the message of the song.

Gramática

▼ Objectives
▶ Read and write about voluntary work
▶ Discuss volunteer opportunities

El presente perfecto del subjuntivo

The present perfect subjunctive refers to actions or situations that may have occurred before the action in the main verb.

Me alegro de que hayas trabajado de voluntario.
I'm glad that you have worked as a volunteer.

Estoy orgullosa de que Julián haya trabajado en el centro de rehabilitación.
I am proud that Julian has worked in the rehabilitation center.

Ojalá que ellos hayan juntado mucho dinero.
I hope that they have collected a lot of money.

Siento que no hayan participado en la campaña.
I'm sorry that you haven't participated in the campaign.

To form the present perfect subjunctive, we use the present subjunctive of the verb *haber* with a past participle. Here are the present perfect subjunctive forms of *trabajar*.

haya trabajado	hayamos trabajado
hayas trabajado	hayáis trabajado
haya trabajado	hayan trabajado

- The present perfect subjunctive uses the same regular and irregular past participles as the other perfect tenses you have learned. To review irregular past participles see pages 214–217.

Más ayuda | **realidades.com** | ▶ *Canción de hip hop* ▶ *Tutorials*

▼34 La bienvenida al comedor

Escribir • Leer

❶ Santiago es el presidente de un comedor de beneficencia. Cada año, da las gracias a las personas que trabajaron allí como voluntarios. Completa lo que dice con el presente perfecto del subjuntivo del verbo apropiado.

| juntar | escribir | decidir | tener | colaborar | organizar | enviar |

Queridos voluntarios:

Me alegro de que ustedes __1.__ trabajar como voluntarios en el comedor. Creo que es justo que los ancianos y la gente sin hogar __2.__ esta oportunidad de recibir alimentos todos los días. Es muy bueno que un voluntario __3.__ fondos para comprar alimentos y espero que nosotros __4.__ para hacer más fácil su trabajo. Ojalá que cuando termine este año, nosotros __5.__ mejor la forma de servir la comida. Estoy contento de que ustedes __6.__ sus comentarios y los __7.__ a la dirección electrónica que les di. Muchas gracias a todos.

❷ Escribe dos frases más que Santiago puede decirles a los voluntarios. Usa el presente perfecto del subjuntivo.

Un comedor de beneficencia

doscientos veintisiete **227**
Capítulo 5

ENRICH YOUR TEACHING

Teacher-to-Teacher

Have students devote a section of their notebook to the subjunctive. This ready reference can include rules and examples on the formation of the various tenses in the subjunctive mood, as well as situations and expressions that require its use.

21st Century Skills

Initiative and Self-Direction Remind students of the various digital tools available in **realidades.com** to help them monitor their own understanding and learning needs, such as the online tutorials with comprehension check exercises and many practice opportunities.

BELLRINGER REVIEW

Before presenting the present perfect subjunctive, have students create sentences using expressions of emotion and the present subjunctive. Examples can be found in *Capítulo* 4 on p. 168.

Gramática

Core Instruction

Standards: 4.1

Resources: Voc. and Gram. Transparency 113

INTERACTIVE WHITEBOARD
Grammar Activities 5-2

Suggestions: Have students use vocabulary from pp. 220–221 in sentences with **Ojalá** and the present perfect subjunctive: *Ojalá que muchos hayan participado en la manifestación.*

▼34 Standards: 1.2

Resources: Answer Keys: Student Edition, p. 70
Focus: Using the present perfect subjunctive in a cloze exercise and in written statements
Suggestions: Have students read the entire message before completing the activity. Ask them to point out verbs of emotion that require the subjunctive.

Answers:
Step 1
1. hayan decidido
2. hayan tenido
3. haya juntado
4. hayamos colaborado
5. hayamos organizado
6. hayan escrito
7. hayan enviado

Step 2
Answers will vary.

Pre-AP* Support

- **Learning Objective:** Interpersonal Writing
- **Activity:** Using *Actividad* 34 as a model, ask students to write an e-mail to thank students at their own school who have a local community organization. Expand the task by asking students to include at least one question for the volunteer/recipient to answer with the communication.
- *Pre-AP* Resource Book:* Comprehensive guide to Pre-AP* writing skill development, pp. 27–38

35
Standards: 1.1,

Focus: Practicing the present perfect subjunctive in a guided conversation

Suggestions: In Step 1, remind students that in most Spanish-speaking countries, people in this situation would address each other using *Ud.* Have them use the *Ud.* forms for their conversations.

Answers will vary.

36
Standards: 1.1, 1.3

Focus: Practicing the present perfect subjunctive in writing and in a guided group discussion

Suggestions: Encourage students to be honest when creating their lists in Step 1. This will contribute to a realistic assessment of the group during the discussion in Step 2.

Answers will vary.

Block Schedule

Actividad 36: Have students work in groups of 4 or 5. On strips of paper, have one student write out the four expressions in *Actividad 36.* Place them face down in one pile. Then have each student write out on three separate strips of paper any subject and any infinitive: *David/trabajar.* Place in a second pile, face down. One student is to select a strip from each pile and create a sentence, receiving a point if the sentence is correct and makes sense. Place strips at the bottom of each pile and continue to play. The winner is the student with the most points.

☑**ASSESSMENT**

Prueba 5-7 with Study Plan (online only)

Prueba: Presente perfecto del subjuntivo
• Prueba 5-7: p. 118

228

▼35 ¿Qué hacen cada día?

Escribir • Hablar

❶ Imagina que eres voluntario(a) de un centro de rehabilitación. Escribe cinco preguntas que puedes hacerle al (a la) director(a) del centro para saber lo que ha pasado y lo que debes hacer.

❷ Trabaja con otro(a) estudiante. Hagan los papeles del (de la) director(a) y el (la) voluntario(a). El (la) director(a) explica lo que no se ha hecho todavía y por qué es importante que se haga.

▶ **Modelo**

A —*¿Los pacientes han hecho sus ejercicios de rehabilitación?*
B —*No sé. Espero que ya los hayan hecho. Es importante que hagan sus ejercicios todos los días.*

▼36 Ayudando a otros

Escribir • Hablar

❶ Haz una lista de trabajos que hayas hecho para ayudar a otros.

Modelo
He atendido a ancianos.
He cocinado para mis catorce primos.

❷ Trabaja con un grupo de estudiantes. Comenten lo que han hecho y escriban una lista de todos los trabajos. Observen la lista y piensen en algunos trabajos que no hayan hecho y que pueden ayudar a la comunidad. Usen las expresiones siguientes para comentar sobre lo que han hecho y lo que no han hecho.

| estoy orgulloso(a) de . . . | me alegro de . . . |
| es una lástima que . . . | me sorprende que . . . |

Modelo
Me alegro de que varios estudiantes hayan donado ropa a la gente sin hogar. Me sorprende que nadie haya trabajado como voluntario en un hogar de ancianos.

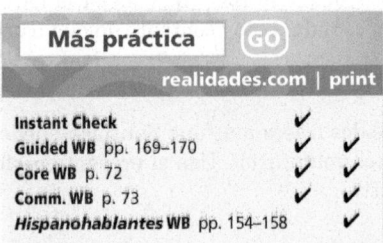

Más práctica	GO	
	realidades.com	print
Instant Check	✔	
Guided WB pp. 169–170	✔	✔
Core WB p. 72	✔	✔
Comm. WB p. 73	✔	✔
Hispanohablantes WB pp. 154–158		✔

228 doscientos veintiocho
Manos a la obra 2

DIFFERENTIATED INSTRUCTION

Advanced Learners/Pre-AP*
Ask students to think of a scene in which something has gone wrong. For example: *Un coche está parado en la calle y le está saliendo humo del motor.* Other students tell what has happened using verbs of emotion and the present perfect subjunctive: *Es una lástima que se haya descompuesto el coche.*

Multiple Intelligences
Visual/Spatial: Ask students to create visuals to help them remember demonstrative pronouns and adjectives. Tell them to include either a caption or speech bubble that shows which word they are illustrating.

| ▼ Objectives

▶ Read and write about volunteer jobs
▶ Discuss preparations for a demonstration
▶ Point out objects

Gramática Repaso

Los adjetivos y los pronombres demostrativos

Remember that you use demonstrative adjectives to point out people or things that are nearby and farther away. A demonstrative adjective always comes before the noun and agrees with it in gender and number.

Me gusta este centro recreativo.
I like this recreation center.

¿Quién donó esa comida?
Who donated that food?

Voy a ayudar a aquellos pacientes.
I'm going to help those patients.

Demonstrative adjectives can also be used as pronouns to replace nouns. To distinguish them from demonstrative adjectives, they have a written accent*.

Me es imposible trabajar para este candidato, pero me encantaría trabajar para ése.
It's impossible for me to work for this candidate, but I would love to work for that one.

¿Ves esas bolsas? Por favor, recoge ésa, pero no recojas aquélla.
Do you see those bags? Please pick up that one, but don't pick up that one over there.

To refer to an idea, or something that has not been identified, use the demonstrative pronouns *esto*, *eso*, or *aquello*. None of them has an accent mark.

Esto es injusto.   *This is unfair.*
Me encantaría eso.   *I would love that.*
¿Qué es aquello?   *What is that (over there)?*

- Here are all the demonstrative adjectives and pronouns.

	Close to you		Closer to the person you are talking to		Far from both of you	
Adjectives	este	estos	ese	esos	aquel	aquellos
	esta	estas	esa	esas	aquella	aquellas
Pronouns	éste	éstos	ése	ésos	aquél	aquéllos
	ésta	éstas	ésa	ésas	aquélla	aquéllas

Éste es un perro marrón.

Ése es un perro blanco.

Aquél es un perro negro.

*Note that accents on demonstrative pronouns are no longer required by Spain's Royal Academy. However, many people continue to use them in their writing for purposes of clarity. Anything written before 2009 will include accents on demonstratives.

Gramática Repaso

Core Instruction

Standards: 4.1

Resources: Voc. and Gram. Transparency 114

INTERACTIVE WHITEBOARD
Grammar Activities 5-2

Suggestions: Have students talk in pairs about classroom objects using demonstrative adjectives and pronouns. Then ask students to make cards for the chapter vocabulary. Two or three cards are needed for each vocabulary item. Place the cards around the room. Students can stand in one position and create a series of sentences that use the vocabulary along with demonstrative adjectives and pronouns: *Trabajo en este centro recreativo. Ese centro recreativo es donde trabaja mi hermano. Me gustaría saber quién trabaja en aquel centro recreativo.*

Note: *According to the Real Academia Española, the use of accent marks is no longer necessary for demonstrative pronouns. The Real Academia suggests that accent marks only be used on demonstrative pronouns as needed to distinguish them from demonstrative adjectives. In this section, we teach students to use a written accent mark on demonstrative pronouns so they learn to recognize and use the two different types of words.*

ENRICH YOUR TEACHING

Teacher-to-Teacher

Write the demonstrative adjectives on note cards. Have students take turns drawing a card and using the demonstrative adjective in a sentence. Sentences should refer to an object whose relative distance makes it clear that the student understands the adjective. Students can also use the demonstrative adjective in a comparison in order to make the meaning clear: *Me gusta más esta obra de arte que aquélla al lado de la puerta.*

Resources: Answer Keys: Student Edition, p. 71

Focus: Practicing demonstrative adjectives and pronouns

Suggestions: Tell students that they must carefully consider accent marks and gender and number agreement as they complete this activity.

Answers:
1. Esta/ Aquélla
2. Éstos/este
3. aquello
4. Aquel/ ése
5. Aquéllas
6. este
7. Éstas
8. esto
9. esas/Ésta
10. Éste

El español en la comunidad

Core Instruction

Standards: 1.2, 3.1

Suggestions: Once students have read the information, ask comprehension questions. For example: *¿Por qué se ofrecen clases de español a bordo del Peace Boat? (Se ofrecen clases de español porque muchos de los participantes no hablan español, pero el barco visita muchos países hispanohablantes.) ¿Cuál es el objetivo principal del Peace Boat? (El objetivo es ayudar a grupos que promueven los derechos humanos, la paz y la protección del medio ambiente.)*

Chapter Project

Students can perform Step 5 at this point. Make audio or video recordings of their presentations for inclusion in their portfolio. (For more information, see p. 200-b.)

▼37 ¿Éste o aquél?

Leer • Escribir

Margarita es voluntaria en el centro de la comunidad. El supervisor del centro le dice lo que tiene que hacer. Completa las siguientes frases con el adjetivo demostrativo o el pronombre demostrativo correcto.

1. *(Esta / Ésta)* lista no es la de los nuevos ciudadanos. *(Aquella / Aquélla)* es la lista.
2. *(Estos / Éstos)* son los fondos que juntó el centro *(este / estos)* mes.
3. Todo *(aquel / aquello)* beneficia al centro que organiza la marcha.
4. *(Aquel / Aquél)* escritorio no es el tuyo, *(esa / ése)* es el tuyo.
5. *(Aquéllas / Esas)* son las donaciones de alimentos que trajo la gente.
6. Debes leer *(esto / este)* artículo sobre el medio ambiente.
7. *(Esas / Éstas)* son las plantas que deben sembrarse en el parque.
8. Tenemos que publicar en nuestro informe *(esto / esos)* que dice el artículo sobre los servicios sociales.
9. No tienes que leer todas *(ésas / esas)* páginas. *(Esta / Ésta)* es la más importante.
10. *(Éste / Este)* es el informe que tienes que leer.

El español en la comunidad

Profesores voluntarios por la paz, los derechos humanos y el medio ambiente

Peace Boat es una organización no gubernamental (ONG) que tiene como objetivo ayudar a grupos que promueven *(promote)* los derechos humanos, la paz y la protección del medio ambiente en distintos países. Para alcanzar su objetivo, *Peace Boat* organiza viajes en un barco alrededor del mundo para visitar países donde se pueda dar ayuda.

Como muchos de los países que el barco visita son hispanohablantes, y muchos de los participantes no hablan español, en el barco se ofrecen clases de español todos los días durante el viaje. Todos los profesores de español de *Peace Boat* son voluntarios. La organización paga solamente el boleto, la comida y las medicinas para los profesores. Todos los pasajeros pueden asistir a las clases, que se ofrecen en un "curso intensivo" para las personas que tienen bastante tiempo para estudiar. Y pueden participar en "clases libres" los pasajeros que no tienen tiempo para estudiar todos los días pero quieren disfrutar y aprender un poquito de español. Es una hermosa manera *(way)* de enseñar español, promover la paz y los derechos humanos y ayudar a proteger el medio ambiente, todo a la misma vez.

DIFFERENTIATED INSTRUCTION

Students with Learning Difficulties

Help students understand demonstrative adjectives and pronouns by making spatial relationships clear. On three cards, write, for example, **esta, esa,** and **aquella.** Place each card beside three similar objects, such as chairs, that are arranged at three different distances from the student. Ask the student to remain in place, point, and say or repeat sentences such as *Esta es una silla. Esa también es una silla. Aquella silla está lejos.*

▼38 Ésta, ésa, aquélla |

Hablar

Imagina que te estás preparando para participar en una manifestación. Habla con un(a) compañero(a) sobre los preparativos (*preparations*). Usa los pronombres demostrativos apropiados.

Estudiante A

1. carteles	4. tambores
2. banderas	5. libros
3. anuncios	6. camisetas de la manifestación

Estudiante B

en el piso	sobre la mesa
en el armario	allí
de color azul	al lado de la puerta

▶ Modelo

artículo / en la página 2 del periódico

A —¿Cuál es el artículo <u>que habla sobre la manifestación</u>?

B —<u>Éste, el que está en la página 2 del periódico.</u>

▼39 A sugerir soluciones |

Escribir • Hablar

1 La clase va a dividirse en dos grupos. Un grupo cree que el trabajo voluntario debe ser obligatorio para la graduación; el otro piensa que no. Cada grupo trata de convencer al otro. Hablen sobre:

- tipos de trabajo
- cuándo deben hacer el trabajo (después de clases, fines de semana, en vacaciones)
- si debe ser parte del currículum o no
- los beneficios que puede tener para el futuro

2 Formen grupos y preparen la representación de una marcha o una manifestación. Escojan la causa y decidan:

- a favor o en contra de qué o de quiénes protestan
- qué exigen o qué resultados esperan
- qué pasará si no consiguen lo que quieren

3 Uno o dos estudiantes pueden representar a reporteros de televisión y entrevistar a los que protestan.

▼ Fondo Cultural | Cuba

Silvio Rodríguez

Silvio Rodríguez es el cantante más importante del "Movimiento de la Nueva Trova", un movimiento musical que apareció en Cuba en los años 60 y tuvo gran influencia en América Latina. Aunque ha escrito canciones de amor, frecuentemente en sus letras habla de los problemas de la sociedad, de lo que cree que es justo o injusto, de las causas que apoya.

- ¿Qué cantante conoces que hable en sus canciones de la sociedad o del medio ambiente?

- ¿Crees que es bueno que los cantantes hablen de problemas sociales en sus canciones? ¿Por qué?

Más práctica

realidades.com | print

Instant Check	✔	
Guided WB pp. 171–172	✔	✔
Core WB pp. 73–74	✔	✔
Comm. WB pp. 66–67, 74–75	✔	✔
Hispanohablantes WB pp. 159–161		✔

Practice and Communicate ⑤

▼38 Standards: 1.1

Resources: Answer Keys: Student Edition, p. 71

Focus: Practicing demonstrative pronouns in a guided conversation

Suggestions: Encourage students to point to the objects mentioned, thus indicating the distance that corresponds to the demonstrative pronoun they have chosen.

Answers will vary. Student B will choose from among the following:

1. Éstos/Ésos/Aquéllos	4. Éstos/Ésos/Aquéllos
2. Éstas/Ésas/Aquéllas	5. Éstos/Ésos/Aquéllos
3. Éstos/Ésos/Aquéllos	6. Éstas/Ésas/Aquéllas

▼39 Standards: 1.1

Focus: Practicing vocabulary and structures through debate and a guided situation

Suggestions: As students do their planning, circulate and help them come up with meaningful ways to use the present perfect subjunctive.

Answers will vary.

Fondo cultural

Standards: 1.1, 1.2, 2.1, 4.2, 5.2

Suggestions: Explain that *trova* means "ballad." A person who sings *trovas* is a *trovador(a)*. This comes from the same Latin root as the English "troubadour."

Answers will vary.

Additional Resources

- Communication Wbk.: Audio Act. 4–5, pp. 66–67
- Teacher's Resource Book: Audio Script, pp. 14–15, Communicative Pair Activity BLM, pp. 24–25
- Audio Program DVD: Cap. 5, Tracks 19–20

✓ASSESSMENT

Prueba 5-8 with Study Plan (online only)

Prueba: Los demostrativos
- Prueba 5-8: p. 119

Examen: Vocabulario y gramática 2
- Examen 2: pp. 120–122
- ExamView: Examen 2

ENRICH YOUR TEACHING

Culture Note

Cuban music has seen a resurgence in popularity in recent years in the United States and Europe. Many different kinds of Cuban music, including **Nueva Trova, son, mambo, rumba, danzón,** and **cha cha chá,** have been a vital cultural force in popular music worldwide for the better part of a century.

21st Century Skills

Technology Literacy Encourage students to go online to learn more about the **Nueva Trova** and **Nueva Canción** movements, and to hear music by artists such as Silvio Rodríguez, Joan Manuel Serrat, or Mercedes Sosa. Have them find lyrics to one song that may deal with a commentary on a social problem. Does the music remind them of other singers they know? What are the similarities or differences?

231

Puente a la cultura

Core Instruction

Standards: 1.2, 3.1

Focus: Reading to learn about the contributions of the Spanish-speaking population of the United States

Suggestions:

Pre-reading: Refer students to the *Estrategia*. Remind them to use their knowledge of cognates, word families, and context clues to keep reading through difficult parts of passages.

Reading: Help students resolve comprehension problems by asking *sí/no* or embedded-answer questions: *Ken Salazar es el Secretario del Interior o senador de Colorado. (Es el Secretario del Interior; antes fue senador.) ¿Linda G. Alvarado es la primera jueza hispana de la Corte Suprema? (No. La primera jueza hispana es Sonia Sotomayor.)*

Post-reading: On the board, begin a concept web with the words **contribuciones de los hispanohablantes** in the center. Use the web as a vehicle to discuss the article. Record in it students' responses about the people mentioned in the article, as well as other information they may supply from their background knowledge.

Country Connection

Core Instruction

Standards: 3.1

Resources: Map Transparency 16

Suggestions: Remind students that Sonia Sotomayor is Puerto Rican. Ask a volunteer to locate Puerto Rico on *Map Transparency* 16. Remind students that the island is the only United States territory where **Cristóbal Colón** actually set foot. He landed there on his second voyage to the Americas in 1493. Puerto Rico is a commonwealth associated with the United States. Large numbers of Puerto Ricans have made permanent homes in Florida, New York City, and elsewhere on the mainland.

Puente a la cultura

Los Estados Unidos . . . en español

Estrategia

Reading for comprehension
Read without stopping at unknown words. Then go back, decide if the words are important, and see if you can guess the meaning. If you do not understand the meaning, then look at the footnotes or a dictionary.

Sonia Sotomayor

232 doscientos treinta y dos
¡Adelante!

Desde el origen de nuestro país, los hispanohablantes han hecho importantes contribuciones. Ya en 1776, el capitán Jorge Ferragut había venido desde España para luchar por la independencia. Hoy día los hispanohablantes son una importante parte de la población[1] y sus contribuciones se pueden observar en todas las áreas de la sociedad.

La población[1]

Según datos de la oficina del censo en el año 2006, la población hispanohablante representa el 14 por ciento del total de la población y es el grupo minoritario más grande de los Estados Unidos. Durante los años noventa, este grupo tuvo un gran crecimiento. El número de estadounidenses que hablan español en el hogar aumentó[2] más del 60 por ciento en la década de los noventa. Según el último censo del año 2000, uno de cada diez estadounidenses, 28 millones de personas, habla español en casa. Como el número de hispanohablantes sigue aumentando cada año, el español tiene cada vez más fuerza e influye en muchos campos del país. Por eso podemos decir que el español es ahora parte importante de la cultura de los Estados Unidos.

La política

El Secretario del Interior Ken Salazar fue también uno de los primeros senadores hispanos de los Estados Unidos. Salazar nació en Colorado. De ahí eran sus antepasados hispanos, que vivieron en el Suroeste desde el siglo XVI, cuando esta región era Nueva España.

Sonia Sotomayor es la primera jueza hispana de la Corte Suprema de los Estados Unidos y la tercera mujer en conseguir este puesto, en el año 2009. Sus padres se mudaron a Nueva York desde Puerto Rico. Sotomayor nació y se crió en el barrio neoyorquino del Bronx, donde hay una gran comunidad puertorriqueña. Estudió derecho en la Universidad de Yale, una de las más prestigiosas del país.

1 population **2** grew

Ken Salazar

Secretary Salazar

DIFFERENTIATED INSTRUCTION

Students with Learning Difficulties

Some students may be intimidated by long reading passages. Provide a jigsawing option for small groups in which each student reads one section of the passage and reports key information to the rest of the group.

Advanced Learners

Ask students to choose one of the people mentioned in the article or another Spanish speaker for further research. Have them present brief oral reports about their choice. Students can also make posters with photos that can be placed in the classroom or around the school.

Hilda Solís, nacida en Los Ángeles de padres inmigrantes, fue la primera mujer hispana que trabajó como miembro del Senado de California y como Secretaria de Trabajo en el gobierno de Obama. La californiana de origen mexicano Rosa Gumataotao es la sexta latina en ocupar el puesto de Tesorera de los Estados Unidos, que obtuvo en el año 2009.

Los negocios[3]

De las 1,000 compañías que la revista *Fortune* considera las más importantes de los Estados Unidos, trece tienen directores(as) hispanohablantes. Algunas de ellas son: ALCOA, Kellogg Co., Wal-Mart y Office Depot.

Además, de cada cinco hispanohablantes en los consejos de administración de esas compañías, una es mujer. Linda G. Alvarado, por ejemplo, además de ser directora general de su propia compañía, Alvarado Construction, es también presidenta de los consejos de administración de otras cinco compañías.

Linda G. Alvarado

Las ciencias

Los hispanohablantes se han destacado[4] también como científicos. Por ejemplo, el Dr. Luis W. Álvarez recibió el Premio Nobel de Física por sus estudios sobre partículas elementales[5] y el Dr. Mario J. Molina ganó el Premio Nobel de Química por sus estudios sobre la capa de ozono.

---

3 business 4 have stood out 5 elementary particles

¿Comprendiste?

1. ¿Puede decirse que la población hispanohablante es una minoría importante en Estados Unidos? ¿Por qué? ¿Qué ha pasado con esta población desde los años noventa?

2. ¿En qué campos trabajan y hacen importantes contribuciones los hispanohablantes de Estados Unidos?

3. ¿Los hispanohablantes participan en la política de Estados Unidos? Da un ejemplo.

Rosa Gumataotao

Escribe tu opinión

Después de leer el artículo, piensa cómo puede servirle aprender español a una persona que no lo habla. Escribe un párrafo en el que expliques cómo el español puede ayudar a esa persona a encontrar un trabajo.

Dr. Mario Molina

Más práctica	GO

realidades.com | print

▶ *Videodocumentario*	✔	
Guided WB p. 173	✔	✔
Comm. WB pp. 76–77	✔	✔
Hispanohablantes WB pp. 162–164		✔
Cultural Reading Activity	✔	

doscientos treinta y tres **233**
Capítulo 5

▼ **¿Comprendiste?** Standards: 1.3

Resources: Answer Keys: Student Edition, p. 72

Focus: Demonstrating reading comprehension

Suggestions: Have students paraphrase the parts of the article they use to support their answers. Point out that for item 3 they must use their critical thinking skills.

Answers:

1. Sí, la población hispanohablante es una minoría importante en los Estados Unidos. Representa el 14 por ciento de la población. Durante los años noventa, esta población aumentó más del 60 por ciento.
2. Además de la cultura y los deportes, los hispanohablantes trabajan y hacen importantes contribuciones en el campo de la política, los negocios y las ciencias.
3. Sí, los hispanohablantes participan en la política de los Estados Unidos. Answers will vary.

▼ **Escribe tu opinión**

Standards: 1.3, 5.2

Focus: Combining learned structures in a written response to a reading

Suggestions: Encourage students to use chapter vocabulary and structures, such as the pluperfect tense and present perfect subjunctive in their paragraphs.

Answers will vary.

Portfolio

Keep students' paragraphs from *Escribe tu opinión* in their portfolios as a writing sample.

▶ **Videodocumentario**

Presentation

Standards: 1.2

Resources: Teacher's Resource Book: Video Script, p. 17; Video Program: Cap. 5

View *Un voluntario en la comunidad* with the class either online in **realidades.com** or using the DVD. See the *Video Teacher's Guide* for additional suggestions.

Additional Resources

Student Resource: Realidades para hispanohablantes, pp. 162–164, Guided Practice Activities, p. 173; Communication Wbk., pp. 76–77

ENRICH YOUR TEACHING

Culture Note

Linda G. Alvarado is a role model in the Hispanic American community and for women in general. Her field of construction is traditionally male, and she has overcome many obstacles in her career. Alvarado began her construction company in 1976 with a loan of $2,500 from her parents. Today it is one of the fastest growing general contracting firms in the country.

21st Century Skills

Information Literacy Have student search the Internet for more information on the individuals featured in this reading. Ask students to identify other Hispanic Americans who have made important contributions to the United States in the areas of politics, business, or the sciences.

5 Integrated Skills

¿Qué me cuentas?

Core Instruction

Standards: 1.1, 1.2, 1.3

Resources: Teacher's Resource Book: Audio Script, p. 15; Audio Program DVD: Cap. 5, Track 21; Answer Keys: Student Edition, p. 72

Focus: Practicing listening and reading comprehension of new vocabulary and grammar; using information to write a cohesive and coherent reaction.

AP* Skills: Integration of listening, reading, and writing to comprehend and synthesize information from spoken and written sources.

Suggestions: For Step 1, use the audio or read the dialogue aloud. Allow students to hear it twice through: the first time to write their answers, the second time to check them.

For Step 2, have students identify points that will allow them to compare the volunteer opportunity presented in the reading to the one they heard about in Step 1.

Encourage students to express their own opinions and to cite specific information from Steps 1 and 2 in their written responses for Step 3.

Answers:
Step 1
1. a	3. b	5. b
2. a	4. a	

Steps 2–3
Answers will vary.

Block Schedule

Have student work in pairs to write ten statements that are *cierto* or *falso* about the brochure in Step 2. Have them partner with another pair and take turns reading their statements. Each pair has to determine whether the other pair's statements are *cierto* or *falso*.

Additional Resources

Student Resource: Realidades para hispanohablantes, p. 165

Integración

¿Qué me cuentas?: En busca de empleo

En tu colegio, ¿es necesario cumplir con un número de horas de servicio comunitario? Escucha una entrevista en una organización que busca voluntarios.

1 🔊)) Vas a escuchar una narración en tres partes. Después de cada parte, vas a oír una o dos preguntas. Escoge la respuesta que corresponda a cada pregunta.

1. a. comedor de beneficencia	b. hogar de niños	c. centro recreativo
2. a. llevarlas a la entrevista	b. pedirlas a los ancianos	c. leerlas
3. a. si tenía responsabilidad	b. si le gustaba ser voluntario	c. si sabía cocinar
4. a. de horario flexible	b. sólo a tiempo parcial	c. fácil
5. a. si donan fondos	b. cuál es el salario	c. ¡Felicitaciones!

2 Ahora lee el folleto sobre otro lugar.

CENTRO COMUNITARIO SAN FELIPE
Ayudamos a nuestra gente

EN EL CENTRO COMUNITARIO SAN FELIPE, SIEMPRE NECESITAMOS VOLUNTARIOS PARA...
+ revisar los alimentos y la ropa que se ha donado
+ repartir alimentos de La Bodega
+ ayudar a la gente
+ ayudar a juntar fondos y donaciones de comida y ropa
+ dar orientación[1] legal y económica
+ donar tiempo, comida o dinero

BUSCAMOS A VOLUNTARIOS QUE SEAN...
+ amables y sinceros
+ organizados y responsables
+ trabajadores
+ bilingües

[1] guidance

En el Centro Comunitario San Felipe ayudamos a la gente de la comunidad con programas de salud y educación, y con orientación legal y económica. También repartimos alimentos y ropa entre la gente más necesitada y ofrecemos un lugar seguro para los jóvenes después del horario escolar. Para educar a la gente, ofrecemos clases de español e inglés. El centro está abierto los siete días de la semana y ayuda a casi 2000 familias.

Si quiere donar fondos, comida, ropa o su tiempo voluntariamente, por favor llame al **805–123–9876.**

3 En una lista, compara y contrasta las dos oportunidades de trabajo voluntario. Luego, escoge un lugar y escribe una carta al director. Explica por qué te gustaría trabajar allí como voluntario y cuánto tiempo puedes dedicar. ¿Qué cualidades o habilidades puedes ofrecer? ¿Qué experiencias anteriores has tenido que te sirven como voluntario? Usa las siguientes expresiones para conectar tus ideas.

me interesaría	en cuanto (*as soon as*)	mientras
me encantaría	para empezar	durante

234 doscientos treinta y cuatro
¡Adelante!

DIFFERENTIATED INSTRUCTION

Heritage Language Learners
Invite students to create a brochure or Web site in Spanish for a volunteer organization in the community, using the brochure in Step 2 as a guide. You may want to present the finished product to the organization for their use.

Students with Learning Difficulties
Students who find it difficult to create their own letter will benefit from working with an advanced learner first. Together they can complete the list in Step 3 before splitting off to write their letters individually.

Presentación oral

La elección de la clase

▶ Demonstrate how to give a speech to be president of your class

▶ Use visual aids to improve your presentation

Tarea
Vas a presentarte como candidato(a) a presidente(a) de la clase. Prepara un discurso para convencer a los estudiantes de que eres el (la) mejor porque has ayudado a los demás y eres responsable. Haz un cartel.

Estrategia

Using visual aids
If you create visual aids such as graphs and charts to support the topic of your speech, they will strengthen your argument while adding visual appeal.

① **Prepárate** Anota en una tabla como la siguiente las razones por las que piensas que eres el (la) mejor candidato(a) para el trabajo.

Cualidades y habilidades	Éxitos importantes	Trabajos realizados	Problemas de la clase	Ideas para resolverlos

② **Practica** Vuelve a leer la información y organízala. Explica tus cualidades y lo que has hecho, los problemas de la clase y tus soluciones. Usa tus notas sólo para practicar. Recuerda:

- expresar tus ideas en forma convincente (a convincing way)
- hablar con voz clara

Modelo
Soy la mejor candidata para presidenta de la clase. Siempre me han preocupado los problemas de mis compañeros. Siempre he ayudado a todos. Tengo muchas ideas para mejorar . . .

③ **Haz tu presentación** Piensa que tus compañeros(as) de clase son los que van a votar a favor del (de la) mejor candidato(a). Usa un cartel u otra ayuda gráfica para apoyar tu presentación.

④ **Evaluación** Tu profesor(a) utilizará la siguiente rúbrica para evaluar tu presentación.

Rubric	Score 1	Score 3	Score 5
How well your information is organized	Your ideas are undeveloped with incorrect or no transitions.	You leave some ideas undeveloped, with some confusing details.	Your ideas are well developed with clear, consistent transitions.
How convincing you are	Your supporting evidence is weak. Your speech is read.	Some of your evidence is convincing. You make some eye contact with audience.	All your evidence is convincing. You have good eye contact and use of gestures.
How effectively you use your visuals	You hardly use visuals, or they don't communicate the message.	You use visuals sometimes, but they're not always effective.	Your visuals are very helpful and are used effectively.

doscientos treinta y cinco 235
Capítulo 5

© **Common Core: Speaking**

Presentación oral
Core Instruction

Standards: 1.2, 1.3, 3.1

Resources: Voc. and Gram. Transparency 4

Focus: Preparing and delivering an oral presentation

Suggestions: Review the task and the four-step approach with students. Before students begin, direct their attention to the *Estrategia*. Encourage them to design their visual aid to be simple, clear, and large enough to be seen by everyone in their audience. Help them organize their information by using *Vocabulary & Grammar Transparency* 4 as a model. You must add a fifth column to the chart.

Portfolio

Make video or audio recordings of student presentations in class, or assign the RealTalk activity so they can record their presentations online. Include the recording in their portfolios.

Pre-AP* Support

- **Learning Objective:** Presentational Speaking
- **Activity:** Remind students to focus on the presentational speaking skills used in this task such as fluency, pronunciation, and comprehensibility.
- *Pre-AP* Resource Book:* Comprehensive guide to Pre-AP* speaking skill development, pp. 39–50

Additional Resources

Student Resource: Realidades para hispanohablantes, p. 166

ENRICH YOUR TEACHING

Teacher-to-Teacher

After students listen to the presentations, have them write a note to name their preferences for the top two candidates and give reasons for their choice. Have them exchange notes with another student. They should respond in writing, telling why they agree or disagree with the writer's preferences.

21st Century Skills

Creativity and Innovation Have students browse video-sharing sites to view nomination speeches for class president by students in Spanish. Remind them that they are "selling" themselves as candidates in this oral presentation. Encourage them to be creative in finding the best way to appeal to the target audience— their classmates.

✓ASSESSMENT

Presentación oral
- Assessment Program: Rubrics, p. T31
  Review the rubric with students. Go over the descriptions of the different levels of performance. After assessing students, help individuals understand how their performance could be improved. (See Teacher's Resource Book for suggestions on using rubrics in assessment.)

Language Arts Connection: Informational Writing

Standards: 3.1

Remind students that in today's busy world, the most important qualities for messages such as the letter they are writing are clarity and brevity. Have them consult reference sources from their Language Arts classes for models of a persuasive cover letter. They can use and adapt information from those models for this assignment.

 Common Core: Writing

Presentación escrita

Core Instruction

Standards: 1.2, 1.3, 3.1, 5.1

Resources: Voc. and Gram. Transparency 12

Focus: Combining learned vocabulary and structures in a written presentation

Suggestions: Begin by explaining the criteria you will use to evaluate students' compositions. (See Step 5, *Evaluación*, in the Student Edition, and *Assessment* on the following page.)

Direct students' attention to the *Estrategia*. Ask them to share additional background information they have learned in Language Arts courses about persuasive writing. Remind them that they also developed some effective persuasion strategies in the *Presentación oral* on the previous page. Use *Vocabulary & Grammar Transparency* 12 to model the organization of the persuasive letter. Adapt the transparency for your purposes by writing your main idea in the center box and using the four outer boxes for the four parts of the letter.

▼ Objectives
▶ Write a cover letter to apply for a job
▶ Include information to persuade the reader

Presentación escrita
La carta para solicitar empleo

Estrategia

Writing to persuade
When you write to persuade, you want to convince someone to do or think the way you do. Here, you are offering to be the best candidate for an opening.
• Think about the needs of the person you are writing to.
• Think of the reasons why you might be the best candidate.
• Organize the reasons and let the person you are writing to know you are the solution.
• Invite your reader to take action.

Quieres pedir trabajo en un centro recreativo. Escribe una carta para solicitar empleo en la que expliques tus cualidades, tu experiencia y las razones por las que te gustaría trabajar allí.

1 Antes de escribir

Piensa en los datos que quieres incluir. Crea una gráfica con la información que debes poner en cada parte. Imagina el nombre de la organización y del gerente al que escribes.

CARTA PARA SOLICITAR EMPLEO A:
Centro Recreativo Avellaneda
Gerente: Sr. Jorge Ríos

SALUDO/INTRODUCCIÓN
Razones por las que le escribo:
He leído el anuncio y me interesa el trabajo. Me gusta ayudar. Me gusta trabajar con niños.

DESARROLLO
Cualidades/Experiencia:
Soy ordenado, puntual y responsable. He trabajado como consejero en un campamento de verano. Había juntado fondos para . . .

CONCLUSIÓN
Tengo las cualidades y la experiencia que se necesitan. Voy a llamarlo la semana que viene.

DESPEDIDA
Atentamente

2 Borrador

Recuerda que la carta es para el gerente del centro recreativo. Escribe tus ideas siguiendo la gráfica. Usa la gramática y el vocabulario de este capítulo.

Modelo

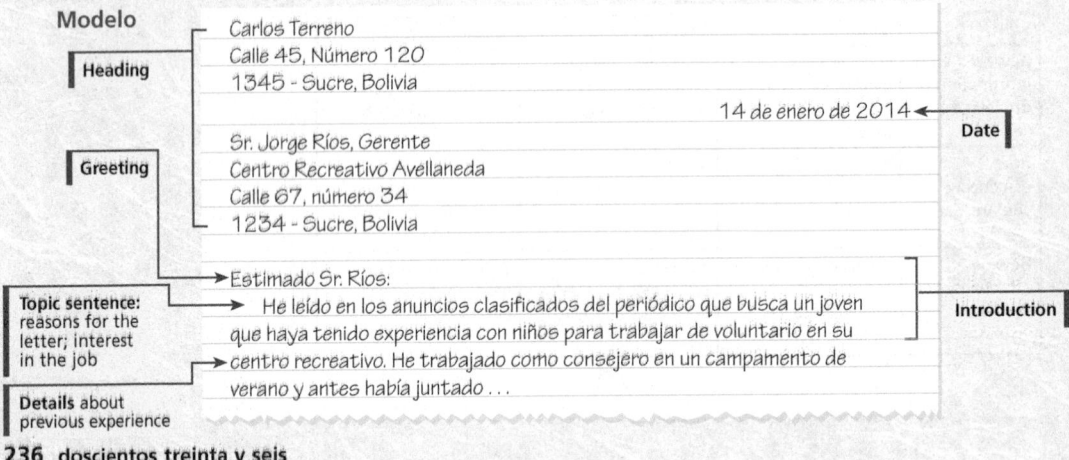

Heading
Carlos Terreno
Calle 45, Número 120
1345 - Sucre, Bolivia

14 de enero de 2014 **Date**

Greeting
Sr. Jorge Ríos, Gerente
Centro Recreativo Avellaneda
Calle 67, número 34
1234 - Sucre, Bolivia

Estimado Sr. Ríos:

Topic sentence: reasons for the letter; interest in the job
He leído en los anuncios clasificados del periódico que busca un joven que haya tenido experiencia con niños para trabajar de voluntario en su centro recreativo. He trabajado como consejero en un campamento de verano y antes había juntado . . . **Introduction**

Details about previous experience

236 doscientos treinta y seis
¡Adelante!

DIFFERENTIATED INSTRUCTION

Students with Special Needs
Allow students with fine motor skill difficulties to dictate their ideas to another student. The second student also benefits from this arrangement, since he or she is exposed to new ideas.

Advanced Learners
Have pairs of students create a humorous skit about a person who lacks the qualities they described in their letters interviewing for a job. Ask them to act out their "How Not to Get a Job" skits for the class.

Details about personal qualities

→ Soy un joven ordenado, puntual y responsable. Además, me gusta ayudar y me interesaría . . . } **Development**

→ Lo llamaré la semana que viene para solicitar una entrevista . . . } **Conclusion:** follow up

Closing

Atentamente,

→ *Carlos Terreno*

Signature

Carlos Terreno

3 Redacción/Revisión

Después de escribir el primer borrador de tu carta, trabaja con otro(a) estudiante para intercambiar los trabajos y leerlos. Digan qué aspectos de las cartas son más efectivos.

Haz lo siguiente: Subraya con una línea los verbos en presente perfecto, con dos los verbos en pluscuamperfecto, y encierra en un círculo los verbos en presente perfecto del subjuntivo. Corrige los errores de verbos, ortografía y concordancia.

> He leído en los anuncios clasificado**s** del periódico
> que busca un joven que ⟨haya tenido⟩ experiencia
> con niños para trabajar como voluntario en su
> *trabajado*
> centro recreativo. He ~~trabaje~~ como consejero en
> *había*
> un campamento de verano y antes ~~habíamos~~
> juntado . . .

4 Publicación

Antes de escribir la versión final, lee de nuevo tu carta y repasa los siguientes puntos:

• ¿Sigue mi carta el formato de una carta para solicitar empleo?

• ¿Puse detalles sobre mis cualidades y mi experiencia de trabajo?

Después de revisar el borrador, escribe una copia en limpio de tu carta.

5 Evaluación

Se utilizará la siguiente rúbrica para evaluar tu presentación.

Rubric	Score 1	Score 3	Score 5
Completion of task	Important parts of your letter are missing.	Minor parts of your letter are missing or incorrect.	All of your information is included and effectively organized.
Ability to persuade	Your lack of information or organization makes the message unclear.	Your message is present, but sometimes unconvincing.	Your choice and organization of information create a clear, convincing message.
Sentence structure/ grammar, spelling, mechanics	Your sentences are run-on or are fragmented with many errors.	You use sentences consistently, but they contain some errors.	Your sentence structure is correct and varied with very few errors.

doscientos treinta y siete **237**
Capítulo 5

ENRICH YOUR TEACHING

21st Century Skills

Communication Students will use their writing skills for the purpose of convincing a prospective employer that they are the best candidate for a particular job. Have students create a list of persuasive words and expressions to use in a cover letter. Ask them to write a list of reasons why they are the perfect candidate for this particular job. Make sure they invite the employer to take action on the job position.

Suggestions (Cont'd):
In Step 2, students should concentrate on how to develop the ideas in the chart from Step 1 and include them in the appropriate sequence in a letter. Explain that the three parts of their chart called *Introducción, Desarrollo,* and *Conclusión* should each become a paragraph in their letter.

For Step 3, encourage students to focus on sentence structure, transitions, use of the pluperfect tense and the present perfect subjunctive, and use of demonstrative adjectives and pronouns. In this step, they should also include and arrange the *Saludo, Despedida,* date, and necessary addresses in their letter. Have them follow the suggestions shown.

Evaluation
Steps 4 and 5 overlap. Students will need evaluation by you, their peers, or self-evaluation to fine-tune and polish their drafts.

Portfolio

Keep students' final drafts in their portfolios as a writing sample.

Pre-AP* Support

• **Learning Objective:** Presentational Writing
• **Activity:** Have students write an e-mail to a prospective employer in which they express their interest in a job posting. Be sure students ask the prospective employer at least one question about the job, and summarize their own qualifications for the job.
• **Pre-AP* Resource Book:** Comprehensive guide to Pre-AP* writing skill development, pp. 27–38

Additional Resources

Student Resource: Realidades para hispanohablantes, p. 167

☑ASSESSMENT

Presentación escrita
• Assessment Program: Rubrics, p. T31
Review the rubric with students. Go over the descriptions of the different levels of performance. After assessing students, help individuals understand how their performance could be improved. (See Teacher's Resource Book for suggestions on using rubrics in assessment.)

▶ Read and understand a Mayan folktale
▶ Use context clues to find meaning of unfamiliar words
▶ Talk about a personal experience and how to turn one's life around

 Common Core: Reading

Lectura

Core Instruction

Standards: 1.2, 2.1, 2.2, 3.1, 3.2

Resources: Voc. and Gram. Transparency 4

Focus: Reading an extended passage

Suggestions:

Pre-reading: Before reading, direct students' attention to the *Al leer* section. Have them copy the graphic organizer from p. 241 and make sure they understand how they will use it. Address any comprehension problems they may have with the three points at the end of *Al leer,* and remind them to focus on these points as they read. Also refer them to the *Estrategia.* In order to answer the question there, ask them to watch for the words **poblado, ramas,** and **deshacerse** as they read.

BELLRINGER REVIEW

Show Fine Art Transparency 51. Have students write a sentence showing something from the Mexican Indian past as reflected in the Rivera painting.

Country Connection

Core Instruction

Standards: 3.1

Resources: Map Transparency 14

Suggestions: After reading the *Al leer* section, refer students to *Map Transparency* 14. Ask a volunteer to point out the Yucatán peninsula. Remind them that this part of Mexico was the home of the great civilization of the ancient Mayas, whose descendents still live there. Ask students to name famous sites with Mayan ruins, such as Chichén Itzá and Tulum in Mexico or Tikal in Guatemala.

Lectura
La Pobreza

Estrategia

Using context clues
If you don't recognize a word in a selection, use other words in the sentence or paragraph to guess its meaning. Which context clues may help you to guess the meaning of words such as *poblado, ramas,* and *deshacerse*?

Al leer

Muchas personas se dedican a tratar de cambiar algo que no les parece bueno o justo. Quieren tener un efecto en la vida de los demás. María Luisa Góngora Pacheco se ha dedicado a conservar la tradición de los pueblos mayas de Yucatán, sus narraciones orales, su teatro popular, su artesanía y su cocina. Vas a leer un cuento escrito por ella.

En este cuento, *La Pobreza,* la autora trata de mostrarnos lo que piensan los mayas sobre la muerte y la pobreza a través de sus propias narraciones orales, que transmiten de padres a hijos.

Antes de leer el cuento, copia la tabla de la página 241. Llena la segunda columna mientras lees y presta atención a los siguientes puntos:

• cómo describe la autora a la Muerte
• la descripción del personaje de la Pobreza
• cómo ve la gente del pueblo a los dos personajes

El señor Aurelio Zumárraga cuenta que hubo una vez cierta viejita cuyo nombre era Pobreza y que vivía en las afueras de la población. En la puerta de su casa había sembrado una mata de huaya[1] y ésta le daba frutos todo el año. Lo que le molestaba a la viejita es que a aquel que veía el fruto le daban ganas de[2] comérselo y sin pedirle permiso se subía a la mata y se anolaba[3] las huayas.

Un día, cuando la viejita llegó al centro del poblado, vio que un viejito pedía limosna, pedía aunque sea le dieran algo para comer en vez de unas monedas, pero nadie lo tomaba en cuenta.

1 guava bush 2 felt like 3 ate

DIFFERENTIATED INSTRUCTION

Heritage Language Learners
Have students ask family members about folk tales from their heritage country, and invite them to share these tales with the class. Some family members might even enjoy visiting the class and sharing these folk tales themselves.

Students with Learning Difficulties
Stop periodically and help students summarize what they have read so far. By breaking up the selection into smaller chunks, you provide students with a better chance for successful reading comprehension.

A la viejita le dio pena verlo en ese estado tan lastimoso y se lo llevó a su casa para darle de almorzar. Cuando el hombrecito terminó de comer, le dijo a la viejita:

—Ahora que ya comí lo que me diste, pídeme lo que quieras, que yo puedo concedértelo[4].

—Buen hombre —dijo la viejita—, lo único que quiero es que le digas a la huaya que no deje bajar al que se suba a sus ramas, hasta que yo se lo mande.

—¡Que se cumpla lo que pides! —contestó el viejito y se fue satisfecho.

La viejita se quedó muy complacida al ver que se cumplía lo prometido por el viejito.

Pasaron muchos años, y un día llegó con la viejita el señor de la Muerte quien le ordenó:

—Ya es tiempo de que vengas conmigo vieja Pobreza, por eso te vine a buscar.

Ella pensó rápidamente la forma de deshacerse de la Muerte y le dijo:

—Me voy contigo, pero primero quiero que bajes unas huayas para que yo anole.

—Bien, en seguida lo haré —contestó la Muerte.

Se dirigieron al árbol y ya debajo, la viejita le dijo a la Muerte:

—Sube hasta allá en lo más alto, ahí se encuentran las más grandes y hermosas huayas, de ésas quiero.

La Muerte, muy segura de sí misma, trepó a la mata, pero no pudo bajarse.

La Pobreza al ver lo que sucedía, se metió a su casa y se desajenó[5] de todo.

Así pasaron muchos años y la Muerte no llegaba a nadie, aunque se enfermara la persona. Los doctores veían con asombro que la viejita Pobreza no moría aun buscando alguna manera para hacerlo.

Un día, uno de los doctores fue a casa de la viejita y lo primero que vio fue la mata llena de frutos, dándole tantas ganas de comer algunos se subió y no pudo bajar. En las ramas encontró al señor de la Muerte y le preguntó:

---

4 grant it **5** washed her hands of

doscientos treinta y nueve **239**
Capítulo 5

ENRICH YOUR TEACHING

Culture Note

María Luisa Góngora Pacheco is one of the most important writers of Mayan culture. She has conducted many activities related to preserving the language, medicines, and traditions of her people. Thanks to her work, Mayan folklore and traditions are enjoying renewed popularity not only in Mexico but internationally.

21st Century Skills

Technology Literacy Have students use the digital technology within **realidades.com** to access extra reading support. Computer corrected activities use different reading strategies to help students build their vocabulary and progress at their own pace through the reading.

Suggestions (Cont'd):

Reading: Allow students time to read the entire selection on their own silently. You might assign this task for homework. This will allow you to capitalize on class time to read it again together with students. When reading together, pause frequently to address comprehension issues that students may bring up and to allow them to fill in their ***Claves del contexto*** charts from p. 241. The following questions and possible thought processes refer to the three words mentioned in the *Estrategia*. Encourage students to use similar reasoning as they complete the rest of the chart.

• p. 238: *¿Qué claves del contexto usaste para comprender la palabra* **poblado**? *(Sé que es un lugar porque la viejita llegó allí. Tiene un centro. Se parece a las palabras* **pueblo** *y* **población**. *Es probablemente un sinónimo de* **pueblo**.)

• p. 239: *¿Qué claves del contexto usaste para comprender la palabra* **ramas**? *(Son una parte de una planta que da frutas. La gente sube a las ramas. Sé que muchos árboles dan frutas y que la gente las sube para recoger las frutas. Entonces* **ramas** *probablemente quiere decir "branches.")*

• p. 239: *¿Qué claves del contexto usaste para comprender la palabra* **deshacerse**? *(A nadie le gusta que le venga el señor de la Muerte. Cuando viene, la viejita piensa rápidamente la forma de* **deshacerse** *de él. Después, engaña (tricks) al señor de la Muerte que se queda en el árbol. Creo que es así que la viejita se* **deshizo** *de él. También la palabra tiene el prefijo* **des-** *y sé que este prefijo quiere decir algo negativo.* **Deshacerse** *debe significar algo como "have nothing to do with" o "get rid of.")*

Teacher-to-Teacher

A successful strategy for teaching reading skills is articulating your thoughts in words, as if you were thinking aloud in order to answer a question. In Spanish, this process not only guides students in how to implement a reading strategy; it provides excellent listening practice.

Suggestions (Cont'd):

Reading: The following questions can be used to help students comprehend the portion of the reading on this page:

¿Piensas que la Muerte habla rápidamente o lentamente? ¿Qué te da esa impresión? (Parece que habla rápidamente. No habla con frases, sino con muchas ideas a la vez, separadas por comas.)

¿Habla formalmente o informalmente con el doctor? ¿Cómo lo sabes? (Le dice "tú." Usa palabras informales.)

¿A quién se refiere el pronombre del complemento indirecto "les" en la frase "Bajen, —les decían"? (a los que están en el árbol)

Según el señor de la Muerte, ¿por qué no puede llevarse a la Pobreza con él al final del cuento? (Tiene demasiado trabajo.)

Post-reading: As students discuss the story and complete the activities in *Interacción con la lectura* on the next page, remind them that the two main characters are meant to represent more than just two inhabitants in a village. Their names, *la Pobreza* and *la Muerte,* are what make the folk tale timeless and larger than life.

Pre-AP* Support

- **Learning Objective:** Presentational Speaking (Cultural Comparison)
- **Background:** This task prepares students for the Spoken Presentational Communication tasks that focus on cultural comparisons.
- **Activity:** Have students prepare a two-minute (maximum) presentation on the following topic: Different views about death between cultures. Students may use the character of *La Muerte,* as portrayed in the reading, as a basis for the comparison. They should then comment on a character from a myth or legend from their own culture, explaining the similarities and differences between the two.
- **Pre-AP* Resource Book:** Comprehensive guide to Pre-AP* speaking skill development, pp. 39–50

Block Schedule

After the class has read the story, create "story experts." Divide the story in four sections and give students numbers 1, 2, 3, or 4. This "expert" is to create five questions about his or her section of the story. Create groups of four students, each with a different "expert." Have them direct their questions to other members of the group.

—¿Qué haces aquí?, todos te andan buscando, pues ya quieren morirse y tú no llegas para llevártelos.

—Mira, lo que pasó fue que esa mentecata[6] de viejita de la casa, me fregó[7], pues vine a buscarla y la muy taimada[8] me dijo que se iría conmigo, pero que antes le bajara unas cuantas huayas. Al subir no pude bajarme y aquí me tienes, y todo aquel que se sube, se queda y hasta tú te quedarás —contestó la Muerte.

—Entonces, a eso se debe que no mueran las personas —dijo el doctor.

—Lo que debemos hacer es bajar —y empezó a gritar: —¡Vengan aquí, vengan aquí, la Muerte está en mi poder, vengan a verla!

Fue tanto lo que gritó y tan fuerte, que la gente de la población se reunió debajo del árbol.

—Bajen —les decían.

—No podemos, todo el que se sube, se queda aquí —contestó el doctor.

Entonces la gente acordó cortar el árbol para que bajaran el doctor y la Muerte. Al momento que lo iban a comenzar a cortar, se asomó la viejita Pobreza.

—¿Qué pretenden hacer, si quieren bajar a los que están en la mata de huaya, por qué no me lo dicen?

—Discúlpenos[9], —dijeron los allí reunidos. La vieja Pobreza se volvió hacia el árbol y le dijo:

—¡Deja que todos bajen!

Cuando todos bajaron, el señor de la Muerte le dijo:

—Vieja Pobreza, por dejarme bajar del árbol, ahora tengo mucho trabajo y no te puedo llevar, otro día será.

Se fue el señor de la Muerte y la Pobreza se quedó en la tierra. Por eso hasta ahora la tenemos con nosotros.

---

6 silly, stupid 7 ruined my plans 8 sly, crafty 9 excuse us

DIFFERENTIATED INSTRUCTION

Multiple Intelligences

Interpersonal/Social: Invite students to discuss ways they can use their interpersonal skills to better the community by working with people of their own age. In small groups, they can brainstorm community needs and possible solutions that they and groups from other schools can help bring about.

Advanced Learners

Students who enjoyed reading this folk tale might wish to use the Internet to find out more about María Luisa Góngora Pacheco and her work preserving the traditions of the Mayas.

Interacción con la lectura

1 Completa la tabla con claves del contexto.

CLAVES DEL CONTEXTO		
palabra desconocida	palabras clave	significado
limosna		
lastimoso		
rama		
satisfecho		
complacida		
deshacerse		
trepó		
acordó		
se asomó		

Más práctica (GO)

realidades.com | print

Guided WB pp. 174–175 ✔ ✔
Comm. WB p. 190 ✔ ✔
Cultural Reading Activity ✔

2 Trabaja con un grupo de estudiantes. Completen sus tablas. Usen las palabras clave que escribieron para decir cuál creen que es el significado de las palabras desconocidas. Escriban el significado de cada palabra en la columna vacía.

3 Comenta con tu grupo lo que escribieron en sus tablas y contesta las preguntas.

• ¿Qué hizo la Pobreza para deshacerse del señor de la Muerte cuando vino a buscarla?

• ¿Cuál era más importante para la vieja Pobreza, la mata de huaya o la Muerte? ¿Por qué?

• ¿Qué significa cuando la autora dice que el señor de la Muerte no se llevó a la Pobreza aunque era vieja?

• Da algunas características del personaje de la Muerte en este cuento. ¿La autora lo presenta como un personaje trágico y serio o no?

4 ¿Conoces otros cuentos o mitos que traten de la Muerte? Escribe un párrafo que diga cómo hablan de ella.

▼ Fondo Cultural | Estados Unidos

Vuelta de hoja La vida de Luis Rodríguez iba por un camino peligroso. A los 7 años, ya era un ladrón. No pasaba de los 13 años, cuando estuvo en un centro de detención juvenil[1] y a los 15, dejó la escuela. Pero a los 18 años "comencé a darle vuelta a mi vida", recuerda Rodríguez. Con ayuda, empezó a trabajar. "Pero a lo largo de todo, leí todo lo que pude. Los libros salvaron mi vida", dice Rodríguez.

En diciembre del 2001, Rodríguez abrió al noreste de Los Ángeles el Café Cultural Tía Chucha, para los jóvenes hispanohablantes y sus familias. Allí tienen charlas de historia y libros, presentaciones musicales y exhibiciones de películas. Rodríguez quiere ayudar a otros jóvenes a desarrollar sus habilidades y a curarse[2] ellos mismos, tal como él se curó. Él es un escritor y activista mexicano-americano que nació en El Paso, Texas. Su padre, Alfonso, un director de escuela en México, fue quien fomentó su amor por los libros.

• ¿Conoces algún centro de la comunidad en tu barrio que te haya ayudado a ti o a algún(a) joven que conoces? ¿Cómo se llama el centro y cómo los(as) ayudó?

• ¿Por qué crees que el café de Rodríguez puede gustarles a los jóvenes? ¿Qué otras cosas crees que puede añadir al café?

1 juvenile detention center 2 to heal

Luis Rodríguez en el Café Cultural Tía Chucha

ENRICH YOUR TEACHING

Culture Note
In addition to being a successful and important community leader, Luis Rodríguez is a renowned writer. He has published memoirs, fiction, nonfiction, children's literature, and poetry. Rodríguez named his café after his aunt, who was an inspiration to him.

21st Century Skills
Initiative and Self-Direction Remind students of the various digital tools available in **realidades.com** to help them monitor their own understanding and learning needs, such as the online tutorials with comprehension check exercises, interactive puzzles, flashcards, and practice tests.

▼ Interacción con la lectura
Standards: 1.1, 1.3, 3.1
Resources: Answer Keys: Student Edition, p. 73

Suggestions: After students share the thought processes they followed to complete the **Claves del contexto** chart, encourage them to go back and read over sections of the story, now that they have a better understanding of the vocabulary.

Answers:
Steps 1, 2, 4
Answers will vary.

Step 3
La Pobreza le dijo al señor de la Muerte que se subiera a la mata de huaya.
Answers will vary for the remaining bulleted questions.

Fondo cultural
Standards: 1.1, 1.2, 5.1, 5.2
Suggestions: After students have read the information silently, ask comprehension questions. For example: *Da unos ejemplos del "camino peligroso" por donde iba Luis Rodríguez durante la primera parte de su vida. (Era ladrón y miembro de una pandilla. Estuvo en un centro de detención juvenil. Se dedicó a la violencia y a las drogas.) ¿Qué ocurre típicamente en el Café Cultural Tía Chucha? (charlas, presentaciones musicales y exhibiciones de películas)*
Answers will vary.

Teacher-to-Teacher
Help students personalize the information about Luis Rodríguez. Use it as a vehicle for discussion about social issues that affect them and your community.

For Further Reading
Student Resource:
• Lecturas 3: "El parque," pp. 14–15
Ana María Matute, "La historia de Nin," pp. 46–50

Additional Resources
Student Resource: Guided Practice: Lectura, pp. 180–181

Repaso del capítulo
Vocabulario y gramática

Review Activities

En el trabajo/Los trabajos/Para la entrevista: Have students prepare their own Spanish definition for each vocabulary item in these categories. Then have teams of two students play against each other in a game of "Password." One student on a team gives his or her partner a definition. The partner must name the vocabulary item defined to earn a point. If he or she cannot, the other team gets a chance at the same definition. The team that correctly matches the greatest number of definitions and vocabulary items wins.

Cualidades y características: Have students work in pairs. One student describes a personality trait of someone he or she knows: *Tengo una hermana que nunca llega tarde.* The partner responds by restating the information using an appropriate adjective: *Así es, tienes una hermana muy puntual.*

Actividades/Acciones: Have students write their own cloze exercises for the items in this category. Explain that, to make a cloze exercise, they use the word or expression correctly in a sentence, then delete the word or expression and replace it with a blank. Ask them to make an answer key to accompany their exercise. Students might enjoy creating their exercises using computer word-processing software. Have partners trade exercises, complete them, and check their work together.

La comunidad: Have students work in pairs and play "Hangman" using the words and expressions in this category.

Expresiones: Students can use these words and expressions as they do the review activities for the other categories.

El presente perfecto: Have students write five sentences in the present perfect tense about the actions of five different people they know or people in the news during the past week. Tell students not to name the people in their sentences, and encourage them to vary the subject each time. Have them share their sentences with other students, who must identify who the subject is: *Hemos ganado el partido de básquetbol contra Wilford Heights. (los miembros del equipo de básquetbol de nuestra escuela)*

en el trabajo
el anuncio clasificado	classified ad
los beneficios	benefits
el / la cliente(a)	client
la compañía	firm / company
el / la dueño(a)	owner
la fecha de nacimiento	date of birth
el / la gerente	manager
el puesto	position
el salario (o el sueldo)	salary
la solicitud de empleo	job application

los trabajos
la computación	computer science
el / la consejero(a)	counselor
el / la mensajero(a)	messenger
el / la niñero(a)	babysitter
el / la repartidor(a)	delivery person
el / la recepcionista	receptionist
el / la salvavida	lifeguard

cualidades y características
agradable	pleasant
dedicado, -a	dedicated
flexible	flexible
injusto, -a	unfair
justo, -a	fair
puntual	punctual
la responsabilidad	responsibility
responsable	responsible

para la entrevista
los conocimientos	knowledge
la entrevista	interview
la habilidad	skill
la referencia	reference
el requisito	requirement

el trabajo
a tiempo completo	full time
a tiempo parcial	part time

actividades
atender	to help, to assist
construir (i → y)	to build
cumplir con	to carry out, to perform
donar	to donate
encargarse(de)(g → gu)	to be in charge of
juntar fondos	to fundraise
presentarse	to apply for a job
reparar	to repair
repartir	to deliver
seguir (+ gerund)	to keep on (doing)
sembrar (ie)	to sow (a seed)
soler (ue)	to usually do something
solicitar	to request

la comunidad
la campaña	campaign
el centro de la comunidad	community center
el centro de rehabilitación	rehabilitation center
el centro recreativo	recreation center
la ciudadanía	citizenship
el / la ciudadano(a)	citizen
el comedor de beneficencia	soup kitchen
los derechos	rights
la gente sin hogar	homeless people
el hogar de ancianos	home for the elderly
la ley	law
la manifestación	demonstration
la marcha	march
el medio ambiente	environment
el servicio social	social service
la sociedad	society

acciones
beneficiar	to benefit
educar	to educate
garantizar	to guarantee
organizar	to organize
proteger	to protect

expresiones
a favor de	in favor of
en contra (de)	against
me es imposible	It is impossible for me. . .
me encantaría	I would love to. . .
me interesaría	I would be interested . . .

DIFFERENTIATED INSTRUCTION

Students with Learning Difficulties
Have students write down words or phrases they are having difficulty remembering. Place these in a hat. Then invite a volunteer to choose two words from the hat and work with a more advanced learner to come up with a sentence using the two words. Students can share their sentences with the class.

Advanced Learners
Invite students to create and trade crossword puzzles using the chapter vocabulary. Tell them they can be creative with their clues, but they must be accurate. You may wish to provide or have students use computer software to make the crossword puzzles.

El presente perfecto

To form the **present perfect tense**, combine the present tense of the verb *haber* with a past participle.

he hablado	hemos hablado
has hablado	habéis hablado
ha hablado	han hablado

To form the past participle of a verb, add *-ado* to the stem of *-ar* verbs and *-ido* to the stem of *-er* and *-ir* verbs.

habl**ar** → habl**ado**   comer → com**ido**   vivir → viv**ido**

Some verbs that have a double vowel in the infinitive (except for *ui*) require an accent mark on the *í* in the past participle.

caer → caído   **oír** → oído

Many Spanish verbs have irregular past participles:

abrir	→	**abierto**	morir	→	**muerto**	romper	→	**roto**
decir	→	**dicho**	poner	→	**puesto**	ser	→	**sido**
escribir	→	**escrito**	resolver	→	**resuelto**	ver	→	**visto**

When using the present perfect tense, place negative words, object pronouns and reflexive pronouns before the form of *haber*.

No he repartido las flores.
Mi profesora me ha escrito un poema.
El dueño se ha ido temprano a la oficina.

El pluscuamperfecto

To form the **pluperfect**, combine the imperfect tense of the verb *haber* with a past participle.

había hablado	habíamos hablado
habías hablado	habíais hablado
había hablado	habían hablado

El presente perfecto del subjuntivo

To form the **present perfect subjunctive**, use the present subjunctive of the verb *haber* with a past participle.

haya trabajado	hayamos trabajado
hayas trabajado	hayáis trabajado
haya trabajado	hayan trabajado

Los adjetivos y los pronombres demostrativos

	Close to you		Closer to the person you are talking to		Far from both of you	
Adjectives	este	estos	ese	esos	aquel	aquellos
	esta	estas	esa	esas	aquella	aquellas
Pronouns	éste	éstos	ése	ésos	aquél	aquéllos
	ésta	éstas	ésa	ésas	aquélla	aquéllas

To refer to an idea, or something that has not been identified, we use the demonstrative pronouns *esto, eso,* or *aquello*.

El pluscuamperfecto: Students can use the sentences they wrote in the previous activity. This time, listeners add a fact about what had happened previously: *Hemos ganado el partido de básquetbol contra Wilford Heights. Antes no habíamos ganado ni un solo partido.*

El presente perfecto del subjuntivo: Have students continue using the same contexts from the previous two activities. This time, they use *Ojalá que* and the present perfect subjunctive to make an additional statement: *Hemos ganado el partido de básquetbol contra Wilford Heights. Antes no habíamos ganado ni un solo partido. Ojalá que nuestro equipo se haya entrenado mejor y no haya sido sólo suerte.*

Los adjetivos y los pronombres demostrativos: Have partners choose three objects to refer to. Pairs take turns giving demonstrations using the demonstrative adjectives and pronouns. They place the objects around the room, stand at opposite ends, and make sentences: *Estas llaves (las que están aquí cerca de mí) son mías. Ésas (las que están cerca de ti)…*

Portfolio

Invite students to review the activities and projects they completed in this chapter. Have them select one or two items that they feel best demonstrate their achievements in Spanish. Include these products in students' portfolios with the Chapter Checklist and Self-Assessment Worksheet.

Additional Resources

Student Resources: Realidades para hispanohablantes, pp. 168–169

Teacher Resources:
• Teacher's Resource Book: Situation Cards, p. 26, Clip Art, pp. 27–34

• Assessment Program: Chapter Checklist and Self-Assessment Worksheet, pp. T49–T50

▶ *¡Pura vida!* is a storyline video that is independent of chapter content and an ideal support for expanding listening skills. The 14 episodes are available within **realidades.com** or on a separate DVD. Student activities and Teacher support are also assignable within **realidades.com**.

ENRICH YOUR TEACHING

Teacher-to-Teacher

Building on activities within the same context, as in the first three activity suggestions on this Teacher's Edition page, is an excellent way to clarify the meaning of verb tenses and moods and show how they interrelate.

Performance Tasks

Standards: 1.1, 1.2, 1.3

Student Resource: *Realidades para hispanohablantes,* pp. 170–171

Teacher Resources: Teacher's Resource Book: Audio Script, p. 16; Audio Program DVD: Cap. 5, Track 23; Answer Keys: Student Edition, p. 73

1. Vocabulario

Suggestions: Encourage students to review the vocabulary from the *A primera vista* sections on pp. 206–209 and 220–223 before they complete the activity.

Answers:

1. b	5. c
2. a	6. a
3. d	7. d
4. b	8. a

2. Gramática

Suggestions: Remind students of the main points of the grammar presentations in *Capítulo* 5:

- the present perfect tense
- the pluperfect tense
- the present perfect subjunctive
- demonstrative adjectives and pronouns

Answers:

1. b	5. c
2. c	6. b
3. a	7. d
4. a	8. a

Preparación para el examen

1 **Vocabulario** Escribe la letra de la palabra o expresión que mejor complete cada frase. Escribe tus respuestas en una hoja aparte.

1. Cuando llenas una solicitud de empleo te piden tu _____.
   a. derecho   c. requisito
   b. fecha de nacimiento d. entrevista

2. Vamos a participar en una _____ para proteger a la gente sin hogar.
   a. campaña   c. rehabilitación
   b. ciudadanía   d. responsabilidad

3. No quiero trabajar todos los días. Necesito un puesto a tiempo _____.
   a. puntual   c. clasificado
   b. completo   d. parcial

4. Una recepcionista debe _____ bien a los clientes.
   a. reparar   c. repartir
   b. atender   d. conseguir

5. ¿Quieres ayudarnos a _____ árboles en el jardín de la comunidad?
   a. educar   c. sembrar
   b. beneficiar   d. solicitar

6. Me gustaría trabajar de _____ en una piscina.
   a. salvavida   c. vendedor
   b. mensajero   d. repartidor

7. Las leyes de nuestro país _____ educar a todos los niños.
   a. benefician   c. rescatan
   b. solicitan   d. garantizan

8. Muchos jóvenes voluntarios _____ casas para la gente sin hogar.
   a. construyen   c. limpian
   b. destruyen   d. protegen

2 **Gramática** Escribe la letra de la palabra o expresión que mejor complete cada frase. Escribe tus respuestas en una hoja aparte.

1. Antes de trabajar en el hogar de ancianos, Pilar _____ en un centro recreativo.
   a. ha trabajado   c. está trabajando
   b. había trabajado d. trabaja

2. Me interesaría este puesto, pero prefiero más _____.
   a. aquella   c. aquél
   b. aquellos   d. aquellas

3. Espero que mi profesora me _____ una buena carta de referencia.
   a. haya escrito   c. ha escrito
   b. había escrito   d. está escribiendo

4. No sé dónde está el gerente. No lo _____ en varias horas.
   a. he visto   c. veía
   b. había visto   d. haya visto

5. Quiero que te encargues de _____ solicitudes de empleo.
   a. estos   c. estas
   b. esto   d. este

6. Espero que ustedes _____ suficientes fondos para el hogar de ancianos.
   a. han juntado   c. habían juntado
   b. hayan juntado   d. juntan

7. "¿Cuántas bicicletas ya _____ este año?", le preguntó a Julio el dueño del taller.
   a. estás reparando c. hayas reparado
   b. reparabas   d. has reparado

8. Cuando llegué al comedor de beneficencia, los voluntarios ya _____ la mesa.
   a. habían puesto   c. van a poner
   b. han puesto   d. hayan puesto

DIFFERENTIATED INSTRUCTION

Heritage Language Learners

Ask students to write down changes that have occurred in their Spanish due to what they have learned in *Capítulo* 5. These might include corrections of grammar or spelling errors, improvements in vocabulary or pronunciation, or elimination of Anglicisms. Have them keep a running list of such changes in their portfolios.

Students with Learning Difficulties

Before asking students to complete each activity on p. 245, review with them the chapter material that pertains to the activity. If students still have difficulty, encourage them to review together in study groups.

Repaso

Más repaso (GO)	realidades.com | print

Instant Check	✔	
Puzzles	✔	
Core WB pp. 75–76		✔
Comm. WB pp. 191, 192–194	✔	✔

Review **5**

En el examen vas a . . .	Éstas son las tareas de práctica que te pueden ser útiles para el examen . . .	Para repasar, ve a tu libro de texto impreso o digital . . .

Interpretive

 3 Escuchar Escuchar a varios estudiantes en entrevistas de trabajo e identificar los empleos que están solicitando

Escucha lo que dicen estos estudiantes en sus entrevistas de trabajo. Presta atención a lo que dicen y di a qué empleo se presentaron Verónica, Ariel, José y Patricia.

pp. 206–209 *A primera vista 1: Vocabulario en contexto*

p. 211 Actividad 9

p. 212 Actividad 11

p. 213 Actividad 12

Interpersonal

 4 Hablar En una feria de trabajo, hablar con un compañero de tu experiencia y hacer preguntas sobre los empleos

Imagina que vas a una feria de trabajo. Di lo que le dirías a un consejero acerca de tus conocimientos y habilidades, en qué te interesaría trabajar y en qué has trabajado antes. También haz preguntas sobre el empleo, por ejemplo: el horario, el sueldo y los beneficios.

p. 211 Actividad 9

p. 212 Actividad 11

p. 212 Actividad 12

p. 215 Actividad 15

p. 216 Actividad 17

Interpretive

 5 Leer Leer y comprender un anuncio clasificado

Lee este anuncio. ¿Qué tipo de empleo se ofrece? ¿Es un trabajo a tiempo completo o a tiempo parcial? ¿Qué conocimientos o habilidades se necesitan?

Recepcionista. Se necesita joven bilingüe, puntual y responsable para atender el teléfono y otros trabajos de oficina. Otros requisitos: saber trabajar con computadoras y tener buenas referencias. Lunes a viernes de 8 a.m. a 5 p.m. Buenos beneficios y salario. Presentarse en nuestras oficinas de la Avenida Bolívar # 534.

p. 209 *A primera vista 1: Vocabulario en contexto*

p. 212 Actividad 11

p. 216 Actividad 16

Presentational

 6 Escribir Escribir una carta para solicitar empleo

Imagina que vas a solicitar empleo. Piensa qué tipo de trabajo es, y escribe una carta para solicitar empleo. En tu carta di (a) por qué te interesa el trabajo, (b) qué cualidades personales tienes por las que serías el (la) mejor para ese puesto y (c) qué experiencia de trabajo tienes.

p. 213 Actividad 13

p. 226 Actividad 33

pp. 236–237 *Presentación escrita*

Comparisons

 7 Pensar Pensar en las contribuciones de los hispanohablantes a los Estados Unidos

¿Cuál es el impacto de algunos hispanohablantes en la cultura de los Estados Unidos? También piensa en cómo les influimos a ellos en sus países, como en la política, los negocios, las artes, las ciencias y el deporte.

p. 226 *Fondo cultural*

pp. 232–233 *Puente a la cultura*

doscientos cuarenta y cinco 245
Capítulo 5

3. Escuchar

Suggestions: Use the audio or read from the script.

Answers:

Verónica: empleada en una tienda de animales
Ariel: voluntario en un hogar de ancianos
José: salvavida
Patricia: recepcionista

4. Hablar

Suggestions: Remind students that in this situation they would most likely address the people to whom they are speaking with **Ud.**

Answers will vary.

5. Leer

Suggestions: Tell students to refer to pp. 206–209 and 220–223 if they have questions about vocabulary in the review.

Answers:

Recepcionista.
Es un trabajo a tiempo completo.
Se necesita ser bilingüe, puntual y responsable. Hay que saber trabajar con computadoras y tener buenas referencias.

6. Escribir

Suggestions: Tell students to use their own cover letters in their portfolios as a model.

Answers will vary.

7. Pensar

Suggestions: Ask students if their perceptions of the Spanish-speaking population have changed in any way because of what they have learned.

Answers will vary.

DIFFERENTIATED ASSESSMENT

CORE ASSESSMENT
- **Assessment Program:** Examen del capítulo 5, pp. 123–126
- **Audio Program DVD:** Cap. 5, Track 24
- **ExamView:** Chapter Test, Test Banks A and B

ADVANCED/PRE-AP*
- **ExamView:** Pre-AP* Test Bank
- **Pre-AP* Resource Book:** pp. 150–152

STUDENTS NEEDING EXTRA HELP
- **Alternate Assessment Program:** Examen del capítulo 5
- **Audio Program DVD:** Cap. 5, Track 24

HERITAGE LEARNERS
- **Assessment Program: Realidades para hispanohablantes:** Examen del capítulo 5
- **ExamView: Heritage Learner Test Bank**

6 Chapter Overview

- **careers, professions, and technology**

Vocabulary
- careers and professions
- plans for the future
- impact of science and technology

Grammar
- future
- future of probability
- future perfect
- uses of direct and indirect object pronouns

Cultural Perspectives
- Chilean surrealist painter Roberto Matta
- living arrangements of young people in Spain
- internships in Washington, D.C., for young Spanish speakers
- the international baccalaureate program
- Spanish and Latin American architects

¡Pura vida!
- Watch an engaging video episode about a group of young people in Costa Rica!

CHAPTER SUPPORT

Bulletin Boards

Theme: *¿Qué nos traerá el futuro?*

Ask students to cut out, copy, or download photos or pictures of projects or things for the future, and people whose careers are related to the future. Cluster photos or pictures according to these themes. Add brief captions to the photos or pictures explaining the project or item for the future.

Hands-on Culture

Recipe: *Gallo pinto*

The national dish of Costa Rica is *gallo pinto*, which is refried rice and beans and is served at breakfast, lunch, or dinner, with fried eggs, sour cream, and hot *tortillas*.

Ingredients:

1 cup white rice
1-3/4 cups water
1 tablespoon olive oil
1 medium onion, diced
1/2 red bell pepper, seeded and diced
1 jalapeño pepper, seeded and minced
2 cloves garlic, minced
1 handful chopped cilantro leaves
16 ounces canned black beans, drained
Salt to taste
1 teaspoon Tabasco sauce
2 tablespoons Worcestershire sauce

Supplies: frying pan, 2 qt. saucepan, serving dish

1. Wash the rice in cold water, drain, and put it in a pot with the water and a pinch of salt. Bring the rice to a boil, stir, cover, and lower the heat to a simmer. Cook the rice until the water is absorbed, about 20 minutes. Let the rice stand for 10 minutes, then fluff it with a fork.

2. Heat the olive oil in a skillet over medium-high heat. Add the onions and peppers and sauté, stirring for 5 minutes. Stir in the garlic and sauté for 2 minutes. Add the cilantro and sauté for 1 minute more.

3. Spoon the rice and beans into the skillet, mix well, and heat everything through. Season the dish to taste with salt and a combination of Worcestershire sauce and Tabasco sauce.

Game

Cosas del futuro

This game practices grammar and vocabulary about the future. Use it toward the end of *Manos a la obra* 2, after students have practiced the chapter vocabulary.

Players: entire class

Materials: paper, pencils, markers, pen

Rules:

1. Divide the class into small groups.
2. Have each group think of an invention for the future, such as a special machine that does homework for students.
3. Ask them to make a drawing of the invention and to write down a clue about its function. The clue could be one word or a phrase.
4. Call one group to come to the front of the class. The group shows their drawing to the class. Meanwhile you write the drawing's clue on the board so everybody can read it.
5. The rest of the students take turns asking the members of the group *sí/no* questions in an attempt to determine what the object is for.

Student 1: ¿Es una máquina?
Group: Sí.
Student 2: ¿Se usa en la escuela?
Group: No.
Student 3: ¿Es para los estudiantes?
Group: Sí.
Student 4: ¿Reemplaza a una máquina que existe en la actualidad?
Group: No.
Student 5: ¿Es una máquina que te hace las tareas?
Group: ¡Sí!

6. When a student correctly guesses what the object is, his or her group gets one point and is the next one to come to the front of the class and show their drawing. Play continues in this manner until every group has had the chance of showing their drawings and answering questions. The group with more points wins the game.

Variation: Instead of drawing the objects, students can write clues in the form of sentences so students guess what the object is.

CHAPTER PROJECT

La evolución de los inventos

Overview: Students create a Web page featuring items that have evolved throughout time and will continue to change in the future. Students should show when each item was invented, what it looked like then, what it looks like now, and what it is going to look like in the future. They should insert a brief description of the changes in the history of each product. Students then present their Web page to the class, describing all the information featured on the page.

Resources: digital or print photos, image editing and page layout software, and/or poster board, colored pencils, markers, glue, scissors, bilingual dictionary

Sequence: (suggestions for when to do each step appear throughout the chapter)

STEP 1. Review instructions so students know what is expected of them. Hand out the "Chapter 6 Project Instructions and Rubric" from the *Teacher's Resource Book*.

STEP 2. Students submit a rough draft of their Web page. Return the drafts with your suggestions. For vocabulary and grammar practice, ask students to work in pairs and present their drafts to each other.

STEP 3. Students create layouts. Encourage students to try different arrangements before writing descriptions. Ask them to use as much of the vocabulary from *Capítulo* 6 as possible in the descriptions. Also, have them use a bilingual dictionary for any words they would like to use but do not yet know.

STEP 4. Students submit a draft of their descriptions. Note your corrections and suggestions, then return the drafts to students.

STEP 5. Students complete and present their Web page to the class. They describe all the information featured on the page.

Options:

1. Students create a poster for their school instead of a Web page.
2. Students write an article for the school newspaper about the inventions.

Assessment:

Here is a detailed rubric for assessing this project:

Chapter 6 Project: *La evolución de los inventos*

RUBRIC	Score 1	Score 3	Score 5
Your evidence of planning	You provide no written draft or page layout.	Your draft was written and layout created, but not corrected.	You show evidence of corrected draft and layout.
Your use of illustrations	You include photos or visuals.	Your photos or visuals were included, but the layout was unorganized.	Your Web page was easy to read, complete, and accurate.
Your presentation	You include little of the required information.	You include most of the required information.	You include all of the required information.

21st Century Skills

Look for tips throughout Chapter 6 to enrich your teaching by integrating 21st Century Skills. Suggestions for the Chapter Project and Culture follow below.

Chapter Project

Modify the Chapter Project with these suggestions:

Encourage Technology Literacy
Encourage students to access a variety of Web sites to use as a model for designing their own Web page. Have them evaluate the layout of various sites to gather ideas for creating their own.

Support Critical Thinking and Problem Solving
As students prepare to start the project, provide them with the handout "Compare and Contrast" to help them organize their ideas about how to describe the evolution of their product from the moment of invention to the present, and projecting to the future.

Foster Creativity and Innovation
Have students be as creative as possible when describing the stages of development of their featured products. How many ways could they present and organize this information using visuals, descriptive text, audio or video footage? How do the products affect the lives of people who use them? How will this change in the future?

Chapter Culture

Develop Flexibility and Adaptability
Direct students to review the information and their answers to the questions in the *Fondo cultural* notes on pages 262, 271, and 287. Promote a discussion about the different cultural perspectives that young people would learn if they participated in these programs. In what ways would they need to adapt to the opportunities provided by them?

▶ **Videodocumentario** View *La tecnología en la carrera de un profesional* online with the class to learn more about a photography professor and his class at the New England School of Photography.

AT A GLANCE

Objectives

- **Listen and read about future plans and predictions**
- **Talk and write about future problems and advances**
- **Explain your career goals for the future**
- **Understand how Hispanic architects are shaping the future**
- **Compare living situations of college graduates from Spain and U.S.**

A ver si recuerdas... ♻

- Career and jobs
- Technology and environment
- **Saber** and **conocer**
- Impersonal **se**

Recycle... ♻

- Combining letters when speaking
- Verbs with irregular participles

Vocabulary

- Professions and careers
- Personal qualities
- Future ideas and actions
- Careers of the future

Grammar

- Future
- Future of probability
- Future perfect tense
- Uses of the direct and indirect pronouns

Culture

- Surrealism in art, p. 251
- Living situations of Spanish young people, p. 257
- Hispanic youth working in Washington, D.C., p. 262
- Technology of the future, pp. 266–267
- International baccalaureate, p. 271
- Life in the future, p. 272
- Architecture in the future, pp. 278–279
- Virtual university in Puerto Rico, p. 287

RESOURCES

FOR THE STUDENT	ONLINE	DVD	PRINT	FOR THE TEACHER	ONLINE	PREEXP	DVD	PRINT
Plan				Interactive TE and Resource DVD	•		•	
				Teacher's Resource Book, pp. 61–119	•		•	•
				Pre-AP* Resource Book, pp. 153–155	•		•	•
				Mapa global interactivo	•			
				Lesson Plans	•			•

A ver si recuerdas PP. 246–249

FOR THE STUDENT	ONLINE	DVD	PRINT	FOR THE TEACHER	ONLINE	PREEXP	DVD	PRINT
Review	*A ver si recuerdas* Study Plan	•			*A ver si recuerdas* Study Plan	•			
	Guided WB, pp. 176–179	•	•	•	Vocabulary and Grammar Transparencies, 116–119	•	•	•	
	Core WB, pp. 77–78	•	•	•	Answer Keys: Student Edition, pp. 75–76	•	•	•	
	Hispanohablantes WB, p. 172			•					

Introducción PP. 250–251

FOR THE STUDENT	ONLINE	DVD	PRINT	FOR THE TEACHER	ONLINE	PREEXP	DVD	PRINT
Present	Student Edition, pp. 250–251	•	•	•	Interactive TE and Resource DVD	•		•	
	DK Reference Atlas	•	•		Teacher's Resource Book, pp. 62–65	•		•	•
	Videonovela: ¡Pura vida!	•	•		Galería de fotos			•	
	¡Pura vida! Video Activities	•			Fine Art Transparencies, 38	•	•	•	
	Hispanohablantes WB, p. 173			•	Map Transparencies, 14, 16, 18, 20, 22	•	•	•	

Vocabulario en contexto PP. 254–255/266–269

FOR THE STUDENT	ONLINE	DVD	PRINT	FOR THE TEACHER	ONLINE	PREEXP	DVD	PRINT
Present & Practice	Student Edition, pp. 254–255/266–269	•	•	•	Interactive TE and Resource DVD	•		•	
	Audio	•	•		Teacher's Resource Book, pp. 66–67, 70–71, 84–93/68–69, 72–73, 84–93	•		•	•
	Flashcards	•	•						
	Instant Check	•			Vocabulary Clip Art	•	•	•	
	Guided WB, pp. 180–188/193–200	•	•	•	Audio Program	•	•	•	
	Core WB, pp. 79–80/84–85	•	•	•	Vocabulary and Grammar Transparencies, 120–123/126–129	•	•	•	
	Comm. WB, pp. 82/86	•	•	•	Answer Keys: Student Edition, pp. 77/84–85	•	•	•	
	Hispanohablantes WB, pp. 174–175/184–185			•					
Assess and Remediate					Pruebas 6–1, 6–5: Assessment Program, pp. 127–128/136–137	•		•	•
					Hispanohablantes, pp. 127–128/136–137	•		•	•

RESOURCES

FOR THE STUDENT	ONLINE	DVD	PRINT	FOR THE TEACHER	ONLINE	PREEXP	DVD	PRINT
Vocabulario en uso PP. 256–259/270–272								
Present & Practice Student Edition, pp. 256–259/270–272	•	•	•	Interactive Whiteboard Vocabulary Activities	•		•	
Instant Check	•			Interactive TE and Resource DVD	•		•	
Comm. WB, pp. 78/80	•	•	•	Teacher's Resource Book, pp. 71, 77–78/73, 80	•		•	•
Hispanohablantes WB, pp. 176–177/186–188			•	Audio Program	•	•	•	
Communicative Pair Activities	•			Videomodelos	•		•	
				Vocabulary and Grammar Transparencies, 4	•	•	•	
				Answer Keys: Student Edition, pp. 78–79/85–86	•	•	•	•
Assess and Remediate				Pruebas 6–2, 6–6 with Study Plans	•			
				Pruebas 6–2, 6–6: Assessment Program, pp. 129–130/138–139	•		•	•
				Hispanohablantes, pp. 129–130/138–139	•		•	•
Gramática PP. 260–265/273–277								
Present & Practice Student Edition, pp. 260–265/273–277	•	•	•	Interactive Whiteboard Grammar Activities	•		•	
Instant Check	•			Interactive TE and Resource DVD	•		•	
Animated Verbs	•			Teacher's Resource Book, pp. 71–72, 79/73–74, 81–82	•		•	•
Tutorial Video: Grammar	•			Audio Program	•	•	•	
Canción de hip hop	•			Videomodelos	•	•	•	
Guided WB, pp. 189–192/201–204	•	•	•	Vocabulary and Grammar Transparencies, 124–125/130–131	•	•	•	
Core WB, pp. 81–83/86–88	•	•	•	Answer Keys: Student Edition, pp. 80–83/86–87	•	•	•	
Comm. WB, pp. 79, 83–85/81, 87–89	•	•	•					
Hispanohablantes WB, pp. 178–183/189–193			•					
Communicative Pair Activities	•							
Assess and Remediate				Pruebas 6–3, 6–4, 6–7, 6–8 with Study Plans	•			
				Pruebas 6–3, 6–4, 6–7, 6–8: Assessment Program, pp. 131, 132/140, 141	•		•	•
				Hispanohablantes, pp. 131, 132/140, 141	•		•	•
				Examen 1, Examen 2: Vocab. y gramática, pp. 133–135/142–144	•		•	•
¡Adelante! PP. 278–287								
Application Student Edition, pp. 278–287	•	•	•	Interactive TE and Resource DVD	•		•	
Online Cultural Reading	•			Teacher's Resource Book, pp. 74, 76	•		•	•
Guided WB, pp. 205–207	•	•	•	Video Program: Videodocumentario	•		•	
Comm. WB, pp. 90–91, 195–196	•	•	•	Video Program Teacher's Guide, Cap. 6	•		•	
Hispanohablantes WB, pp. 194–199			•	Vocabulary and Grammar Transparencies, 2, 4	•		•	
Videodocumentario	•	•		Map Transparency, 14	•	•	•	
Lecturas 3, pp. 38–41			•	Answer Keys: Student Edition, pp. 87–88	•	•	•	
Repaso del capítulo PP. 288–291								
Review Student Edition, pp. 288–291	•	•	•	Interactive TE and Resource DVD	•		•	
Online Puzzles and Games	•			Teacher's Resource Book, pp. 75, 83–93	•		•	•
Core WB, pp. 89–90	•	•	•	Audio Program	•	•	•	
Comm. WB, pp. 197–200	•	•	•	Answer Keys: Student Edition, p. 88	•	•	•	
Hispanohablantes WB, pp. 200–203			•					
Instant Check	•							
Chapter Assessment								
Assess				Examen del capítulo 6: Assessment Program, pp. 145–148	•		•	•
				Alternate Assessment Program, pp. 55–65	•		•	•
				Hispanohablantes, pp. 145–148	•		•	•
				Audio Program, Cap. 6, Examen	•		•	
				ExamView: Test Banks A and B (questions only online)	•		•	
				Heritage Learner Test Bank	•		•	
				Pre-AP* Test Bank	•		•	

REGULAR SCHEDULE (50 MINUTES)

DAY	Warm-up / Assess	Preview / Present / Practice / Communicate	Wrap-up / Homework Options
1	**Warm-up (10 min.)** • Return Examen del capítulo: Capítulo 5	**Repaso (35 min.)** • A ver si recuerdas . . . • Actividades 1, 2, 3, 6, 7	**Wrap-up and Homework Options (5 min.)** • Core Practice 6-1, 6-2
2	**Warm-up (10 min.)** • Homework check	**Chapter Opener (10 min.)** • Objectives • Arte y cultura **Vocabulario en contexto 1 (25 min.)** • Presentation: Vocabulario y gramática en contexto • Actividades 1	**Wrap-up and Homework Options (5 min.)** • Clip Art Vocabulary
3	**Warm-up (10 min.)** • Homework check	**Vocabulario en contexto 1 (30 min.)** • Presentation: Los estudiantes y su futuro • Actividades 2, 3 **Vocabulario en uso 1 (5 min.)** • Interactive Whiteboard Vocabulary Activities • Actividades 4, 5	**Wrap-up and Homework Options (5 min.)** • Core Practice 6-3, 6-4 • Actividad 6 • Prueba 6-1: Vocabulary recognition
4	**Warm-up (10 min.)** • Homework check ✔**Formative Assessment (10 min.)** • Prueba 6-1: Vocabulary recognition	**Vocabulario en uso 1 (25 min.)** • Actividades 7, 8, 9 • Fondo cultural • Ampliación del lenguaje	**Wrap-up and Homework Options (5 min.)** • Actividad 10 • Writing Activities • Prueba 6-2 with Study Plan: Vocabulary production
5	**Warm-up (15 min.)** • Homework check • Communicative Pair Activity • Audio Activity ✔**Formative Assessment (10 min.)** • Prueba 6-2 with Study Plan: Vocabulary production	**Gramática y vocabulario en uso 1 (20 min.)** • Presentation: El futuro • Interactive Whiteboard Grammar Activities • Actividades 11, 12, 13 • Writing Activity	**Wrap-up and Homework Options (5 min.)** • Core Practice 6-5
6	**Warm-up (10 min.)** • Homework check	**Gramática y vocabulario en uso 1 (35 min.)** • Actividades 14, 15 • Fondo cultural • Presentation: El futuro de probabilidad • Interactive Whiteboard Grammar Activities • Actividades 16, 17	**Wrap-up and Homework Options (5 min.)** • Core Practice 6-6, 6-7 • Prueba 6-3 with Study Plan: El futuro
7	**Warm-up (10 min.)** • Homework check ✔**Formative Assessment (10 min.)** • Prueba 6-3 with Study Plan: El futuro	**Gramática y vocabulario en uso 1 (25 min.)** • Actividades 18, 19 • Communicative Pair Activity • En voz alta	**Wrap-up and Homework Options (5 min.)** • Writing Activity • Prueba 6-4 with Study Plan: El futuro de probabilidad
8	**Warm-up (10 min.)** • Homework check ✔**Formative Assessment (10 min.)** • Prueba 6-4 with Study Plan: El futuro de probabilidad	**Vocabulario en contexto 2 (25 min.)** • Presentation: Vocabulario y gramática en contexto • Actividades 20, 21	**Wrap-up and Homework Options (5 min.)** • Clip Art Vocabulary • Examen: Vocabulario y gramática 1
9	**Warm-up (5 min.)** • Homework check ✔**Formative Assessment (30 min.)** • Examen: Vocabulario y gramática 1	**Vocabulario en contexto 2 (10 min.)** • Presentation: Tres campos que tienen futuro • Actividad 22	**Wrap-up and Homework Options (5 min.)** • Actividad 23 • Core Practice 6-8, 6-9 • Prueba 6-5: Vocabulary recognition
10	**Warm-up (20 min.)** • Homework check ✔**Formative Assessment (10 min.)** • Prueba 6-5: Vocabulary recognition	**Vocabulario en uso 2 (15 min.)** • Actividades 24, 25, 26 • Fondo cultural	**Wrap-up and Homework Options (5 min.)** • Actividades 27, 28

REGULAR SCHEDULE (50 MINUTES)

DAY	Warm-up / Assess	Preview / Present / Practice / Communicate		Wrap-up / Homework Options
11	Warm-up (15 min.) • Homework check	Vocabulario en uso 2 (15 min.) • Interactive Whiteboard Vocabulary Activities • Actividad 29 • Writing Activity	Gramática y vocabulario en uso 2 (15 min.) • Presentation: El futuro perfecto • Interactive Whiteboard Grammar Activities • Actividades 30, 32	Wrap-up and Homework Options (5 min.) • Core Practice 6-10 • Prueba 6-6 with Study Plan: Vocabulary production
12	Warm-up (10 min.) • Homework check ✔Formative Assessment (10 min.) • Prueba 6-6 with Study Plan: Vocabulary production	Gramática y vocabulario en uso 2 (25 min.) • Actividad 32 • Presentation: Uso de los complementos directos e indirectos • Interactive Whiteboard Grammar Activities • Writing Activity • Actividades 33, 34 • El español en la comunidad		Wrap-up and Homework Options (5 min.) • Core Practice 6-11, 6-12 • Prueba 6-7 with Study Plan: El futuro de probabilidad
13	Warm-up (10 min.) • Homework check ✔Formative Assessment (10 min.) • Prueba 6-7 with Study Plan: El futuro de probabilidad	Gramática y vocabulario en uso 2 (25 min.) • Actividades 35, 36, 37 • Audio Activity • Writing Activity		Wrap-up and Homework Options (5 min.) • Writing Activity • Prueba 6-8 with Study Plan: Uso de los complementos directos e indirectos
14	Warm-up (10 min.) • Communicative Pair Activity ✔Formative Assessment (10 min.) • Prueba 6-8 with Study Plan: Uso de los complementos directos e indirectos	¡Adelante! (25 min.) • La arquitectura del futuro • ¿Comprendiste? • El futuro de la comunidad • Presentación oral: Step 1		Wrap-up and Homework Options (5 min.) • Examen: Vocabulario y gramática 2
15	Warm-up (5 min.) • Answer questions ✔Formative Assessment (25 min.) • Examen: Vocabulario y gramática 2	¡Adelante! (15 min.) • Presentación oral: Step 2		Wrap-up and Homework Options (5 min.) • Presentación oral: Step 3
16	Warm-up (5 min.) • Homework check	¡Adelante! (40 min.) • Presentación oral: Step 3 (half class) • ¿Qué me cuentas? 1, 2, 3		Wrap-up and Homework Options (5 min.) • Presentación escrita: Steps 1, 2
17	Warm-up (10 min.) • Homework check	¡Adelante! (35 min.) • Presentación oral: Step 3 (half class) • View Video • Video Activities 1, 2, 3 • Presentación escrita: Step 3		Wrap-up and Homework Options (5 min.) • Presentación escrita: Step 4 • Preparación para el examen: 1, 2
18	Warm-up (10 min.) • Homework check	Repaso (10 min.) • Preparación para el examen: Actividades 3, 4 ¡Adelante! (25 min.) • Lectura • Fondo cultural • ¿Comprendiste?		Wrap-up and Homework Options (5 min.) • ¿Comprendiste? • Core Practice: Organizer 6-13, 6-14 • Instant Check
19	Warm-up (15 min.) • Homework check	Repaso (30 min.) • Preparación para el examen: Actividades 5, 6, 7 • Other review		Wrap-up and Homework Options (5 min.) • Examen del capítulo
20	Warm-up (5 min.) • Answer questions ✔Summative Assessment (44 min.) • Examen del capítulo			Wrap-up and Homework Options (1 min.) • A ver si recuerdas: Capítulo 7

BLOCK SCHEDULE (90 MINUTES)

DAY	Warm-up / Assess	Preview / Present / Practice / Communicate	Wrap-up / Homework Options
1	**Warm-up (35 min.)** • Return Examen del capítulo: Capítulo 6 • A ver si recuerdas . . . • Homework check	**Chapter Opener (10 min.)** • Objectives • Arte y cultura **Vocabulario en contexto 1 (30 min.)** • Presentation: Vocabulario y gramática en contexto • Actividad 1 • Presentation: Los estudiantes hablan del futuro • Actividades 2, 3 **Vocabulario en uso 1 (10 min.)** • Interactive Whiteboard Vocabulary Activities • Actividades 4, 5, 6	**Wrap-up and Homework Options (5 min.)** • Core Practice 6-3, 6-4 • Clip Art Vocabulary • Prueba 6-1: Vocabulary recognition
2	**Warm-up (20 min.)** • Homework check • Actividades 7, 8, 9 ✔**Formative Assessment (10 min.)** • Prueba 6-1: Vocabulary recognition	**Vocabulario en uso 1 (55 min.)** • Actividad 10 • Ampliación del lenguaje • Audio Activity • Writing Activity • Communicative Pair Activity	**Wrap-up and Homework Options (5 min.)** • Prueba 6-2 with Study Plan: Vocabulary production
3	**Warm-up (5 min.)** • Homework check ✔**Formative Assessment (10 min.)** • Prueba 6-2 with Study Plan: Vocabulary production	**Gramática y vocabulario en uso 1 (70 min.)** • Presentation: El futuro • Interactive Whiteboard Grammar Activities • Actividades 11, 12, 13, 14, 15 • Fondo cultural • Writing Activity	**Wrap-up and Homework Options (5 min.)** • Actividad 15: Step 3 • Core Practice 6-5 • Prueba 6-3 with Study Plan: El futuro
4	**Warm-up (10 min.)** • Homework check ✔**Formative Assessment (10 min.)** • Prueba 6-3 with Study Plan: El futuro	**Gramática y vocabulario en uso 1 (50 min.)** • Presentation: El futuro de probabilidad • Interactive Whiteboard Grammar Activities • Actividades 16, 17, 18, 19 • En voz alta • Writing Activity • Communicative Pair Activity **Vocabulario en contexto 2 (15 min.)** • Presentation: Vocabulario y gramática en contexto • Actividades 20, 21	**Wrap-up and Homework Options (5 min.)** • Core Practice 6-6, 6-7 • Prueba 6-4 with Study Plan: El futuro de probabilidad • Examen: Vocabulario y gramática 1
5	**Warm-up (10 min.)** • Homework check ✔**Formative Assessment Options (40 min.)** • Prueba 6-4 with Study Plan: El futuro de probabilidad • Examen: Vocabulario y gramática 1	**Vocabulario en contexto 2 (20 min.)** • Presentation: Tres campos que tienen futuro • Actividades 22, 26 **Vocabulario en uso 2 (15 min.)** • Interactive Whiteboard Vocabulary Activities • Actividades 25, 26	**Wrap-up and Homework Options (5 min.)** • Core Practice 6-8, 6-9 • Actividades 27, 28 • Clip Art • Prueba 6-5: Vocabulary recognition
6	**Warm-up (35 min.)** • Homework check • Actividades 26, 29 • Audio Activity • Writing Activity • Communicative Pair Activity ✔**Formative Assessment (10 min.)** • Prueba 6-5: Vocabulary recognition	**Gramática y vocabulario en uso 2 (40 min.)** • Presentation: El futuro perfecto • Interactive Whiteboard Grammar Activities • Actividades 30, 31, 32 • Writing Activities	**Wrap-up and Homework Options (5 min.)** • Core Practice 6-10 • Pruebas 6-6, 6-7 with Study Plans: Vocabulary production, El futuro perfecto

BLOCK SCHEDULE (90 MINUTES)

DAY	Warm-up / Assess	Preview / Present / Practice / Communicate	Wrap-up / Homework Options
7	**Warm-up (10 min.)** • Homework check ✔**Formative Assessment (20 min.)** • Pruebas 6-6, 6-7 with Study Plans: Vocabulary production, El futuro perfecto	**Gramática y vocabulario en uso 2 (40 min.)** • Presentation: El uso de los complementos directos e indirectos • Interactive Whiteboard Grammar Activities • Actividades 33, 34, 35, 36, 37 • Audio Activity • Writing Activity • El español en la comunidad **¡Adelante! (15 min.)** • Presentación oral: Steps 1, 2	**Wrap-up and Homework Options (5 min.)** • Core Practice 6-11, 6-12 • Prueba 6-8 with Study Plan: El uso de los complementos directos e indirectos • Presentación oral: Step 2
8	**Warm-up (15 min.)** • Communicative Pair Activity • Homework check ✔**Formative Assessment (10 min.)** • Prueba 6-8 with Study Plan: El uso de los complementos directos e indirectos	**Gramática y vocabulario en uso 2 (35 min.)** • Presentación oral: Step 3 **¡Adelante! (25 min.)** • Presentation: La arquitectura del futuro • ¿Comprendiste? • El futuro de tu comunidad	**Wrap-up and Homework Options (5 min.)** • ¿Comprendiste? • El futuro de tu comunidad • Examen: Vocabulario y gramática 2
9	**Warm-up (5 min.)** • Homework check ✔**Formative Assessment Options (30 min.)** • Examen: Vocabulario y gramática 2	**¡Adelante! (50 min.)** • ¿Qué me cuentas? 1, 2, 3 • View Video • Video Activities • Presentación escrita: Step 1	**Wrap-up and Homework Options (5 min.)** • Presentación escrita: Step 2 • Preparación para el examen: Actividades 1, 2
10	**Warm-up (20 min.)** • Homework check • Presentación escrita: Step 3	**¡Adelante! (35 min.)** • Lectura • ¿Comprendiste? • Fondo cultural **Repaso (30 min.)** • Preparación para el examen: Actividades 3, 4, 6	**Wrap-up and Homework Options (5 min.)** • Presentación escrita: Step 4 • Core Practice: Organizer 6-13, 6-14 • Instant Check • Preparación para el examen: Actividades 5, 7 • Examen del capítulo
11	**Warm-up (15 min.)** • Homework check ✔**Summative Assessment (45 min.)** • Examen del capítulo	**Theme Game (15 min.)** **A ver si recuerdas – Capítulo 7 (10 min.)** • Presentation: Vocabulario • Presentation: Gramática	**Wrap-up and Homework Options (5 min.)** • A ver si recuerdas – Capítulo 7 • Actividades 1–6 • Core Practice 7-1, 7-2

6 Recycle

Vocabulario Repaso

Core Instruction

Standards: 1.1, 1.2

Resources: Voc. and Gram. Transparency 116

Suggestions: Before presenting the material in this review section, consider testing your students' command of the material by assigning the Study Plan. Students will automatically be given additional practice of the material they have not yet mastered, and you can focus your review based on the class's overall performance on the post-test.

Have students copy the names of the five categories onto their own paper. Show *Vocabulary and Grammar Transparency* 116. With books closed, have students work in pairs and list as many words as they can for each category.

Vocabulario Repaso

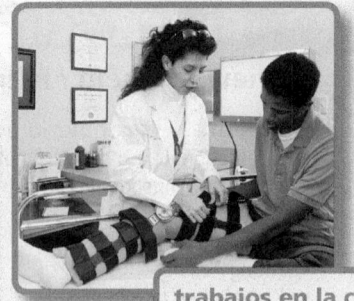

el mundo del espectáculo
el actor, la actriz
el bailarín, la bailarina
el/la cantante
el crítico, la crítica

trabajos en la comunidad
el agricultor, la agricultora
el bombero, la bombera
el cajero, la cajera
el cartero, la cartera
el dependiente, la dependienta
el empleado, la empleada
el/la gerente
el mecánico, la mecánica
el paramédico, la paramédica
el/la policía
el político, la política
el secretario, la secretaria

los estudios
la graduación
la universidad

el mundo de las ciencias y la tecnología
el/la dentista
el enfermero, la enfermera
el médico, la médica
el técnico, la técnica
el veterinario, la veterinaria

el mundo de las artes
el/la artista
el escritor, la escritora
el escultor, la escultora
el pintor, la pintora

1

Standards: 1.1

Resources: Answer Keys: Student Edition, p. 75

Focus: Practicing review vocabulary

Suggestions: Encourage students to use vocabulary and structures from previous chapters in Step 2. For example, they might use the present perfect tense when referring to the experiences needed for a particular profession: *Si alguien ha trabajado mucho con los animales, puede estudiar para ser veterinario(a).*

Common Errors: Some students may use a feminine article when they refer to a male **artista, policía,** or **dentista.** Remind them that although these nouns end in **-a,** they apply to either gender. Students should use them with masculine articles when talking about males: *Conozco a un artista que se llama Guillermo.*

Answers:

Step 1

1. e	**3. a**	**5. c**
2. d	**4. b**	

Step 2

Answers will vary.

▼1 Las profesiones |

Hablar

❶ Trabaja con otro(a) estudiante para emparejar cada actividad o área de trabajo con una profesión.

1. actuar, el teatro
2. los animales, las ciencias naturales
3. cuidar y proteger a la gente
4. los libros, escribir
5. las leyes, las ciencias sociales

a. policía
b. escritor(a)
c. abogado(a)
d. veterinario(a)
e. actor, actriz

❷ Con tu compañero(a), habla de qué cualidades o estudios se necesitan para trabajar en las profesiones de las listas en el *Vocabulario*.

Modelo
investigar / científico(a)
Si te gusta investigar, puedes ser científico.

246 doscientos cuarenta y seis
A ver si recuerdas . . .

Block Schedule

Extend *Actividad* 1 by asking students to write clues or associations for ten additional jobs. Have them read the list to a partner who will try to guess the job being described.

246

DIFFERENTIATED INSTRUCTION

Multiple Intelligences

Bodily/Kinesthetic: Have students play a game of charades in which they physically act out the movements associated with different professions. After the professions have been identified, have all students review by performing the actions while repeating the vocabulary.

Advanced Learners

Have students choose one profession from the *Vocabulario* and prepare a brief oral presentation telling what a person in that profession does, where he or she works, and what skills and studies he or she needs.

Gramática Repaso

Saber vs. conocer

Both *saber* and *conocer* mean "to know."

You use *saber* to talk about knowing facts or information.

Nadie **sabe** la fecha del examen. ¿**Saben** Uds. quién es ese actor?

Saber followed by an infinitive means "to know how to do something."

Por supuesto, yo **sé usar** la computadora. No, mi hermanito no **sabe manejar**.

Conocer means "to know" in the sense of being acquainted or familiar with a person, place, or thing.

Conocemos al Dr. Fernández y a toda su familia. ¿**Conocen** Uds. el jardín zoológico de Mérida?

In the preterite, *conocer* means "to meet someone for the first time."

Conocí a dos críticos que trabajan para el periódico. ¿Los **conociste** en la conferencia de ayer?

Más ayuda **realidades.com** ▶ **Tutorial**

▼2 ¿Qué debe saber?

Hablar

¿Qué es necesario saber hacer en cada profesión? Con tu compañero(a) escoge cuatro profesiones de la lista en la pág. 246. Túrnate con tu compañero(a) para decir qué se debe saber hacer en cada una.

Modelo
periodista
Un periodista debe saber escribir bien.

▼3 ¿Saber o conocer?

Hablar

Túrnate con tu compañero(a) para hacer y contestar preguntas usando *saber* y *conocer*.

▶ **Modelo**

el número de teléfono de (nombre) . . .
A —*¿Sabes el número de teléfono de Alex?*
B —*Sí, lo sé, es 555-1719. / No, no lo sé.*

- la fecha de hoy
- la respuesta
- al profesor (nombre)
- la Ciudad de México
- alguna canción en español
- montar en bicicleta
- alguna mujer de negocios
- a qué hora abre el museo

▼4 La fiesta

Leer • Escribir

Dos amigos hablan en una fiesta. Completa la conversación con el verbo *saber* o *conocer* según corresponda.

A —¿ **1.** quién es esa señora?

B —Es la doctora Rubio. Yo **2.** a sus hijos. Los **3.** el año pasado.

A —¿De veras? ¿Dónde los **4.** ?

B —En la universidad. Ellos **5.** a mi amiga Elena.

A —¿Elena Peña? Yo también la **6.** .

doscientos cuarenta y siete 247
Capítulo 6

ENRICH YOUR TEACHING

Teacher-to-Teacher

Always have a few review targets ready, and use creative ways—informal questions or comments—to elicit them from students as they walk in the door each day. You don't need to do this with all students. One or two comments or questions a day, to different students each time, will have them thinking in Spanish as they come into your classroom.

Recycle **6**

Gramática Repaso
Core Instruction

Standards: 1.4

Resources: Voc. and Gram. Transparency 117

Suggestions: Refer students who are having difficulty with *saber* and *conocer* to the *GramActiva* video from Level 2 Chapter 1B and the online tutorial. Call out words or phrases and have students associate them with the correct verb.

Teacher: *la dirección*
Student: *saber*

▼2 Standards: 1.1

Focus: Reviewing *saber* + infinitive

Suggestions: Encourage students to say more than one thing a person needs to know how to do for each profession.

Answers will vary.

▼3 Standards: 1.1

Resources: Answer Keys: Student Edition, p. 75

Focus: Reviewing *saber* vs. *conocer*

Suggestions: Remind students that Student A's question tells Student B which verb to use.

Answers:

saber	saber
saber	saber
conocer	conocer
conocer	saber

▼4 Standards: 1.3

Resources: Answer Keys: Student Edition, p. 75

Focus: Reviewing *saber* vs. *conocer*

Suggestions: Remind students to make each verb agree in person and number with the subject, and to watch for correct use of tense.

Answers:

1. **Sabes**	4. **conociste**
2. **conozco**	5. **conocen**
3. **conocí**	6. **conozco**

6 Recycle

Vocabulario [Repaso]

Core Instruction

Standards: 1.1, 1.2

Resources: Voc. and Gram. Transparency 118

Suggestions: Ask students to create sentences that use items from at least two of the categories in the *Vocabulario*. For example: *Me gusta mi computadora portátil porque la puedo llevar conmigo y trabajar en casa o en la escuela.*

5 Standards: 1.1, 1.3

Focus: Practicing review vocabulary

Suggestions: As students share their sentences, encourage them to elaborate on each other's comments.

Answers will vary.

Extension: Ask students to say what changes they have made in their personal lives due to the changes in their community: *He tenido que cambiar mi rutina de la mañana. Hoy día es necesario que salga más temprano.*

6 Standards: 1.1

Focus: Practicing review vocabulary

Suggestions: Point out to students that *había* remains singular, even if they are referring to plural objects: *... no había videos.*

Answers will vary.

Vocabulario Repaso

la tecnología

la computadora
la computadora portátil
el correo electrónico
el disco compacto
la página Web
la Red
el salón de chat
el televisor
el video

la ciudad

el apartamento
el barrio
la calle
la casa
la comunidad
el edificio de apartamentos
la gente
el tráfico

el medio ambiente

el agua
el aire
los animales
limpio, -a
la naturaleza
puro, -a
sucio, -a

acciones

beneficiar
cambiar
construir
crear
darse cuenta de
eliminar
mejorar
obtener
preocuparse
proteger
realizar
tener lugar

para comparar

ahora
antes
desafortunadamente
hace . . . que
hasta
más . . . (que)
mejor
menos . . . (que)
peor
pero

▼5 Cambios en mi barrio | 👥

Escribir • Hablar

Haz una lista de cuatro cosas que hayan cambiado en tu barrio o comunidad en los últimos años. Luego escribe frases comparando cómo son las cosas ahora y cómo eran antes. Usa las palabras de la lista. Comparte tus frases con un(a) compañero(a).

Modelo

tráfico

El tráfico en mi comunidad es ahora peor que antes porque hay más gente que vive en el barrio.

▼6 En el pasado | 👥

Hablar

Túrnate con un(a) compañero(a) para decir qué había o no había en los períodos de tiempo indicados. Usen las palabras o expresiones de las listas.

Modelo

Hace 50 años . . .

Hace 50 años había televisión pero no había discos compactos.

1. Hace 40 años . . .
2. En 1975 . . .
3. El año pasado . . .
4. Hace 10 años . . .
5. En 1930 . . .
6. Hace 20 años . . .

248 doscientos cuarenta y ocho
A ver si recuerdas . . .

DIFFERENTIATED INSTRUCTION

Heritage Language Learners

Ask students who have lived in a heritage country to discuss changes that have taken place there as well as in their current community. Have them predict future changes.

Students with Learning Difficulties

Help students organize their sentence ideas for *Actividad* 5. On a piece of paper, have them label two columns *antes* and *ahora.* Ask them to write a simple sentence in each column. Then guide them to connect the two ideas into a complex sentence.

Gramática Repaso

El *se* impersonal

In English you often use *they, you, one,* or *people* in an impersonal or an indefinite sense meaning "people in general." In Spanish you use *se* + the *Ud. /él /ella* or the *Uds. /ellos /ellas* form of the verb.

Se habla español.   **Se** venden computadoras baratas.

• Note that you don't know who performs the action. The word that follows the verb determines whether the verb is singular or plural.

Se creó una página web.   **Se crearon** páginas web.

• When the word following the conjugated verb is an infinitive, the verb form is singular.

Se necesita construir un nuevo edificio.

Más ayuda	realidades.com	▶Tutorial

▼7 Lugares y actividades |

Hablar

Trabaja con otro(a) estudiante para hacer la pregunta *¿Dónde . . . ?* y contestarla. Luego inventen y contesten tres preguntas más con *¿Dónde?*

 **Modelo**

escribir reseñas

A —*¿Dónde se escriben reseñas?*
B —*En el periódico se escriben reseñas.*

1. ver mucha gente tomando el sol
2. no permitir sacar fotos
3. vender ropa barata
4. poder esquiar
5. comer muy bien
6. ¡Respuesta personal!

▼8 En el periódico

Escribir

Trabajas en la sección de anuncios clasificados de un periódico. En una hoja aparte escribe títulos para anuncios usando los siguientes verbos y las palabras de abajo. Recuerda que si la palabra que va después del verbo es plural el verbo debe ir en plural.

vender	reparar	alquilar
necesitar	buscar	comprar

1. un coche
2. computadoras
3. apartamento nuevo
4. personas con experiencia
5. bicicletas usadas
6. joven cortés
7. casas viejas
8. videos y discos compactos

Más práctica	GO

realidades.com | print

A ver si recuerdas with Study Plan	✔	
Guided WB pp. 176–179	✔	✔
Core WB pp. 77–78	✔	✔
Hispanohablantes **WB** p. 172		✔

doscientos cuarenta y nueve **249**
Capítulo 6

ENRICH YOUR TEACHING

Teacher-to-Teacher

As an extension of *Actividad* 8, bring in and photocopy a page from the classified section of a Spanish-language newspaper. Before making copies, scan the ads to make sure no unwanted topics or language are present. Ask students to find examples of the use of the impersonal *se.*

21st Century Skills

Initiative and Self-Direction Direct students to the online tutorials for self-directed review of the grammar topics recycled in this chapter. Students can expand their own learning by reviewing the related English grammar first then proceed to the new Spanish grammar point. Each tutorial is followed by a quick comprehension check.

Gramática

Core Instruction

Standards: 4.1

Resources: Voc. and Gram. Transparency 119

Suggestions: Refer students who are having difficulty with the impersonal *se* to the *GramActiva* video from Level 2 Chapter 7A and the online tutorial. Explain that in most cases the *se* construction can also be compared to the English passive voice. Provide examples, such as "Spanish is spoken here." (*Aquí se habla español.*)

▼7 Standards: 1.1

Resources: Answer Keys: Student Edition, p. 76

Focus: Reviewing impersonal constructions

Common Errors: Students may treat the word **gente** as plural. Remind them that **gente** is always singular and takes singular forms of verbs, adjectives, and articles: *La gente está tomando el sol.*

Answers:

Student B's answers will vary. Student A's questions will use the following verb forms:

1. se ve
2. no se permite
3. se vende
4. se puede
5. se come
6. Answers will vary.

▼8 Standards: 1.3

Resources: Answer Keys: Student Edition, p. 76

Focus: Reviewing impersonal constructions

Suggestions: Remind students that, as in English, Spanish ad titles often omit smaller function words, such as articles.

Answers will vary, but may include:

1. Se vende coche.
2. Se reparan computadoras.
3. Se alquila apartamento nuevo.
4. Se buscan personas con experiencia.
5. Se compran bicicletas usadas.
6. Se necesita joven cortés.
7. Se reparan casas viejas.
8. Se venden videos y discos compactos.

✓ASSESSMENT

A ver si recuerdas with Study Plan (online only)

After reviewing the material on these pages, assign the *A ver si recuerdas* Study Plan to evaluate students' mastery of the material. Additional practice is available online.

Standards for Foreign Language Learning:
Capítulo 6

• To meet the Standards, students will:

Communication

1.1 Interpersonal
• Talk about careers and professions
• Talk about virtual and physical communities
• Talk about past, present, and future changes
• Talk about lifestyles of Spanish youth
• Talk about educational organizations

1.2 Interpretive
• Read and listen to information about careers and professions and necessary qualities for them
• Read about virtual and physical communities
• Read and listen about past, present, future changes
• Read about lifestyles of Spanish youth
• Read about educational organizations
• Read about word families in the world of professions
• Read poetry by Bécquer and fiction by Balzarino
• Read about online Spanish-language newspapers
• Read about speech preparation and compare and contrast essays

1.3 Presentational
• Write and present information orally about careers and professions and necessary qualities for them
• Write and present information orally about past, present, and future changes
• Recite poetry by Gustavo Adolfo Bécquer

Culture

2.1 Practices and Perspectives
• Explain the lifestyles of Spanish youth
• Explain the work of educational organizations
• Explain the readership of online newspapers
• Explain the changing roles of Mexican television
• Explain the perspectives of Spanish-speaking architects

2.2 Products and Perspectives
• Discuss the poetry of Bécquer and fiction of Balzarino
• Discuss the products of Spanish-speaking architects

Connections

3.1 Cross-curricular
• Discuss key facts about Spanish youth
• Discuss key facts about educational organizations
• Discuss key facts about the poetry of Gustavo Adolfo Bécquer and the fiction of Ángel Balzarino
• Discuss employment demographics and futurology
• Discuss Spanish speakers' use of the Internet and T.V.
• Discuss key facts about architecture
• Use Language Arts Strategies: circumlocution, compare and contrast, mapping your speech using main idea and details, coping with unknown words

3.2 Target Culture
• Read a university workshop announcement
• Read poetry by Bécquer and fiction by Balzarino

Comparisons

4.1 Language
• Compare impersonal *se* to the passive in English
• Compare Spanish and English future tenses
• Compare Spanish words to their English counterparts

4.2 Culture
• Compare lifestyles of young people in Spain and U. S.
• Compare the roles of T. V. in Mexico and the U. S.
• Compare distance education in Puerto Rico and U. S.

▼ Chapter Objectives

Communication

By the end of the chapter you will be able to:
• Listen and read about future plans and predictions
• Talk and write about future problems and advances
• Explain your career goals for the future

Culture

You will also be able to:
• Understand how architects from the Hispanic world are shaping the architecture of the future
• Compare the living situations of many Spanish college graduates with those of graduates in the U.S.

You will demonstrate what you know and can do:
• Presentación oral, p. 281
• Presentación escrita, pp. 282–283
• Preparación para el examen, pp. 290–291

You will use:

Vocabulary	Grammar
• Professions and careers	• Future
• Personal qualities	• Future of probability
• Future ideas and actions	• Future perfect tense
• Careers of the future	• Uses of the direct and indirect pronouns

Exploración del mundo hispano

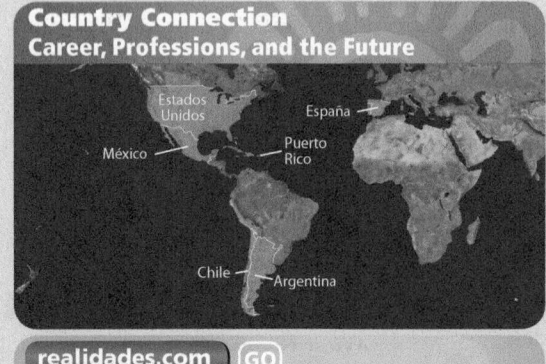

Country Connection
Career, Professions, and the Future

Estados Unidos
España
México
Puerto Rico
Chile
Argentina

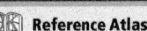
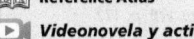

realidades.com **GO**

📖 Reference Atlas
▶ Videonovela y actividades
🌐 **Mapa global interactivo**

250 doscientos cincuenta

ENRICH YOUR TEACHING

Using Backward Design
Have students preview the sample performance tasks on *Preparación para el examen*, p. 291, and connect them to the Chapter Objectives. Explain to students that by completing the sample tasks they can self-assess their learning progress.

Mapa global interactivo
Download the *Mapa global interactivo* files for Chapter 6 and preview the activity. In this activity, you will look at some of the tallest buildings in Mexico City.

El Metropol Parasol
en Sevilla, España

Standards (cont'd)

Communities

5.1 Beyond the School
- Link to Web sites from the Spanish-speaking world
- Describe strategies for obtaining employment and keeping up with employment trends
- Discuss distance education and study abroad

5.2 Lifelong Learner
- Discuss important facts about going to college
- Prepare for the future
- Develop an appreciation for poetry and fiction

 **PresentationExpress™**
See pp. 246c–246d

Chapter Opener
Core Instruction

Resources: Map Transparencies, 14, 16, 18, 20, 22

Suggestions: Introduce students to the chapter theme and objectives.

▶ **Videonovela ¡Pura vida!** View this stand-alone storyline video about five young adults in San José, Costa Rica with your class, either online or on DVD.

Arte y cultura

Standards: 1.1, 1.2, 2.2, 3.1

Resources: Fine Art Transparencies with Teacher's Guide, p. 38

Suggestions: Ask comprehension questions. For example: *¿Qué artistas tuvieron una gran influencia en la obra de Matta?*

Answers will vary but may include Dalí and Picasso.

▶ **TEACHING WITH ART**

Resources: Fine Art Transparencies with Teacher's Guide, p. 38

Arte y cultura | Chile

Matta y el surrealismo El surrealismo fue un movimiento literario y artístico muy importante de la primera mitad *(half)* del siglo XX. Entre sus artistas principales se destaca el pintor chileno Roberto Matta (1911–2002). Matta vivió la mayor parte de su vida en Europa y los Estados Unidos, y sus influencias más importantes fueron Dalí y Picasso. Sus obras se caracterizan por el uso de figuras abstractas, el espacio, la transparencia, el movimiento, la energía y los colores brillantes *(bright)*. Este cuadro es un ejemplo de la pintura surrealista.

- ¿Cómo crees que se diferencia el realismo del surrealismo en la pintura?

"L'Étang de No", (1958), Roberto Matta ▶

L'Étang de No (1958) by Roberto Matta-Echaurren/© Artists Rights Society (ARS), New York/ADAGP, Paris/Musée national d'art moderne, Centre Georges Pompidou/Photo Credit: CNAC/MNAM/Dist. Réunion des Musées Nationaux/Art Resource, NY.

doscientos cincuenta y uno **251**
Capítulo 6

DIFFERENTIATED INSTRUCTION

Digital resources such as the *Interactive Whiteboard* activity banks, *Videomodelos*, additional *Online Activities, Study Plans*, automatically graded *Leveled Workbook*, animated *Grammar Tutorials, Flashcards*, and *Vocabulary and Grammar Videos* will help you reach students of different ability levels and learning styles.

STUDENTS NEEDING EXTRA HELP

Guided Practice Activities
- Flashcards, pp. 180–184, 193–196
- Vocabulary Check, pp. 185–188, 197–200
- Grammar, pp. 189–192, 201–204

HERITAGE LEARNERS

Realidades para hispanohablantes
- Chapter Opener, pp. 172–173
- A primera vista, pp. 174–175, 184–185
- Manos a la obra, pp. 176–184, 186–193
- ¡Adelante!, pp. 194–199
- Repaso del capítulo, pp. 200–203

ADVANCED/PRE-AP*

Pre-AP* Resource Book,
- pp. 153–155

Communications Workbook
- Integrated Performance Assessment, p. 197

Vocabulario en contexto

Core Instruction

Standards: 1.1, 1.2, 5.1

Resources: Teacher's Resource Book: Input Script, p. 66, Clip Art, pp. 84–93, Audio Script, p. 70; Voc. and Gram. Transparencies 120–121; Audio Program DVD: Cap. 6, Tracks 1, 3

Focus: Presenting new vocabulary and using grammar lexically in context

Suggestions: Show *Vocabulary and Grammar Transparencies* 120–121. Say the names of visualized vocabulary items, have students repeat, and ask volunteers to point to the appropriate image on the transparency. For non-visualized vocabulary such as **diseñar, cuidadoso(a),** and **eficiente,** give an explanation and ask students to identify the vocabulary item explained: *Una persona que hace su trabajo con mucho cuidado es una persona … (cuidadosa).*

BELLRINGER REVIEW

Have students choose a word to complete these sentences from the board:
1) *El _____ (dependiente/bombero) ayudó a las víctimas de un incendio.*

2) *Mi padre era _____ (mecánico/gerente) en el almacén El Corte Inglés.*

3) *El _____ (paramédico/agricultor) investigó nuevos métodos de cultivar el maíz.*

4) *La _____ (política/cajera) anunció su plan para reducir el uso de gasolina en la ciudad.*

5) *Espero al _____ (cartero/crítico) que me va a traer el paquete de mis abuelos.*

Block Schedule

Have students work in pairs to draw two illustrations similar to the photos on these pages to represent two additional jobs. Have one pair of students exchange drawings with another group. Each group will write a description for the illustrations using the descriptions on these two pages as models. Have the pairs then read their descriptions to each other.

Vocabulario en contexto

¿Qué planes tienes para el futuro? **Te graduarás de la escuela secundaria** y, ¿qué harás después? En poco tiempo **tomarás decisiones** muy importantes.

Será bueno que hables con un(a) consejero(a), con tus padres o con otras personas sobre este tema. Ellos te pueden ayudar a ver qué profesiones se relacionan con tus intereses y habilidades.

el programa

el científico

3 Te gustan las computadoras. Te gusta resolver problemas y buscar soluciones porque eres emprendedor.

2 Te interesan las finanzas y el dinero. Los hombres y mujeres de negocios confían en ti porque eres honesto e inteligente.

el banquero

la mujer de negocios

1 Te gusta hacer investigaciones científicas en el laboratorio. Eres ordenado y **cuidadoso.** Te importan mucho los detalles.

el hombre de negocios

DIFFERENTIATED INSTRUCTION

Students with Learning Difficulties

Using note cards, have students write words associated with each profession. Tell them not to write the names of the professions. Shuffle the cards and read them aloud. Have students identify the profession associated with each word they hear. Remind them that some words might pertain to more than one profession.

Advanced Learners

Ask students to talk about a person they know whose profession is one of those in the *Vocabulario.* Have them tell the person's profession, some of the activities he or she does, and at least one quality necessary for that type of work.

el redactor

el diseñador

4 Te es fácil escribir y eres cuidadoso. **Además de** escribir, eres **capaz** de leer el trabajo de otros escritores y hacer correcciones.

5 Te interesa la moda y eres capaz de **diseñar** ropa nueva y original. Tienes mucho talento artístico.

la jueza

la abogada

el abogado

el cocinero

6 Te encanta leer sobre la ley. Eres una persona justa y te importan los derechos de los ciudadanos.

7 Te gusta mucho cocinar, eres **eficiente** y algo artístico.

▼1 ¿Con quién debo hablar? | 👥 | 🔊

Escuchar • Escribir • Hablar

1 En una hoja, escribe los números del 1 al 7. Después, escucha lo que necesitan las personas y escribe con qué profesional necesitan hablar.

2 Escribe dos cualidades que se necesitan para cada una de las profesiones que escribiste. Compara tu lista con la de otro(a) estudiante.

doscientos cincuenta y tres 253
Capítulo 6

---

1 Standards: 1.2

Resources: Voc. and Gram. Transparencies 120–121; Teacher's Resource Book: Audio Script, p. 70; Audio Program DVD: Cap. 6, Track 2; Answer Keys: Student Edition, p. 77

Focus: Practicing listening comprehension of new vocabulary

Suggestions: Remind students to listen for key words that will help them determine the answers. Use the audio or read the script. Allow students to listen more than once.

Answers:

Step 1
1. el (la) abogado(a)
2. el (la) banquero(a)
3. el (la) redactor(a)
4. el (la) diseñador(a)
5. el (la) programador(a)
6. el (la) científico(a)
7. el (la) cocinero(a)

Step 2
Answers will vary.

Teacher-to-Teacher

Have pairs of students engage in a written exchange in which they describe their preferred professions and the reasons for their preference.

ENRICH YOUR TEACHING

Culture Note

One of the world's most renowned fashion designers, Oscar de la Renta, is a Spanish speaker. He was born in Santo Domingo, Dominican Republic. As a young man, he left home to study painting in Madrid. There, he started his career in design by drawing for fashion houses. De la Renta worked with accomplished designers in Paris before establishing himself at Elizabeth Arden in New York City. In 1965, de la Renta started his own company, known for fashions, accessories, and fragrances.

Vocabulario en contexto

Core Instruction

Standards: 1.2

Resources: Teacher's Resource Book: Input Script, p. 67, Clip Art, pp. 84–93, Audio Script, pp. 70–71; Voc. and Gram. Transparencies 122–123; Audio Program DVD: Cap. 6, Track 3

Focus: Extending presentation of vocabulary and grammar

Suggestions:

Pre-reading: Have students look at the photos and predict the content of each interview.

Reading: Allow students time to read the interviews silently first. Then play the audio or read the interviews aloud, with students reading along as they listen. Allow them to listen more than once. Another option after silent reading is to have volunteers take turns reading each interview aloud, playing the roles of the two speakers.

Post-reading: To clarify the meaning of new vocabulary, provide synonyms and alternative meanings and ask students to tell which vocabulary item you are talking about: *¿Qué expresión quiere decir "vamos a vivir en otra casa"?* **(nos mudaremos)**

Pre-AP* Support

- **Learning Objective:** Interpretive: Print and Audio
- **Activity:** Have students read the captions on pp. 252–253 the night before. In class the next day, read only a portion of each caption as a dictation. After the students finish writing, point out the selections that you read in the book and have students correct their answers.
- **Pre-AP* Resource Book:** Comprehensive guide to Pre-AP* vocabulary skill development, pp. 51–57

Los estudiantes hablan de su futuro

Estela Pérez

Manolo Sánchez

1 —¿Seguirás estudiando después de terminar la escuela secundaria?

—¡Sí, por supuesto! Para mí lo más importante es tener una buena educación. Soy **ambiciosa**, quiero ganar un buen salario, **así que** estudiaré finanzas. Buscaré trabajo y poco a poco **lograré** conseguir un puesto como directora o **jefa** de una oficina.

—Tu hermana quiere **seguir una carrera** similar, ¿no?

—Sí, ella quiere ser **contadora**. Es muy buena con los números. ¡Ya se encarga del dinero de la familia!

2 —¿Qué harás en cinco años?

—Me gustan los coches, así que **me dedicaré** a la mecánica. Quisiera ser dueño de un taller mecánico. Así no tendré otro jefe y **haré lo que me dé la gana**.

—¿Crees que te quedarás en casa con tus padres?

—Eso depende. Si estoy **casado**, mi esposa y yo **nos mudaremos** a una casa. Si estoy **soltero**, es posible que me quede con mis padres.

Ana María Sosa López

3 —¿Qué harás después de graduarte? Sabemos que eres bilingüe y que has hecho traducciones aquí en la escuela. ¿Serás **traductora**?

—Sí, me gusta **traducir** pero lo que más me interesa es viajar. **Por lo tanto** quiero **desempeñar un cargo** de traductora en **una empresa** que tenga oficinas en varios países.

—¿Te gustará vivir en otro país?

—Sí, porque realizaré mi sueño *(dream)* de viajar y conocer el mundo.

DIFFERENTIATED INSTRUCTION

Heritage Language Learners
Ask students if any of them have considered a career that would utilize their language skills. Some examples might include translator, court interpreter, teacher, international business person, or diplomat. Ask them to share the stories of people they know who utilize two or more languages on the job.

Students with Learning Difficulties
After students have read the interviews, ask them to identify just the questions by pointing to them in the text. Then ask students to provide personal responses to the questions.

Francisco Gómez Durán

Belinda Domínguez

(4) —El consejero te dijo que eres **maduro** y estudioso . . . y sé que te gustan las matemáticas. ¿**Te harás** banquero?

—No. Siempre me han fascinado los castillos históricos y también los edificios modernos. Algún día quiero ser **arquitecto** o **ingeniero.**

—¿De veras? ¿A qué universidad irás el año **próximo**?

—No lo sé todavía. Tengo que investigar para **averiguar** qué universidades ofrecen esas carreras y qué requisitos piden.

(5) —¿Qué crees que harás al terminar la escuela?

—Buscaré empleo. Necesito trabajar un poco y **ahorrar** antes de estudiar.

—¿Para qué estudiarás?

—Estudiaré para ser **peluquera** en un salón de belleza.

▼2 Lo que quieren ser

Leer • Escribir

Escribe la palabra o las palabras que sean necesarias para completar las siguientes frases según lo que dijeron los estudiantes.

1. Estela es _____ y quiere ser _____. Estudiará _____.

2. Manolo se dedicará a la _____. Quiere ser el _____ de un taller mecánico.

3. Ana es _____. Quiere desempeñar un cargo de _____. Su sueño es _____.

4. Francisco es _____ y _____. Dice que será _____ o _____.

5. Belinda buscará _____. Después estudiará para ser _____.

▼3 Planes para el futuro | 🔊

Escuchar

En una hoja escribe los números del 1 al 5. Después, escucha lo que dicen las personas y escribe si es lógico o ilógico. Corrige las oraciones ilógicas.

Más práctica	GO
realidades.com	print

Instant Check	✔	
Guided WB pp. 180–188	✔	✔
Core WB pp. 79–80	✔	✔
Comm. WB p. 82	✔	✔
Hispanohablantes **WB** pp. 174–175	✔	

doscientos cincuenta y cinco **255**
Capítulo 6

Language Input 6

▼**2** Standards: 1.2

Resources: Answer Keys: Student Edition, p. 77

Focus: Writing to demonstrate reading comprehension of new vocabulary

Suggestions: Point out that the sentences in the activity are about the students interviewed. Students can find the answers to each item by referring to the appropriate interview.

Answers:

1. ambiciosa/jefa (directora)/finanzas
2. mecánica/dueño
3. bilingüe/traductora/viajar y conocer el mundo
4. maduro/estudioso/arquitecto/ingeniero
5. empleo/peluquera

▼**3** Standards: 1.2

Resources: Voc. and Gram. Transparencies 122–123; Teacher's Resource Book: Audio Script, p. 71; Audio Program DVD: Cap. 6, Track 4; Answer Keys: Student Edition, p. 77

Focus: Demonstrating listening comprehension of new vocabulary

Suggestions: Point out that there may be more than one way for students to correct the illogical sentences.

Answers:

1. ilógico. Por eso voy a ser mecánico.
2. ilógico. Quiero estar soltera./Por eso me casaré.
3. lógico
4. lógico
5. ilógico. Así que me dedicaré a la medicina.

Chapter Project

Give students copies of the Chapter Project outline and rubric from the Teacher's Resource Book. Explain the task to them, and have them perform Step 1. (For more information, see p. 246-b.)

ENRICH YOUR TEACHING

Culture Note

Traditionally, a workday in Spain or Mexico contained a two-to-three-hour midday break for lunch and *siesta.* Today, multinational corporations are influencing this daily routine. Many firms have adopted a so-called *horario americano,* which resembles the nine-to-five schedule of the United States.

21st Century Skills

Technology Literacy Have students research on the Internet one of the careers mentioned on pp. 254–255. What courses and certifications would be needed to become a professional in those fields? What institutions in their area would provide the necessary training? Have students report their findings to the class.

✓ASSESSMENT

Prueba: Comprensión del vocabulario 1
• Prueba 6-1: pp. 127–128

255

6 Practice and Communicate

Vocabulario en uso

🖥 **INTERACTIVE WHITEBOARD**
Vocabulary Activities 6-1

4 Standards: 1.1, 1.2

Resources: Teacher's Resource Book: Audio Script, p. 71; Audio Program DVD: Cap. 6, Track 5; Answer Keys: Student Edition, p. 78

Focus: Practicing listening comprehension of new vocabulary

Suggestions: Remind students that some of the ads they will hear are missing definite and indefinite articles. Have them listen to the audio more than once.

Answers:

1. jefe; persona madura, con experiencia
2. peluquero; capaz de trabajar rápido, amable y sociable
3. redactor; con experiencia, emprendedor y responsable, capaz de trabajar en equipo
4. cocinero; eficiente y creativo

▼4 Las cualidades necesarias | 👥 | 🔊

Escuchar • Escribir • Hablar

En una hoja, escribe los números del 1 al 4. Escucha los anuncios clasificados y escribe la profesión y la cualidad o las cualidades que se necesitan para cada trabajo. Compara tu lista con la de otro(a) estudiante.

▼5 Los 17 años

Leer

A los 17 años, los jóvenes también tienen nuevas responsabilidades y problemas. Completa lo que dicen estos dos amigos sobre esta edad.

por lo tanto	casado(a)	soltero(a)	además de	próximo

—¿Sabes a qué universidad vas a asistir el año ___1.___, Roberto?

—No lo sé todavía, Luisa. ___2.___ la Universidad San Ignacio, he escrito a cuatro universidades. Todas están lejos de aquí, ___3.___ sé que voy a tener que mudarme.

—Me dicen que en San Ignacio te ayudan a alquilar apartamento si estás ___4.___ porque reconocen que es más difícil para dos personas.

—Pues a mí no me importa eso. Voy a estar ___5.___ hasta cumplir los 30 años.

—¡Yo también!

5 Standards: 1.2

Resources: Answer Keys: Student Edition, p. 78

Focus: Practicing new vocabulary in a cloze exercise

Suggestions: Have students review the vocabulary on pp. 252–255 before completing the activity.

Answers:

1. próximo
2. Además de
3. por lo tanto
4. casado
5. soltero

▼6 ¿Cómo se dice? |  👥 | ♻

Escribir • Hablar

❶ Imagina que te olvidaste de estas palabras. Escribe frases que quieran decir lo mismo.

Modelo
responsable
persona que es capaz de tomar decisiones y desempeñar un cargo

1. amable
2. emprendedor
3. ambicioso
4. honesto
5. capaz
6. maduro
7. cuidadoso
8. puntual

Estrategia

Circumlocution
When you can't remember or don't know a word, you can use circumlocution to describe or exemplify it without naming it (e.g., *the thing you open a door with* for *doorknob*).

❷ Con otro(a) estudiante, decidan qué características deben tener los siguientes profesionales: ingeniero(a), contador(a), hombre / mujer de negocios, mecánico(a), peluquero(a).

6 Standards: 1.1, 1.3, 3.1

Focus: Practicing new vocabulary in a paired matching activity

Recycle: adjectives describing personality

Suggestions: Refer students to the *Estrategia*. Remind them that you often use circumlocution when introducing new vocabulary to the class.

Answers will vary.

DIFFERENTIATED INSTRUCTION

Heritage Language Learners

In addition to definitions, have students brainstorm synonyms for the adjectives in *Actividad* 6. For example: *amable/simpático(a); capaz/talentoso(a).* Invite students to share their synonyms with the class.

Advanced Learners

Ask students to write their own classified ad. In it, they should name the position they are trying to fill and briefly describe the qualities of an ideal candidate.

7 ¿Qué quieres ser?

Hablar

Con un(a) compañero(a) hablen sobre los trabajos que les gustaría o no tener algún día.

▶ Modelo

A —¿Te gustaría ser banquero?

B —Sí, porque *me fascinan los números* y *soy muy cuidadoso.*

o: —¿Yo? ¡Qué va! *No me interesan nada los números.*

Estudiante A

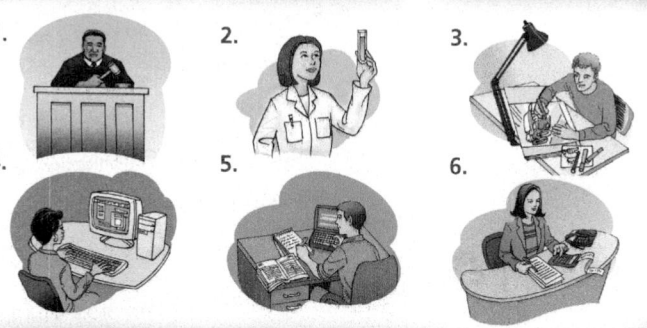

1.
2.
3.
4.
5.
6.

Estudiante B

organizado(a)
eficiente
responsable
creativo(a)
capaz
amable
ambicioso(a)
emprendedor(a)

¡Respuesta personal!

Practice and Communicate 6

7 Standards: 1.1

Resources: Answer Keys: Student Edition, p. 78

Focus: Using new vocabulary and structures in guided dialogues

Suggestions: Encourage students to switch roles and to read each dialogue more than once. Student B's response should be different each time.

Answers will vary. Students will use the following vocabulary:

1. juez
2. científico(a)
3. diseñador(a)
4. programador(a)
5. redactor(a)
6. contador(a)

▼ Fondo Cultural | España

En casa de mamá Según un estudio del Instituto de la Juventud de España, el 75% de los jóvenes españoles menores de 30 años vive con sus padres. ¿Por qué vivirán tantos jóvenes españoles en casa de sus padres? El estudio dice que hay varias razones importantes. En España es bastante difícil para los jóvenes conseguir un empleo que les permita ganar el dinero necesario para vivir solos. Además, no es fácil conseguir una casa o un apartamento barato para mudarse.

Otras personas dicen que el problema es que los jóvenes no quieren tener responsabilidades y por eso prefieren vivir con sus padres. También hay personas que piensan que en la cultura española la familia y los padres son muy importantes para los jóvenes y por eso es difícil para ellos irse a vivir lejos de casa.

- Da dos razones para explicar por qué viven los jóvenes españoles con sus padres.

- ¿Crees que en los Estados Unidos la mayoría de los jóvenes menores de 30 años vive con sus padres? ¿Por qué?

- Compara la situación de los jóvenes españoles y los estadounidenses. ¿Qué tienen en común? ¿Cuál es la diferencia más importante que ves entre ellos?

Fondo cultural

Standards: 1.1, 1.2, 2.1, 3.1, 4.2

Suggestions: After students have read the information, ask: *¿Qué piensas de esta información? ¿A ti te gustaría vivir con tus padres tanto tiempo? ¿Cuáles son los beneficios posibles de este estilo de vida? ¿Cuáles son los puntos negativos?*

Answers:
Una razón es porque es difícil encontrar un empleo que les permita ganar el dinero necesario para vivir solos. Otra es que no es fácil conseguir una casa o un apartamento barato.

Other answers will vary.

BELLRINGER REVIEW

Have students unscramble these words for professions:

tarodnoc
equlupero
zujea
corenico
tordacre

(**Answers:** *contador, peluquero, jueza cocinero, redactor*)

ENRICH YOUR TEACHING

Culture Note

Children in Spain attend elementary school from ages 6 to 12 and secondary school from ages 12 to 16. After secondary school, students may either go on to one to two years of vocational study or complete the **bachillerato,** a two-year course that prepares them for university study.

Teacher-to-Teacher

When students do pair work, such as in *Actividad 7,* encourage them to work with a different partner each time, and avoid the habit of the same partners working together day after day. Working with new partners is a good strategy for keeping students on task.

8 Standards: 1.1, 1.2, 3.2

Resources: Answer Keys: Student Edition, p. 79

Focus: Practicing new vocabulary and structures through reading and response

Suggestions: Assist students as needed with the meaning of any unknown vocabulary.

Answers: Some answers may vary. The following are likely results:

1. Creación e introducción a la poesía argentina
2. Redacción asertiva
3. Expresión teatral
4. Negociación y debate
5. Comunicación persuasiva / Negociación y debate
6. Creación e introducción a la poesía argentina
7. Comunicación persuasiva
8. Danza contemporánea

BELLRINGER REVIEW

Item 3 in Step 2 of *Actividad 9* asks students to make recommendations for which they will need to use the subjunctive. Prepare them for this by asking them to make up sentences with *Es necesario que...* and the subjunctive.

9 Standards: 1.1, 1.2

Focus: Practicing new vocabulary and structures through discussion

Suggestions: Ask groups to appoint a spokesperson to report the results of their discussion to the class.

Answers will vary.

▼8 Talleres de verano |  | ♻

Leer • Hablar

Mira el anuncio sobre los talleres de verano. ¿A qué taller(es) van a asistir las personas que quieran seguir las siguientes carreras? Trabaja con un grupo de tres estudiantes para decidir. Expliquen sus respuestas.

1. escritor(a)   5. hombre / mujer de negocios
2. redactor(a)   6. poeta
3. actor / actriz   7. político(a)
4. abogado(a)   8. bailarín / bailarina

UNIVERSIDAD RODRIGO CABEZAS

DEPARTAMENTO DE ACTIVIDADES CULTURAL

FACULTAD DE HUMANIDADES

TALLERES DE VERANO

6 de diciembre al 12 de febrero

CREACIÓN E INTRODUCCIÓN A LA POESÍA ARGENTINA
Profesor: Fabián Díaz, poeta, doctor en Literatura Argentina

DANZA CONTEMPORÁNEA
Profesor: Lucía Suárez, bailarina y coreógrafa

EXPRESIÓN TEATRAL
Profesor: Javier Jiménez, actor y director

NEGOCIACIÓN Y DEBATE
Profesor: Oliverio Rojas, periodista, licenciado en Comunicación Social

REDACCIÓN ASERTIVA
Profesora: Sarah Vázquez, periodista

COMUNICACIÓN PERSUASIVA
Profesor: Ramón Santiago, actor y dramaturgo

Inscripciones e Informaciones hasta el 2 de diciembre en San Martín 301

▼9 Hablar sobre el trabajo |  | ♻

Leer • Hablar

1 La búsqueda de trabajo es un tema sobre el que todo el mundo tiene diferentes opiniones. Lee la siguiente encuesta *(survey)* que se hizo a un grupo de jóvenes sobre de qué depende encontrar un trabajo.

¿De qué depende encontrar un buen trabajo? ¿Y en segundo lugar?		
	Primer lugar (%)	Segundo lugar (%)
De estar bien preparado.	50	27
De tener buenas recomendaciones.	28	30
De la buena suerte.	16	23
De saber hablar bien.	3	11
De ser guapo(a).	2	7
No sé.	1	2

2 Trabaja con un grupo de estudiantes para hablar de la encuesta y responder a las siguientes preguntas.

1. ¿Están de acuerdo con los resultados de la encuesta? ¿Por qué? Traten de dar ejemplos de algunas personas que conocen.

2. ¿Pueden añadir alguna otra razón a la lista?

3. Si todas estas razones son ciertas, ¿qué recomendaciones pueden darle a una persona que quiera seguir una carrera o comenzar una nueva profesión?

DIFFERENTIATED INSTRUCTION

Multiple Intelligences

Logical/Mathematical: Have groups of students conduct their own polls on the topic of what it takes to find a good job. Have them record their data and present it in the form of a chart. Invite different groups to compare their results.

Students with Learning Difficulties

Distribute props or pictures associated with the professions listed in *Ampliación del lenguaje*. Ask students to say three simple sentences to accompany their props: *Yo soy cocinero(a). Yo cocino. Aquí está la cocina.* Redistribute props among male and female students, so they can practice both masculine and feminine endings.

▼10 Y tú, ¿qué dices? | 💬 _____

Escribir • Hablar

1. ¿A qué se dedican tus padres? ¿Vas a seguir la misma carrera? ¿Por qué?
2. ¿Cuál es el sueño que quieres realizar? ¿Qué quieres lograr en el futuro?
3. ¿Te gustaría mudarte a otra ciudad, otro estado u otro país? ¿Por qué?
4. Imagina que no necesitas ahorrar dinero. ¿A qué te gustaría dedicarte después de graduarte de la universidad?
5. ¿Qué carreras no te gustaría seguir? ¿Por qué?
6. ¿Qué te gustaría hacer con tu tiempo libre?
7. ¿Cuáles son las mayores responsabilidades que tienes a tu edad? ¿Y los problemas? ¿Qué quieres cambiar o lograr en el futuro?

▼ Ampliación del lenguaje

Profesiones

En español hay varios sufijos que indican profesión. Muchas palabras que terminan con los sufijos -or/-ora, -ero/-era, -ario/-aria nombran profesiones que tienen relación con los verbos o sustantivos de los que derivan.

Verbo	Sustantivo	Profesión
vender	venta	vendedor(a)
traducir	traducción	traductor(a)
escribir	escrito	escritor(a)
programar	programa	programador(a)
redactar	redacción	redactor(a)
dirigir	dirección	director(a)
diseñar	diseño	diseñador(a)
	biblioteca	bibliotecario(a)
	carta	cartero(a)
cocinar	cocina	cocinero(a)
	banco	banquero(a)

Lee las palabras de la tabla y escribe ocho frases en las que uses las profesiones y los verbos o sustantivos relacionados.

Modelo
vender / vendedor(a)
Un vendedor trabaja tratando de vender cosas a otras personas.

carta / cartero(a)
Mi tío es cartero. Entrega cartas en las casas y apartamentos de nuestra ciudad.

doscientos cincuenta y nueve **259**
Capítulo 6

Practice and Communicate 6

▼10 Standards: 1.1, 1.3
Focus: Practicing new vocabulary and structures
Suggestions: This activity is ideal as a homework assignment. Encourage students to take the questions seriously and sit in a quiet place to answer them, giving them careful thought. Then invite them to share their answers with the class during a subsequent session.
Answers will vary.

Ampliación del lenguaje
Core Instruction
Standards: 1.2, 1.3, 3.1, 4.1
Focus: Understanding suffixes in nouns that name professions
Suggestions: Ask students to use more than one variation of the word in the same sentence. Encourage them to make it clear from their sentences that they understand the meaning of each word.
Answers will vary.

Additional Resources
• Communication Wbk.: Audio Act. 1, p. 78
• Teacher's Resource Book: Audio Script, p. 71, Communicative Pair Activity BLM, pp. 77–78
• Audio Program DVD: Cap. 6, Track 6

ENRICH YOUR TEACHING

Teacher-to-Teacher
Regularly refer to and isolate word parts such as prefixes and suffixes, and ask students to do the same. Such attention to meaningful chunks of words is an excellent way for language learners to expand their vocabularies. Once students know that suffixes like those shown in the _Ampliación del lenguaje_ indicate professions, they can experiment with them on their own to build new words. Parallels can often be drawn between Spanish and English word parts. For example, the suffixes shown in the _Ampliación del lenguaje_ can be compared to English -er, as in "teacher" or "baker."

✓ASSESSMENT
Prueba 6-2 with Study Plan (online only)
Prueba: Aplicación del vocabulario 1
• Prueba 6-2: pp. 129–130

259

Gramática Repaso

| ▼ Objectives
▶ Discuss and write about plans for the future
▶ Discuss relationships with family and friends in the future

El futuro

You can express the future in Spanish in three ways: by using *ir* + *a* + infinitive, the present tense, or the future tense. In the future tense, all verbs have the same endings. For most verbs, attach the endings to the infinitive.

Here are the future tense forms of the regular verbs *pasar, comer,* and *pedir:*

pasaré	comeré	pediré
pasarás	comerás	pedirás
pasará	comerá	pedirá
pasaremos	comeremos	pediremos
pasaréis	comeréis	pediréis
pasarán	comerán	pedirán

Some verbs have irregular stems in the future tense. Note that their future endings (*-é, -ás, -á, -emos, -éis, -án*) are the same as those of regular verbs.

haber	→	habr-	
poder	→	podr-	
querer	→	querr-	-é
saber	→	sabr-	-ás
poner	→	pondr-	-á
salir	→	saldr-	-emos
tener	→	tendr-	-éis
venir	→	vendr-	-án
decir	→	dir-	
hacer	→	har-	

¿Cómo será la Tierra en 100 años?

Más ayuda | realidades.com | ▶ *Canción de hip hop* ▶ *Tutorials*

Core Instruction

Resources: Voc. and Gram. Transparency 124

INTERACTIVE WHITEBOARD
Grammar Activities 6-1

Suggestions: Ask students to take turns telling about their plans for next summer, using the future tense. If necessary, cue them with questions that elicit verbs of various kinds, including those with the irregular stems shown in the *Gramática.*

▼11 Standards: 1.2

Resources: Answer Keys: Student Edition, p. 80
Focus: Practicing the future tense in a cloze exercise
Suggestions: Remind students to first look over the entire paragraph about Lorena in order to get an idea of its meaning.
Answers:

1. haré	7. podré
2. iré	8. regresaré
3. realizaré	9. llamará
4. Estudiaré	10. diseñaré
5. pasaré	11. tendré
6. visitaré	12. disfrutarán

Extension: Conduct a question-and-answer session with students, using the completed activity as a base.
Teacher: *¿Qué decidió Lorena hoy?*
Student: *Decidió lo que hará el año próximo.*

Block Schedule

Have students work in pairs to practice the different irregular forms of the future. Have one student select an infinitive and then provide different subject pronouns. The partner has to quickly provide the correct verb conjugation. Switch roles with each verb.

▼11 Los sueños

Leer

Lorena escribe en su diario sobre sus experiencias y sueños para el futuro.
Completa este fragmento de su diario con el futuro de los verbos del recuadro.

poder	estudiar	hacer	visitar
pasar	realizar	ir	

disfrutar	regresar	tener	llamar
diseñar			

Hoy, después de regresar del parque, decidí lo que __1.__ el año próximo. Yo __2.__ a una universidad famosa y allí __3.__ mi sueño. __4.__ arquitectura. Después de estudiar, __5.__ unos años en Japón y __6.__ los parques más famosos. Así __7.__ aprender mucho.

Finalmente, __8.__ a este país para crear mi propia empresa. Se __9.__ "Parques y jardines de oriente" y yo __10.__ los jardines. Estoy segura de que __11.__ mucho éxito y muchas personas __12.__ de mis jardines y parques.

DIFFERENTIATED INSTRUCTION

Heritage Language Learners

Have students with exemplary pronunciation model the pronunciation of future verb forms. Ask them to be especially aware of the written accent on the last syllable on all but the *nosotros* forms, and have all students repeat.

Advanced Learners/Pre-AP*

Ask students to talk about habits they or someone they know used to have but now no longer engage in. For the old habit they use the imperfect tense, and for the change they use the future tense: *Antes solía charlar mucho en la cafetería. No charlaré más allí porque no tengo tiempo.*

Practice and Communicate 6

12 En el futuro

Hablar

¿Sabes lo que quieres hacer en el futuro? Pregúntale a otro(a) estudiante sobre sus planes. Después, intercambien papeles.

▶ Modelo

mudarse a otra ciudad para estudiar

A —¿*Te mudarás* a otra ciudad para estudiar en la universidad?

B —*No, iré a la universidad de mi ciudad.*

Estudiante A

1. seguir una carrera después de graduarse
2. dedicarse a hacer trabajo de voluntario
3. averiguar información sobre la carrera de ingeniería
4. ir a ver a un consejero
5. hacer lo que le dé la gana
6. tener un trabajo y ahorrar mucho dinero
7. estudiar finanzas en unos años
8. tomar decisiones importantes para una empresa

Estudiante B

¡Respuesta personal!

13 ¿Qué hará . . . ?

Leer • Escribir

Piensa en personas de tu escuela, familia, comunidad o programa de televisión favorito que correspondan a estas descripciones. ¿Qué harán en el futuro? Usa el futuro de los verbos del recuadro para escribir frases sobre lo que hará cada persona.

hacerse . . .	estudiar para ser . . .	trabajar como / en . . .
tener . . .	lograr ser . . .	mudarse a . . .
dedicarse a . . .	ser . . .	

Modelo
Pinta cuadros muy bonitos.
Santiago será un pintor famoso.

1. Le encanta arreglarles el pelo a sus amigas.
2. Le gusta planear y construir caminos y puentes.
3. Le gustan los animales.
4. Es cuidadoso(a) y escribe muy bien.
5. Le gustan las matemáticas.
6. Me fascina traducir textos.
7. Tiene mucho talento artístico.
8. Le interesan los negocios y las finanzas.

SERVICIOS MUNDIALES, S.A.

Isabela Ruiz
Contadora

Calle Flores, no.85
Caracas, Venezuela
iruiz@serviciosmundiales.ve
Tel: 224-6560
Fax: 224-6586
www.serviciosmundiales.ve

doscientos sesenta y uno **261**
Capítulo 6

ENRICH YOUR TEACHING

Teacher-to-Teacher

Young people are as interested in making New Year's resolutions as many adults. You can take advantage of this custom at any time of the year. An enjoyable way to help them practice using the future tense is to ask them to make a short list of resolutions for the coming week or month. At the end of the time period, check back with students to see whether they kept their resolutions, giving them an opportunity to review the past tenses.

---

12 Standards: 1.1

Resources: Answer Keys: Student Edition, p. 80

Focus: Practicing the future tense in guided dialogues

Suggestions: Point out to students that in the future tense, reflexive and object pronouns are placed in the same position in relation to the verb as they are in other tenses of conjugated verb forms.

Answers: Student B's responses will vary. Student A's questions will use the following verb forms:

1. **Seguirás**
2. **Te dedicarás**
3. **Averiguarás**
4. **Irás**
5. **Harás**
6. **Tendrás**
7. **Estudiarás**
8. **Tomarás**

13 Standards: 1.2, 1.3

Resources: Answer Keys: Student Edition, p. 81

Focus: Practicing the future tense by responding to questions

Suggestions: Tell students to demonstrate their comprehension of new vocabulary by making a logical connection between each cue and the future plans of their chosen person. Remind them that some of their sentences can be negative.

Answers will vary. Third-person, singular future forms of the verbs in the word bank are as follows:

se hará	logrará
tendrá	será
se dedicará	trabajará
estudiará	se mudará

Chapter Project

Students can perform Step 2 at this point. Be sure they understand your corrections and suggestions. (For more information, see p. 246-b.)

▼14 Standards: 1.1

Resources: Answer Keys: Student Edition, p. 81

Focus: Practicing the future tense

Suggestions: Ask Student B to think of real people and to provide an additional detail or two, as the model does.

Answers: Students A and B will use the following verb forms respectively:

1. se escribirán/nos escribiremos
2. asistirán/asistiremos
3. tendrán/tendremos
4. sabrán/sabremos
5. saldrán/saldremos
6. recordarán/recordaremos
7. se dedicarán/nos dedicaremos

▼15 Standards: 1.1, 1.3

Resources: Answer Keys: Student Edition, p. 82

Focus: Practicing the future tense

Suggestions: Tell students to use **nosotros** forms in the left column of the chart in Step 2. The right column will most likely contain a negative statement about one partner and an affirmative one about the other.

Answers: Students will use the following verb forms for Step 1:

me quedaré/me mudaré	viajaré
asistiré/encontraré	me casaré/seguiré
seguiré	tendré

Steps 2–3

Answers will vary.

Fondo cultural

Standards: 1.1, 1.2, 3.1

Suggestions: After students have read the information, ask: *¿Te gustaría trabajar en un programa como éste? ¿Trabajarás para el gobierno en el futuro?*

Answers will vary.

✓ASSESSMENT

Prueba 6-3 with Study Plan (online only)

Prueba: El futuro
• Prueba 6-3: p. 131

262

▼14 Después de . . . |

Hablar

Con un(a) compañero(a), hablen de cómo serán sus relaciones en el futuro usando las frases de abajo. Pueden hablar de sus relaciones con los amigos, la familia, o las personas de la escuela o de la comunidad.

▶ **Modelo**

verse cada semana

A —*En diez años, ¿tus amigos y tú se verán cada semana?*

B —*No, no nos veremos cada semana pero quizás cada mes.*

1. escribirse por correo electrónico
2. asistir a la misma universidad
3. tener mucho en común
4. saber dónde viven sus amigos de la escuela
5. salir juntos los fines de semana
6. recordar todo lo que pasó en la escuela secundaria
7. dedicarse a diferentes intereses

▼15 ¿Cómo será tu vida en el futuro?

Escribir • Hablar

❶ Escribe sobre tu futuro. Incluye la siguiente información:

• quedarse en la misma ciudad o mudarse
• asistir a la universidad o encontrar trabajo
• seguir una carrera
• viajar y adónde
• casarse o seguir soltero(a)
• tener hijos y cuántos

❷ Ahora, compara tus respuestas con las de un(a) compañero(a). Completen una tabla como la siguiente con las semejanzas y las diferencias.

SEMEJANZAS	DIFERENCIAS

❸ Usa la tabla para escribir un párrafo acerca de tu futuro y el futuro de tu compañero(a).

▼ Fondo Cultural | Estados Unidos

Jóvenes hispanohablantes en Washington El *Congressional Hispanic Caucus Institute,* CHCI, selecciona todos los años a unos 50 jóvenes para participar en su programa de pasantías[1]. Los seleccionados trabajan en Washington, D.C., disfrutando de las ventajas de poder observar al gobierno en acción. "CHCI se siente orgulloso de ofrecerles a los mejores representantes de la comunidad hispanohablante la oportunidad de crecer como líderes y miembros de dicha comunidad", dijo la presidenta del instituto, Esther Aguilera.

• ¿Por qué es importante para los estudiantes participar en un programa de pasantías?

_____

[1] internships

Más práctica GO

realidades.com | print

Instant Check	✔	
Guided WB pp. 189–191	✔	✔
Core WB p. 81	✔	✔
Comm. WB p. 83	✔	✔
Hispanohablantes WB pp. 176–180		✔

DIFFERENTIATED INSTRUCTION

Heritage Language Learners

In preparation for the *Gramática* on p. 263, ask students to prepare a short skit portraying a situation in which there is some element of doubt. Instruct them to use the future tense to express this uncertainty at least once in the dialogue. A possible theme might be *¿Dónde estará mi tarea para mañana?*

Students with Learning Difficulties

Before students begin *Actividad* 14, allow them time to make notes on the future forms of the verbs presented. Point out that they will be using the **Uds.** and **nosotros** forms. Give students similar time and guidance for *Actividad* 15.

Gramática

El futuro de probabilidad

In Spanish, you use the future tense to express uncertainty or probability in the present.

¿Qué hora será?
I wonder what time it is.

Serán las seis.
It's probably six o'clock.

Estarán debajo de tu cama.
They must be under your bed.

The English equivalents in these cases are *I wonder, it's probably, it must be,* and so on.

¿Dónde estarán mis zapatos?
Where can my shoes *be?*

| **Más ayuda** | **realidades.com** | ▶ Tutorial |

▼16 Probablemente . . .

Leer • Escribir

En una fiesta, conoces a las siguientes personas y comienzas a imaginarte qué cosas tendrán o qué harán en sus trabajos. Lee las siguientes frases. Escribe una segunda frase relacionada con la primera. Usa la forma correcta de los verbos del recuadro en el futuro para indicar probabilidad.

Modelo
Marcela es escritora.
Tendrá muchos libros.

tener	saber	vender	comprar	trabajar
estudiar	dedicarse	ser	aprender	seguir

1. El Sr. Paz es abogado.
2. Carmen es una mujer de negocios.
3. Andrés quiere ser traductor.
4. La Sra. Dávila es peluquera.
5. Héctor espera ser ingeniero.

6. Los hermanos González son agricultores.
7. Roberto quiere ser diseñador.
8. Margarita quiere ser científica.
9. El Sr. Pérez es juez.
10. Jaime y Elena quieren ser cocineros.

doscientos sesenta y tres 263
Capítulo 6

ENRICH YOUR TEACHING

Teacher-to-Teacher

Making a connection between a grammar point and something in students' everyday lives leads to meaningful language practice and helps students solidify their understanding of the grammar point. Remind students that we frequently make predictions as we look forward to elections, sports events, or award ceremonies.

Choose an upcoming school event, such as a sports match, and ask students to write their predictions about it. Take a survey to see how many of them predict each possible outcome. After the event, ask students to state whether their predictions were correct.

Practice and Communicate ⑥

Gramática (Repaso)

Core Instruction

Standards: 4.1

Resources: Voc. and Gram. Transparency 125

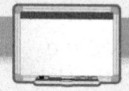

INTERACTIVE WHITEBOARD
Grammar Activities 6-1

Suggestions: Have students talk about the picture using the future tense to express uncertainty: *¿Quién será la persona que está a la derecha? Será….*

▶16 Standards: 1.3

Resources: Answer Keys: Student Edition, p. 82
Focus: Practicing the future tense to express probability or uncertainty
Suggestions: To avoid confusion, remind students that the meaning of the word **conoces** in the first line of the instructions is "to meet someone" rather than "to know someone."

Answers will vary. Students will choose from the following verb forms, depending on the subject of their sentence:
tendrá/tendrán
estudiará/estudiarán
sabrá/sabrán
se dedicará/se dedicarán
venderá/venderán
será/serán
comprará/comprarán
aprenderá/aprenderán
trabajará/trabajarán
seguirá/seguirán

Extension: Once students have completed the activity, challenge them to add another logical sentence about each person. They can use a verb from the word bank or another verb of their choice in the future tense.

Pre-AP* Support

• **Learning Objective:** Interpersonal Speaking
• **Activity:** Have students bring in magazine pictures that show one or more people. Ask them to share with a partner a mini-story using the future of probability to indicate what they believe might be or is probably happening.
• *Pre-AP* Resource Book:* Comprehensive guide to Pre-AP* communication skill development, pp. 10–18, 39–50

En voz alta
Core Instruction

Standards: 1.2, 1.3, 2.2, 3.1, 3.2, 5.2

Resources: Teacher's Resource Book: Audio Script, p. 72; Audio Program DVD: Cap. 6, Track 8

Suggestions: Have students read the information and the poem silently. Help them understand the complicated syntax. For example, point out that **volverán** in the first line is only part of a verb phrase. Ask: *¿Cuáles son las demás palabras que completan esta frase? (a colgar)* Remind them that for effect, poets like Bécquer often invert the positions of subjects and verbs.

Before having students recite the poem, direct their attention to the information in *¿Recuerdas?* Then allow them a few minutes to practice reciting the poem excerpt with a partner.

Common Errors: When working with pronunciation in *¿Recuerdas?*, students may interrupt the elision of the vowel sounds with a glottal stop (a stoppage of air at the back of the throat). Model pronouncing the word groups without interruption and have students repeat.

Extension: Gustavo Adolfo Bécquer is an AP* Literature author. You may want to suggest that students read additional works by this poet.

▼17 Standards: 1.1, 1.3

Resources: Answer Keys: Student Edition, p. 83

Focus: Practicing the future tense

Suggestions: Tell students that their predictions must be at least one complete sentence in length. They need not make all their predictions about the same person or persons.

Answers will vary. The following are third-person singular and plural forms of the verbs in the word bank:

será/serán	realizará/realizarán
logrará/lograrán	hará/harán
trabajará/trabajarán	se mudará/se mudarán
estará/estarán	ahorrará/ahorrarán
se dedicará/se dedicarán	desempeñará/desempeñarán
tendrá/tendrán	podrá/podrán

▼ En voz alta | Talk?

El poeta español Gustavo Adolfo Bécquer nació en Sevilla en 1836. Era hijo de un pintor famoso que murió cuando Bécquer tenía sólo 5 años. Desde joven, Bécquer comenzó a escribir poesía. A los 22 años conoció a Julia Espín, la mujer que inspiró la mayoría de sus famosas *Rimas*. El poeta murió en 1870, a los 34 años de edad.

Bécquer fue quizás el último de los poetas románticos. Sus *Rimas* fueron durante mucho tiempo los poemas de amor más famosos en el mundo hispanohablante.

Lee este fragmento de la "Rima LIII" y luego trata de repetirlo en voz alta.

"Rima LIII"
de Gustavo Adolfo Bécquer

Volverán las oscuras golondrinas[1]
en tu balcón sus nidos[2] a colgar[3],
y otra vez con el ala[4] a sus cristales
        jugando llamarán.

Pero aquellas que el vuelo refrenaban[5] tu hermosura y mi dicha[6] a contemplar, aquellas que aprendieron nuestros nombres . . .
        Ésas . . . ¡no volverán!

---

1 swallows 2 nests 3 hang 4 wing 5 slowed down 6 happiness

¿Recuerdas?

Al hablar en voz alta muchas veces se combinan la última vocal de una palabra con la primera vocal de la siguiente en una sola sílaba. Por ejemplo: *que aprendieron; que el.*

▼17 ¿Dónde estarán en diez años? |

Escribir • Hablar

❶ Haz predicciones sobre tus amigos, profesores, artistas o políticos famosos. Completa la tabla usando por lo menos seis verbos de la lista en futuro.

ser	trabajar	dedicarse	realizar	mudarse	desempeñar
lograr	estar	tener	hacer	ahorrar	poder

¿Cuándo?	Predicción
El próximo año	(Nombre) tendrá...
En cinco años	
En diez años	
En veinte años	

❷ Ahora, habla con un(a) compañero(a) sobre las predicciones que hizo cada uno. Escojan una de ellas, digan si están de acuerdo o no, y vuelvan a contarla añadiendo más detalles. Usen su imaginación y añadan todos los detalles que puedan.

▶ Modelo

en diez años / mujer presidenta
A —*En diez años, una mujer será presidenta de los Estados Unidos.*
B —*Sí, primero será abogada y trabajará para la gente de su estado. Será muy popular.*

264 doscientos sesenta y cuatro
Manos a la obra 1

DIFFERENTIATED INSTRUCTION

Students with Special Needs

Help hearing impaired students appreciate the rhythm and style of *"Rima LIII"* by Gustavo Adolfo Bécquer. After the class has read the poem aloud, ask students to compose a series of rhythmic gestures to accompany the text. Invite everyone to participate in the movements.

Advanced Learners

Ask students to imagine that they will be attending their ten-year high school reunion. Have them use the future tense in as many sentences as they can to describe their classmates as they might appear ten years from now. Monitor for appropriate language usage.

▼18 ¿Qué lograrás?

Escribir

¿Qué harás en las siguientes situaciones? Completa las frases de una manera original usando el futuro.

Modelo
Si ahorro mucho dinero, . . .
Si ahorro mucho dinero, podré viajar a Guinea Ecuatorial.

1. Si consigo el empleo de mis sueños, . . .
2. Si conozco a un(a) chico(a) que me gusta mucho, . . .
3. Si encuentro un millón de dólares en la calle, . . .
4. Si logro entrar en la universidad, . . .
5. Si me ofrecen estudiar en el extranjero, . . .
6. Si mis padres se mudan a otro estado, . . .
7. Si logro tener mi propia empresa, . . .
8. Si me piden trabajar como voluntario(a), . . .

> **Nota**
> Cuando una frase comienza con *si* + presente indicativo, generalmente es seguida de una frase que usa el futuro.

▼19 Los trabajos del futuro |

Leer • Hablar

❶ ¿Qué profesiones serán importantes para el año 2036? Lee el artículo y haz una lista con un(a) compañero(a).

❷ Expliquen de qué hablan las predicciones del artículo. Busquen ejemplos que apoyen estas opiniones.

❸ Escojan dos profesiones y hablen de por qué son o serán importantes. Pueden ser profesiones de ahora o del futuro.

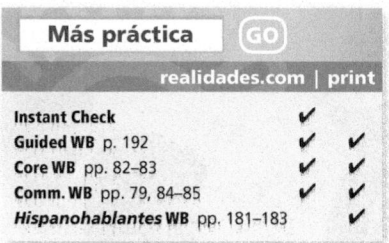

Más práctica	GO
**realidades.com	print**	

Instant Check	✔	
Guided WB p. 192	✔	✔
Core WB pp. 82–83	✔	✔
Comm. WB pp. 79, 84–85	✔	✔
Hispanohablantes WB pp. 181–183		✔

Profesiones del futuro

Según los futurólogos, dentro de treinta años habrá nuevas profesiones que todavía no existen, como los acuicultores (agricultores del mar) y los ludicadores (inventores de programas de juego). Dicen también que los médicos, paramédicos, enfermeros, cocineros y maestros no perderán su importancia. Esto se debe a que las personas no dejarán de enfermarse y siempre necesitarán comer y estudiar. Incluso con el avance del tiempo estas profesiones tendrán más importancia que ahora.

Practice and Communicate ⑥

▼18 Standards: 1.3

Focus: Practicing the future tense

Suggestions: Once students have prepared their answers, encourage them to share them. They can invite others' responses with questions such as *Y tú, ¿qué harás si...?*

Answers will vary.

▼19 Standards: 1.1, 1.2

Resources: Answer Keys: Student Edition, p. 83

Focus: Practicing new vocabulary and structures through reading and discussion about future professions

Suggestions: Before students read the information, have them predict what they think will be important jobs or professions in the future.

Answers:
Step 1
acuicultores, ludicadores, médicos, paramédicos, enfermeros, cocineros y maestros
Steps 2–3
Answers will vary.

Chapter Project

Students can perform Step 3 at this point. (For more information, see p. 246-b.)

Additional Resources

- Communication Wbk.: Audio Act. 2, p. 79
- Teacher's Resource Book: Audio Script, pp. 71–72, Communicative Pair Activity BLM, p. 79
- Audio Program DVD: Cap. 6, Track 7

ENRICH YOUR TEACHING

Culture Note

In addition to writing poetry, Gustavo Adolfo Bécquer composed music, wrote **zarzuelas,** and painted. He was influenced by **coplas,** two-to-three-line poems, usually sung, that were a popular poetic style of the time. Bécquer composed 76 **rimas** in all.

21st Century Skills

Information Literacy Have students search the Internet for more information on Gustavo Adolfo Bécquer and his poetry. Have them find sites where they can listen to the poems from the *Rimas* collection being recited by native speakers.

✔ASSESSMENT

Prueba 6-4 with Study Plan (online only)

Prueba: El futuro de probabilidad
- Prueba 6-4: p. 132

Examen: Vocabulario y gramática 1
- Examen 1: pp. 133–135
- ExamView: Examen 1

| ▼ **Objectives**

▶ Read, listen to, and understand information about
• changes in technology
• the impact of technology on our lives

Vocabulario en contexto

Core Instruction

Standards: 1.1, 1.2, 5.1

Resources: Teacher's Resource Book: Input Script, p. 68, Clip Art, pp. 84–93, Audio Script, p. 72; Voc. and Gram. Transparencies 126–127; Audio Program DVD: Cap. 6, Track 9

Focus: Presenting new vocabulary and using grammar lexically in context

Suggestions: Ask students to look at the seven numbered photos on these pages. Have a volunteer read the titles at the top of the photos. Ask: *¿Esta información se trata de avances tecnológicos o avances artísticos?* **(tecnológicos)** Play the audio or read the text and have students follow along. Point out cognates that will aid in comprehension, such as *inventos, máquinas, satélite, reducir,* and *energía,* among others. Use circumlocution to explain the meaning of other vocabulary: *¿Qué palabra significa el lugar donde se producen cosas como coches?* **(fábrica)**

BELLRINGER REVIEW

Have students complete this sentence on a sheet of paper and be prepared to defend their ideas with the class.

Yo creo que el problema más grande para el futuro es _____.

Block Schedule

Have students work in pairs to write out definitions of five of the words on these two pages. This will practice the skill of circumlocution. Have them work with another pair of students. Each pair will read aloud the definitions. The other pair has to guess the word being described.

Vocabulario en contexto

¿Ya estamos viviendo en el futuro? Hace unos años se hablaba de la llegada del siglo XXI. El siglo XXI ya llegó, y con éste muchos **avances** de la tecnología que cambiarán nuestras vidas.

1 Avances científicos y **tecnológicos**

Muchos trabajos peligrosos son hechos ahora por **máquinas** o robots. Se **predice** que en el futuro menos gente trabajará en **las fábricas**. Habrá más tiempo de **ocio**, o sea que la gente tendrá más tiempo para divertirse o para viajar.

2 Nuevos inventos

Inventos como la televisión digital y la televisión 3D ofrecen imágenes más claras y mejor sonido. En muchas casas, la televisión 3D está **reemplazando** a la televisión tradicional.

3 Realidad virtual

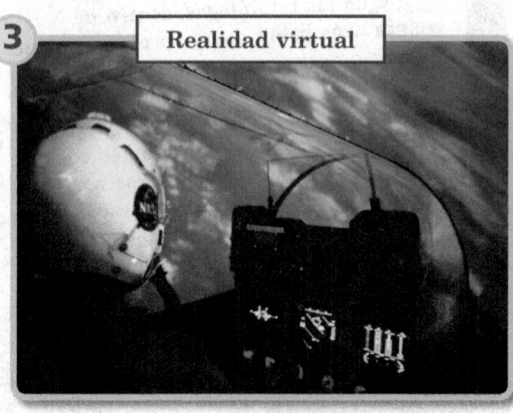

La tecnología llamada realidad virtual permite vivir una experiencia a través de computadoras **como si fuera** real. Esta nueva tecnología ya se usa para entrenar a los pilotos.

Si queremos un futuro mejor, debemos prepararnos desde ahora. ¿Qué podemos hacer?

Hay que tener en cuenta la importancia del medio ambiente.

De hoy en adela debemos dedicar proteger el agu

266 doscientos sesenta y seis
A primera vista 2

DIFFERENTIATED INSTRUCTION

Students with Learning Difficulties

Encourage students to use the photographs on these two pages to help predict the main idea of each paragraph. Ask embedded-answer questions to help them understand the passages: *¿Quién hará muchos trabajos peligrosos en el futuro, la gente o las máquinas?*

Advanced Learners

Have students brainstorm and "invent" a technological advancement that might be possible 100 years from now. Individuals or small groups should describe in detail their prediction and include a drawing that can be shown to the class.

4 Medios de comunicación

Gracias a **aparatos** como el teléfono celular podemos **comunicarnos** desde muchos lugares. Desde que se **inventó** la televisión **vía satélite**, podemos ver imágenes y **enterarnos** inmediatamente de lo que pasa en todo el mundo.

5 Vivienda

El uso de otras **fuentes de energía**, como la energía solar, permitirá calentar las **viviendas** sin **contaminar** el medio ambiente y, además, será mucho más barato.

6 Transporte

Algunas compañías han presentado los primeros coches eléctricos que ayudarán a **reducir** la contaminación del aire.

7 Medicina

los genes

Cada año, los científicos **descubren** más cosas fascinantes sobre el cuidado de la salud. Avances en **la genética** harán posible **curar** muchas de **las enfermedades**, como el cáncer. Algunas enfermedades **desaparecerán** gracias a los nuevos medicamentos, que **prolongarán** la vida de muchas personas.

▼**20** Radio Futura | 🔊 ────────

Escuchar • Escribir

En una hoja de papel escribe los números del 1 al 6. Vas a escuchar lo que se dice en un programa de radio sobre avances científicos que van a ayudar a resolver muchos problemas en el mundo. Escucha cada frase y escribe si es lógica o ilógica. Si la frase no es lógica, corrígela.

▼**21** Avances de la tecnología ────

Escribir

Escribe dos ejemplos de avances que se han logrado en cada una de las siguientes categorías.

- tecnología
- medicina
- medios de comunicación
- vivienda

doscientos sesenta y siete **267**
Capítulo 6

20 Standards: 1.2

Resources: Teacher's Resource Book: Audio Script, p. 72; Audio Program DVD: Cap. 6, Track 10; Answer Keys: Student Edition, p. 84

Focus: Practicing listening comprehension of new vocabulary

Suggestions: Remind students that they are only commenting on whether or not each statement is logical. Whether they agree or not with the future possibilities has no bearing on their answers.

Answers:

1. **lógica**
2. **ilógica**
3. **lógica**
4. **ilógica**
5. **lógica**
6. **lógica**

21 Standards: 1.3

Resources: Answer Keys: Student Edition, p. 84

Focus: Practicing writing of new vocabulary

Suggestions: Invite students to answer with complete sentences if they choose, but to paraphrase the information, rather than stating it verbatim from the *Vocabulario* presentation.

Answers will vary but should contain the following basic information:

- **menos trabajadores en las fábricas; más tiempo de ocio**
- **avances en la genética; algunas enfermedades desaparecerán; la vida de muchas personas se prolongará**
- **nos comunicaremos desde muchos lugares; nos enteraremos inmediatamente de lo que pasa**
- **nuevas fuentes de energía no contaminarán el medio ambiente; serán más baratas**

ENRICH YOUR TEACHING

Culture Note

In 1950, with its population growing rapidly, Mexico City began work on a modern transportation system. The first line of the Mexico City Metro was opened in 1969. Today the system is still expanding and modernizing to meet the needs of the future. Plans are currently in place to introduce light rail lines into the suburbs.

21st Century Skills

Collaboration Have students work in pairs or small groups to compare and consolidate their lists of advances in each category listed in *Actividad* 21. Then have them discuss and decide which are, in their opinion, the most important advances of the last five years in each category.

Vocabulario en contexto

Core Instruction

Standards: 1.1, 1.2, 3.1, 5.1

Resources: Teacher's Resource Book: Input Script, p. 69, Clip Art, pp. 84–93, Audio Script, pp. 72–73; Voc. and Gram. Transparencies 128–129; Audio Program DVD: Cap. 6, Tracks 11–12

Focus: Extending presentation of vocabulary and grammar in context

Suggestions:

Pre-reading: Have students look at the photos and talk about what they see. Ask a volunteer to read the title and the photo captions. Give explanations or ask questions that help clarify the meaning of new vocabulary. For example, point to photo number 1 and say: *Una empresa es una organización que emplea gente. ¿Puedes nombrar algunas empresas de nuestra comunidad?*

Reading: Allow students time to read the information on this and the next page silently first. Then play the audio and have students read along as they listen. Allow them to listen more than once.

Post-reading: Check comprehension by asking questions, including those found in *Actividad 23*.

Pre-AP* Support

- **Learning Objective:** Interpersonal Writing
- **Activity:** Have students write an e-mail to a friend in which they predict what will be the most popular profession of the future. Have students explain whether they would be interested in following this particular career path, and their reasons for it. Be sure students ask their friend their opinion about the profession of the future.
- *Pre-AP* Resource Book:* Comprehensive guide to Pre-AP* writing skill development, pp. 27–38

Tres campos que tienen futuro

Según estudios de los últimos años, para el año 2050 habrá desaparecido la mayoría de los trabajos que ahora existen. Aunque habrá demanda de médicos, abogados y economistas, éstos son los campos con más futuro:

Con el uso de las computadoras y de la Red, la informática es la profesión del futuro. Por todo el mundo, los ingenieros de sistemas y programadores se dedican al desarrollo de nuevos y mejores programas de computación.

Servicios a empresas

Informática

Las empresas en general tendrán menos empleados, pero necesitarán de los servicios de profesionales como vendedores, secretarios y diseñadores gráficos.

Habrá mucho trabajo en hoteles y empresas turísticas. Se necesitarán cocineros, agentes de viaje, camareros y administradores.

Industria de la hospitalidad

DIFFERENTIATED INSTRUCTION

Heritage Language Learners

Ask students if they have ever had occasion to interpret for someone. Ask them to discuss the circumstances that called for an interpreter, as well as comment on the experience. Was it exciting to serve as a bridge between two languages? Was it challenging?

Students with Special Needs

Provide visually impaired students with a partner who can verbally describe the photographs under *Tres campos que tienen futuro.* Instruct the partners to focus on details associated with the profession being discussed.

TRADUCCIONES

○ Traducciones bilingües: inglés-español, español-inglés

○ Especializados en documentos legales, informes de mercadeo, libros científicos

○ Servicio rápido y eficiente

○ Traductores certificados

AGENCIA TRADUCE

Calle 49, número 456
San José, Costa Rica
Tel: 555-5555

www.agenciatraduce.cr

La demanda de traductores **aumentará** porque habrá más **comercio** entre los diferentes países.

Las personas que trabajan en el campo de **mercadeo** desarrollan estrategias **para** vender productos.

UNA DELICIOSA BEBIDA

▼22 Standards: 1.2

Resources: Teacher's Resource Book: Audio Script, p. 73; Audio Program DVD: Cap. 6, Track 13; Answer Keys: Student Edition, p. 85

Focus: Practicing listening comprehension of new vocabulary and structures

Suggestions: Before students listen, make sure they understand the meaning of the word *campo,* since it is a key word in the activity. Give examples of its two most common meanings: *El campo sembrado de maíz es muy bonito. En el campo de la hospitalidad, la gente trabaja en hoteles y restaurantes.*

Answers:
1. el mercadeo
2. la informática
3. la industria de la hospitalidad
4. la traducción
5. los servicios a empresas

▼22 Campos de trabajo | 🔊

Escuchar

Escribe los números del 1 al 5 en una hoja de papel. Escucha la descripción de cada trabajo y escribe a qué campo se refiere.

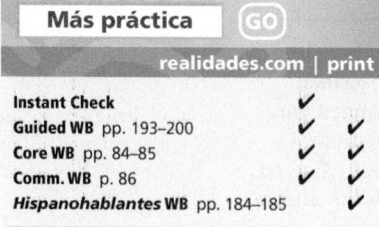

Más práctica	GO
realidades.com	print	

Instant Check	✔	
Guided WB pp. 193–200	✔	✔
Core WB pp. 84–85	✔	✔
Comm. WB p. 86	✔	✔
Hispanohablantes WB pp. 184–185	✔	

▼23 ¿Comprendiste?

Escribir • Hablar

1. ¿Qué empleados(as) se necesitarán para ofrecer servicios a empresas?

2. Según lo que leíste, ¿cuál es la profesión del futuro? ¿Por qué?

3. ¿Por qué se necesitarán más traductores en el futuro?

4. ¿Por qué crees que habrá más demanda de empleados en la industria de la hospitalidad?

5. ¿Puedes describir una estrategia de mercadeo que se usa para vender un producto que conoces?

doscientos sesenta y nueve **269**
Capítulo 6

▼23 Standards: 1.3

Resources: Answer Keys: Student Edition, p. 85

Focus: Writing answers to demonstrate comprehension

Suggestions: Have students answer the questions on their own. Then invite them to share their responses.

Answers:
1. Se necesitarán vendedores(as), secretarios(as) y diseñadores(as) gráficos(as).
2. La informática es la profesión del futuro. Los (Las) ingenieros(as) de sistemas y programadores(as) desarrollarán nuevos y mejores programas de computadora.
3. Se necesitarán más traductores porque habrá más comercio entre los diferentes países.
4–5. Answers will vary.

ENRICH YOUR TEACHING

Culture Note

Some students involved in the **Bachillerato Internacional** go on to special programs of study for careers in interpretation and translation. Students involved in these programs study the difference between *simultaneous* interpretation, listening and speaking at the same time, and *consecutive* interpretation, waiting for pauses every two to three sentences. They also master *phrase* interpretation, which is word-for-word translation, and *summary* interpretation, providing the main idea of what a speaker has said. Students often develop an expertise in a particular field, such as court interpretation or medical translation.

✓ASSESSMENT

Prueba: Comprensión del vocabulario 2
• Prueba 6-5: pp. 136–137

269

6 Practice and Communicate

Manos a la obra 2

| ▼ Objectives
▶ Read about technology and its application
▶ Discuss future technologies
▶ Talk and write about life in the near future

▼24 Standards: 1.2

Resources: Answer Keys: Student Edition, p. 85

Focus: Practicing new vocabulary in a multiple-choice exercise

Suggestions: Remind students to refer back to pp. 266–269 to review the vocabulary, if necessary.

Answers:

1. b	4. b
2. c	5. a
3. a	

▼25 Standards: 1.2

Resources: Answer Keys: Student Edition, p. 86

Focus: Practicing new vocabulary in a cloze exercise

Suggestions: Have students read the entire paragraph before completing it.

Answers:

1. predecir	6. como si fuera
2. el uso	7. los avances
3. reemplazar	8. el campo
4. los inventos	9. tener en cuenta
5. la realidad virtual	

BELLRINGER REVIEW

As you call out these actions, have students respond aloud with the *nosotros* form of the verb in the future:

dar	*ver*
tener	*hacer*
ser	*mudar*
trabajar	

Block Schedule

After completing *Actividad 27,* have students share and summarize the most popular responses to the different questions. Then have students write a short "news report" about the results of this class survey.

Vocabulario en uso

▼24 ¿Nos ayudarán los robots?

Leer

Muchas personas creen que el uso del robot cambiará mucho nuestra vida en el futuro. Completa cada frase con la palabra correcta.

1. En el futuro, ¿nos darán los robots más tiempo para dedicarlo al ____ y al descanso?

   a. uso   b. ocio   c. avance

2. La ____ de las fábricas ya tienen o pronto tendrán robots para hacer gran parte del trabajo allí.

   a. máquina   b. tecnología   c. mayoría

3. La ____ para vender los robots al público será a través de la Red.

   a. estrategia   b. informática   c. vía satélite

4. Veremos robots en muchas ____ también. Los usarán en casas y apartamentos para los trabajos diarios.

   a. demandas   b. viviendas   c. enfermedades

5. Muchas personas que predicen el futuro creen que el robot será uno de los ____ tecnológicos más importantes del siglo.

   a. avances   b. genes   c. campos

▼25 Una vida diferente

Leer

¿Qué piensas acerca de las computadoras? Completa el párrafo con las palabras o expresiones del recuadro.

el uso	reemplazar	predecir	la realidad virtual	los inventos
como si fuera	los avances	el campo	tener en cuenta	

Es imposible __1.__ el futuro, pero no hay duda de que __2.__ de la tecnología va a aumentar. Cada día, los ingenieros de sistemas escriben programas que cambian nuestra vida. Claro, las computadoras nunca van a __3.__ a las personas, pero __4.__ como __5.__, muestran cómo una computadora puede funcionar __6.__ una persona. Pero con todos __7.__ en __8.__ de la informática, es importante __9.__ que las computadoras nunca serán personas.

DIFFERENTIATED INSTRUCTION

Students with Learning Difficulties

Model for students the process of elimination by guiding them to try out each multiple-choice answer in *Actividad* 24. If they are having difficulty with new vocabulary, have them review the *A primera vista* sections to find and reread the words in other contexts.

Advanced Learners/Pre-AP*

Have students tell about the future of their own current field of employment or that of someone they know. They should mention whether or not they think the type of employment will be more or less common in years to come and give reasons for their opinion.

▼26 Las profesiones del mañana |

Leer • Escribir • Hablar

❶ En otro papel, escribe los números del 1 al 8. Escribe la información apropiada para cada espacio en blanco de la tabla.

❷ Con otro(a) estudiante hablen de cuál o cuáles de esos trabajos les gustaría hacer y por qué.

❸ Habla con tu compañero(a) sobre la importancia de estas profesiones ahora y en el futuro.

Industria	Profesión	Servicio / Producto
transporte	ingeniero	1.
medios de comunicación	2.	teléfono celular
finanzas	3.	cajero automático
4.	5.	programa de computación
medicina	6.	7.
8.	mujer de negocios	estrategias para vender productos

▼27 Y tú, ¿qué dices? |

Escribir • Hablar

Imagina que vas a vivir solo(a) durante ocho semanas en un observatorio, en medio del desierto. Haz una lista de los aparatos, la tecnología o los inventos que te gustaría tener allí.

1. ¿Cuáles te parecen más importantes? ¿Cuáles crees que usarás más frecuentemente?

2. ¿Cuáles de esos aparatos o inventos crees que desaparecerán en el futuro? ¿Por qué?

3. ¿Cuáles crees que serán los mejores avances que verás en el futuro?

4. ¿Qué cosas piensas que habrá en el futuro que no te gustarán? ¿Qué crees que se puede hacer para evitarlas?

▼ Fondo Cultural | El mundo hispano

Bachillerato Internacional El Bachillerato Internacional es un programa de estudios común para las escuelas preparatorias de América Latina y otros países. Actualmente[1], más de 2,200 colegios[2] en 141 países forman parte del programa. Tiene una gran ventaja[3] para los estudiantes que cambian de país con frecuencia ya que pueden ir, sin problemas, de un colegio que ofrece Bachillerato Internacional a otro.

Los programas se enseñan en el idioma del país. Por ejemplo, un estudiante de Francia que estudia en España tiene el mismo currículum que el de su país, pero lo aprende en español. El programa empezó en 1968 y es reconocido por universidades de todo el mundo. Busca la excelencia académica, desarrolla el pensamiento crítico y ayuda a la comprensión intercultural entre los jóvenes de todos los países.

_____

1 Currently **2** high schools **3** advantage

• ¿Has oído hablar del Bachillerato Internacional? ¿Conoces alguna escuela que ofrece este programa?

• ¿Qué opinas de un programa de estudios que es igual en todo el mundo? ¿Es buena idea? ¿Por qué? ¿Por qué no?

doscientos setenta y uno **271**
Capítulo 6

ENRICH YOUR TEACHING

Teacher-to-Teacher

Play "Concentration." Prepare twenty notecards. On ten of them, write the name of an area of employment or a profession. On the other ten, write a word or expression that is clearly associated with each area. Example: **el (la) abogado(a)/la ley.** Write the numbers 1–20 in random order on the back of the cards. Tape them to the board in numerical order in a grid. Divide students into two teams. A player from Team A chooses two cards, which are turned over and read aloud. If they match, they are removed from the grid. Team A scores a point and goes again. If the cards don't match, they are returned to their positions and it is Team B's turn.

Practice and Communicate ⑥

▼26 Standards: 1.1

Resources: Voc. and Gram. Transparency 4

Focus: Practicing new vocabulary via note-taking and discussion

Suggestions: Show *Vocabulary and Grammar Transparency* 4 as a reference while students fill in the chart for Step 1.

Answers will vary.

▼27 Standards: 1.3

Focus: Writing answers to demonstrate comprehension of new vocabulary and structures

Suggestions: Point out that questions 1 and 2 deal with the desert observatory situation. Questions 3 and 4 require more open-ended, personal responses.

Answers will vary.

Fondo cultural

Standards: 1.1, 1.2, 3.1, 5.1, 5.2

Suggestions: After students read the information, ask comprehension questions such as the following: *¿Qué tipo de escuela forma parte del Bachillerato Internacional? ¿Cómo beneficia el programa a los jóvenes?*

Common Errors: Some students will assume that ***actualmente*** means the same as the English "actually." Remind them that this is a false cognate and means "currently."

Answers will vary.

Chapter Project

Students can perform Step 4 at this point. Be sure they understand your corrections and suggestions. (For more information, see p. 246-b.)

28 Standards: 1.1, 1.2

Resources: Answer Keys: Student Edition, p. 86

Focus: Practicing new vocabulary in a cloze exercise

Suggestions: Refer students to p. 260 for forms of the future tense.

Answers:

Step 1

1. reemplazarán	6. Nos enteraremos
2. curarán	7. Desaparecerán
3. Nos comunicaremos	8. Inventarán
4. prolongarán	9. aumentarán
5. reducirán	10. descubrirán

Step 2

Answers will vary.

29 Standards: 1.1, 1.2, 3.1

Focus: Demonstrating comprehension of new vocabulary and structures through reading and response

Suggestions: For Step 1, students can read the article in pairs. Ask them to help each other with any comprehension problems they may have.

Answers will vary.

Additional Resources

• Communication Wbk.: Audio Act. 3, p. 80
• Teacher's Resource Book: Audio Script, p. 73, Communicative Pair Activity BLM, p. 80
• Audio Program DVD: Cap. 6, Track 14

☑ ASSESSMENT

Prueba 6-6 with Study Plan (online only)

Prueba: Aplicación del vocabulario 2
• Prueba 6-6: pp. 138–139

272

▼28 Predicciones | 👥

Leer • Hablar

❶ Averigua qué piensan tus compañeros(as) sobre cómo será la vida en 50 años. Completa las siguientes preguntas con el futuro del verbo correcto.

aumentar	comunicarse	curar	desaparecer	descubrir
enterarse	inventar	prolongar	reducir	reemplazar

1. ¿Los robots _____ a los empleados de las fábricas?

2. En el campo de la medicina, ¿_____ a las personas que sufren de cáncer?

3. ¿_____ nosotros con extraterrestres?

4. ¿Nuevas medicinas _____ la vida hasta los cien años?

5. ¿Nuevos métodos tecnológicos _____ la contaminación del aire?

6. ¿_____ nosotros de las causas del cáncer?

7. ¿_____ las enfermedades, como el resfriado común?

8. ¿_____ los ingenieros nuevos aparatos que harán más fáciles los quehaceres diarios?

9. ¿Los autobuses eléctricos _____ el ahorro de gasolina?

10. ¿Los científicos _____ nuevas fuentes de energía en el medio ambiente?

❷ Con otro(a) estudiante preparen respuestas para tres de las preguntas y expliquen por qué dieron esas respuestas.

▼29 Los futurólogos predicen . . . | 👥

Leer • Hablar

❶ Lee estos fragmentos de un artículo sobre la vida en el año 2050.

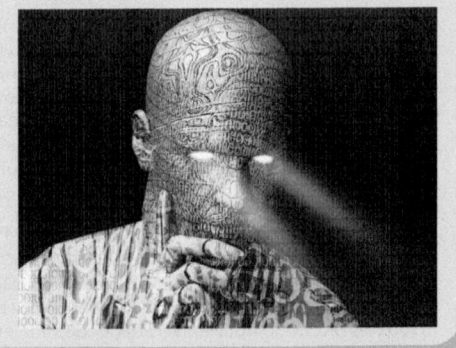

LA VIDA EN EL 2050

Los futurólogos no son adivinos, son científicos que basan sus predicciones en el estado de la ciencia y la sociedad del presente. Predicen que en el 2050 los robots realizarán las tareas de la casa y toda clase de operaciones médicas. La realidad virtual nos permitirá visitar lugares o amigos en el otro lado del mundo, en segundos. La prensa escrita desaparecerá por completo y también los libros y revistas. Las energías limpias pasarán a ser comunes en nuestras vidas. Los carros y el transporte público serán eléctricos además de automáticos. También la realidad virtual tendrá muchas utilidades; por ejemplo, como una herramienta para aprender en las escuelas.

❷ Trabaja con otro(a) estudiante para decir cómo será más fácil la vida y cómo podremos hacer más rápidamente las cosas, según el artículo.

❸ Expliquen por qué son positivos o negativos los cambios que se mencionan en el artículo.

DIFFERENTIATED INSTRUCTION

Heritage Language Learners

Have students exchange papers and edit each other's work for *Actividad* 30. Direct them to focus on the correct placement of accent marks, as well as the correct spelling of past participles. Allow students to discuss their editorial changes with their partners.

Students with Learning Difficulties

Help students divide *Actividad* 28 into several steps. First, have them read over each sentence for meaning. Second, have them identify the subject of the sentence. Third, have them choose the appropriate verb from the word bank. Finally, have them write the correct future verb form in the blank.

Gramática

▼ Objectives
▶ Read about future accomplishments
▶ Discuss inventions and predictions

El futuro perfecto

Use the future perfect tense to express what will have happened by a certain time. To form the future perfect, use the future of the verb *haber* with the past participle of the verb.

Here are all the future perfect tense forms of *inventar*:

habré inventado	habremos inventado
habrás inventado	habréis inventado
habrá inventado	habrán inventado

¿Recuerdas?

Varios verbos tienen participios irregulares, como *escribir, escrito* y *volver, vuelto.* Los participios pasados de los verbos *descubrir* y *resolver* también son irregulares: *descubierto, resuelto.*

Para el año 2050 los científicos habrán descubierto otras fuentes de energía.
By 2050, scientists will have discovered other energy sources.

• The future perfect tense is often used with *dentro de* + time.

Dentro de cinco años, habremos aprendido mucho sobre la genética.
In five years, we will have learned a lot about genetics.

• You also use the future perfect tense to speculate about something that may have happened in the past.
—Laura no me llamó. ¿Qué le habrá pasado?
—Se habrá enterado de que no ibas.

—*Laura didn't call me. What could have happened to her?*
—*Perhaps she found out you were not coming.*

Más ayuda **realidades.com** ▶ *Canción de hip hop* ▶ Tutorials

30 ¿Qué habremos logrado para el año . . . ?

Leer

Imagina que hablas con otros(as) estudiantes sobre lo que habrán logrado dentro de varios años. Completa las siguientes predicciones con el futuro perfecto del verbo correcto.

1. En unos diez años, la mejor estudiante de geología de mi clase _____ (*descubrir / desaparecer*) nuevos materiales de la Luna.

2. Dentro de veinte años, nuestra amiga escritora _____ (*conseguir / permitir*) el Premio Nobel de Literatura.

3. Para las próximas Olimpiadas, mi patinadora favorita _____ (*inventar / reemplazar*) a la campeona mundial.

4. Si sigo estudiando, dentro de dos años _____ (*aumentar / eliminar*) mi vocabulario de español.

5. Dentro de 20 años, probablemente todos nosotros _____ (*prolongar / mudarse*) de casa alguna vez.

6. Dicen mis padres que como trabajamos mucho y somos dedicados, dentro de 15 años _____ (*alcanzar / diseñar*) nuestras metas.

doscientos setenta y tres **273**
Capítulo 6

ENRICH YOUR TEACHING

Culture Note

According to The Second World Assembly on Aging, which met in Madrid in 2002, there will be two billion people over the age of 60 in the world in the year 2050, and for the first time, the number of people over 60 will outnumber those under 14. Ask students to discuss the implications of this trend.

Teacher-to-Teacher

Ask students to write three sentences using the future perfect tense to tell what they will have done one week from now, one month from now, and one year from now.

Practice and Communicate 6

Before presenting the future perfect forms of *haber* in the *Gramática* on this page, review with students the present tense and imperfect forms. Have students use these forms in sentences in the present perfect and past perfect tenses.

Gramática

Core Instruction

Standards: 4.1

Resources: Voc. and Gram. Transparency 130

INTERACTIVE WHITEBOARD
Grammar Activities 6-2

Suggestions: Refer students to the *¿Recuerdas?* Have them list other irregular past participles that they can remember. Point out that all the perfect tenses they have learned so far use the auxiliary verb *haber.* Explain that this verb's conjugated forms are most often used in perfect tenses.

30 Standards: 1.2

Resources: Answer Keys: Student Edition, p. 86
Focus: Using the future perfect tense in a word-choice exercise
Suggestions: Tell students to complete the exercise in steps. First, choose the verb that makes sense. Second, convert the verb to its past participle form. Third, add the appropriate future tense form of *haber* before the participle.

Answers:
1. habrá descubierto
2. habrá conseguido
3. habrá reemplazado
4. habré aumentado
5. nos habremos mudado
6. habremos alcanzado

31 Standards: 1.1, 1.3

Focus: Practicing the future perfect tense through discussion about a fact table

Suggestions: As part of their discussion, ask students to compute the year in which the use of each invention became widespread.

Answers will vary.

32 Standards: 1.1

Focus: Practicing the future perfect tense through discussion in context

Suggestions: As students discuss their predictions, encourage them to choose a secretary for the group who notes down students' comments by category.

Answers will vary.

Extension: After students' discussions, have them report to the class on what other members of their group said. This will elicit third-person forms of the future perfect tense.

✓ASSESSMENT

Prueba 6-7 with Study Plan (online only)

Prueba: El futuro perfecto
• Prueba 6-7: p. 140

▼31 Más y más rápido

Leer • Hablar

Muchas veces, pasan años antes de que la gente empiece a usar los inventos. Lee la tabla siguiente. Con otro(a) estudiante, piensa por qué unos inventos habrán tardado mucho *(taken a long time)* en usarse mientras que otros inventos habrán tardado poco. Escojan cuatro inventos y preparen explicaciones.

▶ **Modelo**

electricidad / 46 años

A —¿Por qué habrán pasado 46 años entre el invento de la electricidad y su uso masivo?

B —Habrá pasado mucho tiempo porque . . .

MÁS Y MÁS RÁPIDO

Invento	Fecha	Años para su uso masivo (widespread)
Electricidad	1873	46
Teléfono	1876	35
Coche	1886	55
Radio	1906	22
Televisión	1927	26
La Red	1991	7
Teléfono inteligente	1992	5
Tableta electrónica	1993	17

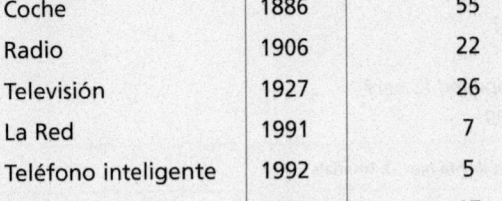

Coche antiguo

▼32 Predicciones para el año 2030

Hablar

En grupos de cuatro, hagan predicciones para el año 2030. ¿Qué habrá pasado en el mundo? ¿Qué pasará? Piensen en sus metas, su escuela, su comunidad, sus viajes de vacaciones, los deportes, la moda y los alimentos.

Modelo

Para el año 2030, habré terminado una carrera y estaré trabajando como abogada.

| Más práctica | GO |

realidades.com | print

Instant Check	✔	
Guided WB pp. 201–202	✔	✔
Core WB p. 86	✔	✔
Comm. WB p. 87	✔	✔
Hispanohablantes **WB** pp. 186–190		✔

274 doscientos setenta y cuatro
Manos a la obra 2

DIFFERENTIATED INSTRUCTION

Students with Learning Difficulties

Guide students to focus on the first sentence or clause of each item in *Actividad* 33. Instruct them to copy the noun that will become an object pronoun in the second part of the item. Then have them convert each noun to the appropriate object pronoun, insert it in the second part of the sentence, and read the entire item aloud.

Advanced Learners

Ask students to use the Internet to investigate other technological advances like those in *Actividad* 31. They might research the creation and widespread use of smartphones, DVDs, e-readers, or tablets. Have them prepare brief reports telling when the device was invented and about what year its use became widespread.

Gramática

▼ Objectives
▶ Read about plans for the future and advances in technology
▶ Talk about people and about giving things to other people

Uso de los complementos directos e indirectos

You already know the direct object pronouns (*me, te, lo, la, nos, os, los, las*) and the indirect object pronouns (*me, te, le, nos, os, les*) in Spanish.

When you use a direct and an indirect object pronoun together, place the indirect object pronoun before the direct object pronoun.

> —Si necesitas un teléfono celular, yo te lo doy. ¿Quién te prestará la computadora?
>
> —Octavio me la prestará.

When the indirect object pronoun *le* or *les* comes before the direct object pronoun *lo, la, los,* or *las*, change *le* or *les* to *se*. In these cases, you often add the prepositional phrase *a Ud., a él, a ella,* etc. or *a* + a noun or a person's name for clarification.

> —¿A quién le comunicarán la noticia del descubrimiento?
>
> —Se la comunicaremos a Carlos.
>
> —José y Adela quieren leer los libros sobre el nuevo invento. ¿Puedes prestárselos?

When you attach two object pronouns to an infinitive, a command, or a present participle, you must add an accent mark to preserve the original stress.

> —Quiero ver las fotos que van a usar para el mercadeo. Dámelas, por favor.
>
> —No puedo dártelas hoy, espera hasta mañana.

▼33 Sobre el futuro

Leer

Carla y Laura quieren estar preparados para el futuro. Completa lo que dicen con los complementos apropiados.

1. Laura quiere que le preste mi libro sobre genética pero no (*se lo / me lo*) _____ voy a prestar.

2. ¿Viste el programa vía satélite sobre la importancia del español en el mundo? (*Se lo / Te lo*) _____ recomiendo.

3. No recibimos la información sobre los nuevos aparatos eléctricos. El gerente de la empresa dice que (*nos la / se la*) _____ enviará la próxima semana.

4. Sé que ustedes comprarán una televisión digital. (*Me la / Se la*) _____ pediré prestada.

5. Quiero leer el artículo sobre informática. ¿(*Me lo / Te lo*) _____ das?

6. Nos explicaron la tarea sobre las nuevas fuentes de energía que habrá en el 2040, pero no (*te la / nos la*) _____ explicaron muy bien.

7. Me compré un programa de realidad virtual. (*Se lo / Te lo*) _____ mostraré cuando vengas a casa.

Una cadena de ADN

Practice and Communicate  6

Gramática [Repaso]

Core Instruction

Resources: Voc. and Gram. Transparency 131

INTERACTIVE WHITEBOARD
Grammar Activities 6-2

Suggestions: On the board or a transparency, cue students with sentences of various types that contain both a direct and an indirect object as nouns. Ask students to restate the sentences, changing the objects to pronouns.

▼**33** Standards: 1.2

Resources: Answer Keys: Student Edition, p. 87

Focus: Practicing combinations of direct and indirect object pronouns

Suggestions: Remind students to use the *se* form of the third-person indirect object pronoun. Point out that Spanish never has the pronoun combinations *le lo, le la, le los,* or *le las.*

Answers:

1. se lo
2. Te lo
3. nos la
4. Se la
5. Me lo
6. nos la
7. Te lo

ENRICH YOUR TEACHING

Teacher-to-Teacher

Using one word per sheet of paper, write the sentence *Juan da el libro a María* and the direct and indirect object pronouns, including *se.* Distribute to students. Say the sentence in English. Students who have the words stand in the correct order. Then say, "Juan gives it to María." The student with *lo* comes up, the one with *el libro* sits down.

21st Century Skills

Creativity and Innovation Have students working in small groups come up with a proposal for a new invention. Their invention can be serious or fanciful, but must be geared towards improving possible future living conditions. Have students share their ideas with the class.

El español en la comunidad

Core Instruction

Standards: 1.2, 5.1

Suggestions: Once students have read the information, ask comprehension questions. For example: *¿Cuál es la idea principal de esta lectura? ¿Cómo ayudan los diarios digitales a los hispanohablantes en los Estados Unidos?*

34 Standards: 1.1

Focus: Practicing combinations of direct and indirect object pronouns

Suggestions: Encourage students to practice alternative placements of object pronouns: *Voy a dársela a Marta./Se la voy a dar a Marta.*

Answers will vary.

35 Standards: 1.1

Focus: Practicing combinations of direct and indirect object pronouns

Suggestions: As students have their group discussions, ask them to be ready to report to the rest of the class on their donation strategy.

Answers will vary.

Pre-AP* Support

• **Learning Objective:** Interpersonal Speaking
• **Activity:** Have students bring to class a donation item such as a CD, a book, etc. Moving around the classroom, have them interact with other students asking if they would like to exchange "gifts" with them. Use this model:
A: *¿Quieres mi disco compacto de Shakira?*
B: *No, gracias. Dáselo a Marcos,* o *Sí, dámelo.*

Following the activity, students can keep the "gift" or, as a class, donate all of the items to a local charity.

• **Pre-AP* Resource Book:** Comprehensive guide to Pre-AP* communication skill development, pp. 10–18, 39–50

El español en la comunidad

Diarios digitales
Las personas hispanohablantes en los Estados Unidos siempre han querido enterarse de las noticias de sus países de origen. Es lógico, allí tienen sus raíces y parte de sus familias. Algunas de las fuentes de información en español más usadas son los periódicos y canales de televisión en español de los Estados Unidos.

Además, gracias a los diarios digitales que hay en la Red, los hispanohablantes pueden leer periódicos de sus países todos los días.

La Red también les ofrece a los estudiantes de español la oportunidad de practicar el idioma y aprender sobre los países hispanohablantes. Pueden saber, por ejemplo, no sólo las noticias importantes de Quito, sino también qué restaurante está de moda, qué película es más popular o qué obra de teatro están poniendo. La Red hace del mundo un lugar verdaderamente pequeño.

▼34 ¿Qué les darás?

Hablar

❶ Imagina que vas a mudarte a un apartamento muy pequeño. Haz una lista de las cosas que no vas a necesitar y que les puedes regalar a tus amigos.

❷ Intercambia tu lista con la de un(a) compañero(a). Tu compañero(a) te va a preguntar a quién le darás cada una de tus cosas.

▶ **Modelo**

la televisión
A —*¿A quién le vas a dar la televisión?*
B —*Voy a dársela a Marta.*

276 doscientos setenta y seis
Manos a la obra 2

▼35 ¿Qué les podemos ofrecer?

Hablar

❶ Tú y tus amigos van a donar cosas a las siguientes personas que las necesitan. Para cada persona, escribe una cosa que le puedes ofrecer.

• un inmigrante que acaba de llegar
• una mujer sin hogar
• una persona de un hogar de ancianos
• un niño de un centro de rehabilitación

Modelo
un paciente de un centro de rehabilitación
unas revistas o una novela

❷ Trabaja con otro(a) estudiante. Hablen de las cosas que pueden ofrecer, cuándo las donarán y cómo las entregarán.

▶ **Modelo**

A —*¿Qué le podemos ofrecer a un paciente de un centro de rehabilitación?*
B —*Le podemos ofrecer unos refrescos.*
A —*¡Buena idea! ¿Cuándo podemos llevárselos?*
B —*Se los podemos llevar este fin de semana.*

DIFFERENTIATED INSTRUCTION

Heritage Language Learners

Ask students who have lived in a heritage country to discuss the role of television there. What are some of the most popular programs? Who are some of the most popular actors or personalities? Ask them to express their opinion on the influence of television. Do they find it positive or negative?

Students with Learning Difficulties

After students have chosen their topics for *Actividad 36,* instruct them to reread sections of the chapter pertaining to that topic. Help them find these sections and suggest that they write down vocabulary and phrases that might be useful to their presentations.

▼36 Las cosas que traerá el futuro |

Hablar • Escribir • Escuchar

❶ Trabaja en un grupo de tres o cuatro estudiantes. Escojan uno de los temas de la lista y hagan predicciones sobre ese tema. Luego, preparen una pequeña presentación para la clase. Mientras escuchan las presentaciones de los demás grupos, tomen notas.

- la vivienda
- la tecnología
- las carreras
- los medios de comunicación
- el ocio
- los alimentos

❷ Con tu compañero(a), usen sus notas para hablar sobre lo que dijeron los demás grupos. Escriban algunas frases que digan si las predicciones de los(as) demás estudiantes son lógicas o ilógicas y por qué.

▼37 Cómo la televisión hizo historia

Leer • Escribir

Pocos avances tecnológicos han tenido una influencia tan grande como la televisión. En México, la televisión ha sido un agente de cambio que ha jugado papeles muy diferentes en distintos momentos históricos.

Conexiones | Las ciencias sociales

La primera transmisión de televisión en México para el público fue el 16 de mayo de 1935, y tuvo lugar en la sede[1] del partido político que gobernó[2] ese país por más de 70 años. Los líderes del partido pensaban que con la televisión en sus manos podían decidir qué ideas, noticias y opiniones iba a recibir el pueblo. Por mucho tiempo, la televisión fue un instrumento de los líderes del país.

1. ¿Por qué se puede decir que la televisión ha tenido una gran influencia en la historia de México?

2. ¿Qué papel juega la televisión en la política de tu país?

1 headquarters 2 ruled

Más práctica	GO

realidades.com | print

Instant Check	✔	
Guided WB pp. 203–204	✔	✔
Core WB pp. 87–88	✔	✔
Comm. WB pp. 81, 88–89	✔	✔
Hispanohablantes WB pp. 191–193		✔

▼36 Standards: 1.1, 1.3

Focus: Using new vocabulary and structures in an oral presentation

Suggestions: As students plan in Step 1, have them brainstorm a list of details associated with their topic that they can use to develop their presentation.

Answers will vary.

▼37 Standards: 1.2, 3.1, 4.2

Resources: Answer Keys: Student Edition, p. 87

Focus: Using new vocabulary and structures to read and respond

Suggestions: Have students read the information silently once. Then ask volunteers to read it aloud in sections. Before students answer the questions, address any reading comprehension issues.

Answers:

1. La televisión fue un instrumento de los líderes políticos. Pensaban que con la televisión podían decidir lo que iba a recibir el pueblo.
2. Answers will vary.

Chapter Project

Students can perform Step 5 at this point. (For more information, see p. 246-b.)

Additional Resources

- Communication Wbk.: Audio Act. 4–5, p. 81
- Teacher's Resource Book: Audio Script, pp. 73–74, Communicative Pair Activity BLM, pp. 81–82
- Audio Program DVD: Cap. 6, Tracks 15–16

ENRICH YOUR TEACHING

Teacher-to-Teacher
Prepare students for *Actividad* 35 by briefly reviewing vocabulary associated with volunteer work and community centers. This can be found in the *A primera vista* 2 section of *Capítulo* 5.

21st Century Skills

Communication Remind students that whenever they do a speaking activity, as in *Actividades* 34 and 35, they will have the opportunity to first watch and listen to native speakers in the *Videomodelos*. This way, they can use a native-speaker model to monitor their own progress.

✔ASSESSMENT

Prueba 6-8 with Study Plan (online only)

Prueba: Uso de los complementos
- Prueba 6-8: p. 141

Examen: Vocabulario y gramática 2
- Examen 2: pp. 142–144
- ExamView: Examen 2

Puente a la cultura

Puente a la cultura
La arquitectura del futuro

Estrategia

Look at Illustrations
Pictures, photographs, and other graphics are often used to emphasize a written message.

You can anticipate what the content of a text will be by examining the illustrations.

The article on this page is about architecture. Look at the photos on these pages and think about the style of the buildings. What might the article be about?

¿Te has preguntado alguna vez cómo serán los edificios del futuro? La mayoría de los arquitectos están de acuerdo en que serán más eficientes, mejores y más inteligentes pero, ¿qué quiere decir eso?

Seguramente, los edificios del futuro usarán menos ladrillo[1] y piedra, pues tendrán materiales como el titanio y las fibras de carbón y grafito[2], siguiendo el ejemplo de los aviones y coches. Cada vez habrá más edificios "inteligentes", en otras palabras, edificios en los que una computadora central controla todos los aparatos y servicios para aprovechar[3] mejor la energía eléctrica, la calefacción y el aire acondicionado en el interior.

El argentino César Pelli es uno de los arquitectos que diseñan edificios futuristas. Una de sus obras más importantes son las Torres Petronas, en Kuala Lumpur, Malasia, consideradas entre los edificios más altos del mundo. Estas torres, con su planta en forma de estrella y construídas de cristal, acero[4] y concreto, tienen un diseño que es a la vez futurista e influenciado por la arquitectura islámica.

---

1 brick 2 titanium, and carbon and graphite fibers 3 to utilize 4 steel

Faro del Comercio, México

Hotel Camino Real, México

Torres Petronas, Malasia

278 doscientos setenta y ocho
¡Adelante!

DIFFERENTIATED INSTRUCTION

Students with Learning Difficulties
Before they read **La arquitectura del futuro,** have students create a chart with the following headings: **nombre del arquitecto, edificio, ciudad, diseño.** After an initial read, have them re-read to find the information necessary to complete the chart.

Advanced Learners
As a group project, have students design and then talk about a futuristic building of their own creation. They should illustrate or discuss how the building will be used, what its appearance will be, and so on.

Otro edificio futurista es el Faro del Comercio, en Monterrey, México, diseñado por el arquitecto mexicano Luis Barragán. La arquitectura de Barragán reúne en un mismo diseño líneas simples y modernas con el uso de colores, texturas y materiales que recuerdan la cultura popular mexicana y los colores de la naturaleza.

Ricardo Legorreta, otro reconocido arquitecto mexicano, ha diseñado el Hotel Camino Real en Polanco, México. La arquitectura de Legorreta se caracteriza por ambientes con diseños geométricos, una armoniosa combinación de espacio y color y un uso funcional y decorativo de la luz.

Un edificio que impresiona por su estilo futurístico es el Milwaukee Art Museum, diseñado por el arquitecto español Santiago Calatrava. Este museo se destaca por su forma única que combina elementos de arte y arquitectura.

Vistas del interior y del exterior del Milwaukee Art Museum

¿Comprendiste?

1. ¿Qué materiales se usarán para construir los edificios del futuro? ¿Por qué crees que se usarán esos materiales?

2. ¿Qué influencias se pueden ver en las Torres Petronas y en el Faro del Comercio? ¿Conoces algún edificio similar? Explica las razones para diseñarlo así.

3. Compara uno de los edificios futuristas de estas páginas con algún edificio moderno que te guste. ¿En qué se parecen? ¿En que se diferencian?

El futuro de tu comunidad

Usa la información del texto y las fotos para hacer predicciones sobre los edificios del futuro de tu comunidad. ¿Cómo será la escuela?, ¿la biblioteca?, ¿el hospital? Escribe un párrafo sobre alguno de esos edificios.

Más práctica GO

realidades.com | print

▶ *Videodocumentario*	✔	
Guided WB p. 205	✔	✔
Comm. WB pp. 90–91, 195	✔	✔
***Hispanohablantes* WB** pp. 194–196		✔
Cultural Reading Activity	✔	

doscientos setenta y nueve **279**
Capítulo 6

ENRICH YOUR TEACHING

Culture Note

César Pelli has also designed many performing arts centers in the United States. The Aronoff Center in Cincinnati features the use of brick and stone, traditional building materials for the area. Pelli's design for the Performing Arts Center of Greater Miami reflects the city's tropical climate and multicultural ambience.

21st Century Skills

Information Literacy Have students search the Internet for more information on the individuals featured in this reading. They can search the keywords: *Santiago Calatrava, César Pelli, Luis Barragán,* and *Ricardo Legorreta.* Ask students to identify other Spanish-speaking architects who have made important contributions in today's world.

¿Qué me cuentas?

Core Instruction

Standards: 1.1, 1.2, 1.3

Resources: Teacher's Resource Book: Audio Script, p. 74; Audio Program DVD: Cap. 6, Track 17; Answer Keys: Student Edition, p. 87

Focus: Practicing listening and reading comprehension of new vocabulary and grammar; using information to write a cohesive and coherent reaction.

AP* Skills: Integration of listening, reading, and writing to comprehend and synthesize information from spoken and written sources.

Suggestions:

For Step 1, use the audio or read the descriptions aloud. Allow students to hear the descriptions twice through: the first time to write their answers, the second time to check them.

For Step 2, have students identify significant details as they read and make appropriate inferences about the type of person that would be best suited for each of the jobs.

For Step 3, encourage students to use each of the suggested expressions, and to support their arguments with specific information from both the listening in Step 1 and the reading in Step 2.

Answers:

Step 1

1. b   2. c   3. a   4. c   5. b   6. b

Steps 2–3

Answers will vary.

Block Schedule

Ask each student to write five false statements about the article. Place the students in pairs. Have them read the sentences to each other with the other student correcting each of the false statements.

Additional Resources

Student Resource: Realidades para hispanohablantes, p. 197

Pre–AP*

| ▼ Objectives

▶ Listen to and read about professional careers
▶ Discuss professions and the necessary qualifications

Integración

¿Qué me cuentas?: Cuando sea mayor

Escucha cómo un profesor describe a sus estudiantes. Anota el nombre de cada estudiante mientras contestas las preguntas. Luego, lee las descripciones de carreras profesionales y decide qué carrera será apropiada para cada estudiante.

1 🔊))) Vas a escuchar una serie de descripciones. Después de cada descripción, vas a oír dos preguntas. Escoge la respuesta correcta para cada pregunta.

1. a. avances tecnológicos   b. programas de dibujos animados   c. productos de mercadeo
2. a. insectos   b. medios de comunicación   c. cómo curar enfermedades
3. a. el mercadeo   b. las comunicaciones   c. la medicina
4. a. una gerente   b. una cocinera   c. una arquitecta
5. a. un disco digital   b. una calculadora   c. un teléfono celular
6. a. una contadora   b. una actriz cómica   c. una abogada

2 Ahora lee este artículo sobre carreras profesionales.

Carreras del futuro

BUSCAR 🔍

⭐ **Arquitecto de viviendas eficientes** En el futuro, se buscarán arquitectos que tengan conocimientos de construcción y que hayan usado nuevas fuentes de energía en sus diseños.

⭐ **Diseñador de juegos virtuales educativos** En el futuro, los diseñadores tendrán que tener experiencia como programadores. Los candidatos ideales serán artísticos pero lógicos y cuidadosos en su trabajo.

⭐ **Vendedores de productos tecnológicos** Se necesitarán representantes amables y emprendedores. Estos vendedores tendrán que buscar nuevos clientes y ofrecerles nuevos productos. Será necesario que sean bilingües o hasta trilingües.

⭐ **Gerente de turismo y hotelería** Se buscarán personas maduras que puedan tomar decisiones. Es importante que se lleven bien con todo tipo de cliente y que tengan un buen sentido de humor.

⭐ **Científico** Las empresas farmacéuticas necesitarán personas que estén informadas sobre los últimos avances tecnológicos de genética y que tengan experiencia en el campo de la medicina.

⭐ **Contador** Las compañías internacionales necesitarán contadores con conocimientos de finanzas y de leyes internacionales. Se buscarán personas capaces de trabajar en forma independiente. Será necesario que tengan experiencia en el extranjero.

3 Trabaja con un(a) compañero(a) y empareja cada estudiante del paso 1 con una carrera del paso 2. Considera estas preguntas: ¿Qué tendrá que estudiar cada estudiante para seguir esa carrera? ¿Qué cualidades y habilidades serán necesarias para esa carrera? Presenten su análisis a la clase. Usen las siguientes expresiones para conectar sus ideas.

| así que | por lo tanto | mientras |
| además que | por eso | aunque |

280 doscientos ochenta
¡Adelante!

DIFFERENTIATED INSTRUCTION

Multiple Intelligences

Have students categorize the six highlighted careers based on the Multiple Intelligences. You may need to explain the categories: linguistic, logical/mathematical, musical/rhythmic, visual/spatial, bodily/kinesthetic, intrapersonal, inter-personal/social, and naturalist. Then, have them write about which career might suit them best and why.

Students with Learning Difficulties

Help students organize information for their oral presentations. Model how to turn each question in the chart into an informative sentence. *¿Quiénes darán las clases? Los estudiantes darán las clases.*

Presentación oral

Mi escuela del futuro

| ▶ **Objectives** | **Aplicación** |

▶ Demonstrate how to give a speech about adapting a school's technology
▶ Map your speech using a main idea and supporting details

Tarea

Imagina que dentro de 10 años regresas a tu escuela y que serás el(la) nuevo(a) director(a). ¿Qué cambios harás para adaptar la escuela a los nuevos avances tecnológicos? Tienes que preparar un discurso para decir lo que harás.

1 Prepárate Responde a las preguntas sobre los cambios que harás en tu escuela. Usa una tabla como ésta.

¿Quiénes darán las clases y cómo las darán?	
¿Qué materias enseñarán?	
¿Qué cambios harás en el edificio?	
¿Cómo harán sus tareas los estudiantes?	
¿Cómo se comunicarán los estudiantes?	

2 Practica Vuelve a leer la información de la tabla. Puedes usar tus notas para practicar, pero no al hablar ante la clase. Recuerda:

- explicar con detalles lo que harás y por qué
- mirar directamente al público al hablar
- usar los tiempos futuros y el vocabulario del capítulo

Modelo

Los estudiantes podrán estudiar desde sus casas. Por las tardes, un robot ayudará a todos los estudiantes con sus tareas. Cada estudiante tendrá una computadora muy avanzada, casi humana . . .

3 Haz tu presentación Imagina que las personas que escuchan no saben cómo será tu escuela en el futuro. Descríbeles con detalles las cosas que harás para adaptar tu escuela a los avances del futuro.

4 Evaluación Tu profesor(a) utilizará la siguiente rúbrica para evaluar tu presentación.

Rubric	Score 1	Score 3	Score 5
How well your information is organized	Your ideas are undeveloped or not addressed at all.	You tend to skip around from idea to idea.	Your ideas are presented in a logical, planned order.
How well you support your main ideas	Your supporting evidence is absent.	Some of your supporting evidence is weak.	All your main ideas are supported with interesting details.
How effectively you deliver your speech	You read your speech. You have no eye contact with the audience and little or no intonation.	You make some eye contact. You use intonation, but not convincingly.	You have good eye contact with the audience. Your intonation helps get the message across.

Estrategia

Mapping your speech using main idea and details

To organize a speech you can *map* it in advance. Think of your presentation as an organized way to communicate your ideas. You should start with an opening statement of the main idea. Then, use the items in the chart you wrote as subtopics. As you speak, introduce each subtopic one at a time, and elaborate on it by adding details. End your presentation with a closing statement that reinforces the main idea or your opinion about it.

Photo courtesy of High Tech High

doscientos ochenta y uno **281**
Capítulo 6

Speaking 6

© Common Core: Speaking

Presentación oral

Core Instruction

Standards: 1.2, 1.3, 3.1

Resources: Voc. and Gram. Transparency 4

Focus: Preparing and delivering an oral presentation

Suggestions: Review the task and the four-step approach with students. Review the rubric (see *Assessment* below) to explain how you will grade the performance task. Before students begin, direct their attention to *Estrategia*. Point out that the chart in Step 1 is one way of mapping a speech. Use *Vocabulary and Grammar Transparency* 4 as a model. Show students how to set up their own charts by copying the questions into the left column. Leave plenty of space between questions and tell students to use that space to write their answers in the right column of their own charts. The answers they write will be the details they use to support each main idea in their speech.

Pre-AP* Support

- **Learning Objective:** Presentational Speaking
- **Activity:** Remind students to focus on the presentational speaking skills used in this task such as fluency, pronunciation, and comprehensibility.
- **Pre-AP* Resource Book:** Comprehensive guide to Pre-AP* speaking skill development, pp. 39–50

Portfolio

Make video or audio recordings of student presentations in class, or assign the RealTalk activity so they can record their presentations online. Include the recording in their portfolios.

Additional Resources

Student Resource: Realidades para hispanohablantes, p. 198

✓ ASSESSMENT

Presentación oral

- Assessment Program: Rubrics, p. T32
  Review the rubric with students. Go over the descriptions of the different levels of performance. After assessing students, help individuals understand how their performance could be improved. (See Teacher's Resource Book for suggestions on using rubrics in assessment.)

ENRICH YOUR TEACHING

Teacher-to-Teacher

e-amigos: Have students send their *e-amigos* a written summary of their *Presentación oral.* Encourage students to defend their suggestions and to respond to those of their *e-amigos.*

21st Century Skills

Creativity and Innovation In preparation for their presentations, have students browse the Internet using keywords such as *futuristic schools* and *future learning.* Encourage students to integrate available images of futuristic school buildings, classrooms, and learning technologies into their presentations to illustrate their visionary plans for their schools.

Language Arts Connection: Expository Writing

Standards: 3.1

Point out to students that there are two ways they can organize their compare and contrast essay. They can tell all about one period of time first, then compare it to the other in another paragraph. Or they can go back and forth between one period of time and the other, showing how they are alike or different in various ways. Remind them that this latter alternative will require them to use more transitions in their writing.

 Common Core: Writing

Presentación escrita

Core Instruction

Standards: 1.2, 1.3, 3.1

Resources: Voc. and Gram. Transparency 2

Focus: Combining learned vocabulary and structures in a written presentation

Suggestions: Begin by explaining the criteria you will use to evaluate students' compositions. (See Step 5, *Evaluación*, in the Student Edition, and *Assessment* on the following page.)

Direct students' attention to the *Estrategia*. Ask them to share additional background information they have learned in Language Arts courses about comparing and contrasting. Use *Vocabulary and Grammar Transparency* 2 to model brainstorming and recording ideas for a comparison and contrast essay.

Pre-AP* Support

- **Learning Objective:** Presentational Writing
- **Pre-AP* Resource Book:** Comprehensive guide to Pre-AP* writing skill development, pp. 27–38

Presentación escrita
El futuro según el presente

| ▼ Objectives
▶ Write a comparison of the past and the present
▶ Use a Venn diagram to organize similarities and differences

Estrategia

Compare and contrast
If you want to compare issues, use signal words to mark their similarities and their differences. You can say, for instance, "*En el pasado había muchas enfermedades, pero hoy, con los avances en la medicina, podemos curarlas*" or "*Antes, los viajes tardaban mucho tiempo, pero ahora tardan sólo unas horas.*" Other expressions are: "*Antes . . . pero ahora . . .*", "*en el pasado, ambos . . . y hoy . . .*", "*ni entonces ni ahora . . . .*"

Signal words give you clues about the structure of the passage.

El futuro es siempre incierto *(uncertain)*. Tenemos una idea de lo que sucederá pero no podemos estar completamente seguros de ello. Podemos hacer predicciones. Para la gente que vivió en tiempos pasados el futuro también fue incierto. Escoge un período del pasado y compáralo con el presente. Escribe un ensayo *(essay)* con tus comparaciones, teniendo en cuenta la pregunta: "¿El futuro será siempre mejor que el presente?"

1 Antes de escribir

Usa un diagrama como éste para anotar las semejanzas y las diferencias *(similarities and differences)* entre el período del pasado que escogiste y el presente.

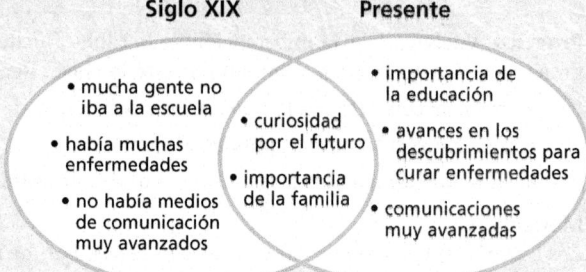

Siglo XIX
- mucha gente no iba a la escuela
- había muchas enfermedades
- no había medios de comunicación muy avanzados

- curiosidad por el futuro
- importancia de la familia

Presente
- importancia de la educación
- avances en los descubrimientos para curar enfermedades
- comunicaciones muy avanzadas

2 Borrador

Escribe tu borrador en forma de ensayo. Comienza con la pregunta de la introducción y presenta las épocas *(time periods)* que vas a describir. Explica las diferencias y semejanzas entre los dos períodos, según lo que escribiste en el diagrama de Venn. Usa expresiones como *pero* y *sin embargo* para comparar y contrastar.

Modelo

Muchas veces nos preguntamos si el futuro será mejor que el presente. Esa pregunta no la podemos responder ahora, porque no sabemos lo que pasará.

Por ejemplo, si comparamos el siglo XIX con el presente, encontraremos que éstos son dos momentos de la historia muy diferentes. La gente del siglo XIX no sabía lo que iba a ocurrir en el futuro; pero nosotros tampoco lo sabemos. En el siglo XIX no había . . .

El mundo siempre tiene problemas diferentes; sin embargo, siempre habrá un futuro. Por eso . . .

Comparison of the past and the present

Introduction to present the topic

Details of the past

Conclusion on how the past and the present are similar

282 doscientos ochenta y dos
¡Adelante!

DIFFERENTIATED INSTRUCTION

Heritage Language Learners

Students may have difficulty correctly placing commas in complex sentences. Have students trade drafts of their essay with a partner and read the drafts aloud. Remind students that in many cases, when they sense a pause in the text, a comma should be inserted.

Advanced Learners

Ask students to imagine they have taken a trip back in time to a point of their choice. Have them explain to a person of that period how one or more aspects of everyday life will have changed. Challenge them to focus on something they take for granted that didn't exist during their chosen period of the past.

3 Redacción/Revisión

Después de escribir el primer borrador de tu ensayo, intercambia tu trabajo con el de otro(a) estudiante. Léanlos y hagan sugerencias sobre cómo mejorarlos. Decidan qué aspectos de los ensayos son más o menos efectivos. Fíjense en cómo el escritor del modelo incluyó detalles en su ensayo. Hagan sugerencias sobre cómo mejorar los ensayos.

Haz lo siguiente: Subraya con una línea los verbos en presente y con dos los verbos en futuro.

- ¿Hay concordancia entre los verbos y el sujeto?
- ¿El presente y el futuro están empleados correctamente?

> nos preguntamos
> Muchas veces preguntamos si el futuro es será
> el presente
> mejor que presente? No sabemos lo que
> pasarán en 50 años. Ignoramos lo que se habrá
> descubierto entonces. Esa pregunta no la
> podemos
> podremos responder ahora, ya que . . .

4 Publicación

Antes de escribir la versión final, lee de nuevo tu borrador y repasa los siguientes puntos:

- ¿Sigue mi ensayo un orden lógico?
- ¿Comparé claramente los dos períodos?
- ¿Añadí detalles a mis descripciones?
- ¿La conclusión es resultado de lo que dice el ensayo?

Después de revisar el borrador, escribe una copia en limpio de tu ensayo.

5 Evaluación

Se utilizará la siguiente rúbrica para evaluar tu presentación.

Rubric	Score 1	Score 3	Score 5
Completion of task	Your main idea is unclear, not stated, or not developed.	Your main idea is stated, but development is weak.	Your main idea is clearly stated and developed.
Development of comparison and contrast	Your essay does not present two time periods for comparison and contrast.	You presented two time periods, but few details are compared or contrasted.	You compared and contrasted time periods clearly with good use of supporting detail.
Sentence structure/ grammar, spelling, mechanics	Your sentences run on or are fragmented with many grammar, spelling, mechanics errors.	You used sentences consistently. You have some grammar, spelling, and/or mechanics errors.	Your sentence structure is correct and varied with few grammar, spelling, mechanics errors.

doscientos ochenta y tres **283**
Capítulo 6

Suggestions (Cont'd):

In Step 2, students should decide on the organization of their essays. Will they make a side-by-side comparison, or will they describe one time period all at once and then compare and contrast the other in a separate paragraph? Explain that the organization strategy they choose depends on how much they have to say about each time period. If they are comparing several details, suggest that they use the latter strategy, focusing on one period at a time, in separate paragraphs.

For Step 3, encourage students to focus on sentence structure, transitions, and use of past, present, and future tenses. Have them follow the suggestions shown.

Evaluation

Steps 4 and 5 overlap. Students will need evaluation by you, their peers, or self-evaluation to fine-tune and polish their drafts.

Portfolio

Keep students' final drafts in their portfolios as a writing sample.

Additional Resources

Student Resource: Realidades para hispanohablantes, p. 199

ENRICH YOUR TEACHING

21st Century Skills

Communication Students will have to use their written language for the purpose of comparing and contrasting a time period in the past with the present. As a warm-up to this task, have students make a list of the Spanish words and expressions they use to discuss similarities and differences between two topics, as well as common transition words and phrases.

✓ ASSESSMENT

Presentación escrita

- Assessment Program: Rubrics, p. T32
  Review the rubric with students. Go over the descriptions of the different levels of performance. After assessing students, help individuals understand how their performance could be improved. (See Teacher's Resource Book for suggestions on using rubrics in assessment.)

Common Core: Reading

Lectura

Core Instruction

Standards: 1.2, 1.3, 2.2, 3.1, 3.2, 5.2

Resources: Voc. and Gram. Transparency 4

Focus: Reading an extended passage

Suggestions:

Pre-reading: Before reading, direct students' attention to the *Al leer* section. Have them copy the graphic organizer from p. 287 and make sure they understand how they will use it. Also refer students to the *Estrategia*. Remind them that, besides using context clues as suggested, they know other strategies to help them understand difficult words and passages: they can use their knowledge of cognates and word families.

Reading: When reading together with students, pause frequently to address comprehension issues they may have and to allow them to fill in their *Elementos del cuento* charts from p. 287. Here are some possible comprehension issues on this page for which you can provide some guidance:

• After students have read the first part of the story, ask: *¿Cuántos personajes están presentes al principio del cuento? ¿Cómo se llaman? ¿Qué relación existe entre ellos? ¿Son miembros de la misma familia? ¿Son amigas? ¿Trabajan juntas? ¿De qué gran cambio están hablando? (Son tres: Rosa, Betty y Carmen; trabajan juntas; hablan del cambio de puesto de Rosa.)*

• *En esta escena, ¿cómo tratan de ayudar Betty y Carmen a Rosa? (Tratan de animarla, de hacerla sentirse mejor.)*

• *Mira las dos primeras preguntas en la sección Al leer. ¿Cómo las puedes contestar ahora?*

BELLRINGER REVIEW

Write these words for parts of a computer on the board:

   teclado   pantalla   ratón

Have students write one sentence for each using the following format:

El/La _____ sirve para_____.

Lectura
Rosa

Estrategia

Coping with unknown words
When you encounter a word you don't know, try to infer its meaning from the context of the sentence. If you can't guess the meaning, skip the word and continue reading. If the word is essential and the reading doesn't help you understand it, look it up in the dictionary.

Al leer

Vas a leer un cuento de Ángel Balzarino, escritor argentino nacido en 1943. Al leer el cuento verás que el autor no nos explica dónde ocurre la acción, ni nos dice claramente quiénes son o qué hacen los personajes. De esta manera, el autor añade un elemento de suspenso. Lee el cuento una primera vez para tener una idea general de lo que pasa. Luego, copia la tabla que aparece al final de la lectura. Mientras lees por segunda vez, completa la tabla. Presta atención a los siguientes puntos:

• quiénes son los personajes

• las emociones de los personajes al principio del cuento

• la importancia de trabajar y la satisfacción de un trabajo bien realizado

• el final sorprendente *(surprising)*

—¡Hoy es el día! —el tono de Rosa expresó cierta zozobra[1], la sensación de una derrota[2] ineludible—. ¿Por qué habrán decidido eso?

—Nadie lo sabe, querida —respondió Betty.

—Así es. Son órdenes[3] superiores —Carmen pareció resignada[4] ante esa realidad—. Simplemente debemos obedecer.

Aunque la explicación resultaba clara y sencilla, no logró convencer a Rosa. Ya nada la consolaría[5]. Ahora sólo deseaba sublevarse[6], expresar abiertamente la indignación que sentía desde hacía una semana, cuando le comunicaron la orden increíble de sacarla de allí.

—¡No quiero separarme de ustedes! —ahora su voz tuvo el carácter de un ruego angustioso[7]—. ¡No puedo aceptarlo!

—Nosotras tampoco lo deseamos, Rosa.

—Posiblemente te lleven a un sitio más importante —dijo Carmen dulcemente, tratando de animarla—. Tus antecedentes son extraordinarios. Sin duda los han tenido en cuenta para esa resolución.

—Por supuesto —confirmó Betty—. ¿Adónde te gustaría trabajar ahora?

Se produjo un largo silencio; embargada[8] por la duda, Rosa demoró[9] una respuesta concreta, como si aún no hubiera contemplado esa posibilidad.

—No lo sé. No tengo ambiciones. Me gusta estar aquí.

—Pero ya estuviste mucho tiempo, ¿no te parece?

---

1 uneasiness, anxiety 2 defeat 3 orders 4 resigned
5 would comfort 6 to revolt 7 anguished plea
8 overwhelmed 9 delayed

DIFFERENTIATED INSTRUCTION

Heritage Language Learners

After students have read the selection for comprehension, assign them the roles of the different characters in the story and have them prepare a dramatic reading. Encourage them to focus on pronunciation and expression.

Students with Learning Difficulties

Some students may have difficulty keeping track of the characters in the story. On a piece of paper, have them copy the names **Rosa, Betty,** and **Carmen.** After reading each paragraph, have them stop and record a key phrase related to the character who has just spoken or been described.

Control de Datos Generales

—Tal vez sí. ¡Cuarenta y tres años! —la pesadumbre[10] de Rosa se transformó de pronto en una ráfaga de orgullo[11]—. Fui la primera que empezó a trabajar en el Control de Datos Generales. Siempre me encargaron las tareas más complicadas. Nunca tuve un problema, nadie me ha hecho una corrección.

—Lo sabemos, Rosa.

—¡Una trayectoria realmente admirable!

—Por eso querrán trasladarte. Necesitarán tus servicios en otra parte. Quizá te lleven al Centro Nacional de Comunicaciones.

Las palabras de Betty reflejaron un vibrante entusiasmo, casi tuvieron una mágica sonoridad[12]. Trabajar en ese lugar constituía un hermoso privilegio. A pesar de ser un anhelo[13] común, todas comprendían que eran remotas las posibilidades de realizarlo, como si debieran recorrer un camino lleno de escollos[14]. Preferían, tal vez para evitar una desilusión, descartar la esperanza[15] de ser escogidas.

---

10 sorrow **11** burst of pride **12** harmony **13** yearning
14 stumbling blocks **15** to leave aside any hope

—A cualquiera le gustaría estar allí —dijo Rosa sin énfasis—. Pero creo que ya soy demasiado vieja.

—Precisamente por eso te habrán escogido —dijo Betty con fervor—. Para trabajar allí se necesita tener mucha experiencia.

—Las cosas están cambiando, Rosa —confirmó Carmen—. Todo se presenta bajo un aspecto nuevo, casi sorprendente. Es un proceso de reestructuración. Ellos parecen decididos a dar a cada cosa el lugar que le corresponde. Sin duda comprendieron que era hora de darte una merecida recompensa[16].

—Quizá tengan razón —dijo Rosa modestamente—. Cuarenta y tres años de eficiente labor tienen un gran significado. Aunque nunca me interesó recibir un premio. Simplemente me dediqué a trabajar de la mejor manera.

—Siempre serás un ejemplo para nosotras, Rosa.

—Nadie será capaz de reemplazarte. Estamos seguras.

—Sin embargo, desearía saber a quién pondrán en mi lugar.

---

16 deserved reward

doscientos ochenta y cinco **285**
Capítulo 6

Suggestions (Cont'd):

Reading: Here are some possible comprehension issues on this page for which you can provide some guidance:

• *Uno de los personajes usa una palabra que se parece a la palabra* trajectory *en inglés. Un sinónimo de la palabra en español es "carrera." ¿Qué palabra es?* (trayectoria)

• *Según dicen los personajes, ¿qué es más prestigioso* (prestigious): *trabajar en el Control de Datos Generales o trabajar en el Centro Nacional de Comunicaciones? ¿Qué partes del texto te ayudan a contestar esta pregunta?* (en el Centro Nacional de Comunicaciones; "un hermoso privilegio"; "A cualquiera le gustaría estar allí.")

• *¿Qué cualidades tiene Rosa como trabajadora?* (es eficiente y dedicada)

• *Ahora, ¿cómo contestas la tercera pregunta en Al leer?* (Los personajes piensan que trabajar bien da mucha satisfacción, tiene importancia y merece un premio.)

Teacher-to-Teacher

When discussing a reading together, ask questions that require students to refer to the text in order to answer them. This causes them to approach the text with a purpose, which is an important reading strategy.

Additional Resources

Student Resource: Guided Practice: Lectura, pp. 206–207

ENRICH YOUR TEACHING

Culture Note

Ángel Balzarino was born in 1943 in Villa Trinidad, Argentina. The recipient of many awards and honors, Balzarino has dedicated his writing to the art and craft of the short story. Given the theme of *Rosa,* it is interesting that many of Balzarino's stories are currently available to read on the Internet.

21st Century Skills

Technology Literacy Have students use the digital technology within **realidades.com** to access extra reading support. Computer corrected activities use different reading strategies to help students build their vocabulary and progress at their own pace through the reading.

Suggestions (Cont'd):

Reading: Here are some possible comprehension issues on this page for which you can provide some guidance:

• *En tus propias palabras, ¿qué pasa en el cuento al principio de esta página? (Alguien se acerca.)*

• *En la seguna columna, ¿qué palabra se parece a la palabra* annihilation *en inglés y tiene el mismo significado? (aniquilación)*

• *¿Con qué van a reemplazar a Rosa, con otra máquina o con un ser humano? (un ser humano)*

Post-reading: Have students discuss the ending of the story and share their thoughts. Did they expect the ending to turn out as it did?

Pre-AP* Support

• **Learning Objective:** Presentational Writing

• **Activity:** Have students focus on the various services that Rosa mentions she has efficiently performed for the company. Then ask each student to imagine that they are a current-day "machine" that will some day be useless. Have each write a brief paragraph arguing several reasons why they should be retained. (Coche: *Siempre lo llevé a su trabajo por la lluvia y la nieve. No gasté mucha gasolina.*) Share with the class.

• *Pre-AP* Resource Book:** Comprehensive guide to Pre-AP* writing skill development, pp. 27–38

Block Schedule

Have students work in groups of three and present this story to the class as a play. Without a narrator (a voice to describe the action), they are to present the dialogue between Rosa, Betty, and Carmen. Ask them to focus on portraying the emotions between the three characters. Have the play end at the line *"¡Mucha suerte en tu nuevo trabajo, Rosa!"*

Las palabras de Rosa quedaron de repente superadas[17] por el ruido de unos pasos cada vez más cercanos; entonces, algo sobresaltadas[18] por esa señal que parecía anunciar una grave amenaza[19], las tres se quedaron a la expectativa.

—¡Allí vienen!

—Sí —Rosa no se preocupó en disimular su consternación—. ¡Ha llegado el momento!

Carmen y Betty se vieron contagiadas[20] por ese estado de ánimo; después, con forzada exaltación, sólo pudieron decir a modo de despedida:

—¡Mucha suerte en tu nuevo trabajo, Rosa!

La puerta se abrió de repente y cuatro hombres jóvenes, de cuerpos esbeltos y vigorosos, entraron en el lugar donde se amontonaban[21] diversas máquinas y pantallas a las que las luces incandescentes les daban un aspecto limpio, reluciente, casi de implacable frialdad[22].

—¿Cuál es? —preguntó uno de ellos.

El Suplente pasó lentamente la vista a su alrededor, en una especie de reconocimiento, hasta que extendió una mano.

—Aquélla. Se la conoce con el nombre de Rosa.

Los tres hombres se acercaron con pasos firmes y decididos hacia la computadora más grande, cuyo material parecía algo deteriorado por el uso y los años.

—¿La llevamos al lugar de costumbre?

—Sí, a la Cámara[23] de Aniquilación.

—Está bien.

Mientras los hombres llevaban la vieja y pesada computadora, el Suplente fue a ocupar su puesto. Entonces no pudo evitar una franca sonrisa de seguridad, de absoluto triunfo al comprender que ya estaba a punto de finalizar la Era de las Máquinas.

---

17 overcome **18** alarmed **19** serious threat **20** infected
21 piled up **22** coldness

23 Chamber

286 doscientos ochenta y seis
   ¡Adelante!

DIFFERENTIATED INSTRUCTION

Heritage Language Learners

Have students debate the following topic with a partner: *La computadora es el avance tecnológico más importante del siglo XX.* Instruct one student to agree with the statement, and the other to disagree. Encourage those who have lived in heritage countries to consider the role of computers there.

Advanced Learners

Ask students to pretend they are writing a longer story about the future. Invite them to write one scene from the story. This could be a dialogue between two or more characters or a description of a futuristic setting.

Interacción con la lectura

1 Llena la tabla con información del cuento.

ELEMENTOS DEL CUENTO

nombre del personaje principal	
dos palabras que describen al personaje	
una frase que dice cuál es el problema	
una frase que dice cuál es el final	

2 Trabaja con un grupo de estudiantes para comentar lo que escribieron en sus tablas.

- ¿Cuál es el problema que se presenta en el cuento? ¿Quién habrá decidido sacar a Rosa de la oficina?

- Carmen dice que quizás lleven a Rosa a un lugar más importante. ¿Lo habrá hecho porque lo cree o para animar a Rosa?

- ¿Cómo apoyan a Rosa sus compañeras? ¿Te parece que así debe ser?

- ¿Cuál será el futuro de Rosa? ¿Por qué habrá dicho que no tiene ambiciones?

- ¿Qué te parece el final del cuento? ¿Te parece optimista o pesimista? Explica por qué.

3 Trabaja con tu grupo para buscar palabras de la lectura que no conocían o no recordaban. Hablen sobre cómo lograron determinar o recordar el significado de esas palabras para entender mejor la lectura.

4 Y tú, ¿qué piensas? ¿Somos en realidad "arquitectos de nuestro propio futuro"? ¿O crees que otras personas deciden todo por nosotros?

▼ Fondo Cultural | Puerto Rico

El Proyecto de la Escuela Virtual de la Universidad de Puerto Rico sigue buscando maestros para un entrenamiento que transformará las clases que se dan a los estudiantes de una futura escuela virtual del Departamento de Educación.

Los interesados deben tener habilidades para el trabajo con computadoras, y tener cuentas (accounts) privadas de acceso a la Red. Se les darán materiales y un poco de dinero a los escogidos. El proyecto durará dos años.

- ¿Crees que en el futuro toda la educación será a distancia?

- ¿Cuáles serán las ventajas (advantages) de estos cursos? ¿Cuáles serán las desventajas?

- ¿Has pensado alguna vez en tomar clases a distancia? ¿Conoces alguna universidad o escuela que las ofrezca?

Instituto de Educación a Distancia, Universidad de Puerto Rico

Más práctica (GO) realidades.com | print

Guided WB pp. 206–207	✔	✔
Comm. WB p. 196	✔	✔
Cultural Reading Activity	✔	

doscientos ochenta y siete **287**
Capítulo 6

ENRICH YOUR TEACHING

Culture Note
Today it is possible to study and travel "virtually." Distance-learning programs allow students to take courses throughout the world. International chat rooms create a place to meet and practice language skills. Many cultural and tourist destinations have their own Web sites.

21st Century Skills

Critical Thinking and Problem Solving Have students discuss the challenges that a foreign language student might face when enrolling in a distance learning program. What are the advantages and disadvantages of learning Spanish in a virtual classroom? How might a distance learning program help them learn Spanish? Are there some skills that they could practice more than others?

Reading 6

▼ Interacción con la lectura
Standards: 1.1, 1.2, 1.3, 3.1

Resources: Answer Keys: Student Edition, p. 88

Suggestions: Point out to students that what they are doing in Step 3 is sharing learning strategies. Provide help as necessary by reminding students of names for the strategies they use, such as *usar claves de contexto, considerar familias de palabras,* or *reconocer cognados.*

Answers:

Step 1
Rosa
vieja, trabajadora
Le comunicaron la orden increíble de sacarla de allí.
Los hombres llevaban la vieja y pesada computadora.

Steps 2–4.
Answers will vary.

Fondo cultural

Standards: 1.1, 1.2, 3.1, 5.1

Suggestions: After students have read the information silently, ask comprehension questions. For example: *¿Está buscando la Universidad de Puerto Rico maestros o estudiantes? (maestros) ¿Será un buen candidato una persona que no tiene computadora? Explica tu respuesta. (No. Un buen candidato tiene que tener habilidades para el trabajo con computadora y acceso a la Red.)*

Answers will vary.

Teacher-to-Teacher

Invite students to tell what they know about existing distance education programs. Encourage them to explain how the programs work and what their advantages and disadvantages are.

For Further Reading

Student Resource: Lecturas 3: "Viaje a las estrellas," pp. 38–41

287

Review Activities

Profesiones y oficios/Sustantivos asociados con el futuro: Have students prepare cards or slips of paper for each vocabulary item in these categories. Divide students into groups and assign each group a section of the vocabulary items. Place the cards or slips from each category into two separate containers. Have students take turns drawing an item from each pile. If there is an obvious connection between the two items drawn, the student makes that connection in a sentence that uses both items. If there is not, the student tells about a connection that might exist in the future. For example: *el (la) peluquero(a)/el aparato* – *Una peluquera usa varios aparatos eléctricos en su trabajo.* *el (la) peluquero(a)/el gen* – *El peluquero del futuro cambiará los genes de sus clientes para que tengan el pelo perfecto.*

Cualidades/Campos y carreras del futuro: Have students use these items in sentences that make it clear they understand their meanings.

Verbos: Have students work in pairs. Partners take turns using a verb in a sentence that either makes sense or doesn't. If the sentence makes sense, the other partner says so and goes to the next verb. If the sentence does not make sense, the partner must explain why it doesn't or correct it so that it does.

Otras palabras y expresiones: Students can use these words and expressions as they go over the review activities for the other categories.

El futuro: Have students pretend they are a wizard from 300 years ago who is very good at making accurate predictions about what life will be like in the twenty-first century. Have them tell about life today: *Cada casa tendrá una caja mágica que da visiones de las cosas que pasan en otras partes del mundo. En vez de leer libros, la gente mirará las imágenes en la caja mágica.*

Repaso del capítulo
Vocabulario y gramática

profesiones y oficios

el / la abogado(a)	lawyer
el / la arquitecto(a)	architect
el / la banquero(a)	banker
el / la científico(a)	scientist
el / la cocinero(a)	cook
el / la contador(a)	accountant
el / la diseñador(a)	designer
la empresa	business
las finanzas	finance
el hombre de negocios, la mujer de negocios	businessman, businesswoman
el / la ingeniero(a)	engineer
el / la jefe(a)	boss
el / la juez(a)	judge
el / la peluquero(a)	hairstylist
el / la programador(a)	programmer
el / la redactor(a)	editor
el / la traductor(a)	translator

cualidades

ambicioso, -a	ambitious
capaz	able
cuidadoso, -a	careful
eficiente	efficient
emprendedor, -a	enterprising
maduro, -a	mature

verbos

ahorrar	to save
aumentar	to increase
averiguar	to find out
comunicarse	to communicate
contaminar	to pollute
curar	to cure
dedicarse a	to dedicate oneself to
desaparecer	to disappear
descubrir	to discover
desempeñar un cargo	to hold a position
diseñar	to design
enterarse	to find out
graduarse (u → ú)	to graduate
hacerse	to become
inventar	to invent
lograr	to achieve, to manage (to)
mudarse	to move to
predecir	to predict
prolongar	to prolong, to extend

reducir (zc)	to reduce
reemplazar	to replace
seguir una carrera	to pursue a career
tomar decisiones	to make decisions
traducir	to translate

sustantivos asociados con el futuro

el aparato	gadget
el avance	advance
el desarrollo	development
la enfermedad	illness
la fábrica	factory
la fuente de energía	energy source
el gen, *pl.* los genes	gene
la genética	genetics
el invento	invention
la máquina	machine
la mayoría	the majority
los medios de comunicación	media
el ocio	free time
la realidad virtual	virtual reality
tecnológico, -a	technological
el uso	use
vía satélite	via satellite
la vivienda	housing

otras palabras y expresiones

así que	therefore
además de	in addition to
casado, -a	married
como si fuera	as though it were
de hoy en adelante	from now on
haré lo que me dé la gana	I'll do as I please
por lo tanto	therefore
próximo, -a	next
soltero, -a	single
tener en cuenta	to take into account

campos y carreras del futuro

el campo	field
la demanda	demand
la estrategia	strategy
la hospitalidad	hospitality
la industria	industry
la informática	information technology
el mercadeo	marketing
el producto	product
el servicio	service

288 doscientos ochenta y ocho
Repaso del capítulo

DIFFERENTIATED INSTRUCTION

Students with Learning Difficulties

To help students reinforce vocabulary comprehension, have them create their own flashcards. On one side of the card, have them write a vocabulary word. On the other side, they can draw a picture or write a Spanish synonym or other clue.

Advanced Learners

Invite students to create a video about a profession of the future. This could be a future version of a profession that exists today or one that is yet unheard of. Have one or more students dramatize the profession while a narrator explains it.

el futuro

To express the future in Spanish, you can use *ir + a* + infinitive, the present tense, or the future. For most verbs, attach the endings *(-é, -ás, -á, -emos, -éis, -án)* to the infinitive.

pasar *to pass*

pasaré	pasaremos
pasarás	pasaréis
pasará	pasarán

comer *to eat*

comeré	comeremos
comerás	comeréis
comerá	comerán

pedir *to ask*

pediré	pediremos
pedirás	pediréis
pedirá	pedirán

Other verbs have irregular stems in the future but have the same endings as the regular verbs.

haber	habr-
hacer	har-
saber	sabr-
tener	tendr-
poder	podr-
decir	dir-
salir	saldr-
querer	querr-
poner	pondr-
venir	vendr-

el futuro de probabilidad

In Spanish the future tense can express uncertainty or probability in the present.

¿Qué hora **será**? *(I wonder what time it is.)*

el futuro perfecto

Use the future perfect tense to express what will have happened by a certain time. To form the future perfect, use the future of the verb *haber* with the past participle of the verb.

pasar *to pass*

ha**bré** pasado	ha**bremos** pasado
ha**brás** pasado	ha**bréis** pasado
ha**brá** pasado	ha**brán** pasado

el uso de los complementos directos e indirectos

The indirect object pronoun goes before the direct object pronoun.

Te los traduciré. (los libros)

In the third person, the indirect objects *le / les* become *se* before the indirect objects *lo / la, los / las.* You can add the prepositional phrase *a Ud., a él, a ella*, etc., or *a* + a noun / name for clarification.

Se los traduciré a ella.

When the object pronouns are attached to an infinitive, a command, or a present participle, you must add an accent mark to keep the stress: *traducírmelos, tradúcemelos, traduciéndomelos.*

El futuro de probabilidad: Have students work in pairs, sitting back to back. One partner performs a simple action that the other can't see. Actions might include writing, holding up a number of fingers, or putting on a hat. The other partner tries to guess the action using the future tense: *¿Escribirás algo? ¿No tendrás unos dedos en el aire? ¿Llevarás puesto tu sombrero?*

El futuro perfecto: Have students make predictions about things that will have happened by the year 2110: *Habremos colonizado otros planetas. Gracias a la genética, todas las enfermedades habrán desaparecido.*

El uso de los complementos directos e indirectos: Have students work in groups of three. Individually, they think of two sentences describing actions that they can perform in the group. Each action should involve a direct object and refer to one or both of the other students as the indirect object. For example: *Les digo un secreto a Uds. dos* or *Le doy mi cuaderno a Mark.* Have them take turns saying their sentences. The other two protest and turn the sentence into a negative command using pronouns: *¡No, no nos lo digas! ¡No, no se lo des!*

Portfolio

Invite students to review the activities, reports and projects they completed in this chapter, including written reports, posters or other visuals, recordings of oral presentations, and other projects. Have them select one or two items that they feel best demonstrate their achievements in Spanish. Include these products in students' portfolios with the Chapter Checklist and Self-Assessment Worksheet.

Additional Resources

Student Resources: Realidades para hispanohablantes, pp. 200–201

Teacher Resources:
• Teacher's Resource Book: Situation Cards, p. 83, Clip Art, pp. 84–93
• Assessment Program: Chapter Checklist and Self-Assessment Worksheet, pp. T49–T50

▶ *¡Pura vida!* is a storyline video that is independent of chapter content and an ideal support for expanding listening skills. The 14 episodes are available within **realidades.com** or on a separate DVD. Student activities and Teacher support are also assignable within **realidades.com**.

ENRICH YOUR TEACHING

Teacher-to-Teacher

Using imperative forms and pronouns are some of the most difficult skills your students have to learn, and yet they are a common part of everyday speech. Provide students with plenty of accurate models and give them every opportunity possible to practice using these structures.

21st Century Skills

Initiative and Self-Direction Remind students of the various digital tools available in **realidades.com** to help them monitor their own understanding and learning needs, especially as a review of the chapter. There are online tutorials with comprehension check exercises, interactive puzzles, flashcards, and self-tests.

Performance Tasks

Standards: 1.1, 1.2, 1.3, 4.2

Student Resource: Realidades para hispanohablantes, pp. 202–203

Teacher Resources: Teacher's Resource Book: Audio Script, p. 75; Audio Program DVD: Cap. 6, Track 19; Answer Keys: Student Edition, p. 88

1. Vocabulario

Suggestions: Encourage students to review the vocabulary from the *A primera vista* sections on pp. 252–255 and 266–269 before they complete the activity.

Answers:

1. b	5. c
2. b	6. c
3. a	7. a
4. a	8. b

2. Gramática

Suggestions: Remind students of the main points of the grammar presentations in *Capítulo* 6:

• the future tense
• the future tense used for probability
• the future perfect tense
• use of direct and indirect object pronouns together

Answers:

1. b	5. a
2. b	6. a
3. c	7. a
4. d	8. d

Preparación para el examen

1 Vocabulario Escribe la letra de la palabra o expresión que mejor complete cada frase. Escribe tus respuestas en una hoja aparte.

1. Tengo que _____ qué cursos ofrecen en la universidad.
   a. desarrollar   c. inventar
   b. averiguar   d. prolongar

2. Después de terminar sus estudios, mi hermano piensa _____ a otro estado.
   a. dedicarse   c. enterarse
   b. mudarse   d. comunicarse

3. Cuando una persona sabe hacer algo bien, se dice que es _____.
   a. capaz   c. madura
   b. entrometida   d. sincera

4. Gracias a _____ como el teléfono celular podemos comunicarnos desde muchos lugares.
   a. aparatos   c. campos
   b. transportes   d. servicios

5. Los avances en la genética harán posible curar _____.
   a. la contaminación   c. las enfermedades
   b. las viviendas   d. el ocio

6. La _____ te permite vivir una experiencia como si fuera real.
   a. vivienda   c. realidad virtual
   b. genética   d. informática

7. A Jorge le gusta resolver problemas y tomar decisiones sin ayuda. Es muy _____.
   a. emprendedor   c. honesto
   b. cuidadoso   d. puntual

8. Creo que _____ me voy a dedicar a la medicina.
   a. así que   c. tener en cuenta
   b. de hoy en adelante d. como si fuera

2 Gramática Escribe la letra de la palabra o expresión que mejor complete cada frase. Escribe tus respuestas en una hoja aparte.

1. El año próximo _____ mi sueño de viajar por todo el mundo.
   a. realicé   c. realizo
   b. realizaré   d. estoy realizando

2. Andrés quiere ser traductor. El año que viene _____ en las Naciones Unidas.
   a. trabaja   c. está trabajando
   b. trabajará   d. trabajaba

3. No tengo reloj. ¿Qué hora _____?
   a. estará   c. será
   b. saldrá   d. era

4. Si necesitas un texto de genética, yo _____ prestaré.
   a. te la   c. se lo
   b. te los   d. te lo

5. ¿Vio usted el programa sobre los inventos del siglo XX? _____ prestaré.
   a. Se lo   c. Me lo
   b. Se la   d. Te la

6. Quiero ver las fotos que sacaste ayer. _____ por favor.
   a. Dámelas   c. Déle
   b. Dáselas   d. Déselas

7. Dentro de 20 años, ya _____ otras fuentes de energía.
   a. habrán descubierto c. descubrieron
   b. han descubierto   d. están descubriendo

8. Para el año 2020, muchos aparatos que ahora se usan ya _____.
   a. han desaparecido   c. están desapareciendo
   b. desaparecen   d. habrán desaparecido

DIFFERENTIATED INSTRUCTION

Heritage Language Learners

Ask students to draft their own set of multiple-choice review questions based on the vocabulary and grammar points of the chapter. Have them trade questions with a partner. Students should not only choose the correct answer, but also proofread their partner's questions for errors.

Students with Special Needs

Give hearing impaired students a transcribed or illustrated version of the conversation in the listening section of the exam. Have students work in pairs and track the appropriate text as the dialogue is played.

Repaso

| Más repaso | GO | realidades.com | print |

Puzzles ✔
Core WB pp. 89–90 ✔ ✔
Comm. WB pp. 197, 198–200 ✔ ✔
Instant Check ✔

Review 6

En el examen vas a . . .	Éstas son las tareas de práctica que te pueden ser útiles para el examen . . .	Para repasar, ve a tu libro de texto impreso o digital . . .

Interpretive

 3 Escuchar Escuchar y comprender una conversación entre dos jóvenes

Félix y Carmen hablan sobre sus planes para el futuro. Escucha su conversación y di (a) qué intereses y habilidades tiene cada uno; (b) cuáles son sus planes para después de graduarse de la escuela secundaria; (c) cuáles son sus sueños para su carrera.

pp. 252–255 *A primera vista 1: Vocabulario en contexto*
p. 253 Actividad 1
p. 255 Actividades 2–3
p. 261 Actividad 12

Interpersonal

 4 Hablar Hablar sobre lo que quieres hacer en el futuro

Imagina que te entrevistas con una consejera que te ayudará a decidir qué carrera debes estudiar y a qué universidad debes ir. Explícale cuáles son tus intereses y cualidades, qué trabajo te gustaría tener, qué sueños quieres realizar, qué quieres lograr, en fin, explícale qué quieres hacer con tu vida.

p. 258 Actividad 9
p. 259 Actividad 10
p. 261 Actividad 12
p. 262 Actividad 15

Interpretive

 5 Leer Leer y comprender las predicciones de un futurólogo

Lee este fragmento del artículo de un futurólogo. ¿Esta persona cree que el futuro será mejor o peor que el presente? ¿Por qué?

En el futuro viviremos en paz, pues en unos años habrá nuevos inventos y aparatos que permitirán una mejor comunicación entre las personas. Además, gracias a ciencias nuevas como la informática y la genética, en 50 ó 60 años no habrá hambre ni enfermedades. Todos vivirán 100 años y trabajarán mucho menos que nosotros.

pp. 266–269 *A primera vista 2: Vocabulario en contexto*
p. 270 Actividad 25
p. 272 Actividades 28, 29
p. 277 Actividad 36

Presentational

 6 Escribir Escribir sobre los avances que habrá en el futuro

Escribe sobre los principales avances y problemas que crees que habrá en los 50 años que vienen. Di dos cosas que crees que habrán ocurrido. ¿Cómo cambiará la vida de la gente? ¿Cuáles serán los problemas más difíciles que tendrán que resolver?

p. 265 Actividad 19
p. 267 Actividad 21
p. 269 Actividad 23
p. 271 Actividad 27
p. 273 Actividad 30
p. 274 Actividades 31–32

Cultures • Comparisons

7 Pensar Pensar en la actitud de algunos jóvenes españoles que prefieren vivir con sus padres al terminar de estudiar

Piensa por qué te gustará o no te gustará vivir con tus padres cuando termines tus estudios. Compara tus razones con las de algunos jóvenes españoles.

p. 257 *Fondo cultural*

doscientos noventa y uno **291**
Capítulo 6

---

3. Escuchar

Suggestions: Use the audio or read from the script.

Answers:
a. **Intereses y habilidades:**
   Félix: finanzas, banca; eficiente, emprendedor
   Carmen: le gustan los libros, es bilingüe
b. **Carmen y Félix piensan seguir estudiando para ser traductora y banquero.**
c. **Sus sueños:**
   Félix: ganar mucho dinero y hacer lo que le dé la gana. Quiere ser banquero.
   Carmen: Quiere ser traductora. Quiere viajar al extranjero y aprender más sobre los países del mundo.

4. Hablar

Suggestions: Point out that this activity requires students to use a variety of tenses. They might use the present tense to talk about their personal qualities and the future tenses and subjunctive mood to tell about their plans for the future.

Answers will vary.

5. Leer

Suggestions: Tell students to refer to pp. 252–255 and 266–269 if they have questions about vocabulary in the review.

Answers:
Esta persona cree que el futuro será mejor que el presente.
Answers will vary.

6. Escribir

Suggestions: After students have completed their writing, ask them how their perceptions of the future have changed since they began *Capítulo* 6.

Answers will vary.

7. Pensar

Suggestions: Encourage students to write down their thoughts in a T-chart with the two columns entitled *A favor de* and *En contra de.*

Answers will vary.

DIFFERENTIATED ASSESSMENT

CORE ASSESSMENT
- **Assessment Program:** Examen del capítulo 6, pp. 145-148
- **Audio Program DVD:** Cap. 6, Track 20
- **ExamView:** Chapter Test, Test Banks A and B

ADVANCED/PRE-AP*
- **ExamView:** Pre-AP* Test Bank
- **Pre-AP* Resource Book,** pp. 153–155

STUDENTS NEEDING EXTRA HELP
- **Alternate Assessment Program:** Examen del capítulo 6
- **Audio Program DVD:** Cap. 6, Track 20

HERITAGE LEARNERS
- **Assessment Program: Realidades para hispanohablantes:** Examen del capítulo 6
- **ExamView:** Heritage Learner Test Bank

7 Chapter Overview

- **myths, legends, and mysterious events**

Vocabulary
- archaeological discoveries and mysteries
- description of objects
- myths and legends

Grammar
- present and present perfect subjunctive after expressions of doubt, uncertainty, or disbelief
- uses of **pero** and **sino**
- subjunctive in adjective clauses

Cultural Perspectives
- prehispanic civilizations as viewed in the art of Diego Rivera
- two wonders of Peru: the Inca Trail and Machu Picchu
- Aztec myths and legends
- contributions of the Mayan and Aztec civilizations
- mysteries of pre-Columbian civilizations

¡Pura vida!
- Watch an engaging video episode about a group of young people in Costa Rica!

CHAPTER SUPPORT

Bulletin Boards

Theme: *Las culturas indígenas latinoamericanas*

Ask students to cut out, copy, or download images of the Aztecs, Mayas, or other indigenous groups in Latin America. Images can include examples of clothing, folk art, crafts, and food. Cluster photos around the name of each group that is chosen.

Hands-on Culture

Music: *Songs from Spain and Latin America*

The fusion of old and new music styles has revived many traditional beats and sounds, such as flamenco, salsa, and cumbia.

Directions:
1. Type out names of Hispanic musical artists and distribute copies to students. Some artists to look for are: Gypsy Kings and Carlos Villalobos (flamenco), Gloria Estefan (salsa), Tito Puente (salsa, boleros, cumbia), and Inti Illimani (Andean).
2. Divide students into four groups. If possible, assign one or two students with strong artistic skills to each group.
3. Ask students to do research about their artist on the Internet and, if possible, record some music clips.
4. Each group types out a fact sheet about their artist with information from the research and makes copies to distribute to the class. They can download the artist's photo and include it in the fact sheet.
5. Each group chooses a leader, who makes a presentation of their artist to the class.
6. The leader reads the fact sheet and plays some music by the artist to the class.

Game

Encuentra dónde estamos

Play this game to review the information about archaeological sites from *Capítulo 7*.

Players: entire class, playing in teams

Materials: slips of paper, a large world map, markers, pins or masking tape

Preparation: Prepare ahead. Draw with different color markers on the map the outlines of Mexico, Peru, Bolivia, Guatemala, and Isla de Pascua. On slips of paper, write the names of different ancient cities and indigenous groups described in *Capítulo 7*, such as *ruinas de Palenque, los aztecas, los mayas, ruinas de Cobá y Tulúm, ciudad de Teotihuacán, cabezas de los olmecas, Chichen Itzá, Líneas de Nazca, estatuas moai, indígenas quichés, ciudad de Machu Picchu, ciudad de Tiahuanaco.* Place the slips of paper in a bag.

Rules:
1. Students should prepare ahead for the game. Ask them to review *Capítulo 7*, paying special attention to the location of the archaeological sites and the indigenous groups described there.
2. Divide the class into teams.
3. Have members of the teams take turns drawing a slip of paper from the bag.
4. If the student can tape the note in the correct place on the map, the team receives 5 points.
5. If he or she can also give cultural, historical, architectural, or other information about that place or indigenous group, the team receives an additional 5 points.
6. The team with the most points when the bag is empty wins.

Variation: Names of indigenous groups from the United States can also be written on the slips of paper. In this case, the outline of the United States should be included.

CHAPTER PROJECT

Cartel de arte indígena

Overview: Students create an illustrated poster to show a piece of indigenous art. They research art of an indigenous group they know from the United States or Latin America and choose one or more images to create an interesting visual composition. Posters should include a message or two and a title. Students then present their poster to the class and describe what the art means, the indigenous group it belongs to, and why they chose those images.

Resources: digital or print photos, image editing and page layout software, and/or pencil, crayons, paint of different colors, poster board, and construction paper

Sequence: (suggestions for when to do each step are found throughout the chapter)

STEP 1. Review instructions so students know what is expected of them. Hand out the "Chapter 7 Project Instructions and Rubric" from the *Teacher's Resource Book*.

STEP 2. Students submit a sketch of their poster. Return the sketches with your suggestions.

STEP 3. Students do layouts setting space for the messages. Encourage them to try different arrangements before drawing their images.

STEP 4. Students submit a draft of the messages and a paragraph for the presentation. Note your corrections and suggestions, then return drafts to students.

STEP 5. Students make a brief presentation of their posters to the class.

Options:

1. Students create computer art using a painting or drawing software.
2. Students make a brief presentation of the indigenous group they chose.

Assessment:

Here is a detailed rubric for assessing this project:

Chapter 7 Project: *Cartel de arte indígena*

RUBRIC	Score 1	Score 3	Score 5
Your evidence of planning	You provide no poster layout or written draft.	You provide a layout and written draft, but they are not corrected.	You show evidence of corrected draft and layout.
Your use of illustrations	You include no art images, or they are not indigenous art.	You include images, but layout is not well organized.	Your poster is carefully done and images are consistent with text.
Your presentation	You include little of the required information.	You include most of the required information.	You include all of the required information.

21st Century Skills

Look for tips throughout Chapter 7 to enrich your teaching by integrating 21st Century Skills. Suggestions for the Chapter Project and Culture follow below.

Chapter Project

Modify the Chapter Project with these suggestions:

Encourage Technology Literacy

Encourage students to go online to their favorite Web sites to choose an indigenous group from the United States or Latin America. Then have them search for museum Web sites to view a variety of artwork from the indigenous group they have chosen.

Foster Creativity and Innovation

Encourage students with artistic interests to expand on the project's task by creating their own version of the indigenous artifacts in their presentation. Interested students can create their own tri-dimensional model of the artifact in different media, such as papier-maché, clay, or other materials, and share with the class their reasons for choosing it.

Enhance Communication

As students prepare to present their project to the class, provide them with the handout "Give an Effective Presentation" to remind them of the importance of body language, tone of voice, eye contact, and other strategies for delivering an effective presentation.

Chapter Culture

Develop Social and Cross-Cultural Skills

Direct the students to the *Fondo cultural* notes on pages 296 and 310. After reviewing the information in the notes, have them consider the similarities and differences between ancient and modern architecture. What functions do large construction projects have in a culture? Have students provide specific examples.

▶ **Videodocumentario** View *¿Cómo se explican los misterios del mundo?* online with the class to learn more about the mysteries behind three ancient sites: Machu Picchu, Chichén Itzá and Teotihuacán.

AT A GLANCE

Objectives

- Listen to and read about archeology and Pre-Columbian legends
- Talk and write about mysterious events
- Provide logical explanations for unexplained phenomena
- Understand the mysteries of past civilizations in Latin America
- Provide reasonable explanations for Pre-Columbian myths

A ver si recuerdas... ♻

- Architecture and materials
- Nature, animals, and places
- Negative constructions
- Adjectives used as nouns

Recycle... ♻

- Pronunciation of diphthong *ue*
- Pronouns *vosotros* and *vosotras*

Vocabulary

- Discoveries
- Myths, legends, and unexplained phenomena
- Expressions of doubt
- Descriptions of the shapes and size of objects
- The universe

Grammar

- Present subjunctive and present perfect subjunctive with expressions of doubt
- Uses of *pero* and *sino*
- Subjunctive with adjective clauses

Culture

- Diego Rivera, p. 297
- Atlantis: Mystery or historical fact?, p. 304
- Inca trail to Machu Picchu, p. 310
- Mayan and Aztec cultures, pp. 314–315
- Aztec calendar, p. 316
- A Quiché legend, p. 318
- Easter Island, the Olmecs, and the Nazca lines, pp. 324–325
- Miguel de Cervantes Saavedra, p. 333

RESOURCES

	FOR THE STUDENT	ONLINE	DVD	PRINT	FOR THE TEACHER	ONLINE	PREEXP	DVD	PRINT
Plan					Interactive TE and Resource DVD	•		•	
					Teacher's Resource Book, pp. 121–177	•		•	•
					Pre-AP* Resource Book, pp. 156–158	•		•	•
					Mapa global interactivo	•			
					Lesson Plans	•			•

A ver si recuerdas PP. 292–295

	FOR THE STUDENT	ONLINE	DVD	PRINT	FOR THE TEACHER	ONLINE	PREEXP	DVD	PRINT
Review	A ver si recuerdas Study Plan	•			A ver si recuerdas Study Plan	•			
	Guided WB, pp. 208–211	•	•	•	Vocabulary and Grammar Transparencies, 133–136	•	•	•	
	Core WB, pp. 91–92	•	•	•	Answer Keys: Student Edition, pp. 90–91	•	•	•	
	Hispanohablantes WB, p. 204			•					

Introducción PP. 296–297

	FOR THE STUDENT	ONLINE	DVD	PRINT	FOR THE TEACHER	ONLINE	PREEXP	DVD	PRINT
Present	Student Edition, pp. 296–297	•	•	•	Interactive TE and Resource DVD	•		•	
	DK Reference Atlas	•	•		Teacher's Resource Book, pp. 122–125	•		•	•
	Videonovela: ¡Pura vida!	•	•		Galería de fotos			•	
	¡Pura vida! Video Activities	•			Fine Art Transparencies, 58	•	•	•	
	Hispanohablantes WB, p. 205			•	Map Transparencies, 14, 15, 19	•	•	•	

Vocabulario en contexto PP. 298–301/312–315

	FOR THE STUDENT	ONLINE	DVD	PRINT	FOR THE TEACHER	ONLINE	PREEXP	DVD	PRINT
Present & Practice	Student Edition, pp. 298–301/312–315	•	•	•	Interactive TE and Resource DVD	•		•	
	Audio	•	•		Teacher's Resource Book, pp. 126–127, 130–131, 145–152/128–129, 132–133, 145–152	•		•	•
	Flashcards	•	•						
	Instant Check	•			Vocabulary Clip Art	•	•	•	•
	Guided WB, pp. 212–220/223–230	•	•	•	Audio Program	•	•	•	
	Core WB, pp. 93–94/98–99	•	•	•	Vocabulary and Grammar Transparencies, 137–140/142–145	•	•	•	
	Comm. WB, pp. 96, 100	•	•	•	Answer Keys: Student Edition, pp. 91/98–99	•	•	•	
	Hispanohablantes WB, pp. 206–207/216–217			•					
Assess and Remediate					Pruebas 7–1, 7–4: Assessment Program, pp. 149–150/157–158	•		•	•
					Hispanohablantes, pp. 149–150/157–158	•		•	•

RESOURCES

FOR THE STUDENT	ONLINE	DVD	PRINT	FOR THE TEACHER	ONLINE	PREEXP	DVD	PRINT
Vocabulario en uso PP. 302–305/316–318								
Present & Practice								
Student Edition, pp. 302–305/316–318	•	•	•	Interactive Whiteboard Vocabulary Activities	•		•	
Instant Check	•			Interactive TE and Resource DVD	•		•	
Comm. WB, pp. 92/94	•	•	•	Teacher's Resource Book, pp. 131, 137–138/133, 140–141	•		•	•
Hispanohablantes WB, pp. 208–209/218–220			•	Audio Program	•	•	•	
Communicative Pair Activities	•			Videomodelos	•		•	
				Answer Keys: Student Edition, pp. 92–94/100–102	•	•	•	
Assess and Remediate								
				Pruebas 7–2, 7–5 with Study Plans	•			
				Pruebas 7–2, 7–5: Assessment Program, pp. 151–152/162	•		•	•
				Hispanohablantes, pp. 151–152/162	•		•	•
Gramática PP. 306–311/319–323								
Present & Practice								
Student Edition, pp. 306–311/319–323	•	•	•	Interactive Whiteboard Grammar Activities	•		•	
Instant Check	•			Interactive TE and Resource DVD	•		•	
Animated Verbs	•			Teacher's Resource Book, pp. 131–132, 139/133–134, 142–143	•		•	•
Tutorial Video: Grammar	•			Audio Program	•	•	•	
Canción de hip hop	•			Videomodelos	•		•	
Guided WB, pp. 221–222/231–234	•	•	•	Vocabulary and Grammar Transparencies, 141	•		•	
Core WB, pp. 95–97/100–102	•	•	•	Map Transparencies, 17, 146–147	•	•	•	
Comm. WB, pp. 93, 97–98/94–95, 101, 201	•	•	•	Answer Keys: Student Edition, pp. 94–97/102–104	•	•	•	
Hispanohablantes WB, pp. 210–215/221–225			•					
Communicative Pair Activities	•							
Assess and Remediate								
				Pruebas 7–3, 7–6, 7–7 with Study Plans	•			
				Pruebas 7–3, 7–6, 7–7: Assessment Program, pp. 153/161, 162	•		•	•
				Hispanohablantes, pp. 153/161, 162	•		•	•
				Examen 1, Examen 2: Vocab. y gramática, pp. 154–156/163–164	•		•	•
¡Adelante! PP. 324–333								
Application								
Student Edition, pp. 324–333	•	•	•	Interactive TE and Resource DVD	•		•	
Online Cultural Reading	•			Teacher's Resource Book, pp. 134, 136	•		•	•
Guided WB, pp. 235–237	•	•	•	Video Program: Videodocumentario	•			
Comm. WB, pp. 104–105, 202	•	•	•	Video Program Teacher's Guide, Cap. 7	•			
Hispanohablantes WB, pp. 226–231			•	Map Transparencies, 20	•	•	•	
Videodocumentario	•	•		Answer Keys: Student Edition, pp. 104–105	•	•	•	
Lecturas 3, pp. 19–21, 30–31			•					
Repaso del capítulo PP. 334–337								
Review								
Student Edition, pp. 334–337	•	•	•	Interactive TE and Resource DVD	•		•	
Online Puzzles and Games	•			Teacher's Resource Book, pp. 134–135, 144–152	•		•	•
Core WB, pp. 103–104	•	•	•	Audio Program	•	•	•	
Comm. WB, pp. 203–207	•	•	•	Answer Keys: Student Edition, p. 105	•	•	•	
Hispanohablantes WB, pp. 232–235			•					
Instant Check	•							
Chapter Assessment								
Assess								
				Examen del capítulo 7: Assessment Program, pp. 165–170	•		•	•
				Alternate Assessment Program, pp. 66–75	•		•	•
				Hispanohablantes, pp. 165–170	•		•	•
				Audio Program, Cap. 7, Examen	•		•	
				ExamView: Test Banks A and B (questions only online)	•		•	
				Heritage Learner Test Bank	•		•	
				Pre-AP* Test Bank	•		•	

REGULAR SCHEDULE (50 MINUTES)

DAY	Warm-up / Assess	Preview / Present / Practice / Communicate	Wrap-up / Homework Options
1	**Warm-up** (10 min.) • Return Examen del capítulo: Capítulo 6	**Repaso** (35 min.) • A ver si recuerdas . . . • Actividades 1, 2, 4, 5, 7	**Wrap-up and Homework Options** (5 min.) • Core Practice 7-1, 7-2
2	**Warm-up** (10 min.) • Homework check	**Chapter Opener** (10 min.) • Objectives • Arte y cultura **Vocabulario en contexto 1** (25 min.) • Presentation: Vocabulario y gramática en contexto • Actividades 4, 5	**Wrap-up and Homework Options** (5 min.) • Clip Art Vocabulary
3	**Warm-up** (10 min.) • Homework check	**Vocabulario en contexto 1** (20 min.) • Presentation: Misterios arqueológicos • Actividad 3 **Vocabulario en uso 1** (5 min.) • Interactive Whiteboard Vocabulary Activities • Actividades 4, 5	**Wrap-up and Homework Options** (5 min.) • Core Practice 7-3, 7-4 • Actividad 8 • Prueba 7-1: Vocabulary recognition
4	**Warm-up** (10 min.) • Homework check ✔**Formative Assessment** (10 min.) • Prueba 7-1: Vocabulary recognition	**Vocabulario en uso 1** (25 min.) • Actividades 6, 7, 9, 10 • Audio Activity • Ampliación del lenguaje	**Wrap-up and Homework Options** (5 min.) • Writing Activities • Prueba 7-2 with Study Plan: Vocabulary production
5	**Warm-up** (15 min.) • Homework check • Communicative Pair Activity ✔**Formative Assessment** (10 min.) • Prueba 7-2 with Study Plan: Vocabulary production	**Gramática y vocabulario en uso 1** (20 min.) • Presentation: Subjuntivo con expresiones de duda • Interactive Whiteboard Grammar Activities • Actividades 11, 12, 13	**Wrap-up and Homework Options** (5 min.) • Core Practice 7-5, 7-6, 7-7
6	**Warm-up** (10 min.) • Homework check	**Gramática y vocabulario en uso 1** (35 min.) • Actividades 14, 15, 16 • Fondo cultural	**Wrap-up and Homework Options** (5 min.) • Actividad 19
7	**Warm-up** (10 min.) • Homework check	**Gramática y vocabulario en uso 1** (35 min.) • Actividades 17, 18, 19 • Writing Activity • Communicative Pair Activity • En voz alta	**Wrap-up and Homework Options** (5 min.) • Writing Activity • Prueba 7-3 with Study Plan: Subjuntivo con expresiones de duda
8	**Warm-up** (10 min.) • Homework check ✔**Formative Assessment** (10 min.) • Prueba 7-3 with Study Plan: Subjuntivo con expresiones de duda	**Vocabulario en contexto 2** (25 min.) • Presentation: Vocabulario y gramática en contexto • Actividades 20, 21	**Wrap-up and Homework Options** (5 min.) • Clip Art Vocabulary • Examen: Vocabulario y gramática 1
9	**Warm-up** (5 min.) • Homework check ✔**Formative Assessment** (30 min.) • Examen: Vocabulario y gramática 1	**Vocabulario en contexto 2** (10 min.) • Presentation: Los mayas y los aztecas • Actividad 22	**Wrap-up and Homework Options** (5 min.) • Core Practice 7-8, 7-9 • Prueba 7-4: Vocabulary recognition
10	**Warm-up** (20 min.) • Homework check ✔**Formative Assessment** (10 min.) • Prueba 7-5: Vocabulary recognition	**Vocabulario en uso 2** (15 min.) • Actividades 23, 24, 25 • Interactive Whiteboard Vocabulary Activities	**Wrap-up and Homework Options** (5 min.) • Actividades 26, 27

REGULAR SCHEDULE (50 MINUTES)

DAY	Warm-up / Assess	Preview / Present / Practice / Communicate	Wrap-up / Homework Options
11	**Warm-up** (15 min.) • Homework check	**Vocabulario en uso 2** (15 min.) • En voz alta • Audio Activity • Writing Activity • Communicative Pair Activity **Gramática y vocabulario en uso 2** (15 min.) • Presentation: *Pero y sino* • Interactive Whiteboard Grammar Activities • Actividades 28, 29	**Wrap-up and Homework Options** (5 min.) • Core Practice 7-10 • Prueba 7-5 with Study Plan: Vocabulary production
12	**Warm-up** (10 min.) • Homework check ✔**Formative Assessment** (10 min.) • Prueba 7-5 with Study Plan: Vocabulary production	**Gramática y vocabulario en uso 2** (25 min.) • Writing Activity 11 • Presentation: El subjuntivo en cláusulas adjetivas • Interactive Whiteboard Grammar Activities • Actividades 30, 31, 32	**Wrap-up and Homework Options** (5 min.) • Core Practice 7-11, 7-12 • Prueba 7-6 with Study Plan: *Pero y sino*
13	**Warm-up** (10 min.) • Homework check ✔**Formative Assessment** (10 min.) • Prueba 7-6 with Study Plan: *Pero y sino*	**Gramática y vocabulario en uso 2** (25 min.) • Actividades 33, 34, 35 • El español en el mundo del trabajo	**Wrap-up and Homework Options** (5 min.) • Writing Activity • Prueba 7-7 with Study Plan: El subjuntivo en cláusulas adjetivas
14	**Warm-up** (10 min.) • Communicative Activity • Audio Activity ✔**Formative Assessment** (10 min.) • Prueba 7-7 with Study Plan: El subjuntivo en cláusulas adjetivas	**¡Adelante!** (25 min.) • Puente a la cultura • ¿Comprendiste? • Investiga • Presentación oral: Step 1	**Wrap-up and Homework Options** (5 min.) • Examen: Vocabulario y gramática 2
15	**Warm-up** (10 min.) • Answer questions ✔**Formative Assessment** (20 min.) • Examen: Vocabulario y gramática 2	**¡Adelante!** (15 min.) • Presentación oral: Step 2	**Wrap-up and Homework Options** (5 min.) • Presentación oral: Step 3
16	**Warm-up** (15 min.) • Homework check	**¡Adelante!** (30 min.) • Presentación oral: Step 3 • ¿Qué me cuentas? 1, 2, 3	**Wrap-up and Homework Options** (5 min.) • Presentación escrita: Steps 1, 2
17	**Warm-up** (10 min.) • Homework check	**¡Adelante!** (35 min.) • Presentación oral: Step 3 • View Video • Video Activities 1, 2, 3 • Presentación escrita: Step 3	**Wrap-up and Homework Options** (5 min.) • Presentación escrita: Step 4 • Preparación para el examen: 1, 2
18	**Warm-up** (10 min.) • Homework check	**¡Adelante!** (25 min.) • Lectura • Interacción • Fondo cultural **Repaso** (10 min.) • Preparación para el examen: Actividades 3, 4	**Wrap-up and Homework Options** (5 min.) • ¿Comprendiste? • Core Practice: Organizer 7-13, 7-14 • Instant Check
19	**Warm-up** (15 min.) • Homework check	**Repaso** (30 min.) • Preparación para el examen: Actividades 5, 6, 7 • Other review	**Wrap-up and Homework Options** (5 min.) • Examen del capítulo
20	**Warm-up** (5 min.) • Answer questions	✔**Summative Assessment** (44 min.) • Examen del capítulo	**Wrap-up and Homework Options** (1 min.) • A ver si recuerdas: Capítulo 8

BLOCK SCHEDULE (90 MINUTES)

DAY	Warm-up / Assess	Preview / Present / Practice / Communicate	Wrap-up / Homework Options
1	**Warm-up** (35 min.) • Return Examen del capítulo: Capítulo 6 • A ver si recuerdas . . . • Homework check	**Chapter Opener** (10 min.) • Objectives • Arte y cultura **Vocabulario en contexto 1** (30 min.) • Presentation: Vocabulario y gramática en contexto • Actividades 1, 2 • Presentation: Misterios arqueológicos • Actividad 3 **Vocabulario en uso 1** (10 min.) • Interactive Whiteboard Vocabulary Activities • Actividades 4, 5	**Wrap-up and Homework Options** (5 min.) • Core Practice 7-3, 7-4 • Clip Art Vocabulary • Prueba 7-1: Vocabulary recognition
2	**Warm-up** (15 min.) • Homework check • Actividades 6, 7 ✔**Formative Assessment** (15 min.) • Prueba 7-1: Vocabulary recognition	**Vocabulario en uso 1** (55 min.) • Actividades 8, 9, 10 • Ampliación del lenguaje • Audio Activity • Writing Activity • Communicative Pair Activity	**Wrap-up and Homework Options** (5 min.) • Prueba 7-2 with Study Plan: Vocabulary production
3	**Warm-up** (5 min.) • Homework check ✔**Formative Assessment** (10 min.) • Prueba 7-2 with Study Plan: Vocabulary production	**Gramática y vocabulario en uso 1** (70 min.) • Presentation: Subjuntivo con duda • Interactive Whiteboard Grammar Activities • Actividades 11, 12, 13, 14, 15, 16 • Fondo cultural	**Wrap-up and Homework Options** (5 min.) • Fondo cultural • Actividad 19 • Core Practice 7-5, 7-6, 7-7
4	**Warm-up** (10 min.) • Homework check	**Gramática y vocabulario en uso 1** (50 min.) • Actividades 17, 18 • Writing Activity • Communicative Pair Activity **Vocabulario en contexto 2** (25 min.) • Presentation: Vocabulario y gramática en contexto • Actividades 20, 21	**Wrap-up and Homework Options** (5 min.) • Prueba 7-3 with Study Plan: El subjuntivo con duda • Examen: Vocabulario y gramática 1
5	**Warm-up** (10 min.) • Homework check ✔**Formative Assessment Options** (40 min.) • Prueba 7-3 with Study Plan: El subjuntivo con duda • Examen: Vocabulario y gramática 1	**Vocabulario en contexto 2** (20 min.) • Presentation: Los mayas y los aztecas • Actividad 22 **Vocabulario en uso 2** (15 min.) • Interactive Whiteboard Vocabulary Activities • Actividades 23, 24, 25	**Wrap-up and Homework Options** (5 min.) • Core Practice 7-8, 7-9 • Actividades 26, 27 • Clip Art • Prueba 7-4: Vocabulary recognition

BLOCK SCHEDULE (90 MINUTES)

DAY	Warm-up / Assess	Preview / Present / Practice / Communicate	Wrap-up / Homework Options
6	**Warm-up (35 min.)** • Homework check • En voz alta • Audio Activity • Writing Activity ✔**Formative Assessment (10 min.)** • Prueba 7-4: Vocabulary recognition	**Gramática y vocabulario en uso 2 (40 min.)** • Presentation: *Pero* y *sino* • Interactive Whiteboard Grammar Activities • Actividades 28, 29 • Writing Activity 11	**Wrap-up and Homework Options (5 min.)** • Core Practice 7-10 • Pruebas 7-5, 7-6 with Study Plans: Vocabulary production, *Pero* y *sino*
7	**Warm-up (10 min.)** • Writing Activity • Communicative Pair Activity ✔**Formative Assessment (20 min.)** • Pruebas 7-5, 7-6 with Study Plans: Vocabulary production, *Pero* y *sino*	**Gramática y vocabulario en uso 2 (40 min.)** • Presentation: Subjuntivo en cláusulas adjetivas • Interactive Whiteboard Grammar Activities • Actividades 30, 31, 32, 33, 34, 35 • El español en el mundo del trabajo **¡Adelante! (15 min.)** • Presentación oral: Steps 1, 2	**Wrap-up and Homework Options (5 min.)** • Core Practice 7-11, 7-12 • Writing Activity 12-13 • Prueba 7-7 with Study Plan: El subjuntivo en cláusulas adjetivas • Presentación oral: Step 2 • Examen: Vocabulario y gramática 2
8	**Warm-up (25 min.)** • Homework check • Writing Activity ✔**Formative Assessment (20 min.)** • Prueba 7-7 with Study Plan: El subjuntivo en cláusulas adjetivas	**¡Adelante! (40 min.)** • Presentación oral: Step 3 • Presentation: Misterios del pasado • ¿Comprendiste?	**Wrap-up and Homework Options (5 min.)** • ¿Comprendiste? • Investiga • Examen: Vocabulario y gramática 2
9	**Warm-up (10 min.)** • Homework check ✔**Formative Assessment (25 min.)** • Examen: Vocabulario y gramática 2	**¡Adelante! (50 min.)** • View Video • Video Activities • ¿Qué me cuentas? 1, 2, 3 • Presentación escrita: Step 1	**Wrap-up and Homework Options (5 min.)** • Presentación escrita: Step 2 • Preparación para el examen: Actividades 1, 2
10	**Warm-up (20 min.)** • Homework check • Presentación escrita: Step 3	**¡Adelante! (35 min.)** • Lectura • Interacción • ¿Comprendiste? • Fondo cultural **Repaso (30 min.)** • Preparación para el examen: Actividades 3, 4, 6	**Wrap-up and Homework Options (5 min.)** • Presentación escrita: Step 4 • Core Practice: Organizer 7-13, 7-14 • Instant Check • Preparación para el examen: Actividades 5, 7 • Examen del capítulo
11	**Warm-up (15 min.)** • Homework check ✔**Summative Assessment (45 min.)** • Examen del capítulo	**Theme Game (15 min.)** **A ver si recuerdas – Capítulo 8 (10 min.)** • Presentation: Vocabulario • Presentation: Gramática	**Wrap-up and Homework Options (5 min.)** • A ver si recuerdas – Capítulo 8 • Actividades 1–6 • Core Practice 8-1, 8-2

7 Recycle

A ver si recuerdas | ◉

▼ **Objectives**
▶ Talk and write about places you visited or would like to visit
▶ Make positive and negative statements

Vocabulario **Repaso**

Core Instruction

Standards: 1.1, 1.2

Resources: Voc. and Gram. Transparency 133

Suggestions: Before presenting the material in this review section, consider testing your students' command of the material by assigning the Study Plan. Students will automatically be given additional practice of the material they have not yet mastered, and you can focus your review based on the class's overall performance on the post-test.

Challenge students to create sentences that use vocabulary from as many categories as possible. For example: *Dentro de un palacio en el bosque, descubrimos una hermosa escultura de piedra.* This can be set up as a game. Students earn a point for every *Vocabulario* item used in a sentence that makes sense. Sentences in which items from all five categories are successfully used earn double, or ten, points. Sentences that don't make sense or are faultily constructed earn no points. The student who earns the most points wins.

▼ **1** Standards: 1.1

Focus: Practicing review vocabulary

Suggestions: In Step 1, encourage students to use the impersonal **se** when telling about what can be found in the various places. Provide a model such as *En la selva tropical de Honduras se pueden encontrar monumentos antiguos.*

Answers will vary.

Block Schedule

Group composition: Divide the class into groups of five. Each student is to begin a paragraph with a sentence that includes one of the negative expressions. Each student passes the paper with the first sentence to the student to his or her left. That student adds a sentence with a negative to the story. Pass to the left, again. Each student in turn adds a sentence to the story. When the paragraph returns to the first writer, have the group read each paragraph aloud to each other and determine the best "story." Have the group read the "best story" aloud for the class.

Vocabulario **Repaso**

materiales
el oro
la piedra
el plástico
la plata
el vidrio

descripciones
antiguo, -a
enorme
hermoso, -a
histórico, -a
impresionante
increíble
moderno, -a

acciones
buscar
dejar
descubrir
encontrar
explicar
impresionar
investigar
olvidar
perder
representar

construcciones
el castillo
el edificio
la escalera
la escultura
la figura
la fuente
el monumento
el palacio
la plaza
el templo

lugares
el bosque
el desierto
el mar
las montañas
el océano
el río
la selva tropical
el valle

▼**1** El viaje ideal | 👥

Escribir • Hablar

❶ Haz una lista de:
• dos lugares que visitaste o te gustaría visitar
• dos construcciones que puedes encontrar en esos lugares
• tres palabras que describan cada lugar

❷ Intercambia tu lista con un(a) compañero(a). Hablen sobre por qué escogieron esos lugares, cómo son y qué se encuentra allí.

292 doscientos noventa y dos
A ver si recuerdas . . .

DIFFERENTIATED INSTRUCTION

Heritage Language Learners

Have students who have lived in a heritage country create a travel brochure for that country. They may choose a place they know there or research another place. Encourage them to use words from the *Vocabulario* in order to create a vivid picture of the place.

Advanced Learners

Have students prepare an oral description of a famous monument. Ask them to give as many details as they can about the monument without naming it. Have them give their descriptions to the class who can guess which monument is being described. They can also tell which descriptive details helped them identify the monument.

Gramática Repaso

Las construcciones negativas

Here are some affirmative and negative words that you already know. Remember that they are antonyms.

AFFIRMATIVE

alguien	someone
algo	something
alguno, alguna *(pron.)*	some
algún, alguna *(adj.)*	some
algunos, algunas *(pron., adj.)*	some
siempre	always
también	also

NEGATIVE

nadie	no one
nada	nothing
ninguno, ninguna *(pron.)*	none, not any
ningún, ninguna *(adj.)*	no, not any
ningunos, ningunas *(pron., adj.)*	none, not any
nunca	never
tampoco	neither, either

- *Alguno, alguna, algunos, algunas,* and *ninguno, ninguna* have the same number and gender as the noun they modify.

- When *alguno* and *ninguno* come before a masculine singular noun, they become *algún* and *ningún*.

- To make a sentence negative in Spanish, put *no* in front of the conjugated verb.

  No pudieron encontrar **nada**.

- If a sentence begins with a negative word, like *nunca* or *nadie*, you don't need to use the word *no* in front of the verb.

  Nunca investigaron bien el interior del templo.

| **Más ayuda** | **realidades.com** | ▶ Tutorials |

▼ 2 ¿Qué pasó?

Hablar

Tu hermano vuelve a casa después de un viaje y quiere saber qué pasó mientras él no estaba. Túrnate con tu compañero(a) para contestar sus preguntas. Todas las respuestas son negativas.

▶ **Modelo**

A —¿Me llamó alguien por teléfono?
B —No, nadie te llamó.

1. ¿Alguien preguntó por mí?
2. ¿Pasó algo interesante?
3. ¿Vino algún amigo a verme?
4. Y Susana, ¿vino a verme?
5. ¿Llegó alguna carta para mí?

▼ 3 Una carta sin noticias

Leer

Laura le escribe a Isabel. Escoge la expresión adecuada para completar su mensaje electrónico.

```
¡Hola Isabel!
¡Qué pena! No tengo __1.__ (algo/nada)
para contarte. He estado muy
ocupada estudiando y no ha pasado
__2.__ (nada/nadie) interesante. No
he visto a __3.__ (alguien/nadie). No
he ido a __4.__ (nada/ninguna) parte.
No he visto __5.__ (ningún/ninguno)
programa de televisión ni __6__
(nada/ninguna) película. ¡Estoy
muy aburrida!
Saludos, Laura
```

doscientos noventa y tres **293**
Capítulo 7

Recycle 7

Gramática Repaso

Core Instruction

Standards: 4.1

Resources: Voc. and Gram. Transparency 134

Suggestions: Refer students who are having difficulty with indefinite and negative expressions to the online tutorials. Have pairs of students practice the words in the *Gramática* by asking negative questions and giving affirmative answers:

A: —¿No ves a nadie en la plaza?

B: —Sí, veo a alguien.

▼ 2 Standards: 1.1

Resources: Answer Keys: Student Edition, p. 90

Focus: Practicing negative constructions

Suggestions: Tell Student B to listen carefully for the affirmative word in the question in order to build the answer around its negative form.

Answers:

Wording of Student B's answers may vary. The following are likely results:

1. No, nadie preguntó por ti.
2. No, no pasó nada interesante.
3. No, ningún amigo vino a verte.
4. No, Susana tampoco vino a verte.
5. No, no llegó ninguna carta (ninguna carta llegó) para ti.

▼ 3 Standards: 1.2

Resources: Answer Keys: Student Edition, p. 90

Focus: Practicing negative constructions

Suggestions: Have students briefly review the *Gramática* before completing the activity and focus on which words are used for people, places, times, count nouns, and mass (collective) nouns.

Answers:

1. nada
2. nada
3. nadie
4. ninguna
5. ningún
6. ninguna

ENRICH YOUR TEACHING

Teacher-to-Teacher

You can review vocabulary or structures that operate in pairs using the round-robin approach. Students need not form a circle; the process can also run up and down rows. To review the words in the *Gramática* on this page, for example, have the first student in a row say one of the words to the second student. The second student gives the opposite and says another word to the third student, and so on:

A: *Nadie.*

B: *Alguien. Siempre.*

C: *Nunca. Tampoco.*

D: *También....*

Vocabulario Repaso

Core Instruction

Standards: 1.1, 1.2

Resources: Voc. and Gram. Transparency 135

Suggestions: Have students make sentences using the expressions in the *para dar tu opinión* category and at least one word from another category. Remind them that when giving opinions, they might be using the subjunctive or indicative.

Vocabulario Repaso

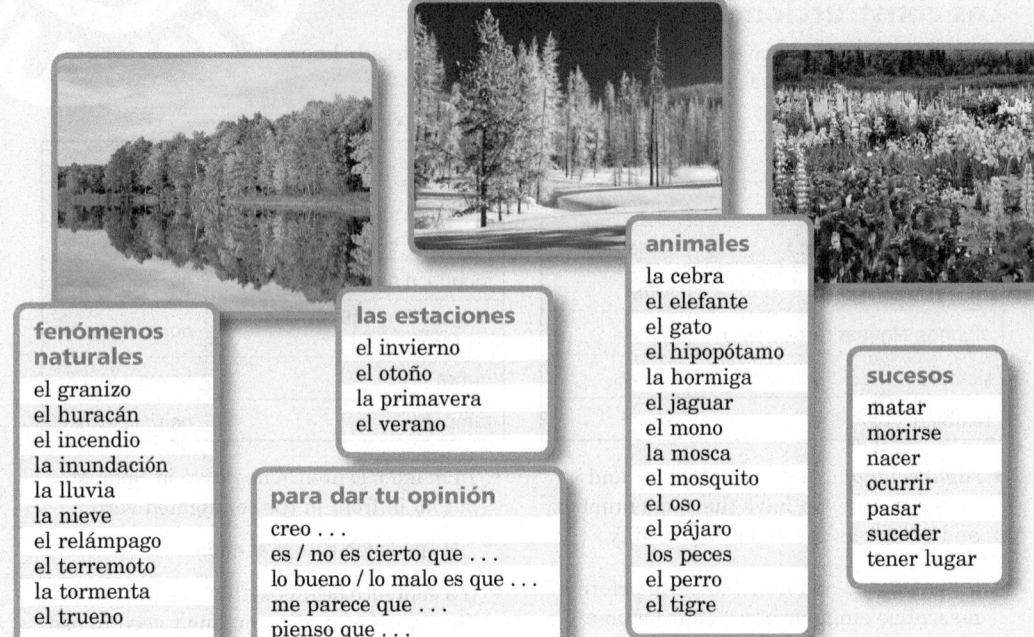

fenómenos naturales

el granizo
el huracán
el incendio
la inundación
la lluvia
la nieve
el relámpago
el terremoto
la tormenta
el trueno

las estaciones

el invierno
el otoño
la primavera
el verano

para dar tu opinión

creo . . .
es / no es cierto que . . .
lo bueno / lo malo es que . . .
me parece que . . .
pienso que . . .

animales

la cebra
el elefante
el gato
el hipopótamo
la hormiga
el jaguar
el mono
la mosca
el mosquito
el oso
el pájaro
los peces
el perro
el tigre

sucesos

matar
morirse
nacer
ocurrir
pasar
suceder
tener lugar

▼4 Standards: 1.1, 1.3

Focus: Practicing review vocabulary

Suggestions: After pairs have worked together, ask students to tell the rest of the class about the animal that their partner chose.

Answers will vary.

Extension: Ask students to talk about any pets they now have or had in the past: *En mi casa tengo un pájaro. Es un canario amarillo que canta.*

▼5 Standards: 1.1

Resources: Answer Keys: Student Edition, p. 90

Focus: Practicing review vocabulary

Suggestions: When students are writing their sentences about weather events, encourage them to use compound sentences with the imperfect and the preterite. Provide a model such as: *Llovía muy fuerte y de repente se oyó un trueno tremendo.*

Answers:

1. b   4. a
2. d   5. c
3. e

▼4 Una descripción | 👥

Hablar • Escribir

Escoge dos animales de la lista. Luego, con un(a) compañero(a), copien en una hoja de papel una tabla como la que sigue. Escriban en la tabla los nombres de los animales que han escogido y las características de cada animal.

Animal favorito
Lugar donde vive
Fenómeno natural que lo afecta
Tu opinión sobre el animal

▼5 Dónde y cuándo | 👥

Trabaja con otro(a) estudiante para emparejar cada descripción con el fenómeno de la naturaleza que corresponde. Luego escoge dos de esos fenómenos que hayan ocurrido recientemente y escribe una frase diciendo cuándo y dónde sucedió cada uno.

1. lluvia, truenos y relámpagos   **a.** trueno

2. luz muy viva producida en una tormenta   **b.** tormenta

3. movimiento de tierra   **c.** huracán

4. ruido fuerte que se oye en una tormenta   **d.** relámpago

5. viento muy fuerte y violento   **e.** terremoto

DIFFERENTIATED INSTRUCTION

Heritage Language Learners

Point out "nonstandard" or regional language use, such as substituting *lo* or *la* for *le* (*Lo hablé* instead of *Le hablé*) or adding *-s* to second-person singular preterite forms (*¿Ya fuistes?*). Explain that regional usage is acceptable in informal settings, but students should rely on "standard" usage in formal writing and speaking.

Students with Learning Difficulties

Write on the board pairs of nouns and adjectives. Have students follow a pattern to use the adjectives as nouns in complete sentences. For example, ***pantalones/negros—*** *¿Pantalones? Yo prefiero los negros.* ***gatos/amarillos—****¿Gatos? Yo prefiero los amarillos.*

Gramática Repaso

Los adjetivos usados como sustantivos

When you talk about two similar things in Spanish you can avoid repeating the noun by using the adjective as a noun.

> ¿Qué prefieres, los edificios antiguos o **los modernos?**
> ¿Quieres un gato blanco o **uno gris?**

- Note that in both cases the noun is dropped in the second part of the sentence, and the definite (*el, la, los, las*) or indefinite article (*un, una, unos, unas*) comes before the adjective.

- The adjective agrees in gender and number just as if the noun were still there; also the indefinite article *un* becomes *uno* when it is not followed by the noun.

> No me gustan los edificios antiguos ni **los modernos.**
> No quiero un gato blanco ni **uno gris.**

- The same applies to a prepositional phrase beginning with *a, de,* or *para.*

> ¿Prefieres las esculturas de la derecha o **las de la izquierda?**
> ¿El informe es para esta semana o **para la próxima?**

A masculine singular adjective can be made into a noun by placing *lo* before it.

> **Lo bueno** del verano es que tenemos vacaciones.

▼6 En el zoológico

Leer

Dos amigos visitan el zoológico. Completa su conversación con *el, la, los, las* o *lo.*

A — ¿Vamos a la sección de los pájaros o a __1.__ de los reptiles?

B — A mí me gusta más __2.__ de los reptiles.

A — ¡Mira ese cocodrilo! ¿No es impresionante?

B — ¿Cuál, __3.__ más grande?

A — No, __4.__ pequeño. ¡Mira sus dientes! Para mí, __5.__ más interesante son los dientes. Y, ¿para ti?

B — A mí, __6.__ que más me interesa es no acercarme demasiado. ¡Me dan mucho miedo!

Más práctica GO	realidades.com	print	
A ver si recuerdas with Study Plan	✔	
Guided WB pp. 208–211	✔	✔
Core WB pp. 91–92	✔	✔
Hispanohablantes WB p. 204		✔

▼7 Madre y niño |

Hablar

Una mamá le ofrece cosas a un niño, pero él quiere algo diferente. Con un(a) compañero(a) hagan los papeles de la mamá y del niño.

▶ Modelo

querer / helado de chocolate / (vainilla)

A —¿Quieres un helado de chocolate?
B —¡No, quiero uno de vainilla!

1. comprar / el globo rojo / (azul)

2. conseguir / un perrito pequeño / (grande)

3. comer / los dulces de fresa / (de limón)

4. ponerse / los pantalones largos / (cortos)

doscientos noventa y cinco **295**
Capítulo 7

Recycle 7

Gramática Repaso

Core Instruction

Resources: Voc. and Gram. Transparency 136

Suggestions: Have students write one sentence in which they talk about two similar things. Ask them to take turns reading their sentences and have volunteers adapt the second part so that an adjective is used as a noun.

▼6 Standards: 1.2

Resources: Answer Keys: Student Edition, p. 90

Focus: Reviewing the use of adjectives as nouns

Suggestions: Remind students to pay attention to the gender and number of the noun they are referring to. Point out that sometimes they must refer to the previous sentence in order to do this.

Answers:

1. la	4. el
2. la	5. lo
3. el	6. lo

▼7 Standards: 1.1

Resources: Answer Keys: Student Edition, p. 91

Focus: Reviewing the use of adjectives as nouns

Suggestions: Encourage Student B to use exaggerated intonation for the child's role. Have pairs of students take turns performing one of the dialogues for the class.

Answers will vary. The following are likely results:

1. A—¿Compras el globo rojo?
   B—¡No, compro el azul!
2. A—¿Consigues un perrito pequeño?
   B—¡No, consigo uno grande!
3. A—¿Comes los dulces de fresa?
   B—¡No, como los de limón!
4. A—¿Te pones los pantalones largos?
   B—¡No, me pongo los cortos!

ENRICH YOUR TEACHING

Teacher-to-Teacher

Ask pairs of students to compare and contrast two pictures of similar items. Point out that they must determine a way to identify each picture. This might be simply the relative positions of the pictures themselves: *la rana de la izquierda* vs. *la de la derecha.*

21st Century Skills

Initiative and Self-Direction Direct students to the online tutorials for self-directed review of the grammar topics recycled in this chapter. Students can expand their own learning by reviewing the related English grammar first then proceed to the new Spanish grammar point. Each tutorial is followed by a quick comprehension check.

✓ ASSESSMENT

A ver si recuerdas with Study Plan (online only)

After reviewing the material on these pages, assign the *A ver si recuerdas* Study Plan to evaluate students' mastery of the material. Additional practice is available online.

295

Capítulo 7 ¿Mito o realidad?

Standards for Foreign Language Learning: *Capítulo 7*

• To meet the Standards, students will:

Communication

1.1 Interpersonal

• Talk about tourist sites, animals, natural phenomena
• Talk about muralist Diego Rivera
• Talk about archaeology and mysteries past and present
• Talk about shapes and measurements
• Talk about the 1938 "War of the Worlds" scare
• Talk about family and community
• Talk about pre-Columbian indigenous civilizations
• Talk about classified ads
• Talk about Cervantes and *Don Quijote de la Mancha*

1.2 Interpretive

• Read about tourist sites, animals, natural phenomena
• Read about muralist Diego Rivera
• Read and listen to information about archaeology and mysteries past and present
• Read about shapes and measurements
• Read about word families
• Read about the 1938 "War of the Worlds" scare
• Read and listen to information about pre-Columbian indigenous civilizations in America
• Read about Feliciano Sánchez Chan and his poetry
• Read about speech preparation and writing a legend
• Read about Cervantes and *Don Quijote de la Mancha*

1.3 Presentational

• Write and present information orally about tourist sites, animals, and natural phenomena
• Write and present information orally about archaeology and mysteries past and present
• Write and present orally about shapes and measurements
• Write and present information orally about a panic like the 1938 "War of the Worlds" scare
• Write about family and community
• Recite poetry by Feliciano Sánchez Chan
• Write about pre-Columbian indigenous civilizations
• Write classified ads and legends
• Write and present information orally about Cervantes and *Don Quijote de la Mancha*

Culture

2.1 Practices and Perspectives

• Describe the perspectives of muralist Diego Rivera
• Describe some practices and perspectives of pre-Columbian indigenous civilizations in America
• Interpret the perspectives of indigenous writers
• Interpret the work of the Academia de Español de Guatemala
• Interpret the perspectives of Miguel de Cervantes

2.2 Products and Perspectives

• Describe the work of muralist Diego Rivera
• Describe the contributions of ancient civilizations
• Discuss the fiction of Miguel de Cervantes

Connections

3.1 Cross-curricular

• Discuss key facts about muralist Diego Rivera
• Discuss key facts about ancient civilizations
• Discuss facts about the "War of the Worlds" scare
• Discuss key facts about Mayan writer Sánchez Chan
• Discuss key facts about Antigua, Guatemala
• Discuss key facts about myths and legends
• Discuss key facts about Cervantes and his times

▼ Chapter Objectives

Communication

By the end of the chapter you will be able to:

• Listen and read about archeology and Pre-Columbian legends
• Talk and write about mysterious events
• Provide logical explanations for unexplained phenomena

Culture

You will also be able to:

• Understand mysteries of past civilizations in Latin America
• Provide reasonable explanations for Pre-Columbian myths

You will demonstrate what you know and can do:

• Presentación oral, p. 327
• Presentación escrita, pp. 328–329
• Preparación para el examen, pp. 336–337

You will use:

Vocabulary

• Discoveries
• Myths, legends, and unexplained phenomena
• Expressions of doubt
• Descriptions of the shapes and size of objects
• The universe

Grammar

• Present subjunctive and present perfect subjunctive with expressions of doubt
• Uses of *pero* and *sino*
• Subjunctive with adjective clauses

Exploración del mundo hispano

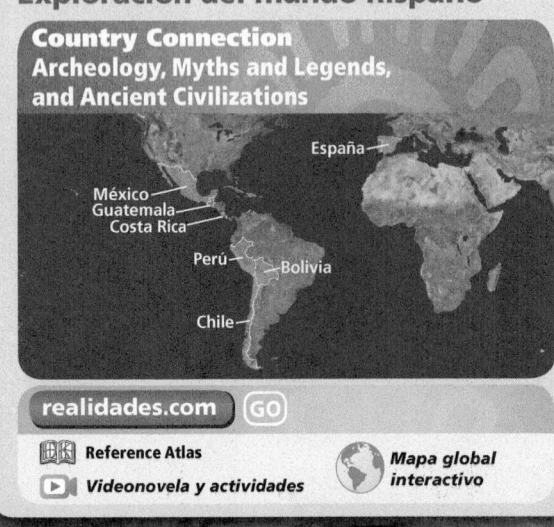

Country Connection
Archeology, Myths and Legends, and Ancient Civilizations

España
México
Guatemala
Costa Rica
Perú
Bolivia
Chile

realidades.com GO

📖 Reference Atlas
▶ Videonovela y actividades
🌎 Mapa global interactivo

296 doscientos noventa y seis

ENRICH YOUR TEACHING

Using Backward Design

Have students preview the sample performance tasks on *Preparación para el examen*, p. 337, and connect them to the Chapter Objectives. Explain to students that by completing the sample tasks they can self-assess their learning progress.

Mapa global interactivo

Download the *Mapa global interactivo* files for Chapter 7 and preview the activities. Activity 1 explores Palenque in Mexico. Activity 2 visits Machu Picchu in Peru. In Activity 3, travel the Inca Trail in Peru. Activity 4 looks at the Aztec and Mayan empires. Activity 5 takes you to Guatemala's rain forests. In Activity 6, visit Easter Island. In Activity 7, discover the Olmec, and in Activity 8, discover the Nazca Lines.

Sitio arqueológico
maya en San Bartolo,
Guatemala

Arte y cultura | México

Diego Rivera, el gran pintor mexicano, basó su
obra en temas políticos y sociales. Siempre tuvo un
gran interés por la historia de su país, y muchas de
sus pinturas representan elementos históricos. Estos
elementos son una forma de honrar y preservar la
herencia (heritage) cultural de las antiguas
civilizaciones prehispánicas. En este caso, se puede
apreciar un detalle del fresco "La civilización
totonaca", que muestra a los jefes de los poztecas
con las pirámides al fondo.

• ¿Qué construcciones indígenas conoces en
los Estados Unidos? ¿Dónde están?

Detalle de "La civilización totonaca",
(1950), Diego Rivera ▶
© 2009 Banco de México Diego Rivera & Frida Kahlo Museums Trust, México,
D.F/Artists Rights Society (ARS), New York. Photo: Corbis.

doscientos noventa y siete **297**
Capítulo 7

Standards (cont'd)
• Use language arts strategies: using illustrations, maintaining
your focus, combining sentences, characters and actions

3.2 Target Culture
• Read poetry by Feliciano Sánchez Chan
• Read fiction by Miguel de Cervantes

Comparisons
4.1 Language
• Compare **pero** and **sino** to English "but" and "but rather"
• Compare Spanish words to their English counterparts

4.2 Culture
• Compare ancient myths with scientific explanations

Communities
5.1 Beyond the School
• Link to Web sites from the Spanish-speaking world

5.2 Lifelong Learner
• Develop an appreciation for fine art and literature

◎ **PresentationExpress™**
See pp. 292c–292d

Chapter Opener
Core Instruction

Resources: Map Transparencies, 14, 15, 19
Suggestions: Introduce students to the
chapter theme and objectives.

▶ **Videonovela** *¡Pura vida!* View this
stand-alone storyline video about five young
adults in San José, Costa Rica with your class,
either online or on DVD.

Arte y cultura

Standards: 1.1, 1.2, 2.1, 2.2, 3.1, 5.2
Resources: Fine Art Transparencies, p. 58
Suggestions: After students read the
information, ask comprehension questions.

▶ **TEACHING WITH ART**
• Fine Art Transparencies, p. 58

DIFFERENTIATED INSTRUCTION

Digital resources such as the *Interactive Whiteboard* activity banks, *Videomodelos*, additional *Online Activities*,
Study Plans, automatically graded *Leveled Workbook*, animated *Grammar Tutorials*, *Flashcards*, and
Vocabulary and Grammar Videos will help you reach students of different ability levels and learning styles.

STUDENTS NEEDING EXTRA HELP
Guided Practice Activities
• Flashcards pp. 212–216, 223–226
• Vocabulary Check, pp. 217–220,
227–230
• Grammar, pp. 221–222, 231–234

HERITAGE LEARNERS
Realidades para hispanohablantes
• Chapter Opener, pp. 204–205
• A primera vista, pp. 206–207, 216–217
• Manos a la obra, pp. 208–215,
218–225
• ¡Adelante!, pp. 226–231
• Repaso del capítulo, pp. 232–235

ADVANCED/PRE-AP*
Pre-AP* Resource Book,
• pp. 156–158
Communications Workbook
• Integrated Performance Assessment,
p. 203

▼ Objectives

▶ Read, listen to, and understand information about
- what archeologists do
- archeological mysteries of other civilizations

Vocabulario en contexto

Core Instruction

Standards: 1.1, 1.2, 3.1

Resources: Teacher's Resource Book: Input Script, p. 126, Clip Art, pp. 145–152, Audio Script, p. 130; Voc. and Gram. Transparencies 137–138; Audio Program DVD: Cap. 7, Tracks 1, 3

Focus: Presenting new vocabulary and using grammar lexically in context

Suggestions: You may want to use the Input Script from the *Teacher's Resource Book* as a source of ideas for presentation of new vocabulary and comprehensible input. Meaning for vocabulary such as *calcular, medir, excavar, pesar,* and *trazar* can be clarified by pantomime. Visualized vocabulary, such as the various forms and measurements, can be taught using TPR commands. Name an object and then have the class repeat the name while a volunteer points to its image on *Vocabulary and Grammar Transparency* 137 or 138.

BELLRINGER REVIEW

Show Fine Art Transparency 58. Remove the transparency from view and read these true/false statements to the class. Have them respond on paper.

1. *La pintura representa una civilización del futuro.*
2. *Hay unos pájaros gigantescos que vuelan en el cielo.*
3. *Los indios preparan una cena muy especial.*
4. *La ropa de los indios es de muchos colores.*
5. *Vemos muchos árboles y ríos en la escena.*

(Answers: F, F, F, V, F)

Vocabulario en contexto

1 66 ¡Hola! Soy Sabrina. El mes pasado, mis compañeros y yo fuimos a visitar **las ruinas de una civilización** que vivió hace muchos siglos. Las civilizaciones antiguas son **pueblos** que **existieron** hace muchos años. ¡Fue muy interesante! 99

2 66 Entre las ruinas se destacaba el **observatorio**. Allí se estudiaban los movimientos de la **Luna** y el Sol y se calculaba el tiempo 99.

3 66 También vimos un monumento de piedra enorme y calculamos que pesaba varias **toneladas**. Es imposible saber qué **función** tenía 99.

4 66 Las paredes de los templos y las **pirámides** tenían **diseños geométricos** muy bonitos 99.

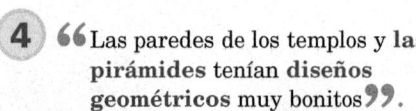

el triángulo   el rectángulo

¿Pesará más de 3 toneladas?   calcular

el diámetro

el círculo

el óvalo

DIFFERENTIATED INSTRUCTION

Advanced Learners

First have students draw a simple design using one or two geometric shapes or lines. Ask them not to show their drawings to anyone. Then have partners sit back-to-back with pencils and pads, looking at their own drawings. Have them take turns using affirmative and negative commands to tell their partner, step by step, how to reproduce their drawing. When finished, have them compare the two drawings and discuss the reasons for any differences between them.

5 ❝También tuvimos la oportunidad de trabajar con **un arqueólogo.** Los arqueólogos estudian los monumentos y las artes de las civilizaciones antiguas. ¡Aprendimos mucho de otras culturas!❞

6 ❝Aprendimos a excavar para buscar cosas del pasado❞.

excavar

7 ❝**Medimos** algunas piedras y **estructuras** como las que se usaron para **construir monumentos**❞.

el ancho

el centímetro

el largo

el alto

8 ❝Pesamos cosas de cerámica❞.

9 ❝También trazamos una línea en la tierra para medir **la distancia** entre dos piedras❞.

trazar

▼1 ¿Qué hicieron? | 🔊

Escuchar

En una hoja de papel escribe los números del 1 al 6. Escucha las frases. Escribe *C* si la frase es cierta o *F* si la frase es falsa.

▼2 Trabajo de arqueólogos | 👥

Hablar

Imagina que trabajaste con un(a) arqueólogo(a). Dile a un(a) compañero(a) lo que hiciste en tu trabajo. Puedes ayudarte usando las ilustraciones de esta página. Por ejemplo: *Excavamos para buscar cosas del pasado.*

doscientos noventa y nueve 299
Capítulo 7

---

1 Standards: 1.2

Resources: Voc. and Gram. Transparencies 137–138; Teacher's Resource Book: Audio Script, p. 130; Audio Program DVD: Cap. 7, Track 2; Answer Keys: Student Edition, p. 91

Focus: Practicing listening comprehension of new vocabulary

Suggestions: Before students listen, point out that the statements they will hear are related directly to the story about Sabrina and her friends on this and the previous page. Use the audio or read the text. Allow students to listen more than once.

Answers:

1. F	4. C
2. F	5. F
3. C	6. C

Extension: Ask students to correct the false statements. Have them do so by changing information, rather than making the false statement negative.

2 Standards: 1.1

Focus: Practicing new vocabulary in a guided conversation

Suggestions: As students talk together, encourage them to use gestures that show that they understand the meaning of the vocabulary items.

Answers will vary.

ENRICH YOUR TEACHING

Culture Note

The largest pyramid in the world by volume is located in Cholula, Mexico, two hours southeast of Mexico City. This colossal structure was only discovered in 1910 during the construction of a nearby building. Grassy vegetation had grown and covered the pyramid, making it look like a huge hill. A church was even built on it. Archaeologists have dug about five miles of tunnels inside the pyramid to study its history. The pyramid consists of several layers of construction that were built over ten centuries. Cholula was conquered by various tribes, including the Olmecs, the Toltecs, and the Aztecs, each building a larger pyramid around the existing one.

Vocabulario en contexto

Resources: Teacher's Resource Book: Input Script, p. 127, Clip Art, pp. 145–152, Audio Script, p. 130; Voc. and Gram. Transparencies 139–140, Map Transparencies, 14, 15, 19; Audio Program DVD: Cap. 7, Track 3

🌐 **Mapa global interactivo, Actividad 1** Explore the Mayan ruins at Palenque in Mexico.

Focus: Extending presentation of vocabulary and grammar

Suggestions:

Pre-reading: Have students read the title and introductory paragraph silently. Ask them to quickly look over the four paragraphs and photos on this page and the next and tell which countries they will be reading about. Have them locate these countries on *Map Transparencies* 14, 15, and 19.

Reading: Allow students time to read the paragraphs silently first. Then play the audio or read the text aloud, with students reading along as they listen. Stop after each paragraph and ask comprehension questions. For example, ask: *¿Pakal es el nombre de un lugar o de una persona? ¿Qué creen algunas personas que es la piedra de la foto?* Remind students to take advantage of cognates such as **evidencia, inexplicable,** and **improbable** to help them understand the reading.

Post-reading: Have interested students do further research on any of the four archaeological mysteries and then report back to the class. Encourage them to do any research necessary in order to find answers that aren't immediately obvious.

🌐 **Mapa global interactivo, Actividad 2** Explore the mountains around Machu Picchu in Peru.

Block Schedule

Have each student write two *Cierto/Falso* statements about each photo using the information provided. In pairs, have students read each statement aloud. The partner has to determine whether it is *cierto* or *falso*.

Misterios arqueológicos

Muchas civilizaciones antiguas construyeron grandes ciudades que son un misterio. No se sabe por qué y para qué se construyeron. Observa las fotos que enviaron los estudiantes de diferentes países explicando qué lugares o cosas misteriosas hay en sus países.

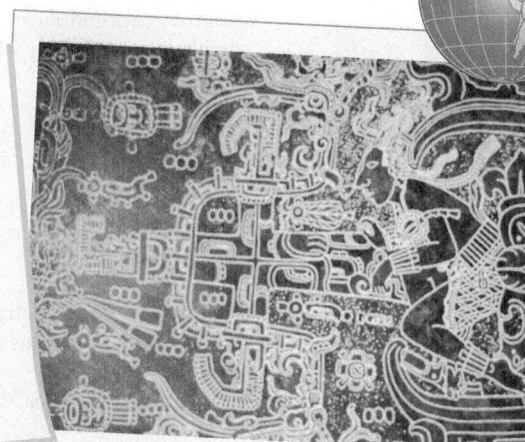

Analía, de Ciudad de México 🌐

Éste es el dibujo que se encontró en la piedra que cubría la tumba del misterioso señor Pakal, en la ciudad de Palenque. El hombre del dibujo parece estar sentado en una nave espacial. Algunas personas creen que esto es una evidencia de la presencia de extraterrestres en los tiempos de los mayas. Es **probable**, ¿no?

José, de Cuzco, Perú 🌐

Éstas son las ruinas de la misteriosa ciudad inca de Machu Picchu. Es posible que los incas hayan construido esta ciudad para protegerse de las invasiones o que haya sido un centro comercial. También es un misterio cómo unieron las piedras de sus muros[1], ya que no usaron argamasa[2]. No se sabe si van a resolver este misterio.

1 walls 2 mortar

300 trescientos
A primera vista 1

DIFFERENTIATED INSTRUCTION

Heritage Language Learners

As students use the new vocabulary, remind them to be careful with spellings of cognates, such as **pirámide.** Also remind them of differences in capitalization rules between English and Spanish: *The Incas* versus **los incas.**

Students with Special Needs

Have partners describe the images in each photo so that visually impaired students can better understand the context of each caption. For example, for the fourth photo: *Vemos a una chica que toca una piedra perfectamente redonda. El diámetro de la piedra debe ser de tres pies, más o menos.*

María, de La Paz, Bolivia

Les envío esta foto de la ciudad de Tiahuanaco, en La Paz. Esta ciudad es un enigma ya que está llena de monumentos construídos con enormes piedras. Los arqueólogos no **dudan** que estas piedras son de un lugar que está a 80 kilómetros de Tiahuanaco. Lo que resulta **inexplicable** es cómo llevaron las piedras de un lugar a otro si no conocían la rueda.

Roberto, de San José, Costa Rica

En Costa Rica sucedió un **fenómeno** muy **extraño**: un día se encontraron piedras perfectamente **redondas** en la costa del Pacífico. Es **improbable** que descubramos de dónde vienen.

▼3 ¿Cuál es el lugar? | 🔊

Escuchar

Escucha las descripciones y escoge la cultura o ciudad que corresponda.

1. a. Canadá   b. Costa Rica   c. Cuzco
2. a. Palenque   b. Honduras   c. Tiahuanaco
3. a. Inca   b. Pakal   c. Machu Picchu
4. a. Machu Picchu   b. Palenque   c. Tiahuanaco
5. a. Palenque   b. Cuzco   c. Machu Picchu

Más práctica	GO	
	realidades.com	print
Instant Check	✔	
Guided WB pp. 212–220	✔	✔
Core WB pp. 93–94	✔	✔
Comm. WB p. 96	✔	✔
Hispanohablantes WB pp. 206–207		✔

trescientos uno 301
Capítulo 7

ENRICH YOUR TEACHING

Culture Note

Thousands of these spherical stones, ranging from a few inches in diameter to eight feet around, have been discovered in Costa Rica. Even the largest of the spheres are so perfect in shape that modern tests show no imperfections. This degree of precision would have required great mathematical ability as well as an advanced knowledge of stoneworking.

21st Century Skills

Technology Literacy Have students research Web sites in Spanish that give more information about the archeological mysteries presented on pages 300–301. What keywords will they use in their search? How can they decide which Web sites will give them reliable and accurate information? Are there other Latin American ruins they have studied in other classes that may help them understand some of these mysteries?

---

3 Standards: 1.2

Resources: Voc. and Gram. Transparencies 139–140; Teacher's Resource Book: Audio Script, p. 131; Audio Program DVD: Cap. 7, Track 4; Answer Keys: Student Edition, p. 91

Focus: Practicing listening comprehension of new vocabulary

Suggestions: Allow students to listen to the audio more than once. Remind them to listen for key words that will guide them toward a correct answer, rather than trying to understand every word.

Answers:

1.	b	3.	b	5.	c
2.	c	4.	b		

Extension: Have students tell as much as they can about the other places listed in numbers 1–5. For example: *Cuzco es una ciudad en Perú. Está cerca de las ruinas de Machu Picchu.*

Pre-AP* Support

- **Learning Objective:** Presentational Speaking
- **Activity:** Have students bring to class a picture of a single object (pre-Columbian statue, rocket ship, bridge, etc.). Taking turns, each student tells the class what his or her picture is and the dimensions of the object *(de ancho, de largo, de alto)*. The next student makes a comparative statement before continuing the activity. *(La Estatua de la Libertad que yo tengo es más alta que el Calendario Azteca que tú tienes.)*
- *Pre-AP* Resource Book:* Comprehensive guide to Pre-AP* vocabulary skill development, pp. 51–57

Teacher-to-Teacher

Many students are intrigued by the mysteries associated with Latin American ruins. Encourage students to share their background knowledge about these places.

Chapter Project

Give students copies of the Chapter Project outline and rubric from the *Teacher's Resource Book.* Explain the task to them, and have them perform Step 1. (For more information, see p. 292-b.)

✔ASSESSMENT

Prueba: Comprensión del vocabulario 1
- Prueba 7-1: pp. 149–150

▶ Talk and read about archeology
▶ Discuss the legend of Atlantis

INTERACTIVE WHITEBOARD
Vocabulary Activities 7-1

4 Standards: 1.2, 3.1

Resources: Answer Keys: Student Edition, p. 92

Focus: Practicing new vocabulary

Suggestions: Remind students that the items are presented as analogies. A single colon means "is to" and a double colon means "as."

Answers:

1. línea
2. medir
3. óvalo
4. astrónomo
5. centímetro
6. triángulo
7. arqueóloga

BELLRINGER REVIEW

Show Voc. and Gram. Transparency 138. Have volunteers tell what action they see represented in each scene beginning with #6.

5 Standards: 1.2

Resources: Answer Keys: Student Edition, p. 92

Focus: Practicing new vocabulary through reading, listing, and discussion

Suggestions: Remind students that reading through the entire announcement first will help them place their answers correctly.

Answers:

1. misterios
2. existen
3. que
4. cubría
5. se excavaron
6. extraños
7. redondas
8. arqueólogos
9. probable

Steps 2–3
Answers will vary.

Vocabulario en uso

▼4 A recordar palabras

Leer • Escribir • Pensar

Completa cada analogía con una palabra correcta del recuadro. Sigue el modelo.

| triángulo | astrónomo | medir | centímetro |
| arqueóloga | línea | óvalo | |

Modelo
cierta : verdad :: inexplicable : *improbable*

1. cortar : papel :: trazar : _____

2. kilo : pesar :: centímetro : _____

3. reloj : círculo :: huevo : _____

4. laboratorio : científico :: observatorio : _____

5. el peso : tonelada :: el largo : _____

6. puerta : rectángulo :: pared de una pirámide : _____

7. enseñar : maestra :: excavar : _____

▼5 ¡A viajar!

Leer • Escribir

❶ Imagina que quieres irte de viaje con tu familia. Completa este anuncio de un viaje arqueológico usando las palabras del recuadro.

redondas	arqueólogos	que
se excavaron	probable	extraños
misterios	cubría	existen

❷ ¿Qué otro misterio arqueológico te gustaría visitar? ¿Por qué?

❸ Haz una lista de tres cosas interesantes que puedes ver en un viaje como éste.

Viaje Arqueológico

Los __1.__ de los mayas

¿Sabías que...

...todavía __2.__ muchas estructuras antiguas __3.__ estaban construidas de piedra?

...la tierra __4.__ muchos monumentos importantes hasta que __5.__ ?

...hay sitios misteriosos y __6.__ con piedras perfectamente __7.__ ?

Explora las ruinas del Yucatán y de Centroamérica con un equipo de __8.__ en la selva tropical. Visita Cobá, uno de los sitios más antiguos de los mayas. Ven a Tulum y disfruta de las aguas azules del Caribe.

¡Es muy __9.__ que te diviertas!

Viajes Paraíso
Calle 55, esquina Lago
Ciudad de México, México

DIFFERENTIATED INSTRUCTION

Students with Learning Difficulties

For *Actividad* 4, explain that to solve an analogy, students must find a word that completes the second pair. The first two words are always related; the second two must be related in the same way. Help students identify the relationship in order to solve the second analogy in each item.

Advanced Learners

Ask students to create more word analogies similar to the ones in *Actividad* 4. Have them refer to previous chapters for vocabulary sets.

▼6 Preguntas de arqueólogos |

Hablar

Un buen arqueólogo se hace muchas preguntas.
Trabaja con un(a) compañero(a) para hablar de
las fotos y los dibujos de los lugares en las páginas
298 a 301. Sigue el modelo.

▶ Modelo

líneas de Nazca / ¿quiénes trazaron?
A —¿Quiénes trazaron las Líneas de Nazca?
B —Los extraterrestres las trazaron, según algunas personas.

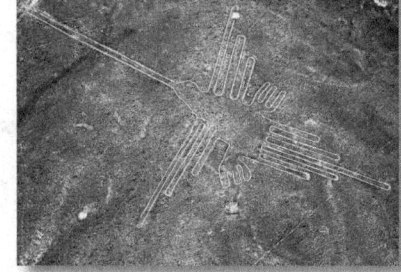
Líneas de Nazca

Estudiante A

1. observatorio / ¿qué calculaban?
2. paredes de los templos / ¿qué tipo de dibujos muestran?
3. el monumento / ¿cuánto pesa?
4. las paredes de la pirámide / ¿qué forma tienen?
5. la evidencia de la presencia de extraterrestres en la región maya / ¿cuál puede ser?
6. las ruinas de Machu Picchu / ¿cuál era el misterio?
7. las piedras misteriosas que se encontraron en Costa Rica / ¿cómo eran?

Estudiante B

triángulo
más de 3 toneladas
cómo unieron las piedras de las paredes
perfectamente redondas
una nave espacial dibujada en una piedra que cubría una tumba
los extraterrestres, según algunas personas
diseños geométricos
el tiempo y el movimiento del Sol y de la Luna

▼7 Juego |

Hablar

Tú y tus compañeros(as) van a jugar al juego de las veinte preguntas.
Cada estudiante piensa en un objeto sin decir lo que es y sus compañeros
tienen que hacerle preguntas que sólo pueden ser contestadas con *sí* o *no*.

Es un objeto redondo.
Tiene números . . .

❶ Cada estudiante escribe una descripción de un objeto de la sala de
clases. Pueden usar las palabras del recuadro.

está hecho(a) de	pesa	mide	el ancho	el alto	el largo
óvalo	círculo	triángulo	rectángulo	redondo	sirve para

❷ Los estudiantes hacen preguntas para identificar el objeto. El (La)
estudiante que identifica el objeto gana dos puntos.

Modelo

¿Tiene el objeto más de 20 centímetros de largo?
¿Tiene forma redonda?

Nota

Para expresar en
español el largo,
ancho o alto de un
objeto, puedes usar
estas mismas palabras
precedidas por la
preposición **de**.

El monumento mide
tres metros **de alto** y
dos metros **de ancho**.

trescientos tres 303
Capítulo 7

Practice and Communicate ⑦

▼6 Standards: 1.1

Resources: Answer Keys: Student Edition, p. 93

Focus: Using new vocabulary and
structures in guided dialogues

Suggestions: Point out to students that
there will be more than one way to ask
and answer the questions. Encourage
them to use their language skills to create
the most clear and efficient questions and
answers possible.

Answers:

Questions and answers will vary. The
following are suggestions:

1. A —¿Qué calculaban en el observatorio?
   B —Calculaban el tiempo y el movimiento del Sol y de la Luna.
2. A —¿Qué tipo de dibujos muestran en las paredes de los templos?
   B —Muestran diseños geométricos.
3. A —¿Cuánto pesa el monumento?
   B —Pesa más de 3 toneladas.
4. A —¿Qué forma tienen las paredes de la pirámide?
   B —Tienen la forma de un triángulo.
5. A —¿Cuál puede ser la evidencia de la presencia de los extraterrestres en la región maya?
   B —Una nave espacial dibujada en una piedra que cubría una tumba puede ser esa evidencia.
6. A —¿Cuál era el misterio de las ruinas de Machu Picchu?
   B —El misterio era cómo unieron las piedras de las paredes.
7. A —¿Cómo eran las piedras misteriosas que se encontraron en Costa Rica?
   B —Eran perfectamente redondas.

▼7 Standards: 1.1

Focus: Using new vocabulary to ask for
and provide descriptions of objects

Suggestions: As students describe and
ask about the objects, encourage them to
include as much new shape and
measurement vocabulary as they can.

Answers will vary.

ENRICH YOUR TEACHING

Teacher-to-Teacher

The game "Twenty Questions" is a tried-
and-true language-teaching strategy. It is easily
adaptable to all sorts of vocabulary and
grammar teaching targets. Any variation that
you can think of for the game (such as

Actividad 7 on this page) will provide students
with excellent real-life language practice. The
game requires students to engage in question
formation and a true exchange of information
within any context you decide to apply.

Leer • Escribir • Hablar

❶ Lee el siguiente artículo sobre el misterio de la Atlántida.

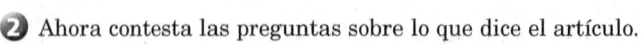

La Atlántida:
¿Un misterio o un hecho histórico?

"Una rica civilización, con unos hermosos edificios, que se hundió[1] y quedó cubierta por el mar en menos de 24 horas". Así describió el filósofo griego Platón a la gran isla de Atlántida, y a la vez, empezó la leyenda del continente perdido.

Muchas personas dicen que fue una civilización imaginaria. Otros creen que existió de verdad.

Según los estudios, es posible que la misteriosa Atlántida no haya estado en el océano Atlántico como pensaba Platón. Es probable que la isla de Creta de Minos haya sido la Atlántida. La civilización de Creta se derrumbó[2], inexplicablemente, en la cumbre[3] de su desarrollo hacia el año 1500 a.C. Esos mismos estudios dicen que por la misma época el volcán Thera, cerca de la isla de Creta, provocó una ola[4] gigantesca que la cubrió por completo.

¿Hay mucho parecido entre el relato de Platón y el fin de Creta? ¿Te parece extraña esta coincidencia? La verdad es que, por ahora, es sólo un misterio más que sigue sin resolverse.

1 sank **2** collapsed **3** peak **4** wave

❷ Ahora contesta las preguntas sobre lo que dice el artículo.

1. ¿De qué trata el artículo?
2. ¿Qué es la Atlántida y qué creen las personas acerca de la Atlántida?
3. ¿Qué sucedió con Creta?
4. ¿En qué se relacionan Creta y la Atlántida?
5. ¿Habías visto o leído antes algo sobre la Atlántida, en películas, documentales, dibujos animados, libros o artículos? ¿Qué explicación se daba allí? ¿Era parecida a la de este artículo?

❸ En grupo, comenten lo que dice la leyenda. ¿Cuántos creen que es cierta? ¿Creen que hay suficiente evidencia de que la Atlántida realmente existió?

304 trescientos cuatro
Manos a la obra 1

▼ **8** Standards: 1.1, 1.2, 1.3, 3.1

Resources: Answer Keys: Student Edition, p. 94

Focus: Practicing new vocabulary and structures through reading and response

Suggestions: First, have students read the article on their own and write their answers to the questions in Step 2. Have them share these answers when they meet in groups for Step 3. Doing so will help them address together any reading comprehension problems they may have.

Answers:

Wording of answers may vary. The following are likely results:

1. Trata del misterio de la Atlántida.
2. Atlántida es el nombre de una antigua civilización que se hundió rápidamente en el mar. Muchas personas creen que la historia de Atlántida es verdad. Otras no la creen.
3. Creta fue completamente cubierta por una ola gigantesca.
4. Los dos lugares fueron destruidos por el mar. La destrucción de los dos lugares ocurrió en la misma época.
5. Answers will vary.

Pre-AP* Support

- **Learning Objective:** Interpretive: Print and Audio
- **Activity:** As a pre-reading activity, divide the students in groups of four. Write the first three questions from *Actividad* 8 on long strips of paper and distribute one strip to each of three of the group members. Have the fourth group member read the article about the *Atlántida* to his or her group members and have each share the answer to his or her question.
- *Pre-AP* Resource Book:* Comprehensive guide to Pre-AP* communication skill development, pp. 10–18, 37–50

DIFFERENTIATED INSTRUCTION

Students with Learning Difficulties

Point out to students that *a.C.* means *antes de Cristo.* Draw a timeline on the board. Label the points *1500 a.C., el año 1 (nacimiento de Jesucristo),* and *20xx* (the current year). Use this visual to demonstrate adding 1,500 years + 2,0(xx) years to determine how many years ago the civilization of Crete was destroyed.

Multiple Intelligences

Logical/Mathematical: As the class completes *Actividad 10,* challenge students to convert answers to the metric system. Remind them that the metric system is used throughout Latin America, Spain, and many other countries. Provide them with the following information: 2.2 pounds = 1 kilogram; 3.3 feet = 1 meter; 1.6 miles = 1 km.

▼9 Compara los misterios | 👥

Hablar • Escribir

❶ Trabaja con un(a) compañero(a). Hagan una lista de los misterios que han estudiado hasta ahora en el capítulo. Añadan otros misterios que conozcan.

❷ Escojan dos misterios y compárenlos. ¿En qué se parecen? ¿En qué se diferencian? Pueden usar un diagrama de Venn como el siguiente para compararlos.

❸ Usando el diagrama de Venn, escriban frases para comparar los misterios.

Machu Picchu   **La Atlántida**

ciudad inca   isla

▼10 Y tú, ¿qué dices? | 💬 _____

Escribir • Hablar

1. ¿Cuánto crees que pesa tu pupitre? ¿Y el escritorio del (de la) profesor(a)? ¿Y un árbol?

2. ¿Qué objeto o edificio en los Estados Unidos tiene el alto de una pirámide? ¿Qué río crees que es el más largo del mundo?

3. ¿Cuál es mayor, el diámetro de la Luna o el de la Tierra? ¿Y qué distancia crees que es mayor, la de la Tierra al Sol o la de la Tierra a la Luna?

4. Busca formas geométricas en la clase. ¿Qué cosas tienen forma de rectángulo, triángulo, círculo u óvalo?

▼ Ampliación del lenguaje

Familias de palabras

Muchas veces podemos averiguar el significado de una palabra si conocemos otras palabras de la misma familia. Observa la relación entre las siguientes palabras. Luego completa las frases.

1. La piedra es muy _____. _____ 20 kilos.
2. Nadie puede _____ ese fenómeno. Es _____.
3. Es _____ que él es el criminal. La _____ lo acusa.
4. Voy a participar en un concurso de _____. Debo _____ un coche súper moderno.

verbo	sustantivo	adjetivo
calcular	la calculadora	
cubrir		cubierto(a)
diseñar	el diseño	
dudar	la duda	dudoso(a)
	la evidencia	evidente
explicar	la explicación	inexplicable
	el fenómeno	fenomenal
funcionar	la función	
medir	la medida	
	el misterio	misterioso(a)
pesar	el peso	pesado(a)

trescientos cinco **305**
Capítulo 7

Practice and Communicate ⑦

▼9 Standards: 1.1, 1.3, 3.1

Focus: Practicing new vocabulary and structures via discussion and note-taking

Suggestions: If students can't name other mysteries in Step 1, suggest well-known ones such as *las predicciones de Nostradamus* or *el Yeti*.

Answers will vary.

▼10 Standards: 1.1, 1.3

Focus: Practicing new vocabulary and structures

Suggestions: As students talk about their answers, they will be making comparisons. Model comparative and superlative structures as necessary.

Answers will vary.

Ampliación del lenguaje
Core Instruction

Standards: 1.2, 3.1

Resources: Answer Keys: Student Edition, p. 94
Focus: Understanding word families
Suggestions: Ask pairs of students to build word families around other verbs such as *expresar* or *impresionar*.

Answers:
pesada; pesa
explicar; inexplicable

Additional Resources
• Communication Wbk.: Act. 1, p. 92
• Teacher's Resource Book: Audio Script, p. 131, Communicative Pair Activity BLM, pp. 137–138
• Audio Program DVD: Cap. 7, Track 5

☑ASSESSMENT

Prueba 7-2 with Study Plan (online only)

Prueba: Aplicación del vocabulario 1
• Prueba 7-2: pp. 151–152

ENRICH YOUR TEACHING

Teacher-to-Teacher
A good way to draw students into a discussion is to use "faulty" questions. A "faulty" question is one that doesn't supply all the information necessary for it to be clearly answered. For example, a question such as: *¿Cuánto pesa un perro?* might elicit further comments, questions, and comparisons such as: *¿Qué clase de perro es?*

21st Century Skills

Critical Thinking and Problem Solving Have students research historical "lost civilizations," such as the Moche in Peru and the Anasazi in New Mexico. What explanations for their disappearance have been proposed? Have students compare them to the beliefs about Atlantis. Why does the idea of a "lost continent" continue to have such an influence in popular imagination, in their opinion?

Gramática

Core Instruction

Standards: 4.1

Resources: Voc and Gram. Transparency 141

INTERACTIVE WHITEBOARD
Grammar Activities 7-1

Suggestions: Ask students to use the expressions in the *Gramática* in sentences with the subjunctive or the indicative, as appropriate. Encourage them to make comments about the mysteries already discussed in the chapter or about current events. If necessary, ask guiding questions such as: *¿Piensas que los extraterrestres estaban presentes en la civilización maya?*

11 Standards: 1.2

Resources: Answer Keys: Student Edition, p. 94

Focus: Practicing the subjunctive with expressions of doubt

Suggestions: Remind students that these are complex sentences with more than one set of subject and verb. Tell them to carefully determine the subject of the subordinate clause before writing each answer, since their verb form must agree in person and number with that subject.

Answers:

1. excaven
2. pueda
3. pesen
4. calculen
5. pese/pesa
6. son

Gramática

El presente y el presente perfecto del subjuntivo con expresiones de duda

To express doubt, uncertainty, or disbelief about actions in the present, you use the present subjunctive. To express doubt, uncertainty, or disbelief about actions in the past, you use the present perfect subjunctive. Recall that the present perfect subjunctive is formed with the present subjunctive of *haber* and a past participle.

doubt, uncertainty		subjunctive
Dudo que . . .		existan los extraterrestres
Es posible que . . .	**+**	*extraterrestrials exist, do exist, will exist*
Es dudoso que . . .		

disbelief		
No creo que . . .	**+**	hayan existido los extraterrestres
Es imposible que . . .		*extraterrestrials existed, have existed*

Expressions of belief, knowledge, or certainty are usually followed by the indicative.

Creo que . . .		
Estoy segura que . . .		
Es evidente que . . .		
Es verdad que . . .	**+**	ésas son ruinas mayas
Sabemos que . . .		
No dudo que . . .		

Más ayuda	**realidades.com**	▶ *Canción de hip hop* ▶ **Tutorials**

▼ 11 Lo dudo

Leer

Jorge está leyendo una revista de arqueología. Completa lo que piensa con el presente del indicativo o el presente del subjuntivo del verbo apropiado.

1. Dudo que los arqueólogos _____ en lugares donde no exista evidencia de otras civilizaciones. *(excavar)*

2. Es improbable que una persona sin experiencia artística _____ trazar los diseños incas. *(poder)*

3. Es posible que las ruinas de los palacios _____ muchas toneladas. *(pesar)*

4. No creo que los científicos _____ el diámetro de una estructura sin ver antes la evidencia. *(calcular)*

5. Es imposible que el antiguo observatorio _____ más que un edificio moderno. Creo que el observatorio _____ menos que un edificio moderno. *(pesar)*

6. Estoy seguro de que los científicos _____ capaces de resolver muchos misterios. *(ser)*

DIFFERENTIATED INSTRUCTION

Students with Learning Difficulties

Point out that these sentences have two clauses, each with its own subject and verb that must agree. Provide models of different subjects with **haber** to form the present perfect subjunctive: *Es imposible que él haya creído esta leyenda. No creo que tú hayas visto un extraterrestre. Es dudoso que haya aterrizado una nave espacial.*

Advanced Learners/Pre-AP*

Have students write three false statements about real-life events: *Shirley sacó una mala nota en el examen de inglés.* Have them exchange sentences with a partner and take turns commenting on each statement using the present perfect subjunctive: *Dudo que haya sacado una mala nota porque estaba muy bien preparada.*

Practice and Communicate 7

▾12 ¿Qué opinas? |

Leer • Hablar

Trabaja con un(a) compañero(a) para dar su opinión sobre la información y las teorías que acaban de leer. Usen frases de las dos columnas.

Modelo
Los extraterrestres vivían en la ciudad de Palenque.
Dudo que los extraterrestres hayan vivido en la ciudad de Palenque.

Columna A

Los seres humanos han transportado las piedras de Tiahuanaco.

Los incas construyeron Machu Picchu para protegerse de las invasiones.

El señor Pakal está sentado en una nave espacial.

Las piedras que se encontraron en Costa Rica son perfectamente redondas.

Atlántida fue en realidad la isla de Creta de Minos.

Columna B

Dudo que . . .

Creo que . . .

Estoy seguro(a) de que . . .

Es imposible que . . .

Es probable / improbable que . . .

▾13 Noticias increíbles |

Leer • Hablar • Escribir

Lee este artículo sobre algo que sucedió en 1938.

❶ Contesta las preguntas.

1. ¿De qué se trataba el programa de radio?

2. ¿Qué causó el pánico?

3. ¿Cree el señor en la calle que existen los extraterrestres?

4. ¿Qué cree la señorita?

❷ Trabaja con un grupo para pensar en un evento o un fenómeno que pueda causar pánico al público hoy día. Escriban entre todos un guión *(script)* de un programa sobre el evento o fenómeno.

❸ "Transmitan" su programa a la clase.

---

31 de octubre, 1938

¡Pánico por supuesta invasión de marcianos!

Programa de radio causó gran revuelo[1]

Orson Welles adaptó y transmitió por radio ayer La guerra de los mundos de H.G. Wells, de manera tan realista que la gente creyó que estaba escuchando las noticias de una invasión extraterrestre. Aquí les damos la opinión del público en las calles cuando todo se aclaró.

Periodista: ¡Señor, señor! ¿Qué cree usted que ha sucedido? ¿Es posible que nos invadan los marcianos?

Señor en la calle: Quizás todos hayamos pensado que era verdad. Pero no creo que una invasión así sea posible.

Periodista: ¿Y usted, señorita?

Chica en la calle: Yo me asusté, pero en realidad, dudo que existan los marcianos.

1 commotion

trescientos siete **307**
Capítulo 7

ENRICH YOUR TEACHING

Teacher-to-Teacher

When students work on group projects, such as the creation of the transmission in *Actividad* 13, monitor them to make sure that everyone is contributing to the best of his or her ability. Whenever possible, allow them to organize themselves according to their skills. It will sometimes be necessary, however, to assign specific tasks to specific students. Those with stronger language skills might be given more of the writing task, for example, while those who are struggling might contribute to the more technical and hands-on parts of the task.

14 Standards: 1.1

Resources: Answer Keys: Student Edition, p. 96

Focus: Practicing the present perfect subjunctive with expressions of doubt

Suggestions: Tell students that Student A may interpret the art in more than one way in order to form the question. Student B should listen carefully and respond using a direct object pronoun that refers to the direct object that Student A used.

Answers:

Direct objects may vary. Direct object pronouns shown in Student B's answers replace the direct objects shown in Student A's questions.

1. A —¿Marcia ya excavó las ruinas?
   B —No, no creo que las haya excavado.
2. A —¿Tú ya pesaste las piedras?
   B —No, no creo que las haya pesado.
3. A —¿Carlos y Raúl ya trazaron las formas geométricas?
   B —No, no creo que las hayan trazado.
4. A —¿Usted ya calculó el diámetro del círculo?
   B —No, no creo que lo haya calculado.
5. A —¿Mateo ya estudió el monumento?
   B —No, no creo que lo haya estudiado.
6. A —¿Teresa y Emilio ya buscaron el templo?
   B —No, no creo que lo hayan buscado.

Block Schedule

After completing *Actividad* 15, divide students into groups of four. Have one student write out each of the expressions on a strip of paper. Place these face down in one pile. Then have students write on a a strip of paper a subject/verb combination: *El arqueólogo/encontrar* and place it in a second pile. One student selects a strip from each pile and creates a sentence combining both elements. The student receives one point if the sentence is correct and logical. Return the strips to the bottom of each pile. Continue play until each student gets three chances to create a sentence. The winner is the student with the most points.

▼14 Los arqueólogos |

Hablar

Imagina que estás trabajando en una excavación arqueológica. Algunos de tus compañeros se olvidaron de hacer sus tareas, y tú quieres confirmar que se han hecho. Observa los dibujos, y con un(a) compañero(a) hagan y contesten preguntas según el modelo.

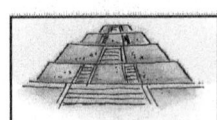

▶ **Modelo**

Pedro / medir
A —¿Pedro ya midió la pirámide?
B —No, no creo que la haya medido.

1. Marcia / excavar

2. tú / pesar

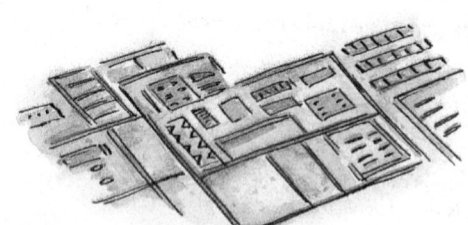

3. Carlos y Raúl / trazar

4. usted / calcular

5. Mateo / estudiar

6. Teresa y Emilio / buscar

DIFFERENTIATED INSTRUCTION

Students with Learning Difficulties

Make sure students understand the scenario of *Actividad* 16. Then have them read the questions in part 2 to set a purpose for listening. Play the interview once for students to get the gist. Have them revisit the questions and answer any that they can. Play the interview two more times so they can listen for any answers they missed.

Students with Special Needs

In order to complete *Actividad* 14, students with visually impaired partners will need to describe the object illustrated for each sentence. For example: *El dibujo es de un pueblo muy antiguo. Parece que lo están excavando.*

▼15 Y tú, ¿qué crees? |

Escribir • Hablar

Escribe tres frases acerca de tu escuela, familia, comunidad o país, y léeselas a otro(a) estudiante. Tu compañero(a) debe responder usando las expresiones del recuadro.

(no) es cierto que	(no) dudar que	(no) creer que
es (im)probable que	es (im)posible que	(no) estar seguro(a) de que

▶ **Modelo**

A —*Creo que nuestro equipo de béisbol puede ganar el campeonato este año.*

B —*Estoy seguro de que nuestro equipo puede ganar el campeonato.*

o: —*Dudo que nuestro equipo pueda ganar este año porque Tomás Álvarez era el mejor jugador y acaba de romperse la muñeca.*

▼16 La civilización misteriosa |

Escuchar • Hablar • Escribir

❶ Un famoso arqueólogo ha descubierto las ruinas de una antigua ciudad de una misteriosa civilización. Escucha la entrevista que le hace una periodista al arqueólogo. Observa el dibujo mientras escuchas la entrevista.

❷ Ahora, contesta las siguientes preguntas según la entrevista.

1. ¿Por qué no cree el Dr. Romero que haya existido esta civilización hace millones de años?

2. ¿El Dr. Romero cree que se puede calcular la edad de las ruinas?

3. ¿Qué formas geométricas se han usado en los diseños de los edificios?

4. Según el Dr. Romero, ¿quiénes fueron los habitantes de esta civilización?

❸ Escribe un párrafo sobre cómo te imaginas tú que haya sido esta misteriosa civilización.

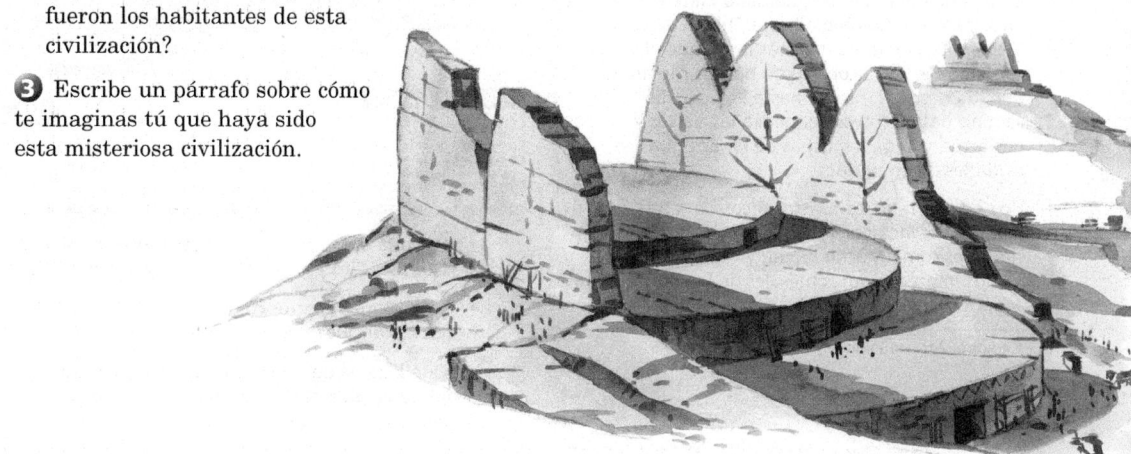

trescientos nueve **309**
Capítulo 7

---

15 Standards: 1.1, 1.3

Focus: Practicing the present perfect subjunctive with expressions of doubt

Suggestions: Suggest that students write some sentences about things they are sure about and some about things they are unsure about. This way, expressions of both doubt and certainty can be used meaningfully in the speaking part of the activity.

Answers will vary.

16 Standards: 1.2, 1.3

Resources: Teacher's Resource Book: Audio Script, pp. 131–132; Audio Program DVD: Cap. 7, Track 7; Answer Keys: Student Edition, p. 97

Focus: Practicing listening comprehension and writing of the subjunctive with expressions of doubt

Suggestions: Play the audio or read from the script. Then allow students two minutes to look over the comprehension questions. Allow them to listen again before they write their answers to the questions.

Answers:

1. Es imposible que la ciudad se haya conservado tan bien por tantos años. Además, dice que los seres humanos están en la Tierra desde hace sólo un millón de años.
2. Sí, está seguro de que se puede calcular.
3. Se han usado círculos, óvalos y rectángulos.
4. Dice que es posible que hayan sido extraterrestres, pero todavía esto no se puede saber.

ENRICH YOUR TEACHING

Teacher-to-Teacher

Students intrigued by the mysteries mentioned in this chapter might wish to create their own "mystery." Encourage them to do so and suggest different formats. Some might write a story or a scene that takes place within a lost civilization. Others might prepare and record a news flash about the discovery of a mysterious object or structure.

21st Century Skills

Communication Have students do research on the Internet about the work of an archeologist working in the field today. Using the information and questions from *Actividad* 16 as a model, have students create a list of questions they would ask him or her. What would they be most interested in finding out during an interview?

17
Standards: 1.1, 1.2

Focus: Practicing the subjunctive with expressions of doubt

Suggestions: Tell students to respond to the questions in Step 1 as though the excursion happened in the past. They should also practice the past tenses in Step 3 when telling about their discoveries.

Answers will vary.

Fondo cultural

Standards: 1.1, 1.2, 3.1, 5.2

Resources: Map Transparency 17; Answer Keys: Student Edition, p. 97

Mapa global interactivo, Actividad 3 Travel the Inca Trail in Peru.

Suggestions: After students read the information, show *Map Transparency* 17. Ask a volunteer to use the transparency to show the extent of the *Camino del Inca* in relation to all of South America. Then ask comprehension questions such as: *¿Por qué recorren hoy en día muchos turistas el Camino del Inca?*

Answers:
- **Los incas construyeron tantos caminos para poder comunicarse con todas las ciudades de su imperio inmenso.**
- **Other answers will vary.**

Chapter Project

Students can perform Step 3 at this point. (For more information, see p. 292-b.)

Teacher-to-Teacher

Have students search the Internet to find the official Peruvian government Web page for Machu Picchu. Have them look for information such as when the site is open, how to get there, and three things they will see when they visit. Have them write a report in Spanish in which they present the information they have learned.

▾17 La misteriosa civilización |

Hablar • Dibujar • GramActiva

1 Imagina que eres un(a) arqueólogo(a) y te envían a trabajar a un lugar misterioso. En grupos pequeños, imaginen cómo fue su viaje. Respondan a las siguientes preguntas. Recuerden que van a inventar una civilización y que deben ser creativos al responder a las preguntas.

1. ¿Adónde fueron? *(desierto, montaña, bosque, mar, playa, etc.)* ¿En qué país estaba ese lugar?

2. ¿Encontraron ruinas? ¿Cómo eran?

3. ¿Qué objetos encontraron? ¿Qué forma tenían esos objetos?

4. ¿Qué estructuras encontraron? ¿Qué creen que representan?

5. ¿Cómo se imaginan que era la civilización? ¿Creen que la crearon extraterrestres?

2 Ahora, dibujen lo que sucedió en el viaje. Pueden ilustrar las respuestas a las preguntas anteriores.

3 Cada grupo debe contar su viaje a la clase mientras muestran los dibujos que hicieron. Los estudiantes deben responderles usando diferentes expresiones del recuadro de gramática de la página 306.

Modelo
Es imposible que las personas de esa civilización hayan sido extraterrestres porque los extraterrestres nunca dejan evidencia.

Fondo Cultural | El mundo hispano

El Camino del Inca Antes de la llegada de los españoles, el imperio¹ inca iba desde lo que es hoy el norte de Chile hasta Colombia. Para poder comunicarse con todas las ciudades de este imperio tan inmenso, los incas construyeron más de 15,000 millas de caminos. El Camino Real, también llamado Camino del Inca, va desde Colombia hasta Chile y tiene 3,250 millas de largo. (Es más largo que el camino más largo construido por los romanos, que iba desde Jerusalén hasta Escocia). El camino pasa a través de montañas, selvas y desiertos, y llega a muchas de las antiguas ciudades del imperio.

Hoy en día, muchos turistas recorren² el Camino del Inca para visitar las ruinas de ciudades como Machu Picchu y también para ver los impresionantes paisajes de la geografía de América del Sur.

_____

1 empire **2** travel (along)

- ¿Por qué construyeron los incas tantos caminos? ¿Qué nos dice esto acerca de la civilización inca?

- ¿Te gustaría recorrer como turista el Camino del Inca? ¿Por qué?

- ¿Qué sistema de caminos o carreteras conoces que se parezca al que construyeron los incas? ¿Para qué se construyó?

310 trescientos diez
Manos a la obra 1

DIFFERENTIATED INSTRUCTION

Students with Learning Difficulties
Provide questions for the last three bulleted items in *Actividad* 18 to guide students in looking for information. For the first of the questions, ask: *¿Qué dice la leyenda? ¿Hay diferentes versiones?* For the second, ask: *¿Qué parte de la leyenda está basada en la verdad? ¿Qué es todavía un misterio?* For the third, ask: *¿Qué crees tú?*

Advanced Learners
Have students read more about the Incan civilization in encyclopedias or on the Internet. Ask them to report two facts about the Incas not mentioned in the *Fondo cultural*.

18 ¿Cómo se explica?

Leer • Escribir • Hablar

¿Te has preguntado alguna vez sobre los misterios? En grupos de tres o cuatro estudiantes van a investigar y presentar ante la clase algunos misterios inexplicables del mundo.

Para decir más

el fantasma	*ghost*
el OVNI	*UFO*
la casa encantada	*haunted house*
el poltergeist	*poltergeist*
el amuleto	*amulet*

❶ Investiguen uno de los misterios que estudiaron en este capítulo u otros fenómenos inexplicables, como el monstruo del Lago Ness o el triángulo de las Bermudas. Deben:

- investigar en periódicos, revistas, libros o en la Red, cuándo, dónde y qué sucedió
- describir los cuentos populares y leyendas que haya sobre ese misterio
- incluir las explicaciones científicas
- dar la opinión que ustedes tienen sobre ese misterio

❷ Luego, hagan una presentación a la clase. Incluyan todo lo que encontraron y sus opiniones. Pueden usar fotos o ilustraciones sacadas de periódicos, revistas o la Red.

19 Machu Picchu

Leer • Escribir

En 1911, el norteamericano Hiram Bingham descubrió unas ruinas en las montañas del Perú. Cuando se excavaron las estructuras cubiertas por la selva, se descubrió una ciudad maravillosa.

Conexiones | La historia

Ubicado[1] a 2,400 metros sobre el nivel del mar, Machu Picchu es uno de los lugares más impresionantes del planeta. Esta ciudad de los incas, de casi un kilómetro de extensión, tenía aproximadamente 1,000 habitantes durante el siglo XV. Su diseño es extraordinario, y sus muros[2], acueductos y observatorios fueron perfectamente construidos sin usar ni cemento ni argamasa[3].

Machu Picchu es considerada uno de los monumentos arquitectónicos y arqueológicos más importantes del mundo, pero la historia y función de Machu Picchu siguen siendo un misterio. Algunos creen que era una fortaleza; otros creen que era un monasterio.

1 located 2 walls 3 mortar

- ¿Por qué es un fenómeno arquitectónico Machu Picchu?
- ¿Cuál se cree que era la función de Machu Picchu?
- Si los incas vivían en el siglo XV, ¿por qué crees que no se descubrieron las ruinas hasta 1911?

Más práctica GO

realidades.com | print

Instant Check	✔	
Guided WB pp. 221–222	✔	✔
Core WB pp. 95–97	✔	✔
Comm. WB pp. 93, 97–98	✔	✔
Hispanohablantes WB pp. 208–215	✔	

trescientos once **311**
Capítulo 7

Practice and Communicate (7)

18 Standards: 1.2, 1.3, 3.1

Focus: Using learned vocabulary and structures to research and report

Suggestions: Encourage students to do the initial research on their own. They can then work together to compile their notes, work them into a report, and decide which visuals to use and how to most effectively use them.

Answers will vary.

19 Standards: 1.1, 1.2, 2.1, 3.1, 5.2

Resources: Answer Keys: Student Edition, p. 97

Focus: Practicing new vocabulary and structures through reading and discussion

Suggestions: Once students have read the information silently, ask comprehension questions before moving on to the discussion questions. For example: *¿Qué palabra en la primera frase es un sinónimo de "encontrado"? (**Ubicado**) Esta palabra nombra una estructura que se parece a un puente para el agua. ¿Qué palabra es? (**el acueducto**)*

Answers:

- **Es un fenómeno arquitectónico porque sus muros, acueductos y observatorios fueron perfectamente construidos sin cemento ni argamasa.**
- **Algunos creen que era una fortaleza; otros creen que era un monasterio.**
- **Answers will vary.**

Additional Resources

- Communication Wbk.: Act. 2, p. 93
- Teacher's Resource Book: Audio Script, p. 131, Communicative Pair Activity BLM, p. 139
- Audio Program DVD: Cap. 7, Track 6

ENRICH YOUR TEACHING

Culture Note

Part of the mystery of Machu Picchu is the skill with which it was constructed. Many of the buildings' stones weigh more than 50 tons. However, they are fitted together so exactly (without mortar) that even a thin knife blade will not fit between them.

21st Century Skills

Information Literacy Have students search the Internet for more information on the Incan civilization using the key words: *el Camino del Inca, Machu Picchu,* and *Cuzco.* Ask students to identify other important archeological sites along *el Camino del Inca.*

✓ ASSESSMENT

Prueba 7-3 with Study Plan (online only)

Prueba: El subjuntivo con expresiones de duda
- Prueba 7-3: p. 153

Examen: Vocabulario y gramática 1
- Examen 1: pp. 154–156
- ExamView: Examen 1

311

Vocabulario en contexto

Standards: 1.1, 1.2, 2.1, 2.2, 3.1, 5.2

Resources: Teacher's Resource Book: Input Script, p. 128, Clip Art, pp. 145–152, Audio Script, p. 132; Voc. and Gram. Transparencies 142–143; Audio Program DVD: Cap. 7, Track 8

Focus: Presenting new vocabulary and using grammar lexically in context

Suggestions: Have students read along as you present the new vocabulary by playing the audio or reading the text aloud. Use the pictures on *Vocabulary and Grammar Transparencies* 142–143 as an aid as you clarify the meaning of new vocabulary. Some vocabulary, such as *leyenda* and *sagrada,* can be taught by explanation: *Una leyenda es una historia muy antigua de una cultura. La historia de Robin Hood es una leyenda inglesa. En nuestra cultura las sinagogas y las iglesias son lugares sagrados.* Other vocabulary, such as *brillaba* and *cualquier* can be taught by demonstration. For *brillar,* for example, look at a light, cover your eyes, squint, and say: *Esa lámpara brilla mucho.* For *cualquier,* present a student with cards as for a card trick and say: *Elige una carta, cualquier carta.* Finally, check comprehension by asking questions. See the Input Scripts in the *Teacher's Resource Book* for specific questions.

Pre-AP* Support

- **Learning Objective:** Interpretive: Print
- **Activity:** As a pre-reading activity for this reading, have students preview the title, the subtitles and the visuals, and then create a list of questions they believe will be answered in the reading. Have students follow along as you read the article out loud. Then, have them confirm their answers by reading the text.
- *Pre-AP* Resource Book:* Comprehensive guide to Pre-AP* reading skill development, pp. 19–26

A primera vista 2 | ◁) | ▭|

▼ **Objectives**
▶ Read, listen to, and understand information about
• myths and legends
• contributions from ancient civilizations

Vocabulario en contexto

¿Cómo se explican los misterios del mundo?

En el mundo de hoy, los científicos desarrollan **teorías** para explicar **cualquier** fenómeno natural. En tiempos antiguos, la gente contaba cuentos para explicar los misterios del **universo** y los fenómenos de la naturaleza. Con el tiempo estos relatos se desarrollaron en **leyendas,** cuentos exagerados basados en personajes o temas históricos. También se crearon **mitos** para explicar los fenómenos de la naturaleza. Los mitos y las leyendas llegaron a formar parte de la cultura de los pueblos.

Uno de estos pueblos, los aztecas, tenía **creencias** muy interesantes para explicar fenómenos naturales como las inundaciones, el fuego y **el origen** del día y de la noche. Es importante comprender que los aztecas tenían muchos **dioses**: un dios del conocimiento y la civilización llamado Quetzalcóatl, un dios de la lluvia, una diosa del agua y una diosa del maíz. Los dioses eran una parte fundamental de la cultura azteca.

312 trescientos doce
A primera vista 2

DIFFERENTIATED INSTRUCTION

Students with Learning Difficulties
Before students begin to read, draw their attention to the boldface words in the text. Remind them that these are all vocabulary words that are listed at the end of the chapter. Encourage students to refer to the chapter vocabulary list as they read, if necessary.

Advanced Learners
On note cards or slips of paper, write several terms, such as *Quetzalcóatl, el mito de la Luna,* and *la creación del Sol.* Once students have read the selection, have them close their books. Place the cards or slips in a container and have students take turns drawing one at a time and explaining it in their own words.

Así es cómo los aztecas explicaban el origen del día y de la noche . . .

"Todos los dioses querían ser el centro del universo, y por eso **compitieron** varias veces para **convertirse** en el Sol. Durante estos **intentos**, destruyeron a **los habitantes de la Tierra** con inundaciones y fuego. El último intento tuvo lugar en Teotihuacán, la ciudad **sagrada** de los dioses. Allí, uno de los dioses saltó al fuego y se convirtió en el Sol. Pero el sol no se movía. Entonces, los demás dioses **se arrojaron** al fuego y el sol pudo moverse por el cielo".

Con estos actos, según los aztecas, también se crearon la Luna y las estrellas, **o sea que** nacieron el día y la noche.

Así es cómo los aztecas explicaban por qué la Luna tiene sombras . . .

"Cuando el sol **apareció**, también apareció la Luna. Los dioses se enojaron porque la Luna **brillaba** tanto como el sol. Así que le arrojaron **un conejo** a la Luna para cubrir su luz".

Según los aztecas, esto explica por qué alguna gente puede ver la imagen de un conejo en la Luna.

▼20 ¿Cómo se explica? | 🔊

Escuchar

Escribe en una hoja de papel los números del 1 al 6. Escucha las frases. Escribe *C* (cierto) o *F* (falso) para cada frase.

▼21 ¿Cómo se creó el Sol según los aztecas?

Leer

Según el relato azteca del origen del mundo, ¿en qué orden sucedieron los siguientes sucesos? Numéralos del 1 al 5.

• Como el Sol no se movía, los otros dioses se arrojaron al fuego.

• Uno de los dioses saltó al fuego y salió el Sol.

• Los dioses destruyeron a los habitantes de la Tierra.

• Los dioses se reunieron en el sitio sagrado de Teotihuacán.

• Se crearon la Luna, el día, la noche y las estrellas.

trescientos trece **313**
Capítulo 7

---

20 Standards: 1.2, 2.1, 2.2, 3.1

Resources: Teacher's Resource Book: Audio Script, p. 132; Audio Program DVD: Cap. 7, Track 9; Answer Keys: Student Edition, p. 98

Focus: Practicing listening comprehension of new vocabulary

Suggestions: Before engaging students in the listening activity, give them a few minutes to read the information on these two pages silently and address any comprehension problems they may still have. Then play the audio or read from the script. Allow students to listen more than once.

Answers:

1. C	4. F
2. F	5. C
3. C	6. F

Extension: Have students correct the answers they marked *falso.* Have them do so by first making the original statement negative, then stating the correct fact: *En los mitos no se explicaban el arte y la cultura de la civilización. Se explicaban los fenómenos naturales.*

BELLRINGER REVIEW

Show the Map Transparency for p. xxi. Point out the locations of *Popocatépetl* and *Iztaccíhuatl.* Ask a volunteer to remind the class which indigenous group of *México* is represented in the legend by these two volcanoes.

21 Standards: 1.2, 2.2, 3.1

Resources: Answer Keys: Student Edition, p. 98

Focus: Practicing reading comprehension and writing of new vocabulary

Suggestions: If students have difficulty ordering the events, model for them how to scan the text on these two pages in order to reference each event.

Answers:
4, 3, 1, 2, 5

ENRICH YOUR TEACHING

Teacher-to-Teacher

Some students may be curious about the notion of the rabbit in the moon. Invite them to share their background knowledge about moon lore, such as the man in the moon or the moon being made of cheese. Encourage students to use a visual to show the position of the rabbit in the moon.

21st Century Skills

Technology Literacy Have students use the digital technology within **realidades.com** to access and manage the audio files, videos, and activities that support learning the new vocabulary. Students can access the eText Audio to follow along with the *¿Cómo se explican los misterios del mundo?* reading, then do additional vocabulary activities.

Vocabulario en contexto

Core Instruction

Standards: 1.1, 1.2, 3.1, 5.2

Resources: Teacher's Resource Book: Input Script, p. 129, Clip Art, pp. 145–152, Audio Script, pp. 132–133; Voc. and Gram. Transparencies 144–145; Audio Program DVD: Cap. 7, Track 10

Mapa global interactivo, Actividad 4 Compare the extent of the Aztec and Mayan empires.

Focus: Extending presentation of vocabulary and grammar in context

Suggestions:

Pre-reading: Ask a volunteer to read aloud the main title. Say: *El título principal nos dice que esta lectura se trata de los mitos de dos culturas. ¿Cuáles son las dos culturas que van a compararse?* **(los mayas y los aztecas)** Point out new vocabulary items that are cognates: *astrónomos, planetas, eclipses,* and *símbolos.*

Reading: Allow students time to read the information on this page and the next silently first. Then play the audio or read the text and have students read along as they listen. Allow them to listen more than once. Demonstrate the meaning of **al igual que** by saying *Al igual que inglés, Uds. también hablan español.* Ask students what verb they think the noun **escritura** comes from. **(escribir)**

Post-reading: Check comprehension by asking questions. See the Input Script in the *Teacher's Resource Book* for specific questions.

BELLRINGER REVIEW

Show Voc. and Gram. Transparency 143. Have students write what is being represented by the symbols in the top circle.

Los mayas y los aztecas

Los mayas y los aztecas eran dos pueblos que existían en México y Centroamérica cuando llegaron los españoles en el siglo XV. Las dos culturas contribuyeron mucho a la civilización mundial de hoy.

Algunos símbolos de la escritura azteca

Los templos

La escritura y los números

Hoy en día, es común que las lenguas *(languages)* del mundo se hablen y se escriban. Pero no ha sido siempre así. Los mayas desarrollaron un sistema de escritura que expresaba la lengua que hablaban. Este sistema tenía cerca de 800 símbolos. La lengua de los mayas se habla todavía en partes de México y Centroamérica. La escritura de los aztecas mezclaba dibujos y símbolos. A veces, el número cinco era el dibujo de una mano, porque la mano tiene cinco dedos.

Los mayas y los aztecas tenían pirámides como parte de su cultura. Como los dioses eran muy importantes, las dos civilizaciones construyeron sus templos sobre las pirámides.

Templo azteca

"El Castillo", un templo maya sobre una pirámide en Chichén Itzá, en México

314 trescientos catorce
A primera vista 2

DIFFERENTIATED INSTRUCTION

Heritage Language Learners

Have students use the Internet to learn more about one of the topics presented in the reading. Invite them to present their findings orally to the class.

Students with Learning Difficulties

Read the introductory paragraph. Then draw students' attention to *Actividad* 22 and the chart that they will fill out after they read. Have students look at the headings in the reading and help them decide in which section they will probably find each piece of information.

Los números y el calendario

Los mayas fueron grandes matemáticos. Descubrieron el concepto del cero, un concepto fundamental en las matemáticas que usamos hoy día. Los aztecas, al igual que los mayas, eran grandes astrónomos. Los mayas observaron los movimientos del Sol desde que salía por la mañana hasta que se ponía por la noche. No sólo estudiaron el Sol, sino también las estrellas, los planetas y la Luna.

Observatorio "El Caracol (snail)", en la ciudad maya de Chichén Itzá

Calendario azteca, también llamado "Piedra del Sol"

Los mayas y los aztecas tenían dos calendarios distintos. Uno, el sagrado, estaba basado en los dioses y la religión. El otro era como el que usamos nosotros, basado en el año solar de 365 días. Los mayas no sabían cómo ocurrían los eclipses, pero creían que cuando el Sol estaba oscuro era porque los dioses estaban enojados.

▼22 ¿Con qué contribuyeron?

Escribir

Después de leer la información de estas páginas, completa el cuadro sobre lo que contribuyeron los mayas y los aztecas.

	Mayas	Aztecas
Astronomía		
Calendario		
Escritura		
Números		
Templos		

Más práctica (GO)

realidades.com | print

Instant Check	✔	
Guided WB pp. 223–230	✔	✔
Core WB pp. 98–99	✔	✔
Comm. WB pp. 99–100	✔	✔
Hispanohablantes WB pp. 216–217		✔

trescientos quince **315**
Capítulo 7

▼22 Standards: 1.2

Resources: Answer Keys: Student Edition, p. 99

Focus: Practicing writing of new vocabulary and structures

Suggestions: Some students may prefer to complete the chart on their own, while others will prefer to work in pairs. Suggest that students paraphrase their answers, instead of copying word for word from the reading.

Answers:

Mayas

Estudiaron los movimientos de las estrellas, los planetas, el Sol y la Luna.
Crearon dos calendarios, uno de los cuales es muy parecido al nuestro.
Desarrollaron un sistema de escritura con cerca de 800 símbolos.
Usaron el cero por primera vez.
Construyeron sus templos sobre las pirámides.

Aztecas

Eran grandes astrónomos.
Tenían dos calendarios, uno solar y otro de los dioses.
Su escritura mezclaba dibujos y símbolos.
Representaban sus números con dibujos.
Construyeron sus templos sobre las pirámides.

ENRICH YOUR TEACHING

Culture Note

The Temple of Kukulkán (plumed serpent god) is the most important structure at Chichén Itzá. The pyramid preserves information about the Mayan calendar. Each of its four sides has 91 steps, which, with the common platform at the top, add up to 365, the number of days in a year. On each side the stairs separate nine terraces into 18 parts, representing the 18 months of the Mayan calendar. Twice a year the pyramid's alignment provides a unique display. Each equinox, the sun hits the steps and creates a shadow that resembles a snake's body slithering down the pyramid; Kukulkán's head rests at the base of the stairs, completing the illusion.

✓ASSESSMENT

Prueba: Comprensión del vocabulario 2
• Prueba 7-4: p. 157–158

315

7 Practice and Communicate

23 Standards: 1.2, 2.1, 2.2, 3.1

Resources: Answer Keys: Student Edition, p. 100

Focus: Demonstrating comprehension of new vocabulary

Suggestions: At first glance, students may think there is more than one correct answer for some items. Encourage them to scan the entire activity first and to use the process of elimination to determine the best answer for each item.

Answers:
1. leyendas
2. astrónomo
3. dioses
4. eclipse
5. conejo
6. símbolos

BELLRINGER REVIEW

Have students complete the following sentences by selecting the appropriate verb and conjugating it in the preterite or imperfect as needed.

*1. Los mayas _____ (construir/desarrollar) un sistema de escritura.
2. Los aztecas _____ (tener/destruir) pirámides como parte de su cultura.
3. Los mayas _____ (descubrir/dibujar) el concepto del cero.
4. La escritura de los aztecas _____ (mezclar/convertir) dibujos y símbolos.*

(**Answers:** 1. desarrollaron 2. tenían 3. descubrieron 4. mezclaba)

24 Standards: 1.2, 2.1, 2.2, 3.1

Resources: Answer Keys: Student Edition, p. 100

Focus: Practicing new vocabulary in a word-choice exercise

Suggestions: Encourage students to scan the complete paragraph before they attempt to write their answers.

Answers:
1. se movían
2. planeta
3. dios
4. símbolos
5. creencia
6. habitantes

Block Schedule

After completing *En voz alta,* have students write a poem about nature modeled after the first verse in *Sueño cuarto (la luz).* Have students read their poem to a small group of students.

316

Vocabulario en uso

▼23 Un poco de todo . . .

Leer

Completa las siguientes frases con las palabras del recuadro.

| conejo | dioses | leyendas | eclipse | astrónomo | símbolos |

1. Los aztecas crearon _____ para explicar el origen del universo.
2. El _____ estudia los planetas y las estrellas desde el observatorio.
3. Las civilizaciones antiguas creían en muchos _____.
4. Durante un _____, la Luna cubre el Sol y la Tierra se queda a oscuras.
5. En la Luna se puede observar la imagen de un _____.
6. La escritura maya tiene una gran cantidad de _____.

▼24 El calendario azteca

Leer

Completa este párrafo con la palabra correcta que describe el calendario azteca.

El calendario azteca fue uno de los objetos más importantes de esa cultura. No sólo mostraba los días, sino que mostraba cómo ___1.___ *(se movían/se convertían)* el Sol, la Luna y el ___2.___ *(estrella/planeta)* Venus. El calendario es una piedra muy grande en forma de círculo y pesa 20 toneladas. En su centro está la cara de Tonatiuh, el ___3.___ *(conejo/dios)* del sol que, rodeada[1] por otros ___4.___ *(símbolos/mitos)*, representa el universo. Los aztecas tenían la ___5.___ *(creencia/línea)* de que para mantener el orden del sistema del universo debían hacer ciertas ceremonias. Por ejemplo, los antiguos ___6.___ *(sistemas/habitantes)* de la Ciudad de México ponían el calendario en posición horizontal como si fuera un espejo del cielo.

_____
1 surrounded

316 trescientos dieciséis
Manos a la obra 2

DIFFERENTIATED INSTRUCTION

Students with Learning Difficulties

Have students break *Actividad* 25 into two tasks. First encourage them to identify which cue in column A matches the one in column B. Once students have identified these pairs, they can concentrate on the structure of their questions and answers.

Advanced Learners

Ask students to research and report interesting facts about our own Gregorian calendar. They can reference the Internet or other sources such as encyclopedias. Suggest that they look for information about such things as the creation of the calendar, the origins of month names, or the purpose of leap year.

▼25 Según la leyenda . . . |

Hablar

Trabaja con tu compañero(a) para hablar sobre lo que están aprendiendo de las civilizaciones antiguas. Sigue el modelo.

▶ **Modelo**

A — *Según una leyenda mexicana, dos volcanes eran antes unos novios, ¿no?*

B —*Sí, se casaron contra los deseos de sus padres.*

Estudiante A

Según una leyenda/un mito/una creencia . . .
1. los dioses hacían muchos intentos para convertirse en el sol
2. unos extraterrestres trazaron las líneas de Nazca
3. los dioses se enojaron porque la luna brillaba tanto como el sol
4. los eclipses ocurrían cuando los dioses estaban enojados
5. los extraterrestres existían en los tiempos de los mayas
6. Atlántida fue una gran civilización en el Mediterráneo
7. Machu Picchu fue un centro comercial importante

Estudiante B

la erupción de un volcán causó su destrucción

los científicos no están seguros del origen de estas ruinas

las trazaron para saber dónde aterrizar (land) sus naves espaciales

mientras, los habitantes de la Tierra fueron destruidos con inundaciones y fuego

le arrojaron un conejo para hacer sombra y cubrir su luz

cubrían la luz del sol con la luna

un dibujo que se encontró en Palenque representa una nave espacial

▼ En voz alta | (Talk?)

En México, muchos escritores contemporáneos de ascendencia maya están escribiendo en el idioma nativo de sus antepasados[1]. Lo hacen para mantener vivos su idioma y su cultura y para conservar los cuentos y las creencias que antes se trasmitían sólo por tradición oral.

Feliciano Sánchez Chan nació en el pequeño poblado de Xaya, Tekax, Yucatán, en 1960. Sus obras *Retazos*[2] *de vida* y *X-Marcela* han sido premiadas en concursos de literatura de la lengua maya.

Escucha el poema de Sánchez Chan y trata de repetirlo en voz alta.
• Nombra tres elementos naturales que se mencionan en el poema. ¿Crees que es importante la naturaleza en la cultura del poeta? ¿Por qué?

_____
1 ancestors 2 snippets

"Sueño cuarto (la luz)"
de Feliciano Sánchez Chan

Soy el trueno que ha venido
con su luz
de eternas profundidades
para alumbrar[3] el camino blanco
por donde transitan tus hijos, Madre.

. . .

El señor fuego es mi hermano mayor.
Hoy he venido
con mis cuatro hermanas:
la lluvia del oriente[4],
la lluvia del poniente[5],
la lluvia del norte
y la lluvia del sur.

. . .

_____
3 to light 4 east 5 west

¿Recuerdas?
In Spanish the diphthong *ue* is pronounced "*we*" as in "wet." Read and pronounce: *trueno, fuego*.

ENRICH YOUR TEACHING

Teacher-to-Teacher

Many books are available on the subject of ancient Latin American civilizations, and many among these contain beautiful pictures of ruins and artists' conceptions of what ancient cities may have been like. If possible, obtain such books from your local library. Have students sit with the books and talk about the pictures, using the vocabulary and structures they are now studying. When searching for books, look under topics such as archaeology and ancient Mesoamerica, as well as under the names of civilizations such as Inca, Maya, Olmec, and Aztec.

▶25 Standards: 1.1, 1.2

Resources: Answer Keys: Student Edition, p. 101

Focus: Practicing new vocabulary and structures via note-taking and discussion

Suggestions: Explain that Student B must read to determine the correct cue and adapt it for his or her response.

Answers will vary. The following answers show the relationship between the comments of both partners:

1. A —Según una leyenda azteca, los dioses hacían muchos intentos para convertirse en el sol.
   B —Sí, y mientras, los habitantes de la Tierra fueron destruidos con inundaciones y fuego.
2. A —Según mucha gente, unos extraterrestres trazaron....
   B —Sí, las trazaron para saber....
3. A —Según un mito azteca, los dioses se enojaron....
   B —Sí, por eso le arrojaron un conejo....
4. A —Según los mayas, los eclipses ocurrían cuando....
   B —Sí, pero nosotros sabemos que cubrían....
5. A —Según mucha gente, los extraterrestres existían....
   B —Sí, porque un dibujo....
6. A —Según mucha gente, Atlántida fue una gran civilización....
   B —Sí, pero la erupción de un volcán....
7. A —Según algunos arqueólogos, Machu Picchu fue....
   B —Sí, pero los científicos no están....

En voz alta
Core Instruction

Standards: 1.2, 1.3, 2.1, 2.2, 3.1, 3.2, 5.2

Resources: Teacher's Resource Book: Audio Script, p. 133; Audio Program DVD: Cap. 7, Track 11; Answer Keys: Student Edition, p. 102

Suggestions: Have students practice reciting with a partner first, then ask volunteers to recite the poem fragment for the class.

Answers:
• el trueno, el rayo, la lluvia; Remainder of answer will vary.

Chapter Project

Students can perform Step 4 at this point. Be sure they understand your corrections and suggestions. (For more information, see p. 292-b.)

26

Standards: 1.3, 3.1

Focus: Practicing writing new vocabulary

Suggestions: Remind students that they are to use their imaginations. Their explanations might resemble those in Mayan or Aztec legends, but they should invent their own.

Common Errors: Students will sometimes confuse *por qué* and *porque.* Remind them that the first is a question and the second an answer. Point out that they can use the accent mark in *por qué* as a reminder, since they know that accent marks appear in question words.

Answers will vary.

27

Standards: 1.2, 1.3, 2.1, 2.2, 3.1, 3.2, 5.2

Resources: Answer Keys: Student Edition, p. 102

Mapa global interactivo, Actividad 5 Look at rain forest habitat in Guatemala.

Focus: Demonstrating comprehension of new vocabulary and structures through reading and response

Suggestions: Have students read through the legend once on their own, then a second time with a partner. During the second reading, partners can help each other with difficult words or sentences.

Answers:
1. Quetzal era el hijo del cacique de una tribu quiché. Chiruma era el hermano del cacique (el tío de Quetzal).
2. Chiruma le robó la pluma de colibrí que lo protegía.
3. La pluma de colibrí es un símbolo de la buena suerte.
4. Quetzal se convirtió en un hermoso pájaro.

Additional Resources

• Communication Wbk.: Audio Act. 3, p. 94
• Teacher's Resource Book: Audio Script, p. 133, Communicative Pair Activity BLM, pp. 140–141
• Audio Program DVD: Cap. 7, Track 12

318

▼26 Mitos y leyendas

Escribir

En los mitos y las leyendas la gente inventa razones para explicar ciertas cosas. Usa tu imaginación para escribir una frase sobre seis de los siguientes fenómenos de la naturaleza. Explica por qué . . .

Modelo
. . . hay truenos
Hay truenos porque los dioses están tocando los tambores.

1. . . . cae lluvia
2. . . . hace viento
3. . . . se pone el sol
4. . . . ocurre un eclipse
5. . . . aparecen sombras
6. . . . brillan las estrellas
7. . . . salta un conejo
8. . . . el agua se convierte en hielo

▼27 Una leyenda quiché | 🌐

Leer • Escribir

Lee esta leyenda de los indígenas quichés de Guatemala sobre el pájaro quetzal, símbolo de la libertad y nombre de su moneda.

Quetzal nunca muere

Quetzal era el hijo del cacique[1] de una tribu[2] quiché[3]. Todos los habitantes lo admiraban y sabían que un día Quetzal se iba a convertir en el jefe de la tribu. Pero Chiruma, el hermano del cacique, estaba celoso de Quetzal.

Cuando Quetzal fue mayor, el adivino[4] le dijo: "No morirás nunca, Quetzal. Vivirás eternamente". Durante una lucha contra otra tribu, Chiruma se dio cuenta de que las flechas[5] que le arrojaban a Quetzal nunca lo herían[6]. Entonces Chiruma pensó que debía tener un amuleto. Esa noche, cuando Quetzal dormía, Chiruma entró en su cuarto y descubrió al lado de Quetzal una pluma de colibrí[7]. Recordó que el colibrí era un símbolo de la buena suerte[8] y robó la pluma.

Cuando murió el cacique, los ancianos escogieron a Quetzal para ser el nuevo jefe. Un día Quetzal caminaba por el bosque cuando de repente apareció un colibrí. El colibrí le dijo a Quetzal: "Soy tu protector y vengo a decirte que alguien quiere matarte".

De pronto oyó un silbido[9] y una flecha penetró en su pecho. Quetzal cayó sobre la hierba[10] verde y murió. Pero los dioses, que habían predicho una vida eterna, lo convirtieron en un hermoso pájaro. Su cuerpo tomó el color del césped, su pecho conservó el color de la sangre y el sol puso en su larga cola[11] muchos colores.

1 chief 2 tribe 3 indigenous people of Guatemala
4 fortune-teller 5 arrows 6 wounded 7 hummingbird's feather
8 luck 9 whistling sound 10 grass 11 tail

¿Comprendiste?

1. ¿Quién es Quetzal? ¿Quién es Chiruma?
2. ¿Qué hizo Chiruma para vengarse *(get revenge)* cuando no lo escogieron para ser el cacique de la tribu?
3. ¿Qué representa el símbolo de la pluma de colibrí?
4. ¿En qué se convirtió Quetzal?

318 trescientos dieciocho
Manos a la obra 2

DIFFERENTIATED INSTRUCTION

Heritage Language Learners

Encourage students to read Spanish-language materials recreationally for at least five to ten minutes per day. Allow them to read a book, magazine, or a newspaper of their choice. As students learn to enjoy reading recreationally in Spanish, they will improve their academic reading skills as well.

Multiple Intelligences

Verbal/Linguistic: Challenge students to pronounce the names of the Aztec gods in the Nahuatl language. When the letters *tl* occur together, they are pronounced as a single consonant, but not as a separate syllable (there is no vowel sound). Have students produce the sound by saying "nightly" without the final /i/ sound.

Gramática

▼ Objectives
▶ Make negative statements
▶ Discuss and read about Aztec gods

Pero y sino

The word *pero* is usually the equivalent of the English conjunction *but*. However, there is another word in Spanish, *sino*, that also means *but*. *Sino* is used after a negative, in order to offer the idea of an alternative: not this, *but rather* that.

No voy a beber jugo de frutas sino agua.

- You can also use *sino* with *no sólo. . . sino también. . . (not only . . . but also)*

Apareció no sólo el sol sino también la luna.

- You use *sino que* instead of *sino* when there is a conjugated verb in the second part of the sentence.

No vendí mis libros sino que los regalé.

| Más ayuda | realidades.com | ▶ Tutorial |

▼28 ¿Qué dice el artículo? _____

Leer

Imagina que estás leyendo diferentes noticias y artículos. Decide si la palabra que completa cada frase es *pero* o *sino*.

1. Hizo varios intentos por convertirse en astrónomo _____ no lo consiguió.
2. No construirán un nuevo observatorio _____ que repararán el viejo.
3. No sólo se ven sombras en la Luna _____ también figuras oscuras.
4. Creía que el lugar era sagrado _____ ahora no estoy seguro.
5. Según la creencia, no fue un solo dios _____ todos.
6. Tenían no sólo información _____ también evidencia importante.

▼29 Dioses de los aztecas | 👥 _____

Leer • Hablar

Lee la lista de los dioses de los aztecas. Trabaja con otro(a) compañero(a) para hacer frases sobre los dioses usando *sino* y *pero*.

Modelo
Quetzalcóatl no sólo era el dios del conocimiento sino también de la civilización. Era el dios de la civilización pero no el dios del fuego.

Los DIOSES importantes de los AZTECAS

Coatlicue– La primera diosa: creó la Luna y las estrellas

Huitzilopochtli– Dios de la guerra y el Sol

Quetzalcóatl– Dios del conocimiento y la civilización

Mictlantecuhtle– Dios de los muertos

Ehecatl– Dios del viento

Tláloc– Dios de la lluvia

Xiuhtecuhtli– Dios del fuego

Más práctica GO	realidades.com	print
Instant Check	✔	
Guided WB pp. 231–232	✔	✔
Core WB p. 100	✔	✔
Comm. WB pp. 101, 201	✔	✔
Hispanohablantes WB pp. 218–222		✔

Practice and Communicate  7

Gramática

Core Instruction

Standards: 4.1

Resources: Voc. and Gram. Transparency 146

INTERACTIVE WHITEBOARD
Grammar Activities 7-2

Suggestions: Provide students with pairs of cues and ask them to make sentences like the models shown in the *Gramática*. Tell them to make their sentences using past tenses. For example *ver la película en el cine/verla en casa: No vi la película en el cine, sino que la vi en casa.*

▼28 Standards: 1.2

Resources: Answer Keys: Student Edition, p. 102
Focus: Using *pero* and *sino* in a word-choice exercise

Suggestions: Remind students that *no sólo* in the first part of a sentence is a hint telling them that they must use *sino también* in the second part.

Answers:

1. pero	4. pero
2. sino	5. sino
3. sino	6. sino

▼29 Standards: 1.2, 2.2, 3.1

Focus: Using *pero* and *sino* in written sentences

Suggestions: Invite pairs of students to share their sentences with others. Encourage them to turn the sharing into a conversation by asking each other questions about the gods:

A —¿Tláloc era el dios del Sol?

B —Tláloc no era el dios del Sol, sino de la lluvia.

Answers will vary.

✓ASSESSMENT

Prueba 7-6 with Study Plan (online only)

Prueba: *Pero y sino*
- Prueba 7-6: p. 161

ENRICH YOUR TEACHING

Teacher-to-Teacher

When talking about ancient civilizations, many unusual words appear, such as the names of gods in *Actividad 29*. Point out that these names come from ancient languages, but their spellings are based on the Spanish alphabet. Help students apply the Spanish phonics skills to sound out the words.

21st Century Skills

Initiative and Self-Direction Remind students of the various digital tools available in **realidades.com** to help them monitor their own understanding and learning needs, such as the online tutorials with comprehension check exercises, animated verbs, and additional grammar practice activities.

Gramática

Core Instruction

Resources: Voc. and Gram. Transparency 147

INTERACTIVE WHITEBOARD
Grammar Activities 7-2

Suggestions: By now, students have seen enough uses for the subjunctive to be able to begin to make subtle associations regarding its meaning. Ask them to give English equivalents for the Spanish models in the *Gramática*. Point out that the subjunctive mood often has the connotation of hypothesis, which can be translated by the English auxiliary verb "might." For this reason, *Busco un libro que tenga un artículo sobre los mayas* can be translated to "I'm looking for a book that might have an article about the Maya."

30 Standards: 1.2

Resources: Answer Keys: Student Edition, p. 103
Focus: Practicing the subjunctive in adjective clauses
Suggestions: Remind students that the subjunctive is used when referring to something that only hypothetically exists. This is true when we refer to things we haven't found or aren't sure of yet. Once we begin talking about something or someone we definitely know of, we use the indicative.
Answers:

1. sea   5. pueda
2. hace   6. guste
3. tiene   7. sirva
4. sepa

Pre-AP* Support

- **Learning Objective:** Interpersonal Writing
- **Activity:** Have students write an e-mail to a friend where they describe the qualities necessary for the perfect Spanish teacher. They can start their e-mail by completing the phrase, *"Busco un profesor de español que…"* and add a series of qualities. Be sure students ask their friend at least one question about their ideal Spanish teacher.
- **Pre-AP* Resource Book:** Comprehensive guide to Pre-AP* writing skill development, pp. 27–38

Gramática

▼ **Objectives**
▶ Provide descriptions of people or things you know or you don't know
▶ Talk and write about a legend you know

El subjuntivo en cláusulas adjetivas

Sometimes you use an entire clause to describe a noun. This is called an adjective clause.

- When you have a specific person or thing in mind, you use the indicative.

  Este libro tiene un artículo que habla sobre los mayas.

- If you don't have a specific person or thing in mind, or if you are not sure the person exists, you use the subjunctive. Sometimes *cualquier(a)* is used in these expressions.

  Busco un libro que tenga un artículo sobre los mayas.
  Escoge cualquier cosa que te guste.

- You also use the subjunctive in an adjective clause when it describes a negative word such as *nadie, nada,* or *ninguno(a)*.

  No hay nadie que conozca los símbolos aztecas.

To refer to something or someone unknown in the past, you can use the present perfect subjunctive.

  Busco a una joven que haya estudiado arqueología.
  No hay nadie que haya visto un extraterrestre.

| **Más ayuda** | **realidades.com** | ▶ *Canción de hip hop* ▶ Tutorial |

▼ 30 El proyecto sobre culturas antiguas

Leer

Un grupo de estudiantes va a hacer un proyecto para representar algunos aspectos artísticos de las culturas antiguas. Están tratando de decidir a quiénes y qué necesitan para hacer su proyecto. Completa las siguientes frases con el presente del subjuntivo o del indicativo.

—Necesitamos encontrar a un estudiante que __1.__ *(ser)* muy artístico para hacer dibujos de los dioses.

—Pues, yo conozco a una chica que siempre __2.__ *(hacer)* dibujos muy bonitos en su cuaderno durante mi clase de inglés.

—Fernando compró un libro que __3.__ *(tener)* unos diseños de la Pirámide del sol. Podemos hacer un modelo de ella. ¿Conocemos a alguien que __4.__ *(saber)* hacer construcciones de cerámica?

—No puedo pensar en ningún estudiante que __5.__ *(poder)* hacer un modelo de la pirámide.

—El calendario azteca es fascinante. Podemos dibujarlo y pintarlo usando cualquier sistema de colores que nos __6.__ *(gustar)*.

—Buena idea. Vamos a buscar un dibujo o una foto que nos __7.__ *(servir)* de modelo.

DIFFERENTIATED INSTRUCTION

Students with Learning Difficulties

Review how to form the present subjunctive and give examples: 1) form the first person singular in the present tense: *hablo, vengo;* 2) take away *o: habl-, veng-;* 3) add "opposite" endings (*-e* for *-ar* verbs and *a* for *-er* and *-ir* verbs): *hable, venga;* 4) make verbs agree with subjects: *que yo hable, que ella venga.*

Advanced Learners/Pre-AP*

Have students write three sentences that set up a situation in which there is a need. Have them trade sentences with a partner, who then makes a suggestion:

A —*Tengo que hacer una investigación sobre el calendario azteca, pero no sé cómo empezar.*

B —*Necesitas encontrar un sitio en el Internet que pueda ayudarte.*

▼31 Investigación sobre las culturas antiguas

Leer • Escribir

Imagina que tienes que investigar acerca de las culturas antiguas. Usa tu imaginación y completa las frases usando la forma correcta del verbo. Añade detalles a cada frase.

Museo Nacional de Antropología, Ciudad de México

Modelo
Busco una biblioteca que (*estar*). . .
Busco una biblioteca que esté cerca de mi casa.

1. Necesito un libro que (explicar). . .
2. Yo sé de un libro que (hablar). . .
3. No hay nadie que (conocer). . .
4. No hay nada que (decir). . .
5. Escogeré cualquier artículo que (gustar). . .
6. Quiero encontrar una página Web que (tener). . .
7. Mi amigo tiene varios artículos que (aparecer). . .
8. Tengo que hablar con las personas que (contribuir). . .

▼32 ¿A quién conoces que sepa . . . ?

Hablar

Trabaja con otro(a) estudiante para identificar a personas de tu escuela o comunidad que hayan hecho o sepan hacer diferentes cosas.

▶ **Modelo**

A —*¿Hay alguien en nuestra escuela que sepa hablar tres idiomas?*

B —*Sí, el padre de Berta sabe hablar español, italiano e inglés.*

o: —*No sé. No conozco a nadie que sepa hablar tres idiomas.*

Estudiante A

1. tener un coche deportivo
2. conocer a una persona famosa
3. haber ganado un campeonato de deportes
4. ser actor / actriz de cine
5. haber vivido en un país extranjero por más de un año
6. contribuir su tiempo como voluntario(a)

Estudiante B

¡Respuesta personal!

trescientos veintiuno **321**
Capítulo 7

▼31 Standards: 1.2, 1.3

Resources: Answer Keys: Student Edition, p. 103

Focus: Practicing the subjunctive in adjective clauses

Suggestions: Remind students to stay within the context of the research project that is set up in the instructions. All of their completed sentences should make sense within that context.

Answers:
Wording of sentences will vary. Students will use the following verb forms:

1.	explique	5.	me guste
2.	habla	6.	tenga
3.	conozca	7.	aparecen
4.	diga	8.	contribuyen

▼32 Standards: 1.1

Resources: Answer Keys: Student Edition, p. 104

Focus: Practicing the subjunctive in adjective clauses

Suggestions: Point out that since Student A is asking if a certain kind of person exists, that person is only hypothetical, and so the subjunctive must be used in the question. If Student B doesn't know of anyone, then such a person remains hypothetical and the subjunctive continues to be used.

Answers:
Students will choose from among the following verb forms. Student A will always use the subjunctive in the question. Student B will use the indicative if he or she knows of a particular person, and the subjunctive if not.

1. tenga/tiene
2. conozca/conoce
3. haya ganado/ha ganado
4. sea/es
5. haya vivido/ha vivido (vivió)
6. contribuya/contribuye

ENRICH YOUR TEACHING

Teacher-to-Teacher

Students tend to have difficulty understanding the subjunctive since it has all but disappeared in English. Give them the example "If I were you...." Since the situation is hypothetical, we don't use the indicative "am." Instead, "were" acts as a vestige of the old English subjunctive.

21st Century Skills

Creativity and Innovation Have students work together to create a list of actions, skills, or experiences to use in *Actividad 32* when asking specifically about the students in the class. "*¿Hay alguien en la clase que sepa...?*" Encourage students to come up with unique questions to ask their classmates.

BELLRINGER REVIEW

Briefly review with students vocabulary associated with jobs and job qualifications. This can be found in the *A ver si recuerdas* and *A primera vista* sections of *Capítulos* 5 and 6.

33 Standards: 1.1, 1.3

Focus: Practicing the subjunctive in adjective clauses

Suggestions: Remind students to use the subjunctive in an adjective clause that modifies someone or something that they are searching for. If an adjective clause modifies something that is already known about, such as a course or a facility at a school, they must use the indicative.

Answers will vary.

El español en el mundo del trabajo

Core Instruction

Standards: 1.2, 5.1

Suggestions: Once students have read the information, ask comprehension questions. For example: *¿Para qué profesiones dan cursos en español?* **(diferentes profesiones, incluyendo guías de turismo)** *En tus propias palabras, describe un paseo típico que da un profesor para guías de turismo.*

▼33 Tu anuncio clasificado |

Escribir • Hablar

❶ Imagina que decides aprender otro idioma o cambiar de trabajo. Escribe un anuncio clasificado para el periódico solicitando un(a) maestro(a) o una escuela de idiomas o pidiendo trabajo.

Modelo
Busco una escuela de idiomas que dé clases de chino.

❷ Ahora, trabaja con otro(a) estudiante para intercambiar los anuncios que hicieron. Cada uno(a) debe responder al anuncio con un mensaje breve.

▶ **Modelo**

A — *Busco una escuela de idiomas que dé clases de chino.*
B — *Yo conozco una escuela que da clases de chino.*

El español en el mundo del trabajo

Antigua, en Guatemala, es una de las ciudades más bellas de América Latina. Está llena de bellos edificios y plazas coloniales. También hay muchas ruinas de edificios antiguos destruidos por los terremotos que ocurren en la región.

En esta ciudad se encuentra la Academia de Español de Guatemala. Allí se dan cursos de español especialmente diseñados para diferentes profesiones.

La escuela tiene un curso muy interesante para guías de turismo. Muchas veces, los estudiantes de este curso salen a pasear por la ciudad mientras el profesor les enseña todas las palabras que deben saber para describir los edificios y las ruinas. Estos estudiantes aprenden a usar el español para hacer un trabajo útil e interesante.

Una calle de Antigua

DIFFERENTIATED INSTRUCTION

Heritage Language Learners
Encourage students to take on the role of editor in *Actividad* 35. As group members suggest potential phrases and sentences, heritage learners can offer more commonly used alternatives.

Students with Learning Difficulties
Remind students that in *Actividad* 33 they are composing an ad for a person or thing that they want to find. They can't be sure that the person or thing exists. So, as explained in the *Gramática* on p. 320, they need to put the verb in the subordinate clause in the subjunctive.

▼34 Juego |

Escribir • Hablar

❶ En grupos, piensen en algún programa de televisión, libro o película que trate sobre extraterrestres o fenómenos inexplicables. Completen una tabla como la siguiente sobre el programa, el libro o la película.

Nombre del programa, libro o película	
Argumento general	
Ejemplos de fenómenos inexplicables	
Personajes	
¿Dónde ocurre?	
¿Cuándo ocurre?	
¿Cuál es el final?	

El monstruo del Lago Ness

❷ Ahora, jueguen a adivinar qué programa de televisión, libro o película escogió cada grupo. Por turnos, cada grupo pasa al frente de la clase y relata de qué trata el programa, el libro o la película que escogió sin dar el título. Pero, para hacer el juego más divertido, tienen que cambiar uno de los elementos que pusieron en sus tablas. Por ejemplo, pueden cambiar el nombre de los personajes principales o el lugar donde ocurre la historia. Gana el grupo que haya adivinado más programas, libros o películas.

▼35 ¿Recuerdas la leyenda? |

Hablar • Escribir

Trabaja con un grupo para escribir con tus propias palabras una leyenda conocida.

❶ Escojan una leyenda que conozcan.

❷ Hagan una tabla con lo siguiente y complétenla con los datos de la leyenda que escogieron.

- el tema
- la situación
- los personajes
- el lugar y la época
- el conflicto
- cómo se resuelve el conflicto

❸ Escriban la leyenda. No se olviden de escribir el título.

❹ Pueden ilustrar la leyenda e incluir música.

> **Estrategia**
> **Cooperative learning**
> You might assign roles to each member of the group. These roles might include:
> - secretary
> - editor
> - illustrator
> - story-teller / presenter

> **Más práctica** GO
> realidades.com | print
>
> | Instant Check | ✔ | |
> | Guided WB pp. 233–234 | ✔ | ✔ |
> | Core WB pp. 101–102 | ✔ | ✔ |
> | Comm. WB pp. 94–95, 102–103 | ✔ | ✔ |
> | Hispanohablantes WB pp. 223–225 | | ✔ |

trescientos veintitrés **323**
Capítulo 7

Practice and Communicate ⑦

▼34 Standards: 1.1, 1.3

Focus: Practicing vocabulary and structures via writing and discussion

Suggestions: Tell students to read the instructions for both steps before they begin their planning in Step 1. This way, they know that they will be using their information in a guessing game and devise more effective ways to disguise their TV show, book, or film.

Answers will vary.

▼35 Standards: 1.1, 1.3, 3.1

Focus: Practicing vocabulary and structures by writing a version of a known legend

Suggestions: Before students begin, refer them to the *Estrategia*. Membership in groups should vary from activity to activity. Encourage students to devise quick, effective, and considerate ways to best use the talents of everyone in a group.

Answers will vary.

Chapter Project

Students can perform Step 5 at this point. Make audio or video recordings of their presentations for inclusion in their portfolios. (For more information, see p. 292-b.)

Additional Resources

- Communication Wbk.: Audio Act. 4–5, pp. 94–95
- Teacher's Resource Book: Audio Script, pp. 133–134, Communicative Pair Activity BLM, pp. 142–143
- Audio Program DVD: Cap. 7, Track 13–14

✓ASSESSMENT

Prueba 7-7 with Study Plan (online only)

Prueba: El subjuntivo en cláusulas adjetivas
- Prueba 7-7: p. 162

Examen: Vocabulario y gramática 2
- Examen 2: pp. 163–164
- ExamView: Examen 2

ENRICH YOUR TEACHING

Culture Note

When assigning *Actividad 35*, tell students an ancient Aztec legend called **La Llorona.** It is still told throughout Mexico and Guatemala today in several versions. Generally, the story is of a beautiful young woman who married a handsome man. They had two children, but eventually the man tired of the woman. The man continued to pay attention to his children but ignored his wife. The woman, crazed with jealousy, killed her children. Struck with remorse, she wandered the town at night, weeping and searching for her lost children. Parents warn their children that if they are out at night, the woman might mistake them for her own and take them away.

Puente a la cultura

Core Instruction

Standards: 1.2, 2.2, 3.1, 5.2

Focus: Reading to learn about ancient civilizations

Suggestions:

Pre-reading: Refer students to the *Estrategia*. Once they have read it, say: *Mira las fotos y los mapas. Basado en ellos, ¿qué predicciones puedes hacer sobre el contenido de esta lectura?* Ask students to write down their predictions in order to return to them later.

Reading: As students read, remind them to use background knowledge, cognates, and context clues to understand unfamiliar words and expressions. Help them resolve comprehension problems by asking **sí/no** or embedded-answer questions.

Post-reading: Ask students to revisit the predictions they made based on the pictures. Ask: *¿Eran tus predicciones correctas? ¿Qué piensas de estos misterios?*

Country Connection

Core Instruction

Standards: 3.1

Mapa global interactivo, Actividad 6
Discover the mysterious statues on Easter Island off the coast of Chile.

Suggestions: Tell students that, although *la Isla de Pascua* is still the official Chilean name for the island (it is a province of Chile), most now refer to it by the name preferred by its inhabitants: Rapa Nui. Show students Rapa Nui on a map. It lies 2,000 miles east of Tahiti and 2,000 miles west of the Chilean coast. Some, including the great Norwegian explorer and archaeologist Thor Hyerdahl, put forth the theory that the ancient inhabitants who placed the famous *moai* were from Peru. This was due to the statues' resemblance to Incan stonework. More recent archaeological evidence, however, leads us to believe that Polynesians discovered the island in about A.D. 400.

Puente a la cultura
Misterios del pasado

▼ Objectives

▸ Read about the mysteries of past civilizations in Latin America
▸ Use illustrations to make predictions about the text
▸ Use different sources to investigate a mystery of the past

Estrategia

Using illustrations
You can preview what you are about to read by looking at the illustrations or photos that accompany the text. You can also look at the illustrations to locate details while reading. Before starting to read, look at the photos on these pages and make a prediction about what the text is about. After you finish reading, check if your prediction was right.

Los *moai*, en la Isla de Pascua

Cuando los europeos llegaron a las Américas en 1492, se encontraron con muchos pueblos indígenas. Hoy día no hay nadie que pueda explicar la desaparición de la cultura de algunos de estos pueblos.

La Isla de Pascua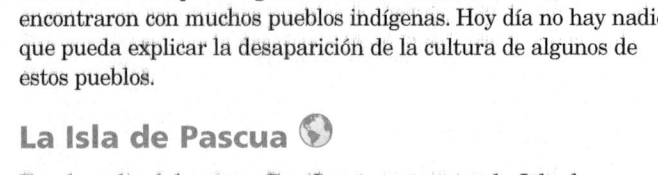

En el medio del océano Pacífico se encuentra la Isla de Pascua, de unos 167 kilómetros cuadrados. Allí se encuentran los *moai*, unas estatuas enormes de piedra que representan enormes cabezas con orejas largas y torsos pequeños. Se encuentran en toda la isla y miran hacia el cielo como esperando a algo o alguien. Pero la pregunta es ¿cómo las construyeron y las movieron los habitantes indígenas a la isla? Se sabe que no conocían ni el metal ni la rueda. Cuando se les pregunta a los habitantes de hoy cómo llegaron las estatuas al lugar, ellos responden: —¡A pie!

Muchos esperan que aparezca la verdad acerca de estas estatuas. Hay quienes dicen que las estatuas representan a los primeros habitantes de la isla, que creen que eran polinesios. Otros dicen que representan a los dioses y muchos creen que eran extraterrestres. Quizás algún día descubramos el misterio de esta pequeña isla.

DIFFERENTIATED INSTRUCTION

Heritage Language Learners
Invite students with exemplary pronunciation to read short sections aloud as a model of fluency and pronunciation.

Advanced Learners
Ask students to research one of the mysteries they read about in the *Puente a la cultura*. Have them present brief oral reports to the class about their chosen mystery.

Los olmecas 🌐

Más de 1,500 años antes de los mayas y 25 siglos antes de los aztecas existieron los olmecas, la primera gran civilización de Mesoamérica. Entre sus ruinas se descubrieron unas cabezas de piedra gigantes que no sólo miden entre dos o tres metros de alto sino que pesan entre 11 y 24 toneladas. Pero en esa zona de México no existen piedras tan grandes. Se supone que[1] los olmecas tuvieron que mover esas piedras más de 129 kilómetros. ¿Cómo lo hicieron? Es un misterio.

Las Líneas de Nazca 🌐

Cabeza olmeca

En 1927, un arqueólogo que recorría[2] el sur del Perú observó unas largas líneas de muchas formas a los lados de la carretera. Observó las líneas desde una meseta, las dibujó en un papel y descubrió que un dibujo tenía la forma de un pájaro volando. Más tarde se encontraron en las pampas de Nazca, al sur del Perú, más de 30 dibujos que representan animales y figuras geométricas y humanas. Lo interesante de estos dibujos es que las formas solamente pueden verse desde el aire. ¿Para qué servían las líneas? ¿Cómo se hicieron?

1 supposedly **2** travelled

¿Comprendiste?

1. ¿Qué son los moai? ¿Qué representan?
2. ¿Qué se descubrió entre las ruinas de los olmecas? ¿Por qué es un misterio?
3. ¿Qué descubrió un arqueólogo que recorría el sur del Perú?
4. ¿Qué representan los dibujos que forman las Líneas de Nazca?
5. ¿Por qué es un misterio las Líneas de Nazca?

Investiga

Busca en la biblioteca o en la Internet información sobre algún otro misterio del pasado, como el hombre de Palenque o la Atlántida. Escribe un pequeño párrafo que describa el misterio y tu opinión sobre el tema.

Líneas de Nazca

Más práctica GO

realidades.com | print

▶ *Videodocumentario*   ✔
Guided WB p. 235   ✔ ✔
Comm. WB pp. 104–105   ✔ ✔
Hispanohablantes WB pp. 226–228   ✔
Cultural Reading Activity   ✔

trescientos veinticinco **325**
Capítulo 7

▼ **¿Comprendiste?** Standards: 1.2, 1.3
Resources: Answer Keys: Student Edition, p. 104
🌐 **Mapa global interactivo, Actividad 7**
Discover the ancient Olmec civililzation.
Focus: Reading comprehension
Suggestions: Have students work in pairs to write their responses.
Answers:
1. **Los moai son unas estatuas enormes de piedra. Representan enormes cabezas con orejas largas y torsos pequeños.**
2. **Entre las ruinas se descubrieron unas cabezas de piedra gigantes. Es un misterio porque en esa zona de México no existen piedras tan grandes.**
3. **El arqueólogo observó unas largas líneas de muchas formas a los lados de la carretera.**
4. **Representan animales y figuras geométricas y humanas.**
5. **Son un misterio porque las formas solamente pueden verse desde el aire.**

🌐 **Mapa global interactivo, Actividad 8**
Discover the mysteries of the Nazca Lines.

▼ **Investiga** Standards: 1.3, 5.1
Focus: Combining learned structures in a written response to a reading
Suggestions: Encourage students to use chapter vocabulary and structures, such as the present perfect subjunctive, *sino,* or adjective clauses, in their paragraphs.
Answers will vary.

Portfolio

Keep students' paragraphs from *Investiga* in their portfolios as a writing sample.

▶ Videodocumentario

Core Instruction

Standards: 1.2

Resources: Teacher's Resource Book: Video Script, p. 136; Video Program: Cap. 7

View *¿Cómo se explican los misterios del mundo?* with the class to learn more about ancient archaeological sites in Mexico and South America. Access the video online in **realidades.com** or use the DVD. See the *Video Teacher's Guide* for suggestions.

Additional Resources

Student Resource: Realidades para hispanohablantes, pp. 226–228; Guided Practice Activities, p. 235; Communication Wbk., pp 104–105

ENRICH YOUR TEACHING

Culture Note
One theory on the origin of the Nazca lines suggests that they indicate positions of the sun, moon, planets, and stars, and that they were used to determine the times of year for planting and harvesting. Another says that the animal figures represent the mountain gods' different animal forms.

21st Century Skills

Critical Thinking and Problem Solving Have students focus on the photographs that accompany the reading *Misterios del pasado*. Then ask students to use the Internet to locate additional images of the stone structures of the Olmec civilization, the *moai* from *Isla de Pascua,* or *las líneas de Nazca*. Have students share their images with the class and make new predictions about these ancient mysteries.

Estados Unidos
MÉXICO
Golfo de México
Océano Pacífico
Olmecas

Ecuador
Brasil
PERÚ
Océano Pacífico
Nazca
Bolivia

¿Qué me cuentas?

Core Instruction

Standards: 1.1, 1.2, 1.3, 2.2, 3.1

Resources: Teacher's Resource Book: Audio Script, p. 134; Audio Program DVD: Cap. 7, Track 15; Answer Keys: Student Edition, p. 105

Focus: Practicing listening and reading comprehension of new vocabulary and grammar; using information to write a cohesive and coherent reaction.

AP* Skills: Integration of listening, reading, and writing to comprehend and synthesize information from spoken and written sources.

Suggestions: For Step 1, use the audio or read the descriptions aloud. Allow students to hear it twice through: the first time to write their answers, the second time to check them.

For Step 2, have students identify significant details as they read and then summarize the main points of the article.

For Step 3, encourage students to use each of the suggested expressions, and to support their arguments with specific information from both the listening in Step 1 and the reading in Step 2.

Answers:
Step1
1. b 2. b 3. a 4. b 5. a 6. b
Steps 2–3
Answers will vary.

Block Schedule

Ask students to draw a 4- to 6-panel story about extraterrestrials on Earth. Encourage creativity! Then place students in groups of four and have them talk about each student's picture sequence. Have students alternate telling about the story with each student contributing one sentence at a time.

Additional Resources

Student Resource: Realidades para hispanohablantes, p. 229

326

Pre–AP*

| ▼ **Objectives**
► Listen to and read descriptions of an archeological investigation
► Write a comparison of two excavations

Integración

¿Qué me cuentas?: Ver para creer

¿Qué civilizaciones existían en las Américas antes de los aztecas, mayas e incas? Primero escucha a una persona que habla sobre una investigación. Anota las respuestas a las preguntas y guárdalas para usarlas en el paso 3.

1 🔊)) Escucha las siguientes descripciones. Después de cada descripción, vas a oír dos preguntas. Escoge la mejor respuesta para cada pregunta.

1. a. del descubrimiento de América
   b. de su trabajo arqueológico

2. a. conocer a un grupo de arqueólogos
   b. las ruinas de un palacio olmeca

3. a. diseños geométricos y símbolos
   b. dibujos de animales

4. a. Leyeron las notas de los olmecas.
   b. Midieron las piedras.

5. a. un hombre misterioso les contó acerca de una leyenda
   b. que nadie sabía que esa estructura existiera

6. a. porque la leyenda decía que ese lugar no existía
   b. porque existía una leyenda y la creencia de que allí vivían extraterrestres

2 Lee este artículo sobre un descubrimiento arqueológico en América del Sur.

América del Sur

CARAL, la ciudad más antigua de las AMÉRICAS

Los descubrimientos de un equipo de arqueólogos peruanos revelaron que las ruinas de Caral en Perú, por muchas décadas ignoradas, pertenecieron a[1] la civilización más antigua de las Américas. La evidencia indica que la ciudad prosperó por cinco siglos, aproximadamente desde el año 2627 a.C. Esto significa[2] que los habitantes de las comunidades alrededor del valle Supe fueron contemporáneos de las civilizaciones antiguas de la Mesopotamia y de Asia, algo que ningún científico pensaba antes.

En el sitio de excavación, los arqueólogos ya desenterraron[3] ocho pirámides públicas, unas plataformas de forma circular que parecen plazas, seis unidades residenciales y cuatro sectores de la ciudad. En total la ciudad cubría un área de 150 ácres y se cree que había sido el centro de control del valle y un importante punto comercial.

Ruinas de Caral, Perú.

[1]belonged to [2]means [3]unearthed

3 Escribe una comparación de las dos excavaciones. ¿Qué encontraron en cada lugar? Mira la foto de Caral y revisa tus notas de la descripción de las ruinas en el paso 1. ¿En qué se parecen o se diferencian? ¿Qué importancia tienen estos descubrimientos? Usa las siguientes expresiones para conectar tus ideas.

| al igual que | antes de | en contraste . . . | es similar a . . . |
| ya que | después de | me parece . . . | es diferente de . . . |

DIFFERENTIATED INSTRUCTION

Heritage Language Learners

Have students periodically watch Spanish-language television programs or videos so that they also, along with their classmates, can benefit from exposure to different accents and language use.

Students with Learning Difficulties

Read the directions to the first task with students. Emphasize that they will: 1) hear a description; 2) hear two questions; 3) choose *a* or *b* to answer each question. Also before listening, have students read each pair of possible answers to help them focus on their listening task. Remind them to listen for one of the two choices.

Presentación oral

Tu descubrimiento científico

▶ Demonstrate how to convince your class of a new scientific theory
▶ Maintain your focus for clarity

Tarea
Eres científico(a) y creaste una teoría para explicar un fenómeno extraño. Tienes que convencer (*convince*) a la clase de que tu explicación tiene sentido.

① Prepárate Completa un organizador gráfico. Escribe a la izquierda el nombre y una descripción del fenómeno inexplicable, y a la derecha tus explicaciones de lo que sucedió. Puedes inventar el fenómeno y las teorías para tratar de explicarlo.

Fenómeno inexplicable: _____

② Practica Vuelve a leer el organizador. Practica tu presentación. Puedes usar tus notas para practicar, pero no al hablar ante la clase. Recuerda:

- explicar claramente de qué fenómeno inexplicable estás hablando
- dar razones convincentes (*convincing*) que traten de explicarlo
- mirar directamente al público al hablar

Modelo
No hay nadie que haya descubierto qué les sucedió a los habitantes de la Atlántida. Yo creo que unos extraterrestres aparecieron en la Atlántida y se convirtieron en sus habitantes. Dudo que el clima les haya gustado, por eso se mudaron a un pueblo de Alaska.

③ Haz tu presentación Haz la presentación de forma convincente para que tus compañeros entiendan el fenómeno y cómo se resuelve. Puedes acompañar tu presentación con un dibujo o un organizador gráfico.

④ Evaluación Tu profesor(a) utilizará la siguiente rúbrica para evaluar tu presentación.

Estrategia

Maintaining your focus
It is important that when you are doing your speech you maintain your focus. Your focus is the message you want to communicate to your audience. Concentrate on the topic of your message and make sure that it is clearly understood by your audience. Avoid adding information not directly related to the topic that might interfere with the purpose of your speech.

Rubric	Score 1	Score 3	Score 5
How well you maintain your focus	Your theory is undeveloped. You miss important ideas.	You present a theory, but your ideas are disorganized.	Your theory is presented in a logical, organized way.
How convincing you are	Your supporting explanations are weak.	Your supporting explanations are somewhat convincing.	You use convincing explanations.
How effectively you deliver your speech	You read your speech and make no eye contact with your audience.	You make some eye contact and you use some intonation.	Your eye contact is good. Your intonation helps get the message across.

trescientos veintisiete 327
Capítulo 7

ENRICH YOUR TEACHING

21st Century Skills

Initiative and Self-Direction Have students review the rubrics on pages 327 and 329. Ask them to work with a partner and discuss why their teacher gives them rubrics; how are they supposed to be used? Have them work with one of the rubrics to start with the outcome, figure out what they have to do to get the best grade possible, and develop a plan to achieve that goal.

© Common Core: Speaking

Presentación oral

Core Instruction
Standards: 1.2, 1.3, 3.1
Resources: Voc. and Gram. Transparency 12
Focus: Preparing and delivering an oral presentation
Suggestions: Review the task and the four-step approach with students. Review the rubric with the class (see *Assessment* below) to explain how you will grade the performance task. Before students begin, direct their attention to the *Estrategia*. Point out that the key to maintaining their focus in a speech or in writing is to organize their ideas first. This is what they should do in Step 1. Show *Vocabulary and Grammar Transparency 12* and have students create a similar chart on their own paper, leaving out the rectangle farthest to the right. Model how to fill in a sample mysterious phenomenon and at least one explanation it. Encourage students to use their imaginations to create their own explanations which, although they may be invented, should be plausible.

Pre-AP* Support

- **Learning Objective:** Presentational Speaking
- *Pre-AP* Resource Book:* Comprehensive guide to Pre-AP* speaking skill development, pp. 39–50

Portfolio
Make video or audio recordings of student presentations in class, or assign the RealTalk activity so they can record their presentations online. Include the recording in their portfolios.

Additional Resources
Student Resource: Realidades para hispanohablantes, p. 230

✓ASSESSMENT

Presentación oral
- Assessment Program: Rubrics, p. T32
  Review the rubric with students. Go over the descriptions of the different levels of performance. After assessing students, help individuals understand how their performance could be improved. (See Teacher's Resource Book for suggestions on using rubrics in assessment.)

Language Arts Connection: Persuasive Writing

Remind students that the subjunctive usually occurs in complex sentences. Point out that the sentences in which they learned to use **sino** in this chapter are compound sentences. Ask them to use their knowledge from their Language Arts courses to talk about the differences between compound and complex sentences.

 Common Core: Writing

Presentación escrita

Core Instruction

Standards: 1.2, 1.3, 3.1
Resources: Voc. and Gram. Transparency 4
Focus: Combining learned vocabulary and structures in a written presentation

Suggestions: Begin by explaining the criteria you will use to evaluate students' compositions. (See Step 5, *Evaluación,* in the Student Edition, and *Assessment* on the following page.)

Direct students' attention to the *Estrategia*. Point out that in *Capítulo 7*, they have learned how to use the present perfect subjunctive and **sino,** as well as the subjunctive in adjective clauses. All three of these are valuable tools they can use to combine sentences more effectively. Then show *Vocabulary and Grammar Transparency* 4. Fill in the left side of the chart on the transparency and model for students how to add one or two pieces of information to the right side when they create their own charts.

Pre-AP* Support

- **Learning Objective:** Presentational Writing
- **Pre-AP* Resource Book:** Comprehensive guide to Pre-AP* writing skill development, pp. 27–38

▼ **Objectives**
▶ **Write a legend about something or someone from the past**
▶ **Combine sentences and use details to add interest to the story**

Presentación escrita

Tu leyenda

Estrategia

Combining sentences
The paragraphs in your story may lose their impact if you use short, choppy sentences. To improve the flow of your paragraphs, combine sentences with conjunctions like *y, o,* or *pero.* For example, *"Todos los habitantes del pueblo conocen la leyenda pero ninguno habla de ella"* is more interesting than *"Todos los habitantes del pueblo conocen la leyenda. Ninguno habla de ella."* Likewise, *"El hombre no tenía ni familia ni amigos"* sounds better than *"El hombre no tenía familia. El hombre no tenía amigos."*

Usa tu imaginación y escribe una leyenda acerca de algún personaje o lugar imaginario. Puedes escribir acerca de una leyenda ya conocida pero añadiéndole detalles propios.

1 Antes de escribir

Responde a las preguntas como ayuda para encontrar ideas para tu leyenda.

- ¿En dónde ocurre la historia?
- ¿Quién o quiénes son los protagonistas de tu historia?
- ¿Cuál es el misterio o fenómeno inexplicable principal? ¿Qué sucede?
- ¿El misterio o fenómeno inexplicable se resuelve?
- ¿Qué título tiene la leyenda?

Recuerda que una leyenda tiene la estructura de un cuento, con una introducción, un desarrollo y un final. Completa la tabla para ordenar tus ideas.

Título de la leyenda	La leyenda del extraterrestre del valle
Introducción	Un hombre estaba dando un paseo por el valle cuando de repente apareció un extraterreste . . .
Desarrollo	Se hicieron amigos y el hombre decidió acompañar al extraterrestre a su planeta . . .
Final	Nunca más se supo del hombre . . .

2 Borrador

Escribe tu borrador utilizando la información de la tabla. Debes añadir todos los detalles que sean posibles y combinar las oraciones para que los párrafos sean más interesantes. La leyenda debe ser misteriosa e interesante. Usa el vocabulario y la gramática que aprendiste en este capítulo.

Modelo

Según cuenta la leyenda, un hombre estaba dando un paseo por el valle del pueblo cuando de repente apareció una figura muy extraña. Tenía una cabeza redonda sin pelo y sus ojos eran muy grandes y ovalados. "Dudo que existan extraterrestres", pensó el hombre en ese momento, "pero ahora no estoy tan seguro". . .

Topic sentence: Sets the story.

Description of a character: What did the stranger look like?

328 trescientos veintiocho
¡Adelante!

DIFFERENTIATED INSTRUCTION

Heritage Language Learners

Before students write final drafts of their legends, have them proofread for correct use of accent marks. Review frequently misspelled words that have homonyms, such as **como/cómo, que/qué, se/sé.**

Advanced Learners

Invite students to have a discussion in Spanish about other ways to create more varied and interesting sentences. Encourage them to talk about other types of subordinate clauses by helping them with vocabulary such as **cláusula adverbial** and **cláusula sustantiva.**

El desconocido se le acercó y le dijo: "Es verdad, soy un extraterrestre, pero no tenga miedo. Yo sólo busco un hombre que quiera ser mi amigo". El hombre le respondió que no tenía amigos pero que podía hacer una excepción. Después de hablar por muchas horas, el extraterrestre le ofreció llevarlo a conocer su planeta. El hombre aceptó la invitación. Entonces . . .

Nunca más se supo del hombre . . .

> **Development:** What happened after the two characters met.

> **Conclusion:** Explains the mystery or leaves it to the reader's imagination.

3 Redacción/Revisión

Después de escribir el primer borrador de la leyenda, trabaja con otro(a) estudiante para intercambiar los trabajos y leerlos. Decidan qué aspectos son más efectivos. Fíjense en cómo el(la) escritor(a) del modelo incluyó detalles en su composición. Cada uno puede sugerir qué cambios hacer para mejorar las leyendas.

Haz lo siguiente: Verifica si usaste correctamente las formas del indicativo y del subjuntivo.

> El desconocido se le acercó y le dijo : "Es
> verdad, ~~sea~~ *soy* un extraterrestre, pero no ~~tienes~~ *tenga*
> miedo. Yo sólo busco un hombre que ~~quiere~~ *quiera*
> ser mi amigo".

4 Publicación

Antes de hacer la versión final, lee de nuevo tu borrador y repasa lo siguiente:

- ¿La leyenda tiene un orden lógico?
- ¿Es interesante la introducción?
- ¿Incluí suficientes detalles que den un ambiente *(feeling)* a la historia?
- ¿Es misterioso el final de la leyenda?

Después de revisar el borrador, escribe tu composición en limpio.

5 Evaluación

Se utilizará la siguiente rúbrica para evaluar tu presentación.

Rubric	Score 1	Score 3	Score 5
Completion of task	Your writing cannot be defined as a legend.	You present an idea for a legend, but you miss important elements.	Your writing is an interesting legend, containing all necessary elements.
Use of varied sentence structure	Your sentences are all the same length.	You combine some sentences but miss some opportunities.	Your sentences are varied, interesting, and effective.
Grammar, spelling, mechanics	Your grammar, spelling, and/or mechanics errors make for difficult reading.	You make some grammar, spelling, and/or mechanics errors.	You make very few grammar, spelling, and/or mechanics errors.

ENRICH YOUR TEACHING

21st Century Skills

Creativity and Innovation Students will have to use their written language for the purpose of creating a new legend. Have students review children's books or other legends they know from their own culture and choose one to adapt into Spanish. Students should retell the story and adapt its main features (characters, location, action) to fit into an ancient Spanish-speaking civilization.

Suggestions (Cont'd)

Once students have a rough draft ready, read through the model on this page together. Help them see how information from the chart on the previous page was incorporated into this draft and to note the additional information that was added. Point out the use of the subjunctive in an adjective clause in the first paragraph: *Yo sólo busco un hombre* **que quiera ser mi amigo.** Encourage them to work toward similar organization, level of detail, and language use as they create their own drafts.

For Step 3, encourage students to experiment with various ways of combining sentences. Have them follow the suggestions shown.

Evaluation

Steps 4 and 5 overlap. Students will need evaluation by you, their peers, or self-evaluation to fine-tune and polish their drafts.

Portfolio

Keep students' final drafts in their portfolios as a writing sample.

Teacher-to-Teacher

e-amigos: Have students send their *e-amigos* the legend they wrote for the *Presentación escrita*. Ask them to include an introduction in which they ask their *e-amigos* to critique the story. Encourage students to express their feelings in the form of constructive criticism. Have students print out their e-mails or send them to you for review.

Additional Resources

Student Resource: Realidades para hispanohablantes, p. 231

☑ ASSESSMENT

Presentación escrita
- Assessment Program: Rubrics, p. T33
  Review the rubric with students. Go over the descriptions of the different levels of performance. After assessing students, help individuals understand how their performance could be improved. (See Teacher's Resource Book for suggestions on using rubrics in assessment.)

329

7 Reading

Common Core: Reading

Lectura

Core Instruction

Standards: 1.2, 2.2, 3.1, 3.2, 5.2

Resources: Voc. and Gram. Transparency 4

Focus: Reading an extended passage

Suggestions:

Pre-reading: Before reading, direct students' attention to the *Al leer* section. Have them begin a T-chart similar to the one on p. 333 and make sure they understand how they will use it. Also refer them to the *Estrategia*. Point out that their T-charts will help them keep track of the characters and their actions.

Reading: When reading together with students, pause frequently to address comprehension issues they may have and to allow them to fill in their charts for *Interacción con la lectura*. Here is an example: Point out that in Spanish, the noun to which a possessive adjective refers is not always immediately obvious. We have to use background knowledge and context clues in order to know. In the first paragraph, we know that **su escudero** means "his, her, or their squire." Since we learned earlier who Sancho Panza is, we can deduce that **su** refers to Don Quijote and not the guards or their prisoners.

Country Connection

Core Instruction

Resources: Map Transparency 20

Suggestions: What was known as La Mancha in Cervantes' day is currently the **comunidad autónoma** called Castilla-La Mancha. Display *Map Transparency* 20 and point out the region on the map. It is a large area in the central part of the country, east and southeast of Madrid. Before the **comunidades autónomas** were created, Spain was divided into smaller provinces named after important cities. Castilla-La Mancha is comprised of five of these older provinces called Guadalajara, Cuenca, Albacete, Ciudad Real, and Toledo.

330

| ¡Adelante! | ▼ Objectives |

▼ Objectives
▶ Read and understand a piece of fiction
▶ Understand the perspective of a character who lives his own fantasy
▶ Read about *Don Quijote*'s author, Miguel de Cervantes Saavedra

Lectura
Fragmento de *Don Quijote de la Mancha*
Capítulo XXII

Estrategia

Characters and actions
Read the passage once through to understand the events of the story. When you have read through once, think about the characters in the story. What are they like? Then, re-read the story and write down the events.

Al leer

El personaje más famoso de la literatura española es Don Quijote de la Mancha, el protagonista de la novela del mismo nombre que escribió Miguel de Cervantes. La historia cuenta que el Quijote leyó tantos libros sobre caballeros andantes (*knights*), que un día perdió el juicio (*lost his mind*) y decidió ser uno de ellos. En la época en que él vive (el siglo XVII) ya no hay caballeros andantes, pero en su imaginación, el Quijote ve a las sirvientas (*maids*) como princesas, las posadas (*inns*) como castillos y los molinos (*windmills*) como gigantes contra los que tiene que pelear. El conflicto entre la fantasía del Quijote y la realidad produce situaciones cómicas que hacen reír.

El fragmento que vas a leer es una adaptación del Capítulo XXII, en el que Don Quijote y su escudero (*squire*) y amigo Sancho Panza se encuentran con unos prisioneros.

Copia la tabla de la página 333. Complétala mientras lees. Ésta te ayudará a contestar las preguntas que aparecen al final.

D on Quijote vio que por el camino venían doce hombres atados[1] con una gran cadena[2] de hierro por el cuello, y todos con esposas[3] en las manos. Venían con ellos dos hombres a caballo y dos a pie. Su escudero Sancho Panza dijo:

—Ésta es una cadena de prisioneros, gente forzada[4] por el rey, que va a las galeras[5].

—¿Cómo gente forzada? —preguntó Don Quijote—. ¿Es posible que el rey haga fuerza a alguien?

—No digo eso —respondió Sancho—, son personas que, por sus crímenes, van condenadas a servir al rey en las galeras por fuerza.

1 tied **2** chain **3** handcuffs **4** forced **5** galleys

330 trescientos treinta
¡Adelante!

DIFFERENTIATED INSTRUCTION

Multiple Intelligences

Bodily/Kinesthetic: Invite students to interpret the excerpt from *Don Quijote* by performing it as a skit for the class. They may use the excerpt as a script, adding inflection and gestures, or they may keep the general idea but improvise the lines. Have students work together to plan and perform their skit.

Students with Learning Difficulties

Have students read through the chart and comprehension questions on p. 333 before they begin to read the excerpt. They can use the questions to set a purpose for reading and to maintain a focus.

—Entonces —contestó Don Quijote— esta gente, aunque los llevan, van de por fuerza, y no porque ellos quieren.

—Así es —dijo Sancho.

—Pues —dijo su amo—, aquí puedo hacer mi tarea: deshacer fuerzas y ayudar a los miserables.

Don Quijote se acercó y le preguntó al primero que por qué crímenes iba a las galeras. Él le respondió que por enamorado.

—¿Por eso no más? —replicó Don Quijote—. Pues, si por enamorados echan a galeras, yo estaría en ellas desde hace tiempo.

—No son los amores como los que usted piensa —dijo el prisionero—; que los míos fueron que quise tanto a una cesta llena de ropa blanca, que la abracé conmigo tan fuertemente que, a no quitármela la justicia por fuerza, aún la tendría.

—Éste, señor, va por músico y cantor—, le dijeron.

—Pues, ¿cómo —repitió Don Quijote—, por músicos y cantores van también a galeras?

Pero uno de los guardas le explicó:

—Señor caballero, cantar es confesar en el tormento[6].

Luego al tercero que le preguntó Don Quijote, éste le dijo:

—Yo voy por cinco años porque me faltaron diez monedas de oro.

—Yo daré veinte de muy buena gana[7] —dijo Don Quijote— por libraros[8] de las galeras.

—Eso me parece —respondió el prisionero— como quien tiene dineros en mitad del mar y se está muriendo de hambre, sin tener adónde comprar lo que necesita. Si hubiera tenido el dinero necesario para cambiar la opinión del juez, hoy estaría paseando por la plaza de Toledo y no camino a las galeras.

Al final venía un hombre con más cadenas que los demás.

—¿Cuál es su crimen? —preguntó Don Quijote.

—Va por diez años por ladrón —replicó el guarda—. Este hombre tiene solo más crímenes que todos los otros juntos. Es el famoso Ginés de Pasamonte.

—Para servir a Dios y al rey, otra vez he estado cuatro años, —respondió Ginés—; y no me pesa mucho ir a ellas, porque allí tendré lugar de acabar de escribir mi libro.

Dijo entonces Don Quijote:

—De todo lo que me habéis dicho, he sacado en limpio que, aunque os han castigado[9] por vuestros crímenes, las penas que vais a padecer[10] no os dan mucho gusto, y que vais a ellas muy de mala gana y muy contra vuestra voluntad. Me parece duro caso hacer esclavos[11] a los que Dios y la naturaleza hizo libres. Estos pobres no han cometido nada contra vosotros, guardias. Pido que los dejéis libres pero si no lo hacen, por fuerza haré que lo hagáis.

---

6 torture 7 willingly 8 *libraros* means *librarlos*; the ending *-os* is the pronoun corresponding to *vosotros* 9 punished 10 to suffer 11 slaves

trescientos treinta y uno **331**
Capítulo 7

Suggestions (Cont'd)

Reading: Here are some possible comprehension issues on this page for which you can provide some guidance:

- Tell students that *su amo* in line five refers to Don Quijote. Explain that *amo* means "master" here.
- Ask students to explain in their own words the real reason why the second prisoner is on his way to the galleys. If necessary, point out how both Spanish and English use the verb *cantar* (to sing) to mean "confess."
- Ask students what the third prisoner means by his analogy in which he refers to the sea. Guide students to understand that Don Quijote's offer of money comes too late for the man, since he's already been convicted of a crime—probably stealing.

Teacher-to-Teacher

Point out that reading a novel in Spanish may not be as difficult as students think. (Although most of those interested in doing so will probably want to start with a shorter and less complex one than *Don Quijote de la Mancha*.) Explain that in this short excerpt from Cervantes, there are indeed unfamiliar words and structures that may make the idea of reading a whole book seem daunting. Remind them that after a chapter or two in a book, however, such problems tend to level off, since the vocabulary used to tell a story doesn't usually keep changing. The hard work involved in reading a novel tends to be limited to the beginning.

Pre-AP* Support

- **Learning Objective:** Presentational Speaking (Cultural Comparison)
- **Background:** This task prepares students for the Spoken Presentational Communication tasks that focus on cultural comparisons.
- **Activity:** Have students prepare a two-minute (maximum) presentation on the following topic: Different views of fantasy vs. reality are reflected in the literature of different times and cultures. Students may use the fragment they read from *Don Quijote de la Mancha* as a basis for the comparison. They should then comment on another work of literature from their own culture that also deals with fantasy vs. reality, explaining the similarities and differences between the two.
- **Pre-AP* Resource Book:** Comprehensive guide to Pre-AP* speaking skill development, pp. 39–50

ENRICH YOUR TEACHING

Culture Note

Don Quijote de la Mancha is the most well-known work of literature in the Spanish language. It has been translated into more than 60 languages. Cervantes' novel is a comic satire, intended to poke fun at the popular chivalric romances of the time. The novel is entertaining, but it also carries a message. The author criticizes the greed, pride, and violence of society at the time. Don Quijote's insanity also demonstrates a form of wisdom. He sees humble people as noble, while the rich and members of the clergy are targets of his wrath.

Suggestions (Cont'd)

Reading: Here are some possible comprehension issues on this page for which you can provide some guidance:

- Refer students to the *¿Recuerdas?* Remind them that verb forms that look unfamiliar to them as they read might be **vosotros** forms.

- If students have difficulty understanding the paragraph that begins **—De gente bien educada...,** explain that Don Quijote sometimes uses archaic syntax when he speaks. Restate the first sentence using modern syntax: *La gente bien educada está siempre agradecida por los beneficios que recibe.*

- Ask students to work together to tell in their own words the sequence of events beginning the moment Don Quijote decides to free the prisoners.

Post-reading: Ask students to talk about the humor in the Cervantes excerpt. Guide them to talk about the situational irony of the character of Don Quijote, totally dedicated to his mission, a mission that has no place in the world in which he lives and which turns him into a clown, no matter how seriously he takes himself. Ask students to draw analogies to such a situation in the present day. For example, Don Quijote might be compared to a man who decides to dress like a cowboy hero and sets out to roam the streets of a modern city on a quest to help the downtrodden.

BELLRINGER REVIEW

Have the class brainstorm famous pieces of world literature that have been made into movies. Discuss briefly whether they most frequently think the book or the film is better. Mention the movie *The Man of La Mancha* made from the musical of the same name.

Block Schedule

After the class has read the excerpt from *Don Quijote,* create "story experts." Divide the story in four sections and give students numbers 1, 2, 3, or 4. This "expert" is to create five questions about his or her section of the story. Create groups of four students, each with a different "expert." Have them ask their questions to other members of the group.

> **¿Recuerdas?**
>
> En el español antiguo, se utilizaban los pronombres personales *vosotros* y *vosotras*, y las formas verbales correspondientes. En la actualidad, estas formas casi no se usan en los países de habla hispana con excepción de España.

Pero los guardias no hicieron caso y le dijeron:

— No ande buscando tres pies al gato[12].

—¡Vos sois el gato, y el ratón, y el bellaco! —respondió Don Quijote furioso y atacó[13] a los guardias. Sancho ayudó a dar la libertad a los prisioneros. Muy sorprendidos y asustados, los guardias se escaparon.

Don Quijote llamó entonces a los prisioneros y así les dijo:

—De gente bien educada es agradecer[14] los beneficios que reciben. Les pido que vayan a la ciudad del Toboso, y allí os presentéis ante la señora Dulcinea del Toboso y le digáis que su caballero, el de la Triste Figura, ha tenido esta famosa aventura.

Respondió por todos Ginés de Pasamonte, y dijo:

—Lo que vuestra merced[15] nos manda, señor y libertador nuestro, es imposible de toda imposibilidad cumplirlo. Lo que podemos hacer es rezar[16] por usted.

—¡No! —dijo Don Quijote furioso.

Pasamonte, que ya se había dado cuenta que Don Quijote no era muy cuerdo[17], empezó con los demás prisioneros a arrojarle piedras a Don Quijote, le quitaron la ropa a Sancho y huyeron[18]. Solos quedaron Sancho y Don Quijote; Don Quijote, muy triste de verse tan malparado[19] por los mismos a quien tanto bien había hecho.

---

12 looking for a problem where there is none **13** attacked **14** to thank **15** archaic usage for *Usted* **16** to pray **17** sane **18** fled **19** left in such a sorry state

332 trescientos treinta y dos
¡Adelante!

DIFFERENTIATED INSTRUCTION

Students with Learning Difficulties

After students read the *¿Recuerdas?*, write on the board verbs from the text in the **vosotros** form. Demonstrate pronunciation of these words by comparing them to words that are familiar to students. For example, the vowels in the last syllables of **presentéis** and **vais** sound much like those in **seis** and **país.**

Advanced Learners

Invite students to read another excerpt from *Don Quijote de la Mancha,* such as his famous battle with the windmill giant, and tell about it in their own words.

Interacción con la lectura

❶ Completa una tabla como la siguiente a medida que lees.

Preguntas	Respuestas
1. ¿Cuál es la situación?	
2. ¿Qué piensa Don Quijote que ocurre?	
3. ¿Qué sucede en realidad?	
4. ¿Qué hace Don Quijote?	
5. ¿Qué resultados tiene su acción?	

❷ Trabaja con otro(a) compañero(a) para comparar la información de las tablas de cada uno(a). Añadan cualquier otro detalle interesante que recuerden.

Más práctica GO

realidades.com | print

Guided WB pp. 236–237	✔	✔
Comm. WB p. 202	✔	✔
Cultural Reading Activity	✔	

¿Comprendiste?

1. ¿Qué cree Don Quijote que es su misión en la vida?

2. Don Quijote escucha las historias de los prisioneros. ¿Cómo reacciona Don Quijote después de escucharlas? ¿Considera que el castigo *(punishment)* de los prisioneros es justo?

3. ¿Por qué quiere Don Quijote que los prisioneros ya libres vayan a ver a la señora Dulcinea? ¿Qué nos dice de su personalidad?

4. Don Quijote ve las cosas de manera diferente que los demás personajes. ¿Crees que él piensa que dice la verdad? ¿Crees que él ve las cosas como son? ¿Crees que Sancho ve las cosas como son?

5. Piensa en algún ejemplo de la vida real en el que dos personas vean una misma cosa de diferente forma. ¿Por qué crees que puede ser eso? Di qué pueden hacer para ponerse de acuerdo.

6. En tu opinión, ¿qué quiere expresar el autor al escribir acerca de Don Quijote?

▼ Fondo Cultural | España

Miguel de Cervantes Saavedra (1547–1616) nació en España, y antes de ser escritor participó en varias guerras. Como soldado *(soldier)*, perdió el uso de la mano izquierda y poco después fue llevado a Argel como esclavo, donde estuvo cinco años. Buscando su libertad *(freedom)* trató de escapar cuatro veces. Un grupo de religiosos lo rescató y pudo regresar por fin a España. Trabajó para el gobierno *(government)* español, pero fue acusado de manejar mal el dinero a su cargo y fue encarcelado durante varios meses. Ya en libertad empezó a escribir novelas y comedias, entre ellas su más famosa novela, *Don Quijote de la Mancha*. Cervantes murió el mismo año que William Shakespeare.

• Da un ejemplo de un conflicto entre la fantasía y la realidad que hayas leído en algún libro. Explica cómo presenta el autor este conflicto y qué crees que quiere decir.

Miguel de Cervantes Saavedra

trescientos treinta y tres 333
Capítulo 7

Interacción con la lectura
Standards: 1.1, 1.2

Suggestions: After students finish and discuss their charts, encourage them to go back and read the excerpt again, now that they have a better understanding of Don Quijote's character and of Cervantes's use of language.

Answers will vary.

¿Comprendiste? Standards: 1.3

Resources: Answer Keys: Student Edition, p. 105

Suggestions: Have students write the answers to the questions on their own first, then use them as a basis for class discussion.

Answers:
1. Don Quijote piensa que su misión es «deshacer fuerzas» y ayudar a los miserables.
2. Don Quijote reacciona con sorpresa y enojo. Piensa que los castigos son injustos.
3. Don Quijote quiere que los prisioneros vayan a decirle a Dulcinea el bien que ha hecho. Answers will vary.
4–6. Answers will vary.

Fondo cultural

Standards: 1.1, 1.2, 2.2, 3.1

Suggestions: After students have read the information silently, ask comprehension questions. For example: *¿Cuál fue la situación de Cervantes en Argel? (Fue llevado allí como esclavo.) ¿Por qué fue encarcelado Cervantes en España durante varios meses? (Lo acusaron de haber manejado mal el dinero a su cargo.) ¿En qué año murió William Shakespeare? (1616)*

Answers will vary.

Additional Resources

Student Resource: Lecturas 3: "Dora," pp. 19–21, "Como el condor se quedó sin plumas en la cabeza," pp. 30–31; Guided Practice: Lectura, pp. 236–237

ENRICH YOUR TEACHING

Culture Note
Miguel de Cervantes Saavedra was shot in his left hand at the battle of Lepanto. He lost the use of this hand and was subsequently nicknamed *el manco* (the maimed) *de Lepanto.* He was proud of both his participation in the battle and his nickname. This nickname is still commonly associated with the author today.

21st Century Skills

Initiative and Self-Direction Remind students of the various digital tools available in **realidades.com** to access reading support. Computer corrected activities employ different strategies to help students build their vocabulary and progress at their own pace through the reading.

Review Activities

Descubrimientos/Mitos y leyendas/Para hablar de los fenómenos inexplicables: Have students number the items in these three categories. Ask them to write these numbers on slips of paper and put them into a hat or other container. Have students take turns drawing four numbers each, writing their numbers down, and then returning the slips to the hat or other container for the next person. Challenge students to write a sentence which uses the four words whose numbers they have drawn. Have them pass the hat more than once. Invite them to share their sentences.

Para describir objetos/Para indicar duda: Have students sketch the ruins of an imaginary ancient civilization and use as many words in this category as they can to label their sketch. Ask them to assume the role of archaeologists and show their sketch to their classmates, describing the ruins and telling what functions the various structures and monuments supposedly served.

El universo: Ask students to create a "size-line" on which they arrange the items in this category in a line from largest to smallest. They should show each item on the "size-line" using a simple sketch or symbol accompanied by a label.

Verbos: Ask students to invent a false definition for each of the verbs. Have them work in pairs and take turns defining the verbs. Students decide each time whether their definition will be the correct one or their invented false one. If the definition is correct, the partner says *Tienes razón.* If it is false, the partner says, for example: *No, trazar no significa "llenar," sino "dibujar."*

Otras palabras/Expresiones: Students can use these words and expressions as they go over the review activities for the other categories.

Additional Resources

Student Resources: Realidades para hispanohablantes, pp. 232–233

Teacher Resources:
- Teacher's Resource Book: Situation Cards, p. 144, Clip Art, pp. 145–152
- Assessment Program: Chapter Checklist and Self-Assessment Worksheet, pp. T49–T50

Repaso del capítulo
Vocabulario y gramática

descubrimientos

el / la arqueólogo(a)	archaeologist
la civilización	civilization
la escritura	writing
la pirámide	pyramid
las ruinas	ruins
sagrado, -a	sacred
el símbolo	symbol

mitos y leyendas

la creencia	belief
el / la dios(a)	god, goddess
la leyenda	legend
el mito	myth
la nave espacial	spaceship
el origen	origin

para hablar de los fenómenos inexplicables

la estructura	structure
la evidencia	proof, evidence
extraño, -a	strange
el fenómeno	phenomenon
la función	function
la imagen	image
inexplicable	inexplicable
el misterio	mystery
misterioso, -a	mysterious
la teoría	theory

para describir objetos

el alto	height
el ancho	width
el centímetro	centimeter
el círculo	circle
el diámetro	diameter
el diseño	design
la distancia	distance
geométrico, -a	geometric(al)
el largo	length
el óvalo	oval
el rectángulo	rectangle
redondo, -a	round
la tonelada	ton
el triángulo	triangle

otras palabras

el conejo	rabbit
cualquier, -a	any
el intento	attempt

para indicar duda

improbable	unlikely
probable	likely

el universo

el / la astrónomo(a)	astronomer
el eclipse	eclipse
el / la habitante	inhabitant
la Luna	moon
el observatorio	observatory
el planeta	planet
el pueblo	people
la sombra	shadow
la Tierra	Earth
el universo	universe

expresiones

al igual que	as, like
o sea que	in other words
sino	but
ya que	because, due to

verbos

aparecer (zc)	to appear
arrojar(se)	to throw (oneself)
brillar	to shine
calcular	to calculate, to compute
convertirse (en)	to turn (into), to become
contribuir (u→y)	to contribute
cubrir	to cover
dudar	to doubt
excavar	to excavate
existir	to exist
medir (e→i)	to measure
pesar	to weigh
ponerse (el sol)	to set (sun)
resolver (o→ue)	to solve
trazar	to trace, to draw

334 trescientos treinta y cuatro
Repaso del capítulo

DIFFERENTIATED INSTRUCTION

Multiple Intelligences

Verbal/Linguistic: Remind students that many words in English come from Latin, with stops in Spanish and French along the way. Have students help their classmates by pointing out meaningful similarities between parts of Spanish and English words, such as "spaceship" and *(nave) espacial,* or "brilliant" and ***brillar.***

Advanced Learners

Have students use their creativity to make an audio or video recording about a group of archaeologists at the moment they discover an important find. Challenge them to use as much as they can of the chapter vocabulary in their script.

El presente y el presente perfecto del subjuntivo con expresiones de duda

Use the present subjunctive after expressions of doubt, uncertainty, or disbelief.

Dudo que haya una nave espacial en el pueblo.

To express doubt, uncertainty, or disbelief about actions in the past, Spanish uses the present perfect subjunctive mode.

Es probable que los arqueólogos hayan encontrado nuevas evidencias.

Expressions starting with *creo, no dudo, estoy seguro(a)* are usually followed by the indicative since they do not express doubt, disbelief or uncertainty.

Estoy seguro de que aquellas piedras pertenecen a los mayas.

Pero y sino

The word *pero* is usually the equivalent of the English conjunction *but*. The word *sino* also means *but. Sino* is used when the idea being conveyed is *not this, but rather* that.

No voy a comer carne sino vegetales.

You can also use *sino* with *no sólo . . . sino también . . .*

Vino no sólo María sino también Ana.

You use *sino que* when there is a conjugated verb in the second part of the sentence.

No salí a pasear sino que me quedé en casa.

El subjuntivo en cláusulas adjetivas

You can use an entire clause to describe a noun. This is an adjective clause. When you have a specific person or thing in mind, you use the indicative.

Busco a la arqueóloga que trabaja con ruinas aztecas.

If you don't have a specific person or thing in mind, or if you are not sure the person exists, you use the subjunctive. To refer to something or someone in the past, you use the present perfect subjunctive.

Necesito un artículo que hable sobre las pirámides.
Busco a un joven que haya estudiado español.

You also use the subjunctive in an adjective clause when it describes a negative word such as *nadie, nada,* or *ninguno(a)*.

No hay nadie que tenga tiempo libre.

You use the subjunctive in an adjective clause when it doesn't describe a specific person or thing, using words such as *cualquier* or *cualquiera*.

Escoge cualquier cosa que quieras.

trescientos treinta y cinco **335**
Capítulo 7

El presente y el presente perfecto del subjuntivo con expresiones de duda: Ask students to think about the mysteries described in *Capítulo* 7 as well as other mysteries and unanswered questions about our world or the universe in general. Have each student write on a slip of paper a statement of opinion about one mystery. Ask them to write their statement as though it were a fact, avoiding expressions of doubt. For example: *Los extraterrestres tenían una presencia en la civilización maya.* Mix the slips of paper. Have students take turns drawing one and giving their own opinion about the mystery, using an expression of certainty or uncertainty: *Es improbable que los extraterrestres hayan tenido una presencia en la civilización maya.*

Pero y sino: Ask students to comment on unexplained phenomena using *sino, sino que,* or *sino también.* For example: *Los extraterrestres no sólo tenían una influencia en la civilización maya sino también en otras civilizaciones.*

El subjuntivo en cláusulas adjetivas: Ask students to pretend they are employment counselors. Have them write two sentences. In the first, they tell what type of position needs to be filled: *Se busca secretaria.* In the second, they tell about a desirable quality or skill needed for the job: *La secretaria tiene que ser organizada.* Have them trade pairs of sentences with a partner, who combines them into a single sentence with an adjective clause: *Se busca una secretaria que sea organizada.*

Portfolio

Invite students to review the activities and projects they completed in this chapter. Have them select one or two items that they feel best demonstrate their achievements in Spanish. Include these products in students' portfolios. Have them include this with the Chapter Checklist and Self-Assessment Worksheet.

ENRICH YOUR TEACHING

Teacher-to-Teacher

Make clear to students the value of using study groups to prepare for exams and other assessment activities. Encourage them to conduct all the activities of the group in Spanish. Besides sharing their knowledge about the vocabulary or grammatical structures under review, students in a study group must also use vital, everyday language necessary for the performance of group activities: taking turns, giving and following commands, offering suggestions and opinions, and so on.

Additional Resources

Teacher Resources:

¡Pura vida! is a storyline video that is independent of chapter content and an ideal support for expanding listening skills. The 14 episodes are available within **realidades.com** or on a separate DVD. Student activities and Teacher support are also assignable within **realidades.com**.

7 Review

Performance Tasks

Standards: 1.1, 1.2, 1.3, 2.1, 2.2, 3.1

Student Resource: Realidades para
hispanohablantes, pp. 234–235

Teacher Resources: Teacher's Resource Book:
Audio Script, pp. 134–135; Audio Program DVD:
Cap. 7, Track 17; Answer Keys: Student Edition,
p. 105

1. Vocabulario

Suggestions: Encourage students to
review the vocabulary from the A *primera
vista* sections on pp. 298–301 and
312–315 before they complete the activity.

Answers:

1. b	5. a
2. d	6. d
3. a	7. d
4. c	8. b

2. Gramática

Suggestions: Remind students of the
main points of the grammar presentations
in *Capítulo 7*:

- the present and present perfect
  subjunctive used with expressions of
  doubt
- the use of **pero** and **sino**
- the subjunctive in adjective clauses

Answers:

1. d	5. d
2. b	6. d
3. c	7. a
4. b	8. c

3. Escuchar

Suggestions: Use the audio or read from
the script.

🔊 **Answers:**

(a) Estudió la civilización de los olmecas.
(b) Excavó una roca con símbolos muy antiguos.
(c) No son símbolos sino letras en un idioma muy
extraño.
(d) El locutor cree que los mitos muchas veces son
realidad.

Preparación para el examen

1 **Vocabulario** Escribe la letra de la palabra o expresión que mejor complete
cada frase. Escribe tus respuestas en una hoja aparte.

1. Un huevo tiene forma de _____ .
   a. triángulo   c. pirámide
   b. óvalo   d. rectángulo

2. El arqueólogo midió _____ de la roca.
   a. el mito y el origen   c. el fenómeno y
   b. el planeta y   el misterio
      el observatorio   d. el ancho y el largo

3. Cada civilización tenía sus teorías sobre el
   _____ del mundo.
   a. origen   c. universo
   b. pueblo   d. habitante

4. Los astrónomos mayas observaban _____
   y los eclipses.
   a. las ruinas   c. los planetas
   b. el símbolo   d. el círculo

5. A un fenómeno extraño e inexplicable lo
   llamamos _____.
   a. misterio   c. evidencia
   b. geométrico   d. estructura

6. El arqueólogo _____ el diámetro del
   calendario azteca.
   a. cubrió   c. pesó
   b. dudó   d. midió

7. A las seis de la tarde se _____ el sol.
   a. excavó   c. calculó
   b. resolvió   d. puso

8. Los astrónomos _____ en la reunión con
   información sobre los planetas.
   a. brillaron   c. se arrojaron
   b. contribuyeron d. existían

2 **Gramática** Escribe la letra de la palabra o expresión que mejor complete
cada frase. Escribe tus respuestas en una hoja aparte.

1. Dudo que _____ naves espaciales en el
   imperio maya.
   a. existió   c. existen
   b. existirán   d. hayan existido

2. Algunos creen que es probable que los
   extraterrestres _____ las Líneas de Nazca.
   a. trazaron   c. trazan
   b. hayan trazado d. tracen

3. La arqueóloga está segura de que esta
   pirámide _____ a la civilización azteca.
   a. pertenecerá   c. pertenece
   b. haya pertenecido d. pertenecerían

4. No conozco a ningún arqueólogo que _____
   el nombre de todos los dioses aztecas.
   a. sabe   c. sabían
   b. sepa   d. supo

5. Necesitan a un científico que _____ la edad
   del templo.
   a. calcula   c. calculo
   b. calculen   d. calcule

6. Es improbable que los aztecas _____ a
   la Luna.
   a. han viajado   c. hayas viajado
   b. viajan   d. hayan viajado

7. No conozco a nadie que _____ para buscar
   ruinas de la cultura azteca.
   a. haya excavado c. han excavado
   b. excava   d. hayan excavado

8. El sol no desapareció _____ que se puso.
   a. también   c. sino
   b. pero   d. sólo

DIFFERENTIATED INSTRUCTION

Heritage Language Learners

Have students review their past exams,
portfolios, and pieces of writing on which you
have given them feedback. Have them identify
errors that they consistently make, including
errors with accent marks and spelling. Guide
them to make notes that will help them to not
repeat these errors as they complete the writing
portion of the exam.

Students with Learning Difficulties

Guide students to use the process of
elimination by first determining which answers
they are sure are incorrect and ignoring them.
Help them begin by eliminating answers that
do not agree in tense, person, or number with
the rest of the sentence.

Repaso

Más repaso GO realidades.com | print

Puzzles ✔
Core WB pp. 103–104 ✔ ✔
Comm. WB pp. 203, 204–207 ✔ ✔
Instant Check ✔

En el examen vas a . . .	Éstas son las tareas de práctica que te pueden ser útiles para el examen . . .	Para repasar, ve a tu libro de texto impreso o digital . . .

Interpretive

 3 **Escuchar** Escuchar y comprender una entrevista con un arqueólogo que acaba de regresar de una excavación

Escucha una entrevista entre un locutor de una estación de radio y la famosa arqueóloga Dra. Cruz, y responde a las siguientes preguntas: (a) ¿Qué civilización estudió? (b) ¿Qué excavó? (c) ¿Cómo explicó lo que encontró? (d) ¿El locutor cree que es un mito o la realidad?

pp. 298–301 *A primera vista 1: Vocabulario en contexto*
p. 299 Actividades 1–2
p. 301 Actividad 3
p. 305 Actividad 9
p. 309 Actividad 16

Interpersonal

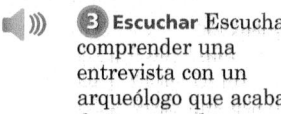 4 **Hablar** Hablar sobre un misterio o fenómeno inexplicable del pasado o del presente

Piensa en un misterio o fenómeno inexplicable que te interese. Descríbelo y sugiere una explicación lógica de por qué existe o se produce dicho misterio o fenómeno.

p. 305 Actividad 9
p. 308 Actividad 14
p. 309 Actividad 16
p. 310 Actividad 17

Interpretive

 5 **Leer** Leer y comprender una leyenda

Lee este relato azteca. Según el relato, ¿cuál es la explicación para el principio de la lluvia? (a) A los dioses les gustaba el templo que los aztecas construyeron. (b) Para que lloviera, siete hombres cantaban cuatro canciones. (c) La Luna apareció por 28 días.

Cuenta el relato que los antiguos aztecas construyeron un templo a los dioses del fuego y de la lluvia en una montaña. Y siete hombres se reunían cuando llegaba el tiempo de sembrar la tierra, llamaban al dios de la lluvia y cantaban cuatro canciones, porque cuatro por siete es 28, y veintiocho días tiene el mes de la Luna. Poco después, comenzaba a llover.

p. 304 Actividad 8
p. 311 Actividad 19
pp. 312–315 *A primera vista 2: Vocabulario en contexto*
p. 313 Actividad 21
p. 318 Actividad 27
pp. 324–325 *Puente a la cultura*

Presentational

 6 **Escribir** Escribir sobre un misterio arqueológico

Escoge una de las ruinas misteriosas de las que se han hablado en este capítulo y escribe un párrafo sobre lo que piensas de ella. ¿Cuál crees que fue el origen y la función de esa construcción? ¿Está relacionada con algún mito o leyenda de esa civilización? ¿Crees que algún día se descubrirán sus misterios?

p. 304 Actividad 8
p. 305 Actividad 9
p. 309 Actividad 16
p. 311 Actividad 18
p. 318 Actividad 27
pp. 324–325 *Puente a la cultura*

Cultures

 7 **Pensar** Pensar en un mito y buscar una explicación posible

Piensa en alguna leyenda o mito que has estudiado en este capítulo. Busca una razón posible para explicar el origen de este mito y la función que tenía.

See *Actividades* referenced above in #6 Escribir p. 337.

trescientos treinta y siete 337
Capítulo 7

4. Hablar
Suggestions: Encourage students to use an expression of doubt or of certainty when giving their explanation for the phenomenon.
Answers will vary.

5. Leer
Suggestions: Tell students to refer to pp. 298–301 and 312–315 if they have questions about vocabulary in the review.
Answers:
b

6. Escribir
Suggestions: Encourage students to use subordinate clauses in their paragraphs in order to make their sentences varied and interesting.
Answers will vary.

7. Pensar
Suggestions: Ask students how their personal opinions regarding unexplained phenomena have changed, if at all, due to what they have learned in *Capítulo* 7. Ask them also to summarize the new information they have learned from the chapter.
Answers will vary.

DIFFERENTIATED ASSESSMENT

CORE ASSESSMENT
- **Assessment Program:** Examen del capítulo 7
- **Audio Program DVD:** Cap. 7, Track 18
- **ExamView:** Chapter Test, Test Banks A and B

ADVANCED/PRE-AP*
- **ExamView Pre-AP* Test Bank**
- **Pre-AP* Resource Book,** pp. 156–158

STUDENTS NEEDING EXTRA HELP
- **Alternate Assessment Program:** Examen del capítulo 7
- **Audio Program DVD:** Cap. 7, Track 18

HERITAGE LEARNERS
- **Assessment Program: Realidades para hispanohablantes:** Examen del capítulo 7
- **ExamView Heritage Learner Test Bank**

8 Chapter Overview

- **interactions between different cultures**

Vocabulary
- fusion of cultures in Spain
- fusion of cultures in the Americas

Grammar
- conditional
- imperfect subjunctive

Cultural Perspectives
- the fusion of different cultures evidenced in the architecture and culture and lifestyles of Spain
- Buenos Aires, a city where cultures, religions, and traditions mix
- the Paraguayan harp and its European origin
- Tex-Mex food, a mixture of two cultures
- the missions of California

¡Pura vida!
- Watch an engaging video episode about a group of young people in Costa Rica!

CHAPTER SUPPORT

Bulletin Boards

Theme: *Mezcla de culturas en España*

Ask students to cut out, copy, or download pictures showing evidence of the exchange between different cultures in Spain. They can include pictures of different architectural structures, musical instruments, writings, mathematical symbols, food, and other examples of how Spain assimilated elements from different cultures.

Hands-on Culture

Craft: *Azulejo de maravilla*

Students will imagine they are creating beautifully decorated *azulejos* (tiles) to be used in the construction of the Alhambra corridors and fountains.

Materials: Internet access or books and magazines about Moorish architecture in Spain (optional), tracing or drawing paper, carbon paper, 2 square or octagonal cardboard or plastic tiles per student, white or beige enamel, paint brushes, permanent markers in a variety of colors and tips

Directions:

1. Students cover each of their tiles with one or two layers of enamel and let it dry overnight.
2. Students either research in the Internet, books, or magazines for examples of Arab designs like the ones used in the tiles of the Alhambra and copy them on tracing paper, or make their own designs on drawing paper.

3. Once the enamel on the tiles dries out, students transfer their designs to each tile by placing a piece of carbon paper on the tile and the design on top of it and tracing with a pencil.
4. Students use colored permanent markers to decorate the tile designs.

Game

Dominó de palabras

This domino game practices vocabulary about cultural exchange during the Spanish conquest of the Americas and the Middle Ages in Spain. Use it after students have practiced the vocabulary from the chapter.

Players: entire class

Materials: index cards, at least five per student, pens or markers

Rules:

1. Distribute five or more index cards to each student. Ask students to draw a vertical line on each card, dividing it in two halves.
2. Ask students to select any words they like from the chapter vocabulary and write them on the cards, one word per half. They can mix and match words on the cards any way they like.
3. Collect the finished "domino" pieces, shuffle them, and redistribute them evenly to the students.
4. Play! Students form a big circle and start playing domino with the cards. The criteria for matching domino halves will be that matching words should fall within the same category or be directly related to each other. This way, *conquista,* could be paired with either *árabes, Cortés, aztecas, reconquistar,* or *soldados;* but *árabes* and *Cortés* could not be paired to each other. *La Giralda, azulejos, maravilla,* and *arco,* can all be paired with each other and with *arquitectura.*
5. Students take turns setting one of their domino pieces on the table and arranging them in creative domino designs. If a student cannot match any of his or her pieces to the free ends of the domino, he or she skips the round and keeps the pieces. The objective is to be the first to set all the pieces on the table.

Variation: Instead of playing traditional domino, in which only one piece can be attached to each free end, students can attach up to three matching words to each word, thus making a multi-lineal design.

CHAPTER PROJECT

Imágenes del encuentro entre culturas

Overview: Students create a poster or slide show about the arrival of the Spaniards or other explorers in the Americas. They can focus on one of the many topics presented on pages 356–358. The poster/slide show must feature labeled photos or illustrations related to the topic they have selected. Students then give an oral presentation describing briefly the culture they are showing and what happened during that period in history.

Resources: digital or print photos, image editing and page layout software, and/or poster board, colored pencils, markers, glue, scissors

Sequence: (suggestions for when to do each step appear throughout the chapter)

STEP 1. Review instructions so students know what is expected of them. Hand out the "Chapter 8 Project Instructions and Rubric" from the *Teacher's Resource Book*.

STEP 2. Students choose their topic and submit a rough sketch of their project. Return the sketches with your suggestions. For vocabulary and grammar practice, ask students to work in pairs and present their drafts to each other.

STEP 3. Students do layouts. Encourage students to try different arrangements before writing descriptions.

STEP 4. Students submit a draft of their descriptions. Note your corrections and suggestions, then return the drafts to students.

STEP 5. Students complete and present their project to the class. They should describe one of the photos or illustrations and give a brief summary of what is shown in the whole poster or slide show.

Options:

1. Instead of a poster or a slide show, students design a Web page with similar information.
2. Students design a timeline beginning with the arrival of the Spaniards in Mexico up to and including the establishment of colonies.

Assessment:

Here is a detailed rubric for assessing this project:

Chapter 8 Project: *Imágenes del encuentro entre culturas*

RUBRIC	Score 1	Score 3	Score 5
Your evidence of planning	You provide no preliminary proposal or descriptions.	Your preliminary proposal and descriptions are not revised.	You show evidence of corrected proposal and descriptions.
Your use of illustrations	Your photos or illustrations are incorrectly labeled.	Your photos or illustrations are disorganized.	Your photos or illustrations are organized. Your presentation is easy to read.
Your presentation	You do not include the required information.	You include most of the required information.	You include all of the required information.

21st Century Skills

Look for tips throughout Chapter 8 to enrich your teaching by integrating 21st Century Skills. Suggestions for the Chapter Project and Culture follow below.

Chapter Project

Modify the Chapter Project with these suggestions:

Encourage Technology Literacy

Encourage students to access their favorite search engine to research the arrival of the Spaniards or other explorers in the Americas. Have them choose one particular explorer that interests them and search for reliable sources for their project. The handout "Search for Information on the Internet" can help them refine their search.

Promote Creativity and Innovation

Have students think about creative ways to organize and present their research. Ask students to come up with creative ways to arrange the information, such as time lines, maps, use of visuals with captions, or text.

Encourage Social and Cross-Cultural Skills

Have students work with partners to discuss the cultural backgrounds they represent. From where are their parents, grandparents, or other family members? What languages or cultural traditions do they use at home? What unique family traditions come from their cultural heritage?

Chapter Culture

Develop Flexibility and Adaptability

Direct students to the information in the *Fondo cultural* on page 362 and *La fusión* on page 358. Have them compare their answers to the questions with classmates and promote a discussion about the fusion of cultures in Latin America. How is Tex-Mex cuisine representative of the fusion of local cultures in the Southwest? What are other examples of cultural fusion in Latin America or the U.S.?

▶ **Videodocumentario** View *Unas herencias ricas* online with the class to learn more about how people of diverse cultural backgrounds can come together to share their cultures.

AT A GLANCE

Objectives

- Listen and read about indigenous cultures
- Talk and write about cultural heritage
- Present a guided city tour
- Understand the historical context of Spanish missions in California
- Express your opinion about cultural exchanges

A ver si recuerdas...

- Buildings, descriptions, and locations
- Conflicts and resolutions
- Interrogative words
- Verbs with changes in the preterite

Recycle... ♻

- The verb **haber** in the preterite
- The preterite of verbs
- Pronunciation of the letter **c** before **a, o,** and **u**

Vocabulary

- Buildings
- The discovery of America
- Cultural exchanges

Grammar

- Conditional
- Imperfect subjunctive
- Imperfect subjunctive with **si**

Culture

- Sevilla, Toledo, and Barcelona, pp. 346–347
- The Paraguayan harp, p. 355
- Aztecs and Hernán Cortés, pp. 356–357
- Spanish colonialism, pp. 358–359
- Empires, p. 361
- Tex-Mex food, p. 362
- The Aztec legend, *El Águila y el nopal,* p. 363
- The missions of California, pp. 370–371
- Aztec words used today, p. 379

RESOURCES

	FOR THE STUDENT	ONLINE	DVD	PRINT	FOR THE TEACHER	ONLINE	PREEXP	DVD	PRINT
Plan					Interactive TE and Resource DVD	•		•	
					Teacher's Resource Book, pp. 179–234	•		•	•
					Pre-AP* Resource Book, pp. 159–161	•		•	•
					Mapa global interactivo	•			
					Lesson Plans	•			•

A ver si recuerdas PP. 338–341

	FOR THE STUDENT	ONLINE	DVD	PRINT	FOR THE TEACHER	ONLINE	PREEXP	DVD	PRINT
Review	A ver si recuerdas Study Plan	•			A ver si recuerdas Study Plan	•			
	Guided WB, pp. 238–241	•	•	•	Vocabulary and Grammar Transparencies, 149–152	•	•	•	
	Core WB, pp. 105–106	•	•	•	Answer Keys: Student Edition, p. 107	•	•	•	
	Hispanohablantes WB, p. 236			•					

Introducción PP. 342–343

	FOR THE STUDENT	ONLINE	DVD	PRINT	FOR THE TEACHER	ONLINE	PREEXP	DVD	PRINT
Present	Student Edition, pp. 342–343	•	•	•	Interactive TE and Resource DVD	•		•	
	DK Reference Atlas	•	•		Teacher's Resource Book, pp. 180–183	•		•	•
	Videonovela: ¡Pura vida!	•	•		Galería de fotos		•		
	¡Pura vida! Video Activities	•			Fine Art Transparencies, 65	•	•	•	
	Hispanohablantes WB, p. 237			•	Map Transparencies, 14, 18, 20, 22	•	•	•	

Vocabulario en contexto PP. 344–347/356–359

	FOR THE STUDENT	ONLINE	DVD	PRINT	FOR THE TEACHER	ONLINE	PREEXP	DVD	PRINT
Present & Practice	Student Edition, pp. 344–347/356–359	•	•	•	Interactive TE and Resource DVD	•		•	
	Audio	•	•		Teacher's Resource Book, pp. 184–185, 188–189, 202–209/ 186–187, 189–190, 202–209	•		•	•
	Flashcards	•	•						
	Instant Check	•			Vocabulary Clip Art	•	•	•	•
	Guided WB, pp. 242–250/253–260	•	•	•	Audio Program	•	•	•	
	Core WB, pp. 107–108/112–113	•	•	•	Vocabulary and Grammar Transparencies, 153–156/158–161	•	•	•	
	Comm. WB, pp. 110/113	•	•	•	Answer Keys: Student Edition, pp. 108/113	•	•	•	
	Hispanohablantes WB, pp. 238–239/248–249			•					
Assess and Remediate					Pruebas 8–1, 8–4: Assessment Program, pp. 171–172/179–180	•		•	•
					Hispanohablantes, pp. 171–172/179–180	•		•	•

RESOURCES

Vocabulario en uso PP. 348–351/360–363

	FOR THE STUDENT	ONLINE	DVD	PRINT	FOR THE TEACHER	ONLINE	PREEXP	DVD	PRINT
Present & Practice	Student Edition, pp. 348–351/360–363	●	●	●	Interactive Whiteboard Vocabulary Activities	●		●	
	Instant Check	●			Interactive TE and Resource DVD	●		●	
	Comm. WB, pp. 106/108	●	●	●	Teacher's Resource Book, pp. 189, 194–195/190–191, 197–198	●		●	●
	Hispanohablantes WB, pp. 240–241/250–252			●	Audio Program	●	●	●	
	Communicative Pair Activities	●			Videomodelos	●		●	
					Fine Art Transparencies, 1–2	●		●	
					Answer Keys: Student Edition, pp. 109–110/114–115	●	●	●	●
Assess and Remediate					Pruebas 8–2, 8–5 with Study Plans	●			
					Pruebas 8–2, 8–5: Assessment Program, pp. 173–174/181–182	●		●	●
					Hispanohablantes, pp. 173–174/181–182	●		●	●

Gramática PP. 352–355/364–369

	FOR THE STUDENT	ONLINE	DVD	PRINT	FOR THE TEACHER	ONLINE	PREEXP	DVD	PRINT
Present & Practice	Student Edition, pp. 352–355/364–369	●	●	●	Interactive Whiteboard Grammar Activities	●		●	
	Instant Check	●			Interactive TE and Resource DVD	●		●	
	Animated Verbs	●			Teacher's Resource Book, pp. 189, 196/191, 199–200	●		●	
	Tutorial Video: Grammar	●			Audio Program	●	●	●	
	Canción de hip hop	●			Videomodelos	●	●	●	
	Guided WB, pp. 251–252/261–264	●	●	●	Vocabulary and Grammar Transparencies, 157/162–163	●	●	●	
	Core WB, pp. 109–111/114–116	●	●	●	Answer Keys: Student Edition, pp. 110–112/115–116	●	●	●	
	Comm. WB, pp. 107, 111–112/108–109, 115, 207	●	●	●					
	Hispanohablantes WB, pp. 242–247, 253–257			●					
	Communicative Pair Activities	●							
Assess and Remediate					Pruebas 8–3, 8–6, 8–7 with Study Plans	●			
					Pruebas 8–3, 8–6, 8–7: Assessment Program, pp. 175/183, 184	●		●	●
					Hispanohablantes, pp. 175/183, 184	●		●	●
					Examen 1, Examen 2: Vocab. y gramática, pp. 176–178/185–187	●		●	●

¡Adelante! PP. 370–379

	FOR THE STUDENT	ONLINE	DVD	PRINT	FOR THE TEACHER	ONLINE	PREEXP	DVD	PRINT
Application	Student Edition, pp. 370–379	●	●	●	Interactive TE and Resource DVD	●		●	
	Online Cultural Reading	●			Teacher's Resource Book, pp. 192–193	●		●	●
	Guided WB, pp. 265–267	●	●	●	Video Program: *Videodocumentario*	●		●	
	Comm. WB, pp. 118–119, 208	●	●	●	Video Program Teacher's Guide, Cap. 8	●		●	
	Hispanohablantes WB, pp. 258–263			●	Map Transparencies, 22	●	●	●	
	Videodocumentario	●	●		Vocabulary and Grammar Transparencies, 4	●	●	●	
	Lecturas 3, pp. 26–29, 36–37			●	Answer Keys: Student Edition, pp. 116–118	●	●	●	

Repaso del capítulo PP. 380–383

	FOR THE STUDENT	ONLINE	DVD	PRINT	FOR THE TEACHER	ONLINE	PREEXP	DVD	PRINT
Review	Student Edition, pp. 380–383	●	●	●	Interactive TE and Resource DVD	●		●	
	Online Puzzles and Games	●			Teacher's Resource Book, pp. 192, 201–209	●		●	●
	Core WB, pp. 117–118	●	●	●	Audio Program	●	●	●	
	Comm. WB, pp. 209–212	●	●	●	Answer Keys: Student Edition, p. 119	●	●	●	
	Hispanohablantes WB, pp. 264–267			●					
	Instant Check	●							

Chapter Assessment

	FOR THE STUDENT	ONLINE	DVD	PRINT	FOR THE TEACHER	ONLINE	PREEXP	DVD	PRINT
Assess					Examen del capítulo 8: Assessment Program, pp. 188–191	●		●	●
					Alternate Assessment Program, pp. 76–86	●		●	●
					Hispanohablantes, pp. 188–191	●		●	●
					Audio Program, Cap. 8, Examen	●		●	
					ExamView: Test Banks A and B (questions only online)	●		●	
					Heritage Learner Test Bank	●		●	
					Pre-AP* Test Bank	●		●	

REGULAR SCHEDULE (50 MINUTES)

DAY	Warm-up / Assess	Preview / Present / Practice / Communicate	Wrap-up / Homework Options
1	**Warm-up (10 min.)** • Return Examen del capítulo: Capítulo 7	**Repaso (35 min.)** • A ver si recuerdas . . . • Actividad 7	**Wrap-up and Homework Options (5 min.)** • Core Practice 8-1, 8-2
2	**Warm-up (10 min.)** • Homework check	**Chapter Opener (10 min.)** • Objectives • Arte y cultura **Vocabulario en contexto 1 (25 min.)** • Presentation: Vocabulario y gramática en contexto • Actividad 1	**Wrap-up and Homework Options (5 min.)** • Clip Art Vocabulary
3	**Warm-up (10 min.)** • Homework check	**Vocabulario en contexto 1 (35 min.)** • Presentation: España: Una gran mezcla de culturas • Actividades 2, 3, 4	**Wrap-up and Homework Options (5 min.)** • Core Practice 8-3, 8-4 • Actividad 6 • Prueba 8-1: Vocabulary recognition
4	**Warm-up (10 min.)** • Homework check ✔**Formative Assessment (10 min.)** • Prueba 8-1: Vocabulary recognition	**Vocabulario en uso 1 (25 min.)** • Interactive Whiteboard Vocabulary Activities • Actividades 5, 7, 8, 9, 10 • Ampliación del lenguaje	**Wrap-up and Homework Options (5 min.)** • Writing Activities • Prueba 8-2 with Study Plan: Vocabulary production
5	**Warm-up (5 min.)** • Homework check ✔**Formative Assessment (10 min.)** • Prueba 8-2 with Study Plan: Vocabulary production	**Gramática y vocabulario en uso 1 (25 min.)** • Presentation: El condicional • Interactive Whiteboard Grammar Activities • Actividades 12, 13, 14 • Writing Activity	**Wrap-up and Homework Options (5 min.)** • Core Practice 8-5
6	**Warm-up (10 min.)** • Actividad 11 • Homework check	**Gramática y vocabulario en uso 1 (35 min.)** • Actividades 15, 16 • Audio or Writing Activity	**Wrap-up and Homework Options (5 min.)** • Core Practice 8-6, 8-7 • Writing Activity • Prueba 8-3 with Study Plan: El condicional
7	**Warm-up (10 min.)** • Fondo cultural • Homework check ✔**Formative Assessment (10 min.)** • Prueba 8-3 with Study Plan: El condicional	**Gramática y vocabulario en uso 1 (10 min.)** • Communicative Pair Activity **Vocabulario en contexto 2 (25 min.)** • Presentation: Vocabulario y gramática en contexto • Actividad 17	**Wrap-up and Homework Options (5 min.)** • Examen: Vocabulario y gramática 1
8	**Warm-up (15 min.)** • Writing Activity • Homework check ✔**Formative Assessment (30 min.)** • Examen: Vocabulario y gramática 1		**Wrap-up and Homework Options (5 min.)** • Writing Activity
9	**Warm-up (5 min.)** • Homework check	**Vocabulario en contexto 2 (25 min.)** • Presentation: La fusión y la herencia • Actividades 18, 19 • Audio and Writing Activities **Vocabulario en uso 2 (15 min.)** • Actividades 21, 22	**Wrap-up and Homework Options (5 min.)** • Core Practice 8-8, 8-9 • Prueba 8-4: Vocabulary recognition
10	**Warm-up (15 min.)** • Actividad 20 • Homework check ✔**Formative Assessment (10 min.)** • Prueba 8-4: Vocabulary recognition	**Vocabulario en uso 2 (20 min.)** • Interactive Whiteboard Vocabulary Activities • Actividades 23, 24, 25	**Wrap-up and Homework Options (5 min.)** • Fondo cultural • Prueba 8-5 with Study Plan: Vocabulary production

REGULAR SCHEDULE (50 MINUTES)

DAY	Warm-up / Assess	Preview / Present / Practice / Communicate	Wrap-up / Homework Options
11	**Warm-up** (10 min.) • Writing Activity • Homework check ✔**Formative Assessment** (10 min.) • Prueba 8-5 with Study Plan: Vocabulary production	**Gramática y vocabulario en uso 2** (25 min.) • Presentation: El imperfecto del subjuntivo • Interactive Whiteboard Grammar Activities • En voz alta • Actividades 26, 27, 29 • Communicative Pair Activity	**Wrap-up and Homework Options** (5 min.) • Actividad 28 • Core Practice 8-10 • Prueba 8-6 with Study Plan: El imperfecto del subjuntivo
12	**Warm-up** (10 min.) • Actividad 30 • Homework check ✔**Formative Assessment** (10 min.) • Prueba 8-6 with Study Plan: El imperfecto del subjuntivo	**Gramática y vocabulario en uso 2** (25 min.) • El español en el mundo del trabajo • Presentation: El imperfecto del subjuntivo con *si* • Interactive Whiteboard Grammar Activities • Actividades 33, 34, 35	**Wrap-up and Homework Options** (5 min.) • Core Practice 8-11, 8-12 • Prueba 8-7 with Study Plan: El imperfecto del subjuntivo con *si*
13	**Warm-up** (20 min.) • Actividades 31, 32, • Homework check ✔**Formative Assessment** (10 min.) • Prueba 8-7 with Study Plan: El imperfecto del subjuntivo con *si*	**Gramática y vocabulario en uso 2** (15 min.) • Communicative Pair Activity	**Wrap-up and Homework Options** (5 min.) • Examen: Vocabulario y gramática 2
14	**Warm-up** (10 min.) • Writing Activity ✔**Formative Assessment** (10 min.) • Examen: Vocabulario y gramática 2	**¡Adelante!** (10 min.) • Presentación oral: Steps 1, 2	**Wrap-up and Homework Options** (5 min.) • Presentación oral: Step 2
15	**Warm-up** (10 min.) • Presentación oral: Step 2	**¡Adelante!** (35 min.) • Presentación oral: Step 3	**Wrap-up and Homework Options** (5 min.) • Las misiones de California • ¿Comprendiste?
16	**Warm-up** (15 min.) • Las misiones de California: ¿Comprendiste? • Homework check	**¡Adelante!** (30 min.) • ¿Qué me cuentas? 1, 2, 3 • View Video • Video Activities 1, 2, 3	**Wrap-up and Homework Options** (5 min.) • Presentación escrita: Steps 1, 2
17	**Warm-up** (10 min.) • Video Activity 4	**¡Adelante!** (15 min.) • Presentación escrita: Step 3 **Repaso** (20 min.) • Preparación para el examen: Actividades 3, 4	**Wrap-up and Homework Options** (5 min.) • Presentación escrita: Step 4
18	**Warm-up** (10 min.) • Homework check	**¡Adelante!** (35 min.) • Lectura • Interacción con la lectura • Fondo cultural	**Wrap-up and Homework Options** (5 min.) • Core Practice: Organizer 8-13, 8-14 • Instant Check
19	**Warm-up** (20 min.) • Preparación para el examen: Actividades 1, 2 • Homework check	**Repaso** (25 min.) • Preparación para el examen: Actividades 5, 6, 7 • Other review	**Wrap-up and Homework Options** (5 min.) • Examen del capítulo
20	**Warm-up** (5 min.) • Answer questions ✔**Summative Assessment** (44 min.) • Examen del capítulo		**Wrap-up and Homework Options** (1 min.) • A ver si recuerdas: Capítulo 9

BLOCK SCHEDULE (90 MINUTES)

DAY	Warm-up / Assess	Preview / Present / Practice / Communicate	Wrap-up / Homework Options
1	**Warm-up** (25 min.) • Return Examen del capítulo: Capítulo 7 • A ver si recuerdas . . . • Actividad 7 • Homework check	**Chapter Opener** (10 min.) • Objectives • Arte y cultura **Vocabulario en contexto 1** (40 min.) • Presentation: Vocabulario y gramática en contexto • Actividad 1 • Presentation: España: Una gran mezcla de culturas • Actividades 2, 3, 4 **Vocabulario en uso 1** (10 min.) • Actividad 7	**Wrap-up and Homework Options** (5 min.) • Core Practice 8-3, 8-4 • Clip Art Vocabulary • Prueba 8-1: Vocabulary recognition
2	**Warm-up** (15 min.) • Actividad 5 • Homework check ✔**Formative Assessment** (10 min.) • Prueba 8-1: Vocabulary recognition	**Vocabulario en uso 1** (60 min.) • Interactive Whiteboard Vocabulary Activities • Actividades 6, 8, 9, 10 • Ampliación del lenguaje • Communicative Pair Activity	**Wrap-up and Homework Options** (5 min.) • Writing Activities • Prueba 8-2 with Study Plan: Vocabulary production
3	**Warm-up** (15 min.) • Writing Activity • Homework check ✔**Formative Assessment** (10 min.) • Prueba 8-2 with Study Plan: Vocabulary production	**Gramática y vocabulario en uso 1** (60 min.) • Presentation: El condicional • Interactive Whiteboard Grammar Activities • Actividades 11, 12, 13, 14, 15, 16 • Fondo cultural • Audio and Writing Activities	**Wrap-up and Homework Options** (5 min.) • Core Practice 8-5, 8-6, 8-7 • Prueba 8-3 with Study Plan: El condicional
4	**Warm-up** (10 min.) • Writing Activity • Homework check ✔**Formative Assessment** (10 min.) • Prueba 8-3 with Study Plan: El condicional	**Gramática y vocabulario en uso 1** (20 min.) • Communicative Pair Activity **Vocabulario en contexto 2** (40 min.) • Presentation: Vocabulario y gramática en contexto • Actividad 17 • Presentation: La fusión y la herencia • Actividades 18, 19	**Wrap-up and Homework Options** (5 min.) • Core Practice 8-8, 8-9 • Examen: Vocabulario y gramática 1
5	**Warm-up** (10 min.) • Actividad 19 • Homework check ✔**Formative Assessment Options** (30 min.) • Examen: Vocabulario y gramática 1	**Vocabulario en contexto 2** (20 min.) • Audio or Writing Activities **Vocabulario en uso 2** (25 min.) • Actividades 21, 22, 23 • En voz alta	**Wrap-up and Homework Options** (5 min.) • Actividades 20, 24 • Prueba 8-4: Vocabulary recognition

BLOCK SCHEDULE (90 MINUTES)

DAY	Warm-up / Assess	Preview / Present / Practice / Communicate	Wrap-up / Homework Options
6	**Warm-up (20 min.)** • Actividad 25 • Homework check ✔**Formative Assessment (10 min.)** • Prueba 8-4: Vocabulary recognition	**Gramática y vocabulario en uso 2 (55 min.)** • Fondo cultural • Presentation: El imperfecto del subjuntivo • Interactive Whiteboard Grammar Activities • Actividades 26, 27, 29, 30 • El español en el mundo del trabajo • Writing Activities	**Wrap-up and Homework Options (5 min.)** • Core Practice 8-10 • Pruebas 8-5, 8-6 with Study Plans: Vocabulary production, El imperfecto del subjuntivo
7	**Warm-up (10 min.)** • Actividad 28 • Writing Activity ✔**Formative Assessment (20 min.)** • Pruebas 8-5, 8-6 with Study Plans: Vocabulary production, El imperfecto del subjuntivo	**Gramática y vocabulario en uso 2 (40 min.)** • Presentation: El imperfecto del subjuntivo con *si* • Interactive Whiteboard Grammar Activities • Actividades 31, 32, 33, 34, 35 **¡Adelante! (15 min.)** • Presentación oral: Steps 1, 2	**Wrap-up and Homework Options (5 min.)** • Presentación oral: Step 2
8	**Warm-up (15 min.)** • Writing Activity • Homework check ✔**Formative Assessment (40 min.)** • Presentación oral: Step 3	**Gramática y vocabulario en uso 2 (15 min.)** • Communicative Pair Activity **¡Adelante! (15 min.)** • Presentation: Las misiones de California	**Wrap-up and Homework Options (5 min.)** • Core Practice 8-11, 8-12 • Prueba 8-7 with Study Plan: El imperfecto del subjuntivo con *si* • Examen: Vocabulario y gramática 2
9	**Warm-up (10 min.)** • Homework check ✔**Formative Assessment Options (30 min.)** • Prueba 8-7 with Study Plan: El imperfecto del subjuntivo con *si* • Examen: Vocabulario y gramática 2	**¡Adelante! (45 min.)** • Las misiones de California • ¿Comprendiste? • ¿Qué me cuentas? 1, 2, 3 • View Video • Video Activities • Presentación escrita: Step 1	**Wrap-up and Homework Options (5 min.)** • Presentación escrita: Step 2 • Preparación para el examen: Actividades 1, 2
10	**Warm-up (20 min.)** • Presentación escrita: Step 3 • Homework check	**¡Adelante! (35 min.)** • Lectura • Interacción con la lectura • Fondo cultural **Repaso (30 min.)** • Preparación para el examen: Actividades 3, 4, 6	**Wrap-up and Homework Options (5 min.)** • Presentación escrita: Step 4 • Core Practice: Organizer 8-13, 8-14 • Instant Check • Preparación para el examen: Actividades 5, 7 • Examen del capítulo
11	**Warm-up (15 min.)** • Homework check ✔**Summative Assessment (45 min.)** • Examen del capítulo	**Theme Game (15 min.)** **A ver si recuerdas – Capítulo 9 (10 min.)** • Presentation: Vocabulario • Presentation: Gramática	**Wrap-up and Homework Options (5 min.)** • A ver si recuerdas – Capítulo 9 • Actividades 1, 2, 3, 6, 8 • Core Practice 9-1, 9-2

Vocabulario Repaso

Core Instruction

Standards: 1.1

Resources: Voc. and Gram. Transparency 149

Suggestions: Before presenting the material in this review section, consider testing your students' command of the material by assigning the Study Plan. Students will automatically be given additional practice of the material they have not yet mastered, and you can focus your review based on the class's overall performance on the post-test.

Ask students to make a map of an imaginary neighborhood. Their map should include labels calling out several of the *construcciones* shown in the *Vocabulario*. Ask them to include some of the terms from the *para describir* and *en la ciudad* categories as well. Have students exchange maps with a partner and ask and answer questions about each other's maps:

A —¿Cómo voy de la vieja sinagoga al nuevo museo?

B —Sal de la sinagoga y sigue por la Avenida Martín. Dobla a la derecha en la Calle del Museo. Camina dos cuadras y verás el museo.

1

Standards: 1.1

Focus: Practicing review vocabulary

Suggestions: Encourage students to invent Spanish names for places and buildings that are known by English names. Their Spanish names should be translations that are direct enough so that their partner can recognize them. If this proves too difficult, allow them to use the English name.

Answers will vary.

Block Schedule

Twenty Questions: Divide the class into groups of four or five to play "Twenty Questions." Each student will assume the identify of a person, living or dead. The group asks up to twenty questions to determine the identity of the mystery person.

Vocabulario Repaso

construcciones

el edificio histórico
la fuente
la iglesia
la mezquita
el monumento
el museo
el palacio
la plaza
el puente
la sinagoga
el teatro

para indicar el lugar

a la derecha
a la izquierda
al lado de
cerca de
debajo de
delante de
detrás de
entre
lejos de

para indicar el tiempo

¿Cuánto tiempo hace que . . . ?
desde
la fecha
hace . . . dos, tres, cuatro años
hace mucho / poco tiempo
recientemente

para describir

antiguo, -a
enorme
grande
horrible
moderno, -a
nuevo, -a
pequeño, -a
viejo, -a

en la ciudad

la avenida
la calle
la cuadra
la esquina

▼**1** En tu ciudad |

Escribir • Hablar

❶ Haz una lista con tres lugares o edificios famosos de tu pueblo, de tu ciudad o de tu estado, por ejemplo: un monumento, una calle, un teatro o una plaza. En una tabla como la siguiente, escribe dónde quedan esos lugares o edificios, cómo son y cuándo los visitaste. Usa las palabras de la lista de vocabulario. NO escribas el nombre de la construcción.

¿Qué es?	¿Dónde queda?	¿Cómo es?	¿Cuándo lo visitaste?
1. [lugar o edificio]			
2. [lugar o edificio]			

❷ Hazle preguntas a otro(a) estudiante sobre los lugares de su lista. Pregúntale sobre la información que escribió y trata de identificar los lugares.

▶ **Modelo**

A —¿Cuándo visitaste el lugar?
B —Lo visité hace un año.

338 trescientos treinta y ocho
A ver si recuerdas . . .

DIFFERENTIATED INSTRUCTION

Heritage Language Learners

Ask students to share the names and types of buildings prevalent in, or specific to, their heritage country. Have them use specific vocabulary to describe some of the noteworthy structures found in their heritage country.

Advanced Learners

Have students write step-by-step directions in order to travel from one place in your community to another. Their directions should be clear and detailed enough so that a person following them would arrive at the destination. Have them read their directions to each other. Ask listeners to identify the destination.

Gramática Repaso

Las palabras interrogativas

Remember that you use interrogative words to ask questions. In Spanish, all interrogative words have a written accent mark.

The interrogative words *¿cómo?*, *¿cuándo?*, *¿dónde?*, *¿adónde?*, *¿qué?*, *¿para qué?*, *¿por qué?* are invariable—they do not change in gender or number.

¿Cuándo vas al museo?   **¿Por qué** vamos a la plaza?

The interrogative words *¿cuál?* / *¿cuáles?*, and *¿quién?* / *¿quiénes?* have both singular and plural forms, but do not change in gender.

¿Cuáles son tus amigos?   **¿Quién** es tu mejor amiga?

The interrogative words *¿cuánto?* / *¿cuántos?* / *¿cuánta?* / *¿cuántas?* agree both in number (singular / plural) and gender (masculine / feminine) with the noun they modify.

¿Cuánto dinero?   **¿Cuántas** horas?

In Spanish, prepositions always precede interrogative words.

¿Para qué hiciste eso?   **¿Con quién** fuiste tú?

Just as in direct questions, interrogative words have a written accent when they are used in indirect questions.

Quiero saber **quiénes** van a la fiesta.   Me preguntó **cuál** era mi mochila.

| **Más ayuda** | realidades.com | ▶ Tutorial |

▼2 ¿Cómo llegamos?

Leer

Dos amigas quieren ir al museo. Completa el diálogo con las palabras interrogativas que correspondan.

A —¿ __1.__ vamos al museo, en autobús o a pie?

B —Depende . . . ¿tú sabes a __2.__ cuadras de aquí está el museo?

A —Creo que a unas veinte . . . ¿ __3.__ no vamos en autobús?

B —Sí, mejor. Estoy cansada. ¿Sabes __4.__ está la parada del autobús?

A —Aquí, pero . . . mira, aquí paran cuatro autobuses. ¿ __5.__ tomamos? ¿A __6.__ le preguntamos?

▼3 Entrevista | 👥

Escribir • Hablar

Tú y tu compañero(a) trabajan para una organización de turismo. Deben entrevistar a los turistas que visitan un centro cultural, un teatro o un museo. Escriban diez preguntas para hacerles a los turistas. Lean sus preguntas a la clase. Pueden representar la entrevista con otros(as) compañeros(as).

Modelo
¿De dónde es usted?
¿Por qué ha venido a . . . ?

Gramática (Repaso)

Core Instruction

Resources: Voc. and Gram. Transparency 150

Suggestions: Refer students who are having difficulty with interrogative words to the online tutorial.

Have students fold a sheet of paper in half to create a flashcard. On one side of the card, have them write a large accent mark. Tell them to leave the other side blank. Say sentences that contain the words reviewed in the *Gramática*. Some of your models should use the words to form questions, and others should use them in subordinate clauses in which no accent is required: *Cuando llegamos al museo, tú no estabas.* Have students flash the accent side their cards if they hear an interrogative word that requires an accent, and the blank side if a similar word they hear requires no accent.

▼2 Standards: 1.2

Resources: Answer Keys: Student Edition, p. 107

Focus: Reviewing interrogative words

Suggestions: Have students scan the entire dialogue for meaning before they begin writing their answers.

Answers:

1. Cómo	4. dónde
2. cuántas	5. Cuál
3. Por qué	6. quién

Extension: Ask pairs of students to practice and present the dialogue for the class.

▼3 Standards: 1.3

Focus: Reviewing interrogative words

Suggestions: Encourage students to ask questions that a tour agency might really ask in order to improve business.

Answers will vary.

ENRICH YOUR TEACHING

Teacher-to-Teacher

Challenge students to write sentences that contain many different types of information. For example: *La plaza vieja está a una distancia de tres cuadras de la plaza nueva. Jorge llegó allí a las seis con su hermana Gloria.* Have them trade sentences with a partner, who writes as many questions as possible about it. Here are some possible questions based on the sample sentences: *¿A qué distancia está la plaza vieja de la plaza nueva? ¿A cuántas cuadras está la plaza vieja de la plaza nueva? ¿Quién llegó a la plaza vieja? ¿Con quién llegó Jorge? ¿A qué hora llegaron Jorge y su hermana?*

8 Recycle

| ▼ Objectives
▶ Discuss a conflict you had
▶ Talk about a movie you saw

Vocabulario Repaso

Core Instruction

Standards: 1.1

Resources: Voc. and Gram. Transparency 151

Suggestions: Ask students to write sentences using each of the verbs in the *reacciones* and *acciones* categories. In each of their sentences, challenge them to use items from at least one of the other categories as well.

4 Standards: 1.1, 1.2, 1.3

Resources: Answer Keys: Student Edition, p. 107

Focus: Practicing review vocabulary

Suggestions: Once students have matched the items and written their definitions, ask them to identify prefixes and suffixes such as *des-* and *-ía* and explain how they are used.

Answers will vary.

1. c   4. a
2. d   5. b
3. e

5 Standards: 1.1, 3.1

Focus: Practicing review vocabulary

Suggestions: As students discuss their word webs, ask them to explain how the solution to the conflict determines how we perceive its causes and reactions. Point out that when a conflict is not yet resolved, there is still confusion as to what its causes are and who is reacting to whom.

Answers will vary.

Vocabulario Repaso

el arte
la artesanía
la creación
la joya
la melodía
el oro
la plata

el comercio
cambiar
comprar
el mercado
pagar
el producto
regatear
vender

reacciones
asustarse
enojarse
estar asustado, -a
estar enojado, -a
ponerse enojado, -a
temer
tener miedo de

acciones
atreverse
capturar
destruir
escaparse
luchar
matar
morirse
refugiarse
salvar

las relaciones
colaborar
comunicarse
el conflicto
desconfiar
llevarse bien / mal
la pelea
pelearse
ponerse de acuerdo
reaccionar
relacionarse

▼4 Definiciones |

Leer • Escribir • Hablar

Empareja cada definición con la palabra correspondiente. Luego, usa las definiciones como modelos y escribe tus propias definiciones de cuatro palabras o expresiones de las listas. Lee tus definiciones a un(a) compañero(a) para ver si puede identificar las palabras apropiadas.

1. arte u obra con una marca personal
2. evitar un peligro
3. no confiar
4. lugar donde la gente compra y vende productos
5. discutir el precio de algo

a. mercado
b. regatear
c. artesanía
d. salvarse
e. desconfiar

▼5 Una vez yo . . . |

Escribir • Hablar

Piensa en un conflicto que hayas tenido en casa o en la escuela. Haz una red de palabras como la que sigue y complétala. Usa las palabras del vocabulario. Compara tu red con las de otros(as) compañeros(as). Hablen sobre las causas de los conflictos y sus soluciones.

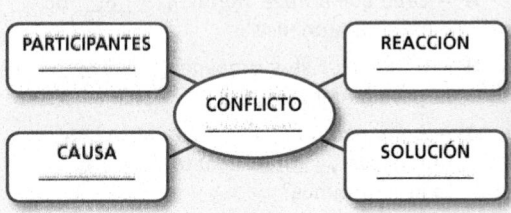

PARTICIPANTES ____
REACCIÓN ____
CONFLICTO ____
CAUSA ____
SOLUCIÓN ____

340 trescientos cuarenta
A ver si recuerdas . . .

DIFFERENTIATED INSTRUCTION

Multiple Intelligences

Interpersonal/Social: Have students choose 8 to 10 words from the *Vocabulario* on pp. 338 and 340. Have them role-play a "walk around the city." Instruct students to meet their "neighbors" and chat about people, places, and reactions. Direct them to use each one of their chosen words before they can "stroll back home."

Students with Learning Difficulties

Students may have difficulty memorizing past forms of irregular verbs, especially verbs with irregular stems. Have students create their own reference cards for each of these verbs. On each card, students should list present, preterite, and imperfect forms. Encourage students to write clearly for quick reference.

Gramática Repaso

Verbos con cambios en el pretérito

Verbs like *oír*, *leer*, and *creer* change the *i* to *y* in the *Ud./él/ella* and *Uds./ellos/ellas* forms: leí, leíste, leyó, leímos, leísteis, leyeron.

Stem-changing -ir verbs like *dormir*, *morir* (o → ue), *sentir*, *preferir* (e → ie), and *pedir*, *repetir* (e → i) have changes in the *Ud./él/ella* and the *Uds./ellos/ellas* form of the preterite.

dormir: durmió, durmieron
sentir: sintió, sintieron

Some verbs, such as *decir*, *traer*, and *traducir* have irregular stems in the preterite but they share the same endings:

decir: dije, dijiste, dijo, dijimos, dijisteis, dijeron
traer: traje, trajiste, trajo, trajimos, trajisteis, trajeron
traducir: traduje, tradujiste, tradujo, tradujimos, tradujisteis, tradujeron

The following verbs also have irregular stems in the preterite and share the following endings:
-e, -iste, -o, -imos, isteis, -ieron.

tener	estar	saber	poner	andar	poder	venir	hacer
tuv-	estuv-	sup-	pus-	anduv-	pud-	vin-	hic-*

*The Ud./él/ella form is *hizo*.

Más ayuda **realidades.com** ▸ Tutorial

¿Recuerdas?

El verbo *haber* en el pretérito se conjuga *hubo*. Se usa para indicar que algo sucedió en el pasado en un momento específico en el tiempo, no algo que sucedía siempre.

Anoche *hubo* luna llena.

---

6 Un día ocupado

Leer

Escribe la forma correcta del pretérito para completar este informe sobre un día en la vida de dos estudiantes.

Ayer, ellos __1.__ (tener) muchas actividades. Primero, __2.__ (andar) un rato por el parque. Después, sus amigos __3.__ (venir) a la casa de visita. Luego, __4.__ (estar) en la biblioteca e __5.__ (hacer) varias tareas para sus clases. __6.__ (leer) un cuento para la clase de inglés y __7.__ (traducir) algunas frases del español al inglés. Al salir, __8.__ (querer) llamar a Pablo e Isabel pero no __9.__ (poder) porque su teléfono no funcionaba. __10.__ (ir) a un café y __11.__ (pedir) unos pasteles con café. ¡Una manera perfecta de descansar después de un día tan ocupado!

7 Al cine

Hablar

Entrevista a tu compañero(a) sobre la última película que fueron a ver sus amigos(as). Túrnense para hacer preguntas y contestarlas. Usen los siguientes verbos: *ir, estar, andar, dormir, preferir, comenzar, terminar*.

Modelo
ir
¿Qué película fueron a ver?

Más práctica GO

realidades.com | print

A ver si recuerdas with Study Plan ✔
Guided WB pp. 238–241 ✔ ✔
Core WB pp. 105–106 ✔ ✔
Hispanohablantes WB p. 236 ✔

trescientos cuarenta y uno **341**
Capítulo 8

Gramática Repaso

Core Instruction

Resources: Voc. and Gram. Transparency 152
Suggestions: Refer students who are having difficulty with the preterite to the *GramActiva* videos from Level 2 Chapters 5A, 5B and 6A, and to the online tutorial. Have students use three different verbs from the *Gramática* in sentences with third-person singular or plural subjects. Ask volunteers to write their sentences on the board and point out the spellings of the irregular verb forms.

6 Standards: 1.2

Resources: Answer Keys: Student Edition, p. 107
Focus: Reviewing irregular preterite verbs
Common Errors: Students may forget to use irregular preterite verb stems. Model the correct forms as necessary.
Suggestions: Remind students to pay particular attention to spelling, since that is the focus of the activity.

Answers:

1. tuvieron	7. tradujeron
2. anduvieron	8. quisieron
3. vinieron	9. pudieron
4. estuvieron	10. Fueron
5. hicieron	11. pidieron
6. Leyeron	

7 Standards: 1.1

Resources: Answer Keys: Student Edition, p. 107
Focus: Reviewing irregular preterite verb forms
Suggestions: Remind students that they are asking about a film their friends saw and should use the **Uds.** verb forms. Point out they should practice careful pronunciation, since many of the irregular verb forms contain spelling changes.

Answers will vary but should include:
fueron, estuvieron, anduvieron, durmieron, prefirieron, comenzaron, terminaron

✔ASSESSMENT

A ver si recuerdas with Study Plan (online only)

After reviewing the material on these pages, assign the *A ver si recuerdas* Study Plan to evaluate students' mastery of the material. Additional practice is available online.

ENRICH YOUR TEACHING

Teacher-to-Teacher

Ask students to talk about the histories of their family or the family of someone they know. Give them a few minutes to prepare what they plan to say. Encourage them to use verbs with irregular preterite forms: *Mis abuelos vinieron de Italia en 1930. Dejaron todo lo que tenían en Italia y trajeron muy poco con ellos.*

21st Century Skills

Initiative and Self-Direction Direct students to the online tutorials for self-directed review of the grammar topics recycled in this chapter. Students can expand their own learning by reviewing the related English grammar first then proceed to the new Spanish grammar point. Each tutorial is followed by a quick comprehension check.

341

Capítulo 8 Encuentro entre culturas

Standards for Foreign Language Learning: *Capítulo* 8

• To meet the Standards, students will:

Communication

1.1 Interpersonal
• Talk about city sights and their relative positions
• Talk about childhood and conflict resolution
• Talk about travel and favorite films
• Talk about Spanish painter Joaquín Sorolla y Bastida
• Talk about cultural and social interaction and fusion
• Talk about Spanish history, including colonial expansion
• Talk about Quechua music

1.2 Interpretive
• Read about city sights and their relative positions
• Read about conflict resolution
• Read about travel and daily activities
• Read about Spanish painter Joaquín Sorolla y Bastida
• Read and listen to information about cultural and social interaction and fusion
• Read about word families
• Read and listen to information about Spanish history
• Read about Quechua music
• Read a story by Elías Miguel Muñoz
• Read an Aztec legend
• Read about Houston's Museo de Salud y Ciencia
• Read about speech and composition preparation

1.3 Presentational
• Present information orally about travel and city sights
• Write about conflict resolution
• Write and present information orally about cultural and social interaction and fusion
• Write and present orally about Spanish history
• Present information orally about childhood

Culture

2.1 Practices and Perspectives
• Interpret cultural and social interaction and fusion
• Interpret cultural influences in Spanish history
• Interpret cultural perspectives in Quechua music

2.2 Products and Perspectives
• Describe the art of Joaquín Sorolla y Bastida and the fiction of Elías Miguel Muñoz
• Discuss cultural and social interaction and fusion
• Discuss Quechua music
• Discuss indigenous legends
• Discuss Spanish history, including colonial expansion

Connections

3.1 Cross-curricular
• Discuss key facts about visual fine art, legends, fiction, music, and cuisine
• Discuss key facts about history and social studies
• Discuss Houston's Museo de Salud y Ciencia
• Use Language Arts strategies: fact and opinion, speaker's purpose, chronological ordering, skipping and guessing

3.2 Target Culture
• Read a story by Miguel Muñoz and an Aztec legend

Comparisons

4.1 Language
• Compare the Spanish to the English conditional
• Compare Spanish use of the imperfect subjunctive with English if/then sentences
• Compare Spanish words to their English counterparts

▼ Chapter Objectives

Communication
By the end of the chapter you will be able to:
• Listen and read about indigenous cultures
• Talk and write about cultural heritage and fusion of cultures in Spain before 1492
• Present a guided city tour

Culture
You will also be able to:
• Understand the historical context of Spanish missions in California
• Express your opinion about cultural exchanges

You will demonstrate what you know and can do:
• Presentación oral, p. 373
• Presentación escrita, pp. 374–375
• Preparación para el examen, pp. 382–383

You will use:

Vocabulary
  • Buildings
  • The discovery of America
  • Cultural exchanges

Grammar
  • Conditional
  • Imperfect subjunctive
  • Imperfect subjunctive with *si*

Exploración del mundo hispano

Country Connection
Cultural Interaction, European Colonization, Culture and Ethnicity in the United States

Estados Unidos
España
México
Ecuador
Perú
Paraguay
Argentina

realidades.com **GO**

📖 Reference Atlas
▶ Videonovela y actividades
🌎 Mapa global interactivo

342 trescientos cuarenta y dos

La mezquita de Córdoba en España es un ejemplo de fusión cultural.

ENRICH YOUR TEACHING

Using Backward Design
Have students preview the sample performance tasks on *Preparación para el examen*, p. 383, and connect them to the Chapter Objectives. Explain to students that by completing the sample tasks they can self-assess their learning progress.

Mapa global interactivo
Download the *Mapa global interactivo* files for Chapter 8 and preview the activities. Use Activity 1 to travel to Spain. In Activity 2, visit Seville, in Activity 3, Toledo, and in Activity 4, Barcelona. In Activity 5, travel to Buenos Aires, Argentina. In Activity 6, travel the route from Río de la Plata to Paraguay. Activity 7 follows the route of Hernán Cortés. In Activity 8, visit California's historic missions. Activity 9 takes you to the Museo de Antropología in Mexico City.

Arte y cultura | España

Joaquín Sorolla y Bastida (1863–1923) fue un pintor español. Su obra refleja una gran habilidad para capturar los efectos de la luz. En este cuadro de Granada, Sorolla y Bastida captura la majestad de la Alhambra y de la Sierra Nevada usando el contraste entre la luz y la sombra.

• ¿Conoces a otros pintores que sean famosos por su uso de la luz? ¿Quiénes son?

▼ "Granada", (1920), Joaquín Sorolla y Bastida
Museo Sorolla, Madrid, Spain/Bridgeman Art Library.

trescientos cuarenta y tres **343**
Capítulo 8

Standards (cont'd)

4.2 Culture
• Compare cultural fusion in the Spanish-speaking world with that in the United States
• Compare Tex-Mex and Latin American food with traditional fare in the United States
• Compare indigenous influence in Latin America with that in the United States

Communities
5.1 Beyond the School
• Link to Web sites from the Spanish-speaking world
5.2 Lifelong Learner
• Develop an appreciation for legends, fiction, and music

PresentationExpress™
See pp. 338c–338d

Chapter Opener
Core Instruction

Resources: Map Transparencies 14, 18, 20, 22

Suggestions: Introduce students to the theme of the chapter and go over the objectives. Point out that they will improve their ability to communicate on the topic of intermixing cultures. Use the transparencies to locate the countries featured.

Videonovela ¡Pura vida! View this stand-alone storyline video about five young adults in San José, Costa Rica with your class, either online or on DVD.

Arte y cultura

Standards: 1.1, 1.2, 2.2, 3.1
Resources: Fine Art Transparencies with Teacher's Guide, p. 65
Suggestions: After students read the information, ask comprehension questions.

DIFFERENTIATED INSTRUCTION

Digital resources such as the *Interactive Whiteboards* activity banks, *Videomodelos*, additional *Online Activities*, *Study Plans*, automatically graded *Leveled Workbook*, animated *Grammar Tutorials*, *Flashcards*, and *Vocabulary and Grammar Videos* will help you reach students of different ability levels and learning styles.

STUDENTS NEEDING EXTRA HELP
Guided Practice Activities
• Flashcards, pp. 242–246, 253–256
• Vocabulary Check, pp. 247–250, 257–260
• Grammar, pp. 251–252, 261–264

HERITAGE LEARNERS
Realidades para hispanohablantes
• Chapter Opener, pp. 236–237
• A primera vista, pp. 238–239, 248–249
• Manos a la obra, pp. 240–247, 250–257
• ¡Adelante!, pp. 258–263
• Repaso del capítulo, pp. 264–267

ADVANCED/PRE-AP*
Pre-AP* Resource Book,
• pp. 159–161
Communications Workbook
• Integrated Performance Assessment, p. 209

Vocabulario en contexto

A primera vista 1 | 🔊 | 🖥️ | ▼ **Objectives**

▶ **Read, listen to, and understand information about**
• **interaction between cultures**
• **fusion of different cultures in Spain before 1492**

Core Instruction

Standards: 1.1, 1.2, 2.2, 3.1, 5.1

Resources: Teacher's Resource Book: Input Script, p. 184, Clip Art, pp. 202–209, Audio Script, p. 188; Voc. and Gram. Transparencies 153–154; Audio Program DVD: Cap. 8, Track 1

🌐 **Mapa global interactivo, Actividad 1**

Explore famous historic sites around Spain.

Focus: Presenting new vocabulary and using grammar lexically in context

Suggestions: Show *Vocabulary and Grammar Transparencies* 153 and 154. Say the names of visualized vocabulary items, have students repeat, and ask volunteers to point to the appropriate image on the transparency. For non-visualized vocabulary such as *asimilaron, maravilla,* and *anteriormente,* use explanation, circumlocution, synonyms, antonyms, or gestures along with exaggerated intonation to clarify meaning: *Anteriormente significa antes. El Gran Cañón es una maravilla natural. La Alhambra en Granada es una maravilla de la arquitectura.* Ask students to point out cognates such as *influencia* and *invadieron* and challenge them to invent Spanish definitions for the words.

BELLRINGER REVIEW

As a class, have the students brainstorm a time line representing five important dates in U.S. history.

Block Schedule

School Year Timeline: Divide the class into groups of three. Have them construct a timeline for the school year placing six significant events on it. Have them provide a brief description as to what happened on each date. Use the timeline on pp. 344–345 as a model.

Vocabulario en contexto 🌐

"Mis compañeros y yo fuimos de viaje a España. Visitamos las ciudades de Córdoba, Granada y Sevilla, y aprendimos mucho sobre la historia. Es interesante que hayan vivido allí **judíos, musulmanes** y **cristianos.** La influencia de cada cultura se puede ver en la **arquitectura** de los edificios y otras construcciones. ¡La mezcla de culturas es fascinante!"

el acueducto

el arc[o]

Acueducto de Segovia

Invasión árabe

La Mezquita de Córdoba

Siglo III a.C. - V d.C.[1]	711	785
El imperio romano dominaba la península. Los romanos trajeron a España la unidad política, vías (calles), acueductos y puentes, y la religión cristiana.	Los árabes vinieron de África, invadieron España y conquistaron gran parte de la península. La ocuparon por casi 800 años.	Los árabes trajeron la religión musulmana a España. Durante la conquista, se construyeron impresionantes mezquitas, como la de Córdoba.

[1] a.C. (*antes de Cristo*) and d.C. (*después de Cristo*) are equivalent to B.C. and A.D. in English.

344 **trescientos cuarenta y cuatro**
A primera vista 1

DIFFERENTIATED INSTRUCTION

Students with Learning Difficulties

Ask students to identify the main idea in each paragraph below the timeline on pp. 344 and 345. Have them copy this main idea onto a card. Direct students to mix the cards, and then put the events back into chronological order.

Advanced Learners

Have students draw on their learning from social studies classes and tell what other countries besides Spain were influenced by the Roman Empire.

▼1 Estilos y culturas | 🔊

Escuchar

Escucha lo que dicen los jóvenes y señala la fotografía que corresponda al lugar del que hablan.

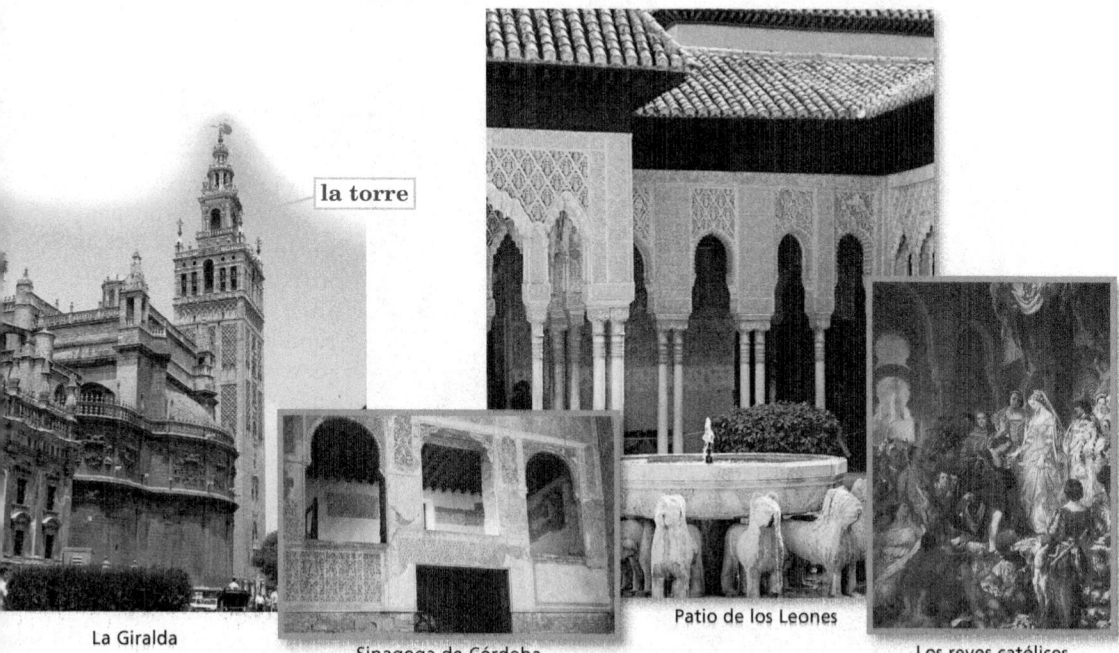

la torre

La Giralda

Sinagoga de Córdoba

Patio de los Leones

Los reyes católicos

Ferdinand and Isabella, Eugenio Deveria (1808-1865) Art Resource, NY.

1248	1315	1377	1492
Cuando los cristianos reconquistaron Sevilla, construyeron la Catedral de Sevilla donde anteriormente había una mezquita musulmana. La única parte de la construcción original que existe todavía es la torre, que se llama la Giralda.	Se construyó la sinagoga de Córdoba, en donde se observa cómo los judíos asimilaron el arte árabe y lo combinaron con sus propias decoraciones.	Los cristianos continuaron la Reconquista. Granada fue la última ciudad que ocuparon los árabes. Al final de esta época, se construyó el Patio de los Leones en la Alhambra, en Granada, que es una maravilla.	Los cristianos expulsaron a los árabes de España. Isabel de Castilla y Fernando de Aragón, "los reyes católicos", gobernaron España. Cristóbal Colón llegó a América.

trescientos cuarenta y cinco **345**
Capítulo 8

1 Standards: 1.2

Resources: Voc. and Gram. Transparencies 153–154; Teacher's Resource Book: Audio Script, p. 188; Audio Program DVD: Cap. 8, Track 2; Answer Keys: Student Edition, p. 108

Focus: Practicing listening comprehension of new vocabulary

Suggestions: Before playing the audio or reading aloud the text, allow students to read over the information on pp. 344–345. Remind them to use familiar key words to help them comprehend what they hear. Allow them to listen more than once.

Answers:
1. el acueducto
2. Sevilla
3. Granada
4. Córdoba, la sinagoga
5. el acueducto
6. Fernando e Isabel de Castilla
7. el mapa de España

ENRICH YOUR TEACHING

Culture Note

The ***Mezquita de Córdoba*** was first built by Abd al-Rahman I in 785 A.D. on the site of the Visigoth Christian Church of St. Vincent, which had replaced a Roman pagan temple. In the sixteenth century, the mosque was converted to a cathedral and its tower was constructed directly over the Islamic Minaret.

21st Century Skills

Information Literacy Have students research Web sites in Spanish that give more information about the historical sites on pp. 344–345. What keywords will they use in their search? How can they decide which Web sites will give them reliable and accurate information? Are there other civilizations they have studied in other classes that may help them understand the fusion of cultures in Spain?

Vocabulario en contexto

Core Instruction

Standards: 1.1, 1.2, 2.1, 2.2, 3.1

Resources: Teacher's Resource Book: Input Script, p. 185, Clip Art, pp. 202–209, Audio Script, pp. 188–189; Voc. and Gram. Transparencies 155–156; Audio Program DVD: Cap. 8, Tracks 3–4

🌐 **Mapa global interactivo, Actividad 2**
Visit famous sites in Seville, Spain.

Focus: Extending presentation of vocabulary and grammar

Suggestions:

Pre-reading: Ask a volunteer to read aloud the main title of the selection, ***Una gran mezcla de culturas.*** To help students understand the reading, say: *Mira las dos páginas. Estos artículos se tratan de tres ciudades españolas. ¿Cuáles son?*

Reading: Allow students time to read the selections silently first. Then play the audio or read the text, with students reading along as they listen. Allow them to listen more than once. Another option is to have students listen and read along first, then have volunteers take turns reading the articles aloud in chunks.

Post-reading: Check comprehension by asking questions. See the Input Scripts in the *Teacher's Resource Book* for specific questions.

▼ 2 Standards: 1.3

Focus: Writing to demonstrate reading comprehension of new vocabulary

Suggestions: Invite students who have appropriate background knowledge to write about places other than those mentioned in the articles.

Answers will vary.

Pre-AP* Support

- **Learning Objective:** Interpersonal Writing
- **Activity:** Have students write an e-mail to a friend in which they choose a Spanish city they want to visit (Sevilla, Toledo, Barcelona or another one). Have them say why they want to visit the city and what they want to see there, making sure they incorporate at least five of the new vocabulary words in their message. Students should ask their friend at least one question about which city they want to visit.
- ***Pre-AP* Resource Book:** Comprehensive guide to Pre-AP* vocabulary skill development, pp. 51–57

España
Una gran mezcla de culturas

El Alcázar Real

balcón

rejas

Sevilla 🌐

En la provincia de Andalucía y su capital, Sevilla, los romanos y los árabes, entre otros grupos, dejaron su huella en la arquitectura. También la dejaron en la gente y en el idioma, al que se asimilaron numerosas palabras árabes. En Sevilla, el Alcázar Real es una construcción de estilo mudéjar, una mezcla de la influencia cristiana y del islam. Tiene arcos con maravillosas decoraciones de azulejos. En el barrio de Triana, muchas de las casas tienen balcones adornados con hermosas rejas de hierro. El viejo barrio de Santa Cruz fue un barrio judío.

▼ 2 Un viaje por España

Escribir

Imagina que tú y tus compañeros van a viajar a España. Escribe tres lugares que te gustaría conocer. Explica por qué te gustaría conocerlos.

346 trescientos cuarenta y seis
A primera vista 1

DIFFERENTIATED INSTRUCTION

Students with Learning Difficulties

Provide students with a graphic organizer to help support understanding of the passages on pp. 346 and 347. Have students create three columns on a piece of paper: *ciudad, culturas, ejemplo de la mezcla de culturas.* Then have them reread the selection to fill in the chart.

Students with Special Needs

Help visually impaired students experience the architecture of the cities portrayed in the photographs on pp. 346 and 347. Assist them in tracing shapes and structures, such as the arches in Sevilla or the tower in Toledo.

Barcelona 🌐

Un ejemplo de cómo se integran las culturas en la época moderna es la ciudad de Barcelona, capital de Cataluña. Por estar cerca de Francia, la población de Cataluña tiene varias formas de expresión de influencia francesa. Una es el idioma catalán, que ha tomado muchas palabras del francés.

Señales en catalán y español

Toledo 🌐

La ciudad de Toledo es ejemplo de la colaboración entre diferentes grupos étnicos. En 1085, el rey Alfonso VI reunió en Toledo a los más importantes científicos y filósofos árabes, judíos y cristianos de la época. En este período se fundó la famosa Escuela de Traductores de Toledo. En ella se traducían al latín los libros que tenían gran demanda en Europa. Más tarde, en el siglo XIII, la ciudad fue el centro cultural de España y de toda Europa.

Otra es la comida, con platos como la butifarra, similar al "saucisson"[1] francés.

[1] cold sausage

▼3 Las culturas de una ciudad 💬👥

Hablar

Conversa con un(a) compañero(a) sobre las diferentes culturas que se ven hoy o que se veían en el pasado en las ciudades de estas páginas.

Modelo

En Toledo había muchas culturas y grupos étnicos que se integraron.

▼4 Construcciones famosas

Escribir

Haz una tabla con tres columnas. Escribe una lista de seis construcciones sobre las que has leído. Di dónde están, cuándo se construyeron y si las construyeron los árabes, los judíos o los cristianos.

Más práctica GO	realidades.com | print
Instant Check	✔
Guided WB pp. 242–250	✔ ✔
Core WB pp. 107–108	✔ ✔
Comm. WB p. 110	✔ ✔
Hispanohablantes WB pp. 238–239	✔

trescientos cuarenta y siete 347
Capítulo 8

▼3 Standards: 1.1

Focus: Demonstrating reading comprehension via discussion

🌐 **Mapa global interactivo, Actividad 3**
Visit famous sites in Toledo, Spain.

Suggestions: Encourage students to paraphrase information about the three cities, rather than reciting parts of the text verbatim. Point out that other places they discuss do not have to be in Spain. Students can discuss any place in which there is a variety of cultures.

Answers will vary.

🌐 **Mapa global interactivo, Actividad 4**
Visit famous sites in Barcelona, Spain.

▼4 Standards: 1.3

Resources: Answer Keys: Student Edition, p. 108

Focus: Demonstrating reading comprehension via note-taking

Suggestions: On the board, create a three-column chart. Label the columns *la construcción, el lugar,* and *la cultura.*

Answers will vary. Students should choose from among the following structures for their lists:

las vías, los puentes, los acueductos
la mezquita de Córdoba
la Giralda de Sevilla
la sinagoga de Córdoba
la Alhambra de Granada
los balcones de Sevilla
la Escuela de Traductores de Toledo

Chapter Project

Give students copies of the Chapter Project outline and rubric from the *Teacher's Resource Book*. Explain the task to them, and have them perform Step 1. (For more information, see p. 338-b.)

✓ ASSESSMENT

Prueba: Comprensión del vocabulario 1
• Prueba 8-1: pp. 171–172

ENRICH YOUR TEACHING

Teacher-to-Teacher

Whenever students record information—while reading, during class discussions, when preparing for tests—encourage them to organize thoughts and information graphically. Help them become familiar with the various types of graphic organizers by regularly modeling their use and working with a variety of them in your teaching.

21st Century Skills

Critical Thinking and Problem Solving
Have students find out more information about the fusion of different cultures in one of the cities mentioned in the reading during a specific period (the XIII century, the last decade). Have students report their findings to the class.

347

▶ Discuss and write about the cities of Toledo, Spain and Buenos Aires, Argentina
▶ Write about the history of Spain
▶ Talk about culture and architecture

Vocabulario en uso

5 Standards: 1.2, 3.1

Resources: Answer Keys: Student Edition, p. 109

Focus: Demonstrating comprehension of new vocabulary

Suggestions: Tell students to complete the activity in three steps: 1. briefly read the word bank and the paragraph, 2. write the answers, 3. read the completed paragraph again.

Answers:
1. unidad
2. ocuparon
3. musulmanes
4. población
5. étnicos
6. judíos
7. maravillas
8. reconquistó
9. única
10. se integraron

6 Standards: 1.3, 2.2

Focus: Practicing new vocabulary via writing

Suggestions: Remind students to present their descriptions of the photo in a logical way. Suggest that they start with the foreground, continue with the background, and save their impressions for last.

Answers will vary.

▼5 ¡Bienvenido a Toledo! |

Leer • Hablar

Completa la siguiente información con las palabras del recuadro. Después, habla con otro(a) compañero(a) y pregúntale si le gustaría visitar Toledo y por qué.

ocuparon	musulmanes	reconquistó	población	étnicos
judíos	maravillas	única	se integraron	unidad

Durante siglos, la ciudad de Toledo ha mantenido su __1.__ mientras recibía la influencia de muchas culturas y religiones. Los romanos entraron en la ciudad en 193 A.C. y la __2.__ . Siglos después, los __3.__ que vinieron desde el sur de España y desde África conquistaron Toledo. Durante la Edad Media (*Middle Ages*), que se extendió aproximadamente desde el año 476 al 1492, Toledo fue un centro intelectual y artístico, con una gran __4.__ formada por varios grupos __5.__ , como musulmanes, __6.__ y cristianos. El palacio musulmán, llamado El Alcázar, originalmente restaurado (*restored*) en el siglo XIII, fue modificado en 1535 como residencia de Carlos V. Es una de las verdaderas __7.__ de la ciudad. Más adelante, durante la Reconquista, el rey Alfonso VI __8.__ la ciudad en 1085 y volvieron a gobernar los reyes cristianos. Toledo no es la __9.__ ciudad de España donde __10.__ muchas culturas y religiones, pero es uno de los mejores ejemplos.

▼6 Un patio español |

Escribir

Observa la foto de un patio en España. Luego, escribe una descripción de lo que ves y tus impresiones. Incluye las palabras siguientes.

azulejos	rejas	influencia
balcón	arquitectura	arco
construcción	maravilloso(a)	musulmán

Patio antiguo, España

DIFFERENTIATED INSTRUCTION

Students with Learning Difficulties

Before students complete *Actividad 5*, have them separate the word choices into the following categories: people, things, descriptions, and actions. As students read through the paragraph, assist them in choosing the correct word by asking what type of word is missing.

Advanced Learners/Pre-AP*

Ask students to write their own fill-in-the-blank vocabulary exercises. These can either be in paragraph form or presented as separate sentences. Have students number each blank and make an answer sheet. Have them exchange their work with a partner, complete each other's exercises, and check their answers together.

▼7 Una breve historia de España |

Leer • Hablar

Para entender bien las culturas de hoy, es importante que conozcas la historia de otros países. Lee la línea cronológica de esta página. Con otro(a) estudiante, habla de la historia de España. Trata de usar todos los verbos siguientes.

invadir	ocupar	asimilarse	llegar	contribuir
reconquistar	gobernar	expulsar	integrarse	dominar

▶ Modelo

A —¿Qué pasó en el año 1085?
B —Los cristianos reconquistaron Toledo.

218 a.C.
Romanos: Conquista de España, construcción de puentes y acueductos

711
Llegada de los musulmanes del África; contribuciones en las matemáticas, las ciencias, el papel, los números que usamos hoy; integración de muchos grupos étnicos en España

1085
Cristianos: reconquista de Toledo

1236
Musulmanes: gobiernan desde La Alhambra de Granada

1492
Reyes Católicos: reconquista y ocupación de Granada; expulsión del último rey musulmán, Boabdil; expulsión de los judíos de España

▼ Ampliación del lenguaje

Palabras árabes

Durante los ochocientos años en que los árabes estuvieron en España, muchas palabras del árabe pasaron a formar parte del español. Muchas de ellas entraron también en otros idiomas de Europa, incluyendo el inglés. Lee las palabras de la tabla y escoge las que mejor completan las frases.

Palabras de origen árabe	
alcázar	¡hola!
algodón	jarabe
alfombra	limón
barrio	mezquita
baño	naranja
café	¡ojalá!
chisme	taza
guitarra	

1. En el _____ donde vivo hay una _____ adonde van los musulmanes.

2. El músico estaba tocando su _____ , pero cuando me vio me saludó diciendo " _____ ".

3. En mi casa tenemos una _____ en el piso que está hecha de _____ .

4. Todas las mañanas, mi mamá bebe una _____ de _____ y un jugo de _____ .

Practice and Communicate 8

7 Standards: 1.1, 1.2, 1.3

Focus: Practicing new vocabulary through reading and discussion

Recycle: Preterite tense verb forms, question formation

Suggestions: Once students have read and discussed the timeline together, open the question-and-answer session up to the whole class.

Answers will vary.

Ampliación del lenguaje
Core Instruction

Standards: 1.2, 3.1

Resources: Answer Keys: Student Edition, p. 109

Focus: Understanding words with Arabic roots

Suggestions: First, address any comprehension issues students may have with the words in the table. Then, ask volunteers to supply definitions for the words.

Answers:

1. **barrio; mezquita**
2. **guitarra; ¡hola!**
3. **alfombra; algodón**
4. **taza; café; naranja**

Extension: Have students work in small groups and add to the list of words with Arabic roots. They can first guess at words they think come from Arabic and then check their guesses in a Spanish dictionary. Show them where to find the basic etymological information (just after the pronunciation) that most unabridged dictionaries provide.

ENRICH YOUR TEACHING

Culture Note

King Boabdil, known as the Boy King or *el Rey Chico,* was the last Islamic ruler of Granada. In 1492, Fernando and Isabel raised the flags of Christian Spain above the Alhambra. In the treaty of surrender, King Boabdil was sent into exile in the countryside along with his mother, Ayesha. Legend has it that as he turned back to look at the city, his mother chastised him severely. Seven years later the treaties were abrogated by Fernando and Isabel. Boabdil fled to Morocco, where he died in poverty.

349

8 Standards: 1.1, 1.2, 2.1, 3.1, 4.2, 5.2

Resources: Answer Keys: Student Edition, p. 109
Mapa global interactivo, Actividad 5
Travel to Buenos Aires, Argentina.

Focus: Practicing new vocabulary and structures through reading and response

Suggestions: First, have students silently read the article and answer questions 1–2 on their own. Invite them to share their answers to these questions in their small groups before they complete the chart for item 3.

Answers:
1. Answers to the first part will vary, but might include: los italianos, ingleses, judíos, rusos, árabes y bolivianos.
2. Es bueno porque hace que una ciudad sea multi-cultural y cosmopolita.
3. Answers will vary.

▼8 Mi Buenos Aires querido | 👥 | 🌐 _____

Leer • Escribir • Hablar

¿Has oído alguna vez hablar de la ciudad de Buenos Aires y su origen?
Lee el siguiente artículo sobre Buenos Aires y contesta las preguntas.

Conexiones | **Las ciencias sociales**

Buenos Aires

Desde que se fundó Buenos Aires en 1536, allí se han mezclado distintas culturas, religiones y tradiciones. Aunque el idioma oficial de Argentina es el español, en la ciudad hay barrios en los que a veces se escucha hablar el italiano, el inglés, el yiddish, el ruso o el árabe y donde se pueden ver mezquitas, sinagogas e iglesias. Anteriormente, la mayoría de los inmigrantes que llegaban a Buenos Aires venían de Europa, pero en los últimos tiempos la mayoría ha llegado de otros países latinoamericanos, sobre todo de Bolivia. Esta inmigración de diferentes grupos étnicos ha hecho de Buenos Aires una ciudad multicultural y cosmopolita. En algunos casos los inmigrantes se han asimilado a la manera de vivir del lugar. Por ejemplo, aunque muchos hablan sus propios idiomas, la mayoría habla también español.

También puedes encontrar que en un mismo barrio se practican las religiones judía, cristiana y musulmana, y se comen platos que vienen de muchos lugares, como la pasta de Italia o los guisos (stews) de España.

Buenos Aires no es la única ciudad de América del Sur con esta mezcla maravillosa de culturas pero es una de las más conocidas por su variedad.

1. ¿Cuáles son algunos de los inmigrantes y grupos étnicos que se establecieron en Buenos Aires?

2. ¿Por qué es bueno que muchas personas de diferentes culturas vivan en una misma ciudad?

3. Trabaja con tres estudiantes. Copien esta tabla, complétenla y comparen su ciudad o comunidad con la ciudad de Buenos Aires.

	Buenos Aires	Mi ciudad / comunidad
¿Dónde está?		
¿Cuál es el idioma oficial?		
¿Qué religiones se practican?		
¿Hay muchos inmigrantes?		
¿De dónde son?		

350 **trescientos cincuenta**
Manos a la obra 1

DIFFERENTIATED INSTRUCTION

Heritage Language Learners
After students have completed the table on p. 350 with reference to Buenos Aires and their own communities, ask them to answer the same questions with reference to their heritage country in general. What are some of the aspects of its culture?

Students with Learning Difficulties
Help students identify key words or phrases in each of the questions on p. 350. Instruct them to locate these words or phrases in the passage. Then have them reread around the key word or phrase to find the answer.

▼9 La cultura en la arquitectura

Leer • Escribir

Puedes aprender sobre otras culturas al observar su arte y su arquitectura. Mira el anuncio y contesta las preguntas.

1. ¿Sobre qué es la exposición *(exhibit)*?

2. ¿De dónde son los arquitectos? ¿Son todos de la misma cultura étnica?

3. ¿Crees que las construcciones que se presentan en la exposición van a ser similares? ¿Por qué? ¿Por qué no?

4. Imagina que puedes dejar una huella en tu comunidad. ¿Qué contribución te gustaría hacer? Haz un folleto como éste que la represente.

Museo Regional del Sur y Museo Histórico Arqueológico
presentan

HUELLAS DE IDENTIDAD:
ASIMILACIÓN CULTURAL EN LA ARQUITECTURA CHILENA

23 de enero–12 de mayo

▸ 5 arquitectos de la época moderna
▸ diversas influencias étnicas
▸ construcciones únicas

Avenida de la Cruz, no. 32
Valparaíso

▼10 Y tú, ¿qué dices? | (Talk!)

Escribir • Hablar

1. ¿Qué cultura(s) representas tú? ¿De dónde eran tus abuelos y bisabuelos *(great-grandparents)*? ¿Qué idioma(s) hablaban? ¿Lo(s) siguen hablando? ¿Por qué?

2. ¿Qué culturas han contribuido a la cultura de los Estados Unidos? ¿Qué huellas han dejado?

3. ¿Alguna vez has tenido que integrarte a una nueva cultura o grupo? ¿Cuándo? ¿Cómo te sentiste? ¿Qué diferencias notaste entre tu manera de ser y la de ellos?

4. Imagina que hay un nuevo estudiante de otro país en tu clase. Di al menos cinco cosas que puedes hacer para ayudarle a integrarse.

trescientos cincuenta y uno 351
Capítulo 8

BELLRINGER REVIEW

Prepare students for the presentation of the conditional tense in the *Gramática* by briefly reviewing the formation of the future tense.

Gramática

Core Instruction

Standards: 4.1

Resources: Voc. and Gram. Transparency 157

INTERACTIVE WHITEBOARD
Grammar Activities 8-1

Suggestions: Ask students to practice the conditional tense by saying what they would do if the principal suddenly announced that school was canceled for the rest of the day.

11

Standards: 1.2

Resources: Answer Keys: Student Edition, p. 110

Focus: Practicing the conditional in a cloze exercise

Suggestions: Remind students to look over the entire paragraph first in order to get an idea of its meaning.

Common Errors: Students will often pronounce conditional tense forms of *querer* exactly like imperfect tense forms. Model the difference in sound between the rolled intervocalic *rr* in the conditional tense and the single *r* in the imperfect tense.

Answers:

1. sería
2. comenzaría
3. irían
4. contribuirían
5. podrían
6. sabrían
7. podrían
8. ayudarían
9. darían

Block Schedule

Divide students into pairs. Give each group two cubes. Have them write six infinitives from the list on p. 352 on one cube and six subject pronouns on the second. Each student "rolls the dice" and gives the conditional for the subjects/verbs on the cube.

Gramática

▸ Write about things you would do
▸ Talk about activities you would do in a new community

El condicional

You use the conditional in Spanish to express what a person *would do* or what a situation *would be like*.

> Me gustaría leer un libro sobre el budismo.   Yo le pediría ese libro a Tomás.

• As with the future tense, you form the conditional by adding the endings to the infinitive. The conditional endings are the same for all verbs. Here are the conditional forms of *hablar, ser,* and *ir*.

hablar		ser		ir	
hablaría	hablaríamos	sería	seríamos	iría	iríamos
hablarías	hablaríais	serías	seríais	irías	iríais
hablaría	hablarían	sería	serían	iría	irían

• All verbs that are irregular in the future tense have the same irregular stems in the conditional.

decir	dir-	poder	podr-	saber	sabr-	tener	tendr-
haber	habr-	poner	pondr-	salir	saldr-	querer	querr-
hacer	har-	componer	compondr-	venir	vendr-	contener	contendr-

Más ayuda   **realidades.com**   ▸ *Canción de hip hop*   ▸ Tutorials

▼11 La Ruta Quetzal

Leer

El año pasado tu amiga participó en la Ruta Quetzal, un viaje que muchos jóvenes hacen por España y América Latina. Tú quieres hacer el viaje el año próximo, y ella te cuenta cómo sería. Completa el párrafo con el condicional del verbo apropiado.

¿Te interesa participar en la Ruta Quetzal? Esta experiencia __1.__ (tener / ser) fantástica para ti. El viaje __2.__ (ocupar / comenzar) en España. Para decidir quiénes __3.__ (ir / poder), tú y los otros estudiantes __4.__ (contribuir / salir) ideas sobre los lugares que se __5.__ (fundar / poder) visitar. Al terminar la experiencia, Uds. __6.__ (saber / fundar) mucho más sobre la integración de la cultura española con la americana y __7.__ (poner / poder) apreciar más las dos culturas. Cuando yo fui, mis padres me dijeron que me __8.__ (ayudar / preferir) a juntar dinero. ¿Te __9.__ (saber / dar) dinero tus padres? ¡No importa! Tienes que ir.

DIFFERENTIATED INSTRUCTION

Heritage Language Learners

Ask students to model speech in the conditional tense. Ask them to speculate on what their life would be like if they were living in a different country. They might focus on their heritage country or another country with which they are familiar.

Advanced Learners

Have students write a paragraph telling what their daily routine would be if they lived in a place very unlike where they are. If you live in a city, have them tell what their routines would be if they lived in the countryside, or vice versa.

▼12 ¡Ganamos! |

Hablar

Tu familia participa en un concurso para ganar una casa que se construiría según el estilo musulmán. Como a tu mamá le encanta este tipo de arquitectura, ella se imagina cómo sería. Habla con otro(a) estudiante para describir su nueva casa. Usen elementos de cada columna.

Modelo
Mi mamá tendría una ventana con un balcón.

Yo	tener	balcón
Nosotros	poner	rejas
Mis hermanos	construir	azulejos
Mi hermano(a)	gustar	flores
Mi mamá (o papá)	querer	fuente
Mis padres	pedir	arcos
¡Respuesta personal!	hacer	torre
	preferir	patio
	¡Respuesta personal!	jardín
		¡Respuesta personal!

▼13 No sabía que en . . . |

Hablar

Piensa en una ciudad que visitaste y en las cosas que encontraste que no te habías imaginado. Escoge entre las cuatro columnas para decir tus frases a un(a) compañero(a).

Modelo
No me había dado cuenta de que vería grupos étnicos tan diferentes.

no podía creer que	haber	cosas tan . . .	divertido
no sabía que	encontrar	grupos étnicos tan . . .	interesante
no me di cuenta de que	ver	construcciones tan . . .	alto
nunca pensé que	comer	la influencia de . . .	impresionante
¡Respuesta personal!	escuchar	música tan . . .	diferente
	visitar	comida tan . . .	similar
	hacer	puntos de interés tan . . .	maravilloso
	¡Respuesta personal!	personas tan . . .	único
		¡Respuesta personal!	¡Respuesta personal!

---

12 Standards: 1.1

Resources: Answer Keys: Student Edition, p. 111

Focus: Practicing the conditional tense in a guided conversation

Suggestions: Point out to students that for the *respuesta personal,* they should use a verb of their own choosing that is different from the rest of those in the chart.

Answers will vary. Students will choose from among the following verb forms:

**tendría/tendríamos/tendrían
pondría/pondríamos/pondrían
construiría/construiríamos/construirían
gustaría/gustarían
querría/querríamos/querrían
pediría/pediríamos/pedirían
haría/haríamos/harían
preferiría/preferiríamos/preferirían**

---

13 Standards: 1.1

Resources: Answer Keys: Student Edition, p. 111

Focus: Practicing the conditional tense in a guided conversation

Suggestions: Remind students to make the adjectives in the fourth column agree in number and gender with the nouns they modify.

Answers will vary. Students will use the following verb forms:

habría	**escucharía**
encontraría	**visitaría**
vería	**haría**
comería	

Pre-AP* Support

- **Learning Objective:** Presentational Writing
- **Activity:** Using *Actividad* 11 as a model, have students write a similar description of a nearby place of interest or well-known historical site. Include a picture, if possible. Share the description with classmates or display in the classroom.
- *Pre-AP* Resource Book:* Comprehensive guide to Pre-AP* writing skill development, pp. 27–38

Chapter Project

Students can perform Step 2 at this point. Be sure they understand your corrections and suggestions. (For more information, see p. 338-b.)

ENRICH YOUR TEACHING

Teacher-to-Teacher

Invite students to use the conditional tense to write a description of the school of their dreams. Ask guiding questions as necessary. For example: *¿Cómo serían las aulas? ¿Qué cursos habría? ¿Cómo serían los profesores? ¿Qué harías durante un día típico? ¿En qué consistirían los almuerzos?* Invite students to share and discuss their completed descriptions.

14 Standards: 1.1

Resources: Answer Keys: Student Edition, p. 112

Focus: Practicing the conditional tense via guided dialogues

Suggestions: Ask students to complete the *Actividad* twice, switching roles. Student B's answers should be different each time.

Answers will vary. Students will use the following verb forms:

1. Viviría
2. podría
3. Sería
4. Tendría
5. encontraría
6. debería

15 Standards: 1.1, 1.3

Focus: Practicing the conditional tense

Suggestions: If students have difficulty thinking of questions, ask them to consider things they like to do, list them, and use the list as a source of ideas for questions.

Answers will vary.

▼14 Conoce nuestra comunidad |

Hablar

Imagina que un(a) estudiante de otro país te hace preguntas para informarse sobre tu comunidad. Trabaja con otro(a) estudiante para hacer los papeles de estudiante y estudiante extranjero(a). Usen el condicional.

▶ Modelo

¿Qué *(tener)* que ponerme para ir a la escuela?
A —¿Qué <u>tendría</u> que ponerme para ir a la escuela?
B —<u>Podrías llevar jeans y una camiseta.</u>

Estudiante A

1. ¿*(Vivir)* en un barrio con muchos o pocos grupos étnicos?
2. ¿A qué lugares *(poder)* ir para ver la vida típica de los jóvenes en tu comunidad?
3. ¿*(Ser)* fácil o difícil asimilarme en tu escuela?
4. ¿*(Tener)* que hablar inglés todo el tiempo?
5. ¿Qué religiones diferentes *(encontrar)*?
6. ¿Qué más *(deber)* hacer para integrarme a la nueva cultura?

Estudiante B

¡Respuesta personal!

▼15 En tu comunidad |

Pensar • Escribir • Hablar

❶ Imagina que acabas de mudarte a otro estado y quieres aprender más sobre tu nueva comunidad. Haz una lista de preguntas que le harías a un(a) joven que vive en esa comunidad.

Modelo
¿Adónde podría ir para encontrar jóvenes de mi edad?
¿Cuál es el equipo de deportes más popular?
¿Cuál es el restaurante más popular entre los jóvenes?

❷ Trabaja con un grupo para escoger un mínimo de seis preguntas. Contesten las preguntas y usen las respuestas para escribir un breve párrafo en el cual describen su comunidad.

Modelo
Si quieres conocer a jóvenes de tu edad, podrías ir a la plaza por la tarde porque allí van muchos chicos después de la escuela.

Plaza Mayor en Antigua, Guatemala

DIFFERENTIATED INSTRUCTION

Heritage Language Learners

Ask students to comment on the musical traditions of their heritage country. Phrase questions so that they may be answered using the conditional tense. You might ask what kinds of instruments one would see, what kinds of sounds one would hear, or what kinds of locations one could visit to listen to music.

Multiple Intelligences

Musical/Rhythmic: Ask students who play a musical instrument to bring their instruments to share with the group. Ask them to research and discuss the history of their instruments, and the cultures in which they are prevalent. Have students play a short selection.

▼16 La música llegó por España

Leer • Hablar

Durante la conquista árabe, España se convirtió en la puerta por donde entraban a Europa las nuevas ideas y descubrimientos.

laúd

Conexiones | La música

Durante la época en que los árabes ocuparon España, Europa recibió muchos instrumentos y conceptos musicales de ese pueblo.

Los árabes fundaron escuelas de música en España. Instrumentos musicales como la guitarra, el órgano y el laúd *(lute)* no se conocían en Europa hasta que los árabes los llevaron a España. Pero quizás la contribución más importante fue el concepto de armonía, que cambió la historia de la música europea.

• ¿Por qué crees que se dice que España era la puerta por donde entraban las nuevas ideas a Europa?

• ¿Cuáles fueron las contribuciones árabes a la música europea?

Fondo Cultural | España • Paraguay

El arpa paraguaya nació cuando se mezclaron dos culturas, la española y la guaraní, en el territorio que sería Paraguay. El arpa es originaria de Egipto y es uno de los instrumentos más antiguos que se conocen. Los exploradores españoles que viajaron por el Río de la Plata en 1526 fueron acompañados de un hombre que tocaba el arpa. Los guaraníes, que amaban la música, adoptaron el arpa, la cambiaron a su manera y la hicieron parte de su vida diaria. El resultado fue maravilloso: un instrumento ligero hecho de madera *(wood)* americana, y frecuentemente, con cuerdas *(strings)* de colores diferentes.

Los paraguayos de hoy enseñan a sus niños a tocar con una técnica propia que pasa de padres a hijos. La música que ha resultado de este instrumento, que llegó con los españoles y que ha sido integrada en la cultura indígena, es muy especial y bella.

• ¿Qué contribuyó España a la música paraguaya? ¿Cómo la han asimilado los guaraníes a su cultura?

• ¿Puedes nombrar un instrumento u otra expresión artística en los Estados Unidos que haya tenido su origen en otra cultura?

Más práctica (GO)

realidades.com | print

Instant Check	✔	
Guided WB pp. 251–252	✔	✔
Core WB pp. 109–111	✔	✔
Comm. WB pp. 107, 111–112	✔	✔
Hispanohablantes WB pp. 240–247		✔

trescientos cincuenta y cinco 355
Capítulo 8

▼16 Standards: 1.1, 1.2, 2.1, 3.1

Resources: Answer Keys: Student Edition, p. 112

Focus: Practicing new vocabulary and structures via reading and response

Suggestions: Have students read the information on their own first, then discuss the questions with a partner. Invite partners to share their responses with the class.

Answers:

• Se dice esto porque España era el país que recibió la mayor cantidad de influencias importantes del mundo árabe.

• Los árabes contribuyeron con instrumentos musicales como la guitarra, el órgano y el laúd. La contribución más importante fue el concepto de armonía.

Fondo cultural

Standards: 1.1, 1.2, 2.1, 2.2, 3.1, 5.2

Suggestions: After students have read the information, ask comprehension questions. For example: *¿Puedes nombrar a un pueblo indígena que vive en Paraguay? (los guaraníes) ¿Qué pasó en 1526? (Los españoles viajaron por el Río de la Plata.)*

Answers:

• España contribuyó con la idea del arpa, un elemento importante de la música paraguaya. Los guaraníes han cambiado los materiales que se usan para construir el arpa. También han adaptado la técnica de tocar ese instrumento.

• Answers will vary.

Resources: Answer Keys: Student Edition, p. 112

Mapa global interactivo, Actividad 6

Travel the route from Río de la Plata to Paraguay.

Additional Resources

• Communication Wbk.: Act. 2, p. 107

• Teacher's Resource Book: Audio Script, p. 189, Communicative Pair Activity BLM, p. 196

• Audio Program DVD: Cap. 8, Track 6

✓ASSESSMENT

Prueba 8-3 with Study Plan (online only)

Prueba: El condicional
• Prueba 8-3: p. 175

Examen: Vocabulario y gramática 1
• Examen 1: pp. 176–178
• ExamView: Examen 1

ENRICH YOUR TEACHING

Culture Note

The harp is thought to have originally evolved from a hunter's bow. Variations can be found throughout the world: the Adunga from Uganda, Celtic harp, Chinese Konghou, Burmese Saung-Gauk, and the Paraguayan harp. The Veracruz harp, common throughout Mexico, came from Spain around the 1500s.

21st Century Skills

Social and Cross-Cultural Skills Have students search for information on the history of other instruments used in traditional Spanish or Latin American music, such as Spanish castanets, the Puerto Rican *cuatro*, or the accordion in Mexican *norteño* bands. Are any similar instruments used in music from their own culture?

Vocabulario en contexto

Core Instruction

Standards: 1.1, 1.2, 2.2, 3.1

Resources: Teacher's Resource Book: Input Script, p. 186, Clip Art, pp. 202–209, Audio Script, pp. 189–190; Voc. and Gram. Transparencies 158–159; Audio Program DVD: Cap. 8, Track 7

🌐 **Mapa global interactivo, Actividad 7**
Travel the route Hernán Cortés followed.

Focus: Presenting new vocabulary and using grammar lexically in context

Suggestions: Ask volunteers to read the main title and the captions on these pages. Invite students to talk about what they see in the pictures. Have students point out cognates such as **europeos, colonia,** and **adoptaran** from among the new vocabulary. Play the audio or read the text and have students follow along. Check comprehension by asking questions. See the Input Script in the *Teacher's Resource Book* for specific questions.

Pre-AP* Support

- **Learning Objective:** Interpretive: Print and Audio
- **Activity:** Distribute Clip Art for new vocabulary presented on pp. 356–357. Have students prepare to retell some of the information in their own words. Then, each selects five of the pieces of clip art that could illustrate their summary. Now working in pairs, have one student tell his or her summary and the other arrange his or her partner's clip art on the desktop in the order it occurs in the summary.
- ***Pre-AP* Resource Book:** Comprehensive guide to Pre-AP* vocabulary skill development, pp. 51–57

Block Schedule

Have each student write six *Cierto/Falso* statements from the information on pp. 356–367. Have them work in pairs and read statements to each other. The partner states whether the statement is *cierto* or *falso* and then corrects the information that is false.

Vocabulario en contexto 🌐

▼ Objectives

▶ Read, listen to, and understand information about
- interaction between cultures
- fusion of different cultures in the Americas after the arrival of the Europeans

Con la llegada de los españoles y otros exploradores europeos a las Américas al final del siglo XV, se produjo **un encuentro** que iba a cambiar para siempre la vida en los dos hemisferios.

La llegada: Los aztecas y Hernán Cortés

1 En el siglo XIII, llegó a la región central de México un grupo de **indígenas** llamados aztecas. Estos indígenas, más tarde llamados ***mexicas***, **establecieron** entre dos lagos la ciudad de Tenochtitlán, la cual llegó a ser la capital de su **imperio.** En esta **tierra** creció el imperio azteca que dominó el centro y el sur de México a finales del siglo XV. El imperio azteca estaba basado en la agricultura, el comercio, la religión y **la guerra.**

Tenochtitlán era una ciudad con una gran población y **una riqueza** increíble.

2 En 1519, el español Hernán Cortés llegó a la costa de México cerca de Veracruz. Desde allí salió para Tenochtitlán con un grupo de **soldados** montados a caballo y con **armas de fuego.** Los aztecas se **rebelaron** contra los españoles, con quienes se **enfrentaron** y **lucharon** en numerosas **batallas.** En 1521, Hernán Cortés logró conquistar al **poderoso** imperio azteca y a su emperador, Moctezuma. Así se creó el gobierno español en las Américas, llamado ***virreinato.*** Éste duró hasta 1821, año en que México ganó su independencia de España.

la batalla

Los aztecas describían a los españoles como seres[1] con dos cabezas, una de hombre y otra de animal, y cuatro patas[2].

---
1 beings **2** legs

DIFFERENTIATED INSTRUCTION

Students with Learning Difficulties
Students may have difficulty with comprehension of the text on pp. 356 and 357. To help organize the information presented, have students find the dates mentioned in sections 1 and 2 of the reading. Then have them create a timeline with a simple caption for each year or century mentioned.

Advanced Learners
Ask students to write paraphrases for each of the four sections on these pages on separate sheets of paper. Collect and mix all the paraphrases. Have students arrange them into sets of four in chronological order and discuss similarities and differences among the different paraphrased versions.

El intercambio

3 **Al llegar** los españoles, se estableció **una colonia** con **el poder** de España, que se llamó Nueva España. Después de poco tiempo, empezó **un intercambio** de mercancías entre Europa y las Américas. Los españoles se llevaron café, chocolate y maíz, hasta entonces **desconocidos** en Europa, y trajeron a Nueva España caballos, pollo y arroz.

las mercancías

la misión

el misionero

4 Los españoles cambiaron muchos aspectos de la vida de los indígenas. Ellos querían que los indígenas **adoptaran** su religión, su **lengua** y su cultura. Muchos religiosos de varias órdenes, como los dominicanos y los franciscanos, llegaron a la colonia. Esos misioneros construyeron misiones para enseñarles a los indígenas su religión. Los españoles también trajeron su arquitectura, su comida y sus tradiciones. Con la poca **semejanza** entre la cultura española y la indígena, el encuentro entre los dos mundos cambió para siempre la historia de las Américas.

▼**17** **Diferentes opiniones** | 🔊 _____

Escuchar

Escribe los números del 1 al 6 en una hoja. Escucha cada frase sobre la historia del encuentro entre los aztecas y los españoles y escribe *C* si es cierta o *F* si es falsa.

trescientos cincuenta y siete **357**
Capítulo 8

---

17 Standards: 1.2

Resources: Teacher's Resource Book: Audio Script, p. 190; Audio Program DVD: Cap. 8, Track 8; Answer Keys: Student Edition, p. 113

Focus: Practicing listening comprehension of new vocabulary

Suggestions: Before students listen, allow them a few minutes to silently read over the information on these two pages. Play the audio or read from the script. Allow students to listen more than once.

Answers:

1. F	4. C
2. F	5. F
3. C	6. C

BELLRINGER REVIEW

Have the students change these present tense verbs to the preterite:

> descubren
> van
> establecen
> construyen
> luchan

(**Answers:** descubrieron, fueron, establecieron, construyeron, lucharon)

Chapter Project

Students can perform Step 3 at this point. (For more information, see p. 338-b.)

ENRICH YOUR TEACHING

Teacher-to-Teacher

Use visuals on these pages to elicit as much language as possible from students. They can describe what they see, practice various tenses to say what happened, is happening, or will happen in a picture, or offer opinions or value statements based on their interpretation of a picture.

21st Century Skills

Technology Literacy Have students use the digital technology within **realidades.com** to access and manage the audio files and activities that support learning the new vocabulary. Students can access the eText Audio to hear the pronunciation of new vocabulary words of *Vocabulario en contexto*, or they can use the Flashcards to study the vocabulary, then do some additional vocabulary activities.

Vocabulario en contexto

Core Instruction

Standards: 1.1, 1.2, 2.1, 2.2, 3.1

Resources: Teacher's Resource Book: Input Script, p. 187, Clip Art, pp. 202–209, Audio Script, p. 190; Voc. and Gram. Transparencies 160–161; Audio Program DVD: Cap. 8, Tracks 9–10

Focus: Extending presentation of vocabulary and grammar in context

Suggestions:

Pre-reading: Point out cognates such as *descendencia, africana,* and *resultado* that will help students better understand the text as they read. Remind students that the information here is an extension of the historical treatment on pp. 356–357.

Reading: Allow students time to read the information on this and the next page silently first. Then play the audio and have students read along as they listen. Allow them to listen more than once.

Post-reading: Check comprehension by asking questions. For example: *¿La celebración del Día de los Muertos es una fusión de elementos de qué religiones? ¿La herencia de Sandra es una fusión de qué tres culturas?*

18 Standards: 1.2

Resources: Answer Keys: Student Edition, p. 113

Focus: Practicing reading comprehension of new vocabulary and structures

Suggestions: Encourage students to review the material presented on pp. 356–359 before completing the activity.

Answers:

1. Se veía la influencia de los españoles, de los indígenas, y de los africanos.
2. Representa la combinación de las religiones católicas e indígenas.
3. La comida representa una mezcla de culturas.
4. La herencia cultural de Sandra representa las tradiciones de los españoles, de los africanos y de los indígenas.

Teacher-to-Teacher

Ask students to discuss how *La fusión* in Mexico has impacted life in the United States.

La fusión

Durante la época colonial (1521–1821) se mezclaron diferentes **razas**, religiones y costumbres. No sólo había gente de **descendencia** europea, sino también indígena y **africana**. Como **resultado** de esta **mezcla**, hay una gran **variedad** de tradiciones y culturas en América.

1 Los indígenas influyeron en las prácticas religiosas cristianas que trajeron los españoles. En la celebración del Día de los Muertos, que tiene lugar el dos de noviembre para recordar a los familiares que han muerto, se combinan elementos de las religiones católicas e indígenas.

Celebración del Día de los Muertos

2 Una de las cosas en que se vio la influencia española fue la comida. Durante la época colonial, la alimentación de los indígenas cambió debido a los productos traídos por los españoles. Es en esta época que aparecen muchos de los platos mexicanos de hoy día. Por ejemplo, el mole poblano, una salsa típica de la cocina mexicana, fue creado por las monjas[1] de una misión utilizando productos mexicanos, asiáticos y europeos.

El mole poblano

1 nuns

▼18 Contestar

Escribir

Contesta las preguntas con la información de las páginas 358–359.

1. En la fusión que tuvo lugar durante la época colonial, ¿se veía la influencia de qué tres tradiciones?

2. ¿La celebración del Día de los Muertos representa la combinación de elementos de qué religiones?

3. ¿Por qué dicen que la comida representa una fusión?

4. ¿Por qué representa la herencia de Sandra lo más noble de la historia de las Américas?

358 trescientos cincuenta y ocho
A primera vista 2

DIFFERENTIATED INSTRUCTION

Heritage Language Learners

Ask students to talk about traditional or typical foods in their heritage country. Ask them to discuss the history of these foods in the culture or in their own families. How did the recipes, ingredients, and traditions begin?

Students with Learning Difficulties

Students may have difficulty with the concept of analogies in *Actividad* 19. Provide students with visual clues to help establish the relationship between the first two words in the analogy. For example, for the first item, *europeo: Europa,* draw a person and a simple map.

La herencia

Esta mezcla de culturas sigue presente hoy en día.

"Me llamo Sandra y vivo en los Estados Unidos. Mi **herencia se compone** de elementos de varias culturas diferentes. **Los antepasados** de mi familia representan lo más noble de la historia de las Américas: los indígenas americanos que vivían aquí desde hace mucho tiempo, los españoles que llegaron a la costa de México en el siglo XVI, y los africanos con sus tradiciones tan ricas. Estoy muy orgullosa de que mi herencia sea de estas tres culturas. Uno de mis **retos** es aprender sobre las contribuciones de estas culturas a mi país"

▼19 Las analogías

Leer • Escribir

Escoge la mejor palabra para completar cada analogía.

africano	europeo	poderoso
luchar	desconocido	lengua

1. europeo: Europa; _____ : África
2. igual : diferente; _____ : débil
3. indígena: azteca; _____ : español
4. escribir : lápiz; _____ : arma
5. justo : injusto; _____ : familiar
6. volver : regresar; _____ : idioma

Más práctica GO

realidades.com | print

Instant Check	✔	
Guided WB pp. 253–260	✔	✔
Core WB pp. 112–113	✔	✔
Comm. WB p. 113	✔	✔
Hispanohablantes WB pp. 248–249		✔

trescientos cincuenta y nueve **359**
Capítulo 8

Language Input 8

19 Standards: 1.2, 3.1

Resources: Answer Keys: Student Edition, p. 113

Focus: Writing answers to demonstrate comprehension

Suggestions: Remind students that the items are presented as analogies. A single colon means "is to" and a double colon means "as."

Answers:
1. africano   4. luchar
2. poderoso   5. desconocido
3. europeo   6. lengua

Extension: After students complete the activity, ask them to point out words that are synonyms, such as *idioma* and *lengua,* and antonyms, such as *familiar* and *desconocido.*

Teacher-to-Teacher

Ask students to work in pairs to discuss how history described in *La herencia* has impacted Sandra's life in the United States.

ENRICH YOUR TEACHING

Culture Note

The Aztecs and the Incas first cultivated the tomato as a crop around 700 A.D. The fruit was brought to Europe by explorers in the sixteenth century. The cuisines of France, Italy, and Spain quickly utilized the new ingredient. The French called it "the apple of love," and the Germans called it "the apple of paradise." As the tomato traveled north, however, its mystery increased. The British actually believed that the tomato was poisonous, a myth that traveled to the American colonies, and was believed by many until the nineteenth century.

✔ **ASSESSMENT**

Prueba: Comprensión del vocabulario 2
• Prueba 8-4: pp. 179–180

359

▶ Discuss cultural heritage and cultural encounters
▶ Talk about fusion of cultures

INTERACTIVE WHITEBOARD
Vocabulary Activities 8-2

20 Standards: 1.1, 1.3, 3.1

Focus: Demonstrating comprehension of new vocabulary

Suggestions: Remind students that a valid definition of a word does not reuse the word or any other form of the word as part of the definition. Encourage them to consider which part of speech each word is before attempting to define it.

Answers will vary.

BELLRINGER REVIEW

Students will hear a combination of the imperfect and preterite tenses in *Actividad* 21. Briefly review the uses of the two tenses. Make statements that use both the imperfect and the preterite tenses. Have students tell why each tense was used.

21 Standards: 1.2, 3.1

Resources: Fine Art Transparencies with Teacher's Guide, p. 2; Teacher's Resource Book: Audio Script, p. 190; Audio Program DVD: Cap. 8, Track 11; Answer Keys: Student Edition, p. 114

Focus: Practicing listening comprehension of new vocabulary and structures

Suggestions: Point out to students that the description they will hear is a running narrative rather than several independent sentences. Show the *Fine Art Transparency* as you play the audio or read from the script. Allow students to listen more than once.

Answers:

1. F; Cortés entró a Tenochtitlán después de que Moctezuma envió a sus mensajeros para invitarlo a entrar en la ciudad.
2. C
3. F; Cortés conoció a Moctezuma en Tenochtitlán.
4. C
5. F; Moctezuma le regaló riquezas importantes a Cortés.

360

Vocabulario en uso

▼20 ¿Qué significa esta palabra? | 👥

Escribir

Trabaja con otro(a) estudiante para escribir definiciones de las palabras siguientes.

Modelo
poderoso
Una persona que es poderosa tiene mucha influencia.

1. la semejanza
2. el imperio
3. la riqueza
4. la batalla
5. el encuentro

6. el resultado
7. la mezcla
8. la mercancía
9. la misión
10. el reto

▼21 Cortés llega a 🔊 Tenochtitlán

Escuchar • Escribir

Escucha una descripción de la entrada de Cortés a Tenochtitlán. Después, lee cada frase y escribe si es cierta (*C*) o falsa (*F*). Si la frase es falsa, vuelve a escribirla para que diga algo cierto.

1. Cortés entró a Tenochtitlán después de una batalla contra los mensajeros de Moctezuma.
2. Los conquistadores no siguieron el camino a Tenochtitlán que les sugirieron los aztecas.
3. Cortés nunca llegó a conocer al líder del imperio azteca.
4. Moctezuma y Cortés se encontraron en un palacio muy grande.
5. Moctezuma le dio armas a Cortés como regalos.

Primera entrada de Hernán Cortés y sus soldados en Tenochtitlán

DIFFERENTIATED INSTRUCTION

Heritage Language Learners

As students write their definitions for the vocabulary words in *Actividad* 20, ask them to also brainstorm a synonym for each word. Then have students discuss the subtle differences in meaning between the original word and its close relation.

Advanced Learners

Have students compare and contrast the two pictures of the encounter between Cortés and Moctezuma that accompany *Actividades* 21 and 22. Encourage them to paraphrase information they heard in *Actividad* 21 in order to talk about the events depicted.

22 ¡A describir el cuadro!

Hablar

Mira este cuadro que representa el encuentro entre Cortés y los representantes de Moctezuma. Describe lo que ves a un(a) compañero(a).

Modelo
Los soldados de Cortés tenían caballos.

Cortés ofrece un banquete a los enviados de Moctezuma

23 ¿Qué es un imperio? 👥

Leer • Escribir • Hablar

¿Sabes qué es un imperio? Lee este párrafo para aprender qué es un imperio y cuáles son sus ventajas y desventajas.

Conexiones | Las ciencias sociales

Un imperio es un grupo importante de territorios que dependen de un mismo gobierno. Los territorios que dependen del gobierno central se llaman colonias. Los ciudadanos de las colonias disfrutan por lo general de los mismos derechos y beneficios que los ciudadanos del país del gobierno central. Sin embargo, esto no ha sido siempre así. Como consecuencia, las colonias se han ido separando del gobierno central, creando sus propios gobiernos.

• ¿Cuáles son las características de un imperio? Trabaja con otro(a) estudiante para hacer una lista usando las palabras del recuadro.

componerse	poder	reto	variedad
riqueza	poderoso	luchar	establecer
invadir	batalla	soldado	intercambio

trescientos sesenta y uno **361**
Capítulo 8

Practice and Communicate 8

24

Standards: 1.2, 2.1, 2.2, 3.1, 3.2

Resources: Answer Keys: Student Edition, p. 114

Focus: Practicing new vocabulary and structures via reading and response

Suggestions: As students read the information silently, ask them to note words or phrases at spots in which they have comprehension problems. Address these problem spots and have students read the material again before answering the questions.

Answers:

1. **Su herencia está formada de tres culturas: la africana, la indígena y la española.**
2. **Sus antepasados son de África, la República Dominicana y España.**
3. **La cultura dominicana ha influido más en su vida.**
4. **Aprende sobre su cultura dominicana cuando visita la República Dominicana. También aprende mucho porque la cultura dominicana ha influido mucho en la Ciudad de Nueva York, donde vive.**
5. **Ella se siente orgullosa de su herencia.**
6. **Answers will vary.**

Fondo cultural

Standards: 1.1, 1.2, 2.1, 2.2, 3.1, 4.2

Suggestions: Before students read the information, ask them to share their background knowledge about Tex-Mex food. Then help them increase their knowledge by asking questions that have answers they will discover as they read. For example: *No sólo dos sino tres culturas han influido en la comida texmex. ¿Cuáles son?*

Answers will vary.

Pre-AP* Support

- **Learning Objective:** Interpretive: Print
- **Activity:** As a pre-reading activity, have students work with a partner who reads one of the two paragraphs in the narration, *Mi herencia africana* silently. Have each student write a one-sentence summary of his or her segment and share with the class.
- **Pre-AP* Resource Book:** Comprehensive guide to Pre-AP* reading skill development, pp. 19–26

▼**24** Una mezcla de culturas

Leer • Escribir

Lee la lectura y contesta las preguntas.

Mi herencia africana

Mi nombre es Noemí y nací en la ciudad de Santo Domingo, en la República Dominicana. Soy resultado de una mezcla de razas y culturas. De mi padre recibí mi herencia africana. Los antepasados de mi madre eran españoles e indígenas. De niña, la cultura dominicana tuvo más influencia en mi vida. Ahora vivo en los Estados Unidos y me encanta ir a la República Dominicana, donde hay mucha riqueza cultural y donde lo paso muy bien con mi familia y mis amigos. Sin embargo, cuando estoy en la República Dominicana quiero volver a los Estados Unidos, porque también me identifico con este país.

Vivo en Nueva York, una ciudad donde se encuentran y se mezclan muchas culturas: la cultura dominicana, la estadounidense y la africana, entre otras. Para mí, en Nueva York es fácil aprender sobre mi herencia cultural. Voy a una iglesia dominicana, escucho cantantes dominicanos y españoles en la radio y voy a festivales de música y presentaciones de arte africano. Las culturas que forman mi herencia han influido mucho en la vida de toda la ciudad. Me siento orgullosa de mi herencia.

1. ¿De cuántas culturas está formada la herencia de Noemí? Di cuáles son.
2. ¿De dónde son los antepasados de la autora?
3. ¿Cuál es la cultura que más ha influido en la vida de la autora?
4. ¿Cómo aprende sobre su cultura dominicana?
5. ¿Cómo se siente ella de su herencia?
6. ¿Hay una variedad de culturas en tu comunidad? Descríbelas.

▼ Fondo Cultural | Estados Unidos • México

¡Qué rica la comida texmex! El estado de Texas está en la frontera con México y allí se encuentran y se mezclan dos culturas, la estadounidense y la mexicana. Algunas personas hablan inglés con acento español o español con palabras del inglés.

La comida texmex es otro resultado de ese encuentro. Es una mezcla de la cocina mexicana y la texana, con influencia de la cocina cajún del Sur de los Estados Unidos. El arroz, los frijoles, el chile y las tortillas de maíz se mezclan con las cebollas texanas y los mariscos del Golfo, para lograr un resultado exquisito.

La comida texmex ya no se encuentra sólo en Texas; en todas las ciudades grandes de los Estados Unidos hay restaurantes de estilo texmex. La próxima vez que veas uno de ellos, no dejes de entrar.

- ¿Has ido a algún restaurante texmex o de comida latinoamericana? Compara la comida que había allí con la que comes generalmente en casa.

DIFFERENTIATED INSTRUCTION

Heritage Language Learners

Have students share their own personal versions of *Una mezcla de culturas* in *Actividad* 24. Ask them to reread the passage, substituting their own information about their heritage country and culture. For example, *Mi nombre es ___ y nací en la ciudad de ___, en ___.*

Multiple Intelligences

Musical/Rhythmic: Divide students into small groups. Have each group rehearse a choral reading of *Calabó y bambú.* Instruct students to create their own rhythmic gestures and percussion accompaniment using hand claps, finger snaps, and knee slaps.

▼ En voz alta | (Talk!)

Muchos poemas y cuentos indígenas pasaron a la forma escrita gracias a las personas bilingües que hablaban el idioma nativo y el español. Estas personas realizaron los escritos durante la colonización de las Américas para conservar la cultura y las creencias que antes se trasmitían por tradición oral.

La leyenda *El águila y el nopal*, redactada hacia el año 1600, explica los orígenes de la ciudad de Tenochtitlán, que hoy en día es la capital del país. Según la leyenda, los mexicas salieron del Norte y, guiados por el dios Huitzilopochtli, viajaron largas distancias buscando la señal que indicaría donde deberían construir su ciudad. El dios les dijo que verían un águila comiendo una serpiente encima de un nopal, un tipo de cactus. El encuentro entre los mexicas y el águila es un hecho de tanta importancia en la historia de México que es el único símbolo en la bandera.

Escucha la leyenda y trata de repetirlo en voz alta.

• ¿Cómo apoya el tema de fusión de culturas esta leyenda?

El Águila y el nopal

Llegaron al sitio donde se
levanta el nopal salvaje
allí al borde de la cueva[1],
y vieron tranquila parada al
Águila en el nopal salvaje:
allí come, allí devora y echa
a la cueva los restos[2] de lo
que come.

Y cuando el Águila vio a los mexicanos,
se inclinó profundamente.
Y el Águila veía desde lejos.
Su nido[3] y su asiento era todo él de cuantas finas
plumas[4] hay; plumas de azulejos, plumas de
aves rojas y plumas de quetzal. . .

Les habló el dios y les dijo:
—¡Ah, mexicanos: aquí sí será! ¡México es aquí!

Y aunque no veían quién les hablaba, se pusieron a
llorar y decían:
—¡Felices nosotros, dichosos[5] al fin:
hemos visto ya dónde ha de ser nuestra ciudad!
¡Vamos y vengamos a reposar aquí!

1 cave 2 remains 3 nest 4 feathers 5 lucky

¿Recuerdas?

Cuando la letra *c* va antes de *a*, *o* y *u*, se pronuncia como la *c* de *cat*.

Cuando la *c* va antes de *e* o de *i*, se pronuncia como la *s* de *Sally*.

Para mantener el sonido de la *c* de *cat* antes de la *e* y la *i*, las palabras se escriben con *qu*: *busqué*, *aquí*.

▼ 25 ¿De dónde venimos? | (Talk!)

Hablar

Trabaja con otro(a) estudiante para contestar las preguntas.

1. ¿Cómo se muestran las diferentes herencias culturales en tu comunidad? ¿Y en los Estados Unidos?

2. Habla de algunas celebraciones que tengan raíces *(roots)* culturales.

3. ¿Cómo se ve la influencia de diferentes herencias en la lengua que hablamos? ¿Puedes pensar en algún ejemplo?

4. ¿Hay influencia indígena en el lugar donde vives? ¿En qué cosas la ves?

El Festival Folklife en San Antonio, Texas

trescientos sesenta y tres **363**
Capítulo 8

En voz alta
Core Instruction

Standards: 1.2, 1.3, 2.1, 2.2, 3.1, 3.2, 5.2

Resources: Teacher's Resource Book: Audio Script, pp. 190–191; Audio Program DVD: Cap. 8, Track 12; Answer Keys: Student Edition, p. 115

Suggestions: Have students read the information and the legend silently. Ask comprehension questions: *¿Cómo se escribieron en español la historia y las leyendas de las culturas indígenas? ¿Qué señal buscaban los mexicas? ¿Qué imagen está en la bandera de México?*

Before having students read the legend aloud, direct their attention to the information in the *¿Recuerdas?* Ask them to identify words with the hard and soft **c** sound and write them in a list. Allow them a few minutes to practice the words with a partner.

Answers may vary: **Esta leyenda azteca ya es parte de la identidad nacional de México y contada en español.**

▼ 25 Standards: 1.1, 1.3, 4.2

Focus: Using new vocabulary and structures in a discussion

Suggestions: After students have answered the questions in item 3, ask *"¿Cómo se ve la influencia de diferentes lenguas en la lengua que hablamos?"* Have students give examples from various languages. Direct attention to the *Fondo cultural* on p. 362 and have students identify words that have passed from Spanish into English. Have students tell you what they learned earlier about the influence of Latin and Arabic on Spanish.

Answers will vary.

Additional Resources

• Communication Wbk.: Audio Act. 3, p. 108
• Teacher's Resource Book: Audio Script, p. 191, Communicative Pair Activity BLM, pp. 197–198
• Audio Program DVD: Cap. 8, Track 13

✓ ASSESSMENT

Prueba 8-5 with Study Plan (online only)

Prueba: Aplicación del vocabulario 2
• Prueba 8-5: pp. 181–182

ENRICH YOUR TEACHING

Culture Note

The legend of *"El Águila y el nopal"* was recorded in the Aztec language of Náhuatl and translated into Spanish by Hernando de Alvarado Tezozómoc, grandson of the Aztec king Moctezuma, in his work the Crónica Mexicayotl. This text chronicles Aztec history and myths up to the early years of the conquest period. The documents were rediscovered in old archives and first published in 1949.

Teacher-to-Teacher

During discussions about cultural influences, play background music that showcases these cultures. Most public libraries have recordings of music from Africa, the Caribbean, and many parts of Latin America. Background music may stimulate the discussion and arouse students' curiosity about its cultural roots.

8 Practice and Communicate

Gramática

Core Instruction

Resources: Voc. and Gram. Transparency 162

INTERACTIVE WHITEBOARD

Grammar Activities 8-2

Suggestions: As you explain the points in the *Gramática*, point out to students the difference between the use of the **presente perfecto del subjuntivo**, which they learned in *Capítulo* 7, and the current lesson, the **imperfecto del subjuntivo.** We use the former when the main clause is in the present tense and expresses doubt or uncertainty about a situation in the past. We use the **imperfecto del subjuntivo** when the main clause is in one of the past tenses.

26 Standards: 1.2, 3.1

Resources: Answer Keys: Student Edition, p. 115

Focus: Practicing the imperfect subjunctive

Suggestions: As students complete the activity, ask them to focus on the clauses that make up each sentence. Remind them that in all cases, the main clause (containing an expression of emotion, doubt, or uncertainty) is in a past tense, thus requiring the imperfect subjunctive in the subordinate clause.

Answers:

1. fuera
2. tuvieran
3. fuera
4. hubiera
5. pudiera
6. supieran

Block Schedule

Play the "Cube Game" with three cubes. In groups of two, give students three cubes. Cube 1: write six infinitives including some irregular verbs from p. 364. Cube 2: six expressions that use the subjunctive. Cube 3: subject pronouns. Have students roll the cubes and provide a sentence combining information on the three cubes: *Mi padre quería que yo estudiara.*

Gramática

▼ Objectives
▶ Express doubts and wishes about family and cultural heritage in the past
▶ Talk about an important event in your childhood

El imperfecto del subjuntivo

You know that you use the subjunctive to persuade someone else to do something, to express emotions about situations, and to express doubt and uncertainty. If the main verb is in the present tense, use the present subjunctive. If the main verb is in the preterite or imperfect, use the imperfect subjunctive.

> Los indígenas dudan que los europeos aprendan su lengua.
> Los indígenas dudaban que los europeos aprendieran su lengua.
>
> El profesor sugiere que aprendamos los nombres de las colonias.
> El profesor sugirió que aprendiéramos los nombres de las colonias.

- To form the imperfect subjunctive, take the *Uds./ellos/ellas* form of the preterite and replace the ending *-ron* with the imperfect subjunctive endings. Here are the forms of the imperfect subjunctive for *cantar, aprender,* and *vivir*.

cantar		aprender		vivir	
cantara	cantáramos	aprendiera	aprendiéramos	viviera	viviéramos
cantaras	cantarais	aprendieras	aprendierais	vivieras	vivierais
cantara	cantaran	aprendiera	aprendieran	viviera	vivieran

- Note that the *nosotros* form has a written accent.

Irregular verbs, stem-changing verbs, and spelling-changing verbs follow the same rule for forming the imperfect subjunctive.

ir: **fueron** → fue-	El rey les dijo que fueran al Nuevo Mundo.
haber: **hubieron** → hubie-	Dudaba que hubiera semejanzas.
pedir: **pidieron** → pidie-	No era necesario que pidieran tantas armas.
construir: **construyeron** → construye-	Los europeos querían que los habitantes construyeran una iglesia.

Más ayuda | **realidades.com** | ▶Tutorials

▼26 Historia de la conquista

Leer

Bernal Díaz del Castillo (1492–1581) escribió uno de los libros más interesantes sobre la conquista de México. Completa estas opiniones de Bernal Díaz del Castillo con el imperfecto del subjuntivo del verbo apropiado.

1. Era impresionante que la capital de los aztecas *(ser / ver)* tan enorme.
2. Era increíble que los edificios de la ciudad *(tener / traer)* torres tan altas.
3. Dudábamos que lo que veíamos *(ser / decir)* verdad.
4. Nos gustó mucho que *(saber / haber)* tantos árboles en los jardines.
5. No podíamos creer que la gente *(creer / poder)* navegar por la ciudad.
6. Nos parecía interesante que los indígenas *(saber / decir)* cultivar el maíz en un lago.

DIFFERENTIATED INSTRUCTION

Students with Learning Difficulties

Students may have difficulty grasping the distinction between the present subjunctive and past subjunctive. Before they attempt *Actividad* 26, provide them with additional examples. Provide a sentence utilizing the subjunctive in the present, discuss its meaning, and then transform that sentence using a past tense and the imperfect subjunctive.

Advanced Learners/Pre-AP*

Ask students to revisit *Actividad* 11 on p. 306 in *Capítulo* 7. Challenge them to change the verbs in each item's main clause to the imperfect or preterite tense, and make the resulting change to the imperfect subjunctive in the subordinate clause.

▼27 Durante la conquista . . .

Leer

Imagina que estuviste presente cuando Cortés llegó a México. Tu trabajo era relatar lo que veías. Completa las siguientes oraciones con el imperfecto del subjuntivo del verbo apropiado.

ser	rebelarse	comprender
establecer	adoptar	

1. Era imposible que los aztecas _____ la lengua de los españoles.

2. Los españoles esperaban que los indígenas _____ sus costumbres inmediatamente.

3. Los reyes querían que las colonias _____ un intercambio de mercancías.

4. Según los aztecas era posible que los españoles _____ enviados por sus antepasados.

5. Los españoles temían que los indígenas _____ contra ellos.

▼28 Nuestras raíces

Escribir

Para la familia de Carlos es muy importante mantener sus raíces. Completa las frases de Carlos de una manera original, usando el imperfecto del subjuntivo de los verbos del recuadro.

hablar	aprender	comer
adoptar	venir	ir
haber	sentirse	abandonar

Modelo
Papá quería que todos nosotros . . . (hablar)
Papá quería que todos nosotros hablaramos la lengua de nuestros antepasados.

1. Mis padres preferían que mis hermanos y yo . . .
2. Mi mamá exigía que todos . . .
3. Mis padres no querían que yo . . .
4. Todos estábamos orgullosos que nuestros antepasados . . .
5. Mi hermana tenía miedo que nuestro hermano . . .
6. A mis abuelos no les gustaba que los jóvenes de la familia . . .
7. Nadie creía que . . .
8. Era importante que todos nosotros . . .

El español en el mundo del trabajo

Salud y ciencia . . . en español

La ciudad de Houston, en Texas, es la cuarta de los Estados Unidos con mayor número de hispanohablantes. Sin embargo, al abrir sus puertas en marzo de 1996, el Museo de Salud de Houston sólo tenía un trabajador bilingüe.

Hoy la situación es muy diferente. El museo tiene profesionales bilingües que ofrecen visitas guiadas en español. También hay videos educativos del museo con subtítulos en español. Además, se publica una guía en español y el servicio telefónico de atención al público tiene menús bilingües.

trescientos sesenta y cinco **365**
Capítulo 8

ENRICH YOUR TEACHING

29 Standards: 1.1

Resources: Answer Keys: Student Edition, p. 115

Focus: Practicing the imperfect subjunctive

Suggestions: Remind Student A to be careful to apply the rules for use of the preterite vs. the imperfect in the independent clause.

Answers will vary. Student B will most often use the **nosotros** forms of the imperfect subjunctive of the given verbs:

respetáramos	fuéramos
adoptáramos	durmiéramos
saliéramos	jugáramos
nos lleváramos	nos despertáramos

Extension: After students complete the activity, ask volunteers to spell aloud the verb forms used by Student B. Remind them to include the necessary accents in the **nosotros** forms as they spell.

BELLRINGER REVIEW

Have students unscramble these words to create logical sentences:

que/mi madre/fuera/yo/niño/quería

el viaje/dudaban/ellos/tanto/costara/que/ a España

(**Answers:** *Mi madre quería que yo fuera niño; Ellos dudaban que el viaje a España costara tanto.*)

30 Standards: 1.1

Focus: Practicing the imperfect subjunctive

Suggestions: Tell students to keep sharpening their skills in the use of the subjunctive by making mental notes as they work on the types of expressions used in the independent clauses of sentences.

Answers will vary.

✓ASSESSMENT

Prueba 8-6 with Study Plan (online only)

Prueba: Imperfecto del subjuntivo
• Prueba 8-6: p. 183

▼29 ¿Qué querían que hicieras? |

Hablar

Piensa en las cosas que esperaban tus familiares u otras personas que hicieras de pequeño(a). Trabaja con otro(a) estudiante para hablar sobre lo que querían esas personas que hiciera cada uno(a) de pequeño(a). Añadan detalles a sus frases.

▶ **Modelo**

los maestros / querer / compartir

A —¿Qué querían <u>los maestros</u> de la escuela primaria?

B —Los maestros querían que <u>compartiéramos</u> los materiales con nuestros compañeros.

Estudiante A

los maestros	querer
mi mamá	esperar
mi papá	pedir
mis padres / abuelos	decir
mi(s) hermano(s)	prohibir
mi(s) hermana(s)	aconsejar
el(la) director(a) de la escuela	sugerir
mi entrenador(a)	exigir
¡Respuesta personal!	

Estudiante B

respetar
adoptar
salir
llevarse bien
ir
dormir
jugar
despertarse
¡Respuesta personal!

▼30 ¿Qué pasó?

Leer • Hablar

Piensa en un momento importante de tu niñez. Según lo que recuerdas, completa las siguientes frases.

1. Yo esperaba que . . .
2. Yo quería que . . .
3. [Nombre de un(a) amigo(a) o un pariente] quería que . . .
4. Era importante que . . .
5. (No) me sorprendió que . . .
6. Me gustó que . . .
7. Me molestó que . . .
8. Me pareció interesante que . . .

Más práctica	GO
	realidades.com	print

Instant Check	✔	
Guided WB pp. 261–262	✔	✔
Core WB p. 114	✔	✔
Comm. WB pp. 114–115, 207	✔	✔
Hispanohablantes WB pp. 250–255		✔

DIFFERENTIATED INSTRUCTION

Heritage Language Learners

Have students do *Actividad 30* with a partner. After completing each sentence, have partners quiz each other on the correct spelling of the past subjunctive form used in the example. Instruct them to write down the verb form once they have agreed on the correct spelling.

Students with Learning Difficulties

Allow students time to brainstorm their responses before completing *Actividad 30*. Instruct them to write down the components of the clauses that they plan to add. For example, *Era importante que... (yo) (escuchar) (a mis padres).* Encourage students to use these notes to formulate their responses.

▼ **Objectives**
▶ Talk about things you could do
▶ Discuss and write about cultural exchange

Practice and Communicate  8

Gramática

El imperfecto del subjuntivo con *si*

Use the imperfect subjunctive after *si* when a situation is unlikely, impossible, or not true.

> Si tuviera tiempo, aprendería más sobre las misiones.
> *If I had time, I'd learn more about the missions.*

> Si viviéramos en México, adoptaríamos las costumbres del país.
> *If we lived in Mexico, we'd adopt the customs of the country.*

> Ese imperio sería más poderoso si tuviera oro.
> *That empire would be more powerful if it had gold.*

• Notice that you use the imperfect subjunctive form after *si*, and the conditional in the main clause.

After *como si* ("as if") you always use the the imperfect subjunctive regardless of the tense of the first verb in the sentence. Notice that the other verb can be in either the present or the past tense.

> Él se vestía como si fuera un rey.
> *He dressed as if he were a king.*

> Hablan como si supieran la lengua desde niños.
> *They speak as if they knew the language since childhood.*

| Más ayuda | realidades.com | ▶ *Canción de hip hop* ▶ Tutorial |

▼31 ¡A pensar!

Leer

Imagina que has ido a ver un espectáculo de bailes tradicionales de diferentes países de América Latina. Completa el texto con el imperfecto del subjuntivo del verbo apropiado.

Si las personas que crearon los bailes __1.__ (*enfrentarse / vivir*) ahora, les gustaría mucho ver a los bailarines interpretarlos. Ellos bailaban como si __2.__ (*estar / establecer*) en una gran fiesta. Las joyas que llevaban brillaban como si __3.__ (*ser / ir*) de oro. Si los antepasados los __4.__ (*ver / adoptar*) bailar, se emocionarían mucho. Si yo __5.__ (*poder / querer*), aprendería más sobre las tradiciones y herencias de los países de América Latina. Me gustaría estudiar sobre los países que no __6.__ (*salir / tener*) muchas semejanzas con el mío.

trescientos sesenta y siete 367
Capítulo 8

Gramática

Core Instruction

Standards: 4.1

Resources: Voc. and Gram. Transparency 163

INTERACTIVE WHITEBOARD
Grammar Activities 8-2

Suggestions: Say clauses in which the verb is in the conditional: ...*todos iríamos para ver el partido*; ...*aprenderías muy rápidamente el español.* Ask volunteers to supply subordinate **(si)** clauses that make sense. Point out the cause-and-effect relationship between the clauses in this type of complex sentence.

▼**31** Standards: 1.2

Resources: Answer Keys: Student Edition, p. 115

Focus: Practicing the imperfect subjunctive with **si**

Suggestions: Have students complete the activity in pairs and discuss their reasoning behind each answer.

Answers:

1. vivieran
2. estuvieran
3. fueran
4. vieran
5. pudiera
6. tuvieran

ENRICH YOUR TEACHING

Teacher-to-Teacher

Have students imagine a situation in which everything goes wrong on what should be a dream vacation. Ask them to work with a partner and come up with as many sentences as they can, saying what they would do if things were different.

21st Century Skills

Initiative and Self-Direction Remind students of the various digital tools available in **realidades.com** to help them monitor their own understanding and learning needs about the imperfect subjunctive, such as the online tutorials with comprehension check exercises, animated verbs, and additional grammar practice activities.

32 Standards: 1.3

Resources: Answer Keys: Student Edition, p. 116

Focus: Practicing the imperfect subjunctive with *si*

Suggestions: If students have difficulty, help them by telling them that they should use the expression *como si* in all the items.

Answers:
1. Antes de la obra el director les habló a los jóvenes como si supieran lo que estaban haciendo.
2. Las armas de los actores brillaron como si fueran de oro.
3. Los jóvenes lucharon como si participaran en una batalla.
4. El actor principal actuó como si fuera un rey de verdad.
5. El jóven que hizo el papel de misionero actuó como si sintiera compasión.
6. La actriz principal actuó como si estuviera enamorada del rey.
7. El público aplaudió como si hubiera visto una obra de teatro de Broadway.

33 Standards: 1.1, 1.3

Focus: Practicing the imperfect subjunctive with *si*

Suggestions: If students need ideas, suggest that they talk about things such as governments, education, the economy, employment, and cultural interaction.

Answers will vary.

▼32 Como si . . .

Escribir

En la escuela Gabriela Mistral los estudiantes están participando en una obra musical sobre la conquista de México. Describe lo que pasó usando expresiones de las dos columnas y el imperfecto del subjuntivo.

Modelo
Los estudiantes actuaron . . . / ser actores profesionales
Los estudiantes actuaron como si fueran actores profesionales.

Columna A	Columna B
1. Antes de la obra el director les habló a los jóvenes . . .	estar enamorada del rey
2. Las armas de los actores brillaron . . .	sentir compasión
3. Los jóvenes lucharon . . .	haber visto una obra de teatro de Broadway
4. El actor principal actuó . . .	ser un rey de verdad
5. El jóven que hizo el papel de misionero actuó . . .	ser de oro
6. La actriz principal actuó . . .	saber lo que estaban haciendo
7. El público aplaudió . . .	participar en una batalla

▼33 Nuestra sociedad

Hablar • Escribir

En grupo hablen sobre las características y los problemas de la sociedad actual. Escriban ocho frases usando el imperfecto del subjuntivo con *si*.

Modelo
Si los jóvenes y los adultos trataran de comprenderse mejor, no habría tantos conflictos sobre la música en nuestras casas.

DIFFERENTIATED INSTRUCTION

Advanced Learners
Have students work in pairs to create two sets of cards. On one set they write only subordinate clauses with *si.* On the other they write corresponding main clauses that make sense with the *si* clauses. Have partners mix the cards in each set and exchange them with another pair of students. Students then match the sentence halves of the cards they have received. Some sentence halves may have more than one match. Have students discuss these instances with those who wrote the cards.

Practice and Communicate ⑧

▼34 Si pudiera . . . | 👥

Leer • Hablar

❶ Lee el siguiente anuncio de una agencia de viajes y completa las frases.

Modelo
Si nada me parara . . .
Si nada me parara, invitaría a mi mejor amigo(a) a un viaje a la Antártida.

❷ Ahora, trabaja con otro(a) estudiante para comparar lo que escribieron.

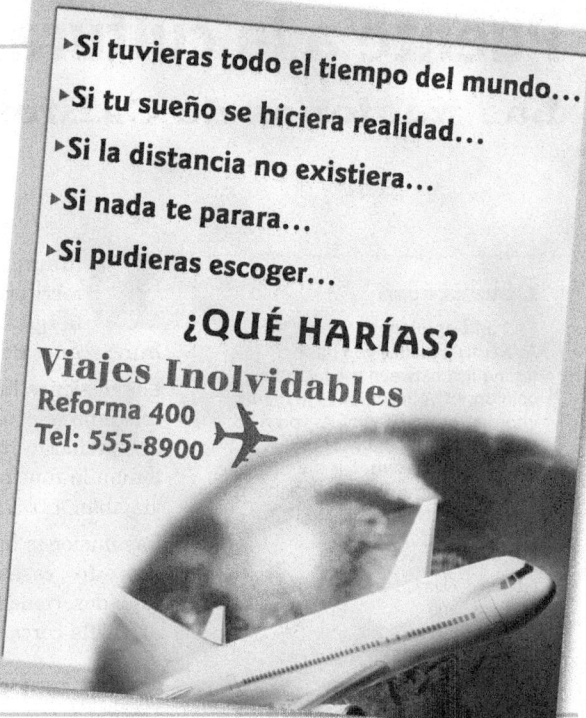

▸Si tuvieras todo el tiempo del mundo...

▸Si tu sueño se hiciera realidad...

▸Si la distancia no existiera...

▸Si nada te parara...

▸Si pudieras escoger...

¿QUÉ HARÍAS?

Viajes Inolvidables
Reforma 400
Tel: 555-8900 ✈

▼35 Encuentros | 👥

Hablar • Escribir

❶ En grupo, van a describir un encuentro de dos culturas del pasado. Pueden tomar ideas de este capítulo o de la clase de estudios sociales. Describan lo siguiente:

- ¿Qué culturas se encontraron?
- ¿Cuándo y dónde fue el encuentro?
- ¿Cómo fue el encuentro?
- ¿Exigía un grupo que el otro hiciera algo?
- ¿Cambió un grupo más que el otro?
- ¿Cuál fue el resultado del encuentro?

❷ Comparen el encuentro sobre el que escribieron con una situación del presente. Analicen qué cosas tienen en común.

Más práctica (GO)

realidades.com | print

Instant Check	✔	
Guided WB pp. 263–264	✔	✔
Core WB pp. 115–116	✔	✔
Comm. WB pp. 108–109, 116–117	✔	✔
***Hispanohablantes* WB** pp. 256–257		✔

trescientos sesenta y nueve 369
Capítulo 8

---

34 Standards: 1.1, 1.2, 1.3

Focus: Practicing the imperfect subjunctive

Suggestions: Point out to students that they should complete all the sentences about themselves, using *yo* as the subject.

Common Errors: Students may mistakenly drop *-ar*, *-ir*, or *-er* infinitive endings when forming the conditional. Remind them that conditional endings are added to the complete infinitive forms of regular verbs.

Answers will vary.

Extension: After students complete step 2, ask them to use third-person forms to report on their partner's responses: *Si nada le parara, mi compañero(a)....*

35 Standards: 1.1

Focus: Practicing the imperfect subjunctive

Suggestions: Encourage students to discuss current world events as they decide on and develop their present-day situation for Step 2.

Answers will vary.

Additional Resources
- Communication Wbk.: Audio Act. 4–5, pp. 108–109
- Teacher's Resource Book: Audio Script, p. 191, Communicative Pair Activity BLM, pp. 199–200
- Audio Program DVD: Cap. 8, Tracks 14–15

Chapter Project
Students can perform Step 5 at this point. Make audio or video recordings of their presentations for inclusion in their portfolios. (For more information, see p. 338-b.)

ENRICH YOUR TEACHING

Teacher-to-Teacher
Help students develop their critical thinking skills. Invite them to research current or recent events for information that will add to class discussions about encounters between different cultures. Besides obtaining information from encyclopedias, newspapers, magazines, personal interviews, and the Internet, they might use information they learned from discussions in their Social Studies courses. Encourage them to synthesize information they glean from a variety of sources, both English and Spanish, in order to verify their facts and develop objective opinions.

✓ASSESSMENT

Prueba 8-7 with Study Plan (online only)

Prueba: Imperfecto del subjuntivo con *si*
- Prueba 8-7: p. 184

Examen: Vocabulario y gramática 2
- Examen 2: pp. 185–187
- ExamView: Examen 2

Puente a la cultura

Core Instruction

Standards: 1.1, 1.2, 2.1, 2.2, 3.1, 5.1, 5.2

Resources: Voc. and Gram. Transparency 4

Focus: Reading to learn about the Spanish missions in California

Suggestions:

Pre-reading: Refer students to the *Estrategia.* Show *Vocabulary and Grammar Transparency* 4 and model setting up a T-chart with the two columns labeled *los hechos* and *las opiniones.* Have students set up a similar chart on their own paper and use it to record facts and opinions as they read the selection.

Reading: As students read, remind them to use background knowledge, cognates, and context clues to understand unfamiliar words and expressions. Help them resolve comprehension problems by asking *sí/no* or embedded-answer questions.

Post-reading: After students have read the selection, allow them to complete their *los hechos/las opiniones* charts and share the information they recorded there. Use the information from the *las opiniones* column as a springboard to discuss the cultural encounter between the Spanish colonizers and the indigenous peoples of California.

Country Connection

Core Instruction

Standards: 3.1

Resources: Map Transparency 22

Mapa global interactivo, Actividad 8

Visit California's historic missions.

Suggestions: Use *Map Transparency* 22 and the map on p. 371 to show the relative location of the **Camino Real.** Explain to students that some of the California missions developed into modern-day cities, the names of which still retain at least part of the name of the original missions. The largest of these are Los Angeles and San Francisco. Smaller cities include Santa Barbara and San Luis Obispo. Other missions, such as San Antonio de Padua, never grew into cities, and today they remain isolated in rural areas.

¡Adelante!

Puente a la cultura
Las misiones de California

▼ Objectives

▶ Read about Spanish missions and learn about their role in California's history

▶ Distinguish between fact and fiction

Estrategia

Fact and opinion
As a critical reader, you must distinguish between the facts and opinions of your source to judge the information's reliability. As you read, try to determine if any of the information presented is the opinion of the author, or whether it is based on facts.

Estatua del Fray *(Brother)* Junípero Serra

Durante el siglo XVIII, los españoles colonizaron el territorio de California. En 1767, el gobierno español y la Iglesia Católica les dieron la tarea a los padres franciscanos de construir misiones y encargarse de ellas.

Las misiones fueron creadas no sólo para enseñar la religión cristiana a los indígenas sino también para enseñarles tareas que pudieran realizar en la nueva sociedad española. Asimismo[1] tenían la función de recibir y alimentar a las personas que viajaban a través del territorio desconocido de California.

Las misiones incluían una iglesia, cuartos para los sacerdotes, depósitos, casas para mujeres solteras, barracas para los soldados, comedores y talleres. Los indígenas casados vivían en una villa cerca de la misión.

---

1 likewise

Misión de San Diego de Alcalá, la más antigua de las misiones

DIFFERENTIATED INSTRUCTION

Students with Learning Difficulties

Provide students with a concept web to help support their comprehension of **Las misiones de California.** Use the question words **¿Qué? ¿Quién? ¿Cuándo? ¿Dónde?** and **¿Por qué?** as the components of the web. After students have read the passage, have them supply information relevant to each of the question words.

Advanced Learners

Invite students to search the Internet for more information about one or more of the missions along the **Camino Real.** Ask them to present the information they find in a brief report to the class. Encourage them to show downloaded photos and share a few facts that are specific to each mission.

Fray Junípero Serra fue escogido por los españoles para fundar las misiones. Serra fundó nueve misiones en California: se encuentran en el Camino Real, una ruta que va desde San Diego hasta la Bahía de San Francisco. Muchas personas recorren hoy el Camino Real para visitar las misiones y aprender sobre su historia.

¿Comprendiste?

1. ¿Para qué fueron creadas las misiones?
2. ¿Qué hizo Fray Junípero Serra?
3. ¿Conoces otros edificios que representen el encuentro entre distintas culturas? Explica tu respuesta.

Más práctica GO	realidades.com	print
▶ Videodocumentario	✔	
Guided WB p. 265	✔	✔
Comm. WB pp. 118–119	✔	✔
Hispanohablantes WB pp. 258–260		✔
Cultural Reading Activity	✔	

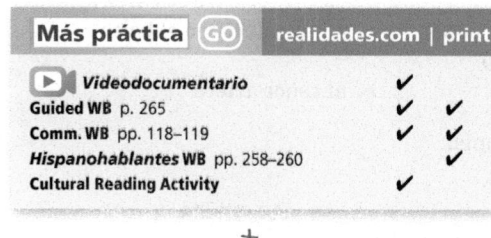

San Rafael
San Francisco de Solano
San José
San Francisco de Asís
Santa Clara
Santa Cruz
San Juan Bautista
San Carlos de Monterey
Soledad
San Antonio
San Miguel
San Luis Obispo
La Purísima   Santa Inés
Santa Bárbara   San Buenaventura
San Fernando Rey
San Gabriel
San Juan Capistrano
San Luis Rey
San Diego

EL CAMINO REAL

Iglesia de la Misión de Santa Bárbara, también llamada "Reina de las Misiones", pues es la más grande de todas

trescientos setenta y uno 371
Capítulo 8

▼ ¿Comprendiste? Standards: 1.2, 1.3

Resources: Answer Keys: Student Edition, p. 116

Focus: Demonstrating reading comprehension

Suggestions: Have students first write answers to the questions on their own. Then ask them to share their answers in a class discussion.

Answers:
1. Fueron creadas para enseñar la religión cristiana a los indígenas y también para enseñarles tareas que pudieron realizar en la nueva sociedad española.
2. Fundó nueve misiones en California.
3. Answers will vary.

▶ Videodocumentario

Core Instruction

Standards: 1.2

Resources: Teacher's Resource Book: Video Script, p. 193; Video Program, Cap. 8

View *Unas herencias ricas* with the class to learn about other examples of cultural fusion in language, food, and art in the Spanish-speaking world. Access the video online in **realidades.com** or use the DVD. See the *Video Teacher's Guide* for additional suggestions.

Teacher-to-Teacher

e-amigos: Have students write their *e-amigos* a description of a building or location in the community that represents another culture. Have them ask if their *e-amigos* are familiar with the place. If so, what do they think of it? Have students print out their e-mails or send them to you for review.

Additional Resources

Student Resource: Realidades para hispanohablantes, pp. 258–260; Guided Practice Activities, p. 265; Communication Wbk., pp. 118–119

ENRICH YOUR TEACHING

Culture Note

Early Spanish influence in California is still very visible and strongly felt today. Most of the early missions are still intact. Many have been completely restored and are open to visitors as museums and as functioning Catholic churches.

21st Century Skills

Critical Thinking and Problem Solving Have students choose a mission from the map of California. Then ask students to use the Internet to locate images of the mission and more information about its founders and its history. Have students share their information with the class and discuss the role of these missions in the history of the state.

¿Qué me cuentas?

Core Instruction

Standards: 1.1, 1.2, 1.3

Resources: Teacher's Resource Book: Audio Script, p. 192; Audio Program DVD: Cap. 8, Track 16; Answer Keys: Student Edition, p. 117

Focus: Practicing listening and reading comprehension of new vocabulary and grammar; using information to write a cohesive and coherent reaction.

AP* Skills: Integration of listening, reading, and writing to comprehend and synthesize information from spoken and written sources.

Suggestions: For Step 1, use the audio or read the descriptions aloud. Allow students to hear it twice through: the first time to write their answers, the second time to check them.

For Step 2, have students identify significant details as they read and then summarize the main points of the article.

Encourage students to express their own opinions and to cite specific information from Steps 1 and 2 in their written responses for Step 3.

Answers:

Step 1

1. b 2. a 3. c 4. b 5. c 6. c

Steps 2–3

Answers will vary.

Additional Resources

Student Resource: Realidades para hispanohablantes, p. 261

Pre–AP*

▼ Objectives
▸ Listen to and read about a legend and an Inca temple
▸ Discuss the relation between indigenous and European cultures

Integración

¿Qué me cuentas?: De leyendas y ciudades

¿Qué resultados trajo el encuentro entre los españoles y los indígenas en las Américas? Escucha una leyenda. Anota las respuestas a las preguntas y guárdalas para usarlas en el paso 3.

1 ◀)) Escucha la leyenda. Después de cada párrafo vas a oír dos preguntas. Escoge la mejor respuesta para cada pregunta.

1. a. una mercancía b. un bolso lleno de oro c. un azulejo
2. a. devolvérselo a su dueño b. llevárselo a su familia c. comprar muchas cosas
3. a. en el bolso no había ninguna moneda b. en el bolso había cuarenta monedas c. faltaban dos monedas en el bolso
4. a. al rey b. al representante del rey c. a sus amigos
5. a. porque le contó su historia b. porque compró pocas cosas con el oro c. porque devolvió el bolso
6. a. al señor español b. al mensajero c. al señor azteca

2 Ahora, lee este artículo sobre una construcción colonial.

Destinos andinos

KORICANCHA: TEMPLO E IGLESIA

El Templo del Sol de Koricancha en la ciudad de Cusco, Perú fue la construcción más impresionante del imperio inca. Estaba decorado totalmente con oro. Había páneles, figuras religiosas y altares de oro, y en el interior había colgado un enorme disco dorado que reflejaba el sol. Durante la conquista, los incas utilizaron gran parte de este oro para pagar la fianza[1] de Atahualpa, el líder capturado por los españoles. Los españoles sacaron lo que quedaba del oro cuando conquistaron Cusco. Después, ellos construyeron el convento y la iglesia de Santo Domingo encima del templo, integrando los muros[2] incaicos de piedra en la base del edificio. El resultado fue una mezcla única de arquitectura colonial.

Vista del muro incaico en la iglesia de Santo Domingo, Cusco.

Peruvian.com

[1] ransom [2] walls

3 Habla con un(a) compañero(a) sobre la relación entre la cultura indígena y la europea en las Américas. ¿Cómo crees que se sentían los indígenas y españoles? ¿Cómo se refleja la fusión de las culturas en la leyenda y en la iglesia? Compara este encuentro entre culturas con lo que pasó en España. Usa las siguientes expresiones para conectar tus ideas.

| antes de | anteriormente | también | durante | para ilustrar |

372 trescientos setenta y dos
¡Adelante!

DIFFERENTIATED INSTRUCTION

Heritage Language Learners

After each oral presentation, ask students to play the part of tourists in the city. Encourage them to ask follow-up questions of the tour guide, and to discuss how this city compares to other cities with which they are familiar, perhaps in their heritage country.

Students with Learning Difficulties

Encourage students to organize and record the information for their oral presentations on index cards. Remind them not to read from their cards, but to refer to their notes during the course of the presentation.

Presentación oral

Una visita a . . .

Objectives
▶ Demonstrate how to give a guided city tour
▶ Identify a purpose to improve your presentation

Tarea
Eres guía turístico(a) en una ciudad multicultural. Planeas una visita a los lugares más importantes de la ciudad.

① Prepárate Escoge la ciudad en la que te gustaría organizar una visita. Completa una tabla con sus características.

nombre de la ciudad	
herencia cultural	
religiones	
restaurantes típicos	
edificios históricos	

Puedes dibujar un plano de la ciudad y marcar con una flecha (arrow) los lugares sobre los que hablarás.

② Practica Vuelve a leer la información que anotaste en la tabla. Practica varias veces tu presentación. Puedes usar tus notas para practicar, pero no al hablar ante la clase. Recuerda:

- describir con detalles la parte de la ciudad de la que hablas
- añadir detalles sobre cómo se relacionan entre sí los diferentes grupos culturales de la ciudad
- mirar directamente al público
- usar el vocabulario y la gramática del capítulo

Modelo
Hoy visitaremos el centro de la ciudad de San Francisco de Quito. La ciudad tiene herencia cultural española e indígena. La religión de sus habitantes es la cristiana, por eso tiene muchas iglesias . . .

③ Haz tu presentación Imagina que tus compañeros de clase son los turistas. Explícales cómo es la ciudad, como si estuvieran allí.

④ Evaluación Tu profesor(a) utilizará la siguiente rúbrica para evaluar tu presentación.

Rubric	Score 1	Score 3	Score 5
How clearly you state your purpose	Your purpose is not stated or evident.	You hint at a purpose but don't clearly state it.	You clearly state your purpose at the beginning.
How well you organize and present information	You give very little information.	You lack important information. You do not organize your information.	Your information is complete, interesting, and well-organized.
How effectively you deliver your speech	Your speech is read. You make no eye contact with the audience.	You make some eye contact with the audience.	You make good eye contact with the audience.

Estrategia

Speaker's purpose
Before giving an oral presentation, you must think what the purpose of your speech is. Do you want to inform, persuade, or entertain your audience?

In this case, your purpose will be to inform. You need your audience—the tourists—to be both interested in the tour and informed. Use interesting facts about the city and present them in an engaging way.

San Francisco de Quito, Ecuador

trescientos setenta y tres **373**
Capítulo 8

Speaking ⑧

ⓒ Common Core: Speaking

Presentación oral

Core Instruction
Standards: 1.2, 1.3, 3.1

Resources: Voc. and Gram. Transparency 4

Focus: Preparing and delivering an oral presentation

Suggestions: Review the task and the four-step approach with students. Review the rubric with the class (see *Assessment* below) to explain how you will grade the performance task. Before students begin, direct their attention to the *Estrategia*. Then ask a volunteer to read the *Modelo* in Step 2. Ask students if they think the speaker's purpose is evident in this sample speech introduction. Tell them that they should not only clarify their purpose in their own minds but make it clear to their audience as well by stating it at the beginning of their speech.

Pre-AP* Support

- **Learning Objective:** Presentational Speaking
- **Activity:** Remind students to gather as many interesting facts about their city in order to make their presentation as informative and interesting as possible. Students should focus on the presentational speaking skills used in this task such as fluency, pronunciation, and comprehensibility.
- **Pre-AP* Resource Book:** Comprehensive guide to Pre-AP* speaking skill development, pp. 39–50

Portfolio
Make video or audio recordings of student presentations in class, or assign the RealTalk activity so they can record their presentations online. Include the recording in their portfolios.

Additional Resources
Student Resource: Realidades para hispanohablantes, p. 262

ENRICH YOUR TEACHING

21st Century Skills

Creativity and Innovation Have students think about the purpose of a guided tour. What are the most interesting features of a city and how would they present them to an audience of fellow students? What are the most interesting ways to promote each visit? Encourage students to be creative in the way they present their city tour using visuals, maps, artifacts, or personal anecdotes.

✓ ASSESSMENT

Presentación oral
- Assessment Program: Rubrics, p. T33
  Review the rubric with students. Go over the descriptions of the different levels of performance. After assessing students, help individuals understand how their performance could be improved. (See Teacher's Resource Book for suggestions on using rubrics in assessment.)

| ▼ **Objectives**

▸ **Narrate a personal experience**
▸ **Order facts chronologically**
▸ **Add details to make a story more interesting**

▼ Language Arts Connection: Expository Writing

Standards: 3.1

Have students consult models of narratives they have encountered in their Social Studies courses, including narratives they themselves may have created. Ask them to focus on how chronological order was used in those narratives and the transitions that were used to connect ideas. Have them incorporate successful organizational strategies from these models into their narrative compositions.

 Common Core: Writing

Presentación escrita

Core Instruction

Standards: 1.2, 1.3, 3.1

Resources: Voc. and Gram. Transparency 4
Focus: Combining learned vocabulary and structures in a written presentation

Suggestions: Begin by explaining the criteria you will use to evaluate students' compositions. (See Step 5, *Evaluación,* in the Student Edition, and *Assessment* on the following page.)

Direct students' attention to the *Estrategia.* Ask them to share additional background information they have learned in Language Arts courses about chronological order. Use *Vocabulary and Grammar Transparency* 4 to model brainstorming and recording ideas for a personal experience narrative. Have students create a similar chart on their own paper, adding a fifth column.

Pre-AP* Support

- **Learning Objective:** Presentational Writing
- **Pre-AP* Resource Book:** Comprehensive guide to Pre-AP* writing skill development, pp. 27–38

Presentación escrita

Mi experiencia con otras culturas

Estrategia

Chronological ordering
Putting events in chronological order means listing them in the order they occurred. This usually means starting with the first event and continuing to the last. You can also use reverse chronological order if it's more appropriate for the story you are telling. Remember to use signal words that indicate chronological order, like *primero, luego, después, segundo, finalmente, por último.*

¿Cómo sería ir a vivir a otro país? ¿Te mudaste de país? ¿Tus padres nacieron en otro país? ¿Conservan en tu familia tradiciones de sus antepasados? ¿Conoces a alguna persona que haya nacido en otro país y esté viviendo aquí? Escribe un episodio *(episode)* autobiográfico sobre una experiencia personal, o inventa una historia. Puedes relatar cómo te sentiste cuando llegaste al país, qué piensas de la integración con otras culturas o qué tradiciones conserva tu familia.

1 Antes de escribir

Piensa en ideas para tu episodio y hazte estas preguntas:

- ¿Con qué claridad recuerdo o me imagino la experiencia?
- ¿Estoy listo(a) para compartirla con otros?
- ¿Qué aprendí o aprendería de la experiencia?

Ordena tus ideas completando una tabla como esta.

Personajes	Lo que sucedió	Época	Lugar	Pensamientos/Sentimientos
yo, mamá, papá, abuela	mudarnos a Estados Unidos	cinco años atrás	Nueva York	• triste por dejar a mis amigos • nervioso por ir a un país desconocido

2 Borrador

Al escribir el borrador, ordena tus ideas lógicamente para que el relato sea fácil de leer. Añade todos los detalles necesarios. Recuerda usar el vocabulario y la gramática de este capítulo.

Modelo

Topic sentence and introductory paragraph: What is the composition about? →

Hace cinco años que vivo con mi familia en los Estados Unidos. Antes vivíamos en México. Tenía muchos amigos allí. Cuando mi papá me dio la noticia de que íbamos a mudarnos a los Estados Unidos, mis amigos no querían que los dejara. Yo les pedí que fueran a . . .

Recuerdo que cuando llegamos a Nueva York me sentía feliz. ← Nuestro apartamento estaba . . .

Details: The writer expresses his or her feelings in the autobiographic composition.

374 trescientos setenta y cuatro
¡Adelante!

DIFFERENTIATED INSTRUCTION

Heritage Language Learners

Ask willing students to serve as interviewees for other students. Encourage them to share their own experiences or those of family members. Have the interviewers show their questions to you first, and remind all participants to conduct these personal interviews with respect and consideration.

Advanced Learners

Invite students to write a short story or dramatic scene. Their story or scene should convey the emotional impact that arises from an encounter between two cultures. Encourage students to limit the number of characters in their story or scene to two or three.

Signal words: The writer uses words that indicate the chronological order of events.

Al principio no sentí mucho la diferencia, pues todas las personas del barrio hablaban español. Era increíble que hasta en los almacenes y los restaurantes hablaban el mismo idioma que yo . . .

Finalmente, me di cuenta de que debía aprender inglés porque . . .

Conclusion: The writer uses a signal word that indicates chronological order.

3 Redacción/Revisión

Después de escribir el primer borrador, trabaja con otro(a) estudiante para intercambiar los trabajos y leerlos. Luego, hagan sugerencias para mejorar sus composiciones.

Haz lo siguiente: Subraya con una línea los verbos en pretérito o en imperfecto y con dos líneas los verbos en imperfecto del subjuntivo.

- ¿Siguieron el plan de la tabla que hicieron?
- ¿Organizaron la información en orden cronológico?

- ¿Están empleados correctamente el pretérito, el imperfecto y el imperfecto del subjuntivo?

Cuando mi papá me <u>dio</u> la noticia de que <u>íbamos</u>

a mudarnos a los Estados Unidos, mis amigos

no <u>querían</u> que los ~~deje~~ *dejara*. Yo les ~~pediré~~ *pedí* que

<u>fueran</u> a . . .

4 Publicación

Antes de crear la versión final, lee de nuevo tu borrador y repasa los siguientes puntos:

- ¿Incluí detalles para expresar mis sentimientos?
- ¿Estoy relatando un episodio interesante?
- ¿Refleja la integración con otras culturas?

Después de revisar el borrador, escribe en limpio tu composición.

5 Evaluación

Se utilizará la siguiente rúbrica para evaluar tu presentación.

Rubric	Score 1	Score 3	Score 5
Completion of task	Your idea is not stated or is unclear. There is little or no development of it.	Your main idea is hinted at, but your development of it is weak.	Your main idea is clear and interestingly developed.
Use of chronological order and transitions	You present too few events and use no transitions.	Some of your events are out of order or lacking helpful transitions.	You sequence events and use effective transitions.
Sentence structure/ grammar, spelling, mechanics	Sentences run on or are fragmented. You make many grammar, spelling, and/or mechanics errors.	You use sentences consistently. You make some grammar, spelling, and/or mechanics errors.	Your sentence structure is correct and varied. You make few grammar, spelling, and/or mechanics errors.

trescientos setenta y cinco **375**
Capítulo 8

Suggestions (Cont'd):

Once students have a rough draft ready, read through the model on this page together. Help them see how information from the chart on p. 374 was incorporated into this draft and to note transitions that were used. Ask them to identify uses of the imperfect subjunctive. Encourage them to work toward a similar level of organization, detail, and language use, even if they have chosen a different chronological order for their own personal experience narratives.

For Step 3, encourage students to focus on sentence structure, transitions, and use of the imperfect subjunctive. Have them follow the suggestions shown.

Evaluation

Steps 4 and 5 overlap. Students will need evaluation by you, their peers, or self-evaluation to fine-tune and polish their drafts.

Portfolio

Keep students' final drafts in their portfolios as a writing sample.

Additional Resources

Student Resource: Realidades para hispanohablantes, p. 263

ENRICH YOUR TEACHING

21st Century Skills

Creativity and Innovation Students will use their written language for the purpose of narrating a personal cross-cultural experience. Have them think of creative ways to express their personal reactions to the experience. How did they feel? What was their first reaction? What did they learn from the experience? They can also include the reaction of others in their narration.

✓ ASSESSMENT

Presentación escrita

- Assessment Program: Rubrics, p. T33
  Review the rubric with students. Go over the descriptions of the different levels of performance. After assessing students, help individuals understand how their performance could be improved. (See Teacher's Resource Book for suggestions on using rubrics in assessment.)

Lectura

Core Instruction

Standards: 1.2, 2.1, 2.2, 3.1, 3.2, 5.2

Resources: Voc. and Gram. Transparency 4

🌐 **Mapa global interactivo, Actividad 9**
Discover the Museo de Antropología in Mexico City.

Focus: Reading an extended passage

Suggestions:

Pre-reading: Before reading, direct students' attention to the *Al leer* section. Have them copy the graphic organizer from p. 379 and make sure they understand how they will use it. If necessary, use *Vocabulary and Grammar Transparency 4* to model setting up a similar chart, leaving one of the columns empty. Explain that **Antes** refers to the point at which the story begins or before, and **Ahora** refers to the end of the story. Point out the relationship between the five questions in *Al leer* and the information in the left column of the chart. Also refer them to the *Estrategia*. Remind them to follow the suggestions there and to read the selection the first time without stopping.

Reading: Allow students time to read the entire selection on their own silently. You might assign this task for homework. This will allow you to capitalize on class time to read it again together with students. When reading together, pause frequently to address comprehension issues they may have and to allow them to fill in their **Cambios en la narración** charts from p. 379. Here are some possible comprehension issues on this page for which you can provide some guidance:

• Explain that the first, italicized paragraph is a summary. It is important to understand this summary of who the characters Daniel and Chalchi are in order to follow the rest of the story.

• *¿En qué tiempo está la narración del cuento, en el presente o en el pasado? (el presente)*

• *¿Daniel se da cuenta de qué cambios en su situación mientras se despierta? (Su ropa y su cama han cambiado.)*

• *¿A quién se parece la mujer que está llamando a Daniel? (Se parece a su novia Chalchi.)*

• *¿Qué nombre es una forma corta de Chalchiunenetl? (Chalchi)*

¡Adelante!

Lectura 🌐
El último sol
Fragmento adaptado

Objectives

▶ Read and understand a story based on historical facts

▶ Use context to guess the meaning of unfamiliar words

▶ Learn about Aztec heritage and borrowed words

Estrategia

Skipping and guessing
When reading for pleasure, you may try to skip unfamiliar words. If the word is truly essential to the meaning of the passage, try to guess the word's meaning. If you guess correctly, the text will make sense!

Al leer

¿Alguna vez has sentido que nadie te entiende? Vas a leer un cuento de Elías Miguel Muñoz, un destacado novelista y cuentista cubano que reside en los Estados Unidos. Al leer este cuento te verás transportado(a) a otro mundo, el mundo del México antiguo, Tenochtitlán. Lee el cuento una primera vez sin pararte. No te preocupes por las palabras que no conozcas. Trata de adivinarlas. Cuando leas el cuento por segunda vez, mira los significados para ver si las entendiste. Mientras lees, presta atención a los siguientes puntos para que puedas llenar la tabla que aparece al final de la lectura:

• quiénes son los personajes
• dónde ocurre la acción, cómo cambia
• cómo cambia la relación de los personajes
• cómo reacciona el narrador
• cómo se siente el narrador al final de la lectura

DANIEL, el protagonista de El último sol es un joven que estudia en la Ciudad de México. A Daniel le encanta compartir pasajes de la historia de México con su novia Chalchi. Un día Daniel se queda dormido y sueña con la Piedra del Sol, el calendario azteca que había visto en el Museo de Antropología. Cuando se despierta, Daniel se encuentra en un mundo diferente . . .

"¡Tozani!" Escucho una voz de mujer que viene de lejos. "¡Tozani!" Trato de despertar, pero me pesan los párpados[1]. Siento mucho frío. "¡Tozani!" La voz se hace más fuerte. Abro por fin los ojos y veo mi cuerpo, casi desnudo. Sólo llevo un taparrabo[2] y estoy acostado en una cama que no es la mía; es un petate[3]. Busco a la dueña de la voz y por fin la veo, parada frente a mí.

—Despierta ya —me dice ella.

Habla un idioma extraño que yo, de una manera también muy extraña, puedo comprender. Sus palabras llegan a mí como filtradas por el aire frío de este cuarto.

—Despierta —repite—. Es hora de ir al lago.

La observo. Es una muchacha joven, hermosa. Tiene el cabello atado atrás, con dos trenzas[4] sobre la frente. Lleva un vestido largo, blanco; en la cintura, un amplio cincho[5] bordado. Sus ojos son de un verde intenso. Se parece tanto a Chalchi que la llamo por ese nombre, Chalchiunenetl, y ella responde . . .

—Sí. Has dormido mucho, Tozani.

—¿Tozani? Yo no me llamo Tozani —le digo, confundido. Y ella me mira sonriendo.

—Levántate ya, esposo.

---

1 eyelids **2** loincloth **3** bedroll **4** braids **5** belt

DIFFERENTIATED INSTRUCTION

Students with Learning Difficulties

Students may be confused by the main character's own confusion in **El último sol.** To help clarify the plot, assign small groups of students different sections of the excerpt. Have each group choose a narrator and the necessary characters. Give students the opportunity to quickly rehearse and present their dramatic interpretation of events.

Students with Special Needs

Provide visually impaired students with partners to describe the illustrations on pp. 377 and 378. Instruct these partners to provide details regarding the setting, calendar, and dress shown. How do these images differ from what Daniel must have been used to?

¡Me ha llamado *esposo*! Miro a mi alrededor y descubro que no estoy en casa de mis padres. Este lugar es mucho más grande; las paredes son blancas y a lo largo de cada una hay tiestos[6] enormes con flores de varios tipos y colores. Los muebles son escasos pero hermosos, de madera densa: un pequeño armario, una mesa baja y dos sillas. Hay una armonía total en este sitio. La puerta que da a la calle está inundada de luz.

¿Dónde estoy?

• • • • • • • • • • •

Trato de ordenar mis pensamientos. Debo estar soñando. Cierro los ojos. Me golpeo la cara para despertar, ¡una, dos, tres veces! Y escucho la voz asustada de Chalchi; sus manos sujetan las mías.

—¡Tozani! —exclama—. ¡¿Qué haces?! ¿Por qué te golpeas?

No puedo contestarle. Algo en la garganta me impide hablar.

—Estabas soñando, esposo —me dice ella, mientras me acaricia.

—¿Soñando? —le pregunto, incrédulo.

—Sí. Pero ya, por fin, empiezas a despertar.

———————————

6 flowerpots

Me muevo. Respiro. Tengo los ojos muy abiertos. Sí. Estoy despierto.

—Cuando regreses del lago, comeremos —me dice Chalchi. Y se va a otro cuarto.

El lago. ¿Qué tendré que hacer en el lago? Me acuesto otra vez en el petate incómodo. ¿Cómo explicar todo esto?

trescientos setenta y siete **377**
Capítulo 8

Suggestions (Cont'd):

Reading: Here are some possible comprehension issues on this page for which you can provide some guidance:

• *En el primer párrafo, hay una palabra que significa lo mismo que harmony en inglés. Adivina qué palabra es. (armonía)*

• *¿Cuáles son los muebles que Daniel ve? (un armario, una mesa y dos sillas) ¿Estos son muchos o pocos muebles? (pocos) Entonces, ¿qué quiere decir la palabra "escasos": "muchos" o "pocos"? (pocos)*

• *¿Por qué no puede hablar Daniel? (Algo en su garganta le impide.) ¿Qué palabra en inglés significa lo mismo que "impide"? (impede)*

BELLRINGER REVIEW

Show Fine Art Transparency 2 for twenty seconds. Remove the transparency and ask the students five true/false statements.

Teacher-to-Teacher

When having students read selections aloud, try assigning roles to volunteers. In this story, you could choose one or more narrators, who rotate reading paragraphs of the narration. Two other volunteers can assume the roles of Daniel-Tozani and Chalchiunenetl.

Additional Resources

Student Resource: Guided Practice: Lectura, pp. 266–267

ENRICH YOUR TEACHING

Culture Note
Built in the center of Lake Texcoco, the Aztec city of Tenochtitlán was one of the biggest metropolitan areas of its era. With causeways linking the city to the mainland, the city featured a number of engineering advances. Aqueducts, sewers, irrigation systems and "floating gardens" were all part of the city's design.

21st Century Skills
Technology Literacy Remind students of the various digital tools available in **realidades.com** to access extra reading support. Computer corrected activities use different reading strategies to help students build their vocabulary and progress at their own pace through the reading.

Suggestions (Cont'd):

Reading: Here are some possible comprehension issues on this page for which you can provide some guidance:

• *¿Cuál es la fecha, exactamente, en el calendario moderno?* (el 29 de junio de 1519)

• *Moctezuma quiere que Daniel-Tozani sea responsable de una misión importante. ¿Qué verbo usa Chalchi que significa "hacer responsable"?* (encomendar)

• *¿Qué expresión usa Chalchi para decir que los seres blancos son altos?* (son grandes de estatura)

Post-reading: Have students complete their **Cambios en la narración** charts, referring to the story as necessary. Ask volunteers to read aloud or paraphrase parts of the story that support their choices for the chart.

Pre-AP* Support

• **Learning Objective:** Interpretive: Print
• **Activity:** Have students create a series of drawings to represent scenes in this story. Use the form of a *códice*. (A *códice* is a book that describes a story with colorful drawings that can be symbols or realistic scenes.) The pages of the book are not separated; each page is long and horizontal, folded like an accordion, between one scene and another. Students should include five scenes. Then, have volunteers tell their story to the class using the *códice* to illustrate it.
• *Pre-AP* Resource Book:* Comprehensive guide to Pre-AP* reading skill development, pp. 19–26

Block Schedule

Expert Groups: After the class has read the story, give each student the number 1, 2, or 3. The story is divided into three sections. Indicate to the students which section they are to focus on. Each student is to write eight questions about their section. Then divide the class into groups of three, with a number 1, 2, and 3 in each group. Have each student read his or her questions starting with the 1s. If a student needs assistance with a particular section, he or she can "ask the expert."

—¡Chalchi! —la llamo, y ella aparece ante mí.

—Estoy amasando *tlaxcalli*[7], preparando tu *atolli*[8]. ¿Por qué no te has ido al lago?

—¡Porque no sé para qué tengo que ir al lago!

—¿Estás soñando otra vez, querido mío? —ella me dice, sonriendo—. Tienes que ir al lago para bañarte, claro. Luego te vestirás de guerra para asistir al Templo Mayor. No olvides que el Reverendo Padre quiere verte.

—¿El Reverendo Padre?

—Sí. El señor emperador, Moctezuma.

—¡¿Quién?!

—Pobre de ti. Ese sueño de anoche te obsesiona.

—¿En qué año estamos, Chalchi?

—Acatl. El año 1-Caña[9], el día de 2-Casas.

Trato de recordar el calendario azteca. Un escalofrío[10] me invade el cuerpo cuando por fin descifro el significado de aquella fecha. *Acatl*, equivalente al año 1519 del calendario cristiano. El día 2-Casas, o sea, el 29, probablemente del mes de junio. Un mes antes de la entrada de Hernán Cortés en Tenochtitlán.

· · · · · · · · · · ·

—Chalchi, ¿por qué quiere verme Moctezuma?

Ella me mira como diciéndome, "despierta ya, querido esposo". Exasperada y sin comprender mi pregunta, me explica:

—El reverendo señor Moctezuma, *Huey-Tlatoani* de los aztecas, quiere encomendarte una misión muy importante . . .

—¿Qué misión es?

—¿Tampoco lo recuerdas? ¡Ese sueño de anoche te ha convertido en otro hombre, Tozani!

—Mi misión tiene que ver con los "dioses blancos", ¿verdad?

—Sí. En la última reunión del consejo gobernante, nuestro emperador decidió enviar una comisión para recibir a los seres blancos, para llevarles regalos y guiarlos hasta nuestra ciudad. El consejo te escogió a ti para encabezar la comisión.

---

7 corn tortillas 8 corn gruel 9 1-Reed, represents a month in the Aztec calendar 10 chill

378 trescientos setenta y seis
¡Adelante!

—Esos seres no son dioses, Chalchi.

—¿Cómo lo sabes?

—Lo sé. Simplemente lo sé.

Chalchi se queda pensativa unos minutos. Luego me dice, agitada:

—Los mensajeros de Moctezuma que han visto a esos seres, cuentan que son grandes de estatura, que tienen la cara cubierta de cabello. Y algunos de ellos tienen cuatro patas enormes y dos cabezas, una de animal y otra de hombre . . .

—Son los españoles, Chalchi —le digo, sabiendo que no me entenderá. Repito: —Son los soldados de Cortés.

—Los soldados . . . ¿de quién?

—De Cortés, un hombre que viene a destruirnos.

—¡No! Moctezuma dice que son dioses. Dice que nuestro creador, Quetzalcóatl, ha regresado para recuperar su reino.

—¡Está loco el emperador!

DIFFERENTIATED INSTRUCTION

Heritage Language Learners

Ask students to choose an interesting and/or important historical event from their heritage country. Have students briefly discuss what it would be like to return to that event. Who would they wish to be? How might their perspective on the event be different given their present-day knowledge?

Advanced Learners

Have students choose one word or expression from the story that they consider new or difficult and write it on a slip of paper. Mix the slips and have students take turns drawing one. Ask them to use background knowledge or reference materials to write a definition or explanation of the item they drew.

Interacción con la lectura

1 Llena la tabla con la información del cuento.

CAMBIOS EN LA NARRACIÓN		
	Antes	Ahora
Nombre de los dos personajes principales		
Cuándo ocurre la acción		
Lugar donde ocurre la acción		
Cuál es la relación entre los personajes		
Cómo se siente el personaje		

2 Trabaja con un grupo de estudiantes para comentar lo que escribieron en sus tablas y contestar las siguientes preguntas.

- ¿Qué le ha ocurrido a Daniel? ¿Cómo lo sabes?
- ¿Cómo es la nueva vida de Daniel?
- ¿Por qué es importante la fecha? ¿Quiénes son esos seres con dos cabezas y cuatro patas?
- ¿Qué tarea le ha encargado el emperador a Daniel?
- ¿Qué sabe Daniel que nadie más sabe?
- ¿Daniel puede cambiar lo que ocurrirá?

3 Trabaja con tu grupo para describir a los personajes en el mundo azteca: ¿Cómo se vestían? ¿Qué comían? Usa el vocabulario de la lectura.

4 Conocemos el final de la historia: Hernán Cortés conquistó el imperio Azteca. ¿Qué crees que hizo Daniel? ¿Trató de prevenir *(warn)* a los demás? ¿Trató de parar a los españoles? Comenta tus ideas con tus compañeros.

Más práctica **GO** realidades.com | print

Guided WB pp. 266–267	✔	✔
Comm. WB p. 208	✔	✔
Cultural Reading Activity	✔	

▼ Fondo Cultural | México

La herencia azteca Aunque el mundo de los aztecas desapareció con la llegada de Hernán Cortés en 1519, en México todavía se siente la herencia azteca en el lenguaje y las costumbres. En México todavía usan petates para acostarse en el campo y los niños toman atole en la merienda y los adultos en las celebraciones. Además, en todo el mundo se usan las palabras tomate, chocolate, chile, coyote. Las otras lenguas americanas de Norteamérica, el Caribe y Sudamérica también han contribuido palabras que se usan hoy en todo el mundo: *caimán, canoa, caribú, cóndor, gaucho, huracán, iglú, iguana, jaguar, maíz, mocasín, papaya, poncho, puma.* Generalmente, estas palabras se refieren a objetos que se desconocían en Europa antes del descubrimiento de América.

- ¿Conoces más palabras como éstas?
- ¿Qué tipos de palabras pasan de una lengua a otra? ¿Por qué?
- ¿Tú usas palabras nuevas o distintas a las que usan los demás? ¿De dónde vienen? ¿Por qué las usas?

Standards: 1.1, 1.2, 3.1

Resources: Answer Keys: Student Edition, p. 118

Suggestions: Explain that the last piece of information in the chart in Step 1, ***Cómo se siente el personaje,*** refers to Daniel-Tozani.

Answers:

Step 1

Daniel/Tozani; Chalchi/Chalchiunenetl
hoy en día/en el año 1519
Ciudad de México/Tenochtitlán
novios/esposos
Answers for how Daniel-Tozani feels will vary.

Step 2

- **Daniel se ha despertado en otro mundo. En la introducción es un joven de la Ciudad de México de hoy en día. De repente se encuentra en el mundo precolonial de los aztecas.**
- **Su vida es muy distinta a la vida de un joven azteca de hace 500 años.**
- **Es una fecha importante porque es un mes antes de la llegada de los europeos. Son soldados españoles montados a caballo.**
- **El emperador ha encargado a Daniel con la tarea de recibir a los europeos.**
- **Daniel sabe que los seres blancos no son dioses sino los españoles.**
- **Answers will vary.**

Steps 3–4
Answers will vary.

Fondo cultural

Standards: 1.1, 1.2, 2.1, 2.2, 3.1

Suggestions: After students have read the information silently, ask them to work in pairs or small groups and develop lists of other words borrowed from indigenous American languages and used in either English or Spanish. Remind them of the many place names in the United States that come from indigenous languages. Encourage them to find out what some of these names mean in their original languages.

Answers will vary.

For Further Reading

Student Resources: Lecturas 3: "Roberto y sus problemas de adaptación," pp. 26–29, "Una carta a Dios," pp. 36–37

ENRICH YOUR TEACHING

Culture Note

Today maize is the third most planted field crop in the world (first and second being wheat and rice). Maize is actually a domesticated grass first cultivated and developed by the Aztecs. A chief staple of their diet, maize also played an important religious role. Of the Aztecs' many gods, ***Xilonen*** was the god of the "young maize ear." The name maize, however, is not an indigenous word. It's thought to have evolved from Columbus' entourage encountering Tahino people, and their ***mahis,*** which means "source of life." ***Mahis*** developed into the word ***maíz.***

Repaso del capítulo

Vocabulario y gramática

Review Activities

Para hablar de construcciones: Ask students to work in pairs to quiz each other. Have them take turns sketching and identifying the various items.

Para hablar del descubrimiento de América: Have students work in groups to create a summary of the discovery and early contact in the Americas. Their summary should include all of the words in the category. Invite them to present their summaries orally. Have the class discuss differences and similarities between the various summaries they hear.

Para hablar del encuentro de culturas: Ask students to prepare brief oral reports about a cultural encounter of their choice, past or present. Encourage each student to base the report on his or her own cultural heritage. Their reports should include as many of the words in the category as possible. Ask students to be prepared to field questions from the audience after their report.

Verbos: Have students choose any five of the verbs and use them in the imperfect subjunctive in complex sentences. Then have students share their sentences.

Otras expresiones y palabras: Students can use these words and expressions as they go over the review activities for the other categories.

Additional Resources

Student Resources: Realidades para hispanohablantes, pp. 264–265

Teacher Resources:

• Teacher's Resource Book: Situation Cards, p. 201, Clip Art, pp. 202–209

• Assessment Program: Chapter Checklist and Self-Assessment Worksheet, pp. T49–T50

para hablar de construcciones

el acueducto	aqueduct
el arco	arch
la arquitectura	architecture
el azulejo	tile
el balcón, *pl.* los balcones	balcony
la construcción	construction
la reja	railing, grille
la torre	tower

para hablar de la llegada a las Américas

anteriormente	before
el arma, *pl.* las armas	weapon
la batalla	battle
la colonia	colony
la conquista	conquest
el imperio	empire
el / la indígena	native
la maravilla	marvel, wonder
la misión	mission
el / la misionero(a)	missionary
la población	population
el poder	power
poderoso, -a	powerful
el reto	challenge
la riqueza	wealth
el / la soldado	soldier
la tierra	land

para hablar del encuentro de culturas

africano, -a	African
el antepasado	ancestor
el / la árabe	Arab
cristiano, -a	Christian
la descendencia	descent, ancestry
desconocido, -a	unknown
el encuentro	meeting
la época	time, era
europeo, -a	European

la guerra	war
el grupo étnico	ethnic group
la herencia	heritage
el idioma	language
la influencia	influence
el intercambio	exchange
el / la judío(a)	Jew
la lengua	language
la mercancía	merchandise
la mezcla	mix
el musulmán, la musulmana	Muslim
el / la romano(a)	Roman
la raza	race
el resultado	result, outcome
la semejanza	similarity
la unidad	unity
la variedad	variety

verbos

adoptar	to adopt
asimilar(se)	to assimilate
componerse de	to be formed by
conquistar	to conquer
dejar huellas	to leave marks, traces
dominar	to dominate
enfrentarse	to face, to confront
establecer (zc)	to establish
expulsar	to expel
fundar(se)	to found
gobernar (ie)	to rule, to govern
integrarse	to integrate
invadir	to invade
luchar	to fight
ocupar	to occupy
rebelarse	to rebel, to revolt
reconquistar	to reconquer

otras expresiones y palabras

al llegar	upon arriving
maravilloso, -a	wonderful
único, -a	only

380 trescientos ochenta
Repaso del capítulo

DIFFERENTIATED INSTRUCTION

Students with Learning Difficulties

Divide students into pairs. Instruct them to use the vocabulary on p. 380 as a guide. One partner should choose a word and read it aloud. The other partner should review the chapter to locate a picture of, or reference to, that word. Have students use the information they have found to formulate a sentence using the word.

Advanced Learners

Have students assume the role of a politician, either local, national, or international. Ask them to prepare and deliver a brief message in which they suggest one or more ways to improve relations between two cultures. Tell them that their message can be created as though it were part of a longer speech.

el condicional

Use the conditional to express what you would do or what a situation would be like.

hablar

hablar**ía**	hablar**íamos**
hablar**ías**	hablar**íais**
hablar**ía**	hablar**ían**

ser

ser**ía**	ser**íamos**
ser**ías**	ser**íais**
ser**ía**	ser**ían**

ir

ir**ía**	ir**íamos**
ir**ías**	ir**íais**
ir**ía**	ir**ían**

Verbs that are irregular in the future tense have the same irregular stems in the conditional.

tener

tendr**ía**	tendr**íamos**
tendr**ías**	tendr**íais**
tendr**ía**	tendr**ían**

future and conditional stems of other irregular verbs:

decir	**dir-**	poder	**podr-**	saber	**sabr-**
haber	**habr-**	poner	**pondr-**	salir	**saldr-**
hacer	**har-**	querer	**querr-**	venir	**vendr-**

el imperfecto del subjuntivo

Use the subjunctive to say what one person asks, hopes, tells, insists, or requires someone else to do. If the main verb is in the preterite or imperfect tense, use the imperfect subjunctive.

cantar

cantar**a**	cantár**amos**
cantar**as**	cantar**ais**
cantar**a**	cantar**an**

aprender

aprendier**a**	aprendiér**amos**
aprendier**as**	aprendier**ais**
aprendier**a**	aprendier**an**

vivir

vivier**a**	viviér**amos**
vivier**as**	vivier**ais**
vivier**a**	vivier**an**

el imperfecto del subjuntivo con *si*

Use the imperfect subjunctive after *si* when a situation is unlikely, impossible, or not true. Use the conditional in the main clause.

   Si hablaras más, tendrías muchos amigos.
   Si Marcos no fuera tan travieso, lo llevaría de paseo.

After *como si* you always use the imperfect subjunctive.

   Ella se sentía como si estuviera en un lugar desconocido.

trescientos ochenta y uno **381**
Capítulo 8

ENRICH YOUR TEACHING

Teacher-to-Teacher

Have students create a practice test covering the vocabulary and grammar structures. Encourage them to use multiple choice, true/false, or short answer questions. Have them exchange tests with a partner or compile the questions and answer them in a game show format.

21st Century Skills

Initiative and Self-Direction Remind students of the various digital tools available in **realidades.com** to help them monitor their own understanding and learning needs as they prepare for chapter tests, such as the online tutorials with comprehension check exercises, interactive puzzles, and flashcards.

El condicional: Tell students that Mateo is a very popular boy. Everyone always needs to talk to him or has something to do with him. Ask students to think of at least two questions concerning Mateo that they might ask a friend, such as: *¿Hablarás con Mateo hoy?* The friend responds using the conditional, saying that he or she would do that thing, but Mateo is not to be found: *Le hablaría, pero no lo encuentro.* Another example might be: *¿Harás tu tarea con Mateo hoy? La haria con él, pero no lo encuentro.* Have partners take turns asking and answering each other's questions.

El imperfecto del subjuntivo: Ask students to think of five wishes they have always had. On the board write the sentence starter *Siempre he querido que....* Have students use the sentence starter five times to write their wishes: *Siempre he querido que el año escolar no fuera tan largo.*

El imperfecto del subjuntivo con si: Challenge students to write comparisons using complex sentences with *como si: Entró en el cuarto como si fuera una reina.* Encourage them to make their comparisons humorous: *Estaba tan alegre como si fuera una tortuga con patines.*

Portfolio

Invite students to review the activities they completed in this chapter, including written reports, posters or other visuals, recordings of oral presentations, and other projects. Have them select one or two items that they feel best demonstrate their achievements in Spanish. Include these products in students' portfolios. Have them include this with the Chapter Checklist and Self-Assessment Worksheet.

Additional Resources

Teacher Resources:

¡Pura vida! is a storyline video that is independent of chapter content and an ideal support for expanding listening skills. The 14 episodes are available within **realidades.com** or on a separate DVD. Student activities and Teacher support are also assignable within **realidades.com**.

Performance Tasks

Standards: 1.1, 1.2, 1.3, 3.1

Student Resource: Realidades para hispano-hablantes, pp. 266–267

Teacher Resources: Teacher's Resource Book: Audio Script, p. 192; Audio Program DVD: Cap. 8, Track 18; Answer Keys: Student Edition, p. 119

1. Vocabulario

Suggestions: Encourage students to review the vocabulary from the *A primera vista* sections on pp. 344–347 and 356–359 before they complete the activity.

Answers:

1. b   5. d
2. c   6. d
3. b   7. b
4. c   8. c

2. Gramática

Suggestions: Remind students of the main points of the grammar presentations in *Capítulo 8*:

• the conditional
• the imperfect subjunctive
• the imperfect subjunctive with *si*

Answers:

1. c   5. a
2. b   6. b
3. c   7. a
4. a   8. d

3. Escuchar

Suggestions: Use the audio or read from the script.

🔊 **Answers:** Wording of answers will vary. The following are likely results:

a. Es famoso por su maravillosa artesanía. Dice que la arquitectura es un resultado de la influencia española durante la colonia.

b. Le impresiona más la variedad de las mercancías. El mercado le recuerda de lo que describió Hernán Cortés en sus Cartas de relación.

c. Encuentra hamacas, joyas de plata y cerámica y también canoas.

d. Lo compara con un mercado de hace siglos.

Preparación para el examen

① Vocabulario Escribe la letra de la palabra o expresión que mejor complete cada frase. Escribe tus respuestas en una hoja aparte.

1. Un ejemplo de un _____ fue el pueblo romano, porque tuvo tanto poder que pudo decidir el futuro de otros pueblos.
   a. misionero   c. arte
   b. imperio   d. arma

2. Empezó un intercambio de _____ entre Europa y las Américas.
   a. riquezas   c. mercancías
   b. banderas   d. libertad

3. Cuando un país invade a otro país y se queda allí por muchos años, decimos que lo _____.
   a. expulsa   c. lucha
   b. ocupa   d. permite

4. Como resultado de la mezcla de españoles, indígenas y africanos hay una gran _____ de culturas en América.
   a. batalla   c. variedad
   b. reja   d. mercancía

5. La Mezquita de Córdoba es un ejemplo de la arquitectura árabe porque tiene muchos _____, igual que la Alhambra, en Granada.
   a. caballos   c. budistas
   b. retos   d. arcos

6. Los misioneros tenían opiniones diferentes sobre _____ de los españoles en la vida de los indígenas.
   a. la semejanza   c. la arquitectura
   b. el azulejo   d. la influencia

7. España era un imperio _____ en la época de la conquista de América.
   a. único   c. débil
   b. poderoso   d. africano

8. Cuando los cristianos reconquistaron Sevilla, muchos árabes se habían _____ con los españoles.
   a. rebelado   c. asimilado
   b. reconquistado d. expulsado

② Gramática Escribe la letra de la palabra o expresión que mejor complete cada frase. Escribe tus respuestas en una hoja aparte.

1. Yo _____ con Luisa por teléfono todos los días si tuviera tiempo, pero estoy muy ocupada.
   a. hablo   c. hablaría
   b. he hablado   d. hablaba

2. Nosotros _____ al balcón, pero hace mucho frío y está lloviendo.
   a. saldremos   c. salíamos
   b. saldríamos   d. saldrían

3. El arquitecto le dijo al dueño de la casa que _____ el azulejo de color amarillo porque era mejor.
   a. compré   c. comprara
   b. compró   d. compras

4. El rey de España lo miró como si _____ que estaba mintiendo.
   a. creyera   c. creía
   b. crea   d. creerá

5. La madre le dijo al niño que _____ a la escuela después de comprar la comida.
   a. vendría   c. vinieron
   b. vienen   d. viene

6. Si _____ todas tus riquezas, te regalaría mis caballos, le dijo el español al indígena.
   a. me das   c. me diste
   b. me dieras   d. me dieron

7. Aprenderíamos otros idiomas, como el chino, si _____ la oportunidad de estudiarlos en la escuela.
   a. tuviéramos   c. tuvieran
   b. tuvimos   d. tuvieras

8. Los misioneros querían que los indígenas _____ su religión.
   a. adoptáramos   c. adoptamos
   b. adoptaron   d. adoptaran

DIFFERENTIATED INSTRUCTION

Heritage Language Learners

Ask students to identify a writing skill that they would like to improve. Examples might include spelling, punctuation, or organization. Have students create a draft of an essay based on the topic on p. 383. Then, have them revise their drafts, focusing on the skill they are trying to improve.

Students with Learning Difficulties

Direct students to focus on the verb(s) in each example of the *Gramática* review. Help them establish the time frame of each sentence. Then, instruct students to choose the verb form that corresponds to both the time frame and meaning of the sentence.

Más repaso [GO] realidades.com | print

Puzzles	✔	
Core WB pp. 117–118		✔
Comm. WB pp. 209, 210–212	✔	✔
Instant Check	✔	

En el examen vas a . . .	Éstas son las tareas de práctica que te pueden ser útiles para el examen . . .	Para repasar, ve a tu libro de texto impreso o digital . . .

Interpretive

3 Escuchar Escuchar y comprender la descripción de una visita a un pueblo indígena

La visitante describe su visita a un pueblo. (a) ¿Por qué es famoso ese pueblo? ¿Qué dice de la arquitectura? (b) ¿Qué le impresiona más? ¿Qué le recuerda el mercado? (c) ¿Qué otras cosas encuentra allí? (d) ¿Con qué compara al pueblo?

pp. 344–347 *A primera vista 1: Vocabulario en contexto*
p. 347 Actividad 4
p. 350 Actividad 8
p. 354 Actividad 15
p. 379 *Interacción con la lectura*

Interpersonal

4 Hablar Presentar una visita guiada para conocer una ciudad

Escoge una ciudad que te guste. Imagina que le hablas de esta ciudad a un recién llegado. Menciona (a) los edificios históricos, (b) las culturas y religiones, (c) una breve historia de la ciudad y (d) lugares donde los jóvenes se divierten.

p. 350 Actividad 8
p. 354 Actividad 15
p. 373 *Presentación oral*

Interpretive

5 Leer Leer y comprender un cuento

Lee este párrafo sobre las aventuras de un indígena azteca y di (a) ¿En qué ciudad crees que se despierta Maco? ¿En qué época sería? (b) ¿Qué lengua habla la gente? (c) ¿Crees que es un sueño o es la realidad?

Un día, Maco, un joven indígena azteca, cerró sus ojos y cuando los abrió se vio en medio de una ciudad muy diferente a la que habitaba. La gente era alta con los cabellos claros. Llevaban ropas largas y zapatos. Hablaban una lengua familiar, parecida a la de las personas que habían llegado a su tierra hacía poco tiempo. La gente lo miraba, pero nadie se paraba a hablarle...

pp. 376–379 *Lectura*

Presentational

6 Escribir Escribir una reseña sobre la herencia cultural

Escribe una reseña sobre qué cosas pueden hacer las familias para mantener sus raíces culturales y las tradiciones de sus antepasados. Sugiere qué pueden hacer para mantener el idioma, las comidas y otras tradiciones familiares.

p. 351 Actividad 9
p. 351 Actividad 10
pp. 374–375 *Presentación escrita*

Cultures

7 Pensar Pensar en ejemplos de intercambio cultural en el mundo de hoy y decir si son positivos o no

Da un ejemplo de un intercambio entre culturas en el mundo de hoy en día. Di por qué crees que ese intercambio es positivo o crea conflictos. ¿Crees que ayuda a que las personas se integren o no?

p. 350 Actividad 8
p. 362 Actividad 24
pp. 370–371 *Puente a la cultura*

trescientos ochenta y tres **383**
Capítulo 8

Review 8

4. Hablar
Suggestions: Encourage students to combine ideas into complex sentences as they describe their city.
Answers will vary.

5. Leer
Suggestions: Tell students to refer to pp. 344–347 and 356–359 if they have questions about vocabulary in the review.
Answers:
a. Cities named should be major Spanish cities. Es la época moderna.
b. La gente habla español.
c. Answers will vary between *sueño* and *realidad.*

6. Escribir
Suggestions: Encourage students to work in pairs or groups to gather ideas for their *reseñas.*
Answers will vary.

7. Pensar
Suggestions: Ask students to consider how their thoughts about cultural fusion have changed, based on what they have learned in *Capítulo* 8.
Answers will vary.

DIFFERENTIATED ASSESSMENT

CORE ASSESSMENT
- **Assessment Program:** Examen del capítulo 8
- **Audio Program DVD:** Cap. 8, Track 19
- **ExamView:** Chapter Test, Test Banks A and B

ADVANCED/PRE-AP*
- **ExamView: Pre-AP* Test Bank**
- **Pre-AP* Resource Book,** pp. 159–161

STUDENTS NEEDING EXTRA HELP
- **Alternate Assessment Program:** Examen del capítulo 8
- **Audio Program DVD:** Cap. 8, Track 19

HERITAGE LEARNERS
- **Assessment Program: Realidades para hispanohablantes:** Examen del capítulo 8
- **ExamView: Heritage Learner Test Bank**

9 Chapter Overview

- **local and global environmental concerns**

Vocabulary
- environmental issues
- endangered species

Grammar
- conjunctions used with the subjunctive and the indicative
- relative pronouns *que, quien, lo que*

Cultural Perspectives
- traffic restrictions in Chile
- ecotourism in Costa Rica
- protection of Magellanic penguins
- endangered species of the Galapagos Islands
- life cycle of the Monarch butterfly

¡Pura vida!
- Watch an engaging video episode about a group of young people in Costa Rica!

CHAPTER SUPPORT

Bulletin Boards

Theme: *Animales en peligro de extinción*

Ask students to cut out, copy, or download photos or pictures of animals in danger of extinction. Place photos around a world map with leader lines from animals to their respective habitats. Add brief captions to the photos or pictures explaining why these animals are in danger of extinction.

Game

En las noticias

Play this game to review *Capítulo 9* vocabulary.

Players: entire class

Materials: index cards, pen

Rules:

1. On index cards, write vocabulary words, expressions, and verbs from *Capítulo 9*. Place the cards in a box.

2. Have a student draw an index card. Ask him / her to begin a story for a news article, using the word on the card in a sentence. Write the sentence on the board. Ask the class to make any corrections.

3. Call on another volunteer to pick a card and to continue the story, doing the same thing. Write the second volunteer's sentence on the board, and have the class make any corrections. Continue in this manner until the class feels the story has reached a logical conclusion. If every student has not had the chance to contribute, begin a second story.

   Student 1: (drew **capa de ozono**) *El problema del agujero en la capa de ozono es cada vez más grave.*

   Student 2: (drew **disminuir**) *Si no disminuimos el uso de aerosoles, podrían producirse más agujeros en la capa de ozono.*

   Student 3: (drew **amenaza**) *Este problema es una amenaza para la vida del planeta.*

Hands-on Culture

Art: *Un adorno móvil de mariposas*

Mobiles of butterflies are a popular decoration in homes throughout the Spanish-speaking world.

Materials: construction paper, pencil, scissors, hole punch, pipe cleaners, thread, large upholstery needle, 3 twigs (about 1 ft long each), markers or crayons, glitter glue or glitter (optional)

1. Fold a piece of construction paper in half and cut along the fold. (This will make 2 butterflies.) You will need to make 4 or more butterflies for the mobile.

2. Fold one of these pieces of paper in half. Draw half of a butterfly along the fold line.

3. Fold a small piece of black or brown paper in half. Draw the body and head of a butterfly on it. Make it the same length as your butterfly. Cut them out. Glue a body on each side of your butterfly.

4. Using a hole punch, make two holes in the butterfly's head. Cut a pipe cleaner in half. Thread it through the holes in the butterfly's head as antennae.

5. Decorate both sides of your butterfly using crayons, markers, glitter, or glitter glue.

6. Using a needle, pull a short length of knotted thread through the balancing point of the butterfly (near its middle). Tie the other end of the thread to the end of a twig.

7. On the other end of the twig, attach another butterfly in the same way.

8. Tie a thread to the middle of this twig and attach it to the end of another twig. Attach a butterfly to the end of this twig.

9. Using a short length of thread, attach what you've made to the end of another twig. Attach a butterfly to the other end of this twig.

10. Tie a longer length of thread to the top twig. If you want the twigs to remain horizontal, tie the thread where the mobile will balance.

CHAPTER PROJECT

Visita un parque nacional

Overview: Students create a digital or print brochure for a national park in Central or South America featuring the flora and fauna of the area, as well as conservation programs sponsored by the park. They should include illustrations of some species found in the area accompanied by a brief description of each. Illustrations can be obtained from magazines, travel brochures, or downloaded from the Web. Students then give an oral presentation of their brochure describing the park and trying to convince their listeners to support the conservation program sponsored by the park.

Resources: digital or print photos, image editing and page layout software, and/or construction paper, magazines, travel brochures, scissors, glue, colored pencils and markers

Sequence: (suggestions for when to do each step appear throughout the chapters)

STEP 1. Review instructions so students know what is expected of them. Hand out the "Chapter 9 Project Instructions and Rubric" from the *Teacher's Resource Book.*

STEP 2. Students submit a rough sketch of their brochure. Return the sketches with your suggestions. For vocabulary and grammar practice, ask students to work in pairs and present their sketches to each other.

STEP 3. Students create layouts. Encourage students to work in pencil first and to try different arrangements before writing the contents of the brochure.

STEP 4. Students submit a draft of their brochure. Note your corrections and suggestions, then return the drafts to students.

STEP 5. Students complete and present their brochure to the class, trying to convince their fellow students to support the conservation program sponsored by the park.

Options:

1. Students create a poster for the national park instead of a brochure.
2. Students write an article for the school newspaper about a national park.

Assessment:

Here is a detailed rubric for assessing this project:

Chapter 9 Project: *Visita un parque nacional*

RUBRIC	Score 1	Score 3	Score 5
Your evidence of planning	You provide no written draft or page layout.	Your draft and layout are provided, but not corrected.	You show evidence of corrected draft and layout.
Your use of illustrations	You include no photos or visuals.	You include photos or visuals, but your layout is disorganized.	Your brochure is easy to read, complete, and accurate.
Your presentation	You include little of the required information.	You include some of the required information. You attempted to convince.	You include all of the required information. You convinced us to support the program.

21st Century Skills

Look for tips throughout Chapter 9 to enrich your teaching by integrating 21st Century Skills. Suggestions for the Chapter Project and Culture follow below.

Chapter Project

Modify the Chapter Project with these suggestions:

Encourage Information Literacy

Encourage students to go online and research national parks in Central or South America. The handout "Search for Information on the Internet" will help them find reliable sources to help them choose a park and find the information and images to use in their brochure.

Promote Creativity and Innovation

Have students be as creative as possible with the layout of their brochure. Ask students to come up with different ways to arrange and label the information, such as flora and fauna, conservation programs, activities to do, things to see, etc.

Foster Media Literacy

Discuss with students the purpose of a brochure. What is the best media to express their message and attract more visitors to the national park? Who is the target audience? What words, expressions, or images would they use to interest potential visitors? What other media might they use?

Chapter Culture

Support Critical Thinking and Problem Solving

Direct students to review the *Fondo cultural* notes on pages 396 and 409. Have them compare with a partner their opinions about the environmental problems in Latin America and the U.S. Promote a discussion about cultural perspectives regarding pollution, endangered animals, or natural environmental disasters.

▶ **Videodocumentario** View *Exploremos la naturaleza fascinante* online with the class to learn more about how several Latin American countries are balancing economic needs and environmental protection.

AT A GLANCE

Objectives

- Listen and read about pollution and other environmental issues
- Talk and write about environmental problems and solutions
- Make suggestions to protect the environment
- Understand the causes of environmental issues in Latin America
- Compare an environmental problem in Latin America with one in the U.S.

A ver si recuerdas...   **Recycle...**

- Recycling and community
- Places and natural phenomena
- Verbs like *gustar*
- Uses of the definite article

- Syllabication

Vocabulary

- Pollution
- Natural resources
- Animals
- The environment

Grammar

- Conjunctions used with the subjunctive and the indicative tenses
- Relative pronouns *que, quien, lo que*

Culture

- Diego Rivera, p. 389
- Puerto Rico, p. 393
- Restrictions on driving cars, p. 396
- Punta Arenas, Chile, p. 406
- National Park of Guanacaste, Costa Rica, p. 407
- Magellanic penguins, p. 409
- Tropical forest of Costa Rica, p. 410
- Galapagos Islands, pp. 416–417
- Monarch Butterfly Festival, p. 425

RESOURCES

FOR THE STUDENT	ONLINE	DVD	PRINT	FOR THE TEACHER	ONLINE	PREEXP	DVD	PRINT
Plan				Interactive TE and Resource DVD	•		•	
				Teacher's Resource Book, pp. 235–290	•		•	•
				Pre-AP* Resource Book, pp. 162–164	•		•	•
				Mapa global interactivo	•			
				Lesson Plans	•			•

A ver si recuerdas PP. 384–387

	ONLINE	DVD	PRINT		ONLINE	PREEXP	DVD	PRINT
Review								
A ver si recuerdas Study Plan	•			A ver si recuerdas Study Plan	•			
Guided WB, pp. 268–271	•	•	•	Vocabulary and Grammar Transparencies, 165–168	•	•	•	
Core WB, pp. 119–120	•	•	•	Answer Keys: Student Edition, pp. 121–122	•	•	•	
Hispanohablantes WB, p. 268			•					

Introducción PP. 388–389

	ONLINE	DVD	PRINT		ONLINE	PREEXP	DVD	PRINT
Present								
Student Edition, pp. 388–389	•	•	•	Interactive TE and Resource DVD	•		•	
DK Reference Atlas	•	•		Teacher's Resource Book, pp. 236–239	•		•	•
Videonovela: ¡Pura vida!	•	•		Galería de fotos			•	
¡Pura vida! Video Activities	•			Fine Art Transparencies, 59				
Hispanohablantes WB, p. 269			•	Map Transparencies, 15, 16, 18	•	•	•	

Vocabulario en contexto PP. 390–393/404–407

	ONLINE	DVD	PRINT		ONLINE	PREEXP	DVD	PRINT
Present & Practice								
Student Edition, pp. 390–393/404–407	•	•	•	Interactive TE and Resource DVD	•		•	
Audio	•	•		Teacher's Resource Book, pp. 240–241, 244–245, 257–265/242–243, 245–246, 257–265	•		•	•
Flashcards	•	•						
Instant Check	•			Vocabulary Clip Art	•	•	•	•
Guided WB, pp. 272–280/285–292	•	•	•	Audio Program	•		•	•
Core WB, pp. 121–122/126–127	•	•	•	Vocabulary and Grammar Transparencies, 169–172/175–178	•	•	•	
Comm. WB, pp. 124/127	•	•	•	Answer Keys: Student Edition, pp. 122–123/129–130	•	•	•	
Hispanohablantes WB, pp. 270–271/280–281			•					
Assess and Remediate				Pruebas 9–1, 9–5: Assessment Program, pp. 193–194/202–203 Hispanohablantes, pp. 193–194/202–203	•		•	•

RESOURCES

Vocabulario en uso PP. 394–397/408–411

FOR THE STUDENT	ONLINE	DVD	PRINT	FOR THE TEACHER	ONLINE	PREEXP	DVD	PRINT
Present & Practice								
Student Edition, pp. 394–397/408–411	•	•	•	Interactive Whiteboard Vocabulary Activities	•		•	
Instant Check	•			Interactive TE and Resource DVD	•		•	
Comm. WB, pp. 120/122	•	•	•	Teacher's Resource Book, pp. 245, 250–251/246–247, 253–254	•		•	•
Hispanohablantes WB, pp. 272–274/282–284			•	Audio Program	•	•	•	
Communicative Pair Activities	•			Videomodelos	•		•	
				Vocabulary and Grammar Transparency, 4	•	•	•	
				Answer Keys: Student Edition, pp. 123–125/130–131	•	•	•	•
Assess and Remediate				Pruebas 9–2, 9–6 with Study Plans	•			
				Pruebas 9–2, 9–6: Assessment Program, pp. 195–196/204–205	•		•	•
				Hispanohablantes, pp. 195–196/204–205	•		•	•

Gramática PP. 398–403/412–415

FOR THE STUDENT	ONLINE	DVD	PRINT	FOR THE TEACHER	ONLINE	PREEXP	DVD	PRINT
Present & Practice								
Student Edition, pp. 398–403/412–415	•	•	•	Interactive Whiteboard Grammar Activities	•		•	
Instant Check	•			Interactive TE and Resource DVD	•		•	
Animated Verbs	•			Teacher's Resource Book, pp. 245, 252/247, 255	•		•	
Tutorial Video: Grammar	•			Audio Program	•	•	•	
Canción de hip hop	•			Videomodelos	•		•	
Guided WB, pp. 281–284/293–294	•	•	•	Vocabulary and Grammar Transparencies, 173–174/179	•	•	•	
Core WB, pp. 123–125/128–130	•	•	•	Answer Keys: Student Edition, pp. 126–128/132	•	•	•	
Comm. WB, pp. 121, 125–126/122–123, 128–131, 213	•	•	•					
Hispanohablantes WB, pp. 275–279/285–289			•					
Communicative Pair Activities	•							
Assess and Remediate				Pruebas 9–3, 9–4, 9–7 with Study Plans	•			
				Pruebas 9–3, 9–4, 9–7: Assessment Program, pp. 197, 198/206	•		•	•
				Hispanohablantes, pp. 197, 198/206	•		•	•
				Examen 1, Examen 2: Vocab. y gramática, pp. 199–201/207–209	•		•	•

¡Adelante! PP. 416–425

FOR THE STUDENT	ONLINE	DVD	PRINT	FOR THE TEACHER	ONLINE	PREEXP	DVD	PRINT
Application								
Student Edition, pp. 416–425	•	•	•	Interactive TE and Resource DVD	•		•	
Online Cultural Reading	•			Teacher's Resource Book, 247–249	•		•	•
Guided WB, pp. 295–297	•	•	•	Video Program: Videodocumentario	•			
Comm. WB, pp. 132–133, 214	•	•	•	Video Program Teacher's Guide, Cap. 9	•			
Hispanohablantes WB, pp. 290–295			•	Map Transparencies, 14, 17	•	•	•	
Videodocumentario	•	•		Vocabulary and Grammar Transparencies, 4–5	•	•	•	
Lectura 3, pp. 16–18, 52–53			•	Answer Keys: Student Edition, pp. 133–134	•	•	•	

Repaso del capítulo PP. 426–429

FOR THE STUDENT	ONLINE	DVD	PRINT	FOR THE TEACHER	ONLINE	PREEXP	DVD	PRINT
Review								
Student Edition, pp. 426–429	•	•	•	Interactive TE and Resource DVD	•		•	
Online Puzzles and Games	•			Teacher's Resource Book, pp. 248, 256–265	•		•	
Core WB, pp. 131–132	•	•	•	Audio Program	•	•	•	
Comm. WB, pp. 215–218	•	•	•	Answer Keys: Student Edition, p. 135	•	•	•	
Hispanohablantes WB, pp. 296–299			•					
Instant Check	•							

Chapter Assessment

FOR THE STUDENT	ONLINE	DVD	PRINT	FOR THE TEACHER	ONLINE	PREEXP	DVD	PRINT
Assess				Examen del capítulo 9: Assessment Program, pp. 210–213	•		•	•
				Alternate Assessment Program, pp. 87–97	•		•	•
				Hispanohablantes, pp. 210–213	•		•	•
				Audio Program, Cap. 9, Examen	•		•	
				ExamView: Test Banks A and B (questions only online)	•		•	
				Heritage Learner Test Bank	•		•	
				Pre-AP* Test Bank	•		•	

REGULAR SCHEDULE (50 MINUTES)

DAY	Warm-up / Assess	Preview / Present / Practice / Communicate	Wrap-up / Homework Options
1	**Warm-up (10 min.)** • Return Examen del capítulo: Capítulo 8	**Repaso (35 min.)** • A ver si recuerdas . . . • Actividades 1–8	**Wrap-up and Homework Options (5 min.)** • Core Practice 9-1, 9-2
2	**Warm-up (10 min.)** • Homework check	**Chapter Opener (10 min.)** • Objectives • Arte y cultura **Vocabulario en contexto 1 (25 min.)** • Presentation: Vocabulario y gramática en contexto • Actividades 1, 2	**Wrap-up and Homework Options (5 min.)** • Clip Art Vocabulary
3	**Warm-up (10 min.)** • Homework check	**Vocabulario en contexto 1 (35 min.)** • Presentation: ¿Cómo cuidas tu planeta?; Puerto Rico: cómo conservar bella la isla • Actividad 3	**Wrap-up and Homework Options (5 min.)** • Core Practice 9-3, 9-4 • Actividad 4 • Prueba 9-1: Vocabulary recognition
4	**Warm-up (10 min.)** • Homework check ✔**Formative Assessment (10 min.)** • Prueba 9-1: Vocabulary recognition	**Vocabulario en uso 1 (25 min.)** • Interactive Whiteboard Vocabulary Activities • Actividades 6, 7, 8, 9	**Wrap-up and Homework Options (5 min.)** • Actividades 5, 10 • Writing Activities • Prueba 9-2 with Study Plan: Vocabulary production
5	**Warm-up (10 min.)** • Homework check ✔**Formative Assessment (10 min.)** • Prueba 9-2 with Study Plan: Vocabulary production	**Gramática y vocabulario en uso 1 (25 min.)** • Fondo cultural • Presentation: Conjunciones que se usan con el subjuntivo y el indicativo • Interactive Whiteboard Grammar Activities • Actividades 11, 12 • Ampliación del lenguaje	**Wrap-up and Homework Options (5 min.)** • Core Practice 9-5
6	**Warm-up (10 min.)** • Actividad 13 • Homework check	**Gramática y vocabulario en uso 1 (35 min.)** • Actividades 14, 15, 16 • Communicative Pair Activity • Presentation: Los pronombres relativos *que, quien y lo que* • Interactive Whiteboard Grammar Activities • Actividad 18	**Wrap-up and Homework Options (5 min.)** • Writing Activity • Prueba 9-3 with Study Plan: Conjunciones que se usan con el subjuntivo y el indicativo
7	**Warm-up (10 min.)** • Actividad 17 • Homework check ✔**Formative Assessment (10 min.)** • Prueba 9-3 with Study Plan: Conjunciones que se usan con el subjuntivo y el indicativo	**Gramática y vocabulario en uso 1 (25 min.)** • Actividad 19 • Communicative Pair Activity	**Wrap-up and Homework Options (5 min.)** • Core Practice 9-6, 9-7 • Prueba 9-4 with Study Plan: Los pronombres relativos *que, quien y lo que*
8	**Warm-up (15 min.)** • Writing Activity • Homework check ✔**Formative Assessment (10 min.)** • Prueba 9-4 with Study Plan: Los pronombres relativos *que, quien y lo que*	**Vocabulario en contexto 2 (20 min.)** • Presentation: Vocabulario y gramática en contexto • Actividades 20, 21	**Wrap-up and Homework Options (5 min.)** • Clip Art Vocabulary • Examen: Vocabulario y gramática 1
9	**Warm-up (5 min.)** • Homework check ✔**Summative Assessment (30 min.)** • Examen: Vocabulario y gramática 1	**Vocabulario en contexto 2 (10 min.)** • Presentation: Punta Arenas • Presentation: El Parque Nacional de Guanacaste	**Wrap-up and Homework Options (5 min.)** • Actividad 22 • Core Practice 9-8, 9-9 • Prueba 9-5: Vocabulary recognition
10	**Warm-up (10 min.)** • Actividad 23 • Homework check ✔**Formative Assessment (10 min.)** • Prueba 9-5: Vocabulary recognition	**Vocabulario en uso 2 (25 min.)** • Interactive Whiteboard Vocabulary Activities • Actividades 26, 27 • Fondo cultural	**Wrap-up and Homework Options (5 min.)** • Actividades 24, 25 • Prueba 9-6 with Study Plan: Vocabulary production

REGULAR SCHEDULE (50 MINUTES)

DAY	Warm-up / Assess	Preview / Present / Practice / Communicate	Wrap-up / Homework Options
11	**Warm-up** (10 min.) • Writing Activity • Homework check ✔**Formative Assessment** (10 min.) • Prueba 9-6 with Study Plan: Vocabulary production	**Vocabulario en uso 2** (25 min.) • Actividades 28, 29 • Communicative Pair Activity	**Wrap-up and Homework Options** (5 min.) • Actividad 30 • Writing Activity
12	**Warm-up** (10 min.) • Homework check	**Gramática y vocabulario en uso 2** (35 min.) • Presentation: Más conjunciones que se usan con el subjuntivo y el indicativo • Interactive Whiteboard Grammar Activities • Actividades 31, 32, 34 • En voz alta	**Wrap-up and Homework Options** (5 min.) • Actividad 33 • Core Practice 9-11, 9-12 • Prueba 9-7 with Study Plan: Conjunciones con el subjuntivo y el indicativo
13	**Warm-up** (10 min.) • Homework check ✔**Formative Assessment** (10 min.) • Prueba 9-7 with Study Plan: Conjunciones con el subjuntivo y el indicativo	**Gramática y vocabulario en uso 2** (25 min.) • Actividades 35, 36, • El español en el mundo del trabajo • Communicative Pair Activity	**Wrap-up and Homework Options** (5 min.) • Examen: Vocabulario y gramática 2
14	**Warm-up** (8 min.) • Writing Activity ✔**Formative Assessment** (30 min.) • Examen: Vocabulario y gramática 2	**¡Adelante!** (10 min.) • Presentación oral: Steps 1, 2	**Wrap-up and Homework Options** (2 min.) • Presentación oral: Step 2
15	**Warm-up** (10 min.) • Presentación oral: Step 2	**¡Adelante!** (35 min.) • Presentación oral: Step 3	**Wrap-up and Homework Options** (5 min.) • Galápagos: el encuentro con la naturaleza • ¿Comprendiste?
16	**Warm-up** (15 min.) • Galápagos: el encuentro con la naturaleza: ¿Comprendiste? • Homework check	**¡Adelante!** (30 min.) • ¿Qué me cuentas? 1, 2, 3 • View Video • Video Activities 1, 2, 3	**Wrap-up and Homework Options** (5 min.) • Presentación escrita: Steps 1, 2
17	**Warm-up** (10 min.) • Video Activity 4	**¡Adelante!** (15 min.) • Presentación escrita: Step 3 **Repaso** (20 min.) • Preparación para el examen: Actividades 3, 4	**Wrap-up and Homework Options** (5 min.) • Presentación escrita: Step 4
18	**Warm-up** (10 min.) • Homework check	**¡Adelante!** (35 min.) • Lectura • Interacción con la lectura • Fondo cultural	**Wrap-up and Homework Options** (5 min.) • Core Practice: Organizer 9-13, 9-14 • Instant Check
19	**Warm-up** (20 min.) • Preparación para el examen: Actividades 1, 2 • Homework check	**Repaso** (25 min.) • Preparación para el examen: Actividades 5, 6, 7 • Other review	**Wrap-up and Homework Options** (5 min.) • Examen del capítulo
20	**Warm-up** (5 min.) • Answer questions ✔**Summative Assessment** (44 min.) • Examen del capítulo		**Wrap-up and Homework Options** (1 min.) • A ver si recuerdas: Capítulo 10

BLOCK SCHEDULE (90 MINUTES)

DAY	Warm-up / Assess	Preview / Present / Practice / Communicate	Wrap-up / Homework Options
1	**Warm-up (35 min.)** • Return Examen del capítulo: Capítulo 8 • A ver si recuerdas . . . • Actividades 4, 5, 7 • Homework check	**Chapter Opener (10 min.)** • Objectives • Arte y cultura **Vocabulario en contexto 1 (30 min.)** • Presentation: Vocabulario y gramática en contexto • Actividades 1, 2 • Presentation: ¿Cómo cuidas tu planeta?; Puerto Rico: cómo conservar bella la isla • Actividad 3 **Vocabulario en uso 1 (10 min.)** • Actividades 7, 8	**Wrap-up and Homework Options (5 min.)** • Core Practice 9-3, 9-4 • Clip Art Vocabulary • Prueba 9-1: Vocabulary recognition
2	**Warm-up (15 min.)** • Actividad 4 • Homework check ✔**Formative Assessment (10 min.)** • Prueba 9-1: Vocabulary recognition	**Vocabulario en uso 1 (60 min.)** • Interactive Whiteboard Vocabulary Activities • Actividades 5, 6, 9, 10 • Communicative Pair Activity	**Wrap-up and Homework Options (5 min.)** • Writing Activities • Prueba 9-2 with Study Plan: Vocabulary production
3	**Warm-up (10 min.)** • Writing Activity • Homework check ✔**Formative Assessment (15 min.)** • Prueba 9-2 with Study Plan: Vocabulary production	**Gramática y vocabulario en uso 1 (60 min.)** • Presentation: Conjunciones con el subjuntivo y el indicativo • Interactive Whiteboard Grammar Activities • Actividades 11, 12, 13, 14, 15 • Ampliación del lenguaje • Audio and Writing Activities	**Wrap-up and Homework Options (5 min.)** • Core Practice 9-5 • Prueba 9-3 with Study Plan: Conjunciones con el subjuntivo y el indicativo
4	**Warm-up (10 min.)** • Actividad 16 • Homework check ✔**Formative Assessment (10 min.)** • Prueba 9-3 with Study Plan: Conjunciones con el subjuntivo y el indicativo	**Gramática y vocabulario en uso 1 (50 min.)** • Presentation: Los pronombres relativos *que, quien* y *lo que* • Interactive Whiteboard Grammar Activities • Actividades 17, 18, 19 • Communicative Pair Activity **Vocabulario en contexto 2 (15 min.)** • Presentation: Vocabulario y gramática en contexto • Actividades 20, 21	**Wrap-up and Homework Options (5 min.)** • Core Practice 9-6, 9-7 • Prueba 9-4 with Study Plan: Los pronombres relativos *que, quien* y *lo que* • Examen: Vocabulario y gramática 1
5	**Warm-up (10 min.)** • Writing Activity • Homework check ✔**Formative Assessment Options (40 min.)** • Prueba 9-4 with Study Plan: Los pronombres relativos *que, quien* y *lo que* • Examen: Vocabulario y gramática 1	**Vocabulario en contexto 2 (20 min.)** • Presentation: Punta Arenas: miedo al sol • Actividad 22 • Presentation: El Parque Nacional de Guanacaste • Actividad 23 **Vocabulario en uso 2 (15 min.)** • Interactive Whiteboard Vocabulary Activities • Actividades 26, 27 • Fondo cultural	**Wrap-up and Homework Options (5 min.)** • Core Practice 9-8, 9-9 • Prueba 9-5: Vocabulary recognition

BLOCK SCHEDULE (90 MINUTES)

DAY	Warm-up / Assess	Preview / Present / Practice / Communicate	Wrap-up / Homework Options
6	**Warm-up** (20 min.) • Actividades 24, 25 • Homework check ✔**Formative Assessment** (10 min.) • Pruebas 9-5: Vocabulary recognition	**Gramática y vocabulario en uso 2** (55 min.) • Actividades 28, 29, 30 • Presentation: Más conjunciones que se usan con el subjuntivo y el indicativo • Interactive Whiteboard Grammar Activities • Actividades 31, 32, 33 • En voz alta • Writing Activities	**Wrap-up and Homework Options** (5 min.) • Core Practice 9-10 • Prueba 9-6 with Study Plan: Vocabulary production
7	**Warm-up** (10 min.) • Homework check ✔**Formative Assessment** (10 min.) • Prueba 9-6 with Study Plan: Vocabulary production	**Gramática y vocabulario en uso 2** (45 min.) • Actividades 34, 35, 36 • El español en el mundo del trabajo • Communicative Pair Activity **¡Adelante!** (20 min.) • Presentación oral: Steps 1, 2	**Wrap-up and Homework Options** (5 min.) • Presentación oral: Step 2
8	**Warm-up** (15 min.) • Writing Activity • Homework check ✔**Formative Assessment** (40 min.) • Presentación oral: Step 3	**¡Adelante!** (30 min.) • Presentation: Galápagos: el encuentro con la naturaleza • ¿Comprendiste?	**Wrap-up and Homework Options** (5 min.) • Core Practice 9-11, 9-12 • Prueba 9-7 with Study Plan: Conjunciones con el subjuntivo y el indicativo • Examen: Vocabulario y gramática 2
9	**Warm-up** (10 min.) • Homework check ✔**Formative Assessment Options** (40 min.) • Prueba 9-7 with Study Plan: Conjunciones con el subjuntivo y el indicativo • Examen: Vocabulario y gramática 2	**¡Adelante!** (35 min.) • ¿Qué me cuentas? 1, 2, 3 • Presentación escrita: Step 1 • View Video • Video Activities	**Wrap-up and Homework Options** (5 min.) • Presentación escrita: Step 2 • Preparación para el examen: Actividades 1, 2
10	**Warm-up** (20 min.) • Presentación escrita: Step 3 • Homework check	**¡Adelante!** (35 min.) • Lectura • Interacción con la lectura • Fondo cultural **Repaso** (30 min.) • Preparación para el examen: Actividades 3, 4, 6	**Wrap-up and Homework Options** (5 min.) • Presentación escrita: Step 4 • Core Practice: Organizer 9-13 9-14 • Instant Check • Preparación para el examen: Actividades 5, 7 • Examen del capítulo
11	**Warm-up** (15 min.) • Homework check ✔**Summative Assessment** (45 min.) • Examen del capítulo	**Theme Game** (15 min.) **A ver si recuerdas – Capítulo 10** (10 min.) • Presentation: Vocabulario • Presentation: Gramática	**Wrap-up and Homework Options** (5 min.) • A ver si recuerdas – Capítulo 10 • Core Practice 10-1, 10-2

Vocabulario Repaso

Vocabulario [Repaso]

Core Instruction

Standards: 1.1, 1.2

Resources: Voc. and Gram. Transparency 165

Suggestions: Before presenting the material in this review section, consider testing your students' command of the material by assigning the Study Plan. Students will automatically be given additional practice of the material they have not yet mastered, and you can focus your review based on the class's overall performance on the post-test.

Number the categories of the *Vocabulario* from 1 to 6, proceeding from left to right on the page: *la basura* is number 1, *la comunidad* is number 2, and so on. Have students roll a numbered cube three times and write down the numbers that they roll. These pertain to the categories of the *Vocabulario*. Ask them to write a sentence using one word from each of the three categories they rolled. Have them roll and write as often as possible in an amount of time that you set.

la basura
la campaña
el centro de reciclaje
la contaminación
el medio ambiente
reciclar
recoger
separar

la comunidad
la avenida
el barrio
la calle
la carretera
la gente
el lago
el parque
la plaza
el pueblo
el río
los vecinos

para reciclar
la botella
el cartón
la lata
el plástico
el vidrio

opiniones
me encanta(n)
me gusta(n)
me importa(n)
me interesa(n)
me molesta(n)
me parece(n)
me preocupa(n)

el tráfico
la ambulancia
el camión
el coche
el peatón
la sirena
la zona escolar
la zona de construcción

actividades
adoptar
arrojar
beneficiar
colaborar
contar con
establecer
evitar
mejorar
obligar
prevenir
reducir

▼1

Standards: 1.1

Focus: Practicing review vocabulary

Suggestions: Allow students to convert some of the sentences they wrote for the *Presentation* above to questions for this *Actividad*.

Answers will vary.

Extension: Have students report to the class about what is important to their partner. Remind them to use third-person verb forms and indirect object pronouns.

▼1 Opiniones | 🗨👥

Escribir • Hablar

¿Te importa el medio ambiente? Escribe cinco preguntas que le puedes hacer a un(a) compañero(a) para saber si le importa a él / ella. Luego, trabaja con tu compañero(a) para hacer preguntas y contestarlas.

▶ **Modelo**

A —¿Te importa reciclar el vidrio?
B —Sí, me importa mucho. Mi familia y yo siempre reciclamos.

▼2 Definiciones | 👥

Escribir • Hablar

Trabaja con otro(a) estudiante para escribir definiciones de las palabras siguientes. Lean sus definiciones a otros estudiantes para ver si pueden identificar las palabras correctas.

1. tráfico   5. peatones
2. carretera   6. evitar
3. arrojar   7. sirena
4. botella   8. vecinos

▼2

Focus: Practicing review vocabulary

Suggestions: Remind students that antonyms sometimes work well to define words. Have them use the sentence starter *Es lo contrario de...* when using an antonym to define a word.

Answers will vary.

DIFFERENTIATED INSTRUCTION

Multiple Intelligences

Visual/Spatial: Have students create a map of a fictional community that is environmentally conscious. Instruct them to include the items listed in *la comunidad, el tráfico,* and *para reciclar.* Have students label the areas and objects shown on their maps using the vocabulary.

Advanced Learners

Have students list five *Vocabulario* items from any of the categories except **opiniones** and exchange lists with a partner. Partners have three minutes to create a drawing that includes all of the items in the list, complete with labels. Then have partners talk about their drawings.

Gramática Repaso

Verbos como *gustar*

You know that *gustar* is used to talk about likes and dislikes. When you use *gustar*, the subject of the sentence is what is liked or disliked. You use the singular form *gusta* when what is liked is a singular noun or an action (an infinitive). You use the plural form *gustan* when what is liked is a plural noun.

Nos **gusta** este barrio.   Le **gusta** trabajar para la comunidad.
Me **gustan** las calles de este barrio.

Use the indirect object pronoun to indicate to whom something is pleasing.

Me gustaría participar en la campaña de reciclaje.

Other Spanish verbs that often follow the same pattern as *gustar* are:

doler	*to ache, to be painful*	importar	*to matter*	parecer	*to seem*
encantar	*to love*	interesar	*to interest*	preocupar	*to worry*
faltar	*to lack, to be missing*	molestar	*to bother*	quedar (bien / mal)	*to fit*

• The personal *a* plus a pronoun or a person's name can be used for emphasis, or to make clear to whom you are referring.

A nosotros nos preocupa la contaminación del aire.
¿Le interesaron **a Sergio** los libros?

Más ayuda	**realidades.com**	▶ Tutorial

3 Escoger

Leer

Un grupo de vecinos escribe una carta al periódico. Escoge las expresiones adecuadas para completarla.

Estimado Sr. Director:
Le escribimos porque __1.__ *(preocupar / interesar)* la interrupción del tráfico en la calle Ramos. Aunque a todos nosotros __2.__ *(importar / interesar)* que se construya un nuevo centro médico, la construcción __3.__ *(importar / molestar)* diariamente. A nosotros no __4.__ *(importar / molestar)* sólo el problema del tráfico, __5.__ *(preocupar / interesar)* también la basura que se está acumulando en el lugar. Favor de mejorar la situación.
Atentamente,
Los vecinos de la calle Ramos

4 Según ellos

Hablar

Tu compañero(a) describe a sus amigos y a su familia usando las palabras siguientes. Responde a lo que dice tu compañero(a) con ejemplos de tu propia experiencia.

▶ **Modelo**

A mi hermano(a) y a mí (molestar) . . .
A —*A nosotros(as) nos molesta el frío.*
B —*A mis hermanos(as) no les molesta nada el frío.*

1. A mí *(molestar)*
2. A mi compañero(a) *(interesar)*
3. A mis amigos(as) *(preocupar)*
4. A mi madre (padre) no *(gustar)*
5. A mí *(faltar)*
6. A mi mejor amigo(a) *(encantar)*

Gramática Repaso

Core Instruction

Standards: 4.1

Resources: Voc. and Gram. Transparency 166

Suggestions: Refer students who are having difficulty with *gustar* to the *GramActiva* video from Level 1 Chapter 1A, and to the online tutorial. Ask students to write three questions they can ask a partner, using three of the verb phrases from the *Gramática*. Have partners take turns asking and answering questions. Then have them report to the class on their partner's answers.

3 Standards: 1.3

Resources: Answer Keys: Student Edition, p. 121
Focus: Practicing verbs like *gustar*
Suggestions: Point out the use of the expressions **Estimado** and **Atentamente** in the salutation and closing of the letter. Remind students that these are good expressions to use in more formal letters.

Answers:
1. nos preocupa
2. nos importa
3. nos molesta
4. nos molesta
5. nos preocupa

4 Standards: 1.1

Resources: Answer Keys: Student Edition, p. 121
Focus: Practicing verbs like *gustar*
Suggestions: Encourage students to listen to each other and to be inventive with their responses. Explain that using the cues to create a natural, flowing conversation is preferable to a rigid A-B-A-B exchange.

Answers will vary. Students will use the following verb forms and indirect object pronouns:

1. me molesta(n)	4. le gusta(n)
2. le interesa(n)	5. me falta(n)
3. les preocupa(n)	6. le encanta(n)

ENRICH YOUR TEACHING

Teacher-to-Teacher

Fill your classroom with posters, advertisements, displays, photos, signs, and anything you can find that corresponds to the environmental theme. Provide students with a center containing articles, suggested Web sites, magazines, and books to browse on the topic.

A classroom environment that is linguistically rich and full of information will enhance learning and provide students with interesting facts and details they can use to contribute to class discussions.

▼ **Objectives**
▶ Talk and write about places and natural phenomena
▶ Refer to people, places and addresses

Vocabulario [Repaso]

Core Instruction

Standards: 1.1, 1.2

Resources: Voc. and Gram. Transparency 167

Suggestions: Have students sit in a circle. Give one student a foam ball and have him or her give a definition of a vocabulary item from one of the lists. That student tosses the ball to another and names a term from a different *Vocabulario* category. Whoever catches the ball gives a brief definition of that term and tosses the ball to another student, and so on.

5 Standards: 1.1

Focus: Practicing review vocabulary

Common Errors: Even with regular review, students may make verbs like *gustar* agree with the indirect object rather than the subject. Remind them that **gustar** means "to please" rather than "to like," and provide models as necessary.

Suggestions: Encourage students to consider all five senses when talking about why they are or are not partial to the various places.

Answers will vary.

6 Standards: 1.2

Resources: Answer Keys: Student Edition, p. 121

Focus: Practicing review vocabulary

Suggestions: Remind students that since the items are headlines, their structure is different from that of complete sentences.

Answers:

1. Incendio; árboles   3. inundaciones; lluvias
2. mosquitos; insectos   4. océano; peces

Vocabulario Repaso

lugares
el bosque
el campo
el desierto
el fondo del mar
las montañas
el océano
el parque nacional
la selva tropical
la sierra
los valles

fenómenos naturales
la explosión
el huracán
el incendio
la inundación
la lluvia
la nieve
el relámpago
el terremoto
la tormenta
el trueno

acciones
capturar
cuidar
eliminar
matar
permitir
prohibir
proteger
rescatar
salvar

animales
el caballo
la cebra
el conejo
el elefante
el gato
el hipopótamo
la hormiga
los insectos
el jaguar
el mono
la mosca
el mosquito
el oso
el pájaro
los peces
el perro
el tigre

▼5 Lugares interesantes | 👥

Hablar • Escribir

Decide con tu compañero(a) qué lugares de la lista les interesan más y cuáles les interesan menos y por qué. Hagan una tabla como la siguiente y compartan los resultados con la clase.

Nos gustan más . . .	Porque . . .	Nos gustan menos . . .	Porque . . .
1. las montañas		1. el desierto	
2. el océano		2. las sierras	

▼6 Titulares | 👥

Leer

Lee con un(a) compañero(a) los siguientes titulares y anuncios de periódicos y luego complétenlos con estas palabras o expresiones.

insectos	océano	mosquitos
árboles	incendio	inundaciones
peces	lluvias	

386 trescientos ochenta y seis
A ver si recuerdas . . .

1. ¡_____ en el bosque! Se quemaron miles de _____.

2. Si quiere que los _____ se mantengan lejos, use el repelente de _____.

3. Grandes _____ en Zamora a causa de las _____ recientes.

4. Una exploración del _____ descubre nuevas especies de _____.

DIFFERENTIATED INSTRUCTION

Heritage Language Learners

Ask students to model additional examples of cases in which the definite article is used in Spanish, but not in English. Then, have students create a short "fill in the blank" exercise for their peers.

Students with Learning Difficulties

Help students reinforce the vocabulary presented on p. 386. Encourage them to create small picture clues for words that are unfamiliar. Ask students to share their picture clues with the group, and have other students guess the word indicated.

Gramática Repaso

Usos del artículo definido

In general, the definite article (*el, la, los, las*) is used in Spanish the same way it is in English. In the following cases, however, it is used in Spanish but not in English.

When people are referred to by name and an accompanying title, preceding the title (but not when people are addressed directly using a title):

La profesora Estévez enseña ciencias.   Buenas tardes, **doctor Zabala**.

Before the name of a street, avenue, park, or other proper names:

Los vecinos de **la calle Ramos** se quejaron.

Before any noun representing an entire species, institution, or general concept:

El perro es el mejor amigo del hombre.   **La educación** es muy importante.

With certain time expressions:

Llegó a **las siete** de la tarde. *(hours)*   Me encanta **la primavera**. *(seasons)*
Van a reunirse **el lunes** próximo. *(days)*   Salió de su país a **los diez años**. *(age)*

When it is an inseparable part of the name of a country, such as *El Salvador* and of some cities, such as *El Cairo, La Habana, El Havre, La Haya, La Paz.*

The words *al* and *del* result from contracting the prepositions *a* and *de* with the article *el*, but there is no contraction when *El* is part of a proper name.

Vamos **al** parque. Venimos **del** bosque.   Vamos a **El Paso**. Venimos de **El Paso**.

▼7 Practicar

Escribir

Con un(a) compañero(a) escriban sustantivos (con su correspondiente artículo definido) que sirvan para completar las frases siguientes.

Modelo
_____ es bueno para la salud.
El aire puro / El ejercicio / El jugo de naranja es bueno para la salud.

1. _____ Romero nos recibirá a las cuatro.

2. _____ es / no es un país de Asia.

3. _____ son / no son muy caros.

4. Generalmente _____ por la tarde practicamos en el club.

▼8 Un diálogo

Leer

Completa los diálogos con artículos definidos o con las contracciones *al* o *del*. Si el artículo no es necesario, deja el espacio en blanco.

1. —Lo siento, ya son _____ siete y debo irme.
   —Claro, Carmen, nos vemos _____ miércoles. Recuerda que es _____ reunión.

2. —¡Mira! Aquí llega _____ doctora López.
   —¿Cómo está, _____ doctora López?

Más práctica	GO

realidades.com | print

A ver si recuerdas with Study Plan ✔
Guided WB pp. 268–271   ✔ ✔
Core WB pp. 119–120   ✔ ✔
Hispanohablantes **WB** p. 268   ✔

trescientos ochenta y siete **387**
Capítulo 9

Gramática Repaso

Core Instruction

Standards: 4.1

Resources: Voc. and Gram. Transparency 168

Suggestions: Refer students who are having difficulty with indefinite articles to the online tutorial. Have students write five sentences or parts of sentences in which they incorrectly use a definite article. Collect their papers and shuffle and redistribute them. Have them correct the errors and discuss their reasoning behind the corrections.

▼7 Standards: 1.1

Resources: Answer Keys: Student Edition, p. 122

Focus: Reviewing the use of definite articles

Suggestions: Ask students which rule from the *Gramática* applies to each use of the definite article.

Answers will vary. Students may use articles and nouns such as the following:
1. El ingeniero/La doctora/La señorita
2. El Salvador/La República Dominicana/Los Estados Unidos
3. Los coches/Los zapatos/Los discos compactos
4. los fines de semana/los sábados/los domingos

▼8 Standards: 1.2

Resources: Answer Keys: Student Edition, p. 122

Focus: Reviewing the use of definite articles

Suggestions: Remind students to read through each item first before attempting to write their answer.

Answers:
1. las; el; la
2. la; leave blank

ENRICH YOUR TEACHING

Teacher-to-Teacher

Applying the correct gender to nouns is one of the more difficult skills that English-speaking learners of Spanish must master. Encourage students to invent their own mnemonic devices for remembering genders. One way is to associate the noun with an oft-heard, tell-tale modifier: **Buenos Aires, Santa Fe, sangre fría.**

21st Century Skills

Initiative and Self-Direction Direct students to the online tutorials for self-directed review of ***gustar*** and similar verbs recycled in this chapter. Students can expand their own learning by reviewing the related English grammar first, then proceed to the new Spanish grammar point. Each tutorial is followed by a quick comprehension check.

✔ASSESSMENT

A ver si recuerdas with Study Plan (online only)

After reviewing the material on these pages, assign the *A ver si recuerdas* Study Plan to evaluate students' mastery of the material. Additional practice is available online.

387

Standards for Foreign Language Learning: *Capítulo* 9

- To meet the Standards, students will:

Communication

1.1 Interpersonal
- Talk about neighborhoods, regions, and weather
- Talk about Diego Rivera, José Martí, and their work
- Talk about environmental issues and endangered species
- Talk about post-high-school plans
- Talk about the Galapagos Islands and butterflies
- Talk about a festival in Michoacán, Mexico

1.2 Interpretive
- Read about neighborhoods, regions, and weather
- Read about Diego Rivera, José Martí, and their work
- Read and listen to information about environmental issues and endangered species
- Read about word families
- Read about the Galapagos Islands, Monarch butterflies, and Magellanic penguins
- Read about **turrones**
- Read about Latin American rescue teams
- Read about a festival in Michoacán, Mexico
- Read about speech prep. and persuasive letters

1.3 Presentational
- Write and present information orally about environmental issues and endangered species
- Write and present information orally about the Galapagos Islands and Monarch butterflies

Culture

2.1 Practices and Perspectives
- Interpret Latin American perspectives and practices regarding the environment and endangered species
- Describe Latin American rescue operations
- Describe Ecuador's policies regarding the Galapagos
- Describe Mexican events spurred by butterfly migration

2.2 Products and Perspectives
- Discuss Diego Rivera, José Martí, and their work
- Describe a Puerto Rican recycling program
- Describe Ecuadorian national parks

Connections

3.1 Cross-curricular
- Discuss key facts about Diego Rivera and José Martí
- Discuss key facts about ecological science, biology, and demographics
- Discuss key geographical facts about Puerto Rico, Chile, Mexico, Costa Rica, and Ecuador
- Discuss key facts about emergency organizations
- Use Language Arts Strategies: using topic sentences, finding good details, good conclusions, context clues

3.2 Target Culture
- Read poetry by José Martí

Comparisons

4.1 Language
- Compare use of Spanish verbs like **gustar** to that of their English counterparts
- Compare Spanish and English pronouns and conjunctions
- Compare Spanish words to their English counterparts

4.2 Culture
- Compare Latin American environmental and recycling problems and programs to those in the United States
- Compare nature-based festivals in Mexico and the U.S.

Capítulo 9 Cuidemos nuestro planeta

▼ Chapter Objectives

Communication
By the end of the chapter you will be able to:
- Listen and read about pollution and other environmental issues
- Talk and write about environmental problems and solutions
- Make suggestions to protect the environment

Culture
You will also be able to:
- Understand the causes of environmental issues in Latin America
- Compare an environmental problem in Latin America with one in the U.S.

You will demonstrate what you know and can do:
- Presentación oral, p. 419
- Presentación escrita, pp. 420–421
- Preparación para el examen, pp. 428–429

You will use:

Vocabulary
- Pollution
- Natural resources
- Animals
- The environment

Grammar
- Conjunctions used with the subjunctive and the indicative tenses
- Relative pronouns *que, quien, lo que*

Exploración del mundo hispano

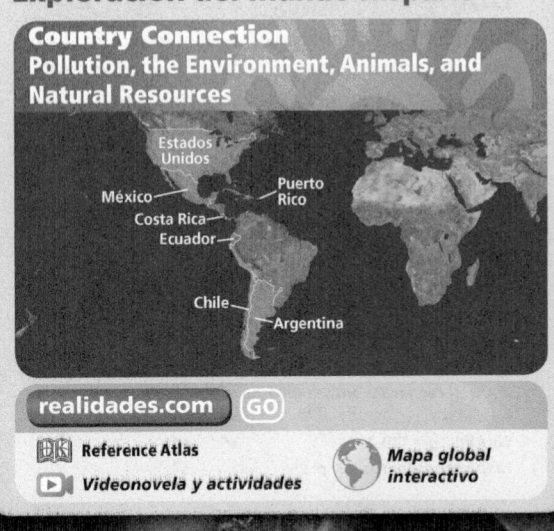

Country Connection
Pollution, the Environment, Animals, and Natural Resources

Estados Unidos
México
Costa Rica
Ecuador
Puerto Rico
Chile
Argentina

realidades.com [GO]

🔖 Reference Atlas
▶ Videonovela y actividades
🌐 Mapa global interactivo

388 trescientos ochenta y ocho

Guacamayas rojas

ENRICH YOUR TEACHING

Using Backward Design
Have students preview the sample performance tasks on *Preparación para el examen*, p. 429, and connect them to the Chapter Objectives. Explain to students that by completing the sample tasks they can self-assess their learning progress.

Mapa global interactivo
Download the *Mapa global interactivo* files for Chapter 9 and preview the activities. Use Activity 1 to explore Santiago, Chile. Activity 2 takes you to Punta Arenas, Chile. In Activity 3, visit penguin nesting areas in Chile and Argentina. In Activity 4, explore the Islas Galápagos. Activity 5 follows monarch butterflies to Mexico.

Arte y cultura | México

Diego Rivera (1886–1957) En 1921, el pintor Diego Rivera conoció a José Vasconcelos, que estaba a cargo del Ministerio de Educación de México. Una de las ideas de Vasconcelos era crear murales en edificios públicos para educar al pueblo. En 1922, Vasconcelos le encomendó (*commissioned*) a Rivera su primer mural. Este mural se llamó "Creación". En este mural Rivera combina elementos de la tradición indígena, como se ve en el dibujo del jaguar, con elementos religiosos e intelectuales basados en el arte clásico europeo.

• ¿Qué otras cosas asocias con la tradición indígena mexicana?

"Creación", (1922–1923), Diego Rivera ▶
© 2009 Banco de México Diego Rivera & Frida Kahlo Museums Trust, México, D.F./Artists Rights Society (ARS), New York. Photo: © Art Resource, NY.

trescientos ochenta y nueve **389**
Capítulo 9

Standards (cont'd)
Communities
5.1 Beyond the School
• Link to Web sites from the Spanish-speaking world
• Describe urban vehicle restriction laws
5.2 Lifelong Learner
• Develop an appreciation for poetry and the visual arts
• Discuss ecological trends and possibilities for community involvement

 **PresentationExpress™**
See pp. 384c–384d

Chapter Opener

Core Instruction

Resources: Map Transparencies 15, 16, 18

Suggestions: Introduce students to the theme of the chapter and go over the objectives. Point out that they will improve their ability to talk and write about environmental concerns.

▶ **Videonovela** *¡Pura vida!* View this stand-alone storyline video about five young adults in San José, Costa Rica with your class, either online or on DVD.

Arte y cultura

Standards: 1.1, 1.2, 2.2, 3.1, 4.1, 5.2

Resources: Fine Art Transparencies with Teacher's Guide, p. 59

Suggestions: After students read the information, ask comprehension questions. For example: *¿Cuál era la idea de José Vasconcelos? (Su idea era crear unos murales para educar al pueblo.)*

Answers will vary.

DIFFERENTIATED INSTRUCTION

Digital resources such as the *Interactive Whiteboard* activity banks, *Videomodelos*, additional *Online Activities*, *Study Plans,* automatically graded *Leveled Workbook,* animated *Grammar Tutorials, Flashcards,* and *Vocabulary and Grammar Videos* will help you reach students of different ability levels and learning styles.

STUDENTS NEEDING EXTRA HELP

Guided Practice Activities
• Flashcards pp. 272–276, 285–288
• Vocabulary Check, pp. 277–280, 289–292
• Grammar, pp. 281–284, 293–294

HERITAGE LEARNERS

Realidades para hispanohablantes
• Chapter Opener, pp. 268–269
• A primera vista, pp. 270–271, 280–281
• Manos a la obra, pp. 272–279, 282–289
• ¡Adelante!, pp. 290–295
• Repaso del capítulo, pp. 296–299

ADVANCED/PRE-AP*

Pre-AP* Resource Book,
• pp. 162–164
Communications Workbook
• Integrated Performance Assessment, p. 215

389

▶ Read, listen to, and understand information about
  • environmental issues
  • what we can do to protect the environment

Vocabulario en contexto

Core Instruction

Standards: 1.1, 1.2, 3.1

Resources: Teacher's Resource Book: Input Script, p. 240, Clip Art, pp. 257–265, Audio Script, p. 244; Voc. and Gram. Transparencies 169–170; Audio Program DVD: Cap. 9, Track 1

Focus: Presenting new vocabulary and using grammar lexically in context

Suggestions: You may want to use the Input Script from the *Teacher's Resource Book* as a source of ideas for presentation of new vocabulary and comprehensible input. While presenting the vocabulary, capitalize on cognates, such as *contaminadas, petróleo,* and *conservar.* Since most of the vocabulary is not visualized, encourage students to use context clues to help themselves understand the meanings of new words and expressions.

BELLRINGER REVIEW

Have students complete this chart from the board:

	Verbo	Sustantivo	Profesión
1.	vender	venta	
2.		baile	bailarín
3.	cocinar		cocinero

Answers: 1. *vendedor* 2. *bailar* 3. *cocina*

Vocabulario en contexto

La **contaminación** del aire, de los ríos y de los mares es un problema gigante. En estas páginas el Dr. Biente contesta algunas preguntas sobre este problema y sobre lo que podemos hacer para ayudar a resolverlo.

1 66 La contaminación es uno de los problemas más **graves** del mundo. Hasta que tomemos **medidas** apropiadas para reducirla, este hermoso planeta estará en peligro 99.

los desperdicios

el veneno

la fábrica

2 —Dr. Biente, en mi barrio hay una fábrica de **pesticidas** y otros productos **químicos** que arroja los desperdicios al río. ¿Cree que es peligroso?

—¡Claro! **Debido a** estas prácticas peligrosas, los peces del río pueden morir en las aguas **contaminadas**. No debemos **echar** desperdicios en los ríos.

3 —Dr. Biente, ¿qué haremos cuando no haya **recursos naturales** tan importantes como el **petróleo**? ¿Cómo podremos usar los coches?

—En el futuro no podremos **depender del** petróleo para producir energía; algún día **se agotará.** Tenemos que **fomentar** el uso de fuentes de energía más eficientes **tan pronto como** sea posible. Creo que en el futuro todos los coches serán eléctricos, pues son **económicos** y limpios.

390 trescientos noventa
A primera vista 1

DIFFERENTIATED INSTRUCTION

Advanced Learners

Have students research a picture or bring in an object that represents one kind of threat to the environment. Ask them to use the picture or object as the basis for a short oral presentation about one kind of pollution. They can tell why they chose that particular picture or object, what kind of environmental problem it represents, their feelings about the seriousness of the problem, and then offer one or more possible solutions to the problem.

4 —La población está **creciendo** y cada día hay más gente en el planeta. ¿Cómo vamos a evitar que haya una **escasez**, o sea, una falta de recursos naturales?

—Es cierto que nos **amenaza** el peligro de la escasez. Por eso todos los seres humanos tenemos que tomar medidas para **conservar** los recursos que tenemos.

5 —¿Y **el gobierno** no puede hacer nada para proteger el medio ambiente?

—El gobierno **está a cargo de** hacer leyes para proteger el ambiente y **castigar** con multas a quienes no las obedezcan. Pero recuerden, no podemos esperar hasta que el gobierno haga algo, nosotros tenemos que cuidar el ambiente cada día.

▼**1 Cómo cuidar el medio ambiente | 🔊** _____

Escuchar

Escribe los números del 1 al 6 en una hoja de papel. Escucha lo que dice cada persona y di si es cierto *(C)* o falso *(F)*.

▼**2 Los consejos del Dr. Biente** _____

Leer

Completa estos consejos con la palabra apropiada.

1. Los *(desperdicios / gobiernos)* no se deben echar en los ríos.

2. Debemos *(agotar / fomentar)* nuevas fuentes de energía.

3. Los gobiernos deben *(tomar medidas contra / depender de)* la contaminación.

4. En el futuro debemos construir menos *(recursos naturales / fábricas)* en las ciudades.

5. El gobierno debe *(estar a cargo de / castigar a)* las personas que echan desperdicios a los ríos.

6. Todos debemos colaborar para *(contaminar / proteger)* el medio ambiente.

trescientos noventa y uno 391
Capítulo 9

---

1 Standards: 1.2

Resources: Teacher's Resource Book: Audio Script, p. 244; Audio Program DVD: Cap. 9, Track 2; Answer Keys: Student Edition, p. 122

Focus: Practicing listening comprehension of new vocabulary

Suggestions: Before students listen, give them a few minutes to review the information on these two pages. Use the audio or read the text. Allow students to listen more than once.

Answers:

1. F   4. C
2. C   5. F
3. C   6. F

Extension: Ask students to correct the false statements. Have them do so by changing information, rather than making the false statement negative. For example: *Los pesticidas no limpian, sino contaminan las aguas de los ríos.*

2 Standards: 1.2

Resources: Answer Keys: Student Edition, p. 123

Focus: Practicing new vocabulary in a word-choice exercise

Suggestions: After students have written their answers, challenge them to explain why the answer they chose makes sense and the other does not. If they cannot do that at this point, allow them to wait until later in the chapter, since the focus here is on vocabulary recognition.

Answers:

1. desperdicios
2. fomentar
3. tomar medidas contra
4. fábricas
5. castigar a
6. proteger

ENRICH YOUR TEACHING

Culture Note

As urbanization and development increase, motor vehicles are quickly becoming the main source of air pollution in Latin America. Air pollution can lead to such health problems as coughing, bronchitis, and lung cancer. The air in Mexico City, for example, was ranked the most contaminated by the World Health Organization.

21st Century Skills

Technology Literacy Have students use the digital technology within **realidades.com** to access and manage the audio files and activities that support learning the new vocabulary. Students can access the eText Audio to hear the pronunciation of new vocabulary words of *Vocabulario en contexto*, or they can use the Flashcards to study the vocabulary, then do some additional vocabulary activities.

Vocabulario en contexto

Core Instruction

Standards: 1.1, 1.2, 3.1, 4.2

Resources: Teacher's Resource Book: Input Script, p. 241, Clip Art, pp. 257–265, Audio Script, pp. 244–245; Voc. and Gram. Transparencies 171–172; Audio Program DVD: Cap. 9, Tracks 3–4

Focus: Extending presentation of vocabulary and grammar

Suggestions:

Pre-reading: Point out that all of the information on this page is a survey, and that the next page contains a separate article. Have students copy the answer grid before taking the survey.

Reading: Have students read the survey questionnaire first and then present the new vocabulary to them. Ask them to cover the **Resultados** part of the survey with a piece of paper, so they are not tempted to read ahead, which may affect their answers. Cover the **Resultados** text on *Vocab. and Gram. Transparency* 171. After the new vocabulary has been presented, ask them to complete the survey and read the **Resultados** part silently. For the article on the next page, play the audio or read aloud as students follow along. Allow them to listen more than once.

Post-reading: Use *Vocab. and Gram. Transparency* 171 to compile students' information from the survey. Use tallies or a percentage to show the results.

Pre-AP* Support

- **Learning Objective:** Interpersonal Writing
- **Activity:** After completing the survey on p. 392, have teams of students tally the results for their group. Then have them draft an e-mail to the director of ICPRO or a similar environmental agency summarizing the results and requesting ideas for conservation initiatives that could be implemented in their own school.
- *Pre-AP* Resource Book:* Comprehensive guide to Pre-AP* vocabulary skill development, pp. 51–57

Block Schedule

After students complete the survey on p. 392, total the responses of the entire class. Discuss how the entire class ranks. Is the class surprised by the results? Why?

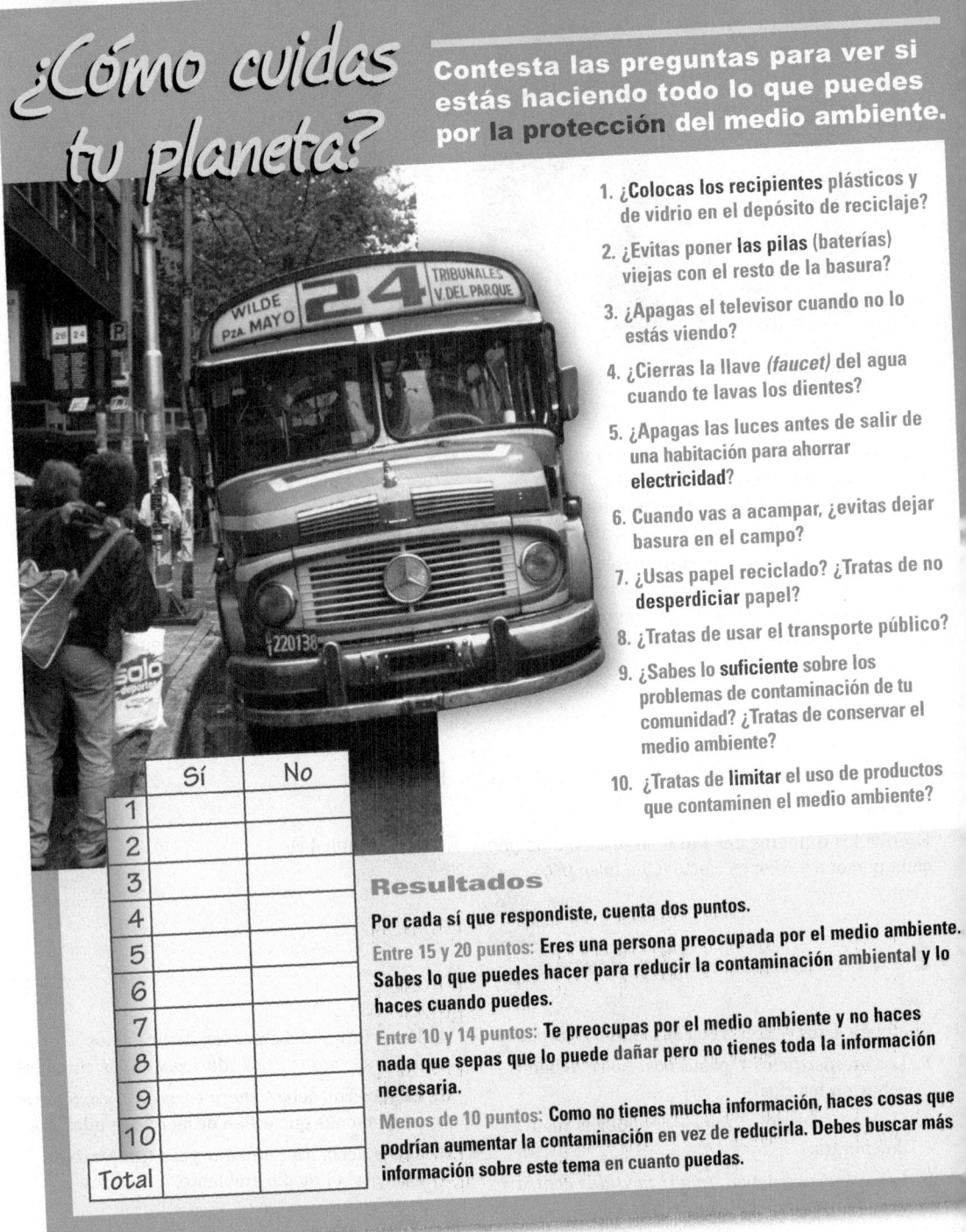

¿Cómo cuidas tu planeta?

Contesta las preguntas para ver si estás haciendo todo lo que puedes por la protección del medio ambiente.

1. ¿**Colocas los recipientes** plásticos y de vidrio en el depósito de reciclaje?
2. ¿Evitas poner **las pilas** (baterías) viejas con el resto de la basura?
3. ¿Apagas el televisor cuando no lo estás viendo?
4. ¿Cierras la llave *(faucet)* del agua cuando te lavas los dientes?
5. ¿Apagas las luces antes de salir de una habitación para ahorrar **electricidad**?
6. Cuando vas a acampar, ¿evitas dejar basura en el campo?
7. ¿Usas papel reciclado? ¿Tratas de no **desperdiciar** papel?
8. ¿Tratas de usar el transporte público?
9. ¿Sabes lo **suficiente** sobre los problemas de contaminación de tu comunidad? ¿Tratas de conservar el medio ambiente?
10. ¿Tratas de **limitar** el uso de productos que contaminen el medio ambiente?

	Sí	No
1		
2		
3		
4		
5		
6		
7		
8		
9		
10		
Total		

Resultados

Por cada sí que respondiste, cuenta dos puntos.

Entre 15 y 20 puntos: Eres una persona preocupada por el medio ambiente. Sabes lo que puedes hacer para reducir la contaminación ambiental y lo haces cuando puedes.

Entre 10 y 14 puntos: Te preocupas por el medio ambiente y no haces nada que sepas que lo puede dañar pero no tienes toda la información necesaria.

Menos de 10 puntos: Como no tienes mucha información, haces cosas que podrían aumentar la contaminación en vez de reducirla. Debes buscar más información sobre este tema en cuanto puedas.

392 trescientos noventa y dos
A primera vista 1

DIFFERENTIATED INSTRUCTION

Heritage Language Learners

Ask students to briefly debate the issues presented in each of the survey questions. Are there reasons one might not turn off a light or use recycled paper? Perhaps there are security or cost concerns. Encourage students to consider possible arguments and discuss them fully.

Students with Learning Difficulties

Assign each of the survey questions on p. 392 to a pair or small group of students. Direct students to act out their question to make its meaning clear. Encourage them to provide two versions of the action. For example, have them act out turning off the faucet, and *not* turning off the faucet.

Puerto Rico:

cómo conservar bella la isla

Como todos sabemos, Puerto Rico es famosa por sus bellos paisajes y sus playas de aguas azules y calientes. Sin embargo, para cuidar esa belleza el gobierno y los habitantes de la isla han tenido que buscar desde hace años nuevas maneras de **deshacerse** de la basura.

Con este objetivo, un grupo de hombres y mujeres de negocios decidió unirse en 1993 para formar el programa Industria y Comercio Pro-Reciclaje (ICPRO). Esta organización se dedica a **promover** programas educativos sobre el ahorro y reciclaje de recursos en escuelas y comunidades alrededor de la isla.

El ICPRO también ha organizado un concurso de artes plásticas llamado "Basurarte" para los jóvenes de escuela secundaria y la universidad. Los jóvenes artistas tratan de hacer obras de arte con materiales recogidos en la basura. Con sus obras de arte, los jóvenes quieren educar a la gente sobre la importancia del reciclaje y el cuidado del medio ambiente.

▼3 ¿Comprendiste?

Escribir

1. ¿Qué han tenido que hacer desde hace años los habitantes y el gobierno de Puerto Rico? ¿Por qué?

2. ¿Qué es ICPRO y a qué se dedica? ¿En tu comunidad hay programas educativos que informen a la gente sobre los beneficios del reciclaje?

3. ¿Qué tipo de concurso organizó el programa ICPRO?

4. ¿Quiénes participaron en ese concurso y para qué lo hicieron?

Más práctica	GO

realidades.com | print

Instant Check	✔	
Guided WB pp. 272–280	✔	✔
Core WB pp. 121–122	✔	✔
Comm. WB p. 124	✔	✔
Hispanohablantes WB pp. 270–271		✔

trescientos noventa y tres **393**
Capítulo 9

ENRICH YOUR TEACHING

9 Practice and Communicate

INTERACTIVE WHITEBOARD
Vocabulary Activities 9-1

4 Standards: 1.2, 3.1

Resources: Answer Keys: Student Edition, p. 123

Focus: Practicing new vocabulary

Suggestions: Remind students that in each item, both possible answers are the correct part of speech, but only one makes sense in the sentence. They must choose their answer based solely on meaning.

Answers:
1. castiga
2. en vez de/la pila
3. contaminado/grave
4. coloca
5. energía
6. escasez/conservar

Extension: After students complete the activity, ask volunteers to summarize what they have learned about some environmental problems and solutions in a few countries.

BELLRINGER REVIEW

Have students brainstorm a list of items that could be recycled.

5 Standards: 1.1, 1.2, 1.3, 3.1

Resources: Answer Keys: Student Edition, p. 124

Focus: Practicing new vocabulary through reading and response

Recycle: *por* and *para,* imperatives

Suggestions: Encourage students to read the entire poster before answering any questions. Have them work with a partner to resolve comprehension problems.

Answers:

Step 1
1. No usar más bolsas de las que se necesitan, comprar productos en recipientes grandes, evitar los productos desechables.
2. Reciclar es devolver a las fábricas todos los materiales que se pueden volver a usar.
3. El objetivo es reducir, reutilizar y reciclar la basura y educar a la gente sobre el reciclaje.

Step 2
Answers will vary.

394

▼ Objectives
▶ Read and write about environmental issues and solutions
▶ Discuss pollution and the shortage of natural resources
▶ Read and write about population growth

Vocabulario en uso

▼4 Problemas y soluciones del medio ambiente

Leer

Lee las siguientes frases que describen problemas del medio ambiente y las soluciones. Escoge la palabra que mejor complete cada frase.

1. En la capital de Chile, se *(castiga / desperdicia)* con una multa a las personas que echan basura en la calle.

2. En España, reciclan los teléfonos celulares *(en vez de / a cargo de)* echarlos a la basura, pero primero se separa *(el veneno / la pila)* del teléfono.

3. En la Ciudad de México, el aire *(contaminado / económico)* es un problema tan *(químico / grave)* que se prohíbe el uso del coche ciertos días de la semana.

4. En Perú, para reciclar, se *(agota / coloca)* el vidrio y el papel en un recipiente especial.

5. Argentina tiene mucho gas natural, que sirve para producir *(desperdicios / energía)*.

6. Debido a la *(escasez / medida)* en la Ciudad de México, hay que *(promover / conservar)* el agua.

▼5 Un cartel ecológico |

Leer • Escribir

1 Lee el cartel y responde a las preguntas.

1. ¿Qué consejos da el cartel para reducir la basura?

2. Según el cartel, ¿qué es reciclar?

3. ¿Cuál es el objetivo de este cartel?

2 Piensa en las tres "R"s de las que habla el cartel. Escribe otros dos consejos sobre cosas específicas que la gente pueda hacer para reducir, reciclar y reutilizar. Piensa en tu propia experiencia y en cosas que se hayan hecho en tu comunidad.

REDUCIR
•No use más bolsas de las que necesita.
•Compre productos en recipientes grandes.
•Evite los productos desechables[1].

RECICLAR
•Reciclar es devolver a las fábricas todos los materiales que se pueden volver a usar, como el cartón y el vidrio.

REUTILIZAR
•Dé a cada producto todo el uso posible antes de considerarlo basura.
•Es importante ser consumidores responsables y pedir a las empresas que vendan productos que se puedan reutilizar.

1 disposable

DIFFERENTIATED INSTRUCTION

Heritage Language Learners

The level of recycling activity and awareness varies greatly depending on country and community. Ask students who have lived in a heritage country to comment on recycling in that country. Were the programs and awareness more or less developed than in their current communities?

Advanced Learners

Invite students to work in a small group to create a Spanish-language poster about environmental programs in your community. If the technology is available in your school, have them generate the poster using computer software. Then they can obtain permission to create multiple copies and post them.

▼**6 Las cosas que contaminan**

Leer • Escribir

En cada grupo de palabras busca algo que contamina el medio ambiente. Después, escribe frases que describan cómo esas cosas contaminan el medio ambiente. Además, sugiere una solución al problema.

Modelo
el petróleo
El petróleo que se usa en los coches contamina mucho.
Tenemos que inventar coches que no usen petróleo.

1. a. el reciclaje   b. las medidas   c. los productos químicos
2. a. el recipiente   b. el gobierno   c. los pesticidas
3. a. el veneno   b. la protección   c. la electricidad
4. a. las verduras   b. la energía   c. la pila
5. a. la población   b. los desperdicios c. los derechos
6. a. la basura   b. lo suficiente   c. el ambiente

▼**7 En el futuro** |

Hablar

Muchos jóvenes se preocupan por el futuro, pues no saben cómo se resolverán los problemas de contaminación y la escasez de recursos naturales que tenemos hoy. Habla sobre este tema con otro(a) estudiante.

fomentar

▶ **Modelo**
A —*En el futuro, ¿crees que se fomentará el uso del transporte público?*
B —*Sí, porque es mucho más económico.*

Estudiante A

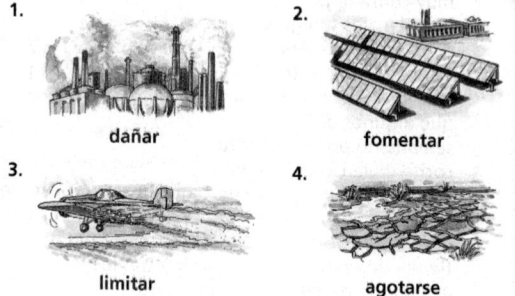

1. dañar
2. fomentar
3. limitar
4. agotarse
5. ¡Respuesta personal!

Estudiante B

económico(a)
grave
medida
escasez
¡Respuesta personal!

trescientos noventa y cinco **395**
Capítulo 9

---

6 Standards: 1.3
Resources: Answer Keys: Student Edition, p. 124
Focus: Practicing new vocabulary
Suggestions: After students make their selections, have them check their work with a partner before writing sentences for the second part of the activity.
Answers: Choices for the first part are as follows. Sentences for the second part will vary:

1. c   4. c
2. c   5. b
3. a   6. a

7 Standards: 1.1
Resources: Answer Keys: Student Edition, p. 125
Focus: Practicing new vocabulary and structures in guided dialogues
Suggestions: As you go over the model with students, point out the use of **porque** as a transition in Student B's response. Encourage students to be creative with their language and vary the way in which they respond to each other's comments.
Answers will vary. Student A will use the following vocabulary and future forms of verbs:

1. las fábricas/dañarán
2. la energía solar/fomentará
3. los pesticidas/se limitarán
4. el agua/se agotará

ENRICH YOUR TEACHING

Culture Note

Extended Producer Responsibility is the concept that a manufacturer's responsibility for the environmental effects of its product does not end when the product is sold. Rather, producers retain a role in the recycling, reuse, or disposal of the product and/or its packaging. In 2000, Peru became the first Latin American country to institute a packaging take-back law. Started in response to a landfill crisis in Germany in 1991, take-back programs require producers to accept responsibility for the waste management of their packaging, even after the product has been sold to and used by the consumer.

8 Standards: 1.1, 1.2, 1.3

Resources: Voc. and Gram. Transparency 4

Focus: Practicing new vocabulary and structures

Recycle: impersonal *se*, pronoun placement

Suggestions: Have students copy the chart to their own paper. Use *Voc. and Gram. Transparency 4* to model adding one other problem to the chart. Leave the right column empty on the transparency.

Answers will vary.

9 Standards: 1.1, 1.3

Focus: Practicing new vocabulary and structures through writing and discussion

Suggestions: Students may wish to consult each other or a bilingual dictionary for pertinent vocabulary to add to the discussion.

Answers will vary.

Fondo cultural

Standards: 1.1, 1.2, 2.1, 3.1, 4.2

Suggestions: After students have read the information, ask comprehension questions. For example: *¿Por qué han establecido la "restricción vehicular" en Santiago? (La han establecido porque el aire está muy contaminado.) Si vives en Santiago y el número de patente de tu coche termina con el 2, ¿irías en coche a la escuela el jueves? (No. La restricción está en efecto.)*

Answers will vary.

Mapa global interactivo, Actividad 1 Explore geographical limits to Santiago, Chile's expansion.

---

8 Para proteger el futuro |  | ♻

Escribir • Hablar

❶ Piensa en los problemas del medio ambiente y lo que se puede hacer para protegerlo. Copia la tabla y complétala con, por lo menos, cuatro problemas.

el problema	lo que se puede hacer	quiénes están a cargo (todos los ciudadanos, el gobierno, las industrias, etc.)
contaminación del océano	no echar basura	los ciudadanos
los desperdicios industriales		

❷ Cuando hayas completado tu tabla, trabaja con otro(a) estudiante. Hablen de las medidas que indicaron en sus tablas y expliquen quiénes deben estar a cargo de tomar esas medidas.

 Modelo

proteger el océano

A —*¿Qué medidas se pueden tomar para proteger el océano de la contaminación?*
B —*No debemos echar basura ni desperdicios al océano.*
A —*¿Quiénes están a cargo de protegerlo?*
B —*Todos los ciudadanos podemos proteger el océano al no echar basura.*

❸ Ahora, hagan una presentación para explicar a la clase los problemas y las soluciones de los que han hablado.

9 Y tú, ¿qué dices? | 🗣

Escribir • Hablar

1. ¿Qué problemas ambientales existen en tu comunidad?

2. ¿Qué medidas toman tú, tu familia y tu comunidad para proteger el medio ambiente? ¿Qué pueden hacer que no estén haciendo ya?

3. Nombra al menos una cosa que quieras . . .
   a. no desperdiciar   c. limitar
   b. promover   d. conservar

4. ¿De qué fuentes de energía depende más tu comunidad? ¿Qué otras fuentes de energía eficientes y económicas están tratando de fomentar?

Fondo Cultural | Chile

Restricción de vehículos
El aire en la ciudad de Santiago de Chile está muy contaminado. El problema es tan grave, que el gobierno ha tenido que establecer la "restricción vehicular". Eso quiere decir que algunos días de la semana no puedes usar tu coche en la ciudad. El día depende del último número de la patente *(license plate)* del coche. Por ejemplo: si miras la tabla del periódico *El Mercurio*, verás que los coches que tienen una patente que termina con los números 3, 4, 5 ó 6 no pueden usarse los lunes.

Día	Terminacie de patent
Lunes	3, 4, 5 y 6
Martes	7, 8, 9 y C
Miércoles	1, 2, 3 y 4
Jueves	5, 6, 7 y 8
Viernes	9, 0, 1 y 2

• ¿Hay algún tipo de restricción vehicular en tu comunidad? Descríbela, y explica qué le pasa a la persona que no la obedezca.

DIFFERENTIATED INSTRUCTION

Heritage Language Learners

Ask students who have lived in a heritage country to discuss the issues of vehicular traffic and water availability in those countries. Are there specific problems or programs in place? If these issues are not at the forefront, are there other, more pressing environmental concerns?

Students with Learning Difficulties

Encourage students to plan out their responses for *Actividad 9*. Before they write their answers, have them record possible ideas in list form. Then, help them use elements of the question and their lists to formulate a complete response.

▼10 La población crece

Leer • Escribir

① Lee la tabla y contesta las preguntas.

1. Según la tabla, ¿en qué siglo creció más la población?

2. ¿Qué problemas crees que ha causado este gran aumento en la población?

② Ahora, lee el artículo siguiente y contesta las preguntas.

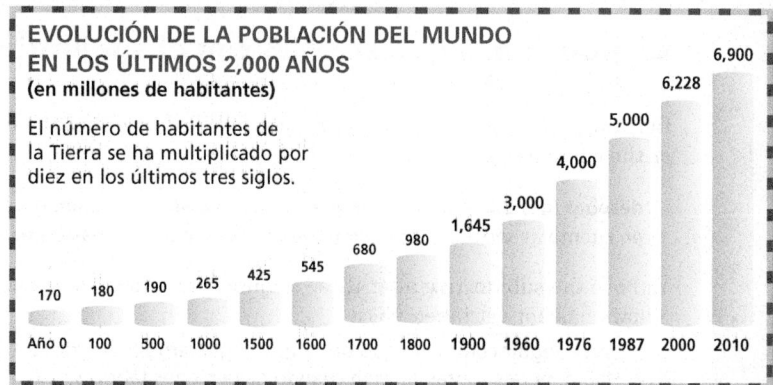

EVOLUCIÓN DE LA POBLACIÓN DEL MUNDO EN LOS ÚLTIMOS 2,000 AÑOS
(en millones de habitantes)

El número de habitantes de la Tierra se ha multiplicado por diez en los últimos tres siglos.

170 — Año 0
180 — 100
190 — 500
265 — 1000
425 — 1500
545 — 1600
680 — 1700
980 — 1800
1,645 — 1900
3,000 — 1960
4,000 — 1976
5,000 — 1987
6,228 — 2000
6,900 — 2010

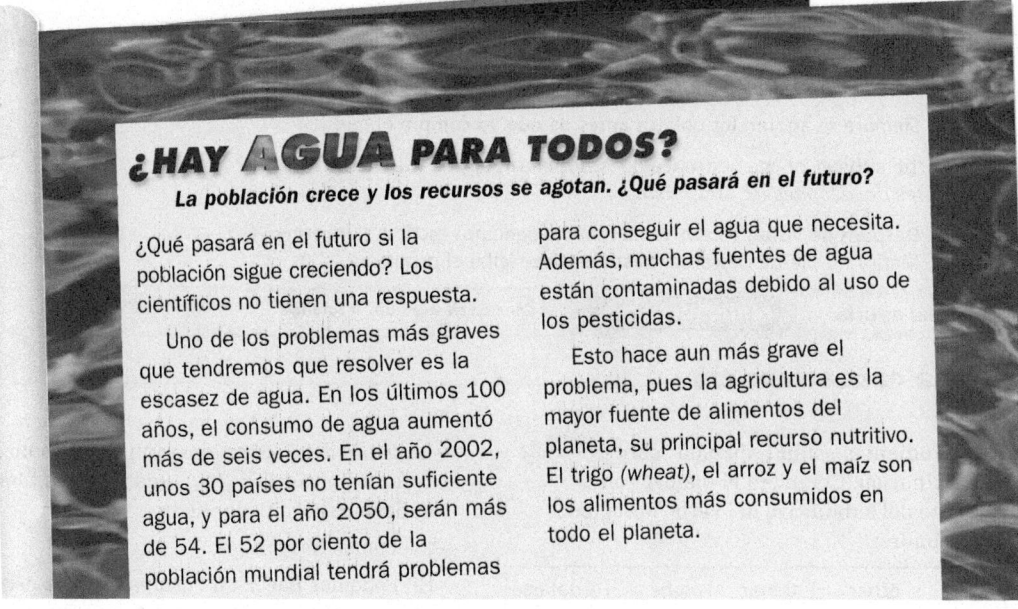

¿HAY AGUA PARA TODOS?

La población crece y los recursos se agotan. ¿Qué pasará en el futuro?

¿Qué pasará en el futuro si la población sigue creciendo? Los científicos no tienen una respuesta.

Uno de los problemas más graves que tendremos que resolver es la escasez de agua. En los últimos 100 años, el consumo de agua aumentó más de seis veces. En el año 2002, unos 30 países no tenían suficiente agua, y para el año 2050, serán más de 54. El 52 por ciento de la población mundial tendrá problemas para conseguir el agua que necesita. Además, muchas fuentes de agua están contaminadas debido al uso de los pesticidas.

Esto hace aun más grave el problema, pues la agricultura es la mayor fuente de alimentos del planeta, su principal recurso nutritivo. El trigo *(wheat)*, el arroz y el maíz son los alimentos más consumidos en todo el planeta.

¿Comprendiste?

1. ¿Cuál será uno de los problemas más graves si la población sigue creciendo?

2. ¿Cuáles son los alimentos más consumidos en todo el planeta?

3. En tu opinión, ¿quién debe tomar medidas para resolver estos problemas: los gobiernos de cada comunidad, los gobiernos de cada país, las Naciones Unidas o los ciudadanos?

trescientos noventa y siete **397**
Capítulo 9

Practice and Communicate ⑨

▼10 Standards: 1.2, 1.3, 3.1

Resources: Answer Keys: Student Edition, p. 125

Focus: Practicing new vocabulary and structures via reading and response

Suggestions: In addition to answering the questions in Step 1, encourage students to comment on the rate of population growth over the years.

Answers:

Step 1
1. La población creció más en el siglo XX.
2. Answers will vary.

Step 2
1. Uno de los problemas más graves será la escasez de agua.
2. Los alimentos más consumidos en el planeta son el trigo, el arroz y el maíz.
3. Answers will vary.

Block Schedule

Inside-Outside Circles. Have students go through the information on pp. 390–397. Have each student create a question and write it on a sheet of paper. Have students count off as 1 or 2. All number 1s form the outside circle. All number 2s form the inside circle, facing out. Each student should be paired. Have each student ask their questions and then the outside circle moves two people to the left. Each partner asks the questions again. Rotate until the class rotates back to the original partner.

Additional Resources

• Communication Wbk.: Act. 1, p. 120
• Teacher's Resource Book: Audio Script, p. 245, Communicative Pair Activity BLM, pp. 250-251
• Audio Program DVD: Cap. 9, Track 5

ENRICH YOUR TEACHING

Culture Note

Because of its geography, Santiago suffers from greater air pollution even compared to cities with similar vehicle emissions levels. Located between two mountain ranges, the Andes and the *Cordillera de la Costa*, the air pollution tends to remain over the city.

21st Century Skills

Information Literacy Have students research Web sites in Spanish that give more information about environmental problems in Latin American cities, such as pollution, scarce natural resources, and population, among others. What keywords will they use in their search? How can they decide which Web sites will give them reliable and accurate information?

✓ASSESSMENT

Prueba 9-2 with Study Plan (online only)

Prueba: Aplicación del vocabulario 1
• Prueba 9-2: pp. 195–196

397

9 Practice and Communicate

▼ Objectives
► Talk and write about events that have happened and that have not yet happened
► Discuss measures that could be taken against pollution

Gramática

BELLRINGER REVIEW

Briefly review with students the formation and use of the subjunctive before beginning the next *Gramática* presentation and series of *Actividades*.

Gramática

Core Instruction

Standards: 4.1

Resources: Voc. and Gram. Transparency 173

INTERACTIVE WHITEBOARD
Grammar Activities 9-1

Suggestions: In random order, call out the conjunctions shown in the *Gramática* and ask volunteers to use them in sentences. Make sure students understand that the two rules given after the word bank apply to all the conjunctions shown in the word bank, not just to those shown in sample sentences.

▼11 Standards: 1.2

Resources: Answer Keys: Student Edition, p. 126

Focus: Practicing the subjunctive and the indicative with time-related conjunctions

Suggestions: Have students read the entire dialogue for meaning before they write their answers.

Answers:
1. tome
2. eche
3. se agoten
4. estén
5. sepan

Chapter Project

Students can perform Step 2 at this point. Be sure they understand your corrections and suggestions. (For more information, see p. 384-b.)

Conjunciones que se usan con el subjuntivo y el indicativo

Certain conjunctions related to time are followed by either the indicative or the subjunctive.

después (de) que *after*	mientras *while, as long as*	cuando *when*
en cuanto *as soon as*	tan pronto como *as soon as*	hasta que *until*

You use the subjunctive after these conjunctions when the action that follows has not yet taken place.

> Van a seguir contaminando hasta que el gobierno los castigue.
> Habrá menos contaminación cuando haya menos fábricas.

You use the indicative after these conjunctions when the action that follows has already taken place or if it occurs regularly.

> Siempre apagamos las luces en cuanto salimos del cuarto.
> La empresa cerró tan pronto como se puso grave el problema.

- The conjunction *antes de que* is always followed by the subjunctive.

> Siempre se agotan los boletos antes de que yo compre el mío.

- If the subject of the sentence does not change, use the infinitive after *antes de*, *después de* and *hasta*:

> Después de visitar (nosotros) la fábrica, debemos escribir el informe.
> Marisa no piensa descansar hasta resolver (ella) el problema.

Más ayuda | **realidades.com** | ► *Canción de hip hop* ► *Tutorials*

▼11 La contaminación

Leer

Dos estudiantes están hablando sobre la contaminación. Completa el diálogo con el presente del subjuntivo del verbo apropiado del recuadro.

estar	echar	tomar	saber	agotarse

—La contaminación es un problema muy grave. Va a seguir aumentando hasta que el gobierno __1.__ medidas serias.

—Sí, seguro. Mientras la gente __2.__ desperdicios en lugares públicos, no vamos a resolver el problema.

—La gente debe saber que tan pronto como los recursos naturales __3.__, no vamos a tener lo suficiente para poder vivir.

—¡Debemos hacer algo!

—Sí. Podemos hacer una campaña en la escuela. Mientras los estudiantes __4.__ en recreo, pueden informarse sobre cómo conservar los recursos naturales.

—Después de que nuestros compañeros __5.__ más sobre el tema, todos van a querer colaborar.

DIFFERENTIATED INSTRUCTION

Students with Learning Difficulties

Lead students through *Actividad* 11 step by step. First, ask them to select the correct verb for the sentence based on meaning. Then, have them create the present subjunctive form of that verb. Last, ask them to explain why the subjunctive is necessary given the conjunction used and the time frame of the sentence.

Advanced Learners

Ask students to write two ways in which people commonly hurt the environment or waste resources. Have them read their sentences to a partner, who responds using a time-related conjunction: A —*Mucha gente no conserva el agua cuando se ducha.* B —*Verdad. Conservaremos el agua tan pronto como desaparezca.*

▶ Ampliación del lenguaje

Familias de palabras

Las familias de palabras son grupos de palabras relacionadas por tener una misma raíz. Lee las familias de palabras de la tabla. Piensa en palabras que conoces que pertenezcan a esas familias. Escribe en una hoja de papel las palabras que faltan para llenar los recuadros.

	Sustantivos	Adjetivos	Verbos
1.	desperdicios	desperdiciado(a)	
2.	contaminación		contaminar
3.		protegido(a)	proteger
4.	amenaza	amenazante	
5.	agotamiento	agotado(a)	
6.	economía		economizar

▼12 ¿Cuándo? |

Hablar

Tu compañero(a) quiere saber cuándo se van a reconocer las amenazas del futuro. Responde a sus preguntas usando las conjunciones *antes de que, cuando, tan pronto como, después de que, mientras, hasta que, en cuanto*.

▶ Modelo

el gobierno *(tomar)* medidas para fomentar la protección de la Tierra / reducir los recursos naturales

A —*¿Cuándo va a tomar medidas el gobierno para fomentar la protección de la Tierra?*

B —*Cuando se reduzcan los recursos naturales.*

Estudiante A

1. las fábricas *(deshacerse)* de los desperdicios sin contaminar
2. voluntarios *(fomentar)* el cuidado de la comunidad
3. *(promoverse)* leyes para proteger los recursos naturales
4. los ciudadanos *(colocar)* los objetos reciclables en lugares apropiados
5. las compañías que producen coches *(limitar)* el uso de petróleo

Estudiante B

castigarlas el gobierno
poder organizarse y recibir fondos
agotarse los recursos naturales
ser fácil y económico hacerlo
dejar de comprar coches ineficientes
tener más influencia los ciudadanos que las empresas
reconocer que el problema es grave

Ampliación del lenguaje
Core Instruction

Standards: 1.2

Resources: Answer Keys: Student Edition, p. 126

Focus: Understanding word families

Suggestions: Ask pairs of students to build word families around other words such as **conservar** or **fábrica**.

Answers:

1. desperdiciar 4. amenazar
2. contaminado(a) 5. agotar
3. protección 6. económico(a)

▼12 Standards: 1.1

Resources: Answer Keys: Student Edition, p. 127

Focus: Practicing the subjunctive and the indicative with time-related conjunctions

Suggestions: Point out that Student B has a choice of more responses than there are questions. Students should choose responses that reflect their opinions and make sense.

Answers will vary. The following are some likely results.

1. A —¿Cuándo van a deshacerse las fábricas de los desperdicios sin contaminar?
   B —Tan pronto como el gobierno las castigue.
2. A —¿Cuándo fomentarán los voluntarios el cuidado de la comunidad?
   B —En cuanto se puedan organizar y recibir fondos.
3. A —¿Cuándo se promoverán leyes para proteger los recursos naturales?
   B —No hasta que tengan más influencia los ciudadanos que las empresas.
4. A —¿Cuándo colocarán los ciudadanos los objetos reciclables en lugares apropiados?
   B —En cuanto sea fácil y económico hacerlo.
5. A —¿Cuándo van a limitar las compañías que producen coches el uso de petróleo?
   B —Después de que se agoten los recursos naturales.

ENRICH YOUR TEACHING

Teacher-to-Teacher

Have students prepare interviews which they can conduct with local business people, merchants, farmers, or community leaders who speak Spanish. Tell students that the purpose of their interviews should be to find out more about what people in your community are doing to protect the environment and conserve natural resources. Ask students to prepare a draft of several questions, then convene in a group to exchange ideas and correct any grammar errors their questions may have. Ask students to conduct their interviews and report back to the class with the results.

13 Standards: 1.2, 1.3, 3.1

Resources: Answer Keys: Student Edition, p. 128

Focus: Practicing the subjunctive and the indicative with time-related conjunctions

Suggestions: Have students read the brochure silently. Ask them to identify and give brief definitions of new vocabulary items it contains.

Answers:

1. La fábrica se deshace de su basura en nuestras aguas y en nuestro aire.
2. El gobierno ha promovido leyes para la protección de la comunidad, pero la fábrica no las obedece.
3. Los ciudadanos pueden dejar de comprar pesticidas y exigir que la fábrica use recipientes adecuados para sus productos químicos.
4. Los ciudadanos pueden participar en una marcha frente a la fábrica, o pueden firmar una petición contra la persona que está a cargo.
5. Answers will vary.

14 Standards: 1.1, 1.3

Focus: Practicing the subjunctive and the indicative with time-related conjunctions

Suggestions: As students make their suggestions in Step 2, encourage them to add comments using verbs of emotion and the subjunctive: *Es importante que hagamos....* Refer them to *Capítulo* 4, p. 154, for information about this use of the subjunctive.

Answers will vary. Students will use subjunctive verb forms after the time-related conjunctions in Step 1.

Pre-AP* Support

- **Learning Objective:** Interpretive: Print and Audio
- **Activity:** As a pre-reading activity, have students work in pairs. One student opens the textbook and reads the article in *Actividad* 13 to the partner. Then the partner opens the textbook and, while covering the article, looks at questions 1–4 as the other re-reads the article. The second student answers the questions aloud. If he or she is not able to answer the questions, the student who reads the article may re-read the particular section of the article where the answer is found. Finally, both students discuss question 5.
- ***Pre-AP* Resource Book:** Comprehensive guide to Pre-AP* communication skill development, pp. 10–18, 39–50

▼13 ¡No a la contaminación!

Leer • Escribir

Lee el siguiente folleto *(brochure)* sobre una fábrica de tu comunidad y responde a las preguntas que aparecen a continuación.

Marcha en contra de la
CONTAMINACIÓN

¿Sabías que la fábrica de pesticidas no respeta el medio ambiente? Contamina el agua del río con los desperdicios y también contamina el aire. Aunque el gobierno ha promovido leyes para la protección de la comunidad, esta fábrica continúa deshaciéndose de su basura en nuestras aguas y en nuestro aire.

Mientras fábricas como ésta no respeten las medidas de protección, van a dañar cada vez más a nuestro planeta. ¡Debemos exigir que la fábrica coloque sus desperdicios en lugares apropiados antes de que sea demasiado tarde! Juntos, podemos fomentar un cambio. ¡Toma medidas para proteger al planeta! ¡Deja de comprar los pesticidas! ¡Exige que la fábrica use recipientes apropiados para sus productos químicos!

Para mostrar tu apoyo, puedes participar en la marcha frente a la fábrica, o puedes firmar una petición en contra de la persona que está a cargo. **La protección de la comunidad depende de ti.**

1. ¿Cómo contamina el medio ambiente la fábrica de pesticidas?
2. ¿Existen leyes para proteger a la comunidad? ¿Las obedece la fábrica?
3. ¿Qué medidas pueden tomar los ciudadanos? Nombra dos medidas.
4. ¿Cómo pueden apoyar la causa los ciudadanos?
5. ¿Puedes pensar en otras maneras de apoyar la causa de la que se habla en el folleto?

▼14 Problemas y soluciones

Escribir • Hablar

❶ Con otro(a) estudiante, escribe cinco frases que identifiquen amenazas en tu comunidad respecto al medio ambiente y soluciones posibles, usando las conjunciones *antes de que, cuando, tan pronto como, después de que, mientras, hasta que.*

Modelo
Los ciudadanos no ahorran electricidad. Hasta que los ciudadanos hagamos un esfuerzo por ahorrar electricidad tendremos problemas.

❷ Cada pareja va a compartir sus ideas con la clase. Para cada problema que se menciona, la clase va a sugerir soluciones.

400 cuatrocientos
Manos a la obra 1

DIFFERENTIATED INSTRUCTION

Heritage Language Learners
Ask students to model the use of the time-related conjunctions in *Actividad* 15. After they have written their responses, have them go back and circle each verb that follows a conjunction. Ask students to confirm and explain why each verb requires the indicative or the subjunctive. Also, have students confirm the spelling of these verb forms.

Students with Learning Difficulties
Encourage students to circle a key word in each of the questions following the brochure in *Actividad* 13. Instruct students to search for these key words in the text to help locate the information required to answer each question.

15 En cuanto podamos . . .

Escribir • Hablar

1 Trabaja con otro(a) estudiante. Imaginen que se reunieron para hablar sobre lo que harán después de graduarse de la escuela. Hagan una lista de cosas que pueden hacer.

Modelo
• ir a la universidad
• buscar un trabajo
• viajar

2 Escojan una idea de su lista y hablen de los pasos necesarios para realizarla, usando las siguientes conjunciones.

después de que	tan pronto como	después de	mientras
cuando	hasta que	en cuanto	

▶ Modelo

ir a la universidad
A —*En cuanto me gradúe iré a la universidad.*
B —*Me quedaré con mis padres hasta que empiecen las clases.*

16 La lluvia ácida

Leer • Hablar

Lee el siguiente artículo sobre la lluvia ácida y contesta las preguntas que aparecen a continuación.

Conexiones | Las ciencias

En más de una docena de países europeos está ocurriendo una corrosión acelerada en los edificios y monumentos históricos. Así, por ejemplo, el Partenón ha sufrido más el efecto de la erosión en los últimos 30 años que durante los 2,400 años anteriores, y en España las pinturas del museo del Prado se han estado deteriorando a causa de la contaminación.

Todo ello es debido a las emisiones de dióxido de azufre (*sulfur*) y óxidos de nitrógeno, que se convierten en ácidos fuertes y atacan tanto a edificios antiguos como nuevos. Los más afectados son los objetos y estructuras de materiales fácilmente degradables, como la piedra caliza (*limestone*) y la arenisca (*sandstone*).

• ¿Qué otros ejemplos de corrosión por lluvia ácida conoces?
• ¿Hay corrosión por lluvia ácida en tu comunidad? Descríbela.

Más práctica	GO	
**realidades.com	print**		
Instant Check	✔	
Guided WB pp. 281–282	✔	✔
Core WB p. 123	✔	✔
Comm. WB p. 125	✔	✔
Hispanohablantes WB pp. 272–277		✔

cuatrocientos uno **401**
Capítulo 9

Practice and Communicate — 9

▼ 15 Standards: 1.1
Focus: Practicing the subjunctive and the indicative with time-related conjunctions
Suggestions: Point out that the future activities in the model are suggestions only. Encourage students to talk about their actual plans after high school.
Answers will vary.

▼ 16 Standards: 1.1, 1.2, 3.1
Focus: Practicing new vocabulary and structures via reading and response
Suggestions: Have students read the information silently. Help them address any comprehension problems they may have. Ask them to share background knowledge they may have about the major causes of acid rain.
Answers will vary.

Block Schedule

After completing p. 401, have students write five *Cierto/Falso* statements about *Actividad* 13 or 15. Ask them to work with a partner and ask each other their questions.

ENRICH YOUR TEACHING

Culture Note
In the Mexico City basin, acid rain is eroding the Aztec ruins of Tenochtitlán. In the Yucatán Peninsula, it is accelerating the erosion of the Mayan ruins. In Peru, it is attacking the Nazca Lines. Projects and studies around the world are dedicated to solving the problem of acid rain, but many of them lack funds.

21st Century Skills
Communication Remind students that whenever they do a speaking activity, as in *Actividad* 15, they will have the opportunity to first watch and listen to native speakers in the *Videomodelos*. This way, they can use a native-speaker model to monitor their own progress.

☑ASSESSMENT
Prueba 9-3 with Study Plan (online only)
Prueba: Conjunciones con el subjuntivo
• Prueba 9-3: p. 197

Gramática

Core Instruction

Standards: 4.1

Resources: Voc. and Gram. Transparency 174

INTERACTIVE WHITEBOARD
Grammar Activities 9-1

Suggestions: Say two short sentences referring to the same thing or person: *La señora Martínez es profesora. Hablé con la señora Martínez ayer.* Ask students to combine the two sentences using a relative pronoun from the *Gramática: La señora Martínez es la profesora con quien hablé ayer.*

17 Standards: 1.2

Resources: Answer Keys: Student Edition, p. 128

Focus: Practicing the relative pronouns *que, quien,* and *lo que*

Suggestions: Suggest that students follow three steps to complete the activity. First, read and understand the sentence. Second, locate the noun that will be replaced by the relative pronoun. Third, choose the correct relative pronoun.

Common Errors: Some students will follow English grammatical logic and use *quien* to refer to people, even when the pronoun doesn't follow a preposition: *Melina es una persona quien conozco.* Remind them that in Spanish, *que* is used to refer to both things and people unless a preposition precedes the relative pronoun: *Melina es una persona que conozco.*

Answers:

1.	que	3.	quien	5.	que
2.	Lo que	4.	que	6.	quienes

18 Standards: 1.1

Focus: Practicing the relative pronouns *que, quien,* and *lo que*

Suggestions: Point out that students are creating complex sentences. The relative pronoun serves as the subject of the subordinate clause. They must supply the verb phrase for that clause.

Answers will vary.

Gramática

▼ **Objectives**
▶ Describe people and issues related to the environment
▶ Read and write about environmental disasters

Los pronombres relativos *que, quien* y *lo que*

You use relative pronouns to combine two sentences or to give clarifying information. The most common relative pronoun in Spanish is *que*. It can mean "that," "which," "who," or "whom," and it may refer either to persons or to things.

> Ésta es la fábrica que visité ayer.
> La fábrica, que hace productos químicos, fomenta la protección del medio ambiente.
> El Sr. Ríos es el profesor que nos llevó a la fábrica.

After a preposition, use *que* to refer to things and *quien(es)* to refer to people.

> No encuentro el papel en que escribí tu dirección.
> El problema del que te hablé ocurrió en otro barrio.
> La señora a quien te presenté trabaja en una fábrica de recipientes.

• Use the relative phrase *lo que* to refer to a situation, concept, action, or object not yet identified.

> No recuerdo lo que me dijo.
> Lo que más me gusta es estar a cargo del proyecto.

Más ayuda | **realidades.com** | ▶**Tutorial**

▼17 El medio ambiente

Leer

Muchas de las noticias del periódico hablan sobre el medio ambiente.
Completa las frases con los pronombres relativos *que, quien(es)* o *lo que*.

1. El gobierno anunció las medidas _____ limitan el uso de pesticidas.

2. _____ más amenaza a la población es la escasez de recursos.

3. La persona de _____ habla el artículo tira los desperdicios en el río.

4. Las medidas _____ fueron tomadas por el gobierno no resuelven los problemas más graves.

5. El petróleo _____ se echa en el océano produce contaminación.

6. Las personas a _____ ayudó el gobierno viven ahora en una zona sin contaminación.

▼18 Lo que a mí me parece es . . .

Hablar

Completa las frases siguientes con tus opiniones personales.

1. Lo que más me molesta de la contaminación es . . .

2. El gobierno es la organización que . . .

3. Nuestros padres son las personas con quienes . . .

4. (Nombres) son las personas que . . .

5. No estoy de acuerdo con lo que . . .

DIFFERENTIATED INSTRUCTION

Advanced Learners/Pre-AP*

On the board, write questions that ask for identifying information that students can supply: *¿Quién es el señor Harler? ¿Qué es la lluvia ácida?* Then answer the questions with complex sentences containing relative pronouns: *El señor Harler es el profesor que enseña matemáticas.*

La lluvia ácida es un problema que destruye los monumentos antiguos. Have students write three similar questions and exchange them with a partner, who answers them using complex sentences with relative pronouns.

▼19 El petróleo | 👥

Leer • Escribir • Hablar

1 En grupo, lean el siguiente artículo sobre el petróleo en el mar.

PETRÓLEO EN EL MAR

En nuestra sociedad, el petróleo y sus derivados son imprescindibles[1] como fuente de energía y para la fabricación[2] de productos químicos, alimentos, medicinas, etc.

Por otro lado, alrededor del 0.1% al 0.2% de la producción mundial de petróleo termina en el mar. Esto produce la contaminación de las aguas y daña el ecosistema marino. Aves[3] y mamíferos mueren constantemente a causa del petróleo en sus cuerpos.

¿Cómo llega el petróleo al mar? El petróleo debe ser transportado muchas millas por el mar hasta llegar al lugar donde se va a usar. En el camino se producen a veces accidentes que pueden ser muy graves. Pero, la mayor parte del petróleo que termina en el mar procede de la tierra, de desperdicios de las casas, automóviles, combustible, fábricas, etc.

En la actualidad[4] se usan productos de limpieza especiales para limpiar el petróleo, pero evitar la contaminación es la única solución verdaderamente aceptable.

---
1 indispensable, essential **2** manufacture
3 Birds **4** currently, today

2 Decidan cuáles son las ideas más importantes del artículo. Escríbanlas en una lista y añadan detalles.

Modelo
Necesitamos el petróleo como fuente de energía.

3 Usen las ideas que anotaron para pensar en una propuesta sobre cómo resolver el problema del petróleo en el mar y en cómo se puede evitar la contaminación de las aguas. Pueden usar la Internet o la biblioteca para investigar sobre el tema.

Modelo
Cuando se transporta el petróleo por mar, se deben usar barcos que sean más modernos.

4 Presenten sus ideas a la clase.

Más práctica	GO
realidades.com	print

Instant Check	✔	
Guided WB pp. 283–284	✔	✔
Core WB pp. 124–125	✔	✔
Comm. WB pp. 121, 126	✔	✔
Hispanohablantes WB pp. 278–279		✔

---

19 Standards: 1.1, 1.2, 1.3, 3.1

Focus: Practicing new vocabulary and structures via reading and response

Suggestions: For Steps 2–3, encourage students to use a graphic organizer, such as a three-column chart, to record the main ideas and important details of the article. They can write their proposed solutions in the third column.

Answers will vary.

Chapter Project

Students can perform Step 3 at this point. (For more information, see p. 384-b.)

Additional Resources

- Communication Wbk.: Act. 2, p. 121
- Teacher's Resource Book: Audio Script, p. 245, Communicative Pair Activity BLM, p. 252
- Audio Program DVD: Cap. 9, Track 6

ENRICH YOUR TEACHING

Culture Note

Oil was first discovered in Venezuela in 1921. In 1960, the country became a founding member of OPEC. In 1976, the oil industry was nationalized. Oil is undoubtedly the lifeblood of the Venezuelan economy. The oil industry accounts for about 80 percent of Venezuela's export earnings.

21st Century Skills

Critical Thinking and Problem Solving
Working in small groups, have students discuss recent oil spill disasters in this country and in the world. Where have the recent oil spill disasters occurred? What companies and countries are involved? What are the biggest problems facing oil companies, environmentalists, and governments?

✓ASSESSMENT

Prueba 9-4 with Study Plan (online only)

Prueba: Pronombres relativos: *que, quien, lo que*
- Prueba 9-4: p. 198

Examen: Vocabulario y gramática 1
- Examen 1: pp. 199–201
- ExamView: Examen 1

Vocabulario en contexto

Core Instruction

Standards: 1.1, 1.2, 3.1

Resources: Teacher's Resource Book: Input Script, p. 242, Clip Art, pp. 257–265, Audio Script, pp. 245–246; Voc. and Gram. Transparencies 175–176; Audio Program DVD: Cap. 9, Track 7

Focus: Presenting new vocabulary and using grammar lexically in context

Suggestions: Have students look over the four numbered reading sections on these pages. Ask questions to help them achieve a general idea of what they will read. For example: *¿Piensas que esta lectura se trata más de la literatura o de las ciencias?* **(las ciencias)** Ask students to describe what they see in the photos. Encourage them to use background knowledge from their science and other courses in this discussion. Use *sí/no* or embedded answer questions to elicit new vocabulary from students. For example, looking at the diagram for section 1, ask: *¿Se atrapa el calor del sol en la tierra o en la atmósfera?* **(en la atmósfera)** Looking at the diagram for section 3, ask: *¿Los problemas del medio ambiente ponen a los animales en peligro de extinción?* **(Sí.)** Then have students read along as you present the new vocabulary by playing the audio or reading the text aloud. Check for comprehension by asking other questions. See the Input Scripts in the *Teacher's Resource Book* for specific questions.

BELLRINGER REVIEW

Have the students complete the sentences from the board with the name of the appropriate animal.

1. *La _____ tiene rayas negras y blancas.*
2. *El _____ es un mamífero muy grande.*
3. *Al _____ le gusta nadar en el océano.*
4. *El mejor amigo del hombre es el _____.*
5. *Cuando hacemos un picnic, las _____ nos visitan.*

(Answers: *cebra; elefante/hipopótamo; pez; perro; hormigas/moscas)*

| ▼ Objectives

▶ Read, listen to, and understand information about
- environmental issues and endangered species
- measures to protect the environment and endangered species

Vocabulario en contexto

¿Has escuchado decir alguna vez que el clima de la Antártida es muy frío o que en el Caribe hace mucho calor? Cada región del planeta tiene su propio clima. La flora y la fauna de cada región, es decir las plantas y los animales que viven en ella, están adaptados a su clima.

1 La actividad de los seres humanos puede cambiar el clima de una región o de todo el planeta. Por ejemplo, el CO_2 que **producen** los automóviles y las plantas generadoras de energía **atrapa** el calor del sol en la **atmósfera**. Este fenómeno, llamado **efecto invernadero**, ha hecho que las temperaturas de muchas regiones aumenten.

la piel

la foca

el ave

la pluma

2 Los seres humanos también pueden causar cambios en las condiciones de vida de un lugar. Cuando se **produce** un **derrame de petróleo**, muchos peces y otros animales marinos de la región pueden morir. **La limpieza** de estos derrames y **el rescate** de los animales de esa región cuesta mucho trabajo y dinero.

DIFFERENTIATED INSTRUCTION

Students with Learning Difficulties

Before students write their definitions for *Actividad* 21, instruct them to locate each word in the reading. Model for students how to use context clues in the reading to come up with a definition for each word.

Advanced Learners

Have students create a large greenhouse effect diagram like the one in section 1 of the reading. Ask them to include labels in their diagram. Have them use the diagram as a visual aid for a brief oral presentation about *el efecto invernadero.*

3 Los cambios en el clima, además de la **caza** y la pesca **excesivas** han puesto muchos animales **salvajes** en **peligro de extinción**. La escasez de alimentos y la **falta** de agua son dos resultados principales de la expansión de las ciudades y de otras actividades humanas. **La selva tropical** es un lugar que ha sido **explotado** sin control. Se han cortado tantos árboles que el número de **especies** que viven allí ha **disminuido**. La **preservación** de todas las especies es nuestra responsabilidad y podemos hacer cambios **con tal que** hagamos un esfuerzo.

Animales en peligro de extinción

el águila calva

la ballena

4 Los científicos dicen que **el recalentamiento global**, es decir, el aumento de las temperaturas en todo el planeta, puede **derretir** la nieve y **el hielo** de los polos y las montañas. Muchas ciudades quedarán bajo el agua **a menos que** detengamos el recalentamiento global.

▼**20** ¿Será cierto? | 🔊
Escuchar • Escribir

Escribe los números del 1 al 6 en una hoja de papel. Escucha cada frase y escribe C *(cierta)* o F *(falsa)*. En el caso de las falsas, vuelve a escribir la frase para que sea cierta.

▼**21** ¿Será cierto? | 👥
Escribir • Hablar

Trabaja con otro(a) estudiante para escribir definiciones de estas palabras y expresiones. Luego, escriban frases usando tres de las palabras y expresiones.

1. el efecto invernadero
2. la caza
3. derretir
4. el rescate
5. disminuir

cuatrocientos cinco 405
Capítulo 9

20 Standards: 1.2

Resources: Voc. and Gram. Transparency 176; Teacher's Resource Book: Audio Script, p. 246; Audio Program DVD: Cap. 9, Track 8; Answer Keys: Student Edition, p. 129

Focus: Practicing listening comprehension of new vocabulary

Suggestions: Display *Voc. and Gram. Transparency* 176 as a reference as students complete the activity. Allow them to listen to the audio once through first. Then play it again, pausing after each item, so they can write their answers.

Answers:

1. **C**
2. **F Si no detenemos el recalentamiento global, muchas ciudades se quedarán bajo el agua.**
3. **F Muchas especies están en peligro de extinción a causa de los cambios en el clima.**
4. **C**
5. **C**
6. **C**

21 Standards: 1.1, 1.3

Resources: Answer Keys: Student Edition, p. 129

Focus: Demonstrating comprehension of new vocabulary

Suggestions: Allow students to use phrases and sentence fragments to define the words and expressions in the first part of the activity. This way they can focus on meaning.

Answers: Sentences and wording of definitions will vary. Definitions should contain the following basic information:

1. **el calor del sol que queda atrapado en la atmósfera**
2. **el acto de seguir a los animales para matarlos**
3. **calentar el hielo para hacerlo líquido**
4. **liberación del peligro**
5. **hacer menos**

ENRICH YOUR TEACHING

Teacher-to-Teacher

Many of your students are already well versed in the area of pollution and other environmental problems. Encourage them to draw on this information and use their Spanish skills and reference materials such as bilingual dictionaries to synthesize it for discussions and writing in Spanish.

21st Century Skills

Critical Thinking and Problem Solving
Divide the class into four teams. Each team will do additional research about one of the environmental issues (greenhouse gases; oil spills; endangered species; global warming) described on pp. 404–405. Have students hold a round table discussion in class to summarize their findings and propose solutions to the problems.

Vocabulario en contexto

Core Instruction

Standards: 1.1, 1.2, 3.1

Resources: Teacher's Resource Book: Input Script, p. 243, Clip Art, pp. 257–265, Audio Script, p. 246; Voc. and Gram. Transparencies 177–178; Audio Program DVD: Cap. 9, Tracks 9–10

Focus: Extending presentation of vocabulary and grammar in context

Suggestions:

Pre-reading: Before reading, point out that *ozono, aerosoles,* and *afecta* are cognates. Show how removing the initial *a-* from the verb *amenazar* makes it closely resemble the English verb "menace," and explain that the meaning is the same. Have volunteers read aloud the titles on this and the next page to help students focus on the main ideas of the two readings.

Reading: Allow students time to read the information on this and the next page silently first. Then play the audio or read the text and have students read along as they listen. Allow them to listen more than once.

Post-reading: Check comprehension by asking questions, including those in *Actividad 22*. See the Input Script in the *Teacher's Resource Book* for other questions.

22 Standards: 1.2, 1.3, 3.1

Resources: Answer Keys: Student Edition, p. 130

Mapa global interactivo, Actividad 2

Look at the proximity of Punta Arenas, Chile to the South Pole.

Focus: Writing answers to demonstrate reading comprehension

Suggestions: Have students answer the questions on their own. Then invite them to share their responses.

Answers

1. La capa de ozono es importante porque nos protege de los rayos ultravioleta del sol. Si no la cuidamos, afectará nuestra vida diaria.
2. Punta Arenas está en Chile. Está en la región con el agujero más grande de la capa de ozono.
3. Los habitantes pueden llevar ropa que protege todo el cuerpo, ponerse anteojos de sol y loción protectora para el sol.
4–5. Answers will vary.

Punta Arenas: Miedo al sol

¿Has oído hablar de **la capa de ozono**? El ozono es un gas que forma una capa en la atmósfera que nos protege de los rayos ultravioleta del sol. A veces esta capa contiene

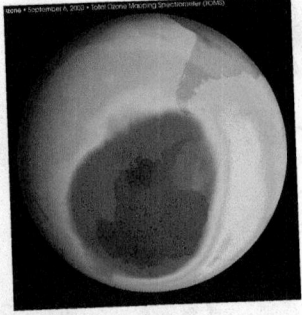

agujeros a causa del uso excesivo de productos que usamos todos los días, como **los aerosoles**. Es importante **tomar conciencia** de este problema, ya que **afecta** nuestra vida diaria.

Punta Arenas, en Chile, es una de las ciudades más cercanas al polo Sur. Y es en esa región donde está el agujero más grande de la capa de ozono.

Desde hace años, los habitantes de Punta Arenas viven bajo **la amenaza** de los rayos ultravioleta y ajustan *(adjust)* sus vidas a

niveles de ozono de la atmósfera. Si las noticias del tiempo indican que los niveles de ozono son muy altos, se recomienda llevar ropa que proteja todo el cuerpo, ponerse anteojos de sol y loción protectora para el sol.

Los científicos no saben aún cómo afectará este fenómeno en el futuro a los habitantes de esta ciudad.

▼22 La amenaza del sol | 🌐

Leer • Escribir

1. ¿Por qué es importante la capa de ozono? ¿Qué pasará si no la cuidamos?

2. ¿Dónde está Punta Arenas? ¿Qué problema hay allí?

3. ¿Qué pueden hacer los habitantes de Punta Arenas para protegerse de los rayos ultravioleta?

4. ¿Cómo crees que se sentirán los habitantes de esa ciudad viviendo bajo esta amenaza todos los días?

5. ¿Qué podemos hacer para que la gente tome conciencia de la importancia que tiene cuidar nuestro medio ambiente?

DIFFERENTIATED INSTRUCTION

Heritage Language Learners

Students may not be familiar with specific scientific vocabulary. Have them read through the passages on pp. 406 and 407 to find terms with which they are not familiar. Then, have them create a simple scientific glossary with explanations of each of these terms.

Students with Special Needs

Help students with visual impairments experience the images of *El Parque Nacional de Guanacaste.* Locate a recording that features some of the sounds one would hear at a Costa Rican nature preserve. These might include the sounds of the weather, birds, and animals.

El Parque Nacional de Guanacaste

En los últimos años se ha hecho muy popular el ecoturismo. Los turistas ecológicos no sólo quieren visitar lugares hermosos, sino que desean aprender sobre la fauna y la flora de la región, las características del terreno *(terrain)* y su clima. Este tipo de turista desea ayudar a cuidar y preservar la naturaleza.

1 Uno de los países que promueve el ecoturismo es Costa Rica. El Parque Nacional de Guanacaste, en la región del Pacífico Norte, por ejemplo, es un refugio para muchos animales y plantas, pero también uno de los lugares favoritos de los ecoturistas. En los años 80, se creó un Programa de Ecoturismo para que los visitantes pudieran disfrutar de los hermosos paisajes mientras participan en los programas educativos.

Lagartija verde, Guanacaste

2 Guanacaste es una **reserva natural** para muchos animales y plantas, pues en sus **tierras** hay varios tipos de bosques. Según los científicos, este parque tiene 3,000 tipos de plantas, 300 especies de aves y mamíferos, como el armadillo, el puma y el mono de cara blanca, y 5,000 especies de mariposas.

▼23 Cuando vaya a Guanacaste . . .

Escribir • Hablar

Haz una lista de los esfuerzos que hacen en un parque nacional de Costa Rica por proteger el medio ambiente. Habla con otro(a) estudiante sobre lo que hacen.

Más práctica	GO
realidades.com | print	

Instant Check	✔	
Guided WB pp. 285–292	✔	✔
Core WB pp. 126–127	✔	✔
Comm. WB pp. 127	✔	✔
Hispanohablantes WB pp. 280–281		✔

cuatrocientos siete **407**
Capítulo 9

▼23 Standards: 1.1, 1.2, 3.1

Focus: Practicing new vocabulary via discussion in context

Suggestions: Explain to students that most of the *esfuerzos* they list and talk about should be a product of their own background knowledge and critical thinking skills.

Answers will vary.

Extension: After students compare and discuss their lists, encourage them to research ecotourism in *El Parque Nacional de Guanacaste* or other *parques nacionales* and collect facts about efforts there to protect wildlife and the environment.

Pre-AP* Support

- **Learning Objective:** Interpersonal Speaking
- **Activity:** Have pairs of students turn their lists from Activity 23 into an interview. One student will play the role of an ecotourism guide from Guanacaste Park. The other will be a tourist interested in finding out details about the park's ecology and the government's conservation initiatives. Encourage students to use information they have learned throughout the chapter to expand the interview. Have students present their dialogues in front of the class.
- *Pre-AP* Resource Book:** Comprehensive guide to Pre-AP* vocabulary skill development, pp. 51–57

Chapter Project

Students can perform Step 4 at this point. Be sure they understand your corrections and suggestions. (For more information, see p. 384-b.)

✓ASSESSMENT

Prueba: Comprensión del vocabulario 2
- Prueba 9-5: pp. 202–203

ENRICH YOUR TEACHING

Culture Note

Although Costa Rica faces the same development concerns as many other countries, including a growing population and high deforestation, the small Central American country has taken a leadership role in the development of ecotourism. With only .03 percent of the world's total land mass, Costa Rica is home to 6 percent of the globe's biodiversity. Currently, national parks and reserves constitute approximately 25 percent of the country's area. Hundreds of thousands of ecotourists visit each year to view, study, and appreciate Costa Rica's natural resources, and these numbers are projected to grow. In 2010 an estimated 2.1 million foreign tourists visited Costa Rica.

24 Standards: 1.2, 1.3, 3.1

Resources: Answer Keys: Student Edition, p. 130

Focus: Demonstrating comprehension of new vocabulary

Recycle: definite articles, relative pronouns

Suggestions: After students have written their answers on their own, suggest that they repeat the activity orally in pairs. One partner reads the definitions in the left column to the other, who has his or her book closed and answers from memory.

Answers:

1. e	5. d
2. g	6. c
3. h	7. b
4. f	8. a

BELLRINGER REVIEW

Use Clip Art (see the *Teacher's Resource Book*) for the animals found on p. 405 and have the students arrange them on their desktop in order of size. Have partners discuss their arrangements.

25 Standards: 1.2, 3.1

Resources: Answer Keys: Student Edition, p. 130

Focus: Practicing new vocabulary in a word-choice exercise

Suggestions: Encourage students to scan the complete conversation before they attempt to write their answers.

Answers:

1. efecto invernadero	5. los aerosoles
2. la atmósfera	6. una amenaza
3. el clima	7. el recalentamiento global
4. la capa de ozono	

Extension: After students have completed the activity, have pairs assume the roles of Tomás and Ana. Ask them to practice speaking the conversation and present all or part of it to the class.

Manos a la obra 2

▼ **Objectives**
▶ Discuss animals and their well-being
▶ Write and talk about tropical forests and endangered animals
▶ Exchange information about environmental concerns

Vocabulario en uso

▼24 Definiciones ambientales | ♻

Leer • Escribir

Indica a qué palabra se refiere cada definición. Luego, escribe un párrafo en el que usas por lo menos tres de las palabras.

1. mamífero *(mammal)* enorme que vive en el agua
2. animal con piel que vive en el mar y en la tierra
3. acción de limpiar
4. cubre el cuerpo del ave
5. hacer o causar algo
6. parar
7. agua sólida
8. ave que representa un símbolo de los Estados Unidos

a. el águila calva
b. el hielo
c. detener
d. producir
e. la ballena
f. la pluma
g. la foca
h. la limpieza

▼25 El efecto invernadero

Leer

Completa esta conversación entre Tomás y Ana con las palabras del recuadro.

una amenaza	el recalentamiento global	la capa de ozono	los aerosoles
el clima	efecto invernadero	la atmósfera	

Tomás: —Hace mucho calor, ¿verdad?

Ana: —Sí, mucho. Tal vez es a causa del __1.__.

Tomás: —¿Qué es eso?

Ana: —Es la producción de gases que atrapan el calor del sol en __2.__. Cuando estos gases aumentan, hay cambios graves en __3.__ del mundo. Hace más calor o llueve más.

Tomás: —Pero __4.__ protege la Tierra de los rayos del sol, ¿verdad?

Ana: —Sí, pero __5.__ y otros productos químicos son __6.__ para la capa de ozono. Ya han creado un agujero en la capa de ozono sobre la Antártida. Un resultado es __7.__ en todas partes del mundo. El sol es tan fuerte en Australia, por ejemplo, que los estudiantes tienen que llevar sombreros especiales para protegerse la cabeza y el cuello.

408 cuatrocientos ocho
Manos a la obra 2

DIFFERENTIATED INSTRUCTION

Students with Learning Difficulties

Have students label the words in *Actividad 24* with one of the following codes: *an (animal), c (cosa),* or *ac (acción)*. Then ask students to determine whether each definition applies to an animal, a thing, or an action. Have them choose the correct word from the smaller group of choices.

Advanced Learners

Have pairs or small groups of students use vocabulary from *Actividades* 24 and 25 to write and present their own conversations. Encourage them to create situations in which the vocabulary would arise naturally, such as a conversation between ecotourists and a park ranger, or between a museum guide and museum goers.

▼26 Peligros |

Escribir • Hablar

❶ Escribe una lista de cinco cosas que pueden afectar la vida y la salud de los animales y de los seres humanos. Puedes usar las palabras del recuadro.

escasez	contaminado(a)	derrame de petróleo	caza excesiva	explotar
derretir	capa de ozono	especie	falta	amenaza

❷ Luego, intercambia tu lista con la de otro(a) estudiante, piensa en qué se puede hacer para solucionar los problemas y habla de tus soluciones con tu compañero(a).

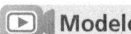 Modelo

la pesca excesiva

A —*La pesca excesiva es una amenaza a la población de peces.*

B —*Podemos establecer leyes en contra de la pesca excesiva.*

26 Standards: 1.1, 3.1

Focus: Practicing new vocabulary and structures via note-taking and discussion

Suggestions: Remind students that the vocabulary in the word bank is there to give them ideas. Encourage them to use the word bank, but to go beyond it as well, and use other pertinent vocabulary they may already know.

Answers will vary.

▼27 Un rescate problemático |

Leer • Pensar • Hablar

Imagina que hay un derrame de petróleo y tienes que llevar a la otra orilla *(bank)* del río a una anaconda, un cocodrilo y un ave. En el barco hay lugar sólo para ti y uno de ellos. Como no puedes dejarlos juntos en ninguna orilla porque la anaconda se comería al cocodrilo o el cocodrilo se comería al ave, ¿cómo podrías rescatar a todos sin problemas? Con un(a) compañero(a), piensen en las soluciones posibles.

27 Standards: 1.1, 1.2, 3.1

Focus: Practicing new vocabulary and structures through problem-solving

Suggestions: Suggest strategies in which students take two animals across, leave one, and return with the other to pick up the third.

Answers will vary.

🌐 Fondo Cultural | Argentina • Chile

Pingüinos magallánicos Los pingüinos magallánicos son los pingüinos más grandes de las zonas templadas. Reciben su nombre de Fernando de Magallanes, quien los vio por primera vez en 1519. Estos pingüinos tienen plumas negras y blancas en la cara, el cuello y el pecho. Viven en las costas rocosas del sur de Argentina y Chile y comen calamares[1] y peces pequeños. Hoy día hay alrededor de 1,800,000 pingüinos magallánicos. Aunque por el momento no están amenazados, las aguas donde comen están expuestas[2] al peligro de derrames de petróleo y algunas veces los pingüinos quedan atrapados en las redes de los pescadores[3].

• ¿Dónde viven los pingüinos magallánicos? ¿Qué comen?

• ¿Qué peligros hay en las aguas donde viven los pingüinos?

---

1 squid **2** exposed **3** fishermen's nets

cuatrocientos nueve **409**
Capítulo 9

Fondo cultural

Standards: 1.1, 1.2, 3.1

Suggestions: After students have read and discussed the information, ask: *¿Qué sabes de los otros animales que viven en la tierra o en el mar en la parte sur de América del Sur? ¿Cómo se llaman? ¿Qué información interesante puedes decir sobre ellos?*

Answers:

• **Viven en las costas rocosas del sur de Argentina y Chile. Comen calamares y peces pequeños.**

• **Las aguas están expuestas al peligro de derrames de petróleo y los pingüinos pueden quedar atrapados en las redes de los pescadores.**

🌐 **Mapa global interactivo, Actividad 3**

Visit penguin nesting areas along the coastlines of Chile and Argentina.

ENRICH YOUR TEACHING

Culture Note

Magellanic penguins are not the only things in the Southern Atlantic to receive the name of Fernando de Magallanes. The Strait of Magellan is the name of the body of water that separates the island of Tierra del Fuego from the tip of South America. Today, ecotours and cruises are available in and around the "land of fire."

Teacher-to-Teacher

Problem-solving activities like *Actividad* 27 are an excellent way to get groups of students speaking in Spanish. Many books are available containing such activities. Although the problems you find will most likely be in English, they can readily be converted and solved in Spanish.

28 Standards: 1.1, 1.2, 1.3, 3.1, 5.2

Resources: Answer Keys: Student Edition, p. 131

Focus: Practicing new vocabulary and structures via reading and response

Suggestions: For the slogans or announcements in Step 3, encourage students to make their message more effective by using poetic devices such as rhyme or alliteration.

Answers:

Step 2

1. **Se cortan los árboles para hacer cosas de madera y tener tierras libres para que coman las vacas.**
2. **El gobierno ayuda al Instituto Costarricense de Turismo.**
3. **Nelly recomienda educar a la gente para que no contamine la atmósfera.**

Step 3

Answers will vary.

Extension: After students have completed the activity, ask pairs of volunteers to perform a dramatic reading of the interview with Nelly Anderson.

▼**28** Las selvas tropicales de Costa Rica | 👥

Leer • Hablar • Escribir

❶ Lee la siguiente entrevista de Nelly Anderson, una estudiante de Costa Rica que se dedica a la preservación de la flora y la fauna de su país.

Entrevista con Nelly Anderson

¿Por qué te interesa la ecología?
Porque Costa Rica tiene muchas especies de plantas y animales salvajes.

¿Cuáles son los problemas que afectan las selvas tropicales y la naturaleza en el mundo?
Muchos países han explotado las selvas sin control. Se cortan los árboles para hacer cosas de madera[1] y tener tierras libres para que coman las vacas[2]. Ahora hay una escasez de recursos naturales.

¿Quién debe ejercer[3] este control?
El gobierno y todos los habitantes de países como Costa Rica. Además, los agricultores no deben cortar tantos árboles y deben respetar la naturaleza.

¿Qué hace el gobierno de Costa Rica ante este problema?
El gobierno ayuda al Instituto Costarricense de Turismo. Los turistas vienen a Costa Rica por su flora y fauna. Por lo tanto, el gobierno trata de fomentar más interés por la ecología.

¿Qué se puede hacer para que los niños y los adultos tomen conciencia del medio ambiente?
Pienso que la gente no tiene suficiente información. Por eso usan productos como aerosoles y pesticidas, que contaminan la atmósfera. Hay que educarlos.

1 wood   2 cows   3 exercise

❷ Contesta las preguntas sobre la entrevista.

1. ¿Por qué se cortan muchos árboles?
2. ¿Qué hace el gobierno de Costa Rica para apoyar la causa de Nelly?
3. ¿Qué recomienda Nelly para que la gente tome conciencia del problema?

❸ Trabaja con un(a) compañero(a) para crear un lema *(slogan)* o un anuncio que ayude a la gente a tomar conciencia de la importancia de no destruir las selvas tropicales.

DIFFERENTIATED INSTRUCTION

Heritage Language Learners

Ask students who have lived in a heritage country if they would volunteer to be interviewed. As the topic, ask them to identify a natural resource or geographic area of the heritage country. Have other students model their questions on those posed to Nelly Anderson in *Actividad* 28.

Multiple Intelligences

Visual/Spatial: Once students have chosen the theme that concerns them the most in *Actividad* 30, have them create a public awareness poster or pamphlet. How could they use art and design to inform the public and improve the situation?

▼29 Para el futuro |

Hablar • Escribir

❶ En grupos de tres o cuatro estudiantes escojan uno de estos temas. Hagan una lista de todas las palabras o expresiones relacionadas con ese tema.

- los derrames de petróleo
- se disminuyen los árboles en las selvas tropicales
- los animales que están en peligro de extinción
- el agujero en la capa de ozono
- el recalentamiento global
- la falta de preservación de la flora del planeta

❷ Luego diseñen un cartel para que la gente de su comunidad tome conciencia del problema que han escogido. Indiquen qué cosas hace la gente diariamente que producen el problema y lo que se puede hacer para mejorar la situación.

Cada vez que usas un vaso de plástico cuando puedes usar un vaso de vidrio, creas basura que no es necesaria.

▼30 Y tú, ¿qué dices? | 💬 | ♻

Leer • Escribir • Hablar

Contesta las preguntas:

1. ¿Puedes nombrar animales en el mundo que estén en peligro de extinción? Usa un diccionario para buscar los nombres en español. ¿Por qué es importante salvar a los animales que están en peligro de extinción?

2. ¿Cómo han cambiado la Tierra las personas? Escribe una lista de cuatro o cinco cosas que han hecho.

3. ¿Qué te preocupa más? Pon en orden la lista de temas, de lo más a lo menos serio, en tu opinión. Después explica por qué te preocupa el tema que escogiste como el más serio.

   a. el recalentamiento global

   b. la amenaza de una guerra nuclear

   c. la destrucción de las selvas tropicales

   d. la caza excesiva de los animales

   e. la falta o escasez de recursos naturales

   f. la contaminación de las aguas

   g. el derretimiento de los glaciares

   h. las nuevas enfermedades

   i. la violencia en la sociedad

4. ¿De qué se preocupan tus compañeros(as)? Haz una encuesta en tu clase para conocer la opinión de los demás estudiantes. Comenta los resultados con el resto de la clase.

Practice and Communicate ⑨

▼29 Standards: 1.1, 1.2, 1.3

Focus: Using new vocabulary and structures in the creation of a poster

Suggestions: Allow students to use and expand upon their slogans or ads from *Actividad 28* in the posters they create here.

Answers will vary.

▼30 Standards: 1.1, 1.2, 3.1

Focus: Practicing new vocabulary and structures

Recycle: present perfect tense

Suggestions: Have groups compile the information that they wrote in item 2. Encourage them to use some of this information, as well as the prioritizing they did in item 3, when they conduct their interviews in item 4.

Answers will vary.

Block Schedule

Total the individual class results for *Actividad* 30, item 3. Determine the top three environmental concerns. Ask students to write whether they agree or disagree with the top choices. Have each student present their opinion to the class.

Additional Resources

- Communication Wbk.: Act. 3, p. 122
- Teacher's Resource Book: Audio Script, pp. 246–247, Communicative Pair Activity BLM, pp. 253–254
- Audio Program DVD: Cap. 9, Track 11

ENRICH YOUR TEACHING

Culture Note

In 1998, the Costa Rican Tourism Institute developed a "Certification for Sustainable Tourism." Tourism companies, from guides to hotels, apply to be rated on a scale from 0 to 5; 0 being unsustainable and 5 being the most sustainable. Companies are rated according to their management of natural, cultural, and social resources.

21st Century Skills

Critical Thinking and Problem Solving Have students work in pairs or small groups to discuss the most serious environmental problems that, in their opinion, will challenge the world most in 50 years. Use the list of environmental concerns in *Actividad* 30, item 3 as a point of departure, then add future concerns to that list.

✓ASSESSMENT

Prueba 9-6 with Study Plan (online only)

Prueba: Aplicación del vocabulario 2
- Prueba 9-6: pp. 204–205

411

9 Practice and Communicate

Gramática

Core Instruction

Standards: 4.1

Resources: Voc. and Gram. Transparency 179

INTERACTIVE WHITEBOARD
Grammar Activities 9-2

Suggestions: Point out to students that here, just as in past *Gramática* presentations concerned with the subjunctive, the key to understanding its use is the concept of hypothetical actions or situations. If a situation has not yet occurred, or is only being considered as a possibility, the subjunctive is used.

31 Standards: 1.2

Resources: Answer Keys: Student Edition, p. 131

Focus: Practicing the subjunctive and the indicative with conjunctions

Suggestions: Ask students to complete the activity on their own. Then have them share their answers and discuss their reasons for choosing the subjunctive or the indicative.

Answers:

1. sepamos
2. se molesten
3. disminuya
4. haya
5. desaparezcan

32 Standards: 1.2, 1.3

Focus: Practicing the subjunctive with conjunctions

Suggestions: Encourage students to refer back to the rules in the *Gramática* as often as necessary in order to complete the activity.

Answers will vary. Students will use subjunctive verb forms in the subordinate clauses.

Gramática

▼ Objectives
▶ Express intentions, purpose, and uncertainty
▶ Discuss intentions to deal with environmental issues

Más conjunciones que se usan con el subjuntivo y el indicativo

The following conjunctions are usually followed by the subjunctive to express the purpose or intention of an action:

a menos que *unless*	para que *so that*
sin que *without*	aunque *although, even though*
con tal (de) que *provided (that)*	

Te doy este libro para que tengas más información sobre la capa de ozono.

If the subject of the sentence does not change, use the infinitive after *para* and *sin*.

No puedes saber el final sin ver la película.

With the conjunction *aunque*, use the subjunctive to express uncertainty. Use the indicative when there is no uncertainty. Compare the following:

Aunque llueve, vamos a la reserva natural.	*Although it is raining, we're going to the nature preserve.*
Aunque llueva, vamos a la reserva natural.	*Although it may rain, we're going to the nature preserve.*

Más ayuda · **realidades.com** · ▶ *Canción de hip hop* ▶ Tutorials

▼31 En el zoológico

Leer • Escribir

Completa las frases sobre el zoológico con el subjuntivo del verbo apropiado.

1. Nos han dado información para que (nosotros) *(producir / saber)* más.

2. El guardia del zoológico limpia el lugar de las focas sin que *(ellas) (molestarse / derretirse)*.

3. Un cartel dice que la ballena azul desaparecerá a menos que su caza *(disminuir / aumentar)*.

4. Aunque *(explotar / haber)* contaminación el río parece limpio.

5. Se construyen reservas para que los animales salvajes no *(desaparecer / afectar)*.

▼32 El rescate

Leer • Hablar

Imagina que se produjo un derrame de petróleo y estás organizando la limpieza y el rescate de animales. Completa las frases de una manera lógica.

1. Nosotros vamos a trabajar hasta tarde con tal de que Uds. . . .

2. No pueden tocarles la piel a las focas a menos que . . .

3. Leonardo y María, Uds. deben limpiar el área sin . . .

4. Vayan a hablar con la gente del barco que lleva petróleo aunque ellos . . .

5. Escribe un informe sobre el rescate para que la gente . . .

DIFFERENTIATED INSTRUCTION

Advanced Learners/Pre-AP*

On separate slips of paper, have students write three subordinate clauses beginning with conjunctions taught in the *Gramática* on this page. If they use **aunque,** allow them to use either the infinitive or the subjunctive in the clause. Collect the strips, mix them, and place them in a container. Have students meet in a circle, take turns drawing one subordinate clause at a time, and completing a complex sentence by inventing a suitable independent clause.

▼33 ¡Delicioso!

Leer • Escribir

Una empresa que crea anuncios para revistas necesita tu ayuda. Completa los anuncios usando la conjunción apropiada de la página 412. Usa como modelo el anuncio sobre el turrón, un alimento dulce en forma de tableta típico de España.

1. El chocolate . . . cómelo _____ te sientas más dulce.

2. ¡No manejes este coche _____ todos lleven su cinturón de seguridad *(seat belts)*!

3. El único teléfono celular que funciona _____ estés bajo tierra.

4. El reloj que sigue funcionando durante un año _____ cambies la pila.

5. ¡Salgan de casa! Vengan de viaje con nosotros . . . ¡_____ tengan un niñero!

¡No conocerás el mejor turrón, a menos que pruebes el turrón Real!

33 Standards: 1.2

Resources: Answer Keys: Student Edition, p. 131

Focus: Practicing the subjunctive with conjunctions

Suggestions: Students will enjoy sharing their responses for these items. After they complete the activity, invite them to do so in round-robin fashion.

Answers

1. para que
2. a menos que
3. aunque
4. sin que
5. Answers will vary.

▼ En voz alta | Talk!

José Martí (1853–1895) fue una de las grandes figuras históricas y literarias de América. Además de escribir poesía, artículos periodísticos y muchísimos ensayos, Martí dedicó su vida a la lucha por la libertad de Cuba. Fue uno de los fundadores del modernismo, un estilo literario que se caracteriza por su interés en la belleza y el estilo. La poesía de Martí es directa y clara. *Versos sencillos,* del cual las siguientes estrofas representan una pequeña parte, refleja la visión que tenía del mundo. Escucha las estrofas y luego contesta las preguntas.

• Según el poema, ¿cómo es el poeta?

• ¿Cómo le da importancia el poeta a la naturaleza en el poema?

De *Versos sencillos,* 1891
José Martí

Yo soy un hombre sincero
de donde crece la palma,
y antes de morirme, quiero
echar mis versos del alma.[1]

Yo vengo de todas partes,
y hacia todas partes voy:
arte soy entre las artes,
en los montes,[2] monte soy.

1 soul 2 forests

¿Recuerdas?

Generalmente se divide una palabra en sílabas después de una vocal o entre las consonantes. Cada línea de estas estrofas de *Versos sencillos* tiene ocho sílabas. Escribe el poema en una hoja de papel y divide las palabras en sílabas.

En voz alta
Core Instruction

Standards: 1.1, 1.2, 2.2, 3.1, 3.2, 5.2

Resources: Teacher's Resource Book: Audio Script, p. 247; Audio Program DVD: Cap. 9, Track 13

Suggestions: After students read the poem, encourage them to write a few lines of poetry to describe themselves and their relationship with nature.

Answers:

• Es un hombre sincero que quiere escribir poesía.
• Dice que, en los montes, el poeta es monte también; por lo tanto, el poeta es parte de la naturaleza.

Extension: José Martí is an AP* Literature author. You may want to suggest that students read additional works by this poet.

ENRICH YOUR TEACHING

Culture Note

Turrón, translated as "nougat," is a Spanish sweet with Arabic origins. The traditional recipe calls for almonds, honey, and eggs. These ingredients can be combined to form ***alicante,*** a hard nougat with whole almonds, or ***jijona,*** a soft nougat with crushed almonds. ***Turrones*** are traditionally eaten at Christmas time, especially after Christmas dinner with coffee. Today, many varieties of the traditional candy are available, including nougats made with peanuts, hazelnuts, coconut, or covered in chocolate.

34 Standards: 1.1

Focus: Practicing the subjunctive with conjunctions

Suggestions: Remind students that the model shows just one possible way to use the cues. Encourage Student A to begin the questions in other ways. Suggest other possibilities, such as: *¿Seremos capaces de parar...?* or *¿Qué se puede hacer con respecto a...?*

Answers will vary. Student B will use the subjunctive after the conjunction.

35 Standards: 1.1, 1.2

Focus: Practicing the subjunctive and the indicative with conjunctions

Suggestions: Point out to students that not all of the subordinate clauses they write must begin with *tú.* It is a given in items 2 and 6, but in the other items they can use different subjects.

Answers will vary. Students will use the subjunctive in the subordinate clauses, with the possible exception of number 5.

Chapter Project

Students can perform Step 5 at this point. Make audio or video recordings of their presentations for inclusion in their portfolios. (For more information, see p. 384-b.)

Teacher-to-Teacher

e-amigos: Have students write their *e-amigos* a list of what they feel are the four most important environmental problems facing their generation. Have them respond to the messages by giving possible solutions to the problems. Have students print out their e-mails or send them to you for review.

Pre-AP* Support

- **Learning Objective:** Presentational Writing
- **Activity:** Have students write a conclusion for the article in *Actividad* 36. Have students include the following in their texts: 1. a statement to summarize the personal opinion of the author on the topic, and 2. a possible long-term solution to the problem.
- **Pre-AP* Resource Book:** Comprehensive guide to Pre-AP* writing skill development, pp. 27–38

▼34 Cómo cuidar el planeta |

Hablar

Imagina que vas a una conferencia sobre cómo cuidar el planeta en que vivimos. En ella se habla sobre diferentes temas ambientales. Trabaja con un(a) compañero(a) para hacer preguntas y respuestas sobre los temas de la conferencia.

▶ **Modelo**

el recalentamiento global / a menos que
A —¿Qué va a suceder con el recalentamiento global?
B —A menos que los gobiernos no tomen conciencia del problema, el recalentamiento global aumentará cada año.

¡Cuidemos el planeta!

Conferencia sobre el medio ambiente

- Oportunidades para hacer trabajo voluntario
- Ideas para tu comunidad
- Nuevos productos para proteger el planeta

sábado 3 de mayo

Proyecto Limpieza

Estudiante A

1. la caza excesiva
2. la destrucción de árboles en la selva tropical
3. la capa de ozono
4. las reservas naturales del planeta
5. la contaminación de los ríos
6. la extinción de algunos animales
7. los derrames de petróleo

Estudiante B

a menos que
para que
sin que
con tal (de) que
aunque
sin

▼35 Ecoturismo en Chile

Leer • Hablar

Imagina que vas a hacer ecoturismo a Chile con un(a) amigo(a). Como él (ella) todavía no ha llegado, le cuentas tus planes por teléfono. Completa las frases de una manera apropiada.

1. Visitaremos varias reservas naturales a menos que . . .
2. No saldré hasta que tú . . .
3. Iremos a una conferencia sobre la capa de ozono con tal que . . .
4. Sacaremos fotos de las especies del lugar para que . . .
5. Nos quedaremos en un pueblo cerca del océano aunque . . .
6. No haré nada sin que tú . . .
7. Planearemos nuestras excursiones en cuanto . . .

414 cuatrocientos catorce
Manos a la obra 2

DIFFERENTIATED INSTRUCTION

Students with Learning Difficulties

Before students read **Victoria parcial para las ballenas** on p. 415, ask them to preview the questions. Have them record a "shorthand" for the main idea of each question. For example:

1) *¿religioso o natural?* 2) *¿Qué dos votaciones?* Remind students to consider these notes as they read the passage.

Advanced Learners

Have students create an adapted version of *Actividad* 35. In their version, ask them to include information about an actual ecotourism spot in Latin America. They can research this information on the Internet.

▼36 Las ballenas en peligro

Leer • Escribir

❶ Lee la noticia del periódico acerca de la reunión anual de la Comisión Ballenera Internacional.

❷ Ahora, responde a las preguntas.

1. En el artículo se habla de un santuario. En este contexto, ¿un santuario es un lugar religioso o un refugio natural?

2. ¿Qué dos votaciones se realizaron en la reunión de la Comisión Ballenera Internacional?

3. ¿Crees que ha sido un hecho positivo que Japón no haya obtenido votos suficientes en la votación?

4. ¿Qué se lograría con la creación del santuario de las ballenas?

5. ¿Has ido alguna vez a un lugar donde se pueda observar a las ballenas? Descríbelo.

Victoria parcial para las ballenas

Con una derrota (defeat) para la ambición de Japón de volver a practicar la caza comercial de ballenas, finalizó la reunión anual de la Comisión Ballenera Internacional. El gobierno de Japón no pudo obtener votos suficientes para que se le permitiera continuar con la caza de ballenas.

En tanto, el proyecto presentado por los gobiernos de Argentina y Brasil de crear un Santuario Ballenero del Atlántico Sur no obtuvo el 75% de los votos necesarios en la votación para ser aprobado.

Desde hace más de tres años las organizaciones ecológicas trabajan para lograr la creación de un santuario en el Atlántico Sur que ofrecería la protección que las ballenas necesitan y beneficiaría a las actividades científicas, educativas y turísticas en la región.

El español en el mundo del trabajo

Rescatista internacional en Sudamérica

En los países de habla hispana existen brigadas de rescate que ayudan a las víctimas de tragedias como, por ejemplo, la de los 33 mineros que quedaron atrapados en una mina el 5 de agosto de 2010 en Copiapó, Chile. Para desempeñar (perform) este trabajo se necesita entrenamiento, equipo y conocimiento del idioma para comunicarse y coordinarse con los demás rescatistas (rescuers). No importa cuál sea la especialidad del rescatista: primeros auxilios, excavación, demolición o control de incendios, hablar español le permite al rescatista trabajar en equipo con las otras organizaciones nacionales. Hoy en día, existen numerosos grupos, tanto oficiales como no oficiales, que desempeñan esta labor tan importante.

• ¿Conoces a algún grupo de rescatistas?

• ¿Te gustaría trabajar como rescatista?

Más práctica   GO

realidades.com | print

Instant Check	✔	
Guided WB pp. 293–294	✔	✔
Core WB pp. 128–130	✔	✔
Comm. WB pp. 122–123, 128–131, 213	✔	✔
Hispanohablantes WB pp. 282–289		✔

Practice and Communicate 9

▼36 Standards: 1.1, 1.2, 3.1

Focus: Practicing new vocabulary and structures via reading and response

Suggestions: Have students note down their ideas for responses to the questions on their own. Tell them their notes do not have to be in the form of complete sentences. Have them use these notes as they discuss the questions with a partner or in a group.

Answers:

1. En este contexto, un santuario es un refugio natural.
2. Se votó para que no se permitiera a Japón continuar con la caza de ballenas y sobre un proyecto para crear un santuario ballenero.
3–5. Answers will vary.

▼ El español en el mundo del trabajo

Core Instruction

Standards: 1.1, 1.2, 3.1, 5.2

Suggestions: Once students have read the information, ask comprehension questions. For example: ¿Cuáles son algunas especialidades de los rescatistas? (Son primeros auxilios, excavación, demolición y control de incendios.)

Answers will vary.

Additional Resources

• Communication Wbk.: Act. 4–5, pp. 122–123
• Teacher's Resource Book: Audio Script, p. 247, Communicative Pair Activity BLM, p. 255
• Audio Program DVD: Cap. 9, Tracks 12–14

ENRICH YOUR TEACHING

Culture Note

In 1998, Brazil and Argentina proposed a South Atlantic whale sanctuary, stretching from the equator to Antarctica, and from South America to Africa. Before whaling, there were 100,000 humpbacks in these waters, but due to exploitation the numbers dwindled to 10,000. Today, after strong recovery efforts, there are close to 60,000 humpbacks in the South Atlantic.

21st Century Skills

Creativity and Innovation Have students working in small groups come up with a creative idea for a product to protect the planet, as announced in the conference brochure in Actividad 34. Have a representative from each group describe the benefits of their environmentally-friendly product as if they were participants in the conference.

✔ASSESSMENT

Prueba 9-7 with Study Plan (online only)

Prueba: Más conjunciones con el subjuntivo
• Prueba 9-7: pp. 206

Examen: Vocabulario y gramática 2
• Examen 2: pp. 207–209
• ExamView: Examen 2

Puente a la cultura

Core Instruction

Standards: 1.2, 3.1

Focus: Reading to learn about the Galapagos Islands

Suggestions:

Pre-reading: Refer students to the *Estrategia* and have them read the topic sentences from the selection in order to better understand the information. Ask them to share background knowledge they may have about the function of topic sentences from their Language Arts courses.

Reading: Help students resolve comprehension problems by asking *sí/no* or embedded-answer questions: *En el siglo XVI, ¿los barcos españoles fueron atacados por los piratas ingleses o por los piratas peruanos? (por los piratas ingleses) ¿El exceso de tortugas es uno de los problemas que enfrenta las islas Galápagos? (No, pero un problema es el exceso de la población humana.)*

Post-reading: Ask volunteers to tell in their own words about the important details that support the topic sentence in each paragraph of the selection.

Country Connection

Core Instruction

Standards: 3.1

Resources: Map Transparency 17

Mapa global interactivo, Actividad 4
Explore the Islas Galápagos off the coast of Ecuador.

Suggestions: Ecuador's official name for the Galapagos Islands is the **Archipiélago de Colón.** Before the historical events presented on these pages, it is thought that people from the northern part of the Incan Empire, the Chimu, were present here. The islands were "discovered" by Europeans in 1535, when the Bishop of Panama's ship was blown off course on its way to Peru. The archipelago consists of eight major islands, thirteen smaller ones, and forty islets. Besides the turtles mentioned in the reading selection, the islands are famous for their iguanas, of which there are two types: the sea iguana and the land iguana (pictured on p. 417).

¡Adelante!

Puente a la cultura 🌐

Galápagos: El encuentro con la naturaleza

▼ Objectives
► Read about the history of the Galapagos Islands
► Learn about the endangered species of the Galapagos
► Use topic sentences to increase comprehension

Estrategia

Using topic sentences to orient you
In this text, you will read about the history of a particular place. As you read, notice how the topic sentence of each paragraph helps orient you. Each topic sentence contains a date, and the paragraph then discusses a particular period in history. As you read, think about what other information the topic sentence provides to set the scene for the rest of the paragraph.

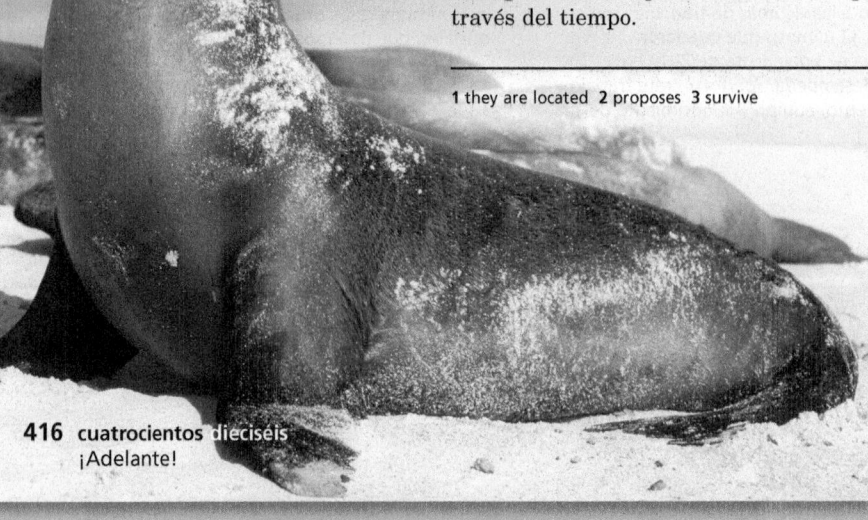

416 cuatrocientos dieciséis
¡Adelante!

Las islas Galápagos son un archipiélago de más de cincuenta islas que se encuentran en el Océano Pacífico a 800 kilómetros de la costa del Ecuador. Estas islas, que forman una provincia del Ecuador, son de origen volcánico y se ubican[1] directamente en la línea ecuatorial. Las islas son famosas por sus tortugas gigantes, que pueden vivir más de 100 años.

A finales del siglo XVI los piratas ingleses se establecieron en el archipiélago para atacar los barcos españoles que traían riquezas del Perú. Los piratas descubrieron que la carne de las tortugas gigantes era una excelente fuente de alimentos. Además, las tortugas podían vivir en los barcos, sin comida ni agua, por muchos meses.

A finales del siglo XVIII llegaron los balleneros. Pronto comenzaron a cazar las tortugas con la misma velocidad con que cazaban las ballenas. Se cree que mataron alrededor de 200,000 tortugas.

En 1835, un joven inglés de 22 años llamado Charles Darwin llegó a las islas en el barco HMS *Beagle* y pasó cinco semanas estudiando su fauna. Las ideas centrales de su libro fundamental, *El origen de las especies*, nacieron a partir de su viaje en el *Beagle*. La teoría propone[2] que las tortugas son las especies más fuertes que sobreviven[3] a través del tiempo.

1 they are located 2 proposes 3 survive

DIFFERENTIATED INSTRUCTION

Students with Learning Difficulties
Assign each paragraph of the reading to a small group of students. Direct each group to create a picture based on the main idea of their paragraph. Then, have students arrange their pictures by date to create a pictorial timeline of the reading's main ideas.

Advanced Learners
Ask students to research a Galapagos animal on the Internet. Have them present brief oral reports in which they present a few interesting facts about their chosen animal.

En 1935 el gobierno ecuatoriano decidió establecer una reserva natural de flora y fauna en las islas. En esa época, 3 de las 14 especies de tortugas habían desaparecido junto con algunos mamíferos y aves del lugar. En 1959 se creó la Fundación Charles Darwin para las islas Galápagos. Su trabajo de investigación y protección de los animales logró salvar varias especies que estaban por desaparecer.

El turismo organizado comenzó en 1970, pero se han implementado estrictas reglas para el cuidado de la fauna del lugar. Hoy en día las islas enfrentan muchos problemas, como el exceso de población y la falta de recursos del gobierno ecuatoriano para proteger su flora y fauna. Pero muchos colaboran para preservar este lugar único . . . y sus tortugas gigantes.

¿Comprendiste?

1. Usando las frases que empiezan cada párrafo, dibuja una línea de tiempo identificando los períodos de tiempo en la historia de las islas Galápagos de los que habla el artículo.

2. ¿A qué país pertenecen las islas Galápagos? ¿Dónde se encuentran?

3. ¿Por qué se establecieron en Galápagos los piratas ingleses?

4. ¿Qué logró la Fundación Charles Darwin para las islas Galápagos?

5. ¿Qué problemas enfrentan hoy en día las islas?

Más práctica	GO

realidades.com | print

▶ *Videodocumentario*	✔	
Guided WB p. 295	✔	✔
Comm. WB pp. 132–133,	✔	✔
Hispanohablantes **WB** pp. 290–292		✔
Cultural Reading Activity	✔	

**Islas Galápagos
ECUADOR**

cuatrocientos diecisiete **417**
Capítulo 9

ENRICH YOUR TEACHING

Culture Note
The Galapagos Islands are part of Ecuador's national park system. The human population lives in roughly five percent of the islands' area that is not a park. One of the main challenges facing the wildlife of the islands today is the introduction by humans of animals such as pigs and goats, which destroy natural habitats, and rats, which prey on the young of wild animals.

21st Century Skills
Information Literacy Have students research Web sites in Spanish that give more information about the Galapagos Islands. Have them find photos of the unique endangered species that live there. What keywords will they use in their search? How can they decide which Web sites will give them reliable and accurate information?

▼ **¿Comprendiste?** Standards: 1.2, 1.3

Resources: Answer Keys: Student Edition, p. 133

Focus: Demonstrating reading comprehension

Suggestions: Have students write their responses to the questions on their own. For item 1, ask them to write a brief identifying detail at each point on their time line.

Answers:

1. Siglo XVI, piratas ingleses descubren las tortugas gigantes; siglo XVIII, llegada de los balleneros; 1835, llegada de Charles Darwin; 1935, creación de la reserva natural; 1959, Fundación Charles Darwin para las islas Galápagos; 1970, comienzo del turismo organizado

2. Las islas Galápagos forman una provincia del Ecuador. Se ubican directamente en la línea ecuatorial en el Océano Pacífico, a 800 kilómetros de la costa del Ecuador.

3. Los piratas ingleses se establecieron en Galápagos porque querían atacar los barcos españoles que traían riquezas del Perú.

4. La Fundación Charles Darwin logró salvar varias especies que estaban por desaparecer.

5. Hoy en día las islas enfrentan muchos problemas, como el exceso de población y la falta de recursos del gobierno ecuatoriano para proteger su flora y fauna.

Portfolio
Keep students' responses to the ¿Comprendiste? questions in their portfolios as a writing sample.

▶ Videodocumentario

Core Instruction

Standards: 1.2

Resources: Teacher's Resource Book: Video Script, p. 249; Video Program, Cap. 9

View *Exploremos la naturaleza fascinante* with the class to learn more about the economic use and environmental protection of natural resources in the Spanish-speaking world. Access the video online in **realidades.com** or use the DVD. See the *Video Teacher's Guide* for additional suggestions.

Additional Resources
Student Resource: Realidades para hispanohablantes, pp. 290–292; Guided Practice Activities, p. 295; Communication Wbk., pp. 132–133

¿Qué me cuentas?

Core Instruction

Standards: 1.1, 1.2, 1.3

Resources: Teacher's Resource Book: Audio Script, pp. 247–248; Audio Program DVD: Cap. 9, Track 15; Answer Keys: Student Edition, p. 134

Focus: Practicing listening and reading comprehension of new vocabulary and grammar; using information to write a cohesive and coherent reaction.

AP* Skills: Integration of listening, reading, and writing to comprehend and synthesize information from spoken and written sources.

Suggestions: For Step 1, use the audio or read the descriptions aloud. Allow students to hear the descriptions twice through: the first time to write their answers, the second time to check them.

For Step 2, have students identify significant details as they read and then summarize the main points of the article.

Have students review the rules on pages 398 and 412 before they begin Step 3. Encourage them to use each of the suggested expressions in their written responses.

Answers:
Step 1
1. b 2. a 3. a 4. b 5. b 6. a
Steps 2–3
Answers will vary.

Additional Resources

Student Resource: Realidades para hispanohablantes, p. 293

Block Schedule

You might record the presentations and have each student watch his or her presentation at a later time. Have each student evaluate the presentation from the perspective of being effective:

Good eye contact, clear speaking voice, convincing tone of voice.

Pre–AP* | ▼ **Objectives**

Integración

▶ Listen to and read about a vacation that teaches you about global warming
▶ Write about the environment and how to take care of it

¿Qué me cuentas?: Unas vacaciones inolvidables

¿Cómo cambió de opinión Catalina después de sus vacaciones? Primero escucha la narración. Anota las respuestas a las preguntas y guárdalas para el paso 3.

1 🔊 Escucha estas descripciones. Después de cada párrafo vas a oír dos preguntas. Escoge la mejor respuesta para cada una.

1. a. Se quemó en una fogata en una excursión de cámping.
   b. Se quemó en el sol.
2. a. Le explicó que en esa zona existía un agujero en la capa de ozono.
   b. Le explicó que en esa zona existía el efecto invernadero.
3. a. Le aconsejó que se cubriera el cuerpo si iba a la playa.
   b. Le aconsejó que se quedara en el mar si iba a la playa.
4. a. Catalina fue a la playa con sus amigas y llevó crema protectora.
   b. Catalina pasó unos días sin ir a la playa.
5. a. Empezó a pensar que la crema protectora para el sol era muy buena.
   b. Empezó a pensar en el medio ambiente.
6. a. Decidió proteger más el medio ambiente.
   b. Decidió usar más recursos naturales en su comunidad.

2 Ahora lee el artículo que Catalina escribió para su periódico escolar.

Recalentamiento global

Para que no se produzca más daño a la capa de ozono, es necesario que eliminemos el uso de productos como los aerosoles. Pero hay otros factores que amenazan la capa de ozono: el recalentamiento global y el efecto invernadero causado por los gases que se quedan en la atmósfera, sobre todo el dióxido de carbono. Este gas se queda en la parte inferior de la atmósfera y atrapa el calor. Esto contribuye al recalentamiento global. Y cuanto menos calor pasa de la parte inferior a la parte superior de la atmósfera —donde está la capa de ozono— la parte superior más se enfría. Resulta que mientras más se enfríe, más se dañará la capa de ozono.

El uso de energía produce dióxido de carbono. Por eso cada uno de nosotros debe reducir la energía que usamos. O sea, reducir nuestra "huella de carbono".[1]

A la derecha se indican las fuentes mayores de uso de energía en el país y en las viviendas. ¿Cómo puedes ayudar y usar menos energía?

[1] carbon footprint, [2] heating and cooling, [3] water heater

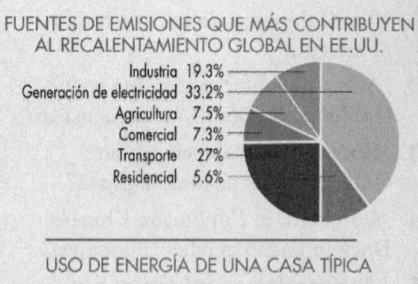

FUENTES DE EMISIONES QUE MÁS CONTRIBUYEN AL RECALENTAMIENTO GLOBAL EN EE.UU.

Industria 19.3%
Generación de electricidad 33.2%
Agricultura 7.5%
Comercial 7.3%
Transporte 27%
Residencial 5.6%

USO DE ENERGÍA DE UNA CASA TÍPICA

Calefacción y enfriamiento[2] 49%
Otros 8%
Luz 7.5%
Aparatos electrónicos 7%
Calentador de agua[3] 13%
Lavador & secador de ropa 5%
Refrigerador 5%
Lavaplatos 5%

3 Escribe un artículo sobre la experiencia que motivó a Catalina a estudiar sobre el medio ambiente y las recomendaciones que ella hace. ¿Qué pueden hacer tú y tus compañeros y por qué? Usa las expresiones para conectar tus ideas.

| antes de que | tan pronto como | hasta que | sin que | para que |

418 cuatrocientos dieciocho
¡Adelante!

DIFFERENTIATED INSTRUCTION

Multiple Intelligences

Interpersonal/Social: Encourage students to follow through on the topics of their oral presentations. Have students form action teams based on their areas of interest, and give them an opportunity to bring their message to the wider school audience through posters or announcements.

Students with Learning Difficulties

Students may have difficulty recalling and utilizing new vocabulary. Refer them to the vocabulary lists on pp. 384 and 386. Have students identify and copy words that would be useful to their oral presentations.

Presentación oral 🗨

Campaña para limpiar la comunidad

▶ Demonstrate how to organize a campaign to keep your community clean

▶ Use details to improve your presentation

Tarea
Vas a organizar una campaña para limpiar tu comunidad. Tienes que convencer a tus compañeros de que es necesario mantener limpia la ciudad para evitar la contaminación. Haz un discurso persuasivo para presentar tus ideas.

① **Prepárate** Completa una red de palabras como la siguiente.

¿Por qué hay que mantener limpia la comunidad?

> ### Estrategia
>
> **Finding good details**
> When giving a speech, you need to include appropriate details in order to make sense when talking about your topic. Interesting details add color and life to what you talk about and give it more substance. A good way to choose the right details to include is to ask these questions: *Who? What? Where? Why? When? How?*

② **Practica** Vuelve a leer la red de palabras. Practica tu presentación para recordar los detalles. Puedes usar tus notas para practicar. Recuerda:

- explicar cada razón usando vocabulario del capítulo
- presentar un plan a tus compañeros de lo que deben hacer
- mirar al público y hablar con voz clara y persuasiva

Modelo
Existen muchas razones para que mantengamos limpia nuestra comunidad. Es importante que sepamos que la contaminación se puede evitar. Cada uno de nosotros puede contribuir con la tarea.

③ **Haz tu presentación** Imagina que tus compañeros de clase van a ayudar a limpiar la comunidad. Explícales por qué es importante.

④ **Evaluación** Tu profesor(a) utilizará la siguiente rúbrica para evaluar tu presentación.

Rubric	Score 1	Score 3	Score 5
How well you organize information	The information you present is not well organized.	Your information is somewhat organized but hard to follow.	Your information is well organized and easy to follow.
How well you use details	You do not include details that make your speech interesting.	Your details are too few; some do not belong with your main idea.	Your details are interesting and support your main idea.
How effectively you deliver your speech	You read your speech and make no eye contact with your audience.	You make some eye contact, and you use some intonation.	Your eye contact is good. Your intonation helps you persuade.

ENRICH YOUR TEACHING

21st Century Skills

Initiative and Self-Direction Have students review the rubrics on pp. 419 and 421. Have them work in partners and discuss why their teacher gives them rubrics; how are they supposed to be used? Have them work with one of the rubrics to start with the outcome, figure out what they have to do to get the best grade possible, and develop a plan to achieve that goal.

ⓒ Common Core: Speaking

Presentación oral

Core Instruction

Standards: 1.1, 1.2, 1.3, 3.1, 5.1
Resources: Voc. and Gram. Transparency 5
Focus: Preparing and delivering an oral presentation

Suggestions: Review the task and the four-step approach with students. Review the rubric with the class (see *Assessment* below) to explain how you will grade the performance task. Before students begin, direct their attention to the *Estrategia*. Remind them of how the inclusion of details made for interesting reading in the *Puente a la cultura* section on pp. 416–417. Show *Vocab. and Gram. Transparency* 5 and have students create a similar word web on their own paper. Model how to include some details related to the topic that would make for an interesting and persuasive speech, i.e. details about a litter problem or a clean-up program at your school.

Pre-AP* Support

- **Learning Objective:** Presentational Speaking
- **Pre-AP* Resource Book:** Comprehensive guide to Pre-AP* speaking skill development, pp. 39–50

Portfolio

Make video or audio recordings of student presentations in class, or assign the RealTalk activity so they can record their presentations online. Include the recording in their portfolios.

Additional Resources

Student Resource: Realidades para hispanohablantes, p. 294

✓ASSESSMENT

Presentación oral

- Assessment Program: Rubrics, p. T34
  Review the rubric with students. Go over the descriptions of the different levels of performance. After assessing students, help individuals understand how their performance could be improved. (See Teacher's Resource Book for suggestions on using rubrics in assessment.)

| ▼ Objectives

▶ Write a petition letter to an oil company
▶ Give reasons and details to explain why the petition is being made
▶ Use the conclusion to draw your main ideas together

Language Arts Connection: Persuasive Writing

Standards: 3.1

Encourage students to draw on background knowledge they have from their Language Arts courses about introductions and conclusions in formal speaking and writing. Remind them that introductions and conclusions act as signposts to prepare the reader for the information presented and to summarize the information so it is easier to remember.

 Common Core: Writing

Presentación escrita

Core Instruction

Standards: 1.3, 3.1

Resources: Voc. and Gram. Transparency 4

Focus: Combining learned vocabulary and structures in a written presentation

Suggestions: Begin by explaining the criteria you will use to evaluate students' compositions. (See Step 5, *Evaluación,* in the Student Edition, and *Assessment* on the following page.)

Direct students' attention to the *Estrategia*. Remind them that an effective conclusion of a composition or letter almost always restates the main idea in other words. For this assignment, it should also help persuade. Then show *Vocabulary & Grammar Transparency* 4. Model filling in information like that shown in the chart on this page, and have students follow along on their own paper. Have them continue adding ideas to their charts that will help them develop their own compositions. Encourage them to do some outside research in order to find additional facts and interesting details that will improve their compositions.

Pre-AP* Support

- **Learning Objective:** Presentational Writing
- **Pre-AP* Resource Book:** Comprehensive guide to Pre-AP* writing skill development, pp. 27–38

Presentación escrita

Cuidemos nuestros océanos

Estrategia

Good conclusions
It's always a good idea to end what you write with a good conclusion that draws your main ideas together. For example, your conclusion can review ideas you introduced earlier and give a few sentences that tie them together. Your conclusion can also summarize your main idea in other words, or it can close with an interesting comment that leaves your reader wanting to know more about your topic.

Trabajas como voluntario(a) en una asociación para la preservación de los océanos. Tienes que escribir una carta a una empresa petrolera para que tome conciencia de los problemas que producen los derrames de petróleo y qué cosas se pueden hacer para evitarlos. Puedes concentrarte en los problemas que producen en su flora y fauna y las consecuencias para las personas.

1 Antes de escribir

Completa una tabla como la siguiente para reunir datos sobre los problemas que producen los derrames de petróleo en las aguas de los océanos.

Problemas que causan los derrames	Cómo se pueden evitar
• destrucción de las plantas • contaminación del alimento de los peces •	• tener cuidado • tomar conciencia de los peligros •

2 Borrador

Escribe tu borrador. Explica cómo afectan los derrames de petróleo a los océanos y qué se puede hacer para evitarlos. Añade todos los detalles necesarios. Recuerda que debes usar el vocabulario y la gramática de este capítulo.

Modelo

Estimado Sr. López:

Mi nombre es Enrique Lomas y trabajo como voluntario en una asociación para la preservación de los océanos. Le escribo esta carta para que ustedes tomen conciencia de lo importante que es la preservación de las aguas de nuestro planeta y de su flora y fauna. — **Topic sentence:** set the purpose of the letter.

Details: add information about the topic. → Es importante que se eviten los derrames de petróleo en los océanos antes de que sea demasiado tarde. Los derrames de petróleo destruyen y contaminan los animales y las plantas que viven en los océanos. Esto afecta también a las personas …

Mi intención con esta carta es comunicarles que mientras la vida en los océanos no sea respetada no vamos a poder… — **Conclusion:** ties everything together.

420 cuatrocientos veinte
¡Adelante!

DIFFERENTIATED INSTRUCTION

Heritage Language Learners

Students may have difficulty organizing their writing into formal, cohesive paragraphs. Have students write the topic sentence of each paragraph they plan to include at the top of an index card. Then have them add supporting details below. Remind them that each card will constitute one paragraph.

Advanced Learners

Encourage students to experiment with more than one attempt at a concluding paragraph for their letters. They might simply summarize the ideas presented in the body of the composition, restate the introduction in other words, or ask a question or two that will keep their readers thinking about the implications of what they have said.

③ Redacción/Revisión

Después de escribir el primer borrador, trabaja con otro(a) compañero(a) para intercambiar los trabajos y leerlos. Decidan qué aspectos son más efectivos. Luego, hagan sugerencias para mejorar sus composiciones. Fíjense si:

• ¿Se usó correctamente el subjuntivo o el indicativo después de las conjunciones?

• ¿Hay concordancia (agreement) entre los sujetos y los verbos?

• ¿Existen errores de ortografía?

En caso de algún error, corríjanlo.

Le escribo esta carta para que ustedes
~~tomen~~ tomar conciencia de lo importante
que ~~son~~ es la ~~preservasión~~ preservación de las aguas de
nuestro planeta y de su flora y fauna.

④ Publicación

Antes de hacer la versión final, lee de nuevo tu borrador y repasa los siguientes puntos:

• ¿Muestra la carta mi punto de vista respecto al tema?

• ¿Incluí detalles para expresar lo que pienso?

• ¿Refleja la importancia de comprender el problema?

• ¿Presenta una conclusión interesante?

Después de revisar el borrador, escribe una copia en limpio de tu composición.

⑤ Evaluación

Se utilizará la siguiente rúbrica para evaluar tu presentación.

Rubric	Score 1	Score 3	Score 5
Completion of task	Important parts of your letter are missing.	Parts of your letter are missing or disorganized.	You include and organize all the parts needed for a persuasive letter.
Effective conclusion	Your letter lacks an effective conclusion.	Your letter has a conclusion, but it is not effective.	You include an effective conclusion that helps persuade your readers.
Grammar, spelling, mechanics	You make many errors in grammar, spelling, and punctuation.	You make some errors in grammar, spelling, and punctuation.	You make very few errors in grammar, spelling, and punctuation.

Suggestions (Cont'd):

In Step 2, students should concentrate on how to develop and organize their ideas from the chart from Step 1 into an effective sequence. This is also the step in which they should focus on an effective conclusion for their persuasive letter. Encourage them to work toward organization, level of detail, and language use similar to that shown in the model.

For Step 3, encourage students to experiment with various ways of combining sentences. Remind them that this often entails use of the subjunctive. Have them follow the revision suggestions shown.

Evaluation

Steps 4 and 5 overlap. Students will need evaluation by you, their peers, or self-evaluation to fine-tune and polish their drafts.

Portfolio

Keep students' final drafts in their portfolios as a writing sample

Additional Resources

Student Resource: Realidades para hispanohablantes, p. 295

ENRICH YOUR TEACHING

21st Century Skills

Communication Students will use their written language for the purpose of petitioning a corporation about an environmental problem. They will need to use formal language in a business letter format. Have them work in small groups and determine the desired format for a business letter and the appropriate language to use when addressing a company's representative. What is a proper way to begin and end a business letter?

✓ ASSESSMENT

Presentación escrita

• Assessment Program: Rubrics, p. T34

Review the rubric with students. Go over the descriptions of the different levels of performance. After assessing students, help individuals understand how their performance could be improved. (See Teacher's Resource Book for suggestions on using rubrics in assessment.)

> ▶ Read about the Monarch butterfly
> ▶ Use context clues to figure out the meaning of a word
> ▶ Discuss festivals dedicated to the fauna and flora

© Common Core: Reading

Lectura

Core Instruction

Standards: 1.2, 3.1

Resources: Voc. and Gram. Transparency 4
Focus: Reading an extended passage
Suggestions:

Pre-reading: Before reading, direct students' attention to the *Estrategia* and *Al leer* sections. Have them begin a T-chart similar to the one on p. 425 and make sure they understand how they will use it. Point out that their T-charts will help them keep track of important details related to the points listed in *Al leer.* Have a volunteer read the subtitles of the passage aloud, so that the class can get an idea of how the information about Monarch butterflies will be presented.

Reading: Allow students time to read the selection on their own silently. Consider assigning this task for homework. This will allow you to capitalize on class time to read it again together with students. When reading together, pause frequently to address comprehension issues they may have and to allow them to fill in their **Mariposa monarca** charts from p. 425. Ask comprehension questions to help them focus on the main idea and important details in sections of the reading. Suggestions for these begin on the next page.

Country Connection
Core Instruction

Standards: 3.1

Resources: Map Transparency 14
🌐 **Mapa global interactivo, Actividad 5**
Follow monarch butterfly migrations to Mexico.

Suggestions: The state of Michoacán lies to the west of the state of México, (where Ciudad de México is located). Since it extends from the center of Mexico to the Pacific coast, Michoacán has a variety of climactic zones and terrains. It is primarily an agricultural and livestock-raising zone, specializing in lemons, corn, cotton, sugar cane, beef cattle, and pigs. The capital of Michoacán is Morelia, a city with a population of nearly one million.

Lectura
La mariposa monarca

Estrategia

Context clues
It is impossible to know the meaning of every word you read, but by developing your guessing ability, you will be able to understand enough to guess at the total meaning of a sentence, paragraph, or essay. Sometimes you can discover the meaning of a word from other words, punctuation, or sentences in the paragraph. These clues are often called context clues.

Al leer

Vas a leer un artículo sobre la mariposa monarca. Como ocurre casi siempre en los textos de no ficción, encontrarás palabras relacionadas con el tema de las mariposas que quizás no conozcas. Recuerda que debes tratar de determinar su significado a partir del contexto antes de consultar el diccionario o pedir ayuda a otra persona. Antes de leer, copia la tabla que aparece al final de la lectura. Mientras lees, complétala para que puedas contestar las preguntas sobre la lectura. Presta atención a los siguientes puntos:

- la migración de la mariposa monarca
- características que diferencian a esta mariposa de las demás
- los problemas que amenazan a la mariposa monarca

422 cuatrocientos veintidós
¡Adelante!

Tres cuartas partes de los animales que viven en la tierra son insectos. De todos los insectos, quizás el más hermoso sea la mariposa monarca. Este insecto, además de ser increíblemente bello, es un importante agente polinizador[1] y un factor de equilibrio ecológico.

Las mariposas, en general, viven alrededor de 24 días; sin embargo, la mariposa monarca puede llegar a vivir 8 meses, es decir, 12 veces más que las otras especies de mariposas. Además, es muy resistente a las condiciones del clima.

---

1 pollen carrier

DIFFERENTIATED INSTRUCTION

Heritage Language Learners

Ask students to read **La mariposa monarca** aloud. Have them model pronunciation, and encourage them to follow the rules of punctuation in their reading. They should briefly pause at each comma, and pause a bit longer at each period.

Students with Learning Difficulties

Students may have difficulty organizing the wealth of information provided in the non-fiction passage. Have them create their own concept webs around the theme of **La mariposa monarca.** As they encounter interesting facts in the reading, instruct them to record the information on their webs.

Llegada a México

Cada año, millones de mariposas monarca vuelan desde Canadá, lugar de donde provienen[2], hasta México. Llegan a fines de octubre a la zona entre Michoacán y el Estado de México y a mediados[3] de abril comienzan el viaje de regreso al norte. Es un viaje de más de 4,000 kilómetros.

En el camino, las mariposas se alimentan de asclepias[4], unas plantas que contienen una sustancia que es venenosa para otras especies. Esta sustancia le da a la mariposa un sabor y un olor desagradables, y esto le sirve de protección contra otros animales. La mariposa monarca también ayuda a la asclepia, pues es su agente de polinización.

Las condiciones de las montañas michoacanas son ideales para las mariposas: hay mucho oxígeno, están protegidas del viento y la temperatura es casi siempre agradable. Por otra parte, gracias a que los millones de mariposas que llegan a esta zona son agentes de polinización, hay una gran variedad de plantas en esta región.

Hibernación

Durante mucho tiempo se pensó que la mariposa monarca pasaba el invierno en zonas tropicales; pero nadie sabía adónde iban. Fue un misterio hasta 1975, en que después de décadas de investigación se encontró su lugar de hibernación. Para sorpresa de muchos, estaba en una zona donde las temperaturas normales están cerca de cero grados centígrados, en una región boscosa[5] entre valles y montañas. Esta región tiene una altitud promedio[6] de 3,300 metros sobre el nivel del mar, y se encuentra en la majestuosa Sierra Madre de México, entre Michoacán y el Estado de México.

Como la mariposa es un insecto de sangre fría, puede ajustar[7] la temperatura de su cuerpo al medio ambiente, lo que le permite conservar una gran cantidad de energía y grasa para su largo viaje de regreso.

Migración

Las mariposas monarca deben migrar en invierno porque el clima de Canadá es extremadamente frío durante esa estación. Para asegurar su sobrevivencia[8], las mariposas comienzan a desplazarse[9] al sur a medida que se acerca el invierno. Al llegar a las zonas de hibernación entre los estados de México y Michoacán, las mariposas buscan los lugares con la mejor temperatura para hibernar.

---

2 come from 3 in the middle of 4 milkweed

5 wooded 6 average 7 to adjust 8 survival 9 travel

La ruta de *las mariposas monarca*

CANADÁ
ESTADOS UNIDOS
MÉXICO

Suggestions (Cont'd):

Reading: Here are some possible comprehension issues on pp. 422–423 for which you can provide some guidance:

p. 422

- After reading the first sentence of the selection, ask a volunteer to write on the board the numerical percentage of earth's animals that are insects. (75%)
- After reading the second paragraph, ask a volunteer to write an arithmetical sentence that shows the calculation of how long a Monarch butterfly lives compared to most other butterflies. (Possible response: 24 días mariposa típica X 12 veces más = 288 días ó 9.6 meses.)

p. 423

- *¿De dónde vienen las mariposas monarca? (de Canadá)*
- *¿En qué meses del año se quedan las mariposas monarca en su lugar en México? (desde octubre hasta abril)*
- *¿A los demás animales les gusta comer las mariposas monarca? (No. Las mariposas tienen un sabor y un olor desagradables para los demás animales.)*
- *¿Qué fue un misterio hasta 1975 sobre las mariposas monarca? (el lugar donde se hibernan)*
- *¿Cuál tiene más influencia sobre la hibernación de las mariposas monarca, la presión atmosférica o la temperatura? (la temperatura)*

Pre-AP* Support

- **Learning Objective:** Interpretive: Print
- **Activity:** Have students work in groups of five. Assign each student in the group one of the five subtitled sections of this article. Ask that they create three multiple-choice questions for their section. While sitting in a circle, each student passes their three questions to the person on their left. The person assigned the first section, *Llegada a México*, reads the section aloud to the group. The person to his or her left asks one of the three questions to each of the other three students. Rotate around the circle in the same way until all sections have been read and all questions answered.
- *Pre-AP* Resource Book:* Comprehensive guide to Pre-AP* reading skill development, pp. 19–26

ENRICH YOUR TEACHING

Teacher-to-Teacher

Monarch butterflies are present in many parts of the United States during one part of the year or another. Invite students to talk about personal sightings of Monarch butterflies. If milkweed grows nearby, ask volunteers to bring in samples and tell where they found them. Interested students may wish to create a *Centro de mariposas monarca* in which they display photos and other information.

21st Century Skills

Technology Literacy Remind students of the various digital tools available in **realidades.com** to access extra reading support. Computer corrected activities use different reading strategies to help students build their vocabulary and progress at their own pace through the reading.

El número de mariposas que llega a los diferentes refugios del Estado de México y Michoacán está entre los 100 y los 140 millones, de acuerdo con las condiciones de su hábitat de verano en Canadá y los Estados Unidos.

Sobrevivir[10] el invierno es una tarea difícil para las monarcas. También es importante el papel que juegan los depredadores[11], aves y pequeños mamíferos, ya que de las mariposas muertas el 50% muestra mutilaciones y señales de ataque. La mortalidad natural en invierno se acerca al 35% aunque cambia de acuerdo a las condiciones del clima.

Refugios

Los refugios son lugares donde se reúnen las monarcas para pasar el invierno y reproducirse; se trata de bosques localizados en las laderas de las montañas y que están resguardados[12] del aire polar y de los cambios del clima. Los refugios se localizan entre los 2,700 y 3,200 metros de altitud sobre el nivel del mar, dependiendo de las condiciones del clima de cada año.

---

10 to survive **11** predators **12** protected

Peligros

El 20 de mayo de 2001 hubo un incendio en la zona entre el Estado de México y Michoacán en donde se reproduce la mariposa monarca. A pesar de los esfuerzos, se quemaron más de 500 hectáreas de la reserva natural. Afortunadamente las mariposas no sufrieron daños, pues habían emigrado a Canadá desde marzo.

En febrero de 2003 el diario *The New York Times* informó que una tormenta de invierno en la zona de hibernación había causado la muerte de miles de mariposas. Sin embargo, los científicos habían podido comprobar[13] que un año después la población de mariposas parecía haber recuperado[14] su nivel de años anteriores.

En los últimos años, el mayor problema de las monarcas es la desaparición[15] de su hábitat. El uso de pesticidas en las cosechas[16] agrícolas y la tala[17] de árboles hacen que desaparezca la planta asclepias, donde estas mariposas ponen huevos.

Las mariposas monarca son insectos bellos, útiles y resistentes. Debemos hacer todo lo posible para proteger los increíbles habitantes que comparten este planeta con nosotros.

---

13 to prove **14** recovered **15** disappearance **16** crops **17** tree felling

424 cuatrocientos veinticuatro
¡Adelante!

DIFFERENTIATED INSTRUCTION

Interacción con la lectura

1 Trabaja con un grupo de estudiantes para comentar lo que escribieron en sus tablas.

- ¿En qué se diferencia la mariposa monarca de las demás mariposas?
- ¿Conoces otros animales que migran para pasar el invierno en otras zonas? ¿En qué se diferencian esos animales de las mariposas monarca?
- ¿Por qué podemos decir que las mariposas monarca no son solamente hermosas sino también muy útiles?
- ¿Cuáles son los principales problemas que enfrentan las mariposas monarca? ¿Qué podemos hacer para protegerlas?

2 Trabaja con tu grupo para buscar palabras de la lectura que no conocían. Hablen sobre cómo lograron determinar el significado de esas palabras para entender la lectura.

3 Y tú, ¿qué piensas? ¿Crees que las mariposas monarca son animales extraordinarios o no? ¿Qué otro animal conoces que te parece extraordinario? Habla de ese animal a tu grupo.

Mariposa monarca	
¿Dónde vive?	
¿Cuánto tiempo vive?	
¿De qué se alimenta?	
Otras características importantes	
¿Qué peligros la amenazan?	

Más práctica GO

realidades.com | print

Guided WB pp. 296–297	✔	✔
Comm. WB p. 214	✔	✔
Cultural Reading Activity	✔	

Fondo Cultural | México

Festival Cultural de la Mariposa Monarca Desde hace más de 15 años, en los pueblos de Michoacán cercanos a los lugares donde hibernan las mariposas monarca, se celebra el Festival Cultural de la Mariposa Monarca. El Festival tiene como objetivo promover las artes de esos pueblos y el ecoturismo en la región oriental del estado de Michoacán.

La fiesta incluye música, danza, pintura y artesanías. La sede central del festival es Angangueo, ciudad que se hizo famosa desde que en 1976 se descubrió cerca de allí el primer santuario de las mariposas monarca. Durante los 16 días del festival, los artesanos trabajan en las plazas de los pueblos y venden sus obras a los visitantes.

- ¿Conoces algún festival que celebre la flora o fauna de tu región? Si es así, descríbelo.

cuatrocientos veinticinco **425**
Capítulo 9

Interacción con la lectura

Standards: 1.1, 1.2, 1.3, 3.1

Resources: Answer Keys: Student Edition, p. 134

Suggestions: As students work together in Step 2, ask them to use their combined knowledge and context clues to resolve comprehension problems. Encourage them to use dictionaries as a last resort.

Answers:

Step 1

- **La mariposa monarca se diferencia de las demás mariposas porque vive 12 veces más que las otras especies. Además es muy resistente a las condiciones del clima.**
- **Answers will vary.**
- **Las mariposas monarca no son solamente hermosas sino también muy útiles porque son un importante agente polinizador y un factor de equilibrio ecológico.**
- **Los principales problemas que enfrentan son el clima, los depredadores y los incendios. The remainder of this answer will vary.**

Steps 2-3

- **Answers will vary.**

Fondo cultural

Standards: 1.1, 1.2, 2.1, 3.1, 4.2

Suggestions: After students have read the information and answered the question, invite them to draft a letter to festival organizers in Mexico, telling them about a festival in your area that celebrates some plant or animal. In their letter, they should compare and contrast features of the *Festival Cultural de la Mariposa Monarca* and your local festival.

Answers will vary.

For Further Reading

Student Resource: Lecturas 3: "Los cuatro gatos," pp. 16–18, "A mi amigo," pp. 52–53

ENRICH YOUR TEACHING

Culture Note

One of the greatest threats to the Monarch butterfly is to its natural environment. The forests in Michoacán offer a unique ecosystem. Hanging from fir trees, the Monarchs achieve the perfect temperature for their winter hibernation. Unfortunately, this forest ecosystem only constitutes 2% of the total forest area in Mexico. In addition, there are people who depend on the logging and development of these areas for economic reasons. In 1986, the *Reserva de la Biosfera Mariposa Monarca* created two zones within the butterfly's habitat. In the "nuclear zone," no logging is allowed; in the "buffer zone," only limited logging is permitted.

Review Activities

Sobre la contaminación/Sobre el medio ambiente: Have students prepare their own Spanish definition for each vocabulary item in these categories. Then have teams of two students play against each other in a game of "Password." One student on a team gives his or her partner a definition. The partner must name the vocabulary item defined to earn a point. If he or she cannot, the other team gets a chance at the same definition. The team that correctly matches the greatest number of definitions and vocabulary items wins.

Sobre los recursos naturales: On their own, have students write three other words or expressions that are clearly associated with each item in this category. For example, for **la protección,** a student might write **un santuario ballenero, una ley,** and **una reserva natural.** Have students conduct the next part of the activity in round-robin fashion. One student says a word that he or she has written. The next student says which **recursos naturales** word it is associated with and explains the association.

Animales/Sobre los animales: Have students create their own fill-in-the-blanks exercises for these words. Tell them to create answer keys as well. Have them exchange exercises with a partner, complete each other's exercise, and check their answers together.

Otras palabras y expresiones: Students can use these words and expressions as they go over the review activities for the other categories and in the grammar review activities on the next page.

Verbos: Ask students to perform actions that they think portray the meanings of the verbs. Those watching must guess which verb is being acted out. Some verbs, such as **derretir** and **castigar** will be easy and fun to act out. Others like **fomentar** and **promover** present more of a challenge.

Repaso del capítulo
Vocabulario y gramática

sobre la contaminación

el aerosol	aerosol
la contaminación	pollution
contaminado, -a	polluted
el derrame de petróleo	oil spill
el desperdicio	waste
la fábrica	factory
el pesticida	pesticide
el petróleo	oil
la pila	battery
químico, -a	chemical
el recipiente	container
el veneno	poison

sobre los recursos naturales

económico, -a	economical
la protección	protection
el recurso natural	natural resource
suficiente	enough

verbos

afectar	to affect
agotar(se)	to exhaust, to run out
amenazar	to threaten
atrapar	to catch, to trap
castigar	to punish
colocar	to put, place
conservar	to preserve
crecer	to grow
dañar	to damage
depender de	to depend on
derretir	to melt
deshacerse de	to get rid of
desperdiciar	to waste
detener	to stop
disminuir	to decrease, to diminish
echar	to throw (away)
explotar	to exploit, to overwork
fomentar	to encourage
limitar	to limit
producir	to produce
promover (ue)	to promote

sobre los animales

la caza	hunting
(en) peligro de extinción	(in) danger of extinction, endangered
la piel	skin
la pluma	feather
salvaje	wild

otras palabras y expresiones

el agujero	hole
la amenaza	threat
a menos que	unless
con tal que	provided that, as long as
debido a	due to
la electricidad	electricity
en cuanto	as soon as
la escasez	shortage
estar a cargo de	to be in charge of
excesivo, -a	excessive
la falta	lack
el gobierno	government
grave	serious
la limpieza	cleaning
tan pronto como	as soon as
tomar conciencia de	to become aware of
tomar medidas	to take steps (to)

sobre el medio ambiente

la atmósfera	atmosphere
la capa de ozono	ozone layer
el clima	weather
el efecto invernadero	greenhouse effect
el hielo	ice
la preservación	conservation
el recalentamiento global	global warming
el rescate	rescue
la reserva natural	nature preserve
la selva tropical	tropical forest
la tierra	land

animales

el ave	bird
el águila calva, *pl.* las águilas calvas	bald eagle
la ballena	whale
la especie	species
la foca	seal

426 cuatrocientos veintiséis
Repaso del capítulo

DIFFERENTIATED INSTRUCTION

Heritage Language Learners
Have students provide examples of sentences utilizing each of the conjunctions reviewed on p. 427. Ask them to explain why they used the indicative or the subjunctive following each conjunction. Then have them write down their examples focusing on the spelling of the appropriate verb forms.

Advanced Learners
Invite students to create and exchange word-search puzzles using the chapter vocabulary. Remind them that the words hidden in their grids of letters can be written vertically, horizontally, or diagonally. Remind them to blend in the Spanish letters **ñ** and **ll** throughout their word-search grids.

Conjunciones que se usan con el subjuntivo y el indicativo

Certain conjunctions related to time are followed by either the indicative or the subjunctive.

en cuanto	tan pronto como	cuando
mientras	hasta que	después (de) que

You use the subjunctive after these conjunctions when the action that follows has not yet taken place. You use the indicative with these conjunctions when the action that follows has already taken place or if it occurs regularly.

Van a producir petróleo **hasta que** se agote.
En cuanto salgo del cuarto, siempre apago las luces.

• The conjunction *antes de que* is always followed by the subjunctive.

Pon el helado en el refrigerador **antes de que** se derrita.

• If the subject of a sentence does not change, use the infinitive after *antes de, después de, hasta.*

Después de salir del trabajo, voy a visitar a mi amigo Juan.

Más conjunciones que se usan con el subjuntivo y el indicativo

The following conjunctions are usually followed by the subjunctive to express the purpose or intention of an action:

a menos que	para que	sin que	con tal (de) que	aunque

No haré la limpieza de la casa **a menos que** me ayudes.

• If the subject of the sentence does not change, use the infinitive after *para* and *sin.*

Debemos dejar de usar aerosoles **para** detener la destrucción de la capa de ozono.

• With the conjunction *aunque*, use the subjunctive to express uncertainty. Use the indicative when there is no uncertainty.

Aunque produzcan más petróleo no podrán depender de este recurso por mucho tiempo.
No quiero ver ese programa sobre las ballenas **aunque** todos dicen que es muy bueno.

Los pronombres relativos que, quien y lo que

You use relative pronouns to combine two sentences or to give clarifying information. The most common relative pronoun in Spanish is *que*. It can mean "that," "which," "who," or "whom," and it may refer either to persons or to things.

El artículo **que** salió en el periódico habla sobre la contaminación.

After a preposition, use *que* to refer to things and *quien(es)* to refer to people.

El problema **del que** te hablé es muy grave.   La persona **de quien** te hablé se llama Adriana.

Use the relative phrase *lo que* to refer to a situation, concept, action, or object not yet identified.

Te cuento **lo que** me explicó el científico.

cuatrocientos veintisiete **427**
Capítulo 9

ENRICH YOUR TEACHING

Teacher-to-Teacher

Play "Concentration." Prepare twenty note cards. On ten, write an indicative form of one of the verbs from the list on p. 426. On the other ten, write a the corresponding subjunctive form. A sample pair might be **coloca/coloque.** Number the cards randomly 1–20 on the reverse side. Tape them to the board in numerical order in a grid.

Divide students into two teams. A player from Team A chooses two cards, which are turned over and read aloud. If they match, they are removed from the grid. Team A scores a point and goes again. If the cards don't match, they are returned to their positions and it is Team B's turn.

Conjunciones que se usan con el subjuntivo y el indicativo: In this activity, students can review the conjunctions from both the first and second grammar explanations on this page. On their own, have students use each of the eleven conjunctions in a written sentence. Tell them to use the subjunctive or indicative incorrectly in about half of their sentences and to randomly mix these incorrect sentences in with the rest. Then have students trade papers. Ask them to mark the correct sentences they see with a **C,** and to correct any errors they see in the use of the subjunctive versus the indicative. Have them read the corrected sentences aloud to their partners and explain the corrections they made.

Los pronombres relativos que, quien y lo que: Have students use the pronouns to create definitions of the chapter vocabulary on the previous page. For example: *Una selva tropical es un bosque cerca del ecuador que recibe una gran cantidad de lluvia. Los senadores son unas personas a quienes podemos escribir sobre la protección del medio ambiente. Crecer es lo que hacen las plantas en la primavera.*

Portfolio

Invite students to review the activities and projects they completed in this chapter. Have them select one or two items that they feel best demonstrate their achievements in Spanish. Include these products in students' portfolios with their Chapter Checklist and Self-Assessment Worksheet.

Additional Resources

Student Resources: Realidades para hispanohablantes, pp. 296–297

Teacher Resources:
• Teacher's Resource Book: Situation Cards, p. 256, Clip Art, pp. 257–265
• Assessment Program: Chapter Checklist and Self-Assessment Worksheet, pp. T49–T50

▶ ***¡Pura vida!*** is a storyline video that is independent of chapter content and an ideal support for expanding listening skills. The 14 episodes are available within **realidades.com** or on a separate DVD. Student activities and Teacher support are also assignable within **realidades.com**.

Performance Tasks

Standards: 1.1, 1.2, 1.3, 3.1

Student Resource: Realidades para hispanohablantes, pp. 298–299

Teacher Resources: Teacher's Resource Book: Audio Script, p. 248; Audio Program DVD: Cap. 9, Track 17; Answer Keys: Student Edition, p. 135

1. Vocabulario

Suggestions: Encourage students to review the vocabulary from the *A primera vista* sections on pp. 390–393 and 404–407 before they complete the activity.

Answers:

1. b	5. b
2. c	6. d
3. b	7. a
4. a	8. b

2. Gramática

Suggestions: Remind students of the main points of the grammar presentations in *Capítulo 9*:

- conjunctions that use the subjunctive and the indicative
- the relative pronouns *que, quien,* and *lo que*

Answers:

1. a	5. d
2. a	6. a
3. d	7. c
4. a	8. b

3. Escuchar

Suggestions: Use the audio or read from the script.

🔊 **Answers:**

(a) El problema de la contaminación de los ríos.
(b) Que el gobierno tome las medidas apropiadas para castigar a las fábricas que continúan echando desperdicios al agua.

Preparación para el examen

① **Vocabulario** Escribe la letra de la palabra o expresión que mejor complete cada frase. Escribe tus respuestas en una hoja aparte.

1. Muchos animales salvajes están en peligro de _____ a causa de la caza.
   a. preservación   c. población
   b. extinción   d. amenaza

2. El uso excesivo de _____ puede destruir la capa de ozono.
   a. venenos   c. aerosoles
   b. derrames   d. recipientes

3. Es muy peligroso cuando las fábricas arrojan _____ al río.
   a. peces   c. recursos
   b. desperdicios   d. medidas

4. ¿Qué haremos cuando se acaben los recursos naturales como _____?
   a. el petróleo   c. el terreno
   b. la energía   d. el clima

5. El número de ballenas ha disminuido a causa de _____ de petróleo.
   a. la contaminación c. la piel
   b. los derrames   d. la electricidad

6. Hay que buscar nuevas maneras de _____ de la basura.
   a. depender   c. promover
   b. castigar   d. deshacerse

7. El _____ es un fenómeno que ocurre cuando las temperaturas suben.
   a. efecto invernadero   c. producto químico
   b. derrame de petróleo d. medio ambiente

8. Muchos se dedican a la caza de las focas para usar sus _____.
   a. alimentos   c. plumas
   b. pieles   d. dientes

② **Gramática** Escribe la letra de la palabra o expresión que mejor complete cada frase. Escribe tus respuestas en una hoja aparte.

1. No van a parar de tirar desperdicios hasta que los _____.
   a. castiguen   c. castigaran
   b. castigaron   d. castigan

2. Mientras la gente no _____ conciencia de los problemas de la contaminación, no podrán disminuirla.
   a. tome   c. haya tomado
   b. tomará   d. toma

3. Después de _____ los ríos, tendremos que tomar medidas para reducir el número de fábricas.
   a. limpiemos   c. limpiaremos
   b. limpiamos   d. limpiar

4. Mientras no _____ leyes más justas no voy a contribuir a su campaña.
   a. promuevan   c. promoviendo
   b. promueven   d. promovieron

5. Allí está el refugio de vida silvestre _____ visitamos el año pasado.
   a. quien   c. lo que
   b. del que   d. que

6. _____ más le molesta a la gente es el recalentamiento global.
   a. Lo que   c. Que
   b. El que   d. En que

7. La señora _____ te hablé trabaja en una reserva natural.
   a. a quien   c. de quien
   b. del que   d. que

8. Siempre _____ las luces en cuanto salimos de casa.
   a. apaguemos   c. apagaron
   b. apagamos   d. apaguen

DIFFERENTIATED INSTRUCTION

Heritage Language Learners

Encourage students to review the standard format for a business or professional letter on p. 421. Discuss how a letter to the editor of a newspaper or to an environmental group would differ in form and content from a casual letter to a friend or family member.

Students with Learning Difficulties

Have students identify and copy the conjunction used in each sentence of the *Gramática* review. Have them refer to the chart on p. 427 to review the rules for each conjunction. Then direct them to apply the appropriate rule to select the correct choice.

Más repaso GO realidades.com | print

Puzzles	✔	
Core WB pp. 131–132		✔
Comm. WB pp. 215, 216–218	✔	✔
Instant Check	✔	

En el examen vas a . . .	Éstas son las tareas de práctica que te pueden ser útiles para el examen . . .	Para repasar, ve a tu libro de texto impreso o digital . . .

Interpretive

 3 Escuchar Escuchar y comprender unas descripciones sobre la contaminación del medio ambiente

Escucha a una persona que llama al locutor de un programa popular en la radio. Quiere expresar sus opiniones sobre los problemas y las soluciones del medio ambiente. Identifica a) el problema que menciona, y b) la solución que sugiere.

pp. 390-393 *A primera vista 1: Vocabulario en contexto*
p. 396 Actividades 8–9

Interpersonal

 4 Hablar Hacer unas sugerencias sobre cómo proteger el medio ambiente de la comunidad

Trabajas para un centro comunitario y te piden que hables con un grupo de jóvenes sobre cómo proteger el medio ambiente en sus vidas personales. Diles qué hacer en a) casa, b) la escuela y c) la comunidad.

p. 394 Actividad 5
p. 396 Actividades 8–9
p. 400 Actividad 13
p. 419 *Presentación oral*

Interpretive

 5 Leer Leer y comprender declaraciones sobre los problemas del medio ambiente

Lee este artículo sobre un reciente derrame de petróleo y di a) ¿dónde tuvo lugar el derrame?, b) ¿por qué ha sido un desastre para el turismo?, c) ¿qué medidas deberían tomarse para prevenir estos accidentes?

El derrame de petróleo cerca de la costa de Galicia, en España, ha causado grandes problemas para el turismo y el trabajo en la región. El gobierno ha gastado millones de euros en la limpieza de las playas y el rescate de la fauna marina. Miles de peces y otras especies marinas han desaparecido. A menos que no haya leyes más estrictas para prevenir desastres de este tipo, la vida marina y el turismo seguirán amenazados.

pp. 404–407 *A primera vista 2: Vocabulario en contexto*
p. 410 Actividad 28
p. 415 Actividad 36

Presentational

 6 Escribir Escribir una carta al periódico sobre los problemas del medio ambiente

Eres miembro de un grupo que se encarga de la protección del ambiente y tienes que escribir una carta a los jóvenes de tu zona para que tomen conciencia de lo que pueden hacer para proteger la comunidad. Describe por lo menos dos problemas y explica las consecuencias si no se toman las medidas necesarias. Al final, diles qué pueden hacer ellos para ayudar.

p. 394 Actividad 5
p. 396 Actividad 9
p. 400 Actividad 14
p. 411 Actividad 29
pp. 420–421 *Presentación escrita*

Comparisons

 7 Pensar Pensar en los problemas ecológicos globales

Piensa en uno de los problemas y su solución mencionados en el capítulo. Descríbelo y piensa si en los Estados Unidos existe o no ese problema y cómo lo resolverías tú.

pp. 390–393; 404–407
p. 397 Actividad 10
p. 403 Actividad 19

cuatrocientos veintinueve 429
Capítulo 9

---

4. Hablar
Suggestions: Encourage students to use in their answer at least one of the conjunctions studied in this chapter that take either the subjunctive or the indicative.

Answers will vary.

5. Leer
Suggestions: Tell students to refer to pp. 390–393 and 404–407 if they have questions about vocabulary in the review.

Answers:
a. **El derrame tuvo lugar cerca de la costa de Galicia, en España.**
b. **Ha causado grandes problemas para el turismo porque ha ensuciado las playas.**
c. **Debe haber leyes más estrictas para prevenir desastres de este tipo.**

6. Escribir
Suggestions: Remind students of what they learned about effective conclusions in this chapter's *Presentación escrita*. Have them apply that learning to their writing here.

Answers will vary.

7. Pensar
Suggestions: Encourage students to review current events on the Internet or in your local newspaper in light of what they have learned about the environment in *Capítulo 9*.

Answers will vary.

DIFFERENTIATED ASSESSMENT

CORE ASSESSMENT
- **Assessment Program:** Examen del capítulo 9, pp. 210–213
- **Audio Program DVD:** Cap. 9, Track 18
- **ExamView:** Chapter Test, Test Banks A and B

ADVANCED/PRE-AP*
- **ExamView:** Pre-AP* Test Bank
- **Pre-AP* Resource Book,** pp. 162–164

STUDENTS NEEDING EXTRA HELP
- **Alternate Assessment Program:** Examen del capítulo 9
- **Audio Program DVD:** Cap. 9, Track 18

HERITAGE LEARNERS
- **Assessment Program: Realidades para hispanohablantes:** Examen del capítulo 9
- **ExamView:** Heritage Learner Test Bank

10 Chapter Overview

- **rights and responsibilities**

Vocabulary
- rights and responsibilities at home and in school
- rights in society guaranteed by the Constitution

Grammar
- passive voice
- present perfect subjunctive and imperfect subjunctive
- pluperfect subjunctive
- conditional perfect

Cultural Perspectives
- find out what young people think about their rights and world problems
- interpret cultural perspectives on rights and responsibilities
- heroes of the Latin American independence movement

¡Pura vida!
- Watch an engaging video episode about a group of young people in Costa Rica!

CHAPTER SUPPORT

Bulletin Boards

Theme: *Derechos y deberes*

Have students work in pairs to brainstorm about their rights and duties at home, at school, and with their friends, and then collect magazine clippings to illustrate them. The class then arranges the information on the bulletin board under *Derechos* and *Deberes*.

Hands-on Culture

Recipe: *Queso fundido*

This is an authentic recipe to help you celebrate Mexican Independence Day. This delicious fondue takes only about 20 minutes to make. It serves six and can be served on *tortillas* or scooped up with chips.

Ingredients:

1 lb. Mexican *queso Cacique* or any other *queso blanco* (light white cheese), cut into small chunks
3 to 4 cloves garlic, minced
juice of 4 limes, or 1/4 cup lime juice
6 to 8 drops of Tabasco, or other hot pepper sauce

Directions:

1. Slowly melt cheese in a medium saucepan over slow heat. Stir continuously with a wooden spoon.
2. When almost melted, add the garlic, lime, and Tabasco, and heat through.
3. Serve immediately with *tortillas* or chips.

Game

Derechos contra obligaciones

Play this game to review the objectives and the vocabulary from *Capítulo* 10.

Players: entire class

Materials: pens, paper, a stopwatch

Rules:

1. Divide the class into two teams: *los derechos* and *las obligaciones. Los derechos* team generates a list of rights of parents, children, and teachers. *Las obligaciones* group generates a list of responsibilities for those same categories.
2. Teams have ten minutes to generate their lists.
3. When time is up, toss a coin to determine which team begins the game.
4. The team member who plays first tells a *derecho/obligación* from the list. For example, a *derechos* player says: *Un niño tiene derecho a jugar todos los días.*
5. The member of the opposite team should tell an obligation the same child should have. For example, *Un niño debe cumplir con sus deberes de la escuela todos los días.*
6. Play continues until a team is stumped and cannot think of a reply.
7. No repeated sentences are allowed.

Variation: Apply the game to rights of animals, communities, or countries.

CHAPTER PROJECT

Web pages for *Club Los Ruidosos*

Overview: Students work in teams of four to create illustrated pages for a Web site of fans and members of a music-sharing club. The home page should include an introduction and an index to three pages.

Resources: digital or print photos, image editing and page layout software; if computers are not available, poster boards, magazines, markers, glue, scissors

Sequence: (suggestions for when to do each step appear throughout the chapter)

STEP 1. Review instructions so students know what is expected of them. Hand out the "Chapter 10 Project Instructions and Rubric" from the *Teacher's Resource Book*.

STEP 2. Students submit sketches of their Web pages. Return the sketches with your suggestions.

STEP 3. Students do layouts of Web pages. Encourage them to try different arrangements before adding illustrations.

STEP 4. Students submit a draft of the texts for each page. Note your corrections and suggestions, then return drafts to students.

STEP 5. Students complete and present their Web pages to the class, reading and / or describing all the information featured in the pages.

Option:
Students create Web pages for a club of book fans.

Assessment:
Here is a detailed rubric for assessing this project:
Chapter 10 Project: *Web pages for Club Los Ruidosos*

RUBRIC	Score 1	Score 3	Score 5
Your evidence of planning	You provide no layout or written draft.	Your layout and written draft are provided, but not corrected.	You show evidence of corrected draft and layout.
Your use of illustrations	You include no images and little of the required information.	You include images, but your layout is disorganized.	Your Web pages are carefully done and images are consistent with text.
Your presentation	You include little of the required information.	You include most of the required information.	You include all the required information.

21st Century Skills

Look for tips throughout Chapter 10 to enrich your teaching by integrating 21st Century Skills. Suggestions for the Chapter Project and Culture follow below.

Chapter Project
Modify the Chapter Project with these suggestions:

Support Technology Literacy
Encourage students to access a variety of Web sites to use as a model for the design of their own music-sharing club site. Have them evaluate the format, organization, use of visuals and text, and layout of various sites to gather ideas. What is the best way to attract fans to their music-sharing club?

Encourage Initiative and Self-Direction
Have students develop their own timeline for accomplishing different stages of the project. They should study the rubric in order to figure out in advance the grammar and vocabulary tools they will need to successfully accomplish the tasks. The hand out "Solve Problems" can help them develop a plan of action.

Foster Collaboration
Encourage students to work together in small groups and assume shared responsibility for researching and creating their Web site project. Provide them with the handout "Work in Teams" to help them organize their group and divide the tasks.

Chapter Culture

Develop Social and Cross Cultural Skills
Direct students to review the *Fondo cultural* notes on pages 443 and 453. Promote a discussion about young people's different cultural perspectives about their student rights and responsibilities or the importance of a good education.

▶ **Videodocumentario** View *Gran trabajo para la comunidad* online with the class to learn more about a Latino political organization in Massachusetts.

10 ¿Cuáles son tus derechos y deberes?

Objectives
- Listen and read about rules and government
- Write about rights and responsibilities
- Talk about citizen and animal rights
- Understand the historical context of the Latin American independence movement
- Express your opinion on children's rights

A ver si recuerdas...
- Rights and obligations
- People and organizations
- Conflicts and solutions
- Preterite vs. imperfect
- Verbs with different meanings in the imperfect and preterite tenses

Recycle...
- Pronunciation of diphthong *ue*
- Pronouns *vosotros* and *vosotras*

Vocabulary
- Rights and responsibilities
- At home and at school
- Citizens' and people's rights

Grammar
- Passive voice
- Present perfect subjunctive and imperfect subjunctive
- Pluperfect subjunctive
- Conditional perfect

Culture
- Francisco de Goya, p. 435
- *Consulta infantil y juvenil 2000*, p. 443
- Teenagers and world problems, pp. 450–451
- José Vasconcelos, politician and educator, p. 453
- Juan Lovera, painter, p. 455
- Latin American heroes, pp. 462–463
- Domitila Barrios de Chungara, p. 471

RESOURCES

	FOR THE STUDENT	ONLINE	DVD	PRINT	FOR THE TEACHER	ONLINE	PREEXP	DVD	PRINT
Plan					Interactive TE and Resource DVD	•		•	
					Teacher's Resource Book, pp. 291–351	•		•	•
					Pre-AP* Resource Book, pp. 165–167	•		•	•
					Mapa global interactivo	•			
					Lesson Plans	•			•
A ver si recuerdas PP. 430–433									
Review	*A ver si recuerdas* Study Plan	•			*A ver si recuerdas* Study Plan	•			
	Guided WB, pp. 298–301	•	•	•	Vocabulary and Grammar Transparencies, 181–184	•	•	•	
	Core WB, pp. 133–134	•	•	•	Answer Keys: Student Edition, pp. 136–137	•	•	•	
	Hispanohablantes WB, p. 300			•					
Introducción PP. 434–435									
Present	Student Edition, pp. 434–435	•	•	•	Interactive TE and Resource DVD	•		•	
	DK Reference Atlas	•	•		Teacher's Resource Book, pp. 292–295	•		•	•
	Videonovela: ¡Pura vida!	•	•		Galería de fotos			•	
	¡Pura vida! Video Activities	•			Fine Art Transparencies, 31	•	•	•	
	Hispanohablantes WB, p. 301		•		Map Transparencies, 14, 16, 18, 20	•	•	•	
Vocabulario en contexto PP. 436–439/448–451									
Present & Practice	Student Edition, pp. 436–439/448–451	•	•	•	Interactive TE and Resource DVD	•		•	
	Audio	•	•		Teacher's Resource Book, pp. 296–297, 300–301, 316–324/298–299, 302–303, 316–324	•		•	•
	Flashcards	•	•						
	Instant Check	•			Vocabulary Clip Art	•	•	•	•
	Guided WB, pp. 302–310/315–322	•	•	•	Audio Program	•	•	•	
	Core WB, pp. 135–136/140–141	•	•	•	Vocabulary and Grammar Transparencies, 185–188/191–194	•	•	•	
	Comm. WB, pp. 138/141	•	•	•	Answer Keys: Student Edition, pp. 137–138/142–143	•	•	•	
	Hispanohablantes WB, pp. 302–303/312–313		•						
Assess and Remediate					Pruebas 10–1, 10–5: Assessment Program, pp. 215–216/224–225	•		•	•
					Hispanohablantes, pp. 215–216/224–225	•		•	•

RESOURCES

FOR THE STUDENT	ONLINE	DVD	PRINT	FOR THE TEACHER	ONLINE	PREEXP	DVD	PRINT
Vocabulario en uso PP. **440–443/452–455**								
Present & Practice — Student Edition, pp. 440–443/452–455	•	•	•	Interactive Whiteboard Vocabulary Activities	•		•	
Instant Check	•			Interactive TE and Resource DVD	•		•	
Comm. WB, pp. 134/136	•	•	•	Teacher's Resource Book, pp. 301, 307–308/303, 311–312	•		•	•
Hispanohablantes WB, pp. 304–306/314–316			•	Audio Program	•	•	•	
Communicative Pair Activities	•			Videomodelos	•		•	
				Vocabulary and Grammar Transparencies, 4	•	•	•	
				Answer Keys: Student Edition, pp. 138–139/143–144	•	•	•	•
Assess and Remediate				Pruebas 10–2, 10–6 with Study Plans	•			
				Pruebas 10–2, 10–6: Assessment Program, pp. 217–218/226–227	•		•	•
				Hispanohablantes, pp. 217–218/226–227	•		•	•
Gramática PP. **444–447/456–461**								
Present & Practice — Student Edition, pp. 444–447/456–461	•	•	•	Interactive Whiteboard Grammar Activities	•		•	
Instant Check	•			Interactive TE and Resource DVD	•		•	
Animated Verbs	•			Teacher's Resource Book, pp. 301–302, 309–310/303–304, 313–314	•		•	•
Tutorial Video: Grammar	•			Audio Program	•	•	•	
Canción de hip hop	•			Videomodelos	•	•	•	
Guided WB, pp. 311–315/323–326	•	•	•	Vocabulary and Grammar Transparencies, 189–190/195–196	•	•	•	
Core WB, pp. 137–139/142–144	•	•	•	Answer Keys: Student Edition, pp. 140–142/144–147	•	•	•	
Comm. WB, pp. 135, 139–140/137, 142–145	•	•	•					
Hispanohablantes WB, pp. 307–311/317–321			•					
Communicative Pair Activities	•							
Assess and Remediate				Pruebas 10–3, 10–4, 10–7, 10–8 with Study Plans	•			
				Pruebas 10–3, 10–4, 10–7, 10–8: Assessment Program, pp. 219, 220/228, 229	•		•	•
				Hispanohablantes, pp. 219, 220/228, 229	•		•	•
				Examen 1, Examen 2: Vocab. y gramática, pp. 221–223/230–232	•		•	•
¡Adelante! PP. **462–471**								
Application — Student Edition, pp. 462–471	•	•	•	Interactive TE and Resource DVD	•		•	
Online Cultural Reading	•			Teacher's Resource Book, pp. 304, 306	•		•	•
Guided WB, pp. 327–329	•	•	•	Video Program: Videodocumentario	•		•	
Comm. WB, pp. 146–147, 219–220	•	•	•	Video Program Teacher's Guide, Cap. 10	•		•	
Hispanohablantes WB, pp. 322–327			•	Map Transparencies, 17	•	•	•	
Videodocumentario	•	•		Vocabulary and Grammar Transparencies, 4	•	•	•	
Lecturas 3, pp. 32–35			•	Answer Keys: Student Edition, pp. 148–149	•	•	•	
Repaso del capítulo PP. **472–475**								
Review — Student Edition, pp. 472–475	•	•	•	Interactive TE and Resource DVD	•		•	
Online Puzzles and Games	•			Teacher's Resource Book, pp. 305, 315–324	•		•	•
Core WB, pp. 145–146	•	•	•	Audio Program	•	•	•	
Comm. WB, pp. 221–224	•	•	•	Answer Keys: Student Edition, p. 150	•	•	•	
Hispanohablantes WB, pp. 328–331			•					
Instant Check	•							
Chapter Assessment								
Assess				Examen del capítulo 10: Assessment Program, pp. 233–236	•		•	•
				Alternate Assessment Program, pp. 98–108	•		•	•
				Hispanohablantes, pp. 233–236	•		•	•
				Audio Program, Cap. 10, Examen	•		•	
				ExamView: Test Banks A and B (questions only online)	•		•	
				Heritage Learner Test Bank	•		•	
				Pre-AP* Test Bank	•		•	

REGULAR SCHEDULE (50 MINUTES)

DAY	Warm-up / Assess	Preview / Present / Practice / Communicate	Wrap-up / Homework Options
1	**Warm-up** (10 min.) • Return Examen del capítulo: Capítulo 9 • Homework check	**Repaso** (35 min.) • A ver si recuerdas . . . • Actividades 1–8	**Wrap-up and Homework Options** (5 min.) • Core Practice 10-1, 10-2
2	**Warm-up** (10 min.) • Homework check	**Chapter Opener** (10 min.) • Objectives • Arte y cultura **Vocabulario en contexto 1** (25 min.) • Presentation: Vocabulario y gramática en contexto • Actividades 1, 2	**Wrap-up and Homework Options** (5 min.) • Clip Art Vocabulary
3	**Warm-up** (10 min.) • Homework check	**Vocabulario en contexto 1** (35 min.) • Presentation: Derechos • Actividades 3, 4 **Vocabulario en uso 1** (25 min.) • Actividades 5, 6	**Wrap-up and Homework Options** (5 min.) • Core Practice 10-3, 10-4 • Actividad 4 • Prueba 10-1: Vocabulary recognition
4	**Warm-up** (10 min.) • Homework check • Audio or Writing Activity ✔**Formative Assessment** (10 min.) • Prueba 10-1: Vocabulary recognition	**Vocabulario en uso 1** (25 min.) • Interactive Whiteboard Vocabulary Activities • Actividades 7, 8, 9, 10 • Fondo cultural	**Wrap-up and Homework Options** (5 min.) • Actividad 11 • Writing Activities • Prueba 10-2 with Study Plan: Vocabulary production
5	**Warm-up** (15 min.) • Homework check • Communicative Activity ✔**Formative Assessment** (10 min.) • Prueba 10-2 with Study Plan: Vocabulary production	**Gramática y vocabulario en uso 1** (20 min.) • Presentation: La voz pasiva • Interactive Whiteboard Grammar Activities • Actividades 12, 13 • Writing Activity	**Wrap-up and Homework Options** (5 min.) • Core Practice 10-5
6	**Warm-up** (10 min.) • Homework check	**Gramática y vocabulario en uso 1** (35 min.) • Presentation: El presente y el imperfecto del subjuntivo • Interactive Whiteboard Grammar Activities • Actividades 14, 15, 16, 17	**Wrap-up and Homework Options** (5 min.) • Core Practice 10-6, 10-7 • Writing Activity • Prueba 10-3 with Study Plan: La voz pasiva
7	**Warm-up** (10 min.) • Homework check ✔**Formative Assessment** (10 min.) • Prueba 10-3 with Study Plan: La voz pasiva	**Gramática y vocabulario en uso 1** (25 min.) • Writing Activity • Communicative Pair Activity • En voz alta	**Wrap-up and Homework Options** (5 min.) • Writing Activity • Prueba 10-4 with Study Plan: El presente y el imperfecto del subjuntivo
8	**Warm-up** (10 min.) • Homework check ✔**Formative Assessment** (10 min.) • Prueba 10-4 with Study Plan: El presente y el imperfecto del subjuntivo	**Vocabulario en contexto 2** (25 min.) • Presentation: Vocabulario y gramática en contexto • Actividades 18, 19	**Wrap-up and Homework Options** (5 min.) • Clip Art Vocabulary • Examen: Vocabulario y gramática 1
9	**Warm-up** (5 min.) • Homework check ✔**Formative Assessment** (30 min.) • Examen: Vocabulario y gramática 1	**Vocabulario en contexto 2** (10 min.) • Presentation: Jóvenes por el desarrollo y la paz • Actividades 20, 21	**Wrap-up and Homework Options** (5 min.) • Actividad 22 • Core Practice 10-8, 10-9 • Prueba 10-5: Vocabulary recognition
10	**Warm-up** (20 min.) • Homework check ✔**Formative Assessment** (10 min.) • Prueba 10-5: Vocabulary recognition	**Vocabulario en uso 2** (20 min.) • Interactive Whiteboard Vocabulary Activities • Actividades 23, 24, 25 • Fondo cultural	**Wrap-up and Homework Option–s** (5 min.) • Actividades 29, 30

REGULAR SCHEDULE (50 MINUTES)

DAY	Warm-up / Assess	Preview / Present / Practice / Communicate	Wrap-up / Homework Options
11	Warm-up (10 min.) • Homework check	Vocabulario en uso 2 (20 min.) • Actividades 26, 27, 28 • Audio Activity • Writing Activity Gramática y vocabulario en uso 2 (15 min.) • Presentation: El pluscuamperfecto del subjuntivo • Interactive Whiteboard Grammar Activities • Actividades 31, 32	Wrap-up and Homework Options (5 min.) • Core Practice 10-10 • Prueba 10-6 with Study Plan: Vocabulary production
12	Warm-up (10 min.) • Homework check • Communicative Pair Activity ✔**Formative Assessment (10 min.)** • Prueba 10-6 with Study Plan: Vocabulary production	Gramática y vocabulario en uso 2 (25 min.) • Actividades 33, 34 • Writing Activity • Presentation: El condicional perfecto • Interactive Whiteboard Grammar Activities • Actividades 35, 36	Wrap-up and Homework Options (5 min.) • Core Practice 10-11, 10-12 • Prueba 10-7 with Study Plan: El pluscuamperfecto del subjuntivo
13	Warm-up (10 min.) • Homework check ✔**Formative Assessment (10 min.)** • Prueba 10-7 with Study Plan: El pluscuamperfecto del subjuntivo	Gramática y vocabulario en uso 2 (25 min.) • Actividades 35–40 • Audio Activity • Writing Activity	Wrap-up and Homework Options (5 min.) • Prueba 10-8 with Study Plan: El condicional perfecto
14	Warm-up (10 min.) • Communicative Pair Activity ✔**Formative Assessment (10 min.)** • Prueba 10-8 with Study Plan: El condicional perfecto	¡Adelante! (25 min.) • Puente a la cultura: Héroes de América Latina • ¿Comprendiste? • Cronología • Presentación oral: Step 1	Wrap-up and Homework Options (5 min.) • Examen: Vocabulario y gramática 2
15	Warm-up (5 min.) • Answer questions ✔**Formative Assessment (25 min.)** • Examen: Vocabulario y gramática 2	¡Adelante! (15 min.) • Presentación oral: Step 2	Wrap-up and Homework Options (5 min.) • Presentación oral: Step 3
16	Warm-up (5 min.) • Homework check	¡Adelante! (30 min.) • Presentación oral: Step 3 (half class) • ¿Qué me cuentas? 1, 2, 3	Wrap-up and Homework Options (5 min.) • Presentación escrita: Steps 1, 2
17	Warm-up (10 min.) • Homework check	¡Adelante! (35 min.) • Presentación oral: Step 3 (half class) • View Video • View Activities 1, 2, 3 • Presentación escrita: Step 3	Wrap-up and Homework Options (5 min.) • Presentación escrita: Step 4 • Preparación para el examen: 1, 2
18	Warm-up (10 min.) • Homework check	Repaso (10 min.) • Preparación para el examen: Actividades 3, 4 ¡Adelante! (25 min.) • Lectura • Interacción • ¿Comprendiste? • Fondo cultural	Wrap-up and Homework Options (5 min.) • ¿Comprendiste? • Core Practice: Organizer 10-13, 10-14 • Instant Check
19	Warm-up (15 min.) • Homework check	Repaso (30 min.) • Preparación para el examen: Actividades 5, 6, 7 • Other review	Wrap-up and Homework Options (5 min.) • Examen del capítulo
20	Warm-up (5 min.) • Answer questions ✔**Summative Assessment (45 min.)** • Examen del capítulo		

BLOCK SCHEDULE (90 MINUTES)

DAY	Warm-up / Assess	Preview / Present / Practice / Communicate	Wrap-up / Homework Options
1	**Warm-up (35 min.)** • Return Examen del capítulo: Capítulo 9 • A ver si recuerdas . . . • Homework check	**Chapter Opener (10 min.)** • Objectives • Arte y cultura **Vocabulario en contexto 1 (30 min.)** • Presentation: Vocabulario y gramática en contexto • Actividades 1, 2 • Presentation: Derechos • Actividades 3, 4 **Vocabulario en uso 1 (10 min.)** • Interactive Whiteboard Vocabulary Activities • Actividades 5, 6, 7	**Wrap-up and Homework Options (5 min.)** • Core Practice 10-3, 10-4 • Clip Art Vocabulary • Prueba 10-1: Vocabulary recognition
2	**Warm-up (15 min.)** • Homework check • Actividades 8, 9 ✔**Formative Assessment (10 min.)** • Prueba 10-1: Vocabulary recognition	**Vocabulario en uso 1 (60 min.)** • Actividades 10, 11 • Fondo cultural • Ampliación del lenguaje • Audio Activity • Writing Activity • Communicative Pair Activity	**Wrap-up and Homework Options (5 min.)** • Prueba 10-2 with Study Plan: Vocabulary production
3	**Warm-up (5 min.)** • Homework check ✔**Formative Assessment (10 min.)** • Prueba 10-2 with Study Plan: Vocabulary production	**Gramática y vocabulario en uso 1 (70 min.)** • Presentation: La voz pasiva • Interactive Whiteboard Grammar Activities • Actividades 12, 13 • Presentation: El presente y el imperfecto del subjuntivo • Interactive Whiteboard Grammar Activities • Actividades 14, 15 • Writing Activity	**Wrap-up and Homework Options (5 min.)** • Core Practice 10-5 • Prueba 10-3 with Study Plan: La voz pasiva
4	**Warm-up (10 min.)** • Homework check ✔**Formative Assessment (10 min.)** • Prueba 10-3 with Study Plan: La voz pasiva	**Gramática y vocabulario en uso 1 (50 min.)** • Actividades 16, 17 • En voz alta • Writing Activity • Communicative Pair Activity **Vocabulario en contexto 2 (15 min.)** • Presentation: Vocabulario y gramática en contexto • Actividades 18, 19	**Wrap-up and Homework Options (5 min.)** • Core Practice 10-6, 10-7 • Prueba 10-4 with Study Plan: El presente y el imperfecto del subjuntivo • Examen: Vocabulario y gramática 1
5	**Warm-up (10 min.)** • Homework check ✔**Formative Assessment Options (40 min.)** • Prueba 10-4 with Study Plan: El presente y el imperfecto del subjuntivo • Examen: Vocabulario y gramática 1	**Vocabulario en contexto 2 (20 min.)** • Presentation: Jóvenes por el desarrollo y la paz • Actividades 20, 21, 22 **Vocabulario en uso 2 (15 min.)** • Interactive Whiteboard Vocabulary Activities • Actividades 23, 24	**Wrap-up and Homework Options (5 min.)** • Core Practice 10-8, 10-9 • Actividad 25 • Clip Art • Prueba 10-5: Vocabulary recognition

BLOCK SCHEDULE (90 MINUTES)

DAY	Warm-up / Assess	Preview / Present / Practice / Communicate	Wrap-up / Homework Options
6	**Warm-up** (35 min.) • Homework check • Fondo cultural • Actividades 26, 27, 28 • Audio Activity • Writing Activity • Communicative Pair Activity ✔**Formative Assessment** (10 min.) • Pruebas 10-5: Vocabulary recognition	**Gramática y vocabulario en uso 2** (40 min.) • Presentation: El pluscuamperfecto del subjuntivo • Interactive Whiteboard Grammar Activities • Actividades 31, 32, 33, 34 • El español en la comunidad	**Wrap-up and Homework Options** (5 min.) • Actividades 29, 30 • Core Practice 10-10 • Pruebas 10-6, 10-7 with Study Plans: Vocabulary production, El pluscuamperfecto del subjuntivo
7	**Warm-up** (10 min.) • Homework check ✔**Formative Assessment** (20 min.) • Pruebas 10-6, 10-7 with Study Plans: Vocabulary production, El pluscuamperfecto del subjuntivo	**Gramática y vocabulario en uso 2** (40 min.) • Presentation: El condicional perfecto • Interactive Whiteboard Grammar Activities • Actividades 35, 36, 37, 38, 39, 40 • Audio Activity • Writing Activity **¡Adelante!** (15 min.) • Presentación oral: Steps 1, 2	**Wrap-up and Homework Options** (5 min.) • Core Practice 10-11, 10-12 • Prueba 10-8 with Study Plan: El condicional perfecto • Presentación oral: Step 2
8	**Warm-up** (15 min.) • Homework check • Communicative Pair Activity ✔**Formative Assessment** (20 min.) • Prueba 10-8 with Study Plan: El condicional perfecto	**¡Adelante!** (35 min.) • Presentación oral: Step 3 **¡Adelante!** (15 min.) • Presentation: Héroes de América Latina • ¿Comprendiste?	**Wrap-up and Homework Options** (5 min.) • ¿Comprendiste? • Cronología • Examen: Vocabulario y gramática 2
9	**Warm-up** (10 min.) • Homework check ✔**Formative Assessment** (30 min.) • Examen: Vocabulario y gramática 2	**¡Adelante!** (45 min.) • ¿Qué me cuentas? 1, 2, 3 • Presentación escrita: Step 1 • View Video • Video Activities	**Wrap-up and Homework Options** (5 min.) • Presentación escrita: Step 2 • Preparación para el examen: Actividades 1, 2
10	**Warm-up** (20 min.) • Homework check • Presentación escrita: Step 3	**¡Adelante!** (35 min.) • Lectura • Interacción • ¿Comprendiste? • Fondo cultural **Repaso** (30 min.) • Preparación para el examen: Actividades 3, 4, 6	**Wrap-up and Homework Options** (5 min.) • Presentación escrita: Step 4 • Core Practice: Organizer 10-13, 10-14 • Instant Check • Preparación para el examen: Actividades 5, 7 • Examen del capítulo
11	**Warm-up** (20 min.) • Homework check ✔**Summative Assessment** (45 min.) • Examen del capítulo	**Theme Game** (25 min.)	

10 Recycle

Vocabulario Repaso

Vocabulario Repaso

Core Instruction

Standards: 1.1, 1.2

Resources: Voc. and Gram. Transparency 181

Suggestions: Before presenting the material in this review section, consider testing your students' command of the material by assigning the Study Plan. Students will automatically be given additional practice of the material they have not yet mastered, and you can focus your review based on the class's overall performance on the post-test.

Have students copy the names of the five categories to their own paper. Show *Voc. and Gram. Transparency 181*. With books closed, have students work in pairs and list as many words and expressions as they can remember in each category.

la sociedad

la comunidad
la costumbre
los/las demás
la escuela
la familia
el hermano, la hermana
los padres
la sociedad
el vecino, la vecina

condiciones

la edad
injusto, -a
justo, -a
libre
mayor
menor

derechos y obligaciones

el derecho
la injusticia
la ley
las medidas
la obligación
las reglas
la responsabilidad
la seguridad
las tareas

actividades

alcanzar
beneficiar
conseguir
cumplir (con)
disfrutar (de)
encargarse (de)
luchar
obtener
proteger

expresiones

a favor
de niño
de pequeño
en contra
(me) parece justo/injusto
se permite
se prohíbe

1

Standards: 1.1, 1.2, 1.3

Resources: Answer Keys: Student Edition, p. 136

Focus: Practicing review vocabulary

Suggestions: Remind students to consider parts of speech when completing the matching activity. Explain that a definition beginning with a verb is most likely matched with a verb; one that begins with a noun is mostly likely matched with a noun.

Answers:

1. f. proteger
2. d. injusto
3. e. los vecinos
4. c. permitir
5. a. cumplir
6. b. la ley
7. g. encargarse

2

Standards: 1.1, 1.3

Focus: Practicing review vocabulary

Suggestions: Point out to students that when listing permitted or prohibited activities, they can use either the impersonal *se* or *estar* + past participle: *se prohíbe/está prohibido.*

Answers will vary.

Block Schedule

Have students write five questions, each using a different vocabulary word from the organizer. Have them ask a partner the questions.

▼1 Emparejar | 👥

Hablar • Escribir

Trabaja con otro(a) estudiante para emparejar cada definición con la palabra correspondiente. Luego, escoge 4 palabras y escribe un cuento.

1. cuidar a alguien de cualquier tipo de peligro
2. lo contrario de justo
3. las personas que viven en el mismo barrio
4. lo contrario de prohibir
5. hacer lo que se debe
6. la regla establecida por una autoridad
7. tomar la responsabilidad de hacer algo

a. cumplir
b. la ley
c. permitir
d. injusto
e. los vecinos
f. proteger
g. encargarse

▼2 Actividades | 👥

Escribir • Hablar

Haz una lista de tres actividades que se prohíban y tres actividades que se permitan en tu casa o en tu escuela. Compara la lista con la de un(a) compañero(a). Escriban una frase entre los (las) dos para expresar su opinión. Compartan su oración con la clase.

Modelo
En la escuela se prohíbe hablar mientras la profesora habla.
Nos parece justo para mantener el orden en la clase.

DIFFERENTIATED INSTRUCTION

Heritage Language Learners

After the class writes their accounts of experiences in *Actividad* 4, have them exchange papers. Ask students with strong grammar skills to identify errors they see in their partners' work without correcting them. Then have the writers revise their work based on this feedback.

Advanced Learners

Challenge students to create sentences that use vocabulary from as many categories as possible. For example: *En mi familia, los niños mayores disfrutan de más derechos que los niños menores.*

Gramática Repaso

Pretérito vs. imperfecto

Remember that when speaking in Spanish about the past, you can use either the preterite or the imperfect, depending on the sentence and the meaning you want to convey. Compare:

> El sábado pasado me **permitieron** llegar tarde a casa.
> De niño nunca me **permitían** llegar tarde.

Use the preterite:
- to tell about past actions that happened and are complete.

  > Las mujeres **protestaron** para obtener los mismos derechos.

- to give a sequence of actions in the past.

  > **Llegamos** al restaurante, **nos sentamos** y **comimos.**

Use the imperfect:
- to tell about habitual actions in the past.

  > Ellas no **tenían** los mismos derechos que los hombres.

- to give background details such as time, location, weather, mood, age, and physical and mental descriptions.

  > **Era** tarde, **hacía** frío, **estábamos** cansados y **teníamos** hambre.

- when two or more actions are taking place simultaneously in the past.

  > Mientras nosotros **comíamos,** mis hermanos **se peleaban.**

Use the preterite and the imperfect together when an action (preterite) interrupts another that is taking place in the past (imperfect).

> **Estábamos comiendo** cuando **llegó** mi hermano.

Más ayuda realidades.com ▶Tutorial

▼3 Completar

Leer

Esteban se asustó ayer por la noche al volver a su casa. Para saber qué le pasó, completa estas frases con el tiempo verbal correcto.

Ayer __1.__ *(eran / fueron)* las once de la noche cuando Esteban __2.__ *(regresó / regresaba)* a su casa. __3.__ *(Estaba / Estuvo)* muy oscuro y no se __4.__ *(vio / veía)* nada. De repente __5.__ *(se escuchó / se escuchaba)* un extraño ruido en la noche. Esteban __6.__ *(salió / salía)* corriendo y __7.__ *(se escondió / se escondía)* detrás de un árbol. ¿ __8.__ *(Fue / Era)* un fantasma quien __9.__ *(se acercó / se acercaba)*? ¡No! __10.__ *(Fue / Era)* un gato que __11.__ *(tuvo / tenía)* hambre y __12.__ *(buscó / buscaba)* algo para comer.

▼4 Relatar | 👥

Escribir • Hablar

Con un(a) compañero(a) escribe un relato sobre algo que les haya sucedido, usando el pretérito y el imperfecto. Primero, escojan algo en lo que los (las) dos participaron. Luego, formen frases sobre:
- la causa de lo que sucedió
- la hora de llegada y una descripción del ambiente
- qué hacía la gente
- algo que pasó

Compartan su relato con otros(as) compañeros(as).

Modelo
Era el cumpleaños de [nombre] y él (ella) hizo una fiesta.

cuatrocientos treinta y uno **431**
Capítulo 10

Gramática Repaso

Core Instruction

Resources: Voc. and Gram. Transparency 182

Suggestions: Refer students who are having difficulty with preterite vs. imperfect contrast to the *GramActiva* videos from Level 2 Chapters 4B, 5A, and 5B, and to the online tutorial. Have students write three sentences using past tenses. Encourage them to use more than one verb in each sentence. Have them take turns reading their sentences aloud and explaining their reason for using the preterite tense or the imperfect tense in each case.

3 Standards: 1.2

Resources: Answer Keys: Student Edition, p. 136

Focus: Practicing the preterite tense vs. the imperfect tense

Suggestions: Have students number the rules in the *Gramática* from 1 to 6. As they complete *Actividad* 3, have them write the rule number that applies beside each sentence.

Answers:

1. eran
2. regresó
3. Estaba
4. veía
5. se escuchó
6. salió
7. se escondió
8. Era
9. se acercó
10. Era
11. tenía
12. buscaba

4 Standards: 1.1, 1.3

Focus: Practicing the preterite tense vs. the imperfect tense

Suggestions: Before students begin writing, encourage them to decide which tense they think should be used with each of the four cues that are given. Point out that the verbs in the clues provide some guidance on which tenses they should use.

Answers will vary.

ENRICH YOUR TEACHING

Teacher-to-Teacher

Correct use of the imperfect tense vs. the preterite tense is a difficult skill for language learners to master. Remind them that mastery comes through patience and practice. Whenever students are engaged in oral communication, correct errors that they may make by modeling the correct usage and having them repeat. Better yet, create a cue card with *imperfecto* written on one side and *pretérito* on the other. Flash the appropriate side of this card when you hear an error, and have the student self-correct.

Vocabulario Repaso

Core Instruction

Standards: 1.1, 1.2

Resources: Voc. and Gram. Transparency 183

Suggestions: Ask students to create sentences that use items from at least three of the categories in the *Vocabulario*. For example: *El juez resolvió el problema entre los dos ciudadanos.*

---

5 Standards: 1.2

Resources: Answer Keys: Student Edition, p. 136

Focus: Practicing review vocabulary

Suggestions: Have students read the sentences first and make tentative decisions about how they will use the words in the word bank. Remind them to complete the items about which they are the most certain first.

Answers:

1. manifestación
2. habitantes; gobierno
3. víctimas; juez
4. campaña; población
5. beneficios

---

6 Standards: 1.1, 3.1

Focus: Practicing review vocabulary

Suggestions: As students discuss their conflicts in Step 2, remind them to use the preterite and the imperfect tenses appropriately.

Answers will vary.

Vocabulario Repaso

expresiones

decir la verdad
tener la culpa
tener razón

personas y organizaciones

la campaña
el ciudadano, la ciudadana
la gente
el gobierno
el/la habitante
la manifestación
la organización
la población
la reunión
el sistema

profesiones

el abogado, la abogada
el juez, la jueza
el/la policía

soluciones

los beneficios
la confianza
confiar
garantizar
obedecer
perdonar
resolver
reunirse
solicitar

conflictos

acusar
arrestar
capturar
el conflicto
desconfiar
limitar
mentir
molestar
la pelea
pelearse
el problema
quejarse
rebelarse
temer
la víctima

▼ 5 Titulares

Leer

Estos titulares y anuncios aparecieron recientemente en los periódicos. Léelos y luego complétalos con las palabras que siguen.

campaña	gobierno	beneficios
juez	habitantes	víctimas
manifestación	población	

1. ¡Arrestaron a quince personas en la _____ de ayer!
2. El conflicto entre los _____ del valle causa problemas al _____.
3. Las _____ del accidente aparecen ante *(before)* el _____.
4. La _____ de limpieza de la plaza Tribunales cuenta con el apoyo de la _____ de ese lugar.
5. Los ciudadanos quieren garantizar _____ para los ancianos.

▼ 6 Un conflicto |

Escribir • Hablar

❶ Piensa en un conflicto que haya sucedido en tu familia, escuela o comunidad recientemente. Luego, copia esta tabla en una hoja y complétala.

¿Quiénes participaron?	¿Qué hicieron?	¿Por qué?	¿Tenían o no razón?
_____	_____	_____	_____

❷ Usando la información que escribiste en la tabla, cuéntale a otro(a) estudiante la historia del conflicto.

DIFFERENTIATED INSTRUCTION

Students with Learning Difficulties

Students may have difficulty establishing the contexts in *Actividades* 7 and 8. Give them the opportunity to act out the events described in both activities. This will help them grasp each situation, which will in turn help them choose correct answers.

Advanced Learners

Ask students to model using the vocabulary in context. Give them time to think about the words, then ask them to create a fictional story about a courtroom scene that uses as many of the words as possible.

Gramática Repaso

Verbos con distinto sentido en el pretérito y en el imperfecto

A few Spanish verbs have different meanings in the imperfect and the preterite tenses.

	IMPERFECT	PRETERITE
saber	*knew* ¿**Sabías** que Ángel Suárez había ganado las elecciones?	*found out, learned* Sí, lo **supe** esta mañana por el periódico.
conocer	*knew (somebody)* Mi padre lo **conocía** cuando era pequeño.	*met (somebody) for the first time* Ellos se **conocieron** en la escuela.
(no) querer	*wanted to* Mi hermana **quería** ir a la manifestación.	*tried to* Yo también **quise** hacerlo pero no pude.
	didn't want to No **querían** decirle la verdad a su familia.	*refused to* No **quisieron** decirle la verdad a su familia.
poder	*was able to, could* Ella **podía** encontrar la solución en un minuto.	*managed to, succeeded in* Ella **pudo** encontrar la solución en un minuto.

▼7 Completar

Leer

Dos amigos hablan sobre sus actividades. Completa esta conversación con el pretérito o el imperfecto del verbo apropiado.

conocer	poder	querer	saber

A — ¿Pudiste estudiar el sábado por la tarde?

B — No, no __1.__ . Pablo y Agustín estuvieron en casa toda la tarde.

A — ¡Ah! Pablo es el chico que yo __2.__ el verano pasado, ¿no?

B — No, tú no lo __3.__ .

A — Bueno, yo __4.__ conocerlo, pero no __5.__ conocerlo en persona. Lo __6.__ por teléfono.

B — ¿Tú hablaste por teléfono con él? ¡Yo nunca lo __7.__ ! A mí él nunca me dijo nada.

▼8 Escoger

Leer

Completa la carta con el verbo que corresponda.

Querido diario:

Hoy __1.__ (conocí/conocía) a un chico guapísimo. Julia y yo __2.__ (quisimos/queríamos) ir al cine, pero no __3.__ (pudimos/podíamos). No había más entradas para la película que __4.__ (quisimos/queríamos) ver. Al salir nos encontramos con el chico guapísimo. Yo no lo __5.__ (conocí/conocía), pero Julia me contó que ella lo __6.__ (conoció/conocía) en una fiesta. Él __7.__ (quiso/quería) ir a tomar algo pero Julia no __8.__ (quiso/quería).

Más práctica GO	realidades.com | print

A ver si recuerdas with Study Plan	✔	
Guided WB pp. 298–301	✔	✔
Core WB pp. 133–134	✔	✔
Hispanohablantes **WB** p. 300		✔

Gramática Repaso

Core Instruction

Standards: 4.1

Resources: Voc. and Gram. Transparency 184

Suggestions: Have students write question-and-answer dialogues practicing the verbs in the preterite tense: —¿Jorge escribió su composición? —Quiso escribirla pero dice que era demasiado difícil.

▼7 Standards: 1.2

Resources: Answer Keys: Student Edition, p. 137

Focus: Reviewing verbs with different meanings in the preterite/imperfect tenses

Common Errors: Some students may spell preterite forms of **querer** with *-c-* instead of *-s-* in the middle. On the board, model as necessary the correct spellings of the forms of this irregular verb.

Suggestions: Remind students that the items in the activity are part of a dialogue. They need to keep track of the meaning of what has already been said in order to better know which verb form to use.

Answers:

1. **pude**	5. **pude**
2. **conocí**	6. **conocí**
3. **conociste**	7. **sabía**
4. **quería**	

▼8 Standards: 1.2

Resources: Answer Keys: Student Edition, p. 137

Focus: Reviewing verbs with different meanings in the preterite/imperfect tenses

Suggestions: Remind students to read the entire diary entry before attempting to write their answers.

Answers:

1. **conocí**	4. **queríamos**	7. **quería**
2. **queríamos**	5. **conocía**	8. **quiso**
3. **pudimos**	6. **conoció**	

✓ ASSESSMENT

A ver si recuerdas with Study Plan (online only)

After reviewing the material on these pages, assign the *A ver si recuerdas* Study Plan to evaluate students' mastery of the material. Additional practice is available online.

ENRICH YOUR TEACHING

Teacher-to-Teacher

A great way to get students on-task at the beginning of the class is to put a short written exercise on an overhead transparency. Stand at the door as students enter and hand them copies of the accompanying activity to complete and have them begin immediately. These should be short activities.

21st Century Skills

Initiative and Self-Direction Direct students to the online tutorials for self-directed review of the grammar topics recycled in this chapter. Students can review the related grammar first and then proceed to the new Spanish grammar point. Each tutorial is followed by a quick comprehension check.

Capítulo
10 ¿Cuáles son tus derechos y deberes?

Standards for Foreign Language Learning: *Capítulo* 10

• To meet the Standards, students will:

Communication
1.1 Interpersonal
• Talk about rights, responsibilities, the role of government
• Talk about Goya, Barrero, Lovera, and their work
• Talk about Peruvian schools and a Mexican referendum
• Talk about famous people who fought for justice
• Talk about heroes of Latin American independence

1.2 Interpretive
• Read and listen to information about problems, rights, responsibilities, and the role of government
• Read about Goya, Barrero, Lovera, and their work
• Listen to information about Peruvian schools
• Read about a Mexican referendum
• Read about the suffix *-miento*
• Read about famous people who fought for justice
• Read about Spanish-language campaigns in the U.S.
• Read about heroes of Latin American independence
• Read about Barrios de Chungara's struggle for justice

1.3 Presentational
• Write and present information orally about problems, rights, responsibilities, and the role of government
• Recite poetry by Hilario Barrero
• Write a news report
• Write and present orally about famous people
• Write about heroes of Latin American independence
• Write about Barrios de Chungara's struggle for justice

Culture
2.1 Practices and Perspectives
• Interpret the cultural perspectives of important artists
• Interpret student rights in Spain and Peru
• Interpret the vision of José Vasconcelos
• Interpret the perspectives of heroes of Latin America

2.2 Products and Perspectives
• Discuss the work of Goya, Barrero, Lovera
• Discuss Latin American independence movements
• Discuss a book about Domitila Barrios de Chungara

Connections
3.1 Cross-curricular
• Discuss key facts about art, poetry and literature
• Discuss key social and geographical facts about many Latin American countries and Spain
• Discuss key facts about civics and social studies
• Use Language Arts Strategies

3.2 Target Culture
• Read a pamphlet from Spain
• Read a transcript of an interview with a Peruvian student
• Read poetry by Hilario Barrero
• Read a testimonial by Domitila Barrios de Chungara

Comparisons
4.1 Language
• Compare the passive voice in Spanish and English
• Compare the use of *como si* with "as if"

▼ Chapter Objectives

Communication
By the end of the chapter you will be able to:
• Listen and read about rules and government
• Write about rights and responsibilities
• Talk about citizen and animal rights

Culture
You will also be able to:
• Understand the historical context of the Latin American independence movement
• Express your opinion on children's rights

You will demonstrate what you know and can do:
• Presentación oral, p. 465
• Presentación escrita, pp. 466–467
• Preparación para el examen, pp. 474–475

You will use:

Vocabulary	Grammar
• Rights and responsibilities	• Passive voice
• At home and at school	• Present perfect subjunctive and imperfect subjunctive
• Citizens' and people's rights	• Pluperfect subjunctive
	• Conditional perfect

Exploración del mundo hispano

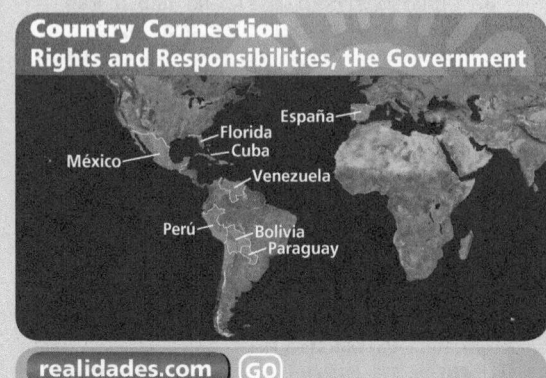

Country Connection
Rights and Responsibilities, the Government

España
Florida
Cuba
México
Venezuela
Perú
Bolivia
Paraguay

 realidades.com GO

 Reference Atlas
 Videonovela y actividades
 Mapa global interactivo

434 cuatrocientos treinta y cuatro

Manifestación de jóvenes en Lima, Perú

ENRICH YOUR TEACHING

Using Backward Design
Have students preview the sample performance tasks on *Preparación para el examen*, p. 475, and connect them to the Chapter Objectives. Explain to students that by completing the sample tasks they can self-assess their learning progress.

Mapa global interactivo
Download the *Mapa global interactivo* files for Chapter 10 and preview the activities. In Activity 1, look at the countries liberated by Bolívar, Martí, and Hidalgo. In Activity 2, travel to the mountains of Bolivia.

Arte y cultura | España

Escenas de la vida La obra de Francisco de Goya (1746–1828) cubrió un período de más de 60 años. En su juventud, cuando pintó este cuadro, Goya aceptó felizmente el mundo tal como era.

Años más tarde, Goya comenzó a sentirse desilusionado con la gente y la sociedad. Como resultado, pintó escenas que criticaban la política de la época. Su selección de temas es evidencia de que creía en el derecho del artista de pintar el mundo tal como lo veía.

• ¿Crees que un artista debe tener el derecho de pintar lo que le dé la gana? ¿Por qué? ¿Por qué no?

"El baile a orillas del Manzanares", (1777),
Francisco de Goya y Lucientes ▶
© 2003 SCALA/Art Resource, New York.

cuatrocientos treinta y cinco **435**
Capítulo 10

Preview 10

Standards (cont'd)
• Compare the Spanish conditional perfect with English
• Compare Spanish words with their English counterparts

4.2 Culture
• Compare student rights and responsibilities in Spain and Mexico with those in the United States
• Compare Venezuelan historical art with that of the U.S.
• Compare Latin American independence movements
• Compare a Bolivian civil rights movement with one in the United States

Communities
5.1 Beyond the School
• Link to Web sites from around the Spanish-speaking world

5.2 Lifelong Learner
• Develop an appreciation for visual art, and literature
• Discuss the individual's place in society

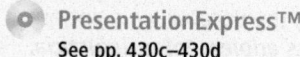 **PresentationExpress™**
See pp. 430c–430d

Chapter Opener
Core Instruction

Resources: Map Transparencies 14, 16, 18, 20
Suggestions: Introduce students to the theme and objectives of the chapter.

▶ **Videonovela ¡Pura vida!** View this stand-alone storyline video about five young adults in San José, Costa Rica with your class, either online or on DVD.

Arte y cultura

Standards: 1.1, 1.2, 2.1, 2.2, 3.1
Resources: Fine Art Transparencies with Teacher's Guide, p. 31
Suggestions: After students read the information, ask: *¿Cómo comenzó a sentirse Goya durante la segunda parte de su vida?*

▶ **TEACHING WITH ART**
Resources: Fine Art Transparencies with Teacher's Guide, p. 31

DIFFERENTIATED INSTRUCTION

Digital resources such as the *Interactive Whiteboard* activity banks, *Videomodelos*, additional *Online Activities*, *Study Plans*, automatically graded *Leveled Workbook*, animated *Grammar Tutorials*, *Flashcards*, and *Vocabulary and Grammar Videos* will help you reach students of different ability levels and learning styles.

STUDENTS NEEDING EXTRA HELP
Guided Practice Activities
• Flashcards, pp. 302–306, 315–318
• Vocabulary Check, pp. 307–310, 319–322
• Grammar, pp. 311–314, 323–326

HERITAGE LEARNERS
Realidades para hispanohablantes
• Chapter Opener, pp. 300–301
• A primera vista, pp. 302–303, 312–313
• Manos a la obra, pp. 304–311, 314–321
• ¡Adelante!, pp. 322–327
• Repaso del capítulo, pp. 328–331

ADVANCED/PRE-AP*
Pre-AP* Resource Book,
• pp. 165–167
Communications Workbook
• Integrated Performance Assessment, p. 221

435

Vocabulario en contexto

Core Instruction

Standards: 1.1, 1.2

Resources: Teacher's Resource Book: Input Script, p. 296, Clip Art, pp. 316–324, Audio Script, p. 300; Voc. and Gram. Transparencies 185–186; Audio Program DVD: Cap. 10, Track 1

Focus: Presenting new vocabulary and using grammar lexically in context

Suggestions: You may want to use the Input Script from the *Teacher's Resource Book* as a source of ideas for presentation of new vocabulary and comprehensible input. While presenting the vocabulary, point out cognates, such as *adolescentes, injusticia, libertad, respeto,* and *tolerancia.* Since most of the vocabulary is not visualized, encourage students to use context clues to help themselves understand the meanings of new words and expressions.

Block Schedule

Divide the class into two sections. Have students from one half work in groups of three and create three additional *derechos de los adolescentes.* Have the other half work in threes and write three additional *derechos de los padres.* Ask each group to present their statements to the groups. Write different *derechos* on the board and have the class vote on the best three.

Culture Note

In a UNICEF-sponsored series of youth opinion polls conducted from 1999-2001, Latin Americans from ages 9 to 18 said they were most concerned with access to education, violence in their communities, and social justice.

| ▼ Objectives

▶ Read, listen to, and understand information about
  • children's rights at home, at school, and in society
  • parents' rights

Vocabulario en contexto

Los adolescentes sienten a veces que tienen tantos deberes o responsabilidades como los adultos, pero menos derechos que los niños. ¿Crees que los problemas de Laura son comunes entre los adolescentes de hoy?

Laura: ¿Puedo ir a la fiesta el sábado?

Madre: El sábado vamos a ver a tu abuela.

Laura: ¡Es una injusticia! Tengo 16 años y no tengo libertad para decidir qué voy a hacer el sábado. . .

Ustedes dicen que quieren mi felicidad, pero no sé hasta qué punto es justo que me traten como a una niña, de ese modo no soy feliz.

Padre: Laura, claro que queremos que seas feliz y que sientas nuestro apoyo. Para nosotros también es difícil saber cómo tratar a una chica de 16 años.

Laura: Pero, ¿por qué tienen que obligarme a ir a casa de la abuela un sábado por la noche?

Creo que tengo una idea para resolver este asunto.

DERECHOS DE LOS ADOLESCENTES

▶ IRÉ SIEMPRE DONDE YO QUIERA IR.

▶ PODRÉ USAR LA ROPA QUE YO QUIERA.

▶ NADIE PODRÁ PROHIBIRME QUE ME PINTE EL PELO DE CUALQUIER COLOR.

▶ HABLARÉ POR TELÉFONO CON MIS AMIGAS TODO EL TIEMPO QUE SEA NECESARIO.

▶ NADIE ME PROHIBIRÁ NAVEGAR EN LA RED.

▶ NADIE ENTRARÁ EN MI CUARTO SIN PERMISO.

DIFFERENTIATED INSTRUCTION

Advanced Learners

Ask students to work in a small group to compare and contrast the rights and responsibilities they and their classmates have at home. They can begin by telling about their own rights and responsibilities in round-robin fashion, and then commenting on similarities and differences among them. Encourage them to compile information on the group in a T-chart with the two headings *nuestros derechos en casa* and *nuestras responsabilidades en casa.* Invite the group to share their findings with the rest of the class.

Derechos de los padres

Padre: Ana, nosotros nunca hemos maltratado a Laura. . . ambos queremos su felicidad. ¿Por qué está tan enojada con nosotros?

Madre: Pedro, si tú tuvieras 16 años, ¿no te sentirías como ella?

Padre: Quizás. Pero creo que debe tratarnos con respeto y tolerancia. ¿O es que los padres no tenemos derechos?

1. Nos dirás siempre adónde vas.

2. Si te vas a cambiar el color del pelo, pedirás permiso.

3. Estableceremos un horario para hablar por teléfono.

4. Estableceremos un horario para usar la Red.

5. Mantendrás tu cuarto ordenado y limpio.

Laura: Papá, creo que mi lista de derechos es muy adecuada, ¿verdad?

Padre: Pues yo también hice una lista, pero de los derechos de los padres. ¿Qué te parece?

▼1 Los derechos de cada uno
Escuchar

Escribe los números del 1 al 5 en una hoja de papel. Escucha cada frase y escribe *C* (cierta) o *F* (falsa).

▼2 Lo mejor de las listas
Hablar

Piensa si estás de acuerdo con las listas que escribieron Laura y su papá. De ambas listas, escoge cuatro frases con las que estés de acuerdo y di por qué estás de acuerdo. Habla con otro(a) estudiante sobre tus opiniones.

cuatrocientos treinta y siete **437**
Capítulo 10

---

1 Standards: 1.2

Resources: Voc. and Gram. Transparencies 185–186; Teacher's Resource Book: Audio Script, p. 300; Audio Program DVD: Cap. 10, Track 2; Answer Keys: Student Edition, p. 137

Focus: Practicing listening comprehension of new vocabulary

Suggestions: Remind students to listen for key words that will help them determine the answers. Use the audio or read the script. Allow students to listen more than once.

Answers:

1. C	4. C
2. F	5. C
3. C	

2 Standards: 1.1

Resources: Voc. and Gram. Transparencies 185–186

Focus: Practicing new vocabulary in a guided conversation

Suggestions: Use the instructions to clarify the meaning of *ambos(as).* Point to both lists on *Voc. and Gram. Transparencies* 185–186 and say: *Voy a seleccionar de ambas listas. Esto quiere decir que voy a usar las dos listas y seleccionar un número total de cuatro frases.*

Answers will vary.

ENRICH YOUR TEACHING

Culture Note

Many families in Spanish-speaking countries still take the time to discuss daily events, make plans, and resolve conflicts in a conversation around the table after dinner. There is even a name for this custom of after-dinner conversation: *la sobremesa.* Depending on the household, dessert and coffee may remain on the table during *la sobremesa,* or other foods, such as fruit or cheeses, may be served. On special days, when guests are invited to the house, *la sobremesa* may last for hours. *Una sobremesa* after a Sunday lunch, for example, may last right into dinnertime!

Vocabulario en contexto

Core Instruction

Standards: 1.1, 1.2, 2.1, 2.2, 3.1, 3.2

Resources: Teacher's Resource Book: Input Script, p. 297, Clip Art, pp. 316–324, Audio Script, pp. 300–301; Voc. and Gram. Transparencies 187–188; Audio Program DVD: Cap. 10, Tracks 3–4

Focus: Extending presentation of vocabulary and grammar

Suggestions:

Pre-reading: Explain to students that the readings on these two pages are separate and will be read and discussed individually. Before beginning, write on the board **responsabilidades = deberes** and say: Estas dos palabras son sinónimos. *En estas lecturas se usan "deberes."*

Reading: After students read the brochure on this page, have them complete *Actividad 3* before they go on to read the article on p. 439 and complete *Actividad 4*.

Post-reading: After an initial reading of each of the selections, clarify the meaning of new vocabulary as necessary. Point out cognates such as **satisfactoria** and **abusos.** Ask a volunteer to read aloud the definition for **estado** that is included in the article on p. 439. **(todas las instituciones del gobierno)** Use circumlocution, synonyms, antonyms, and demonstrations to teach the meanings of other non-visualized words and expressions.

3 Standards: 1.2, 1.3, 3.1, 4.2

Focus: Practicing new vocabulary via note-taking and discussion

Suggestions: Encourage students to add to their discussion other pertinent student rights and responsibilities that the Spanish brochure does not address.

Answers will vary.

Derechos y deberes en la escuela

En todas las escuelas, los estudiantes tienen ciertos derechos y deberes. Sin embargo, no en todos los países, ni en todas las escuelas, son iguales. Por ejemplo, en tu escuela, ¿hay un **código de vestimenta** o todo el mundo puede llevar la ropa que más le guste? Y **en cuanto a los armarios** de los estudiantes, ¿los maestros tienen derecho a registrarlos?

Para resolver estas preguntas de manera **satisfactoria**, el gobierno en España estableció una ley de los derechos y deberes de los estudiantes.

▼3 Los derechos en tu escuela

Hablar • Escribir

Con otro(a) estudiante, comenta los derechos y deberes de los estudiantes españoles. Hablen de los derechos y deberes que tienen ustedes en su escuela y escríbanlos en una hoja de papel. Luego, compárenlos con los de los estudiantes en España.

Los estudiantes tienen el deber de:

- cumplir y respetar los horarios para el desarrollo de las actividades de la escuela
- respetar la autoridad de los maestros
- respetar el derecho al estudio de sus compañeros
- respetar la libertad de expresión y pensamiento de sus compañeros
- no discriminar a ningún o ninguna estudiante por motivos personales o sociales
- cuidar y utilizar correctamente las escuelas; ayudarlas a funcionar bien
- participar en la vida y funcionamiento de las escuelas

Los estudiantes tienen derecho a:

- recibir una enseñanza gratuita
- no ser discriminados por causas personales o sociales
- votar por sus representantes en el Consejo Escolar
- gozar de libertad de expresión y pensamiento
- reunirse y utilizar las escuelas para actividades educativas

438 cuatrocientos treinta y ocho
A primera vista 1

DIFFERENTIATED INSTRUCTION

Advanced Learners

Invite students to convert their notes from *Actividad 3* into an "official" **Panfleto de los deberes y derechos de los estudiantes** for your school. They can use the Spanish brochure as a model. If they have computer software available to them, encourage them to design the pamphlet for reproduction and posting in the classroom or, with permission, in other parts of the school. Interested students may want to bring the contents of their pamphlet before your school's student council for consideration.

El gobierno y los derechos de la niñez

El estado, o sea todas las instituciones del gobierno, son responsables de aplicar las leyes que protegen a la niñez. Los gobiernos deben:

1. Garantizar que los niños y adolescentes vivan en **paz.**

2. Garantizar que los niños no **estén sujetos a maltratos** ni **abusos** por parte de las personas que se encargan de ellos.

3. Dar ayuda a los niños que sufren de mucha **pobreza.**

4. Prohibir que se discrimine por **razones** de raza, nacionalidad o sexo.

5. Reconocer **la igualdad** de derechos ante la ley.

▼4 La felicidad de los más jóvenes

Escribir

1. Según el documento, ¿qué derechos debe garantizar el gobierno para los niños?

2. Indica dos cosas que, según el documento, el gobierno debe prohibir.

3. ¿Qué quiere decir "reconocer la igualdad de todas las personas ante la ley"? ¿Por qué es importante?

Más práctica	GO
realidades.com	print

Instant Check	✔	
Guided WB pp. 302–310	✔	✔
Core WB pp. 135–136	✔	✔
Comm. WB p. 138	✔	✔
Hispanohablantes WB pp. 302–303	✔	

cuatrocientos treinta y nueve **439**
Capítulo 10

BELLRINGER REVIEW

Briefly review the formation of the subjunctive with students before they read the article on this page and complete *Actividad* 4.

▼**4** Standards: 1.2, 1.3, 3.1

Resources: Answer Keys: Student Edition, p. 138

Focus: Practicing reading comprehension of new vocabulary

Suggestions: Encourage students to paraphrase information from the article in order to answer the questions.

Answers:

1. El gobierno debe garantizar que los niños y adolescentes vivan en paz y que no estén sujetos a maltratos ni abusos por parte de las personas que los cuidan.

2. El gobierno debe prohibir que se discrimine por razones de raza, nacionalidad o sexo. También debe prohibir los maltratos y abusos de los niños y adolescentes.

3. Answers will vary.

Pre-AP* Support

- **Learning Objective:** Presentational Writing
- **Activity:** Have students write a blog about the rights and responsibilities of the students in their school. Have them complete the phrases, *Los estudiantes tienen el deber de:* and *Los estudiantes tienen derecho a:* with their lists of action items. Have them use vocabulary words in their lists of student rights and responsibilities.
- **Pre-AP* Resource Book:** Comprehensive guide to Pre-AP* writing skill development, pp. 27–38

Chapter Project

Give students copies of the Chapter Project outline and rubric from the *Teacher's Resource Book.* Explain the task to them, and have them perform Step 1. (For more information, see p. 430-b.)

ENRICH YOUR TEACHING

Culture Note

Many schools and organizations in Spanish-speaking countries post information about student rights and responsibilities on the Internet. Examples include: "that students' freedom of choice as well as their religious, moral, and ideological convictions be respected" and "that students respect the right of their classmates to study."

21st Century Skills

Information Literacy Have students research Web sites in Spanish that give more information about student rights in Latin America and the U.S. What keywords will they use in their search? How can they decide which Web sites will give them reliable and accurate information? Which countries have an official set of student rights?

✓ASSESSMENT

Prueba: Comprensión del vocabulario 1
• Prueba 10-1: pp. 215–216

10 Practice and Communicate

▼ Objectives

▶ Listen to and talk about students' rights and responsibilities at school
▶ Discuss social issues in your country
▶ Write and draw about people's rights and responsibilities

Vocabulario en uso

INTERACTIVE WHITEBOARD
Vocabulary Activities 10-1

▼5

Standards: 1.2, 1.3, 3.1

Resources: Answer Keys: Student Edition, p. 138

Focus: Demonstrating comprehension of new vocabulary by sorting

Suggestions: Tell students that for some items, such as **el deber,** there may be a rationale for placing them in either category.

Answers will vary. The following are likely results. Some items have been placed in both categories:

lo positivo
la libertad, el respeto, la felicidad, el deber, la tolerancia, el apoyo, gratuito(a), la paz, la igualdad, adecuado(a)
lo negativo
el abuso, el deber, discriminar, maltratar, sufrir, el maltrato, la injusticia, adecuado(a)

Extension: After they complete the activity, ask students to explain their reasoning behind the placement of items such as **el deber, el apoyo,** and **adecuado(a).**

▼6

Standards: 1.1, 1.2, 2.1, 3.1

Resources: Teacher's Resource Book: Audio Script, p. 301; Audio Program DVD: Cap. 10, Track 5; Answer Keys: Student Edition, p. 139

Focus: Practicing new vocabulary through reading, listening, and responding

Suggestions: Play the audio or read the script once through entirely. Allow students to listen again, pausing after each item, so they can write their answers. Allow them to listen a third time to check their answers.

Answers:

1. **Los colegios del estado son gratuitos.**
2. **Cada escuela tiene su propio uniforme.**
3. **Son centros médicos pequeños. Ofrecen consultas y dan vacunas.**

▼5 Lo positivo y lo negativo

Leer • Escribir

En una hoja de papel, copia esta tabla. Lee las palabras y escríbelas en la columna apropiada. Luego, escribe frases con tres de las palabras.

lo positivo	lo negativo

la libertad	el respeto	la felicidad	el abuso
el deber	discriminar	la tolerancia	el apoyo
maltratar	sufrir	el maltrato	gratuito(a)
la paz	la injusticia	la igualdad	adecuado(a)

▼6 Entrevista con una joven peruana | ◀))

Leer • Escuchar • Escribir

❶ Lee esta entrevista con Viviana Gallegos, una adolescente del Perú.

Una entrevista con

Viviana Gallegos...

¿Qué nacionalidad tienes?
Soy peruana.

¿Es gratuita la enseñanza en Perú?
Hay colegios privados y colegios del estado. Los colegios del estado son gratuitos.

¿Hay un código de vestimenta en las escuelas?
Sí, tenemos que usar uniformes. Cada escuela tiene su uniforme. Unos uniformes son más bonitos que otros.

¿Hay servicios médicos adecuados para todos los ciudadanos?
Sí, se llaman postas médicas. Son centros médicos pequeños. Ofrecen consultas con médicos y dan vacunas (*vaccines*). Ambos servicios son gratuitos.

En la Plaza de Armas, Cuzco, Perú

❷ Ahora, escucha las preguntas y contéstalas en clase.

DIFFERENTIATED INSTRUCTION

Heritage Language Learners
Ask students who have lived in a heritage country if they would let others interview them on the topic of schools and the educational system in the heritage country. Interviewers can base their questions on the interview with Viviana Gallegos in *Actividad* 6.

Students with Learning Difficulties
Help students grasp the abstract concepts listed in *Actividad* 8. Provide them with photographs or icons that represent each of the issues described. For example, a photograph of people protesting might represent **la libertad de expresión y pensamiento.**

▼7 Los derechos en nuestra escuela |

Leer • Escribir • Hablar

Túrnate con un(a) compañero(a) para indicar si estás de acuerdo o no con las frases siguientes sobre tu escuela, y explícale por qué. Tu compañero(a) va a tomar apuntes sobre lo que dices, y luego ambos van a compartir sus ideas con la clase.

1. No es necesario seguir un código de vestimenta en esta escuela.

2. Los adolescentes deben tratar a los maestros con más respeto y, de ese modo, respetar su autoridad.

3. En nuestras clases, los chicos tienen más libertad que las chicas.

4. La enseñanza en esta escuela es adecuada para prepararme para lo que voy a hacer en el futuro.

5. Todos los estudiantes tienen derecho a gozar de libertad de expresión.

6. Los profesores deben tener la autoridad y el deber de registrar los armarios.

7. Todos los estudiantes deben estar sujetos a las mismas reglas.

Estos estudiantes de Paraguay trabajan en un proyecto para la escuela.

▼8 En nuestro país | | ♻

Escribir • Hablar

❶ Piensa en los siguientes temas sociales. En tu opinión, ¿cuál es el más importante? ¿Y el menos importante? Ponlos en orden de importancia.

1. la libertad de expresión y pensamiento

2. la igualdad entre los hombres y las mujeres

3. cómo tratar a los animales

4. los servicios médicos

5. el apoyo a los niños

6. la pobreza

7. las reglas para manejar

8. los deberes del estado

❷ Dile tu opinión a un(a) compañero(a) sobre los temas mencionados en la parte anterior. Usa las palabras del recuadro.

adecuado(a)	satisfactorio(a)	injusticia	en cuanto a
abuso	respeto	gratuito(a)	ambos(as)

▶ **Modelo**

la alimentación

A —*La alimentación en nuestro país es satisfactoria.*

B —*Pues yo no estoy de acuerdo. La gente come demasiada comida basura y . . .*

cuatrocientos cuarenta y uno **441**
Capítulo 10

7 Standards: 1.1, 1.2, 1.3

Focus: Using new vocabulary in a contextualized discussion

Suggestions: Remind students that when they report on their pair work, they will change verb forms frequently in order to tell about what their partner said.

Answers will vary.

8 Standards: 1.1, 1.2

Focus: Using new vocabulary in a contextualized discussion

Recycle: conjunctions that take the subjunctive or the indicative

Suggestions: For Step 1, tell students to copy each item entirely for writing practice, rather than using numbers to order the items.

Answers will vary.

ENRICH YOUR TEACHING

Teacher-to-Teacher

Invite students who have cameras to create photo essays about student rights and responsibilities in your school. They can take pictures of their friends studying, participating in extracurricular activities, having lunch in the cafeteria, taking breaks, making visits to their lockers, interacting with faculty and administration, and so on. Have them assemble the photos in a visual display, complete with a title, a brief statement about the purpose of the display, and a caption for each photo, explaining how it represents a student right or responsibility.

Resources: Voc. and Gram. Transparency 4

Focus: Practicing new vocabulary via note-taking and discussion

Suggestions: This activity can be conducted with the whole class. Use *Voc. and Gram. Transparency* 4 to begin the chart, and have students follow along on their own paper. Use guiding questions to elicit from students the information to record on the chart. Record it there yourself or have a volunteer do so as the class follows along.

Answers will vary.

10 Standards: 1.1

Focus: Practicing new vocabulary through discussion

Suggestions: Encourage students to use background knowledge they have gained in their Language Arts or Social Studies classes to answer the questions.

Answers will vary.

Ampliación del lenguaje
Core Instruction

Standards: 1.2, 3.1

Resources: Answer Keys: Student Edition, p. 139

Focus: Understanding the suffix *-miento*

Suggestions: After students complete the chart, encourage them to experiment using *-miento* to form other nouns from verbs. They can use a dictionary to check their work.

Answers:

Chart

3. pensamiento	6. comportamiento
4. mejoramiento	7. descubrimiento
5. conocimiento	8. movimiento

Sentences
1. descubrimiento; descubrir
2. mejorar; mejoramiento

---

9 Derechos y responsabilidades | 👥

Hablar • Escribir

❶ Ser adolescente quiere decir tener muchos derechos pero también responsabilidades. En grupo, completen una tabla como la siguiente con los derechos y responsabilidades que tienen los adolescentes.

❷ ¿Cómo se comparan los derechos y responsabilidades de los adolescentes con los de los adultos? Usen sus tablas para responder.

Derechos	Responsabilidades
1.	1.
2.	2.
3.	3.

10 Y tú, ¿qué dices? | 🗨

Escribir • Hablar

1. ¿Por qué crees que hay códigos de vestimenta en muchas escuelas? ¿Crees que es buena idea tener un código de vestimenta? ¿Por qué?

2. Describe el asunto de tu comunidad que sea más importante para ti. ¿Cómo se debe resolver ese asunto?

3. En tu opinión, ¿por qué la gente discrimina? ¿Tiene motivos personales? Explica.

4. ¿Hasta qué punto piensas que en nuestra sociedad hay igualdad?

▼ Ampliación del lenguaje

El sufijo *-miento*

Un sustantivo que termina en el sufijo *–miento* tiene como base un verbo. Para formar sustantivos, a los verbos en infinitivo que terminan en *-ar*, quítales la *r* y añádeles el sufijo *-miento* (*tratar* → *trat**amiento***), y a los que terminan en *-er* y en *-ir*, quítales la terminación y agrégales una *i* antes del sufijo (*vencer* → *venc**imiento***). Los sustantivos con *-miento* son masculinos. Copia la tabla y escribe los sustantivos. Luego, completa las frases.

verbo	sustantivo
1. funcionar	funcionamiento
2. nacer	nacimiento
3. pensar	
4. mejorar	
5. conocer	
6. comportar	
7. descubrir	
8. mover	

1. El ____ de la electricidad hizo que la vida de mucha gente fuera más fácil. Pero ____ la electricidad tomó mucho tiempo.

2. Muchos científicos trabajan juntos para ____ el medio ambiente. El ____ del medio ambiente es importante.

442 cuatrocientos cuarenta y dos
Manos a la obra 1

DIFFERENTIATED INSTRUCTION

Heritage Language Learners
Ask students who have lived in a heritage country to comment on the issue of equality in that country. Do they feel equality exists? If not, along which lines do inequalities appear? Invite all students to compare these descriptions to the situation in their present community.

Students with Learning Difficulties
Before students speak about their opinions in *Actividad* 10, give them the opportunity to brainstorm and plan their responses. Suggest that students write down a few notes on each of the topics.

▼11 Una tarjeta especial

Escribir • Dibujar

Vas a entrar en un concurso para hacer tarjetas que digan algo sobre los derechos y las responsabilidades de la gente. Dibuja una tarjeta y añádele un deseo o derecho. Usa el vocabulario de este capítulo.

Modelo

Es importante que todos los ciudadanos voten en las elecciones del estado.

▼Fondo Cultural | México

Consulta (referéndum) infantil y juvenil 2000 En este hecho histórico del 2 de julio de 2000, día de la votación para presidente de México, casi 4 millones de niños y adolescentes votaron para dar sus opiniones sobre la familia, la escuela y el país.

Mira las gráficas para comparar lo que dijeron los niños y los adolescentes sobre el respeto en las escuelas y lee la tabla de abajo que muestra las opiniones de los adolescentes.

• ¿Son ustedes respetados en la escuela?

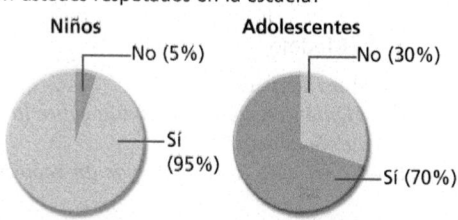

Niños
No (5%)
Sí (95%)

Adolescentes
No (30%)
Sí (70%)

DEPOSITE AQUÍ SU VOTO

IFEG

Adolescentes	Sí	No
¿Son tomados en cuenta en su familia?	95%	5%
¿Son tomados en cuenta en la comunidad?	83%	17%
¿Son tomados en cuenta en el país?	61%	39%
¿Participan en las decisiones del país?	32%	68%
¿Hay igualdad entre hombres y mujeres en el país?	37%	63%

• ¿Por qué crees que la opinión de los niños y de los adolescentes sobre la escuela era diferente?

• Compara lo que dijeron los adolescentes mexicanos sobre el respeto en las escuelas con lo que piensan tus compañeros(as). ¿Crees que ellos opinan lo mismo? ¿Por qué?

Practice and Communicate 10

▼11 Standards: 1.3

Focus: Practicing new vocabulary

Suggestions: Encourage students to research greeting card stores or the Internet to find creative ideas for their cards.

Answers will vary.

Fondo cultural

Standards: 1.1, 1.2, 2.1, 3.1, 4.1

Suggestions: After students have read the information, ask: *¿Quiénes votaron en la consulta? (niños y adolescentes) Según las gráficas, ¿hay más o menos adolescentes que niños que piensan que son respetados en la escuela? (menos) ¿Cuánto menos? (casi el 25 por ciento menos)*

Answers will vary.

Additional Resources

• Communication Wbk.: Act. 1, p. 134
• Teacher's Resource Book: Audio Script, p. 301, Communicative Pair Activity BLM, pp. 307–308
• Audio Program DVD: Cap. 10, Track 6

ENRICH YOUR TEACHING

Teacher-to-Teacher

The **Consulta infantil y juvenil 2000** was considered a success by its organizers and by the Mexican press. All ballots contained **sí/no** questions that varied according to the age groups, as well as one open-ended question that read: **Yo quiero que en México nunca más haya....**

21st Century Skills

Creativity and Innovation As an expansion of *Actividad* 11, have students write an e-mail to their local representative in Congress in which they express their concerns about student rights and responsibilities. Have them take a stand on an issue that is important to them.

✓ASSESSMENT

Prueba 10-2 with Study Plan (online only)

Prueba: Aplicación del vocabulario 1
• Prueba 10-2: pp. 217–218

10 Practice and Communicate

Gramática

Core Instruction

Standards: 4.1

Resources: Voc. and Gram. Transparency 189

INTERACTIVE WHITEBOARD
Grammar Activities 10-1

Suggestions: Ask questions about what students do to elicit the passive voice:
—¿Por quién fue cerrada la puerta? —La puerta fue cerrada por (nombre).

12 Standards: 1.2, 1.3

Resources: Teacher's Resource Book: Audio Script, pp. 301–302; Audio Program DVD: Cap. 10, Track 8; Answer Keys: Student Edition, p. 140

Focus: Practicing the passive voice

Suggestions: Pause the audio after each item, so students can write their answers.

Answers:
1. un perro; fue maltratado; su dueño
2. varios jóvenes; fueron discriminados; no se sabe
3. los dueños de una fábrica; fueron acusados; no se sabe
4. dos adolescentes; fueron obligados; no se sabe
5. la víctima; fue apoyada; los abogados
6. un hombre; fue criticado; otros ciudadanos
7. los criminales; fueron perdonados; el juez
8. una empleada; fue acusada; el dueño de la compañia

13 Standards: 1.1

Resources: Answer Keys: Student Edition, p. 141

Focus: Practicing the passive voice

Suggestions: Have students switch roles, so everyone has a chance to practice.

Answers: Passive subjects will vary. The following are possible results.
1. —¿Quién curó a los niños?
   —Fueron curados por....
2. —¿Quién respetó la igualdad?
   —La igualdad fue respetada por....
3. —¿Quién aplicó las leyes?
   —Las leyes fueron aplicadas por....
4. —¿Quién leyó el discurso?
   —El discurso fue leído por....

✓ ASSESSMENT

Prueba 10-3 with Study Plan (online only)

Prueba: La voz pasiva con *ser*
• Prueba 10-3: p. 219

444

Gramática

La voz pasiva: *ser* + participio pasado

In a sentence, the subject usually performs the action. This is called active voice. Sometimes, the subject does not "do" the action but rather has the action "done to it" or receives the action. This is called passive voice.

> Santiago estableció las reglas del club.
> Las reglas del club fueron establecidas por Santiago.

In Spanish, like in English, you form the passive voice by using *ser* + past participle. Since the past participle is an adjective, it agrees in number and gender with the subject.

> Las reglas son aplicadas por el estado.

• If you mention "who" or "what" performs the action, you use *por* to mean "by."

• You often use the impersonal *se* when the subject is unknown.

> Se necesita una persona para trabajar en el centro comunitario.

Más ayuda | **realidades.com** | ▶ *Canción de hip hop* ▶ Tutorials

▼12 Las noticias del día | 🔊

Escuchar • Escribir • Hablar

Imagina que enciendes la radio y escuchas las noticias del día. Para cada frase que escuches, llena una tabla como ésta. Después, usa tus notas para contar de nuevo las noticias.

¿Quién(es) fue(ron) afectado(s)?	¿Qué le(s) pasó?	¿Por quién(es)?
un niño	fue asustado	un oso
1.		

Modelo
Un niño fue asustado por un oso que había escapado del zoológico.

▼13 ¿Quién lo hizo? |

Hablar

Con un(a) compañero(a), comenta por quién o quiénes fueron hechas estas cosas. Sigue el modelo.

▶ **Modelo**

escribir / artículo

A —¿Quién escribió el artículo sobre la adolescencia?
B —El artículo fue escrito por un reportero.

Estudiante A
1. curar / niños
2. respetar / igualdad
3. leyes / aplicar
4. leer / discurso
5. entrevistar / adolescentes
6. (nombre) / escoger
7. promover / paz
8. evitar / injusticias

Estudiante B
autoridades
gobierno
estudiantes
maestro(a)
médico(a)
reportero(a)
juez

Más práctica (GO)

realidades.com | print

Instant Check	✔	
Guided WB pp. 311–312	✔	✔
Core WB p. 137	✔	✔
Comm. WB p. 139	✔	✔
Hispanohablantes WB pp. 304–308	✔	

444 cuatrocientos cuarenta y cuatro
Manos a la obra 1

DIFFERENTIATED INSTRUCTION

Students with Learning Difficulties

Before students make their choices in *Actividad 14*, first have them identify the verb in the main clause of each sentence. Second, ask them to determine the tense based on that verb. Third, have them choose the correct answer based on that tense.

Advanced Learners/Pre-AP*

Have students prepare brief news reports about current events. Tell them to use at least one sentence in the passive voice for each report.

Gramática

▼ **Objectives**

▶ Discuss and read about school and students' responsibilities

▶ Discuss and write about life as a teenager today

El presente y el imperfecto del subjuntivo

Use the present or the present perfect subjunctive when the verb in the main clause is in the:

Present	Espero que hayan votado.
Command form	Dile que vote mañana en las elecciones.
Present perfect	No hemos establecido ninguna regla que sea injusta.
Future	El sistema funcionará mejor cuando se cambien las leyes.

Use the imperfect subjunctive when the verb in the main clause is in the:

Preterite	Mi mamá me pidió que tratara con más respeto a mi hermano.
Imperfect	Mis padres querían que mi hermano y yo nos lleváramos bien.
Pluperfect	El profesor nos había exigido que ambos tuviéramos más tolerancia.
Conditional	Al jefe le gustaría que los empleados llegaran a tiempo.

Más ayuda **realidades.com** ▶ Tutorials

▼14 Responsabilidades como estudiante

Leer

Imagina que hablas con un adulto acerca de las responsabilidades que tenía cuando iba a la escuela. Completa el párrafo con el tiempo correcto del subjuntivo de los verbos.

Cuando era joven, el director de la escuela quería que los estudiantes __1.__ *(sigan / siguieran)* un código de vestimenta. A mí no me gustaba que __2.__ *(tenga / tuviera)* que usar ropa especial para ir a clases. Yo quería que nosotros __3.__ *(gocemos / gozáramos)* de la libertad de vestirnos de cualquier manera, como ahora. ¡Tú tienes suerte! Los maestros no pueden prohibir que __4.__ *(lleves / llevaras)* pantalones rotos ni zapatos viejos. Siempre me ha sorprendido que ahora los maestros no __5.__ *(obliguen / obligaran)* a los estudiantes a sentarse cuando empieza la clase. Es curioso que tampoco les __6.__ *(pidan / pidieran)* la tarea todos los días. En mis clases era común que todas las semanas nos __7.__ *(den / dieran)* un examen, y de ese modo, hacían que __8.__ siempre *(estudiáramos / estudiemos)*. También querían que los estudiantes __9.__ *(hagamos / hiciéramos)* proyectos especiales después de la escuela. Pero hoy es diferente. Este sistema de enseñanza menos formal funciona bien, a menos que los jóvenes __10.__ *(se rebelen / se rebelaran)*. Ojalá no __11.__ *(pase / pasara)* eso. Sería triste que los estudiantes __12.__ *(sufran / sufrieran)* por una falta de organización en la escuela.

▼13 (cont'd)

5. —¿Quién entrevistó a los adolescentes?
   —Los adolescentes fueron entrevistados por....
6. —¿Quién escogió...?
   —...fue escogido por...
7. —¿Quién promovió la paz?
   —La paz fue promovida por....
8. —¿Quién evitó las injusticias?
   —Las injusticias fueron evitadas por....

BELLRINGER REVIEW

Before completing the next *Gramática* presentation and accompanying series of activities, briefly review with students the formation of the imperfect subjunctive.

Gramática

Core Instruction

Focus: Voc. and Gram. Transparency 190

INTERACTIVE WHITEBOARD
Grammar Activities 10-1

Suggestions: Have students invent sentences to demonstrate their understanding of each of the rules for use of the present subjunctive, present perfect subjunctive, and imperfect subjunctive.

▼14 Standards: 1.2

Resources: Answer Keys: Student Edition, p. 142

Focus: Using various tenses in the subjunctive

Suggestions: Remind students to focus on the verb in the main clause of each sentence in order to determine which tense to use in the subordinate clause.

Answers:

1. siguieran	7. dieran
2. tuviera	8. estudiáramos
3. gozáramos	9. hiciéramos
4. lleves	10. se rebelen
5. obliguen	11. pase
6. pidan	12. sufrieran

ENRICH YOUR TEACHING

Teacher-to-Teacher

Have students interview a family member from an earlier generation about similarities and differences between family dynamics when they were adolescents and now. Ask students to report on the comments. To practice the subjunctive, include that person's value judgments or opinions.

21st Century Skills

Initiative and Self-Direction Remind students of the various digital tools available in **realidades.com** to help them monitor their own understanding and learning needs about the present and imperfect subjunctive, such as the online tutorials with comprehension check exercises, animated verbs, and additional grammar practice activities.

15 Standards: 1.1

Focus: Using various tenses in the subjunctive

Suggestions: Tell students to use one of the words or expressions from Column B in the sentence about the past as well as in the one about the present.

Answers will vary.

16 Standards: 1.1, 1.3

Focus: Using various tenses in the subjunctive

Suggestions: Students can begin their preparation in Step 1 by writing a key word or two about something they would like to ask their interview subject. Then they can determine which verbs they will use and begin to construct the questions.

Answers will vary.

Pre-AP* Support

- **Learning Objective:** Interpersonal Writing
- **Activity:** Have students write an e-mail to a friend in which they give their opinion on the most important issue facing teenagers today. They can start their e-mail by completing the phrase, "*Nos importa que...*" with their most important issue. Be sure students ask their friend at least one question about important issues facing them.
- **Pre-AP* Resource Book:** Comprehensive guide to Pre-AP* writing skill development, pp. 27–38

Block Schedule

Cube Game with *Actividad* 15: Divide the class into groups of three. Give each group two game cubes or two small six-sided boxes. Have students write on each side of one cube a word from Column A. Then have them write one verb from Column B on each side of the other box. Have each student roll the cubes and create a sentence combining the words that show face-up on the cubes.

Teacher-to-Teacher

e-amigos: Have students write their *e-amigos* describing the basic needs of teenagers. Ask them to respond to the messages by outlining the steps required to satisfy at least two of those needs. Have students send their e-mails to you for review.

446

▼15 Los primeros años . . . |

Hablar

¿Cómo fueron tus primeros años de escuela? Con un(a) compañero(a), comparen las responsabilidades que tenían en sus primeros años de escuela con las que tienen ahora. Usen palabras de las dos columnas.

Modelo
Antes, la maestra prefería que yo hiciera la tarea con mis padres. Ahora, mis profesores quieren que haga la tarea solo(a).

Columna A	Columna B
mis padres	exigir
mis maestros(as)	dudar
mis profesores(as)	aconsejar
mis amigos(as)	ser común que
mi entrenador(a)	querer
mis hermanos(as)	sugerir
mis compañeros(as) de clase	preferir
	recomendar
	ser importante que

▼16 Una biografía |

Escribir • Hablar

Imagina que tienes que escribir una biografía de un(a) compañero(a).

1 Escribe cinco preguntas que le puedes hacer a tu compañero(a) sobre su niñez y sobre cómo es diferente hoy por las experiencias que ha tenido.

▶ **Modelo**

A —*¿De qué tenías miedo cuando eras niño(a)?*
B —*Tenía miedo de que mis padres me castigaran.*
A —*Y ahora, ¿de qué tienes miedo?*
B —*Ahora tengo miedo de que las clases de la universidad sean más difíciles.*

2 Haz las preguntas a tu compañero(a) y toma apuntes mientras las contesta. Luego, intercambien papeles.

3 Usa tus notas para escribir una biografía breve.

446 cuatrocientos cuarenta y seis
Manos a la obra 1

DIFFERENTIATED INSTRUCTION

Heritage Language Learners

Before partners complete *Actividad* 16, ask students who have lived in a heritage country to serve as models. Ask questions that highlight the differences between childhood in the heritage country and childhood in the United States.

Multiple Intelligences

Musical/Rhythmic: In small groups, have students rehearse choral readings of Hilario Barrero's ***Subjuntivo.*** Discuss how punctuation, word choice, and line breaks impact the rhythm of the poem. Have students compare and contrast the different interpretations they hear.

▼17 Los adolescentes en el mundo de hoy | 👥

Hablar • Escribir

Tu clase va a escribir un informe sobre los adolescentes de hoy.

❶ Para juntar información, trabajen en grupos de cuatro estudiantes y completen las siguientes frases con tres diferentes respuestas.

• Nos importa que . . .   • Nos sorprende que . . .   • Queremos que . . .

• Nos alegramos de que . . .• Es una lástima que . . .   • Nos molesta que . . .

❷ Compartan sus respuestas con los otros grupos. Escojan las respuestas que más se repitieron y digan en qué orden de importancia las colocarían.

❸ Ahora, imaginen que pueden hablar con las autoridades del gobierno para informarles cómo se sienten ustedes como adolescentes. Deben presentarles una propuesta *(proposal)* sobre cuáles son los temas más importantes para los adolescentes. Escríbanlos en forma de frase, dando buenas razones de por qué son importantes.

Modelo

Nos parece injusto que no podamos votar hasta los 18 años. Tenemos . . .

▼ En voz alta | 🗣️

Escucha el poema que escribió Hilario Barrero (Toledo, 1948–), un escritor, traductor y poeta español que vive en Nueva York y también da clases en una universidad. Trata de repetir el poema en voz alta. Luego, contesta las preguntas.

• ¿Por qué dice el poeta que el maestro les roba su tiempo a los estudiantes?

• ¿Crees que los estudiantes están interesados en lo que les quiere enseñar el profesor? Repite alguna de las frases del poema para dar un ejemplo.

• ¿Te parece que para el autor es fácil o difícil enseñar a los estudiantes? ¿Por qué?

"Subjuntivo"
de Hilario Barrero

Y tener que explicar de nuevo el subjuntivo,
. . . cuando lo que desean es (. . .)
y olvidarse del viejo profesor que les roba
su tiempo inútilmente.
Mientras copian los signos del lenguaje,
emotion, doubt, volition, fear, joy . . .,
y usando el subjuntivo de mi lengua de humo[1]
mi deseo es que tengan un amor como el nuestro,
pero sé que no escuchan la frase
que les pongo para ilustrar su duda
ansiosos como están de usar el indicativo.
(. . .)

_____

1 smoke

Más práctica GO   realidades.com | print

	✔	
Instant Check		
Guided WB pp. 313–314	✔	✔
Core WB pp. 138–139	✔	✔
Comm. WB pp. 135, 140	✔	✔
Hispanohablantes WB pp. 309–311		✔

17 Standards: 1.1, 1.3

Focus: Using various tenses in the subjunctive

Suggestions: For Step 1, ask: *¿En qué tiempo estarán los verbos que escriben Uds?* (en el presente o el presente perfecto del subjuntivo)

Answers will vary.

En voz alta
Core Instruction

Standards: 1.1, 1.2, 1.3, 2.1, 2.2, 3.1, 3.2, 5.2

Resources: Audio Program DVD: Cap. 10, Track 9

Suggestions: Before students read the poem, prepare them by saying: *Este poema se trata de los pensamientos de un profesor de español.* When they recite the poem, encourage them to use expression appropriate to the professor's thoughts.

Answers will vary.

Chapter Project

Students can perform Step 2 at this point. Be sure they understand your corrections and suggestions. (For more information, see p. 430-b.)

Additional Resources

• Communication Wbk.: Act. 2, p. 135
• Teacher's Resource Book: Audio Script, p. 301, Communicative Pair Activity BLM, pp. 309–310
• Audio Program DVD: Cap. 10, Track 7

ENRICH YOUR TEACHING

Culture Note

Hilario Barrero's poetry has won awards and been published in numerous anthologies and literary magazines. Besides writing poetry and teaching Spanish, Barrero has translated to Spanish the poetry of Robert Frost, Jane Kenyon, and Donald Hall, among others.

21st Century Skills

Collaboration In preparation for *Actividad* 17, have students clearly define and assign the tasks for each person in their group. Teams work well together if they know what they want to accomplish and when each person has an equal role.

✔ ASSESSMENT

Prueba 10-4 with Study Plan (online only)

Prueba: El presente y el imperfecto del subjuntivo
• Prueba 10-4: p. 220

Examen: Vocabulario y gramática 1
• Examen 1: pp. 221–223
• ExamView: Examen 1

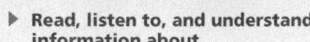
▶ Read, listen to, and understand information about
• individual rights in society
• the role of government

Vocabulario en contexto

Core Instruction

Standards: 1.1, 1.2, 3.1

Resources: Teacher's Resource Book: Input Script, p. 298, Clip Art, pp. 316–324, Audio Script, p. 302; Voc. and Gram. Transparencies 191–192; Audio Program DVD: Cap. 10, Track 10

Focus: Presenting new vocabulary and using grammar lexically in context

Suggestions: Have students read along as you present the new vocabulary by playing the audio or reading the text aloud. Use the pictures on *Voc. and Gram. Transparencies* 191–192 and questions with embedded answers to elicit the vocabulary from students: *¿La igualdad es esencial para que tengamos justicia o injusticia? (justicia) ¿Lo contrario de inocente es acusado o culpable? (culpable)* Check for comprehension by asking other questions. See the Input Scripts in the *Teacher's Resource Book* for specific questions.

Vocabulario en contexto

¿Te preguntaste alguna vez de dónde vienen tus derechos? **La garantía** de decir lo que piensas, de reunirte con otros, y de sentirte tranquilo(a) forman parte de la Constitución de los Estados Unidos. Son parte de las diez primeras enmiendas[1] que se añadieron a la Constitución en 1791 para garantizar la libertad de expresión y otros derechos **fundamentales**.

[1] amendments

"La libertad de expresión es la base de una sociedad democrática. Debemos proteger la libertad de prensa, de modo que todos tengamos acceso a los diferentes puntos de vista que se expresan en los medios de comunicación".

La igualdad es esencial si queremos tener una sociedad libre y con justicia para todos. Hay que asegurar que todas las personas, en todo el mundo, lleguen a gozar de los mismos derechos.

DIFFERENTIATED INSTRUCTION

Students with Learning Difficulties
Before students read or listen to the text on pp. 448–449, ask them to preview the passages to look for cognates. Some examples might include **garantía, fundamentales, justicia,** or **democrática.** Discuss how these words can help students decipher meaning from the text.

Advanced Learners
Have students search newspapers, magazines, and the Internet for pictures of such things as the Bill of Rights, trials, juries, defendants, and judges. Have them work together in a group to assemble these visuals into a display, complete with captions and labels, about individual rights and the role of government.

"Debido a que todos gozamos de derechos, la policía no puede detener a una persona sin acusarla de un crimen específico. Tampoco puede registrar la casa del acusado sin un documento que indique que es sospechoso de haber violado la ley".

"La Declaración garantiza los derechos del acusado a tener un juicio rápido y público, a ser juzgado por un jurado imparcial del estado y a no recibir castigos crueles".

la testigo

"El acusado es inocente hasta que se muestre, con testigos y pruebas, que es culpable".

el acusado

▼18 Los derechos del pueblo | 🔊

Escuchar • Escribir

Escribe los números del 1 al 6 en una hoja de papel. Escucha lo que dicen estos jóvenes y en cada caso escribe *C* (cierto) o *F* (falso). Vuelve a escribir las frases falsas, de manera que sean ciertas.

▼19 Tus derechos

Escribir

Escribe una lista de los tres derechos que te parecen más importantes para que una sociedad sea democrática. Puedes usar los que aparecen en estas páginas u otros que conozcas.

18 Standards: 1.2

Resources: Teacher's Resource Book: Audio Script, p. 302; Audio Program DVD: Cap. 10, Track 11; Answer Keys: Student Edition, p. 142

Focus: Practicing listening comprehension of new vocabulary

Suggestions: Allow students to silently review the material on these two pages before they complete the listening activity. Use the audio or read from the script. Allow students to listen more than once.

Answers:
1. C
2. F La libertad de prensa es necesaria para tener acceso a los puntos de vista de los medios de comunicación.
3. F Es necesario asegurar que haya igualdad en la sociedad.
4. C
5. F Las personas son inocentes hasta que se muestre que son culpables.
6. C

19 Standards: 1.3

Focus: Writing new vocabulary in a list

Suggestions: Point out to students that they need not use the word *derecho* in each item in their list. Have them study the material on these two pages as a model for how to express various rights.

Answers will vary.

cuatrocientos cuarenta y nueve **449**
Capítulo 10

ENRICH YOUR TEACHING

Teacher-to-Teacher

The constitutions of Spain and Latin American countries are readily available on the Internet. Have students choose, or assign them, a constitution to study. They can compare its structure and contents to the United States Constitution, find out which rights it guarantees, analyze verb tenses used in the text, and so on.

21st Century Skills

Information Literacy Have students search the Internet for information in Spanish about civil rights and the U.S. Constitution. Have them search the U.S. government Web sites to see what information is available in Spanish or in other languages. What other Web sites may provide similar information, and from what point of view?

Vocabulario en contexto

Core Instruction

Standards: 1.1, 1.2

Resources: Teacher's Resource Book: Input Script, p. 299, Clip Art, pp. 316–324, Audio Script, pp. 302–303; Voc. and Gram. Transparencies 193–194; Audio Program DVD: Cap. 10, Tracks 12–13

Focus: Extending presentation of vocabulary and grammar in context

Suggestions:

Pre-reading: Present the readings on this and the next page one at a time, along with their respective activities.

Reading: Allow students time to read each presentation silently first before they listen to the audio.

Post-reading: Check comprehension by asking questions. See the *Teacher's Resource Book* for specific questions.

▼**20** Standards: 1.3

Focus: Writing new vocabulary in a list

Suggestions: Encourage students to think of problems they consider important and list them with the problems on this page.

Answers will vary.

Pre-AP* Support

- **Learning Objective:** Interpersonal Speaking
- **Activity:** Have students focus on one problem presented on this page and allow them two minutes to think of a specific way they would propose to solve it. Then have students work in pairs and tell each other the problem they have chosen along with their proposed solution. Allow each student to talk for one minute. Request that they offer suggestions to each other to improve their mini-talk.
- ***Pre-AP* Resource Book:** Comprehensive guide to Pre-AP* vocabulary skill development, pp. 51–57

Block Schedule

Have students work in pairs and rank the problems from most to least serious. Have each group report back on their top four. Use the results to create a class summary.

Jóvenes por el desarrollo y la paz

Los jóvenes tienen gran fuerza en el mundo de hoy. El desarrollo de los países depende, entre otras cosas, de la participación de los jóvenes. Hay organizaciones internacionales, como la Red de Jóvenes y Estudiantes, que reúnen grupos de jóvenes de todo el mundo. Allí **intercambian** sus ideas y hacen **propuestas** sobre los diferentes **modos** de resolver sus propios problemas y los de otros jóvenes.

Manifestación por la paz en España

▼**20** Problemas de los jóvenes

Escribir

Haz una lista de los problemas que tienen los jóvenes de hoy. Empieza con los que creas que son más importantes y termina con los menos importantes.

A **medida que** participan en estas reuniones, los jóvenes aprenden a respetar la diferencia de opiniones de otros grupos. Juntos **proponen** soluciones a sus problemas y a los problemas del mundo.

Éstos son algunos problemas que enfrentan los jóvenes:

- **las desigualdades** sociales, económicas y políticas
- **el desempleo**
- la discriminación por sexo
- los jóvenes sin hogar
- los conflictos **mundiales**
- la contaminación ambiental
- las enfermedades, el hambre y la mala nutrición
- los problemas en la familia
- la **falta de** oportunidades de educación y entrenamiento

450 **cuatrocientos cincuenta**
A primera vista 2

DIFFERENTIATED INSTRUCTION

Heritage Language Learners

Ask students who have lived in a heritage country to share their views on the biggest problems facing the youth in that country. Are the issues similar to or different from those faced by young people in the United States?

Students with Learning Difficulties

Ask students to provide each other with brief definitions or explanations of each of the issues listed on p. 450. For example: *¿Qué es el desempleo? ¿Cuáles son algunos ejemplos de problemas en la familia?*

¿Qué proponen los jóvenes?

Lydia, de San Luis Obispo, California. Ella quiere ser representante ante la Organización de las Naciones Unidas. ▶

❝ **En lugar de** pensar sólo en nosotros mismos, somos responsables de hablar por los jóvenes del mundo que llevan una vida difícil. Ellos también tienen derecho a lograr sus **aspiraciones** ❞.

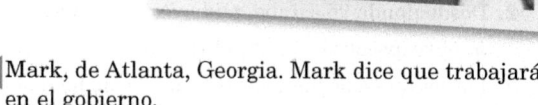

◀ Mark, de Atlanta, Georgia. Mark dice que trabajará en el gobierno.

❝ **El fin** de la democracia es que tengamos más libertad para expresar sin miedo lo que **opinamos**. La libertad de expresión es **un valor** democrático fundamental ❞.

Yamiko y Alicia, de Providence, Rhode Island. Ellas quieren ser consejeras de estudiantes. ▶

❝ Si la gente se reúne con fines **pacíficos** e intercambia opiniones cuando no está de acuerdo, puede encontrar soluciones a muchos problemas. Así, habrá menos guerras y también menos problemas en las escuelas ❞.

▼21 Hagamos algo | 🔊

Escuchar

Escucha las frases. Después de oír cada frase, di quién de los estudiantes de esta página crees que dijo cada cosa.

▼22 Y tú, ¿qué propones?

Escribir

Imagina que te invitan a representar a los jóvenes de tu país, o de otro país que conozcas, en alguna organización internacional. Escribe cinco problemas y cinco propuestas que harías para mejorar las condiciones de los jóvenes de ese país.

Más práctica	GO	
realidades.com | print		
Instant Check	✔	
Guided WB pp. 315–322	✔	✔
Core WB pp. 140–141	✔	✔
Comm. WB p. 141	✔	✔
Hispanohablantes **WB** pp. 312–313	✔	

cuatrocientos cincuenta y uno **451**
Capítulo 10

▼21 Standards: 1.2

Resources: Teacher's Resource Book: Audio Script, p. 303; Audio Program DVD: Cap. 10, Track 14; Answer Keys: Student Edition, p. 143

Focus: Practicing listening comprehension of new vocabulary

Suggestions: Remind students that the comments they will hear are by the four people shown on this page.

Answers:
1 Lydia
2 Mark
3. Yamiko y Alicia
4. Mark
5. Lydia

▼22 Standards: 1.3

Focus: Practicing new vocabulary through writing in context

Suggestions: Once students have written their five problems and solutions, invite them to share them in a class discussion.

Answers will vary.

Chapter Project
Students can perform Step 3 at this point. (For more information, see p. 430-b.)

ENRICH YOUR TEACHING

Culture Note
La Red de Jóvenes y Estudiantes, mentioned on p. 450, belongs to the Mexican section of Amnesty International, and some of its campaigns are operated through that organization. Their mission is to encourage youth involvement in the promotion and defense of human rights. Each year, Amnesty International unites the energy and ideas of young Mexicans of *la Red* with other young people all over the world in a unified action. They call attention to one place in the world in which human rights are in jeopardy and put pressure on authorities and organizations in that place to respect human rights.

☑**ASSESSMENT**

Prueba: Comprensión del vocabulario 2
• Prueba 10-5: pp. 224–225

Manos a la obra 2

▼ Objectives
▶ Read and write about justice
▶ Express your opinions about rights and responsibilities
▶ Discuss and write about democracy

INTERACTIVE WHITEBOARD
Vocabulary Activities 10-2

Vocabulario en uso

▼23 Standards: 1.2

Resources: Answer Keys: Student Edition, p. 143

Focus: Demonstrating comprehension of new vocabulary

Suggestions: Make sure students are given adequate writing practice by having them write the entire answer and not just the corresponding letter.

Answers:

1. c   5. a
2. b   6. b
3. a   7. c (a)
4. c

▼24 Standards: 1.2, 1.3

Resources: Answer Keys: Student Edition, p. 143

Focus: Demonstrating comprehension of new vocabulary

Suggestions: After students have completed the activity, have them share their work, reading each item as a complete sentence.

Answers:

1. dar a cada persona lo que es de esa persona
2. cuando todos participan en el gobierno de un país
3. cuando la policía le quita la libertad a una persona porque cree que es sospechosa
4. las da el estado cuando asegura derechos para todos sus ciudadanos
5. las cosas que los ciudadanos pueden hacer o exigir de acuerdo con la ley
6. no respetar una ley

▼23 En la sala de justicia

Leer

¿Quién dijo cada frase en la sala de justicia?

1. Hay que prometer decir la verdad, sólo la verdad.
   - a. el inocente
   - b. el juicio
   - c. el juez

2. Desde donde yo estaba, pude ver muy bien lo que hizo el criminal.
   - a. el sospechoso
   - b. el testigo
   - c. la acusada

3. Lo siento, señor juez, pero esa mujer no ha dicho la verdad. Yo no lo hice.
   - a. el acusado
   - b. el jurado
   - c. la víctima

4. No hay suficiente información. ¡El acusado es inocente!
   - a. la justicia
   - b. la policía
   - c. la abogada

5. Sí, soy inocente. ¡Tienen que creerme!
   - a. el acusado
   - b. el juicio
   - c. el castigo

6. Hemos decidido quién es culpable.
   - a. el inocente
   - b. el jurado
   - c. la acusada

7. El jurado deberá juzgar al acusado con justicia.
   - a. el juez
   - b. los valores
   - c. la prensa

▼24 ¿Qué quieren decir?

Leer • Escribir

Para poder defender nuestros derechos, es importante saber lo que quieren decir las palabras de la Declaración de derechos. Empareja cada palabra con su significado. Luego, escribe dos frases usando cuatro palabras de la primera columna.

1. la justicia   dar a cada persona lo que es de esa persona
2. democrático(a)   no respetar una ley
3. detener   las cosas que los ciudadanos pueden hacer o exigir de acuerdo con la ley
4. las garantías   cuando todos participan en el gobierno de un país
5. los derechos   cuando la policía le quita la libertad a una persona porque cree que es sospechosa
6. violar   las da el estado cuando asegura derechos para todos sus ciudadanos

452 cuatrocientos cincuenta y dos
Manos a la obra 2

DIFFERENTIATED INSTRUCTION

Students with Learning Difficulties

Assign students the roles outlined in *Actividad* 23, and provide each character with a label card. Ask them to stand at the front of the class, holding their label card. Read the quotes from the activity and ask students to call out the character who would say those words.

Advanced Learners

Have students write sentences containing the unused words from *Actividad* 23. Ask them to read their sentences to each other and listen to make sure the words are used correctly.

☀ El Sol

Santiago, 23 de septiembre

Presidente asegura derechos a todos los niños.

▼25 ¿Que dicen los titulares? | 👥

Escribir • Hablar

❶ Usa elementos de cada columna para escribir titulares *(headlines)*.

1. la Organización de las Naciones Unidas	detener	puntos de vista con fines pacíficos
2. la policía	votar	competencia mundial de atletismo
3. el Congreso	asegurar	garantías y derechos de los ciudadanos
4. el juez	proponer	el castigo del culpable
5. la declaración	reunirse	los valores democráticos
6. el presidente del club atlético	defender	los sospechosos
7. el grupo para la defensa de los niños	intercambiar	el derecho a la educación y la alimentación

❷ Imagina que eres reportero(a). Trabaja con otro(a) estudiante para escribir tres frases sobre uno de los titulares.

▼ Fondo Cultural | México

Políticos y educadores ¿Sabías que muchos líderes políticos en los países hispanohablantes fueron educadores o maestros? Un político famoso, el mexicano José Vasconcelos (1882–1959), también fue educador, además de filósofo, abogado, historiador y escritor. Después de luchar en la Revolución Mexicana, fue rector de la Universidad Nacional y creó la Secretaría de Educación Pública. La dividió en cuatro departamentos: el de Escuelas, para desarrollar la enseñanza técnica y científica; el de Bibliotecas, para promover la lectura en todo el país; el de Bellas Artes, para desarrollar la cultura artística; y el de Enseñanza indígena para enseñar a los indígenas a leer ya que no tenían acceso a la educación. En su época, miles de campesinos y obreros aprendieron a leer y a escribir y se dio el más importante avance de la educación en México. Los estudiantes lo llamaron "Maestro de la juventud de América".

Vasconcelos, además, creó la orquesta sinfónica de México y promovió la pintura mural y la obra de los grandes muralistas Diego Rivera y José Clemente Orozco.

José Vasconcelos

• ¿Por qué es importante que los políticos sean maestros?

---

25 Standards: 1.1, 4.1

Focus: Practicing new vocabulary via guided writing

Suggestions: Remind students that the structure of a *titular* is different from that of a complete sentence. Point out the model *titular* at the top of the page, and ask them to use it as a model.

Answers will vary.

Fondo cultural

Standards: 1.1, 1.2, 3.1

Suggestions: After students have read and discussed the information, ask comprehension questions. For example: *¿Cuáles eran las profesiones de José Vasconcelos? (político, educador, filósofo, abogado, historiador, escritor) ¿Cuáles eran los cuatro departamentos de la Secretaría de Educación Pública que él creó? (los departamentos de Escuelas, Bibliotecas, Bellas Artes y Enseñanza indígena)*

Answers will vary.

ENRICH YOUR TEACHING

Culture Note

José Vasconcelos considered it one of his most important missions as a leader to reach out to the indigenous peoples of Mexico through education. As part of this mission, he started the "muralist movement," which helped launch the artistic careers of Diego Rivera, José Clemente Orozco, and Alfaro Siqueiros.

21st Century Skills

Information Literacy Have students do further research about José Vasconcelos and his accomplishments in education, art, and government in Mexico. Ask them to look up a list of his major writings. What do the titles indicate about Vasconcelos' interests and concerns as educator and politician?

26 Standards: 1.2

Resources: Teacher's Resource Book: Audio Script, p. 303; Audio Program DVD: Cap. 10, Track 15; Answer Keys: Student Edition, p. 144

Focus: Practicing listening comprehension of new vocabulary

Suggestions: Before students listen, tell them that they will hear five separate, short news reports. Encourage them to write their responses in their own words.

Answers: Wording of answers will vary. The following contain the main ideas:
1. **está acusado de tratar de robar un banco.**
2. **pidiendo una solución al problema del tráfico.**
3. **fueron a varios países para hablar de los derechos y los valores democráticos.**
4. **de la tienda Alegría.**
5. **castigaría a quien viole la ley contra el ruido.**

27 Standards: 1.1

Focus: Practice new vocabulary in discussions around themes

Recycle: subjunctive with verbs of emotion or doubt

Suggestions: Have students take turns being the one to launch each interchange.

Answers will vary.

28 Standards: 1.1, 1.3

Focus: Practice new vocabulary via an oral news report

Recycle: preterite and imperfect tenses

Suggestions: Encourage students to present their report as though it were part of a real news program. The narrator should introduce the witness.

Answers will vary.

▼26 Escucha la radio |

Escuchar • Escribir

A veces parece que las noticias siempre son malas. Escucha la radio y completa las frases para hacer un resumen de las noticias.

1. En Santa Ana, un grupo de personas ...
2. En Ciudad Luna, hubo una manifestación ...
3. Representantes de la organización mundial Los Amigos ...
4. Desaparecieron 200 cajas de juguetes ...
5. El alcalde Marino dijo que ...

▼27 ¿Qué opinas? o "la libertad de opinión" | | ♻

Leer • Hablar

Trabaja con otro(a) estudiante. Usa tu derecho a la libertad de opinión y di si estás de acuerdo o no con las siguientes frases. Usa expresiones como: *creo que, me parece que, me preocupa que, dudo que.*

▶ **Modelo**

(no) proteger los derechos fundamentales
A —*Debemos proteger los derechos fundamentales.*
B —*Creo que debemos proteger los derechos fundamentales para no perderlos.*

1. (no) detener a los sospechosos
2. los testigos de un crimen (no) ayudar a la víctima
3. (no) ser culpables los padres de jóvenes desobedientes
4. (no) apoyar la participación de jóvenes en manifestaciones pacíficas
5. (no) luchar contra la falta de justicia en otros países
6. (no) construir más carreteras
7. (no) controlar lo que pueden hacer los jóvenes
8. (no) proponer soluciones pacíficas

▼28 El noticiero | ♟ | ♻

Hablar • Escribir

Con un(a) compañero(a), escribe un breve reportaje sobre "el misterio de la desaparición de una bicicleta" para el programa de noticias. Describe lo que pasó e incluye un comentario de un testigo. Pueden usar las palabras del recuadro. Presenten su reportaje a otra pareja. Uno(a) es reportero(a) del noticiero y otro(a) es testigo.

el / la testigo	culpable	en lugar de	sospechoso(a)
inocente	detener	el punto de vista	opinar

454 cuatrocientos cincuenta y cuatro
Manos a la obra 2

DIFFERENTIATED INSTRUCTION

Students with Learning Difficulties
For *Actividad* 28, help students first note down ideas for events involved in the theft of a bicycle. Have them use a flow chart or other graphic organizer for this purpose. Ask what would happen: first the discovery that the bicycle is missing, then asking family members or neighbors, and so on. Guide them to use the vocabulary in the word bank.

Students with Special Needs
You may need to provide impaired students with a copy of the script in order for them to complete listening activities like *Actividad* 26.

▼29 Momentos históricos |

Leer • Hablar

En todas las épocas hay artistas que representan momentos históricos de la vida de sus países y de sus héroes. Uno de esos momentos es cuando se firman *(sign)* documentos fundamentales, como las declaraciones de independencia y las constituciones. Lee sobre un pintor de la historia de Venezuela y contesta las preguntas.

Conexiones | Las artes

Juan Lovera (1776–1841) es un pintor que inició el género de pintura histórica en Venezuela. En su obra, "El 5 de julio de 1811", retrata a más de cien personajes y deja testimonio de un suceso de gran importancia para Venezuela, la firma de la declaración de independencia de España. La pintura muestra con detalles y de manera fiel a los hechos la ropa y la posición de los criollos *(native born)* de esa época. Además de los dibujos de cada uno de los personajes principales, tiene escritos sus nombres. Esta obra muestra la misión de las artes para preservar la historia.

"El 5 de julio de 1811", Juan Lovera, (Venezuela)

• ¿Por qué piensas que las pinturas eran más importantes testimonios históricos antes que ahora?

• ¿Recuerdas alguna pintura que muestre un momento de la historia de los Estados Unidos?

▼30 Y tú, ¿qué respondes? |

Hablar • Escribir

❶ Imagina que estás en tu clase de educación cívica. Conversa y contesta estas preguntas con un(a) compañero(a):

1. En tu opinión, ¿qué debe garantizar el gobierno a los ciudadanos?

2. ¿Qué debe garantizar el(la) director(a) de tu escuela a los(as) estudiantes?

3. ¿Conoces países donde no respetan el punto de vista de la gente? ¿Puedes mencionar algunos de esos países?

4. ¿El desempleo existe en todos los países del mundo? ¿Cómo crees que afecta a las familias que sufren debido al desempleo?

5. ¿Qué organizaciones mundiales conoces que tengan fines pacíficos? Descríbelas.

6. ¿Conoces países que aseguran una educación gratuita para los ciudadanos?

❷ Escribe un párrafo sobre lo que significa para ti la democracia de los Estados Unidos.

cuatrocientos cincuenta y cinco 455
Capítulo 10

Practice and Communicate 10

▼29 Standards: 1.1, 1.2, 2.2, 3.1, 4.2
Focus: Practicing new vocabulary via reading and response
Suggestions: Have students read the information about Juan Lovera in pairs and help each other with any comprehension problems they may have.
Answers will vary.

▼30 Standards: 1.1, 1.3
Focus: Practicing new vocabulary
Recycle: subjunctive, country names
Suggestions: For Step 2, encourage students to consider and comment on their partner's opinions as well as their own.
Answers will vary.

Block Schedule
After completing *Actividad 30 #2*, have each student write on the board one statement from his or her paragraph. Use these ideas as a brainstorm. Have each student take these ideas and write a new paragraph. Select the top two paragraphs and send them to a local Spanish newspaper to be published or submit them to the school literary magazine.

Additional Resources
• Communication Wbk.: Act. 3, p. 136
• Teacher's Resource Book: Audio Script, p. 303, Communicative Pair Activity BLM, pp. 311–312
• Audio Program DVD: Cap. 10, Track 16

✓ASSESSMENT
Prueba 10-6 with Study Plan (online only)
Prueba: Aplicación del vocabulario 2
• Prueba 10-6: pp. 226–227

ENRICH YOUR TEACHING

Culture Note
Juan Lovera is Venezuela's most outstanding artist of the school known as *arte republicana,* which portrayed historical events. He eventually became known as *El pintor de los Próceres.* His paintings on a grand scale like *El 5 de julio de 1811* are known for their composition and perspective.

21st Century Skills
Communication As a warm-up to *Actividad* 30, have students brainstorm a list of expressions in Spanish they would use when giving their personal opinion or when taking a stand on an important issue. What words or expressions do they use to persuade others to agree with them? Have them choose one of the questions in this activity, then prepare to debate the issue with their classmates.

455

Gramática

Gramática

Core Instruction

Standards: 4.1

Resources: Voc. and Gram. Transparency 195

INTERACTIVE WHITEBOARD

Grammar Activities 10-2

Suggestions: On the board, write sentence frames consisting of a verb in the preterite, the imperfect, or the past perfect tense, followed by **que,** followed by an infinitive. The three parts should be able to work together as building blocks for a complex sentence. Here are some examples:

dudó + que + terminar

quería + que + invitar

habíamos pedido + que + servir

Challenge students to put the parts together to make complex sentences using the pluperfect subjunctive. Tell them they can use whatever subject they wish in the subordinate clause. The above frames might result in sentences like the following:

Papá dudó que Benito hubiera terminado el maratón antes de la puesta del sol.

Yo quería que tú me hubieras invitado.

Habíamos pedido que Ud. nos hubiera servido antes.

El pluscuamperfecto del subjuntivo

You use the pluperfect subjunctive to describe actions in the past, when one action takes place before the other. In such cases, the action that takes place before is in the pluperfect subjunctive, and the action that takes place after is in the preterite, the imperfect or the pluperfect of the indicative.

> Carlos se sorprendió que su amigo hubiera comprado todos los materiales.
> Esperaba que hubieran ido a la fiesta con los niños.
> Yo había querido que mis hermanos hubieran venido a la casa de la abuela.

You form the pluperfect subjunctive using the past subjunctive of *haber* + the past participle of the verb.

hubiera salido	hubiéramos salido
hubieras salido	hubierais salido
hubiera salido	hubieran salido

- You also use the pluperfect subjunctive when the verb in the main clause is in the conditional.

> ¿Sería posible que Teresa hubiera terminado el informe?

- Note that since the expression *como si* (as if) always refers to something that is contrary to the truth, or unreal, it must always be followed by the subjunctive, either the imperfect subjunctive or the pluperfect subjunctive.

> Estaba tan cansada como si hubiera corrido todo el día.
> Sergio descansa como si no tuviera nada que hacer.

Más ayuda | **realidades.com** | ▶ **Tutorials**

Resources: Answer Keys: Student Edition, p. 144

Focus: Practicing the pluperfect subjunctive

Suggestions: In addition to forming the pluperfect subjunctive for the correct verb, encourage students to think about the time relationships in the sentences.

Answers:

1. hubiera detenido
2. hubieran destruido
3. hubiera castigado
4. hubieran sido
5. hubiera garantizado
6. hubiera opinado
7. hubiera robado
8. hubiera sabido

▼**31** **Las noticias del día**

Leer

Imagina que estás leyendo el periódico. Completa las siguientes frases con la forma correcta del verbo en el pluscuamperfecto del subjuntivo.

1. Fue una sorpresa que el gobierno _____ (detener / proponer) a tantas personas en el aeropuerto.

2. Los ciudadanos se sorprendieron que los aerosoles _____ (opinar / destruir) tanto el medio ambiente.

3. Los estudiantes dudaban que la policía _____ (castigar / asegurar) al presidente de la universidad.

4. Los testigos esperaban que las noticias _____ (estar / ser) más positivas.

5. Los ciudadanos de ese país esperaban que el gobierno _____ (garantizar / juzgar) la libertad de prensa y de expresión.

6. Me sorprendía que el juez _____ (opinar / violar) de esa manera.

7. ¿Sería verdad que el actor _____ (juzgar / robar) el coche de su novia?

8. El testigo desapareció como si _____ (saber / violar) algo acerca del acusado.

456 cuatrocientos cincuenta y seis
Manos a la obra 2

DIFFERENTIATED INSTRUCTION

Advanced Learners

On separate slips of paper, have students write three subordinate clauses beginning with conjunctions taught in the *Gramática* on this page. If they use **aunque,** allow them to use either the indicative or the subjunctive in the clause. Collect the strips, mix them, and place them in a container. Have students meet in a circle, take turns drawing one subordinate clause at a time, and completing a complex sentence by inventing a suitable main clause.

▼32 En tu comunidad |

Hablar

Imagina que te encuentras con un(a) amigo(a) y conversan sobre las cosas que sucedieron en tu barrio. Trabaja con un(a) compañero(a). Tu compañero(a) te dice lo que pasó en el barrio y tú le respondes cómo te hizo sentir, usando un verbo de emoción y el pluscuamperfecto del subjuntivo.

▶ **Modelo**

Roberto / celebrar su cumpleaños
A —*Roberto celebró su cumpleaños.*
B —*Me alegré mucho que hubiera celebrado su cumpleaños.*

Estudiante A

1. la abuela de Pedro / enfermarse
2. los hijos de Ana / cambiarse de escuela
3. la familia Ortiz / irse de viaje
4. el dueño del supermercado / acusar al vecino
5. los padres de Luisa/ comprarse una casa

Estudiante B

Me alegré . . .
Fue una lástima . . .
Me sorprendió . . .
Me enojó . . .
Fue maravilloso . . .

El español en la comunidad

El español y las campañas electorales

Cada día más, en las campañas electorales en los Estados Unidos los candidatos dedican tiempo a comunicarse en español con la comunidad hispanohablante. Además de que ya hay boletas para votar traducidas al español, en las elecciones para presidente del 2008, por ejemplo, los candidatos usaron la radio, la televisión y páginas de Internet en español para trasmitir sus

Marco Rubio, Senador de los EE. UU. por Florida

mensajes y dar entrevistas en español. Pero esta idea no es nueva; el presidente John F. Kennedy fue el primero que grabó mensajes en español durante su campaña, en 1960.

Como la población de hispanohablantes está creciendo en los Estados Unidos, se espera que durante las campañas presidenciales próximas, los candidatos usarán aún más el español para convencer *(convince)* a los hispanohablantes de votar por ellos. Es probable que entonces quienes puedan hablar los dos idiomas, ¡tendrán más posibilidades de ganar!

El bilingüismo es importante en las campañas electorales de varios países del mundo.

ENRICH YOUR TEACHING

Culture Note

Business leaders and politicians from the Spanish-speaking community in the United States have made great progress in broadcasting their messages in the past thirty years. Besides many Spanish-language media tools, such as radio stations and TV channels at their disposal throughout the country, there is also Hispanic Heritage Month. It runs from September 15 to October 15 of each year and celebrates contributions to United States society from anyone in the Spanish-speaking community. It was originally approved by Congress as National Hispanic Heritage Week in 1968, and was expanded to an entire month in 1988.

Practice and Communicate 10

▼32 Standards: 1.1

Resources: Answer Keys: Student Edition, p. 145

Focus: Practicing the pluperfect subjunctive

Suggestions: Make sure both partners have a chance to assume the role of Student B.

Answers: Student B's choices of verbs of emotion will vary. The following are likely results:

1. —La abuela de Pedro se enfermó.
   —Fue una lástima que ella se hubiera enfermado.
2. —Los hijos de Ana se cambiaron de escuela.
   —Me sorprendió que ellos se hubieran cambiado de escuela.
3. —La familia Ortiz se fue de viaje.
   —Fue maravilloso que ellos se hubieran ido de viaje.
4. —El dueño del supermercado acusó al vecino.
   —Me enojó que él lo hubiera acusado.
5. —Los padres de Luisa se compraron una casa.
   —Fue maravilloso que ellos se hubieran comprado una casa.

▼ El español en la comunidad

Core Instruction

Standards: 1.2, 3.1, 5.1

Suggestions: Once students have read the information, ask comprehension questions. For example: *¿De qué manera se comunican los candidatos con la comunidad? (Hay boletas para votar traducidas al español. Usan la radio, la televisión y el Internet para transmitir sus mensajes. Se entrevistan en programas de la televisión en español.)*

Answers will vary.

Chapter Project

Students can perform Step 4 at this point. Be sure they understand your corrections and suggestions. (For more information, see p. 430-b.)

457

▼33 Standards: 1.1

Resources: Answer Keys: Student Edition, p. 146

Focus: Practicing the pluperfect subjunctive

Suggestions: Conduct the activity with the whole class, calling on volunteers randomly for each item.

Answers:

1. El vecino actuó como si no le hubiera importado nada.
2. El contador respondió como si hubiera estado loco.
3. La vendedora pareció como si hubiera escondido algo.
4. La dueña habló como si se hubiera enojado con la vendedora.
5. El cliente se rió como si se hubiera asustado con las preguntas.

▼34 Standards: 1.1, 1.3, 3.1

Focus: Practicing the pluperfect subjunctive

Suggestions: Encourage students to check back to the rules in the *Gramática* as often as necessary in order to complete the activity. Remind them that the most likely way to use the pluperfect subjunctive is to talk about the reactions others had to what their famous person did or said.

Answers will vary.

▼33 El culpable

Escribir

Imagina que eres un(a) detective que investigó un robo en una tienda. Entrevistaste a diferentes personas y su comportamiento fue muy sospechoso. Usa la expresión *como si* y el pluscuamperfecto del subjuntivo para explicar cómo actuaron.

Modelo

el chofer *(reaccionar)* / estar enojado con la dueña
El chofer reaccionó como si hubiera estado enojado con la dueña.

1. el vecino *(actuar)* / no importarle nada
2. el contador *(responder)* / estar loco
3. la vendedora *(parecer)* / esconder algo
4. la dueña *(hablar)* / enojarse con la vendedora
5. el cliente *(reírse)* / asustarse con las preguntas

▼34 Por una sociedad mejor

Hablar • Escribir

❶ En grupo, investiguen sobre la vida de una persona famosa que luchó o que lucha por una sociedad más justa. Pueden buscar información en la biblioteca o en la Red. La persona puede ser:

• un(a) presidente(a)
• un(a) escritor(a)
• un(a) pintor(a)
• un héroe o una heroína
• un(a) científico(a)

❷ Preparen un cuestionario sobre la vida de la persona que escogieron, por ejemplo, dónde nació, cómo fue su niñez, a qué se dedicaba, cuáles eran o son sus razones para luchar por una sociedad mejor, qué logró hacer. Escriban en una hoja de papel aparte las respuestas a las preguntas del cuestionario.

Modelo

¿Cómo reaccionó el país cuando se murió Lincoln?
El país se sorprendió de que el presidente Lincoln hubiera muerto.

❸ Intercámbiense los cuestionarios entre los grupos para responderlos. Luego, devuélvanlos al grupo que los hizo para que revise las respuestas.

❹ Corrijan las respuestas y compartan su información sobre la persona famosa con el resto de la clase.

Más práctica	**GO**	
*realidades.com	print*		
Instant Check	✔	
Guided WB pp. 323–324	✔	✔
Core WB p. 142	✔	✔
Comm. WB pp. 142–143	✔	✔
***Hispanohablantes* WB** pp. 314–319		✔

458 cuatrocientos cincuenta y ocho
Manos a la obra 2

DIFFERENTIATED INSTRUCTION

Heritage Language Learners

For *Actividad* 34, encourage students who have lived in a heritage country to suggest famous persons from that country for their group to investigate. They can provide valuable cultural insight on the famous person's achievements.

Advanced Learners

Have students use the pluperfect subjunctive to tell about three outstanding events in their lives and their reactions—or the reactions of others—to those events. Provide an example, such as: *Mis padres no pudieron creer que yo hubiera ganado el concurso de poesía.*

Gramática

▼ Objectives
▶ Express what would or should have happened
▶ Discuss possible outcomes
▶ Exchange information about animal rights

El condicional perfecto

You use the conditional perfect to express what would or should have happened at some point in the past.

Y tú, ¿qué habrías dicho en esa situación?
And you, what would you have said in that situation?

Yo le habría dado un buen consejo.
I would have given him(her) good advice.

You form the conditional perfect using the conditional of *haber* + the past participle of the verb.

habría trabajado	habríamos trabajado
habrías trabajado	habríais trabajado
habría trabajado	habrían trabajado

• The conditional is used with *si* clauses to say what might have been if things had been different. In these sentences you use the past perfect subjunctive and the conditional perfect together.

Si hubiera sabido que estabas interesada, te habría invitado a la reunión.
If I had known you were interested, I would have invited you to the meeting.

Si no hubieran venido a este país, no los habrías conocido.
If they hadn't come to this country, you would not have met them.

Más ayuda **realidades.com** ▶ *Canción de hip hop* ▶ *Tutorials*

▼35 Lo habrían hecho pero, . . .

Leer

Muchas personas quieren resolver problemas, pero no siempre pueden. Completa las frases con el condicional perfecto del verbo apropiado.

1. Yo *(participar / detener)* en la reunión, pero no pude porque estaba enferma.

2. Los profesores *(obligar / asegurar)* el respeto a los derechos de los estudiantes si hubieran ido a la manifestación.

3. Si las personas no hubieran actuado de una manera tan sospechosa, la policía no los *(detener / intercambiar)*.

4. Si yo fuera el profesor, *(decir / proponer)* otro código de vestimenta.

5. Si ellos no hubieran tenido problemas, no *(aceptar / sufrir)* nuestra ayuda.

6. Si hubiera tenido problemas como tú, yo *(buscar / asegurar)* el apoyo de mis padres.

7. Creo que con un buen traductor, la confusión entre los dos países *(proponerse / resolverse)*.

Practice and Communicate 10

Gramática

Core Instruction

Standards: 4.1

Resources: Voc. and Gram. Transparency 196

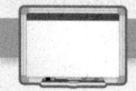

INTERACTIVE WHITEBOARD
Grammar Activities 10-2

Suggestions: To help students become familiar with using the past perfect subjunctive and the conditional perfect together, write on the board English sentences like the examples in the second part of the *Gramática* and have students translate them to Spanish.

▼35 Standards: 1.2

Resources: Answer Keys: Student Edition, p. 146
Focus: Practicing the conditional perfect
Common Errors: Some students will confuse verb forms of ***haber*** when working with the past perfect subjunctive and the conditional perfect. Write the forms of ***haber*** for the former tense on the left side of the board and those for the latter tense on the right side, and allow students to refer to them as they complete the activities.

Suggestions: Once students have written the answers on their own, invite them to take turns reading the completed sentences aloud.

Answers:

1. habría participado
2. habrían asegurado
3. habría detenido
4. habría propuesto
5. habrían aceptado
6. habría buscado
7. se habría resuelto

ENRICH YOUR TEACHING

Teacher-to-Teacher

If you use a predictable system for calling on volunteers, such as going up and down rows, some students will determine which item they are going to be held responsible for and "drop out" of the activity until it is their turn. When conducting activities together with the whole class, randomize the way you choose volunteers.

21st Century Skills

Initiative and Self-Direction Remind students of the various digital tools available in **realidades.com** that can provide extra practice with verb conjugations. Students can access grammar tutorial with comprehension check exercises and additional grammar practice activities.

36 Standards: 1.3

Resources: Answer Keys: Student Edition, p. 147

Focus: Practicing the pluperfect subjunctive and conditional perfect

Suggestions: Encourage students to use humor in some of their responses.

Answers will vary. Students will use *habría* in all main clauses, since they are talking about themselves. Pluperfect subjunctive forms for the subordinate *(si)* clauses follow:

1. hubiera estado
2. hubiera perdido
3. hubiera llegado
4. hubiera ganado
5. hubiera sido
6. hubiera empezado
7. hubiera encontrado
8. hubiera tenido
9. hubiera visto
10. hubiera tenido

37 Standards: 1.1

Resources: Answer Keys: Student Edition, p. 147

Focus: Practicing the pluperfect subjunctive and conditional perfect

Recycle: past participle formation, reflexive verbs

Suggestions: Encourage students to answer honestly and completely in order to practice useful, real-world vocabulary.

Answers will vary. Students will use the following pluperfect subjunctive forms:

1. hubieras ido
2. hubieras perdido
3. hubiera ocurrido
4. te hubieran invitado
5. te hubiera detenido
6. hubiera desaparecido
7. te hubieras enterado
8. te hubieran ignorado

38 Standards: 1.1, 1.3

Focus: Practicing the conditional perfect

Suggestions: For Step 2, encourage students to talk about their partners as well as themselves in order to practice different verb forms.

Answers will vary.

Chapter Project

Students can perform Step 5 at this point. Make audio or video recordings of their presentations for inclusion in their portfolios. (For more information, see p. 430-b.)

460

▼36 ¿Qué habrías hecho?

Escribir

Imagina que te sucedieran las siguientes cosas. Escribe frases sobre lo que habrías hecho si hubieras estado en estas situaciones.

Modelo
ser testigo
Si hubiera sido testigo en un juicio, me habría olvidado de todo lo que sabía.

1. estar acusado
2. perder (una cosa)
3. llegar tarde
4. ganar un premio
5. ser sospechoso(a)
6. empezar a trabajar
7. encontrar (una cosa)
8. tener derecho a (algo)
9. ver un extraterrestre
10. tener conocimiento de (una cosa)

▼37 ¿Qué habría hecho yo? | |

Hablar

Habla con un(a) compañero(a) de lo que habrías hecho si hubieran pasado las siguientes cosas. Usen la información para hacer la pregunta *¿Qué habrías hecho si . . .?* y contéstenla.

▶ Modelo

mudarse nuevos vecinos a tu barrio
A —*¿Qué habrías hecho si se hubieran mudado nuevos vecinos a tu barrio?*
B —*Yo habría ido a conocerlos.*

1. (no) ir de vacaciones
2. perder mucho dinero
3. ocurrir un accidente en la calle
4. invitarte a ir a una fiesta
5. detenerte la policía
6. desaparecer tu coche
7. enterarte de un crimen
8. ignorarte tus amigos

▼38 Cómo me habría gustado |

Hablar • Escribir

❶ ¿Qué habrías hecho para mejorar la vida de los jóvenes de tu país y del mundo en el siglo XX? Trabaja con otro(a) estudiante para hacer una lista. Habla de los siguientes temas:
• la escuela
• la comunidad
• los países pobres
• el gobierno

Modelo
Yo habría quitado el código de vestimenta para dar más libertad a los estudiantes.

❷ Ahora, cada pareja debe presentar sus ideas a la clase. La clase debe hacer comentarios y preguntas sobre las ideas.

DIFFERENTIATED INSTRUCTION

Students with Learning Difficulties

Use English and basic physical demonstrations to point out to students the cause-and-effect nature of situations that require the conditional perfect. For example, drop a piece of chalk and say, "The chalk broke. Why? Because I dropped it. If I hadn't dropped the chalk, it wouldn't have broken."

Advanced Learners/Pre-AP*

Invite students to talk about how things would have turned out differently if certain events had or had not happened in the past. Encourage them to mention world as well as local events: *Si no hubieran inventado el Internet, yo no me habría comunicado tanto con mi tía de España.*

▼39 En otro país |

Escribir • Hablar

❶ Imagina cómo habría sido tu vida si hubieras nacido en otro país. Piensa en un país que te interese. Investiga cómo vive la gente en ese lugar. Escribe un párrafo describiendo cómo habría sido tu vida en ese país.

Modelo
Si yo hubiera nacido en España, habría hablado español. Me habría gustado la comida con pescado y mariscos, así como . . .

❷ Trabaja con otro(a) estudiante. Lean los párrafos que escribieron y digan por qué eligieron ese lugar. Añadan detalles de ese país, como el clima, los lugares que pueden visitar, la comida, el idioma y la música.

Madrid, España

▼40 Por los derechos | de los animales

Leer • Escribir • Hablar

❶ Lee el siguiente folleto que se repartió en una manifestación en España a favor de los derechos de los animales.

❷ Responde a las siguientes preguntas sobre el folleto.

1. Según el folleto, ¿cuál es la situación de los perros en España? ¿Cómo ayudan los suizos?

2. ¿Cuál habría sido tu reacción si hubieras recibido este folleto?

3. ¿Qué opinas sobre los derechos de los animales? ¿Piensas que todos los animales deben gozar de los mismos derechos? ¿Por qué?

❸ En grupo, comparen sus respuestas a las preguntas anteriores. Piensen qué otras cosas se podrían hacer para proteger a los animales. Hagan un folleto para proponer sus ideas y explicar por qué la gente debe cuidar a los animales.

> ### Situación de los perros en España
>
> Estoy obligado a escribir esto, después de toda la información que he recibido sobre el maltrato que dan a muchos animales en España. Ahora vivo en Zurich (Suiza), y me sorprende que la gente de este país tenga que solucionar nuestros problemas. Cada semana, llegan perros de España que son salvados de su sacrificio o rescatados de alguna otra situación difícil.
>
> Por favor, firmen esta petición de apoyo.
>
> Amante de los animales 🐾

Más práctica GO

realidades.com | print

Instant Check	✔	
Guided WB pp. 325–326	✔	✔
Core WB pp. 143–144	✔	✔
Comm. WB pp. 137, 144–145	✔	✔
Hispanohablantes WB pp. 320–321		✔

Practice and Communicate 10

▼39 Standards: 1.1, 1.2, 1.3

Focus: Practicing the conditional perfect

Suggestions: In Step 2, encourage students to make suggestions to their partner on what else he or she might have done: *Habrías visitado la ciudad de...; Habrías ido a un concierto de....*

Answers will vary.

▼40 Standards: 1.1, 1.2, 1.3, 2.1

Focus: Practicing new vocabulary and structures via reading and response

Suggestions: Display students' leaflets from Step 3 around the classroom.

Answers will vary.

Pre-AP* Support

- **Learning Objective:** Presentational Writing
- **Activity:** As a variation for *Actividad* 39, ask that students write the paragraph describing how their life would have been if they had been born in another time. However, do not include the time period referenced. Then, have students read their paragraph to a partner and allow the partner to guess the time period.
- **Pre-AP* Resource Book:** Comprehensive guide to Pre-AP* communication development, pp. 27–38, 39–50

Additional Resources

- Communication Wbk.: Act. 4–5, p. 137
- Teacher's Resource Book: Audio Script, pp. 303–304, Communicative Pair Activity BLM, pp. 313–314
- Audio Program DVD: Cap. 10, Tracks 17–18

✔ ASSESSMENT

Prueba 10-8 with Study Plan (online only)

Prueba: El condicional perfecto
- Prueba 10-8: pp. 229

Examen: Vocabulario y gramática 2
- Examen 2: pp. 230–232
- ExamView: Examen 2

ENRICH YOUR TEACHING

Culture Note
The notion of animal rights has been gaining popularity. Animal rights groups in Spanish-speaking countries include *Alternativa de la Liberación Animal* in Spain, *Ánima* and *Asociación para la Defensa de los Derechos del Animal* in Argentina, and Mexico's *Conservación de Mamíferos Marinos de México.*

21st Century Skills

Critical Thinking and Problem Solving Have students write a blog about animal rights in this country. Have students complete the phrase, *Los animales tienen el derecho a:* or *Los animales no tienen derecho a:* with their list of action items. Have them use vocabulary from this chapter and apply it to animals. Have students take sides and see which side has a stronger argument.

461

Puente a la cultura

Core Instruction

Standards: 1.1, 1.2, 2.1, 2.2, 3.1, 4.1

Focus: Reading to learn about heroes of Latin American independence

Suggestions:

Pre-reading: Refer students to *Estrategia*. Then, based on a brief survey of the selection's main title, subtitles, pictures, and captions, ask: *Si vamos a crear una línea cronológica, ¿de qué se tratará: la historia social y política en América Latina o el desarrollo de las artes en América Latina?* (la historia social y política en América Latina)

Reading: Encourage students to read through the entire passage once silently, without stopping at problem words or to ask questions. Then, for the second time through, ask volunteers to read sections aloud. Remind students to use background knowledge, cognates, and context clues to help them understand unfamiliar words and expressions as they read.

Post-reading: Ask students to paraphrase the main accomplishments of each of the three heroes mentioned in the reading.

Country Connection

Core Instruction

Standards: 3.1

Resources: Map Transparency 17

🌐 **Mapa global interactivo, Actividad 1**

Look at the countries liberated by Simón Bolívar, José Martí, and Miguel Hidalgo.

Venezuela's large size and latitudinal location result in a variety of topographies and climates. The country has four main climactic zones, all of which fall under the main category of "tropical." These include rain forest (a large part of the Amazon) in the south, savannah in the center and northwest, semi-arid tropical regions along the coasts, and highlands. The different areas—some of them huge—as well as the difficulty of overland travel, have given rise to many different indigenous cultures throughout the country. These, along with strong Spanish and African influences, are what create Venezuela's incredibly rich blend of dialects, foods, music, and folklore.

¡Adelante!

Puente a la cultura 🌐

Héroes de América Latina

Estrategia

Creating a timeline
Graphic aids are always useful to show data in a visual way. *Timelines* are graphic aids used to organize data in chronological order. Use them when you have historical information to organize and compare.

Durante la época colonial, España dominaba un territorio desde California hasta el Cabo de Hornos, al extremo sur de Sudamérica. Este territorio tenía aproximadamente 17 millones de habitantes y estaba dividido en cuatro virreinatos, o unidades políticas. Los representantes de la Corona[1] española controlaban no sólo la política en las colonias sino también los impuestos[2], el comercio, y así la vida de los habitantes.

Simón Bolívar

Los habitantes de las colonias en América criticaban a España por su gran poder, pero en 1808, la monarquía española tuvo una crisis. Al sentir que la monarquía estaba débil, los criollos, o hijos de españoles nacidos en América, se rebelaron contra la Corona, iniciando así un movimiento de independencia en las colonias. Este movimiento resultó en la independencia de los países de América Latina.

Aquí hablamos de tres de los héroes de este movimiento. Aunque la historia de cada uno es my diferente, sus sueños de crear naciones independientes en América son muy similares.

Simón Bolívar: El Libertador de América

Simón Bolívar (1783–1830) nació en Caracas, Venezuela. Su sueño era liberar las colonias españolas y unirlas en una gran patria[3]. Casi lo logró en 1819 cuando, después de muchos éxitos militares, creó la República de la Gran Colombia y fue su presidente. La Gran Colombia incluía los territorios que hoy forman Colombia, Venezuela, Panamá y Ecuador. Hacia 1826, Bolívar ya era también jefe supremo del Perú y presidente de Bolivia. Pero Bolívar murió sin realizar su sueño. Nunca pudo unir las repúblicas hispanoamericanas ya que había divisiones entre ellas. Bolivia se independizó en 1825 y Venezuela se separó de Colombia.

---

1 (Spanish) crown 2 taxes 3 homeland

DIFFERENTIATED INSTRUCTION

Students with Learning Difficulties

Help students focus on the theme of national heroes by asking them to talk briefly about heroes they know of from United States history. Connect this to the reading by saying: *En América Latina también hay héroes. Ellos lucharon por la independencia de sus países. Esta lectura se trata de ellos.*

Advanced Learners

Ask students to do further research on one of the figures from the selection, or on another of their choice from Latin American history, such as José de San Martín.

José Martí: El apóstol de la independencia cubana

Además de gran poeta e intelectual, José Martí (1853–1895) es el héroe nacional y el apóstol de la independencia de Cuba. Desde los dieciséis años, ya participaba en la vida política y estuvo en prisión por haber escrito en publicaciones contra las autoridades coloniales españolas. Lo deportaron a España y de allí, fue a Nueva York, donde escribió la mayoría de sus obras. Luego, fundó el Partido Revolucionario Cubano en 1892. Regresó a Cuba cuando comenzó la guerra por la independencia en 1895 y murió en una batalla.

Miguel Hidalgo: El precursor de la independencia de México

Miguel Hidalgo se destaca en la historia de México como uno de los precursores de la independencia de ese país. Muchos lo criticaron porque era miembro del clero y tenía ideas revolucionarias. En 1810, durante un sermón, llamó al pueblo a luchar. Miles de indígenas que habían sufrido largos años de maltrato y explotación, decidieron seguirlo junto con los criollos. Miguel Hidalgo y su representante, el general Allende, organizaron el movimiento que llevó a la independencia en 1821.

José Martí

Miguel Hidalgo

¿Comprendiste?

1. ¿En qué siglo se iniciaron los movimientos de independencia de las naciones hispanohablantes de América y cuáles fueron sus causas?

2. ¿Qué tienen en común los héroes del artículo? Da dos ejemplos.

3. Menciona dos héroes de otros países y di quiénes eran y qué hicieron.

4. Compara el movimiento de independencia de los Estados Unidos con el de las naciones hispanohablantes. Di cuáles son sus semejanzas y diferencias.

Cronología de la independencia latinoamericana

Copia la línea cronológica y complétala con la información del texto que leíste.

1808	1810	1819	1821	1825	1826	1895
____	Movimiento de independencia de México	____	____	Independencia de Bolivia	____	____

Más práctica	**GO**

realidades.com | print

▶ *Videodocumentario*	✔	
Guided WB p. 327	✔	✔
Comm. WB pp. 146–147	✔	✔
Hispanohablantes **WB** pp. 322–324	✔	
Cultural Reading Activity	✔	

cuatrocientos sesenta y tres **463**
Capítulo 10

▼ **¿Comprendiste?** Standards: 1.1, 1.2, 1.3, 2.1, 2.2, 3.1, 4.2

Resources: Answer Keys: Student Edition, p. 148

Focus: Demonstrating reading comprehension

Suggestions: Before discussing, have students write the answers on their own.

Answers:
1. Se iniciaron en el siglo XIX.
2. La causa de Bolívar era unir a las colonias en una gran patria. La de Martí era la independencia de Cuba. Hidalgo luchaba contra la esclavitud y por los derechos de los indígenas.
3. Answers will vary.

▼ **Cronología de la independencia latinoamericana** Standards: 1.2, 1.3

Resources: Answer Keys: Student Edition, p. 148

Focus: Demonstrating reading comprehension

Suggestions: Have students complete their time lines together in pairs or groups.

Answers will vary, but should include:
1808: Rebelión de los criollos latinoamericanos
1819: Creación de la República de la Gran Colombia por Bolívar
1821: Organización del movimiento independentista mexicano
1826: Bolívar: jefe supremo en Perú, presidente en Bolivia
1895: Muere José Martí

Portfolio

Keep students' responses and their time lines in their portfolios as writing samples.

▶ Videodocumentario

Core Instruction

Standards: 1.2

Resources: Teacher's Resource Book: Video Script, p. 306; Video Program: Cap. 10

View *Gran trabajo para la comunidad* to learn about a political organization for the Spanish-speaking community. Access the video online in **realidades.com** or use the DVD. See the *Video Teacher's Guide* for additional suggestions.

Additional Resources

Student Resource: Realidades para hispanohablantes, pp. 322–324; Guided Practice Activities, p. 327; Communication Wbk., pp. 146–147

463

ENRICH YOUR TEACHING

Culture Note
José Martí was unwelcome in many countries because of his political outspokenness. He had a variety of jobs, including editor, journalist, and foreign correspondent for several magazines. He even worked as a Spanish teacher at New York's Central High School. The popular song *Guantanamera* is based on Martí's poetry.

21st Century Skills

Critical Thinking and Problem Solving To expand on their knowledge of Latin American independence movements, have student research the role played by women such as Manuela Sáenz or Mariana Bracetti in these struggles. Have students compare them to female figures in their own culture who have played similar historical roles.

¿Qué me cuentas?

Core Instruction

Standards: 1.1, 1.2, 1.3

Resources: Teacher's Resource Book: Audio Script, p. 304; Audio Program DVD: Cap. 10, Track 19; Answer Keys: Student Edition, p. 149

Focus: Practicing listening and reading comprehension of new vocabulary and grammar; using information to write a cohesive and coherent reaction.

AP* Skills: Integration of listening, reading, and writing to comprehend and synthesize information from spoken and written sources.

Suggestions: For Step 1, use the audio or read the script aloud. Allow students to hear it twice through: the first time to write their answers, the second time to check them.

For Step 2, have students identify significant details as they read and then summarize the main points of the article.

Encourage students to express their own opinions and to cite specific information from Steps 1 and 2 in their written responses for Step 3.

Answers:

Step1

1. b   2. a   3. b   4. a   5. c   6. c

Steps 2–3

Answers will vary.

Additional Resources

Student Resource: Realidades para hispanohablantes, p. 325

▼ Objectives

▶ Listen to and read about the legal system in Mexico
▶ Compare the old and new Mexican legal systems with the current legal system in the U.S.

Integración

¿Qué me cuentas?: Justicia para todos

Compara el sistema legal de México con el sistema de los Estados Unidos. Primero escucha la conversación. Anota las respuestas a las preguntas y guárdalas para usarlas en el paso 3.

1 Escucha el siguiente diálogo entre Sergio y su padre. Después de cada sección del diálogo vas a oír tres preguntas. Escoge la mejor respuesta para cada pregunta.

1. a. a una propuesta   b. a un juicio   c. a un castigo
2. a. un jurado, un   b. una secretaria y   c. un representante del estado
      juez y testigos   dos policías
3. a. un libro   b. un video   c. una obra de teatro
4. a. gozarían de igualdad   b. todos serían culpables   c. no podría haber testigos
5. a. el juez   b. el abogado   c. el estado
6. a. es interesante   b. es entretenido   c. es muy necesario

2 Ahora lee sobre el sistema legal de México.

México Hoy   17 de junio

Reforma del sistema de los juicios legales

México, D.F. — El presidente Felipe Calderón firmó un cambio a la constitución de México. Es un cambio legal que tardó muchos años en hacerse realidad. Con este cambio los acusados de un crimen en México serán inocentes frente a la justicia hasta que se compruebe que son culpables en un juicio legal. También los juicios seguirán un procedimiento oral. Anteriormente habían seguido un procedimiento escrito en el que el juez leía las evidencias escritas sobre el caso a puertas cerradas sin la presencia del acusado y del público. Un caso legal de forma escrita se tardaba hasta 6 a 8 meses. Con la reforma, el juez escuchará el caso legal delante del acusado, los abogados y el público. De esta manera, la duración de un caso se reducirá a sólo 2 o 3 meses.

Con la reforma, más gente llegará a los edificios de las cortes como éste en Guadalajara, México.

3 En parejas, comparen el sistema legal antiguo de México con el sistema nuevo. Luego, conversen sobre cuál de los dos sistemas se parece más al sistema estadounidense que describen Sergio y su padre. Consideren estas preguntas: ¿Creen que una persona acusada bajo el sistema antiguo de México hubiera sido considerada culpable o inocente antes del juicio? ¿Y ahora? ¿Qué sistema trata mejor a los acusados y asegura sus derechos? ¿Qué ventajas y desventajas habrían en un juicio escrito y cerrado? ¿Y en un juicio abierto? Usen las siguientes expresiones para conectar sus ideas.

| cuando | con tal que | antes de |
| mientras | aunque | después de |

DIFFERENTIATED INSTRUCTION

Students with Learning Difficulties

For the *Presentación* oral, allow students the option of describing rules and regulations your school already has.

Students with Special Needs

Make a recording of the article in Step 2 of *¿Qué me cuentas?* for visually impaired students. They can then perform the task on their own, including for homework.

Presentación oral 🗨

Los derechos de los estudiantes

Objectives
▶ Demonstrate how to present new rules and rights for your school
▶ Make a plan to improve your performance

Tarea
El director de la escuela ha decidido que los estudiantes propongan qué reglas y derechos les gustaría tener en su escuela. Prepara un discurso para presentar tu propuesta.

❶ Prepárate Completa una tabla como la siguiente con las reglas y los derechos que quieres proponer.

Reglas de la escuela	Derechos de los estudiantes

> **Estrategia**
>
> **Think, plan, then speak**
> Before proposing a list of rules, think about what you're going to include. Make a plan and use a table or graphic to organize your thoughts. Then, speak using the information that you have gathered.

❷ Practica Vuelve a leer la información que anotaste en la tabla. Practica varias veces tu discurso. Presenta razones por las que crees que estos derechos y reglas son beneficiosos. Usa tus notas para practicar, pero no al hablar ante la clase. Recuerda:

- explicar cada regla y derecho en forma clara y persuasiva
- presentar las razones por las que serían beneficiosos
- mirar directamente al público y hablar con voz clara

Modelo
Los estudiantes deberíamos tener derecho a vacaciones más largas. Si hubiéramos tenido antes más tiempo para relajarnos, habríamos aprendido más y mejor. También la escuela debería tener derecho a exigir que . . .

❸ Haz tu presentación Imagina que tus compañeros son los que van a analizar las reglas y los derechos que propongas. Debes convencerlos de que tu propuesta beneficiará tanto a los estudiantes como a los profesores.

❹ Evaluación Tu profesor(a) utilizará la siguiente rúbrica para evaluar tu presentación.

Rubric	Score 1	Score 3	Score 5
How well you use organizers	Your speech includes no organizers.	You use one or more organizers, but they contain little useful information.	You use organizers effectively to plan your speech.
How convincing you are	You miss important arguments. Your arguments are weak.	You present some convincing arguments.	You present convincing arguments.
How effectively you deliver your speech	You read your speech and make no eye contact with your audience.	You make some eye contact, and you use some intonation.	Your eye contact is good. Your intonation helps get your message across.

cuatrocientos sesenta y cinco **465**
Capítulo 10

Presentación oral

Core Instruction
Standards: 1.2, 1.3, 3.1

Resources: Voc. and Gram. Transparency 4

Focus: Preparing and delivering an oral presentation

Suggestions: Review the task and the four-step approach with students. Review the rubric with the class (see *Assessment* below) to explain how you will grade the performance task. Before students begin, direct their attention to the *Estrategia*. Show *Vocabulary and Grammar Transparency* 4 and have students create a similar word chart on their own paper. Model how to include in the chart an idea or two for proposed student rules and rights. Encourage them to use other graphic organizers as well, such as concept webs, that they may find beneficial in developing their speeches. Remind them that they will submit and be evaluated on their use of one or more organizers.

Pre-AP* Support

- **Learning Objective:** Presentational Speaking
- *Pre-AP* Resource Book:* Comprehensive guide to Pre-AP* speaking skill development, pp. 39–50

Portfolio
Make video or audio recordings of student presentations in class, or assign the RealTalk activity so they can record their presentations online. Include the recording in their portfolios.

Additional Resources
Student Resource: Realidades para hispanohablantes, p. 326

✓ASSESSMENT

Presentación oral
- Assessment Program: Rubrics, p. T34
  Review the rubric with students. Go over the descriptions of the different levels of performance. After assessing students, help individuals understand how their performance could be improved. (See Teacher's Resource Book for suggestions on using rubrics in assessment.)

ENRICH YOUR TEACHING

21st Century Skills

Communication As a warm-up to the *Presentación oral,* have students brainstorm a list of expressions in Spanish that they would use when proposing new school rules and advocating student rights. What expressions can be used to convince or persuade the audience to agree? Have students list the verbs they would use, then conjugate them in the conditional.

Language Arts Connection: Expository Writing

Standards: 3.1

Encourage students to draw on background knowledge they have from their Language Arts courses about introductions used in writing. Remind them that an effective introduction provides readers with a context for what is to follow—a kind of mental "shelf" on which to place the information they will read. Without an effective introduction, an essay is bound to quickly lose readers' attention.

 Common Core: Writing

Presentación escrita

Core Instruction

Standards: 1.2, 1.3, 3.1

Resources: Voc. and Gram. Transparency 4

Focus: Combining learned vocabulary and structures in a written presentation

Suggestions: Begin by explaining the criteria you will use to evaluate students' compositions. (See Step 5, *Evaluación,* in the Student Edition, and *Assessment* on the following page.)

Direct students' attention to the *Estrategia.* Suggest than another idea for a snappy introduction for this particular essay might be to include an interesting comment from one of the people interviewed. Such a comment should catch readers' attention and give an idea of what the subject of the essay will be. Then show *Voc. and Gram. Transparency* 4. Model filling in part of a column with information like that shown in the chart on this page. Have students begin a similar columnar chart on their own paper. Tell them to use one column for the responses of each person that they interview, and to interview at least two people.

Pre-AP* Support

- **Learning Objective:** Presentational Writing
- **Pre-AP* Resource Book:** Comprehensive guide to Pre-AP* writing skill development, pp. 27–38

| ▼ Objectives

▶ Write an editorial essay for a newspaper
▶ Present other people's opinions about a subject
▶ Use an interesting fact to capture the audience's attention

Presentación escrita

¿Cuáles son sus derechos?

Estrategia

Snappy introductions
An interesting introduction will get your reader involved in your essay immediately. One good way to begin is to ask a question to pique his or her curiosity. Another way to hook your reader is to start with an interesting fact or incident related to your story.

Entrevista a: Ingrid Ramírez

1. ciudadana de los Estados Unidos
2. maestra en Nueva York
3. derecho a la libertad de expresión, libertad de prensa, libertad de religión
4. "Trabajo, me expreso y viajo libremente; tengo la religión que quiero".
5. muy buena situación con respecto a otros países

Entrevista a: Jorge Ríos

1. ciudadano de los Estados Unidos
2. mecánico en Miami
3. derecho a la libertad de decir lo que uno quiere
4. "Puedo tener una vida cómoda, trabajar y viajar".
5. mejor situación que en otros países

Eres reportero(a) y tienes que hacer un ensayo editorial sobre lo que saben los ciudadanos de los Estados Unidos acerca de los derechos y las garantías que tienen según la Constitución. Puedes entrevistar *(interview)* a personas de diferentes edades y usar sus respuestas en tu ensayo.

1 Antes de escribir

Usa estas preguntas en tus entrevistas. Escrib las respuestas en una tabla como la del model

1. ¿Es ciudadano(a) de los Estados Unidos?
2. ¿A qué se dedica?
3. ¿Sabe qué derechos y garantías tiene?
4. ¿Cómo usa usted sus libertades?
5. ¿Cómo compara su situación en este país co respecto a otros países?

2 Borrador

Escribe tu borrador. Presenta las opiniones de las personas entrevistadas. Añade todos los detalles necesarios. Recuerda usar el vocabulario y la gramática de este capítulo.

Modelo

Snappy introduction uses a question to get the readers' attention
→ Nuestra Constitución determina los derechos y las garantías que tienen los ciudadanos de este país. Pero, ¿sabe realmente la gente de qué tratan esos derechos y garantías? La mayoría de nosotros vivimos sin preguntarnos qué habría sido de nuestra vida si no se hubieran creado los derechos de los ciudadanos . . .

Examples of how people think about the topic
→ Por ejemplo Ingrid, una maestra de Nueva York, dice que goza de sus libertades ya que trabaja, se expresa y viaja libremente . . .

Conclusion ties everything together
→ Al igual que Ingrid, muchas personas que hubieran vivido en este país en las últimas décadas, habrían . . .

DIFFERENTIATED INSTRUCTION

Students with Learning Difficulties

Suggest that students interview their Social Studies teachers for the *Presentación escrita.* If possible, meet with the teachers beforehand and tell them what type of research students are doing, so that they can provide guidance to students during the interviews.

Advanced Learners

Have students prepare and present orally their own Spanish paraphrases of the ten amendments to the United States Constitution in the Bill of Rights.

3 Redacción/Revisión

Después de escribir el primer borrador, trabaja con otro(a) compañero(a) para intercambiar los trabajos y leerlos. Decidan qué aspectos son más interesantes. Luego, hagan sugerencias para mejorar sus composiciones y corregir los errores.

• ¿Se usó correctamente el pluscuamperfecto del subjuntivo y el condicional perfecto?

• ¿Existen errores de ortografía?

> mayoría
> La ~~mayorías~~ de nosotros vivimos sin
>   habría
> preguntarnos qué ~~habrían~~ sido de nuestra
>   hubieran
> vida si no se ~~hubiera~~ creado los derechos
> de los ciudadanos . . .

4 Publicación

Antes de hacer la versión final, lee de nuevo tu borrador y repasa los siguientes puntos:

• ¿Presenta el ensayo una idea clara sobre el tema?

• ¿Incluí opiniones de otras personas para explicar el tema?

• ¿Muestra el ensayo la importancia del tema?

• ¿Presenta una conclusión interesante?

Después de revisar el borrador, escribe una copia en limpio de tu composición.

5 Evaluación

Se utilizará la siguiente rúbrica para evaluar tu presentación.

Rubric	Score 1	Score 3	Score 5
Completion of task	Important parts of your essay are missing.	Information in your essay is disorganized and hard to follow.	You include and organize all the parts needed for an effective essay.
Effective introduction	Your essay lacks an introduction.	You attempt an introduction, but it is not effective.	Your introduction is effective, attracting and orienting readers.
Grammar, spelling, mechanics	You make many errors in grammar, spelling, and punctuation.	You make some errors in grammar, spelling, and punctuation.	You make very few errors in grammar, spelling, and punctuation.

Writing 10

Suggestions (Cont'd):

For Step 1, encourage students to interview at least one Spanish-speaking person, if possible. Help them agree upon effective English translations of the five interview questions to use when interviewing people in English. Remind them that they must convert the information gained in English interviews to Spanish.

In Step 2, students should concentrate on developing the information they obtained in their interviews into a rough draft. This is also the step in which they should focus on an effective introduction for their essay. Encourage them to work toward organization, level of detail, and language use similar to that shown in the model.

For Step 3, encourage students to experiment with various ways of combining sentences. Suggest that they use the pluperfect subjunctive and the conditional perfect at least once by mentioning how some aspect of United States society would have developed differently without the rights guaranteed by the Constitution and the Bill of Rights.

Evaluation

Steps 4 and 5 overlap. Students will need evaluation by you, their peers, or self-evaluation to fine-tune and polish their drafts.

Portfolio

Keep students' final drafts in their portfolios as a writing sample.

Additional Resources

Student Resource: Realidades para hispanohablantes, p. 327

ENRICH YOUR TEACHING

21st Century Skills

Flexibility and Adaptability Students will use their written language for the purpose of writing an editorial essay. For this, they will need to play several roles; first they will gather information as they interview people about their opinions on their Constitutional rights, then they will present these opinions in an editorial essay and provide their own conclusion. Remind students that they will need to adapt to these different roles in the project.

✓ ASSESSMENT

Presentación escrita
• Assessment Program: Rubrics, p. T35
Review the rubric with students. Go over the descriptions of the different levels of performance. After assessing students, help individuals understand how their performance could be improved. (See Teacher's Resource Book for suggestions on using rubrics in assessment.)

© Common Core: Reading

Lectura

Core Instruction

Standards: 1.2, 2.1, 3.1, 3.2, 5.2

Resources: Voc. and Gram. Transparency 4

Focus: Reading an extended passage

Suggestions:

Pre-reading: Before reading, direct students' attention to the *Estrategia* and *Al leer* sections. Have them copy the T-chart on p. 471 to their own paper and make sure they understand how they will use it. Explain that, since this reading is based on an oral account, the language used is more informal than in other readings. Point out as examples of this the use of **Bueno** at the outset of the reading and the frequent use of informal and creative diminutives, such as **otrita** and **cajoncito** in the first paragraph. Ask students to pay attention to other examples of informal language as they read.

Reading: When reading together with students, pause frequently to address comprehension issues they may have and to allow them to fill in their charts from p. 471. Here are some suggestions for providing comprehension guidance on this page:

• Ask: *¿En qué año empieza la historia?* (1954)

• Ask: *En tus propias palabras, describe qué verías si la joven Domitila y sus hermanas te pasaran en la calle delante de la escuela.*

Country Connection

Core Instruction

Standards: 3.1

Resources: Map Transparency 17

🌐 **Mapa global interactivo, Actividad 2**

Travel to the mountains of Bolivia.

Suggestions: After students have read the *Al leer* section, show *Map Transparency 17* and ask a volunteer to point out Bolivia. Explain to students that historically mining was the most important attraction that the country held for Europeans. At the end of the sixteenth century, for example, the city of Potosí was the largest urban center in South America, due to its surrounding silver mines. Those mines are now depleted.

468

Lectura

Si me permiten hablar . . .
Testimonio de Domitila Barrios, por Moema Viezzer
(Fragmento)

▸ Read and understand an autobiographical account
▸ Understand the author's reasons for writing the selection
▸ Read about a Bolivian social activist and give your opinion about social rights movements

Estrategia

Investigate the author's reasons

Authors must decide which materials are most appropriate for describing the events they want to include in the narration of their experiences. The setting, the selection of special memories and how they affected the author's life, the use of particular details to describe feelings and personal opinions and the inclusion of anecdotes to liven up the narration will give you clues to the author's reasons for writing.

Al leer

Este fragmento es parte de una historia oral basada en las experiencias de Domitila Barrios de Chungara en las minas de cobre *(copper mines)* de Bolivia que fue recogida y escrita por Moema Viezzer. En este fragmento, Domitila cuenta cómo tenía que luchar para quedarse en la escuela y continuar su educación. Su testimonio revela a una joven cuyo coraje y determinación lograron vencer los obstáculos y prejuicios que formaban parte de la vida diaria de las mujeres en los pueblos mineros. Mientras lees este relato, presta atención a los siguientes puntos y luego completa la tabla que aparece en la página 471 con la siguiente información:

• el ambiente de pobreza en el hogar de la protagonista
• los errores que cometió y cómo logró superarlos
• los obstáculos que tuvo que enfrentar
• la actitud del padre de Domitila

Bueno, en el 54 me fue difícil regresar a la escuela después de las vacaciones, porque nosotros teníamos una vivienda que consistía en una pieza pequeñita donde no teníamos patio y no teníamos dónde ni con quiénes dejar a las wawas[1]. Entonces consultamos al director de la escuela y él dio permiso para llevar a mis hermanitas conmigo. El estudio se hacía por las tardes y por las mañanas. Yo tenía que combinar todo: casa y escuela. Entonces yo llevaba a la más chiquita cargada y a la otra agarrada de la mano y Marina llevaba las mamaderas[2] y las mantillas[3] y mi hermana la otrita llevaba los cuadernos. Y así todas nos íbamos a la escuela. En un rincón teníamos un cajoncito donde dejábamos a la más chiquita mientras seguíamos estudiando. Salía de la escuela, tenía que cargarme la niñita, nos íbamos a la casa y tenía yo que cocinar, lavar, planchar, atender a las wawas. Me parecía muy difícil todo eso. ¡Yo deseaba tanto jugar! Y tantas otras cosas deseaba, como cualquier niña.

Dos años después, ya la profesora no me dejó llevar a mis hermanitas porque ya metían bulla[4]. Mi padre no podía pagar a una sirvienta, pues no le alcanzaba su sueldo ni para la comida y la ropa de nosotras. En la casa, por ejemplo, yo andaba siempre descalza, usando los zapatos solamente para ir a la escuela.

---

1 small children **2** baby bottles **3** swaddling clothes **4** made noise

468 cuatrocientos sesenta y ocho
¡Adelante!

DIFFERENTIATED INSTRUCTION

Heritage Language Learners

When the class reads the Bolivian slang term **wawas,** ask students to mention other slang terms for children that they may know. They may wish to comment on other elements of Domitila Barrios' informal style of narration, as well.

Students with Learning Difficulties

Write a paragraph-by-paragraph paraphrase of the reading selection for students, using language suitable to their level. Consider jigsawing this task and assigning paragraphs or sections to interested Advanced Learners.

Bueno, como la profesora me había dado aquella orden, entonces yo empecé a irme sola a la escuela. Echaba llave a la casa y tenían que quedarse las wawas en la calle, porque la vivienda era oscura, no tenía ventana y les daba mucho terror cuando se la cerraba. Era como una cárcel[5], solamente con una puerta. Y no había dónde dejar a las chicas, porque en ese entonces vivíamos en un barrio de solteros, donde no había familias, puros hombres vivían allí.

Entonces mi padre me dijo que dejara la escuela, porque ya sabía leer y leyendo podía aprender otras cosas. Pero yo no acepté y me puse fuerte[6] y seguí yendo a la escuela.

Mi padre gestionó[7] en la empresa minera de Pulacayo para que le diera una vivienda con patiecito, porque era muy difícil vivir donde estábamos. Y el gerente, a quien mi papá le arreglaba sus trajes, ordenó que le diera una vivienda más grande con un cuarto, una cocina y un corredorcito donde se podía dejar a las chicas.

Sufríamos hambre a veces y no nos satisfacían los alimentos porque era poco lo que podía comprar mi papá. Ha sido duro vivir con privaciones y toda clase de problemas cuando pequeñas. Pero eso desarrolló algo en nosotras: una gran sensibilidad, un gran deseo de ayudar a toda la gente. Nuestros juegos de niños siempre tenían algo relacionado con lo que vivíamos y con lo que deseábamos vivir. Además, en el transcurso de nuestra infancia habíamos visto eso: mi madre y mi padre, a pesar de que teníamos tan poco, siempre estaban ayudando a algunas familias de Pulacayo. Entonces, cuando veíamos pobres por la calle mendigando[8], yo y mis hermanas nos poníamos a soñar. Y soñábamos que un día íbamos a ser grandes, que íbamos a tener tierras, que íbamos a sembrar y que a aquellos pobres les íbamos a dar de comer.

Y bueno, así era nuestra vida. Yo tenía entonces 13 años. Mi padre siempre insistía en que no debía seguir en la escuela. Pero yo le iba rogando[9], rogando y seguía yendo. Claro, siempre me faltaba material escolar[10]. Entonces, algunos maestros me comprendían, otros no.

---

5 jail **6** got stubborn **7** negotiated **8** begging
9 pleading **10** school supplies

Suggestions (Cont'd):

Reading: Here are some suggestions for providing comprehension guidance on this page:
• After reading the first paragraph ask: *¿Qué expresión significa que Domitila cerraba la puerta de la casa con llave?* (Echaba llave a la casa.)
• After reading the third paragraph, say: *Recuerda que el padre de Domitila era sastre* (tailor). *¿Cómo le ayudó a su padre influir al gerente de la mina?* (El padre podía influir al gerente porque le arreglaba sus trajes.)
• After reading the fourth paragraph, ask: *¿Qué expresión significa "durante nuestra infancia"?* (en el transcurso de nuestra infancia)

cuatrocientos sesenta y nueve **469**
Capítulo 10

ENRICH YOUR TEACHING

Culture Note

Bolivia offers many attractions for tourists. There is the capital La Paz, with all its record-breaking statistics, including world's highest large city, world's highest capital, and world's highest major airport. Even higher in the Andes is **el lago Titicaca,** the highest lake in the world and one of the earliest centers of human population in South America. One of the reasons for this is because its waters cause local temperatures to be more moderate, allowing for cultivation of wheat and maize at much higher altitudes than usual. But Bolivia isn't all mountainous. It also contains part of the Amazon rainforest, an area called Beni, which is about the size of the United Kingdom.

Suggestions (Cont'd):

Reading: Here are some suggestions for providing comprehension guidance on this page:

• After reading the second paragraph, write on the board in English:

A. "In the sixth grade I had a great teacher who knew how to understand me."

B. "In the sixth grade I had a great teacher who learned how to understand me."

Then ask: *¿Cuál es la mejor traducción de la primera frase de este párrafo, A o B? ¿Por qué? (B. El pretérito de saber quiere decir "learned.")*

• After reading the first column, ask: *¿Qué significa la expresión "a la salida": "en la puerta del aula" o "después de la clase"? (después de la clase)*

• After reading the second column, ask: *¿Creían los vecinos de Domitila en educar a las niñas? (No. Creían que no se debe eseñar a leer a las mujeres.)*

• *¿Tenía Domitila un hermano? ¿Qué parte del texto te lo dice? (No tenía hermano. "cinco mujeres, ningún varón")*

Post-reading: When students finish reading, ask: *¿Qué inferencia podemos hacer al fin de la historia? ¿Qué decidió hacer el maestro de Domitila? (Parece que decidió darle a Domitila el material escolar que necesitaba.)* Then ask them to go back and identify other examples of informal language they can find in the reading.

▼ **Interacción con la lectura** Standards: 1.1, 1.2, 1.3

Suggestions: Have students work together to complete their charts in Step 1. Encourage them to help each other paraphrase the pertinent parts of the text.

Answers will vary.

Additional Resources

Student Resource: Guided Practice: Lectura, pp. 328–329

El problema es que habíamos hecho un trato[11] mi papá y yo. Él me había explicado que no tenía dinero, que no me podía comprar material, que no podía dar nada para la escuela. Y de ahí que me arreglaba como podía. Y por eso tenía yo problemas.

En el sexto curso tuve como profesor a un gran maestro que me supo comprender. Era un profesor bastante estricto, y los primeros días que no llevé el material completo, me castigó severamente. Tuve que irme a la casa, llorando. Pero al día siguiente, volví. Y de la ventana miraba lo que estaban haciendo los chicos.

En uno de esos momentos, el profesor me llamó.

—Seguramente no ha traído su material —me dijo. Yo no podía contestar y me puse a llorar.

—Entre. Ya pase, tome su asiento. Y a la salida se ha de quedar usted.

A la salida me quedé y entonces él me dijo:

—Mira, yo quiero ser tu amigo, pero necesito que me digas qué pasa con vos[12]. ¿Es cierto que no tienes tu mamá?

Vista de La Paz, Bolivia

—Sí, profesor.

—¿Cuándo se murió?

—Cuando estaba todavía en el primer curso.

—Y tu padre, ¿dónde trabaja?

—En la policía minera, es sastre[13].

—Bueno, ¿qué es lo que pasa? Mira, yo quiero ayudarte, pero tienes que ser sincera. ¿Qué es lo que pasa?

Yo no quería hablar, porque pensé que iba a llamar a mi padre como algunos profesores lo hacían cuando estaban enojados. Pero el profesor me hizo otras preguntas y entonces le conté todo. También le dije que podía hacer mis tareas, pero que no tenía mis cuadernos, porque éramos bien pobres y mi papá no podía comprar y que, años atrás, ya mi papá me había querido sacar de la escuela porque no podía hacer ese gasto más. Y que con mucho sacrificio y esfuerzo había yo podido llegar hasta el sexto curso. Pero no era que mi papá no quisiera, sino porque no podía, porque, incluso, a pesar de toda la creencia que había en Pulacayo de que a la mujer no se le debía enseñar a leer, mi papá siempre quiso que supiéramos por lo menos eso.

Sí, mi papá siempre se preocupó por nuestra formación[14]. Cuando murió mi mamá, la gente nos miraba y decía: "Ay, pobrecitas, cinco mujeres, ningún varón . . . ¿Para qué sirven? . . . Mejor si se mueren". Pero mi papá muy orgulloso decía: "No, déjenme a mis hijas, ellas van a vivir". Y cuando la gente trataba de acomplejarnos[15] porque éramos mujeres y no servíamos para gran cosa, él nos decía que todas las mujeres tienen los mismos derechos que los hombres. Y decía que nosotras podíamos hacer las hazañas[16] que hacen los hombres. Nos crió siempre con esas ideas. Sí, fue una disciplina muy especial. Y todo eso fue muy positivo para nuestro futuro. Y de ahí que nunca nos consideramos mujeres inútiles.

El profesor comprendía todo esto, porque yo le contaba. E hicimos un trato de que yo le iba a pedir todo el material que necesitaba. Y así pude terminar mi último año escolar.

---

11 deal **12** with you **13** tailor **14** education **15** make us feel bad **16** feats

DIFFERENTIATED INSTRUCTION

Heritage Language Learners
Ask students who have lived in heritage countries to share what they know about student-teacher relations in schools there.

Advanced Learners
Invite students to compare Domitila Barrios Chungara's account with readings from past *Capítulos*. Can they find a similar theme of overcoming obstacles in the other readings? What are the obstacles? How are they overcome?

Interacción con la lectura

① Completa la tabla siguiente para investigar por qué Domitila Barrios de Chungara escribió este relato autobiográfico.

Razones de Domitila	Ejemplos
describir las condiciones en que ella y su familia vivían	vivienda pobre, pasar hambre
analizar sus errores para prevenirlos en el futuro	
explicar su actitud frente a los obstáculos que tenía que enfrentar	
explicar el comportamiento de sus maestros	
explicar el comportamiento de su padre	

② Trabaja con otro(a) compañero(a) para analizar la información de las tablas de cada uno(a). Comenten cuáles son las razones principales que llevaron a Domitila Barrios de Chungara a escribir este relato.

¿Comprendiste?

1. ¿Por qué dice Domitila que le fue difícil regresar a la escuela después de las vacaciones de 1954?

2. Según Domitila, ¿qué aspecto positivo surgió de las privaciones que ella y su familia tuvieron que pasar?

3. ¿Cuál era la actitud del pueblo de Pulacayo hacia las mujeres?

4. ¿Qué piensas de la actitud del padre hacia los derechos de las mujeres?

5. ¿Piensas que Domitila logró superar los obstáculos que tuvo que enfrentar? Explica tu respuesta.

Más práctica GO

realidades.com | print

Guided WB pp. 328–329	✔	✔
Comm. WB pp. 219–220	✔	✔
Cultural Reading Activity	✔	

▼ Fondo Cultural | Bolivia

Domitila Barrios De Chungara (1937–) se crió en Pulacayo, un pueblo minero de Bolivia. Recogió sus memorias de este pueblo en su obra *Si me permiten hablar . . .* Desde muy pequeña, Domitila estaba consciente del sufrimiento de su pueblo. Su ambición era mejorar las condiciones de vida de los campesinos y mineros de Bolivia. En 1952 se casó con un minero y empezó a participar en el Comité de Amas de Casa *(Homemakers)* del Distrito Minero Siglo XXI, y después, fue nombrada su Secretaria General. Su participación en las protestas contra las injusticias del gobierno causó que la encarcelaran *(jailed)*. Después tuvo que exiliarse *(go into exile)* en Europa. A pesar de estas experiencias, Domitila sigue su campaña por los derechos humanos y fue nominada para el Premio Nobel de la Paz en 2005.

- ¿Has participado alguna vez en un movimiento que se dedica a luchar por los derechos de la gente? ¿Qué motivo tuviste para hacerlo? Si no lo has hecho, ¿te gustaría participar en el futuro?

Mujeres mineras protestan en Bolivia.

cuatrocientos setenta y uno **471**
Capítulo 10

ENRICH YOUR TEACHING

471

Review Activities

Sobre tus derechos y responsabilidades/ Sobre los derechos de los ciudadanos/Sobre los derechos de todas las personas: On strips of paper, have students write a phrase or sentence using each word in these three categories. You can divide this task among small groups. Students' phrases or sentences should connote either a right or a responsibility. For example: *que los niños no sufran* or *Gozamos de una prensa libre.* Collect all strips and place them in a container. Have students sit in a circle. They take turns drawing one slip at a time, reading it aloud, and stating whether the phrase or sentence connotes a *derecho* or a *responsabilidad.*

En el hogar: Have students work in pairs and play *hangman* using the words and expressions in this category.

En la escuela: Play charades using the words and expressions in this category. Write them on slips of paper and place them in a container. Students take turns drawing an expression and getting its meaning across to the others any way they can without speaking or writing. Use body language and strategies of traditional charades such as tugging at the ear to mean *suena como* or holding up two fingers to mean *dos palabras*—or invent your own rules.

Otros adjetivos y expresiones: Students can use these words and expressions in the grammar review activities on the next page.

Additional Resources

Student Resources: Realidades para hispanohablantes, pp. 328–329

Teacher Resources:
- Teacher's Resource Book: Situation Cards, p. 315, Clip Art, pp. 316–324
- Assessment Program: Chapter Checklist and Self-Assessment Worksheet, pp. T49–T50

▶ *¡Pura vida!* is a storyline video that is independent of chapter content and an ideal support for expanding listening skills. The 14 episodes are available within **realidades.com** or on a separate DVD. Student activities and Teacher support are also assignable within **realidades.com**.

472

Repaso del capítulo
Vocabulario y gramática

sobre tus derechos y responsabilidades

aplicar (las leyes)	to apply (the law)
discriminado, -a	discriminated
discriminar	to discriminate
funcionar	to function
gozar (de)	to enjoy
maltratar	to mistreat
obligar	to force
sufrir	to suffer
tratar	to treat
votar	to vote

en el hogar

el abuso	abuse
el / la adolescente	adolescent
el apoyo	support
la libertad	liberty
la niñez	childhood
la pobreza	poverty

en la escuela

el armario	locker
la autoridad	authority
el código de vestimenta	dress code
el deber	duty
la enseñanza	teaching
la igualdad	equality
el maltrato	mistreatment
el motivo	cause
el pensamiento	thought
la razón	reason
el respeto	respect

otros adjetivos y expresiones

adecuado, -a	adequate
ambos	both
de ese modo	in that way
en cuanto a	with respect to, as for
estar sujeto(a) a	to be subject to
gratuito, -a	free (no cost)
satisfactorio, -a	satisfactory

sobre los derechos de los ciudadanos

el / la acusado(a)	accused, defendant
asegurar	to assure
el castigo	punishment
la desigualdad	inequality
el desempleo	unemployment
detener	to detain
el estado	the state
la felicidad	happiness
fundamental	fundamental, vital
la injusticia	injustice
el juicio	judgement
el jurado	jury
la justicia	justice
juzgar	to judge
la paz	peace
la prensa	the press
la propuesta	proposal
sospechoso, -a	suspicious
el / la testigo	witness
la tolerancia	tolerance
violar	to violate

sobre los derechos de todas las personas

la aspiración	aspiration
el fin	purpose
la garantía	guarantee
la igualdad	equality
intercambiar	to exchange
libre	free
mundial	worldwide
opinar	to think
pacífico, -a	peaceful
proponer	to propose, to suggest
el punto de vista	point of view
el valor	value

otros adjetivos y expresiones

a medida que	as
ante	before
culpable	guilty
democrático, -a	democratic
de modo que	so, so that
el modo	the way
en lugar de	instead of
la falta de	lack of
inocente	innocent
llegar a	to reach, to get to

472 cuatrocientos setenta y dos
Repaso del capítulo

DIFFERENTIATED INSTRUCTION

Students with Learning Difficulties

For additional vocabulary practice, have students make vocabulary flashcards for the vocabulary words. Tell them to write the word on one side of the card, and on the other to include a photo, sketch, synonym, antonym, or whatever other clue helps them remember the word. Have pairs of students quiz each other using their cards.

Advanced Learners

Invite students to create and trade crossword puzzles using the chapter vocabulary. Tell them they can be creative with their clues, but they must be accurate. You may wish to provide or have students use computer software to make the crossword puzzles.

La voz pasiva: *ser* + participio pasado

Form the passive voice by using *ser* + past participle. The past participle is an adjective, so it agrees in number and gender with the subject. However, use the impersonal *se* when the subject is unknown.

Las reglas son aplicadas por el estado.   Se necesita una persona para trabajar con nosotros.

El presente y el imperfecto del subjuntivo

Use the present subjunctive when the verb in the main clause is in the present, present perfect, command or future tense.

Dile que vote mañana en las elecciones.   Armando cantará cuando se lo pidan.
No hemos dicho que ella sea nuestra amiga.

Use the imperfect subjunctive when the verb in the main clause is in the preterite, imperfect, pluperfect or conditional.

Mi maestra me pidió que bailara.   El adolescente había tratado que nos conociéramos.
El presidente quería que todos votaran.   Le gustaría a mamá que llegáramos a tiempo.

pluscuamperfecto del subjuntivo

Use the pluperfect subjunctive when the verb of the main clause is in the preterite, the imperfect or the pluperfect of the indicative.

Esperaba que hubieran ido a la fiesta con los niños.
Carlos no pensó que Juan hubiera intercambiado su pluma.
Había querido que la prensa hubiera dicho la verdad.

To form the pluperfect subjunctive use the past subjunctive of *haber* + the past participle of the verb.

hubiera	salido	hubiera	salido	hubierais	salido
hubieras	salido	hubiéramos	salido	hubieran	salido

Also use the pluperfect subjunctive when the verb in the main clause is in the conditional.

¿Sería posible que él hubiera terminado la tarea?

After the expression *como si* (as if), use either the imperfect subjunctive or the pluperfect subjunctive.

Estaba tan alegre como si hubiera dormido.   El niño descansa como si no tuviera nada que hacer.

El condicional perfecto

Form the conditional perfect using the conditional of *haber* + the past participle of the verb.

habría	trabajado	habría	trabajado	habríais	trabajado
habrías	trabajado	habríamos	trabajado	habrían	trabajado

In sentences with *si* clauses, use the past perfect subjunctive and the conditional perfect together.

Si hubieras ido a la fiesta, te habrías divertido.   Si hubieran venido aquí, no habrían estudiado.

ENRICH YOUR TEACHING

Teacher-to-Teacher

As students read more and more in Spanish, help them improve their skills in dictionary use by offering this suggestion. Tell them that each time they look up a word in their own dictionary, they should place a small dot beside the entry. If they look up a word and find a dot already there, they know this is the second time they have looked up the word. If they see two dots beside a word, they know it is one that they need frequently, and they should take steps to internalize it.

La voz pasiva: ser + participio pasado:
Ask students to write five sentences that contain a transitive verb and a direct object. Have them exchange sentences with a partner, who converts them to the passive voice: *Tina leyó un libro sobre los derechos de la gente./Un libro sobre los derechos de la gente fue leído por Tina.*

El presente y el imperfecto del subjuntivo: Ask students to write two opinions they have about rights and responsibilities. Encourage them to begin each opinion with an expression that requires the subjunctive and to sign their opinions. For example: *Es importante que el gobierno asegure la protección de los niños—Pedro.* Have them place these in a "time capsule." Pretend that 100 years have passed and the class is opening the time capsule. Students read the opinions, converting them to the past tense: *Pedro dijo que era importante que el gobierno asegurara la protección de los niños.*

El pluscuamperfecto del subjuntivo: Have students write humorous expressions using *como si* and the pluperfect subjunctive: *La muchacha bailó como si hubiera tenido alitas en los tobillos.*

El condicional perfecto: Have students write five things to tell a partner that he or she should have done. For example: *Deberías haber ido a la fiesta.* Ask them to take turns reading their statements to a partner, who asks *¿Por qué?* The first student then responds with a suitable sentence using the conditional perfect: *Habrías bailado mucho.*

Portfolio

Invite students to review the activities they completed in this chapter, including written reports, posters or other visuals, recordings of oral presentations, and other projects. Have them select one or two items that they feel best demonstrate their achievements in Spanish. Include these products in students' portfolios. Have them include this with the Chapter Checklist and Self-Assessment Worksheet.

10 Review

Performance Tasks

Standards: 1.1, 1.2, 1.3, 3.1

Student Resource: Realidades para hispanohablantes, pp. 330–331

Teacher Resources: Teacher's Resource Book: Audio Script, p. 305; Audio Program DVD: Cap. 10, Track 21; Answer Keys: Student Edition, p. 150

1. Vocabulario

Suggestions: Encourage students to review the vocabulary from the *A primera vista* sections on pp. 436–439 and 448–451 before they complete the activity.

Answers:

1. c   5. a
2. d   6. a
3. c   7. c
4. b   8. b

2. Gramática

Suggestions: Remind students of the main points of the grammar presentations in *Capítulo* 10:

• the passive voice
• the present and imperfect subjunctive
• the pluperfect subjunctive
• the conditional perfect

Answers:

1. d   5. a
2. c   6. d
3. c   7. c
4. a   8. d

3. Escuchar

Suggestions: Use the audio or read from the script.

🔊)) **Answers:**

a. un deber
b. podrán votar
c. serán castigados
d. Answers will vary.

Preparación para el examen

1 **Vocabulary** Escribe la letra de la palabra o expresión que mejor complete cada frase. Escribe tus respuestas en una hoja aparte.

1. El _____ de las opiniones de los demás ayuda a que la gente viva de manera pacífica.
   a. valor   c. respeto
   b. código de vestimenta d. maltrato

2. Antes, era muy difícil recibir las noticias _____ si vivías en un pueblo pequeño.
   a. inocentes   c. enseñanzas
   b. propuestas   d. mundiales

3. La justicia y la paz son _____ que tienen los países de todo el mundo.
   a. democráticas   c. aspiraciones
   b. injusticias   d. castigos

4. A medida que le hacían preguntas, el sospechoso de _____ la ley se asustaba más.
   a. intercambiar   c. opinar
   b. violar   d. proponer

5. En los libros que usan los abogados encontrarás frecuentemente las palabras juicio, _____ y juzgar.
   a. jurado   c. desempleo
   b. armario   d. felicidad

6. Cuando pasan de _____ , muchos adolescentes creen que pueden hacer todo sin avisar a sus padres.
   a. la niñez   c. la injusticia
   b. la pobreza   d. la libertad

7. La policía tiene _____ de detener a las personas cuando existe un motivo.
   a. la igualdad   c. el deber
   b. la tolerancia   d. el pensamiento

8. _____ guardar para sus estudios el dinero que ganó con el premio, lo gastó en divertirse.
   a. A pesar de   c. Ante
   b. En lugar de   d. Debido a

2 **Gramática** Escribe la letra de la palabra o expresión que mejor complete cada frase. Escribe tus respuestas en una hoja aparte.

1. Luis no esperaba que su jefe lo _____ a quedarse trabajando toda la noche.
   a. obligará   c. habrá obligado
   b. habían obligado   d. hubiera obligado

2. Las leyes que prohiben maltratar a los animales _____ en muchas ciudades.
   a. aplicarán   c. están aplicadas
   b. son aplicados   d. son aplicadas

3. Si _____ una educación adecuada, todos los jóvenes se habrían graduado.
   a. tienen   c. hubieran tenido
   b. tenían   d. han tenido

4. La acusada hablaba sobre el asunto como si _____ la autoridad para acusar a otros durante su propio juicio.
   a. hubiera gozado de   c. habría gozado de
   b. han gozado de   d. ha gozado de

5. Dile al candidato que te _____ que va a luchar contra la desigualdad.
   a. asegure   c. asegura
   b. asegurará   d. ha asegurado

6. Si _____ sujeto a todos los problemas que sufrió ese adolescente, tu punto de vista sería muy distinto.
   a. estabas   c. hubiste estado
   b. estás   d. hubieras estado

7. Ambos estudiantes le pidieron al profesor que _____ de convencer a toda la clase para que votaran por su candidata.
   a. tratará   c. tratara
   b. hubiera tratado   d. trataría

8. Su amigo le _____ el apoyo que necesitaba si él no lo hubiera tratado así.
   a. sería dado   c. había dado
   b. habrá dado   d. habría dado

474 cuatrocientos setenta y cuatro
Preparación para el examen

DIFFERENTIATED INSTRUCTION

Students with Learning Difficulties

Refer students to their portfolios. Have them look at chapter exams from past chapters. Lay three or four exams side-by-side and point out the similarities in structure between them. Remind students that knowing how a test is laid out helps them know what to expect next and reduces stress.

Advanced Learners

Provide students with additional vocabulary practice by asking them to use the incorrect answers from performance task 1 in sentences.

Más repaso GO   realidades.com | print

	✔	
Puzzles		✔
Core WB pp. 145–146		✔
Comm. WB pp. 221, 222–224	✔	✔
Instant Check	✔	

En el examen vas a . . .	Éstas son las tareas que te pueden ser útiles para el examen . . .	Para repasar, ve a tu libro de texto impreso o digital . . .
Interpretive		
3 Escuchar Escuchar y comprender la descripción de las reglas de un club deportivo	Responde a las preguntas sobre las reglas del Club Deportivo Veloz. (a) ¿Respetar el código de vestimenta es un derecho o un deber de los miembros? (b) ¿Qué significa que los miembros tendrán derecho de opinar? (c) ¿Qué les pasa a los que no obedecen las reglas? (d) ¿Crees que hay igualdad entre los derechos y los deberes de los miembros? Di por qué.	**pp. 436–439** *A primera vista 1: Vocabulario en contexto* **p. 437** Actividad 2 **p. 442** Actividad 9 **p. 465** *Presentación oral*
Presentational		
4 Hablar Hacer una presentación para explicar por qué los animales también tienen derechos	Haz una presentación a los jóvenes del barrio sobre lo que deben hacer para cuidar a los animales. Incluye (a) una explicación de los problemas que sufren los animales, (b) qué derechos deberían tener, (c) lo que pueden hacer los jóvenes para protegerlos.	**p. 438** Actividad 3 **p. 461** Actividad 40 **p. 465** *Presentación oral*
Interpretive		
5 Leer Leer y comprender un párrafo de un ensayo editorial	Lee un párrafo de un ensayo editorial sobre el mar y Chile. (a) ¿Qué solución propone el autor para desarrollar al país? (b) ¿Quién es el libertador de Chile? (c) ¿De qué depende Chile? *Ante lo que he dicho antes, propongo que hagamos una campaña para que Chile vuelva a mirar hacia el mar como solución para desarrollar al país. Para terminar, debemos recordar a nuestro libertador, Don Bernardo O'Higgins, quien dijo que el pueblo de Chile, "desde siempre y para siempre, depende del mar".*	**pp. 448–451** *A primera vista 2: Vocabulario en contexto* **p. 455** Actividad 29 **pp. 468–471** *Lectura*
Presentational		
6 Escribir Escribir un cuestionario sobre cómo hacer uso de un parque	En un parque sembraron césped y flores y construyeron un camino para bicicletas, pero la gente no está de acuerdo en cómo usarlos. Escribe un cuestionario para preguntarles cómo habrían usado el parque si hubiera sido de ellos. Incluye (a) el horario, (b) las obligaciones y los derechos, (c) lo que debe garantizar la ciudad.	**p. 438** Actividad 3 **p. 442** Actividad 9 **p. 447** Actividad 17 **p. 460** Actividades 36–38 **pp. 436–437** *A primera vista 1*
Cultures		
7 Pensar Decir de qué derechos deberían gozar los niños	Piensa en lo que leíste sobre Domitila Barrios de Chungara y di tres derechos que deberían tener todos los niños del mundo.	**p. 439** *A primera vista 1* **p. 439** Actividad 4 **pp. 468–471** *Lectura*

4. Hablar

Suggestions: Encourage students to use sentences in which they say what will happen to the animals if they are not cared for and protected.

Answers will vary.

5. Leer

Suggestions: Tell students to refer to pp. 436–439 and 448–451 if they have questions about vocabulary in the review

Answers:

(a) Propone una campaña para que el país use el mar.
(b) Don Bernardo O'Higgins
(c) Chile depende del mar.

6. Escribir

Suggestions: Remind students of what they learned about effective introductions in this chapter's *Presentación escrita*. Have them apply that learning to their writing here.

Answers will vary.

7. Pensar

Suggestions: Encourage students to review the reading on pp. 468–470 before they make their recommendations.

Answers will vary.

DIFFERENTIATED ASSESSMENT

CORE ASSESSMENT

- **Assessment Program:** Examen del capítulo 10, pp. 233–236
- **Audio Program DVD:** Cap. 10, Track 22
- **ExamView:** Chapter Test, Test Banks A and B

ADVANCED/PRE-AP*

- **ExamView Pre-AP* Test Bank**
- **Pre-AP* Resource Book,** pp. 165–167

STUDENTS NEEDING EXTRA HELP

- **Alternate Assessment Program:** Examen del capítulo 10
- **Audio Program DVD:** Cap. 10, Track 22

HERITAGE LEARNERS

- **Assessment Program: Realidades para hispanohablantes:** Examen del capítulo 10
- **ExamView Heritage Learner Test Bank**

Vocabulario adicional

realidades.com GO

 Bilingual Visual Dictionary

Capítulo 1

El equipo para ir de cámping

el abrelatas can opener

la balsa raft

el bote inflable inflatable boat

la cantimplora canteen

la caña de pescar fishing rod

el casco helmet

el chaleco salvavidas life jacket

los fósforos matches

la leña firewood

el remo oar, paddle

Para indicar cuándo sucede algo

el amanecer dawn

el atardecer dusk

el mediodía noon

la puesta del sol sunset

la salida del sol sunrise

Expresiones para los deportes

empatar to tie (a game)

la cancha (sports) field

el podio podium

Capítulo 2

Los materiales

la acuarela watercolor

el barro clay

el caballete easel

el lienzo canvas

el óleo oleo (paint)

la témpera tempera

Las expresiones de teatro

la escenografía set design

la iluminación lighting

la ovación ovation

poner en escena (una obra) to stage (a play)

el telón curtain

la utilería props

el vestuario wardrobe

Los instrumentos musicales

el arpa harp

el contrabajo double bass

la flauta flute

el instrumento de cuerda string instrument

el instrumento de percusión percussion instrument

el instrumento de viento wind instrument

el violoncelo cello

La literatura

la autobiografía autobiography

la biografía biography

el ensayo essay

la estrofa stanza

la ficción fiction

la prosa prose

la rima rhyme

Capítulo 3

Las expresiones para la salud

el análisis clínico laboratory test

el / la especialista specialist

el estetoscopio stethoscope

el medicamento medicine

los minerales minerals

la presión arterial blood pressure

los primeros auxilios first aid

la respiración breathing

el síntoma symptom

el termómetro thermometer

Las máquinas de ejercicio

la caminadora treadmill

la máquina de remar rowing machine

la máquina de subir escaleras stair climber

las pesas libres free weights

Los condimentos

la mayonesa mayonnaise

la mostaza mustard

la salsa de tomate ketchup

Otro tipo de comidas

los fideos noodles

Capítulo 4

Los estados de ánimo

ansioso, -a anxious

abrumado, -a overwhelmed

agotado, -a exhausted

rendido, -a worn out

Las relaciones con los demás

agradecer to thank

chismear to gossip

disculpar to excuse

insultar to insult

opinar to give / to have an opinion

querer (a alguien) to love (someone)

soportar to tolerate

Capítulo 5

Expresiones para el empleo y trabajo voluntario

comunitario, -a community related

la destreza skill

los estudios (cursados) studies (completed)

el patrón / la patrona boss

los recursos humanos human resources

el / la supervisor(a) supervisor

sin fines de lucro nonprofit

Capítulo 6

Otras profesiones

el / la aprendiz apprentice

el / la camarógrafo(a) cameraman, camerawoman

el / la cirujano(a) surgeon

el /la intérprete interpreter

el / la jardinero(a) gardener

el / la modista(a) dressmaker, designer

el /la oculista eye doctor

Las ciencias

la astronomía astronomy

la física physics

la química chemistry

La tecnología

la energía nuclear nuclear energy

el facsímil fax

la fotocopiadora copier

inalámbrico, -a wireless

el microscopio electrónico electronic microscope

el rayo / la luz láser laser beam / light

el telescopio telescope

Capítulo 7

La arqueología

abandonar to abandon

el / la antropólogo(a) anthropologist

avanzado, -a advanced

los datos data, information

la desaparición disappearance

descifrar to decipher

desenterrar to unearth

la evolución evolution

el / la geólogo(a) geologist

el jeroglífico hieroglyph

la prueba proof

el significado meaning

surgir to arise

Para hablar del universo

la constelación constellation

la galaxia galaxy

intergaláctico, -a intergalactic

el sistema solar solar system

Otras formas geométricas

el cuadrado square

la circunferencia circumference

el cubo cube

la esfera sphere

la rueda wheel

Capítulo 8

La arquitectura

la capilla chapel

la cúpula dome

el muro wall

la muralla (de la ciudad) wall (of a city)

Expresiones para la historia de América

la armadura armor

las armas de fuego firearms

el arribo arrival

cabalgar to ride a horse

la carabela caravel

el escudo shield

la lanza spear

la nave (a vela) sailboat

la pólvora gunpowder

unificar to unify

el yelmo helmet

Capítulo 9

Expresiones sobre el cuidado del planeta

la atmósfera atmosphere

la biosfera biosphere

descomponer(se) to decompose

los desechos industriales industrial waste

el /la ecólogo(a) ecologist

la erosión erosion

la radioactividad radioactivity

radiactivo,-a radiactive

la superpoblación overpopulation

la sustancia substance

la tala de bosques felling of forests

Capítulo 10

Las leyes y los derechos

apelar to appeal

el congreso congress

la Declaración de Derechos Bill of Rights

la democracia democracy

los derechos civiles civil rights

los derechos humanos human rights

encarcelar to put in jail

las enmiendas amendments

el himno nacional national anthem

la monarquía monarchy

la patria homeland

el patriotismo patriotism

el senado senate

Resumen de gramática
Grammar Terms

Adjectives describe nouns: *a **red** car.*

Adverbs usually describe verbs: *He read it **quickly**.* Adverbs can also describe adjectives or other adverbs: ***very** tall, **quite** well.*

Articles are words in Spanish that can tell you whether a noun is masculine, feminine, singular, or plural. In English, the articles are ***the, a,*** and ***an.***

Commands are verb forms that tell people to do something: ***Work!***

Comparatives compare people or things: *more . . . than.*

Conditional tense is used to express what a person would do or what a situation would be like: *I **would like** to write a book.*

Conjugations are verb forms that add endings to the stem in order to tell who the subject is and what tense is being used: *escribo, escribiste.*

Conjunctions join words or groups of words. The most common ones are ***and, but,*** and ***or.***

Direct objects are nouns or pronouns that receive the action of a verb: *I read **the book.** I read **it.***

Future tense is used to talk about actions in the future: *Tomorrow we **will begin** working.*

Gender in Spanish tells you whether a noun, pronoun, or article is masculine or feminine.

Imperfect tense is used to talk about actions that happened repeatedly in the past; to describe people, places, and situations in the past; to talk about a past action or situation where no beginning or end is specified; and to describe an ongoing action in the past.

Imperfect progressive tense is used to describe something that was taking place over a period of time in the past: *He **was skiing** when he broke his leg.*

Indicative mood refers to present, past or future actions or states based on reality: *It **snowed** all night. It's **snowing** right now. **Will it snow** tomorrow?*

Indirect objects are nouns or pronouns that tell you to whom / what or for whom / what something is done: *I gave **him** the book.*

Infinitives are the basic forms of verbs. In English, infinitives have the word "to" in front of them: ***to walk.***

Interrogatives are words that ask questions: ***What** is it? **Who** is he?*

Nouns name people, places, or things: ***students, Mexico City, books.***

Number tells you if a noun, pronoun, article, or verb is singular or plural.

Past participles are verb forms that are used with forms of *haber* to form compound tenses: *He **escrito** una carta.* When a participle is used with *estar*, it functions as an adjective: *La mesa **está puesta.***

Prepositions show relationship between their objects and another word in the sentence: *He is **in** the classroom.*

Present tense is used to talk about actions that always take place, or that are currently happening: *I always **take** the bus; I **study** Spanish.*

Present perfect tense is used to say what a person *has done: We **have seen** the new movie.*

Present progressive tense is used to emphasize that an action is happening *right now: I **am doing** my homework; he **is finishing** dinner.*

Preterite tense is used to talk about actions that were completed in the past: *I **took** the train yesterday.*

Pronouns are words that take the place of nouns: ***She** is my friend.*

Reflexive verbs are used to say that people do something to or for themselves: *I **wash my** hair.* Reflexive verbs often describe a change in emotional or physical state, and express the idea that someone "gets" or "becomes": *They **became** angry.*

Subjects are the nouns or pronouns that perform the action in a sentence: ***John** sings.*

Subjunctive mood is used to say that one person influences the actions of another: *I **recommend that you study** more.* It is also used after verbs and expressions of doubt or uncertainty: *It's **possible that there's** enough food.*

Verbs show action or link the subject with a word or words in the predicate (what the subject does or is): *Ana **writes;** Ana **is** my sister.*

Nouns, Number, and Gender

Nouns refer to people, animals, places, things, and ideas. Nouns are singular or plural. In Spanish, nouns have gender, which means that they are either masculine or feminine.

Singular Nouns	
Masculine	Feminine
libro	carpeta
pupitre	casa
profesor	noche
lápiz	ciudad

Plural Nouns	
Masculine	Feminine
libros	carpetas
pupitres	casas
profesores	noches
lápices	ciudades

Definite Articles

El, la, los, and *las* are definite articles and are the equivalent of "the" in English. *El* is used with masculine singular nouns; *los* with masculine plural nouns. *La* is used with feminine singular nouns; *las* with feminine plural nouns. When you use the words *a* or *de* before *el,* you form the contractions *al* and *del: Voy* **al** *centro; Es el libro* **del** *profesor.*

Masculine		Feminine	
Singular	**Plural**	**Singular**	**Plural**
el libro	los libros	la carpeta	las carpetas
el pupitre	los pupitres	la casa	las casas
el profesor	los profesores	la noche	las noches
el lápiz	los lápices	la ciudad	las ciudades

Indefinite Articles

Un and *una* are indefinite articles and are the equivalent of "a" and "an" in English. *Un* is used with singular masculine nouns; *una* is used with singular feminine nouns. The plural indefinite articles are *unos* and *unas.*

Masculine		Feminine	
Singular	**Plural**	**Singular**	**Plural**
un libro	unos libros	una revista	unas revistas
un baile	unos bailes	una mochila	unas mochilas

Pronouns

Subject pronouns tell who is doing the action. They replace nouns or names in a sentence. Subject pronouns are often used for emphasis or clarification: *Gregorio escucha música.* **Él** *escucha música.*

A *direct object* tells who or what receives the action of the verb. To avoid repeating a direct object noun, you can replace it with a *direct object pronoun.* Direct object pronouns have the same gender and number as the nouns they replace: *¿Cuándo compraste* **el libro?** *Lo* *compré ayer.*

An *indirect object* tells to whom or for whom an action is performed. *Indirect object pronouns* are used to replace an indirect object noun: **Les** *doy dinero. (I give money to them.)* Because *le* and *les* have more than one meaning, you can make the meaning clear, or show emphasis, by adding *a* + the corresponding name, noun, or pronoun: **Les** *doy dinero a* **ellos.**

When two object pronouns are used together, the indirect object pronoun comes before the direct object pronoun: *Si necesitas este libro,* **te lo** *doy.*

The indirect object pronoun *le* or *les* becomes *se* before the direct object pronoun *lo, la, los,* or *las: María quiere escuchar esta canción.* **Se la** *voy a cantar.*

A *reflexive pronoun* is used to show that someone does an action to or for themselves. Each reflexive pronoun corresponds to a different subject and always agrees with the subject pronoun: *Todos los días* **me ducho** *y* **me arreglo** *el pelo.*

The personal a

When the direct object is a person, a group of people, or a pet, use the word *a* before the object. This is called the "personal *a*": *Visité* **a** *mi abuela. Busco* **a** *mi perro, Capitán.*

Subject Pronouns		Direct Object Pronouns		Indirect Object Pronouns		Reflexive Pronouns		Objects of Prepositions	
Singular	**Plural**	**Singular**	**Plural**	**Singular**	**Plural**	**Singular**	**Plural**	**Singular**	**Plural**
yo	nosotros, nosotras	me	nos	me	nos	me	nos	(para) mí, conmigo	nosotros, nosotras
tú	vosotros, vosotras	te	os	te	os	te	os	(para) ti, contigo	vosotros, vosotras
usted (Ud.),	ustedes (Uds.),	lo, la	los, las	le	les	se	se	Ud.	Uds.
él, ella	ellos, ellas							él, ella	ellos, ellas

Adjectives

Words that describe people and things are called adjectives. In Spanish, most adjectives have both masculine and feminine forms, as well as singular and plural forms. Adjectives must agree with the noun they describe in both gender and number. When an adjective describes a group including both masculine and feminine nouns, use the masculine plural form.

Masculine	
Singular	Plural
alto	altos
inteligente	inteligentes
trabajador	trabajadores
fácil	fáciles

Feminine	
Singular	Plural
alta	altas
inteligente	inteligentes
trabajadora	trabajadoras
fácil	fáciles

Shortened Forms of Adjectives

When placed before masculine singular nouns, some adjectives change into a shortened form.

bueno	→	buen chico
malo	→	mal día
primero	→	primer trabajo
tercero	→	tercer plato
grande	→	gran señor

One adjective, **grande,** changes to a shortened form before any singular noun: *una **gran** señora, un **gran** libro.* In these cases, **gran** means "great."

Possessive Adjectives and Pronouns

Possessive adjectives are used to tell what belongs to someone or to show relationships. Like other adjectives, possessive adjectives agree in number with the nouns that follow them.

Only *nuestro* and *vuestro* have different masculine and feminine endings. *Su* and *sus* can have many different meanings: *his, her, its, your,* or *their.*

The long forms of possessive adjectives agree in number and gender with the noun. They are used for emphasis and come *after* the noun. They may also be used without a noun:

Singular	Plural
mi	mis
tu	tus
su	sus
nuestro, -a	nuestros, -as
vuestro, -a	vuestros, -as
su	sus

*¿Esta chaqueta es **tuya**? Sí, es **mía**.*

Singular	Plural
mío/mía	míos/mías
tuyo/tuya	tuyos/tuyas
suyo/suya	suyos/suyas
nuestro/nuestra	nuestros/nuestras
vuestro/vuestra	vuestros/vuestras
suyo/suya	suyos/suyas

Possessive pronouns use the long form of possessive adjectives preceded by the definite article. *Tu cuarto es grande.* ***El mío** es pequeño.*

Demonstrative Adjectives and Pronouns

Demonstrative adjectives are used to point out people or things that are nearby and farther away. A demonstrative adjective agrees in gender and number with the noun that follows it.

Use *este, esta, estos, estas* ("this" / "these") before nouns that name people or things that are close to you. Use *ese, esa, esos, esas* ("that" / "those") before nouns that name people or things that are at some distance from you.

	Close to you		Closer to the person you are talking to		Far from both of you	
Adjectives	este	estos	ese	esos	aquel	aquellos
	esta	estas	esa	esas	aquella	aquellas
Pronouns	éste	éstos	ése	ésos	aquél	aquéllos
	ésta	éstas	ésa	ésas	aquélla	aquéllas

Use *aquel, aquella, aquellos,* or *aquellas* ("that one [those] over there") before nouns that name people or things that are far from both you and the person you are speaking to.

Demonstrative adjectives can be used as pronouns to replace nouns. Accents are no longer required on demonstrative pronouns as of 2010. Anything written before 2009 will include accents on demonstratives.

Interrogative Words

You use interrogative words to ask questions. When you ask a question with an interrogative word, you put the verb before the subject. All interrogative words have a written accent mark.

¿Adónde?	¿Cuándo?	¿Dónde?
¿Cómo?	¿Cuánto, -a?	¿Por qué?
¿Con quién?	¿Cuántos, -as?	¿Qué?
¿Cuál?	¿De dónde?	¿Quién?

Comparatives and Superlatives

Comparatives Use *más . . . que* or *menos . . . que* to compare people or things: *más interesante que . . . , menos alta que . . . .*

When talking about number, use *de* instead of *que: Tengo más de cien monedas en mi colección.*

To compare people or things that are equal, use *tan . . . como: tan popular como . . . . Tanto / tanta . . . como* is used to say "as much as" and *tantos / tantas . . . como* is used to say "as many as": *tanto dinero como . . . tantas amigas*

como . . . . Tanto and *tanta* match the number and gender of the noun to which they refer.

Superlatives Use this pattern to express the idea of "most" or "least."

el
la + *noun* + más / menos + *adjective*
los
las

Es la chica más seria de la clase.
Son los perritos más pequeños.

Several adjectives are irregular when used with comparisons and superlatives.

older	mayor
younger	menor
better	mejor
worse	peor

Affirmative and Negative Words

To make a sentence negative in Spanish, *no* usually goes in front of the verb or expression. To show that you do not like either of two choices, use *ni . . . ni.*

Alguno, alguna, algunos, algunas and *ninguno, ninguna* match the number and gender of the noun to which they refer. *Ningunos* and *ningunas* are rarely used. When *alguno* and *ninguno* come before a masculine singular noun, they change to *algún* and *ningún.*

Affirmative	Negative
algo	nada
alguien	nadie
algún	ningún
alguno, -a, -os, -as	ninguno, -a, -os, -as
siempre	nunca
también	tampoco

Adverbs

To form an adverb in Spanish, *-mente* is added to the feminine singular form of an adjective. The *-mente* ending is equivalent to the "-ly" ending in English. If the adjective has a written accent, such as *rápida, fácil,* and *práctica,* the accent appears in the same place in the adverb.

general	→ generalmente
especial	→ especialmente
fácil	→ fácilmente
feliz	→ felizmente
rápida	→ rápidamente
práctica	→ prácticamente

Past Participles

Past participles are used with forms of the verb *haber* to form compound tenses: **Había escrito** *un poema muy hermoso.* They can also be used as adjectives: *El espejo estaba* **roto**.

To form a past participle, add *-ado* to the root of *-ar* verbs and *-ido* to the root of *-er* and *-ir* verbs.

Some past participles are irregular.

decorar	decor**ado**	conocer	conoc**ido**	preferir	prefer**ido**

abrir: abierto	morir: muerto
cubrir: cubierto	poner: puesto
decir: dicho	resolver: resuelto
descubrir:	romper: roto
descubierto	ver: visto
escribir: escrito	volver: vuelto
hacer: hecho	

Por and para

Both *por* and *para* are prepositions. Their usages are quite different.

Use *por* to indicate:	
length of time or distance	Caminamos **por** dos horas.
where an action takes place	El perro corría **por** la playa.
an exchange	Le doy diez pesos **por** ese dibujo.
an action on behalf of someone or something	Vamos a la marcha **por** la paz.
a means of communication or transportation	Lo vimos **por** televisión.

Use *por* in certain expressions:
por ejemplo
por eso (tanto)
por la (mañana, tarde, noche)
por favor
por lo general
por primera (segunda, tercera, última) vez
por supuesto

Use *para* to indicate:	
purpose	Como frutas **para** obtener vitaminas.
destination	Hace una hora salieron **para** la playa.
a point in time	**Para** mañana ya tendrás lo que encargaste.
use	¿Dónde hay una cuchara **para** sopa?
opinion	**Para** los niños el helado es muy rico.

Pero and sino

The word *pero* is usually the equivalent of the English conjunction *but*. The word *sino* also means *but*.

Sino is used after a negative, to convey the idea of an alternative: "not this, but rather that."

No compré pastel *sino* helado.

Yo can also use *sino* with *no sólo . . . sino* también.

Me regaló *no sólo* dulces *sino* también flores.

You use *sino que* when there is a conjugated verb in the second part of the sentence.

No fuimos a la ciudad *sino que* salimos a navegar.

Relative Pronouns *que*, *quien*, and *lo que*

You use relative pronouns to combine two sentences or to give clarifying information. The most common relative pronoun in Spanish is *que*. It can mean *that, which, who,* or *whom,* and it may refer either to persons or to things.

El artículo **que** *salió en el periódico habla sobre la contaminación.*

> After a preposition, use *que* to refer to things and *quien(es)* to refer to people.
>
> > El problema **del que** te hablé es muy grave.
> > La persona **de quien** te hablé se llama Adriana.
>
> Use the relative phrase *lo que* to refer to a situation, concept, action, or object not yet identified.
>
> > Te cuento **lo que** me explicó el científico.

Conjunctions Used with the Subjunctive and the Indicative

Certain conjunctions related to time are followed by either the indicative or the subjunctive:

> | antes de que | tan pronto como | cuando | en cuanto |
> | después (de) que | hasta que | mientras | |
>
> You use the subjunctive after these conjunctions when the action that follows has not yet taken place. You use the indicative with these conjunction when the action that follows has already taken place or if it occurs regularly.
>
> > Van a producir petróleo **hasta que** se agote.
> > **En cuanto** salgo del cuarto, siempre apago las luces.
>
> The conjunction *antes de que* is always followed by the subjunctive.
>
> > Pon el helado en el refrigerador **antes de que** se derrita.
>
> If the subject of a sentence does not change, use the infinitive after *antes de, después de* and *hasta*.
>
> > Voy a salir **después de** terminar la tarea.

The following conjunctions are usually followed by the subjunctive to express the purpose or intention of an action:

> | a menos que | para que | sin que |
> | a fin de que | aunque | con tal (de) que |
>
> No haré la limpieza de la casa **a menos que** me ayudes.
>
> If the subject of the sentence does not change, use the infinitive after *para* and *sin*.
>
> > Debemos dejar de usar aerosoles **para** detener la destrucción de la capa de ozono.
>
> With the conjunction *aunque*, use the subjunctive to express uncertainty. Use the indicative when there is no uncertainty.
>
> > **Aunque** produzcan más petróleo, no podrán depender de este recurso por mucho tiempo.
> > No quiero ver ese programa sobre las ballenas **aunque** todos dicen que es muy bueno.

Verbos

Regular Verbs

Here are the conjugations for regular -*ar*, -*er*, and -*ir* verbs in the indicative (present, preterite, imperfect, future, and conditional) and the present and imperfect subjunctive.

Infinitive Present Participle Past Participle	Present		Preterite		Imperfect	
estudiar	estudio	estudiamos	estudié	estudiamos	estudiaba	estudiábamos
estudiando	estudias	estudiáis	estudiaste	estudiasteis	estudiabas	estudiabais
estudiado	estudia	estudian	estudió	estudiaron	estudiaba	estudiaban
correr	corro	corremos	corrí	corrimos	corría	corríamos
corriendo	corres	corréis	corriste	corristeis	corrías	corríais
corrido	corre	corren	corrió	corrieron	corría	corrían
vivir	vivo	vivimos	viví	vivimos	vivía	vivíamos
viviendo	vives	vivís	viviste	vivisteis	vivías	vivíais
vivido	vive	viven	vivió	vivieron	vivía	vivían

Present Progressive and Imperfect Progressive

Progressive tenses are formed with a form of *estar* and the present participle.

Present Progressive	Present Participle	Imperfect Progressive	Present Participle
estoy		estaba	
estás		estabas	
está	estudiando	estaba	estudiando
estamos	corriendo	estábamos	corriendo
estáis	viviendo	estabais	viviendo
están		estaban	

Reflexive Verbs

Infinitive and Present Participle	Present	Preterite	Subjunctive
lavarse	me lavo	me lavé	me lave
lavándose	te lavas	te lavaste	te laves
	se lava	se lavó	se lave
	nos lavamos	nos lavamos	nos lavemos
	os laváis	os lavasteis	os lavéis
	se lavan	se lavaron	se laven

Regular Verbs (continued)

Future		Conditional		Present Subjunctive		Imperfect Subjunctive	
estudiaré	estudiaremos	estudiaría	estudiaríamos	estudie	estudiemos	estudiara	estudiáramos
estudiarás	estudiaréis	estudiarías	estudiarías	estudies	estudiéis	estudiaras	estudiarais
estudiará	estudiarán	estudiaría	estudiaría	estudie	estudien	estudiara	estudiaran
correré	correremos	correría	correríamos	corra	corramos	corriera	corriéramos
correrás	correréis	correrías	correríais	corras	corráis	corrieras	corrierais
correrá	correrán	correría	correrían	corra	corran	corriera	corrieran
viviré	viviremos	viviría	viviríamos	viva	vivamos	viviera	viviéramos
vivirás	viviréis	vivirías	viviríais	vivas	viváis	vivieras	vivierais
vivirá	vivirán	viviría	vivirían	viva	vivan	viviera	vivieran

Perfect Tenses

Perfect tenses are formed with an auxiliary verb *(haber)* and a past participle.

Present Perfect		Pluperfect		Future Perfect		Present Perfect Subjunctive		Past Perfect Subjunctive		Conditional Perfect	
he		había		habré		haya		hubiera		habría	
has	estudiado	habías	estudiado	habrás	estudiado	hayas	estudiado	hubieras	estudiado	habrías	estudiado
ha	corrido	había	corrido	habrá	corrido	haya	corrido	hubiera	corrido	habría	corrido
hemos	vivido	habíamos	vivido	habremos	vivido	hayamos	vivido	hubiéramos	vivido	habríamos	vivido
habéis		habíais		habréis		hayáis		hubierais		habríais	
han		habían		habrán		hayan		hubieran		habrían	

Stem-changing Verbs

Here is a list of stem-changing verbs. Only conjugations with changes are shown.

Infinitive in -*ar*

Infinitive	Present Indicative		Present Subjunctive	
pensar (e→ie)	pienso	pensamos	piense	pensemos
	piensas	pensáis	pienses	penséis
	piensa	piensan	piense	piensen
Verbs like **pensar:** calentar, comenzar, despertar(se), empezar, recomendar, tropezar				
contar (o→ue)	cuento	contamos	cuente	contemos
	cuentas	contáis	cuentes	contéis
	cuenta	cuentan	cuente	cuenten
Verbs like **contar:** acostar(se), almorzar, costar, encontrar(se), probar(se), recordar				
jugar (u→ue)	juego	jugamos	juegue	juguemos
	juegas	jugáis	juegues	juguéis
	juega	juegan	juegue	jueguen

Infinitive in -*er*

Infinitive	Present Indicative		Present Subjunctive	
entender (e→ie)	entiendo	entendemos	entienda	entendamos
	entiendes	entendéis	entiendas	entendáis
	entiende	entienden	entienda	entiendan
Verbs like **entender:** encender, perder				
devolver (o→ue)	devuelvo	devolvemos	devuelva	devolvamos
past participle:	devuelves	devolvéis	devuelvas	devolváis
devuelto	devuelve	devuelven	devuelva	devuelvan
Verbs like **devolver:** mover(se), resolver, torcer(se), volver (past participle: **vuelto**)				

Stem-changing Verbs (continued)

Infinitive in -ir

	Indicative		Preterite		Subjunctive	
	Present		**Preterite**		**Present**	
pedir (e→i) (e→i)	pido	pedimos	pedí	pedimos	pida	pidamos
present participle: pidiendo	pides	pedís	pediste	pedisteis	pidas	pidáis
	pide	piden	pidió	pidieron	pida	pidan
Verbs like pedir: conseguir, despedir(se), repetir, seguir, servir, vestir(se)						
preferir (e→ie) (e→i)	prefiero	preferimos	preferí	preferimos	prefiera	prefiramos
present participle:	prefieres	preferís	preferiste	preferisteis	prefieras	prefiráis
prefiriendo	prefiere	prefieren	prefirió	prefirieron	prefiera	prefieran
Verbs like preferir: divertir(se), hervir, mentir, sugerir						
dormir (o→ue) (o→u)	duermo	dormimos	dormí	dormimos	duerma	durmamos
present participle:	duermes	dormís	dormiste	dormisteis	duermas	durmáis
durmiendo	duerme	duermen	durmió	durmieron	duerma	duerman
Verbs like **dormir**: morir(se) (past participle: **muerto**)						

Spelling-changing Verbs

These verbs have spelling changes in the present, preterite, and/or the subjunctive tenses. The spelling changes are indicated in boldface.

Infinitive Present Participle Past Participle	Present		Preterite		Subjunctive	
almorzar (z→c) almorzando almorzado	See stem-changing verbs		**almorcé** almorzaste almorzó	almorzamos almorzasteis almorzaron	**almuerce** **almuerces** **almuerce**	**almorcemos** **almorcéis** **almuercen**
buscar (c→qu) buscando buscado	See regular -ar verbs		**busqué** buscaste buscó	buscamos buscasteis buscaron	**busque** **busques** **busque**	**busquemos** **busquéis** **busquen**
comunicarse (c→qu) comunicándose	See reflexive verbs		See reflexive verbs and **buscar**		See reflexive verbs and **buscar**	
conocer (c→zc) conociendo conocido	**conozco** conoces conoce	conocemos conocéis conocen	See regular -er verbs		conozca conozcas conozca	conozcamos conozcáis conozcan
creer (i→y) creyendo creído	See regular -er verbs		creí creíste creyó	creímos creísteis creyeron	See regular -er verbs	
empezar (z→c) empezando empezado	See stem-changing verbs		empecé empezaste empezó	empezamos empezasteis empezaron	See stem-changing verbs	
enviar (i→í) enviando enviado	**envío** **envías** **envía**	enviamos enviáis **envían**	See regular -ar verbs		envíe envíes envíe	enviemos enviéis envíen
escoger escogiendo escogido	**escojo** escoges escoge	escogemos escogéis escogen	See regular -er verbs		escoja escojas escoja	escojamos escojáis escojan
esquiar (i→í) esquiando esquiado	See **enviar**		See regular -ar verbs		See **enviar**	
jugar (g→gu) jugando jugado	See stem-changing verbs		**jugué** jugaste jugó	jugamos jugasteis jugaron	See stem-changing verbs	
leer (i→y) leyendo leído	See regular -er verbs		See **creer**		See regular -er verbs	
obedecer (c→zc) obedeciendo obedecido	See **conocer**		See regular -er verbs		See **conocer**	

Spelling-changing Verbs (continued)

Infinitive Present Participle Past Participle	Present		Preterite	Subjunctive	
ofrecer (c→zc) ofreciendo ofrecido	See **conocer**		See regular *-er* verbs	See **conocer**	
pagar (g→gu) pagando pagado	See regular *-ar* verbs		See **jugar**	**pague** **pagues** **pague**	**paguemos** **paguéis** **paguen**
parecer (c→zc) pareciendo parecido	See **conocer**		See regular *-er* verbs	See **conocer**	
practicar (c→qu) practicando practicado	See regular *-ar* verbs		See **buscar**	See **buscar**	
recoger (g→j) recogiendo recogido	**recojo** recoges recoge	recogemos recogéis recogen	See regular *-er* verbs	See **escoger**	
sacar (c→qu) sacando sacado	See regular *-ar* verbs		See **buscar**	See **buscar**	
tocar (c→qu) tocando tocado	See regular *-ar* verbs		See **buscar**	See **buscar**	

Irregular Verbs

These verbs have irregular patterns.

	1		2		3		4	
Infinitive Present Participle Past Participle		Present		Preterite		Imperfect		
dar	doy	damos	di	dimos	daba	dábamos		
dando	das	dais	diste	disteis	dabas	dabais		
dado	da	dan	dio	dieron	daba	daban		
decir	digo	decimos	dije	dijimos	decía	decíamos		
diciendo	dices	decís	dijiste	dijisteis	decías	decíais		
dicho	dice	dicen	dijo	dijeron	decía	decían		
estar	estoy	estamos	estuve	estuvimos	estaba	estábamos		
estando	estás	estáis	estuviste	estuvisteis	estabas	estabais		
estado	está	están	estuvo	estuvieron	estaba	estaban		
haber	he	hemos	hube	hubimos	había	habíamos		
habiendo	has	habéis	hubiste	hubisteis	habías	habíais		
habido	ha	han	hubo	hubieron	había	habían		
hacer	hago	hacemos	hice	hicimos	hacía	hacíamos		
haciendo	haces	hacéis	hiciste	hicisteis	hacías	hacíais		
hecho	hace	hacen	hizo	hicieron	hacía	hacían		
ir	voy	vamos	fui	fuimos	iba	íbamos		
yendo	vas	vais	fuiste	fuisteis	ibas	ibais		
ido	va	van	fue	fueron	iba	iban		
oír	oigo	oímos	oí	oímos	oía	oíamos		
oyendo	oyes	oís	oíste	oísteis	oías	oíais		
oído	oye	oyen	oyó	oyeron	oía	oían		
poder	puedo	podemos	pude	pudimos	podía	podíamos		
pudiendo	puedes	podéis	pudiste	pudisteis	podías	podíais		
podido	puede	pueden	pudo	pudieron	podía	podían		
poner	pongo	ponemos	puse	pusimos	ponía	poníamos		
poniendo	pones	ponéis	pusiste	pusisteis	ponías	poníais		
puesto	pone	ponen	puso	pusieron	ponía	ponían		

Irregular Verbs (continued)

	5 Future		6 Conditional		7 Present Subjunctive		8 Imperfect Subjunctive
daré	daremos	daría	daríamos	dé	demos	diera	diéramos
darás	daréis	darías	daríais	des	deis	dieras	dierais
dará	darán	daría	darían	dé	den	diera	dieran
diré	diremos	diría	diríamos	diga	digamos	dijera	dijéramos
dirás	diréis	dirías	diríais	digas	digáis	dijeras	dijerais
dirá	dirán	diría	dirían	diga	digan	dijera	dijeran
estaré	estaremos	estaría	estaríamos	esté	estemos	estuviera	estuviéramos
estarás	estaréis	estarías	estaríais	estés	estéis	estuvieras	estuvierais
estará	estarán	estaría	estarían	esté	estén	estuviera	estuvieran
habré	habremos	habría	habríamos	haya	hayamos	hubiera	hubiéramos
habrás	habréis	habrías	habríais	hayas	hayáis	hubieras	hubierais
habrá	habrán	habría	habrían	haya	hayan	hubiera	hubieran
haré	haremos	haría	haríamos	haga	hagamos	hiciera	hiciéramos
harás	haréis	harías	haríais	hagas	hagáis	hicieras	hicierais
hará	harán	haría	harían	haga	hagan	hiciera	hicieran
iré	iremos	iría	iríamos	vaya	vayamos	fuera	fuéramos
irás	iréis	irías	iríais	vayas	vayáis	fueras	fuerais
irá	irán	iría	irían	vaya	vayan	fuera	fueran
oiré	oiremos	oiría	oiríamos	oiga	oigamos	oyera	oyéramos
oirás	oiréis	oirías	oiríais	oigas	oigáis	oyeras	oyerais
oirá	oirán	oiría	oirían	oiga	oigan	oyera	oyeran
podré	podremos	podría	podríamos	pueda	podamos	pudiera	pudiéramos
podrás	podréis	podrías	podríais	puedas	podáis	pudieras	pudierais
podrá	podrán	podría	podrían	pueda	puedan	pudiera	pudieran
pondré	pondremos	pondría	pondríamos	ponga	pongamos	pusiera	pusiéramos
pondrás	pondréis	pondrías	pondríais	pongas	pongáis	pusieras	pusierais
pondrá	pondrán	pondría	pondrían	ponga	pongan	pusiera	pusieran

Irregular Verbs (continued)

1	2		3		4	
Infinitive **Present Participle** **Past Participle**	**Present**		**Preterite**		**Imperfect**	
querer queriendo querido	quiero quieres quiere	queremos queréis quieren	quise quisiste quiso	quisimos quisisteis quisieron	quería querías quería	queríamos queríais querían
saber sabiendo sabido	sé sabes sabe	sabemos sabéis saben	supe supiste supo	supimos supisteis supieron	sabía sabías sabía	sabíamos sabíais sabían
salir saliendo salido	salgo sales sale	salimos salís salen	salí saliste salió	salimos salisteis salieron	salía salías salía	salíamos salíais salían
ser siendo sido	soy eres es	somos sois son	fui fuiste fue	fuimos fuisteis fueron	era eras era	éramos erais eran
tener teniendo tenido	tengo tienes tiene	tenemos tenéis tienen	tuve tuviste tuvo	tuvimos tuvisteis tuvieron	tenía tenías tenía	teníamos teníais tenían
traer trayendo traído	traigo traes trae	traemos traéis traen	traje trajiste trajo	trajimos trajisteis trajeron	traía traías traía	traíamos traíais traían
venir viniendo venido	vengo vienes viene	venimos venís vienen	vine viniste vino	vinimos vinisteis vinieron	venía venías venía	veníamos veníais venían
ver viendo visto	veo ves ve	vemos veis ven	vi viste vio	vimos visteis vieron	veía veías veía	veíamos veíais veían

Irregular Verbs (continued)

5		6		7		8	
Future		Conditional		Present Subjunctive		Imperfect Subjunctive	
querré	querremos	querría	querríamos	quiera	queramos	quisiera	quisiéramos
querrás	querréis	querrías	querríais	quieras	queráis	quisieras	quisierais
querrá	querrán	querría	querrían	quiera	quieran	quisiera	quisieran
sabré	sabremos	sabría	sabríamos	sepa	sepamos	supiera	supiéramos
sabrás	sabréis	sabrías	sabríais	sepas	sepáis	supieras	supierais
sabrá	sabrán	sabría	sabrían	sepa	sepan	supiera	supieran
saldré	saldremos	saldría	saldríamos	salga	salgamos	saliera	saliéramos
saldrás	saldréis	saldrías	saldríais	salgas	salgáis	salieras	salierais
saldrá	saldrán	saldría	saldrían	salga	salgan	saliera	salieran
seré	seremos	sería	seríamos	sea	seamos	fuera	fuéramos
serás	seréis	serías	seríais	seas	seáis	fueras	fuerais
será	serán	sería	serían	sea	sean	fuera	fueran
tendré	tendremos	tendría	tendríamos	tenga	tengamos	tuviera	tuviéramos
tendrás	tendréis	tendrías	tendríais	tengas	tengáis	tuvieras	tuvierais
tendrá	tendrán	tendría	tendrían	tenga	tengan	tuviera	tuvieran
traeré	traeremos	traería	traeríamos	traiga	traigamos	trajera	trajéramos
traerás	traeréis	traerías	traeríais	traigas	traigáis	trajeras	trajerais
traerá	traerán	traería	traerían	traiga	traigan	trajera	trajeran
vendré	vendremos	vendría	vendríamos	venga	vengamos	viniera	viniéramos
vendrás	vendréis	vendrías	vendríais	vengas	vengáis	vinieras	vinierais
vendrá	vendrán	vendría	vendrían	venga	vengan	viniera	vinieran
veré	veremos	vería	veríamos	vea	veamos	viera	viéramos
verás	veréis	verías	veríais	veas	veáis	vieras	vierais
verá	verán	vería	verían	vea	vean	viera	vieran

Affirmative and Negative Commands

To form an affirmative *tú* command, use the present-tense indicative *Ud. / él / ella* form. This rule also applies to stem-changing verbs. Some verbs have an irregular affirmative *tú* command.

To form a command with *Ud.*, remove the *-s* from a negative *tú* command form. To form a command with *Uds.*, replace the *-s* of a negative *tú* command with an *-n*.

Regular and stem-changing verbs, and verbs ending in *-car, -gar,* and *-zar*

Infinitive	Tú	Negative tú	Usted	Ustedes
estudiar	estudia	no estudies	(no) estudie	(no) estudien
volver	vuelve	no vuelvas	(no) vuelva	(no) vuelvan
abrir	abre	no abras	(no) abra	(no) abran
sacar	saca	no saques	(no) saque	(no) saquen
llegar	llega	no llegues	(no) llegue	(no) lleguen
cruzar	cruza	no cruces	(no) cruce	(no) crucen

Irregular verbs

Infinitive	Tú	Negative tú	Usted	Ustedes
decir	di	no digas	(no) diga	(no) digan
hacer	haz	no hagas	(no) haga	(no) hagan
ir	ve	no vayas	(no) vaya	(no) vayan
mantener	mantén	no mantengas	(no) mantenga	(no) mantengan
poner	pon	no pongas	(no) ponga	(no) pongan
salir	sal	no salgas	(no) salga	(no) salgan
ser	sé	no seas	(no) sea	(no) sean
tener	ten	no tengas	(no) tenga	(no) tengan
venir	ven	no vengas	(no) venga	(no) vengan

Placement of Pronouns with Commands

Attach reflexive or object pronous at the end of affirmative commands. With negative commands, place them after the word *no*.

Toma esas vitaminas.
*¡Tóma**las** ahora mismo!*
*No **las** tomes.*

Expresiones útiles para conversar

Making an Apology

Perdóname. Forgive me.

Lo siento mucho. I'm very sorry.

Fue un malentendido. It was a misunderstanding.

Hagamos las paces. Let's make up.

Reconciliémonos. Let's reconcile.

Te pido perdón. I'm asking for your forgiveness.

Estoy equivocado, -a. I'm wrong.

Pongámonos de acuerdo. Let's come to an agreement.

Yo tengo la culpa. It's my fault.

Talking about Friendship

Tenemos mucho en común. We have a lot in common.

Te acepto tal como eres. I accept you just the way you are.

Tengo celos. I'm jealous.

No me hace caso. He / She doesn't pay any attention to me.

Sólo piensa en sí mismo, -a. He / She only thinks about himself / herself.

Confío en ti. I trust you.

Cuento contigo. I count on you.

Sé guardar un secreto. I can keep a secret.

Resolvamos este conflicto. Let's resolve this conflict.

Tenemos una diferencia de opinión. We disagree.

Me identifico contigo. I identify with you.

De hoy en adelante . . . From now on . . .

Ten en cuenta . . . Keep in mind . . .

Tengo derecho a . . . I have a right to . . .

Expressing Disagreement

Qué va. No way.

Yo no fui. I didn't do it.

No es cierto que . . . It's not true that . . .

No es verdad que . . . It's not true that . . .

No estoy de acuerdo. I disagree.

Me parece que no tienes razón. I think you're wrong.

Expressing Interest

Me es posible. I can.

Me gustaría . . . I'd like to . . .

Me encantaría . . . I'd love to . . .

Expressing Certainty or Possibility

Es cierto que . . . It's true that . . .

Estoy seguro, -a que . . . I'm sure that . . .

Es probable que . . . It's probable that . . .

Puede ser que . . . It's possible that . . .

Es posible que . . . It's possible that . . .

Es evidente que . . . It's clear that . . .

Quizás . . . Perhaps . . .

Expressing Doubt or Uncertainty

Dudo que . . . I doubt that . . .

No creo que . . . I don't think that . . .

No estoy seguro, -a que . . . I'm not sure that . . .

Es imposible que . . . It's impossible that . . .

Talking about How You Feel Physically

Me siento fatal. I feel awful.

Me caigo de sueño. I'm exhausted.

Estoy resfriado, -a. I have a cold.

Tengo tos. I have a cough.

Estornudo mucho. I'm sneezing a lot.

Tengo gripe. I have the flu.

Tengo fiebre. I have a fever.

Tengo alergia a . . . I'm allergic to . . .

Talking about How You Feel Emotionally

Estoy en la luna. I'm daydreaming.

No puedo concentrarme. I can't concentrate.

No aguanto más. I can't take it anymore.

Estoy de buen humor. I'm in a good mood.

Estoy de mal humor. I'm in a bad mood.

Estoy estresado, -a. I'm stressed out.

Me preocupo por . . . I'm worried about . . .

Me emociono mucho. I'm very emotional.

Estoy orgulloso, -a de . . . I'm proud of . . .

Estoy animado, -a. I'm excited.

Tengo confianza en mí mismo, -a. I have confidence in myself.

Me vuelvo loco, -a. I'm going crazy.

He cambiado de opinión. I've changed my mind.

Me doy cuenta de que . . . I realize that . . .

Me vuelvo . . . I'm getting / becoming . . .

Haré lo que me dé la gana. I'll do whatever I want.

Talking about Personal Goals

Alcancé mi meta. I achieved my goal.

Hice un esfuerzo. I made an effort.

Salí campeón. I won (I was the winner).

¡Felicitaciones! Congratulations!

Eres mi fuente de inspiración. You're my inspiration.

Describing Things or People

Se parece a . . . It / He / She looks like . . .

Suena a . . . It / He / She sounds like . . . .

Está basado, -a en . . . It's based on . . .

Se destaca. It / He / She stands out.

Está a cargo de . . . He / She is in charge of . . .

Vocabulario español-inglés

The *Vocabulario español-inglés* contains all active vocabulary from the text, including vocabulary presented in the grammar sections.

A dash (—) represents the main entry word. For example, **pasar la** — after **la aspiradora** means **pasar la aspiradora.**

The number following each entry indicates the chapter in which the word or expression is presented. A Roman numeral (I) indicates that the word was presented in REALIDADES 1. A Roman numeral (II) indicates that the word was presented in REALIDADES 2.

The following abbreviations are used in this list: *adj.* (adjective), *dir. obj.* (direct object), *f.* (feminine), *fam.* (familiar), *ind. obj.* (indirect object), *inf.* (infinitive), *m.* (masculine), *pl.* (plural), *prep.* (preposition), *pron.* (pronoun), *sing.* (singular).

A

a to (*prep.*) (I)

— **... le gusta(n)** he / she likes (I)

— **... le encanta(n)** he / she loves (I)

— **casa** (to) home (I)

— **causa de** because of (II)

— **favor de** in favor of (5-2)

— **la derecha (de)** to the right (of) (I)

— **la izquierda (de)** to the left (of) (I)

— **la parrilla** on the grill (II)

— **la una de la tarde** at one (o'clock) in the afternoon (I)

— **las ocho de la mañana** at eight (o'clock) in the morning (I)

— **las ocho de la noche** at eight (o'clock) in the evening, at night (I)

— **mano** by hand (II)

— **medida que** as (10-2)

— **menos que** unless (9-2)

— **menudo** often (I)

— **pesar de** despite (10-2)

— **mí también.** I do (like to) too. (I)

— **mí tampoco.** I don't (like to) either. (I)

¿— **qué hora?** (At) what time? (I)

— **tiempo** on time (II)

— **tiempo completo** full time (5-1)

— **tiempo parcial** part time (5-1)

— **través de** through (2-1)

— **veces** sometimes (I)

— **ver.** Let's see. (I)

abdominales crunches (3-2)

abierto, -a open (II)

el **abogado, la abogada** lawyer (II, 6-1)

abordar to board (II)

abrazar(se) to hug (II)

el **abrigo** coat (I)

abril April (I)

abrir to open (I)

abstracto, -a abstract (2-1)

el **abuelo, la abuela** grandfather, grandmother (I)

los **abuelos** grandparents (I)

aburrido, -a boring (I)

aburrir to bore (I)

aburrirse to get bored (II)

me aburre(n) it bores me (they bore me) (I)

el **abuso** abuse (10-1)

acabar de + *inf.* to have just... (I)

el **accidente** accident (II)

el **aceite** cooking oil (II)

aceptar to accept (4-1)

— **tal como (soy)** to accept (me) the way (I am) (4-1)

acercarse a to approach (1-1)

acompañar to accompany (II)

aconsejar to advise (3-2)

acostarse (o → ue) to go to bed (II)

las **actividades extracurriculares** extracurricular activities (II)

el **actor** actor (I)

la **actriz,** *pl.* **las actrices** actress (I)

la **actuación** acting (II)

actuar to perform (2-2)

el **acueducto** aqueduct (8-1)

acuerdo:

Estoy de —. I agree. (I)

No estoy de —. I don't agree. (I)

el **acusado, la acusada** accused (10-2)

acusar to accuse (4-2)

adecuado, -a adequate (10-1)

además de in addition to, besides (II, 6-1)

¡Adiós! Good-bye! (I)

la **adolescencia** adolescence (10-1)

el / la **adolescente** adolescent (10-1)

¿Adónde? (To) where? (I)

adoptar to adopt (8-2)

la **aduana** customs (II)

el **aduanero, la aduanera** customs officer (II)

el **aeropuerto** airport (II)

el **aerosol** aerosol (9-2)
afectar to affect (9-2)
afeitarse to shave (II)
el **aficionado, la aficionada**
fan (II)
afortunadamente fortunately
(II)
africano, -a African (8-2)
la **agencia de viajes** travel
agency (II)
el / la **agente de viajes** travel
agent (II)
agitado, -a agitated (II)
agosto August (I)
agotar(se) to exhaust, to run
out (9-1)
agradable pleasant (5-1)
el **agricultor, la agricultora**
farmer (II)
el **agua** *f.* water (I)
el **— de colonia** cologne (II)
el **aguacate** avocado (II)
aguantar to endure, to tolerate
(3-2)
el **águila calva,** *pl.* **las águilas**
calvas bald eagle (9-2)
el **agujero** hole (9-2)
ahora now (I)
ahorrar to save (II, 6-1)
el **aire acondicionado** air
conditioner (II)
el **ajedrez** chess (II)
el **ajo** garlic (II)
al *(a + el),* **a la** to the (I)
— aire libre outdoors (II)
— amanecer at dawn (1-1)
— anochecer at dusk (1-1)
— final at the end (II)
— horno baked (II)
— igual que as, like (7-2)
— lado de next to (I)
— llegar upon arriving (8-2)
— principio at the beginning

(1-2)
alcanzar to reach (1-2)
alegrarse to be delighted (4-1)
alegre happy (II)
la **alergia** allergy (3-1)
la **alfombra** rug (I)
algo something (I)
¿— más? Anything else? (I)
el **algodón** cotton (II)
alguien someone, anyone (II)
algún, alguno, -a some (II)
— día some day (II)
algunos, as any (II)
la **alimentación** nutrition,
feeding (3-1)
los **alimentos** food (3-1)
allí there (I)
una vez — once there (1-1)
el **almacén,** *pl.* **los almacenes**
department store (I)
almorzar (o → ue) to have
lunch (II)
el **almuerzo** lunch (I)
en el — for lunch (I)
alquilar to rent (II)
alrededor de around (II)
alto, -a tall (I); high (II)
el **alto** height (7-1)
amable kind, nice (4-1)
amanecer:
al — at dawn (1-1)
amarillo, -a yellow (I)
ambicioso, -a ambitious (6-1)
ambos both (10-1)
la **ambulancia** ambulance (II)
la **amenaza** threat (9-2)
amenazar to threaten (9-1)
la **amistad** friendship (4-1)
el **amor** love (II)
añadir to add (II)
anaranjado, -a orange (I)
ancho, -a wide (II)
el **ancho** width (7-1)

el **anciano, la anciana** elderly
man, elderly woman (I)
los **ancianos** the elderly (I)
andar to walk, to move (1-1)
el **anillo** ring (I)
animado, -a excited (1-2)
el **animador, la animadora**
cheerleader (II)
el **animal** animal (I)
el **aniversario** anniversary (II)
anoche last night (I)
anochecer:
al — at dusk (1-1)
ante before (10-1)
los **anteojos de sol** sunglasses (I)
el **antepasado, la antepasada**
ancestor (8-2)
anteriormente before (8-1)
antes de before (I, II)
el **antibiótico** antibiotic (3-1)
antiguo, -a old, antique (II)
anunciar to announce (II)
el **anuncio** announcement (II)
el **— clasificado** classified ad
(5-1)
el **año** year (I)
el **— pasado** last year (I)
¿Cuántos —s tiene(n)...?
How old is / are...? (I)
Tiene(n)...—s. He / She is /
They are...(years old). (I)
apagar to put out *(fire)* (II); to
turn off (II)
el **aparato** gadget (6-2)
aparecer (zc) to appear (1-1,7-2)
el **apartamento** apartment (I)
aplaudir to applaud (II)
el **aplauso** applause (2-2)
aplicar (las leyes) to apply
(the law) (10-1)
apoyar(se) to support, to back
(each other) (4-1)
el **apoyo** support (10-1)

aprender (a) to learn (I)
— **de memoria** to memorize (II)

apretado, -a tight (II)

apropiado, -a appropriate (3-1)

aproximadamente approximately (II)

aquel, aquella that one (over there) (II)

aquellos, aquellas those (over there) (II)

aquí here (I)

el / la **árabe** Arab (8-1)

el **árbol** tree (I)

el **arco** arch (8-1)

los **aretes** earrings (I)

el **argumento** plot (II)

el **arma,** *pl.* **las armas** weapon (8-2)

el **armario** closet, locker (I, II, 10-1)

la **armonía** harmony (4-2)

el **arqueólogo, la arqueóloga** archaeologist (7-1)

el **arquitecto, la arquitecta** architect (II, 6-1)

la **arquitectura** architecture (8-1)

arreglar (el cuarto) to straighten up (the room) (I)

arreglarse (el pelo) to fix (one's hair) (II)

arrestar to arrest (II)

arrojar (se) to throw (7-2)

el **arroz** rice (I)

el **arte:**
la clase de — art class (I)
la obra de — work of art (2-1)
las artes the arts (II)
las — marciales martial arts (II)

la **artesanía** handicrafts (II)

el **artículo** article (II)

el / la **artista** artist (II)

artístico, -a artistic (I)

asado, -a grilled (II)

asar to grill (II)

el **ascensor** elevator (II)

asco:
¡Qué —! How awful! (I)

asegurar to assure (10-2)

así this way (1-1)
— **que** therefore (6-1)

el **asiento** seat (II)

asimilar(se) to assimilate (8-1)

asistir a to attend (II)

la **aspiración** aspiration (10-2)

la **aspirina** aspirin (3-1)

el **astrónomo, la astrónoma** astronomer (7-2)

el **asunto** matter (10-1)

asustado, -a frightened (II)

asustar to scare (1-1)

atender to help, to assist (5-1)

atento, -a attentive (II)

el / la **atleta** athlete (II)

la **atmósfera** atmosphere (9-2)

la **atracción,** *pl.* **las atracciones** attraction (I)

atrapar to catch, trap (9-2)

atreverse to dare (4-2)

atrevido, -a daring (I)

la **audición,** *pl.* **las audiciones** audition (II)

el **auditorio** auditorium (II)

aumentar to increase (6-2)

aunque despite, even when (3-1)

el **autobús,** *pl.* **los autobuses** bus (I)

la **autoridad** authority (10-1)

el **autorretrato** self-portrait (2-1)

el / la **auxiliar de vuelo** flight attendant (II)

el **avance** advance (6-2)

el **ave** bird (9-2)

la **avenida** avenue (II)

averiguar to find out (6-1)

el **avión** airplane (I)

¡Ay! ¡Qué pena! Oh! What a shame / pity! (I)

ayer yesterday (I)

la **ayuda** help (II)

ayudar to help (I)

el **azúcar** sugar (I)

azul blue (I)

el **azulejo** tile (8-1)

bailar to dance (I)

el **bailarín, la bailarina** dancer (II)

el **baile** dance (I)

bajar to go down (II)

bajar (información) to download (I)

bajo, -a short *(stature)* (I); low (II)

la planta baja ground floor (I)

el **balcón,** *pl.* **los balcones** balcony (8-1)

la **ballena** whale (9-2)

el **banco** bank (II)

la **banda** (musical) band (II)

la **bandera** flag (I)

el **banquero, la banquera** banker (6-1)

bañarse to take a bath (II)

el **baño** bathroom (I)

el traje de — swimsuit (I)

barato, -a inexpensive, cheap (I)

el **barco** boat, ship (I)

el **barrio** neighborhood (I)

¡Basta! Enough! (II)

el **básquetbol:**

jugar al — to play basketball (I)

bastante enough, rather (I)

basura:

sacar la — to take out the trash (I)

la **batalla** battle (8-2)

batir to beat (II)

el / la **bebé** baby (II)

beber to drink (I)

las **bebidas** drinks (I)

béisbol:

jugar al — to play baseball (I)

bello, -a beautiful (II)

beneficiar to benefit (5-2)

los **beneficios** benefits (II, 5-1)

besar(se) to kiss (II)

la **biblioteca** library (I)

bien well (I)

— educado, -a well-behaved (II)

pasarlo — to have a good time (1-1)

bienvenido, -a welcome (II)

bilingüe bilingual (II)

los **binoculares** binoculars (1-1)

el **bistec** steak (I)

blanco, -a white (I)

los **bloques** blocks (II)

la **blusa** blouse (I)

la **boca** mouth (I)

la **boda** wedding (II)

el **boleto** ticket (I)

el **bolígrafo** pen (I)

los **bolos:**

jugar a los — to bowl (II)

la **bolsa** bag, sack (I)

el **bolso** purse (I)

el **bombero, la bombera** firefighter (II)

bonito, -a pretty (I)

el **bosque** wood, forest (II, 1-1)

las **botas** boots (I)

el **bote:**

pasear en — to go boating (I)

el — de vela sailboat (II)

la **botella** bottle (I)

el **brazo** arm (I)

brillar to shine (7-2)

la **brújula** compass (1-1)

bucear to scuba dive, to snorkel (I)

bueno (buen), -a good (I)

Buenas noches. Good evening. (I)

Buenas tardes. Good afternoon. (I)

Buenos días. Good morning. (I)

buscar to look for, to search (for) (I)

la **búsqueda** search (II)

hacer una — to do a search (II)

el **buzón,** *pl.* **los buzones** mailbox (II)

C

el **caballo:**
    montar a — to ride horseback (I)

la **cabeza** head (I)

cada día every day (I)

la **cadena** chain (I)

caer granizo to hail (1-1)

caerse to fall (II)
    — de sueño to be exhausted, sleepy (3-2)
    (yo) me caigo I fall (II)
    (tú) te caes you fall (II)

el **café** coffee; café (I)

la **caja** box (I); cash register (II)

el **cajero, la cajera** cashier (II)
    el — automático ATM (II)

el **calambre** cramp (3-2)

los **calcetines** socks (I)

el **calcio** calcium (3-1)

la **calculadora** calculator (I)

calcular to calculate, to compute (7-1)

el **caldo** broth (II)

la **calefacción** heat (II)

calentar (e → ie) to heat (II)

caliente hot (II)

la **calle** street, road (I)

calor:
    Hace —. It's hot. (I)
    tener — to be warm (I)

la **cama** bed (I)
    hacer la — to make the bed (I)

la **cámara** camera (I)
    la — digital digital camera (I)

el **camarero, la camarera** waiter, waitress (I)

el **camarón,** *pl.* **los camarones** shrimp (II)

cambiar to change, to exchange (II)
    — de opinión to change one's mind (4-1)

caminar to walk (I)

la **caminata** walk (II)
    dar una — to take a walk (II)

el **camión,** *pl.* **los camiones** truck (II)

la **camisa** shirt (I)

la **camiseta** T-shirt (I)

el **campamento** camp (I)

la **campaña** campaign (5-2)

el **campeón, la campeona,** *pl.* **los campeones** champion (II)

el **campeonato** championship (II)

el **campo** countryside, field (I, 6-2)

el **canal** (TV) channel (I)

la **canción,** *pl.* **las canciones** song (I, II)
    canoso: pelo — gray hair (I)
    cansado, -a tired (I)

el / la **cantante** singer (II)
    cantar to sing (I)

la **capa de ozono** ozone layer (9-2)
    capaz able (6-1)
    capturar to capture (II)

la **cara** face (II)
    cara a cara face-to-face (I)
    caramba good gracious (II)

el **carbohidrato** carbohydrate (3-1)
    cariñoso, -a loving, affectionate (4-1)

la **carne** meat (I)
    la — de res beef (II)

el **carnet de identidad** I.D. card (II)
    caro, -a expensive (I)

la **carpeta** folder (I)
    la — de argollas three-ring binder (I)

la **carrera** race (II, 1-2); career (II)

la **carretera** highway (II)

la **carta** letter (I, II)
    echar una — to mail a letter (II)

el **cartel** poster (I)

la **cartera** wallet (I)

el **cartero, la cartera** mail carrier (II)

el **cartón** cardboard (I)

la **casa** home, house (I)
    a — (to) home (I)
    en — at home (I)
    — de cambio money exchange (II)

casado, -a married (6-1)

casarse (con) to get married to (II)

casi almost (I, II)

castaño:
    pelo — brown (chestnut) hair (I)

castigar to punish (9-1)

el **castigo** punishment (10-2)

el **castillo** castle (II)

la **catedral** cathedral (II)

catorce fourteen (I)

la **causa** cause (II)

la **caza** hunting (9-2)

la **cebolla** onion (I)

celebrar to celebrate (I)

celos:
    tener celos to be jealous (4-1)

celoso, -a jealous (4-1)

la **cena** dinner (I)

centígrado
    el grado — centigrade degree (3-1)

el **centímetro** centimeter (7-1)

el **centro** center, downtown (I, II)
    el — comercial mall (I)
    el — de la comunidad community center (5-2)

el **— de reciclaje** recycling center (I)

el **— de rehabilitación** rehabilitation center (5-2)

el **— recreativo** recreation center (5-2)

cepillarse (los dientes) to brush (one's teeth) (II)

el **cepillo** brush (II)

el **— de dientes** toothbrush (II)

la **cerámica** pottery (2-1)

cerca (de) close (to), near (I)

el **cerdo** pork (II)

la **chuleta de —** pork chop (II)

el **cereal** cereal (I)

la **ceremonia** ceremony (1-2)

la **cereza** cherry (II)

cero zero (I)

cerrado, -a closed (II)

cerrar to close (II)

el **certificado** certificate, diploma (1-2)

la **cesta** basket (II)

el **champú** shampoo (II)

la **chaqueta** jacket (I)

charlar to chat (II)

el **cheque:**

cobrar un — to cash a check (II)

el **— de viajero** traveler's check (II)

el **— personal** personal check (II)

la **chica** girl (I)

el **chico** boy (I)

chismoso, -a gossipy (4-1)

chocar con to crash into, to collide with (II)

la **chuleta de cerdo** pork chop (II)

el **cielo** sky (II)

cien one hundred (I)

las **ciencias:**

la **clase de — naturales** science class (I)

la **clase de — sociales** social studies class (I)

el **científico, la científica** scientist (II, 6-1)

(es) cierto (it is) true (II)

cinco five (I)

cincuenta fifty (I)

el **cine** movie theater (I)

la **cinta adhesiva** adhesive tape (II)

el **cinturón,** *pl.* **los cinturones** belt (II)

el **círculo** circle (7-1)

la **cita** date (II)

la **ciudad** city (I)

la **ciudadanía** citizenship (5-2)

el **ciudadano, la ciudadana** citizen (5-2)

la **civilización** civilization (7-1)

claro, -a light *(color)* (II)

la **clase** class (I)

la **sala de clases** classroom (I)

¿Qué — de...? What kind of...? (I)

clásico, -a classical (2-2)

el **cliente, la clienta** client (5-1)

el **clima** weather (9-2)

el **club,** *pl.* **los clubes** club (II)

el **— atlético** athletic club (II)

cobrar un cheque to cash a check (II)

el **coche** car (I)

la **cocina** kitchen (I)

cocinar to cook (I)

el **cocinero, la cocinera** cook (6-1)

el **código de vestimenta** dress code (10-1)

el **codo** elbow (II)

colaborar to collaborate (4-2)

la **colección,** *pl.* **las colecciones** collection (II)

coleccionar to collect (II)

el **colegio** secondary school, high school (II)

la **colina** hill (II)

el **collar** necklace (I)

colocar to put, place (9-1)

la **colonia** colony (8-2)

el **color,** *pl.* **los colores** (I)

¿De qué — ...? What color...? (I)

la **comedia** comedy (I)

el **comedor** dining room (I)

el **— de beneficencia** soup kitchen (5-2)

el **comentario** commentary (II)

comenzar (e → ie) to start (II)

comer to eat (I)

cómico, -a funny, comical (I)

la **comida** food, meal (I)

la **— basura** junk food (3-1)

como like, as (I)

— si fuera as though it were (6-2)

¿Cómo?:

¿— eres? What are you like? (I)

¿— es? What is he / she like? (I)

¿— está Ud.? How are you? *formal* (I)

¿— estás? How are you? *fam.* (I)

¿— lo pasaste? How was it (for you)? (I)

¿— se dice...? How do you say...? (I)

¿— se escribe...? How is...spelled? (I)

¿— se hace...? How do you make...? (II)

¿— se llama? What's his / her name? (I)

¿— se va a...? How do you go to...? (II)

¿— te llamas? What is your name? (I)

¿— te queda(n)? How does it (do they) fit you? (I)

¡Cómo no! Of course! (II)

la **cómoda** dresser (I)

cómodo, -a comfortable (II)

la **compañía** firm, company (5-1)

compartir to share (I)

el **compás** rhythm (2-2)

la **competencia** competition (II)

competir (e → i) to compete (II)

complicado, -a complicated (I, II)

componerse de to be formed by (8-2)

el **comportamiento** behavior (4-2)

la **composición,** *pl.* las **composiciones** composition (I)

comprar to buy (I)

  — recuerdos to buy souvenirs (I)

comprender to understand (I)

comprensivo, -a understanding (4-1)

la **computación** computer science (5-1)

la **computadora** computer (I)

  la — portátil laptop computer (I)

  usar la — to use the computer (I)

comunicarse to communicate (I, 6-2)

  (tú) te comunicas you communicate (I)

  (yo) me comunico I communicate (I)

la **comunidad** community (I)

con with (I)

  — destino a going to (II)

  — mis / tus amigos with my / your friends (I)

— tal de que provided that (9-2)

¿— qué se sirve? What do you serve it with? (II)

¿— quién? With whom? (I)

concentrarse to concentrate (3-2)

el **concierto** concert (I)

el **concurso** contest (II)

  el — de belleza beauty contest (II)

el **conductor, la conductora** driver (II)

el **conejo** rabbit (7-2)

confianza trust (4-1)

  — en sí mismo, -a self-confidence (3-2)

confiar (i → í) to trust (4-1)

el **conflicto** conflict (4-2)

congelado, -a frozen (II)

el **conjunto** band (2-2)

conmigo with me (I)

conocer to know, to be acquainted with (I, II)

los **conocimientos** knowledge (5-1)

la **conquista** conquest (8-1)

conquistar to conquer (8-1)

conseguir (e → i) to obtain (II)

el **consejero, la consejera** counselor (5-1)

el **consejo** advice (3-2)

consentido, -a spoiled (II)

conservar to conserve (II, 9-1)

considerado, -a considerate (4-1)

la **construcción** construction (8-1)

construir (i → y) to build (5-2)

el **consultorio** doctor's / dentist's office (II)

el **contador, la contadora** accountant (II, 6-1)

la **contaminación** pollution (II, 9-1)

contaminado, -a polluted (II, 9-1)

contaminar to pollute (6-2)

contar (chistes) (o → ue) to tell (jokes) (II)

  — con to count on (4-1)

contener to contain (3-1)

contento, -a happy (I)

contestar to answer (II)

contigo with you (I)

contra against (II, 1-2)

  en — (de) against (5-2)

contribuir (u → y) to contribute (7-2)

convertirse (en) to turn (into), to become (7-2)

el **corazón** heart (3-2)

la **corbata** tie (I)

el **coro** chorus, choir (II)

el **correo** post office (II)

el **correo electrónico** e-mail (I)

  escribir por — to write e-mail (I)

correr to run (I)

cortar to cut (I, II)

  — el césped to mow the lawn (I)

  —se to cut oneself (II)

  —se el pelo to cut one's hair (II)

cortés, *pl.* **corteses** polite (II)

las **cortinas** curtains (I)

corto, -a short *(length)* (I)

  los pantalones —s shorts (I)

la **cosa** thing (I)

costar (o → ue) to cost (I)

  ¿Cuánto cuesta(n)...? How much does (do)...cost? (I)

la **costumbre** custom (II)

crear to create (I)

  — una página Web to create a Web page (II)

crecer to grow (9-1)

la **creencia** belief (7-2)

creer:

   Creo que... I think... (I)

   Creo que no. I don't think so. (I)

   Creo que sí. I think so. (I)

el **crimen** crime (II)

el / la **criminal** criminal (II)

el **cristiano, la cristiana** Christian (8-1)

criticar to criticize (4-2)

el **crítico, la crítica** critic (II)

el **cruce de calles** intersection (II)

cruzar to cross (II)

el **cuaderno** notebook (I)

la **cuadra** block (II)

el **cuadro** painting (I)

¿Cuál? Which? What? (I)

   ¿— es la fecha? What is the date? (I)

la **cualidad** quality (4-1)

cualquier, -a any (7-2)

¿Cuándo? When? (I)

¿Cuánto?:

   ¿— cuesta(n)...? How much does (do)...cost? (I)

   ¿— tiempo hace que...? How long (has)...? (II)

   ¿Cuántos, -as? How many? (I)

   ¿—s años tiene(n)...? How old is / are...? (I)

cuanto:

   en — a with respect to, as for (10-1)

   en — as soon as (9-1)

cuarenta forty (I)

cuarto, -a fourth (I)

   y — quarter past *(in telling time)* (I)

el **cuarto** room (I)

cuatro four (I)

cuatrocientos, -as four hundred (I)

cubrir to cover (7-1)

la **cuchara** spoon (I)

la **cucharada** tablespoon(ful) (II)

el **cuchillo** knife (I)

el **cuello** neck (II)

la **cuenta** bill (I)

   tener en — to take into account (6-2)

la **cuerda** rope (II)

el **cuero** leather (II)

cuidadoso, -a careful (6-1)

cuidar a to take care of (II)

culpable guilty (10-2)

el **cumpleaños** birthday (I)

   ¡Feliz —! Happy birthday! (I)

cumplir años to have a birthday (II)

cumplir con to carry out, to perform (5-1)

el **cupón de regalo,** *pl.* **los cupones de regalo** gift certificate (II)

curar to cure (6-2)

el **curso:**

   tomar un curso to take a course (I)

D

la **danza** dance (2-2)

dañar to damage (9-1)

dar to give (I)

   — + *movie or TV program* to show (I)

   — de comer al perro to feed the dog (I)

   — puntadas to stitch *(surgically)* (II)

   — un discurso to give a speech (II)

   — un paseo to take a walk, to stroll (1-1)

   — una caminata to take a walk (II)

dar(se) la mano to shake hands (II)

darse cuenta de to realize (1-2)

de of, from (I)

   — acuerdo. OK. Agreed. (II)

   — algodón cotton (II)

   — cuero leather (II)

   ¿— dónde eres? Where are you from? (I)

   — ida y vuelta round trip (II)

   — la mañana / la tarde / la noche in the morning / afternoon / evening (I)

   — lana wool (II)

   — negocios business (II)

   — niño as a child (II)

   — oro gold (II)

   — pequeño as a child (II)

   — plata silver (II)

   — plato principal as a main dish (I)

   — postre for dessert (I)

   — prisa in a hurry (II)

   ¿— qué color...? What color...? (I)

   ¿— qué está hecho, -a? What is it made of? (II)

— **repente** suddenly (II)

— **seda** silk (II)

— **sólo un color** solid-colored (II)

— **tela sintética** synthetic fabric (II)

¿— **veras?** Really? (I)

— **vez en cuando** once in a while (II)

debajo de underneath (I)

deber should, must (I)

el **deber** duty (10-1)

debido a due to (9-1)

débil weak (3-2)

decidir to decide (I)

décimo, -a tenth (I)

decir to say, to tell (I)

— **la verdad** to tell the truth (II)

¿**Cómo se dice...?** How do you say...? (I)

dime tell me (I)

¡**No me digas!** You don't say! (I)

¿**Qué quiere —...?** What does...mean? (I)

Quiere — ... It means... (I)

Se dice... You say..., people say... (I)

las **decoraciones** decorations (I)

decorar to decorate (I)

dedicado, -a dedicated (5-1)

dedicarse a to dedicate oneself to (6-1)

el **dedo** finger (I)

Déjame en paz. Leave me alone. (II)

dejar to leave, to let (II)

— **de** to stop (doing something) (1-1)

— **huellas** to leave marks, traces (8-1)

no dejes don't leave, don't let (II)

delante de in front of (I)

delicioso, -a delicious (I)

la **demanda** demand (6-2)

los / las **demás** others (I)

demasiado too (I)

democrático, -a democratic (10-2)

el / la **dentista** dentist (II)

dentro de inside (II)

depende it depends (II)

depender de to depend on (9-1)

el **dependiente, la dependienta** salesperson (I)

deportista athletic, sports-minded (I)

derecha:

a la — (de) to the right (of) (I)

derecho straight (II)

el **derecho** *(study of)* law (II)

los **derechos** rights (5-2)

el **derrame de petróleo** oil spill (9-2)

derretir to melt (9-2)

desafortunadamente unfortunately (1-2)

desanimado, -a discouraged (1-2)

desaparecer to disappear (6-2)

desarrollar to develop (3-2)

el **desarrollo** development (6-2)

el **desayuno** breakfast (I)

en el — for breakfast (I)

descansar to rest, to relax (I)

la **descendencia** descent, ancestry (8-2)

desconfiar to mistrust (4-1)

desconocido, -a unknown (8-2)

descubrir to discover (6-2)

los **descuentos:**

la tienda de — discount store (I)

desde from, since (II)

desear to wish (I)

¿**Qué desean (Uds.)?** What would you like? *formal* (I)

desempeñar un cargo to hold a position (6-1)

el **desempleo** unemployment (10-2)

el **desfile** parade (II)

deshacerse de to get rid of (9-1)

el **desierto** desert (II, 1-1)

la **desigualdad** inequity (10-2)

desobediente disobedient (II)

el **desodorante** deodorant (II)

desordenado, -a messy (I)

despacio slowly (II)

el **despacho** office, study (home) (I)

despedirse (e → i) de to say good-bye (II)

el **despertador** alarm clock (I)

desperdiciar to waste (9-1)

el **desperdicio** waste (9-1)

despertarse (e → ie) to wake up (II)

después (de) afterwards, after (I)

destacar(se) to stand out (2-2)

la **destrucción** destruction (II)

destruir (i → y) to destroy (II)

el / la **detective** detective (II)

detener to detain (10-2), to stop (9-2)

detrás de behind (I)

devolver (o → ue) (un libro) to return (a book) (II)

el **día** day (I)

Buenos —s. Good morning. (I)

cada — every day (I)

el — festivo holiday (II)

¿**Qué — es hoy?** What day is today? (I)

todos los —s every day (I)

el **diámetro** diameter (7-1)

la **diapositiva** slide (I)

dibujar to draw (I)

el **diccionario** dictionary (I)

diciembre December (I)

diecinueve nineteen (I)

dieciocho eighteen (I)

dieciséis sixteen (I)

diecisiete seventeen (I)

los **dientes** teeth (II)

    cepillarse — to brush one's teeth (II)

    el cepillo de — toothbrush (II)

la **dieta** diet (3-1)

diez ten (I)

la **diferencia de opinión** difference of opinion (4-2)

difícil difficult (I)

digital:

    la cámara — digital camera (I)

dime tell me (I)

el **dinero** money (I)

    — en efectivo cash (II)

el **dinosaurio** dinosaur (II)

el **dios, la diosa** god, goddess (7-2)

la **dirección,** *pl.* **las direcciones** direction (II)

    la — electrónica e-mail address (I)

directo, -a direct (II)

el **director, la directora** (school) principal (II)

el **disco compacto** compact disc (I)

    grabar un — to burn a CD (I)

discriminado, -a discriminated (10-1)

discriminar to discriminate (10-1)

el **discurso** speech (II)

discutir to discuss (II)

el **diseñador, la diseñadora** designer (II, 6-1)

diseñar to design (6-1)

el **diseño** design (7-1)

disfrutar de to enjoy (II)

disminuir (i→y) to decrease, to diminish (9-2)

la **distancia** distance (7-1)

divertido, -a amusing, fun (I)

divertirse (e → ie) to have fun (II)

doblar to turn (II)

doce twelve (I)

el **documento** document (I)

doler (o → ue) to hurt (I, II)

el **dolor** pain (II)

dominar to dominate (8-1)

domingo Sunday (I)

donar to donate (5-2)

dónde:

    ¿—? Where? (I)

    ¿De — eres? Where are you from? (I)

dormido, -a asleep (II)

dormir (o → ue) to sleep (I)

    —se to fall asleep (II)

    el saco de — sleeping bag (1-1)

el **dormitorio** bedroom (I)

dos two (I)

los **/ las dos** both (I)

doscientos, -as two hundred (I)

el **drama** drama (I)

la **ducha** shower (II)

ducharse to take a shower (II)

dudar to doubt (II, 7-1)

el **dueño, la dueña** owner (II, 5-1)

dulce sweet (II)

los **dulces** candy (I)

durante during (I)

durar to last (I, II)

el **durazno** peach (II)

duro, -a hard (1-2)

E —————

echar to throw (away) (9-1)

    — una carta to mail a letter (II)

el **eclipse** eclipse (7-2)

ecológico, -a ecological (II)

económico, -a economical (II, 9-1)

la **edad** age (3-1)

el **edificio de apartamentos** apartment building (II)

la **educación física:**

    la clase de — physical education class (I)

educar to educate (5-2)

efecto:

    el — invernadero greenhouse effect (9-2)

los **efectos especiales** special effects (II)

eficiente efficient (II, 6-1)

egoísta selfish (4-1)

el **ejercicio:**

    hacer — to exercise (I)

    ejercicios aeróbicos aerobics (3-2)

el *m. sing.* the (I)

él he (I)

la **electricidad** electricity (II, 9-1)

los **electrodomésticos:**

    la tienda de — household-appliance store (I)

electrónico, -a:

    la dirección — e-mail address (I)

elegante elegant (II)

eliminar to eliminate (II, 1-2)

ella she (I)

ellas *f.* they (I)

ellos *m.* they (I)

emocionado, -a excited, emotional (II)

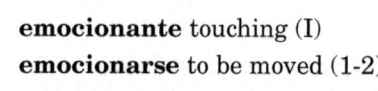

emocionante touching (I)

emocionarse to be moved (1-2)

el empate tie (II)

empezar (e → ie) to begin, to start (I, II)

el empleado, la empleada employee (II)

emprendedor, -a enterprising (6-1)

la empresa business (6-1)

en in, on (I)

— + *vehicle* by, in, on (I)

— casa at home (I)

— contra (de) against (5-2)

— cuanto as soon as (9-1)

— cuanto a with respect to (10-1)

— la...hora in the...hour (class period) (I)

— la Red online (I)

— lugar de instead of (10-2)

— medio de in the middle of (II)

— punto exactly (II)

¿— qué puedo servirle? How can I help you? (I)

— realidad really (II)

— seguida right away (II)

— vez de instead of (10-1)

enamorado, -a de in love with (II)

enamorarse (de) to fall in love (with) (II)

encantado, -a delighted (I)

encantar to please very much, to love (I)

a él / ella le encanta(n) he / she loves (I)

me encantaría I would love to... (5-2)

me / te encanta(n)... I / you love... (I)

encargarse (de) (g → gu) to be in charge (of) (5-1)

encender (e → ie) to turn on, to light (II)

encima de on top of (I)

encontrar (o → ue) to find (II)

el encuentro meeting (8-2)

la energía energy (II, 3-1)

la fuente de — energy source (6-2)

enero January (I)

la enfermedad illness (6-2)

el enfermero, la enfermera nurse (II)

enfermo, -a sick (I)

enfrentarse to face, to confront (8-2)

enlatado, -a canned (II)

enojado, -a angry (II)

enojarse to get angry (II)

enorme enormous (II)

la ensalada salad (I)

la — de frutas fruit salad (I)

ensayar to rehearse (II)

el ensayo rehearsal (II)

la enseñanza teaching (10-1)

enseñar to teach (I)

entender (e → ie) to understand (II)

enterarse to find out (6-2)

entonces then (I)

la entrada entrance (II), ticket (2-2)

entrar to enter (I)

entre among, between (II)

la entrega de premios awards ceremony (1-2)

entregar to turn in (II)

— la tarea a tiempo to turn in homework on time (II)

el entrenador, la entrenadora coach, trainer (II)

el entrenamiento training (1-2)

entrenarse to train (1-2)

la entrevista interview (II, 5-1)

entrevistar to interview (II)

entrometido, -a meddlesome, interfering (4-1)

entusiasmado, -a excited (II)

el entusiasmo enthusiasm (2-2)

enviar to send (I, II)

la época time, era (8-1)

equilibrado, -a balanced (3-1)

el equipaje luggage (II)

facturar el — to check luggage (II)

el equipo team (II)

el — de sonido sound (stereo) system (I)

el — deportivo sports equipment (II)

¿Eres...? Are you...? (I)

es is; (he / she / it) is (I)

— cierto it's true (II)

— el (number) de (month) it is the... of... (in telling the date) (I)

— el primero de (month). It is the first of... (I)

— la una. It is one o'clock. (I)

— necesario. It's necessary. (I)

— un(a)... It's a... (I)

la escala stopover (II)

escalar to climb (a rock or mountain) (1-1)

la escalera stairs, stairway (I); ladder (II)

escaparse to escape (II)

la escasez shortage (9-1)

la escena scene (II)

el escenario stage (2-2)

escoger to choose (II)

esconder(se) to hide (oneself) (II)

escribir: to write (I)

¿Cómo se escribe...? How is...spelled? (I)

— **cuentos** to write stories (I)

— **por correo electrónico** to write e-mail (I)

— **un informe sobre...** to write a report about...

Se escribe... It's spelled... (I)

el **escritor, la escritora** writer (II, 2-2)

el **escritorio** desk (I)

la **escritura** writing (7-2)

escuchar música to listen to music (I)

la **escuela primaria** primary school (I)

la **escuela técnica** technical school (II)

el **escultor, la escultora** sculptor (2-1)

la **escultura** sculpture (2-1)

ese, esa that (I, II)

de ese modo in that way (10-1)

eso:

por — that's why, therefore (I)

esos, esas those (I, II)

el **espacio** (outer) space (II)

los **espaguetis** spaghetti (I)

la **espalda** back (II)

el **español:**

la clase de — Spanish class (I)

especial special (II)

especialmente especially (I)

la **especie** species (9-2)

el **espectáculo** show (2-2)

el **espejo** mirror (I)

esperar to hope (for) (4-1); to wait (II)

la **esposa** wife (I)

el **esposo** husband (I)

el **esquí acuático** water-skiing (II)

esquiar to ski (I)

la **esquina** corner (II)

Está hecho, -a de... It is made of... (II)

establecer (zc) to establish (8-2)

la **estación,** *pl.* **las estaciones** season (I)

la — de servicio service station (II)

el **estadio** stadium (I)

el **estado** state (10-1)

el **estante** shelf, bookshelf (I)

estar to be (I)

¿Cómo está Ud.? How are you? *formal* (I)

¿Cómo estás? How are you? *fam.* (I)

— + *present participle* to be + *present participle* (I)

— **a cargo de** to be in charge of (9-1)

— **basado, -a en** to be based on (II)

— **de buen / mal humor** to be in a good / bad mood (3-2)

— **de moda** to be in fashion (II)

— **en la luna** to be daydreaming (3-2)

— **en línea** to be online (I)

— **enamorado, -a de** to be in love with (II)

— **equivocado, -a** to be mistaken (4-2)

— **orgulloso / orgullosa de** to be proud of (1-2)

— **resfriado, -a** to have a cold (3-1)

— **seguro, -a** to be sure (II)

— **sujeto, -a a** to be subject to (10-1)

Estoy de acuerdo. I agree. (I)

No estoy de acuerdo. I don't agree. (I)

la **estatua** statue (II)

la **estatura** height (3-1)

este, esta this (I, II)

esta noche this evening (I)

esta tarde this afternoon (I)

este fin de semana this weekend (I)

el **estilo** style (II)

estirar to stretch (3-2)

el **estómago** stomach (I)

estornudar to sneeze (3-1)

estos, estas these (I, II)

Estoy de acuerdo. I agree. (I)

la **estrategia** strategy (6-2)

estrecho, -a narrow (II)

la **estrella (del cine)** (movie) star (II)

el **estrés** stress (3-2)

estresado, -a stressed out (3-2)

la **estructura** structure (7-1)

el / la **estudiante** student (I)

estudiar to study (I)

estudioso, -a studious (I)

la **estufa** stove (II)

estupendo, -a stupendous, wonderful (II)

europeo, -a European (8-2)

la **evidencia** proof, evidence (7-1)

el **evento especial** special event (II)

evitar to avoid (3-1)

exagerado, -a outrageous (II)

exagerar to exaggerate (2-2)

examinar to examine, to check (II)

excavar excavate (7-1)

excesivo, -a excessive (9-2)

exigir to demand (3-2)

existir to exist (7-1)

el **éxito** success (II)

tener — to be successful (II)

la **excursión,** *pl.* **las excursiones** excursion, short trip (II)

la **experiencia** experience (I)

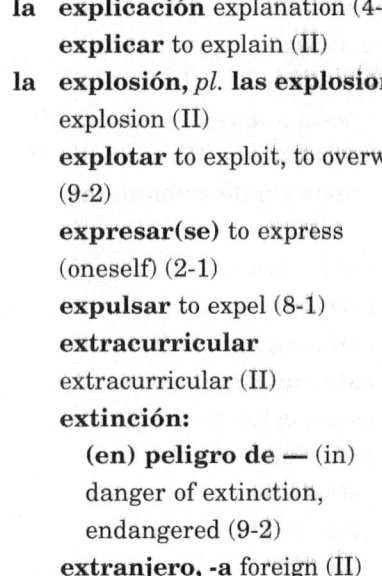

la **explicación** explanation (4-2)

explicar to explain (II)

la **explosión,** *pl.* **las explosiones** explosion (II)

explotar to exploit, to overwork (9-2)

expresar(se) to express (oneself) (2-1)

expulsar to expel (8-1)

extracurricular extracurricular (II)

extinción:

  (en) peligro de — (in) danger of extinction, endangered (9-2)

extranjero, -a foreign (II)

extraño, -a strange (7-1)

el / la **extraterrestre** alien (II)

F _____

la **fábrica** factory (6-2)

fácil easy (I)

facturar (el equipaje) to check (luggage) (II)

la **falda** skirt (I)

la **falta** lack (9-2)

  la — de lack of (10-2)

faltar to be missing (I)

famoso, -a famous (II, 2-1)

fantástico, -a fantastic (I)

la **farmacia** pharmacy (II)

fascinante fascinating (I)

fascinar to fascinate (II)

favorito, -a favorite (I)

febrero February (I)

la **fecha:**

  ¿Cuál es la —? What is the date? (I)

  la — de nacimiento date of birth (5-1)

la **felicidad** happiness (10-1)

¡Felicidades! Congratulations! (II)

¡Felicitaciones! Congratulations! (1-2)

felicitar to congratulate (II)

¡Feliz cumpleaños! Happy birthday! (I)

fenomenal phenomenal (II)

el **fenómeno** phenomenon (7-1)

feo, -a ugly (I)

la **fibra** fiber (3-1)

la **fiebre** fever (3-1)

la **fiesta** party (I)

  la — de sorpresa surprise party (II)

la **figura** figure (2-1)

el **fin,** *pl.* **los fines** purpose (10-2)

el **fin de semana:**

  este — this weekend (I)

  los fines de semana on weekends (I)

las **finanzas** finance (6-1)

flexible flexible (5-1)

flexionar to flex, to stretch (3-2)

flexiones:

  hacer — to do push-ups

flojo, -a loose (II)

la **flor,** *pl.* **las flores** flower (I)

la **foca** seal (9-2)

la **fogata** bonfire (II)

fomentar to encourage (9-1)

el **fondo** background (2-1)

el **fósforo** match (II)

la **foto** photo (I)

la **fotografía** photography (II)

el **fotógrafo, la fotógrafa** photographer (II)

el **fracaso** failure (II)

frecuentemente frequently (II)

el **fregadero** sink (II)

freír (e → í) to fry (II)

las **fresas** strawberries (I)

fresco, -a fresh (II)

los **frijoles** beans (II)

el **frío:**

  Hace —. It's cold. (I)

  tener — to be cold (I)

frito, -a fried (II)

fue it was (I)

  — un desastre. It was a disaster. (I)

el **fuego** fire (II)

los **fuegos artificiales** fireworks (II)

la **fuente** fountain (II); source (II)

  la — de energía energy source (6-2)

  la — de inspiración source of inspiration (2-1)

fuera (de) outside (II)

fuerte strong (3-1)

la **fuerza** strength (3-2)

la **función** function (7-1)

funcionar to function, to work (II, 10-1)

fundamental fundamental, vital (10-2)

fundar to found (8-1)

furioso, -a furious (II)

el **fútbol:**
  jugar al — to play soccer (I)

el **fútbol americano:**
  jugar al — to play football (I)

el **futuro** future (II)

G

el **galán** leading man (II)

la **galleta** cookie (I)

ganar to win; to earn *(money)* (II)

  — **se la vida** to make a living (II)

la **ganga** bargain (II)

el **garaje** garage (I)

la **garantía** guarantee (10-2)

garantizar to guarantee (5-2)

la **gasolina** gasoline (II)

gastar to spend (II)

el **gato** cat (I)

el **gel** gel (II)

el **gen** *pl.* **los genes** gene (6-2)

generalmente generally (I)

generoso, -a generous (II)

la **genética** genetics (6-2)

¡Genial! Great! (I)

la **gente** people (I)
  la — **sin hogar** homeless people (5-2)

geométrico, -a geometric(al) (7-1)

el / la **gerente** manager (II, 5-1)

el **gesto** gesture (2-2)

la **gimnasia** gymnastics (II)

el **gimnasio** gym (I)

el **globo** balloon (I)

gobernar (ie) to rule, to govern (8-1)

el **gobierno** government (9-1)

el **gol** goal *(in sports)* (II)
  meter un — to score a goal (II)

el **golf:**
  jugar al — to play golf (I)

la **gorra** cap (I)

gozar (de) to enjoy (10-1)

grabar to record (II)
  — **un disco compacto** to burn a CD (I)

gracias thank you (I)

gracioso, -a funny (I)

el **grado centígrado** centigrade degree (3-1)

la **graduación,** *pl.* **las graduaciones** graduation (II)

graduarse (u → ú) to graduate (II, 6-1)

los **gráficos** computer graphics (I)

grande large (I)

el **granizo** hail (1-1)
  caer — to hail (1-1)

la **grapadora** stapler (II)

grasoso, -a greasy (II)

gratuito, -a free (10-1)

grave serious (II, 9-1)

la **gripe** flu (3-1)

gris gray (I)

gritar to scream (II)

el **grupo étnico** ethnic group (8-1)

los **guantes** gloves (I)

guapo, -a good-looking (I)

guardar (un secreto) to keep (a secret) (4-1)

la **guardería infantil** day-care center (II)

la **guerra** war (II, 8-2)

el / la **guía** guide (II)

la **guía** guidebook (II)

los **guisantes** peas (I)

gustar:
  a él / ella le gusta(n) he / she likes (I)
  (A mí) me gusta... I like to... (I)
  (A mí) me gusta más... I like to...better (I prefer to...) (I)
  (A mí) me gusta mucho... I like to...a lot (I)
  (A mí) no me gusta... I don't like to... (I)
  (A mí) no me gusta nada... I don't like to...at all. (I)
  Le gusta... He / She likes... (I)

Me gusta... I like... (I)

Me gustaría... I would like... (I)

Me gustó. I liked it. (I)

No le gusta... He / She doesn't like... (I)

¿Qué te gusta hacer? What do you like to do? (I)

¿Qué te gusta hacer más? What do you like to do better / prefer to do? (I)

Te gusta... You like... (I)

¿Te gusta...? Do you like to...? (I)

¿Te gustaría...? Would you like...? (I)

¿Te gustó? Did you like it? (I)

H _____

haber to have *(as an auxiliary verb)* (II)

había there was / there were (II)

la **habilidad** skill (5-1)

la **habitación,** *pl.* las **habitaciones** room (II)

  la **— doble** double room (II)

  la **— individual** single room (II)

el / la **habitante** inhabitant (7-2)

el **hábito alimenticio** eating habit (3-1)

hablar to talk (I)

  — por teléfono to talk on the phone (I)

habrá there will be (II)

hacer to do (I)

  hace + *time expression* ago (I)

  Hace + *time* **+ que...** It has been... (II)

  Hace calor. It's hot. (I)

  Hace frío. It's cold. (I)

  Hace sol. It's sunny. (I)

  — bicicleta to use a stationary bike (3-2)

  — caso to pay attention, to obey (4-2)

  — cinta to use a treadmill (3-2)

  — ejercicio to exercise (I)

  — el papel de to play the role of (II)

  — escala to stop over (II)

  — flexiones to do push-ups (3-2)

  — gimnasia to do gymnastics (II)

  — la cama to make the bed (I)

  — la maleta to pack the suitcase (II)

  — las paces to make peace

with (4-2)

  — ruido to make noise (II)

  — un esfuerzo to make an effort (1-2)

  — un picnic to have a picnic (II)

  — un proyecto to do a project (II)

  — un viaje to take a trip (II)

  — un video to videotape (I)

  — una búsqueda to do a search (II)

  — una gira to take a tour (II)

  — una parrillada to have a barbecue (II)

  — una pregunta to ask a question (II)

haz *(command)* do, make (I)

¿Qué hiciste? What did you do? (I)

¿Qué tiempo hace? What is the weather like? (I)

(tú) haces you do (I)

(yo) hago I do (I)

hacerse to become (6-1)

hacia toward (1-1)

hambre:

  Tengo —. I'm hungry. (I)

la **hamburguesa** hamburger (I)

haré lo que me dé la gana I'll do as I please (6-1)

la **harina** flour (II)

has visto you have seen (II)

hasta until (II); as far as, up to (II)

  — luego. See you later. (I)

  — mañana. See you tomorrow. (I)

hay there is, there are (I)

  — que one must (I)

haya *(subjunctive)* there is, there are (II)

he visto I have seen (II)

el **helado** ice cream (I)

la **herencia** heritage (8-2)

herido, -a injured (II)

el **herido, la herida** injured person (II)

el **hermanastro, la hermanastra** stepbrother, stepsister (I)

el **hermano, la hermana** brother, sister (I)

los **hermanos** brothers, brother(s) and sister(s) (I)

hermoso, -a beautiful (1-1)

el **héroe** hero (II)

la **heroína** heroine (II)

hervir (e → ie) (e → i) to boil (II)

el **hielo** ice (9-2)

el **hierro** iron (3-1)

el **hijo, la hija** son, daughter (I)

los **hijos** children, sons (I)

histórico, -a historical (II)

el **hockey** hockey (II)

hogar:

    el **— de ancianos** home for the elderly (5-2)

    la gente sin — homeless people (5-2)

la **hoja de papel** sheet of paper (I)

¡Hola! Hello! (I)

el **hombre** man (I)

    el **— de negocios** businessman (II, 6-1)

el **hombro** shoulder (II)

honesto, -a honest (4-1)

la **hora:**

    en la... — in the...hour (class period) (I)

    ¿A qué —? (At) what time? (I)

el **horario** schedule (I)

la **hormiga** ant (II)

el **horno** oven (II)

    al — baked (II)

horrible horrible (I)

el **horror:**

    la película de — horror movie (I)

el **hospital** hospital (I)

la **hospitalidad** hospitality (6-2)

el **hotel** hotel (I)

hoy today (I)

    de — en adelante from now on (6-2)

    hubo there was (II)

el **hueso** bone (II)

los **huevos** eggs (I)

el **humo** smoke (II)

el **huracán,** *pl.* **los huracanes** hurricane (II)

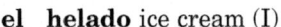

I

ida y vuelta round trip (II)

identificarse con to identify oneself with (2-2)

el **idioma** language (II)

la **iglesia** church (I)

ignorar to ignore (4-2)

igual: al — que as, like (7-2)

la **igualdad** equality (10-1)

igualmente likewise (I)

la **imagen** image (2-1)

impaciente impatient (I)

el **imperio** empire (8-1)

importante important (I)

importar: me importa(n) it matters (it's important) / they matter to me (II)

impresionante impressive (I)

impresionar to impress (1-1)

improbable unlikely (7-1)

el **incendio** fire (II)

incluir to include (3-1)

increíble incredible (I)

el / la **indígena** native (8-2)

la **industria** industry (6-2)

inexplicable inexplicable (7-1)

infantil childish (I)

la **influencia** influence (8-1)

influir (i → y) to influence (2-1)

la **información** information (I)

la **informática** information technology (6-2)

el **informe** report (I, II)

el **ingeniero, la ingeniera** engineer (II, 6-1)

el **inglés:**

    la clase de — English class (I)

el **ingrediente** ingredient (II)

la **injusticia** injustice (10-1)

injusto, -a unfair (5-2)

inmediatamente immediately (II)

inocente innocent (10-2)

inolvidable unforgettable (I)

inscribirse to register (1-2)

la **inscripción** registration (1-2)

insistir en to insist (II)

la **inspección,** *pl.* **las inspecciones de seguridad** security checkpoint (II)

inspirar to inspire (2-1)

integrarse to integrate (8-1)

inteligente intelligent (I)

el **intento** attempt (7-2)

intercambiar to exchange (10-2)

el **intercambio** exchange (8-2)

el **interés** interest (II)

interesante interesting (I)

interesar to interest (I)

 me interesa(n) it interests me (they interest me) (I)

 me interesaría I would be interested... (5-2)

la **interpretación** interpretation (2-2)

interpretar to interpret (2-2)

íntimo, -a intimate (4-1)

la **inundación,** *pl.* **las inundaciones** flood (II)

invadir to invade (8-1)

inventar to invent (6-2)

el **invento** invention (6-2)

investigar to investigate (II)

el **invierno** winter (I)

la **inyección,** *pl.* **las inyecciones** injection, shot (II)

ir to go (I)

 — a + *inf.* to be going to + *verb* (I)

 — a la escuela to go to school (I)

 — a pie to go on foot (II)

 — de cámping to go camping (I)

 — de compras to go shopping (I)

 — de pesca to go fishing (I)

 — de vacaciones to go on vacation (I)

¡Qué va! No way! (4-2)

¡Vamos! Let's go! (I)

el **itinerario** itinerary (II)

la **izquierda:**

 a la — (de) to the left (of) (I)

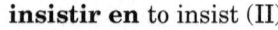

J

el **jabón** soap (II)

el **jarabe** syrup (3-1)

el **jardín** garden, yard (I)

los **jeans** jeans (I)

el **jefe, la jefa** boss (6-1)

joven *adj.* young (I)

el / la **joven** young man, young woman (I)

los **jóvenes** young people (II)

las **joyas (de oro, de plata)** (gold, silver) jewelry (II)

la **joyería** jewelry store (I)

las **judías verdes** green beans (I)

el **judío, la judía** Jew(ish) (8-1)

jueves Thursday (I)

el **juez, la jueza,** *pl.* **los jueces** judge (II, 6-1)

el **jugador, la jugadora** player (II)

jugar (a) (u → ue) to play *(games, sports)* (I)

 — a los bolos to bowl (II)

 — al básquetbol to play basketball (I)

 — al béisbol to play baseball (I)

 — al fútbol to play soccer (I)

 — al fútbol americano to play football (I)

 — al golf to play golf (I)

 — al tenis to play tennis (I)

 — al vóleibol to play volleyball (I)

 — videojuegos to play video games (I)

el **jugo:**

 el — de manzana apple juice (I)

 el — de naranja orange juice (I)

el **juguete** toy (I)

el **juicio** trial (10-2)

julio July (I)

junio June (I)

juntar fondos to fundraise (5-2)

juntarse to join (II)

juntos, -as together (4-1)

el **jurado** jury (10-2)

la **justicia** justice (10-2)

justo, -a fair (5-2)

juzgar to judge (10-2)

L _____

la the *f. sing.* (I); it, her *f. dir. obj. pron.* (I)

los **labios** lips (II)

el **laboratorio** laboratory (I, II)

el **lado:**

    al — de next to (I)

el **ladrón, la ladrona,** *pl.* **los ladrones** thief (II)

el **lago** lake (I)

la **lámpara** lamp (I)

la **lana** wool (II)

el **lápiz,** *pl.* **los lápices** pencil (I)

largo, -a long (I)

el **largo** length (7-1)

las the *f. pl.;* them *f. dir. obj. pron.* (I)

    — dos, los dos both (I)

lástima:

    ¡Qué —! What a shame! (II)

lastimarse to hurt oneself (II)

la **lata** can (I)

lavar to wash (I)

    — el coche to wash the car (I)

    — la ropa to wash the clothes (I)

    — los platos to wash the dishes (I)

    —se la cara to wash one's face (II)

le (to / for) him, her, it, *(formal)* you *sing. ind. obj. pron.* (I)

    — gusta... He / She likes... (I)

    — traigo... I will bring you... (I)

    No — gusta... He / She doesn't like... (I)

la **lección,** *pl.* **las lecciones de piano** piano lesson (class) (I)

la **leche** milk (I)

la **lechuga** lettuce (I)

el **lector DVD** DVD player (I)

leer revistas to read magazines (I)

lejos (de) far (from) (I)

la **lengua** language (8-2)

lentamente slowly (II)

la **leña** firewood (II)

les (to / for) them, *(formal)* you *pl. ind. obj. pron.* (I)

la **letra** lyrics (2-2)

el **letrero** sign (II)

levantar pesas to lift weights (I)

levantarse to get up (II)

la **ley** law (II, 5-2)

la **leyenda** legend (7-2)

la **libertad** liberty (10-1)

libre free (10-2)

la **librería** bookstore (I)

el **libro** book (I)

la **liga** league (II)

limitar to limit (9-1)

la **limonada** lemonade (I)

limpiar el baño to clean the bathroom (I)

la **limpieza** cleaning (9-2)

limpio, -a clean (I)

la **línea:**

    estar en — to be online (I, II)

    la — aérea airline (II)

la **linterna** flashlight (1-1)

la **liquidación,** *pl.* **las liquidaciones** sale (II)

listo, -a ready (II)

llamar:

    — por teléfono to call on the phone (II)

    ¿Cómo se llama? What's his / her name? (I)

    ¿Cómo te llamas? What is your name? (I)

    Me llamo... My name is... (I)

la **llave** key (II)

el **llavero** key chain (I)

la **llegada** arrival (II)

llegar to arrive

al — upon arriving (8-2)
— **a** to reach, to get to (10-2)
— **tarde** to arrive late (II)
llenar (el tanque) to fill (the tank) (II)
lleno, -a full (3-1)
llevar to wear (I); to take, to carry, to bring (I)
llevarse bien / mal to get along well / badly (II)
llorar to cry (II)
llover (o → ue) to rain (II)
Llueve. It's raining. (I)
la **lluvia** rain (II)
lo que what (II)
lo it, him *m. dir. obj. pron.* (I)
— **siento.** I'm sorry. (I)
el **locutor, la locutora** announcer (II)
lograr to achieve (6-1)
los the *m. pl.* (I); them *m. dir. obj. pron* (I)
— **dos, las dos** both (I)
— **fines de semana** on weekends (I)
— **lunes, los martes...** on Mondays, on Tuesdays... (I)
luchar to fight (II, 8-2)
luego then (II)
el **lugar** place (I)
en — de instead of (10-2)
tener — to take place (1-2)
la **Luna** the Moon (II, 7-1)
lunes Monday (I)
los lunes on Mondays (I)
la **luz,** *pl.* **las luces** light (I)

M

la **madrastra** stepmother (I)
la **madre (mamá)** mother (I)
maduro, -a mature (6-1)
el **maíz** corn (II)
mal bad, badly (I)
pasarlo — to have a bad time (1-1)
el **malentendido** misunderstanding (4-2)
la **maleta** suitcase (II)
malo, -a bad (I)
maltratar to mistreat (10-1)
el **maltrato** mistreatment (10-1)
manejar to drive (II)
la **manera** way, manner (II, 3-1)
la **manifestación** demonstration (5-2)
la **mano** hand (I)
darse la — to shake hands (II)
mantener:
para — la salud to maintain one's health (I)
la **mantequilla** butter (I)
la **manzana** apple (I)
el jugo de — apple juice (I)
mañana tomorrow (I)
la mañana:
a las ocho de la — at eight (o'clock) in the morning (I)
de la — in the morning (I)
el **maquillaje** make-up (II)
la **máquina** machine (6-2)
el **mar** sea (I)
la **maravilla** marvel, wonder (8-1)
maravilloso, -a wonderful (8-1)
la **marca** brand (II)
la **marcha** march (5-2)
los **mariscos** shellfish (II)
marrón brown (I)
martes Tuesday (I)
los martes on Tuesdays (I)
marzo March (I)

más:
¿Qué —? What else? (I)
— **...que** more...than (I)
— **de** more than (I)
— **o menos** more or less (I)
matar to kill (II)
las **matemáticas:**
la clase de — mathematics class (I)
los **materiales** supplies, materials (II)
mayo May (I)
la **mayonesa** mayonnaise (II)
mayor, *pl.* **mayores** *adj.* older (I)
los **mayores** grown-ups (II)
la **mayoría** the majority (6-2)
me me *dir. obj. pron.,* (to / for) me *ind. obj. pron.* (I)
— **aburre(n)** it / they bore(s) me (I)
— **encantaría** I would love to... (5-2)
— **es imposible** It is impossible for me... (5-2)
— **estás poniendo nervioso, -a.** You are making me nervous. (II)
— **falta(n)...** I need... (I)
— **gustaría** I would like (I)
— **gustó.** I liked it. (I)
— **interesa(n)** it / they interest(s) me (I)
— **interesaría** I would be interested... (5-2)
— **llamo...** My name is... (I)
— **importa(n)** it matters (it's important) / they matter to me (II)
— **parece** it seems to me (II)
— **queda(n) bien / mal.** It / They fit(s) me well / poorly. (I)

— quedo en casa. I'm staying at home. (I)

¿— trae...? Will you bring me...? *formal* (I)

el **mecánico, la mecánica** mechanic (II)

la **medalla** medal (1-2)

media, -o half (I)

y — thirty, half past (I)

mediano, -a medium (II)

la **medicina** medicine (II)

el **médico, la médica** doctor (II)

el **medio ambiente** environment (II, 5-2)

los **medios de comunicación** media (6-2)

medir (e → i) to measure (7-1)

mejor:

el / la —, los / las —es the best (I)

—(es) que better than (I)

mejorar to improve (II, 4-2)

la **melodía** melody (2-2)

el **melón,** *pl.* **los melones** melon (II)

menor younger (I)

menos:

a — que unless (9-2)

más o — more or less (I)

— ...que less / fewer...than (I)

— de less / fewer than (I)

el **mensajero, la mensajera** messenger (5-1)

mentir (e → ie) to lie (II)

el **menú** menu (I)

menudo:

a — often (I)

el **mercadeo** marketing (6-2)

el **mercado** market (II)

la **mercancía** merchandise (8-2)

la **merienda** snack (3-1)

el **mes** month (I)

la **mesa** table (I)

poner la — to set the table (I)

la **mesita** night table (I)

la **meta** goal (1-2)

meter:

meter un gol to score a goal (II)

el **metro** subway (II)

la **mezcla** mix (8-2)

mezclar to mix (II)

la **mezquita** mosque (I)

mi, mis my (I)

mí:

a — también I do (like to) too (I)

a — tampoco I don't (like to) either (I)

para — in my opinion, for me (I)

el **micrófono** microphone (2-2)

el **microondas** microwave (II)

el **miedo: tener — (de)** to be scared (of), to be afraid (of) (I)

el **miembro** member (II)

ser miembro to be a member (II)

mientras (que) while (II)

miércoles Wednesday (I)

mil thousand (I)

militar *(adj.)* military (II)

un millón de / millones de a million / millions of (II)

mío, -a, -os, -as mine (II)

mirar to look (at) (I)

la **misión** mission (8-2)

el **misionero, la misionera** missionary (8-2)

mismo, -a same (I)

pensar en sí — to think of oneself (4-2)

el **misterio** mystery (7-1)

misterioso, -a mysterious (7-1)

el **mito** myth (7-2)

la **mochila** bookbag, backpack (I)

los **modales** manners (II)

el **modo** the way (10-2)

de ese — in that way (10-1)

de — que so, so that (10-2)

mojado, -a wet (II)

molestar to bother (II)

el **momento:**

un — a moment (I)

la **moneda** coin (II)

el **mono** monkey (I)

las **montañas** mountains (I)

montar:

— a caballo to go (horseback) riding (I)

— en bicicleta to ride a bicycle (I)

— en monopatín to skateboard (I)

el **monumento** monument (I)

morado, -a purple (I)

morirse to die (II)

la **mosca** fly (II)

la **mostaza** mustard (II)

mostrar (ue) to show (2-1)

el **motivo** cause (10-1)

la **moto acuática** personal watercraft (II)

moverse (o → ue) to move (II)

el **movimiento** movement (2-1)

mucho, -a a lot (I)

— gusto pleased to meet you (I)

muchos, -as many (I)

mudarse to move (house) (6-1)

los **muebles** furniture (II)

muerto, -a dead (II)

la naturaleza muerta still life (2-1)

la **mujer** woman (I)

la — de negocios businesswoman (II, 6-1)

las **muletas** crutches (II)

la **multa** ticket (II)

mundial worldwide (10-2)

el **mundo** world (II)

la **muñeca** doll (II); wrist (II)

el **muñeco** action figure (II)

el **mural** mural (2-1)

el **músculo** muscle (II, 3-2)

el **museo** museum (I)

el **músico, la música** musician (II)

el **musulmán, la musulmana** Muslim (8-1)

muy very (I)

— **bien** very well (I)

N _____

nacer to be born (II)

nada nothing (I)

(A mí) no me gusta — ... I don't like to...at all. (I)

nadar to swim (I)

nadie no one, nobody (II)

la **naranja:**

el **jugo de** — orange juice (I)

la **nariz,** *pl.* **las narices** nose (I)

la **natación** swimming (II)

natural:

la **reserva** — nature preserve (9-2)

la **naturaleza** nature (II, 1-1)

la — **muerta** still life (2-1)

la **nave espacial** spaceship (7-1)

navegar to sail, to navigate (II)

— **en la Red** to surf the Web (I, II)

necesario:

Es —. It's necessary. (I)

necesitar:

necesitas you need (I)

necesito I need (I)

los **negocios** business (II)

el **hombre de** — businessman (II, 6-1)

la **mujer de** — businesswoman (II, 6-1)

negro, -a black

el **pelo** — black hair (I)

nervioso, -a nervous (II)

nevar (e → ie) to snow (II)

Nieva. It's snowing. (I)

ni...ni neither...nor, not...or (I)

ningún, ninguno, -a no, none (II)

el **niñero, la niñera** babysitter (5-1)

la **niñez** childhood (10-1)

el **niño, la niña** young boy, young girl (I)

los **niños** children (I)

el **nivel** level (3-1)

No comas. Don't eat. (II)

No dejes Don't leave, don't let (II)

No escribas. Don't write. (II)

No estoy de acuerdo. I don't agree. (I)

No hables. Don't speak. (II)

¡No me digas! You don't say! (I)

no...todavía not yet (II)

la **noche:**

a las ocho de la — at eight (o'clock) in the evening, at night (I)

Buenas —**s.** Good evening. (I)

de la — in the evening, at night (I)

esta — this evening (I)

nos us *dir. obj. pron.,* (to / for) us *ind. obj. pron.* (I)

¡— vemos! See you later! (I)

nosotros, -as we (I)

la **nota** grade, mark (in school) (II)

sacar una buena — to get a good grade (II)

el **noticiero** newscast (II)

novecientos, -as nine hundred (I)

noveno, -a ninth (I)

noventa ninety (I)

noviembre November (I)

el **novio, la novia** boyfriend, girlfriend (I)

la **nube** cloud (II)

nuestro, -a, -os, -as our (I)

nueve nine (I)

nuevo, -a new (I)

el **número** shoe size (II)

nunca never (I)

nutritivo, -a nutritious (3-1)

O _____

o or (I)

  — sea que in other words (7-2)

obedecer to obey (II)

obediente obedient (II)

obligar to force (10-1)

la **obra:**

  la **— de arte** work of art (2-1)

  la **— de teatro** play (I)

observar to observe (II)

el **observatorio** observatory (7-1)

obtener to obtain, to get (1-2)

ochenta eighty (I)

ocho eight (I)

ochocientos, -as eight hundred (I)

el **ocio** free time (6-2)

octavo, -a eighth (I)

octubre October (I)

ocupado, -a busy (I)

ocupar to occupy (8-1)

ocurrir to occur (II)

ofender to offend (II)

la **oficina** office (II)

ofrecer to offer (II)

el **oído** ear (3-1)

oír to hear (II)

ojalá I wish (4-1)

el **ojo** eye (I)

la **olla** pot (II)

el **olor** odor (II)

olvidarse de to forget about (II)

  no te olvides de don't forget about (II)

once eleven (I)

opinar to think (10-2)

la **oportunidad** opportunity (II)

ordenado, -a neat (I)

organizar to organize (5-2)

el **origen** origin (7-2)

el **oro** gold (II)

la **orquesta** orchestra (II)

os you *pl. fam. dir. obj. pron.,* (to / for) you *pl. fam. ind. obj. pron.* (I)

oscuro, -a dark (II)

el **oso de peluche** teddy bear (II)

el **otoño** fall, autumn (I)

otro, -a other, another (I)

otra vez again (I)

el **óvalo** oval (7-1)

¡Oye! Hey! (I)

ozono:

  la **capa de —** ozone layer (9-2)

P _____

la **paciencia** pacience (II)

  tener — to be patient (II)

paciente *adj.* patient (I)

pacífico, -a peaceful (10-2)

el **padrastro** stepfather (I)

el **padre (papá)** father (I)

los **padres** parents (I)

pagar (por) to pay (for) (I)

la **página Web** Web page (I)

el **país** country (I)

el **paisaje** landscape (1-1)

el **pájaro** bird (I)

la **palabra** word (II)

el **palacio** palace (II)

la **paleta** palette (2-1)

el **palo de golf** golf club (II)

el **pan** bread (I)

  el **— tostado** toast (I)

la **pantalla** (computer) screen (I)

los **pantalones** pants (I)

  los **— cortos** shorts (I)

las **papas** potatoes (I)

  las **— fritas** French fries (I)

el **papel** role (II)

  el **— picado** cut-paper decorations (I)

  hacer el — de to play the role of (II)

la **hoja de —** sheet of paper (I)

la **papelera** wastepaper basket (I)

para for (I)

  — + *inf.* in order to (I)

  — la salud for one's health (I)

  — mantener la salud to maintain one's health (I)

  — mí in my opinion, for me (I)

  ¿— qué sirve? What's it (used) for? (I)

  — ti in your opinion, for you (I)

parado, -a to be standing (2-1)

el **paramédico, la paramédica**

paramedic (II)

parar to stop (II)

pararse to stand up (2-2)

parecer:

  me parece que it seems to me (II)

  ¿Qué te parece? What do you think? / How does it seem to you? (II)

  parecerse a to look, to seem (like) (2-2)

la **pared** wall (I)

los **parientes** relatives (II)

el **parque** park (I)

  el — de diversiones amusement park (I)

  el — nacional national park (I)

la **parrilla** grill (II)

el / la **participante** participant (1-2)

  participar (en) to participate (in) (II)

el **partido** game, match (I)

el **pasajero, la pasajera** passenger (II)

el **pasaporte** passport (II)

  pasar to pass, to go (II)

  ¿Cómo lo pasaste? How was it (for you)? (I)

  — la aspiradora to vacuum (I)

  — tiempo con amigos to spend time with friends (I)

  ¿Qué pasa? What's happening? (I)

  ¿Qué te pasó? What happened to you? (I, II)

  pasarlo bien / mal to have a good time / bad time (1-1)

el **pasatiempo** pastime (II)

  pasear en bote to go boating (I)

el **pasillo** aisle (II)

el **paso** step (2-2)

la **pasta dental** toothpaste (II)

  pastel *adj.* pastel (colors) (II)

el **pastel** cake (I)

los **pasteles** pastries (I)

las **pastillas** pills (II)

  patinar to skate (I)

los **patines** skates (II)

el **patio de recreo** playground (II)

el **pavo** turkey (II)

la **paz** peace (II, 10-1)

  hacer las paces to make peace (with) (4-2)

el **peatón,** *pl.* **los peatones** pedestrian (II)

el **pecho** chest (3-1)

el **pedazo** piece, slice (II)

  pedir (e → i) to order, to ask for (I)

  — ayuda to ask for help (II)

  — prestado, -a (a) to borrow (from) (II)

  — perdón to ask for forgiveness (4-2)

el **peine** comb (II)

  pelar to peel (II)

la **pelea** fight (4-2)

  pelearse to fight (II)

la **película** film, movie (I)

  la — de acción action film (II)

  la — de ciencia ficción science fiction movie (I)

  la — de horror horror movie (I)

  la — policíaca detective movie, mystery (I)

  la — romántica romantic movie (I)

  ver una — to see a movie (I)

peligro:

  (en) peligro de extinción (in) danger of extinction, endangered (II, 9-2)

peligroso, -a dangerous (II)

pelirrojo, -a red-haired (I)

el **pelo** hair (I, II)

  el — canoso gray hair (I)

  el — castaño brown (chestnut) hair (I)

  el — negro black hair (I)

  el — rubio blond hair (I)

la **pelota** ball (II)

el **peluquero, la peluquera** hairstylist (6-1)

el **pensamiento** thought (10-1)

  pensar (e → ie) to plan, to think (I)

  — en sí mismo(a) to think of oneself (4-2)

peor:

  el / la —, los / las —es the worst (I)

  —(es) que worse than (I)

pequeño, -a small (I)

perder (e → ie) to lose (II)

  — el equilibrio to lose one's balance (1-1)

perderse to get lost (1-1)

Perdón. Excuse me. (I)

perdonar to forgive (4-2)

perezoso, -a lazy (I)

el **perfume** perfume (I)

el **periódico** newspaper (I)

el **permiso de manejar** driver's license (II)

permitir to permit, to allow (II)

pero but (I)

el **perrito caliente** hot dog (I)

el **perro** dog (I)

la **persona** person (I)

el **personaje principal** main character (II)

  pesar to weigh (7-1)

  a — de despite (10-2)

pesas:

  levantar — to lift weights (I)

el **pescado** fish (as a food) (I)

el **peso** weight (3-1)

el **pesticida** pesticide (9-1)

el **petróleo** oil (9-1)

　　el **derrame de —** oil spill (9-2)

el **pez,** pl. **los peces** fish (II)

picante spicy (II)

picar to chop (II)

el **picnic** picnic (II)

el **pie** foot (I)

la **piedra** rock (II)

la **piel** skin (9-2)

la **pierna** leg (I)

la **pila** battery (9-1)

el / la **piloto** pilot (II)

la **pimienta** pepper (I)

el **pincel** brush (2-1)

pintarse (las uñas) to paint, to polish (one's nails) (II)

el **pintor, la pintora** painter (II)

la **pintura** painting (2-1)

la **piña** pineapple (II)

la **piñata** piñata (I)

la **pirámide** pyramid (7-1)

la **piscina** swimming pool (I)

el **piso** story, floor (I)

　　primer — second floor (I)

　　segundo — third floor (I)

la **pizza** pizza (I)

planear to plan (II)

el **planeta** planet (7-2)

la **planta** plant (II)

la **planta baja** ground floor (I)

el **plástico** plastic (I)

la **plata** silver (II)

el **plátano** banana (I)

el **plato** plate, dish (I)

　　de — principal as a main dish (I)

　　el — principal main dish (I)

la **playa** beach (I)

la **plaza** plaza (II)

la **pluma** feather (9-2)

la **población** population (8-1)

pobre poor (I)

pobrecito, -a poor thing (II)

la **pobreza** poverty (10-1)

poco:

　　un — (de) a little (I)

poder to be able to (I)

　　(tú) puedes you can (I)

　　(yo) puedo I can (I)

el **poder** power (8-2)

　　poderoso, -a powerful (8-2)

el **poema** poem (2-2)

el / la **poeta** poet (2-2)

el / la **policía** police officer (II)

policíaca:

　　la película — detective movie, mystery (I)

la **política** politics (II)

el **político, la política** politician (II)

el **pollo** chicken (I)

poner to put, to place (I)

　　pon (command) put, place (I)

　　— la mesa to set the table (I)

　　— una multa to give a ticket (II)

　　(tú) pones you put (I)

　　(yo) pongo I put (I)

ponerse to apply, to put on (clothing, make up, etc.) (II); to become (II)

　　— de acuerdo to reach an agreement (4-2)

　　— el sol to set (the sun) (7-2)

por for (how long) (II); by, around, along, through (II)

　　— ejemplo for example (II)

　　— eso that's why, therefore (I)

　　— lo general in general (II)

　　— lo tanto therefore (6-1)

　　¿— qué? Why? (I)

　　— supuesto of course (I)

　　—...vez for the...time (II)

porque because (I)

portarse bien / mal to behave well / badly (II)

la **posesión,** pl. **las posesiones** possession (I)

el **postre** dessert (I)

　　de — for dessert (I)

la **práctica** practice (II)

practicar deportes to play sports (I)

práctico, -a practical (I)

el **precio** price (I, II)

predecir to predict (6-2)

preferir (e → ie) to prefer (I)

　　(tú) prefieres you prefer (I)

　　(yo) prefiero I prefer (I)

la **pregunta** question (II)

　　hacer una — to ask a question (II)

el **premio** prize (II)

la **prensa** the press (10-2)

preocuparse worry (3-2)

preparar to prepare (I)

　　—se to get ready (II)

la **presentación,** pl. **las presentaciones** presentation (I)

el **presentador, la presentadora** presenter (II)

presentarse to apply for a job (5-1)

la **preservación** conservation (9-2)

prestar atención to pay attention (II)

la **primavera** spring (I)

primer (primero), -a first (I)

　　— piso second floor (I)

　　el — plano foreground (2-1)

el **primo, la prima** cousin (I)

los **primos** cousins (I)

prisa hurry (II)

tener — to be in a hurry (II)

probable likely (7-1)

probar (o → ue) to taste, to try (II)

probarse (o → ue) to try on (II)

el **problema** problem (I)

producir to produce (9-2)

el **producto** product (6-2)

la **profesión,** *pl.* **las profesiones** profession (II)

el **profesor, la profesora** teacher (I)

el **programa** program, show (I)

   el **— de concursos** game show (I)

   el **— de dibujos animados** cartoon (I)

   el **— de entrevistas** interview program (I)

   el **— de estudios** course of studies (II)

   el **— de la vida real** reality program (I)

   el **— de noticias** news program (I)

   el **— deportivo** sports program (I)

   el **— educativo** educational program (I)

   el **— musical** musical program (I)

el **programador, la programadora** programmer (6-1)

prohibir:

   se prohíbe it is forbidden (II)

prolongar to prolong, to extend (6-2)

promover (ue) to promote (9-1)

pronto soon (II)

   tan — como as soon as (9-1)

la **propina** tip (II)

propio, -a own (I)

proponer to propose, to suggest (10-2)

la **propuesta** proposal (10-2)

la **protección** protection (9-1)

proteger to protect (II, 5-2)

la **proteína** protein (3-1)

próximo, -a next (6-1)

el **proyecto** project (II)

   el **— de construcción** construction project (I)

el **público** audience (II)

el **pueblo** people (7-1); town (II)

puedes:

   (tú) — you can (I)

puedo:

   (yo) — I can (I)

el **puente** bridge (II)

la **puerta** door (I)

   la **— de embarque** departure gate (II)

   pues well *(to indicate pause)* (I)

el **puesto** position (5-1); food stand (II)

la **pulsera** bracelet (I)

el **reloj** watch (I)

las **puntadas** stitches (II)

   dar — to stitch *(surgically)* (II)

el **punto de vista** point of view (10-2)

puntual punctual (II, 5-1)

el **pupitre** desk (I)

puro, -a pure (II)

Q

que who, that (I)

qué:

   ¿Para — sirve? What's it (used) for? (I)

   ¡— + *adj.!* How...! (I)

   ¡— asco! How awful! (I)

   ¡— buena idea! What a good / nice idea! (I)

   ¿— clase de...? What kind of... ? (I)

   ¿— desean (Uds.)? What would you like? *formal* (I)

   ¿— día es hoy? What day is today? (I)

   ¿— es esto? What is this? (I)

   ¿— hiciste? What did you do? (I)

   ¿— hora es? What time is it? (I)

   ¡— lástima! What a shame! (II)

   ¿— más? What else? (I)

   ¿— pasa? What's happening? (I)

   ¡— pena! What a shame / pity! (I)

   ¿— quiere decir... ? What does...mean? (I)

   ¿— tal? How are you? (I)

   ¿— tal es...? How is (it)...? (II)

   ¿— te gusta hacer? What do you like to do? (I)

   ¿— te gusta hacer más? What do you like to do better / prefer to do? (I)

   ¿— te parece? What do you think? / How does it seem to you? (I, II)

   ¿— te pasó? What happened to you? (I, II)

¿— tiempo hace? What's the weather like? (I)

¡— va! No way! (4-2)

quedar to fit, to be located (I, II)

quedarse to stay (II)

el **quehacer (de la casa)** (household) chore (I)

quejarse to complain (3-2)

quemar(se) to burn (oneself), to burn up (II)

querer (e → ie) to want (I)

¿Qué quiere decir...? What does...mean? (I)

Quiere decir... It means... (I)

quisiera I would like (I)

(tú) quieres you want (I)

(yo) quiero I want (I)

¿Quién(es)? Who? (I)

químico, -a chemical (9-1)

quince fifteen (I)

quinientos, -as five hundred (I)

quinto, -a fifth (I)

el **quiosco** newsstand (II)

quisiera I would like (I)

quitar to take away, to remove (II)

— el polvo to dust (I)

quizás maybe (I)

R ⎯⎯⎯⎯⎯⎯⎯⎯⎯⎯

la **radiografía** X-ray (II)

rápidamente quickly (I, II)

la **raqueta de tenis** tennis racket (II)

un rato a while (1-1)

el **ratón,** *pl.* **los ratones** (computer) mouse (I)

la **raza** race (8-2)

razón reason (10-1)

tener — to be correct (I)

reaccionar to react (4-2)

la **realidad virtual** virtual reality (6-2)

realista realistic (I)

realizar to perform, to accomplish (2-2)

rebelarse to rebel, to revolt (8-2)

el **recalentamiento global** global warming (9-2)

la **recepción** reception desk (II)

el / la **recepcionista** receptionist (5-1)

la **receta** prescription (II); recipe (II)

recetar to prescribe (II)

recibir to receive (I)

reciclar to recycle (I)

recientemente recently (II)

el **recipiente** container (9-1)

recoger to collect, to gather (I)

recomendar (e →ie) to recommend (II)

reconciliarse to become friends again (4-2)

reconocer (c → zc) to admit, recognize (4-2)

reconquistar to reconquer (8-1)

recordar (o → ue) to remember (II)

el **rectángulo** rectangle (7-1)

los **recuerdos** souvenirs (I)

comprar — to buy souvenirs (I)

el **recurso natural** natural resource (9-1)

la **Red:**

en la — online (I)

navegar en la — to surf the Web (I)

el **redactor, la redactora** editor (6-1)

redondo, -a round (7-1)

reducir (zc) to reduce (II, 6-2)

reemplazar to replace (6-2)

la **referencia** reference (5-1)

el **refresco** soft drink (I)

el **refrigerador** refrigerator (II)

refugiarse to take shelter (1-1)

el **refugio** refuge, shelter (1-1)

regalar to give (II)

el **regalo** gift, present (I)

regatear to bargain (II)

registrar to inspect, to search *(luggage)* (II)

la **regla** rule (II)

regresar to return (I)

regular okay, so-so (I)

la **reina** queen (II)

reírse (e → í) to laugh (II)

la **reja** grate (8-1)

relajar(se) to relax (3-2)

el **relámpago** lightning (1-1)

el **reloj** clock (I)

el — pulsera watch (I)

reparar to repair (5-1)

el **repartidor, la repartidora** delivery person (5-1)

repartir to deliver (5-1)

el **repelente de insectos** insect repellent (1-1)

repetir (e → i) to repeat (II)

el **reportero, la reportera** reporter (II)

el / la **representante**
representative (1-2)

representar to represent (2-1)

el **requisito** requirement (5-1)

la **res** cattle (II)

rescatar to rescue (II)

el **rescate** rescue (9-2)

la **reseña** review (2-2)

la **reserva natural** nature preserve (9-2)

la **reservación,** *pl.* **las reservaciones** reservation (II)

reservado, -a reserved, shy (I)

resolver (o → ue) to resolve (4-2); to solve (II)

respetar to respect (II)

el **respeto** respect (10-1)

respirar to breathe (3-2)

la **responsabilidad** responsibility (5-2)

responsable responsible (5-1)

el **restaurante** restaurant (I)

el **resultado** result, outcome (8-2)

resultar to result, to turn out (II)

el **reto** challenge (8-2)

el **retraso** delay (II)

el **retrato** portrait (2-1)

la **reunión,** *pl.* **las reuniones** meeting, gathering (II)

reunirse (u → ú) to meet (II)

el **rey** king (II)

rico, -a rich, tasty (I)

el **río** river (I)

la **riqueza** wealth (8-2)

el **ritmo** rhythm (2-2)

robar to rob, to steal (II)

la **roca** rock (1-1)

la **rodilla** knee (II)

rojo, -a red (I)

el **romano, la romana** Roman (8-1)

romántico, -a:
la **película —** romantic movie (I)

romper to break (I)
—se to break, to tear (II)

la **ropa:**
la **tienda de —** clothing store (I)

rosado, -a pink (I)

roto, -a broken (II)

rubio, -a blond (I)

el **ruido** noise (II)

las **ruinas** ruins (II, 7-1)

s

sábado Saturday (I)

saber to know (how) (I, II)
(tú) sabes you know (how to) (I)
(yo) sé I know (how to) (I)

el **sabor** taste (II)

sabroso, -a tasty, flavorful (I)

el **sacapuntas,** *pl.* **los sacapuntas** pencil sharpener (I)

sacar:
— fotos to take photos (I)
— la basura to take out the trash (I)
— un libro to take out, to check out a book (II)
— una buena nota to get a good grade (II)

el **saco de dormir** sleeping bag (1-1)

sagrado, -a sacred (7-2)

la **sal** salt (I)

la **sala** living room (I)
la **— de clases** classroom (I)
la **— de emergencia** emergency room (II)

el **salario** (*o* el **sueldo**) salary (II, 5-1)

la **salchicha** sausage (I)

la **salida** exit (II); departure (II)

salir to leave, to go out (I)
— campeón, campeona to become the champion (1-2)

el **salón de belleza,** *pl.* **los salones de belleza** beauty salon (II)

los **salones de chat** chat rooms (II)

la **salsa** salsa, sauce (II)
la **— de tomate** ketchup (II)

saltar:
— a la cuerda to jump rope (II)
— una comida to skip a meal (3-1)

la **salud**:

para la — for one's health (I)

para mantener la — to maintain one's health (I)

saludable healthy (3-1)

saludar(se) to greet (II)

salvaje wild (9-2)

salvar to save (II)

el / la **salvavida** lifeguard (5-1)

la **sandía** watermelon (II)

el **sándwich de jamón y queso** ham and cheese sandwich (I)

la **sangre** blood (II)

la **sartén** frying pan (II)

satélite:

vía satélite via satellite (6-2)

satisfactorio, -a satisfactory (10-1)

se abre opens (II)

se cierra closes (II)

se me olvidó I forgot (II)

se murieron they died (II)

se prohíbe... it's forbidden... (II)

se puede you can (II)

sé:

(yo) — I know (how to) (I)

el **secador** blow dryer (II)

secarse to dry (II)

seco, -a dry (II)

el **secretario, la secretaria** secretary (II)

el **secreto** secret (4-1)

sed:

Tengo —. I'm thirsty. (I)

la **seda** silk (II)

seguir (e → i) to follow, to continue (II)

— (+ gerund) to keep on (doing) (5-1)

— una carrera to pursue a career (II, 6-1)

según according to (I)

— mi familia according to my family (I)

segundo, -a second (I)

— piso third floor (I)

seguro, -a sure (II)

seis six (I)

seiscientos, -as six hundred (I)

el **sello** stamp (II)

la **selva tropical** tropical rainforest (II, 9-2)

el **semáforo** stoplight (II)

la **semana** week (I)

este fin de — this weekend (I)

la — pasada last week (I)

los fines de — on weekends (I)

sembrar (ie) to plant (5-2)

la **semejanza** similarity (8-2)

el **sendero** trail (II)

sentado, -a to be seated (2-1)

el **sentimiento** feeling (2-1)

sentirse (e → ie) to feel (II)

— fatal to feel awful (3-2)

la **señal** sign (II)

la — de parada stop sign (II)

señor (Sr.) sir, Mr. (I)

señora (Sra.) madam, Mrs. (I)

señorita (Srta.) miss, Miss (I)

separar to separate (I)

septiembre September (I)

séptimo, -a seventh (I)

ser to be (I)

¿Eres...? Are you...? (I)

es he / she is (I)

fue it was (I)

no soy I am not (I)

— miembro to be a member (II)

soy I am (I)

ser:

será it, he, she will be (II)

serio, -a serious (I)

el **servicio** service (6-2)

el — social social service (5-2)

la **servilleta** napkin (I)

servir (e → i) to serve, to be useful (I)

¿En qué puedo —le? How can I help you? (I)

¿Para qué sirve? What's it (used) for? (I)

sirve para it is used for (I)

sesenta sixty (I)

setecientos, -as seven hundred (I)

setenta seventy (I)

sexto, -a sixth (I)

si if, whether (I)

sí yes (I)

siempre always (I)

siento:

Lo —. I'm sorry. (I)

la **sierra** sierra, mountain range (1-1)

siete seven (I)

el **siglo** century (2-1)

siguiente next, following (II)

la **silla** chair (I)

la — de ruedas wheelchair (II)

el **símbolo** symbol (7-2)

simpático, -a nice, friendly (I)

sin without (I)

— duda without a doubt (II)

— embargo however (1-2)

la **sinagoga** synagogue (I)

sincero, -a sincere (4-1)

sino but (7-2)

el **sitio Web** Web site (I)

sobre about (I)

sociable sociable (I)

la **sociedad** society (5-2)

¡Socorro! Help! (II)

el **software** software (I)

el **sol**:

Hace —. It's sunny. (I)

los anteojos de — sunglasses (I)

tomar el — to sunbathe (I)

solar solar (II)

el / la soldado soldier (8-2)

soler (ue) to usually do something (5-1)

solicitar to request (5-1)

la solicitud de empleo job application (5-1)

sólo only (I)

solo, -a alone (I)

soltero, -a single (6-1)

la sombra shadow (7-2)

Son las... It is... *(in telling time)* (I)

sonar (ue) (a) to sound like (2-2)

sonreír (e → í) to smile (II)

la sopa de verduras vegetable soup (I)

sorprender(se) to (be) surprise(d) (4-1)

la sorpresa surprise (II)

sospechoso, -a suspicious (10-2)

el sótano basement (I)

soy I am (I)

su, sus his, her, your *formal*, their (I)

subir to go up (II)

suceder to occur (1-1)

sucio, -a dirty (I)

la sudadera sweatshirt (I)

el suelo ground, floor (II)

sueño:
  tener — to be sleepy (I)

el suéter sweater (I)

suficiente enough (9-1)

sufrir to suffer (10-1)

sugerir (e → ie) to suggest (II)

el supermercado supermarket (II)

supuesto:
  por — of course (I)

el surf de vela windsurf (II)

T _____

tal:
  ¿Qué — ? How are you? (I)

tal vez maybe, perhaps (II)

talentoso, -a talented (I)

la talla size (II)

el taller workshop (2-1)

también also, too (I)
  a mí — I do (like to) too (I)

el tambor drum (2-2)

tampoco:
  a mí — I don't (like to) either (I)

tan so (II)
  — + *adj.* so + *adj.* (II)
  — + *adj.* **+ como** as + *adj.* + as (II)
  — pronto como as soon as (9-1)

el tanque tank (II)

el tanteo score (II)

tanto so much (I)
  por lo — therefore (6-1)

tantos, -as + *noun* **+ como** as much / many + *noun* + as (II)

tarde late, afternoon (I)
  a la una de la — at one (o'clock) in the afternoon (I)
  Buenas —s. Good afternoon. (I)
  de la — in the afternoon (I)
  esta — this afternoon (I)
  llegar — to arrive late (II)

la tarea homework (I)

la tarjeta card (I, II)
  la — de crédito credit card (II)
  la — de embarque boarding pass (II)
  la — postal postcard (II)

la taza cup (I)

te you *sing. dir. obj. pron.*, (to / for) you *sing. ind. obj. pron.* (I)

¿— gusta...? Do you like to...? (I)

¿— gustaría...? Would you like...? (I)

¿— gustó? Did you like it? (I)

— importa(n) it matters (it's important), they matter to you (II)

— ves (bien) you look (good) (II)

el té tea (I)
  el — helado iced tea (I)

el teatro theater (I)
  la obra de — play (2-1)

el teclado (computer) keyboard (I)

el técnico, la técnica technician (II)

la tecnología technology / computers (I)
  la clase de — technology / computer class (I)

tecnológico, -a technological (6-2)

la tela sintética synthetic fabric (II)

la telenovela soap opera (I)

el televisor television set (I)

el tema subject (2-1)

temer to fear (4-1)

el templo temple, Protestant church (I)

temprano early (I)

el tenedor fork (I)

tener to have (I)
  ¿Cuántos años tiene(n)...? How old is / are...? (I)
  — calor to be warm (I)
  — celos to be jealous (4-1)
  — cuidado to be careful (II)
  — en común to have in common (4-1)
  — en cuenta to take into account (6-2)

— **éxito** to succeed, to be successful (II)

— **frío** to be cold (I)

— **la culpa** to be guilty (4-2)

— **lugar** to take place (1-2)

— **miedo (de)** to be scared (of), to be afraid (of) (I)

— **paciencia** to be patient (II)

— **prisa** to be in a hurry (II)

— **razón** to be correct (I)

— **sueño** to be sleepy (I)

Tengo hambre. I'm hungry. (I)

Tengo que... I have to... (I)

Tengo sed. I'm thirsty. (I)

Tiene(n)...años. He / She is / They are...(years old). (I)

el **tenis:**

jugar al — to play tennis (I)

la **teoría** theory (7-2)

tercer (tercero), -a third (I)

terminar to finish, to end (I)

el **terremoto** earthquake (II)

el / la **testigo** witness (10-2)

ti you *fam. after prep.*

¿Y a —? And you? (I)

para — in your opinion, for you (I)

el **tiempo:**

a — on time (II)

a — completo full time (5-1)

a — parcial part time (5-1)

el — libre free time (I)

pasar — con amigos to spend time with friends (I)

¿Qué — hace? What's the weather like? (I)

la **tienda** store (I)

la — de acampar tent (1-1)

la — de descuentos discount store (I)

la — de electrodomésticos household-appliance store (I)

la — de ropa clothing store (I)

Tiene(n)...años. He / She is / They are...(years old). (I)

la **Tierra** Earth (II, 7-2); **la tierra** land (8-2)

las **tijeras** scissors (II)

tímido, -a timid (II)

típico, -a typical (II)

el **tío, la tía** uncle, aunt (I)

los **tíos** uncles, aunt(s) and uncle(s) (I)

tirar to spill, to throw away (II)

no tires don't spill, don't throw away (II)

la **toalla** towel (II)

el **tobillo** ankle (II)

tocar la guitarra to play the guitar (I)

el **tocino** bacon (I)

todavía still (II)

todo el mundo everyone (II)

todos, -as all (I)

— los días every day (I)

la **tolerancia** tolerance (10-1)

tomar to take, to drink (3-1)

— conciencia de to become aware of (9-2)

— decisiones to make decisions (6-1)

— el sol to sunbathe (I)

— lecciones to take lessons (II)

— un curso to take a course (I)

los **tomates** tomatoes (I)

la **tonelada** ton (7-1)

tonto, -a silly, stupid (I)

torcerse (o → ue) to twist, to sprain (II)

la **tormenta** storm (II)

la **torre** tower (8-1)

la **tortuga** turtle (II)

la **tos** cough (3-1)

trabajador, -ora hardworking (I)

trabajar to work (I)

el **trabajo** work, job (I)

el — voluntario volunteer work (I)

traducir to translate (6-1)

el **traductor, la traductora** translator (6-1)

traer:

Le traigo... I will bring you... (I)

¿Me trae...? Will you bring me...? *formal* (I)

el **tráfico** traffic (II)

el **traje** suit (I)

el — de baño swimsuit (I)

tranquilo, -a calm (II)

tratar to treat (10-1)

— de to try to (II)

tratarse de to be about (II)

travieso, -a naughty, mischievous (II)

trazar to trace, to draw (7-1)

trece thirteen (I)

treinta thirty (I)

treinta y uno thirty-one (I)

tremendo, -a tremendous (I)

el **tren** train (I)

el — eléctrico electric train (II)

tres three (I)

trescientos, -as three hundred (I)

el **triángulo** triangle (7-1)

el **triciclo** tricycle (II)

triste sad (I)

el **trofeo** trophy (1-2)

la **trompeta** trumpet (2-2)

tropezar (e → ie) (con) to trip (over) (II)

el **trueno** thunder (1-1)
tu, tus your (I)
tú you *fam.* (I)
el / la **turista** tourist (II)
tuyo, -a, -os, -as yours (II)

Ud. (usted) you *formal sing.* (I)
Uds. (ustedes) you *formal / informal pl.* (I)
¡Uf! ugh!, yuck! (I)
último, -a the last / final (II)
un, una a, an (I)
— **poco (de)** a little (I)
la **una:**
a la — at one o'clock (I)
único, -a only (8-1)
la **unidad** unity (8-1)
la **universidad** university (II)
el **universo** universe (7-2)
uno one (I)
unos, -as some (I)
las **uñas** nails (II)
usado, -a used (I)
usar la computadora to use the computer (I)
el **uso** use (6-2)
usted (Ud.) you *formal sing.* (I)
ustedes (Uds.) you *formal / informal pl.* (I)
las **uvas** grapes (I)

las **vacaciones:**
ir de — to go on vacation (I)
vacío, -a empty (3-1)
valiente brave (II)
el **valle** valley (II, 1-1)
el **valor** value (10-2)
¡Vamos! Let's go! (I)
vanidoso, -a vain, conceited (4-1)
la **variedad** variety (8-2)
varios, -as various, several (II)
el **vaso** glass (I)
el **vecino, la vecina** neighbor (II)
veinte twenty (I)
veintiuno (veintiún) twenty-one (I)
la **vela** sail (II)
vencer to beat (1-2)
la **venda** bandage (II)
el **vendedor, la vendedora** vendor (II)
vender to sell (I)
el **veneno** poison (9-1)
venir to come (I)
la **ventana** window (I)
la **ventanilla** (airplane) window (II)
ver to see (I)
a — ... Let's see... (I)
¡Nos vemos! See you later! (I)
— **la tele** to watch television (I)
— **una película** to see a movie (I)
el **verano** summer (I)
veras:
¿De —? Really? (I)
la **verdad** truth (II)
¿Verdad? Really? (I)
verde green (I)
el **vestido** dress (I)
vestirse (e → i) to get dressed (II)

el **veterinario, la veterinaria** veterinarian (II)

la **vez,** *pl.* **las veces:**

    a veces sometimes (I)

    en — de instead of (10-1)

    otra — again (I)

    una — allí once there (1-1)

    vía satélite via satellite (6-2)

    viajar to travel (I)

el **viaje** trip (I)

la **víctima** victim (II)

la **vida** life (II)

el **video** video (I)

los **videojuegos:**

    jugar — to play video games (I)

el **vidrio** glass (I)

    viejo, -a old (I)

    viernes Friday (I)

el **vinagre** vinegar (II)

    violar to violate (10-2)

la **violencia** violence (II)

    violento, -a violent (I)

    visitar to visit (I)

    — salones de chat to visit chat rooms (I, II)

la **vitamina** vitamin (3-1)

la **vivienda** housing (6-2)

    vivir to live (I)

    vivo, -a bright *(color)* (II); living, alive (II)

el **vóleibol:**

    jugar al — to play volleyball (I)

el **voluntario, la voluntaria** volunteer (I)

    volver (o → ue) to return (II)

    —se loco, -a to go crazy (II)

    volverse (ue) to become (2-1)

    vosotros, -as you *fam. pl.* (I)

    votar to vote (10-1)

la **voz,** *pl.* **las voces** voice (II)

el **vuelo** flight (II)

    vuestro, -a, -os, -as your (I)

Y

  y and (I)

    ¿**— a ti?** And you? (I)

    — cuarto quarter past (I)

    — media thirty, half-past *(in telling time)* (I)

    ¿**— tú?** And you? *fam.* (I)

    ¿**— usted (Ud.)?** And you? *formal* (I)

  ya already (I, II)

    — que because, due to (7-1)

el **yeso** cast (II)

  yo I (I)

  ¡Yo no fui! It was not me! (4-2)

el **yoga** yoga (3-2)

el **yogur** yogurt (I)

Z

las **zanahorias** carrots (I)

la **zapatería** shoe store (I)

los **zapatos** shoes (I)

el **zoológico** zoo (I)

English–Spanish Vocabulary

The *English-Spanish Vocabulary* contains all active vocabulary from the text, including vocabulary presented in the grammar sections.

A dash (—) represents the main entry word. For example, **to play —** after **baseball** means **to play baseball.**

The number following each entry indicates the chapter in which the word or expression is presented. A Roman numeral (I) indicates that the word was presented in REALIDADES 1. A roman numeral II indicates the word was presented in REALIDADES 2.

The following abbreviations are used in this list: *adj.* (adjective), *dir. obj.* (direct object), *f.* (feminine), *fam.* (familiar), *ind. obj.* (indirect object), *inf.* (infinitive), *m.* (masculine), *pl.* (plural), *prep.* (preposition), *pron.* (pronoun), *sing.* (singular).

A

a, an un, una (I)
a little un poco (de) (I)
a lot mucho, -a (I)
a while un rato (1-1)
able capaz (6-1)
able:
  to be — to poder (o → ue) (I)
about sobre (I)
abstract abstracto, -a (2-1)
abuse el abuso (10-1)
to **accept** aceptar (4-1)
  — (me) the way (I am)
    aceptar tal como (soy) (4-1)
accident el accidente (II)
to **accompany** acompañar (II)
to **accomplish** realizar (2-2)

according to según (I)
  — my family según mi familia (I)
accountant el contador, la contadora (II, 6-1)
to **accuse** acusar (4-2)
accused el acusado, la acusada (10-2)
to **achieve** lograr (6-1)
acquainted:
  to be — with conocer (I, II)
acting la actuación (II)
action figure el muñeco (II)
actor el actor (I)
actress la actriz, *pl.* las actrices (I)
to **add** añadir (II)
address:
  e-mail — la dirección electrónica (I)
adequate adecuado, -a (10-1)
adolescence la adolescencia (10-1)
adolescent el / la adolescente (10-1)
to **adopt** adoptar (8-2)
advance el avance (6-2)
advice el consejo (3-2)
to **advise** aconsejar (3-2)
aerobics ejercicios aeróbicos (3-2)
aerosol el aerosol (9-2)
to **affect** afectar (9-2)
affectionate cariñoso, -a (4-1)
afraid:
  to be — (of) tener miedo (de) (I)
African africano, -a (8-2)
after después de (I)
afternoon:
  at one (o'clock) in the afternoon a la una de la tarde (I)

  Good —. Buenas tardes. (I)
  in the — de la tarde (I)
  this — esta tarde (I)
afterwards después (I)
again otra vez (I)
against contra (II, 1-2), en contra de (5-2)
age la edad (3-1)
agitated agitado, -a (II)
ago hace + *time expression* (I)
agree:
  I —. Estoy de acuerdo. (I)
  I don't —. No estoy de acuerdo. (I)
Agreed. De acuerdo. (II)
air conditioner el aire acondicionado (II)
airline la línea aérea (II)
airplane el avión (I)
airport el aeropuerto (II)
aisle el pasillo (II)
alarm clock el despertador (I)
alien el / la extraterrestre (II)
alive vivo, -a (II)
all todos, -as (I)
allergy la alergia (3-1)
almost casi (I, II)
alone solo, -a (I)
along por (II, II)
already ya (I)
also también (I)
always siempre (I)
am:
  I — (yo) soy (I)
  I — not (yo) no soy (I)
ambitious ambicioso, -a (6-1)
ambulance la ambulancia (II)
among entre (II)
amusement park el parque de diversiones (I)
amusing divertido, -a (I)
ancestor el antepasado, la antepasada (8-2)

ancestry la descendencia (8-2)

and y (I)

— **you?** ¿Y a ti? *fam.* (I);
¿Y tú? *fam.* (I);
¿Y usted (Ud.)? *formal* (I)

angry enojado, -a (II)

to get — enojarse (II)

animal el animal (I)

ankle el tobillo (II)

anniversary el aniversario (II)

another otro, -a (I)

to announce anunciar (II)

announcement el anuncio (II)

announcer el locutor, la locutora (II)

to answer contestar (II)

ant la hormiga (II)

antibiotic el antibiótico (3-1)

antique antiguo, -a (II)

any algunos, -as (II); cualquier, -a (7-2)

anyone alguien (II)

Anything else? ¿Algo más? (I)

apartment el apartamento (I)

— **building** el edificio de apartamentos (II)

to appear aparecer (zc) (1-1, 7-2)

to applaud aplaudir (II)

applause el aplauso (2-2)

apple la manzana (I)

— **juice** el jugo de manzana (I)

to apply for a job presentarse (5-1)

to apply (the law) aplicar (las leyes) (10-1)

to approach acercarse a (1-1)

appropriate apropiado, -a (3-1)

approximately aproximadamente (II)

April abril (I)

aqueduct el acueducto (8-1)

Arab el / la árabe (8-1)

arch el arco (8-1)

archaeologist el arqueólogo, la arqueóloga (7-1)

architect el arquitecto, la arquitecta (II, 6-1)

architecture la arquitectura (8-1)

Are you...? ¿Eres...? (I)

arm el brazo (I)

around por (II); alrededor de (II)

to arrest arrestar (II)

arrival la llegada (II)

to arrive late llegar tarde (II)

art class la clase de arte (I)

article el artículo (II)

artist el artista, la artista (II)

artistic artístico, -a (I)

arts las artes (II)

martial — las artes marciales (II)

as como (I), al igual que (7-2), a medida que (10-2)

— **a child** de niño (II); de pequeño (II)

— **a main dish** de plato principal (I)

— **far as, up to** hasta (II)

— **soon as** en cuanto, tan pronto como (9-1)

— **though it were** como si fuera (6-2)

as much / many + *noun* + as tantos, -as + *noun* + como (II)

as + *adj.* + as tan + *adj.* + como (II)

to ask for pedir (e → i) (I)

to — forgiveness pedir perdón (4-2)

— **help** pedir ayuda (II)

to ask a question hacer una pregunta (II)

asleep dormido, -a (II)

aspiration la aspiración (10-2)

aspirin la aspirina (3-1)

astronomer el astrónomo, la astrónoma (7-2)

to assimilate asimilar(se) (8-1)

to assist atender (5-1)

to assure asegurar (10-2)

at:

— **dawn** al amanecer (1-1)

— **dusk** al anochecer (1-1)

— **eight (o'clock)** a las ocho (I)

— **eight (o'clock) at night** a las ocho de la noche (I)

— **eight (o'clock) in the evening** a las ocho de la noche (I)

— **eight (o'clock) in the morning** a las ocho de la mañana (I)

— **home** en casa (I)

— **one (o'clock)** a la una (I)

— **one (o'clock) in the afternoon** a la una de la tarde (I)

— **the beginning** al principio (1-2)

— **the end** al final (II)

— **what time?** ¿A qué hora? (I)

ATM el cajero automático (II)

atmosphere la atmósfera (9-2)

attempt el intento (7-2)

to attend asistir a (II)

attentive atento, -a (II)

athlete el / la atleta (II)

attraction(s) la atracción, *pl.* las atracciones (I)

audience el público (II)

audition la audición, *pl.* las audiciones (II)

auditorium el auditorio (II)

August agosto (I)

aunt la tía (I)

aunt(s) and uncle(s) los tíos (I)

authority la autoridad (10-1)

autumn el otoño (I)

avenue la avenida (II)

avocado el aguacate (II)

to avoid evitar (3-1)

awards ceremony la entrega de premios (1-2)

B

baby el / la bebé (II)

babysitter el niñero, la niñera (5-1)

back la espalda (II)

to back (each other) apoyarse (4-1)

background el fondo (2-1)

backpack la mochila (I)

bacon el tocino (I)

bad malo, -a (I); mal (I)

badly mal (I)

bag la bolsa (I)

baked al horno (II)

balanced equilibrado, -a (3-1)

balcony el balcón, pl. los balcones (8-1)

bald eagle el águila calva, pl. las águilas calvas (9-2)

ball la pelota (II)

balloon el globo (I)

banana el plátano (I)

band (musical) la banda (II), el conjunto (2-2)

bandage la venda (II)

bank el banco (II)

banker el banquero, la banquera (6-1)

bargain la ganga (II)

to bargain regatear (II)

baseball:

 to play — jugar al béisbol (I)

basement el sótano (I)

basket la cesta (II)

basketball:

 to play — jugar al basquétbol (I)

bathroom el baño (I)

battery la pila (9-1)

battle la batalla (8-2)

to be ser (I); estar (I)

 He / She is / They are... (years old). Tiene(n)... años. (I)

How old is / are...? ¿Cuántos años tiene(n)...? (I)

to — + present participle estar + present participle (I)

to — a member ser miembro (II)

to — able to poder (o → ue) (I)

to — about tratarse de (II)

to — acquainted with conocer (I)

to — afraid (of) tener miedo (de) (I)

to — based on estar basado, -a en (II)

to — born nacer (II)

to — cold tener frío (I)

to — correct tener razón (I)

to — daydreaming estar en la luna (3-2)

to — delighted alegrarse (4-1)

to — exhausted caerse de sueño (3-2)

to — formed by componerse de (8-2)

to — going to + verb ir a + inf. (I)

to — guilty tener la culpa (4-2)

to — in a good / bad mood estar de buen / mal humor (3-2)

to — in charge of encargarse (5-1), estar a cargo de (9-1)

to — in fashion estar de moda (II)

to — in love with estar enamorado, -a de (II)

to — jealous tener celos (4-1)

to — located quedar (I, II)

to — mistaken estar equivocado, -a (4-2)

to — moved emocionarse (1-2)

to — online estar en línea (I)

to — proud of estar orgulloso, -a de (1-2)

to — **scared (of)** tener miedo (de) (I)

to — **sitting** sentado, -a (2-1)

to — **sleepy** tener sueño (I), caerse de sueño (3-2)

to — **standing** parado, -a (2-1)

to — **subject to** estar sujeto, -a a (10-1)

to — **sure** estar seguro, -a (II)

to — **surprised** sorprenderse (4-1)

to — **useful** servir (I)

to — **warm** tener calor (I)

beach la playa (I)

beans los frijoles (II)

bear el oso (I)

to **beat** batir (II), vencer (1-2)

beautiful bello, -a (II), hermoso, -a (1-1)

beauty salon el salón de belleza, *pl.* los salones de belleza (II)

because porque (I), ya que (7-1)

— **of** a causa de (II)

to **become** ponerse (II), volverse (ue) (2-1), hacerse (6-1), convertirse (en) (7-2)

to — **aware of** tomar conciencia de (9-2)

to — **friends again** reconciliarse (4-2)

to — **the champion** salir campeón / campeona (1-2)

bed la cama (I)

to **make the** — hacer la cama (I)

bedroom el dormitorio (I)

beefsteak el bistec (I)

before antes de (I), anteriormente (8-1), ante (10-1)

to **begin** empezar (e → ie) (I)

to **behave well / badly** portarse bien / mal (II)

behavior el comportamiento (4-2)

behind detrás de (I)

belief la creencia (7-2)

belt el cinturón, *pl.* los cinturones (II)

to **benefit** beneficiar (5-2)

benefits los beneficios (II, 5-1)

best:

the — el / la mejor, los / las mejores (I)

better than mejor(es) que (I)

between entre (II)

bicycle:

to ride a — montar en bicicleta (I)

bilingual bilingüe (II)

bill la cuenta (I)

binder:

three-ring — la carpeta de argollas (I)

binoculars los binoculares (1-1)

bird el pájaro (I), el ave (9-2)

birthday el cumpleaños (I)

Happy —! ¡Feliz cumpleaños! (I)

black hair el pelo negro (I)

block la cuadra (II)

blocks los bloques (II)

blond hair el pelo rubio (I)

blood la sangre (II)

blouse la blusa (I)

blow dryer el secador (II)

blue azul (I)

to **board** abordar (II)

boat el barco (I)

sail— el bote de vela (II)

boating:

to go — pasear en bote (I)

to **boil** hervir (e → ie) (II)

bone el hueso (II)

bonfire la fogata (II)

book el libro (I)

bookbag la mochila (I)

bookshelf el estante (I)

bookstore la librería (I)

boots las botas (I)

to **bore** aburrir (I)

it / they bore(s) me me aburre(n) (I)

to get bored aburrirse (II)

boring aburrido, -a (I)

to **borrow (from)** pedir prestado, -a (a) (II)

boss el jefe, la jefa (6-1)

both los dos, las dos (I), ambos (10-1)

to **bother** molestar (II)

bottle la botella (I)

to **bowl** jugar a los bolos (II)

box la caja (I)

boy el chico (I)

young — el niño (I)

boyfriend el novio (I)

bracelet la pulsera (I)

brand la marca (II)

brave valiente (II)

bread el pan (I)

to **break** romper (I); romperse (II)

breakfast el desayuno (I)

for — en el desayuno (I)

to **breathe** respirar (3-2)

bridge el puente (II)

bright *(color)* vivo, -a (II)

to **bring** traer (I); llevar (I)

I will — you... Le traigo... (I)

Will you — me... ? ¿Me trae... ? (I)

broth el caldo (II)

brother el hermano (I)

brothers; brother(s) and sister(s) los hermanos (I)

brown marrón (I)

— **(chestnut) hair** el pelo castaño (I)

brush el cepillo (II), el pincel (2-1)

tooth— el cepillo de dientes (II)

to brush (one's teeth) cepillarse (los dientes) (II)

to build construir (i → y) (5-2)

to burn a CD grabar un disco compacto (I)

to burn (oneself), to burn up quemar(se) (II)

bus el autobús, *pl.* los autobuses (I)

business los negocios (II), la empresa (6-1)

  —**man** el hombre de negocios (II, 6-1)

  —**woman** la mujer de negocios (II, 6-1)

busy ocupado, -a (I)

but pero (I), sino (7-2)

butter la mantequilla (I)

to buy comprar (I)

  — **souvenirs** comprar recuerdos (I)

by por (II)

  — + *vehicle* en + *vehicle* (I)

  — **hand** a mano (II)

C _____

café el café (I)

cake el pastel (I)

calcium el calcio (3-1)

to call:

  to — on the phone llamar por teléfono (II)

to calculate calcular (7-1)

calculator la calculadora (I)

calm tranquilo, -a (II)

camera la cámara (I)

  digital — la cámara digital (I)

camp el campamento (I)

campaign la campaña (5-2)

can la lata (I)

can:

  I — (yo) puedo (I)

  you — (tú) puedes (I)

candy los dulces (I)

canned enlatado, -a (II)

cap la gorra (I)

to capture capturar (II)

car el coche (I)

carbohydrate el carbohidrato (3-1)

card la tarjeta (I)

  credit — la tarjeta de crédito (II)

  post— la tarjeta postal (II)

cardboard el cartón (I)

career la carrera (II)

careful cuidadoso, -a (6-1)

carrots las zanahorias (I)

to carry llevar (I)

  — **out** cumplir con (5-1)

cartoon el programa de dibujos animados (I)

cash el dinero en efectivo (II)

  to cash a check cobrar un cheque (II)

cash register la caja (II)

cashier el cajero, la cajera (II)

cast el yeso (II)

castle el castillo (II)

cat el gato (I)

to catch atrapar (9-2)

cathedral la catedral (II)

cattle la res (II)

cause la causa (II), el motivo (10-1)

CD:

  to burn a — grabar un disco compacto (I)

to celebrate celebrar (I)

center, downtown el centro (I, II)

centigrade degree el grado centígrado (3-1)

centimeter el centímetro (7-1)

century el siglo (2-1)

cereal el cereal (I)

ceremony la ceremonia (1-2)

certificate el certificado (1-2)

chain la cadena (I)

chair la silla (I)

  wheel— la silla de ruedas (II)

challenge el reto (8-2)

champion el campeón, la campeona, *pl.* los campeones (II)

to become the — salir campeón, campeona (1-2)

championship el campeonato (II)

to change cambiar (II)

  to — one's mind cambiar de opinión (4-1)

channel *(TV)* el canal (I)

to chat charlar (II)

chat rooms los salones de chat (II)

cheap barato, -a (I)

check:

  to cash a — cobrar un cheque (II)

  traveler's — el cheque de viajero (II)

personal — el cheque personal (II)

to **check (luggage)** facturar (el equipaje) (II)

to **check out a book** sacar (II)

cheerleader el animador, la animadora (II)

chemical químico, -a (9-1)

cherry la cereza (II)

chess el ajedrez (II)

chest el pecho (3-1)

chicken el pollo (I)

childhood la niñez (10-1)

childish infantil (I)

children los hijos (I); los niños (I)

to **chop** picar (II)

chore:

   household — el quehacer (de la casa) (I)

chorus, choir el coro (II)

to **choose** escoger (II)

Christian el cristiano, la cristiana (8-1)

church la iglesia (I)

  Protestant — el templo (I)

circle el círculo (7-1)

citizen el ciudadano, la ciudadana (5-2)

citizenship la ciudadanía (5-2)

city la ciudad (I)

civilization la civilización (7-1)

class la clase (I)

classical clásico, -a (2-2)

classified ad el anuncio clasificado (5-1)

classroom la sala de clases (I)

clean limpio, -a (I)

to **clean the bathroom** limpiar el baño (I)

cleaning la limpieza (9-2)

client el / la cliente / a (5-1)

to **climb (a rock or mountain)** escalar (1-1)

clock el reloj (I)

to **close** cerrar (II)

close (to) cerca (de) (I)

closed cerrado, -a (II)

closes se cierra (II)

closet el armario (I)

clothing store la tienda de ropa (I)

club el club, *pl.* los clubes (II)

  athletic — el club atlético (II)

coach el entrenador, la entrenadora (II)

coat el abrigo (I)

coffee el café (I)

coin la moneda (II)

cold:

  It's —. Hace frío. (I)

  to be — tener frío (I)

to **collaborate** colaborar (4-2)

to **collect** recoger (I)

to **collect** coleccionar (II)

collection la colección, *pl.* las colecciones (II)

to **collide with** chocar con (II)

cologne el agua de colonia (II)

colony la colonia (8-2)

color:

  What — ... ? ¿De qué color ... ? (I)

  —s los colores (I)

comb el peine (II)

to **come** venir (I)

comedy la comedia (I)

comfortable cómodo, -a (II)

comical cómico, -a (I)

commentary el comentario (II)

to **communicate** comunicarse (I, 6-2)

  I — (yo) me comunico (I)

  you — (tú) te comunicas (I)

community la comunidad (I)

  — center el centro de la comunidad (5-2)

compact disc el disco compacto (I)

  to burn a — grabar un disco compacto (I)

company la compañía (5-1)

compass la brújula (1-1)

to **compete** competir (e → i) (II)

competition la competencia (II)

to **complain** quejarse (3-2)

complicated complicado, -a (I, II)

composition la composición, *pl.* las composiciones (I)

to **compute** calcular (7-1)

computer la computadora (I)

  — graphics los gráficos (I)

  — keyboard el teclado (I)

  — mouse el ratón (I)

  — screen la pantalla (I)

  — science la computación (5-1)

  —s / technology la tecnología (I)

  laptop — la computadora portátil (I)

  to use the — usar la computadora (I)

conceited vanidoso, -a (4-1)

to **concentrate** concentrarse (3-2)

concert el concierto (I)

conflict el conflicto (4-2)

to **confront** enfrentarse (8-2)

to **congratulate** felicitar (II)

Congratulations! ¡Felicidades! (II), ¡Felicitaciones! (1-2)

to **conquer** conquistar (8-1)

conquest la conquista (8-1)

conservation la preservación (9-2)

to **conserve** conservar (II)

considerate considerado, -a (4-1)

construction la construcción (8-1)

  — project el proyecto de construcción (I)

to **contain** contener (3-1)

container el recipiente (9-1)

contest el concurso (II)

beauty — el concurso de belleza (II)

to **contribute** contribuir (u → y) (7-2)

cook el cocinero, la cocinera (6-1)

to **cook** cocinar (I)

cookie la galleta (I)

cooking oil el aceite (II)

corn el maíz (II)

corner la esquina (II)

correct:

to be — tener razón (I)

to **cost** costar (o → ue) (I)

How much does (do)... —? ¿Cuánto cuesta(n)? (I)

cotton el algodón (II)

cough la tos (3-1)

counselor el consejero, la consejera (5-1)

to **count on** contar con (4-1)

country el país (I)

countryside el campo (I)

course:

to take a — tomar un curso (I)

— of studies el programa de estudios (II)

cousin la prima, el primo (I)

—s los primos (I)

to **cover** cubrir (7-1)

cramp el calambre (3-2)

to **crash into** chocar con (II)

to **create** crear (I)

to — a Web page crear una página Web (II)

crime el crimen (II)

— movie la película policíaca (I)

criminal el / la criminal (II)

critic el crítico, la crítica (II)

to **criticize** criticar (4-2)

to **cross** cruzar (II)

crunches los abdominales (3)

crutches las muletas (II)

to **cry** llorar (II)

cup la taza (I)

to **cure** curar (6-2)

curtains las cortinas (I)

custom la costumbre (II)

customs la aduana (II)

customs officer el aduanero, la aduanera (II)

to **cut** cortar (I, II)

to — oneself cortarse (II)

to — one's hair cortarse el pelo (II)

to — the lawn cortar el césped (I)

cut-paper decorations el papel picado (I)

D _____

to **damage** dañar (9-1)

dance el baile (I), la danza (2-2)

to **dance** bailar (I)

dancer el bailarín, la bailarina (II)

dangerous peligroso, -a (II)

to **dare** atreverse (4-2)

daring atrevido, -a (I)

dark oscuro, -a (II)

date:

What is the —? ¿Cuál es la fecha? (I)

date la cita (II)

date of birth la fecha de nacimiento (5-1)

daughter la hija (I)

day el día (I)

every — todos los días (I); cada día (I)

What — is today? ¿Qué día es hoy? (I)

day-care center la guardería infantil (II)

dead muerto, -a (II)

December diciembre (I)

to **decide** decidir (I)

to **decorate** decorar (I)

decorations las decoraciones (I)

to **decrease** disminuir (9-2)

to dedicate oneself to dedicarse a (6-1)

dedicated dedicado, -a (5-1)

delay el retraso (II)

delicious delicioso, -a (I)

delighted encantado, -a (I)

to **deliver** repartir (5-1)

delivery person el repartidor, la repartidora (5-1)

demand la demanda (6-2)

to **demand** exigir (3-2)

democratic democrático, -a (10-2)

demonstration la manifestación (5-2)

dentist el / la dentista (II)

department store el almacén, *pl.* los almacenes (I)

departure gate la puerta de embarque (II)

to **depend on** depender de (9-1)

deodorant el desodorante (II)

descent la descendencia (8-2)

desert el desierto (II, 1-1)

design el diseño (7-1)

to **design** diseñar (6-1)

designer el diseñador, la diseñadora (II, 6-1)

desk el pupitre (I); el escritorio (I)

despite aunque (3-1), a pesar de (10-2)

dessert el postre (I)

 for — de postre (I)

to **destroy** destruir (i → y) (II)

destruction la destrucción (II)

to **detain** detener (10-2)

detective el / la detective (II)

detective movie la película policíaca (I)

to **develop** desarrollar (3-2)

development el desarrollo (6-2)

diameter el diámetro (7-1)

dictionary el diccionario (I)

Did you like it? ¿Te gustó? (I)

to **die** morirse (II)

diet la dieta (3-1)

difference of opinion la diferencia de opinión (4-2)

difficult difícil (I)

digital camera la cámara digital (I)

to **diminish** disminuir (9-2)

dining room el comedor (I)

dinner la cena (I)

dinosaur el dinosaurio (II)

diploma el certificado (1-2)

direct directo, -a (II)

direction la dirección, *pl.* las direcciones (II)

dirty sucio, -a (I)

to **disappear** desaparecer (zc) (6-2)

disaster:

 It was a —. Fue un desastre. (I)

discount store la tienda de descuentos (I)

discouraged desanimado, -a (1-2)

to **discover** descubrir (6-2)

to **discriminate** discriminar (10-1)

to **discuss** discutir (II)

dish el plato (I)

 as a main — de plato principal (I)

 main — el plato principal (I)

disobedient desobediente (II)

distance la distancia (7-1)

to **do** hacer (I)

 — *(command)* haz (I)

 — you like to ... ? ¿Te gusta ... ? (I)

 I — (yo) hago (I)

 to — a project hacer un proyecto (II)

 to — a search hacer una búsqueda (II)

 to — gymnastics hacer gimnasia (II)

 to — push-ups hacer flexiones (3-2)

 to — the laundry lavar la ropa (I)

 you — (tú) haces (I)

 What did you —? ¿Qué hiciste? (I)

doctor el médico, la médica (II)

doctor's / dentist's office el consultorio (II)

document el documento (I)

dog el perro (I)

 to feed the — dar de comer al perro (I)

doll la muñeca (II)

to **dominate** dominar (8-1)

to **donate** donar (5-2)

Don't eat. No comas. (II)

Don't leave, Don't let No dejes (II)

Don't speak. No hables. (II)

Don't write. No escribas. (II)

door la puerta (I)

to **doubt** dudar (II, 7-1)

to **download** bajar (información) (I)

drama el drama (I)

to **draw** dibujar (I)

dress el vestido (I)

 — code el código de vestimenta (10-1)

dresser la cómoda (I)

to **drink** beber (I), tomar (3-1)

drinks las bebidas (I)

to **drive** manejar (II)

driver el conductor, la conductora (II)

driver's license el permiso de manejar (II)

drum el tambor (2-2)

dry seco, -a (II)

to **dry** secarse (II)

due to ya que (7-1), debido a (9-1)

during durante (I)

to **dust** quitar el polvo (I)

duty el deber (10-1)

DVD player el lector DVD (I)

E _____

e-mail:
  — address la dirección electrónica (I)
  to write — escribir por correo electrónico (I)
ear el oído (3-1)
early temprano (I)
to **earn** *(money)* ganar (II)
Earth la Tierra (II, 7-2)
earthquake el terremoto (II)
earrings los aretes (I)
easy fácil (I)
to **eat** comer (I)
eating habit el hábito alimenticio (3-1)
eclipse el eclipse (7-2)
ecological ecológico, -a (II)
economical económico, -a (II, 9-1)
editor el redactor, la redactora (6-1)
to **educate** educar (5-2)
educational program el programa educativo (I)
efficient eficiente (II, 6-1)
eggs los huevos (I)
eight ocho (I)
eight hundred ochocientos, -as (I)
eighteen dieciocho (I)
eighth octavo, -a (I)
eighty ochenta (I)
either tampoco (I)
  I don't (like to) — a mí tampoco (I)
elbow el codo (II)
elderly man, woman el anciano, la anciana (I)
the elderly los ancianos (I)
electricity la electricidad (II, 9-1)
elegant elegante (II)

elevator el ascensor (II)
eleven once (I)
to **eliminate** eliminar (II, 1-2)
else:
  Anything —? ¿Algo más? (I)
  What —? ¿Qué más? (I)
emergency room la sala de emergencia (II)
empire el imperio (8-1)
employee el empleado, la empleada (II)
empty vacío, -a (3-1)
to **encourage** fomentar (9-1)
to **end** terminar (I)
endangered (en) peligro de extinción (9-2)
to **endure** aguantar (3-2)
energy la energía (II, 3-1)
  — source la fuente de energía (6-2)
engineer el ingeniero, la ingeniera (II, 6-1)
English class la clase de inglés (I)
to **enjoy** disfrutar de (II), gozar (de) (10-1)
enormous enorme (II)
enough bastante (I), suficiente (9-1)
Enough! ¡Basta! (II)
to **enter** entrar (I)
enterprising emprendedor, -a (6-1)
enthusiasm el entusiasmo (2-2)
entrance la entrada (II)
environment el medio ambiente (II, 5-2)
equality la igualdad (10-1)
era la época (8-1)
to **escape** escaparse (II)
especially especialmente (I)
establish establecer (zc) (8-2)
ethnic group el grupo étnico (8-1)
European europeo, -a (8-2)
even when aunque (3-1)

evening:
  Good —. Buenas noches. (I)
  in the — de la noche (I)
  this — esta noche (I)
every day cada día (I), todos los días (I)
everyone todo el mundo (II)
evidence la evidencia (7-1)
exactly en punto (II)
to **exaggerate** exagerar (2-2)
to **examine, to check** examinar (II)
to **excavate** excavar (7-1)
excessive excesivo, -a (9-2)
exchange el intercambio (8-2)
to **exchange** cambiar (II)
to **exchange** intercambiar (10-2)
excited entusiasmado, -a, emocionado, -a (II), animado, -a (1-2)
excursion, short trip la excursión, *pl.* las excursiones (II)
Excuse me. Perdón. (I)
to **exercise** hacer ejercicio (I)
to **exhaust** agotar(se) (9-1)
to **exist** existir (7-1)
exit la salida (II)
to **expel** expulsar (8-1)
expensive caro, -a (I)
experience la experiencia (I)
to **explain** explicar (II)
explanation la explicación (4-2)
to **exploit** explotar (9-2)
explosion la explosión, *pl.* las explosiones (II)
to **express (oneself)** expresar(se) (2-1)
to **extend** prolongar (6-2)
extinction:
  in danger of — en peligro de extinción (9-2)
extracurricular extracurricular
  — activities las actividades extracurriculares (II)
eye el ojo (I)

F

face la cara (II)

to **face** enfrentarse (8-2)

face-to-face cara a cara (I)

factory la fábrica (6-2)

failure el fracaso (II)

fair justo, -a (5-2)

fall el otoño (I)

to **fall** caerse (II)

    I — (yo) me caigo (II)

    to — asleep dormirse (II)

    to — in love (with)
    enamorarse (de) (II)

    you — (tú) te caes (II)

famous famoso, -a (II, 2-1)

fan el aficionado, la aficionada (II)

fantastic fantástico, -a (I)

far (from) lejos (de) (I)

farmer el agricultor, la agricultora (II)

to **fascinate** fascinar (II)

fascinating fascinante (I)

fast rápidamente (I)

father el padre (papá) (I)

favorite favorito, -a (I)

to **fear** temer (4-1)

feather la pluma (9-2)

February febrero (I)

to **feed the dog** dar de comer al perro (I)

to **feel** sentirse (e → ie) (II)

    to — awful sentirse fatal (3-2)

feeling el sentimiento (2-1)

fever la fiebre (3-1)

fewer:

    — ...than menos... que (I)

    — than... menos de... (I)

fiber la fibra (3-1)

field el campo (6-2)

fifteen quince (I)

fifth quinto, -a (I)

fifty cincuenta (I)

fight la pelea (4-2)

to **fight** luchar (II, 8-2), pelearse (II)

figure la figura (2-1)

to **fill (the tank)** llenar (el tanque) (II)

film la película (I)

final último, -a (II)

finance las finanzas (6-1)

to **find** encontrar (o → ue) (II)

    — out averiguar (6-1), enterarse (6-2)

finger el dedo (I)

to **finish** terminar (I)

fire el incendio (II); el fuego (II)

firefighter el bombero, la bombera (II)

firewood la leña (II)

fireworks los fuegos artificiales (II)

firm la compañía (5-1)

first primer (primero), -a (I)

fish el pescado (I); el pez, *pl.* los peces (II)

    to go —ing ir de pesca (I)

to **fit:**

    It / They —(s) me well / poorly. Me queda(n) bien / mal. (I)

five cinco (I)

five hundred quinientos, -as (I)

to **fix (one's hair)** arreglarse (el pelo) (II)

flag la bandera (I)

flashlight la linterna (1-1)

flavorful sabroso, -a (I)

to **flex** flexionar (3-2)

flexible flexible (5-1)

flight el vuelo (II)

flight attendant el / la auxiliar de vuelo (II)

flood la inundación, *pl.* las inundaciones (II)

floor el piso (I); el suelo (II)

    ground — la planta baja (I)

    second — el primer piso (I)

    third — el segundo piso (I)

flour la harina (II)

flower la flor, *pl.* las flores (I)

flu la gripe (3-1)

fly la mosca (II)

folder la carpeta (I)

to **follow** seguir (e → i) (II)

following siguiente (II)

food la comida (I), los alimentos (3-1)

food stand el puesto (II)

foot el pie (I)

football:

    to play — jugar al fútbol americano (I)

for para (I)

    — breakfast en el desayuno (I)

    — lunch en el almuerzo (I)

    — me para mí (I)

    — you para ti (I)

for (how long) por (II)

    — example por ejemplo (II)

    — the ... time por ... vez (II)

forbidden:

    It is — . Se prohíbe. (II)

to **force** obligar (10-1)

foreground el primer plano (2-1)

forest el bosque (II, 1-1)

to **forget about** olvidarse de (II)

    don't — no te olvides de (II)

to **forgive** perdonar (4-2)

fork el tenedor (I)

fortunately afortunadamente (II)

forty cuarenta (I)

to **found** fundar (8-1)

fountain la fuente (II)

four cuatro (I)

four hundred cuatrocientos, -as (I)

fourteen catorce (I)

fourth cuarto, -a (I)

free gratuito, -a (10-1), libre (10-2)

free time el tiempo libre (I), el ocio (6-2)

French fries las papas fritas (I)

frequently frecuentemente (II)

fresh fresco, -a (II)

Friday viernes (I)

fried frito, -a (II)

friendly simpático, -a (I)

friendship la amistad (4-1)

frightened asustado, -a (II)

from de (I); desde (II)

  — now on de hoy en adelante (6-2)

  Where are you —? ¿De dónde eres? (I)

frozen congelado, -a (II)

fruit salad la ensalada de frutas (I)

frying pan la sartén (II)

full lleno, -a (3-1)

  — time a tiempo completo (5-1)

fun divertido, -a (I)

function la función (7-1)

to **function, to work** funcionar (II, 10-1)

fundamental fundamental (10-2)

to **fundraise** juntar fondos (5-2)

funny gracioso, -a (I); cómico, -a (I)

furious furioso, -a (II)

furniture los muebles (II)

future el futuro (II)

G _____

gadget el aparato (6-2)

game el partido (I)

game show el programa de concursos (I)

garage el garaje (I)

garden el jardín (I)

garlic el ajo (II)

gasoline la gasolina (II)

to **gather** recoger (I)

gathering la reunión, *pl.* las reuniones (II)

gel el gel (II)

gene, genes el gene, *pl.* los genes (6-2)

generally generalmente (I)

generous generoso, -a (II)

genetics la genética (6-2)

geometric(a) geométrico, -a (7-1)

gesture el gesto (2-2)

to **get** obtener (1-2)

  to — a good grade sacar una buena nota (II)

  to — along well / badly llevarse bien / mal (II)

  to — dressed vestirse (e → i) (II)

  to — lost perderse (1-1)

  to — married (to) casarse (con) (II)

  to — ready prepararse (II)

  to — rid of deshacerse de (9-1)

  to — up levantarse (II)

gift el regalo (I)

gift certificate el cupón de regalo, *pl.* los cupones de regalo (II)

girl la chica (I)

  young — la niña (I)

girlfriend la novia (I)

to **give** dar (I); regalar (II)

  to — a speech dar un discurso (II)

  to — a ticket poner una multa (II)

glass el vaso (I); el vidrio (I)

global warming el recalentamiento global (9-2)

gloves los guantes (I)

to **go** ir (I); pasar (II)

  Let's —! ¡Vamos! (I)

  to be —ing to + *verb* ir a + *inf.* (I)

  to — to bed acostarse (o → ue) (II)

  to — boating pasear en bote (I)

  to — camping ir de cámping (I)

  to — crazy volverse loco (II)

  to — down bajar (II)

  to — fishing ir de pesca (I)

  to — on foot ir a pie (II)

  to — on vacation ir de vacaciones (I)

  to — out salir (I)

  to — shopping ir de compras (I)

  to — to school ir a la escuela (I)

  to — up subir (II)

goal *(in sports)* el gol (II); la meta (1-2)

  to score a — meter un gol (II)

god, goddess el dios, la diosa (7-2)

going to con destino a (II)

gold el oro (II)

golf:

  — club el palo de golf (II)

  to play — jugar al golf (I)

good bueno (buen), -a (I)

  — afternoon. Buenas tardes. (I)

  — evening. Buenas noches. (I)

  — gracious caramba (II)

  — morning. Buenos días. (I)

Good-bye! ¡Adiós! (I)

good-looking guapo, -a (I)

gossipy chismoso, -a (4-1)

to **govern** governar (8-1)

government el gobierno (9-1)

grade *(in school)* la nota (II)

  to get a good — sacar una buena nota (II)

to **graduate** graduarse (u → ú) (II, 6-1)

graduation la graduación, *pl.* las graduaciones (II)

grandfather el abuelo (I)

grandmother la abuela (I)

grandparents los abuelos (I)

grapes las uvas (I)

grate la reja (8-1)

gray gris (I)

  — hair el pelo canoso (I)

greasy grasoso, -a (II)

Great! ¡Genial! (I)

green verde (I)

  — beans las judías verdes (I)

  —house effect el efecto invernadero (9-2)

  to greet saludar(se) (II)

to **grill** asar (II)

grill la parrilla (II)

grilled asado, -a (II)

ground floor la planta baja (I)

ground el suelo (II)

to **grow** crecer (9-1)

grown-ups los mayores (II)

guarantee la garantía (10-2)

to **guarantee** garantizar (5-2)

guide el / la guía (II)

guidebook la guía (II)

guilty culpable (10-2)

guitar:

  to play the — tocar la guitarra (I)

gym el gimnasio (I)

gymnastics la gimnasia (II)

H ───────────

hail granizo (1-1)

  to hail caer granizo (1-1)

hair el pelo (I)

  black — el pelo negro (I)

  blond — el pelo rubio (I)

  brown (chestnut) — el pelo castaño (I)

  gray — el pelo canoso (I)

hair stylist el peluquero, la peluquera (6-1)

half media, -o (I)

  — past y media *(in telling time)* (I)

ham and cheese sandwich el sándwich de jamón y queso (I)

hamburger la hamburguesa (I)

hand la mano (I)

  to shake —s darse la mano (II)

handicrafts la artesanía (II)

happiness la felicidad (10-1)

happy contento, -a (I); alegre (II)

  — birthday! ¡Feliz cumpleaños! (I)

harmony armonía (4-2)

hardworking trabajador, -ora (I)

to **have** tener (I)

  I — to... tengo que + *inf.* (I)

  to — a barbecue hacer una parrillada (II)

  to — a birthday cumplir años (II)

  to — a cold estar resfriado, -a (3-1)

  to — a good / bad time pasarlo bien / mal (1-1)

  to — a picnic hacer un picnic (II)

  to — fun divertirse (e → ie) (II)

  to — in common tener en común (4-1)

  to — just... acabar de + *inf.* (I)

  to — lunch almorzar (o → ue) (II)

to **have** haber *(as an auxiliary verb)* (II)

he él (I)

he / she is es (I)

He / She is / They are... (years old). Tiene(n) ... años. (I)

head la cabeza (I)

health:

  for one's — para la salud (I)

  to maintain one's — para mantener la salud (I)

healthy saludable (3-1)

to **hear** oír (II)

heart el corazón (3-2)

heat la calefacción (II)

to **heat** calentar (e → ie) (II)

height la estatura (3-1), el alto (7-1)

Hello! ¡Hola! (I)

help la ayuda (II)

to **help** ayudar (I), atender (5-1)

  How can I — you? ¿En qué puedo servirle? (I)

her su, sus *possessive adj.* (I); la *dir. obj. pron.* (I); le *ind. obj. pron.* (I)

here aquí (I)

heritage la herencia (8-2)

hero el héroe (II)

heroine la heroína (II)

Hey! ¡Oye! (I)

to **hide (oneself)** esconder(se) (II)

high alto, -a (II)

high school el colegio (II)

highway la carretera (II)

hill la colina (II)

him lo *dir. obj. pron.* (I); le *ind. obj. pron.* (I)

his su, sus (I)

historical histórico, -a (II)

hockey el hockey (II)

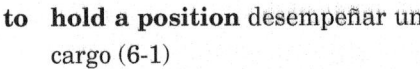

to **hold a position** desempeñar un
cargo (6-1)

hole el agujero (9-2)

holiday el día festivo (II)

home: la casa (I)

at **—** en casa (I)

— for the elderly el hogar de
ancianos (5-2)

— office el despacho (I)

(to) — a casa (I)

homeless people la gente sin
hogar (5-2)

homework la tarea (I)

honest honesto, -a (4-1)

to **hope (for)** esperar (4-1)

horrible horrible (I)

horror movie la película de
horror (I)

horseback:

to ride — montar a caballo (I)

hospital el hospital (I)

hospitality la hospitalidad (6-2)

hot caliente (II)

— dog el perrito caliente (I)

It's **—.** Hace calor. (I)

hotel el hotel (I)

hour:

in the ... — en la ... hora *(class
period)* (I)

house la casa (I)

household:

— appliance store la tienda
de electrodomésticos (I)

— chore el quehacer (de la
casa) (I)

housing la vivienda (6-2)

how!

— + *adj.!* ¡Qué + *adj.*! (I)

— awful! ¡Qué asco! (I)

How? ¿Cómo? (I)

— are you? ¿Cómo está Ud.?
formal (I); ¿Cómo estás?
fam. (I); ¿Qué tal? *fam.* (I)

— can I help you? ¿En qué
puedo servirle? (I)

— do you go to...? ¿Cómo se
va...? (II)

— do you make ...? ¿Cómo se
hace ...? (II)

— do you say... ? ¿Cómo se
dice... ? (I)

— does it (do they) fit (you)?
¿Cómo te queda(n)? (I)

— does it seem to you? ¿Qué
te parece? (II)

— is ... spelled? ¿Cómo se
escribe ...? (I)

— is (it)...? ¿Qué tal es...? (II)

— long...? ¿Cuánto tiempo hace
que...? (II)

— many? ¿Cuántos, -as? (I)

— much does (do) ... cost?
¿Cuánto cuesta(n) ... ? (I)

— old is / are ... ? ¿Cuántos
años tiene(n) ... ? (I)

— was it (for you)? ¿Cómo lo
pasaste? (I)

however sin embargo (1-2)

to **hug** abrazar(se) (II)

hundred:

one — cien (I)

hungry:

I'm **—.** Tengo hambre. (I)

hunting la caza (9-2)

hurricane el huracán, *pl.* los
huracanes (II)

to **hurt** doler (o **→** ue) (I, II)

to **hurt oneself** lastimarse (II)

hurry prisa (II)

to be in a — tener prisa (II)

husband el esposo (I)

I

I yo (I)

— am soy (I)

— am not no soy (I)

— do too a mí también (I)

— don't either a mí tampoco (I)

— don't think so. Creo que
no. (I)

— forgot se me olvidó (II)

— have seen he visto (II)

— 'll do as I please haré lo
que me dé la gana (6-1)

—'m hungry. Tengo hambre. (I)

—'m sorry. Lo siento. (I)

—'m thirsty. Tengo sed. (I)

— stay at home. Me quedo en
casa. (I)

— think ... Creo que ... (I)

— think so. Creo que sí. (I)

— will bring you ... Le traigo
... (I)

— wish ojalá (4-1)

— would like Me gustaría (I);
quisiera (I)

— would be interested ... Me
interesaría ... (5-2)

— would love to ... Me
encantaría ... (5-2)

ice el hielo (9-2)

ice cream el helado (I)

iced tea el té helado (I)

I.D. card el carnet de identidad
(II)

to **identify oneself with**
identificarse con (2-2)

if si (I)

to **ignore** ignorar (4-2)

illness la enfermedad (6-2)

image la imagen (2-1)

immediately inmediatamente
(II)

impatient impaciente (I)

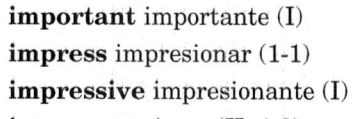

important importante (I)
impress impresionar (1-1)
impressive impresionante (I)
to **improve** mejorar (II, 4-2)
in en (I)
  — **addition to** además de (6-1)
  — **danger of extinction** (en) peligro de extinción (II)
  — **favor of** a favor de (5-2)
  — **front of** delante de (I)
  — **general** por lo general (II)
  — **love with** enamorado, -a de (II)
  — **my opinion** para mí (I)
  — **other words** o sea que (7-2)
  — **order to** para + *inf.* (I)
  — **that way** de ese modo (10-1)
  — **the ... hour** en la ... hora (class period) (I)
  — **the middle of** en medio de (II)
  — **your opinion** para ti (I)
include incluir (3-1)
to **increase** aumentar (6-2)
incredible increíble (I)
industry industria (6-2)
inequity la desigualdad (10-2)
inexpensive barato, -a (I)
inexplicable inexplicable (7-1)
influence la influencia (8-1)
to **influence** influir (i → y) (2-1)
information la información (I)
  — **technology** la informática (6-2)
ingredient el ingrediente (II)
inhabitant el / la habitante (7-2)
injection, shot la inyección, *pl.* las inyecciones (II)
injured herido, -a (II)
injured person el herido, la herida (II)
injustice la injusticia (10-1)
innocent inocente (10-2)

insect repellent el repelente de insectos (1-1)
inside dentro de (II)
to **insist** insistir en (II)
to **inspect** registrar (II)
to **inspire** inspirar (2-1)
instead of en vez de (10-1), en lugar de (10-2)
to **integrate** integrarse (8-1)
intelligent inteligente (I)
interest el interés (II)
to **interest** interesar (I)
  it / they interest(s) me me interesa(n) (I)
interesting interesante (I)
interfering entrometido, -a (4-1)
to **interpret** interpretar (2-2)
interpretation la interpretación (2-2)
intersection el cruce de calles (II)
interview la entrevista (II, 5-1)
  — **program** el programa de entrevistas (I)
to **interview** entrevistar (II)
intimate íntimo, -a (4-1)
to **invade** invadir (8-1)
to **invent** inventar (6-2)
invention el invento (6-2)
to **investigate** investigar (II)
iron el hierro (3-1)
is es (I)
  he / she — es (I)
  it — true es cierto (II)
it la, lo *dir. obj. pron.* (I)
  — **depends** depende (II)
  — **fits (they fit) me well / poorly.** Me queda(n) bien / mal. (I)
  — **has been...** Hace + *time* + que... (II)
  — **is ...** Son las *(in telling time)* (I)

  — **is forbidden...** Se prohíbe... (II)
  — **is impossible for me...** Me es imposible... (5-2)
  — **is made of...** Está hecho, -a de... (II)
  — **is one o'clock.** Es la una. (I)
  — **is the ... of ...** Es el *(number)* de *(month) (in telling the date)* (I)
  — **is the first of ...** Es el primero de *(month).* (I)
  — **seems to me** me parece que (II)
  — **was** fue (I)
  —**was not me!** ¡Yo no fui! (4-2)
  — **was a disaster.** Fue un desastre. (I)
  —**'s a ...** es un / una ... (I)
  —**'s cold.** Hace frío. (I)
  —**'s hot.** Hace calor. (I)
  —**'s necessary.** Es necesario. (I)
  —**'s raining.** Llueve. (I)
  —**'s snowing.** Nieva. (I)
  —**'s sunny.** Hace sol. (I)
it / he / she will be ser: será (II)
itinerary el itinerario (II)

J

jacket la chaqueta (I)
January enero (I)
jealous celoso, -a (4-1)
jeans los jeans (I)
jewelry (gold, silver) las joyas (de oro, de plata) (II)
jewelry store la joyería (I)
Jew(ish) el judío, la judía (8-1)
job el trabajo (I)
  — application la solicitud de empleo (5-1)
to **join** juntarse (II)
judge el juez, la jueza, *pl.* los jueces (II, 6-1)
to **judge** juzgar (10-2)
juice:
  apple — el jugo de manzana (I)
  orange — el jugo de naranja (I)
July julio (I)
to **jump (rope)** saltar (a la cuerda) (II)
June junio (I)
junk food la comida basura (3-1)
jury el jurado (10-2)
just:
  to have — ... acabar de + *inf.* (I)
justice la justicia (10-2)

K

to **keep (a secret)** guardar un secreto (4-1)
to **keep on (doing)** seguir (+ present participle) (5-1)
ketchup la salsa de tomate (II)
key la llave (II)
key chain el llavero (I)
keyboard (computer) el teclado (I)
to **kill** matar (II)
kind:
  What — of ... ? ¿Qué clase de ... ? (I)
kind amable (4-1)
king el rey (II)
to **kiss** besar(se) (II)
kitchen la cocina (I)
knee la rodilla (II)
knife el cuchillo (I)
to **know** saber (I); conocer (I, II)
  I — (yo) conozco (I)
  I — (how to) (yo) sé (I)
  you — (tú) conoces (I)
  you — (how to) (tú) sabes (I)
knowledge los conocimientos (5-1)

L

laboratory el laboratorio (I)
lack la falta (9-2)
ladder la escalera (II)
lake el lago (I)
lamp la lámpara (I)
language el idioma (II)
land la tierra (8-2)
landscape el paisaje (1-1)
language la lengua (8-2)
laptop computer la computadora portátil (I)
large grande (I)
last último, -a (II)
last:
  — night anoche (I)
  — week la semana pasada (I)
  — year el año pasado (I)
to **last** durar (I)
late tarde (I)
to **arrive —** llegar tarde (II)
later:
  See you — ¡Hasta luego!; ¡Nos vemos! (I)
to **laugh** reírse (e → í) (II)
laundry:
  to do the — lavar la ropa (I)
law *(study of)* el derecho (II)
law la ley (II, 5-2)
lawyer el abogado, la abogada (II, 6-1)
lazy perezoso, -a (I)
leading man el galán (II)
league la liga (II)
to **learn** aprender (a) (I)
leather el cuero (II)
to **leave** salir (I), dejar (II)
  don't — no dejes (II)
  to — marks / traces dejar huellas (8-1)
  Leave me alone. Déjame en paz. (II)

left:

   to the — (of) a la izquierda (de) (I)

leg la pierna (I)

legend la leyenda (7-2)

lemonade la limonada (I)

length el largo (7-1)

less:

   — ... than menos ... que (I)

   — than menos de (I)

to let dejar (II)

   don't — no dejes (II)

Let's go! ¡Vamos! (I)

Let's see ... A ver ... (I)

letter la carta (I, II)

   to mail a — echar una carta (II)

lettuce la lechuga (I)

level el nivel (3-1)

liberty la libertad (10-1)

library la biblioteca (I)

to lie mentir (e → ie) (II)

life la vida (II)

lifeguard el / la salvavida (5-1)

to lift weights levantar pesas (I)

to light encender

light *(color)* claro, -a (II)

light la luz, *pl.* las luces (I)

to light encender (e → ie) (II)

lightning el relámpago (1-1)

like como (I)

to like:

   Did you — it? ¿Te gustó? (I)

   Do you — to ...? ¿Te gusta ... ? (I)

   He / She doesn't — ... No le gusta ... (I)

   He / She —s ... Le gusta ... (I); A él / ella le gusta(n) ... (I)

   I don't — to ... (A mí) no me gusta ... (I)

   I don't — to ... at all. (A mí) no me gusta nada ... (I)

   I — ... Me gusta ... (I)

   I — to ... (A mí) me gusta ... (I)

   I — to ... a lot (A mí) me gusta mucho ... (I)

   — to ... better (A mí) me gusta más ... (I)

   I —d it. Me gustó. (I)

   I would — Me gustaría (I); quisiera (I)

   What do you — to do? ¿Qué te gusta hacer? (I)

   What do you — to do better / prefer to do? ¿Qué te gusta hacer más? (I)

   What would you — ? ¿Qué desean (Uds.)? (I)

   Would you —? ¿Te gustaría? (I)

   You — ... Te gusta ... (I)

likely probable (7-1)

likewise igualmente (I)

to limit limitar (9-1)

lips los labios (II)

to listen to music escuchar música (I)

little:

   a — un poco (de) (I)

to live vivir (I)

living vivo, -a (II)

living room la sala (I)

locker el armario (I, II, 10-1)

long largo, -a (I)

to look:

   to — (at) mirar (I)

   to — for buscar (I)

   to — like parecerse a (2-2)

loose flojo, -a (II)

to lose perder (e → ie) (II)

   — one's balance perder el equilibrio (1-1)

lot:

   a — mucho, -a (I)

to love encantar (I)

   He / She —s ... A él / ella le encanta(n) ... (I)

   I / You — ... Me / Te encanta(n)... (I)

love el amor (II)

loving cariñoso, -a (4-1)

low bajo, -a (II)

luggage el equipaje (II)

   to check — facturar el equipaje (II)

lunch el almuerzo (I)

   for — en el almuerzo (I)

lyrics la letra (2-2)

M

machine máquina (6-2)
madam (la) señora (Sra.) (I)
magazines:
 to read — leer revistas (I)
majority la mayoría (6-2)
mail:
 — carrier el cartero, la cartera (II)
 —box el buzón, *pl.* los buzones (II)
 to — a letter echar una carta (II)
main:
 — character el personaje principal (II)
 — dish el plato principal (I)
 as a — dish de plato principal (I)
to **maintain one's health** para mantener la salud (I)
to **make:**
 — *(command)* haz (I)
 to — a living ganarse la vida (II)
 to — an effort hacer un esfuerzo (1-2)
 to — decisions tomar decisiones (6-1)
 to — the bed hacer la cama (I)
 to — noise hacer ruido (II)
 to — peace with hacer las paces (4-2)
 You are making me nervous. Me estás poniendo nervioso, -a. (II)
make-up el maquillaje (II)
mall el centro comercial (I)
man el hombre (I)
 business— el hombre de negocios (II)
 elderly — el anciano (I)
manager el / la gerente (II, 5-1)

manner la manera (II)
manners los modales (II)
many muchos, -as (I)
 How —? ¿Cuántos, -as? (I)
March marzo (I)
march la marcha (5-2)
mark *(in school)* la nota (II)
 to get a good — sacar una buena nota (II)
market el mercado (II)
marketing el mercadeo (6-2)
married casado, -a (6-1)
marvel la maravilla (8-1)
match el partido (I); el fósforo (II)
materials los materiales (II)
mathematics class la clase de matemáticas (I)
matter el asunto (10-1)
mature maduro, -a (6-1)
May mayo (I)
maybe quizás (I)
mayonnaise la mayonesa (II)
me me *dir. obj. pron., ind. obj. pron.* (I)
 for — para mí (I), me (I)
 it matters / they matter to — me importa(n) (II)
 it seems to — me parece que (II)
 — too a mí también (I)
 to — me (I)
 with — conmigo (I)
meal la comida (I)
to **mean:**
 It —s ... Quiere decir ... (I)
 What does ... —? ¿Qué quiere decir ... ? (I)
to **measure** medir (i) (7-1)
meat la carne (I)
mechanic el mecánico, la mecánica (II)
medal la medalla (1-2)

media los medios de comunicación (6-2)
medicine la medicina (II)
medium mediano, -a (II)
meddlesome entrometido, -a (4-1)
to **meet** reunirse (u → ú) (II)
meeting la reunión, *pl.* las reuniones (II), el encuentro (8-2)
melody la melodía (2-2)
melon el melón, *pl.* los melones (II)
to **melt** derretir (9-2)
member el miembro (II)
 to be a — ser miembro (II)
to **memorize** aprender de memoria (II)
menu el menú (I)
merchandise la mercancía (8-2)
messenger el mensajero, la mensajera (5-1)
messy desordenado, -a (I)
microphone el micrófono (2-2)
microwave el microondas (II)
military *(adj.)* militar (II)
milk la leche (I)
million un millón (II)
 —s of millones de (II)
mine mío, -a, -os, -as (II)
mirror el espejo (I)
Miss (la) señorita (Srta.) (I)
missing:
 to be — faltar (I)
mission la misión (8-2)
missionary el misionario, la misionaria (8-2)
to **mistreat** maltratar (10-1)
mistreatment el maltrato (10-1)
to **mistrust** desconfiar (4-1)
misunderstanding el malentendido (4-2)
mix la mezcla (8-2)
to **mix** mezclar (II)

moment:

  a — un momento (I)

Monday lunes (I)

  on —s los lunes (I)

money el dinero (I)

money exchange la casa de cambio (II)

monkey el mono (I)

month el mes (I)

monument el monumento (I)

moon la Luna (II)

more:

  — ... than más ... que (I)

  — or less más o menos (I)

  — than más de (I)

morning:

  Good —. Buenos días. (I)

  in the — de la mañana (I)

mosque la mezquita (I)

mother la madre (mamá) (I)

mountain range sierra (1-1)

mountains las montañas (I)

mouse (computer) el ratón (I)

mouth la boca (I)

to move moverse (o → ue) (II), andar (1-1); *(house)* mudarse (6-1)

  movement el movimiento (2-1)

  movie la película (I)

  action — la película de acción (II)

  — theater el cine (I)

  to see a — ver una película (I)

to mow the lawn cortar el césped (I)

Mr. (el) señor (Sr.) (I)

Mrs. (la) señora (Sra.) (I)

much:

  so — tanto (I)

mural el mural (2-1)

muscle el músculo (II)

museum el museo (I)

music:

  to listen to — escuchar música (I)

  —al program el programa musical (I)

musician el músico, la música (II)

Muslim el musulmán, la musulmana (8-1)

must deber (I)

  one — hay que (I)

mustard la mostaza (II)

my mi (I); mis (I)

  — name is ... Me llamo ... (I)

mysterious misterioso, -a (7-1)

myth el mito (7-2)

mystery la película policíaca (I); el misterio (7-1)

N

name:

  My — is ... Me llamo ... (I)

  What is your —? ¿Cómo te llamas? (I)

  What's his / her —? ¿Cómo se llama? (I)

nails las uñas (II)

napkin la servilleta (I)

narrow estrecho, -a (II)

native el / la indígena (8-2)

naughty travieso, -a (II)

national park el parque nacional (I)

natural preserve la reserva natural (9-2)

natural resource el recurso natural (9-1)

nature la naturaleza (II, 1-1)

near cerca (de) (I)

neat ordenado, -a (I)

necessary:

  It's —. Es necesario. (I)

neck el cuello (II)

necklace el collar (I)

to need

  I — necesito (I)

  I — ... Me falta(n) ... (I)

  you — necesitas (I)

neighbor el vecino, la vecina (II)

neighborhood el barrio (I)

neither ... nor ni ... ni (I)

nervous nervioso, -a (II)

never nunca (I)

new nuevo, -a (I)

news program el programa de noticias (I)

newscast el noticiero (II)

newspaper el periódico (I)

newsstand el quiosco (II)

next siguiente (II), próximo (6-1)

  — to al lado de (I)

nice simpático, -a (I), amable (4-1)

night:
  at — de la noche (I)
  last — anoche (I)

night table la mesita (I)

nine nueve (I)

nine hundred novecientos, -as (I)

nineteen diecinueve (I)

ninety noventa (I)

ninth noveno, -a (I)

No way! ¡Qué va! (4-2)

nobody nadie (II)

noise el ruido (II)

none ningún, ninguno, -a (II)

nose la nariz, *pl.* las narices (I)

not:
  — yet no...todavía (II)
  — ... or ni ... ni (I)

notebook el cuaderno (I)

nothing nada (I)

November noviembre (I)

now ahora (I)

nurse el enfermero, la enfermera (II)

nutrition la alimentación (3-1)

nutritious nutritivo, -a (3-1)

O _____

obedient obediente (II)

to **obey** obedecer to (II); hacer caso (4-2)

observatory el observatorio (7-1)

to **observe** observar (II)

to **obtain** conseguir (e → i) (II), obtener (1-2)

to **occupy** ocupar (8-1)

to **occur** ocurrir (II), suceder (1-1)

o'clock:
  at eight — a las ocho (I)
  at one — a la una (I)

October octubre (I)

odor el olor (II)

of de (I)
  — course por supuesto (I)
  What is it made —? ¿De qué está hecho, -a? (II)

to **offend** ofender (II)

to **offer** ofrecer (II)

office (home) el despacho (I)

office la oficina (II)

often a menudo (I)

Oh! What a shame / pity! ¡Ay! ¡Qué pena! (I)

oil el petróleo (9-1)
  — spill el derrame de petróleo (9-2)

okay regular (I)

old viejo, -a (I); antiguo, -a (II)
  He / She is / They are ... years —. Tiene(n) ... años. (I)
  How — is / are ... ? ¿Cuántos años tiene(n) ... ? (I)
  —er mayor, *pl.* mayores (I)

on en (I)
  — Mondays, on Tuesdays ... los lunes, los martes ... (I)
  — the grill a parrilla (II)
  — time a tiempo (II)
  — top of encima de (I)
  — weekends los fines de semana (I)

once there una vez allí (1-1)

one uno (un), -a (I)
  at — (o'clock) a la una (I)
  — hundred cien (I)
  — must hay que (I)

onion la cebolla (I)

online en la Red (I)
  to be — estar en línea (I)

only sólo (I), único, -a (8-1)

to **open** abrir (I)

open abierto, -a (II)

opens se abre (II)

opinion:
  in my — para mí (I)

opportunity la oportunidad (II)

or o (I)

orange anaranjado, -a (I)
  — juice el jugo de naranja (I)

orchestra la orquesta (II)

to **order** pedir (e → i) (I)

to **organize** organizar (5-2)

origin el origen (7-2)

other otro, -a (I)

others los / las demás (I)

our nuestro(s), -a(s) (I)

outcome el resultado (8-2)

outdoors al aire libre (II)

outer space el espacio (II)

outrageous exagerado, -a (II)

outside fuera (de) (II)

oval el óvalo (7-1)

oven el horno (II)

to **overwork** explotar (9-2)

own propio, -a (I)

owner el dueño, la dueña (II, 5-1)

ozone layer la capa de ozono (9-2)

P

to **pack the suitcase** hacer la maleta (II)

pain el dolor (II)

to **paint (one's nails)** pintarse (las uñas) (II)

painter el pintor, la pintora (II)

painting el cuadro (I), la pintura (2-1)

palace el palacio (II)

palette la paleta (2-1)

pants los pantalones (I)

paper:
  sheet of — la hoja de papel (I)

parade el desfile (II)

paramedic el paramédico, la paramédica (II)

parents los padres (I)

park el parque (I)
  amusement — el parque de diversiones (I)
  national — el parque nacional (I)

part time a tiempo parcial (5-1)

participant el / la participante (1-2)

to **participate (in)** participar (en) (II)

party la fiesta (I)
  surprise — la fiesta de sorpresa (II)

to **pass** pasar (II)

passenger el pasajero, la pasajera (II)

passport el pasaporte (II)

pastel *(colors)* pastel *adj.* (II)

pastime el pasatiempo (II)

pastries los pasteles (I)

patience la paciencia (II)

patient paciente (I)
  to be — tener paciencia (II)

to **pay (for)** pagar (por) (I)

to **pay attention** prestar atención (II)
  — to hacer caso a (4-2)

peace la paz (II, 10-1)

peaceful pacífico, -a (10-2)

peach el durazno (II)

peas los guisantes (I)

pedestrian el peatón, *pl.* los peatones (II)

to **peel** pelar (II)

pen el bolígrafo (I)

pencil el lápiz, *pl.* los lápices (I)
  — sharpener el sacapuntas, *pl.* los sacapuntas (I)

people la gente (I); el pueblo (7-1)
  elderly — los ancianos (I)

pepper la pimienta (I)

to **perform** realizar (2-2); actuar (2-2); cumplir con (5-1)

perfume el perfume (I)

to **permit, to allow** permitir (II)

person la persona (I)

personal watercraft la moto acuática (II)

pesticide el pesticida (9-1)

pharmacy la farmacia (II)

phenomenal fenomenal (II)

phenomenon el fenómeno (7-1)

phone:
  to talk on the — hablar por teléfono (I)

photo la foto (I)
  to take —s sacar fotos (I)

photographer el fotógrafo, la fotógrafa (II)

photography la fotografía (II)

physical education class la clase de educación física (I)

piano lesson (class) la lección de piano (I)

picnic el picnic (II)

piece el pedazo (II)

pills las pastillas (II)

pilot el / la piloto (II)

piñata la piñata (I)

pineapple la piña (II)

pink rosado, -a (I)

pizza la pizza (I)

place el lugar (I)

to **place** poner (I), colocar (9-1)

to **plan** pensar (e → ie) (I)

plant la planta (II)

to **plant** sembrar (5-2)

plastic el plástico (I)

plate el plato (I)

play la obra de teatro (I)

to **play** jugar (a) (u → ue) *(games, sports)* (I); tocar *(an instrument)* (I)
  to — baseball jugar al béisbol (I)
  to — basketball jugar al básquetbol (I)
  to — football jugar al fútbol americano (I)
  to — golf jugar al golf (I)
  to — soccer jugar al fútbol (I)
  to — sports practicar deportes (I)
  to — tennis jugar al tenis (I)
  to — the guitar tocar la guitarra (I)
  to — the role of hacer el papel de (II)
  to — video games jugar videojuegos (I)
  to — volleyball jugar al vóleibol (I)

player el jugador, la jugadora (II)

playground el patio de recreo (II)

plaza la plaza (II)

pleasant agradable (5-1)

to **please very much** encantar (I)

pleased to meet you mucho gusto (I)

plot el argumento (II)

poem el poema (2-2)

poet el / la poeta (2-2)

point of view el punto de vista (10-2)

poison el veneno (9-1)

police officer el / la policía (II)

to **polish (one's nails)** pintarse (las uñas) (II)

polite cortés, *pl.* corteses (II)

politician el político, la política (II)

to **pollute** contaminar (6-2)

polluted contaminado, -a (II, 9-1)

pollution la contaminación (II, 9-1)

pool la piscina (I)

poor pobre (I)

— **thing** pobrecito, -a (II)

population la población (8-1)

pork el cerdo (II)

— **chop** la chuleta de cerdo (II)

portrait el retrato (2-1)

position el puesto (5-1)

possession la posesión, *pl.* las posesiones (I)

post office el correo (II)

poster el cartel (I)

pot la olla (II)

potatoes las papas (I)

pottery la cerámica (2-1)

poverty la pobreza (10-1)

power el poder (8-2)

powerful poderoso, -a (8-2)

practical práctico, -a (I)

practice la práctica (II)

to **predict** predecir (6-2)

to **prefer** preferir (e → ie) (I)

I — (yo) prefiero (I)

I — to ... (a mí) me gusta más ... (I)

you — (tú) prefieres (I)

to **prepare** preparar (I)

to **prescribe** recetar (II)

prescription la receta (II)

present el regalo (I)

presentation la presentación, *pl.* las presentaciones (I)

presenter el presentador, la presentadora (II)

to **preserve** conservar (9-1)

press la prensa (10-2)

pretty bonito, -a (I)

price el precio (I)

principal *(of a school)* el director, la directora (II)

primary school la escuela primaria (I)

prize el premio (II)

problem el problema (I)

to **produce** producir (9-2)

product el producto (6-2)

profession la profesión, *pl.* las profesiones (II)

program el programa (I)

programmer el programador, la programadora (6-1)

project el proyecto (II)

to **prolong** prolongar (6-2)

to **promote** promover (ue) (9-1)

proposal la propuesta (10-2)

to **propose** proponer (10-2)

proof la evidencia (7-1)

protein la proteína (3-1)

Protestant church el templo (I)

to **protect** proteger (II, 5-2)

protection la protección (9-1)

provided that con tal que (9-2)

punctual puntual (II, 5-1)

to **punish** castigar (9-1)

punishment el castigo (10-2)

pure puro, -a (II)

purple morado, -a (I)

purpose el fin, *pl.* los fines (10-2)

purse el bolso (I)

to **pursue a career** seguir una carrera (II, 6-1)

to **put** poner (I), colocar (9-1)

— *(command)* pon (I)

I — (yo) pongo (I)

to — on *(clothing, make-up, etc.)* ponerse (II)

to — out *(fire)* apagar (II)

you — (tú) pones (I)

pyramid la pirámide

Q

quality cualidad (4-1)

quarter past y cuarto (I)

queen la reina (II)

question la pregunta (II)

to ask a — hacer una pregunta (II)

quickly rápidamente (I)

R

rabbit el conejo (7-2)

race la carrera (II, 1-2), la raza (8-2)

rain la lluvia (II)

to rain llover (o → ue) (II)

  It's —ing. Llueve. (I)

rather bastante (I)

to reach alcanzar (1-2), llegar a (10-2)

  — an agreement ponerse de acuerdo (4-2)

to react reaccionar (4-2)

to read magazines leer revistas (I)

ready listo, -a (II)

realistic realista (I)

reality program el programa de la vida real (I)

to realize darse cuenta de (1-2)

Really? ¿Verdad? (I); ¿De veras? (I)

really en realidad (II)

reason la razón (10-1)

to rebel rebelarse (8-2)

receptionist el recepcionista, la recepcionista (5-1)

to receive recibir (I)

recently recientemente (II)

reception desk la recepción (II)

recipe la receta (II)

to recommend recomendar (e → ie) (II)

to reconquer reconquistar (8-1)

to record grabar (II)

recreation center el centro recreativo (5-2)

rectangle el rectángulo (7-1)

to recycle reciclar (I)

recycling center el centro de reciclaje (I)

red rojo, -a (I)

  — -haired pelirrojo, -a (I)

to reduce reducir (zc) (II), (6-2)

reference la referencia (5-1)

refrigerator el refrigerador (II)

refuge el refugio (1-1)

to register inscribirse (1-2)

registration la inscripción (1-2)

rehabilitation center el centro de rehabilitación (5-2)

rehearsal el ensayo (II)

to rehearse ensayar (II)

relatives los parientes (II)

to relax descansar (I), relajar(se) (3-2)

to remember recordar (o → ue) (II)

to rent alquilar (II)

to repair reparar (5-1)

to repeat repetir (e → i) (II)

to replace reemplazar (6-2)

report el informe (I)

reporter el reportero, la reportera (II)

to represent representar (2-1)

representative el / la representante (1-2)

to request solicitar (5-1)

requirement el requisito (5-1)

rescue el rescate (9-2)

to rescue rescatar (II)

reservation la reservación, pl. las reservaciones (II)

reserved reservado, -a (I)

to resolve resolver (o → ue) (4-2)

respect el respeto (10-1)

to respect respetar (II)

responsibility la responsabilidad (5-2)

responsible responsable (5-1)

to rest descansar (I)

restaurant el restaurante (I)

result el resultado (8-2)

to result resultar (II)

to return regresar (I, II)

  to — a book devolver (o → ue) (un libro) (II)

review la reseña (2-2)

to revolt rebelarse (8-2)

rhythm el ritmo, el compás (2-2)

rice el arroz (I)

rich rico, -a (I)

to ride:

  to — a bicycle montar en bicicleta (I)

  to — horseback montar a caballo (I)

right:

  to the — (of) a la derecha (de) (I)

  — away en seguida (II)

rights los derechos (5-2)

ring el anillo (I)

river el río (I)

road la calle (I)

to rob robar (II)

rock la piedra (II), la roca (1-1)

role el papel (II)

  to play the — of hacer el papel de (II)

Roman romano, -a (8-1)

romantic movie la película romántica (I)

room el cuarto (I); la habitación, pl. las habitaciones (II)

  double occupancy — la habitación doble (II)

  single occupancy — la habitación individual (II)

  to straighten up the — arreglar el cuarto (I)

rope la cuerda (II)

round redondo, -a (7-1)

round-trip ida y vuelta (II)

ruins las ruinas (II, 7-1)

rug la alfombra (I)

rule la regla (II)

to rule gobernar (8-1)

to run correr (I)

  to — out agotar(se) (9-1)

s _____

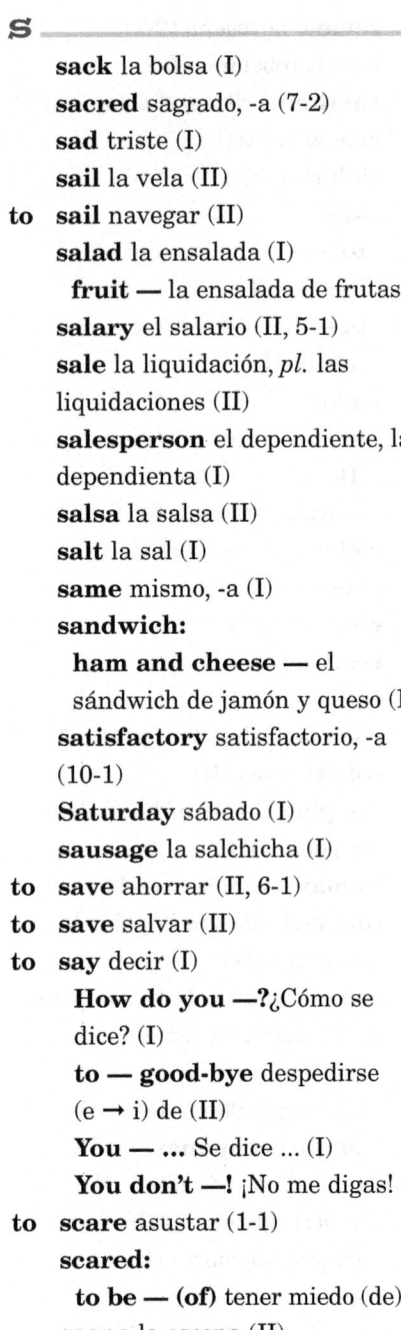

sack la bolsa (I)

sacred sagrado, -a (7-2)

sad triste (I)

sail la vela (II)

to sail navegar (II)

salad la ensalada (I)

  fruit — la ensalada de frutas (I)

salary el salario (II, 5-1)

sale la liquidación, *pl.* las liquidaciones (II)

salesperson el dependiente, la dependienta (I)

salsa la salsa (II)

salt la sal (I)

same mismo, -a (I)

sandwich:

  ham and cheese — el sándwich de jamón y queso (I)

satisfactory satisfactorio, -a (10-1)

Saturday sábado (I)

sausage la salchicha (I)

to save ahorrar (II, 6-1)

to save salvar (II)

to say decir (I)

  How do you —?¿Cómo se dice? (I)

  to — good-bye despedirse (e → i) de (II)

  You — ... Se dice ... (I)

  You don't —! ¡No me digas! (I)

to scare asustar (1-1)

scared:

  to be — (of) tener miedo (de) (I)

scene la escena (II)

schedule el horario (I)

science:

  — class la clase de ciencias naturales (I)

  — fiction movie la película de ciencia ficción (I)

scientist el científico, la científica (II, 6-1)

scissors las tijeras (II)

to score (a goal) meter un gol (II)

score el tanteo (II)

to scream gritar (II)

screen:

  computer — la pantalla (I)

to scuba dive bucear (I)

sculpture escultura (2-1)

sculptor el escultor, la escultora (2-1)

secret el secreto (4-1)

sea el mar (I)

seal la foca (9-2)

to search (for) buscar (I)

search la búsqueda (II)

  to do a — hacer una búsqueda (II)

  to — *(luggage)* registrar (II)

season la estación, *pl.* las estaciones (I)

seat el asiento (II)

second segundo, -a (I)

  — floor el primer piso (I)

secretary el secretario, la secretaria (II)

security checkpoint la inspección, *pl.* las inspecciones de seguridad (II)

to see ver (I)

  Let's — A ver ... (I)

  — you later! ¡Nos vemos!; Hasta luego. (I)

  — you tomorrow. Hasta mañana. (I)

  to — a movie ver una película (I)

to seem like parecerse a (2-2)

self-confidence confianza en sí mismo, -a (3-2)

self-portrait el autorretrato (2-1)

selfish egoísta (4-1)

to sell vender (I)

to send enviar (I, II)

to separate separar (I)

September septiembre (I

serious serio, -a (I), grave (9-1)

to serve servir (e → i) (I)

service el servicio (6-2)

  — station la estación de servicio (II)

to set (sun) ponerse (el sol) (7-2)

  to set the table poner la mesa (I)

seven siete (I)

seven hundred setecientos, -as (I)

seventeen diecisiete (I)

seventh séptimo, -a (I)

seventy setenta (I)

shadow la sombra (7-2)

shake hands dar(se) la mano (II)

shame:

  What a —! ¡Qué lástima! (II)

shampoo el champú (II)

to share compartir (I)

to shave afeitarse (II)

she ella (I)

sheet of paper la hoja de papel (I)

shelf el estante (I)

shellfish los mariscos (II)

shelter el refugio (1-1)

to shine brillar (7-2)

ship el barco (I)

shirt la camisa (I)

  T— la camiseta (I)

shoe store la zapatería (I)

shoes los zapatos (I)

shoe size el número (II)

short bajo, -a *(stature);* corto, -a *(length)* (I)

shortage la escasez (9-1)

shorts los pantalones cortos (I)

should deber (I)

shoulder el hombro (II)

show el programa (I); el espectáculo (2-2)

to **show +** *movie or TV program* dar (I); mostrar (ue) (2-1)

shower la ducha (II)

shrimp el camarón, *pl.* los camarones (II)

shy reservado, -a (I)

sick enfermo, -a (I)

sierra la sierra (1-1)

sign el letrero (II); la señal (II)

  stop — la señal de parada (II)

silk seda (II)

silly tonto, -a (I)

silver la plata (II)

similarity la semejanza (8-2)

since desde (II)

sincere sincero, -a (4-1)

to **sing** cantar (I)

singer el / la cantante (II)

single soltero, -a (6-1)

sink el fregadero (II)

sir (el) señor (Sr.) (I)

sister la hermana (I)

site:

  Web **—** el sitio Web (I)

six seis (I)

six hundred seiscientos, -as (I)

sixteen dieciséis (I)

sixth sexto, -a (I)

sixty sesenta (I)

size la talla (II)

to **skate** patinar (I)

to **skateboard** montar en monopatín (I)

skates los patines (II)

to **ski** esquiar (I)

skill la habilidad (5-1)

skin la piel (9-2)

to **skip (a meal)** saltar (una comida) (3-1)

skirt la falda (I)

sky el cielo (II)

to **sleep** dormir (I)

sleeping bag el saco de dormir (1-1)

sleepy:

  to be — tener sueño (I)

slice el pedazo (II)

slide la diapositiva (I)

slowly lentamente (II); despacio (II)

small pequeño, -a (I)

to **smile** sonreír (e → í) (II)

smoke el humo (II)

snack la merienda (3-1)

to **sneeze** estornudar (3-1)

to **snorkel** bucear (I)

to **snow:** nevar (e → ie) (II)

  It's —ing. Nieva. (I)

so tan (II), de modo que (10-2)

  — + *adj.* tan + *adj.* (II)

  — much tanto (I)

  so-so regular (I)

  — that de modo que (10-2)

soap el jabón (II)

soap opera la telenovela (I)

soccer:

  to play — jugar al fútbol (I)

sociable sociable (I)

social service el servicio social (5-2)

social studies class la clase de ciencias sociales (I)

society la sociedad (5-2)

socks los calcetines (I)

soft drink el refresco (I)

software el software (I)

solar solar (II)

soldier el / la soldado (8-2)

solid-colored de sólo un color (II)

to **solve** resolver (o → ue) (II)

some unos, -as (I); algún, alguno, -a (II)

  some day algún día (II)

someone alguien (II)

something algo (I)

sometimes a veces (I)

son el hijo (I)

  —s; —(s) and daughter(s) los hijos (I)

song la canción, *pl.* las canciones (I,II)

soon pronto (II)

sorry:

  I'm —. Lo siento. (I)

sound (stereo) system el equipo de sonido (I)

to **sound like** sonar (ue) a (2-2)

soup:

  vegetable — la sopa de verduras (I)

soup kitchen el comedor de beneficencia (5-2)

source la fuente (II)

  — of inspiration la fuente de inspiración (2-1)

souvenirs los recuerdos (I)

  to buy — comprar recuerdos (I)

spaceship la nave espacial (7-1)

spaghetti los espaguetis (I)

Spanish class la clase de español (I)

special especial (II)

  special effects los efectos especiales (II)

  special event el evento especial (II)

  species la especie (9-2)

speech el discurso (II)

to **spell:**

  How is ... spelled? ¿Cómo se escribe ... ? (I)

  It's spelled ... Se escribe ... (I)

to **spend** gastar (II)

to **— time with friends** pasar tiempo con amigos (I)

spicy picante (II)

to **spill** tirar (II)

don't — no tires (II)

spoiled consentido, -a (II)

spoon la cuchara (I)

sports:

— equipment el equipo deportivo (II)

— -minded deportista (I)

— program el programa deportivo (I)

to play — practicar deportes (I)

spring la primavera (I)

stadium el estadio (I)

stage el escenario (2-2)

stairs, stairway la escalera (I)

stamp el sello (II)

to **stand:**

— out destacarse (2-2)

— up pararse (2-2)

stapler la grapadora (II)

star:

movie — la estrella (del cine) (II)

to **start** empezar (e → ie) (I); comenzar (e → ie) (II)

state el estado (10-1)

statue la estatua (II)

to **stay:** quedarse (II)

I — at home. Me quedo en casa. (I)

steak la carne de res (II), el bistec (I)

to **steal** robar (II)

step el paso (2-2)

stepbrother el hermanastro (I)

stepfather el padrastro (I)

stepmother la madrastra (I)

stepsister la hermanastra (I)

stereo system el equipo de sonido (I)

still todavía (II)

still life la naturaleza muerta (2-1)

to **stitch** (*surgically*) dar puntadas (II)

stitches las puntadas (II)

stomach el estómago (I)

to **stop** parar (II), detener (9-2)

— doing something dejar de (1-1)

— over hacer escala (II)

stoplight el semáforo (II)

stopover la escala (II)

store la tienda (I)

book— la librería (I)

clothing — la tienda de ropa (I)

department — el almacén, *pl.* los almacenes (I)

discount — la tienda de descuentos (I)

household-appliance — la tienda de electrodomésticos (I)

jewelry — la joyería (I)

shoe — la zapatería (I)

stories:

to write — escribir cuentos (I)

storm la tormenta (II)

story el piso (I)

stove la estufa (II)

straight derecho (II)

to **straighten up the room** arreglar el cuarto (I)

strange extraño, -a (7-1)

strategy la estrategia (6-2)

strawberries las fresas (I)

street la calle (I)

strength la fuerza (3-2)

stress el estrés (3-2)

stressed out estresado, -a (3-2)

to **stretch** estirar (3-2)

to **stroll** dar un paseo (1-1)

strong fuerte (3-1)

structure la estructura (7-1)

student el / la estudiante (I)

studious estudioso, -a (I)

to **study** estudiar (I)

stupendous estupendo, -a (II)

stupid tonto, -a (I)

style el estilo (II)

subject el tema (2-1)

subway el metro (II)

success el éxito (II)

to be —ful tener éxito (II)

suddenly de repente (II)

to **suffer** sufrir (10-1)

sugar el azúcar (I)

to **suggest** sugerir (e → ie) (II), proponer (10-2)

suit el traje (I)

suitcase la maleta (II)

summer el verano (I)

to **sunbathe** tomar el sol (I)

Sunday domingo (I)

sunglasses los anteojos de sol (I)

sunny:

It's —. Hace sol. (I)

supermarket el supermercado (II)

supplies los materiales (II)

support el apoyo (10-1)

to **support (each other)** apoyarse (4-1)

sure seguro, -a (II)

to **surf the Web** navegar en la Red (I)

surprise la sorpresa (II)

suspicious sospechoso, -a (10-2)

sweater el suéter (I)

sweatshirt la sudadera (I)

sweet dulce (II)

to **swim** nadar (I)

swimming la natación (II)

swimsuit el traje de baño (I)

symbol el símbolo (7-2)

synagogue la sinagoga (I)

synthetic fabric la tela sintética (II)

syrup el jarabe (3-1)

T

T-shirt la camiseta (I)

table la mesa (I)

  to set the — poner la mesa (I)

to take llevar (I), tomar (3-1)

  to — a bath bañarse (II)

  to — a course tomar un curso (I)

  to — a shower ducharse (II)

  to — a tour hacer una gira (II)

  to — a trip hacer un viaje (II)

  to — a walk dar una caminata (II), dar un paseo (1-1)

  to — away quitar (II)

  to — care of cuidar a (II)

  to — into account tener en cuenta (6-2)

  to — lessons tomar lecciones (II)

  to — out the trash sacar la basura (I)

  to — photos sacar fotos (I)

  to — place tener lugar (1-2)

  to — shelter refugiarse (1-1)

talented talentoso, -a (I)

to talk hablar (I)

  to — on the phone hablar por teléfono (I)

tall alto, -a (I)

tank el tanque (II)

taste el sabor (II)

to taste probar (o → ue) (II)

tasty sabroso, -a (I); rico, -a (I)

tea el té (I)

  iced — el té helado (I)

to teach enseñar (I)

teacher el profesor, la profesora (I)

teaching la enseñanza (10-1)

team el equipo (II)

to tear romperse (II)

technical school la escuela

técnica (II)

technician el técnico, la técnica (II)

technological tecnológico, -a (6-2)

technology / computers la tecnología (I)

technology / computer class la clase de tecnología (I)

teddy bear el oso de peluche (II)

teeth los dientes (II)

  to brush one's — cepillarse los dientes (II)

television:

  to watch — ver la tele (I)

television set el televisor (I)

to tell decir (I)

  — me dime (I)

  to — jokes contar (chistes) (o → ue) (II)

  to — the truth decir la verdad (II)

temple el templo (I)

ten diez (I)

tennis:

  to play — jugar al tenis (I)

tent la tienda de acampar (1-1)

tennis racket la raqueta de tenis (II)

tenth décimo, -a (I)

thank you gracias (I)

that que (I); ese, esa (I)

  —'s why por eso (I)

that one (over there) aquel, aquella (II)

the el, la, los, las (I)

  — best el / la mejor, los / las mejores (I)

  — worst el / la peor, los / las peores (I)

theater el teatro (I)

  movie — el cine (I)

their su, sus (I)

them las, los *dir. obj. pron.* (I), les *ind. obj. pron.* (I)

then entonces (I)

then luego (II)

theory la teoría (7-2)

there allí (I)

  — is / are hay (I); haya *(subjunctive)* (II)

  — was hubo (II)

  — was / — were había (II)

  — will be habrá (II)

therefore por eso (I), así que (6-1), por lo tanto (6-1)

these estos, estas (I)

they ellos, ellas (I)

they died se murieron (II)

thief el ladrón, la ladrona, *pl.* los ladrones (II)

thing la cosa (I)

to think pensar (e → ie) (I), opinar (10-2)

  I don't — so. Creo que no. (I)

  I — ... Creo que ... (I)

  I — so. Creo que sí. (I)

  to — of oneself pensar en sí mismo, -a (4-2)

  What do you — (about it)? ¿Qué te parece? (I)

third tercer (tercero), -a (I)

third floor el segundo piso (I)

thirsty:

  I'm —. Tengo sed. (I)

thirteen trece (I)

thirty treinta (I); y media *(in telling time)* (I)

thirty-one treinta y uno (I)

this este, esta (I)

  — afternoon esta tarde (I)

  — evening esta noche (I)

  — way así (1-1)

  — weekend este fin de semana (I)

What is — ? ¿Qué es esto? (I)

those esos, esas (I)

those (over there) aquellos, aquellas (II)

thought el pensamiento (10-1)

thousand:

  a — mil (I)

threat la amenaza (9-2)

to threaten amenazar (9-1)

three tres (I)

three hundred trescientos, -as (I)

three-ring binder la carpeta de argollas (I)

through por (II), a través de (2-1)

to throw arrojar(se) (7-2)

  to — away tirar (II), echar (9-1)

thunder el trueno (1-1)

Thursday jueves (I)

ticket el boleto (I), la entrada (2-2)

ticket la multa (II)

tie la corbata (I); el empate (II)

tight apretado, -a (II)

tile el azulejo (8-1)

time la época (8-1)

time:

  At what —? ¿A qué hora? (I)

  free — el tiempo libre (I)

  on — a tiempo (II)

  to spend — with friends pasar tiempo con amigos (I)

  What — is it? ¿Qué hora es? (I)

timid tímido, -a (II)

tip la propina (II)

tired cansado, -a (I)

to a *prep.* (I)

  in order — para + *inf.* (I)

  — the a la, al (I)

  — the left (of) a la izquierda (de) (I)

  — the right (of) a la derecha (de) (I)

toast el pan tostado (I)

today hoy (I)

together juntos, -as (4-1)

tolerance la tolerancia (10-1)

to tolerate aguantar (3-2)

tomatoes los tomates (I)

tomorrow mañana (I)

  See you —. Hasta mañana. (I)

ton la tonelada (7-1)

too también (I); demasiado (I)

  I do (like to) — a mí también (I)

  me — a mí también (I)

toothbrush el cepillo de dientes (II)

toothpaste la pasta dental (II)

top:

  on — of encima de (I)

touching emocionante (I)

tourist el / la turista (II)

toward hacia (1-1)

towel la toalla (II)

tower la torre (8-1)

town el pueblo (II)

toy el juguete (I)

to trace trazar (7-1)

traffic el tráfico (II)

trail el sendero (II)

train el tren (I)

  electric — el tren eléctrico (II)

to train entrenarse (1-2)

training el entrenamiento (1-2)

trainer el entrenador, la entrenadora (II)

to translate traducir (zc) (6-1)

translator el traductor, la traductora (6-1)

transparent tape la cinta adhesiva (II)

to trap atrapar (9-2)

to travel viajar (I)

  travel agency la agencia de viajes (II)

  travel agent el / la agente de viajes (II)

to treat tratar (10-1)

tree el árbol (I)

tremendous tremendo, -a (I)

trial el juicio (10-2)

triangle el triángulo (7-1)

tricycle el triciclo (II)

trip el viaje (I)

to trip (over) tropezar (e → ie) (con) (II)

trophy el trofeo (1-2)

tropical rain forest la selva tropical (II, 9-2)

truck el camión, *pl.* los camiones (II)

true:

  it's true es cierto (II)

trumpet la trompeta (2-2)

trust la confianza (4-1)

to trust confiar (i → í) (4-1)

truth la verdad (II)

to try on probarse (o → ue) (II)

to try to tratar de (II)

Tuesday martes (I)

  on —s los martes (I)

turkey el pavo (II)

to turn doblar (II)

  to — in entregar (II)

  to — in homework on time entregar la tarea a tiempo (II)

  to — into convertirse en (7-2)

  to — off apagar (II)

  to — on encender (e → ie) (II)

  to — out resultar (II)

turtle la tortuga (II)

TV channel el canal (I)

twelve doce (I)

twenty veinte (I)

twenty-one veintiuno (veintiún) (I)

to twist torcerse (o → ue) (II)

two dos (I)

two hundred doscientos, -as (I)

typical típico, -a (II)

U

Ugh! ¡Uf! (I)
ugly feo, -a (I)
uncle el tío (I)
uncles; uncle(s) and aunt(s) los tíos (I)
underneath debajo de (I)
to **understand** comprender (I); entender (e → ie) (II)
understanding comprensivo, -a (4-1)
unemployment el desempleo (10-2)
unfair injusto, -a (5-2)
unfortunately desafortunadamente (1-2)
unity la unidad (8-1)
universe el universo (7-2)
university la universidad (II)
unforgettable inolvidable (I)
unknown desconocido, -a (8-2)
unless a menos que (9-2)
unlikely improbable (7-1)
until hasta (II)
upon arriving al llegar (8-2)
us nos *dir. obj. pron.* (I)
   (to / for) — nos *ind. obj. pron.* (I)
to **usually do something** soler (ue) (5-1)
use el uso (6-2)
to **use:**
   to — a stationary bike hacer bicicleta (3-2)
   to — a treadmill hacer cinta (3-2)
   to — the computer usar la computadora (I)
   What's it —d for? ¿Para qué sirve? (I)
used usado, -a (I)
   it's — for sirve para (I)
useful:
   to be — servir (I)

V

vacation:
   to go on — ir de vacaciones (I)
to **vacuum** pasar la aspiradora (I)
vain vanidoso, -a (4-1)
valley el valle (II), (1-1)
value el valor (10-2)
variety la variedad (8-2)
various varios, -as (II)
vegetable soup la sopa de verduras (I)
vendor el vendedor, la vendedora (II)
very muy (I)
   — well muy bien (I)
veterinarian el veterinario, la veterinaria (II)
via satellite via satélite (6-2)
victim la víctima (II)
video el video (I)
video games:
   to play — jugar videojuegos (I)
to **videotape** hacer un video (I)
vinegar el vinagre (II)
to **violate** violar (10-2)
violence la violencia (II)
violent violento, -a (I)
virtual reality la realidad virtual (6-2)
to **visit** visitar (I)
   to — chat rooms visitar salones de chat (I)
vital fundamental (10-2)
vitamin la vitamina (3-1)
voice la voz, *pl.* las voces (II)
volleyball:
   to play — jugar al vóleibol (I)
volunteer el voluntario, la voluntaria (I)
   — work el trabajo voluntario (I)
to **vote** votar (10-1)

W

to **wait** esperar (II)
waiter, waitress el camarero, la camarera (I)
to **wake up** despertarse (e → ie) (II)
to **walk** caminar (I), andar (1-1)
   to take a — dar una caminata (II)
wall la pared (I)
wallet la cartera (I)
to **want** querer (e → ie) (I)
   I — (yo) quiero (I)
   you — (tú) quieres (I)
war la guerra (II, 8-2)
warm:
   to be — tener calor (I)
was fue (I)
to **wash** lavar (I)
   to — the car lavar el coche (I)
   to — the clothes lavar la ropa (I)
   to — the dishes lavar los platos (I)
   to — one's face lavarse la cara (II)
waste el desperdicio (9-1)
to **waste** desperdiciar (9-1)
wastepaper basket la papelera (I)
watch el reloj pulsera (I)
   to watch television ver la tele (I)
water el agua (I)
watermelon la sandía (II)
waterskiing el esquí acuático (II)
way la manera (II, 3-1), el modo (10-2)
we nosotros, -as (I)
weak débil (3-2)
wealth la riqueza (8-2)
to **wear** llevar (I)

weapon el arma, *pl.* las armas (8-2)

weather el clima (9-2)
  What's the — like? ¿Qué tiempo hace? (I)

Web:
  to surf the — navegar en la Red (I)
  — page la página Web (I)
  — site el sitio Web (I)

Wednesday miércoles (I)

wedding la boda (II)

week la semana (I)
  last — la semana pasada (I)

weekend:
  on —s los fines de semana (I)
  this — este fin de semana (I)

to weigh pesar (7-1)

weight el peso (3-1)

welcome bienvenido, -a (II)

well bien (I); pues … *(to indicate pause)* (I)
  very — muy bien (I)
  — -behaved bien educado, -a (II)

wet mojado, -a (II)

whale la ballena

What? ¿Cuál? (I)
  — a shame! ¡Qué lástima! (II)
  — are you like? ¿Cómo eres? (I)
  (At) — time? ¿A qué hora? (I)
  — color … ? ¿De qué color … ? (I)
  — day is today? ¿Qué día es hoy? (I)
  — did you do? ¿Qué hiciste? (I)
  — do you like to do better / prefer to do? ¿Qué te gusta hacer más? (I)
  — do you like to do? ¿Qué te gusta hacer? (I)
  — do you think (about it)?

¿Qué te parece? (I, II)
  — does … mean? ¿Qué quiere decir … ? (I)
  — else? ¿Qué más? (I)
  — happened to you? ¿Qué te pasó? (I, II)
  — is she / he like? ¿Cómo es? (I)
  — is the date? ¿Cuál es la fecha? (I)
  — is this? ¿Qué es esto? (I)
  — is your name? ¿Cómo te llamas? (I)
  — kind of … ? ¿Qué clase de… ? (I)
  — time is it? ¿Qué hora es? (I)
  — would you like? ¿Qué desean (Uds.)? (I)
  — 's happening? ¿Qué pasa? (I)
  — 's his / her name? ¿Cómo se llama? (I)
  — 's it (used) for? ¿Para qué sirve? (I)
  — 's the weather like? ¿Qué tiempo hace? (I)

what!:
  — a good / nice idea! ¡Qué buena idea! (I)
  — a shame / pity! ¡Qué pena! (I)

what lo que (II)

When? ¿Cuándo? (I)

Where? ¿Dónde? (I)
  — are you from? ¿De dónde eres? (I)
  (To) —? ¿Adónde? (I)

whether si (I)

Which? ¿Cuál? (I)

while mientras (que) (II)
  once in a — de vez en cuando (II)

white blanco, -a (I)

who que (I)

Who? ¿Quién? (I)

Why? ¿Por qué? (I)

wide ancho, -a (II)

width el ancho (7-1)

wife la esposa (I)

wild salvaje (9-2)

Will you bring me … ? ¿Me trae … ? (I)

window la ventana (I)

window *(airplane)* la ventanilla (II)

windsurf el surf de vela (II)

winter el invierno (I)

with con (I)
  — me conmigo (I)
  — my / your friends con mis / tus amigos (I)
  — respect to en cuanto a (10-1)
  — whom? ¿Con quién? (I)
  — you contigo (I)
  What do you serve it —? ¿Con qué se sirve? (II)

without sin (I)
  — a doubt sin duda (II)

witness el / la testigo (10-2)

woman la mujer (I)
  business— la mujer de negocios (II)
  elderly woman la anciana (I)

wonder la maravilla (8-1)

wonderful estupendo, -a (II), maravilloso, -a (8-1)

wood el bosque (1-1)

wool la lana (II)

word la palabra (II)

work el trabajo (I)
  — of art la obra de arte (2-1)
  volunteer — el trabajo voluntario (I)

to work trabajar (I)

workshop el taller (2-1)

world el mundo (II)

worldwide mundial (10-2)

to worry preocuparse (3-2)

worse than peor(es) que (I)

worst:

the — el / la peor, los / las peores (I)

Would you like? ¿Te gustaría? (I)

wrist la muñeca (II)

to write:

to — e-mail escribir por correo electrónico (I)

to — stories escribir cuentos (I)

writer el escritor, la escritora (II, 2-2)

writing la escritura (7-2)

X

X-ray la radiografía (II)

Y

yard el jardín (I)

year el año (I)

He / She is / They are ... —s old. Tiene(n) ... años. (I)

last — el año pasado (I)

yellow amarillo, -a (I)

yes sí (I)

yesterday ayer (I)

yoga el yoga (3-2)

yogurt el yogur (I)

you fam. sing. tú (I); formal sing. usted (Ud.) (I); fam. pl. vosotros, -as (I); formal and informal pl. ustedes (Uds.) (I); fam. after prep. ti (I); sing. dir. and ind. obj. pron. te (I); sing. formal dir. obj. pron. lo, la (I); pl. fam. ind. obj. pron. os (I); ind. obj. pron. le, les (I)

And —? ¿Y a ti? (I)

for — para ti (I)

it matters (it's important), they matter to — te importa(n) (II)

to / for — fam. pl. os (I)

to / for — fam. sing. te (I)

with — contigo (I)

— can se puede (II)

— don't say! ¡No me digas! (I)

— have seen has visto (II)

— know conocen (II)

— look (good) te ves (bien) (II)

— say ... Se dice ... (I)

young joven (I)

— boy / girl el niño, la niña (I)

— man el joven (I)

— people los jóvenes (II)

— woman la joven (I)

—er menor, pl. menores (I)

your fam. tu (I); fam. pl. tus, vuestro(s), -a(s) (I); formal su, sus (I)

yours tuyo, -a, -os, -as (II)

yuck! ¡Uf !(I)

Z

zero cero (I)

zoo el zoológico (I)

Grammar Index

Structures are most often presented first in *A primera vista*, where they are practiced lexically in conversational contexts. They are then explained in a *Gramática* section or are placed as reminders in a *¿Recuerdas?* or *Nota*. Lightface numbers refer to the pages where these structures are initially presented lexically or, after explanation, where student reminders occur. Lightface numbers also refer to pages that review structures first presented in Level 2. **Boldface numbers** refer to pages where new structures are explained.

Acknowledgments

Maps All maps created by XNR Productions.

Photographs Every effort has been made to secure permission and provide appropriate credit for photographic material. The publisher deeply regrets any omission and pledges to correct errors called to its attention in subsequent editions.

Unless otherwise acknowledged, all photographs are the property of Pearson Education, Inc.

Photo locators denoted as follows: Top (T), Center (C), Bottom (B), Left (L), Right (R), Background (Bkgd)

Cover (L) Image Source/Getty Images; (CL) Tom Mackie/Alamy Images; (CR) ©Jan A. Csernoch/Alamy Images; (R) Kevin Schafer/Alamy Images

Front Matter vii (TR) Alamy, (BR, BC) NASA, (BL) StockTrek/SuperStock; **xix** Petra Fiedler/Fotolia; **xx** (Bkgd) ©José Fuste Rage/Corbis, (Inset) Shutterstock; **xxi** (Inset) ©John Elk III; **xxii** (BL) Steve Kaufman/Bettmann/Corbis, (Bkgd) Taxi/Getty Images; **xxiv** (BL) Image Bank/Getty Images, (Bkgd) Stone Allstock/Getty Images; **xxvi** (Bkgd) ©Ed Simpson; **xxviii** (Bkgd) Dennis Degnan/Bettmann/Corbis; **xxx** (BL) ©AFP/Getty Images, (Bkgd) ©Michelle Chaplow/Corbis; **xxxi** (BC) The Image Works; **xxxii** (C, Bkgd) ©John Elk III; **xxxiii** ©James Quine/Alamy Images; **xxxiv** ALEJANDRA BRUN/AFP/Getty Images/NewsCom

2 (TL) ©Michael Newman/PhotoEdit, (TR) ©Richard Hutchings/PhotoEdit; **4** (TR) ©Michelle D. Bridwell/PhotoEdit; **6** (TC) ©Tracy Frankel/Getty Images, (TR) Andreas Pollok/Getty Images; **8** (BR) ©Ted Foxx/Alamy, (CL) Amy Strycula/Alamy Images, (TR) Jim West/Alamy Images; **13** ©Travelshots/Alamy Images; **14** (T) ©Aurora Photos/Alamy Images, (BL) Getty Images; **15** ©David Frazier/The Image Works; **16** (T) ©Image Source; **18** (C) ©Al Bello/Getty Images, (TL) ©Joe McBride/Corbis, (TR) Latin Focus; **20** ©Prisma Bildagentur AG/Alamy Images; **21** (Inset) Paisaje chileno by Matilde Pérez. Used by permission of Museo de Arte Contemporáneo de la Universidad de Chile/Artists Rights Society (ARS), NY; **22** (BR) Mark Herreid/Fotolia, Brent Winebrenner/Lonely Planet Images/NewsCom, (CL) Daniel Pangbourne/©DK Images, (BL) DK Images, (BC) Steve Gorton/©DK Images, (CR) Tim Ridley/©DK Images; **23** (BL) ©Andrea Jemolo/Corbis, (TL) ©Blaine Harrington III/Alamy Images, (BR) ©Prisma Bildagentur AG/Alamy Images, (BC) e54/ZUMA Press/NewsCom; **26** (BR) Corbis, (BL) Daniel Pangbourne/©DK Images, (BC) DK Images, (BC) Steve Gorton/©DK Images, (BC) Susanna Price/©DK Images, (BL) Tim Ridley/©DK Images; **27** (R) Shutterstock; **29** ©Luke Dodd/Photo Researchers, Inc.; **30** ©Gregory D. Dimijian/Photo Researchers, Inc.; **34** ©Jacques Jangoux/Photo Researchers, Inc.; **35** ©SeBuKi/Alamy Images; **36** (C) ©Benn Mitchell; **41** (B) ©blickwinkel/Alamy Images, (CR) Corbis; **45** (TR, CR) ©AP Photo, (BR) ©Tanya Constantine/Alamy; **48** (BL) ©leandro hermida/Alamy Images, (BR) ©Roberto Reyes Ang, (BC) Bridgeman Art Library; **49** (CR) ©Jennie Hart/Alamy Images, (BC) ©Roberto Reyes Ang, (TR) Dave King/©DK Images; **50** ©Jborzicchi /Dreamstime LLC; **51** ©Golden Pixels LLC/

Alamy; **54** ©Jeremy Woodhouse/SuperStock; **57** (B) ©Marco Regalia/Shutterstock; **62** (TC) ©Réunion des Musées Nationaux/Art Resource, NY, (C) San Antonio de Oriente (1957) by José Antonio Velásquez/Art Museum of the Americas; **64** (CC) ©LondonPhotos — Homer Sykes/Alamy Images, (TL) ©Richard Hutchings/PhotoEdit, (TR, TC) ©Tony Freeman/PhotoEdit; **66** (Bkgd) Jeremy Graham/dbimages/Alamy Images; **67** (Inset) Scala/Art Resource, NY; **68** (BL) ©Bob Daemmrich/Daemmrich Photography, (CL) Naturaleza muerta (1999)/©Alfonso Fernández; **69** (TR) Art Resource, NY, (BL) Dutch Interior I (1928) by Joan Miró/Scala/Art Resource, NY, (BR) Pair of Lovers With Almond Blossom Games (1975) by Joan Miró/James Blassi/Artists Rights Society (ARS), NY, (TL) The Farm (1922) by Joan Miró/Artists Rights Society (ARS), NY; **70** (C) Dina Bursztyn, (R) Lady Dreams/Dina Bursztyn; **71** (TL) Corbis, (C) INBA/Banco de México/Corbis, (CR) Nickolas Muray, Diego Rivera and Wife, Frida Kahlo, ca. 1930s, gelatin silver print, 24.1 × 16.3 cm./©Nickolas Muray Photo Archives/Gift of the Muray Family. /Courtesy George Eastman House, (CL) Nicolás Osorio Ruiz, (TL) SCALA/Art Resource, NY; **73** (BR) Eric Lessing/Art Resource, NY, (TR) Naturaleza muerta (1999)/©Alfonso Fernández; **74** (B) Dennis Hallinan/Alamy Images, (TR) SuperStock; **75** (TR) Scala/Art Resource, NY; **77** (BR) ©2009 VEGAP, Madrid/Artists Rights Society (ARS), NY; **78** ©Schalkwijk/Art Resource, NY; **80** (R) Collection Walker Art Center, Minneapolis; **81** (BR) ©Beth Dixson, (TR) Bettmann/Corbis; **82** (CL) Photofest; **83** (TR) ©Rubberball/SuperStock, (BL) Alamy Images, (BR) Daemmrich Photography, (TR) eStock Photo; **84** (Inset) Agencia el Universal/El Universal de México/NewsCom, (C) DANIEL GARCIA/AFP/Getty Images/NewsCom; **85** (T) ©Martin Valigursky/Alamy, (CL) AFP/Getty Images; **86** (B) ©David Friedman/Reuters/Landov LLC; **91** ©LOOK Die Bildagentur der Fotografen GmbH/Alamy Images; **93** (BR) ©1988, W. Chasen/©Wayne H. & Alan D. Chasan, (T) Kolesnikova Natalia Itar-Tass Photos/NewsCom, (BR) Krzysztof Dydynski/Lonely Planet Images; **94** (BC) Art Resource, NY, (L) NewsCom; **95** (TR) ©Erich Lessing/Art Resource, NY, (BR) Bridgeman Art Library; **96** (L) Naturaleza muerta con sopa verde (Still Life with Green Soup) (1972) by Fernando Botero/Courtesy Marlborough Gallery, NY; **97** (B) ©Everett Collection Inc./Alamy Images, (T) ©United Archives GmbH/Alamy Images; **101** ©Dana White/PhotoEdit; **102** ©Spencer Grant/PhotoEdit; **103** d17/ZUMA Press/NewsCom; **108** ©Michelle D. Bridwell/PhotoEdit; **110** (TR) ©Michael Newman/PhotoEdit, (TL) HIRB/Index Stock/PhotoLibrary Group, Ltd.; **112** ©Craig Lovell/Eagle Visions Photography/Alamy Images; **113** (Inset) ©D.R. Rufino Tamayo/Herederos/México/2010/Fundación Olga y Rufino Tamayo, A.C./Christie's Images/Corbis; **120** (B) ©Patsy Michaud/Shutterstock; **123** ©Bob Daemmrich/The Image Works, Inc.; **124** (TR) ©Helen Norman/Corbis, (BR) Corbis; **132** NewsCom; **133** (BL) ©John Alves/Mystic Wanderer Images, (TR) ©Michael Newman/PhotoEdit; **134** Radosław Brzozo/Fotolia; **135** (BL) ©PhotoAlto/Alamy; **139** Shadd/St. Petersburg Times/NewsCom; **140** (BL) ©DK Images, (BR) ©John Neubauer/PhotoEdit, (TL) ©Peter E. Spier/National Geographic Image Collection; **141** (CR, BR) ©Erich Lessing/Art

Resource, NY, (TR) ©Macduff Everton/Corbis; **142** ©Foodcollection/Getty Images; **143** ©Michael Newman/ PhotoEdit; **147** (BR) Steve Gorton/©DK Images; **148** (BR) ©Michael Prince/Corbis, (TL) Getty Images; **149** David R. Frazier/Danita Delimont "Danita Delimont Photography"/ NewsCom; **154** (TL) Deklofenak/Fotolia, (TR) Syda Productions/Shutterstock, (C) ©Arch White/Alamy; **158** ©Blend Images/Alamy; **159** (Inset) Madre e hijo (Mother & Child) (1907) by Pablo Picasso/Art Resource, NY; **161** (TL) ©Jennie Hart/Alamy Images, (CR) Daemmrich Photography, (BL) Thinkstock; **162** (TR) ©Lawrence Manning/Corbis, (BR) ©Tim O'Hara/Corbis; **167** Corbis; **169** Ghislain & Marie David de Lossy Cultura/NewsCom; **170** ©Blend Images/Alamy; **176** Michael Newman/PhotoEdit, Inc.; **177** ©Myrleen Ferguson Cate/PhotoEdit; **178** Juan Ignacio Ortega/NewsCom; **179** Wolfgang Dietze/Carmen L. Garza; **183** KENNELL KRISTA/ SIPA/NewsCom; **185** (B) ©Jack Hollingsworth/Corbis; **186** (B) ©Tony Freeman/PhotoEdit, (CL) Mother and Child (1926) by Diego Rivera/Art Resource, NY; **187** (TR) ©Bill Ross/Corbis, (BL) ©Kelly-Mooney Photography/Corbis; **188** ©Mike Kemp/ Rubberball/Jupiter Images; **189** ©John Henley/Corbis; **192** (R) ©Kurt Stier/Corbis; **193** Latin Focus; **194** Woman in Spanish Costume (La salchichona) (1917) by Pablo Picasso/Giraudon/ Art Resource, NY; **195** (BR) ©Philip Scalia/Alamy Images; **200** (TL) ©Steve Skjold/PhotoEdit; **202** Hero Images Inc./ Alamy, (CR) ©James Shaffer/PhotoEdit, (TC) ©Jeff Greenberg/ PhotoEdit; **204** ©Jeff Greenberg/Alamy Images; **205** (Inset) Christie's Images/Corbis; **212** (R) Alamy Images; **213** Corbis; **215** Photoaisa; **216** ©Allstar Picture Library/Alamy Images; **219** ©2010 Banco de México Diego Rivera & Frida Kahlo Museums Trust, México, D.F./Artists Rights Society (ARS)/ Detroit Institute of the Arts/Bridgeman Art Library; **223** (R) ©ERproductions Ltd./Getty Images, (CL) ©Michael Newman/ PhotoEdit; **226** (BR) Jimmy Dorantes/Latin Focus; **227** ©SW Productions/Brand X/Corbis; **228** ©Dwayne Newton/PhotoEdit; **230** (B) ©Associated Press, (TR) ©Spencer Grant/PhotoEdit; **231** ©AP Photo; **232** b21ZUMA Press/NewsCom, (BR) CD1 WENN Photos/NewsCom; **233** (BR) Agencia el Universal GDA Photo Service/NewsCom, (TR) Courtesy of Linda Alvarado/ Alvarado Construction Inc., NewsCom; **234** ©LATIN PHOTO; **235** Alamy Images; **241** (B) Luiz Rodríguez/Tía Chucha's Centro Cultural; **246** (TL) ©Bob Daemmrich/The Image Works, (TR) Corbis; **248** (TL) ©Carolyn Brown/Getty Images, (R, C) Shutterstock; **250** ©Right Perspective Images/Alamy Images; **251** (Inset) L'Etang de No (1958) by Roberto Matta-Echaurren/©Artists Rights Society (ARS), New York/ADAGP, Paris/Musée National d'Art Moderne, Centre Georges Pompidou/Photo Credit: CNAC/MNAM/Dist. Réunion des Musées Nationaux/Art Resource, NY; **254** (TR) ©Bob Daemmrich/The Image Works, (TL) Stephen Coburn/Fotolia, (TL) Blend Images/Alamy; **255** (TR) Caro/Alamy Images, (TL) moodboard/Alamy; **257** ©Sue Cunningham Photographic/ Alamy Images; **262** ©CHCI; **265** Alamy Images; **266** (BC) ©Bil Aron/PhotoEdit, Inc., (BR) ©Michael Newman/PhotoEdit, Inc., (BL) Alamy Images, (TL) Glowimages/NewsCom; **267** (BL) Alamy Images, (BR) Guy Croft SciTec/Alamy Images; **268** (CR) ©John Madere/Corbis, (Bkgd) takito/Shutterstock; **269** (Bkgd)

Matt Antonio/Shutterstock, The Image Works, Inc.; **270** ©The Shadow Robot Company; **271** Xinhua/Photoshot/NewsCom; **272** Carol and Mike Werner/Alamy Images; **274** ©Kent News & Pictures/Corbis; **275** RM/Corbis; **276** Alex Segre/Alamy Images, (BL) UpperCut Images/Alamy; **277** ©NMPFT/Topham/ The Image Works; **278** (BR) ©Jan Butchofsky-Houser/Corbis, (BC) ©Randy Faris/Corbis, (BL) ©Sergio Pitamitz/Corbis; **279** (TR, B) ©Joseph Sohm; Visions of America/Corbis; **281** Courtesy of High Tech High; **287** Corbis; **292** (TC) ©Danny Lehman/Corbis, (R) Anthony Haigh/Alamy Images, (L) Sean White/Design Pics/NewsCom; **294** (TR) ©Adam Jones/ Dembinsky Photo Associates, (TC) ©Darrell Gulin/Dembinsky Photo Associates, (TL) ©Rod Planck/Dembinsky Photo Associates; **296** ©Danita Delimont/Alamy Images; **297** (Inset) La civilización Totonaca (1950) by Diego Rivera/©Charles & Josette Lenars/Corbis;
300 (TL) ©Bill Bachmann/PhotoEdit, (TR) DDB Stock Photography; **301** (CL) ©Buddy Mays/Alamy Images, (TR) ©Chris Lisle/Corbis; **303** (TR) ©Kevin Schafer/Corbis; **304** ©Michael Nicholson/Corbis; **311** ©Bill Bachmann/PhotoEdit; **314** (TR) akg/Bildarchiv Steffens/NewsCom, (TL) Charles Lenars/Corbis, (B) NewsCom; **315** (TR) ©Gianni Dagli Orti/ Corbis, (CL) Shutterstock; **316** ©Gianni Dagli Orti/Corbis; **318** ©Kevin Schafer/Getty Images; **319** Gianni Dagli Orti/ Corbis; **321** ©John Neubauer/PhotoEdit; **322** ©Terrance Klassen/AGE Fotostock; **323** (TR) ©Vo Trung Dung/Corbis; **324** (BL) ©James L. Amos/Corbis, (B) Corbis; **325** (CR) ©Charles & Josette Lenars/Corbis, (TR) ©Gianni Dagli Orti/ Corbis; **326** ©Pasquale Sorrentino/Photo Researchers, Inc.; **327** Corbis; **330** ©Francis G. Mayer/Corbis; **333** ©The Granger Collection, NY; **338** Shutterstock; **340** (TR) ©Carl & Ann Purcell/Corbis, (TL) ©Mark Antman/The Image Works, (C) Prisma Bildagentur AG/Alamy Images; **342** ©HP Canada/ Alamy Images; **343** (Inset) Granada (1920) by Joaquín Sorolla y Bastida/Bridgeman Art Library; **344** (CL) ©Patrick Ward/ Corbis, (CR) ©Paul Almasy/Corbis; **345** (CL) ©Stephanie Colasanti/Corbis, (C) AGE Fotostock, (CR) Barry Mason/ Alamy, (CR) Ferdinand and Isabella by Eugene Deveria/Art Resource, NY; **346** (C) ©John and Lisa Merrill/Corbis, (Bkgd) ©Paul Almasy/Corbis, (BL) Getty Images; **347** (Bkgd) ©Paul Almasy/Corbis, (CR) ©Stephanie Maze/Corbis, (TL) DDB Stock Photography; **348** ©Charlie Waite/Getty Images; **349** (CL) ©Macduff Everton/Corbis, (R) Jon Arnold Images Ltd./Alamy; **350** Bernardo Galmarini/Alamy Images; **351** (CL) ©John Warburton-Lee/Danita Delimont/Alamy Images; **353** ©Michael Newman/PhotoEdit; **354** Tim Graham/Corbis; **355** (TR) ©Spencer Grant/PhotoEdit, (BR) Getty Images, (T) NewsCom; **358** (CR) ©Monica Stevenson/Getty Images, (TR) ©Tony Freeman/PhotoEdit; **360** ©Giraudon/Art Resource, NY; **361** (TR) ©Michael Zabe/Art Resource, NY, (CR) ©Snark/Art Resource, NY; **362** ©Mike & Carol Werner/©Carol and Mike Werner; **363** (CR) ©Bob Daemmrich/The Image Works, (BC) Daemmrich Photography; **365** Stephen Finn/Alamy Images; **366** ©Myrleen Ferguson/PhotoEdit; **367** ©Rudi Von Briel/ PhotoEdit; **368** ©Jeff Greenberg/PhotoEdit; **369** ©William Whitehurst/Corbis; **370** (B) ©Philip James Corwin/Corbis, (BL) ©Richard Cummins/Corbis; **371** (B) ©John Elk III, (TR)

Página de Cultura

"Si me permiten hablar...testimony de Domitila Barrios" by Moema Viezzer from SI ME PERMITEN HABLAR. Siglo XXI Editores, México, 1976. Reprinted by permission of the author.

Random House

Excerpts from CUANDO ERA PUERTORRIQUEÑA by Esmeralda Santiago, introducción y traducción copyright © 1994 by Random House, Inc. Used by permission of Vintage Español, division of Random House, Inc.

Sony/ATV Music Publishing LLC

"Será entre tú y yo" © 1996 Sony/ATV Music Publishing LLC, Insignia Music. All rights administered by Sony/ATV Music Publishing LLC, 8 Music Square West, Nashville, TN 37203. All rights reserved. Used by permission.

Tangoshow.com

"Museo Vivo del Tango" from www.tangoshow.com

Note: Every effort has been made to locate the copyright owner of material reproduced in this component. Omissions brought to our attention will be corrected in subsequent editions.